ENCYCLOPEDIA OF WORLD TRAVEL

VOLUME I

Encyclopedia of
WORLD TRAVEL

Second Revised Edition

VOLUME I

UNITED STATES · CANADA
MEXICO · CENTRAL AMERICA · BERMUDA
THE BAHAMAS · THE CARIBBEAN
SOUTH AMERICA

Edited by NELSON DOUBLEDAY
and C. EARL COOLEY

Revised by MARJORIE ZELKO
and DIANA POWELL WARD

DOUBLEDAY & COMPANY, INC. GARDEN CITY, NEW YORK

ISBN: 0-385-06120-X
LIBRARY OF CONGRESS CATALOG CARD NUMBER 73–76221

PRINTED IN THE UNITED STATES OF AMERICA

Foreword

TRAVELING to the ends of the earth is within the reach of nearly everyone; no longer is a trip to Asia or Africa beyond the realm of possibility. With people's appetites for travel and discovery increasingly whetted by the expanding network of communications covering all parts of the globe, year-round vacations are planned and itineraries written that would have boggled the mind and pocketbook several years ago. In short, the travel industry has become one of the largest and most vital businesses in the world today.

As countries the world over compete for the tourist trade, books, magazines, tipping guides, brochures, and pamphlets flood the market in increasing numbers. The job of searching out and absorbing all this material is a formidable and frustrating task. Aware of the acute need for one definitive source book on travel information for every state and country in the world, Doubleday brought out the Encyclopedia of World Travel in 1961.

The product of 20 contributing editors and a large Doubleday editorial staff, this two-volume set, which has sold over 350,000 copies, has been a mainstay of the tourist industry since its publication. In 1967, a new, completely revised edition was published. Now in 1973, due to the ever-changing and developing nature of our fast-paced world, with new nations emerging and new tourist attractions becoming available, another extensive revision of the Encyclopedia has been completed.

The editorial staff involved in these revisions worked closely with state and national tourist boards, consulates, and United Nations missions in order to ensure that this would be the most comprehensive, up-to-date travel reference possible. We want to give special thanks to Thomas B. and Judy H. Manton of the China-America Relations Society in New York for revising the section on China.

Each map has been thoroughly examined by Douglas Waugh, former chief cartographer of the American Geographical Society, who not only added place names and other revisions where necessary, but has supplied new maps where the situation warranted. For each revision, the photographs were carefully screened, with dated ones discarded and current ones added, to assure each country the best possible representation.

Recognizing its extensive value for school and home reference use, the Encyclopedia was specifically designed to include sections on agriculture and industry, a capsule history of each country, as well as travel information on the land, weather, major cities, sports, national holidays and special events, dining and shopping.

Whether planning an itinerary for a trip this year or reading for the enjoyment of expanding your knowledge of people and places, we feel sure the Encyclopedia will fulfill the requirement of being the most complete, current source of travel information available today.

Marjorie Zelko

Diana Powell Ward

Contents

Part Two: CANADA

PART THREE: MEXICO, CENTRAL AMERICA, BERMUDA, THE BAHAMAS

PART FOUR: THE CARIBBEAN

PART FIVE: SOUTH AMERICA

Table of Maps

VOLUME I

United States

New England

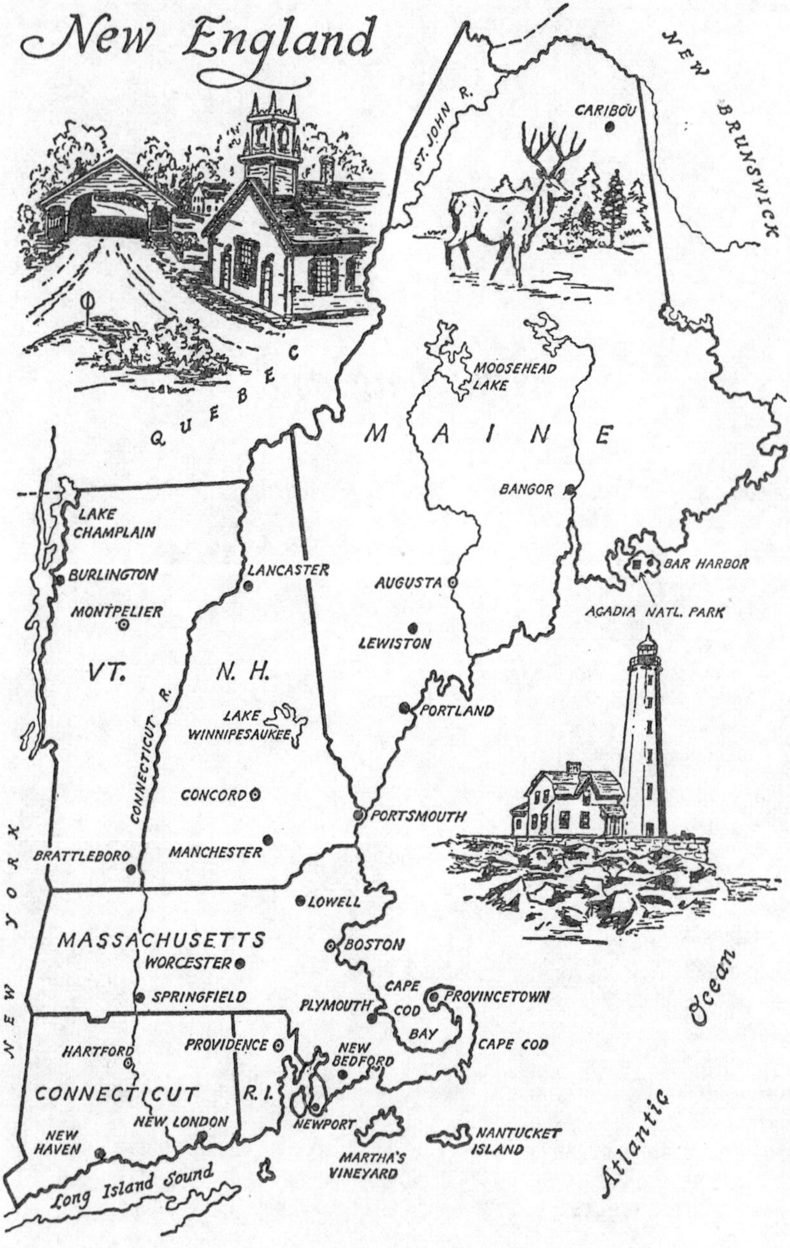
New England
QUEBEC
NEW BRUNSWICK
ST. JOHN R.
CARIBOU
MAINE
MOOSEHEAD LAKE
BANGOR
BAR HARBOR
ACADIA NATL. PARK
AUGUSTA
LEWISTON
PORTLAND
LAKE CHAMPLAIN
BURLINGTON
MONTPELIER
LANCASTER
VT.
N. H.
CONNECTICUT R.
LAKE WINNIPESAUKEE
CONCORD
PORTSMOUTH
MANCHESTER
BRATTLEBORO
NEW YORK
LOWELL
MASSACHUSETTS
BOSTON
WORCESTER
SPRINGFIELD
CAPE COD BAY
PROVINCETOWN
PLYMOUTH
CAPE COD
HARTFORD
PROVIDENCE
NEW BEDFORD
CONNECTICUT
R. I.
NEW LONDON
NEW HAVEN
NEWPORT
NANTUCKET ISLAND
MARTHA'S VINEYARD
Long Island Sound
Atlantic Ocean

New England

In the extreme northeast corner of the United States six of our oldest states form one of the most homogeneous and clearly defined regions in the whole country. Everyone is familiar with the New England States —Maine, New Hampshire, Vermont, Massachusetts, Rhode Island, and Connecticut. Four were among the 13 colonies, the other two among the first new states in the Union.

Originally populated by Indians of the Algonquian Nation, this region of rugged mountains, and watered, apart from the swift-flowing mountain streams, by only a single major river, New England did not appear a particularly auspicious place for the Pilgrim Fathers and their successors to build a new home. Despite the poor farming, the fishing was excellent, and the forests rich in game and timber. The small, rapidly falling rivers supplied power for sawmills and for the factories which the practical and inventive "Yankees" (a mysterious nickname given by the Dutch) were soon running. As the factories multiplied people flocked to work in them—French-Canadians from Quebec, Irish and English from Great Britain, many nationalities from Europe.

New England today is highly industrialized and urbanized, yet it preserves much of its old early-American flavor. Its fishing fleet still brings in enormous catches of cod, mackerel, and haddock, nowadays frozen and sold across the country. The picturesque fishing ports are favored haunts of artists, both amateur and professional. Lovely old villages are still distinguished by the famous "New England" commons and "New England" churches—graceful and white, surmounted sometimes by a square bell tower, sometimes by a slender spire.

Hundreds of covered bridges preserve the rustic charm of horse-and-buggy days, and also the memory of an engineering revolution. Examine the interior of a covered bridge and you will find an ingenious structural system, developed by Yankee carpenter-engineers of a century and a half ago, and later adapted for most of the world's steel railroad bridges.

No region has more landmarks of America's struggle toward nationhood. Plymouth Rock marks the place where the Pilgrims landed after making the Mayflower Compact, America's first written instrument of democratic government. Successive waves of English colonists quickly made New England the most populous part of North America. Boston became the leading city of the New World, and presently the chief center of colonial resistance to British rule. Faneuil Hall, Old North Church, the battlefields of Lexington and Concord, Bunker Hill, and many more carefully preserved sites and buildings commemorate the outbreak of the Revolution.

Perhaps even more fascinating reminders of the past are the excellent restorations of whole towns and industries of New England's early days: Old Sturbridge Village, Massachusetts; the seaport of Mystic, Connecticut; the Saugus Iron Works near Boston; Shelburne, Vermont, and others which show the visitor how our forefathers lived and worked.

The fine highway network winds through some of the country's most beautiful scenery–the wooded slopes of the Green Mountains of Vermont, the White Mountains of New Hampshire, the Berkshires of Massachusetts and Connecticut, the forest-covered primeval wilderness of Maine. The single large river, the Connecticut, flowing south from the Canadian border to Long Island Sound, and dividing Vermont from New Hampshire, provides New England's only sizable area of good farmland.

Fishing, including surf-casting and deep-sea fishing, is the outstanding summer sport, although there are dozens of fine golf courses and many beaches both on the ocean and on the inland lakes. Hiking the mountain trails is a favorite summer pastime. The coastal waters are ideal for boating, and schooner cruising is available around the islands off the Maine shore.

The mountain slopes and heavy annual snowfall have made New England as famous for winter as for summer fun. Ski resorts of every size and type are available, while tobogganing, ice-boating, and skating are also popular.

For the exploratory diner New England offers a wide assortment of dining places, many in settings of exceptional beauty, often featuring local specialties–Maine lobster, fish chowder, Boston baked beans and brown bread, Indian pudding, blueberries and cranberries. For the antique collector, too, New England is a notable hunting ground.

Maine

Maine, the largest of the New England states (it contains more than half the area of all New England), fills the northeast corner of the United States below Canada. Among the United States, it is thirty-ninth in size. With about a million people, most of whom live in small towns and villages, it is third in population among the New England states and thirty-eighth among the states of the Union. The shape of Maine is immensely irregular. On the northeast and north is the Canadian province of New Brunswick. On the north and west the Canadian province of Quebec, south of which is the only straight-line border, with New Hampshire opposite. The whole southeast coast of Maine is cut with deep bays and inlets, fringed with hundreds of islands. Though the total straight-line length of Maine from northeast to southwest is 332 miles, the actual shoreline is 3,478 miles, all immensely rugged and picturesque. Along the Maine Atlantic Coast is the easternmost point in the continental United States, **West Quoddy Head.** The farthest east town in the United States, **Lubec,** is also on the Maine coast. Maine's state tree is the white pine, the state bird the chickadee, the state flower, the pine cone and tassel.

THE LAND. The surface of Maine is a dramatic contrast between land and water. The land is hilly, low granite peaks toward the coast, rising higher toward the west, where the ranges are an extension of the White Mountains of New Hampshire. Among the mountains are hundreds of lakes, some of them, like **Moosehead,** quite large. The highest mountain in the state is **Mount Katahdin** (5,268 feet), in Maine's great north-central wilderness, a vast mountain region of primitive forests, set with hundreds of lakes, many of them connected by channels. There are no roads through it, and the only access to it is by plane or boat.

Most of the people live in towns and villages on or close to the coast. Along the shore are more than 1,000 islands. The largest, **Mount Desert Island,** contains New England's only national park, **Acadia,** and is the highest point on the eastern coast. Maine's longest river, flowing south into the Atlantic, is the Penobscot. Others are Androscoggin, the Kennebec, the Saco, and in the far north the big, beautiful St. John that divides Maine from New Brunswick.

Much of the state is forest land—almost 17.5 million acres, with more than 2,500 lakes—a wilderness resource which makes the state a paradise for sportsmen.

THE CLIMATE. Maine's annual precipitation is between 35 and 45 inches, much of it falling as snow during winter months. Summers are short, relatively cool, winters cold and long. The coastal areas are more temperate, with Portland having an average January temperature of 21 degrees, an average July temperature of 68 degrees. Weather changes are often sudden and severe. Northern forest areas have winter periods with temperatures below zero. The best time for a visit to Maine, except for winter sports, is during the summer months, from mid-June to mid-September.

THE PEOPLE. Maine's coast was known and explored as early as 1496, and it is believed probable that Norse navigators sailed along the coast as early as the eleventh century. The Cabots are known to have reached the shore of Maine as early as 1498, and a settlement was made on the Maine coast as early as 1604.

In the beginning, Maine was considered to be a part of the colony of Massachusetts and remained a part of the Massachusetts area until 1820. It was admitted to the Union that same year, as the twenty-third state. From that time on, the population grew slowly but steadily, with the development of ship-building and lumbering.

At the beginning of the nineteenth century, the population of Maine was predominantly English, Scottish, and

Scotch-Irish, plus scattered settlements of French from Canada and Acadian-French stock from the Maritime Provinces of Canada. During the early years of the nineteenth century, the original Yankee stocks were supplemented by a slow but steady migration of Irish and Germans. Following them came Swedish settlers to live and work in the forests. Their enthusiasm for the new land brought settlers from other Scandinavian areas–Finns, Norwegians, and Icelanders–to engage in fishing, shipping, and lumbering. The growth of Maine's cities has brought in scattered groups from southern European areas–Italians, Greeks, Syrians–but the people of Maine today are still predominantly Scotch-Irish, with a generous proportion of French. Many of the French live in northern counties, working in mills and potato fields and often attending French churches and French schools. Early settlers in Maine were competent craftsmen, as they were through nearly all of New England. They built the graceful, simple frame dwellings and public buildings, the charming small churches that are still to be seen along Maine's coast. Later, the descendants of the early craftsmen began to design and build more pretentious and elaborate buildings. Builders erected dozens of covered bridges which span Maine's streams and rivers, almost a trademark of New England character.

AGRICULTURE. Though most of Maine's farmlands are restricted to the few level valley areas, and more than half of its farms are of the subsistence type–wood lot and pasture–the state does have important specialty crops. The chief of these is potatoes, in which Maine leads all states but Idaho, grown in the fertile Aroostook valley in the north-central part of the state. There, potato fields flowering in the early summer attract visitors, and later, towns in the area celebrate the potato harvest with festivals.

Another important specialty crop is blueberries, of which Maine grows about 90 percent of all those sold in the United States. They grow chiefly among the hills and valleys of the southeastern part of the state and are an indigenous crop. Other farm products produced in commercial quantities are apples, sweet corn, peas, and beans. Poultry raising is one of the most important farm businesses.

Supplementing crops from Maine's farms are the harvest from its coastal waters. Maine is nationally famous for several specialties, the most important being lobster, which dwellers in Maine say is the finest in the world. More than 20 million pounds of them are trapped and sold each year. Another marine harvest is soft-shell clams, with Maine producing 30 percent of all sold in the United States. A third is sardines and **Eastport** is the base for a large fleet.

INDUSTRY. The chief products of Maine's factories and mills derive raw material from the forests of the state. The commercially useful trees are chiefly white pine, spruce, balsam, fir, some maple and ash. There are sawmills and pulp and paper mills throughout the state; also factories which convert timber into finished products as diverse as canoes, snowshoes, and toothpicks. The building of small ships and boats is also important.

CITIES. Maine is essentially a region of small cities, towns, and villages. No city in the state exceeds 100,000 in population, and only one has more than 50,000 people. Among the state's approximately 1,800 settled places, less than 100 have more than 1,000 population, and most of these have less than 5,000 people.

AUGUSTA (population about 22,000), a hub of highways and capital of the state, straddles the Kennebec River at the head of navigation, some 50 miles northeast of Portland. Though not a resort city, Augusta has several attractions, including the handsome **state capitol,** constructed of Maine granite, and nearby **Blaine House,** the Governor's official home, once the residence of James G. Blaine, who was a presidential nominee in 1884. Nearby is a 20-

acre park with one of the state's best collections of trees and plants. Augusta is an important manufacturing center, with one of the oldest and the largest of Maine's many cotton textile mills.

BANGOR, 45 miles north of Camden, on a bypass of U.S. 1, is Maine's third largest city (population about 33,000). It was once a bustling seaport and center for shipbuilding at the head of Tidewater on the big Penobscot River.

BAR HARBOR is, for most visitors to Maine, the most interesting and rewarding city. On the eastern shore of rugged Mount Desert Island, it is about 40 miles southeast of Bangor and some ten air miles from the mainland. With a population of about 4,000, it is one of the oldest and most fashionable resort communities in the East. The city is devoted almost entirely to providing resort facilities for the summer visitor, but it does have one important institution, the **Jackson Memorial Laboratory,** for the study of cancer. Bar Harbor is the western and United States terminus for an international ocean ferry linking Maine with Nova Scotia. Several sightseeing cruises of the bay to the east and north are based on Bar Harbor.

Immediately behind Bar Harbor is **Acadia National Park,** the first national park to be established east of the Mississippi. It has more than 41,000 acres in several sections, most of them on Mount Desert Island, including the highest point on the Atlantic Coast, 1,528 feet. The park has many miles of well-maintained and superbly scenic highways.

BATH, about 25 miles northeast of Portland, near the coast and the mouth of the Kennebec River, is a handsome, historic old town, famed for shipbuilding. During the heyday of sailing ships, it made more of them than any city in the country. Bath is a convenient base for exploring several rocky, picturesque promontories that extend south into the sea, with a variety of resort establishments and communities.

CAMDEN, with a population of about 4,000, is one of the most attractive coastal communities in the East. Forty-five miles northeast of Bath, it has a rugged, highly scenic shore setting, and is one of the few coastal cities which provides facilities for both winter sports and summer visitors. Camden is the home port for a fleet of vessels that provide a unique summer holiday opportunity–schooner-cruising along the coast.

PORTLAND, with a population of about 65,000, is not only Maine's largest city, but one of the most historic and interesting towns in New England. It has a commanding position at the southwestern end of Casco Bay, in the southeast corner of the state, and is the chief city of a heavily populated coastal region. Maine's coastal turnpike has its northern terminus in Portland, which is a hub of highways, including U.S. 1 linking all of Maine's coastal cities.

Portland is both a major commercial port and the chief city of a large resort region which extends along the coast and west to the New Hampshire border. Several interesting sights relate to the poet Henry Wadsworth Longfellow (who was born in Portland), including the house where he lived, now maintained as a shrine. There is also a statue of the poet and a **Longfellow Square.** Near the Longfellow House is a small but excellent **historical museum,** with many Maine relics. Portland is a terminus for sightseeing trips by boat in Casco Bay.

South of Portland, along the shore, is a chain of resort communities, the most celebrated of which is the public beach resort called **Old Orchard.** Northwest of Portland is one of Maine's most important summer resort districts, developed around **Sebago Lake.**

SPORTS AND RECREATION. Maine, particularly the coastal area, is one of the chief resort regions of the country, with many facilities for the diversion of the visitor.

Maine's coastal waters provide boating of unique potential and variety.

Cruising the coast among the thousands of islands has been the traditional summer pastime for boating enthusiasts for many years. Maine's northern wilderness area, with its vast forests, mountains, and thousands of lakes, of which the most famous is rugged **Moosehead Lake,** offers sportsmen a unique opportunity for hunting and fishing in one of the few great wilderness regions left in the United States.

In addition to Maine's national park, **Acadia,** there are a number of state parks in areas of scenic interest. Other sights include a number of historic buildings, several small but good museums.

SPECIAL EVENTS. **Winter carnivals,** held in January and February, are main events in Fryeburg, Fort Fairfield, Rumford, Camden, Bangor, and Presque Isle. Other popular events are **regattas,** taking place in Boothbay Harbor, Casco Bay, and Kennebunkport in July; **Potato Blossom Festival,** Aroostook County, mid-July; **Lobster Festival,** Winter Harbor, in August. Maine's outstanding event of the year is the **Maine State Fair,** in Lewiston in early September.

New Hampshire

With a land and water area of some 9,300 square miles, New Hampshire is third in size among the New England states, forty-fourth in size in the United States. With a population of about 722,000, it is fifth among the New England states and forty-second in the United States. The shape of New Hampshire is that of an irregular, narrow triangle with its base to the south, its stubby tip to the north. Among the New England states, it is the central state of a northern tier. The Province of Quebec is to the north, separated from New Hampshire by a winding land border. A straight-line land border on the east separates the state from its neighbor, Maine. Part of the eastern border in the south is the Atlantic Ocean, made possible by a narrow corridor to the sea between Maine and Massachusetts. The entire southern border, arrow-straight except in the extreme eastern part, is the state of Massachusetts. The winding course of the Connecticut River, rising in Canada, is the western border, with Vermont on the western shore.

New Hampshire is nearly 200 miles north to south, and an extreme east to west width of 93 miles, with the narrowest part of the state along the Canadian border. The state flower is the purple lilac, the state tree the white birch, of which New Hampshire has more than any other state. The state bird is the purple finch. The name of the state is a direct transplant from England–the county, Hampshire. Its nickname, the "Granite State," is appropriate, for New Hampshire has one of the largest and richest quarries of granite in the country. New Hampshire was the first state to declare its independence from England and to adopt a state constitution. It was one of the original 13 colonies, and was ninth among them to ratify the Constitution.

THE LAND. Except for the narrow strip of New Hampshire facing the sea in the southeast corner, most of the rest of the state is either hilly or mountainous. New Hampshire's **White Mountains,** which extend from the Canadian border south to well below the center of the state, are the highest, most celebrated, most impressive in New England. Among their several ranges are eight peaks over a mile high, with **Mount Washington,** 6,288 feet, the highest point in New England. Most of the mountains are forested, cut by deep valleys or notches. They provide New Hampshire with fine resort facilities year round. Among the mountains are some of the finest ski slopes in the country, served by winter sports resorts that draw business from all over the East and Canada.

New Hampshire has more than 1,300 lakes, many of them quite large. The largest, and perhaps the most famous, is called the most beautiful lake in New England, **Lake Winnipesaukee,** with deeply cut forested shores and more than 300 islands.

New Hampshire shares its principal river, the Connecticut, with Vermont, to the west. It grows wider and more peaceful as it flows south to the Massachusetts line, with dams providing power for commercial purposes and water areas for recreation.

The wind velocity at the crest of Mount Washington has been recorded as high as 231 mph, the highest on record for any state.

THE CLIMATE. The climate of New Hampshire provides relatively short, cool, pleasant summers and long, severe winters, usually with a great deal of snow. Several of the mountain slopes of northern New Hampshire provide good spring skiing into April. Annual rainfall ranges from 50 inches in the mountains to about 35 inches in the south near the coast. Snowfall along the coast is about 50 inches a year, but in the mountains it averages 150 inches. In Concord, the capital, in the southeast, the January average temperature is 22 degrees, the July average 70 degrees. But in Berlin, in the northern mountains, the average January temperature is 14 degrees, the average July temperature 66. Except for winter sports, the best time for a visit to New Hampshire is summer and early fall. During the fall the state is famed for brilliant autumn coloring.

THE PEOPLE. An Englishman named Captain Martin Pring is the first European known to have explored any part of New Hampshire. He landed on the coast in 1603. Champlain, the French explorer, followed him two years later, and a few years after that, the renowned Captain John Smith came to the area.

The first permanent settlements were made at Dover and Little Harbour (now town of Rye) around 1623. Other settlements were established along the coast and in the southern part of the state, chiefly along rivers where the falls provided power for village mills and for sawmills which used the fine timber. Like their neighbors Maine to the north and Massachusetts to the south, most of those who lived in New Hampshire looked to the sea for their livelihood. Shipbuilding and ocean commerce were important, and New Hampshire's sea captains were among the more skilled and famous of their day.

Until about the middle of the nineteenth century, almost everyone living in New Hampshire was of British origin. Nearly every town, except those with Indian names, had names borrowed from England, such as Plymouth, Bristol, Concord, Manchester, Colebrook, Bath, Albany, and many more.

But about the middle of the nineteenth century, building of railways and the exploitation of vast forest reserves started an industrial boom. New factories making textiles and shoes needed workers for machines. Consequently a flood of French-Canadian workers came from the north, settling in the cities, while keeping their own culture and traditions. In a few communities of New Hampshire today there are French-Catholic schools where classes are conducted partly in French.

Forty percent of the population even now is of the original British or Yankee stock, industrious people, skilled in the use of tools and in design. Many of the dwellings and public buildings, built during the Colonial period and during the early years of the nineteenth century, were beautifully designed and of great charm: village churches and meetinghouses; some handsome Colonial mansions in the larger cities, particularly the seaport of Portsmouth. Over its narrow, fast-flowing small rivers, New Hampshire built covered bridges, many still in use today. Some of the finest examples of architecture in New Hampshire are buildings on the campuses of the state's historic colleges, reflecting the English heritage and adapting the architecture of the Georgian period with superb results.

AGRICULTURE. Among the commercial crops, New Hampshire has none of importance in the national picture.

Subsistence farming is the rule, with small plots devoted chiefly to dairying, fruits, and truck crops. The chief field crop is hay.

INDUSTRY. One of New Hampshire's most important industries, providing a special opportunity for sightseeing, is the exploitation of huge deep veins of fine granite.

Other New Hampshire industries, once dominated by water-powered textile mills, include metalworking, manufacture of electrical and electronic parts, often produced in modernistic new factories built in the open country. Older plants still make quantities of shoes and textiles and many products derived from the state's forest resources, from paper to wooden furniture. Most of the manufacturing plants of the state, except those deriving their raw material from the forests, are in the south and central parts.

CITIES. New Hampshire has no large cities and few medium-sized ones. No city is over 100,000 in population, and only one, Manchester, has more than 50,000 people. Among some 730 settled areas, about 680 have less than 1,000 inhabitants, and an additional 78 towns have 2,500 or less. But much of the charm of New Hampshire lies in the relatively high proportion of pleasant small towns and villages.

CONCORD, the capital of New Hampshire, is 45 miles from the coast on the west bank of the Merrimack River. With a population of about 30,000, it is one of the larger cities of the state. Chief point of interest is the **state capitol,** built of granite from local quarries, in beautifully landscaped grounds near the center of town. In the building and on the grounds are memorials to distinguished New Hampshire citizens such as Daniel Webster and Franklin Pierce, the state's only U. S. President.

Worth seeing nearby is an **exhibit of native handicrafts** maintained by the League of New Hampshire Arts and Crafts. One of Concord's most notable industries is the **Rumford Press,** a huge printing establishment which produces millions of copies of several national magazines. In nearby Bow the **homestead of Mary Baker Eddy,** who founded the Christian Science faith, is marked by a granite pyramid.

CONWAY, with its neighbor North Conway a few miles upstate, is a shopping center in the heart of the **White Mountain National Forest.** Here are year-round resorts, some of the finest ski and winter sports areas in the country. **Mount Washington,** the crest 6,288 feet (highest point in New England), is reached by a historic and picturesque cog railway, first of its kind in the world.

HANOVER, on the western edge of the state (population 8,000) is the home of **Dartmouth College,** oldest college in New Hampshire. The campus, with its Georgian buildings and spacious tree-lined green, which it shares with the town, is regarded as one of the most handsome in the country. An annual event is Dartmouth's **winter carnival,** held each February, which attracts nation-wide attention. The new, $7 million **Hopkins Center** for creative and performing arts should be visited.

LACONIA, about 40 miles north of Concord, is the service and shopping center for an important resort district which has grown up around **Lake Winnipesaukee,** largest and most beautiful lake in New Hampshire. The lake shore is lined with resort facilities for the visitor, and the lake area is becoming an increasingly important winter sports center. Laconia is not far from an important New Hampshire shrine, the cottage **home of Daniel Webster,** outside of Franklin, about 15 miles southwest of town.

MANCHESTER, 17 miles south of Concord on the Merrimack River, is New Hampshire's largest city and its chief industrial community. Many of the city's 90,000 residents work in the mills and factories which line the river and formerly drew power from it. Manchester once claimed to have the world's largest textile mills. Though some of them have now moved to other parts of the country, textiles are still made there, as well as shoes and many other products. One good small **art gallery**, and an **institute of arts and sciences** which exhibits craft products are interesting to visit.

NORTH WOODSTOCK, about 35 miles west of Conway, is the closest town to New Hampshire's most celebrated natural wonder—the **Great Stone Face** or the Profile, a rugged face 50 feet high made by the shape of a cliff at Franconia Notch. The area is an important winter sports region. Cannon Mountain Tramway, just north of the Profile, lifts passengers more than 2,000 feet in seven and a half minutes.

PORTSMOUTH has been New Hampshire's only seaport since clipper days. A handsomely set small city, with a population of about 25,000, Portsmouth is in the southeastern part of the state on the Piscataqua River opposite southern Maine. It is now a chief resort center for the coast region of New Hampshire and service center for a large U.S. naval base across the river in Maine. The small city has great charm, with some notable streets lined with fine old houses, relics of its seagoing past. The most famous of these is the **John Paul Jones House,** home of the naval hero while his fighting ship, the *Ranger,* was being outfitted in the nearby yards. An offbeat but pleasant sightseeing trip by boat can be taken from Portsmouth on a steamer to the tiny cluster of islands called **Isles of Shoals,** a few miles offshore.

The coast of New Hampshire, about 18 miles southwest of the city, is lined with resort communities linked by a pleasant coastal highway. Of them, the most important are **Rye** and **Hampton beaches,** each with a state park.

Portsmouth is the nearest city to the charming town of **Exeter,** 20 miles to the southwest, which has grown up around the campus of historic **Phillips Exeter Academy,** first opened in 1783. The campus, with towering, graceful elms, has several buildings noted for their nearly perfect adaptation of Georgian architecture.

SPORTS AND RECREATION. Along the coast to the south of Portsmouth, around the shores of Lake Winnipesaukee and throughout the White Mountains are a wide range of sports facilities. The lake provides excellent boating and fishing, and has several fine beaches. Trout fishing is especially good in the mountains, where there are also hundreds of miles of hiking trails. In all areas there are golf courses, many of which are used for championships.

Although New Hampshire draws thousands of summer visitors, it is more well-known for the number and quality of its winter sports facilities. Recreation areas in the White Mountains offer skiing, tobogganing, snowshoe hiking, sledding, and winter picnics.

SPECIAL EVENTS. Focal points of winter activity are **winter carnivals,** held yearly at Manchester and the University of New Hampshire at Durham as well as at Dartmouth, and the **World's Sled Dog Championships,** held annually on the last weekend in February in Laconia.

Vermont

Vermont holds down the northwest corner of New England, and is second in size among the New England states, with 9,609 square miles. It is forty-third in area among the states of the United States, but in population Vermont, with about 445,000 people, is the smallest of the New England states and forty-ninth in population in the states of the Union.

Vermont is roughly rectangular in shape, wider in the north than in the south. The longest border is across the north, about 100 miles, and the greatest north-south distance of the state is 160 miles. The narrowest east-west dimension is the Massachusetts border, only 36 miles wide.

Vermont's state tree is the sugar maple, which accounts for one of the state's most important products, maple syrup. The state bird is the hermit thrush, state flower, the red clover. The name Vermont is a corruption of two French words meaning "green mountain," given it by the French explorers who first saw the area. Although not one of the 13 colonies, Vermont was the next state admitted to the Union, in 1791.

THE LAND. Vermont has three important natural features, two of which it shares with adjoining areas. East is the course of the Connecticut River, which becomes larger, more important and useful as it flows south toward Massachusetts. Dams in it provide power and recreational opportunity. Exclusively Vermont's are the **Green Mountains,** superb range of forested mountains which extend the length of the state from Canada to Massachusetts, containing peaks and ridges rising to more than 4,000 feet. **Mount Mansfield,** 4,393 feet, is the highest point in the state. Much of the mountain area is within **Green Mountain National Forest,** giving the state a unique recreational feature both winter and summer. Running the length of the mountain range along the crest of the ridges is a famous hiking path, the **Long Trail.**

The third important feature is **Lake Champlain,** one of the most beautiful lakes in the country, 125 miles long, varying in width from a half-mile to twenty miles. Actually, it is a flooded valley between mountain ranges, with the Adirondacks rising from its western shore, the Green Mountains from its eastern shore. The Vermont shore of the lake is lined with summer colonies, linked by stretches of scenic highway.

Eastern Vermont, stretching west from the Connecticut River, is chiefly a region of rolling hills and upland areas. Among them are most of the state's farmlands.

The **Connecticut River** is Vermont's only large river. Several small ones, none navigable, flow into the Connecticut. In addition to Lake Champlain, there are a few fairly large and attractive lakes in scattered sections of the state.

THE CLIMATE. Vermont's climate is humid, with annual rainfall from 35 to 45 inches, much of it accounted for by winter snows, up to 120 inches in the Green Mountain area. They provide some of the finest skiing in the East. Winters are long and cold, with subzero temperatures not uncommon. Summers are cool and sunny, with temperatures both winter and summer more moderate in the southern part. In Rutland, in the south, January average is about 20 degrees, July average about 70 degrees. In Burlington, to the north, the January average is about 18 degrees, the July average about 68 degrees. Except for winter sports, for which Vermont has some of the best facilities in the East, the pleasantest time for a visit is summer, from about mid-June to early September.

THE PEOPLE. The first Europeans to visit the state were French. Samuel de Champlain, for whom Lake Champlain is named, explored that body of water in 1609, and a few years later the French tried to establish a military post. But the first permanent settlement did not occur until 1724, when a frontier fort was built by Englishmen from Massachusetts near the present site of Brattleboro. Thereafter, almost all of Vermont's settlement was made by people of English stock from New Hampshire, Massachusetts, and New York. Their descendants account for the majority of the present permanent population. However, during the nineteenth century, there were small streams of migration from areas of Europe and the British Isles. An early group were Irish, who came to help build the railways and open the marble quarries. Later (and still continuing) came French from Canada to the north, to work in textile mills, so that in several textile towns in the northern part of the state there are now French schools and churches and French is a community language. In a few towns there are Welsh settlers, who worship in churches celebrated for stately music. In the quarry regions are many skilled Scottish and Italian stonecutters. In the early years of settlement Vermonters were farmers, but in recent years native Vermonters have tended to abandon their farms and move to the cities. Many Vermont farms have been acquired by artists and writers from New York City and other urban areas, who consider a Vermont farm a perfect sanctuary.

AGRICULTURE. Most of Vermont's farms are small and many are of the subsistence type. There are less than four million acres in farmlands, of which only about a million acres are in crops. The most important farming activity is dairying; making hay and corn for silage are also important. In the Connecticut River Valley potatoes are grown commercially, and Vermont turkeys, which have a national market, are an important specialty product. But the most celebrated of all Vermont's farm products is maple syrup, of which the state produces more than 600,000 gallons a year from more than two and a half million maple trees, its grade and character rigorously maintained by law. Maple products are among the best gift buys in the state.

INDUSTRY. Vermont leads the nation in the production of marble and granite, with quarries and the mills for finishing the quality stone an interesting sightseeing novelty for visitors. Marble centers are in the western part of the state, the granite being quarried in the eastern slopes of the Green Mountains, in and around Barre. Most of the stone goes into monuments and buildings. Other mineral resources are asbestos, produced from the country's largest asbestos deposits; talc; and small but commercially workable deposits of limestone and soapstone.

Most mills and factories of Vermont, in addition to those devoted to shaping quarry products, concentrate on making precision machinery and machine tools, lumber and wood products, paper, textiles (chiefly woolens), and plastics. There are many small handicraft shops, most producing handloomed fabrics and novelty woodenware.

CITIES. Vermont is almost entirely a state of picturesque small towns and villages. No city in the state exceeds 50,000 in population, and only one is larger than 25,000. The state has close to 700 communities with less than 1,000 residents. But for the visitor much of the charm of the state lies in the fact that it has no big urban center, and that hundreds of the Vermont villages have distinctive character. A number of the larger towns are important both for the sights and facilities they have and as bases in areas of interest.

BARRE, six miles from Montpelier, with a population of about 10,000, is one of the world's largest granite-producing centers. Worth seeing are the granite plants where huge blocks are cut, shaped, polished, and carved. Some of the large quarries lie chiefly south of the city, with probably the largest of the world at **Graniteville,** three miles southeast.

About midway between Burlington and Montpelier, north of the main highway, is Vermont's most celebrated winter sports area, on the slopes of and near Mount Mansfield (altitude 4,393 feet), highest peak in the Green Mountains.

BENNINGTON, on the west, is actually two towns with a combined population of over 14,000. In the valley is a relatively modern, congested industrial center of little interest, but on the hill to the west, Old Bennington has some fine houses and monuments which mark the Battle of Bennington, an engagement in the Revolutionary War. Among the houses is the oldest frame house in Vermont, built in 1762. East of Bennington, winding through the mountains, is a scenic mountain road, leading to Brattleboro, 42 miles away. **Brattleboro,** offering little of interest or facility for the visitor, is an industrial center, with a population of about 12,000.

BURLINGTON, with a population of over 38,000, is Vermont's largest city, as well as one of the most interesting and attractive. It has a commanding setting along the crest of bluffs overlooking Lake Champlain, and a pleasant park provides fine views of the lake and of the Adirondack Mountains on the western shore. The **University of Vermont,** chartered in 1791, is one of the oldest colleges in the country. It spreads over rolling hills in the eastern part of the town, has some buildings of interest, including a museum with a good collection of Oriental art. Seven miles south of Burlington, on the lake shore, at the village of **Shelburne,** there is an unusual museum with a group of reconstructed buildings from pioneer days, a covered bridge, and a former lake steamer.

MONTPELIER, capital of Vermont, is one of the smallest state capitals in the country, with a population of less than 9,000. It is an important insurance city, with one company having its headquarters in the state's largest office building. A large granite-finishing center for quarried stone is nearby, with several buildings of granite worth noting (especially the **state capitol** and nearby **supreme court building).**

RUTLAND, about 60 miles south of Burlington on the western slopes of the Green Mountains, is Vermont's second largest city. It has a population of about 19,000, and is the principal center for Vermont's important marble quarrying and finishing business. Worth seeing are several buildings and monuments of gleaming white marble. Rutland is near one of the most attractive mountain villages in the East, the town of **Woodstock,** set in the eastern slopes of the Green Mountains, 45 miles away. It has some notable Colonial buildings, an oval village green, and a celebrated covered bridge. For winter sports fans it claims to be the oldest ski center in the country, with ski trails, slopes, and jumps all around. It is also the nearest point to a Vermont shrine in the tiny village of **Plymouth,** a few miles west, the homestead where Calvin Coolidge was born, including a new museum.

STOWE, chief center in the winter sports area, is a village of about 2,000 permanent residents, though in the winter months it may have three or four times that many visitors. The area around Stowe has an unusually long winter season, with exceptionally heavy falls of snow. It boasts some of the finest ski trails in the East, with an aerial chair lift four and a half miles long, one of the longest and the highest in the world, to the crest of **Mount Mansfield.** The region is a summer resort section, when a toll road to the crest of Mount Mansfield is open to cars.

SPORTS AND RECREATION. Though Vermont's fame is as a winter sports center, the state has much quiet interest for the summer visitor. The Green Mountains stretch the length of the state, studded with small resorts laced with mountain trails, including the celebrated Long Trail. The mountains offer excellent stream **fishing** (fly casting), and, in the northern part of the state, lake fishing for trout.

The west shore of Lake Champlain is lined with small resorts and good beaches. The lake has fine fishing, with boats, gear and guides widely available. It is one of the best and most interesting boating areas in the East. Sightseeing trips on the lake can be taken from several centers, particularly Burlington.

For the mobile sightseer, Vermont has scenic highway stretches with dramatic mountain backdrops. There are good small museums, attractive and highly photogenic small villages. More than 60 state parks and forests, all of which offer picnic facilities, most of them—**bathing, boating, camping,** and **fishing,** are in the mountain area and along the shore of Lake Champlain.

SPECIAL EVENTS. As in Maine and

New Hampshire, many of Vermont's important events take place during the winter season. **Ski competitions** are held from January to March at resorts near Middlebury, Waitsfield, Brattleboro, Stowe, Manchester, and Rutland. Other interesting events are the **Lumberjack Roundup** at Lake Dunmore in mid-August; **forest festivals** throughout the state in October; and **foliage tours** in Bennington, Woodstock, Cabot, Calais, Stowe, Danville, and Walden.

Massachusetts

Among the New England states, Massachusetts is fourth in size, with slightly more than 8,200 square miles, and is forty-fifth in size among the states of the Union. Though relatively small in area, Massachusetts is a giant in population, with over five million people, more than half the total for New England and ranking tenth in the United States.

Massachusetts is a central New England state, with its borders touching all of the other six states in the area except Maine. Most of it is a horizontal panel with an extreme breadth of 110 miles and a total length of 190 miles from east to west. To its west is New York State, along the northern border are Vermont and New Hampshire, and on the south are Connecticut and Rhode Island. On its eastern side, facing the Atlantic Ocean, the panel spreads into a gaping mouth, which is the great harbor of Boston. The jaw of the mouth is the curious hook of Cape Cod.

The state flower of Massachusetts is the rare plant known as trailing arbutus, or mayflower. The name, Massachusetts, derives from a combination of Indian words meaning "the place of the great mountain." Massachusetts' nickname is "Bay State" or "Old Colony State," and the state bird is the chickadee. Massachusetts was one of the original 13 colonies, the sixth to become a state of the Union.

THE LAND. The surface of Massachusetts is divided into three areas: the western uplands, which lie west of the Connecticut River; the central uplands, an area of rolling hills east of the river; and the coastal area. The western highlands are a southern extension of the Green Mountains of Vermont to the north, running north to south through the state in parallel wooded ranges, both playgrounds and centers of regional culture. Among them, crests rise to more than 3,000 feet, with **Mount Graylock,** the highest point in the state, 3,491 feet. Called the **Berkshire Hills,** they are lived-in mountains, with many resorts and recreational areas. Between the two upland areas of Massachusetts, stretching north to south, is a fertile region called **Pioneer Valley,** where the Connecticut River flows. Scattered through the valley on both sides of the river are 70 towns and cities, including several of Massachusetts' famed college towns. The central upland area of rolling hills contains some of Massachusetts' best farmland area. It has one distinctive feature—a large lake, called **Quabbin Reservoir,** one of the largest artificial bodies of water in the nation used only for domestic water supply. Authentic dinosaur tracks are a scientific curiosity of the region.

The natural features of eastern Massachusetts include the rocky promontory called **Cape Ann.** South of this is a succession of harbors, including those of **Salem** and **Boston,** the latter one of the finest natural harbors on the Atlantic Coast. Some distance below Boston is **Plymouth Harbor,** and just below that the strange, crooked arm of **Cape Cod,** a huge sandspit of low, rolling hills covered with scrub pine. In the Atlantic below Cape Cod are two celebrated coastal islands, both important resort areas, **Martha's Vineyard** and **Nantucket,** triangular in shape and similar in character. Below Cape Cod, the Massachusetts shore swings sharply to the west, has several harbors. One is the old whaling base of **New Bedford,** protected from the open sea by a chain of offshore islands called the **Elizabeth Islands.**

In addition to Quabbin Reservoir, Massachusetts has hundreds of small natural lakes. Of the rivers in Massachusetts, the largest and most important is the Connecticut, although it belongs only in part to Massachusetts.

THE CLIMATE. The climate of Massachusetts, though more temperate than northern areas of New England, is relatively humid, with annual rainfall of from 40 to 45 inches, somewhat heavier in summer than winter. Winter snows are often quite heavy and snowstorms come on abruptly—sudden weather changes are likely to occur throughout the year. Summer temperatures are often quite hot, making late spring through early fall the most pleasant time for a visit. The average January temperature in Boston is 29 degrees; the average July temperature, 72 degrees. In the Berkshire Hills, along the western side of the state, both winter and summer temperatures are somewhat lower than along the coast.

THE PEOPLE. Although the actual settlement of Massachusetts did not begin until the Pilgrims landed in 1620, the coastal area of the state had been known and explored long before that. It is fairly well established that Norsemen landed on the Massachusetts coast as early as 1000, and it is certain that the English navigator, John Cabot, arrived a few years after Columbus discovered the New World. Cape Cod had been explored and named 18 years before the Pilgrims landed there, but with the settlement of the Pilgrims, first at Cape Cod and then at Plymouth, the permanent settlement of all New England began in earnest. Salem was established in 1626, Boston in 1630.

Many of the early settlers looked to the sea for survival, and began to develop commercial fishing and build ships that could carry cargoes all over the world. Boston became an international port and a center for trade and manufacture, the greatest in New England, and for a time the most important in the Colonial world. Fleet sailing vessels, built in the yards of Massachusetts, carrying Yankee captains and crews, developed profitable trade with the rest of the world, particularly the Orient. At the same time, shops and factories were started. In 1814, the first power loom in the United States was established at Waltham to revolutionize the textile industry, and Massachusetts became a great textile center. Among citizens of Massachusetts were able craftsmen and designers. One, Paul Revere, was a pioneer in the development of metalcraft—a great Massachusetts metalworking company today bears his name. During the early half of the nineteenth century, most of the migration to Massachusetts from across the seas came from western Europe, Britain and Ireland. Today Boston has a larger Irish population than any city in the country except New York. The continued industrialization of Massachusetts began to draw workers from other countries of Europe.

But long before the migrations of foreign peoples to Massachusetts began, Massachusetts had become a political and cultural hub of the New World. Its development in the arts, in politics, and in industry has been steady, and today Massachusetts is a leader in all three areas.

AGRICULTURE. Massachusetts is not generally regarded as an agricultural state, as most of its farms are small, and much of the farmland area is woodland and pasture. In the west, dairying is important, and hay, corn, potatoes, and oats are produced in commercial quantities. The Connecticut River Valley farms produce tobacco, grown under shade, which is used for cigar wrappers, while cranberries and quantities of vegetables are grown in boglands on and near Cape Cod. The Cape also produces strawberries, while apples, generally in small orchard tracts, are grown throughout the state.

Massachusetts leads all of New England in the catch of commercial fish, and Boston has one of the largest fishing fleets in the country. The port of Gloucester to the north is also important. The catch includes cod, haddock, mackerel, halibut, sea and river herring, flounder, shad, bluefish, lobster, and shellfish.

INDUSTRY. Among the states of the Union, Massachusetts has a unique preeminence in industry and manufacture. Some of the earliest and most successful factories in the country were developed in Massachusetts, and today the number of products produced in the mills and factories of the state defies listing. Among the products are fabrics of all kinds, particularly wool, worsted, and cotton goods. Also important in the national production pattern are machinery, machine tools, fabricated metal products, paper, chemicals, furniture, rubber products, and electrical equipment. Boston, the great industrial hub of the state, alone has more than 2,000 factories which turn out products as diverse as razor blades and electronic accessories. Boston ranks near the top among cities in the country in shoes, textiles, and in food products. In recent years, Boston, and the cluster of important manufacturing cities which surround it, has forged ahead rapidly as a center for technical research, leading to a whole new group of manufactured products, particularly in the field of electronics. Boston is also an important financial and insurance center, and has the world's largest fish-freezing plant.

CITIES. Although Massachusetts has hundreds of pleasant small towns and villages, it is essentially an urban state; more than 84 percent of all its residents live in cities. There are four cities in the state with more than 100,000 population, and one of these, Boston, is the tightly built core of an urban area in which about four million people live. In addition to having more and larger cities than any other state in New England, Massachusetts has many that are of special interest to the visitor. Some of them are unique both in setting and character. Of all the cities of Massachusetts, the most important one for the visitor, from nearly every standpoint, is the metropolis of Boston.

BOSTON is physically the smallest in area among big American cities. Within the city limits of about 47 square miles live around 640,000 people, but almost no one thinks of Boston proper as the limit of the city. Metropolitan Boston includes about 100 communities that cluster around the great central harbor, all closely linked to the core of Boston itself by a network of highways, bridges, tunnels, rail lines. Among them are cities such as Brookline, birthplace of **John Fitzgerald Kennedy.**

The physical pattern of Boston involves three irregular triangles, with the apex of each at the harbor. The southern triangle has the Charles River on the north, the harbor to the east, and downtown Boston at its tip. Cambridge dominates the second triangle, with historic **Bunker Hill** on the harbor at its tip. The third triangle lies to the east, and is called East Boston.

Of the whole of Boston, the part of greatest interest for the visitor is the older downtown section near the harbor. There the pattern of old, winding narrow streets is both complex and confusing, and results in most visitors getting lost without the help of a detailed map. On a hill near its center is Boston's most distinguished building, the historic gold-domed **State House.** It faces **Boston Common,** one of the oldest and most interesting public parks in the country. Fashionable **Beacon Hill** lies to the west of the State House along Beacon Street. West of the Common lies Boston's **Public Garden,** with a lake famed for its swan boats, and massive beds of flowers seasonally changed. Beyond the Public Garden, along the Charles River, lies the historic, once fashionable district called **Back Bay.**

Few cities in the country offer the visitor more sights to see than Boston. They include buildings and monuments of all kinds, closely related to the city's long and colorful past, many of them of national significance, several of great architectural interest. Boston is also a fine base for visiting many nearby places of interest.

A sightseeing must for most visitors is the **State House** on Beacon Hill,

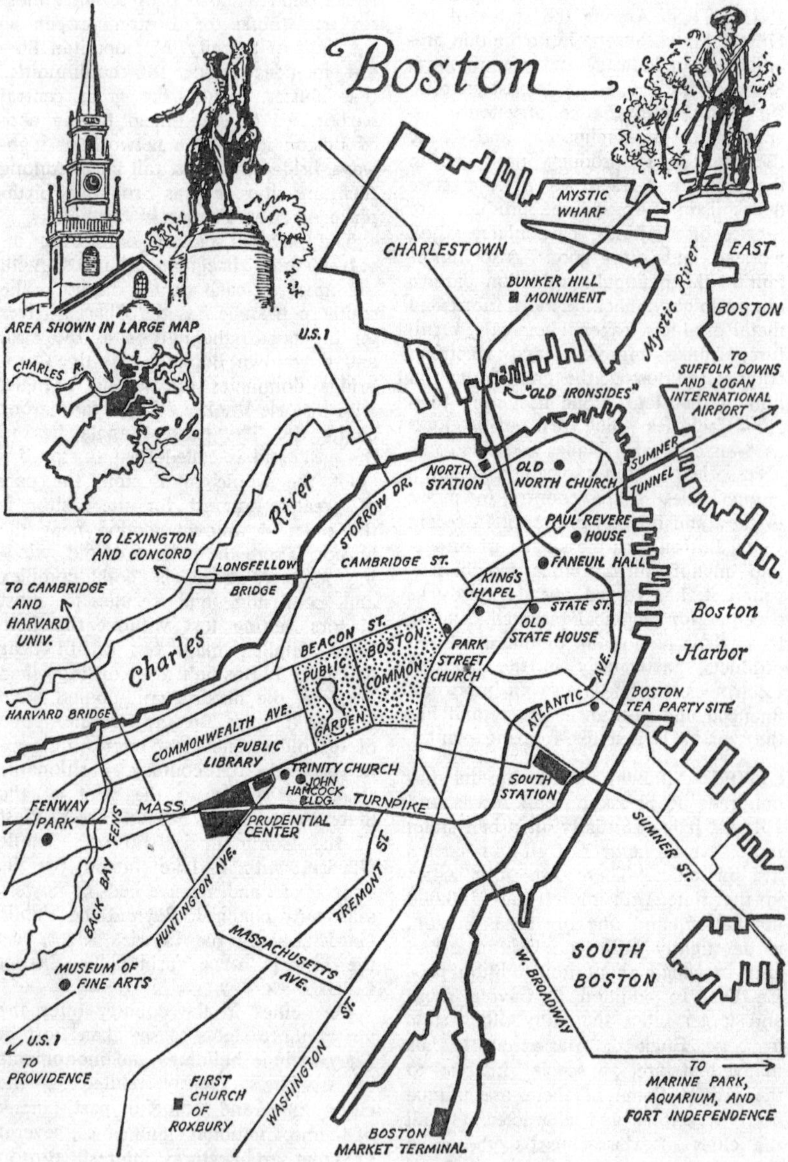
Boston
AREA SHOWN IN LARGE MAP
CHARLES R.
U.S.1
CHARLESTOWN
MYSTIC WHARF
BUNKER HILL MONUMENT
Mystic River
EAST BOSTON
TO SUFFOLK DOWNS AND LOGAN INTERNATIONAL AIRPORT
"OLD IRONSIDES"
NORTH STATION
OLD NORTH CHURCH
SUMNER TUNNEL
STORROW DR.
River
PAUL REVERE HOUSE
FANEUIL HALL
TO LEXINGTON AND CONCORD
LONGFELLOW BRIDGE
CAMBRIDGE ST.
KING'S CHAPEL
STATE ST.
OLD STATE HOUSE
TO CAMBRIDGE AND HARVARD UNIV.
Boston Harbor
BEACON ST.
BOSTON COMMON
PUBLIC GARDEN
PARK STREET CHURCH
Charles
ATLANTIC AVE.
BOSTON TEA PARTY SITE
HARVARD BRIDGE
COMMONWEALTH AVE.
PUBLIC LIBRARY
TRINITY CHURCH
JOHN HANCOCK BLDG.
SOUTH STATION
FENWAY PARK
MASS.
TURNPIKE
PRUDENTIAL CENTER
FENS
SUMNER ST.
HUNTINGTON AVE.
TREMONT ST.
BACK BAY
MASSACHUSETTS AVE.
SOUTH BOSTON
W. BROADWAY
MUSEUM OF FINE ARTS
U.S.1
TO PROVIDENCE
FIRST CHURCH OF ROXBURY
WASHINGTON ST.
BOSTON MARKET TERMINAL
TO MARINE PARK, AQUARIUM, AND FORT INDEPENDENCE

started in 1795, one of the city's handsomest and most historic buildings. A particular novelty is Boston's great sacred codfish in the **Hall of Representatives.** Most visitors find a leisurely stroll through **Boston Common** facing the State House rewarding, as well as a walk along Beacon Street and through nearby **Louisburg Square.** Not far from the State House is **Old North Church,** oldest church building in Boston. From its spire, Paul Revere received the light signal that started him on his historic ride. Not far away is **Faneuil Hall,** at Dock Square, built in 1742 as a city market, first one of its kind in the country. In the same area is the oldest wooden frame house in Boston, the **Paul Revere House,** believed to have been built in 1660. Nearby churches of interest include **King's Chapel,** two blocks east of the State House, the first Protestant-Episcopal church in New England, with a burial ground beside it containing graves going back to 1630, among them tombs of many eminent dead. Another church, the **Park Street Church,** just a block south of the State House, has one of the loveliest spires anywhere. The graveyard which adjoins it contains the graves of such noted sons of Massachusetts as Paul Revere and Samuel Adams.

Flanking the Charles River, about a half-mile west of Beacon Hill, is a handsome, relatively modern park worth visiting, called the **Esplanade.** At the north end of it, overlooking the river, is one of the most remarkable museums anywhere, the new **Museum of Science,** first in the country to combine natural history, science, industry, public health, and a planetarium. Relatively modern sights of interest west of the Public Garden and the Back Bay district are in the **Copley Square** area, with Boston's distinguished **public library** and historic **Trinity Church.** Nearby is the **John Hancock Building,** Boston's tallest building, new and striking in design, with an observation deck on top that offers a fine view.

Still farther west is the group of sights and facilities that draw visitors from all over the world. They include the **Christian Science headquarters** buildings, including the mother church and the **Christian Science Monitor** publishing headquarters. Nearby is Boston's **Museum of Fine Arts,** one of the great museums of the country. Boston's second highest building, 52-story **Prudential Tower,** is located in the Back Bay area. Set on a 31-acre site, the **Prudential Center,** in which the Tower is located, also includes a 1,000-room hotel, banking facilities, restaurants, and shops.

Sights near Boston's harbor include the **Bunker Hill Monument,** 220 feet high, in the section known as **Charlestown,** marking the site of the Battle of Bunker Hill. Nearby, in the **Boston Navy Yard,** is exhibited the fighting ship *Constitution,* known as "Old Ironsides."

CAMBRIDGE, opposite Boston across the Charles River to the north, has two great universities. One is **Harvard,** the first college to be established in the country. Among its hundreds of buildings are several of distinguished design. In them are fine museums, including the world's best collection of botanically accurate glass flowers. Not far away is the **Massachusetts Institute of Technology,** generally referred to as M.I.T., with a large campus and many buildings. One of the world's greatest scientific and technical schools, it has exhibits in those fields open to visitors. Of special interest are the **M.I.T. chapel** and **The Kresge Auditorium.**

CONCORD, a few miles west of Lexington, is a residential town of great charm, and like Lexington has an important historic site—the Revolutionary battleground where was fired "the shot heard round the world." Also like Lexington, Concord has beautiful old homes, one the home of Ralph Waldo Emerson. There is a fascinating antiquarian museum and just outside the town is **Walden Pond,** where Henry David Thoreau lived and wrote.

On the fringe of metropolitan Boston to the northeast is a recently reconstructed exhibit of unusual interest, the **Saugus Iron Works,** an authentic restoration of the seventeenth-century original, America's first facility for making iron and steel.

GLOUCESTER, home of one of the biggest fishing fleets in the country, manned chiefly by Portuguese, is chief community of an important resort region. Resort communities are on the coast of **Cape Ann** all around it.

LEXINGTON, to the northwest of metropolitan Boston, with a population of about 31,000, is a quiet, residential suburb with a historic heart. Millions of visitors flock to it to see the village green, **site of the Battle of Lexington,** the first engagement of the Revolutionary War. Worth seeing nearby are old and beautiful houses dating from Colonial days.

NEW BEDFORD, 36 miles southwest of Plymouth, is an industrial city, known for textiles, which has a population of more than 100,000. It is important to the visitor because of its association with whaling days, fully shown in a fine **whaling museum** and with a scale model of a famed whaling vessel.

PITTSFIELD, the chief city in the Berkshire Hills, on Massachusetts' western edge, has a population of about 57,000, and is both an industrial and a cultural center. Its plants produce paper, textiles and electrical products. The pleasant mountain slopes in and around the town have long been home for writers and musicians and the setting for small summer resorts. A fashionable one nearby is **Lenox,** where a summer music festival is staged at **Tanglewood.**

PLYMOUTH, about 40 miles southeast of Boston, has a permanent population of about 18,000, but draws more than 100,000 visitors each year to see its special historic relics. These include **Plymouth Rock,** where the Pilgrims are believed to have stepped ashore from the sea, and various monuments, buildings, and exhibits, including Plymouth Plantation, with a replica of the Pilgrim vessel, the *Mayflower,* and reconstructions of pioneer dwellings.

SALEM, about 14 miles northeast of Boston on the coast, facing a large harbor, is one of the most picturesque towns in New England. Notorious for the witch trials, it was famous as a seaport during sailing days, and as the home of Nathaniel Hawthorne, who made famous the town's celebrated **House of Seven Gables.** Salem has a fine small museum, and a number of houses distinguished for architecture and historical interest. Interesting to see is **Pioneer Village,** where early houses have been reconstructed. About 15 miles northeast of Salem, on the southern side of the rocky, picturesque Cape Ann peninsula, is Massachusetts' fishing port, Gloucester.

SPRINGFIELD, the largest city to the south, is an industrial center for the manufacture of machinery, metal products, and chemicals. North of Springfield are several college towns. About ten miles north, near Holyoke, is **South Hadley,** home of **Mount Holyoke College,** oldest women's college in the United States. A few miles beyond Holyoke is **Northampton,** home of **Smith College;** northeast of there is **Amherst,** site of **Amherst College** and the **University of Massachusetts.** About 20 miles farther north is industrial **Greenfield,** which makes nuts, bolts, and fine cutlery. West of Greenfield is **Williamstown,** home of **Williams College,** and to the south, **Deerfield** is a pioneer village of great charm.

WORCESTER is another important industrial city, 40 miles west of Boston, and linked to it by main highways including the Massachusetts Turnpike. More than 500 factories in Worcester produce a variety of products including watch springs, rugs, abrasives, machine tools, and textiles. It has a nationally famous art museum, with a distinguished collection, and a special museum featuring arms and armor.

Several charming small towns and

villages include **Sandwich** on Cape Cod, one-time home of the nation's largest glass industry; the reconstruction of a pioneer village just west of **Sturbridge,** about 30 miles east of Springfield; the fashionable resort town of **Great Barrington** in the Berkshire Hills, as well as **Stockbridge,** a few miles to the north. The home and studio of Daniel Chester French and many more are scattered over the state and on the islands of Nantucket and Martha's Vineyard, which have **Nantucket** and **Edgartown.**

SPORTS AND RECREATION. Few states in the country offer more variety, diversion, and recreation than Massachusetts, which has four special resort districts. In the west are the **Berkshire Hills,** with dozens of small resorts set among wooded slopes and in the high valleys, popular both with summer visitors and as centers for winter sports.

Northeast of Boston is the rocky, granitic peninsula of **Cape Ann** with historic towns and some of the oldest resorts in the East. Southeast of Boston, starting just south of Plymouth and extending for about 100 miles, is the arc of **Cape Cod.** On the Cape, one of the most popular beach and recreation areas in the country, visitors can have the quiet and seclusion of the National Seashore, or the charm and bustle of **Provincetown, Hyannis,** or several other resort towns.

South of Cape Cod and connected to it by ocean ferry are two celebrated resort islands, **Martha's Vineyard,** and, to the west and farther out to sea, **Nantucket.** All the shore resorts of Massachusetts offer beaches, boating, and fishing.

Massachusetts has more than 60 state parks and recreational areas, most of them in scenic regions. Nearly all provide picnicking and fishing, many boating and bathing.

SPECIAL EVENTS. One of the most anticipated yearly events is the **Berkshire Festival of the Boston Symphony Orchestra,** held each July and August at Tanglewood Music Shed. Among the other annual observances are **Winter Carnival,** Greenfield, in January; **Patriot's Day,** commemorated in Boston, Concord, and Lexington on April 19; **Boston Arts Festival,** June; **Jacob's Pillow Dance Festival,** Becket, July through September; **yacht races,** Edgartown, Quincy, Marblehead, and other coastal towns, July and August; **Pilgrim Thanksgiving Day,** Plymouth, November; **Forefathers' Day,** marking the landing of the Pilgrims at Plymouth, December 21.

Rhode Island

Among the states of New England and the nation, Rhode Island is the smallest. It is about 1,200 square miles in area, of which some 150 square miles are water. In that area live about 920,000 people. Fourth largest in population in New England, and thirty-ninth in the United States, Rhode Island is the second most densely settled state, with over 800 people for each square mile of land.

Rhode Island is in the southern tier of the New England states. Its neighbors are, on the north and east, Massachusetts; on the west, Connecticut. To the south is the open sea, to which Rhode Island has access by Narragansett Bay, one of the great harbors of the world.

In dimension Rhode Island is 48 miles north to south, 37 miles east to west. The name of the state derives from the island of Rhodes, largest island in Narragansett Bay, so named by the mariner, Verrazano, who discovered it in 1524. He thought it looked like the Greek island of Rhodes. The state flower of Rhode Island is the violet, the state tree the red maple, the state bird the chicken, the Rhode Island Red. A state monument has been erected to it at Adamsville.

THE LAND. Narragansett Bay spreads from Providence south to the coast 28 miles away, varying in width from two to twelve miles. In the bay are several big islands, the largest, Rhode Island, having the state's historic resort city of Newport. Other islands include Conanicut and Prudence.

From the western side of Narragansett Bay, low rolling hills rise toward the Connecticut line. The highest point in the state is only a little more than 800 feet. In the hills to the north there are a few small lakes, natural and man-made. The seacoast of Rhode Island, from Watch Hill in the west to beyond Newport in the east, is a succession of sandspits, cliffs and barrier beaches backed by salt ponds and lagoons. Ten miles offshore is Block Island, linked to the mainland by ferry. Although Rhode Island is 67 percent woodland, most of it is not suitable for commercial development. The largest of its rivers is the Blackstone, which flows into Narragansett Bay at the capital city of Providence.

THE CLIMATE. Rhode Island's climate is more mild than is general throughout New England although its humidity is average. Its proximity to the sea tends to temper weather. The state has approximately 40 inches of annual rainfall, fairly well distributed throughout the year. Winter snowfalls are not usually heavy. The range of temperature varies about ten degrees throughout the state, with Providence having a January average of 29 degrees, a July average of 72 degrees. The most pleasant time for a visit is from early spring to late fall.

THE PEOPLE. Though the coast of Rhode Island was discovered as early as 1524, settlement of the state did not occur until Roger Williams, banished from the Massachusetts Bay Colony, migrated south in 1636 and selected the site of the present city of Providence as a place for settlement. For many years after that the unique religious freedom which Williams maintained attracted special settlers, including Quakers and Jews, primarily from England and Holland. As a result, one of the most historic and beautiful buildings in the area is the oldest Jewish Synagogue in the United States. In the early days, shipbuilding and seafaring activities based on the superb protected water of Narragansett Bay predominated. Newport became a big seaport, with Newport captains engaging in the "triangular trade": rum, Negro slaves, and molasses. The first suggestion of Rhode Island's future importance as an industrial area came with the establishment of the first United States cotton mill, in 1790. It presaged the growth of a huge textile industry developed within the next generation.

As late as the middle of the nineteenth century, more than 95 percent of the people in Rhode Island were of British stock. Then, as industry began to boom, other foreign strains came to Rhode Island to work in new, fast-developing mills. One large group was Italian, an ethnic strain that accounts for about 16 percent of the state's present population. Another large group was French-Canadian. They established French-speaking districts, sent their children to French schools. A particular French-Canadian community is the city of Woonsocket. In the middle of the nineteenth century came large numbers of Irish, to be followed by Poles and, still later, Portuguese immigrants. An unusual foreign group is a colony of Syrians, skilled as weavers of damask, who have come within recent years to work in textile mills.

The notable examples of architectural design which the state has were built by the early English settlers, the English people of the Colonial period, and by the very rich and socially prominent who developed Newport as an opulent resort community. Some of the best examples of both in Newport include Colonial mansions of the Georgian period, several notable churches, including the Touro Synagogue, oldest in the country. Also in Newport are the flamboyant summer "cottages" of the very rich, copied from French châteaux and European palaces. Some homes, including **The Breakers, Marble House,** and **The Elms,** are open to summer visitors.

AGRICULTURE. Farming in Rhode Island is relatively unimportant, with 104,000 acres devoted to it. Of these, much is pasture land, involving substantial dairying. Rhode Island's most notable single farm activity is poultry-raising, originating with the famous red hen which bears the state's name. Miscellaneous crops include hay, potatoes, corn, fruits of various kinds.

Rhode Island's harvest of the sea includes commercial quantities of lobsters, hard-shell clams (or quahaugs), scallops, flounder, bluefish, herring, swordfish.

INDUSTRY. Rhode Island leads the nation in costume jewelry manufacture, and it has more industrial workers in proportion to the total population than any other state. Providence, with the communities around it, is one of the great industrial districts of the world. The textiles produced in the district include woolens, worsted, cotton, silk, rayon. Other manufactured goods are machinery, machine tools, rubber goods, silverware, and food products. A specialty product is fishing tackle. One city, Pawtucket, just outside of Providence, contains the oldest textile mill in the country. Nearby is a plant which is the oldest and one of the biggest makers of baking powder in the country. One of the most important activities in Rhode Island is based on several large naval installations, chiefly in and near Newport at Quonset Point.

CITIES. From the standpoint of the visitor, Rhode Island has only two important cities. They are the capital, **Providence,** center of a huge industrial area, and **Newport,** a resort and great naval town. Eight cities have a population of more than 25,000, while four have more than 50,000. The state is essentially urban in character.

NEWPORT crowds the tip of slender Rhode Island, 25 miles south of Providence by water, 30 by highway. The city has a permanent population of about 34,000 people (exclusive of Navy personnel), most of whom are engaged in service activities relating to the two facets of Newport's character, its resort facilities and a service center for the United States Navy. Sites of interest in the town include several buildings of unusual architectural character, the historic **Newport Casino,** and several of the great mansions, which, though no longer lived in, are open to visitors and reveal in their design and furnishings a pattern of life which no longer exists. Of these, the most celebrated is the Vanderbilt mansion called **The Breakers.** Newport has good beaches, well-known **cliff walk,** and a three-mile-long footpath, offering fine sea views.

Other towns or districts of Rhode Island which offer some special interest for the visitor include **Narragansett,** an old and famous beach resort long identified with its wealthy summer colonists. It is near Port Judith, from which a summer ferry connects with offshore **Block Island,** an isolated resort island which supports a commercial fish industry. West along the coast is the resort town of **Watch Hill,** an old, fashionable community with a fine beach. Summer colonies and beach communities stretch along the shore to the east, offering surf bathing and fishing in the ocean, fishing and swimming in sheltered salt-water pools.

PROVIDENCE, with a population of more than 180,000, is the capital of Rhode Island and second city of size in New England. It is one of the country's oldest cities, settled in 1636 by Roger Williams. The city and many of its streets (i.e., Hope, Peace, Faith, Friendship) were named as an expression of religious feeling. The **State House** has a commanding setting on a hill; and the **Old State House** is a building both historically and architecturally interesting. The **First Baptist Meetinghouse** in the country and the campus of **Brown University,** oldest college in Rhode Island and seventh oldest in the country, are of interest. Near Providence, to the north and east, are two race tracks. **Roger Williams Park,** two miles south, has unusual scenic and recreational facilities.

SPORTS AND RECREATION. Newport, though a famous resort, is not a tourist area in the usual sense due to its lack of facilities for the average summer visitor. New motels in adjoining Middletown are making the area more available, however. Other resorts along the coast are all quite small, deriving their patronage chiefly from local residents or people living in inland areas such as New York, New Jersey, and Connecticut.

In the area of **deep-sea fishing,** Rhode Island offers a sports facility of substantial character. Most sought-after are swordfish and the giant bluefin tuna. **Block Island** is the fishing center, with boats and tackle available at various shore points at and around **Narragansett Bay** (Galilee, near Point Judith, has southern New England's largest fleet of charter boats). Although the community of **Newport** is of great sightseeing interest, other scattered monuments and sites should be visited. They include the **birthplace of Gilbert Stuart,** distinguished early Colonial artist, located in **Saunderstown; Old Slater Mill** in **Pawtucket,** a museum in the state's oldest mill, dedicated to the textile industry. Both Providence and Newport have fine examples of early architecture, especially the latter community, which contains many lavishly elegant mansions.

SPECIAL EVENTS. Rhode Island's two best-known events are the **Newport Music Festivals** in July–August and the **America's Cup Races,** international yacht race between British and American competitors. Also, the **Winter Sports Carnival** at Providence in February; the **Newport-Bermuda Yacht Race** and the **Newport-Annapolis Yacht Race,** in June on alternating years; and the **New York Yacht Club Races** at Newport, August 6.

Connecticut

With an area of about 5,000 square miles, Connecticut is fifth in size among the states of New England, and forty-eighth in the United States. Only Rhode Island and Delaware are smaller. But in population Connecticut, with over 3 million people, is second in size among the New England states, next to Massachusetts, and twenty-fourth in the United States.

In position, Connecticut is the most southern of the New England states, filling the southwest corner of the New England area, next to New York, on the west. From the north-south New York border, a narrow neck of Connecticut extends almost to the New York City line. The northern boundary is Massachusetts, eastern boundary Rhode Island, and on the south is the irregular shore of Long Island Sound.

In dimensions, Connecticut is approximately 100 miles east-west, and 50 miles from north to south, making an irregular rectangle. The name of the state is an adaptation of an Indian word, meaning "beside the tidal river," presumably the Connecticut River, which took its name from the area. Connecticut has no outstanding nickname, but the one most commonly applied is the "Nutmeg State," said to derive from the habit Connecticut peddlers had of making nutmegs out of wood. The state flower is the mountain laurel, the state bird, the American robin, and the state tree the white oak. One of the original 13 colonies, Connecticut was the fifth admitted to the United States.

THE LAND. The natural features of Connecticut include areas of fairly rugged wooded hills, three important rivers, and an irregular, deeply indented coast line with some good beaches and harbors. The highland areas are in the east and the west, separated by the valley of the Connecticut River. In the west the hills become almost low mountains, with crests of ridges rising to more than 2,000 feet. The highest peak in the state is Mount Frissell, in the northwest corner, with a summit 2,380 feet. The western hills are a southern extension of the Berkshire Hills in Massachusetts.

The three rivers are, from west to east, the Housatonic, draining the western highland region, coming to the sea just east of Bridgeport. The central river is the beautiful Connecticut, most important river in New England. It is tidal for many miles above its mouth near Old Saybrook, and is navigable for small craft as far as Windsor Locks and for large craft as far north as Hartford. The eastern river is the Thames, named for England's river but pronounced differently. It comes to the sea at the port of New London, is navigable north to Norwich.

One of the most attractive physical features of Connecticut is the coast with its succession of harbors, inlets, and beaches, a chain of important towns and villages linked by an old and famous highway, U.S. 1.

Over two million acres of hardwood forest make up two-thirds of the state's entire land area. Much of the rest, with the exception of the Connecticut Valley, is used for subsistence farms.

THE CLIMATE. Connecticut's climate is humid, rainfall ranging from 42 to 48 inches, scattered throughout the year. Proximity to the sea and the sheltering barrier of the western hills tends to give most of the state more moderate temperature winter and summer than the rest of New England. Hartford, in the approximate center of the state, has a January average of 26 degrees and a July average of 73 degrees. Spring comes earlier in Connecticut and fall later than in most of New England. Except for occasional severe winter storms, the state is pleasant year round. The best time for a visit is from early spring through late fall.

THE PEOPLE. Connecticut's coast was discovered by a Dutchman named Adriaen Block in 1614. A few years later, the Dutch from New York tried to establish a colony at the present site of Hartford, but it lasted only a few years. For many years after that, most settlers of Connecticut were of English origin, coming either from England direct or migrating south from other areas of New England. The first permanent English colony was made by colonists from Massachusetts in 1633, at the present site of Windsor. Early residents turned to the sea for their livelihood and for many years the coastal harbors of Connecticut were busy with Connecticut ships. But competition from other areas and the War of 1812 took the bloom off shipping profits, and restless Yankees of Connecticut turned to other fields, especially industry.

By 1840 Connecticut had become a leading industrial state, with a great shortage of labor for its mills and factories, requiring factory owners to seek European labor. The first to come were large groups of Irish. Their descendants represent a substantial proportion of the people of Connecticut today. The second group were Germans. So many of them came that their descendants today outnumber the descendants of English stock. A third group were French Canadians, to work in textile mills. A fourth group were Scandinavians, chiefly skilled mechanics and machinists. The final migration was made up of large numbers of Italians, who settled in growing metropolitan areas. Today people of Italian descent represent a substantial part of the population.

But the only groups of people who left important physical evidence of their work and activity in Connecticut were the English and Scotch residents who dominated the population during the first half of the nineteenth century. They left the state a rich architectural heritage, including dozens of charming churches, most of them white frame and slender-spired. They built hundreds of pleasant simple houses, from two-room cottages that were the original salt-box dwellings to gracious mansions of the Greek revival period, financed by the growing wealth of Connecticut's industrial leaders. Among public buildings, Connecticut borrowed the talents of the distinguished Massachusetts designer, Bulfinch, for its old State House in Hartford. Much later, Connecticut's builders began to adopt the French Gothic form for its public buildings, with notable examples of it rising on college campuses, particularly Yale and Trinity.

AGRICULTURE. Connecticut is not an important agricultural state. Its rolling, rock-studded hills make farming difficult and soil is generally poor.

But Connecticut does have some specialized and important farm products. The chief is tobacco, grown under shade in the Connecticut Valley. It is so valuable as a commercial crop that Connecticut can claim a higher dollar value per acre for a crop than any state in the country. Other commercial crops are potatoes, also grown in the Connecticut Valley, apples and other fruits from orchards scattered over the state. Poultry farming is the biggest general farming activity in the state. One unusual specialization is Rock Cornish hens, breeding of which was perfected in Connecticut.

Connecticut has no important mineral resources, but at one time Connecticut quarries produced an unusual type of sandstone of a peculiar brown color, popular 100 or more years ago. It accounts for thousands of buildings in New York City today, the celebrated brownstone fronts.

INDUSTRY. Leading industries include firearms, hats, clocks, typewriters, jet engines for aircraft, brass goods, ball bearings, silverware, and pins. The value added by manufacture is higher on a per capita basis in Connecticut than in any other state. There are more big insurance companies in Connecticut, chiefly in Hartford, than anywhere else in the world. Connecticut was the first state to apply Eli Whitney's principle of interchangeable parts to manufacture, an idea which has spread to all the great mass production industries of the nation. Connecticut's great industrial concentration has led to city specialization. Waterbury is known for brass, New Haven for firearms, and Hartford for aircraft engines, typewriters, and insurance.

CITIES. Connecticut has an almost perfect balance between urban areas and rural life. No city is large, and at no place within the state are you far from open country. But though there is no metropolis in Connecticut, there are quite a number of moderate-sized cities. Ten have populations over 50,000. Five cities have populations in excess of 100,000.

BRIDGEPORT, about 20 miles southwest of New Haven, most industrial city in Connecticut, claims to have made the first sewing machine, and is now a center for machines and metalworking, including firearms, brass products and electrical specialties.

HARTFORD, capital and largest city, population about 160,000, is the insurance capital of the world, with the home offices of more large companies than any other city. It produces more typewriters than any other city, is important in the manufacture of airplane motors, and is the packing and warehouse center for Connecticut's tobacco industry. Hartford claims an oddly diverse list of national firsts: first children's magazine, first newspaper to maintain continuous publication, first published cookbook, first standard inch, and first pneumatic tire. Things worth seeing include the **state capitol grounds,** with several buildings set in a pleasantly landscaped area. The grounds are studded with monuments and memorials of various kinds. Nearby is the **old state house,** built in 1796, a fine example of civic architecture. Several large insurance headquarters, most notable being **Aetna-Life,** the largest building of Colonial design anywhere, should be visited, as should **Constitution Plaza,** a downtown redevelopment area which has attracted nationwide attention.

NEW HAVEN, with a population of over 137,000, fills an irregular triangle, facing a shallow but useful harbor. New Haven is the location of **Yale University,** situated on a large campus built around a handsome green near the center of town. Considered one of the most attractive universities in the East, its Gothic **Harkness Tower,** and its celebrated **Bowl,** first and one of the most famous stadiums, are known for their architecture and should be visited.

NEW LONDON. Also on the coast, to the east of New Haven, is Connecticut's oldest and most important port, New London. It has a population of about 31,000, and an impressive setting at the mouth of the wide Thames River. The whole history of New London has been related to the sea. During the Revolution, it was the headquarters for privateers, and later became one of the great whaling ports, rivaling New Bedford in Massachusetts. It is the home of the **Coast Guard Academy,** which has an attractive campus overlooking the river. Across the river, in the suburb of **Groton,** the United States Navy maintains its huge submarine base. They include an increasing fleet of atomic-powered submarines, made in the Electric Boat Division of the General Dynamics Corporation.

The old seaport of **Mystic** on the Mystic River, has one of the most unique exhibits in New England, the **Mystic Seaport and Marine Museum.** It contains exhibits of celebrated ships, including the celebrated whaling ship, *Charles W. Morgan,* seafaring gear, and relics from everywhere, including the finest collection of model ships.

Many of Connecticut's smaller towns and villages offer special interest to the visitor, chiefly along the coast. These include coastal villages like the charming old port of **Southport,** just west of Bridgeport. Its fine old houses, many of them beautifully restored, are relics of the day when Southport was an important ocean port and shipping center. An inland village of interest is the small town of **Ridgefield,** eight miles south of Danbury, in the western hills. A handsome residential town with some historic old buildings, its main street is regarded as one of the most attractive town streets in the country. **Litchfield,** just south of Torrington, in the western side of the state has a village church noted for the grace of its Colonial design, a historic Colonial tavern, and fine old dwellings.

The western neck of Connecticut, which extends for 20 miles west from the main body of the state toward New York City, is filled with suburban communities along the shore, with dozens of residential areas and estates scattered through the hills to the north. Of these, the largest is **Stamford,** an important commuter base and residential and industrial center. West of it, on the shore, is **Greenwich,** one of the richest and fastest growing suburban centers in the East, almost entirely a residential community, with opulent estates, large and small, flanking highways in all directions from the city center.

SPORTS AND RECREATION. The coast has many good beaches. Most coastal towns have facilities for offshore **fishing,** but the most popular ocean activity of Connecticut is **yachting.** Most Connecticut coast towns have good small boat harbors, facilities for renting craft, with more boating events and regattas occurring during the season than in any other section of the East. Offshore fishing is also good. The lakes scattered through the western hills offer limited boating and fishing and have a few beaches. The **Yale Bowl,** at New Haven, draws big crowds for **football** in the fall, and the Thames River is the setting each June for the celebrated **boat race** between Yale and Harvard.

SPECIAL EVENTS. The **American Shakespeare Festival,** held each summer in Stratford, is one of Connecticut's best-known events. Also interesting are **Rose Sunday,** held in Hartford, mid-June; **Barnum Festival,** Bridgeport, in July; **American Dance Festival,** New London, mid-August; and the **New Haven Antique Show,** in October.

The Middle Atlantic States

Middle Atlantic States

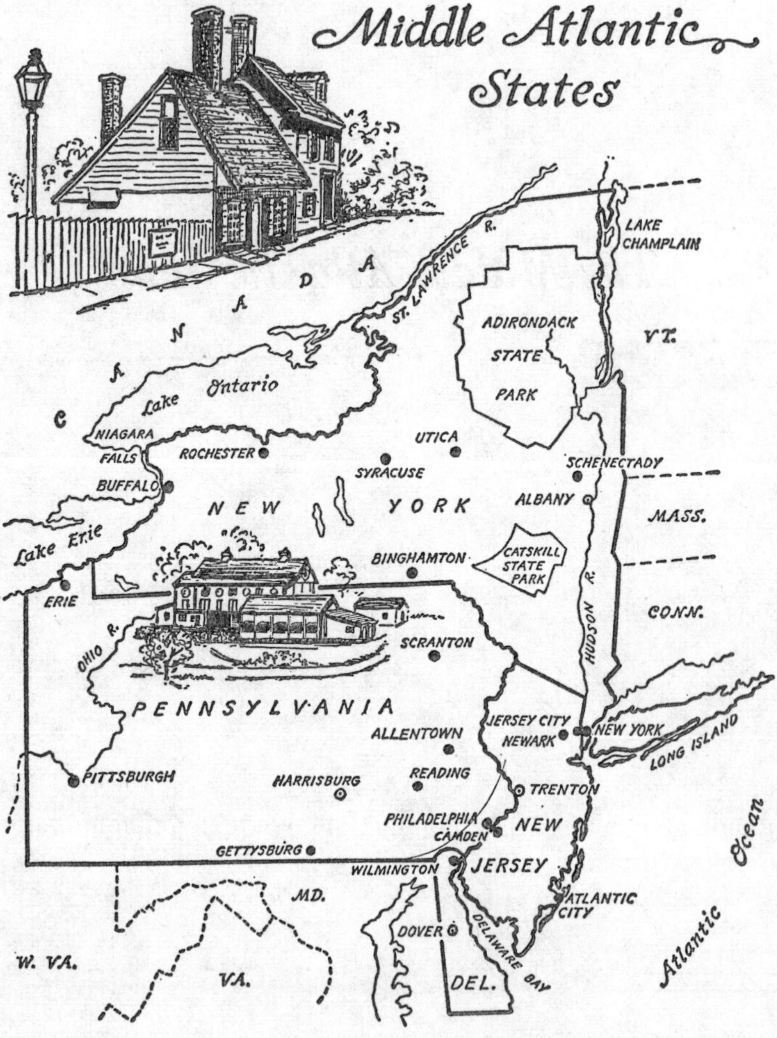

CANADA
ST. LAWRENCE R.
LAKE CHAMPLAIN
ADIRONDACK STATE PARK
VT.
Lake Ontario
NIAGARA FALLS
ROCHESTER
UTICA
SYRACUSE
SCHENECTADY
BUFFALO
NEW YORK
ALBANY
MASS.
Lake Erie
BINGHAMTON
CATSKILL STATE PARK
ERIE
OHIO R.
SCRANTON
HUDSON R.
CONN.
PENNSYLVANIA
JERSEY CITY
NEWARK
NEW YORK
LONG ISLAND
ALLENTOWN
PITTSBURGH
READING
HARRISBURG
TRENTON
PHILADELPHIA
CAMDEN
NEW JERSEY
GETTYSBURG
WILMINGTON
MD.
ATLANTIC CITY
DOVER
DELAWARE BAY
W. VA.
VA.
DEL.
Atlantic Ocean

The Middle Atlantic States

Along the Atlantic coast between New England and the South lie four states—New York, New Jersey, Pennsylvania, and Delaware—whose total area represents only a thirtieth of the U.S. land surface, but which contain nearly a fifth of the population. This busy, populous seaboard region includes the nation's largest city (New York), its fourth largest (Philadelphia), and six other cities (Pittsburgh, Buffalo, Newark, Rochester, Jersey City, and Syracuse) of over 200,000. Three-fourths of the entire population of the region live in cities. Probably for most visitors, the chief attraction is these cities, and above all New York, with its theaters, art galleries, museums, night clubs, concert halls, dance stages, and the most varied collection of good restaurants of every description in the Western Hemisphere.

The mines and factories of this industrialized belt produce a large proportion of the nation's steel and coal, its clothes and furniture, its chemicals and scientific instruments. Yet though the eastern coastal plain is a virtually solid metropolitan belt of industrial centers and suburbs, the four states also provide handsome countryside—mountains, woods, lakes, rolling hills, and valleys. The Catskills, Adirondacks, Poconos, and other Appalachian ranges offer some of the finest recreation and resort areas in the world. Side by side with the urban centers stretch miles of the world's richest farmland. Delaware is famous for its broilers, Pennsylvania for its buckwheat and mushrooms, New York for its apples and wine grapes, New Jersey for its garden vegetables, berries, and fruits.

It is a region rich in history. All four states were among the original 13, and are dotted with roadside plaques commemorating Colonial and Revolutionary events. Washington and his army spent nearly the entire war in this area, and reminders of the winters in Valley Forge, Pennsylvania and in Morristown, New Jersey, at the crossing of the Delaware, and of several battlefields can be seen. Philadelphia's Independence Square preserves the memories of the Declaration of Independence and the Constitutional Convention, as well as the embattled sessions of the Continental Congress. But the most extensive historical site in the region dates from another crisis in our history. The battlefield of Gettysburg is preserved as a national military park.

On the scenic side are the Hudson River Palisades above New York City, where West Point stands; the narrow, deep-water Finger Lakes of central New York State; the Adirondacks and Catskills of New York, and the Poconos of Pennsylvania. The splendid stretches of ocean shore of Long Island, New Jersey, and Delaware are dotted with beaches, including Atlantic City's world-famed Boardwalk, scene of the Miss America pageant. But the visitor who sees nothing else is certain to want to visit Niagara Falls, one of the world's great natural wonders.

The region is rich, too, in man-made wonders. The Empire State Building, which was the world's tallest (102 stories) for more than 30 years, is only one of more than a dozen super-skyscrapers (the newest, the World Trade Center, is the tallest in New York). The Verrazano-Narrows Bridge, under which the ocean liners steam into New York Harbor, longest-span bridge of any type in the world, is the queen of a galaxy of long-span bridges in and around New York and Philadelphia—the George Washington, the Hell Gate Arch, the Delaware Memorial, and many more. The Robert Moses Power Plant at Niagara Falls adds a notable man-made wonder to a famous natural one.

Equally remarkable are a number of structures designed for entertainment and cultural purposes: Shea Stadium, the Guggenheim Museum (designed by Frank Lloyd Wright) in New York, and numerous other museums, art galleries, theaters, industrial exhibits, and sports arenas in New York, Philadelphia, Pittsburgh, and other cities.

Besides first-class spectator accommodations for all major seasonal sports, there are well-stocked fishing streams, beautiful lakes, and a widening choice of ski slopes in northern Pennsylvania and New York. An unusual attraction is the caves and vineyards of New York State's champagne country.

The area is equally rich in its heritage of Americans from all countries and of many religions, from New York's cosmopolitan millions to Pennsylvania's Quakers and the picturesque Mennonites, Amish, and Dunkers of Lancaster County.

The climate is generally mild, with hot summers along the coastal plain and the lowlands, and below-zero winters in the mountains.

New York

New York can be any kind of state the visitor wants it to be. There is speed, glitter, excitement in the City; moccasined quiet in the Adirondack woods; superior hunting in the Catskills; fishing in the Finger Lakes, and skiing on Whiteface Mountain.

THE LAND. New York is the only state bordering both the Atlantic Ocean and the Great Lakes. Its area, over 49,000 square miles, makes it the largest of the four states in this region. New York has a 127-mile Atlantic coastline, with 371 miles on Lakes Ontario and Erie. Its highest mountains are the Adirondacks in northeastern New York (Mount Marcy, 5,344 feet, is the highest point in the state).

Waterways are important means of transportation to New York. The Hudson and the Mohawk are the chief rivers, followed by the Genesee and Oswego. Of more than 8,000 lakes, the best-known are the Finger Lakes, which make central New York a major water-recreation area.

THE CLIMATE. Temperatures vary greatly with altitude and surface of the land, with the coastal areas having the hottest summers, mildest winters, and least snow, and the Adirondack Highlands receiving the heaviest snows, coldest winters, and coolest summers. Average temperatures along the coastal plain are 32 degrees in January, and 76 degrees in July. In the Adirondacks they average 18 degrees in January and 64 degrees in July.

Precipitation varies between 32 and 45 inches yearly, including melted snow.

THE PEOPLE. Though Verrazano did a bit of exploring locally on behalf of the French in 1524, no one established strong territorial claims before Henry Hudson piloted the *Half Moon* up the river which bears his name in 1609. The Dutch, for whom he was sailing, founded trading posts at New Amsterdam and at Fort Nassau, 150 miles north. Settlement began in earnest in 1624, and the trading posts and the land along the river began to flourish.

In 1664 the Duke of York by a bloodless coup took over the Dutch lands for Charles II of England. Names changed all along the line: New Netherlands became New York as did the city of New Amsterdam; Fort Orange, formerly Nassau, finally became Albany. Thus the British started their 110-year rule.

The French who had claimed Lake Champlain began a steady harassment from the north—sometimes with Indian help, sometimes without. But in spite of the loss of settler scalps in what were later known as the French and Indian Wars, the British colonies continued to prosper. Gradually the colonists set up basic concepts of freedom. Under the Charter of Liberties and Privileges (1683) they were guaranteed a representative assembly with control over taxation. Freedom of speech and the press was won at the John Peter Zenger trial in 1735. It was at Albany in 1754 that the first Colonial Congress adopted a Plan of Union incorporating these principles and taking a first positive step toward uniting all 13 colonies.

New York's strategic location made it the ground on which one third of the Revolution's battles were fought. Burgoyne's defeat at the Battle of Saratoga in 1777 turned the tide of war in the colonists' favor.

New York adopted its first constitution with three basic branches of government—legislative, executive and judicial—in 1777, 12 full years before the federal government worked out the form of its own. In the same year, George Clinton was installed as the state's first governor.

During the War of 1812, the joint land-lake victory of General Macomb and Commodore Macdonough at Plattsburgh broke the strength of British attacks from the north.

In 1825, under Governor DeWitt Clinton, nephew of the first Governor Clinton, New York's Erie Canal was opened, providing low-cost transportation from the Great Lakes to the At-

New York City

lantic and encouraging new industries all the way from New York to Buffalo.

The same water-level route proved ideal for railroad building, which cemented New York City's position as the nation's "front door." The communications industry came to center in this capital of business and finance facing the Atlantic and Europe, and in the twentieth century New York has become the nation's cultural capital as well. The decision to build the United Nations Headquarters in New York has given it the role of diplomatic capital of the globe, unique among the world's cities.

More than 18 million people live in New York, where there are some of the largest foreign-born groups in the country (including Italians, Russians, Germans, Poles, and Puerto Ricans). More than 900,000 Puerto Ricans are residents of New York City.

AGRICULTURE. Farming, though only 4 percent of the people are engaged in it, is a leading source of income. Among the most important products are dairy and poultry, beef cattle, calves, fruits, and vegetables. New York is second only to Wisconsin in milk production, and is a leader in production of butter and cheese. The grapes grown in the Finger Lakes district sustain New York's large wine industry.

INDUSTRY. New York turns out over $25 billion in manufactured products each year, leading all states in the value of manufactured goods. Its most important industries, in order of size and output, are clothing, printing and publishing, metal processing, food processing, and a variety of other industries including chemicals, transportation equipment, appliances, and machinery.

Because of this wealth of industry, New York is a leader in transportation, with some 411 landing fields, 34 railroad companies, and over 104,000 miles of roads. New York is the nation's most important seaport, handling annual imports of 34 million tons, and exports of eight million tons.

CITIES. New York has over 60 incorporated cities, ranging in size from 3,000 (Sherrill) to about 8,000,000 (New York City). Other cities with populations above 100,000 are Albany, Buffalo, Rochester, Syracuse, and Yonkers.

NEW YORK CITY is almost anything they say: friendly, cold; beautiful, ugly; cosmopolitan, provincial. But nobody ever calls it dull.

Everywhere, any time of day, there's something going on: a skyscraper going up; a giant liner steaming out of the harbor; ticker tape snowing down on a visiting celebrity. Fashionable shoppers crowd Fifth Avenue; peddlers rattle their carts along the Lower East Side. Artists studios and galleries dot the area of "Soho," south of Houston Street; Broadway thrives as the nightlife capital of the country.

Buses are sluggish but friendly. Subways are crowded but quick (in five minutes you cover more ground than you could in a half hour's public transportation in most other cities). And it's a great town for walking: up Madison Avenue, across Central Park, around Times Square, in the Wall Street canyons on Sunday. Guided walking tours in various parts of the city are offered by the Museum of the City of New York.

Sightseeing boats leave the end of West 42nd Street and Battery Park for two-and-one-half-hour cruises around the island, April to November. Even though the **Verrazano-Narrows Bridge,** world's longest single span suspension bridge, joins Brooklyn and Staten Island, the ferry ride over and back is still very popular, and only costs a nickel. Boats sail from South Ferry near Battery Park.

Starting in downtown Manhattan, **Battery Park,** on the southern tip of the island, includes remnants of **Castle Clinton,** built in 1807, where Jenny Lind once sang. There is also a wide promenade along the waterfront, while nearby, boats leave for the **Statue of Liberty** or **Staten Island.**

Not far away at 54 Pearl Street, **Fraunces Tavern** (1719) was the scene of Washington's farewell to the officers of the Continental Army in 1783. The first floor is a restaurant and the museum upstairs displays Revolutionary relics and Washington memorabilia.

Wall Street, the nation's financial capital, was the city's northern boundary three centuries ago; and there *was* a wall built along it by order of Peter Stuyvesant. The original **Trinity Church,** at the head of Wall Street on Broadway, was built in 1697; the present building dates from 1846. Alexander Hamilton and Robert Fulton are buried in the churchyard.

The **New York Stock Exchange,** 11 Wall Street, is a fascinating and confusing market place for the world's stocks, bonds and securities. The visitors' gallery, open from 10 A.M. to 3:30 P.M. on weekdays, overlooks the trading floor. Receptionists explain the activities below.

Federal Hall National Memorial, across the street, was formerly the U.S. Sub-Treasury built on the site of the first United States Capitol, where Washington was inaugurated.

Nearby, on Church Street, are the twin towers of the **World Trade Center** (110 stories).

Up Broadway from Wall Street stands the **Woolworth Building,** the 60-story neo-Gothic skyscraper that was for years the tallest in the world. Nearby, **City Hall,** a century and a half old, is still a complex but impressive mass of civic architecture. Most of the city's business is transacted around **Foley Square,** north of City Hall. Ringing the Square are the **Municipal Building,** the **U. S. Court House,** the **New York County Court House,** the **State Office Building,** and the **City Health, Hospital** and **Sanitation Department Building.** East of the Square is **Brooklyn Bridge,** for long after its completion in 1883 the world's longest suspension span. Its promenade is one of the city's best sightseeing walks.

Northeast of Foley Square is **Chinatown,** a 30-acre sector of narrow streets, Oriental restaurants, small shops offering exotic foodstuffs and trinkets.

Uptown and west is **Greenwich Village,** traditional refuge of writers, artists, and students, known for its informal atmosphere. **Washington Square,** at the foot of Fifth Avenue, location of the famous **Washington Arch** designed by Stanford White, is one of the meeting places of the Village. Open-air art shows are held around the area in the spring and fall. The campus of **New York University's** main division lines the east and south sides of the Square. A walk around the Village should include cobbled, gas-lit MacDougal Alley; West 4th Street's craft shops; espresso shops on MacDougal Street and in Minetta Lane; New York's narrowest house, nine and one-half feet wide—once the home of Edna St. Vincent Millay—at 75½ Bedford Street.

Travel east of the Square to the **East Village** (Lower East Side), one of the most vital multi-racial, multi-lingual communities in the country.

Between the Village and midtown Manhattan is the **Theodore Roosevelt House,** 28 East 20th Street, birthplace of the twenty-sixth President. Furnished as it was 100 years ago, it is now a National Historic Site.

The Flatiron Building, the city's first skyscraper (1902), was shaped to fit the triangular block cut where Broadway crosses Fifth Avenue at 23rd Street.

The **Little Church Around the Corner**—officially, the Episcopal Church of the Transfiguration—Fifth Avenue and 29th Street, is a small stone church in a garden where many, many people, a number of them celebrities, are married every year.

The **Empire State Building,** Fifth Avenue and 34th Street, 102 stories, is one of the world's tallest buildings; the view from the top—especially on a clear night—is well worth the price of admission.

Pennsylvania Station, on Seventh Avenue and 33rd Street, New York terminus for the Pennsylvania and Long Island Railroads, has had its railway facilities compressed into the lower level. It has been replaced above by the **Madison Square Garden Center.** Formerly located at 50th Street and Eighth Avenue, the Garden contains a 22,000-seat arena, a forum, cinema, bowling alley, and many other attractions. A 29-story office building is adjacent to the Garden, connected by a four-lane private mall.

The **post office,** opposite Madison Square Garden Center on Eighth Avenue, is the largest in the country. The famous legend that runs the length of the façade is based on Herodotus' report on the messengers of the Persian Empire. It reads: "Neither snow nor rain nor heat nor gloom of night stays these couriers from the swift completion of their appointed rounds."

The **Metropolitan Opera Company** formerly located at 39th on Broadway in the old Metropolitan Opera House, now performs in its new opera house, located at Lincoln Center, during the September–April season. Especially noteworthy are paintings by Marc Chagall which are found inside the entrance.

The **New York Public Library,** Fifth Avenue and 42nd Street, its entrance guarded by the famous stone lions, is one of the world's great libraries with over 14 million books, manuscripts and other items. There are regular exhibits of rare books, manuscripts, and pictures. Free concerts are given in Bryant Park just behind the library daily all summer long.

Grand Central Terminal, built in 1913, with a complex of tracks underneath it, is interesting for its great main room (the ceiling is a sky-map) and the pedestrian tunnels that link the terminal with three neighboring hotels, several nearby office buildings and the Yale Club.

Times Square, actually the intersection of Broadway and Seventh Avenue at 42nd Street, has come to mean the entire district along Broadway from 42nd Street up to Columbus Circle at 59th. This part of New York—a collection of shops, hotels, shooting galleries, bars, movies, restaurants and people—never sleeps. At night, brilliant advertising signs called "spectaculars" and bright marquees keep Times Square as light as noon. This district is the theatrical heart of the country, with legitimate theaters on the side streets east and west of Broadway. A moving electric sign around the Allied Chemical Tower keeps the latest news flashing continuously.

The **United Nations' Headquarters,** directly across town on the East River (42nd to 48th Street), is dominated by the majestic slab of glass, marble and aluminum that houses the Secretariat. Other buildings in the group: the Conference Building, the General Assembly and the Library. Guided parties leave the main information desk every few minutes from 9:15 A.M. to 4:45 P.M. daily on hour-long tours which—when possible—show the U.N. members in action.

Park Avenue is a wide boulevard of fashionable apartment houses and clubs and also an avenue of ultra-modern architecture. Cases in point: **Lever House,** 390 Park, composed chiefly of green-tinted glass with a restful ground-floor arcade; and the **Seagram Building,** 375 Park, first bronze skyscraper in the world, with a wide fountained plaza (free tours every Tuesday afternoon). Other interesting buildings along the Avenue: **St. Bartholomew's,** a handsome Byzantine-style church, behind which is the **General Electric Building,** and the famous **Waldorf-Astoria Hotel** filling the block between 49th and 50th streets.

Fifth Avenue is for shopping (real and window), at Bergdorf-Goodman, Bonwit Teller, Tiffany, Saks Fifth Avenue, Lord & Taylor, B. Altman and a wealth of other splendid stores and specialty shops. At 50th Street stands **St. Patrick's Cathedral,** seat of the Roman Catholic Archdiocese of New York, a twin-spired Gothic edifice planned in 1850 and completed in 1888. Notable: its fine stained-glass windows and great bronze entrance doors.

Across Fifth Avenue from St. Patrick's is **Rockefeller Center.** The Center proper extends from 48th to 51st Street and from Fifth Avenue to the Avenue of the Americas; and new buildings are on the way up all around. Among the Center's most prominent structures: the **RCA Building** (N.B.C.'s radio and television studios are inside), the **Associated Press Building,** the **Exxon Building,** the **Time-Life Building, Radio City Music Hall** (the Rockettes' stage show is a visitor's must) and the **International Building** (the Atlas statue in front is a favorite photographers' focus point). There are about 20 restaurants and 200 shops, many lining the underground concourse that links all the buildings together. A promenade, with changing floral exhibits, leads to the sunken Plaza. Surrounded by the flags of the United Nations and watched over by the huge Prometheus statue, the Plaza is an umbrella-shaded outdoor restaurant in summer and an ice-skating rink from late September to May.

One-hour guided Rockefeller Center tours leave a lounge on the RCA building concourse at frequent intervals all day long. Tours conclude on the **Observation Roof of the RCA Building,** 850 feet above the street, for a wide-angle view of New York.

The **Museum of Modern Art,** not far from Rockefeller Center on 53rd Street between Fifth Avenue and the Avenue of the Americas, is a strikingly modern building housing notable exhibits of contemporary paintings, sculpture, photography and other modern art forms. Revivals of important motion pictures are shown twice a day, and a cafeteria overlooking the sculpture garden serves lunch and tea.

Uptown, **Carnegie Hall,** at Seventh Avenue and 57th Street, is former home of the New York Philharmonic and current home of the American Symphony Orchestra. For years it has been regarded as the foremost concert hall in the country.

The **New York Coliseum** on Columbus Circle is a huge exhibition center where display shows such as the International Flower Show and the National Motor Boat Show are held. Four different expositions can be staged in it at the same time. Also on Columbus Circle, the **Gallery of Modern Art** houses contemporary art exhibits, including the Huntington Hartford collection, and is itself a handsome new white marble building.

Lincoln Center for the Performing Arts, located on Broadway between 62nd and 66th Streets, is a complex of striking modern buildings designed to house opera, concerts, recitals, dance and drama. Principal buildings are **Avery Fisher Hall** (home of the New York Philharmonic), **Metropolitan Opera House, New York State Theater, New York Public Library at Lincoln Center: Library & Museum of the Performing Arts, Vivian Beaumont Theater,** and **The Juilliard Building.**

The boundaries of **Central Park**—59th Street to 110th Street, Fifth Avenue to Central Park West—enclose 860 acres with lakes, woods, a zoo, bridle paths, statues, gardens and playgrounds. Band concerts and summer dances are held on the Mall, and the Wollman Memorial is a skating rink—roller in summer, ice in winter.

Established on the park grounds is the **Metropolitan Museum of Art,** Fifth Avenue and 82nd Street, which houses the most extensive collection of art in the Western Hemisphere. In addition to European and American paintings and sculpture, especially interesting exhibits include the Hall of Arms and Armor; the exhibit of ancient Egyptian, Greek and Roman art; the American Wing with re-created interiors of early Colonial rooms; the Costume Institute and the Junior Museum.

Up Fifth Avenue at 89th Street is the once controversial **Guggenheim Museum,** its building designed by Frank Lloyd Wright, devoted to twentieth-century painting and sculpture. In contrast to this avant-garde structure, the **Frick Museum,** 1 East 70th Street, is a classic and elegant building, housing one of the best private collections of paintings—chiefly eighteenth-century British and French classical—to be found anywhere in the world. Nearby, at 75th Street and Madison Avenue, is the new, modern structure designed by Marcel Breuer which is home of the **Whitney Museum of American Art.**

Across Central Park, between 79th and 81st streets on Central Park West, is the **American Museum of Natural History,** devoted to such natural science exhibits as the North American Forests; jungle beasts—lions, elephants and others—against realistic backgrounds; and impressively reconstructed dinosaurs. At 81st Street, the **Hayden Planetarium** offers "sky shows" dramatizing the movements of the planets, the stars and the universe.

Away across town on the East River, **Carl Schurz Park** (84th to 89th Street) includes a wide esplanade overlooking the river traffic as well as **Gracie Mansion** (1799), official residence of the Mayor of New York.

In the **Harlem** area of Manhattan are **Columbia University** with campus extending from 116th to 120th Street between Broadway and Amsterdam Avenue; the Episcopal **Cathedral of St. John the Divine** (112th Street and Amsterdam), in size second only to St. Peter's in Rome; and **Riverside Drive** (72nd to 181st Street), a fine place to take a long high look at the Hudson. Notable along the Drive are the **Soldiers' and Sailors' Monument,** 89th Street, honoring Northern Civil War troops, and **Grant's Tomb,** 122nd Street. Across the Drive from Grant's Tomb is **Riverside Church,** an interdenominational French Gothic building of impressive size. The 22-story tower contains a 72-bell carillon, the world's largest; an observatory near the top offers a dramatic view of the city.

The **Roger Morris-Jumel Mansion,** West 160th Street at Edgecomb Avenue, is a meticulously restored Colonial house built in 1765 that has served as a headquarters for Washington and a home for Aaron Burr. It is now a museum, open every day but Monday.

The **Cloisters,** in Fort Tryon Park, Northern Avenue and Cabrini Circle, is a fascinating museum of medieval art in a building composed of elements of monasteries dating from the Middle Ages. The setting is a handsome park with spectacular views of the Hudson, the Palisades and the George Washington Bridge.

Yankee Stadium, at 161st Street and River Avenue, is the 70,000 seat home of the New York Yankees baseball team and a leading sports center of the world.

At 181st Street and University Avenue, on the uptown campus of New York University, is the **Hall of Fame for Great Americans,** a semi-circular colonnade sheltering bronze busts and biographical tablets dedicated to distinguished citizens.

Fordham University, eminent Catholic college, is located on a 70-acre campus with impressive Gothic buildings at Fordham Road and Third Avenue. Nearby is **Bronx Park,** 700 acres of wooded land, home of the famous **New York Botanical Gardens:** lawns, flower-bordered paths, beds displaying more than 12,000 different plant species. Also in the park: America's biggest zoo, second only to London's in the world—the **New York Zoological Park** or **Bronx Zoo.** Outstanding features: the African Plains, where lions and antelope play; the Lion House; the Elephant House; the World of Darkness; the new World of Birds building; and a Children's Zoo where children can play with small animals. Adults are not admitted unless accompanied by a child.

THE BOROUGHS OF QUEENS AND BROOKLYN claim three well-known sports centers: **Forest Hills West Side Tennis Club** (Queens), with a stadium seating 15,000, where championship tennis tournaments are held; large, modern **Aqueduct Race Track;** and **Shea Municipal Stadium** (Flushing Meadow Park, Queens), which seats 55,000 for baseball (the New York Mets), and 60,000 for football (the New York Jets), all seats with unobstructed views. New York's two great airports—**La Guardia** and **Kennedy International Airport** at Idlewild—are both located in Queens.

Brooklyn Heights, the historic tree-lined residential neighborhood overlooking the East River, has an esplanade from which there is a breathtaking view of the Manhattan skyline.

Prospect Park (main entrance: Flatbush Avenue and Eastern Parkway), more than 500 acres of woods, meadows and lakes, is one of the handsomest city parks. In-park attractions include the **Brooklyn Museum,** an active art center with outstanding collections of primitive, Egyptian, Oriental and American art; **Brooklyn Botanic Garden,** 50 acres of gardens, including a "touch-taste-smell" garden for the blind; greenhouse displays, native and exotic trees and shrubs; **Lefferts Homestead,** a Dutch Colonial farmhouse built in 1777; the **Quaker Cemetery,** dating from 1662.

Sheepshead Bay is a noted deep-sea fishing center with a number of very good sea-food restaurants lining its shore. To the west is **Coney Island,** the raucous granddaddy of all beach amusement parks. The **New York Aquarium** is located at the end of the boardwalk.

LONG ISLAND, east of Brooklyn and Queens, is a vacationland of resort communities and small charming towns. Its farms produce vegetables and the famous Long Island ducks; clams, oysters and scallops are gathered offshore. There are 14 state parks on Long Island and many miles of sandy shore line—particularly at **Jones Beach, Fire Island** and the **Hamptons.**

The home of Theodore Roosevelt, **Sagamore Hill,** near Oyster Bay, is furnished as it was when he lived there. **Vanderbilt Museum,** near Centerport, displays the elaborate furnishings and miscellaneous collections of William K. Vanderbilt. South of these, near Huntington, is the shingled cottage where **Walt Whitman** was born. The new **Nassau Coliseum** is a great sports center.

STONY BROOK, on a bay of Long Island Sound, is a unique community, a completely reconstructed (not restored) eighteenth-century village with village green, inn and gristmill. Other points of interest: the **Suffolk Museum** and its Carriage House annex; **State University at Stony Brook. Setauket** is a truly unspoiled eighteenth-century village nearby. Worth seeing: the **Caroline Church of Brookhaven,** built in 1729, now carefully restored; **Thompson House,** a circa-1700 salt box.

RIVERHEAD is the chief city of Suffolk County and the shipping center for Long Island vegetables (cauliflower and potatoes, for example). Sights to see: the **Suffolk County Historical Society Museum** and the **county court house.**

SAG HARBOR, once a great whaling port, has preserved its fine sea captains' homes. The house once owned by a whale-ship builder is now a **Whaling Museum.**

SOUTHAMPTON AND EAST HAMPTON are shore resorts with a large artists' colony. Worth seeing: **Hollyhock House,** a shingled cottage built in 1645; a 1700-built cottage, once the residence of **John Howard Payne** who wrote "Home Sweet Home," and behind it, the only windmill on Long Island still working.

MONTAUK, at the tip of Long Island, is a favorite sport-fishing center with many motels, hotels, marinas, and a tall white lone-standing office building. On a rugged promontory lookout to the Atlantic is dependable **Montauk Lighthouse.**

THE HUDSON VALLEY REGION, from New York's city limits to Albany and the upstate towns beyond, embodies history as old as Hudson's first landfall, as recent as northern Westchester's new atomic electric plant. On the lighter side there are legends: **Rip van Winkle** in the Catskills, the Headless Horseman larruping through Tarrytown. There are Shaker dwellings, Huguenot homes and headquarters Washington slept in. And, to vary the historic-house pattern, there are game preserves, and the river itself for boating.

ALBANY, capital of New York State, lies some 150 miles north of New York City. It is the oldest United States city still operating under its original charter. Among the city's important sites: the **state capitol,** between State Street and Washington Avenue, housing the legislature, a governor's hearing room, a relic room, and a number of offices; the **state education building** (across Washington Avenue from the Capitol) with the **state library and museum;** the **Court of Appeals Building** (Eagle and Pine streets); the **Governor Alfred E. Smith State Office Building.** The **Albany Institute of History and Art** (125 Washington Avenue) has a particularly fine collection of Dutch Colonial furnishings and housewares. The **First Church in Albany** (Reformed), in existence continuously since 1642, is the second oldest Protestant church organization in the country. Two Albany houses are especially interesting: the **Schuyler Mansion,** home of Alexander Hamilton's father-in-law, General Philip Schuyler, and the **Ten Broeck Mansion** built in 1797, a handsome example of Federalist architecture.

BEAR MOUNTAIN, part of Palisades Interstate Park, offers open-air sports facilities plus an inn and cottages. Five nature museums on the premises are maintained in cooperation with the American Museum of Natural History. There is skiing (with lifts and jumping competitions) in winter.

CROTON, several miles north of Tarrytown, has its own fine restoration: **Van Cortlandt Manor,** where Washington, Rochambeau, Lafayette and Franklin all visited. The house and gardens are now open to the public.

GOSHEN, west of Monroe, is home of a world-famous harness racing track and the **Hall of Fame of the Trotter,** stocked with engravings and exhibits straight out of Currier & Ives.

HYDE PARK (vicinity): **Franklin Delano Roosevelt's ancestral home,** now a national historic site on which he and his wife are buried, and his home, books and mementos are preserved. Also in the neighborhood: the elaborate **Vanderbilt Mansion** with Renaissance mantels, Venetian chairs, Medici tapestries and other decorative objets d'art. Once home of Frederick W. Vanderbilt, a grandson of "the Commodore," it, too, is now a national historic site open to the public.

KATONAH has preserved the **house of John Jay,** president of the Continental Congress, first chief justice of the United States and a governor of New York. Built in 1801, it became a state historic site in 1958. Its library is particularly interesting.

KINGSTON, once a Dutch trading post, achieved permanent-settlement status in 1658, became New York's first capital in 1777. The first State Constitution was drafted here. The old **Senate House and Museum,** Clinton Avenue and North Front Street, built in 1676, has been restored, refurnished and opened to the public. In the cemetery of the **Old Dutch Church** on Main Street, George Clinton, first governor, is buried.

MONROE, due west of Bear Mountain, is the site of the **Old Museum Village** of Smith's Clove. Exhibits in 30 reconstructed Colonial buildings trace the history of 100 or more commonplace articles—handbags, harmoniums, what have you—from Colonial times to the present.

NEWBURGH, north of West Point, has two Revolutionary headquarters: those of General Knox in the **John Ellison House** (1754), and those of General Washington—his last before the Continental Army disbanded and went home—in the small stone **Hasbrouck House** at Liberty and Washington streets. Both are open to the public.

The chief attractions of **Beacon,** just across the river from Newburgh, are the **incline railway** that clambers up Beacon Mountain for a 75-mile view from the top, and the **Madam Brett Homestead,** built in 1709.

POUGHKEEPSIE is the site of **Clinton House,** a stone home associated with George Clinton, first Governor of the state. Across the Hudson and just a bit north at **New Paltz** is a cluster of five stone houses—Huguenot-built between 1692 and 1712; the **Jean Hasbrouck** and **Colonel Josiah Hasbrouck houses** are open to the public all year round. The others are open on **Stone House Day** in August.

SARATOGA SPRINGS, due north of Albany, is a famous old spa and a gay racing town "in season" (August for flat races). There are trotting races at the Raceway from late May through September. Other local sights: the modernized **Saratoga Spa State Park,** with swimming pools and championship golf course; the **National Museum of Racing; Congress Park and Casino,** a lavishly landscaped one-time gambling palace, now a historical museum.

SCHENECTADY, at the Hudson end of the Mohawk River, is home to **Union College** as well as the giant General Electric organization. Its city museum houses a splendid natural history section.

SCHUYLERVILLE, named for General Philip Schuyler, is the site of his country estate and of the Saratoga Battle Monument. **Saratoga National Historical Park,** the site of General Burgoyne's defeat in 1777, is just south of the town.

TARRYTOWN, on the river's east bank, has Washington Irving's busily gabled home, **Sunnyside,** restored to its former pleasantly musty charm and now sheltering a wealth of Irving mementos.

Additional stops in North Tarrytown: the **Old Dutch Church** erected in the late seventeenth century by Frederick Philipse; **Sleepy Hollow Cemetery** where Washington Irving, Andrew Carnegie and William Rockefeller are buried.

WARWICK, south of Goshen, keeps its historical society collection in **"Shingle House,"** a 1764 salt box built by Daniel Burt. The **Warwick Valley Museum** concentrates on early furniture (some fine Queen Anne and Duncan Phyfe), guns and sports equipment.

WEST POINT became the United States Military Academy in 1802. Though there is no regular guide service, visitors are welcome during daylight hours. Principal tour stops: Michie Stadium, where the Army plays its home games; Fort Clinton, an antique defense post, north and east of the Plain; Trophy Point, where a part of the chain stretched across the Hudson to jam British shipping is preserved; the military museum; the Cadet Chapels (Catholic and non-sectarian); the Post Cemetery and Old Cadet Chapel. Weather permitting, parades are held every Saturday of the academic year at 1:10 P.M., except on home-game football weekends when the marching starts at 11:45 A.M.

WOODSTOCK, northwest of Kingston just inside the Catskill Forest Preserve, is a year-round resort and artists' colony. Highmount, in a western part of the forest, is site of the **Belleayre Mountain Ski Center** (chair lifts, T-bar lifts, ski lodge).

YONKERS. **Philipse Manor** is one of the Valley's truly distinguished estate houses, built by the Philipse family between 1682 and 1745. Restored and maintained by the state, it houses the Cochran collection of presidential portraits. The **Hudson River Museum** is a handsome old stone mansion exhibiting every imaginable kind of local curio —from minerals to muskets.

Across the river, a few miles north at Tappan, the **DeWindt Mansion**—another early (1700) Dutch home—was Washington's local headquarters in 1780 and again in 1783.

NORTHERN NEW YORK is a land of lakes, mountains and deep, quiet forests covering more than 8,000 square miles. Its southeastern section lies almost wholly within the Adirondack Park reservation, and at its northwest edge is the new **St. Lawrence Seaway.** In summer, there's swimming, land sports and fishing; in winter, excellent skiing.

ALEXANDRIA BAY, below Ogdensburg, is the main gateway to the St. Lawrence's principal play area: the **Thousand Islands** (of which, by actual count, there are nearly 1,800). Some—Cedar and Mary islands, for example—are state parks with camping facilities. Launch tours out of Alexandria Bay take in most of the Canadian and American sights; some make stopovers at Boldt's castle, abandoned in 1902 after an expenditure of $2 million.

AUSABLE CHASM, famous mile-and-a-half-long gorge, is northeast of Lake Placid near Lake Champlain. Spring, summer and fall, a walk-and-boat tour shows visitors the twisting river, its rapids and falls walled in by sheer 100-to-200-foot cliffs.

The **St. Lawrence Seaway** that brings deep-water shipping to the Great Lakes runs from Ogdensburg, New York, north and east of **Massena.** Massena has five "overlook" points within viewing distance of the Eisenhower and Snell Locks, the Wiley-Dondero Ship Canal, the Long Sault Dam, Barnhart Island Bridge, Robert Moses State Park, and the Moses-Saunders Power Dam.

LAKE GEORGE (village), shopping center and sportsmen's departure point, sits at the southern tip of the long (32 miles), narrow lake of the same name. To the west–around Luzerne, Stony Creek and Warrensburg–lies New York State's dude ranch country. Camping sites, public and private, are centered around the village of Bolton's Landing. East of Lake George Village are **Lake George Beach** and **Battleground State Park** and **Fort William Henry,** a restored British-built pre-Revolutionary fort.

Near the south end of Lake Champlain are **Ticonderoga** and its namesake fort. Built by the French in 1755, it was called Fort Vaudreuil, then Fort Carillon. The British, who seized it in 1759, gave it its present Indian-born name. Its most famous tenants were Ethan Allen and his Green Mountain Boys, whose Revolutionary attack so surprised the resident British forces that they surrendered without shedding blood. The **Fort,** restored in keeping with the original French plans, now houses a collection of weapons, uniforms and utensils.

LAKE PLACID, east of Saranac, glamor queen of the area, was the location of the 1936 Winter Olympics, and now has a bobsled run (the only one in the Western Hemisphere), an ice arena, and a ski jump for sports enthusiasts. Excellent facilities for riding, tennis, golf, and lake sports in summer and skiing on **Whiteface Mountain** in winter make the area popular all year round. Whiteface's twin chair lift runs as a sightseeing attraction during the summer. For the earthbound, a scenic highway also makes the Whiteface climb, and an elevator inside the mountain ascends the last few hundred feet.

OLD FORGE, on the Fulton Chain of Lakes, anchors a series of famous woods-lake resorts that stretch north and east into the mountains. Old Forge itself, set in big hunting and fishing country, is take-off point for a classic multi-lake canoe trip that follows the eight Fulton Lakes north, continues through Raquette, Forked and Long lakes for 100 miles.

THE VILLAGE OF SARANAC LAKE is actually on Lake Flower, half a mile below Lower Saranac Lake. The local year-round program includes winter skiing on nearby Mount Pisgah. Chief local monument is the **Robert Louis Stevenson Memorial Cottage,** where the writer spent the 1887–88 winter.

CENTRAL NEW YORK, quilted with farms and orchards, is a 115-mile-wide patch of historic country between Amsterdam on the east and Oswego on the west. On the north it takes in its own small corner of Lake Ontario; its southern section–running down to the Pennsylvania border–includes most of James Fenimore Cooper's Leatherstocking Country. The **Mohawk Valley**–only water-level pass through the Appalachians between Maine and Georgia–carries not only the river, but the New York State Barge Canal, the wide new New York Thruway and the New York Central's Buffalo-bound tracks.

AMSTERDAM, on the Mohawk, once turned out more square miles of carpet per year than any place else in the country. The city was founded by Sir William Johnson, one-time Superintendent of Indian Affairs for His Majesty in all of North America. His home, old **Fort Johnson,** just west of town, is now headquarters of the Montgomery County Historical Society and a museum of Indian relics. **Guy Park Manor** in Amsterdam was built for Sir William's daughter and son-in-law.

Nearby, at Auriesville, stands the **Shrine of our Lady of Martyrs,** scene of the torture and death of three French Jesuit missionaries, and birthplace of Kateri Tekakwitha, who may be the first North American-born saint.

COOPERSTOWN, another ten miles south and east, is located at the south tip of Otsego Lake. Founded in 1786 by Judge William Cooper, James Fenimore's father, the town is best-known for the **National Baseball Hall of Fame and Museum,** opened in 1939 (General Abner Doubleday "invented" the game here). Also in Cooperstown are **Farmers' Museum** (early American farming and household equipment, reconstructed Village Crossroads); **Fenimore House** (Cooper memorabilia and Hall of Life masks); the **Indian Museum;** and the **Woodland Museum.**

OSWEGO, near the east end of Lake Ontario, is a port and manufacturing town at the northern terminus of the State Barge Canal. Local interest points: star-shaped **Fort Ontario,** battled over by French, British and Americans, now restored as a state shrine; **Oswego County Historical Society Museum** with a Louis XV medal commemorating the French victory in 1756.

SYRACUSE, south of Oneida Lake, in the center of the state, majors in manufacturing (air conditioners, electronic equipment, plows, pottery and so on). It is also home to **Syracuse University.** Sightseeing stops: **Onondaga Lake Park** with a replica of Fort Ste. Marie de Gannentaha—the old French post which was the area's first building, the ancient Jesuit well, a Salt Museum, the **Canal Museum** with a fine collection of Erie Canal mementos; **Mills Rose Garden,** a lavishly flowered tract within Thornden Park; **Everson Art Museum,** and **Lowe Art Center.**

THE FINGER LAKES-GENESEE REGION reaches from Lake Otisco (actually an auxiliary digit, east of the Finger Lakes proper) to Rochester and the Genesee River in the west. Its northern portion —just below Lake Ontario—is truck farming and garden country. The Finger Lakes themselves—Skaneateles, Owasco, Cayuga, Seneca, Keuka and Canandaigua—with a sprinkling of smaller lakes—Honeoye, Lamoka, Waneta, Cayuta and Otisco—form a fine big fresh-water playland. At their southern tips lie New York's wine-grape counties.

CANANDAIGUA is northernmost and chief city on Canandaigua Lake. Historical attractions: relics and manuscripts (including the Indians' copy of the 1794 Pickering Treaty) preserved by the **Ontario County Historical Society;** the **Granger Homestead** with beautifully paneled doors, handsome woodwork, china, silver. Sports lures: The new Finger Lakes Race Track; swimming, boating, good fishing, and a large amusement park.

CORNING, west of Elmira, has glass as its main attraction—from the earliest Egyptian museum pieces to super-practical modern kitchenware. The free **Corning Glass Center** tour covers all these and a visit to the Steuben factory to watch artisans hand-fashion glass objects.

ELMIRA, where Mark Twain lived, lies south of the Finger Lakes just north of the Pennsylvania border. On the **Elmira College** campus stands his study, built in the shape of a riverboat's pilothouse. His grave is in Woodlawn Cemetery.

GENEVA, on the northern end of Seneca, the biggest Finger Lake, is a farming and nursery center. Fishing is one of its prime sports attractions. There are swimming and boating facilities at **Seneca Park** on the lake. **Watkins Glen,** at Seneca's southern tip, takes its name from a sheer-walled neighborhood gorge with shaped rocks and spectacular waterfalls. Part of one of the oldest state parks, it has camping sites, and an olympic-size swimming pool. The **International Grand Prix Road Race** for sports cars is held here annually.

ITHACA, at the lower tip of Cayuga, is chiefly renowned as the home of **Cornell University.** Sightseeing stops: the **Andrew Dickson White Museum of Art;** the **University Clock Tower;** the **University Library; Anabel Taylor Hall,** campus interfaith center with remarkable revolving altar; the tiny **Lua A. Minns Memorial Gardens.** There are student-conducted tours. Non-collegiate attractions include the **DeWitt Historical Museum** and **Stewart Park** on the lake.

PALMYRA, southeast of Rochester, was the birthplace of Mormonism. Founder **Joseph Smith's** boyhood home in Palmyra is open to the public. Other Mormon shrines include the **Sacred Grove,** the **Martin Harris Farm** and the **Peter Whitmer Home.**

ROCHESTER has grown up where the Genesee River meets Lake Ontario. It is, primarily, a manufacturing town with industry bringing it not only cameras but culture in the form of the endowed Eastman-Rochester Symphony and the Eastman School of Music. Worthwhile museums: the **Rochester Museum of Arts and Sciences** (history, science, nature, industry, education); **Memorial Art Gallery** (University of Rochester); the **Bevier Memorial Art Gallery** of the Rochester Institute of Technology (special collections, September through May). **George Eastman House** exhibits tell photography's story. Well-tended parks are another local specialty. Several local plants offer factory tours.

WESTERN NEW YORK takes in the land beyond Rochester all the way west to Lake Erie and includes two of the state's most spectacular sites: **Niagara Falls** and **Allegany State Park.**

BUFFALO, 20 miles southeast of the falls, is western New York's metropolis. Founded by the French in the late seventeenth century, it has known its greatest growth since the Erie Canal opened up in 1825. The **Buffalo Historic Society,** which should be visited, is housed in the only building remaining from the 1901 Pan American Exposition. Other cultural stops: **Albright Art Gallery** in Delaware Park, where paintings, library and sculpture court are housed in the classic Greek manner; **Buffalo Museum of Science** in Humboldt Park; **South Park Conservatory** (rare specimens of plant life) at the end of McKinley Parkway; and **Delaware Park Zoo.**

CHAUTAUQUA INSTITUTE, near Jamestown, is where a summer population of nearly 10,000 (winter's total runs between 400 and 500) holds lakeside seminars on arts, music, crafts, theater, dance, adult education and religion; concerts, opera, drama and lectures.

NIAGARA FALLS, on the Niagara River, shared by New York and Ontario, is probably the most-visited, most-honeymooned-near attraction in the country. The two sections—Canadian (curved, called "Horseshoe"; 186 feet high, over 2,500 feet wide) and American (straight; 193 feet high, 1,000 feet wide)—are separated by **Goat Island.** A good spot from which to get a top-side perspective on both is the 282-foot observation tower near the American Falls. From the island, an elevator descends to the **Cave of the Winds. Maid of the Mist** diesel powerboats carry passengers to the base of the Falls for a front-and-center view (waterproofs provided). **Devil's Hole** and **Whirlpool State Parks** are on the American side. The **Viewmobile,** an awning-covered motor train, stops at all vantage points.

OLD FORT NIAGARA—about 14 miles above the falls near Youngstown at the mouth of the Niagara River—was constructed by the French in 1726. Now a historic shrine, its restored military assets include 52 mounted cannon (Louis XV models), a drawbridge, a hot shot furnace and five of the original buildings.

SPORTS AND RECREATION. New York has an outstanding system of 82 public parks, preserving scenic areas and providing statewide facilities for picnicking, camping, swimming, hiking, fishing and other sports. The New York State Conservation Department, State Campus, Albany, New York 12226, has full details. Largest state parks are described here.

On Long Island: **Bethpage State Park,** 1,500 acres near Farmingdale; golf, tennis, riding, picnicking; athletic field, clubhouse, restaurant. **Fire Island State Park,** 1,000 acres of beach on the Atlantic Ocean, reached by ferry from Bay Shore; fishing, boating, swimming, picnicking. **Heckscher State Park,** 1,500 acres near Islip; beach swimming, picnicking; playgrounds. **Hither Hills State Park,** more than 1,700 acres west of Montauk; camping, fishing, swimming, picnicking. **Jones Beach,** 2,400 acres of Atlantic Ocean shore; roller skating, paddle tennis, ping-pong, fishing, pool and surf swimming, picnicking; playgrounds, restaurants, outdoor entertainment. **Sunken Meadow State Park,** 1,266 acres near Kings Park, features swimming and picnicking, as do eight other Long Island parks.

In the Hudson Valley region: **Bear Mountain State Park,** 4,900 acres on Hudson River near West Point; winter sports, hiking, boating, archery, tennis, swimming; inn, museums. **Catskill Forest Preserve,** 237,000 acres in the Catskill Mountains; camping, fishing, swimming, picnicking; Belleayre Ski Center. **Harriman State Park,** 40,000 acres, 45 miles up the Hudson from New York; camping, fishing, swimming, picnicking; playgrounds. **John Boyd Thacher State Park,** 1,100 acres near Albany; camping, hiking, swimming, picnicking. **Saratoga Spa State Park,** 1,300 acres; golf, picnicking, swimming; mineral springs, baths. **Taconic State Park,** 3,900 acres near Copake Falls; camping, fishing, swimming, picnicking; cabins.

In northern New York: **Adirondack Forest Preserve,** an immense two-and-one-quarter-million-acre recreation area with lakes, woods and the state's highest peaks; winter sports, camping, hunting, fishing, boating, swimming, picnicking. **Wellesley Island State Park,** over 2,600 acres on the St. Lawrence River near Alexandria Bay; camping, fishing, swimming, picnicking; cabins.

In central New York: **Gilbert Lake State Park,** nearly 1,600 acres near Oneonta; camping, fishing, boating, swimming, picnicking; cabins.

In the Finger Lakes-Genesee region: **Robert H. Treman State Park,** almost 1,000 acres near Ithaca; camping, hiking, fishing, swimming, picnicking; cabins.

In western New York: **Allegany State Park,** 58,000 acres from Salamanca to the Pennsylvania line; winter sports, camping, swimming, picnicking; cabins. **Letchworth State Park,** over 13,000 acres, near Portageville; swimming, picnicking; restaurant, cabins, inn, museum and the 17-mile Genesee Gorge.

SPECIAL EVENTS. **Chinese New Year's Festival,** New York, late January or early February; **St. Patrick's Day Parade,** New York, March 17; **Easter Parade,** New York, Easter Sunday; **International Flower Show,** New York, early March; **Miss New York State Pageant,** Kingston, early July; **tulip festival,** Albany, mid-May; **Greenwich Village Spring Outdoor Art Exhibit,** New York, May; **lilac festival,** Rochester, late May; **rose festival,** Newark, mid-June; county fairs throughout the state, mid-July through September; **Mormon Pageant,** Palmyra, early August; **Old Stone House Day,** New Paltz, early August; **Shaker Museum Festival,** Old Chatham, early August; **Woodsmen's Field Days,** Tupper Lake, August; **New York State Exposition,** Syracuse, Labor Day week; **Scottish Games,** Altamont, early September; **Greenwich Village Fall Outdoor Art Show,** New York, September; **Thanksgiving Day Parade,** New York, late November.

On the sporting side: **NCAA College Basketball Tournament,** New York, March; **New York Yankees** and **New York Mets professional baseball,** New York, April through September; **horse racing,** Aqueduct (Long Island) and Saratoga; **harness racing,** Yonkers (April to December) and Roosevelt Raceway on Long Island (summer and fall); **New York Giants** and **New York**

Jets professional football, New York, early fall through December; **college football** at Columbia University (New York), Cornell (Ithaca), U. S. Military Academy (West Point) in fall; **National Horse Show,** New York, November; **New York Knickerbockers, Nets,** and **Harlem Globetrotters professional basketball,** New York, winter; **New York Rangers** and **Islanders professional ice hockey,** New York, winter.

New Jersey

Only three states are smaller than New Jersey, but no state produces a greater variety of manufactured goods—from dolls to drugs, chemicals, and machinery.

THE LAND. Except for a 48-mile land border with New York on the north, New Jersey is surrounded by water—the Hudson River and Atlantic Ocean on the east, Delaware Bay on the southwest, and the Delaware River on the west. Covering 7,836 square miles, most of New Jersey's soil, except for the salt marshes and sandy soil in the Atlantic coastal area, makes excellent farmland. The state is primarily flat, with low hills and plains. High Point is the tallest peak, at 1,803 feet.

THE CLIMATE. Although New Jersey, due to its long coastline, is susceptible to violent storms sweeping in from the Atlantic, its climate is basically mild. Temperatures average 70–76 degrees in July and 26–34 degrees in January. Snowfall averages 42 inches yearly in the north and 17 inches in the south. Rainfall averages 42 inches annually.

THE PEOPLE. The land between the Delaware and the Hudson that is now New Jersey was, before settlers arrived, occupied by peaceful Indians, called Delawares, after their home valley, by the white men, and known among themselves as Leni-Lenape—"the original people." The Dutch set up a trading post at Bergen in 1618, and Cornelius Mey, another Dutchman after whom Cape May was named, sailed up the Delaware to establish Fort Nassau near where Gloucester City stands today. There were small Swedish settlements on the Delaware and the Maurice River. Aside from these intrusions, the Delawares still had the land to themselves.

When a change of power did come, the atmosphere was still placid. In 1664, Charles II granted his brother the Duke of York extensive New World holdings including what later became New Jersey. The Dutch gave up their claim without a fight. The land on the west side of the Hudson was granted to John Berkeley, Baron of Stratton, and Sir George Carteret. It was Sir George, who had made himself something of a hero defending the Isle of Jersey, who was responsible for the territorial name.

English colonization progressed rapidly, as Calvinists, Congregationalists and Presbyterians moved in to civilize the eastern half of the state. In the west, on lands sold him by Berkeley, John Fenwick, a Quaker, established the first Friends' settlement in America at Salem. (Title was later sold to William Penn.) Philip Carteret, a cousin of Sir George, was appointed to govern the entire area.

Upon her succession in 1702, Queen Anne required proprietors to surrender all rights of government to the throne, and the halves of New Jersey were united in a single royal province. Even this change made no appreciable difference in the colony's day-to-day life.

It was not till some 70 years later that Revolutionary rumblings disturbed the peace. The first Provincial Congress that assembled in New Brunswick in 1774 appointed delegates to the Continental Congress at Philadelphia. On July 2, 1776, it deposed the last royal governor and adopted a combined state constitution and declaration of independence. As far as New Jersey was concerned, the Revolution was on.

From that time until Cornwallis' surrender at Yorktown in 1781, New Jersey knew no peace. The state became "the pathway of the Revolution." Washington and his army crossed and recrossed it four times, shivering out two winters at Morristown. Tories took the Pine Barrens and waged harassing guerrilla warfare from there. A hundred engagements, three of them (Monmouth, Trenton, and Princeton) major battles, were fought on New Jersey soil.

New Jersey was the third state to ratify the Constitution in 1787, and the state capital was established at its present site, Trenton, in 1790. In the War of 1812, a New Jersey man, Captain James Lawrence, gave the Navy its motto: "Don't give up the ship!"

Most of the state's post-Revolutionary energies, however, have been concentrated on peace and profitable progress. Along with individual coups (Edison's lamp, his phonograph, his movies; Holland's submarine), there have been group giant steps—the development of large industrial cities, like Paterson, and grander agricultural schemes such as the huge frozen food operation at Bridgeton.

AGRICULTURE. Leading farm products in this heavily agricultural state are poultry and dairy produce (most important area of agriculture); vegetables, fruits, and field crops (through extensive truck farming); and nursery products. Farmers in New Jersey produce an average annual income of $223 per acre, the highest gross income per acre in the country.

INDUSTRY. Because of its excellent transportation facilities and water power, New Jersey has developed into one of the leading manufacturing states in the country. Aiding its growth is the fact that few of the factories rely on nearby raw materials.

More than 11,000 manufacturing plants, many located between Fort Lee and Trenton, employ over 80,000 workers. Chief industries are chemicals, pharmaceuticals, and allied products (New Jersey factories lead the nation in this area), machinery, metal processing, china, and automobiles. Industrial research in the state accounts for 15 percent of the nation's total.

CITIES. Only one of New Jersey's seven cities with more than 100,000 residents—Atlantic City—has no large manufacturing facilities. The others, Trenton, Camden, Newark, Jersey City, Paterson, and Elizabeth, are all important centers of industry and commerce.

NORTHERN NEW JERSEY has at least one of almost every kind of town. The industrial giants—Jersey City, Elizabeth, Newark, Paterson—cluster in its southeast corner across the river from New York. Northeast of those lie Morristown, Madison, Caldwell and towns like them—all with historic claims to fame. North and west, in the lakes and the mountains, some villages live for pleasure (and the tourist in pursuit of it); others are centers for men who trap for a living. Scattered on both sides of U. S. Route 1, a road that runs between Jersey City and Trenton, dividing North Jersey from South, lie the commuter towns that owe Monday-to-Friday allegiance to New York or Philadelphia.

CALDWELL, south of Paterson, was Grover Cleveland's birthplace; his home is now a museum and open to the public. South of Caldwell, suburban **Montclair** has an art museum worth visiting, and across the Orange Mountains in **West Orange, Edison Laboratory** is a national monument (where a nickel in the "juke box" buys one play-through of the inventor's favorite cylinder record, "I'll Take You Home Again, Kathleen"). In Pleasantdale, there is a beautifully equipped recreation area (swimming, tennis, golf, horseback riding) called **South Mountain Reservation.**

ELIZABETH boasts a total of 23 pre-Revolutionary houses (they're marked with plaques showing Washington on horseback). Among them: the **Boudinot Mansion, Boxwood Hall,** home of Elias Boudinot, first president of the Continental Congress.

HACKENSACK, east of Paterson, is the site of the **Baron von Steuben House,** Washington's headquarters in 1780. Later presented to the baron in payment of New Jersey's share of the nation's debt to him, it is now a Colonial museum. The **Dey Mansion** at Mountain View, west of Paterson, was another occasional Washington command post.

In the lake country at the state's northern border, **Ringwood Manor House,** once Peter Cooper's home, in Ringwood Manor State Park, displays Revolutionary relics. Near Sussex in another state park, **High Point,** a summit-perched observation tower offers visitors a two-state view of the surrounding mountain country. Handsome highland landscapes are also preserved in **Stokes State Forest** and **Swartswood State Park,** both within 20 miles west and south of Sussex.

LAMBERTVILLE on the Delaware, one of a number of Washington headquarters in the Trenton vicinity, is famous for its summer "music circus." Hopewell, to the east, has a worthwhile history museum. At **Washington Crossing,** a few miles south, the General made his Christmas-night trip across the Delaware to surprise the Hessians at Trenton six miles below.

MORRISTOWN, where the Continental army spent two winters (1777 and 1779–80), was considered to have been as cold and hard on the troops as was the 1777–78 winter at Valley Forge. Washington's headquarters in the **Ford Mansion,** a historic museum (interesting weapons collection, dioramas of significant Revolutionary events); **Fort Nonsense** (so called because, as far as anyone can discover, it was constructed just to keep soldiers busy); and the **Jockey Hollow** preserve (officers' hut, reconstructed Continental army hospital and Wick House, a restored circa-1770 farmhouse), make up the **Morristown National Historical Park.** Other historic stops: **Campfield House** (Olyphant Place) where Alexander Hamilton courted Betsy Schuyler, and the **Speedwell Iron Works,** which made supplies for the Continental army.

NEWARK brews six million barrels of beer a year, thereby earning itself the title of "Milwaukee of the East." It also makes the country's finest gold jewelry, and boasts one notable Gothic monument—the **Catholic Cathedral of the Sacred Heart**—patterned after France's basilica at Rheims.

NEW BRUNSWICK, 16 miles northeast of Princeton, is the site of **Rutgers,** New Jersey's state university. Other points of interest are **Buccleuch Mansion,** a Colonial museum, and **Mettler's Woods,** an imposing 65-acre tract of primeval forest.

PATERSON, founded in 1791 on a spot selected by Alexander Hamilton to take maximum advantage of the powerful Passaic Falls, was the first planned industrial city in the United States. On the historic side, it boasts two good museums: the **Paterson Museum,** resting place of J. P. Holland's first submarine; and **Lambert Castle,** an impressive Victorian pile in the Garret Mountain Reservation, now the **Passaic County Historical Society Museum.**

PLAINFIELD, home to a number of important industrial firms, remains primarily residential. In 1777 Washington reportedly visited its **Nathaniel Drake House** (now a museum of the local historical society) and—also reportedly—spied out British troop movements from nearby **Washington Rock State Park. Edison State Park** in Menlo Park has a memorial tower and museum.

Washington's trail leads northwest to Morristown through **Springfield** (where the "fighting parson," Reverend James Caldwell, once fired hymnals at the onrushing British), Chatham and Madison, New Jersey's rose-growing center where the **Hartley Dodge Memorial** houses a worthwhile art exhibit.

PRINCETON, to the east, is home to the university of the same name;

Nassau Hall (1756) on Nassau Street is its oldest building; its **chapel** is the largest at any American university. Notable non-collegiate structures in the neighborhood: **Morven,** a pre-Revolutionary home, now official residence of the governor of New Jersey; **Berrien House,** six miles north at Rocky Hill, where Washington wrote and delivered his farewell address to the army.

SOUTHERN NEW JERSEY is seashore—more than 120 Atlantic-washed miles of it. It is also history at Trenton and Monmouth, pine-and-scrub-oak wilderness around Batsto, truck gardening near Bridgeton, oyster farming at Bivalve. Settled by Quakers on the one side (west) and sun-worshipers on the other, its cities and towns offer all sorts of things to do and see.

Starting with southern New Jersey's northeast corner, Monmouth County mixes history with shore sports. **Red Bank** is its shopping center (also a yachting, ice-boating, fishing, crabbing and eeling headquarters). **Middletown,** to the north, has a good Colonial museum. The **Battle of Monmouth,** in which Molly Pitcher won fame as a heroic water-girl, was waged between Freehold and Tennent where a handsome old church can be seen. The **Village Inn** at **Englishtown** was standing at the time. The **Monmouth County Historical Association Museum** at Freehold displays battle relics along with other early Americana; has a junior museum stocked with toys, miniature furniture, dolls, costumes and firearms. At **Allaire,** the furnace and forge that operated in its heyday as a bog ironworks still stand among the deserted nineteenth-century village buildings. Now a state park, the village has been restored as a full-scale museum.

A similar ironworks-turned-ghost-town, Batsto, is located in the Pine Barrens near the center of the state's southern section. Part of the **Wharton Tract of State Forest Park and Water Reserve,** it is open to visitors sun-up to sun-down.

Other inland points of interest: **Farmingdale,** where a small community of Kalmuk (Mongol) refugees have established their Buddhist temple in a cinder-block garage; **Lakewood,** where a former Rockefeller estate is now a county park; and **Lakehurst Naval Air Station,** famous mooring for lighter-than-air craft, and its adjoining military reservation, **Fort Dix.**

When traveling in Monmouth or Ocean counties, the ocean is scarcely ever more than a shell's throw away. Scattered along the 127-mile stretch between Atlantic Highlands and Cape May are more than 50 boardwalk-lined resorts. Some are huge hotel and motel operations; others are family cottage colonies. In some, night brings forth nothing more boisterous than strollers on the boardwalk. At others—**Atlantic City,** for instance—it lights up all kinds of excitement: name dance bands, diving horse exhibitions, penny-arcade spectaculars.

From north to south, some of the best-known resorts are the following:

ASBURY PARK has a full mile of boardwalk, fine hotels, beaches and five large swimming pools. Along the beach front are game arcades, amusement-park rides, an ice-skating rink.

ATLANTIC CITY, about 20 miles south of Long Beach Island, is the largest of the resort cities—an oasis of hotels and motels plus a full complement of amusement piers, fine seafood restaurants and salt-water taffy factories—most of them open year round. One of Atlantic City's most well-known and anticipated events is the **Miss America Pageant,** held each year in late summer. Another acclaimed attraction is the super-modern **State Marina.** Ventnor, Margate (home of an elephant-shaped "hotel"), Longport and Ocean City are all pleasantly subdued family variations on the Atlantic City theme. The **Somers Mansion Museum,** at Somers Point on the mainland opposite Ocean City, traces Jersey Shore history through its exhibits.

BORDENTOWN, between Burlington and Trenton, specializes in historic buildings: **St. Joseph's Mission** on the former estate of Napoleon's brother, Joseph Bonaparte; the home of **Francis Hopkinson,** signer of the Declaration of Independence; the brick school where **Clara Barton,** Red Cross founder, once taught; the **Thomas Paine House,** home of the Revolutionary writer. West and a little north of Bordentown is **Crosswicks,** site of the most renowned of many Friends' meetinghouses in the state.

BURLINGTON, northeast of Camden, is another Quaker-settled community (1677). The **Revell House** on East Pearl Street was built in 1685; the **Quaker Schoolhouse,** in 1792. **James Fenimore Cooper** was born at 457 South High Street, now headquarters of the **Burlington County Historical Society.** Next door to the Cooper house is the birthplace of **James Lawrence,** "Don't give up the ship" naval hero.

CAMDEN, facing Philadelphia across the Delaware, was the last **home of Walt Whitman.** The house he lived in on Mickle Street is now a shrine; his tomb is in Harleigh Cemetery at Haddon Avenue and Vesper Boulevard. Camden's historical collections are housed in **Charles S. Boyer Memorial Hall,** Euclid Avenue and Park Boulevard.

CAPE MAY, at the shore's southern tip, was the country's very first ocean resort. Its chief charm: a combination of full-scale boardwalk-beach operation and tree-shaded residential streets. There are fishing, tennis, golf and horseback riding facilities nearby. **Cape May Court House,** a separate community about ten miles up the peninsula, has a historical museum filled with antique whaling implements, glass, costumes, Indian relics and genealogical material.

GREENWICH, on an inlet near the mouth of the Delaware River, not to be outdone by Boston, staged its own "tea party" when, in 1774, citizens dressed as Indians burned a shipload of the East India Company's finest in a local vacant lot. The **Richard Wood Mansion** (historical exhibits) is open Sunday afternoons. At Hancock's Bridge, ten miles north, **Hancock House,** scene of a Revolutionary massacre, is now a state-aided museum.

HADDONFIELD has its own collection of Colonial mementos, furniture, and costumes on exhibition at the **Historical Society Building** on Kings Highway. The town's **Indian King Tavern,** was built in 1750 and was a meeting place for the New Jersey legislature in 1777.

POINT PLEASANT is a large ocean-fishing center (200 party and charter boats on call); its mile of boardwalk is lined with amusements and good seafood restaurants. Miss New Jersey Seafood Princess is crowned at the Point every August. On the north tip of Long Beach Island, slightly less than halfway down the coast, red and white **Barnegat Light** stands in a state picnic preserve; first lit in 1858, it was replaced by a lightship in 1927. Just north of it is **Island Beach State Park,** one of New Jersey's newest (for fuller information, see *Sports and Recreation*).

The rest of 19-mile-long Long Beach Island is shared by the summer communities of Loveladies, Harvey Cedars, Surf City, Ship Bottom, the Beach Havens and Holgate. All pride themselves on a lack of commercialized boardwalk, instead offering sun and surf for guests.

SALEM, founded in 1675, was part of the New World property purchased by John Fenwick from John Berkeley, Baron of Stratton in 1674, and as such, part of the first Quaker colony on the continent; the venerable **Salem Oak** and the old **Friends' Meeting House** still stand.

SPRING LAKE is a fashionable spot with a famous hotel and a number of pleasant guest houses. The beach offers surf and sunning; the lake, good fresh-water fishing (pickerel, sunfish, black bass, trout).

STONE HARBOR, some 20 miles farther south, is a yachting center with a sandy protected beach, facilities for golf, tennis and other sports. The **Wildwoods** offer good fishing (deep sea, surf and pier), a boardwalk full of shops and amusement centers.

TRENTON, primarily an industrial city, also has several historic landmarks: **Trent House,** home of Justice William Trent who named and laid out the city, an impressive brick mansion, painstakingly restored; **Friends' Meeting House,** the original portion of which was built in 1739; the **Old Barracks,** handsome Colonial buildings erected to shelter British troops through the winter of 1758 during the French and Indian Wars. The **Trenton Battle Monument,** 155 feet tall, stands where Washington's troops opened fire on the British December 26, 1776; an elevator carries sightseers to a lookout post on top. The **state capitol,** built in 1792 and substantially added to since, displays an interesting collection of battle flags; the **state museum, library** and **state cultural center** are in the adjoining buildings. The **War Memorial,** dedicated to soldiers and sailors of all wars, includes a theater and assembly hall.

SPORTS AND RECREATION. New Jersey's parks and forests range from solidly forested hunting preserves in the north of the state to a narrow spit of sandy beach-island paralleling the southern coast. Almost all are equipped with picnicking places, many offer fishing and swimming. Campsites and cabins–where they are available–may be reserved by contacting the Forest or Park Officers in charge at specific locations. Following is a north-to-south summary of principal out-of-door playlands and facilities they offer.

In northern New Jersey: **Palisades Interstate Park,** some 50,000 acres in New Jersey and New York, the New Jersey sector beginning at Fort Lee and following the Hudson's Palisades to the New York border; fishing, boating, picnicking; playgrounds. **Ringwood Manor State Park,** nearly 600 acres in northern Passaic County, including the big old homestead of the Cooper and Hewitt families; river fishing, picnicking; museum. **High Point State Park,** 12,000-acre site near Sussex in the Kittatinny Mountains, highest in New Jersey; camping, hiking, fishing, swimming, picnicking; summer restaurant, cabins, lodge, observation tower. **Stokes State Forest,** over 14,000 mountainous acres adjoining High Point near Branchville with impressive views from Sunrise Mountain; camping, hunting, hiking on **Appalachian Trail** (snowshoes or skis in winter), fishing, swimming, picnicking; cabins, trailer sites. **Swartswood State Park,** 1,200 acres west of Newton, including Big Swartswood Lake and the hemlock land around it; swimming, boating, fishing, picnicking; boat liveries. **Hopatcong State Park,** 100-acre landing and water-sports area near Ledgewood on Lake Hopatcong, the state's largest; fishing, swimming, picnicking. **Musconetcong State Park,** 300 acres–nearly all of them in and under Lake Musconetcong–near the town of Netcong; fishing, swimming. **Saxton Falls State Park,** nine-acre site on the old Morris Canal near Hackettstown; river fishing, swimming. **Stephens State Park,** about 125 acres just north of Hackettstown; river fishing, picnicking. **Hacklebarney State Park,** 569-acre site in a beautiful Black River gorge southwest of Chester; fishing, picnicking. **Jenny Jump State Forest,** almost 1,000 acres of woodland high up on Jenny Jump Mountain near the Delaware Water Gap; camping, hunting, picnicking. **Voorhees State Park,** 400 acres in the hills of Hunterdon County north of High Bridge; picnicking; playfield. **Washington Rock State Park,** 36-acre site in the Watchung Mountains near Dunellen where, tradition holds, Washington came to watch British troop movements below; picnicking. **Washington Crossing State Park,** over 750 acres eight miles north of Trenton, commemorates the general's trans-Delaware trip; picnicking; museum. **Abram S. Hewitt** and **Norvin Green forests,** both near the state's north-central border, are open for hunting in season. Northern New Jersey also has two privately developed ski areas: at **Schooley's Mountain** near Hackettstown and in **Rockaway Township** south of Newfoundland; a third ski center is located near **Newton.**

In southern New Jersey: **Cheesequake State Park,** about 1,000 acres of picturesque wood and marshland on Cheesequake Creek near Perth Amboy; swimming, picnicking. **Ocean County Park,** 440-acre deer refuge, once a Rockefeller estate near Lakewood; lake boating, swimming, picnicking; golf driving and archery ranges. **Lebanon State Forest,** 27,000 wooded acres with ponds east of Camden; camping, hunting, swimming, picnicking; cabins. **Island Beach State Park,** 2,600 acres of sandy beach on a spit below Seaside Park; fishing, swimming (Memorial Day to September 15), picnicking. **Barnegat Lighthouse State Park,** 31 acres surrounding the historic old beacon off the shore opposite Barnegat (post office: New Gretna); fishing, picnicking. **Penn State Forest,** over 3,000 acres of pleasant coastal plain southeast of Chatsworth; hunting, fishing, swimming, picnicking. **Bass River State Forest,** 9,000-acre preserve due north of New Gretna; camping, hunting, fishing, swimming, picnicking; cabins. **Green Bank State Forest,** almost 2,000 acres along the Mullica River at Greenbank; hunting, fishing, swimming, picnicking. **Fort Mott State Park,** 100-acre fortification site three miles northwest of Salem; fishing, swimming, picnicking. **Parvin State Park,** 1,000 acres of lake, river and woodland west of Vineland; camping, hiking, fishing, boating, swimming, picnicking; cabins. **Belleplaine State Forest,** 11,000 acres in Cape May and Cumberland counties southeast of Millville; hunting, fishing, swimming, picnicking.

SPECIAL EVENTS. **Washington's Birthday Celebrations,** North Hackensack (von Steuben House) and Elizabeth (Boxwood Hall), February 22; **Easter fashion promenades,** Atlantic City and Asbury Park, Easter Sunday; **Miss New Jersey pageant,** Wildwood, mid-June; **Antique auto parade,** Ocean City, late June; **Hydrangea Festival,** Atlantic City, July; **Victorian weekend open house tours,** Cape May County, mid-July; **Baby Parade,** Ocean City, mid-August; **Miss New Jersey Seafood Princess Contest,** Point Pleasant, mid-August; **Flemington Fair,** Flemington, first week in September; **Miss America Pageant,** Atlantic City, first full week in September; **New Jersey State Fair,** Trenton, last week in September; **Coin show,** Monmouth club, Asbury Park, mid-October; **Re-enactment of Delaware Crossing,** Washington Crossing, December 25.

On the sporting side: **Horse racing** at Garden State Park, Camden, late April through May, and October through early November; at Monmouth Park, Oceanport, June through early August; at Atlantic City Race Course, August through early October; **Goldthwait Cup Regatta,** Lake Carnegie, Princeton, May; **Tuna Tournament,** Atlantic City, last weekend in June; **Fishing Tournament,** Seaside Heights, summer to mid-December; **harness racing,** Freehold, mid-August and September; **striped bass contest,** Long Beach Island, mid-September to mid-November; **college football** at Princeton and Rutgers (New Brunswick), fall.

Pennsylvania

Since pre-Declaration days, the promise of independence has drawn people to Pennsylvania. Its development has been rapid and successful, due in large part to the interest and enthusiasm of Pennsylvania's settlers.

THE LAND. Covering a total of 45,333 square miles, Pennsylvania lies in the center of the Appalachians. It is bordered by Delaware, Maryland, and West Virginia on the south, West Virginia and Ohio on the west, Lake Erie and New York on the north, and New York and New Jersey on the east. Its principal waterways are the Delaware, Lehigh, Schuylkill, Susquehanna, Juniata, Allegheny, and Monongahela rivers.

Much of the state is hilly or mountainous, especially in the Appalachian Plateau and the Appalachian Ridge.

THE CLIMATE. In Pennsylvania, temperatures are usually moderate, with little variance between weather in the eastern and western parts of the state. Average January temperatures are between 26 degrees and 32 degrees; in July they range from 70 to 76 degrees. Yearly rainfall varies from 34 inches to 51 inches in western Pennsylvania, and 40 to 46 inches in the eastern half.

THE PEOPLE. Although Henry Hudson's 1609 stopover in Delaware Bay had established their claim to the lands that lined the Delaware River, the Dutch did little to colonize the country beyond establishing trading posts here and there. It was Johan Printz with a Swedish delegation who put down the first permanent roots at a village called New Gottenburg on Tinicum Island. In 1655, the Dutch annexed the Swedish settlements including Fort Christina (later, Wilmington, Delaware) as well as Printz's community. In 1664, the British took over the land.

In 1681, all the land between the 41st and 43rd latitudes and extending west five degrees from the Delaware River line was granted to William Penn. It was in honor of Penn the elder that the country was christened "Penn's Woods," which is to say Pennsylvania.

In 1682 Penn received a supplementary grant of the Lower Counties (land that was to become Delaware and part of Maryland). He also crossed the Atlantic, landed at Upland (now Chester), set up a temporary capital, laid plans for a new one at Philadelphia, traded with the Indians, established a General Assembly which, before the year was out, had drafted and adopted a "Frame of Government" as well as several "Great Laws" spelled out by Penn.

The most important provision in all this legislation—and one that was emphasized again in the "Charter of Privileges" Penn drew up in 1701 which served the state as a constitution until after the Revolution—was the one that guaranteed religious tolerance. It drew to the new colony not only Penn's fellow Quakers, but an industrious crop of Germans and, in the years that followed, thousands like them.

The pre-Revolutionary years were characterized by Indian troubles and growing irritation with the British Colonial policy, and when war did come, Philadelphia was at the heart of it. In 1774, the First Continental Congress convened there to protest the Stamp Act. The Second Continental Congress met in 1775 and 1776 to draw up the Declaration of Independence and set up the first federal government. When the British captured Philadelphia, the legislators took up temporary residence in York, where they drafted the Articles of Confederation. In 1789, the Constitution was adopted in Philadelphia, which also became the country's capital until the government moved south to Washington's new city on the Potomac.

In spite of its pacific Quaker heritage, Pennsylvania has found itself in the thick of every war ever fought on United States territory. Both Fort Necessity and Fort Duquesne were important in the French and Indian Wars. Washington's bitterest winter encampment was at Valley Forge, and from Pennsylvania he launched his Christmas attack on the Hessians across the Delaware. Peace had no more than started to settle in when first the Whiskey Rebellion (1794), then the Hot-Water Rebellion (1798) boiled up on Pennsylvania soil. In the War of 1812, a Pennsylvanian admiral named Perry launched Pennsylvanian ships from a Pennsylvanian port (Erie) to fight the Battle of the Great Lakes. Civil War battles crossed into Pennsylvania three times and the last—the Battle of Gettysburg—turned the tide of the war.

Today Pennsylvania's population stands at more than 11 million, with 71 of each 100 persons living in cities. Of the state's foreign-born population, most came from Italy, Poland, Russia, and Germany.

AGRICULTURE. More than two-fifths of the state is used for farming and for pasturing of livestock, with over 100,000 farms spread throughout the state.

Leading field crops are corn and hay (largely fed to livestock), potatoes, tobacco, buckwheat, mushrooms, and cigar-filler tobacco. Other products include grapes (grown in the Lake Erie lowlands), apples and peaches, cherries, and tomatoes. Pennsylvania is a leader in production of eggs, milk, and dairy cattle.

INDUSTRY. Pennsylvania is one of the leading manufacturing states in the country, ranking first in iron and steel products and in the output of pig iron and steel. These industries are located predominantly at Pittsburgh, Johnstown, Bethlehem, Lebanon, Coatesville, Steelton, and Morrisville.

There are over 19,000 plants in the state, turning out products such as plastics, machinery, textiles, clothing, and food products. Railroad cars and locomotives are built largely of steel, and more glass is produced in Pennsylvania than in any other state.

CITIES. There are five cities with more than 100,000, and another nine with populations of 50,000 to 100,000. Pennsylvania's urban population is 71 percent of the total, its rural population 29 percent.

EASTERN PENNSYLVANIA. In this part of the state, rolling countryside and wandering streams contrast markedly with the fast pace of large cities like Philadelphia. A variety of attractions, including New Hope, bring thousands of visitors to this region yearly.

ALLENTOWN makes silk, fabrics, machinery, housewares, and cement (the original Portland fields are near here). Washington hid the Liberty and Christ Church bells in **Allentown's Zion Reformed Church** on Hamilton Street just before Philadelphia fell to the British. **Trout Hall** (4th and Walnut streets) is the handsome home built in 1770 by James Allen, founder of the town. Other places of interest: **Allentown Art Museum; Trexler Memorial Park** (its November Chrysanthemum Show is a big event); and the **Trexler-Lehigh County Game Preserve.**

BETHLEHEM, about 40 miles north of Philadelphia, was founded by Moravians in 1741. Their staunch stone buildings are still among the city's handsomest. The women's campus of **Moravian College** dates back to 1785; nearby **Gemein House** (Heckewelder Street) was the first Moravian stone house, while **Bell House** was the first home of the girls' boarding school; it is now a Moravian residence. The old **Chapel** (1751) is now used only for weddings and other very special occasions. Guided tours of the Moravian section are available. Bethlehem is also the home of **Lehigh University** and important iron and steelworks.

EASTON, 11 miles northeast of Bethlehem, is the seat of **Lafayette College.** Also notable: the **home of George Taylor,** Declaration of Independence signer; the **First United Church of Christ,** where Indian treaties were negotiated. **Nazareth,** northwest of Easton, is another Moravian settlement with several good stone Moravian buildings: **gray Cottage,** a school and the oldest Moravian building in America; **Whitefield House,** now the **Moravian Historical Society;** and **Nazareth Hall,** a fine stone mansion on Hall Square, now a children's home.

NEW HOPE, center of Bucks County's flourishing artists' colony, is on the Delaware River just above a reconstructed section of the old Delaware Canal. At Doylestown, 12 miles west, stand the **Bucks County Historical Society** (antique and historical collections, library) and **Fonthill,** the former Henry C. Mercer home, with displays of art, Americana and the Moravian Pottery and Tile Works (daily tours).

PHILADELPHIA, the city founded by William Penn in 1682, is the beginning of eastern Pennsylvania. Any American with a grammar school education can picture certain things about it clearly: the Liberty Bell, Independence Hall, Ben Franklin with a loaf of bread under his arm (the picture is pre-Revolutionary), Thomas Jefferson editing the Declaration of Independence by candlelight.

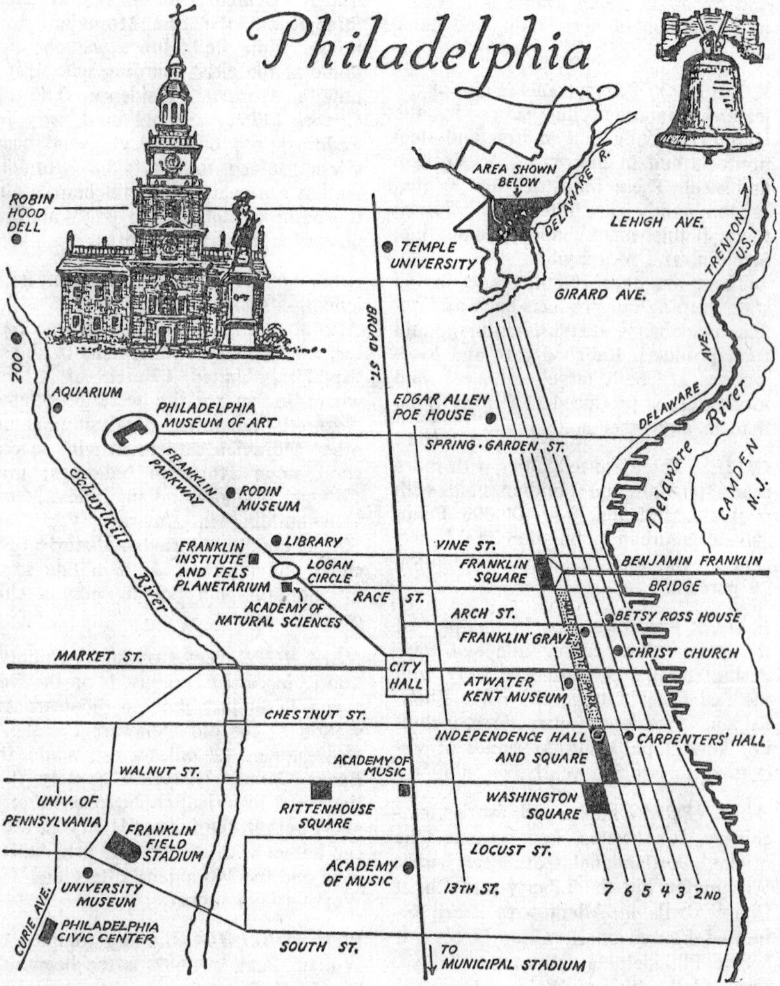

Philadelphia
AREA SHOWN BELOW
DELAWARE R.
ROBIN HOOD DELL
TEMPLE UNIVERSITY
LEHIGH AVE.
TRENTON
U.S. 1
GIRARD AVE.
ZOO
BROAD ST.
AQUARIUM
EDGAR ALLEN POE HOUSE
PHILADELPHIA MUSEUM OF ART
SPRING · GARDEN ST.
DELAWARE AVE.
Delaware River
FRANKLIN PARKWAY
RODIN MUSEUM
CAMDEN N.J.
Schuylkill River
LIBRARY
FRANKLIN INSTITUTE AND FELS PLANETARIUM
LOGAN CIRCLE
VINE ST.
FRANKLIN SQUARE
BENJAMIN FRANKLIN BRIDGE
RACE ST.
ACADEMY OF NATURAL SCIENCES
ARCH ST.
BETSY ROSS HOUSE
FRANKLIN GRAVE
CHRIST CHURCH
MARKET ST.
CITY HALL
ATWATER KENT MUSEUM
MALL STATE PARK
CHESTNUT ST.
INDEPENDENCE HALL AND SQUARE
CARPENTERS' HALL
ACADEMY OF MUSIC
WALNUT ST.
WASHINGTON SQUARE
UNIV. OF PENNSYLVANIA
RITTENHOUSE SQUARE
FRANKLIN FIELD STADIUM
LOCUST ST.
ACADEMY OF MUSIC
UNIVERSITY MUSEUM
13TH ST.
7 6 5 4 3 2ND
CURIE AVE.
PHILADELPHIA CIVIC CENTER
SOUTH ST.
TO MUNICIPAL STADIUM

Independence Hall,
Philadelphia, Pennsylvania

Countryside and covered bridge, Vermont

Paul Revere statue and Old North Church, Boston, Massachusetts

Lighthouse at Pequot Point, New London, Connecticut, dating from 1760

Campus of Dartmouth College in Hanover, New Hampshire

New York State Theatre and Metropolitan Opera House, Lincoln Center, New York City

Old Ironsides, Boston, Massachusetts

Atlantic City, New Jersey

Trophy Point,
West Point, New York

Second Day's Battlefield,
Gettysburg, Pennsylvania

1,000-foot American Falls at Niagara Falls, New York

Twin towers of the World Trade Center, New York City

Harkness Tower, Yale University, New Haven, Connecticut

Provincetown, Cape Cod, Massachusetts

Lake Winnipesaukee, New Hampshire

Maple-sugaring in northern Vermont

"The Breakers," Newport, Rhode Island

The harbor at Newport, Rhode Island

Bar Harbor, Maine

Lobster traps, New Harbor, Maine

Superficially at least, present-day Philadelphia seems slow-moving by comparison, a place where everyone seems thoroughly satisfied with life as it is and has been.

Traditionally, in the prosperous green reaches of the suburbs, there are fox hunts and cricket matches. Men from the right old families cherish memberships in the Philadelphia Club and the "State in Schuylkill" luncheon society. Men and women contribute to family charities, work hard for 200-year-old causes they believe in deeply, which is why the American Philosophical Society founded by Benjamin Franklin is still one of the most respected of North American intellectual organizations and why Philadelphia's **Art Museum** is among the world's most distinguished.

Solid Quaker grounding in the good sense of restraint may make Philadelphia seem less than lively to outsiders. Yet in their quietly cultivated way, its citizens have moved ahead to build up a manufacturing output which ranks third among all United States cities and a port that is one of the country's largest with some 50 miles of developed water front. Their urban renewal plan has become a model for slum-clearance projects everywhere. And though Philadelphians revere **Independence Hall** (with typical understatement, most old-liners refer to it as "the State House"), the heart of their city is the handsome new Penn Center of which the architecture may be most accurately described as multi-windowed modern. Both sides of the city—its vigorous Colonial past and its lively present—are well worth looking into.

Exploration begins with **Independence National Park,** a group of Colonial buildings most of which are centered around Independence Square at 6th and Chestnut streets. (Tour it in daylight, come back for a night look when the 56 gas lamps—one for each Declaration signer—are lit.) There is the old State House, now officially called Independence Hall, where the Declaration of Independence and the Constitution were signed, where George Washington accepted command of the Continental Armies and the Liberty Bell is preserved. Flanking it are **Congress Hall,** home of Congress from 1791 to 1800, and the **Second Bank of the United States,** which turned Customs House in 1845 and is now a museum. **Carpenters' Hall,** where the First Continental Congress met, and the **First United States Bank,** set up by Alexander Hamilton, are also part of the Independence Square group. **Christ Church** (2nd between Market and Arch streets), where Washington and Franklin worshiped; its **graveyard,** where Franklin and his wife Deborah are buried; **Gloria Dei** (Old Swedes') **Church** (Swanson at Christian Street and Delaware Avenue), one of the oldest in the state; and the **Deshler-Morris House** (5442 Germantown Avenue), where Washington lived in 1793 and 1794, are all administered by the same National Park authority.

Philadelphians have restored a number of other historic Colonial houses—some quaint, some handsome. Several lining **Elfreth's Alley** between Front and 2nd streets may be visited on Fete Day, the first Saturday in June. **Betsy Ross' house** (239 Arch Street near Independence Square), where the first American flag was made, is all of two windows wide. **Edgar Allan Poe** wrote some of his eeriest stories while living at **530 North 7th Street.** The magnificently landscaped home of America's first botanist (Elmwood Avenue, west of 54th Street) is called **Bartram's Gardens. Powel House** (244 South 3rd Street) is a handsome Revolutionary mansion. Others of its kind—**Strawberry Mansion, Woodford Mansion, Mount Pleasant, Cedar Grove** and **Sweetbriar Mansion**—all authentically restored, refurnished and open to visitors—are in **Fairmount Park** at the northwest end of the city. Another park landmark: the cabin Grant occupied during the last days of the Civil War.

There are several worthy old churches within strolling distance of Independence Square: **St. Joseph's Church** (321 Willings Alley) was founded in 1733, the first Roman Catholic church in the city; **Old St. Mary's Church** (4th

Street above Spruce), founded in 1763, was the second and became the first Roman Catholic cathedral in 1808; **St. George's Methodist Church** (235 North 4th Street) is the oldest continuously used Methodist church in the world.

Philadelphia's museums are many and excellent. The Philadelphia **Museum of Art** (end of Benjamin Franklin Parkway) ranks with the finest in the world. The **Pennsylvania Academy of the Fine Arts** (Broad and Cherry streets) has an especially good collection of American portraits. The **Benjamin Franklin Memorial** and **Franklin Institute** (20th Street and Benjamin Franklin Parkway) houses a fascinating group of science exhibitions. **Fels Planetarium** shares the institute building. The **University of Pennsylvania Museum** (near the university at 33rd and Spruce streets) contains outstanding studies of ancient and primitive man. Other exhibitions of note: the **Drexel Institute Art Gallery** (nineteenth-century German and French artists, antique American and European furniture); the **Rodin Museum** (sculpture); the **Philadelphia Art Alliance** (sculpture, painting); the **Samuel S. Fleisher Art Memorial** (art objects, ecclesiastical art); the **Rosenbach Galleries** (art objects, books, manuscripts); the **Atwater Kent Museum** (American folk art, history); the **Academy of Natural Sciences** (oldest natural history museum in the country); the **Wagner Free Institute of Science;** the **Historical Society of Pennsylvania** (manuscripts, newspapers, portraits); the **American Swedish Historical Museum;** the **Commercial Museum** (raw materials and manufactured goods from all over the world); and the **Botanical Gardens** (37th Street and Hamilton Walk).

The Philadelphia Orchestra, one of the world's great, makes its home at the **Academy of Music.**

The **City Hall,** from which today's Philadelphia is run, offers guided tours and a view from the William Penn Tower. The **New Custom House** (2nd and Chestnut streets) houses other federal offices—including the secret service and treasury. **U. S. Mint tours** (16th and Spring Garden streets) follow a penny from copper to finish. *The Evening and Sunday Bulletin* (30th and Market streets) offers guided trips through its newspaper plant. And visitors can also arrange to tour the **Philadelphia Navy Yard** (League Island) by applying in advance to the Security Department. A standard two-hour city bus tour covers the most important territory, costs about two dollars.

Within an afternoon's drive of mid-Philadelphia lie all sorts of historic and scenic spots worth the excursion time. To the west there is the **Governor Printz Park** in Essington, site of the capital of New Sweden, first permanent European settlement in Pennsylvania. The **Morton Homestead,** a seventeenth-century Swedish log cabin, is just a few minutes away. **Chester,** the nearest sizeable town, settled by Swedes and Finns, boasts a number of interesting historical houses and giant industrial plants. At **Chadds Ford,** south of West Chester, is **Brandywine Battlefield Historical Monument,** site of a severe setback for Washington and Lafayette in 1777. **Longwood Gardens,** a few miles farther on, are a du Pont donation to the beauty of the local countryside; they take every imaginable form—formal and natural, indoor and outdoor, land and water. Fountains are a specialty, and there are operettas and pageants presented in the open-air theater during the summer.

Philadelphia's famous **"Main Line"** suburbs—Ardmore, Haverford, Bryn Mawr and so on—follow the route of the Paoli Local railroad tracks north and west of the city. **Valley Forge State Park** (also northwest of Philadelphia) enshrines the scene of Washington's bitter 1777–78 winter encampment; remains of entrenchments, chinked-up log cabins, the old camp schoolhouse and Washington's sturdy stone headquarters—Pott's House—still stand. Washington Memorial Chapel, a Museum of American History, Patriot's Hall and a National Memorial Arch have been added to house the relics and honor the men who suffered through the long winter. Four-hour guided tours cost about four dollars round trip from Philadelphia.

At Tullytown, northeast of Philadelphia, is **Pennsbury Manor,** a reconstruction of William Penn's elegant Bucks County estate from which he commuted to the city via six-oared barge.

SCRANTON, another growing manufacturing town, turns out Geiger counters, organs, luggage, jet-fighter assemblies, and lace. It was once a leading coal-mining center. Local scenic wonder: **Nay Aug Park** with lakes, flowers, falls and a zoo.

STROUDSBURG, due north of Easton, is capital of the Pocono vacation country, filled with gentle wooded hills well-stocked with hotels, trout streams and even a dude ranch or two. Among best-known resort towns: **Pocono Manor, Mount Pocono, Mountainhome, Cresco, Bushkill,** and **Buck Hill Falls.** Three miles due east of Stroudsburg is the deep green **Delaware Water Gap.**

WASHINGTON CROSSING STATE PARK—connected by bridge to its New Jersey namesake—is seven and a half miles south of New Hope on the Delaware River. Its chief monuments are the original **ferry house** and **Taylor Mansion** where Washington made plans for his surprise Christmas raid on the Hessians at Trenton. Nearby are **Bowman's Hill Observation Tower** and memorial flagstaff (on the site of a Continental army lookout station), the **Thompson-Neely House** (1701) and an old grist-mill.

WILKES-BARRE is today a manufacturing and hard-coal mining town, though industry now employs ten times as many persons as does decreasingly active coal mining. On July 2, 1778, it was the scene of the Wyoming Massacre, led by Tory Colonel "Indian" Butler and "Queen Esther," a part-Seneca. Exhibits in the **Wyoming Historical** and **Geological Society headquarters** (69 South Franklin Street) tell the story. **Swetland Homestead,** not far from town, is an early nineteenth-century home, restored, and refurnished.

THE PENNSYLVANIA-DUTCH COUNTRY, a beguiling tourist area, lies along the southeastern border. Two stops along the way from Philadelphia to Lancaster, its center: **Pottstown** (visit **Pottsgrove,** restored home of the city founder); and **Hopewell Village,** an eighteenth-century ironworks now maintained as a historic site by the National Park Service.

HERSHEY, the "chocolate town," halfway between Cornwall and Harrisburg, offers tours of the candy and cocoa plant, the large **Hershey Museum** (furniture, music boxes and assorted Penn-Dutch treats), the patterned **Hershey Park** and **Gardens,** in bloom eight months of the year. Main streets: Chocolate and Cocoa avenues.

LANCASTER, ten miles east of the Susquehanna, was official capital of Pennsylvania from 1799 to 1812; today it is the unofficial capital of the pretty and productive Pennsylvania-Dutch country. The surrounding land—the state's most fertile—is farmed by the bonneted and bearded "Plain People"—Amish, Mennonite and Brethren. Among its early American memorabilia: **Trinity Lutheran Church** (1734); **Wheatland,** home of President James Buchanan; **Willson Memorial Building** with its historical museum. **Franklin and Marshall College** was founded here in 1853.

Stops on a Pennsylvania-Dutch expedition: one of the five **farmers' markets** (Tuesday, Friday or Saturday), piled high with produce and Penn-Dutch delicacies (schnitz, souse, shoofly pie); the **Amish farm and house** (five miles east of town on U. S. Route 30), furnished in the "old order" style; the **Farm museum of Landis Valley** (three miles north off U. S. Route 222); the semi-monastic **Cloister** founded by a society of Seventh Day Baptists at Ephrata; the **Pretzel House** and **Moravian settlement buildings** at **Lititz.**

Half-day guided tours of the Pennsylvania-Dutch country originate in Lancaster, cost about five dollars.

MANHEIM, north of Lancaster, still pays one-rose-a-year rent to a descend-

Gettysburg Battlefield

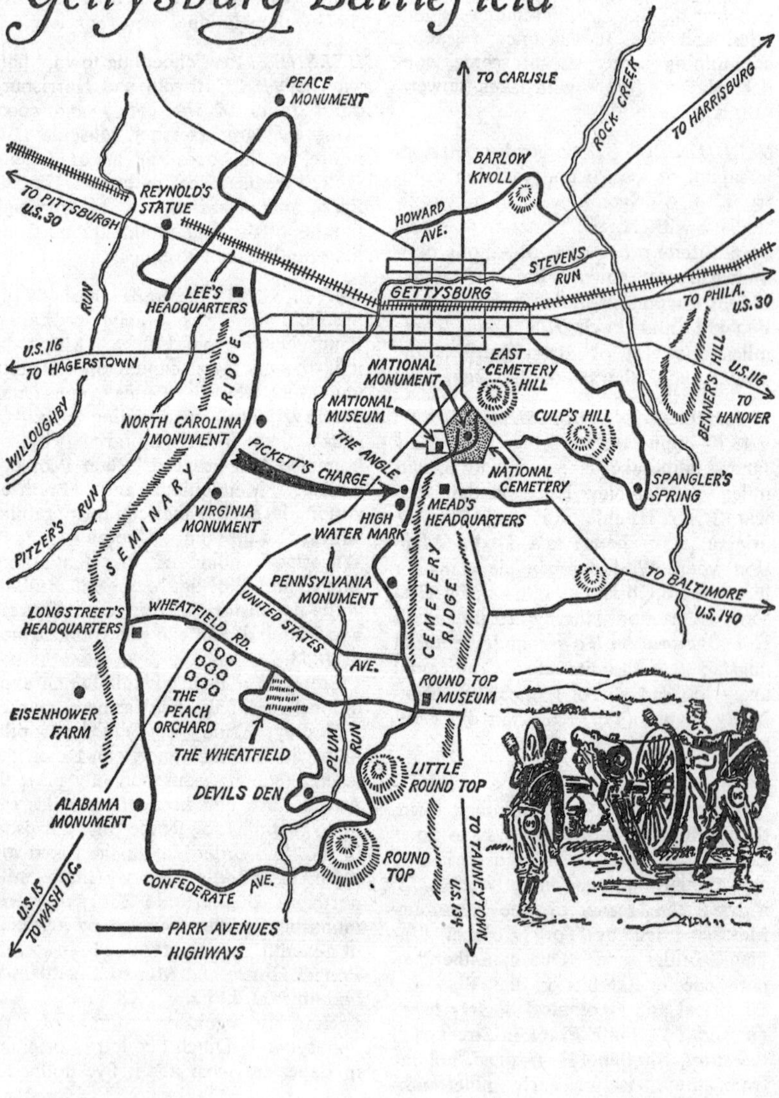

PEACE MONUMENT
TO CARLISLE
ROCK CREEK
TO HARRISBURG
BARLOW KNOLL
REYNOLD'S STATUE
TO PITTSBURGH U.S. 30
HOWARD AVE.
STEVENS RUN
GETTYSBURG
TO PHILA. U.S. 30
LEE'S HEADQUARTERS
RUN
U.S. 116 TO HAGERSTOWN
RIDGE
NATIONAL MONUMENT
EAST CEMETERY HILL
BENNER'S HILL
U.S. 116 TO HANOVER
NATIONAL MUSEUM
WILLOUGHBY
NORTH CAROLINA MONUMENT
CULP'S HILL
PICKETT'S CHARGE
THE ANGLE
NATIONAL CEMETERY
SPANGLER'S SPRING
SEMINARY
RUN
PITZER'S
VIRGINIA MONUMENT
HIGH WATER MARK
MEAD'S HEADQUARTERS
PENNSYLVANIA MONUMENT
CEMETERY RIDGE
TO BALTIMORE U.S. 140
LONGSTREET'S HEADQUARTERS
WHEATFIELD RD.
UNITED STATES AVE.
EISENHOWER FARM
THE PEACH ORCHARD
ROUND TOP MUSEUM
THE WHEATFIELD
PLUM RUN
LITTLE ROUND TOP
ALABAMA MONUMENT
DEVILS DEN
ROUND TOP
TO TANNEYTOWN U.S. 134
U.S. 15 TO WASH D.C.
CONFEDERATE AVE.
PARK AVENUES
HIGHWAYS

ant of Baron Stiegel who founded the town. A ceremony, called the **Feast of Roses,** is held each June in **Zion Lutheran Church.**

READING is home to some 700 factories, which turn out products from full-fashioned hosiery to giant pretzels. To be seen: the **Lincoln Homestead,** about six miles southeast of town, built by Abraham's great-grandfather Mordecai in 1733; **Daniel Boone's birthplace** about nine miles southeast; **Bushong's covered bridge** across the Schuylkill; and the **Pagoda,** a Japanese lookout tower perched on Mount Penn at the eastern edge of the city.

Stop-offs north of Reading: **Crystal Cave,** three miles west of Kutztown; and **Hawk Mountain Sanctuary,** 11 miles north of Hamburg, one of the few in the world set aside for birds of prey.

South of Reading, at Morgantown, the **Grace Mine**—one of Bethlehem Steel's newest completely air-conditioned iron-ore producers—runs conducted tours for visitors.

CENTRAL PENNSYLVANIA, for descriptive purposes, is bounded on the east by the Susquehanna River, on the west by the mountain-rimmed western edge of Somerset, Cambria, Clearfield, Elk and McKean counties.

CARLISLE, a 200-year-old town west of Harrisburg, was home for two of the 56 signers of the Declaration of Independence (James Wilson and George Ross), was occupied by General Jenkins' Confederate Cavalry during the Civil War, and was site of the first non-reservation school for Indians in the States. Its showplaces are mainly historic: **Carlisle Barracks,** built in Revolutionary days, now the U. S. Army War College with museum attachment; the **First Presbyterian Church,** where Carlisle citizens rallied to second the motion for independence in 1776; the **grave of Molly Pitcher** (on South Street), who moved west after doing her Revolutionary best at New Jersey's Battle of Monmouth; **Dickinson College,** founded in 1773; and the **Hamilton** and **J. Herman Bosler Memorial libraries,** each sheltering a number of honorable historic relics.

GETTYSBURG, site of the decisive Union victory that ended the South's last offensive, lies in the apple-farming country west of York. Its chief attraction for visitors is, of course, the battlefield, now a national military park. Across from the gate, a privately-owned museum charts the battle on a big electric-lit map. Within the park itself, car tours with licensed guides take about two hours to cover the 2,300 monuments and markers and the five observation towers laid out along the 26 miles of roadway on the 25-square-mile reservation which includes the **cemetery,** the **Eternal Light Peace Memorial** and the **headquarters of both generals** (Meade and Lee).

HARRISBURG, capital of the state, is the hub of the region, sitting on the Susquehanna's eastern bank, with the Blue Mountains ringing it on the west and north. South of Harrisburg lies a corner of historic and prospering farm country. On the other side of the mountains to the north: the forested **Northern Tier Country,** handsome summer vacation land, good fall hunting territory (bear, deer, wild turkey), a well-developed ski country.

Harrisburg has been capital of Pennsylvania since the Legislature was moved up from Lancaster in 1812. Once it was called Louisborg in honor of Louis XVI. However, John Harris, Jr., son of its founding father, refused to sell land to the state government until the city had been rechristened and its present name made official. Sights to see: the **state capitol,** gold-domed gray, in 13 acres of park, with a number of architectural refinements including a staircase patterned after that of the Paris Grand Opera; the **state museum** on Capitol Hill, exhibiting the original Penn Charter and a Battle-of-Gettysburg painting peopled by life-sized figures; the **Dauphin County Historical Society** and **Fort Hunter Museum** with collections of early Colonial pewter, furniture, costumes and toys.

JOHNSTOWN, in the central section's mountainous southwest corner, is a big steel city, which has been repeatedly devastated by floods (for a spectacular view ride the steep "incline plane" from the city center to the top of its residential plateau); and **Altoona,** a railroad center since pre-Civil War days, is located near the famous horseshoe curve of the Pennsylvania's tracks.

STATE COLLEGE is a town at the geographic center of Pennsylvania's midsection, and the home of the **Pennsylvania State University.** Chief attractions are the **Land Grant Mural** in the hall of **Old Main,** the museum in the **Mineral Industries Building,** the **Helen Eakin Eisenhower Chapel,** and the 50,000-seat, all-steel football stadium.

YORK, an industrial town in a corner of Penn-Dutch farm country south of Harrisburg, was Colonial capital from September, 1777, to June, 1778, while Philadelphia was occupied by the British. During its residence, the Congress adopted the Articles of Confederation and proclaimed the first national Thanksgiving Day. Current attractions: lively **Pennsylvania-Dutch farmers markets;** the **Quaker Meeting House,** used for worship since 1765; the **Historical Society museum and reference library.** One strictly present-day sight: the **Weight-Lifters Hall of Fame** on Ridge Avenue. At Red Lion, southwest of York, **Laucks Craft and Farm Museum** (open Sundays and holidays) features exhibits of antique farm equipment and conveyances, live demonstrations of farmland skills—weaving, spinning, wagon-making and so on.

WESTERN PENNSYLVANIA is a land full of coal and oil and furnaces blasting out steel. It is also a country with sailable lakes, cool woods and many historic towns.

ERIE, on Lake Erie, was first inhabited by the Eriez Indians, then by the French, who built Fort de la Presque Isle on the Peninsula across from the present city and Fort le Boeuf near Waterford, 15 miles south. In 1759 the French abandoned the area and the British took over only to be driven away by Pontiac and his Indian forces three years later. In 1795, a new settlement was laid out, this one the permanent site of Pennsylvania's only Great Lakes port. In 1812, it was headquarters for Oliver Hazard Perry's American lake fleet which was also built in Erie with whatever local materials were handy. Worth seeing: the U.S.S. *Niagara,* a reconstructed version of Perry's flagship, and the prow of the U.S.S. *Wolverine,* first iron-hulled warship built and launched at Erie (1843) —both permanently installed at the foot of State Street; the **Land Lighthouse** (1818), one of the first on the Great Lakes. The **Old Customs House** (State Street) started life as a bank, is now headquarters for the Erie Historical Society; **Wayne Blockhouse,** erected over the grave of General "Mad Anthony" Wayne, is a replica of the fort building in which he died. The **Public Museum** (6th and Chestnut) specializes in local history.

PITTSBURGH's settlement began in 1754 with a detachment of Virginia troops who were ousted by the French, who were, in turn, routed by the British in 1758. The French fort had been called Duquesne; the British named theirs Fort Pitt in honor of the then Prime Minister of England. Indian resistance slowed the settlement's growth until General Anthony Wayne managed to subdue them in 1795. Pittsburgh's industries and population have been growing ever since. Soot and smoke were once its trade-marks. Recently, due to a determined urban renewal program and rigid smoke control, the smog around the new stainless-steel skyscrapers and parks has lifted. The following sights now can be seen more clearly: the **Blockhouse** (Penn Avenue), once part of Fort Pitt, Pittsburgh's only pre-Revolutionary building; the **Golden Triangle,** symbol of the new Pittsburgh—new park and tall new buildings where the Monongahela and the Allegheny converge to form the Ohio River; **Gateway Center,** a spectacular 15-acre office-hotel-and-apartment development, also part of the urban renewal scheme; **Carnegie Institute,** one-building home of fine arts galleries, a natural history museum (over five million specimens), lecture rooms, halls of music and architecture and sculpture, plus the **Central Carnegie Library of Pittsburgh;** the University of Pittsburgh's 42-story skyscraper, **Cathedral of Learning,** the **University Chapel,** the **Stephen Collins Foster Memorial Auditorium; Phipps Conservatory** with 12 blooming greenhouses. Pittsburgh's "incline plane" carries commuters and visitors up to the **City View Observation Deck** on Grandview Avenue, Mount Washington. **Buhl Planetarium** (Federal and West Ohio streets) offers two "sky shows" a day; and the **West Park Conservatory-Aviary** displays tropical birds in naturalistic settings.

WASHINGTON, southwest of Pittsburgh, is the seat of **Washington and Jefferson College,** the birthplace of William Holmes McGuffey who wrote the famous elementary readers. **Uniontown,** at the foot of the Blue Ridge Mountains, is a big soft-coal-and-coke center. Southwest of Uniontown are the **grave of General Braddock** (near Farmington) and the reconstructed **Fort Necessity** where, in 1754, George Washington met his first defeat at the hands of the French and the Indians.

SPORTS AND RECREATION. Pennsylvanians have not only kept "Penn's Woods," they have added to them. The forested land that covers over half of the state actually shelters more wildlife today than it did when William Penn roamed it. The state goal of a park within 25 miles of every resident is not far off. New parks open every year—all with built-in picnic places, most with camping, fishing and swimming sites. The Division of Recreation, Department of Forests and Waters, Harrisburg, Pennsylvania, handles requests for information and camping reservations. Reading north to south, some of the best-known recreation areas, both public and private are the following:

In eastern Pennsylvania: **Elk Mountain Ski Center,** 24 miles north of Scranton, with slopes, trails, cross-country, T-bar lift, rope tows. **Promised Land State Park,** shore and woodland at the edge of Lake Wallenpaupack ten miles north of Canadensis; camping, fishing, boating, swimming, picnicking; trailer sites, cabins. **George W. Childs State Park,** acres of woods with waterfalls west of Dingman's Ferry; fishing, picnicking. **Big Boulder Ski Area,** ten miles east of White Haven, with slopes, trails, cross-country, T-bar lift, tows. **Hickory Run State Park,** more than 3,000 acres of Pocono country north of Jim Thorpe; camping, fishing, swimming, picnicking; tent and trailer sites. **French Creek State Park,** 6,000 acres of woods and rolling country 14 miles southeast of Reading; camping, fishing, swimming, picnicking.

In central Pennsylvania: **Zippo Ski Slope** near Bradford, with slopes, trails, cross-crountry, tows at night and on weekends. **Denton Hill State Park,** between Galeton and Coudersport, first state-maintained ski venture, with slopes, trails, cross-country, Poma lifts. **Colton Point State Park,** more than 500 acres, three miles southwest of Ansonia, along the west rim of the Pine Creek Gorge they call "the Grand Canyon of Pennsylvania"; camping, picnicking. **Hills Creek State Park,** 140-acre lake site northwest of Mansfield; camping, fishing, boating, swimming, picnicking. **World's End State Park,** 1,900 acres of mountain creek country, nine miles north of Eagles Mere; tenting, fishing, swimming, picnicking; cabins. **Little Pine State Park,** north of Waterville; camping, fishing, boating, swimming. **Mount Rainsares Natural Monument,** 50-acre reservoir southeast of Lock Haven—once part of lands owned by Maria Cristina of Spain; fishing, picnicking; observation tower. **Parker Dam State Park,** over 500 acres on a man-made lake north of Clearfield; camping, fishing, boating, swimming, picnicking; cabins. **Black Moshannon State Park,** 2,100-acre preserve with a 250-acre lake, ten miles east of Philipsburg; camping, fishing, boating, swimming, picnicking;

cabins. **Poe Valley State Park,** 760-acre remote mountain area about six miles south of Coburn; camping, fishing, swimming, picnicking. **Snyder-Middleswarth State Park,** five miles west of Troxelville, part of Bald Eagle State Forest; fishing, picnicking. **Skimont,** five miles east of State College; slopes, tows, lifts, lodge. **Bear Meadows Natural Monument,** 550 acres of wooded swampland southeast of Boalsburg; fishing, picnicking. **Blue Knob State Park,** 5,600-acre site north of Bedford with magnificent mountain view; camping, hiking, fishing, picnicking. **Camp T. Frank Soles,** ten miles west of Somerset; ski slopes, trails, cross-country, Poma lift. **Laurel Hill State Park,** 3,800 acres of mountain country complete with forests and streams, twelve miles west of Somerset; camping, hiking, fishing, boating, swimming, picnicking. **Shawnee State Park,** 3,500 acres of hill country with 450-acre lake about nine miles west of Bedford; camping, fishing, boating, swimming, picnicking. **Cowan's Gap State Park,** 1,300-acre lake-and-shore playground, eight miles northeast of McConnellsburg; camping, fishing, boating, swimming, picnicking; cabins. **Caledonia State Park,** 1,400-acre tract near Chambersburg, with an ancient iron furnace site; camping, fishing, picnicking; swimming pool, golf course, trailer area.

In western Pennsylvania: **Pennsylvania State Park** at Erie, seashore-like acres with seven miles of sand beach on Presque Isle Peninsula facing the city; fishing, boating, swimming, picnicking; **Oliver Hazard Perry Memorial. Camp Mystic Ski Area,** five miles north of Cambridge Springs, slopes, cross-country, week-end tows. **Chapman State Park** with a ten-acre lake in Allegheny National Forest west of Clarendon; camping, fishing, swimming, picnicking. **Pymatuning State Park,** 1,000-acre play area north of Jamestown at the southwest end of vast Pymatuning Lake; camping, fishing, boating, swimming. **Cook Forest State Park,** 6,800 acres of timbered wildlife sanctuary at Cooksburg; camping, riding, fishing, swimming, picnicking; cabins, inn, observation tower. **Clear Creek State Park,** named for a fine trout stream, 12 miles north of Brookville; camping, fishing, swimming, picnicking; cabins. **Raccoon Creek State Park,** good green retreat in the mining country near Frankfort Springs; camping, hiking, fishing, swimming, picnicking. **Keystone State Park,** a tract of nearly 800 acres south of New Alexandria; camping, fishing, swimming, picnicking. **Seven Springs Ski Area,** 11 miles south of Donegal, with slopes, trails, cross-country, Poma lifts, tows. **Fort Necessity State Park,** 300-acre historic site with stockaded fort replica, ten miles southeast of Uniontown; camping, picnicking.

A special attraction of this state are the Pennsylvania Dutch (including Mennonites, Amish, Dunkards, and River Brethren), known for their hearty, delicious foods. Especially outstanding are cakes made from scraps of pie dough, relishes, jellies, homemade apple butter, *shmierkase* (creamy version of cottage cheese), *Schnitz und Knepp* (apples simmered with ham and molasses), shoofly pie, and a variety of other desserts.

SPECIAL EVENTS. **Mummers Parade,** Philadelphia, January 1; **State Farm Show,** Harrisburg, mid-January; **Poor Richard Celebration,** Philadelphia, January 17; **Arbor Day,** throughout state, early April; **Flower Show,** Philadelphia, March; **Somerset County Maple Festival,** Meyersdale, early April; **Bach Festival,** Bethlehem, May; **Dogwood Celebration,** Phoenixville, May; **Miss Pennsylvania Pageant,** West Chester, June; **Rittenhouse Square Clothesline Art Exhibition,** Philadelphia, first week in June; **Laurel Festival,** Poconos, second week in June; **Pennsylvania State Laurel Festival,** Wellsboro, mid-June; **Flag Day,** Philadelphia, June 14; **Pennsylvania Dutch Days,** Kutztown, early July; **Independence Day Festivities,** Philadelphia, July 4; **Allegheny County Fair,** Pittsburgh, late August; **Pennsylvania State Fair,** Harrisburg, September; **Fall Flower Show,** Pittsburgh, October; **Chrysanthemum Show,** Allentown, November; **Star of Bethlehem**

lighting, South Mountain, Bethlehem, December.

On the sporting side: **Philadelphia Phillies** and **Pittsburgh Pirates professional baseball,** mid-April through September; **college football** at University of Pennsylvania (Philadelphia), Pennsylvania State University (University Park), Lehigh (Bethlehem), Lafayette (Easton), University of Pittsburgh, Duquesne and Carnegie Tech (all Pittsburgh), fall; **Army-Navy Football Game,** Philadelphia, late November; **Philadelphia Eagles** and **Pittsburgh Steelers professional football,** early fall through December; **professional ice hockey** in Philadelphia and Pittsburgh, winter; **boxing** and **wrestling,** Philadelphia Arena, all year.

Delaware

Delaware, the smallest of the Middle Atlantic states, is known as "The First State" (because it was first to ratify the Constitution), "The Blue Hen State" (for its Revolutionary War record), and "The Home of Corporations" (because a state law makes it easy for businesses to incorporate in Delaware).

THE LAND. With a total of 2,370 square miles, Delaware is smaller than any state except Rhode Island. It is bordered by New Jersey, the Delaware River, Delaware Bay, and the Atlantic Ocean on the east; Maryland on the south and west; and Pennsylvania on the north. Water forms an important part of Delaware's economy, especially the Delaware River, which links the state with the Atlantic, and Delaware Bay, which provides an abundance of seafood.

THE CLIMATE. Temperatures rarely vary from one end of Delaware to the other. In January they average 33 degrees, and in July, 76 degrees. Rainfall is about 45 inches a year, with 18–22 inches of snow falling in the north, and 14–17 inches in the south.

THE PEOPLE. Delaware, a three-county state only 96 miles long and 35 miles across at its widest point, is tenth in per capita income in the country.

The Dutch established their claim to the land through the 1609 voyage of Henry Hudson and those of Hendricksen and Mey, who followed him in 1613–14. (Coinciding explorations in and around New Amsterdam led to the now-confusing naming of New York's west-side river. At the time it seemed quite logical; to a captain navigating both, New York's was the North River; Delaware's, the South.)

Captain Peter Heyes led the first group of settlers from Hoorn in the Netherlands. Their ship, *The Whale,* landed at Zwaanendael (Swan Valley) near the present city of Lewes in 1631. A year later the town and everyone in it had been wiped out by Indians.

The Swedish, who, under the leadership of Peter Minuit, landed farther north near what is now Wilmington, were considerably more successful. They built Fort Christina, named it for the young Swedish queen and prospered. In consequence, the Dutch set up a Swede-watching post called Fort Casimir (now New Castle) a very few miles away. The Swedish Governor Johan Rising seized Casimir in 1654, and the New Amsterdam Dutch under Peter Stuyvesant recaptured it and also took Fort Christina in 1655. The parcel passed into British hands in 1664 along with the northern Dutch colony and was named Delaware after Thomas West, Lord de la Warr, one-time royal governor of Virginia.

In 1681, after his agents had reported that his Pennsylvania territory would be dangerously landlocked without it, title passed to William Penn—a circumstance that accounts for the Quaker good sense which is still the heritage of many Delaware families. Then while Penn and Lord Baltimore wrangled over whose lands were whose, the lower counties were left to defend themselves against privateers from the sea and in land-based Colonial wars (among these was the obscure conflict known as the War of Jenkins' Ear, 1739–42). Of necessity, the lower counties united. They set up their own legislature in 1704 and proclaimed Delaware's boundaries in 1775 after the 1763–68 surveys of Mason and Dixon.

Came the Revolution and Caesar Rodney made his ride (easily as famous locally as that of Paul Revere), carrying Delaware's decisive vote for the Declaration of Independence to Philadelphia on July 2, 1776. Delaware sent a remarkable total of almost 4,000 to the Revolutionary War; they were nicknamed "the Blue Hen's Chickens" after the gamecocks they took along with them. The only Revolutionary battle on Delaware soil was fought at Cooch's Bridge near Newark in 1777. Later that year, the British did capture Wilmington; a fact which caused the state capital to be moved from New Castle south to safer Dover.

With characteristic willingness to stand and be counted, Delaware was the first state of the original 13 to ratify the Constitution (December 7, 1787). In the War of 1812 when the British Captain Beresford fired on Lewes the ammunitionless defenders showed their resourcefulness (also characteristic) by returning his fire with his own cannon balls, sent him flying so fast for Bermuda he forgot to take on fresh water. When the Civil War came along, Delaware, though a slave-holding state, contributed seven regiments to the Union victory force.

In 1785 Oliver Evans of Newport, Delaware, built the first automatic flour-milling machinery. In 1802 Eleuthère Irenée du Pont built his first powder mill on the Brandywine. And north Delaware's fantastic industrial growth began in earnest. Thanks to hospitable tax and business laws, hundreds of firms now make their international headquarters in Dover. For years the southern part of the state, still primarily agricultural, lived in the same sort of pleasant semi-isolation that Maryland's East Shore enjoyed.

Delaware's population stands at over 542,000, and it is forty-sixth among the 50 states in number of residents.

AGRICULTURE. Poultry plays such an important role in the state's economy that broilers raised in Sussex County alone account for half of the state's farm income. Dairy products, especially milk, are also leading income-producers. Crops include vegetables, melons, apples, peaches, and strawberries.

INDUSTRY. Over one-third of the persons employed in Delaware's manufacturing plants are working in some segment of the chemical industry. Chemical research operations are among the largest in the world. End products from nylon and paint pigments are produced, but the state is most widely known as a headquarters for management.

Food processing is also important, especially for chickens and for produce coming from nearby farms.

CITIES. Wilmington, Delaware's only large city, contains about two-thirds of the entire state's population. There are several large towns, however, including Dover, New Castle, Newark, and Seaford.

DOVER, Delaware state capital since 1777, boasts the second oldest **state house**—after Maryland's—in use today. The **Hall of Records** two blocks east preserves the state's most important documents, including the original Royal Grant from Charles II and Penn's order for laying out of the town. Also of interest: **Christ Church** (where Caesar Rodney, the Signer, is buried) and the **Delaware State Museum.** Six miles south is the **mansion** that belonged to **John Dickinson,** "penman of the Revolution." At Frederica, a few miles farther south, is **Barratt's Chapel** (1780), a stern beshuttered building known as "the Cradle of Methodism in America."

LEWES is a resort town with an inviting expanse of breakwater-protected beach, good fishing and crabbing. Two reminders of earlier days: **Zwaanendael Museum,** named after the first Dutch settlement and preserving Colonial and Revolutionary relics, and **St. Peter's Church** where many early settlers are buried. A string of bay-front resorts north of Lewes—among them, **Broadkill, Prime Hook, Fowler** and **Slaughter beaches**—are notable fishing spots.

Rehoboth Beach, on the Atlantic shore south of Lewes, is a beach resort with a family air and a large following among Washington-based legislators. At **Dagsboro**—south again—stands **Prince George's Chapel** and, in its graveyard, a monument to General John Dagworthy for whose family the town was named. **Bethany Beach** and **Fenwick Island** are other peaceful ocean resorts with good beaches, swimming, and surf fishing.

Woodland Ferry, a quaint two-car cable-run operation crossing the Nanticoke River, is located near Seaford. **Patty Cannon House,** in nearby Reliance, was the site of a tavern run by that lady, a locally notorious kidnapper of slaves.

MIDDLETOWN, 14 miles south of Newark, has a handsome Church of England Mission, **Old St. Anne's** (1768). Nearby Odessa boasts the **Old Drawyers Presbyterian Church** (1773), the elegant Georgian **David Wilson House** (1769), and **Corbit-Sharp Mansion** (1772).

NEWARK, nine miles northwest of New Castle, is the seat of the **University of Delaware,** née New Ark College in 1833. **Welch Tract Church** is an early Baptist meetinghouse hit by cannon fire during the Revolution. **Cooch's Bridge,** about two miles south, where the Cooch homestead (1760) still stands, was scene of the only Revolutionary War battle fought on Delaware soil (1776).

The **Chesapeake and Delaware Canal** crosses the state just below Pea Patch Island in the Delaware River where old **Fort Delaware**—now a state park—stands. (A regular summer boat service carries visitors to and from the park.)

NEW CASTLE, less than three miles south of Wilmington—formerly called Fort Casimir, then New Amstel—was founded by the Dutch in 1651. Handsome early houses have been restored around the old Green. Sights worth seeing: **Amstel House;** the **old court house,** Delaware's first capitol and state house; the **Old Dutch House,** believed to be oldest in the state (late 1600's); **Immanuel Church** (circa 1703), with silver presented by Queen Anne; and the tiny ticket office, roughly the size of a phone booth, of the old **Frenchtown railroad,** one of the country's first steam lines.

WILMINGTON, the state's largest and northernmost city, has grown up where the Christina River flows into the Delaware. Encompassing the site of the earliest permanent settlement in the state and the seat of the du Pont chemical empire, its homes and public buildings represent every chapter of Delaware history from its Swedish beginnings to its bustling American present. Of historical interest: **Fort Christina State Park,** including "the Rocks" where the first settlers landed and a handsome monument by Carl Milles presented by the Swedish government in 1938, three-hundredth anniversary of their landing; **Old Swedes Church,** now the Episcopal Church of the Holy Trinity, built in 1698 and said to be the oldest continuously active church in the country; **Rodney Square** with a spirited equestrian statue of Caesar Rodney; **Claymont Blockhouse,** a few miles northeast of Wilmington, built by Swedish Governor Johan Rising in 1654, later captured by both the Dutch and the British; **Wilmington's Old Town Hall,** dated 1798, now headquarters for the Historical Society of Delaware and exhibiting Colonial and Revolutionary War relics, portraits and furnishings; the old **Bank of Delaware Building** (1812), present home of the Delaware Academy of Medicine. The **Hagley Museum,** in an old textile mill on grounds once the site of the du Pont Powder Yards, tells the story of early Delaware industry. Henry Francis du Pont's former home, **Win-**

terthur, is now a private museum covering the American scene between 1640 and 1849; except during the special spring showing (late April through May), reservations are required for half- and full-day tours (Address: Museum, Winterthur, Delaware). One of Wilmington's most interesting present-day buildings, the **Delaware Art Center,** specializes in works of regional artists.

SPORTS AND RECREATION. Delaware's forests and parks are small but comfortably equipped. Most offer pleasant picnicking; a few, full facilities for overnight camping. In addition to permitting public fishing on state-owned ponds, several streams in northern New Castle County are being stocked with fresh-water trout. Public waterfowl areas at **Woodland Beach, Little Creek, Prime Hook,** and **Assawoman Bay** are open to hunters. Complete hunting and fishing information is available from the Fish and Game Commission, Dover, Delaware, while the State Development Department, Dover, has details on camping and trailer areas. The following are the principal spots:

Brandywine Springs Park, west of Wilmington; play areas, softball, picnicking. **Ellendale State Forest,** wooded site south of Milford; picnicking. **Redden State Forest,** two-section reservation east and west of Route 113 near Redden; picnicking, lodge for civic groups. **Indian River Inlet Park,** miles of state-owned ocean and bay shore line south of Dewey Beach; fishing, swimming, picnicking. **Trap Pond,** 965 acres with pine groves and lake; trailer and tent camping, fishing, boating, swimming, picnicking.

SPECIAL EVENTS. **Wesley College Antique Show and Sale,** Dover, February; **Swedish-Colonial Day,** Fort Christina Monument, Wilmington, March 29; **New Castle Antique Show,** New Castle, late April; **Museum-Garden Tour,** Winterthur Museum near Wilmington, five weeks starting late April; **Delaware Festival of Arts,** statewide, May; **Old Dover Days,** Dover, first May weekend; **Wilmington Garden Day,** Wilmington, first May Saturday; **Wilmington Flower Market,** Wilmington, second May Friday and Saturday; **A Day in Old New Castle,** New Castle, third May Saturday; **Kent-Sussex Fair,** Harrington, last full week in July; **Cottage Tour of Art,** Rehoboth Beach, third week in August.

On the sporting side: **University of Delaware college baseball,** Newark, spring; **flat and steeplechase racing,** Delaware Park, Stanton, May 29 through July 25; **harness racing,** Brandywine Raceway near Wilmington, starting in July, and at Kent and Sussex Raceway, Harrington, 30 days from about September 15; **University of Delaware college football,** Newark, fall; **University of Delaware college basketball,** Newark, winter.

The Mid-South

The Mid-South

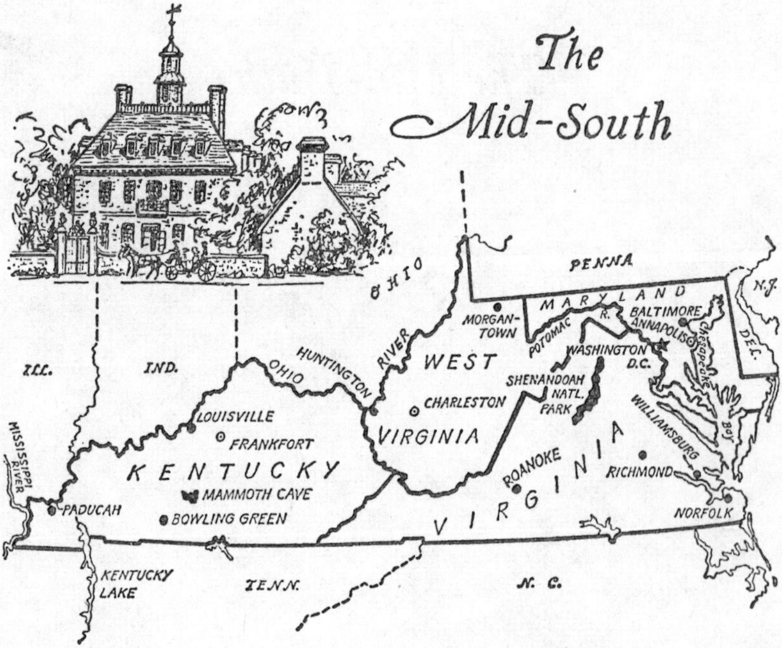

The Mid-South

From the first permanent English settlement in America, founded at Jamestown in 1607, slowly grew a large and prosperous colony named Virginia, stretching west to the Mississippi River. Ultimately it was carved into three states–Virginia, West Virginia, and Kentucky. Virginia and its small neighbor Maryland contributed the land that makes up the District of Columbia. These four states and the site of the national capital comprise a geographic region called the Mid-South.

It is the only region of the United States equally rich in historic souvenirs from the two great crises of American history–the Revolution and the Civil War. In the Old Capitol at Williamsburg, Patrick Henry made his inflammatory speech against George III in 1765, concluding with the words, "If this be treason, make the most of it!" Sixteen years later, and just thirteen miles away, Cornwallis surrendered at Yorktown. Four of the new nation's first five Presidents were born in Virginia. Two of their homes–Washington's at Mount Vernon and Jefferson's at Monticello–are famous landmarks today. The Colonial and Revolutionary period lives, too, in the magnificent restorations of Williamsburg, Yorktown, and Jamestown, as well as in the lovingly preserved great private houses, such as Carrollton and Kenmore, Clayton Court and Farmington. In contrast to these stately mansions is the Abraham Lincoln Birthplace National Historic Site at Hodgenville, Kentucky. A birthplace of a different sort is at Paris, Kentucky, where a restored tavern marks the invention of bourbon whiskey.

From the same Yorktown peninsula and stretching west to the Mississippi, many of the bloodiest battles of the Civil War were fought–Bull Run, the Seven Days' Battles, Fredericksburg, Chancellorsville, the Wilderness. Other history lives here too. Over the Wilderness Road through the Alleghenies Daniel Boone led the pioneers west into "the dark and bloody ground" of Kentucky, an area preserved in pioneer cabins and restorations. Beautiful old stone-arch bridges still mark the famed Cumberland Road, or National Pike, that followed.

History is by no means the only attraction of the Mid-South. Scattered generously through country that yields some of the world's choicest tobacco, fastest horses, and finest whiskeys are hundreds of vacation sites offering scenic wonders and sports pleasures. Off Maryland lie some of the country's best fishing waters. Virginia's beaches attract millions of sun seekers, while the state and national parks along the state's western edge provide camping, hunting, fishing, and outdoor-living facilities for hundreds of thousands of people.

An unusual vacation experience is the opportunity to drive a car over and under the ocean, via the 17-mile-long Chesapeake Bay Bridge-Tunnel, one of the engineering wonders of the world, consisting of 12 miles of concrete trestle, two mile-long tunnels under the navigation channels of the bay, two high-level bridges, and four artificial islands.

West Virginia is famous for its "spas," including White Sulphur and Berkeley, where Washington "took the waters," and the state's own vast expanse of public recreation lands. Kentucky's vacation assets include the fabled caves of the southeastern part of the state and the giant resort area around Kentucky Lake, not to mention the Kentucky Derby, probably the nation's premier single-day sporting event. The famed stud farms around Lexington are open to visitors.

An unusual vacation spot of the region is Mammoth Cave, and the other spectacular caves of southeastern Kentucky. Outdoor drama is a specialty, both in Virginia and Kentucky. "The Common Glory" at Williamsburg, "The Book of Job" in Pine Mountain State Park, and "Wilderness Road" at Berea, Kentucky, are among the most popular.

But the chief cultural center of the region is unquestionably Washington. The National Capitol, besides being a striking piece of architecture, is the repository of the nation's democratic political history. In the Smithsonian Institution, also in Washington, can be found scientific and technical history, from the Wright Brothers' plane to spacecraft of astronauts. Of a number of art galleries in Washington and Baltimore, the outstanding is the National Gallery, with collections ranging from Italian Renaissance to modern French.

Baltimore is the cuisine capital of the Mid-South, and seafood is its chief specialty, although excellent regional cooking can be found throughout Virginia and Kentucky.

District of Columbia

Washington, D.C. is unique in that it was created with the distinct purpose of establishing a home for the nation's government. Its magnificent buildings and monuments, its lack of heavy industry, the fact that one-third of all employed persons work for the government, its international flavor—all contribute to this great metropolis and make it one of the most important tourist areas in the country. The unusual pattern of streets, with wide avenues leading to the central capital like spokes on a wheel, has a rich history, as do the memorials, malls, and other areas of the city.

HISTORY. In 1790, after much controversy between the northern and southern states, George Washington chose a site for the United States capital city on the banks of the Potomac. Original plans called for exactly 100 square miles of District of Columbia, a ten-by-ten-mile square taken from the states of Maryland and Virginia. In 1791, purchase of land from private owners was completed. Land in hand, Washington and an ingenious young Frenchman, Major Pierre Charles L'Enfant, set up planning headquarters in a small stone cottage in Georgetown.

L'Enfant's vision was big and beautiful—great avenues, expansive parks and at least one boulevard a full 400 feet wide. Plans were progressing nicely and buildings were on their way up (Washington himself laid the Capitol cornerstone in 1792) when Major L'Enfant's enthusiasm for spaciousness ran away with him. He demanded that a wealthy and influential District citizen move his impressive home out of the path of an onrushing boulevard, and, after the angry words that ensued, Washington was forced to ask for the major's resignation.

Still, present-day Washington owes much of its beauty to the young Frenchman. The basic concept was his but preserving it has not been easy. For one thing, not all heads of government have shared L'Enfant's reverence for clear-spaced grandeur. Andrew Jackson, for example, is rumored to have planted the great gray Treasury Building directly in the way of a planned White House-Capitol vista with an arbitrary wave of his cane. For another, government buildings have suffered chronic lack-of-funds construction stoppages. Though work on the Capitol began in 1792, the permanent 4,500 ton cast-iron dome was not in place for Lincoln's 1861 inaugural; work on the later-built Washington Monument stood still for 20 years—a fact permanently reflected in its final two-toned marble facing.

For many years the District development kept well within its original boundaries. In fact, 50 years after its original purchase, Virginia's land was returned, unused, to its original owners. The transaction left Washington its present total of 69 square miles, eight of them under water. In this century government is big business and a whole new Washington population has pushed out to the city limits, spilled over into Maryland and Virginia suburbs.

In all its history, Washington has suffered only one foreign invasion: the British raid in 1814 when the White House and Capitol were burned. The District's official population is about 756,000 (counting "transient" members of Congress and suburb dwellers, it is pegged unofficially closer to two and a half million).

SEEING WASHINGTON. The **monuments to Presidents Washington, Lincoln** and **Jefferson** are first stops for most District visitors. The **Washington obelisk** (precisely 555 feet 5⅛ inches high; 55 feet square at the base) is said to be the tallest masonry structure in the world. Sitting in a great green field near Constitution Avenue at the end of the 15th Street extension, it was opened in 1888 after several construction delays; one, a 20-year halt, caused the color-change in the marble facing a third of the way to the top. Most people take the elevator up, walk down the 898 spiraled steps to read the carved inscriptions on

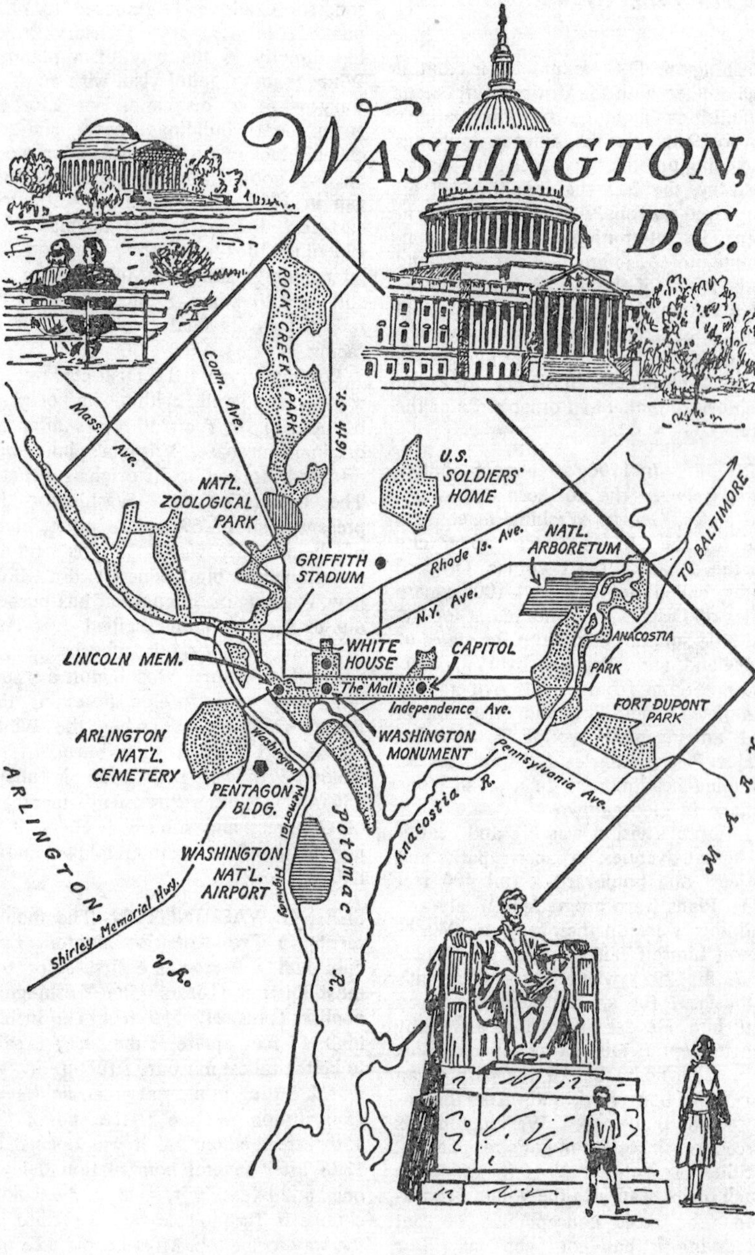

WASHINGTON, D.C.
ROCK CREEK PARK
Conn. Ave.
16th St.
Mass. Ave.
NAT'L. ZOOLOGICAL PARK
U.S. SOLDIERS' HOME
Rhode Is. Ave.
NAT'L. ARBORETUM
TO BALTIMORE
GRIFFITH STADIUM
N.Y. Ave.
WHITE HOUSE
CAPITOL
ANACOSTIA PARK
LINCOLN MEM.
The Mall
Independence Ave.
FORT DUPONT PARK
MARYLAND
ARLINGTON NAT'L. CEMETERY
WASHINGTON MONUMENT
Washington Memorial Highway
Pennsylvania Ave.
Anacostia R.
PENTAGON BLDG.
Potomac R.
WASHINGTON NAT'L. AIRPORT
ARLINGTON, VA.
Shirley Memorial Hwy.

stones donated by states, foreign countries, and organizations.

The **Lincoln Memorial,** built like a Greek temple, faces the Washington Monument across a long reflecting pool. The 19-foot statue of the seated Lincoln by Daniel Chester French looks as though it had been carved from a single block of marble; it is actually 28 separate pieces. The Memorial, opened in 1922, has the President's Second Inaugural and Gettysburg addresses inscribed on the walls.

The **Jefferson Memorial** is newest of the three; it was opened in 1943. Pantheon-shaped like his home, Monticello, it shelters a 19-foot statue, quotations from the Declaration of Independence, and other Jeffersonian documents.

The **John F. Kennedy Center for the Performing Arts,** theatrical complex on the Potomac River, has four major facilities: an Opera House, Concert Hall, Eisenhower Theatre, and a film theatre.

Next on most itineraries is the **Capitol,** the 285-foot-domed building 88 feet above sea level on Capitol Hill. Its design is the work of an amateur who submitted prize plans in a contest in 1792. Washington laid the cornerstone in 1793, but due to several financial crises (Maryland held a state lottery to help out in one), the 19-foot Freedom statue was not lifted to the dome-top nor was construction completed until 1863. Inside, the guides tour visitors through a maze of pillars, corridors, stairways, and paintings showing scenes from American history, the muraled Rotunda, the Old Supreme Court Chamber (once the Senate Chamber), the miniature subway that carries senators to their office building, the Statuary Hall (one statue from each state), and, when Congress is not in session, the Senate floor, the President's Room, the Vice President's Room, the Senators' Reception Room, the Congressional dining rooms and barber shops. When the Senate is in session, visitors may watch from the Visitors' Gallery; those presenting cards from their senators get choice seats. Constituents call on individual congressmen at the three **House Office Buildings** (the newest of these is the modern, spacious **Sam Rayburn House Office Building**), or the **Senate Office Buildings.** Pleasant stop on the way to or from the halls of Congress: the **Capitol Botanic Garden** (First Street and Independence Avenue) which specializes in citrus, tropical fruit trees and orchids.

The **White House,** 1600 Pennsylvania Avenue, has been white only since 1817 when it was painted to conceal the smoke scars left when the British set fire to it during the War of 1812. The cornerstone was laid in 1792. John Adams, first President to live there, became a resident in 1800. In 1949, President Truman moved out to **Blair House** (Pennsylvania Avenue west of Lafayette Square), now the President's official guest house, so that a $5,761,000 renovation could be completed; he returned in 1952 after the mansion had been completely rebuilt within its original walls. The regular White House tour visits the Lobby, the State Dining Room and the gold-and-white East Reception Room as well as the Green, Blue and Red rooms.

At the south end of the White House lawn—officially, the "Presidential Park"—is the **Ellipse,** a huge public playing field almost constantly in use. Across from the White House front door is **Lafayette Square,** one of Washington's best-known parks, populated by exceedingly friendly pigeons, squirrels and an equestrian statue of Andrew Jackson.

The **United States Information Bureau,** just across E Street from the Department of Commerce, is maintained to bring visitors up to date on official and unofficial places of interest.

The **Supreme Court Building,** just east of the Capitol, is one of Washington's handsomest. The nine carved figures on its white marble portico symbolize the nine justices who sit two weeks of each month, October through May. When court is in session, any member of the public may claim one of the 144 courtroom seats on a first-come basis. At other times the courtroom is open to sightseers. The **Library of Congress** (across from the Court on East Capitol Street) with its Annex stores more than six million books and a huge miscellany of maps, prints, newspapers, manuscripts and documents in a five-and-a-half-acre area. Its most prized possessions, the Declaration of Independence, the Constitution and a 1455 Gutenberg Bible are on display. North of the Library Annex on East Capitol, the **Folger Shakespeare Library,** owned and administered by Amherst College, contains close to 150,000 volumes by or about Shakespeare.

The **Government Printing Office,** North Capitol between G and H streets, open to visitors, is the world's largest printing plant. **National Archives,** northwest of the Capitol, fills the block between 7th and 9th streets, Pennsylvania and Constitution avenues. It houses government records of permanent value, including the World War II Japanese and German surrender documents. Next door on Pennsylvania Avenue, the **Department of Justice** offers an excellent tour. Starting from Room 5634, groups are shown crime and crime-prevention exhibits, and finish with an F.B.I. demonstration. The **Department of Commerce Building,** between Pennsylvania and Constitution avenues, 14th and 15th streets, contains offices as well as the country's oldest public aquarium. The **Department of the Interior,** another giant block building on E to C streets between 18th and 19th, houses several special museums which are concerned with national parks, native American arts and crafts. The museums are open throughout the week. Via morning and afternoon tours at the **Bureau of Engraving and Printing** (entrance on 14th Street near the Washington Channel) outsiders can watch money and stamps being made.

The United States Government maintains a number of museums. Most famous is the **Smithsonian Institution,** affectionately known as "the nation's attic." Among its thousands of possessions are Mamie Eisenhower's wedding dress, a working model of a 1928 Willys engine and a cat (stuffed) that, in life, survived a fall from the top of the Washington Monument. However, the major feature of the Smithsonian is the **Museum of History and Technology** at 14th and Constitution Avenue, N.W. The Institute, originally endowed by an Englishman who never set foot in the United States, also administers several other museums including the **Museum of Arts and Industries,** which contains an exciting collection of space technology, and the **National Zoological Park** at Rock Creek. The old **National Museum** is now part of the Smithsonian. The new **National Museum,** usually referred to as the Natural History Museum, is on Constitution Avenue between 9th and 12th streets. Its exhibits include a fine group of wild animals collected by Theodore Roosevelt.

A number of wealthy families have endowed Washington's art museums. Most famous is the **National Gallery of Art** (between 7th and 4th streets on Constitution Avenue), often spoken of as the Mellon Gallery, after Andrew Mellon, who donated the money to build it. Among its fine collections is the very extensive Chester Dale group of nineteenth-century French painters. The **Freer Gallery,** facing Independence Avenue east of 12th Street, is noted for Asiatic works and its Peacock Room designed by Whistler. The **Corcoran Gallery,** 17th Street north of E Street, specializes in American painting, prints and sculpture. The **Phillips Gallery** shows modern painters. The **Dumbarton Oaks Museum** in Georgetown has a definitive collection of Byzantine and early Christian art.

Many organizations maintain Washington headquarters. Some attract the general public almost as much as they do their own special-interest groups. Visitors stop at the main building of the **Pan American Union** (17th Street and Constitution Avenue) to admire its Latin American design, its Aztec garden and patio, its handsome Hall of the Americas. The museum at **American Red Cross Headquarters** (17th between E and D streets) has a number of interesting exhibits. For a dollar, any visitor can look up his family tree in the genealogy library of the D.A.R.'s **Continental Hall** (17th between C and D streets); there are also furniture and glass collections, concerts in the Daughters' **Constitution Hall** next door. The **Octagon House** (18th Street and New York Avenue) is intriguing because of its eight-sided floor plan, its history (Madison lived there when he was burned out of the White House) and the exhibits assembled there by its owners, the American Institute of Architects. Girl Scouts, their leaders, and others, drop in at the **Little House** (18th and E streets) to see the Juliette Lowe mementos. The large **National Geographic Society** building (17th and L) contains a museum and a large number of exhibits, including equipment from the Mount Everest expedition. All are open to the public. Also available are guided tours at **The House of the Temple** (Scottish Rite)—also on outer 16th Street.

"Embassy Row," once a term designating a mansion-lined stretch of Massachusetts Avenue northwest of Dupont Circle, no longer has meaning. Today, embassies are scattered throughout the outer northwest section.

West of 16th Street and north of M Street is **Georgetown,** now part of the District, but a well-to-do town in its own right before Washington was in blueprints. Today it is chiefly residential with cobbled streets and Colonial houses worth an afternoon's browsing. Among them: **Washington's Headquarters** (3049 M Street N.W.), the stone cottage where he and L'Enfant laid out the city plans; the **Robert Todd Lincoln House** (3014 N Street N.W.), built about 1800; **Dumbarton House** (2715 Q Street N.W.), headquarters of the **National Society of Colonial Dames** and open to the public. **Georgetown University** is at 37th and O streets N.W.

Washington National Cathedral (the Cathedral of St. Peter and St. Paul, Protestant Episcopal) is high on Mount St. Albans at the junction of Massachusetts and Wisconsin avenues. Started in 1907, it will be one of the largest Gothic churches in the world when completed. **Catholic University** and the **National Shrine of the Immaculate Conception,** dedicated in 1959, are east of 16th Street at Michigan Avenue and Harewood Road.

Rock Creek Park, also in Georgetown, is the District's beautiful 1,800-acre recreation ground with scenic drives, the splendid **National Zoological Park** (with world's finest bird house), a nine-hole golf course, tennis courts, picnic groves, and bridle paths. The formal gardens at **Dumbarton Oaks Park** overlook Rock Creek. **Anacostia Park** lines both banks of the Anacostia River on the eastern edge of the city; its northern end has been left in its natural state; the southern part has three nine-hole golf courses, tennis courts, and assorted playing fields. **Kenilworth Aquatic Gardens**—the world's most extensive collection of water lilies, lotus, iris, and other water-thriving plants—is part of Anacostia Park. **Fort Dupont Park,** a mostly-wooded tract east of Anacostia, has picnic places, hiking and riding trails. At the southern end of the District are the **Potomac Parks, East and West.** West includes most of the territory on which the presidential memorials stand and the **Tidal Basin** (swan- and pedal-boat rides). East Potomac Park is on a point of land bounded on the west by the river, on the east by **Washington Channel,** the city's commercial port area. On park premises are three nine-hole golf courses; fishing, swimming, picnicking and bike-riding facilities. East Potomac's double cherry trees bloom two weeks later than the single blossoms that grow around the Tidal Basin.

Reaching the **Pentagon** on the Virginia side of the river involves crossing the **Arlington Memorial Bridge** and negotiating a few deeply involved cloverleaf traffic patterns. This is the world's largest office building, housing the entire administrative staff of the U.S. military establishment.

Also on the Virginia side of the Potomac, **Arlington National Cemetery** is visited annually by thousands of persons, many paying tribute to the late President John Fitzgerald Kennedy, assassinated November 22, 1963. His simple grave, high on a hill overlooking the capital, is marked by a flame which burns day and night, and can be seen across the Potomac from the **Lincoln Memorial.** The cemetery was originally part of Robert E. Lee's estate, the **Lee Mansion,** now a national shrine open to the public. On the cemetery's 400 acres are the graves of 70,000 soldiers and former military men, and the **Tomb of the Unknown Soldier.** The **Memorial Amphitheater** has a chapel and trophy room where medals awarded the Unknown Soldier are displayed. The **Lee home** is now a national shrine. In the same area are Washington's ever-expanding **National Airport** and **National Capital Park Waterfowl Sanctuary,** known as Roaches Run. Also on the Virginia side is **Dulles International Airport,** largest civil airport in the U.S.

A number of sightseeing firms offer a four-hour tour of the District's high spots. The four-hour steamer trip from Washington to **Mount Vernon** is one of the pleasantest ways to spend a sunny week-end afternoon. Another is to take the leisurely flat-bottomed-boat ride up the restored Chesapeake & Ohio Canal to **Maryland's Great Falls Park.** Complete information on tours, sights, and maps may be obtained at the Washington Convention and Visitors Bureau.

SPORTS AND RECREATION. In addition to making use of the many park facilities, visitors attend National Football League contests of the Washington Redskins played at Robert Francis Kennedy Stadium.

SPECIAL EVENTS. The **Presidential Inauguration,** January 20, takes place every four years; **Cherry Blossom Festival,** Tidal Basin, timed according to predicted blooming date, usually early April; **The Pageant of Peace,** featuring the National Christmas Tree, opens about December 20 and runs through January 1.

Maryland

Maryland, home of Annapolis, the United States Naval Academy; Baltimore, one of the nation's great ports; and "The Star-Spangled Banner," is known as the *Old Line State* because of its soldiers' heroic stand during the Revolutionary War. Its many historic sights, excellent beaches and fishing make it a popular vacation area.

THE LAND. With a total of 10,577 square miles, Maryland is forty-second in size of the 50 states. **Chesapeake Bay,** running northeast to south, divides the state into the Western Shore and the Eastern Shore, and gives Maryland many of its excellent harbors. Western Maryland is a district of hills, mountains, valleys, and plateaus; the eastern section is relatively low and flat. The highest point in the state, which borders Pennsylvania, Delaware, Virginia, and West Virginia, is **Backbone Mountain,** 3,360 feet above sea level.

THE CLIMATE. Maryland's summers are hot (July temperatures average around 76 degrees) and the winters are generally mild (temperatures range from 25 to 44 degrees in January). The climate is relatively humid, though much less so at the shore. Precipitation averages 43 inches throughout the year.

THE PEOPLE. Maryland began in 1634 when a pair of small ships, the *Ark* and the *Dove,* dropped anchor just above the mouth of the Potomac River. The settlers were led by Leonard Calvert, brother of Cecil, then Lord Baltimore. The land they settled and named for their queen, Henrietta Maria, had been granted George Calvert, first Lord Baltimore, by Charles I of Great Britain two years before. The town they founded, St. Mary's City, was, therefore, capital of a sort of private country, of which the Calvert family were sole owners.

Though their power was absolute, the Calverts must have seemed alarmingly liberal to their seventeenth-century contemporaries. From the beginning, their settlers were allowed to elect their own governor; the Calverts themselves were Roman Catholics but people of all religions were welcomed in the colony.

The state capital was moved to Annapolis in 1694. And in 1729, after two previous unsuccessful tries, the city of Baltimore was founded and became the colony's shipping and shipbuilding center.

Charles Carroll of Carrollton was best known of the four Maryland men who signed the Declaration of Independence. But his fellow colonists were reluctant to relinquish their long-held powers to the Continental Congress. However, it was at Annapolis that the 1783–84 session of the federal legislature ratified the treaty with Britain that ended the Revolution and recognized the United States as an independent power.

The War of 1812 is remembered in Maryland for the bombardment of Fort McHenry. The British never did capture Baltimore (though they burned Washington one month earlier), and Francis Scott Key, a local lawyer interned on a British ship in the harbor, composed "The Star-Spangled Banner" —presumably "by the dawn's early light." It became the country's national anthem in 1931.

In 1830, the opening of the B&O Railroad made Baltimore the nation's first railroad center. Mount Clare Station is still a city landmark. A few years later, the world's first telegraphic message "What hath God wrought?"—was decoded by a Baltimore receiver in 1844.

Today, Maryland, which has steadily developed its industry, agriculture, and tourist trade, is a state with over 4 million residents, seventeenth in size in the nation.

AGRICULTURE. Farmland covers over half the state, with each of the 25,000 farms averaging around 153 acres. Livestock and their products are the top moneymakers, especially broiler hens. Chief crops are tobacco, grown in southwestern Maryland; corn, soybeans, apples, cucumbers, hay, and wheat. Total gross income for agriculture is over $379 million.

INDUSTRY. Maryland is highly industrialized, its most important products being primary metals, food products, and transportation equipment. Chemicals and allied products, and electrical machinery are other leading industries. Natural resources, especially fish from the coastal areas (crab, striped bass, clams, oysters), and mineral deposits on the Western Shore contribute to the state's growing economy.

CITIES. Baltimore and Annapolis are the state's two best-known cities, though many others, located in southern, eastern, and western Maryland, are interesting to visit.

BALTIMORE is the state's largest city and the country's sixth largest port. It has been a transportation center from the day the first Baltimore & Ohio locomotive chugged across the city limits in 1830. It is, of course, still B&O headquarters; along its 45 miles of waterfront ships arrive from everywhere, set sail for anywhere. **Friendship International Airport,** located at the edge of the city, was among the world's first jet-scale airports.

Residents claim Baltimore has more public monuments and memorial statuary than any other American city; visitors report that its parks and fine old Colonial homes are among the nation's handsomest. Among famous local products: terrapin chowder or stew, red-brick "row houses" with marble steps stacked like sugar cubes, sharp-tongued essayist H. L. Mencken and the Duchess of Windsor.

Start on Mount Vernon Place with Baltimore's own **Washington's Monument,** an imposing marble column with the President standing 16 feet tall on top; via stairs inside you can travel 168 feet up for a lookout view of the city. Historical stops in the neighborhood: the **Walters Art Gallery** at Charles and Centre streets which shelters the Star-Spangled Banner manuscript; the **Maryland Historical Society,** 201 West Monument Street, with a fine library and elegant period rooms; the **Cathedral of the Assumption** at Cathedral and Mulberry streets, first Roman Catholic cathedral in the United States.

South and east is the **Civic Center,** an impressive string of modern municipal buildings that line downtown Fayette Street. Just around the corner on North Holliday Street is the **Peale Museum.** Founded by one of the painting Peale brothers as an art gallery, it now houses a civic history collection. At the **Shot Tower,** an ancient stack at Fayette and Front streets, lead bullets were once manufactured by ladling drops of molten metal from the top into cold-water tanks on the ground. The **Flag House Museum** where Mary Pickersgill stitched the stars on the flag that became Key's "spangled banner" is four blocks south of the Tower at Pratt and Albemarle.

Johns Hopkins Medical Center is at Monument Street and Broadway, northeast of the Civic Center.

The **University of Maryland's** city campus (schools of medicine, pharmacy, dentistry and law. Other divisions are at College Park near the District of Columbia) is south and west of the Civic Center nearer the harbor. **Edgar Allan Poe,** who once lived in the neighborhood at 203 Amity Street, is buried in **Westminster Graveyard** on Green Street. From there, **Mount Clare Station,** first railroad station in the country, now the Baltimore & Ohio's official museum, is south and west again. **Bailey's Roundhouse** at Howard and Ostend shelters another splendid collection of early locomotives, among them the famous little engine, "Tom Thumb."

In a gentler mood, **Mount Clare Mansion,** one of the city's loveliest, has been restored by the Maryland Colonial Dames and welcomes visitors daily. The address: Carroll Park, southwest of the University.

From the center of town, go to **Fort McHenry National Monument** which guards the harbor. Its present treasures: the 1812 restorations, the firearms collection, Star-Spangled Banner souvenirs. Another harbor point: the **U. S. Frigate Constellation** (Pier 4 at Pratt Street), the nation's oldest warship, launched in 1797, now a maritime museum.

Many sights worth seeing lie in the city's north sections. Among them: **Druid Park,** a large woodsy preserve with lake, forest walks, bridle paths, and an admirable zoo; the heroic **Francis Scott Key Monument** at Lanvale and Eutaw Place; **Johns Hopkins University** (note Gilman Hall and Homewood, once a Carroll residence, now the administration building); the **Baltimore Museum of Art** (lovingly restored rooms, Colonial crafts, as well as excellent Oriental and modern French collections); **Pimlico Race Track,** home of the Preakness.

Guided bus tours of Baltimore leave regularly from Mount Vernon Place. In summer, there are daily cruises across **Chesapeake Bay** to **Tolchester.**

SOUTHERN MARYLAND counties are the oldest in the state. The first settlers planted tobacco, still the section's chief crop. It is quiet farming land—with oxen still yoked to plows and carts here and there. Its place names recall its early inhabitants, Indian (Wicomico, Nanjemoy, Patuxent) and British (Calvert, Newport, Cheltenham), its past and present love of gentle living (Marshall Hall, Charlotte Hall, Seat Pleasant).

Southern Maryland is an almost-peninsula washed by Chesapeake Bay on the east, the Potomac River on its south and west sides. To explore it, start at **Annapolis.**

ANNAPOLIS today is capital of its state, site of the United States Naval Academy, and home of St. John's College, third oldest in the country (founded as King William's School in 1696).

The United States Naval Academy (known simply as "The Academy" to residents) is an island of French Renaissance architecture surrounded by the Severn River, the Dewey and Santee boat basins. Its anchor-embellished **Bancroft Hall** is the world's largest dormitory. At the entrance stands a bronze figurehead of Tecumseh, Academy "god," who sees to it midshipmen get passing grades in return for a tribute of pennies.

The **Naval Museum** preserves a number of treasured trophies. Naval hero John Paul Jones rests in the **Chapel crypt.** While there is no guide service provided, the reservation is open to civilians from nine to five every day. Midshipmen muster on Bancroft Hall Terrace at 12:05 weekdays (weather permitting); 12:15, Saturdays; 12:30, Sundays; in fall and spring there are dress parades on Worden Field Wednesdays at 3:25.

The white-domed Georgian **State House,** which dates from 1772, is the oldest capitol in use in the country today. Inside, guided tours cover early paintings, the rooms where the treaty recognizing American independence was signed and the chamber in which Washington resigned his U. S. Army commission. Out front: an imposing statue of Civil War Justice Taney and a small fierce iron cannon believed to be from the *Ark* or the *Dove,* ships that carried the state's first settlers.

Behind the State House stands the restored **Treasure House,** oldest public building in Maryland. One block northwest is **St. Anne's Church** with a silver communion service donated by William III back in 1695.

From State House Circle narrow cobbled streets lead to some of the handsomest Georgian homes in the country. In October **Heritage Week,** almost all of them are open to the public. Among those that welcome visitors all year long are the **Chase House** (one-time residence of Samuel Chase who signed the Declaration of Independence, now a home maintained by the Episcopal Church); the **Richard Carvel House** which dates back to 1751; the **Hammond Harwood House** (exquisite entrance, interior woodwork); and the eighteenth-century **Brice House.**

ST. MARY'S, the first capital, is 60 miles south of Annapolis. The **Old State House** is a reproduction of the actual building erected near but not on the original site. **Trinity Church** is still standing nearby (it was built in 1829 with some of the original State House bricks). The **Leonard Calvert Monument** marks the spot where he bought the colony's land from the Indians' king Yaocomico. The **Freedom of Conscience Monument** commemorates "An Act Concerning Religion" which guaranteed Marylanders unrestricted worship in 1649.

Other relics of early Maryland: the tiny wooden church at **St. Inigoes,** some miles south of St. Mary's City, home of the oldest Roman Catholic congregation in the United States; **Cross Manor,** thought to be the state's earliest house, just south of St. Inigoes; **Port Tobacco,** today only a plaque overlooking land that rolls down to the Potomac, once a major export town. Nearby are four of Maryland's great estates: **La Grange, Mulberry Grove, Havre de Venture, Rose Hill,** and the home of **Daniel of St. Thomas Jennifer,** a signer of the Constitution.

Benedict, due east of Port Tobacco on the Patuxent River, was the place the British landed on their way to sack Washington during the War of 1812.

Point Lookout on the southernmost tip of the Peninsula has facilities for swimming, hunting and fishing; and **Solomons Island** at the mouth of the Patuxent is a famous yacht and boatbuilding center. The **Cliffs of Calvert,** where geologic formations from 40 to 110 feet high are filled with fossils of sharks, whales, and crustaceans dating back 50 million years, should be visited.

WESTERN MARYLAND starts in the east as rich farmland (a fact the United States Department of Agriculture took advantage of when it established its big research center at **Beltsville**), runs to orchard crops—apples, peaches, pears—around Westminster and Frederick. Its western panhandle ends in the Alleghenies, a rugged section which the state has dedicated to state park and forest areas, preserving thereby not only some very handsome woodlands, but some of the best bass and trout waters in the East. The state's northern edge is the Mason-Dixon Line. Its southern boundary follows the serpentine course of the Potomac.

In its southern corner lie the prosperous suburbs Chevy Chase, Bethesda and Silver Springs. **College Park** is home to the principal schools of the University of Maryland.

From east to west, **Westminster,** Carroll County seat, has two colleges—**Western Maryland** and **Westminster Theological Seminary.**

Frederick was home to Whittier's strong-minded heroine Barbara Fritchie (her house, reconstructed on Patrick Street, is now a museum). **Francis Scott Key** lived in Frederick and the American flag flies over his tomb in **Mt. Olivet Cemetery** day and night. Mrs. Fritchie is buried here also. Of interest: three old covered bridges on country roads outside of town. In 1767, at the **Court Square,** the first organized community resistance to British rule in the colonies took place. The local citizens burned the **Stamp Act** in effigy. Nearby is Monocacy Civil War Battlefield.

BOONSBORO lies south of Hagerstown. Near it are Maryland's **Washington Monument**—a canister-shaped stone tower hand-built by local farmers, the first architectural tribute ever paid the President—and the **Crystal Grottoes.** Not far away, at Sharpsburg, is **Antietam Battlefield,** scene of the bloodiest single day of the Civil War. Today it is a national monument comprised of a cemetery for those who fell, the field itself, a library and a museum.

Fort Frederick, once-sturdy French and Indian War battlements, was built in 1756 as part of the frontier chain. Its museum displays Indian artifacts and rusted weapons.

CUMBERLAND, some 50 miles west of Hagerstown, is where General Braddock (British) maintained a Revolutionary headquarters in the catacomb-like caves under **Emanuel Episcopal Church,** which stands on land then occupied by Fort Cumberland. The city is an industrial and coal-shipping center.

HAGERSTOWN, about 30 miles northwest of Frederick, was named for Jonathan Hager who laid it out in 1762. Among other industries it boasts an aircraft plant and one of the largest pipe organ factories in the world (guided tours provided).

EASTERN SHORE residents live on the peninsula east of Chesapeake Bay, linked to "continental Maryland" by the **Chesapeake Bay Bridge.**

The Eastern Shore is mostly flat, rich farmland. Its towns are more apt to be old than big. Off its jigsaw-cut shores, there is a variety of sea life—oysters, crabs, terrapin, game fish—to be caught for pleasure and profit. Toward the south, broiling chickens are now big business.

CAMBRIDGE, Dorchester county seat, is another food-packing and shipping town. Nearby and notable: charming old (1690) **Trinity Church** at Church Creek, eight miles south; the fishing and crabbing fleets and the old **Friends Meeting House** in Easton, 15 miles north; the ancient white oak protected by **Wye Oak State Park,** 14 miles north; the hamlet of Tilghman, on **Tilghman's Island,** headquarters for sports fishermen; **Blackwater National Wildlife Refuge.**

CHESTERTOWN, due south of Havre de Grace, on the peninsula proper, is the site of the first school ever to award an honorary degree to General George Washington—**Washington College.** In the town's **Emanuel Church,** the Protestant Episcopal Church of the United States declared its independence from the Church of England. **Kent Island,** holding up one end of the Chesapeake Bay Bridge, is site of the first settlement in Maryland.

HAVRE DE GRACE, 35 miles northeast of Baltimore at the head of Chesapeake Bay, is the city that cans and ships much of the produce raised on the Eastern Shore. Notable spots in the vicinity: **Aberdeen Proving Ground** (southwest), a huge Army weapons-testing center; **Conowingo Dam** (north), a mile-long structure holding back the Susquehanna and providing power for a huge hydroelectric system.

OCEAN CITY is Maryland's only Atlantic resort, perched on a sandy stretch of land paralleling the coast. A hospitable row of shingled resort hotels, boardwalk and white sand beach. Marlin fishing is popular.

SALISBURY, on the Wicomico River, is Maryland's second largest port, a center for industries (food-packing, bricks, lumber), home of **Maryland State Teachers College.** There are some lovely old homes along the river. **Maryland State College** (a branch of the University) is at **Princess Anne,** 12 miles south, where the **Washington Hotel** has been open to guests ever since 1797.

SPORTS AND RECREATION. State parks and forests are among Maryland's top travel assets. Camping reservations should be made in advance by writing the superintendent of a particular park or the Department of State Forests and Parks, Annapolis.

In the Baltimore area: **Sandy Point State Park,** 700 acres of beach land at the western end of the Chesapeake Bay Bridge; picnicking, fishing, swimming, crabbing, boating, bird study, field trials; amusement center. **Patapsco State Park,** 1,500 acres of river country 11 miles west of Baltimore; picnicking, camping, fishing, horseback riding, marked nature trails, swimming.

In southern Maryland: **Cedarville State Forest,** 3,500 acres of piny woods five miles southeast of Brandywine; camping, hunting, picnicking. **Doncaster State Forest,** 1,400-acre pine woodlands one and a half miles east of Doncaster; picnicking, hunting, hiking, limited camping.

In the Eastern Shore area: **Elk Neck State Park,** nearly 1,000 acres fronting on the Elk River and Chesapeake Bay ten miles south of Northeast; salt-water swimming, boating, picnicking, camping; cabins. **Pocomoke State Forest,** over 12,000 acres five miles northeast of Pocomoke City; picnicking, camping, hiking, fishing, hunting.

In western Maryland: **Big Run,** a section of **Savage River State Forest** five miles east of New Germany; camping, picnicking. **Catoctin Recreational Demonstration Area, "Shangri-La"** site 16 miles north of Frederick (rechristened **Camp David** during the Eisenhower administration); fishing, camping, picnicking. **Dans Mountain State Park,** picnicking, hiking. **Deep Creek Lake,** huge man-made lake on a mountain-top 30 miles northeast of Oakland; boating, swimming, fishing, winter sports. **Fort Frederick State Park,** with eighteenth-century battlements on the route of the old Chesapeake & Ohio Canal five miles south of Clear Spring; camping, fishing, boating, picnicking; museum. **Gambrill State Park,** 1,100 acres of hill country six miles northwest of Frederick; picnicking; tearoom. **Green Ridge State Forest,** 25,000-acre preserve 15 miles east of Cumberland; undeveloped campsites, rough trails; camping, fishing, hunting, picnicking. **Herrington Manor Recreation Area,** 53-acre lake site five miles northwest of Oakland; swimming, fishing, boating, picnicking, camping; fully equipped cabins. **New Germany Recreation Area** in 51,000-acre **Savage River State Forest** southeast of Grantsville; camping, fishing, swimming, winter sports, hunting; fully equipped housekeeping cabins. **Potomac State Forest,** 12,000 acres split in two wooded, river-cut sections east of Oakland; camping, picnicking, hiking, fishing, hunting. **Seneca Creek State Park,** 2,000 acres three miles west of Gaithersburg which has excellent camping, picnicking, hiking, fishing, nature-study facilities. **Swallow Falls Recreation Area,** 7,000 acres high in the Alleghenies eight miles northwest of Oakland; camping, fishing, hunting, picnicking. **Washington Monument State Park,** setting for first tower dedicated to the first President; picnicking, lookout.

In addition to these, there are ten **Game and Inland Fish Commission Lands** set aside as public shooting areas in Allegany, Dorchester, Garrett, Somerset, Washington and Worcester counties.

SPECIAL EVENTS. **Maryland Day Celebration,** state-wide, March 25; **Maryland House and Garden Pilgrimage,** three weeks in late April and early May; **Spring Flower Mart,** Mount Vernon Place, Baltimore, mid-May; **June Week, U. S.** Naval Academy, Annapolis, early June; **Defenders' Day,** all-state holiday with re-enactment of the War of 1812 bombardment at Fort McHenry, September 12; **Autumn Glory Time,** Garrett County, western Maryland, first two weeks in October; **Heritage Weekend** (balls, hunt breakfasts, dinners, tours celebrating Colonial history), Annapolis, late October; **Toytown Parade,** Baltimore, Thanksgiving Day.

Annapolis Yacht Club Spring Races, last weekend in May; **Maryland Hunt Cup Race,** spring; **Baltimore Yacht Club Regatta,** July fourth weekend; **Oxford Boat Race,** Gibson Island, mid-August; **Chesapeake Bay Fishing Fair,** late August; **Ocean City White Marlin Tournament,** September. Several tournaments for **jousting,** Maryland's official sport, are held during the year.

Virginia

The Virginia image is definite, immediate, and real. The pillared mansions welcome visitors; tobacco grows by the fieldful.

There is a sense of continuity with the past. Families of the eastern part of the state are directly descended from those who first came to Virginia to establish a new aristocracy. In the mountains to the west, the language of the people is essentially Elizabethan English. Virginia's favorite recipes for fried chicken, baking-powder biscuits, pumpkin pie, and gingerbread have been handed down from the earliest colonists.

Virginia has been significantly involved in most of American history—the state has contributed Washington, Jefferson, Patrick Henry, John Marshall, Madison, Monroe, the Harrisons and the Lees to America.

THE LAND. Virginia is famous for its beautiful scenery, especially the **Blue Ridge Mountains** and the **Shenandoah Valley.** Its area totals 40,817, and it has a 342-mile coastline. Mount Rogers is the highest point in the state, at 5,729 feet. Virginia is bordered by Maryland, Washington, D.C. (the Potomac River), North Carolina, Tennessee, Kentucky, and West Virginia.

THE CLIMATE. There are few extremes in temperature in Virginia, the averages running 32–50 degrees in January and 69–87 degrees in July, depending on location. Snowfall ranges between 25–30 inches in the western mountains, but as little as 5–10 inches falls in the Tidewater area.

THE PEOPLE. In 1584, Sir Walter Raleigh found a new plant—tobacco—and laid a foundation for the economic future of the land he had discovered and named Virginia in honor of his monarch, the Virgin Queen.

The first colonizers, Captain John Smith and company, settled at Jamestown in 1607. Although they suffered from repeated attacks of swamp fever and Indians (one of their number, John Rolfe, married Pocahontas, but the redmen remained hostile), they persevered, cultivating tobacco and developing politically. They formed the first legislative assembly in America, the Virginia House of Burgesses, in 1619.

That same year, the first slave was brought to the New World by a Virginian. The event was followed by growth of private fortunes and of a landed aristocracy supported by a plantation economy. By the middle of the eighteenth century, Williamsburg, capital of the Colony since 1699, had become rich and powerful.

The upper class had time for discussion, for development of ideas and independent thinking. A remarkable group of leaders emerged: the eloquent Patrick Henry; Washington; the versatile Thomas Jefferson; Madison and Monroe, whose impression on our political philosophy is apparent even today.

Strong leadership resulted in independent action. When the Colonies revolted against England, Virginians helped frame the Declaration and became leaders of the Revolution. General Cornwallis surrendered his British army at Yorktown, Virginia on October 19, 1781, and the new nation was born with Virginians again as leaders. Four of the first five presidents were from Virginia.

The paradox inherent in Virginia's history—fighters for freedom, whose economy was dependent on the slavery their ancestors introduced—finally led to tragedy. Virginia was not in favor of secession from the Union, but when President Lincoln called for volunteers to quell the secession movement in 1861, Virginia formed her own volunteer army, led by Robert E. Lee.

The bitterest fighting of the Civil War took place on Virginia soil. Richmond, the Confederate capital, was attacked six times. The city never surrendered although Grant's final siege broke the back of Southern resistance and led to Lee's surrender at Appomattox Court House, Virginia, on April 9, 1865. That the unequal struggle lasted as long as it did was largely due to the military genius of two men born in Virginia territory—Lee and "Stonewall" Jackson.

After the war, the ravaged state began again, with nothing, to rebuild her fortunes. She developed industrial and agricultural diversity. Today tobacco is still important to Virginia, but so are coal, textiles, apples, lumber, and ships.

Over 4.5 million persons live in Virginia, making it the fourteenth in population in the country. The majority live in urban areas.

AGRICULTURE. Virginia is best-known as a tobacco-producing state, even though all the tobacco is grown on a small segment of the state's farmland. Livestock, dairying, and poultry raising provide the majority of Virginia's farm income (which totals over $563 million yearly). Virginia's Smithfield hams are famous. Leading field crops, after tobacco, are corn, hay, soybeans, and peanuts.

INDUSTRY. Virginia's industrial development has been rapid since 1930, and today the value of manufactured goods is 76 percent of all goods produced in the state. A combination of good transportation and land, coal and natural resources, and a growing population have spurred this growth. Most important areas of manufacturing are chemical products, processed foods, tobacco products, textiles, machinery, and clothing. Virginia is also a leading fishing state.

CITIES. Richmond, Virginia's capital and capital of the Confederacy from May 1861 to April 1865, and Norfolk, the largest city, are popular with visitors. But because of the number of historic events which took place throughout the state, many small towns should also be visited.

NORTHERN VIRGINIA stretches from the suburbs of Washington on the Potomac across the fox-hunting country of the Piedmont to the western mountains dotted by Shenandoah apple orchards and forested mountain playgrounds.

ALEXANDRIA, just across the river from Washington, D.C., was surveyed by George Washington. Both he and Robert E. Lee belonged to **Christ Church,** which was built in 1767 and has been holding services ever since. Washington was also a member of the **Friendship Fire Engine Company** (South Alfred Street) where today there is an exhibit of early fire-fighting equipment. **Carlyle House** (North Fairfax Street) is a carefully restored Virginia mansion (1752); the **Stabler-Leadbetter Apothecary** (107 South Fairfax Street) opened in 1792, is now a pharmaceutical museum. **Gadsby's** famous **Tavern** (132 North Royal Street), built in 1752, was Washington's recruiting headquarters for the French and Indian Wars; later a gathering place for Revolutionary leaders. Appropriately, the most prominent landmark in Alexandria is the **George Washington Masonic National Memorial,** a 333-foot granite tower high above the river.

From Alexandria, the Mount Vernon Memorial Highway follows the Potomac nine miles south to **Mount Vernon.** This, the country home of George Washington, is one of the most beautiful examples of Colonial architecture in the United States. It is complete with kitchens, dairy, smokehouse, stables, greenhouse, laundry, spinning house, slaves' quarters, and little round schoolhouse. Much of the original furniture and many of Washington's possessions, books, letters, swords, clothing—even his false teeth—are on display. On a hillside near the house is the tomb where George and Martha Washington are buried.

West of Alexandria is **Manassas National Battlefield Park,** commemorating the two Civil War battles that are usually called the First and Second Battles of Bull Run. On **Henry House Hill,** a 1,600-acre park, is a museum, open every day, with various exhibits, including a diorama and an electric map that traces troop movements. Jackson's stubborn stand on that hill against McDowell's Union forces earned him the name "Stonewall."

CHARLOTTESVILLE, home of the **University of Virginia,** was visited by three Presidents—Jefferson, Madison, and Monroe—in 1818 when the cornerstone was laid for the University. The original buildings were planned by Jefferson, notably the symmetrically impressive Rotunda. His famous serpentine walls are only one brick thick yet satisfactorily strong thanks to their self-supporting curves. Charlottesville's **Old Courthouse** on Courthouse Square was also designed by Jefferson, as was **Ash Lawn,** the simple house set in ancient shaped boxwood hedges, home of James Monroe five miles from town. Designed and built in 1799, it is open to the public.

Michie Tavern, on the road to Monticello, is an interesting pre-Revolutionary inn, built in 1735, with authentically refurbished ballroom, "keeping hall," dining room and tap bar.

FRONT ROYAL is the northern gateway to **Shenandoah National Park** (see "Sports and Recreation"), a 75-mile-long section of the beautiful Blue Ridge Mountains, where scenic highways and trails wind along ridges and valleys, streams, waterfalls and fields of flowers. Near Front Royal are **Skyline Caverns** and **Crystal Caverns,** major limestone caves.

Farther south in the Blue Ridge country, several important caves can be found. In **Luray Caverns,** Virginia's largest, subterranean lakes reflect stalactites, and special lighting enables visitors to photograph the interior with any kind of camera. **Endless Caverns,** noted for vivid coloring, have never been fully explored. The **Caverns of Melrose,** near Harrisonburg, were once used as a Civil War encampment, and soldiers' names can still be seen in the walls.

ORANGE, northeast of Charlottesville, is an area of fine old Virginia homes, a number of which Thomas Jefferson helped to design. Most notable of these is **Montpelier,** five miles west of Orange, the large, beautiful mansion of James Madison, built in 1790. Neither the house nor the formal gardens behind it are open, but the nearby cemetery containing the **graves of James and Dolly Madison** may be visited.

On a mountaintop near Waynesboro, west of Charlottesville, sits unique **Swannanoa,** a totally unexpected Italian marble palace surrounded by formal gardening and sheltering a collection of paintings and sculpture.

STAUNTON, a Shenandoah Valley community founded in 1728, is most famous as the **birthplace of Woodrow Wilson.** The house where he was born (24 North Coalter Street) displays mementos of his career.

Not far from Staunton are a number of outstanding attractions. To the north stand the **Natural Chimneys,** odd stone towers, 100 feet high, pierced with tunnels. To the southwest are **Hot Springs** and **Warm Springs,** historic watering places within five miles of each other. Hot Springs is an imposing resort with 17,000 landscaped acres of grounds, three golf courses, riding trails, tennis courts, swimming pools, a ski slope, skating rink, and its own trout streams.

Farther down the Shenandoah Valley from Staunton is **Lexington,** a hallowed Confederate shrine where both Lee and "Stonewall" Jackson are buried—Jackson in **Old Lexington Cemetery** and Lee in the **Lee Memorial Chapel** on the campus of **Washington and Lee Univer-**

sity. Adjoining Washington and Lee is the **Virginia Military Institute,** "West Point of the South," and site of the **General George C. Marshall Research Library and Museum.**

Across the Blue Ridge is **Charlottesville,** a small city of great charm, situated in Albemarle County, a region of peach and apple orchards and rolling hills crowned with fine old homes. Jefferson designed the most important buildings in the area. **Monticello,** his classically designed mansion three miles southeast of Charlottesville, houses many of his ingenious inventions—dumb-waiters, hidden stairways, a clock operated by cannonball weights. Its gardens and interior are open to the public every day.

WINCHESTER, near the northern end of the Shenandoah Valley, is another place important in George Washington's career. He started out from Winchester as Lord Fairfax's surveyor, built **Fort Loudoun** here for the protection of the frontier, and was elected to the Virginia House of Burgesses from Winchester. His office is preserved in a cabin at Cork and Braddock streets. During the Civil War, Winchester was fought over continually, changed hands 73 times. Both **"Stonewall" Jackson's headquarters** and **Sheridan's headquarters** are marked, and guided tours may be arranged through the Chamber of Commerce. Other historic Winchester sites are: **Red Lion Tavern,** an inn belonging to Indian fighter Peter Lauck and the **tomb of Lord Fairfax.** Winchester, now Virginia's apple center, is the location of the annual **Shenandoah Apple Blossom Festival.**

THE TIDEWATER is laced through by four wide Virginia rivers—the Potomac, the Rappahannock, the York and the James—all emptying into Chesapeake Bay. Many of America's earliest settlements were established on Tidewater land, now a region of farms, Colonial towns, battlefields, churches and imposing plantation homes.

Gunston Hall, on the Potomac a few miles below Mount Vernon, was built by George Mason, author of Virginia's Declaration of Rights.

FREDERICKSBURG, farther south on the Rappahannock River, was a political and cultural center in Colonial and Revolutionary times. Nearly 40 of its pre-1776 buildings are still standing. The town is closely identified with George Washington (his mother and sister lived there); John Paul Jones, who rested there between ships; and James Monroe, who first practiced law in Fredericksburg. (In his Charles Street museum-office, many of his furnishings, letters and mementos are preserved.) **Kenmore,** on Washington Avenue, built in 1752, was home to Colonel Fielding Lewis and Betty Washington Lewis, George Washington's only sister. Visitors are served tea and gingerbread made from the recipe of Mary Washington, George's mother, who lived in a simple white clapboard cottage nearby at Lewis and Charles streets.

Fredericksburg also saw major Civil War action. A visitors' center at Lafayette Boulevard and Sunken Road gives information and directions, has a museum containing a Civil War diorama, relief maps, firearms, photographs and a military library. Guided groups tour the following **Civil War battlefields** in the neighborhood: **Fredericksburg, The Wilderness** (15 miles west), **Spotsylvania Court House** (5 miles southwest) and **Chancellorsville** (15 miles west).

George Washington's birthplace, 38 miles east of Fredericksburg, is maintained as a national monument. The original buildings were destroyed by fire in 1779, and a Georgian Colonial brick house that suggests the style of the original now stands on the spot, furnished with authentic period pieces. The Washington family plot, where George Washington's great-grandfather, grandfather, father and 28 other members of the family are buried, is there.

Stratford Hall, on a bluff overlooking the Potomac near Baynesville, was once home of the Lees—Richard Henry, Francis Lightfoot and Robert E. Today the plantation is still in full operation. Hams are cured, the gristmill grinds out meal and—in summer—visitors can stay for southern-cooked meals.

IRVINGTON, at the mouth of the Rappahannock, is a resort and fishing center. **Christ Church,** near town, is called "King" Carter's Church after the planter who built it in 1732. Carter owned 300,000 acres in the vicinity, and he ran his domain like a feudal lord. One of his mansions, **Sabine Hall** (1730), still stands 30 miles northwest of Irvington, and his descendants still live there and maintain the estate as a working plantation.

Across Chesapeake Bay is the Eastern Shore peninsula which Virginia shares with Maryland and Delaware. Best-known of the commercial and sport-fishing ports perched on the long sandy strip of Virginian land is **Chincoteague,** famous for excellent beaches, oysters, and the pygmy ponies that roam the neighboring salt marshes. Every year on **"Pony Penning Day"** in July, the ponies are rounded up for auction.

Chesapeake Bay Bridge-Tunnel, recently completed, stretches 17.5 miles across the lower Chesapeake Bay, connecting the lower tip of Virginia's eastern shore with the southern Virginia mainland. Consisting of 12 miles of concrete trestle, two one-mile tunnels, two steel bridges, and four man-made islands, it cuts north–south driving time to 25 minutes (compared with the previous two-hour ferry ride).

Cape Charles, near the south tip of the eastern shore, has very good beach and fishing facilities. Five miles from Cape Charles is **Arlington House,** built before 1680; it is the original home of the Custis family, Martha Washington's first in-laws.

SOUTHWESTERN VIRGINIA is rolling farmland—chiefly tobacco country. Farther west the fields turn to hills, and beyond that the **Blue Ridge Mountains** rise in peaceful, wooded beauty. Finally, at Virginia's western tip, the **Cumberland Gap,** historic pass through which thousands of pioneers followed Daniel Boone to the West, cuts through the rugged ridges of the Appalachians. The summit of **Pinnacle Mountain** surveys an impressive three-state panorama.

In the neighborhood of **Norton,** Appalachian Mountain mining center, two natural phenomena are of particular interest. **High Knob,** a 4,152-foot peak in Jefferson National Forest, looks out over rugged mountains and valleys and the neighboring states of West Virginia, Kentucky and Tennessee. (On a clear day, add North Carolina.) **Natural Tunnel** is a 900-foot geological oddity that is used by both the Southern Railroad and Stock Creek to short-cut through Powell Ridge. The **Southwest Virginia State Museum,** a remodeled mansion with local-interest exhibits, is southwest of Norton at **Big Stone Gap,** home town of John Fox, Jr., who wrote "The Trail of the Lonesome Pine."

Southwest Virginia's nationally famous **Barter Theatre at Abingdon** has been adopted as Virginia's official State Theater. Started during the Depression, when livestock and other goods were accepted in exchange for tickets, its players now produce Broadway and experimental dramas at Abingdon throughout the summer and tour the United States from September to April. **Abingdon,** itself, is a town of beautiful old buildings, a center for artists and craftsmen, and home of the **Virginia Highlands Festival.**

Forest headquarters are in **Roanoke.**

U.S. Route 11 passes over **Natural Bridge.** A 215-foot-high limestone span over Cedar Creek, Natural Bridge has been a tourist attraction since the days when Jefferson owned it and built a cabin there for visitors. Every summer night, the bridge plays backdrop for a **pageant** called **"The Story of Creation."**

LYNCHBURG, east of the bridge, was founded in 1757 by John Lynch as a ferry crossing on the James River. Lynch built the first tobacco warehouse in the United States (1791), and his city is today one of the leading dark-tobacco markets in the world. Tobacco auctions along Commerce Street may be visited during the fall and winter.

Near Lynchburg are **Poplar Forest,** a distinguished house designed by

Thomas Jefferson (1806), and the handsomely landscaped campus of **Sweet Briar Women's College.**

To the east of Lynchburg is **Appomattox Court House National Historical Park,** scene of Lee's surrender to Grant on April 9, 1865. The **McLean House,** where the surrender took place, the **Old Court House, Appomattox Tavern** and other buildings are reconstructed. Markers show positions of troops as well as Grant's and Lee's headquarters.

Also nearby are two other tobacco centers, **Danville** and **South Boston,** where bright-leaf tobacco auctions are held from September to December.

SOUTHERN VIRGINIA, the active heart of the state, is the location of **Richmond,** Virginia's political and industrial capital and former capital of the Confederacy. At the mouth of the James River is **Hampton Roads**—one of the world's great harbors—with the ports of **Norfolk, Portsmouth** and **Newport News.**

NORFOLK's best-known attraction is the **Norfolk Naval Station,** followed by the 100-acre **"Gardens-by-the-Sea."** The Gardens contain more than 100,000 azaleas, camellias, rhododendron, and other plants and flowers that flourish there all year round. Also in Norfolk is **General Douglas MacArthur Memorial,** located in the stately century-old courthouse building, where the General's body rests, and his personal memorabilia can be seen.

Myers House, Norfolk, is a beautiful example of Federal Georgian architecture, built in 1792. On display are the original furniture, glass, silver, china and Gilbert Stuart paintings.

OLD POINT COMFORT, historic resort town at the tip of the Virginia Peninsula, is the site of **Fort Monroe,** a moated fortification built in 1834 and still in use. Jefferson Davis was held prisoner in the fort for two years after the Civil War. The room he occupied, and the adjoining room full of material on the battle of the *Monitor* and the *Merrimac* and related Civil War exhibits, is now a museum that may be visited by arrangement.

PETERSBURG was founded in 1645. In the cemetery of **Blandford Church** (1735) are the graves of soldiers of six wars.

Five of Virginia's most distinguished plantations can be found near Petersburg, along the James River. Rich in ante-bellum atmosphere are **Shirley** (1740), built by the Carter family; **Westover** (1730), a classic mansion designed by William Byrd II; **Evelynton,** the Byrd family seat; **Sherwood Forest,** home of President John Tyler; **Berkeley** (1726), ancestral home of the Harrison family. (Benjamin Harrison, signer of the Declaration of Independence, and William Henry Harrison, ninth President and grandfather of the twenty-third President, were born there.)

RICHMOND began as a trading post in 1637 and during the Revolution was the site of two of the four Virginia Conventions attended by Washington, Jefferson, Richard Henry Lee, George Wythe and Thomas Marshall.

In the classic **state capitol**—the central section of which was designed by Thomas Jefferson in 1785—stands Houdon's famed statue of Washington. Other historic buildings open to visitors include the **Lee House,** the **John Marshall House, Jefferson Davis' "White House,"** the **Edgar Allan Poe Museum,** and **St. John's Church** (1741) where Patrick Henry made his "liberty or death" speech.

Southeast of the city, the **Richmond National Battlefield Park** preserves forts, breastworks and other landmarks of Civil War battles. Other sites in the neighborhood include **Petersburg National Military Park** with mementos of Grant's 1864–65 siege and **Fort Sedgwick,** built by Federal troops to support the siege of Petersburg.

VIRGINIA BEACH, due east of Norfolk, is one of the most popular seaside resorts along the Atlantic.

Near Suffolk is the eerily beautiful amphibious wilderness, called the **Great Dismal Swamp** since before the time George Washington explored it in 1764. Larger than the whole state of Rhode Island, this jungle of gnarled cypress and hanging moss has an abundance of deer, bear, duck, and fish. Canals make many parts accessible to boats, and a three-hour boat tour is available from Chesapeake.

WILLIAMSBURG, farther east on the peninsula that lies between the James and York rivers, is a unique community where America's Colonial past has become a living reality. The Colonial capital of Virginia, Williamsburg has been restored as it was; shopkeepers and artisans wear authentic eighteenth-century clothes and work with eighteenth-century tools. Outstanding among the many buildings, both original and restored, are the **Governor's Palace;** the **Old Capitol** (where Patrick Henry thundered, "If this be treason, make the most of it!"); the **Raleigh Tavern; Bruton Parish Church** (Washington, Jefferson, and Monroe prayed here); the **Public "Gaol,"** where Blackbeard's pirates were imprisoned; and the **craft shops** (bootmaker, bakery, bookbindery, weaver, wig-maker, blacksmith, apothecary, silversmith, milliner, cabinetmaker). **Carter's Grove,** stately plantation where patriots such as Washington and Jefferson enjoyed its gracious elegance, should be visited. See the film at the Information Center and consult the attendants on an itinerary for the area. **The College of William and Mary,** chartered in 1693, is located in Williamsburg.

Jamestown, six miles south of Williamsburg, is the site of the first permanent English settlement in America. The only standing relic is the ivy-covered ruin of a 1639 church, although statues of **John Smith** and **Pocahontas** have been erected. Exhibits at **Jamestown Festival Park,** constructed in 1957 for a celebration of the 350th anniversary of the first landing, include a reconstructed fort, a working replica of the glass factory of 1608 and full-sized replicas of the three ships (*Susan Constant, Godspeed* and *Discovery*) that carried the original Colonists.

YORKTOWN. Thirteen miles of scenic Colonial Parkway link Williamsburg and Yorktown, where Lord Cornwallis surrendered to Washington on October 19, 1781. Interesting to visit are **Moore House,** where surrender terms were drafted; **York Hall,** with two Revolutionary cannon balls embedded in one of its walls; the **Swan Tavern Group**—a restored tavern, kitchen, smokehouse and stable. **Battlefield** tours start at the Visitors' Center and take in the reconstructed fortifications, the marked site of Washington's headquarters, the positions of the armies and other exhibits.

Around **Hampton Roads** are clustered cities devoted to ships and the sea. Hampton is the center of a big commercial fishing industry; the **Newport News Shipbuilding and Dry Dock Company** is the largest private shipyard in the world; **Norfolk Navy Yard** is one of the oldest and largest naval shipyards anywhere. In addition, there are attractive seashore resorts.

The **Mariner's Museum,** set in an 800-acre park on the James River five miles north of Newport News, is outstanding as a storehouse of nautical material. It contains maps, pictures, ship models and a library of over 40,000 volumes and manuscripts.

Just north of it is another unusual museum, the **James River Golf Museum,** with exhibits tracing the history of golf since the sixteenth century.

SPORTS AND RECREATION. Well-kept recreation areas in all parts of the state make lakes, forests and mountains readily accessible to vacationists. Most are open daily 9 A.M. to 10 P.M. Reservations for camping, cabins or lodges should be made through Commissioner of Parks, Virginia Department of Conservation and Development, Richmond.

Skyline Drive and **Blue Ridge Parkway:** These linked highways parallel the Appalachian Trail through the spectacular mountain scenery of **Shenandoah National Park,** the **George Washington National Forest** and part of the **Jefferson National Forest.** Below Roanoke, the Blue Ridge Parkway continues south to the **Great Smoky Mountains National Park** in North Carolina. Along this highway chain are numerous facilities for making motor trips.

Northern Virginia: **Westmoreland State Park,** 1,300 acres on the Potomac River; **Douthat State Park,** 5,000 acres of mountain-lake country near Clifton Forge.

Southwest Virginia: **High Knob Recreation Area,** near Norton; **Bark Camp and Recreation Area,** south of Tacoma; **Hungry Mother State Park,** 2,100 acres with lake and sand beach; **Claytor Lake State Park,** southwest of Radford, on the banks of a 20-mile lake created by the New River Dam; **Fairy Stone State Park** (its name comes from oddly shaped local crystals that supposedly bring good luck), a 5,000-acre wooded tract with a large lake; **Cave Mountain Recreation Area** in Jefferson National Forest, southeast of Natural Bridge.

Southeast Virginia: **Staunton River State Park,** 700 acres on the shore of the reservoir formed by the John H. Kerr Dam near South Boston; **Appomattox-Buckingham State Forest,** 19,000 acres; **Cumberland State Forest,** 16,000 acres containing two lakes; **Goodwyn Lake Recreation Area,** south of Burkeville; **Pocahontas State Park,** 7,000-acre tract of woods 15 miles southwest of Richmond.

SPECIAL EVENTS. **Lee-Jackson Day,** January 19; **Antiques Forum,** Williamsburg, January; **International Azalea Festival,** Norfolk and vicinity, late April; **Historic Garden Week** in Virginia, tours through private homes and gardens, state-wide, last full week in April; **Shenandoah Apple Blossom Festival,** Winchester, early May; **Prelude to Independence,** Williamsburg, May 15 through July 4; **Barter Theatre Season,** Abingdon, April through October; **Chincoteague Wild Pony Round-up,** Chincoteague Island, last Wednesday and Thursday in July; outdoor dramas (**"The Common Glory"** at Williamsburg) nightly, except Sunday in July and August; **Lotus Festival,** Virginia Beach, late July; **Virginia Highlands Arts and Crafts Festival,** Abingdon, August 1 to 15; **Norfolk Fair,** Norfolk, September; **State Fair of Virginia,** Richmond, October; **National Tobacco Festival,** Richmond, late October.

Sporting events include **Hunter Trials,** Middleburg, spring; **Virginia Salt Water Fishing Tournament,** ocean, rivers and Chesapeake Bay, May 1 through November 30; **Deep Run Hunt Races,** Atlantic Rural Exposition Grounds, Richmond, May; **Virginia Gold Cup Race,** Warrenton, May; **Natural Chimneys Jousting Tournament,** horseback contests held annually since 1821, Mount Solon, third Saturday in August; **East Coast Surfing Championships,** Virginia Beach, late August; **Warrenton Horse Show,** early September.

West Virginia

To a businessman today, West Virginia connotes industry, especially coal mines, but to early visitors to the area, George Washington and Thomas Jefferson, and to many others since their day, the state has meant natural beauty on a scale rarely found elsewhere in the East.

THE LAND. West Virginia's land borders are among the most irregularly shaped of any state. It goes almost as far west as Columbus, Ohio, and its eastern boundaries are only 50 miles from Washington, D.C. Pennsylvania and parts of western Maryland are on the north, and Virginia makes up most of the southern border. West Virginia, at 1,500 feet, has the highest elevation of any state east of the Mississippi. Its excellent black soil and wealth of minerals and coal are the chief natural resources.

THE CLIMATE. Temperatures in the summer in West Virginia average 74 degrees throughout the state, although 68 degrees is average for the mountain areas. In January they rarely fall below 29 degrees in the mountains, and are in the mid-30's in the valley areas. Rainfall averages 44 inches yearly, with snowfall varying from 20 to 35 inches throughout the state.

THE PEOPLE. Among earliest known residents of this land were the Adena and Hopewell Indians. Mounds attributed to them can be seen in the state, notably at Moundsville, in the Northern Panhandle, and in the Great Kanawha Valley in southern West Virginia. The earliest white men to come through the mountains from the East in the seventeenth and eighteenth centuries often encountered Indian hunting parties, who long had visited the area in pursuit of game. Few Indians were regularly resident here, however.

Morgan Morgan, who located in the Bunker Hill section of the Eastern Panhandle in 1731, is credited with being the first permanent settler. Others trickled in after him, mostly Germans, Welsh and Scots-Irish. Coal was discovered in 1742, an event of major consequence for the state.

In 1749 George II of England granted half a million acres between the Ohio and the Monongahela Rivers to the Ohio Company, but prior to this the French had laid claim to all the Ohio Valley.

Early development of the western lands of Virginia, later to be West Virginia, included surveys made by George Washington for Lord Fairfax, whose vast estate included what is now the Eastern Panhandle of the state.

In 1768 Charles Washington, brother to George, laid out the city of Charles Town, which was named after him. The Town of Bath, better known as Berkeley Springs today, had been established two years earlier, 40 miles northwest of the site of Charles Town.

John Brown's ill-fated raid on the United States arsenal at Harper's Ferry in 1859, a prelude to the Civil War, resulted in Brown's execution at Charles Town.

The Civil War made West Virginia a state. After the Commonwealth of Virginia seceded from the Union, in 1861, representatives of western counties which had opposed secession had a series of meetings. In the "Second Wheeling Convention" these representatives adopted a "Declaration of Rights" which branded the secession ordinance illegal, and reorganized the government of Virginia. Francis Pierpont was chosen governor.

On June 20, 1863, West Virginia was formally admitted to the Union. The area was not without Confederate sympathizers, however. Two who were to play dramatic roles in the conflict were natives of the Mountain State, General Thomas J. "Stonewall" Jackson and Belle Boyd, renowned Confederate spy.

The first land battle of the Civil War actually occurred in West Virginia, at Philippi, where Yanks and Rebels clashed for control of the Baltimore & Ohio Railroad. Fighting thereafter resulted in gradual expulsion of Southern forces from West Virginia.

Wheeling was the first capital of West Virginia. In 1870 the capital was moved to Charleston, where, after a short return to Wheeling in 1877, it finally settled in 1885.

The population of West Virginia is over 1.7 million, ranking it thirty-fourth in population among the 50 states.

AGRICULTURE. With about 44,000 farms in the state, agriculture plays a vital part in West Virginia's economy. Excellent bluegrass, good for grazing all-year-round, enables livestock to be bred in large numbers. Sheep, hogs, and poultry are also important.

Apples, cherries, grapes, and peaches are leading fruits, while corn, barley, hay, and potatoes are among the vegetables grown.

Fine woods can be cut from West Virginia's extensive forests. Wood products are a large contributor to the state's industry.

INDUSTRY. In addition to forest products, West Virginia is most well-known for its chemical industries, iron and steel production, glass and pottery, textiles, and metal products. Industrial centers are largely in the Northern Panhandle near Wheeling.

West Virginia is also one of the most important mining states, and is best known for its wealth of coal, natural gas, limestone, petroleum, and salt.

CITIES. West Virginia's large cities, which are industry-based, are located in the areas where manufacturing is important. More West Virginians live in small towns or rural areas, however, and there are 230 of these towns with less than 5,000 residents.

EASTERN WEST VIRGINIA contains some of the state's most beautiful country, oldest homes, and fascinating historic sites. Monongahela National Forest, within this area, contains more than 800,000 acres. It includes Blackwater Falls and Watoga state parks, the Seneca State Forest, and Spruce Knob, highest point (4,862 feet) in the state. Additional attractions are the Smoke Hole and Cranberry Glades, Hills Creek Falls, the Cass Scenic Railroad, Seneca Caverns, Seneca Rocks, and Summit Lake.

BERKELEY SPRINGS, the nation's oldest spa, is at the Eastern Panhandle's northern edge. Its famous baths were patronized by George Washington and his contemporaries. The town itself is named "Bath," after Bath, England, famed for its waters. The post office name, Berkeley Springs, honors Norborne Berkeley, royal governor of Virginia, 1768=70. The springs are now owned by the state.

CHARLES TOWN, in the extreme eastern section, contains many old Washington homes restored to former elegance. Most famous of these are **Happy Retreat, Harewood, Beallair,** and **Claymont Court.** Dolley Payne Todd and James Madison, later President of the United States, were married at Harewood in 1794. The ruins of **St. George's Chapel,** where George Washington worshiped, are two miles west of town. **Jefferson County Courthouse,** where John Brown was convicted of treason, stands at George and Washington streets. Two racetracks, **Shenandoah Downs** and **Charles Town** are open all year round.

HARPERS FERRY, at the confluence of the Potomac and Shenandoah rivers, has the **Harpers Ferry National Historical Park,** which includes **John Brown's Fort,** earthworks and gun emplacement, relics of Civil War battles. Here also is a natural rock "bench," a vantage point for what Thomas Jefferson once described as "one of the most stupendous scenes in nature"—the view of the blending rivers.

MARTINSBURG, about 15 miles northwest, a great apple center, boasts magnificent old homes. **Bunker Hill,** southwest of Martinsburg, was the home of Morgan Morgan, the state's first permanent settler. **Shepherdstown,** east of Martinsburg, dating from the early 1700's, is said to be the oldest town in West Virginia. Originally chartered as Mecklenburg, the present name was adopted in 1867, honoring the founder, James Shepherd. Here in 1787 James Rumsey first publicly exhibited his steamboat, for which the state has erected a monument.

PETERSBURG, near the eastern tip of the Monongahela National Forest, is the location of the legendary "Fox and Ox" rocks, so-called because at certain times the 800-foot-high cliffs appear to be carved to resemble those animals. Near Riverton and Mouth of Seneca, to the southwest, is the spectacular **Seneca Rocks,** 900 feet high; the **Smoke Hole Recreation Area, Seneca Caverns** and **Spruce Knob,** the state's highest point.

ROMNEY, on the south branch of the Potomac, chartered in 1762, was the scene of recurring conflict during the Civil War—it changed hands 56 times. The **Confederate Monument in Indian Mound Cemetery** was one of the first in the country (1867). Natural attractions include startlingly perpendicular cliffs rising 300 feet from the river, and the Nathaniel and Short Mountain Hunting Areas.

CENTRAL WEST VIRGINIA, directly south of the state's Mason-Dixon Line boundary, rises rather abruptly from the Ohio Valley. A crisscross of mountains, ravines, and streams, it is heavily underlaid with coal. Fertile farmlands lie along the West Fork, Buckhannon, and Tygart river valleys.

CLARKSBURG, 25 miles southwest of Fairmont, has historic importance as the birthplace of General Thomas J. "Stonewall" Jackson, of Civil War renown. Clarksburg, a rich manufacturing center, boasts the **Benedum Civic Center** and is a principal tourist crossroads. Nearby, Jacksons Mill is the site today of the **West Virginia 4-H Camp,** and a favorite spot for tourists. Weston also is notable for the largest hand-cut stone structure in the world, the main unit of Weston State Hospital. Nearby is Watters Smith Memorial State Park, a pioneer farm (late 1700's) preserved intact.

FAIRMONT, 19 miles south of Morgantown, turns out glass products, precision machinery, and sheet aluminum. It is the center of a coal area which produces more than 30 million tons annually. One mechanized mine here, the **Loveridge,** is credited with having the deepest shaft in active operation in the state, 732 feet. The Loveridge yields 8,376 tons of coal on the average day. Fairmont products are distributed worldwide; **Fairmont State College** is located here.

MORGANTOWN, northernmost city in central West Virginia, is the seat of **West Virginia University,** including a modern medical center. Morgantown produces handmade glass, plumbing fixtures, and coal from the Scotts Run Field. Northeast of the city are **Mont Chateau State Park, Coopers Rock State Forest,** and **Cheat Lake.**

MOUNDSVILLE, 12 miles south of Wheeling, has the largest conical burial mound in America—the **Grave Creek Mound.** The West Virginia Archeological Society maintains a "prehistory museum" adjacent to this mound. At glass plants in Moundsville, New Martinsville, and Williamstown, farther south on the Ohio River, visitors may observe every step in the handcrafting of table and stemware.

PARKERSBURG, also a river city, grew up near the site of frontier Fort Neal. Its chief concerns are industrial (synthetic fibers, glass, iron, steel). Historic spots in the neighborhood include **Blennerhassett Island,** where Hiram Blennerhassett and Aaron Burr plotted their visionary western "kingdom," and **Centennial Cabin** in City Park, which displays pioneer goods and documents.

POINT PLEASANT, where the Great Kanawha River joins the Ohio, was the scene of the defeat of Indians under the Shawnee Chief Cornstalk by General Andrew Lewis in 1774. A granite shaft in **Tu-Endie-Wei Park** commemorates the battle, and the log **Mansion House Inn,** oldest building in the Kanawha Valley, exhibits souvenirs.

WHEELING has more than 200 manufacturing establishments and is an important steel center. The "commercial hub of the Great Ohio Valley," the city also is an important historical, educational, and recreational center. The last battle of the Revolution occurred here at Fort Henry (named for Patrick Henry) in 1782. In 1861 representatives of many western counties of Virginia met at Wheeling to set up "The Restored Government of Virginia." Relics of these historic moments are on display in the **Oglebay Park Mansion House Museum.** Park buildings house art, drama, and music workshops. Oglebay Park also features the "Frontier Travel Gallery," displaying early vehicles of transportation, from the old Conestoga Wagon to the sternwheel steamboat. **Wheeling College, Linsly Military Institute,** and **Mount de Chantal Academy** are located here.

SOUTHERN WEST VIRGINIA extends from northwest to southeast, roughly parallel to the state's southern boundary. It is mostly coal country, with industrial Huntington, second largest city, at the westernmost end, and a number of famous old spas—**White Sulphur Springs, Sweet Springs, Salt Sulphur Springs,** and **Pence Springs**—at the other.

Lewisburg, also in the southeast, is host to the annual West Virginia State Fair. Other points of interest at Lewisburg include the **Old Stone Church,** dating from 1796, and **Daywood Art Gallery,** featuring paintings, engravings, china, and glass.

CHARLESTON, state capital and largest city, lies along the Kanawha River, equidistant from Point Pleasant and Huntington. The capitol, on the site of old Fort Lee, was built in 1932 at a cost of $10 million. Guides show its splendid interior—crystal chandeliers, great bronze doors, and much magnificent Danby Marble. **The Capitol Museum** displays the Beckley Table, on which the Declaration of Independence was signed; a rifle used by Lewis Wetzel, famous Indian fighter; Aaron Burr's spectacles, and a 35-star flag flown at Gettysburg when Lincoln spoke. Industrially, Charleston produces chemicals and synthetics, but also has diversified manufacturing.

MILTON, 18 miles east of Huntington, is the home of **Blenko Glass,** one of the few places in the world where handmade cathedral glass is produced, a process which visitors may view, step by step. Colonial Williamsburg glassware also is produced here.

WILLIAMSON, near the Kentucky border 111 miles southwest of Charleston, features a building made entirely of coal, headquarters for the city's chamber of commerce. Almost due east of Williamson is Beckley, with an exhibition coal mine entered from within the city itself, where visitors may view activities involved in extracting coal from the depths of earth. The **Stotesbury Coal Town Museum,** also near Beckley, displays objects illustrative of the entire development of the coal mining industry, and offers handcrafted articles for sale. Hinton, 25 miles from Beckley, is the site of the Bluestone Reservoir, Bluestone State Park. Ronceverte, between Hinton and White Sulphur Springs, lists **Organ Cave** as a stellar attraction. In this cavern saltpeter was made during the Civil War—old hoppers used in the process can be seen. Visitors to the Bluefield area, in the extreme southern end of the state, may drive their automobiles through the **Pocahontas Exhibition** (coal) **Mine,** although they will see more on foot. Two scenic panoramas lure visitors, Skyland Overlook atop East River Mountain, and a towering stone formation in Pinnacle Rock State Park. At Skyland visitors may ride the miniature **Ridge Runner Railroad** to view breathtaking mountain scenery.

SPORTS AND RECREATION. Most of West Virginia's state parks and forests are mountain-set, and feature **hiking, bridle trails, picnic grounds,** and **scenic views**—overlooks and panoramas. Many have cabins and **campsites** for tents and trailers. Playgrounds, swimming pools, and fishing areas are usual. **Trout fishing** is legal throughout the year. Provision is made in many for **hunting** deer, bear, and such small game as grouse and wild turkey, in season. Three of the state parks—Blackwater Falls, Cacapon, and Mont Chateau—offer all-year, overnight accommodations. Others generally are open from late March until early December. Literature containing additional information may be obtained from the Division of State Parks and Recreation, Department of Natural Resources, State Capitol, Charleston, West Virginia 25305. Application may be made to the same authority for reservations.

Tomlinson Run State Park, 1,383 acres at Pughtown, near the tip of the Northern Panhandle, is a well-known facility. Nearby is **Newell,** which has the largest single pottery factory in the world, and **Waterford Park,** scene of thoroughbred **racing** in season. **Oglebay Park,** 957-acre facility operated by the City of Wheeling and developed over a period of 40 years "along the most modern principles of park planning," is West Virginia's chief recreational (also educational) attraction.

Cacapon State Park, 5,800 acres near Berkeley Springs, is where four states may be seen from Prospect Rock, on the park's 2,208-foot Cacapon Moun-

National Parks & Forests in Eastern United States

tain. A variety of facilities are available. The historic **Fairfax Stone Monument,** marking a survey made in 1746 of lands in the vast estate of Lord Fairfax, now the base for the boundary line between West Virginia and Maryland, is located in nearby Tucker County.

Blackwater Falls State Park, 1,679 acres just southeast of Davis, is named for a magnificent waterfall almost six stories in height.

Renowned pre-Civil War spa, Lee White Sulphur Springs, is within the bounds of 3,680-acre **Lost River State Park. Watoga State Park,** 10,057 acres southwest of Huntersville, Pocahontas County, surrounded by **Monongahela National Forest,** includes the 400-acre **Brooks Memorial Arboretum;** deer and other interesting wildlife, as well as sports and camping facilities. **Calvin Price State Forest,** 9,482 acres adjoining Watoga; deer, small game hunting, and fishing. **Seneca State Forest,** 11,503 acres near Marlinton, and **Droop Mountain Battlefield State Park,** 285 acres near Droop, Pocahontas County (site of the state's most extensive Civil War engagement) are well-equipped parks.

Cass Scenic Railroad, in Pocahontas County, affords a thrilling ride up Cheat Mountain to Bald Knob, second highest point in the state, on a restored lumber railroad, the train powered by an authentic steam locomotive.

The whole of **Monongahela National Forest** is in eastern West Virginia, and this area also includes that portion of the George Washington National Forest which is in West Virginia.

Fifteen developed tent and trailer campsites lying within these National Forest boundaries are **Bear Heaven, Big Rock, Blue Bend, Brandywine Lake, Camp Run, Cranberry, Horseshoe, Lake Sherwood, Pocahontas, Seneca, Smoke Hole, Spruce Knob Lake, Stuart, Summit Lake,** and **Wolf Gap.**

CENTRAL WEST VIRGINIA. **Coopers Rock State Forest,** 13,043 acres near Morgantown, distinguished by an awesome hanging cliff, affords a breathtaking view of the Cheat River Gorge and encircling mountains, plus ruins of a pre-Revolutionary iron furnace and powder mill; winter sports, hunting, fishing, play and picnic grounds, tent camping. **Tygart Lake State Park,** 1,805 acres south of Grafton and Holly River State Park, 7,592 acres of varied flora and abundant wildlife in Webster County are also popular. **Watters Smith Memorial State Park,** 278 acres near Clarksburg and Weston, includes buildings and grounds of a pioneer farm of the late 1700's preserved intact. Also to be visited are **Cedar Creek State Park,** 2,034 acres of beautiful woodland near Glenville and **North Bend State Park,** 1,405 acres with distinctive rock formations near Cairo, Ritchie County.

SOUTHERN WEST VIRGINIA. **Carnifex Ferry Battlefield State Park,** 156 acres near Summersville, contains the site of a significant Civil War engagement; museum in Patteson House showing cannonhole battle scars; play and picnic grounds, trails and a spectacular overlook above a gorge of the Gauley River.

Grandview State Park, 878 acres near Beckley, has an overlook of the New River Canyon, 1,400 feet below. Civil War historical drama, **"Honey in the Rock,"** is presented here nightly (except Mondays) during summer months. **Stephens Lake,** a recreation area of 2,400 acres near Beckley, includes 303 acres of water surface, 16 acres of shoreline with a 1,000-foot beach, and many other features. **Bluestone State Park,** 1,346 acres bordering on Bluestone Reservoir, is near Hinton.

Other popular parks in southern West Virginia are **Camp Creek State Forest,** 5,897 acres near Princeton; **Panther State Forest,** 7,810 acres near Iaeger; **Kanawha State Forest,** 6,597 acres; **Babcock State Park,** 3,277 acres near Clifftop; and **Cabwaylingo State Forest,** 8,036 acres.

SPECIAL EVENTS. **Historic Homes and Gardens Tours,** Charles Town, Harpers Ferry, Martinsburg and Shepherdstown, late April; **Creative Arts Festival,** Charleston, late April or early May; **Webster County Nature Tour,** late April or early May, in Webster Springs area; **Wildflower Pilgrimage,** Blackwater Falls State Park, in May; **Strawberry Festival,** Buckhannon, in June; **West Virginia's Birthday,** observed statewide, June 20; **Folk Festival,** Glenville, late June or early July; **Mountain State Art and Craft Fair,** Cedar Lakes, early in July; **West Virginia State Poultry Festival,** at Moorefield, in July; **Moundsville Corn Festival,** at Moundsville, in August; **West Virginia State Fair,** at Lewisburg, in August; **Hardy County House and Garden Tour,** both in September; **Buckwheat Festival,** Kingwood, late in September; **Mountain State Forest Festival,** Elkins, early October; **Black Walnut Festival,** Spencer, October; **Chrysanthemum Show,** Oglebay Park in Wheeling, early November; **Glass Show,** Weston, late November or early December.

Sports events include **Alpine Festival,** Davis, late January or early February; **West Virginia Ski Meet, Mont Chateau Cup Races,** and **West Virginia Ice Skating Meet,** Coopers Rock State Forest, in January; **White Water Weekend,** Petersburg, in April; **Tygart Lake Spring Regatta,** Grafton, late May or early June; **Antique Car Show,** Nitro, in August; **New Martinsville Inboard Regatta,** at New Martinsville, and **West Virginia State Water Festival,** at Hinton, both in September; **Charleston Championship Boat Races,** at Charleston, October.

Kentucky

Kentucky, *The Bluegrass State,* gets its nickname from the lush grass, containing blue-gray blossoms, which grows on Kentucky soil. This grass, as well as Thoroughbred racehorses and rich tobacco, have made Kentucky famous.

THE LAND. Water provides the border for Kentucky on two sides—the **Ohio River** on the north and the **Mississippi River** on the west. This Ohio River boundary is the traditional border between northern and southern states. Many lakes, including two created by the Tennessee Valley Authority, dot the state. **Black Mountain,** in southwestern Kentucky, is 4,145 feet high—the state's highest point.

THE CLIMATE. Kentucky's climate is generally warm and rainy—excellent for growing fine tobacco and grass. In January, temperatures rarely drop below 38 degrees, and in July they rarely rise above 77. Rain is heaviest in southern Kentucky, with total precipitation averaging around 48 inches a year.

THE PEOPLE. The first Kentuckians entered what was then Fincastle County, Virginia, through the Cumberland Gap in the Alleghenies. Dr. Thomas Walker was the first white settler, near Barbourville in 1750. Daniel Boone, with the help of his "axe men," blazed the Wilderness Road and set up headquarters at Boonesboro in 1775.

James Harrod established Kentucky's first permanent settlement at Harrodsburg in 1774. By 1775 there were enough people present to open the first legislature west of the Alleghenies, which in 1776 declared Kentucky County separate from Fincastle and set up a new county seat at Harrodsburg.

New settlements sprang up and prospered. The village George Rogers Clark founded on the Ohio in 1778 was called Louisville in honor of Louis XVI of France and the help he gave the embattled colonists during the Revolution. In 1779 a hunting party from Harrodsburg built a fort and blockhouse at a place they named Lexington after the Revolutionary battlefield in Massachusetts. (In 1776 several prehistoric Mound Builder mummies were discovered in a series of ancient catacombs under the city site.)

Kentucky petitioned for statehood in 1790, was admitted as the fifteenth state in 1792. Her citizens had founded the first college west of the Alleghenies, Transylvania at Lexington, in 1780; later they added the first medical school, the first law school, the first normal school and the first library. The *Kentucky Gazette,* the first newspaper on its side of the mountains, was published in 1787. The West's first railroad, the Lexington and Ohio, was built in 1830–32.

During the Civil War, Kentucky's struggles dramatized those of a "border state." She supplied both the North and the South with Presidents (Lincoln had been born at Hodgenville; Jefferson Davis, at Fairview). A special convention claiming to represent 65 counties voted secession; the regular legislature never did. Bloody battles were fought on Kentucky soil, especially in the eastern part of the state; the most severe, the Confederate defeat at Perryville in 1862.

Since the war, Kentuckians have made their border status an asset, preserved the pleasantest of Southern life—the fine old Kentucky homes, lush bluegrass farms, the ingrained respect for leisure—and combined it with a Northern-bred progressiveness (such as the huge Kentucky Lake Development, Louisville's impressive symphony).

The population today is over 3.1 million, of which the majority lives in rural areas.

AGRICULTURE. Kentucky's natural resources, especially an abundance of rich soil, have led to the development of a healthy farm economy which now accounts for a fourth of the value of goods produced. Tobacco outranks all other crops in value, earning more than a third of Kentucky's farm income. Dark tobacco grows in an area in the southern part of the state known as the **black patch.** Livestock, notably cows and calves, are also important. Thoroughbred racehorses raised near Lexington are possibly Kentucky's best-known product.

INDUSTRY. Over 65 percent of the value of goods produced in Kentucky comes from manufacturing or processing. Kentucky leads the nation in the production of whiskey, with principal distilleries located in Louisville, Lexington, Bardstown, and Owensboro. Other important manufacturing areas are chemicals and allied products, electrical machinery, tobacco products, and meats. Although most of Kentucky's electric power comes from coal and other fuels, a sharp drop in coal demand has affected the economic growth of the eastern portion of the state.

CITIES. Louisville, Lexington, and the Ashland-Huntington area contain close to a third of Kentucky's population. Frankfort, the state capital, Covington, Owensboro, Paducah, Ashland, and Newport are other large cities.

EASTERN KENTUCKY is, for the most part, mountain country—handsome but rugged and sparsely settled. There is considerable coal mining around Harlan in its southeastern corner and a few pioneer monuments here and there (**Walker's cabin** at **Barbourville,** for example), but most of the sights worth seeing come under the heading of natural wonders like the "moonbow" at **Cumberland Falls** or the deep-walled **"Breaks of Cumberland"** near **Pikeville.**

Ashland, on the Ohio, forms a triple-city industrial team with Ironton, Ohio, and Huntington, West Virginia; uses nearby natural resources (coke, oil, natural gas, limestone, clays, shale) to process steel, oil, coal, coke, bricks and leather. A major freight depot, it was named for Henry Clay's homestead in Lexington.

Southwest of Ashland are two notable subterranean sights: **Cascade Caves** (with underground river and waterfall) and **Carter Caves** (with natural bridge).

U. S. Highway 23 goes south into Kentucky's easternmost section. Union General Garfield made his Battle of Middle Creek headquarters at Prestonsburg. From this neighborhood, Kentucky's Route 15 connects with the new four-lane Mountain Parkway, crossing west to **Winchester** and **Cumberland National Forest** headquarters. South of Winchester lie **Richmond** (site of a Wilderness Road marker, a Confederate victory and—in the **library of Eastern Kentucky State College**—an extensive exhibit of Kentuckiana) and **Berea,** with its famous mountain college (over-

Stud Farms in Kentucky

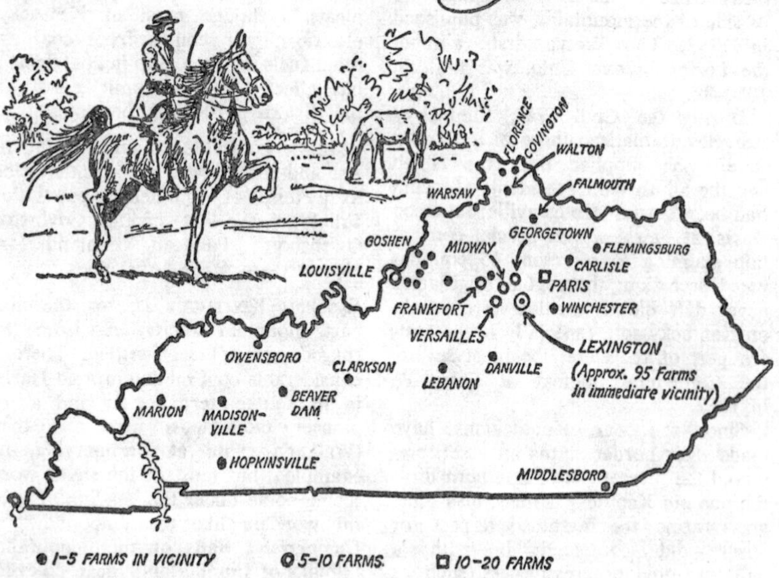

night accommodations are available at the student-staffed **Boone Tavern** in downtown Berea).

Still farther south—on U. S. Highways 25 and 25E—are **London, Corbin,** and **Pineville,** where the **Mountain Laurel Queen** is crowned each spring.

CENTRAL KENTUCKY is the region where visions strummed up by chords of "My Old Kentucky Home" become real for most non-Kentuckians. Bourbon ages in charred oak kegs, flat hands of burley tobacco hang drying in the sheds. This was the Bluegrass country of the great Thoroughbred Man O'War.

COVINGTON is almost exclusively industrial. From Covington, the Ohio bends west then south to **Carrollton.** Worth seeing: **General Butler State Park** and the old brick **Butler home** there, now handsomely refurnished and restored. Near Mount Olivet is the **park memorial** to the **Bloody Battle of Blue Licks,** last western clash of the Revolution. A cemetery on the grounds and a museum full of prehistoric relics, Indian mementos, glass and gun collections should be visited.

DANVILLE lies on a southeast tangent from Harrodsburg. Its **Constitution Square,** where the first constitutional convention was held, has been restored as a state park; the **Dr. Ephraim McDowell House** on Second Street commemorates the work of the pioneer surgeon; the **Isaac Shelby Memorial** to the state's first governor is in the Shelby burial grounds five miles south.

From Harrodsburg the main crescent route travels southwest to **Perryville,** then west to **Springfield (Lincoln Homestead State Park** with the Thomas Lincoln House, Nancy Hanks' log cabin and a museum), northwest to **Bardstown. "Federal Hill,"** in the same neighborhood, is the "Old Kentucky Home" where Stephen Foster wrote the song; his desk and spinet are still there. **St. Joseph's Cathedral** holds a number of art masterpieces (a Murillo and a Rubens, among others) presented to the church by Louis Philippe of France.

FRANKFORT has been state capital since 1792. Its highlights: the **capitol building** (the dome was modeled after that on Napoleon's tomb); the **Governor's Mansion** on the banks of the Kentucky; the **Old State House** (Greek Revival architecture outside, library and museum of the Kentucky Historical Society within); **Frankfort Cemetery,** where Daniel and Rebecca Boone are buried; and the **Corner of Celebrities** (homes of 24 men of national prominence).

The crescent route starts at Lexington and passes through **Shakertown** (where that sect's stone guest house and dwelling houses still stand) on its way to **Harrodsburg,** oldest permanent settlement in Kentucky. Its sightseeing stops: **Pioneer Memorial State Park** with the **Lincoln Marriage Temple** and a replica of Fort Harrod enclosing a school and settlers' cabins partially furnished with Boone relics; **Old Mud Meeting House; Boone's Cave,** four miles east of town.

LEXINGTON, unofficial capital of the Bluegrass country, lies 20 miles southwest of Paris. Thoroughbred farms in the vicinity, including **Calumet, Greentree** and **C. V. Whitney's,** are open to visitors daily—Man O'War's grave and statue are on **Man O'War Farm.** Other claims to fame: handsome homes such as **"Ashland,"** Henry Clay's home; **"Hopemont,"** home of the Confederate General John Hunt Morgan; **Mary Todd's home** and her grandfather Levi's **"Ellerslie"**; fine schools, including the **University of Kentucky,** built on land once part of Clay's "Ashland" estate, and **Transylvania University,** oldest west of the Alleghenies. Additional interest points: **Keeneland Race Course,** where trotting races and horse sales are held; **Lexington Cemetery** with its 100-foot monument to Henry Clay. Nearby is **"White Hall,"** home of **Cassius Marcellus Clay,** the great abolitionist.

LOUISVILLE, at the western tip of the crescent, is the seat of Jefferson County, commercial and artistic capital of the state. The Louisville Orchestra has a distinguished record of modern symphonic firsts. There is a good collection of painting and sculpture at the **J. B. Speed Memorial Museum** on the University of Louisville campus; regional art and pottery at the **Little Gallery;** regional art displays at the **Art Center Gallery.** In addition to books, the **Louisville Free Public Library's** lending stock includes moving-picture films, long-playing records, framed prints, and musical scores. Louisville is the place where the Toonerville Trolley, Mrs. Wiggs of the Cabbage Patch and chewing gum were invented. Worth seeing: **Churchill Downs** (Central Avenue), where the Derby is run; the **Louisville Barge Canal,** bypassing the Falls of the Ohio, home of the U. S. Coast Guard's only inland station; the **American Printing House for the Blind** (Frankfort Avenue), largest Braille publishers in the world; the **University of Louisville** (Third and Shipp); the four municipal parks—**Shawnee, Iroquois, Cherokee** and **Seneca.** Historic sites include **"Farmington,"** on the Bardstown road, a charming Federal-style residence designed by Thomas Jefferson; **Zachary Taylor National Cemetery** and **Monument,** and **Cave Hill Cemetery,** where George Rogers Clark is buried; plaques marking the spots where Clark established his first settlement (foot of Twelfth Street) and where Fort Nelson once stood (Seventh and Main). The **Filson Club** (Breckinridge Street) houses an extensive collection of Kentuckiana.

Fort Knox, where the country stores its gold, is about 12 miles southwest of Louisville. Its war-trophy museum is named for World War II General Patton.

The Kentucky Turnpike, a wide new toll road, spans the 40 miles from Louisville, south to **Elizabethtown,** and Interstate 65 continues on from that point. The **Brown-Pusey Community House** is over a century old, and was once a stagecoach inn. At **Hodgenville,** a few miles southeast, **Abraham Lincoln Birthplace National Historic Site** includes part of the farm on which he was born, and an imposing marble shrine over his birthplace cabin.

The mighty **Mammoth Caves** lie about 40 miles due south of Elizabethtown in a national park of their own; tours take one-and-one-half to seven hours.

PARIS is the seat of Bourbon County. Bourbon whiskey was invented here and quaffed at **Duncan Tavern,** which stands—restored by the Kentucky Daughters of the American Revolution—on the Paris Public Square. Neighborhood stops: the **Claiborne** and **Stoner Creek studs,** Thoroughbred breeding farms; and **Cane Ridge Meeting House,** where the Disciples of Christ sect held its first meeting.

WESTERN KENTUCKY is tobacco and farming country. Its largest towns lie along the winding course of the Ohio on the north or along U. S. Route 68, which parallels the bottom edge of the state. Its most spectacular triple feature: **Kentucky Lake,** made by the Kentucky Dam, largest in the Tennessee Valley Authority's string; **Lake Barkley,** formed by Barkley Dam just a few miles from Kentucky Dam; and the large **Land Between the Lakes National Recreation Area,** separating the two lakes.

HENDERSON, center for industry, oil, and agriculture (corn, soybeans, tobacco), is the town where John James Audubon spent nine years of his life. The land near his steam mill has been made a state park, with an **Audubon Museum** nearby.

PADUCAH, still farther west on the Ohio, is the birthplace of humorist Irvin S. Cobb and Indian Chief Paduke for whom the city was named.

Thirty-eight miles southwest of Paducah near Wickliffe, on U. S. Route 60, there is an ancient buried city called **King Mounds.** The **Columbus-Belmont Battlefield,** now a state park, is about 20 miles farther south.

The **Kentucky Dam** and **Kentucky Dam Village State Park** are about 20 miles southeast of Paducah near Gilbertsville. The large **Kentucky Lake** stretches south and slightly east, with **Kenlake State Park** on its western shore about halfway down toward the Tennessee line.

East from the lake are **Hopkinsville** (tobacco and livestock markets), **Fairview** (351-foot Jefferson Davis Monument with elevator to lookout perch inside), and **Bowling Green,** where the Kentucky Building at **Western Kentucky State College** contains a museum and a 16,000-volume library of Kentucky history.

The last passenger-carrying sternwheeler on the river, the Greene Line's *Delta Queen,* makes seven-day Ohio River and Kentucky Lake cruises in summer; for information, consult the Line's headquarters in Cincinnati.

SPORTS AND RECREATION. Kentucky's natural wonders include caves, sandstone bridges, mountains, lakes. Her public parks and forests are built around the most spectacular of these as well as on land important in the lives of her particular heroes. Outdoor facilities at most of them are open from April through October. For information on camping facilities, contact the superintendents of individual areas or the Department of Parks, Frankfort, Kentucky.

In Kentucky's eastern mountains: **Carter Caves State Park,** 1,000 acres of caves, cliffs, cascading streams, and other scenic wonders between Olive Hill and Grayson. **Natural Bridge State Park,** more than 1,300 acres setting off the bridge and other spectacular stone formations near Slade, southeast of Lexington. **Buckhorn Lake State Park,** nearly 750 acres northwest of Hazard. **Jenny Wiley State Park,** a 1,700-acre lakeside site northeast of Prestonsburg. **Breaks Interstate Park,** a two-state (Kentucky and Virginia) park near Pikeville built around "The Breaks of the Sandy," a magnificent mountain gorge; trails, picnicking. **Levi Jackson Wilderness Road State Park,** some 800 acres south of London, preserving a number of interesting pioneer buildings. **Rock Creek Natural Area,** nearly 200 acres of rugged timber tract in Cumberland National Forest, 22 miles southwest of London. **Cumberland Falls State Park,** 1,720 acres southwest of Corbin, with a splendid waterfall, 125 feet wide, and the only resident moonbow this side of South Africa. **Pine Mountain State Park,** 2,500 acres just south of Pineville. **Cumberland Gap National Historical Park,** 20,000-acre area, is at the point where Kentucky, Virginia and Tennessee meet.

In central Kentucky: **General Butler State Park,** 800 acres just east of Carrollton, containing the handsome brick Butler home. **Blue Licks Battlefield State Park,** 100-acre monument to "the last battle of the Revolution," between Paris and Maysville. **Otter Creek Park,** 2,400-acre wildlife refuge southwest of Louisville. **Bernheim Forest,** a 14,000-acre tract of rocky, wooded "knobland," 17 miles northwest of Bardstown, complete with arboreta, nature trails and a nature museum. **Herrington Lake,** formed by Dix Dam near Shakertown. **Lincoln Homestead State Park,** north of Springfield, with three early buildings on the first Lincoln landholdings in Kentucky. **Mammoth Cave National Park,** 51,000 wooded acres encircling the famous underground limestone formations west of Cave City; scenic cruises on the Green River, cave tours and boat trips on underground Echo River. **Lake Cumberland State Park,** 3,000 acres on the lake of the same name, 12 miles southwest of Jamestown; and **General Burnside Island State Park,** on an island in the same lake near Burnside. **Wisdom Fishing Camp** and **Illwill Creek Picnic Area,** seven miles west of Albany on Dale Hollow Reservoir.

In western Kentucky: **Kentucky Dam Village State Park,** 1,200-acre all-age playground near Gilbertsville; **Kentucky Woodlands National Wildlife Preserve,** 68,000 acres in Lyon and Trigg counties on Kentucky Lake west of Cadiz, sanctuary for game and waterfowl. **Kenlake State Park,** 1,800-acre stretch along the west shore of the lake the TVA built near Hardin. **Pennyrile Forest State Park,** in a 15,000-acre woodland south of Dawson Springs, and **John James Audubon State Park,** a 645-acre wildflower and bird sanctuary north of Henderson. **Rough River Dam State Park,** 377 acres with a 35-mile-long lake, between Leitchfield and Hardinsburg.

SPECIAL EVENTS. **Garden club tours and open houses** in Louisville, Lexington, and central Kentucky, one late May weekend; **mountain laurel festival,** Pineville, late May; **outdoor dramas** ("The Stephen Foster Story" at Bardstown; Shakespeare in Central Park, Louisville; Pioneer Playhouse at Danville; and "The Book of Job" at Pineville), late June through late August or early September; **Mountain Music Festival,** Slade, July 4; **Kentucky State Fair,** Louisville, mid-August; **Daniel Boone Festival,** Barbourville, late October; **Kentucky Highlands Folk Festival,** Prestonsburg; **Autumn Song Festival,** Elkhorn City, early September.

Sporting events include **horse** sales (spectators welcome), Keeneland at Lexington, spring, summer, and fall; **Keeneland Spring Race Meet,** Lexington, three weeks in April; **annual steamboat race** between "Belle of Louisville" and "Delta Queen," **Derby Trial** and **Kentucky Derby,** at Louisville, first Saturday in May and the preceding week; **Churchill Downs Racing,** Louisville, three weeks in April and May; **Madison Regatta,** early July, on Ohio River in Milton; **Miles Park Race Meet,** Louisville (Kentucky's longest Thoroughbred racing season), daily from mid-May to mid-July; **Fairgrounds Speedway Trotting Races,** Louisville, weekends in summer; **Watkins Cup Regatta,** Hardin, October; **Keeneland Fall Race Meet,** Lexington, October; **Churchill Downs Fall Race Meet,** Louisville, late October and early November; **University of Kentucky Invitational Basketball Tourney,** Lexington, mid-December.

The South

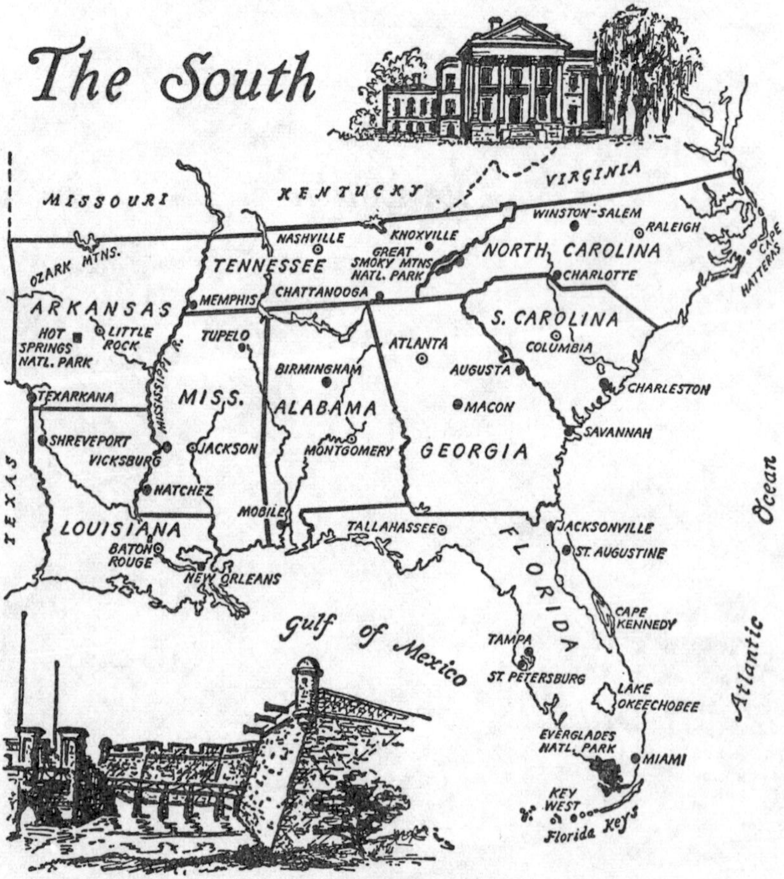
The South
MISSOURI
KENTUCKY
VIRGINIA
WINSTON-SALEM
RALEIGH
NASHVILLE
KNOXVILLE
GREAT SMOKY MTNS. NATL. PARK
NORTH CAROLINA
CAPE HATTERAS
OZARK MTNS.
TENNESSEE
CHARLOTTE
ARKANSAS
MEMPHIS
CHATTANOOGA
S. CAROLINA
HOT SPRINGS NATL. PARK
LITTLE ROCK
TUPELO
ATLANTA
COLUMBIA
MISSISSIPPI R.
BIRMINGHAM
AUGUSTA
CHARLESTON
TEXARKANA
MISS.
ALABAMA
MACON
SAVANNAH
SHREVEPORT
VICKSBURG
JACKSON
MONTGOMERY
GEORGIA
TEXAS
NATCHEZ
MOBILE
TALLAHASSEE
JACKSONVILLE
LOUISIANA
FLORIDA
ST. AUGUSTINE
BATON ROUGE
NEW ORLEANS
Atlantic Ocean
Gulf of Mexico
CAPE KENNEDY
TAMPA
ST. PETERSBURG
LAKE OKEECHOBEE
EVERGLADES NATL. PARK
MIAMI
KEY WEST
Florida Keys

The South

Although the South was the earliest part of the United States to be settled by Europeans, it is only within the last few decades that its rich history, its equable climate, its food, entertainment, and hospitality have made it an important tourist area. The nine states of the South run the gamut from mile-high forested mountain peaks to rolling farmlands to palm-shaded subtropical beaches. The system of dams that harness its mighty rivers for electric power also provide fresh-water boating, swimming, and fishing. The thousands of miles of Atlantic and Gulf coasts offer ocean sailing and fishing waters, with a wealth of sheltered harbors. State and private preserves furnish hunters with more abundant game today than in the days before the white man set foot here.

Many recreational areas have been set aside by both the federal and the various state governments, notably two large national parks, Great Smokies and The Everglades, and the Cape Hatteras National Seashore Recreational Area—one of the few reservations of its kind in America.

The Appalachians have mild summer weather, southern Florida has balmy winters, although travelers should bring both light and warm clothing if they plan to visit any part of the South during the mid-winter months. Only Key West, at the threshold of the tropics, is entirely free of frost. Advance warnings and precautions have reduced the toll of seasonal hurricanes, but they remain a menace from May to November. Born at sea, the hurricane is likely to roar inland in late August or September.

The first explorers and colonizers of this vast region were Spanish. Ponce de León's exploration of both Florida coasts was followed by Hernando de Soto's 4,000-mile trek into the interior, in which he penetrated the future states of Georgia, Tennessee, Alabama, and Mississippi before discovering and crossing the Mississippi River. In 1565 the first permanent settlement of the future United States by Europeans was accomplished by the Spaniards at St. Augustine. The ancient fortifications, the Plaza, and the original narrow streets preserve St. Augustine's heritage to this day.

Farther west a French settlement took root at New Orleans early in the eighteenth century. Here the famed Vieux Carré keeps alive historic memories. Early English settlements at Charleston, Savannah, Wilmington, and elsewhere also survive. Nearly a score of historic sites associated with the American Revolution and the Civil War are now national historical parks, open free to the public. Less formal reminders of a part of the American past are the many fine examples of the South's distinctive types of architecture: the plantation manor house, with tall pillars and portico in front, and driveway shaded by pines and magnolia; the numerous rambling, unpainted, one-story wooden frame houses raised only slightly from the ground and almost surrounded by a screen porch covered with honeysuckle; the humble chinked-log cabins of the field hands and sharecroppers. Old city homes are likely to be large and rambling, of brick or timber, nondescript as far as formal architecture is concerned, yet characteristic.

Dining is one of the major pleasures of visiting the South. Most of the traditional "Southern" cooking originated in Virginia and the Carolinas, though it is now found throughout the region. New Orleans specializes in Creole cookery–French with overtones of Spanish, Indian, and African. Key West and Tampa offer Latin-American specialties. But besides these three regional varieties, the sophisticated hotels of Miami and Miami Beach offer almost every kind of food prepared by expert chefs of many nationalities.

In the French Quarter of New Orleans the adventurous diner can find such native delicacies as cream of avocado soup, *pompano en papillote* (fish cooked and served in a paper bag), oysters Rockefeller, frogs' legs, *canapé marguery,* shrimp Arnaud, jambalaya, *grillades,* and pecan pralines.

In the more widespread "Southern cooking" category come such specialties as crab gumbo, terrapin soup, hush puppies, beaten biscuits, black-eyed peas, and chili. In the small country towns the traveler may sample other distinctively Southern foods–turnip greens, hog jowl, country ham, grits, corn pone, candied yams, chitterlings, hominy, and pecan pie.

Florida's native dishes include the conch stew and key lime pie of Key West, and savory turtle and crawfish dishes. In Tampa, try tortillas, tamales, chicken and yellow rice Valenciana, chicken Acosta, and Spanish bean soup.

North Carolina

Leading tobacco producer in the United States, North Carolina is known as the *Tar Heel State* because, during the Civil War, her troops threatened to put down tar to stop South Carolina confederates from retreating, leaving North Carolina to fight alone. North Carolina is also the home of Cape Hatteras, the "Graveyard of the Atlantic," so-called because many ships, caught in Atlantic storms, were wrecked off its coast.

THE LAND. **Mount Mitchell,** the highest peak in eastern North America at 6,684 feet above sea level, lies to the east of Asheville, outside the Great Smoky Mountains National Park. The highest peak in the Blue Ridge, however, is **Grandfather Mountain,** near Linville.

North Carolina is bordered by Virginia, the Atlantic Ocean, South Carolina, Georgia, and Tennessee. It is mountainous in the western and central portions (location of the Blue Ridge and the Piedmont), but relatively level along the eastern coast. Main rivers in the state are the **Roanoke,** the **Neuse,** and the **Tar.**

THE CLIMATE. Temperatures in North Carolina range from 67–88 degrees in July to 31–51 in January, the warmer temperatures being along the coast. Rainfall is moderate, averaging around 44 inches yearly. The state, since 1900, has received nearly one hurricane a year.

THE PEOPLE. The first known white man to explore North Carolina was Verrazano, who came in the service of France in 1524. De Soto and others followed, as did Sir Walter Raleigh of England, who set up the first English colony in 1587. (This settlement, known as the Lost Colony, was wiped out by 1590.)

Colonization developed slowly but steadily during the seventeenth and early eighteenth centuries, though harmony with the Indians was deeply damaged when the Tuscarora Indians massacred settlers between the Neuse and Pamlico rivers in 1711. North Carolina participated in the colonial wars with the French and Indians, and was the scene of several engagements of the Revolutionary War. She was a leader of the movement to include a Bill of Rights in the United States Constitution, delaying ratification until the first ten amendments were drafted.

North Carolina was one of the last states to secede and side with the Confederate States during the Civil War, rejoining the Union in 1868. Since that date, the state's development has been rapid, especially in the growth of tobacco and cotton, and in the establishment of strong industries. Today her population is more than 5 million, twelfth among all the states.

AGRICULTURE. The coastal plain and the Piedmont are North Carolina's chief farming areas. Here the state grows more flue-cured or bright tobacco than any other area, and it manufactures more than half of the nation's total of cigarettes. Visitors are welcome at most plants where cigarettes are made (in Winston-Salem, Greensboro, Durham, and Reidsville). Also entertaining are the tobacco auctions held at huge warehouses throughout the tobacco-growing regions.

Other leading crops are corn and cotton, followed by peanuts, hay, and truck crops.

INDUSTRY. North Carolina is the nation's leader in furniture production. Chief city is High Point, especially noted for its manufacture of the Gainsborough Portrait Chairs. There are nearly 90 furniture factories in the vicinity, as well as the Southern Furniture Exposition Building, where four markets, held annually, attract some 25,000 buyers. Famous North Carolina textiles are made chiefly in Charlotte and the nearby fabric-making mill towns of Kannapolis, Belmont, and Gastonia.

Pulp and paper production, as well as processing of foods and tobacco, adds to North Carolina's high industrial income.

CITIES. Largest city is Charlotte, located in the southern part of the state. Greensboro, Winston-Salem, and Raleigh, the capital, are also important. The majority of North Carolina residents live in small towns or rural areas, many of which are interesting to visit.

ASHEVILLE, the county seat of Buncombe County, is the metropolis of the highlands and the shopping center for area resorts. A bustling city with skyscrapers, hotels, and shops, it is a center for marketers of homespun woolens, silver, leather work, and native pottery.

BREVARD is a music center, its **Transylvania Music Camp and Festival** attracting talented teenagers and music lovers from many states.

Chimney Rock affords one of North Carolina's most spectacular views, while **Blowing Rock,** when the wind is high, will return hats and other light objects tossed off its overhanging cliff. Ripley pictured Blowing Rock as the only place in the world where "snow falls upside down."

CHARLOTTE. Both the town and its county, Mecklenburg, were named for Queen Charlotte of Mecklenburg-Schwerin, German wife of Britain's George III, but its citizens were among the first to rebel against ever-increasing taxes and the Crown's interference in local affairs. News of Lexington and Concord aroused great patriotic fervor in Charlotte, where, on May 20, 1775, the "Mecklenburg Declaration" was drawn up, courageously signed, and sent to England. May 20 is still observed as a state holiday in North Carolina.

Today Charlotte is famed as the capital of "Textile Land." And as a distribution center for automobiles, machinery, groceries, meat, household appliances, and other products, Charlotte ranks second only to Atlanta in the Southeast.

The **American Cotton Manufacturers Institute** now has its headquarters in Charlotte. Its **Coliseum** has one of the world's largest aluminum domes, beneath which 13,500 fans can gather for ice-hockey games. Nearby **Lake Catawba** offers boating, water skiing and superb bass fishing.

DURHAM. This noted tobacco manufacturing center has modern skyscrapers that contrast sharply with the classic Gothic spires of its university. Spreading tobacco factories and huge warehouses are symbols of the city's chief source of wealth.

The city has other industries, including hosiery and cotton-textile mills, and it is also an important medical center.

ELIZABETH CITY. Yachtsmen usually stop at Elizabeth City for fueling and provisioning. Here the Intracoastal Waterway emerges from the Dismal Swamp, and continues southward via the Pasquotank River and Albemarle Sound. Small-boat owners may cruise within marked and sheltered waters from Delaware Bay almost to Key West, Florida.

The Coast Guard base at Elizabeth City is worth a visit. It is equipped with both planes and helicopters, always ready for rescue work along the treacherous Outer Banks.

FAYETTEVILLE. Dating from 1739 when the area was settled by Highland Scots, the city was the first of many in America to be named for Lafayette. Famous area landmarks are **Market House,** surmounted by a tower whose clock has run accurately since 1838; and **Fort Bragg,** ten miles west of Fayetteville, one of the largest military reservations in the United States.

GREENSBORO, located in the north-central part of the Piedmont, has one of the largest denim mills in the world, as well as cigarette and rayon plants. Here, the short-story writer William Sydney Porter (O. Henry) was born. The **Greensboro Historical Museum,** including an O. Henry Memorial, is open daily except Saturdays and Mondays.

Guilford Courthouse National Mili-

tary Park, near Greensboro, is unusual in that it commemorates an American defeat during the Revolution. Here, on March 15, 1781, Lord Cornwallis trounced Colonial forces under General Nathanael Greene, but the British were so weakened as a result that they soon afterward took the road to Yorktown and final surrender.

The park, which contains about 150 acres, includes the major portion of the battlefield, a few miles northwest of Greensboro, near U. S. Highway 220.

INDIAN COUNTRY. Just south of the Great Smokies lies the largest Indian reservation east of Wisconsin. Although less than 15 percent of the **Qualla Reservation's Cherokees** are full-blooded, their lands are held in common for the tribe, under the supervision of the Office of Indian Affairs, in Washington. Almost 4,000 Indians live in the area.

Indian handicraft and souvenirs are exhibited and sold in the community of Cherokee; **Oconoluftee Indian Village** is a re-created 200-year-old Cherokee community where craftsmen demonstrate their skills.

KITTY HAWK. The northern end of the North Carolina banks rises in spectacular dunes, the highest along the Atlantic seaboard. These restless sand mountains constantly shift with the winds. One huge dune, **Kill Devil Hill,** however, has been securely anchored with wire-grass sod. On its summit a stately granite pylon recalls one of the great events of all time—man's conquest of the air in 1903.

The actual location of Kill Devil Hill at the time the Wright Brothers made the first "powered, controlled and sustained flight by man in a heavier-than-air craft" is now a low spot some distance away, but it is marked, too, by a smaller monument. The initial flight lasted only 12 seconds, but it changed the course of history.

From the summits of Kitty Hawk's huge dunes unfold sweeping vistas of the storm-tossed Atlantic on one side and the placid waters of Albemarle Sound on the other.

NEW BERN. The little Neuse River port of New Bern is one of the earliest of Colonial capitals. **Tryon Palace,** built by the royal governor, William Tryon, has been restored to its former elegance. Costumed hostesses act as guides for visitors to this splendid building, with its background of rebellion, hangings and high living.

RALEIGH. Like Washington, D.C., Raleigh is a made-to-order capital. Its inland site, near the geographical center of the state, was selected as early as 1788, during the Hillsboro convention, at the time North Carolina rejected the Federal Constitution because it then had no Bill of Rights.

The first **capitol** was replaced in 1833 by the present imposing structure, a fine example of Greek Revival architecture. Within the beautiful grounds are statues of famous North Carolinians, including the three Presidents of the United States born in the state. Nearby is the new **state legislative building,** first ever built by a state for the exclusive use of its legislative branch of government.

The **North Carolina Museum of Art,** in Raleigh, houses a collection of old masters valued at more than $7 million, including works of Rubens, Rembrandt, Goya, Sully, Peale and others. The Spanish still-life collection is outstanding. An unusual feature of the museum is its pictures of English people and scenes coinciding with Colonial North Carolina. Nearby are the **Hall of History,** the **Museum of Natural History** and the **state library.**

Largely due to the influence of the school of design at North Carolina State College, the state has pioneered in modern architecture. An outstanding example of advanced design is the **J. S. Darton Arena,** on the state fairgrounds outside the city, whose parabolic arch is continually being adapted to other forms of construction, including private dwellings.

North Carolina State College at Raleigh, **Duke University** at Durham, and the **University of North Carolina,** at Chapel Hill, call themselves a "research triangle," dedicated not only to the education of the state's leaders of tomorrow, but also to providing greatly needed research for industry, agriculture, and other vital activities of the state.

ROANOKE. The first Raleigh expedition arrived in 1584 at an island they called Roanoke, but today there is no trace of this mere landing and departure, which preceded the arrival of the first Jamestown settlers by 23 years.

Three Raleigh expeditions came to naught, and the last one, sent out in 1587, disappeared completely. This was the famous "Lost Colony" of 100 men, women and children, including the newborn Virginia Dare, the first English native of America. Several expeditions were sent by Raleigh's group to search for them, but the only clue they found were the letters "CRO" blazed on a tree.

Today, at the **Fort Raleigh National Historical Site,** each summer evening, from late June until Labor Day, **"The Lost Colony,"** dramatizes some of the highlights of the venture on the actual ground trod by the pioneers of Roanoke Island.

The site also includes the settlement areas of 1585 and 1587, and restoration of the "new fort in Virginia," as this part of North Carolina was originally known. Not far away, reached by a free ferry and hard surface road, is **Cape Hatteras,** and the tallest tower (over 190 feet) lighthouse in the United States.

WILMINGTON. Although it is several miles inland, up the Cape Fear River, Wilmington is one of North Carolina's two chief seaports. Its exciting past includes the fitting out of many fast Confederate blockade-runners during the Civil War.

Today Wilmington is an important port, accessible by a 34-foot channel. Cotton and turpentine, once the city's chief exports, have given way to manufactured goods, refinery products, paper, textiles, textile fibers, and lumber.

A few miles northwest of Wilmington, on a branch of the Cape Fear River, is a national military park commemorating one of the most significant battles in the American Revolution. The engagement of **Moore's Creek Bridge,** fought on February 27, 1776, was a major factor in preventing a full-scale British invasion of the South in the opening phases of the war. Further, it not only supplied a needed stimulus for the country as a whole in the movement toward independence, but the victory also prompted North Carolina's decision, on April 12, 1776, to instruct her delegates in the Continental Congress to vote for independence. This was the first colony to take such action.

Today you may reach the picturesque site of the battle via U. S. Highway 421 and State Highway 210. Markers along the trail relate the battle story as it unfolded.

WINSTON-SALEM. The hyphenated metropolis of Winston-Salem dates only from 1913, but the older parts of Salem date back to 1766, and industrial Winston to 1849. Salem, founded by Moravians from Pennsylvania, has many well-preserved Colonial structures, including an inn, shops and dwellings clustered about the venerable campus of **Salem College,** dating from 1802. Old Salem celebrates Christmas and Easter in the traditional Moravian manner. The **annual Easter sunrise services** of the **Moravian Church,** held in "God's Acre" (the Salem cemetery), attract thousands.

Winston-Salem, with its tobacco factories, electrical, textile, electronics and furniture industries, is one of the most diversified manufacturing communities in North Carolina.

SPORTS AND RECREATION. The **Cape Hatteras** and **Cape Lookout National Seashores** includes many miles of storm-swept Outer Banks. Game fishermen come here in quest of blue marlin, tuna, and sailfish. Beaches near Wilmington include Wrightsville, Carolina, Wilmington, Kure, and **Fort Fisher. Great Smoky Mountains National Park,** straddling the North Carolina-Tennessee line, is a popular recreation area.

The Piedmont is the best area in the state for **golf.** Within a radius of five miles, there are ten excellent 18-hole courses, most famous at **Pinehurst** and **Southern Pines.** The annual North-South Invitation is held at Pinehurst, and the International Ryder Cup matches were played on its Number Two course.

At both Southern Pines and at **Tryon,** farther west, spring hunt **races** and **horse shows** top off the winter training of steeplechasers and hunters.

SPECIAL EVENTS. Among the state's annual events are the **North Carolina Azalea Festival,** held in Wilmington, early April; **Garden Tour,** Charlotte, mid-March. **"May Holiday,"** held in Winston-Salem during the first week in May, includes an eighteenth-century flower fair and a home-garden tour. An outdoor drama of the frontier days of Daniel Boone, **"Horn in the West,"** is presented in Boone each night except Monday from June until Labor Day. Another drama, this one about Cherokee life and called **"Unto These Hills,"** is given by Mountainside Theatre between June and Labor Day in the large Indian reservation south of the Great Smokies. North Carolina's **State Fair** is held in Raleigh each October.

South Carolina

This state, named for King Charles I of England, is smallest of all the southern states, but is one of its industrial leaders. South Carolina's nickname is the *Palmetto State,* its flower, the carolina (yellow) jessamine.

THE LAND. The lay of the land—low and swampy near the coast, rising to hills and mountains in the west—has led to the nicknames, "Low Country" and "Up Country." South Carolina's area is 31,055 square miles, making it fortieth of all states, and its highest point is Sassafras Mountain, 3,560 feet above sea level. Along the state's Atlantic coastline are many bays and inlets, as well as small islands. Principal rivers are the **Pee Dee** and the **Santee.**

THE CLIMATE. Because of its proximity to the coast, the eastern half of the country is warm and humid, though drier toward the western section. Temperatures range between 70–92 degrees in summer, and drop to 35–58 in the winter. Rainfall averages 46 inches yearly, with most falling in the mountains. Very light amounts of snow fall, rarely more than a few inches.

THE PEOPLE. Spanish explorers were the only people interested in what is now South Carolina until the 1600's, when England claimed the entire North American mainland and gradually began colonizing. It was not until 1680 that English proprietors established a settlement near Charles Town (the spelling was changed to its present form in 1783). King George I bought back the land from the proprietors in 1729, and divided North Carolina from South Carolina. But these actions did little to help or protect the settlers, and in the 1760's, when unrest was developing in the other colonies, South Carolina responded and fought actively. Many Revolutionary War battles were fought on her soil.

South Carolina, the sixth state of the Union to ratify the Constitution, was a strong supporter of state's rights, and bitterly opposed federal tariffs. When a depression hit in the 1820's and the government set up trade restrictions, South Carolina adopted an ordinance of nullification and did not follow the tariff restrictions until after 1833.

She was the first state to secede from the Union when the controversy over slavery arose, and it was in Charleston that the first shots of the Civil War were fired. Over a fourth of South Carolina's troops were killed in action.

More economic hardships were felt during Reconstruction, but through expansion of her textile industry and use of hydroelectric power, she was able ultimately to build a strong industrial economy. As it developed, South Carolina's population grew, and today there are over 2.5 million residents. Yet even today the majority live in rural areas.

AGRICULTURE. Tobacco and cotton are South Carolina's chief crops, followed by soybeans, peaches, and corn. Only 19 percent of the value of goods produced in the state come from agriculture, and only a fourth of the land is used for farming (another fourth is covered with forests). More hogs are raised in South Carolina than any other animal.

INDUSTRY. Almost 80 percent of South Carolina's economy is industrial, with textiles leading all other products. Cotton fabrics are the most important, with over 2.5 million bales of cotton used yearly. Key textile towns are Greenville, Greenwood (which also makes textile machinery), and Lancaster (where seven plants, owned by Springs Cotton Mills, turn out over six million yards of cotton fabrics a week). Orlon is manufactured at Camden, and there is a large installation of the Atomic Energy Commission on the Savannah River.

CITIES. Chief cities in South Carolina (with more than 50,000 population) are Columbia, Greenville, and Charleston. Towns of interest include Spartanburg and Beaufort.

BEAUFORT. Around Beaufort, on the winding back roads, a number of **"tabby ruins"** can be found. These old buildings are made of an unusual construction material–crushed oyster shells. Beaufort is the home port of much of South Carolina's shrimp, and the scene of yearly **yacht regattas.**

At nearby **St. Helena Island** live Gullah Negroes, who still retain many of the customs of their African ancestors and speak a distinctive dialect of their own. **Old Fort Frederick,** the largest tabby fort in America, recalls that the French once attempted a settlement at Port Royal, near the present Parris Island Marine Base.

CHARLESTON. With its fine sheltered harbor, protected by fortified islands, Charleston early became the metropolis of the Carolinas, which at first included both North and South Carolina. It lost none of its wealth and influence when the Carolinas separated early in the eighteenth century, even though the capital of South Carolina was removed to inland Columbia in 1786.

Between the Revolution and the Civil War, Charleston's social life was unmatched for brilliance and gaiety anywhere in the South, and it became the social and financial center of the rich plantation system. First rice, then indigo, and finally cotton and tobacco sustained the city's prosperity.

With the firing of the first Confederate shells on Fort Sumter, however, an era abruptly came to an end. By 1863 the Federal navy controlled all important Atlantic coastal ports, except Charleston and Wilmington. In two months during 1863, 21 Confederate vessels slipped out of Charleston, and 15 came in, escaping the blockade. During most of the war Charleston was bottled in, and was finally captured by Union forces in 1865.

Charleston narrowly escaped the fate of Columbia, which was burned. General Sherman had orders from the War Department in Washington to annihilate this birthplace of secession, but fortunately he turned aside to intercept one of the last remaining armies in the South, under General Joseph E. Johnston, and Charleston was spared.

Even die-hard Yankees can rejoice today that Charleston's fine public buildings and old homes, with their piazzas and walled gardens; **Cabbage Row,** inspiration for "Porgy and Bess"; the old **Dock Street Theatre,** the **Heyward-Washington House, Rainbow Row** along East Battery, and scores of others were not put to the torch.

Rainbow Row is so-called because each house is painted a different color –blue, green, yellow, pink, or brown. In the early morning the shrill cries of the street vendors echo melodiously in the narrow streets nearby. The **Dock Street Theatre,** with its iron-grilled balcony, opened on February 12, 1736, the first building in America designed solely for theatrical purposes. Twice burned and rebuilt, it is still in operation today.

In downtown Charleston is the **Old Slave Market Museum.** So is the old gallows, on which 49 pirates died in one month in 1718. A reminder of when the Jolly Roger flew off the Carolina coast is the old **Pirate House,** near St. Philip's gate. **St. Philip's Episcopal Church,** erected more than a century ago, carried a mariner's light in its steeple to guide blockade-runners, and was often a target for Federal bombardment. Fortunately, the gunners were not very accurate, for the beautiful edifice still remains practically unscarred.

Now a restored national monument, **Fort Sumter** is reached by a delightful three-and-a-half-mile voyage in a boat operating on convenient schedules from the battery.

The **National Monument** today commemorates both the "first shot" of 1861 and the resolute Confederate defense of 1863–65, two years of almost continuous attack by the Union fleet.

The tour of the fort has been recently lengthened, and now includes the newly uncovered right-flank gunrooms, in addition to those of the left flank. Additional markers give interesting historical data, so that the visitor may make his own "self-guided" tour. However, guide service is available free on weekdays from 8 A.M. to 4:30 P.M. and on weekends during the hours of the boat-tour visits.

Visitors should allow several days for the beautiful old plantation gardens in the vicinity of **Charleston.** A dozen or more are open to the public from February to April, when they are at the height of their glory, but some of them continue to blossom almost the entire year.

Among the most famous of the **"low country" gardens** are **Brookgreen, Magnolia, Middleton, Cypress,** and **Belle Isle.** The better known inland gardens include **Edisto, Lamis, Kalmia, Swan Lake** and **Dunndell.**

Dating from 1741, Middleton is the oldest landscaped garden in the United States. Cypress's three-centuries-old cypress trees grow in a lake which once was a reservoir for a rice plantation. Belle Isle was the birthplace of Francis Marion, the Revolution's daring "Swamp Fox."

COLUMBIA. Bronze stars on the side of the imposing stone building which houses the state legislature mark shell-hits during Sherman's visit in 1865. The **state capitol** was the only building on Main Street that survived the burning of the city.

Today Columbia bears no other visible scars of the conflict. As a manufacturing city specializing in textiles, lumber, building stone and printing, it is one of the South's busiest industrial centers. Its **free farm market,** a sight for visitors, is the largest in the Southeast.

The **University of South Carolina** is the third state university organized in the United States. Here, too, is the **boyhood home of President Woodrow Wilson,** now a museum, and the **grave of Anne Pamela Cunningham,** the courageous woman who was responsible for the restoration of Mount Vernon.

The **Battle of King's Mountain** and the **Battle of the Cowpens** were both American victories in the early days of the colonies. These were startling triumphs of untrained American frontiersmen over elite British regulars and Tories. About 140 engagements of the Revolution were fought on South Carolina soil, most of these being indecisive skirmishes. Only one, at Camden, was a major American defeat.

DORCHESTER. Another promising historical site lies beneath a tangle of forest and vines about 18 miles up the Ashley River from Charleston. This is the almost forgotten **Puritan village of Dorchester,** founded by New Englanders who came here in 1696, seeking a milder climate and fresh prospects for conversion. The town died out and was deserted shortly after the Revolution. The 48-acre site has been fenced in, to protect it from souvenir hunters, and historians plan to proceed with archaeological exploration.

GREENVILLE, the third largest South

Carolina community, is also a ranking textile center. Its busy looms weave nearly everything from heavy duck to the finest silks, and visitors are welcome to see the fabrics being made.

Greenville's weavers can handle many combinations of the new synthetic fibers with cotton and wool. Well-known plants which produce margarine are open to the public.

SPARTANBURG. The boll weevil drove farmers in the neighborhood of Spartanburg from cotton to peaches. The area now produces half of the South Carolina peach crop, and threatens to surpass the output of Georgia. Because fresh peaches must be picked, packed and rushed to market within a few days, peach-harvest time is a hectic week. The city is also an important railroad car repair and textile center.

SPORTS AND RECREATION. **Myrtle Beach,** near Georgetown, is the state's largest and best seaside resort. Also in that area are several state parks. **Lake Murray,** formed by the Saluda Dam near Columbia, covers 84 miles, providing **boating, swimming,** and **fishing.**

For horse-lovers, **Camden** is especially popular. This year-round resort features **polo, flat racing, fox hunts, drag races,** and **steeplechases.**

SPECIAL EVENTS. **Drag Hunts** (artificial fox scents are used) in Camden and Aiken, January through March; **Plantation Tours,** Low Country, April; **Confederate Memorial Day,** statewide, May 10; **Carolina Cup Steeplechase,** Camden, spring; **Carolina Summer Jazz Festival,** July 4; **Junior Davis Cup Tennis Match,** Clinton, summer; and the **Southern 500 stock car race,** Darlington, Labor Day.

Georgia

Georgia, long famous for its cotton, peaches, and magnolia trees, has developed into one of the nation's leading industrial states. The largest state in area east of the Mississippi, with a population that has passed four million, Georgia has been nicknamed the *Empire State of the South.*

THE LAND. Located to the south of the Carolinas and Tennessee, Georgia is mountainous in the northern sections, but flattens out to rolling hills and plains toward the south. **Brasstown Bald Mountain** (4,784 feet) is the state's highest point. Its mountains are the southern tip of the Appalachians and the Blue Ridge. One of the most well-known rivers (but by no means one of the largest) is the Suwannee, made famous by Stephen Foster's song, "Old Folks at Home." **Little Grand Canyon,** near Lumpkin, is an unusual sight, for erosion has deeply scarred the Piedmont, exposing great cliffs and canyon-like gullies of rainbow-hued clays.

THE CLIMATE. Georgia has an average annual temperature of 61.4 degrees, and receives about 47 inches of precipitation yearly. Temperatures all year round are good for traveling (in summer they range from 70–87 degrees, and in winter from 37–52 degrees).

THE PEOPLE. Conflicting claims between Spain and England marked the early years of Georgia's development. Ultimately England retained control, and in 1754 Georgia—named for King George II—became a royal province. Its life as such was short, the Revolutionary War quickly forcing Georgia to abandon its neutral position and join the other colonies. She was the fourth to ratify the Constitution in 1788.

Between the Revolutionary and Civil Wars Georgia established its strong cotton industry, based on slave labor. One of the first states to secede, Georgia fought with the South, suffering severe damage during Sherman's march to the sea.

The war left Georgia's economy severely damaged. The Reconstruction period and subsequent years of political upheaval did not aid recovery.

But after the turn of the century, industry began to grow steadily. Cotton, whose intensive cultivation had damaged the soil, was supplemented by tobacco, livestock, and heavy industries. Despite the boll weevil attacks on cotton crops during the early 1920's, Georgia's economy has grown rapidly.

AGRICULTURE. Cotton now thrives in all parts of the state, due to the warm climate, plentiful rainfall, and careful use of fertilizer. Another important product is tobacco, followed by corn and other grain crops.

More peanuts are grown in Georgia than in any other state. Georgia peaches, world famous for their flavor and quality, are grown around Thomasville, south of Augusta, and in Peach County.

Georgia is the second largest producer of chickens in the nation and a major supplier of hogs.

INDUSTRY. Manufacturing, chiefly the production of cotton cloth and other textiles, accounts for 70 percent of Georgia's income. Georgia is a leader in the production of timber and wood products, such as turpentine, and produces nylon and rayon cord for automobile tires.

Other key industries are related to cotton and peanut products, such as cooking fat, soap, peanut butter, and peanut oil. Mining is also important, and Georgia is the leading producer of kaolin (a clay used in making china, paint, and paper), bauxite, barite, marble, zirconium, and granite. Georgia is also one of the top shrimp-fishing states.

CITIES. Atlanta is the state's largest, most important city, followed (in order of population) by Columbus, Macon, Savannah, Albany, and Augusta.

ANDERSONVILLE. North of Americus, the **Andersonville Prison Park and National Cemetery** poignantly recalls the infamous prison stockade where thousands of Union prisoners of war perished during the latter stages of the Civil War. Old escape tunnels can still be seen.

ATHENS is the home of the **University of Georgia,** which claims to be the first chartered state university. A city associated with many cotton products–tire cord, hosiery, overalls, and cottonseed oil–Athens has many historic mansions, including that of Henry W. Grady, the South's "silver-tongued orator" and statesman.

ATLANTA, capital of Georgia, has a population of around 500,000. Its history can be seen in the **Cyclorama,** a modern building housing a huge circular and very realistic painting of the battle action which took place around Atlanta during the Civil War. This building is in **Grant Park,** southeast of the center of the city. In the cyclorama building is the locomotive "Texas," which took part in one of the strangest and most exciting episodes of the war.

In 1837 a railroad surveyor named Stephen Harriman Long drove a stake into the ground near what is now known as Five Points, the heart of the financial district. This became the turn-around point of the state's first railroad, and the small town which grew there was called Terminus. Later the name was changed to Marthasville, and, in 1847, to Atlanta. But the city did not become the state capital until, tentatively, in 1868, and permanently, by popular vote, in 1877.

Today Atlanta is the "headquarters-city" of the entire southeastern region. Great national business and industrial firms maintain more than 3,300 branch, district and division offices here. In addition, "government" itself is an important business in Atlanta.

This is the second highest *large* city (Denver is first) in the United States. With an altitude of 1,050 feet, its climate is one of the most equable in the United States.

Georgia's **capitol** has a dome covered with Georgia gold, but its most interesting section is the **State Museum of Natural History,** on the fourth floor.

Georgia Tech, a leading engineering school, has brought football as well as scholastic fame to the city, which also has an important institutional complex of higher learning, **Atlanta University.**

Underground Atlanta is a fascinating

complex of shops, restaurants, and museums.

Atlanta gave inspiration to two famous authors. Here was the setting for Margaret Mitchell's historical novel "Gone With the Wind," and you will find many of the places she mentions, such as Peachtree Street, very much in existence. "Tara Plantation" was purely imaginary, although several old mansions in the vicinity of Atlanta meet the general description. On Gordon Street you will find **"Wren's Nest,"** home of Joel Chandler Harris, author of the popular "Uncle Remus" stories.

A short distance east of Atlanta rises **Stone Mountain,** North America's largest exposed granite formation, and one of the world's natural wonders. Just below its 1,686-foot summit, an imposing memorial to the Confederacy was carved in the living rock by Gutzon Borglum, sculptor also of the Black Hills Memorial. **Six Flags Over Georgia,** an amusement park to the west of Atlanta offers rides, live shows, and many exhibits and historical attractions, plus spectacular flowers and landscaping. To the south, **Indian Springs Park** has been a favorite spa since 1800.

AUGUSTA lies 125 miles from the mouth of the Savannah River, yet it is a seaport for barges and shallow-draft ships which conduct much commerce with Savannah and other coastal cities and towns. The second oldest city in Georgia, it was the capital from 1786–96. Like Savannah, Augusta was established by James E. Oglethorpe, founder of Georgia.

Today Augusta is one of the leading cotton markets of the world, and a busy industrial city, making textiles, bricks, feed, fertilizers, and iron. But its present fame derives from the superb **National Golf Course** of the **Augusta Country Club,** scene of the annual **Masters Invitation Tournament.**

BLAKELY, known for the quantity of peanuts grown annually, has a monument to the peanut in the town. A fine museum at **Kolomoki Mounds State Park** displays relics from Indian burial mounds.

GREENSBORO. A **state park** and **museum** in Greensboro has much valuable information about the political aspects of the Confederacy, and of its little known Vice-President, Alexander Stephens. Greensboro was Stephens' home. To the south is Milledgeville, capital of Georgia from 1804–67. Many fine old classic revival houses are still standing.

MACON's chief attraction is one of the largest collections of the remains of early Indian civilizations in the United States. Six successive occupations, by different Indian cultural groups, can be recognized here, extending possibly from 8000 B.C. to about A.D. 1717. **Ocmulgee National Monument,** which embraces nearly 700 acres of this historic site, is three miles south of Macon.

In the monument's museum is the whole story of the first aboriginal tribes, who migrated to this hospitable region.

Most unusual of the restored portions of Ocmulgee is a nearby **"earth lodge,"** a circular, earth-covered room where important tribal matters once were settled. This council room is entered through a low, narrow passage. Within, 47 clay benches are set back against the circular wall of a room 40 feet in diameter. A raised clay platform, shaped in the form of a crude eagle, stands opposite the entrance. The floor and walls are original, only the roof being added by Park Department experts to give a better idea of how Ocmulgee's "master farmers" met in solemn council over 1,000 years ago.

SAVANNAH. In the original part of the old city the tree-shaded streets and small parks still follow the plan laid out by Oglethorpe when the construction of Savannah was begun on a 40-foot bluff overlooking the Savannah River. For, although Savannah is an important seaport, its wharves and docks lie about 18 miles inland.

Some of the fine homes, such as the **Pirates' House,** which in Colonial times was a seamen's grogshop, and the beautiful **Pink House,** built about 1771 as a private residence, have become fashionable restaurants.

The **Telfair Academy of Arts and Sciences,** originally one of Savannah's great homes, is now a permanent art museum. The **Owens-Thomas House,** also a museum, is an outstanding example of a nineteenth-century Regency mansion, with a formal garden and authentic furnishings.

Another fine Regency home is the **birthplace of Juliette Gordon Low,** founder of the Girl Scouts in 1912. Completely restored, the Low mansion is now a National Girl Scout Memorial. **Christ Episcopal Church** dates from the founding (1733) of Georgia. Here John Wesley opened one of the first Protestant Sunday schools in North America. The present church building, with its classic tall columns, was erected in 1840.

General Sherman's famous march from Atlanta to the sea ended in Savannah, and the **"Green House"** used by the Union general as his headquarters is now the parish house of St. John's Episcopal Church. It is a magnificent example of an ante-bellum home.

Fort Pulaski, which fell to Union soldiers in 1861, is located near Savannah. Open daily, it is in excellent repair, and includes two drawbridges with perfect arches, barracks, and cannon.

Savannah has an unusually interesting **custom house,** with, among other exhibits, a model of the packet ship *Savannah,* first steam-propelled vessel to cross the Atlantic. It left Savannah in 1819. **Forsyth Park and Parade** has many of the flowering trees, bushes and plants, native and foreign, which flourish in the Savannah climate—roses, coleus, palmettos, oleanders, jasmines, cacti, magnolias, and live oaks draped with Spanish moss.

Moving southward from Savannah, the visitor comes to **Brunswick,** whose name is linked with a well-known stew. From here, a side road strikes out over the tidal marshes to the **Golden Isles,** Jekyll, St. Simons, Tybee, and Sea Island, offering swimming, fishing, and golf. **Fort Frederica,** a national monument, once was the base from which the British fought the Spaniards in Florida.

Neither completely succeeded, but Fort Frederica's final role, following the Treaty of Aix-la-Chapelle (1748), as neutral ground, meant that the Spaniards henceforth would look southward, and the English settlements north of it would no longer be harassed. In 1763, when Florida was ceded to England, the reason for Frederica's existence as a fortification was gone, and it fell into ruin.

Westward from Brunswick on U. S. Highway 84 you can tap the edge of Okefenokee Swamp, one of the largest swamplands in the United States, located at Waycross. **Okefenokee Swamp Park** offers boat tours into a land of fantastic beauty.

TATE. The official end of the Appalachian Trail, a hiker's route that follows the mountains from Maine to Georgia, is the summit of **Mount Oglethorpe** near Tate, which has the world's largest deposit of marble. This is rugged country and the winding roads disclose breath-taking vistas of mountains, canyons and beautiful lakes bordered by tall pines, oaks, and maples. Warm Springs is the site of the 5,000-acre **Franklin D. Roosevelt State Park.** The late President came often to Warm Springs to rest and take treatments in the healing waters which have helped so many stricken by polio. The **"Little White House,"** where the President worked, has been kept exactly as it was when Roosevelt died there April 12, 1945.

SPORTS AND RECREATION. There are many well-known resorts in Georgia, **Sea Island** and **St. Simons** being among the most famous. **Thomasville,** one of the oldest resorts in the South, specializes in **quail hunting, fishing, golf,** and many other outdoor sports. **Golf, fishing, bird study, swimming, square dancing,** and **flower trails** of azalea, holly, magnolia, and rhododendron are features of the 2,500-acre **Ida Cason Callaway Gardens** at Pine Mountain.

Parks of special interest are **Amicalola Falls State Park,** which has one of the highest waterfalls in the East; **Kenesaw Mountain National Battlefield Park,** scene of one of the Confederate army's last stands to save Atlanta; **Chickamauga National Military Park,** 8,200 acres in northwest Georgia with a museum containing war mementos; and **Veteran's Memorial State Park** near Cordele.

SPECIAL EVENTS. Annual activities of special interest to visitors include **Georgia Day,** February 12; **Masters Golf Tournament,** held on Augusta's National Golf Course in mid-April; **Thomasville Rose Show,** last Friday in April; **Watermelon Festival** in Cordele, July; **Georgia Mountain Fair,** in Hiawassee, August; **Pulaski Day,** in Savannah, October 11, and the **Holiday Festival** near Pine Mountain, December 22–31.

Florida

Florida, *The Sunshine State,* contains the oldest remnants of the white man's civilization in the continental United States, and some parts of it, especially the Everglades, are as untamed as they were centuries ago. But Florida is best known today for its excellent climate, its orange groves, palm trees, and relaxed atmosphere which have made it one of the leading tourist states in the country.

THE LAND. Florida has, next to Alaska, the longest coastline of any state in the Union, and no spot in its 58,560 square miles is more than 100 miles from the sea. From north to south, Florida measures some 465 miles, and along its northern border is almost as wide. Its Gulf and Atlantic coastline extends 1,350 miles. The highest point, in Walton County, is a hillock of 345 feet. There are few navigable rivers, but there are about 30,000 lakes and ponds.

THE CLIMATE. Florida's climate ranges from humid subtropical at the southern tip to temperate in the northern areas. Even in midsummer, the heat is alleviated by cooling Atlantic and Gulf breezes. Temperatures in summer average about the same throughout the state (83 degrees), but in winter, Miami averages 67 degrees while temperatures drop to 56 in northern Florida. Rainfall averages 53 inches, with some coming from the hurricanes whose paths cut across Florida.

THE PEOPLE. In 1513 Ponce de León, in search of the "Fountain of Youth," landed on Florida's eastern coast, but it wasn't until 1559–65 that the first attempts at European colonization were made. One settlement at Pensacola failed, as did the Huguenot colony, but by 1565 a firm foothold was established in St. Augustine.

Ceded to Great Britain by Spain in 1763 (in exchange for Cuba), Florida was returned to its previous owners in 1783.

Western Florida was invaded by Andrew Jackson, on an expedition against the Seminole Indians in 1818. Finally, in 1819 Florida was acquired from Spain by treaty. In 1845 Florida acquired statehood, but seceded to join the Confederacy in 1861. Only one major battle was fought on Florida soil.

After being readmitted to the Union in 1868, Florida grew rapidly. Settlers poured in, citrus groves were developed, swamplands were drained, and resorts were opened. Two severe hurricanes and the Depression interrupted the boom. But after World War II, when Florida's location made it important to the armed forces, the state expanded, brought in new industry, and developed into one of the country's outstanding resort areas. Its population has grown to over six million, with many more during the winter months.

AGRICULTURE. Citrus fruits and nuts are the leading farm income-producers, with Florida growing nearly one-third of the world's oranges (much is marketed as frozen juice), practically all the tangerines, limes, and non-

Hawaiian coconuts, and over two-thirds of the nation's grapefruit.

Truck farming is important, second only to California in value of produce. Tomatoes, celery, and most early vegetables are best income-producers. Florida is also a leading commercial fishing state.

INDUSTRY. In spite of the high value of agricultural crops and the importance of tourism, manufacturing accounts for the majority of income in Florida.

Food processing, especially in the area of citrus and vegetables, is one of the state's top industries, followed by chemicals, paper and paper products, and fabrication of metals. Phosphate is mined in central Florida.

CITIES. Geographically, historically, and in terms of attractions for visitors, Florida has nine distinct sections, each with its individual features and cities—Northwest, North, Upper East Coast, Indian River Region, Central, West Coast, the Everglades, Lower East Coast, and the Keys.

NORTHWEST FLORIDA

PANAMA CITY. Eastward toward Panama City stretches one of Florida's finest beaches, a dazzling white carpet against a background of pale green shallows and the deep blue of the Gulf of Mexico. At the **Gulfarium,** near Fort Walton Beach, trained porpoises, giant sea turtles and other underwater inhabitants put on an entertaining water show. **Eglin Field,** 12 miles north, is one of the largest U.S. military reservations. General Doolittle's Tokyo raiders of World War II trained on the field, where today military power demonstrations are put on in which the Air Force shows off its newest weapons systems and aircraft.

PENSACOLA retains many aspects of early Spanish times in its street names and quaint houses. But it is actually a bustling industrial city, with one of the nation's finest natural harbors and a waterfront that is most interesting when the red-snapper and shrimp boats unload their catches. At the nearby **U. S. Naval Air Station** the Navy trains its fledgling pilots. Within its yard are the ruins of old **Fort San Carlos,** a former Spanish stronghold, and **Fort Barrancas. Fort Pickens State Park** contains old battlements, cannon and a cell block dating from 1829, where Geronimo, famed Apache, was long imprisoned.

NORTH FLORIDA. North Florida is very "southern" in character and the customs and traditions are less changed than in sections farther south.

This section of the state, popular for hunting and fresh-water fishing, extends from the Apalachicola River on the west nearly to the St. Johns River, and southward to the mouth of the Suwannee. Farming is the chief activity, with good harvests of cotton, sweet potatoes, peanuts and tobacco. Tung trees, whose nuts produce an oil used in varnish, brighten the landscape in spring with their gay blossoms.

GAINESVILLE. Of particular interest to visitors for its Indian artifacts, mounted birds of Florida, and relics of early state history is the **Florida State Museum** in downtown Gainesville, and the floral displays and buildings of the 1500-acre **University of Florida** campus.

TALLAHASSEE, Florida's capital city, still maintains its picturesque antebellum air, with massive live oaks and magnolias draped with Spanish moss, shading its quiet streets. **Big Bend Pioneer Village and Junior Museum,** containing a replica of a North Florida farm of the 1880's, is popular with visitors, as is **Killearn Gardens State Park.**

The region's most famous stream is the Suwannee River, whose name was immortalized in song by Stephen Foster.

UPPER EAST COAST. The Upper East Coast area extends from the St. Mary's River or Georgia boundary south to Edgewater and Sanford, including the valley of the St. Johns River, once the water highway into the interior and one of the few rivers that flows northward for most of its course.

DAYTONA AND ORMOND BEACHES. Daytona Beach is famous for its 23-mile hard-packed sand beach, upon which visitors can drive their cars. In the same area, Ormond Beach first gained fame as the winter home of John D. Rockefeller.

JACKSONVILLE. With over 500 factories manufacturing products from canned goods and paper to chemicals and ships, Jacksonville is the industrial capital of Florida. Located on the banks of the St. Johns River, it is a major Atlantic port, even though it is 20 miles from the sea.

MARINELAND. Although Marineland oceanarium, where fish and other marine creatures may be seen, is the area's main attraction, the **Lightner Museum of Hobbies,** the **St. Augustine Alligator Farm,** and Ponce de León's reputed **"Fountain of Youth"** should be visited.

ST. AUGUSTINE. Here are preserved such venerable structures as the **Castillo de San Marcos,** oldest masonry fort in the United States, complete with moat, battlements, and dungeons; the **"Oldest House,"** and narrow streets lined with typically Spanish mansions.

INDIAN RIVER REGION. "Indian River" looks like a river but it is actually a lagoon, or series of narrow inlets, behind the barrier islands along a large section of Florida's east coast. At Daytona Beach it is called the Halifax River and at Palm Beach, Lake Worth. But most of its length, from New Smyrna Beach on the north to Stuart on the south, carries the name "Indian River."

CAPE KENNEDY. Titusville, Cocoa, Rockledge and Melbourne have become "boom towns" since the expansion of the **Air Force Missile Test Center** and **Patrick Air Force Base** on nearby Cape Kennedy, from which America's astronauts have taken off on their history-making flights. Visitors are often allowed to visit the test center, and usually there are local notices of scheduled launchings. The larger rockets and missiles can be observed roaring off into space from Cocoa Beach or Titusville Beach.

The first national wildlife refuge in the United States is on **Pelican Island,** near Sebastian. South of Vero Beach on U. S. Highway 1, the **McKee Jungle Gardens** lives up to its name with an exotic collection of orchids, royal and coconut palms, and other tropical vegetation.

CENTRAL FLORIDA. Central Florida extends roughly from Ocala on the north to Lake Placid and Arcadia on the south, and is the broad backbone of the peninsula. In prehistoric times, when most of Florida was still covered by the sea, Central Florida was an island. Old beachheads can still be observed where the ridge flattens out to the east and south into lush pasturage, now grazed by white-faced Herefords, oddly-humped Brahmans, and those aristocrats of the cattle world, the King Ranch's Santa Gertrudis. In recent years Florida has become one of the leading beef-cattle states in the nation, and its dairy herds have also increased.

For the visitor interested in Southern ranching, many show farms are open in the vicinity of **Ocala, Lake Wales,** and **Kissimmee** (the "Kow Kapital," where a rodeo is held annually).

LAKE WALES. Much of Florida's orange crop is now shipped north as frozen concentrate, and visitors can see how this is done at several plants in or near Lake Wales. Here soars the celebrated **Singing Tower** at **Mountain Lakes Sanctuary,** the second highest point in Florida. Its carillon concerts amid a setting of serene beauty have drawn millions of music lovers since the sanctuary was opened in 1923.

ORLANDO, largest city of central Florida, offers both greyhound and harness racing in winter. **Winter Park,** a quiet residential town revolving around the activities of **Rollins College,** attracts many visitors interested in art, music and literature. **Walt Disney World** is an enormous recreation complex outside the city.

SEBRING. Visitors who enjoy seeing alligators, deer, raccoons and other wildlife in a natural setting will want to stop at **Highlands Hammock State Park** near Sebring. Raised wooden walkways provide safe access to cypress swamps where they live.

SILVER SPRINGS AND CYPRESS GARDENS. The area also possesses two of Florida's most famous and popular tourist attractions: Silver Springs, with its glass-bottomed boats, and Cypress Gardens, a lush setting for thrilling water-ski drills and ballets.

WEST COAST. The West Coast may be said to begin at Cedar Key and extend southward to Naples. All up and down this bright shore of the Gulf of Mexico the fishing is superb—snook, sea trout and redfish in protected inside waters; mackerel and bonito in the Gulf; red snapper and grouper over the banks; and tarpon.

CEDAR KEY was the busiest town on the West Coast of Florida when it was the end-of-the-line for the only railroad from the north, and passengers took ships there to reach other West Coast cities and Key West. Completion of a direct line to Tampa, in 1884, ended Cedar Key's prosperity, but Florida artists and photographers today love the atmosphere and setting of this old ghost town.

Near Cedar Key, Dunnellon's **"Rainbow Springs,"** Homosassa's **"Giant Fish Bowl,"** and **Weeki Wachee Springs underwater ballet** all are worth visiting.

FORT MYERS derives much of its income from the gladiolus industry, but to visitors its greatest attraction is the former **winter home** and workshop of **Thomas A. Edison,** famed inventor. Fishermen know it as a prime area for tarpon and snook.

Offshore, and reached by a bridge, the famous shell-collecting islands of **Sanibel** and **Captiva** bask in the sun.

ST. PETERSBURG, known for the long green benches that line the downtown sidewalks, is a town for young and old alike. Its beaches on the Gulf of Mexico have developed considerably in recent years. In addition, a new **Aquatarium,** containing the world's largest salt water marine-life tank; the multimillion-dollar **Bayfront Center,** including a marina, auditorium, and arena; and **Criswell's Money Museum,** which displays bank safety devices, should be visited.

With the completion of the **"Sunshine Skyway,"** a toll highway and lofty bridge over the mouth of Tampa Bay, St. Petersburg has a direct connection with lower West Coast cities.

SARASOTA. The state-owned **Ringling Museum of Art,** with its superb collection of Rubens, and the **John Ringling residence,** now a museum, are of particular interest. **"Horn's Cars of Yesterday"** and **"Music Box Arcade"** are nostalgic attractions.

TAMPA, metropolis of the West Coast, is perhaps Florida's most cosmopolitan city. Cigars, Tampa's best known product, are made in **Ybor** (pronounced "ee-bore") **City,** the Latin section, also famous for its excellent Spanish restaurants.

Tampa is also a very sports-conscious city, with five golf courses, training camps for two major-league teams and a spring horse-racing meet at nearby "Sunshine Park."

The **University of Tampa,** in Plant Park, occupies the old Tampa Bay Hotel, an incredible structure of rococo Moorish architecture. Also in Tampa is the state-supported **University of South Florida.**

TARPON SPRINGS, home of the Greek sponge fleet, is one of the most fascinating cities on the West Coast. Colorful boats of the sponge fishermen are favorite subjects, too, of artists and photographers.

THE EVERGLADES. The Everglades region is the largest single area of its kind in Florida, and contains the **Everglades National Park,** third largest of Federal reservations. Highway entrance to the Park is at **Florida City.**

It is not a swamp, although there are

some swampy areas. The Indians called it "River of Grass," an appropriate term, because, over most of the Everglades, water moves slowly southward to the Gulf, like a great shallow river. Sometimes it is concealed by tall grasses, and hammocks of cypress, mangrove, and other vegetation.

The Everglades region, which begins a little north of Lake Okeechobee and Palmdale, and extends to the Gulf, might be compared to the shallow bowl of a gigantic spoon. The rim consists of ridges of limestone, wider on the east coast than on the west. Along these ridges the coastal resorts have been built. Between them, the land drains from the area of Lake Okeechobee, toward the point of the spoon, into a maze of waterways and marshes which shred the southwestern coast.

Everglades is the western gateway to the **Ten Thousand Islands,** and for **boat tours** of the **Audubon Society** to spectacular bird rookeries deep in the mangrove swamps.

Tamiami Trail, cutting across the heart of the Everglades region, was 12 years in the making. Tons of muck and limestone rock had to be moved to obtain a firm roadbed, well above flood waters. A parallel canal now provides some of the best fresh-water fishing in Florida.

Along the Tamiami Trail one may see unusual birds or a lonely Indian poling his dugout canoe—perhaps even an alligator. At intervals, there are **Seminole Indian villages.** The area's greatest thrill is an **air-boat ride** in a small scow, pushed through the grasslands at bone-chilling speed by means of an airplane propeller.

LOWER EAST COAST. The Gulf Stream helps to maintain an equable year-around climate on both land and sea, and makes this the most nearly tropical region on the mainland of the United States.

Here flourish the graceful coconut, the stately royal palm, and such exotic fruits as the avocado, mango, sapote, guava, and the oriental litchi. While frost is not unknown, and coats are sometimes needed on winter nights, the days are almost always warm.

FORT LAUDERDALE claims the largest municipal marina or yacht basin in the world, with docking and other facilities for a multitude of small boats. Its fine beach is open free to the public. Sight-seeing boats offer **"jungle cruises"** far back in the Everglades.

LAKE WORTH boasts the state's largest shuffleboard club, and its own city beach. Southward along the coast, Route A1A hugs the beach, a favorite spot for surf fishing.

Nearby **Boca Raton** has a lavish hotel-club, with its own golf course.

MIAMI AND MIAMI BEACH. Miami was the original settlement of south Florida and today is the largest and busiest city in the state. The city was incorporated in 1896 and had only 500 voters. Miami Beach was then a deserted sandspit, which could be reached only by boats.

While the city of Miami is still an important resort, its imposing skyline of tall buildings indicates that it is also the commercial, industrial and transportation center of south Florida, and an important U.S. port of entry from the Caribbean and South America, by air and by sea.

Miami Beach, however, symbolizes most completely the playground and recreation center which has become world-famous. Glittering, incredible, unique, it is dedicated almost entirely to the feeding, housing, sunning, and entertaining of visitors.

Miami Beach has no cemeteries, no streetcars, no industries, no railroads, not even an airport. Within its 87 narrow blocks from north to south there are more than 45,000 hotel and motel rooms and over 100,000 apartment houses.

The Miami area has much to offer the sports lover: **horse racing** at tropical **Hialeah,** and **Gulfstream parks** (November to April); **greyhound racing** at West Flagler, Biscayne and Miami Beach kennel clubs (November to June); and the pro-football powerhouse, the **Miami**

Miami and Miami Beach

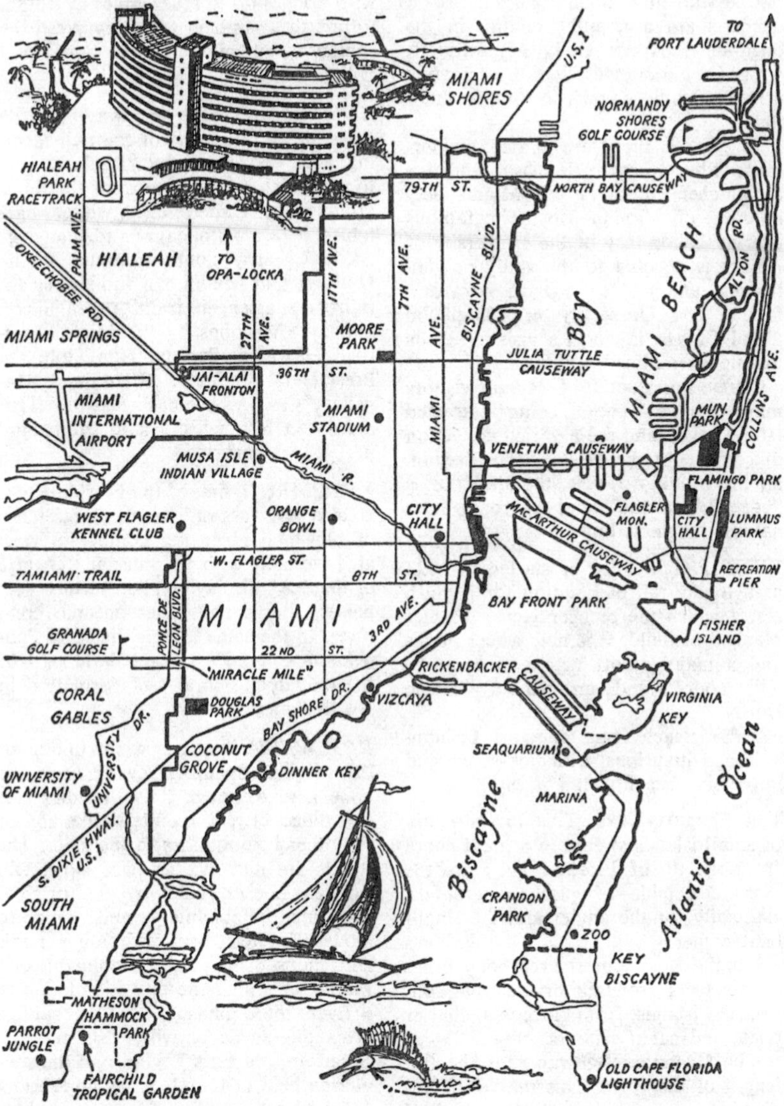

TO FORT LAUDERDALE
U.S. 1
MIAMI SHORES
NORMANDY SHORES GOLF COURSE
HIALEAH PARK RACETRACK
79TH ST.
NORTH BAY CAUSEWAY
PALM AVE.
OKEECHOBEE RD.
HIALEAH
TO OPA-LOCKA
17TH AVE.
7TH AVE.
BISCAYNE BLVD.
ALTON RD.
MIAMI BEACH
Bay
MIAMI SPRINGS
27TH AVE.
MOORE PARK
MIAMI AVE.
JULIA TUTTLE CAUSEWAY
JAI-ALAI FRONTON
36TH ST.
COLLINS AVE.
MIAMI INTERNATIONAL AIRPORT
MIAMI STADIUM
MUN. PARK
VENETIAN CAUSEWAY
MUSA ISLE INDIAN VILLAGE
MIAMI R.
FLAMINGO PARK
WEST FLAGLER KENNEL CLUB
ORANGE BOWL
CITY HALL
FLAGLER MON.
MAC ARTHUR CAUSEWAY
CITY HALL
LUMMUS PARK
W. FLAGLER ST.
TAMIAMI TRAIL
8TH ST.
RECREATION PIER
PONCE DE LEON BLVD.
MIAMI
BAY FRONT PARK
3RD AVE.
FISHER ISLAND
GRANADA GOLF COURSE
22ND ST.
"MIRACLE MILE"
RICKENBACKER CAUSEWAY
CORAL GABLES
DOUGLAS PARK
BAY SHORE DR.
VIZCAYA
VIRGINIA KEY
UNIVERSITY DR.
COCONUT GROVE
SEAQUARIUM
Ocean
UNIVERSITY OF MIAMI
DINNER KEY
MARINA
Biscayne
Atlantic
S. DIXIE HWAY. U.S. 1
CRANDON PARK
SOUTH MIAMI
ZOO
KEY BISCAYNE
MATHESON HAMMOCK PARK
PARROT JUNGLE
FAIRCHILD TROPICAL GARDEN
OLD CAPE FLORIDA LIGHTHOUSE

Dolphins. There are many other attractions.

The **Vizcaya Dade County Art Museum,** in the old James Deering Estate, is a replica of a fifteenth-century Italian palace with huge formal gardens. Band concerts are a popular feature in the open-air **Bayfront Park** amphitheater, while **Orchid Jungle** offers a fascinating array of tropic blooms in a native habitat.

In Miami, there are skilled taxidermists who mount prize fish, and for fishwatchers there is the **Miami Seaquarium** on Virginia Key. The famous **Marine Laboratory** of the University of Miami is devoted to the study of subtropical and tropical marine flora and fauna. The **University of Miami,** in Coral Gables, is worth a visit to see its unique streamlined buildings.

A few miles south of Miami, visitors may observe venom being extracted from snakes, and see a varied collection of serpents at the **Miami Serpentarium.** At the **Monkey Jungle,** the spectator is "caged" and the monkeys roam in a natural jungle setting.

WEST PALM BEACH started in 1893 as a lonely railroad station for a plush resort which the pioneer Henry Flagler planned to build. It is now a metropolis and a major resort with a fine public golf course and an annual Sailfish Derby.

Palm Beach itself remains fashionable and luxurious, with fine shops and impressive beachfront homes.

THE FLORIDA KEYS. This lovely chain of small islands sweeps in a great curve from the tip of Florida. They are the most delectable of pleasure grounds, especially for the angler and the small-boat owner.

On the Keys almost everybody fishes —from piers, from the bridges that connect the islands, from rowboats, charter boats and cabin cruisers.

The **Overseas Highway** runs the full length of the Keys. This marvel of engineering was built upon the roadbed and piers originally laid down as an extension of the Florida East Coast Railroad. The railroad had been built at fantastic cost, but was abandoned following the hurricane of 1935.

As a public works project, the Overseas Highway was constructed to provide a toll-free road, 100 miles long and with bridges up to seven miles in length, to link the mainland with Key West, the southernmost city in the continental United States.

HOMESTEAD, the gateway to the Keys, lies in the heart of the rich farming area known as the "Redland District," which produces most of the limes grown in the United States, winter vegetables, avocados, papayas and mangoes. At the nearby South Campus of the **University of Miami** is a full-size steam railroad passenger train, operated on Sunday afternoons by the Miami Railroad Historical Society. Here, too, the Presidential Pullman, "Ferdinand Magellan," from whose back platform Truman won his "whistle stop campaign" in 1948, is enshrined.

KEY LARGO, first of the Florida Keys, is also the largest. Beautiful stretches of blue and green sea come into view at Tavernier, with its unusual **"Theatre of the Sea,"** displaying giant turtles, porpoises, sharks and other oceanic creatures. In the same area is the **John Pennekamp Coral Reef State Park,** part of the only living coral reef formation in North America.

KEY WEST's name is a corruption of the original Spanish *Cayo Huesto,* or bone key. Although it is Florida's second oldest city, it is quite unlike any of the other communities in the state. The streets are narrow, the pace slow. Old wooden houses, built by the original seafaring inhabitants, stand next to modern motels with swimming pools and shops displaying the colorful souvenirs for which the city is noted.

Even more unusual are the **sponge pier,** the **turtle crawls, fish market, aquarium, old Fort Taylor,** and the **submarine base** at the U. S. Naval Station, which also has been a winter retreat for several Presidents.

Those who like Spanish and Latin-American dishes and seafoods will enjoy fish cooked "Key West style." The conch (pronounced "konk") chowder, turtle steak, green turtle soup, crawfish, jumbo shrimp, stone crabs, and lime pie should be sampled.

MARATHON is the second largest city on the Keys, with a marina that caters to cruising yachtsmen, charter boats, and even treasure-seekers, probing the sunken wrecks of old Spanish galleons on the offshore reefs. Small-boat owners can moor their craft at the door of cottage "botels" for weekends or longer. When the shrimp boats are in it is interesting to see this "pink gold" being unloaded and processed for shipment to Northern markets.

Between Marathon and Key West, tiny deer, not much bigger than a large dog, which are native to the Keys and now protected by law, are often seen.

SPORTS AND RECREATION. Florida is a sports lover's paradise, especially for those who prefer water sports such as **swimming, surfing, water-skiing, deep-sea fishing,** and **boating.** Ideal weather, especially in southern Florida, makes all outdoor sports possible for most of the year. Also popular are **golf, horse racing, greyhound racing, tennis, jai alai,** and spring training of several major league baseball teams.

All forms of entertainment—from underwater ballets and water shows to night clubs and concerts—can be found throughout the state, with the greatest concentration in the Miami area.

SPECIAL EVENTS. One of Florida's most well-known events is the **Orange Bowl** football game, played in Miami on New Year's Day. Other occasions include the **Florida State Fair and Gasparilla Festival,** Tampa, in February; **"Black Hills Passion Play,"** presented near Lake Wales each winter; **"Pageant of Light,"** in Fort Myers in February (honors the birthday of Thomas A. Edison); **Florida International Grand Prix Sports Car Twelve-hour Races,** held near Sebring in March; **Tarpon Tournament,** Tampa, June–July; and the **All Florida Championship Rodeo,** Arcadia, July.

Alabama

In spite of Alabama's nickname, *The Heart of Dixie* (for its central location among the southern states), its southern tip, Mobile Bay, has made Alabama a major shipping state. Alabama is famous for its lush gardens, cotton, and rapidly growing steel industry.

THE LAND. Twenty-ninth in size of all the states, Alabama's area is 51,609 square miles, it has a 53-mile coastline, and its highest point is **Cheaha Mountain,** at 2,407 feet. In spite of this mountain, most of the state is less than 500 feet above sea level. Alabama's coastal plain in the eastern section of the state is low and swampy, sloping down to lush Mobile Bay. Near the Bay is the wiregrass area, known for farming. Another top farming area is the Black Belt. Chief rivers are the Mobile, Alabama, Tombigbee, Coosa, and the Chattahoochee.

THE CLIMATE. Alabama's location gives it a mild climate throughout the year. In January temperatures rarely fall below 43 degrees, and in July they average 82 degrees. Snowfall is rare, with rain varying from 53 inches in the north to 68 inches along the coast.

THE PEOPLE. Following early explorations by Piñeda (1519) and De Soto (1540) the land which is now Alabama was disputed among France, Spain, and Great Britain, with all except the Mobile area becoming part of the United States after the Revolutionary War. The Mobile area was seized from Spain by the United States during the War of 1812. Shortly thereafter, following several battles with the Creek Indians in 1814, their land was surrendered to the United States, giving the Alabama territory its present dimensions with the exception of a northern Indian reservation.

Alabama achieved statehood in 1819, the capital being established at Huntsville, then moved to Cahaba and Tuscaloosa.

During the 1850's, the poorly managed state bank, a drought, and epidemics of yellow fever put Alabama in economic difficulty. This was compounded by the Civil War (the first capital of the Confederacy was located in Montgomery) and Reconstruction.

With the development of the iron and steel industry, especially around Birmingham, Alabama slowly recovered and expanded. Textiles and lumber were also important, and with World War I, the shipbuilding industry was established in Mobile.

There are now close to 3.5 million residents in Alabama, the majority living in urban areas.

AGRICULTURE. Livestock, poultry, and dairy products are Alabama's highest income-producers (60 percent of the total farm income). Cotton, which used to be the state's chief crop, has been replaced by corn in many areas, and hay, wheat, oats, and soybeans are also grown. Peanuts and pecans are important to the economy, as are strawberries, blackberries, and pears.

Fishing for seafood, red snapper, oysters, and mullets nets more than four million pounds of fish from the Gulf of Mexico annually.

INDUSTRY. The metal industry is Alabama's most important, accounting for $572 million yearly. Iron and steel mills are located in Birmingham, Anniston, Bessemer, and Gadsden.

Clothing and textiles, a $353-million industry, centers in the Piedmont. Also important are forest products (paper, pulp, furniture), meat and food packing, and rubber products.

Many of Alabama's manufacturing concerns were able to grow rapidly because of the extensive Tennessee Valley Authority hydroelectric power.

CITIES. Huntsville, Mobile, Montgomery, Birmingham, Gadsden, and Tuscaloosa are Alabama's chief cities, with Birmingham being the largest.

BIRMINGHAM. High up on the top of Red Mountain stands a majestic iron statue of Vulcan, god of the forge, symbol of this iron-and-steel community and the largest city in Alabama. Birmingham is a "southern Pittsburgh," and the heart of the largest industrial area in the South.

This industrial center is the scene of the annual **Alabama State Fair** (predominantly agricultural) held during late September or early October.

Like Pittsburgh, Birmingham is also a cultural center, with its own **Civic Symphony Orchestra,** established in 1932, and a **Little Theatre,** presenting performances each winter season.

BRIDGEPORT. Near here is **Russell Cave National Monument** showing a detailed record of human occupancy from about 7000 B.C. to A.D. 1650.

CULLMAN. The unique **Ave Maria Grotto** is located on the campus of **St. Bernard College,** a boarding and day school for young men conducted by the Benedictine monks near Cullman.

In miniature are clustered over 125 of the famous shrines, buildings and churches of the world, from the days of the Roman Empire up to and including World War II. All of them are the creations of a single Benedictine monk—Brother Joseph, O.S.B. A native of Landshut, Bavaria, Brother Joseph came to Alabama in 1892.

HUNTSVILLE, in northeastern Alabama, is the historic city where the constitutional convention of the Alabama Territory was held in 1819, and the state government first established. The original state legislature met here, but Huntsville's bid to become the state capital lost to Cahaba, because of the latter's more central location.

Today Huntsville is a city of about 137,000, known chiefly for its progressive space facilities at **Monte Sano Observatory** and **Redstone Arsenal,** which includes **George C. Marshall Space Flight Center** and the **Army Missile Command and Ordnance Guided Missile School.** A mixture of stately old homes on shaded lawns, and modern, new buildings such as the **Huntsville Center of the University of Alabama** provide interesting contrast for visitors.

Washington Monument with Capitol in background, Washington, D.C.

Mount Vernon, Virginia

Thoroughbred farms, Bluegrass region of Kentucky

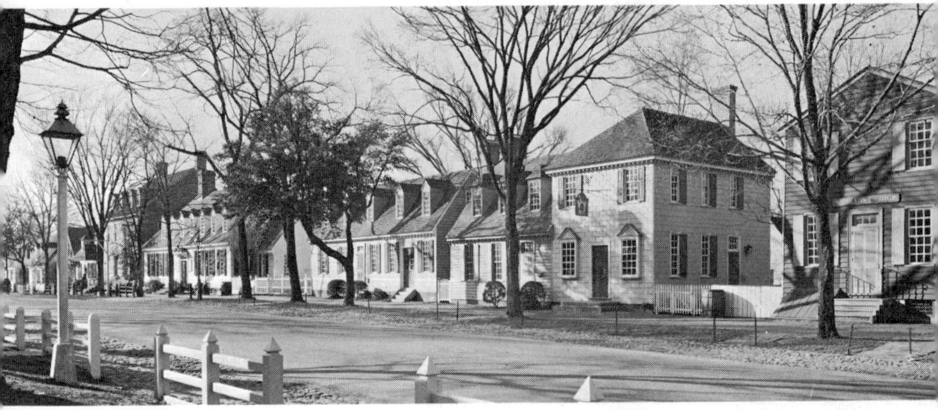

Duke of Gloucester Street, Colonial Williamsburg, Virginia

John F. Kennedy Center for The Performing Arts, Washington, D.C.

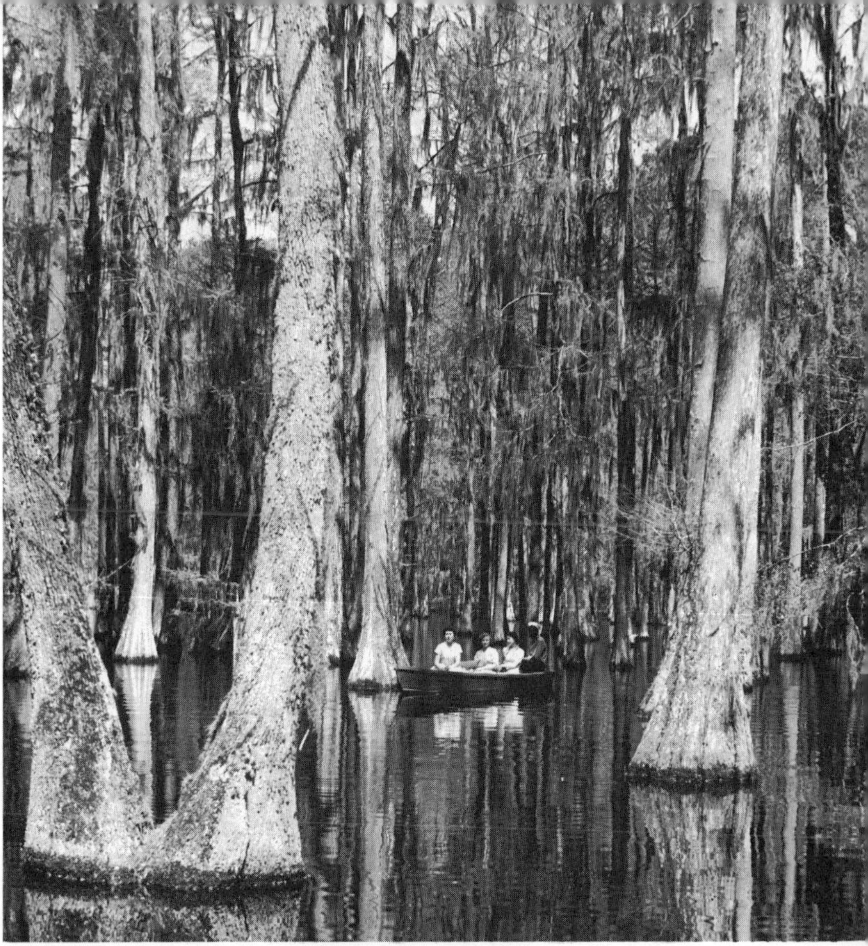

Cypress Gardens,
Charleston, South Carolina

Franklin Roosevelt's
Little White House,
Warm Springs, Georgia

"Jumping" porpoises at Marineland of Florida

Governor's mansion, Tallahassee, Florida

Stanton Hall, antebellum mansion in Natchez, Mississippi

Lookout Mountain, Chattanooga, Tennessee

Mynelle's Gardens, Jackson, Mississippi

Burnham Harbor, Chicago, Illinois

Tuskegee Institute, Alabama

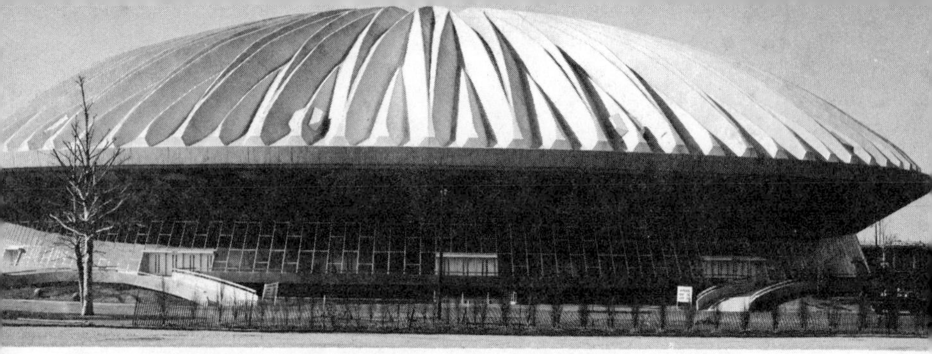

University of Illinois' Assembly Hall, Urbana, Illinois

The Henry Ford Museum, Dearborn, Michigan

In August the city is host to many religious leaders during its annual **Catholic Festival.**

IVY GREEN is the **birthplace of Helen Keller.** The simple white cottage in **Tuscumbia,** built in 1820, has been preserved as a monument to the woman who, when only two years old, was stricken with an illness that left her both blind and deaf. The story of how she overcame these handicaps has been an inspiration to millions. The garden includes the old outdoor pump where she first learned the word "water."

MOBILE. Mobile's present site dates from 1710, and for several years it prospered as the capital of French Louisiana territory. When the capital was moved to New Orleans, Mobile had a precarious time, but it recovered under American rule, and even suffered less than most Southern cities during and after the Civil War.

The **Azalea Trail** is a flower festival held annually in February or early March. The trail, 17 miles long, is a specially-marked route through the city and suburbs, showing beautiful specimens of azaleas ranging in color from pure white through pink and scarlet to deep purple, and in size from century-old plants 30 feet high to dwarf Japanese varieties. The trail begins at **Bienville Square,** a public park downtown named for the founder of Mobile.

Around Mobile, Mobile Bay gives the city access to the Gulf of Mexico, and makes Alabama a maritime state.

The east side of Mobile Bay has long been known as the **"Province of Baldwin"**—just a more elegant way of saying Baldwin County. At Fairhope, America's pioneer single tax colony was founded by a group of Iowans, Ohioans, and Pennsylvanians, who came to practice the teachings of Henry George. Here, too, a school of Organic Education did much to influence progressive education.

Far down on a sandspit, overlooking the entrance to Mobile Bay, the ancient parapets of **Fort Morgan** carry five flagpoles, bearing the emblems which have waved over this early stronghold since it was built during the War of 1812, as Fort Bowyer. Now a state park and picnic grounds, markers recall that Farragut, in 1864, worked his way through mined waters ("Damn the torpedoes, full speed ahead") to silence its guns and bottle up blockade-runners.

On the west side of the channel leading into Mobile Bay lies sunny **Dauphin Island,** a seaside resort, accessible to Mobile by a $4 million causeway. Its **Fort Gaines** dates from 1822, and is also now a picturesque state park.

A mild climate, bright sunshine, gentle Gulf breezes and abundant rainfall have made the Mobile area a great and natural garden. Many of its showiest flowers and plants have come from far places, but some thrive better here than they do in their native soil.

Most spectacular of the garden showplaces around Mobile is **Bellingrath,** along the west side of Mobile Bay. Admission fees go to the support of the gardens, and to a group of churches and colleges, among them a Negro institution at **Tuscaloosa.** Bellingrath Gardens are incredibly lovely, particularly in the late winter and early spring, in a setting of unsurpassed natural beauty.

Another enchanting garden in the Mobile area is **Clarke's,** 12 miles from downtown. Here trees—gums, maples, beeches, dogwoods, oaks—and migrating birds are almost as much of an attraction as great colorful banks of the flowers of the Gulf region. **Long Gardens** on Tuthill Lane is a spectacular formal garden, with azaleas and camellias displayed around a sunken pool.

MONTGOMERY was the first capital of the Confederate States of America, and is often referred to as the "Cradle of the Confederacy." Here, in the **state capitol,** met the first Congress of the Confederacy, which enacted the Articles of Secession. Not far away stands the original **White House of the Confederacy,** where Jefferson Davis and his family lived during their brief stay in the city.

The **World War Memorial Building** is a modern (1940) structure built to house the Alabama State Department of Archives and History. Alabama was the first state to establish a historical agency by law as a branch of the executive department. Its manuscript collection is outstanding and has been growing steadily since the legislature in 1939 provided a full-time employee to obtain old diaries, letters, and records which should be preserved.

There is also a **general museum,** an **Indian museum,** and an exhibit of memorabilia on the state's early contacts with the French. The **Museum of Fine Arts** contains some excellent murals depicting early Indian life. Elegant **Alabama State Chamber of Commerce home** in Montgomery, built in 1848, is furnished with antiques and original pieces, and is open to the public.

Some of Alabama's most magnificent ante-bellum homes and gardens can be found in the rolling countryside around Montgomery. **Jasmine Hill,** a beautiful privately-owned garden, is open to the public free of charge.

SELMA. At nearby Selma, the **Sturdivant Home,** built by Colonel Edward M. Watts around 1850, remains one of the classic examples of plantation mansions. It was designed by a cousin of General Robert E. Lee, and all of its furniture was specially imported from France. It is now a museum, open to the public.

Northeast of Selma, on the Tallapoosa River near Alexander City, is **Horseshoe Bend National Military Park,** site of the battle in 1814 where General Andrew Jackson defeated the Creeks and helped pave the way for the Treaty of Ghent.

TUSCALOOSA is best known today as the home of the **University of Alabama.** It was once an Indian settlement which took its odd name from two words in the Choctaw Indian language—"tusko," meaning warrior, and "loosa," meaning black. Under the guidance of federal Indian agents, "Black Warrior Town" prospered as a trading post until the Indians revolted in 1813, and U.S. troops under General John Coffee captured and burned the town. With Coffee was the celebrated scout, Davy Crockett. New settlers arrived and the capital was moved from Cahaba.

As the state capital, Tuscaloosa prospered greatly from 1826–46, when the capital was again moved (to Montgomery). Long rows of beautiful water oaks were planted along its broad avenues, giving Tuscaloosa the nicknames "City of Oaks" and the "Druid City." Development of mineral resources in the vicinity has brought new wealth, and replaced the city's dependence upon the cotton market's whims and fluctuations.

Most of the original buildings of the University of Alabama were burned during the Civil War, but the **Gorgas Home,** built in 1829, and the **Gorgas Oak,** favorite rendezvous of Alabama students, were spared. The U. S. Bureau of Mines maintains a research laboratory on the campus, and not far away, the **Museum of Natural History** contains a splendid display of artifacts and burial ornaments of the early Indian civilization found at nearby **Moundville,** one of the most impressive mound groups in the South. **Mound State Monument,** 17 miles south of Tuscaloosa, has a museum containing additional relics, and 34 square or oval mounds, one of which is 58 feet high and covers one-and-a-quarter acres at its base.

TUSKEGEE, home of **Tuskegee Institute** is also the location of the **George Washington Carver Museum.** The Museum contains records of the famous scientist's contributions to agronomy and dioramas of important achievements by other black people.

WARRIOR. One of the most beautiful caverns in the area is **Rickwood,** at Warrior, just north of Birmingham. Here have been found fossil remains millions of years old, and species of fish which have become blind because they never saw light. **Cathedral Caverns,** near Grant, claims to possess the largest stalagmite in the world.

Alabama also has several natural bridges, one of the most beautiful being near **Jasper.** Here a stream, with the aid of springs, wore away soft shale, leaving a hard sandstone cap and two arches draped with ferns. The walls of the valley are covered with mountain laurel, snowball bushes and giant magnolias.

SPORTS AND RECREATION. **Hunting** is one of Alabama's most popular sports. The Mississippi Valley is the main flyway for migratory waterfowl such as wood ducks, mallards, and canvasbacks, and quail, rabbit, fox, and squirrel can be hunted in fall. Another important sport is **fishing,** both in the Gulf of Mexico and on inland lakes. Well-known beach areas are at Mobile Bay, the Gulf Shore, and on Dauphin Island.

SPECIAL EVENTS. Mobile's **Mardi Gras** is second only to that of New Orleans in colorful pageantry, gaiety, and festivities. As in New Orleans, Mardi Gras is held in February or March during the week ending on Shrove Tuesday. **America's Junior Miss Pageant,** the search for the nation's ideal high school senior, is held during the azalea-blooming season, with entries from all 50 states.

Other annual events are the **Air Carnival,** held at Birmingham Municipal Airport, early June, and the **United Sacred Harp Singing Convention,** Birmingham Municipal Auditorium, late August.

Mississippi

More than two million people, the majority of them from rural areas, live in Mississippi. Well-known trademarks of the state are its magnolia blossoms, its cotton, and the Mississippi River, which flows along its western border.

THE LAND. Aside from the Gulf Coast, which extends over the eastern half of the state, the most clearly defined part of Mississippi is the Delta, a leaf-shaped plain lying in the northwestern corner. It is about 200 miles long, and its greatest width is 85 miles, an area of great soil fertility.

Mississippi's coastline runs for 44 miles along the Gulf of Mexico, with towns on the coast including Gulfport, Biloxi, and Pascagoula. The Mississippi (near which levees stand to prevent flood damage), Yazoo, Pearl, and Big Black are the state's leading rivers.

THE CLIMATE. Summers are long in Mississippi, with temperatures averaging 82 degrees on the Gulf of Mexico and often higher in the interior. However, cool breezes from the Gulf and frequent showers cool the land considerably.

Snow is rare in the southern part of Mississippi, but does fall in the north, where winter temperatures average 48 degrees. The state occasionally lies in the path of hurricanes traveling north from the Gulf.

THE PEOPLE. De Soto, the Spanish explorer, was the first European to set foot on this region of the Chickasaw, Choctaw, and Natchez Indians. In 1682, La Salle claimed the Mississippi Valley for France, and settlements were made near present-day Ocean Springs, Natchez, and Mobile. By the Treaty of Paris after the French and Indian War, Mississippi passed to Great Britain and then to the United States following the Revolution.

In 1803, with the Louisiana Purchase, the Mississippi River became part of the United States. Statehood was granted to Mississippi in 1817, with the capital established at Jackson in 1822. Gradually Indian territory was turned over to the state, and its cotton industry started. It was during this period that the magnificent ante-bellum mansions were built and plantation life flourished.

Mississippi seceded from the Union early in 1861 and supplied close to 80,000 troops to the Confederacy. The Vicksburg campaign was fought mainly on Mississippi soil.

After the war Mississippi was readmitted to the Union in 1870. Despite heavy economic losses of the war and Mississippi River floods, the state's agricultural growth proceeded. During the 1920's, boll weevil attacks ruined cotton crops, forcing many farmers to develop other crops, notably pecans, rice, sweet potatoes.

AGRICULTURE. Cotton is Mississippi's leading crop, accounting for 40 percent of the state's farm income. It is largely grown in the Delta, where some of the world's richest alluvial soil can be found. Also important are corn, soybeans, tung nuts, and a variety of grains.

Due to its excellent pastures and abundance of grain, Mississippi has developed into an important livestock-raising state. Truck farming is another key area of agriculture.

INDUSTRY. Papermaking and food processing bring in the most industrial income for Mississippi. More than two million cords of pulpwood are used in papermaking each year. The food processing centers, especially for cheese and meats, are near the Black Belt. Seafood processors are nearer the coast.

The chemical industry has grown rapidly in Mississippi, as have shipbuilding, metal producing, and clothing. Mining for petroleum and natural gas adds another $210 million annually to the state's income.

CITIES. Jackson, the capital, is Mississippi's largest and most important city. Others include Greenville, Vicksburg, Natchez, and Pascagoula, which has developed rapidly because of its shipbuilding industry.

BILOXI is definitely a fisherman's town. Its harbor is always crowded with boats, bringing in cargoes of shrimp, fish, oysters, and other seafoods. When the ships dock, whether day or night, shrieking whistles from freezing plants and canneries summon the town's workers to dockside, for cargoes must be unloaded and processed with utmost speed to remain fresh.

In the Gulf, a string of picturesque islands borders the Mississippi coastline. **Deer Island** provides a stage for a spectacular display of fireworks for Biloxi citizens on the Fourth of July. Farther out, on **Ship Island,** one of the stout brick fortresses built to defend this coast just before the Civil War can be found. It is called **Fort Massachusetts,** in honor of Federal General Benjamin Butler's home state, and was used as a prison for captured Confederate prisoners of war.

Biloxi's **lighthouse,** much photographed by visitors, is the only such beacon in the center of a busy four-lane highway, U.S. 90, which here follows close to the beach.

Some intimate glimpses of the last 12 years of Jefferson Davis' life can be obtained at **Beauvoir,** his home outside of Biloxi, which has been faithfully and almost entirely restored, even to the prayerbook of Mrs. Davis on her bedside table. With his wife's help, Mr. Davis wrote at Beauvoir his "Rise and Fall of the Southern Confederacy."

COLUMBUS. At Friendship Cemetery, in Columbus, Memorial Day had its origin on April 26, 1866, when ladies of the town met and marched in procession to the burial ground, where they cleared and decorated with flowers the graves of both Confederate and Union soldiers. This act inspired Francis Miles Finch's poem "The Blue and the Gray." April 26th is still observed as Memorial Day in four Southern states, but the rest of the nation has accepted May 30th, a date first selected in 1869, for the decoration of the graves of the honored dead.

Columbus has a **garden and home pilgrimage** in early April which is second only to that of Natchez in color and pageantry. In addition to a special tour, including 15 stately mansions, there is an outstanding antique show, featuring priceless heirlooms rarely seen by the public. **Holly Springs,** once known as the "Athens of the South," re-creates its past glory in late April, when ten old homes and numerous other historic shrines beckon lovers of the authentic Old South. **Cedarhurst,** at Holly Springs, is particularly worth visiting. Built in 1857, Cedarhurst has some exquisite iron grillwork and Venetian glass, showing French-Gothic influence. Hoop-skirted belles serve as hostesses.

Two Civil War battlefields—**Brice's Cross Roads** and **Tupelo**—are national battlefield sites, and another—**Ackia**—is a national monument. Tupelo marks the climax of a series of operations designed by General Sherman to protect his line of supply during the long Atlanta campaign. At Brice's Cross Roads, Confederate General Nathan Bedford Forrest won a tactical victory over superior enemy forces.

GULFPORT came into being in 1887, as a deep-sea outlet for the timber brought from the forest areas a few miles inland. Now it is a state-owned port and a major shipping point for Latin American and world markets.

JACKSON. South-central Mississippi includes Jackson, the state's capital and largest city. Because much of Mississippi's recent oil development has taken place in this region, Jackson seems more like a modern bustling metropolis than most of the other cities. The state museum in the old **capitol** gives an excellent insight into the early history of the state. The city's **wildlife museum** and **municipal zoo,** where the monkey island is a unique feature, are also well worth visiting.

NATCHEZ. One of the most colorful parts of the nation is the **Natchez Territory** of southwest Mississippi. This group of counties, which has been under the rule of five nations, is rich in reminders of the Old South. Much of the home architecture and gardens of a bygone day, as well as many antebellum customs, are still evident in this section which is also rapidly developing many modern ways. Yet its citizenry have been careful not to mar the beauty that makes this lovely section of Mississippi so appealing.

As early as 1800, explorers, trappers and pioneers were pouring down the famed **Natchez Trace** to Natchez, and boatmen who had brought cargoes on rafts down the Ohio, Missouri and Mississippi were returning overland via the same wilderness path. Later, when cotton became the principal crop of the area, Natchez developed as a seaport. Land owners and shipping magnates built mansions and estates which are still in an excellent state of preservation.

The best time to see Natchez is in March, during the pilgrimage to some 30 magnificent mansions and gardens. Among them are **Stanton Hall,** the most palatial home in Natchez and today the headquarters of the Pilgrimage Garden Club.

Rosalie, built in 1820, was used as the headquarters of General Grant during his occupation of Natchez. Behind the house lies the site of old Fort Rosalie, which is now the property of the Mississippi Daughters of the American Revolution. Even older is **Connelly's Tavern,** built during the Spanish rule in 1795 on Ellicott's Hill. Here Aaron Burr and Blennerhassett met to plan their defense, following their arrest for treason in 1807.

OCEAN SPRINGS, on the east side of the Bay of Biloxi, occupies the site of **Old Biloxi,** the first European settlement in the lower Mississippi River Valley, founded by d'Iberville, in 1699. The waterfront is extraordinarily beautiful. Once this little town was the capital of the whole vast wilderness drained by the Mississippi, but after the government was moved to Mobile around 1710, the settlement eked out a bare subsistence until 1880 by fishing and charcoal-making. Since then catering to tourists and raising pecans have brought it a comfortable income.

The nearby **Shearwater Pottery,** named for a variety of seagull found along the Gulf Coast, produces various clay products which are sold throughout the United States. The glazes and designs are quite distinctive, including gulls, pelicans, fish, crabs, and figurines.

OXFORD is the seat of the **University of Mississippi** and the lifetime home of Nobel prize novelist William Faulkner.

PASCAGOULA, near the Alabama border, is a leading industrial city, known for the submarines and other ships built by Ingalls, shipbuilders. The town pioneered in all-welded seagoing vessels, and is now producing nuclear-powered underseas craft.

A local curiosity in Pascagoula is **"Singing River,"** which emits mysterious sounds caused by underground currents, marsh gas, and movement of sand. The **"Old Spanish Fort,"** which resembles an old ranch house, dates from 1718 and is the oldest structure in the lower Mississippi Valley region.

PASS CHRISTIAN was once a "Newport of the South," its comfortable old hotels and beachside homes attracting the planters of Louisiana, Alabama and Mississippi, and the aristocrats of New Orleans. Today everyone can still enjoy the area's famous Creole dishes. The town is also noted for its antique shops, and the **"Dixie White House,"** which acquired its name when President Woodrow Wilson visited there in 1913.

PORT GIBSON, not far away, is a pleasant town which General Grant found "too beautiful to burn." Its landmark is the **First Presbyterian Church,** whose steeple-peak bears a hand "pointing to heaven." Built in 1855 with slave labor, the church's interior is lighted by elegant chandeliers from the famous old river steamboat *Robert E. Lee.*

Grant did not burn it, but a fire of unknown origin in 1890 finally destroyed **Windsor,** considered the handsomest house in Mississippi. Even in ruins its 22 gigantic Corinthian columns are impressive. Symbols of a lost era, they rise starkly from the underbrush of the ghost town of Rodney, near Port Gibson.

VICKSBURG. Most of the Delta's attractions for the visitor are at the southern end, in and around the historic river port of Vicksburg, which sprawls over the highest of a line of picturesque bluffs overlooking the junctions of the Mississippi River and the Yazoo Canal.

The Spaniards, as far back as 1790, first recognized the military advantages of these cliffs commanding the waterway, and built a fort there called Nogales, named for the many walnut trees that grew on it. During the Civil War, Vicksburg, as the last rebel stronghold on the river, became the "Gibraltar of the Confederacy." With its fall, after a spectacular siege of 47 days and nights, the fate of the Confederacy was sealed.

Vicksburg National Military Park and Cemetery is one of the largest and best-marked battlefield areas in the United States. Via parkways, the whole length of the defense line of fortifications (along Confederate Avenue), and the plan of attack (along Union Avenue) can be followed.

Like Gettysburg, Vicksburg's battlefield has some spectacular memorials, including statues honoring northern as well as southern leaders. To understand this significant siege the visitor should first call at the museum, in the park headquarters on Confederate Avenue, adjacent to U. S. Highway 80, and obtain, free, an official map and historical leaflet summarizing the action.

The **steamboat "Sprague,"** the largest stern-wheeler ever built, is now a unique riverboat museum. Each March, the **Showboat Players** present an old-fashioned melodrama, "Gold in the Hills," in the ship's auditorium.

When, in 1879, Congress created the Mississippi River Commission to improve navigation, prevent floods and promote river commerce, headquarters were placed in St. Louis. But after the 1927 flood, principal offices of the Commission were concentrated in Vicksburg.

The **U. S. Waterways Experiment Station** is five miles out of Vicksburg, with operating scale-models of the Mississippi and other rivers. From nine to four on weekdays, visitors can watch skilled engineers working on flood control and navigation problems, trying to find means of keeping shifting river channels open without constant dredging, and studying wave and tide action. The model of the Mississippi is the largest of its type in the world. A fifth of a mile long, it represents every twist, turn and backwater of the mighty river for 600 miles—from Helena, Arkansas, to Donaldson, Louisiana.

SPORTS AND RECREATION. Water-sports lovers can find many beaches and resorts in Mississippi, especially along the coast of the Gulf of Mexico where there is a 26-mile-long white sand beach. The oldest yacht club in the South is at Pass Christian, and Pickwick Lake, in the northeastern corner of the state, is a popular resort for fishermen, swimmers, and yachtsmen. Islands off the coast provide protected waters perfect for sailboat racing (every Saturday and Sunday from May until mid-September). Large and small-mouth bass, bream, and crappie can be caught all year round in the Mississippi Delta, and surf fishing is at its best off Ship Island near Biloxi.

SPECIAL EVENTS in Mississippi include the **Fox Hunter's Meet,** in Gulfport, February; annual **Shrimp Festival** and blessing of the fleet, Biloxi, early June; annual **Regatta and Deep-Sea Fishing Rodeo,** Gulfport, early July; **sailboat races,** Biloxi, September; and the **Mississippi-Alabama State Fair,** in Meridian, October.

Louisiana

Because of its strategic location where the Mississippi River spills into the Gulf of Mexico, Louisiana is one of the nation's most important shipping states. Although paddle-wheel steamers have been replaced by tugs and oceangoing ships, tourists find Louisiana—and its most historic city, New Orleans—a charming state with a unique old-world atmosphere.

THE LAND. Louisiana has a land area of 48,523 square miles, and a 397-mile coastline. All of the land is relatively flat, the highest point, **Driskill Mountain,** being only 535 feet above sea level. This low land, often marshy but always fertile, has been responsible for Louisiana's prosperous farming industry. The Mississippi Delta, formed at the river's mouth, contains the most fertile soil in the state.

In addition to the Mississippi River, the Atchafalaya and Red (branches of the Mississippi), Black, Ouachita, and Sabine rivers are also important.

THE CLIMATE. Louisiana, with 53 inches of rain annually, is one of the wettest states in the country. Hot and humid in summer, temperatures in southern Louisiana run into the eighties in July and rarely fall below 50–55 in January.

THE PEOPLE. The first permanent Louisiana settlement was made by French colonists on the Red River at Natchitoches in 1714. New Orleans was founded four years later, and in 1762 the region passed to Spain.

Under Spanish rule Louisiana prospered and developed its sugar industry, which was in a flourishing state by 1803 when Louisiana went to the United States as part of the Louisiana Purchase. Its present dimensions were virtually determined when Congress created the Territory of Orleans. This territory was renamed Louisiana and admitted to the Union in 1812.

For 58 years Louisiana developed rapidly, with settlers pouring in, and the port of New Orleans expanding enormously.

But the Civil War, in which Louisiana seceded and joined the Confederacy, left the state economically ruined. Union forces occupied New Orleans in 1862, and later the rest of the state. Not until the beginning of the 20th century did the economy recover. Railroads then came in, commerce resumed growth, and eventually oil was discovered. Today Louisiana is one of the South's industrial leaders.

AGRICULTURE. Almost one-third of the sugar raised in the United States is grown in Louisiana. Louisiana also grows more sweet potatoes and yams than any other state, and is a leading supplier of rice and corn. Other chief crops are white potatoes, strawberries, and truck crops such as beans, tomatoes, okra, and cabbage.

INDUSTRY. Petroleum is one of Louisiana's biggest businesses, with refineries located at Baton Rouge, Shreveport, and several other cities. Rice processing is another key industry, centered around Crowley. Also important are chemicals, pulp and paper production, and furniture manufacturing. Commercial fishing brings in over $30 million yearly.

CITIES. New Orleans is the largest city. Others, in order of size, include Shreveport, Baton Rouge (the capital), Lake Charles, Lafayette, and Monroe.

ALEXANDRIA, Louisiana's seventh largest city, lies in the geographic center of the state. It has a young appearance, largely because the town was almost completely destroyed by fire during the Civil War. Its home gardens show luxuriant bloomings of magnolia, japonica, camellia, azalea, yaupon, and wisteria.

Not far away, **Leesville** and **Winnfield** celebrate **forest festivals** in the early autumn, recalling that once this whole rich farming area was covered with dense forest growth.

BATON ROUGE. To the west, toward the Mississippi River, the towering white shaft of the **Louisiana capitol,** in Baton Rouge, reputedly the tallest (450 feet) and most unusual state legislature building in America, can be seen on the skyline.

The new capitol towers over the old **statehouse,** built in 1849, a castellated Gothic structure which stands on a bluff overlooking the Mississippi River. Mark Twain, in his "Life on the Mississippi," termed the venerable building a "little sham castle" and blamed its exotic design on Sir Walter Scott, who had "run people mad, a couple of generations ago, with his medieval romances."

Like New Orleans, Baton Rouge is a deep-water port for freighters of many oceanic lines. Ships drawing up to 35 feet here exchange cargoes with diesel-towed barges from Pittsburgh, Chicago, Minneapolis, and St. Louis. Baton Rouge is also the busy shopping center for a large cotton, sugar-cane, and cattle-raising area.

Louisiana State University and **Southern University** are the two major schools in the city.

CROWLEY. Rice, one of Louisiana's top agricultural commodities, comes into its own during the **International Rice Festival,** staged in Crowley in October. Unique with this celebration is the **"Frog Derby,"** when two-pound Louisiana jumbos compete in broad-jumping contests and other events. Most of the frogs come from **Rayne,** where pedigreed frogs are raised for some of the nation's finest restaurants, as well as for biological laboratories and research centers.

The Crowley Festival also features an international duck calling contest, a cooking competition featuring Creole delicacies, a selection of a "Rice Queen," and demonstrations of Acadian handicrafts.

LAKE CHARLES, while inland, is Louisiana's nearest major port to the sea (37 miles from the Gulf of Mexico). It is an interesting combination of a Louisiana-French community and a Texas-type of town. Visitors are admitted to its big rice mill, the only plant of its kind, where they may see cellulose being made from rice hulls, formerly used only as fuel. Also near Lake Charles, cotton is compressed into bales at the **Lake Charles Cotton Compress.**

MORGAN CITY, one of the state's principal fishing ports, holds a **shrimp festival** in early September. Blessing of the shrimp fleet, a ceremony dating from shortly after the arrival of the Acadians from Nova Scotia in the eighteenth century, is accompanied by a water pageant, when shrimp boats festooned with balloons and bunting parade along the winding Atchafalaya River. Visitors are offered a colorful series of parades, tableaux, and water races, and restaurants vie with one another to serve shrimp and other delicious seafood specialties.

NEW IBERIA is renowned for its famous Tabasco or pepper sauce, which is distilled from tiny red peppers, in a small factory near Avery Island. At

New Iberia, too, an annual **sugar-cane festival** is held in September, with parades, balls, and the selection of a "Sugar Queen." Visitors may join in the traditional *fais do-do,* or street dance, to the accompaniment of Acadian music.

For visitors interested in the breeding of foreign cattle, the **Iberia Experimental Station** near New Iberia can be visited.

NEW ORLEANS, a hub of transportation by air, land, or sea, is a gateway to Latin America. Its harbor is one of the busiest and most colorful in the nation, and though more than 100 miles from the nearest salt water, the **port of New Orleans** ranks second only to New York in dollar value of cargo. Its concrete, deep-water, quay-type wharves can berth more than 100 ships at a time.

Not only does the port handle some 4,000 sailings a year, but it boasts the fastest turn-around for ships in the country. Wharves are built to parallel the shore, making for easier maneuverability of ships, and all quaysides are united by the publicly owned **Public Belt Railroad,** which operates 135 miles of track.

In addition to its port, New Orleans has a new municipally owned **Union Passenger Terminal,** combining six railroad stations; and **Moisant International Airport,** handling around 800,000 air travelers each year.

On the waterfront visitors can see the flags of every maritime nation, and hear ship crews and longshoremen shouting in many tongues. Sea gulls cry overhead, and the smell of coffee, spices, tarred ropes, and oil smoke blend in the breeze. Tugboats chug by with incredible tows of barges, and the deep sirens of ferryboats vie with the horns of diesel switch engines.

New Orleans is a leading U.S. cotton, coffee, and banana port, with one out of every four domestically consumed cups of coffee and one out of every four bananas being imported here. Its grain elevators handle tons of wheat, corn, rye, and barley. Largest is the **Public Grain Elevator,** which can handle some five-and-a-half million bushels at a time.

A short distance upstream from this elevator is the **Foreign Trade Zone,** the second to be opened in the United States. In this "free port," produce not bound for this country may be stored, packaged or processed and sent on its way, without being subject to U.S. customs duties.

There are three airports for scheduled airlines, commercial and private aviation and military use serving the city, as well as railroad, bus and freight lines.

International House combines a club and an international chamber of commerce with an agency which offers expert guidance to any importer or exporter who wishes to buy, sell, ship, or establish trade contacts in any part of the world. A foreign businessman, arriving in New Orleans, can have a temporary office, the services of a bilingual secretary, and the aid of foreign trade experts—all absolutely free.

To the average tourist, however, the new **International Trade Mart** at the foot of Canal Street on the Mississippi River, has the greater appeal. Products from every state in the Union and from 25 foreign countries are set out for inspection in modern, air-conditioned showrooms. In this unique global market you will find household wares and toys from Japan, the latest fashions from Paris, tweeds and woolens from Britain, cheeses from Holland, more cheese and watches from Switzerland, cutlery from Germany, and all kinds of goods from the U.S.A.

The famed **French Market** is where housewives, restaurateurs, and others who appreciate good eating and cooking, come for the ingredients of gourmet meals. A market place when Choctaw Indians traded with the earliest settlers, here can be found delectable seafoods, meats and vegetables.

For travelers in a hurry for a meal, try a New Orleans institution, the "Po' Boy Sandwich," a length of toasted French bread, stuffed with roast beef, lettuce, tomatoes, coleslaw and other ingredients. Or stop at a New Orleans oyster bar, and down a dozen delicious

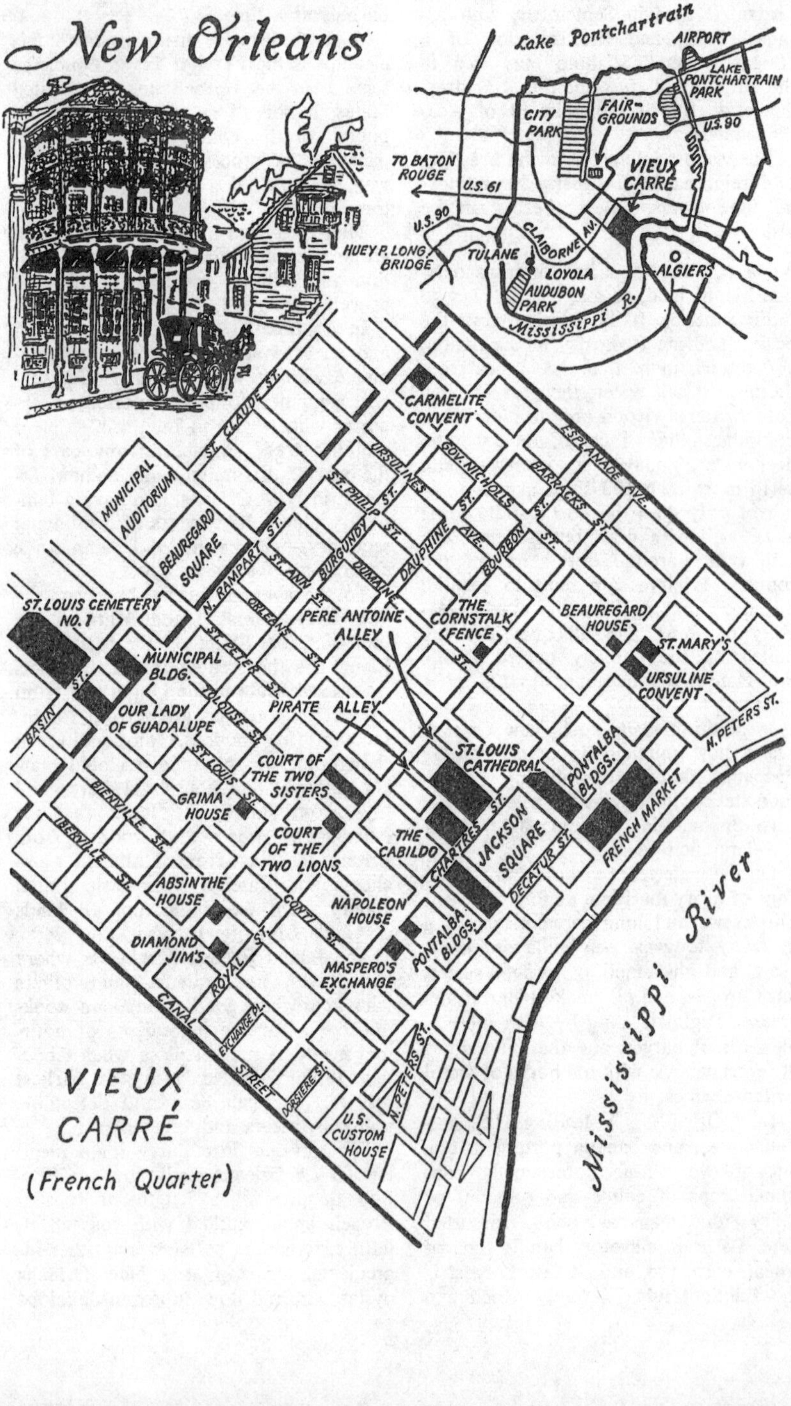
New Orleans
Lake Pontchartrain
AIRPORT
LAKE PONTCHARTRAIN PARK
CITY PARK
FAIR-GROUNDS
U.S. 90
TO BATON ROUGE
U.S. 61
VIEUX CARRÉ
U.S. 90
HUEY P. LONG BRIDGE
TULANE
CLAIBORNE AV.
LOYOLA
AUDUBON PARK
ALGIERS
Mississippi R.
CARMELITE CONVENT
ST. CLAUDE ST.
URSULINES ST.
GOV. NICHOLLS ST.
ESPLANADE AVE.
BARRACKS ST.
MUNICIPAL AUDITORIUM
BEAUREGARD SQUARE
ST. PHILIP ST.
N. RAMPART ST.
ST. ANN ST.
BURGUNDY ST.
DUMAINE ST.
DAUPHINE AVE.
BOURBON ST.
ST. LOUIS CEMETERY NO. 1
ORLEANS ST.
PERE ANTOINE ALLEY
THE CORNSTALK FENCE
BEAUREGARD HOUSE
ST. MARY'S
URSULINE CONVENT
MUNICIPAL BLDG.
ST. PETER ST.
BASIN ST.
OUR LADY OF GUADALUPE
TOULOUSE ST.
PIRATE ALLEY
N. PETERS ST.
ST. LOUIS ST.
COURT OF THE TWO SISTERS
ST. LOUIS CATHEDRAL
PONTALBA BLDGS.
BIENVILLE ST.
GRIMA HOUSE
COURT OF THE TWO LIONS
THE CABILDO
CHARTRES ST.
JACKSON SQUARE
DECATUR ST.
FRENCH MARKET
IBERVILLE ST.
ABSINTHE HOUSE
CONTI ST.
NAPOLEON HOUSE
PONTALBA BLDGS.
Mississippi River
DIAMOND JIM'S
ROYAL ST.
MASPERO'S EXCHANGE
CANAL STREET
EXCHANGE PL.
DORSIERE ST.
N. PETERS ST.
U.S. CUSTOM HOUSE
VIEUX CARRÉ
(French Quarter)

oysters with crackers and a glass of beer.

But New Orleans is a place for leisurely eating, and there are scores of hotels and restaurants where that can be done well. In addition to the internationally known restaurants, many of the smaller, less expensive eating places, as in Paris, turn out excellent dishes.

Two things are outstanding about Creole cooking. One is the prevalence of seafood and the multiple ways it is served in New Orleans. The other is the universal and expert use of piquant herbs. Specialties of the city are gumbo, grillades, red beans and rice, oysters Rockefeller, *pompano en papillotes* (fish cooked and served in a special paper bag), and pecan pralines. New Orleans also claims the origin of several specialty drinks, including the sazerac cocktail, the Ramos gin fizz, and café brûlot.

Café brûlot deserves special mention because the serving of it is something of a New Orleans ritual. Several special utensils are needed—a ladle, a metal bowl, and a metal tray. Into the bowl go spices—cinnamon, cloves, and sometimes allspice and aloes—orange and lemon rind, sliced thin, and sugar plus cognac or brandy. An alcohol burner under the bowl ignites the brandy. When the fire dies out, a quart of dark-roast drip coffee is added, and served.

In the **Vieux Carré** or French Quarter, every house and shop, within a few squares of each other, has its special history. City fathers, while guarding the old-world charm of this cosmopolitan quarter, also encourage restoration in the Vieux Carré. Here, on Bourbon Street, home of jazz, is the historic **Old Absinthe House,** built in 1806, and the blacksmith shop of **Lafitte,** the pirate.

On one side of **Basilica of St. Louis, King of France,** most famous of Louisiana churches, you will find the handsome stone **Presbytère,** or church building, and on the other side the state building, or **Cabildo,** now the **Louisiana State Museum.** Its colonnade at night is still lighted by gas lamps. "Orleans Alley," better known as **"Pirates Alley,"** is a favorite subject for artists. Another famous but narrow street is **"Exchange Alley,"** location of the fencing academies. Ten deadly duels a day were once not uncommon at a favorite spot like the **Dueling Oaks in City Park.**

Most Vieux Carré houses turn their backs on the streets and open out onto flagstoned, flower-filled patios shaded by palms and banana plants. In this private world the family has morning breakfast, the housewife does chores, and cool drinks are served on a summer's evening.

Canal Street—Broadway of the Crescent City—is perhaps the widest street in America. While the "Street Car Named Desire" has been replaced by a modern bus, the destination is still the same, Desire Street—which now has a low-income housing project of the same name. Basin Street and the blues are still synonymous terms.

A **sight-seeing steamer** which makes a 30-mile harbor trip twice a day, departs from Eads Plaza, at the foot of Canal Street. This boat, the *S/S President* affords a close-up of the varied river traffic, the picturesque communities on the west bank of the river, the oil, salt and sulphur docks, sugar refineries, cottonseed oil mills, the **U. S. Naval Repair Base, Army Storehouses,** and the **U. S. Immigration Station.**

Chalmette, site of the Battle of New Orleans, January 8, 1815, is where American and British forces met in bloody combat *after* the treaty of peace, ending the war of 1812, was signed at Ghent on December 24, 1814—the news not reaching the United States in time.

A 100-foot monument and an interesting visitors' center will be found in the restored **Beauregard House,** once owned by Judge Rene Beauregard, son of the Confederate general.

New Orleans' levees are thick, high and strong, holding the mighty Mississippi within its present limits. But they get a powerful assist in times of flood from the **Bonnet Carré floodway,** above the city, which pours excess water into a back channel leading into **Lake Pontchartrain,** one of the largest natural fresh-water lakes in the United States.

OPELOUSAS, once the Spanish Colonial district capital of southwestern Louisiana, is today a town where the French touch shows in appearance, customs and manners. Opelousas celebrates the growth of yams, or sweet potatoes in October, with a **"Yambilee"** featuring an elaborate pageant, glittering floats, and other festivities over a three-day period.

The "Yambilee" includes the usual selection of a "Yam Queen," parades, and the display of quaint French costumes of the Teche country. English has replaced French as the court language of Opelousas' St. Landry parish courthouse, although French is still sometimes necessary.

ST. MARTINVILLE. Westward, along Bayou Teche between Morgan City and Lafayette and parallel to U. S. Highway 90, lies the picturesque **Acadian country,** where most of the Acadians exiled from Nova Scotia originally settled nearly two centuries ago. Their descendants, the "Cajuns," still speak a language which is basically French. Here many Old World civic and religious customs prevail.

St. Martinville is a quaint old French town with subtropical trimmings, and the locale of Longfellow's "Evangeline." Near the **St. Martin Catholic Church,** the Mother Church of the Acadians, are located the **Evangeline Oak** and the **Evangeline Monument.**

In the museum of the nearby **Longfellow-Evangeline State Park** are many poignant mementos of the era when whole families were uprooted and separated in one of the most tragic transplantings in history.

Avery Island, and nearby Jefferson Island, both inland, stand over a huge mass of solid salt about three miles in diameter and extending more than seven miles down into the earth. The salt mines at Jefferson, Weeks Island, and the Carey Salt Company are usually open to visitors, Monday through Friday.

SHREVEPORT, in the northwestern corner of the state, is an important cotton and oil center, and a bustling retail and wholesale marketing center for the whole Red River Valley area, extending well into Oklahoma.

Shreveport is one of the wealthiest cities for its size in America. Its original citizens represented the intermixture of almost all European stocks, as well as some Mexican, Syrian and even Chinese.

In Shreveport is held the **State Fair,** during a ten-day period in late October and early November with amusements, an elaborate State Fair Revue, and other extravaganzas.

SPORTS AND RECREATION. **Hunting and fishing** are among the most popular outdoor sports, with facilities found throughout Louisiana. About 30 miles north of Baton Rouge is Audubon Memorial Park, the beautiful reservation where John James Audubon came to paint birds.

Grand Isle, south of New Orleans on the Gulf of Mexico, is one of the state's best surf-bathing beaches. The Isle is also noted for excellent fishing.

SPECIAL EVENTS. The festive **Mardi Gras** season in New Orleans is one of the outstanding annual events in the country. The season is generally touched off on the twelfth night after Christmas, and the fiesta tempo is rapidly accelerated until Mardi Gras (Fat Tuesday), 40 days before Easter. Then the Lord of Misrule reigns over subjects mad with carefree abandon, and there is a continuous masquerade, beginning at dawn and lasting until midnight.

Parade is the key to Mardi Gras, with each year's procession carrying out a theme, such as Sinbad the Sailor, Tales of the South Pacific, or Great Stories of the Sea. Winding along a prearranged route, it ends at the municipal auditorium, on the site of old Congo Square.

Other events in Louisiana include **tours of homes and gardens** along the 27-mile azalea trail in Lafayette, mid-March; **Southeastern Indian Festival,** Baton Rouge, late March; **Spring Fiesta of New Orleans,** New Orleans, April; **New Orleans Jazz Festival,** New Orleans, April; **World Champion Pirogue**

Races, Lafitte, May (native boatmen race in pirogues–dugouts made from hollowed-out cottonwood and cypress logs); **Jambalaya Festival**, Gonzales, early June.

Also interesting are the **Dairy Festival and Livestock Show**, Hammond, May; **"Tarpon Rodeo,"** three days at Grand Isle in July when fishermen try their luck at catching swordfish, pompano, flounder, and redfish; **Louisiana Livestock Show and Dixie Horse Show Jubilee**, Baton Rouge, November; and the **Oil Exposition**, Jennings, November.

Arkansas

Hot springs and lush forests are the trademarks of Arkansas. Less well-known is the fact that the only diamond field in North America lies within Arkansas' 53,104 square miles, where nearly two million people live.

THE LAND. The Ozark Mountains run across the northwest section of the state, sloping down to rolling hills and valleys, then swampy areas in the southeast. In this southeastern corner are some of the most versatile timbers grown in the country. The highest point in the state is **Magazine Mountain**, at 2,753 feet. In addition to the Mississippi, important rivers include the Ouachita, the Arkansas, St. Francis, Red, and the White.

THE CLIMATE. Temperatures vary considerably from north to south, although the entire state has a rainy, but warm climate. In July, temperatures range from 78 degrees in the northwest to 82 degrees in the lower areas, and in January, they average 36–42 degrees. Rainfall averages around 48 inches a year.

THE PEOPLE. Arkansas' early history parallels that of Mississippi and Louisiana, with the first actual settlement being made in 1686 at the mouth of the Arkansas River.

Following the Louisiana Purchase, present-day Arkansas was part of the Missouri Territory until 1819 when the government set up the Arkansas Territory. Statehood followed in 1836.

Arkansas was divided on the question of slavery, and when the Civil War broke out, initially voted to remain in the Union. When the United States asked for troops, however, she refused and seceded. For a time, the state had rival Union and Confederate governments.

Reconstruction was an especially bitter period in Arkansas, but slowly the state recovered, with strong new economic developments in mining, farming, and lumbering. Today Arkansas is expanding economically and its population is growing, especially in urban and surrounding areas.

AGRICULTURE. Cotton, soybeans, and rice are Arkansas' most important crops, the last two prospering because the low, flat land is easily irrigated. Almost half of the state's gross income comes from agriculture, augmented considerably by livestock (broilers, cattle, eggs, milk, hogs). Other farm crops are peaches, wheat, and tomatoes. The state has over 20 million acres of trees, many planted by farmers.

INDUSTRY. Manufacturing is becoming increasingly important to Arkansas' economy. Food processing, including canned goods, animal feeds, and soft drinks, is the most prosperous industry, followed by lumber, paper, publishing, oil refining, and chemicals. Petroleum is Arkansas' most valuable mineral, and almost all of the nation's bauxite comes from Arkansas.

CITIES. The majority of Arkansas' residents live in small towns and rural areas. Little Rock, the capital, is the state's largest city (about 132,000), followed by Pine Bluff, Fort Smith, and Hot Springs.

ARKANSAS POST. Not far from the junction of the Arkansas and White rivers is **Arkansas Post National Monument.** Here the French explorer, Henri de Tonti, founded the first settlement west of the Mississippi in 1686. Later the community became the first capital of Arkansas Territory. The *Arkansas Gazette,* oldest newspaper west of the Mississippi, was first published here.

Today Arkansas Post is a ghost town, but an old mud-chinked log cabin in the park area gives an idea of how the first Arkansans lived. Just northeast of the park is the large **White River National Wildlife Refuge.**

FAYETTEVILLE, far up in almost the northwest corner of the state, is surrounded by the picturesque ridges of the Ozark hill country. Here is located the **University of Arkansas,** an **experimental station** and a large **veterans hospital. Hatchet Hall,** once a school for young prohibitionists, taught by Carrie Nation, is now a museum. A wood veneer plant in Fayetteville turns out sheets of walnut only 1/28th of an inch thick. It also cuts sweet gum and sycamore.

FORT SMITH, with its busy factories and shops, was once a military outpost on the Oklahoma border, guarding pioneer settlers against Indian attack. A stout log fort was built here in 1818. The old commissary, a stone building erected in 1839, alone survives, and is now a museum.

"Hanging Judge" Isaac Parker, who condemned 151 persons to the gallows during the rough and tumble days when this area was the true frontier, is buried in **Fort Smith National Cemetery.** Visitors can see his courtroom downtown. Today Fort Smith, one of the leading manufacturing cities of Arkansas, turns out glass, fine furniture and a variety of other products.

HOT SPRINGS is the only city in America surrounded by a national park. The thermal waters of its 47 springs are world-renowned for their therapeutic values.

Hot Springs Mountain, which rises like a stage backdrop behind the town, is the source of the thermal water, which is piped to all the elaborate establishments on Central Avenue's bathhouse row. The average patient is immersed only 15 minutes. He or she then drinks hot mineral water to perspire faster, and gets a massage, rubdown and shower. Other forms of hydrotherapy are applied for rheumatism, arthritis and paralysis.

Not all those who come to Hot Springs to "take the waters" are sick or afflicted. Most visitors find it an excellent place to rest, eat good food, go to night clubs or watch the horse races at nearby **Oaklawn Track.**

Near the town of **Murfreesboro** in Pike County are located the only diamond-producing fields in North America. Although no longer commercially mined, the Pike County diamond fields are a popular tourist attraction. Tourists may hunt diamonds on a finders keepers basis, and many gem and commercial stones are found each year.

LITTLE ROCK, on the winding Arkansas River, stands where the Ouachita foothills meet the alluvial plains to the east. Once this was the head of navigation for shallow-draft steamboats which, before the coming of the railroads, carried much commerce between Little Rock and New Orleans.

Little Rock contains three buildings which in turn have housed its Legislature. The first of these, today a restoration, was built in 1820–24, and was the meeting place of the last Territorial Legislature in 1835. The second Statehouse, now the **Old State House,** dates from 1833, and was remodeled in 1885. The third, the present imposing stone **capitol,** was completed in 1915.

The Arkansas Territorial Capitol Restoration is the result of years of careful and extensive research to restore the buildings as they were and to secure authentic furnishings for each of them. The project includes a number of houses and utility buildings, and the **home of William E. Woodruff,** founder of the *Arkansas Gazette,* oldest newspaper published west of the Mississippi, and the print shop he built in 1824.

Among the pieces of original furniture in the Woodruff house are a table and crib made from a cedar tree which grew on the little rock (*Petite Roche*) that gave its name to the pioneer settlement. It was the first rock of any size to be seen by the early French explorers as they moved up through the marshy plains along the Arkansas River in 1722.

Little Rock itself is a pleasant city of tree-lined streets and garden suburbs, and is the one big shopping center and bright-light spot between Memphis and Dallas.

The **Arkansas Museum of Natural History and Antiquities,** the **birthplace** of **General Douglas MacArthur,** and the **Arkansas Arts Center** contain many items of interest. The **Governor's Mansion,** of Georgian Colonial architecture, was completed in 1950.

Not far beyond the city limits are the big open pits which produce bauxite, the source of aluminum, and barite, used in drilling for oil.

PINE BLUFF, to the west, is the second oldest city in the state, and an important cotton ginning center. At nearby **Lonoke** is one of the world's largest fish hatcheries, open to the public.

De Soto and the early French explorers described Arkansas as a green land of almost solid forest. The homesteaders burned off valuable hardwoods to clear farmland. With the expansion of the railroads, more acres were stripped by get-rich-quick lumbermen.

Today, thanks to sensible forest protection by the state and federal governments, and the cooperation of private enterprises, some kind of timber growth covers nearly two-thirds of the state again. One of the best places to see good forest operations is at **Crossett,** which calls itself "The Forestry Capital of the South." In addition to board lumber, Crossett produces kraft paper, charcoal, turpentine, acetic acid, tar creosote, from what were once considered waste (tops of trees, crooked limbs, bark).

TEXARKANA, a city divided between Arkansas and Texas, is an important trading center for a prosperous two-state area of cattle ranches and oil production. But Arkansas' biggest oil refineries are farther east at El Dorado, where the first big oil gushers stampeded the state in 1921–22. At Stamps visitors can see blocks of yellow sulphur, refined from ill-smelling hydrogen-sulphide natural gas.

WASHINGTON was known as "the jumping-off place for Texas," during the hectic period when the Texas Revolution was in the making. Here, in a tavern, met such notables as Steven F. Austin, Sam Houston, James Bowie and Davy Crockett. And here, James Black, the village blacksmith, fashioned the first of the famous Bowie knives for James Bowie. Old Hempstead County Courthouse, built in 1833, served as temporary state capitol for a short period during the Civil War.

SPORTS AND RECREATION. Western Arkansas forests such as Ouachita and the Boston Mountains are excellent **hunting** and **fishing** country. Also good for those sports are the cypress bayous in southeastern Arkansas. In this area, Lake Chicot State Park offers camping, fishing, and swimming in Lake Chicot or the Mississippi River.

Eureka Springs, near the Missouri border, is a health resort in the "Little Switzerland" district. Built on steep hillsides, the town has no cross streets. Two man-made lakes, Bull Shoals Lake and Norfolk Lake, are popular for fishing and swimming.

SPECIAL EVENTS. Most towns in Arkansas have a fair, folk festival, or farm show at some time during the year. Best-known of these is the **Arkansas State Livestock Show,** held in Little Rock in October. Other popular events include the **Oil Jubilee** in Magnolia, March; **Arkansas Arts Festival,** Little Rock, April; **Arkansas Folk Festival,** Mountain View, April; **Outboard Speedboat Regatta** on Lake Hamilton in Hot Springs, July 4; **National Cotton Picking Contest,** Blytheville, October; and the **World Championship Duck Calling Contest,** held in Stuttgart, in November.

Tennessee

Tennessee is one of the true pioneering states in the country. Daniel Boone, in 1775, blazed a trail through the Cumberland Gap to open up the territory for settlers. More recently, seeking new ways to harness water, the state pioneered in the extensive use of dams to furnish electric power and control floods.

THE LAND. The **Blue Ridge and Appalachian Mountains** are located in eastern Tennessee. The land levels off to a broad plain in the west.

The highest point in the state, **Clingmans Dome,** is located in the Blue Ridge and rises to a height of 6,643 feet. **Roan Mountain,** which also rises more than 6,000 feet, is famous for its rare flowers, including purple rhododendrons (*catawba rhododendron*). In the Cumberlands, to the west of the Appalachians, are vast gulfs, lofty overlooks, deep gorges, and hundreds of waterfalls.

The three largest rivers are the Mississippi, Tennessee, and Cumberland.

THE CLIMATE. Because it has a fairly warm, humid climate, Tennessee receives only four to six inches of snow yearly in the west, and around ten inches in the east. Temperatures range from 70–90 degrees in July (higher in the western sections), and from 30–48 degrees in January.

THE PEOPLE. De Soto of Spain discovered the Mississippi River near Memphis in 1541. His party raided several Indian villages, moved on, and no explorers returned to the region until 1673. That year two Englishmen as well as two Frenchmen explored the Tennessee River Valley.

Battles among the Indians (Cherokees, Chickamaugas, and Chickasaws lived in Tennessee), French, Spanish, and English over control of the land raged for the next 80 years, and with the end of the French-Indian War, France turned the land over to Great Britain.

At this point the area began opening up to settlers. Although it was part of the North Carolina colony, the mountains made governing difficult. In 1775 a group called the Transylvania Company bought a large area of land from the Cherokees, hiring Daniel Boone to blaze a trail through the Cumberland Gap. Davy Crockett, the state's favorite son, was born on the new land a few years later.

Several Revolutionary War battles were fought in Tennessee, although the major conflict was with the Indians, who did not give up all of their land until 1818.

Tennessee became the sixteenth state in the Union in 1796, and its development was accelerated by its three future Presidents, Andrew Jackson, James K. Polk, and Andrew Johnson.

When the Civil War broke out, Tennessee was divided on whether to secede or remain in the Union, and was the last to finally join the Confederacy. The Battle of Shiloh, at which the Union won a bloody victory, was a key battle in the war, and was one of many to take place on Tennessee soil.

Andrew Johnson, the only Southern senator who did not secede with his state, became Abraham Lincoln's Vice President in 1865, and President when Lincoln was assassinated later that year.

Reconstruction in Tennessee was especially difficult because of the vast destruction. Gradually land was cleared, crops planted, and industry developed, but a yellow fever epidemic in the 1870's set back recovery.

Industrial expansion aided Tennessee's steady growth in the twentieth century. The Tennessee Valley Authority brought new wealth to the state through conservation and increased water power. Today there are more than 3.9 million residents in the state, with a growing percentage living in urban areas.

AGRICULTURE. More than 130,000 farms are located throughout the state. Over half of Tennessee's farm income comes from raising livestock, especially purebred Jersey cattle. Tennessee Walking Horses, raised in the Nashville Basin, have become famous.

Crops include cotton, tobacco, soybeans, corn, and truck crops such as beans, potatoes, corn, strawberries, and tomatoes.

INDUSTRY. Manufacturing is by far Tennessee's leading source of income. Chemicals are produced with a value of $765 million yearly; metals and metal products are manufactured in Chattanooga, Nashville, and Louisville. Textiles (including related industries such as hoisery, blankets, and work clothes) are a key industry, and food products are packed in several cities.

Research centers, including 24 maintained by the TVA, carry on industrial research in many areas. Tennessee's mines are known for zinc, phosphate, bituminous coal, and stone (Tennessee is a leading producer of marble).

CITIES. Memphis is Tennessee's largest city, followed by Nashville, Knoxville, and Chattanooga. Many of Tennessee's most interesting sights are located in small towns and state parks, making all parts of the state interesting to visit.

CHATTANOOGA. **Lookout Mountain** rises 2,000 feet above the city of Chattanooga, and is a part of the **Chattanooga and Chickamauga National Military Park,** the first and largest park of its kind in the United States.

Lookout was the scene of the celebrated "Battle Above the Clouds" during the Civil War, and is also famous for strange rock formations, caves and waterfalls. One cave, 1,120 feet underground, is reached by elevator. Within it is a colorfully-lighted waterfall which drops a sheer 145 feet.

The summit of Lookout Mountain may be reached by a winding highway, or by what is reputed to be the world's steepest passenger incline-railway, an amazing mile's ride. **Chickamauga Lake,** formed by a TVA dam, begins just north of Chattanooga, and extends for 59 miles. The military park is composed of separate areas, all reached by paved highways: **Chickamauga Battlefield,** in Georgia: **Point Park** and the **Battlefield of Lookout Mountain,** and **Orchard Knob,** in Chattanooga; a chain of small reservations on **Missionary Ridge;** and **Signal Point,** on Signal Mountain.

COLUMBIA. A simple brick house with large shutters was the home of James K. Polk, one of three Tennesseans who occupied the White House. It was during his administration that the Mexican War was fought and the United States acquired most of its southwestern domain.

GATLINBURG has become a handicraft capital and a favorite convention city. The **Sky Lift** is a spectacular way of ascending **Crockett Mountain,** "the Grandstand of the Great Smokies." At nearby **Pigeon Forge,** six miles from Gatlinburg, a horse-operated mill grinding clay for handmade pottery can be visited.

GREENEVILLE, founded in 1783, became the capital of the short-lived "Free State of Franklin," and later the home of Andrew Johnson, the seventeenth President of the United States. His house, tailor shop and a museum comprise a **national monument,** open to the public. The **Davy Crockett Tavern** and **Pioneer Museum** commemorate the pioneer famed in song and story, who was born in nearby Morristown.

KNOXVILLE, largest city of the upper Tennessee Valley, lies in a region of great scenic beauty where the French Broad and Holston rivers unite to form the Tennessee. This bustling modern shopping and industrial center is also the headquarters for the Tennessee Valley Authority, two of whose major units, **Norris Dam** and **Norris Lake,** lie a short distance northwest of the city. A marker on the courthouse lawn recalls that the Treaty of Holston (1791) by which the Cherokees relinquished their claims to much of what is now Tennessee was signed on that spot.

Knoxville also is the seat of the **University of Tennessee,** whose library contains many fine works of art.

MARYVILLE-ALCOA, twin cities about 15 miles south of Knoxville, have one of the world's largest aluminum plants. And only a short distance west lies the mountain city of **Oak Ridge,** the original home of atomic power.

Although production areas cannot be visited, tours of the **American Museum of Atomic Energy,** operated for the U. S. Atomic Energy Commission, are worth taking. Skilled guides explain more than 30 exhibits showing atomic energy processes from the ore mine to the production of power. There is no admission charge.

MEMPHIS, the largest city of Tennessee, in the southwest corner of the state on the Mississippi, is a commercial and shopping center, a convention city, transportation hub, educational center, and has passed along several famous "blues" songs. One-fourth to one-third of the nation's cotton is sold here.

On **Beale Street,** famed in song and story, W. C. Handy wrote "The Memphis Blues," "The St. Louis Blues," "Beale Street Blues" and other immortal songs. Modern Beale Street (actually named Beale Avenue) has come a long way from its boisterous and bawdy past. Today it is a well-behaved, but still colorful shopping district.

On the **stern-wheeler "Memphis Queen II"** tourists can get a close-up view of the three great bridges that here span the Mississippi, the $50 million dam which forms the only still-water harbor on the Mississippi, and the barge traffic. Some of these diesel-propelled tows (they are really *pushed*) are the longest vessels afloat.

Visitors are welcome to step into the old buildings along **Front Street** and watch brokers and buyers haggle over cotton-piled tables. Equally interesting is the **Cotton Exchange,** on Front Street, where a somewhat brisker trade takes in cotton "futures."

NASHVILLE. The replica of the Parthenon in **Centennial Park** is actually the second one on the same site. The first was built of wood and plaster for the Tennessee Centennial of 1897, celebrating Tennessee's admission to statehood. It won such wide acclaim that it was permanently remodeled in concrete in the period from 1921 to 1931. Like the ancient temple, it is 288 feet long, 101 feet wide, and 65 feet high.

Tennessee's **state capitol** rises from a hill overlooking the central business district of Nashville. Its magnificent porticos, after the Erectheum which stood near the Parthenon at Athens, have Ionic columns, 4 feet in diameter and 33 feet high, with a cupola 205 feet high.

The capitol's tall tower is a reproduction of another gem of Greece's golden age, a monument called the "Lantern of Demosthenes," built by Lysistrates. On a Doric base rests the round part or lantern, and attached to its outer circumference are eight columns of Corinthian design. A fine library and museum, plus numerous markers and monuments of historical significance, combine to make a visit to the capitol grounds worth while.

In 1780, the pioneer James Robertson established a settlement on the west bank of the Cumberland River, destined to become the capital of Tennessee. Named for General Francis Nash, North Carolina Revolutionary War hero killed in the Battle of Germantown, the town was first known as Nashborough. Nashville did not become the permanent capital of Tennessee, however, until 1843.

On **First Avenue,** north of Broadway, are authentic replicas of the frontier stockade, cabins, and blockhouses which protected the founders of Nashville and their families. In the cabins are many articles of ingenious design such as bootjacks, bullet molds, piggin, dug-out cradles, handmade furniture and many utensils that give a good idea of how the early families lived.

It is a short and pleasant drive from Nashville to **The Hermitage,** the plantation home of Andrew Jackson. Built in 1835 by Jackson himself, the beautiful mansion with its tall white columns and broad verandas ranks in historic interest with Washington's Mount Vernon and Jefferson's Monticello.

Nashville's outstanding educational

institutions include **Vanderbilt University, Meharry Medical College, Tennessee State University, George Peabody College for Teachers, Fisk University, David Lipscomb College, Trevacca College, Scarritt College for Christian Workers, American Baptist Theological Seminary, Aquinas Junior College,** and a branch of the University of Tennessee.

Educators and teachers will find particularly interesting Nashville's **Joint University Library,** which is operated by Peabody, Vanderbilt and Scarritt, the first large cooperative university library project in America. The program has been extended to an interchange of courses, one of the most significant advances in higher education in recent years.

Among Nashville's 500 manufacturing industries are country music recordings, printing and publishing, boots and shoes, rayon and cellophane, heaters, stoves, ranges, food products, hosiery and textiles, fabricated metal products.

NATCHEZ TRACE was an important early overland trail linking Nashville with the lower Mississippi River at Natchez. It became a post road in 1800, and was the route of General Jackson's men to and from the Battle of New Orleans.

Late in the nineteenth century the original Trace fell victim to railroad expansion, and disappeared into a few fragments of local roads. In 1938, however, Congress created the **Natchez Trace Parkway** as a unit of the national park system.

Near the Hohenwald, on the old Trace, is a **national monument to Meriwether Lewis,** who with William Clark first carried the American flag across the continent to the Pacific.

STONE'S RIVER, near Murfreesboro, marked the beginning of a two-year campaign that finally cut the Confederacy in two. While both sides claimed victory, casualties amounted to almost a third of the approximately 80,000 men engaged. The **Haxen Brigade Monument,** erected on the battlefield in early 1863, is believed to be the oldest Civil War memorial.

SPORTS AND RECREATION. **Shiloh National Military Park,** popular historic spot, was the scene of a major Civil War battle. Another interesting park is **Fort Donelson National Military Park.**

In the northwest corner of the state is **Reelfoot Lake,** formed by a violent earthquake in 1811. It has become one of the nation's finest natural fish hatcheries, and is popular for bird lovers as well. Reelfoot, a 14,000-acre lake, has facilities for **boating, fishing,** and **camping,** as do most of the parks and lakes throughout the state.

SPECIAL EVENTS. Memphis' **Cotton Carnival,** held each May, is highlighted by the arrival of the Cotton King and Queen on a brightly illuminated Mississippi River barge. Fireworks brighten the bluffs as the barge arrives with its entourage.

A **Tennessee Walking Horse Celebration** is held in Shelbyville in late August; **Robert E. Lee's birthday** is celebrated throughout the state January 19; and a **Catfish Derby** is held in Savannah every July.

The Midwest

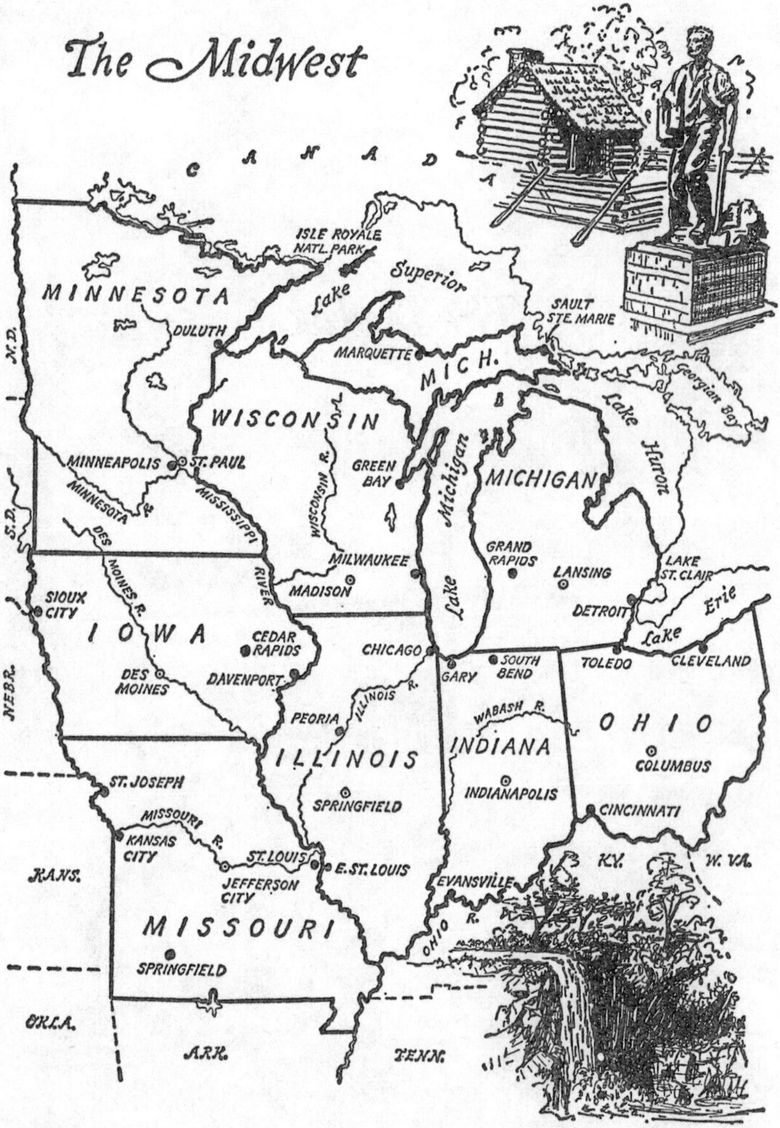
The Midwest
CANADA
ISLE ROYALE NATL. PARK
Lake Superior
SAULT STE. MARIE
MINNESOTA
DULUTH
MARQUETTE
MICH.
Georgian Bay
WISCONSIN
Lake Huron
N.D.
MINNEAPOLIS
ST. PAUL
GREEN BAY
MICHIGAN
Lake Michigan
MINNESOTA R.
MISSISSIPPI
WISCONSIN R.
S.D.
DES MOINES R.
RIVER
MILWAUKEE
GRAND RAPIDS
LANSING
LAKE ST. CLAIR
MADISON
SIOUX CITY
DETROIT
Lake Erie
IOWA
CEDAR RAPIDS
CHICAGO
NEBR.
DES MOINES
DAVENPORT
GARY
SOUTH BEND
TOLEDO
CLEVELAND
ILLINOIS R.
WABASH R.
PEORIA
OHIO
INDIANA
ILLINOIS
COLUMBUS
ST. JOSEPH
INDIANAPOLIS
SPRINGFIELD
CINCINNATI
MISSOURI R.
KANSAS CITY
ST. LOUIS
E. ST. LOUIS
KY.
W. VA.
KANS.
JEFFERSON CITY
EVANSVILLE
OHIO R.
MISSOURI
SPRINGFIELD
OKLA.
ARK.
TENN.

The Midwest

Though the Midwest is often fuzzily defined, the most meaningful delimitation comprises the eight states of the Great Lakes and upper Mississippi Valley: Michigan, Wisconsin, Minnesota, Ohio, Indiana, Illinois, Iowa, and Missouri. This large block, measuring 800 miles from east to west and 750 from north to south, contains 50 million people, over a quarter of the U.S. population.

The region is broad and flat, with many clusters of rolling hills, but no mountains. The northern stretch is studded with lakes and surviving patches of the magnificent forest the first explorers found. Craggy and wild Isle Royale, in Lake Superior, is the site of the only national park, but state parks preserve many beautiful wilderness and dune areas. The climate ranges from the record-breaking below-zero points in northern Minnesota, Wisconsin, and Michigan, where winters are long and snowy, to sunny southern Missouri, where winters are mild, summers scorching.

Early French explorers and fur trappers dotted the whole area with French names—Eau Claire, Terre Haute, Detroit, Fond du Lac, St. Louis, and many more. Vincennes, Indiana, was the scene of George Rogers Clark's Revolutionary War victory which helped insure that the vast region would be part of the new United States. The end of the war was the signal for a tremendous immigration from the eastern seaboard. Ohio became a state in 1803, the same year that the Louisiana Purchase gave the vast trans-Mississippi area, including Minnesota and Iowa, to the Union.

The stream of migrants from the eastern side of the Appalachians was soon swollen by immigrants from Europe, especially Germans. Cincinnati, St. Louis, Milwaukee, and other Midwest cities today bear a strong German imprint. The Irish potato famine sent another wave, to be followed later by Italians, Poles, Scandinavians, and others, in many instances establishing ethnic islands unmistakable to this day—Holland, Michigan; Swiss City, Indiana.

The first-generation pioneers who cut down the forests of the Midwest were followed by pioneers in other fields—inventors of new techniques of living. William Holmes McGuffey, president of Ohio University, published the famed McGuffey's Readers from which generations of Americans learned to read. In Kokomo, Indiana, Elwood Haynes built America's first automobile, and in Dayton, Ohio, Orville and Wilbur Wright invented the airplane. Cyrus McCormick's mechanical reaper helped make midcontinental America the world's richest agricultural region.

At the same time, major coal, oil, and gas deposits, plus fabulous iron ore ranges, stimulated an unparalleled industrial development, which was facilitated by the wealth of navigable waters. The opening of the St. Lawrence Seaway in 1959 gave Midwest industry and agriculture a direct link to the world market.

Scattered through the Midwest are fascinating samples of a succession of American architectural styles—solid, snug pioneer log cabins, many preserved in park areas; New England-type homes and streets, brought in by the first wave of settlers; Colonial and Greek Revival mansions along the Ohio River, built by migrants from Virginia and the Carolinas; covered bridges by the hundreds, especially in Indiana and Ohio; in the wintry north, homes built by Scandinavian settlers like those they had left in Sweden and Norway; and public buildings and homes by famed architects Louis Sullivan and Frank Lloyd Wright. A collection of the varied architecture of the region may be seen at Henry Ford's Greenfield Village near Detroit.

The Midwest is a great vacationland, with both summer and winter outdoor sports. A highway network ranging from Interstate expressways to country lanes takes the visitor to hunting and camping grounds, to fishing, boating, and swimming on rivers and lakes. For fishermen: catfish and trout in the rivers; bass, pike, perch, bluegill, crappie in the smaller lakes; lake trout, whitefish, bass, pickerel, and the giant fighting muskellunge on the Great Lakes. For hunters, throughout the region and subject to local limits: grouse, quail, pheasant, rabbit, squirrel, with deer plentiful in Michigan, Minnesota, and Wisconsin and excellent duck hunting in certain areas. Winter sports flourish in the northern regions of the same tier of states, with winter carnivals, ski tournaments, iceboat races, speed skating, even ice-harness racing and dog-team derbies.

Ohio

Ohio, most eastern of the midwestern states, is seventh in size among the states of the Midwest, with more than 41,000 square miles, but is second (after Illinois) in population. Ohio's location is both central and strategic. Along most of its northern border is the southern shore of Lake Erie. At the western end of Lake Erie the border becomes a land border, with Michigan to the north. On the east are Pennsylvania and West Virginia. The southern border is the winding course of the Ohio River from which the state takes its name (it is an Indian word meaning great). Kentucky and West Virginia lie to the south of the river. The ruler-straight western border is Indiana.

The shape of Ohio is almost a rectangle, dished in on the northern side, bulging out in a series of scallops (great bends of the Ohio River) on its southern side. The state measures slightly more than 200 miles east and west, north and south.

Ohio was the seventeenth state to be admitted to the Union. It is thirty-fifth in size, sixth in population. The buckeye is the state tree and Ohio is known as the *"Buckeye State."* The state flower is the scarlet carnation, the state bird, the cardinal.

THE LAND. The eastern flank of Ohio is made up of tumbling hills, from 900 to 1,400 feet in height, western foothills of the great Allegheny ranges. Toward the center of the state the hills subside into pleasantly rolling, fertile land. The northern edge, along Lake Erie, is a level plain, part of a former lake bed. The southern edge is a hilly plateau, from which ravines and gorges break sharply down to the Ohio River. In the south the small rivers, none of navigational importance, drain into the Ohio; in the north they drop into Lake Erie. The rolling central plain has the state's highest point, Campbell Hill, 1,550 feet high, a remnant of glacial action.

In the northeast corner of the state is a hill area studded with small lakes, both natural and man-made. The hill slopes have vineyards and orchards.

Ohio originally had nearly 30 million acres of hardwood forests, though they were cut down to clear land for farms, and provide timber for building. Now the state has in scattered patches about five million acres of forest land and woods (about 1.5 million of it within national forest reserves). The farms that replaced the forest, however, now spread over about 17 million acres, making Ohio one of the great agricultural regions of the country.

THE CLIMATE. Ohio's climate is called continental, with from 35 to 39 inches of rainfall scattered throughout the year and fairly well distributed over the state. Cleveland in the north has an average January temperature of about 28 degrees, and a July average of about 71 degrees; while Cincinnati in the south has a January average of 33 degrees, a July average of 76. There is a snow belt along the shore of Lake Erie where fairly heavy snowfalls are likely to occur in winter. The hottest part of the state in summer is around Cincinnati. Ohio is most pleasant in the late spring, summer and early fall.

THE PEOPLE. Ohioans like to claim that in its population pattern and in the origins of the people who settled in Ohio it is the most typically American of all states, with people from every other eastern state and many foreign countries in a balanced ethnic pattern. But the earliest Ohioans were prehistoric Indians called the Mound Builders, and the first explorers were French, seeking furs. They found them, but they could not hold the land. Making alliances with the Indians, British soldiers and explorers from the English colonies along the Atlantic seaboard built wilderness garrisons (some later to become cities) and held the land against the French.

Following the American Revolution, Ohio was organized as a part of the Northwest Territory (roughly the present area of the Midwest). And with the war's end settlement of Ohio began. The first settlement was at Marietta,

near the Ohio River, in 1788, with Cincinnati founded the same year.

Twelve years after the first settlement, and three years before Ohio became a state, the area had a population of more than 45,000. They came chiefly from three regions: New England, Pennsylvania and Kentucky. Among them was a man called Johnny Appleseed, whose passion for orchards was to give the fields cut from the forests a springtime pattern of flowering trees, and still gives Ohio high rank among apple-producing states.

Many settlers in the early years were Scotch-Irish from the mountains of Virginia and North Carolina. Many of them had been soldiers of the Revolution with grants of virgin land from a grateful government unable to pay them in money.

Sometimes there were whole villages of log cabins. One which has been restored and rebuilt is **Schoenbrunn,** in eastern Ohio, which was a settlement of Moravian Germans.

The opening of the Erie Canal in 1825 offered a new and easy route for the settlement of Ohio, with thousands of families moving in from northern New York and New England. In 1830 the population of the young state was nearly a million.

At about the same time a great wave of Germans moved into Ohio. They established the first organ factory, the first bank, first woolen and flour mills. Many of them settled in Cincinnati, giving that booming center the distinctive Germanic character it has today.

Poles, Czechoslovakians, Rumanians, Yugoslavs, Lithuanians, and Bulgarians settled in the new cities along the shore of Lake Erie that were turning ore from Minnesota, coal and gas from Ohio into iron and steel.

At the turn of the century the pattern of population was set in its present form, with more than four million people representing most nations of Europe and many areas of the eastern United States fused in a balanced and distinctively American mold. Today over ten million persons live in Ohio.

AGRICULTURE. Farm production, with 9 million acres used for crops and the balance for grazing and wood lots, is highly diversified. The chief crop is corn, grown largely in western Ohio, where hog raising is also important. Other crops include hay, wheat, potatoes, sugar beets, soybeans, tobacco, and in the northeast, grape vineyards.

INDUSTRY. More rubber goods, automobile tires (both made in Akron) and clay products are manufactured in Ohio than in any other state. It is also a leader in steel and iron production, and in mining of rock salt and coal (which is the state's chief mineral resource, found in eastern and southern Ohio). Papermaking is another important industry in the southern part of the state, and Ohio is second only to Pennsylvania in the making of coke. Ohio is first in machine tools, cutlery, glassware, business machines, playing cards, pottery, electrical machinery, and dishwashers.

CITIES. Though Ohio has an unusually large number of large and important cities (eight have more than 100,000 population), equally important are more than 3,500 communities of less than 1,000 population.

AKRON, 30 miles southeast of Cleveland, has a population of over 275,000 and is the chief producer of rubber goods in the world. The city is also the U.S. center for lighter-than-air craft and has an enormous air dock built to accommodate such giant dirigibles as the **Akron** and **Macon,** both of which were constructed here. Each year Akron draws big crowds to the **Blossom Music Center,** the largest structure of its kind in the world. The **International Soap Box Derby** is held in Akron also.

ATHENS, 35 miles west of **Marietta** (Ohio's first settlement), in the southeast part of the state, has a population of about 23,000. It is the site of **Ohio University,** oldest (1804) college in the entire Northwest Territory. On the pleasant campus are towering elms, a

memorial to William McGuffey, one-time president of the institution.

CANTON, 20 miles southeast of Akron, has a population of more than 110,000 and is an important steel producing center. Among its special products are roller bearings and diesel engines. President William McKinley, who was born in Niles, is buried in a handsome, massive tomb in Canton.

CINCINNATI, with a population of about 452,000, is situated in the extreme southwest corner of the state, on the Ohio River opposite Kentucky. It is the second largest city in Ohio (after Cleveland), and was the first big city to be settled (1788). Built on a series of terraces rising from the river, the present city climbs over and around hills that spread north, east and west. It began as an important port on the Ohio River and has become one of the great transportation centers of the country for rail, highway, and air travel. The city's railway terminal is notable for its design.

Cincinnati products include soap, watches, printing ink, paper, playing cards, machine tools. Things to see include the **Taft House Museum, Eden Park,** with a fine zoo, and scene of summer opera performances, the **Cincinnati Art Museum.** The city's symphony orchestra is one of the best in the country. A state park, to the west, contains the **tomb of President William H. Harrison.**

CLEVELAND, about 125 miles northeast of Columbus, has a population of more than a million, is the largest city in Ohio, seventh largest in the country. It is a chief port on the Great Lakes, south shore of Lake Erie, and one of the main highway and rail hubs in the Midwest. Cleveland's huge industrial complex includes some of the country's biggest steel mills, foundries, oil refineries, machine shops, fabricating plants of all types. Its products include electrical equipment, machine tools, automobile parts, and chemicals.

Interesting sights include a **new civic center** on the lake shore, the **Western Reserve Historical Society Museum,** the **Cleveland Museum of Art,** the **Cleveland Cultural Gardens, Lake View Cemetery** with the tomb of President Garfield, the **civic theater,** a **zoo,** and **horticultural gardens,** and the world-famous **Cleveland Symphony Orchestra.** Just east is **Nela Park,** a research center for the General Electric Company, which offers tours to visitors.

COLUMBUS, on the Scioto River, 70 miles northeast of Dayton and 125 miles southeast of Cleveland, is the centrally located state capital. It has a population of about 540,000, third largest in the state. Columbus is an important hub of railways and highways, a big distribution and manufacturing center, and the trading center for a rich area. The large campus of **Ohio State University** is on the north side of town. The city's products include paper, foundry supplies, aircraft (North American Aviation), auto parts, glass, footwear, clothing. In addition to the **capitol building,** a notable example of Greek Revival architecture, and the university campus, the **Ohio State Museum** and **Ohio Historical Center** are worth seeing.

DAYTON, 45 miles north of Cincinnati in the Miami Valley, has a population of about 243,000. Though the city's fame is derived from aviation (it was the home of the Wright brothers, who invented the airplane, and is today the chief U.S. aviation center), its industries include machine tools, cash registers, refrigerators, air-conditioning equipment, and paper. Interesting sights include a **museum** in the **home of poet Paul Laurence Dunbar;** the **Dayton Art Institute;** the **graves of the Wright brothers** and **Dunbar,** located in a nearby cemetery; and the **city's first courthouse,** of Greek Revival architecture.

OXFORD, near the Indiana state line, has a population of approximately 15,000, and possesses something of the atmosphere of an English country town. Its principal attraction is the big campus of **Miami University,** with a few historic buildings, including the **William Holmes**

McGuffey home and a **museum of McGuffey memorabilia.**

TOLEDO, about 90 miles west of Cleveland on Lake Erie, is an important Great Lakes port and a center for rail traffic, handling big shipments of coal and oil. The city has a population of about 383,000 and spreads over both banks of the Maumee River, just east of its mouth at Lake Erie. Plants turn out automobile parts, glass, electrical equipment, steel. Tourist attractions include the **art museum;** a **Roman Catholic cathedral,** notable for its design; and a zoo. Monuments just west in the Maumee Valley mark the pioneer battle of **Fallen Timbers** and the sites of two pioneer forts, **Miamis** and **Meigs.**

YOUNGSTOWN, just west of the Pennsylvania state line, 65 miles southeast of Cleveland and linked to it by the Ohio Turnpike, has a metropolitan area population of over 500,000. It is the hub of an industrial district making and processing pig-iron, steel, coke, chemicals, and cement. The **Butler Art Institute** is small but interesting.

SPORTS AND RECREATION. Most popular sports in Ohio are those which take place on or around the state's many lakes. Well-known recreation areas include Lake Erie, Buckeye Lake, Lake Hope, and man-made reservoirs–Berlin, Mosquito Creek, and Senecaville. Spectator sports, which have nationwide followings, are **professional football,** played by the Cleveland Browns; **college football,** especially at Ohio State University; and **professional baseball,** with two major-league teams–the Cleveland Indians and Cincinnati Reds.

SPECIAL EVENTS. The boys' **All-American Soap Box Derby** is held in Akron in August. Also well known is the **Ohio State Fair,** held in Columbus the week before Labor Day. Other interesting events are the **International Festival,** Toledo, early May; **Bach Festival,** at Baldwin-Wallace College in Berea, June; and the **Jackson Apple Festival,** September.

Indiana

Of the eight Midwestern states, Indiana, with about 36,000 square miles, is the smallest, but its five million population ranks it fourth in the Midwest.

Indiana is bordered by Michigan, Lake Michigan, Ohio, the Ohio River, Kentucky, the Wabash River, and Illinois.

Indiana is roughly rectangular. The north-south dimension is about 280 miles, along the western side, with the width of the state east-west almost uniformly 160 miles.

Although it is called the *"Hoosier State,"* no one knows why. The state flower is the peony, the state bird is the cardinal, the state tree the tulip tree (yellow poplar). Indiana was the nineteenth state admitted to the Union.

THE LAND. Indiana is divided into three quite different regions. In the northeast are rolling hills set with hundreds of lakes. Both the lakes and the hills are of glacial origin. Through the center of the state stretches an almost level, once grassy plain, now productive farmland. Most of the southern third is rugged–knobby, steeply sloped hills rising above narrow valleys, once completely covered by a superb hardwood forest. A few patches of the primeval forest are preserved here and there in park areas and farm wood lots.

In the north is the sandy shore of Lake Michigan, shared now by resort towns, state park areas (which preserve a completely unique region of giant sand dunes), and the nation's heaviest concentration of diversified industry, the great iron and steel producing district of the Calumet. Under the limestone hills of the southern section are hundreds of miles of caverns, including **Wyandotte Cave,** the third largest in the country. Muck land in the north, once thought a useless swamp, has rich and deep soil.

The famed Wabash River, rising in the northeast, flows west and south to join the Ohio at the southwest corner of the state. A tributary of the Wabash, wholly within the state, gained national fame when a battle was fought on its banks. When General William Henry Harrison, who defeated the Indian chief, Tecumseh, became a presidential candidate, the river's name, Tippecanoe, became a part of his campaign slogan ("Tippecanoe and Tyler too"—John Tyler, the vice-presidential candidate succeeding Harrison when the latter died after a month in office). The highest point of the state, in the southeast, is 1,257 feet; the lowest, on the Ohio River, is 320 feet.

THE CLIMATE. The climate of Indiana is marked by sharply defined seasons, sometimes sudden weather changes. Rainfall, fairly high and spread throughout the year, averages about 40 inches. Winter temperature ranges from about 29 degrees in the north to about 35 in the south, though winter periods of zero weather and heavy snowfalls are not uncommon. Summer averages range from about 73 to 86 degrees, sometimes over 100 degrees. Humidity is often high.

THE PEOPLE. The French, moving in from Canada and across the Great Lakes, were the first Europeans to explore Indiana. The first settlement was a French trading post called Vincennes, fortified in 1732 on the Wabash, but the French left no marks on the land except names of places such as Terre Haute, La Porte, Vincennes. By the second half of the eighteenth century control had passed to the British and settlers from the British colonies were beginning to filter in, coming down the Ohio and across Kentucky, becoming a steady stream after the end of the Revolutionary War. As in Ohio, many were former soldiers who held land grants in lieu of pay. They cleared fields, built pioneer settlements, and lived in log cabins. One pioneer family named Lincoln had come from Kentucky with their young son, Abraham. Soon after they came, the mother, Nancy Hanks, died and the boy Abraham helped his father bury her in the forest. The grave is one of the most touching memorials of pioneer days in the Midwest today. Not far from it to the north is a complete pioneer village with stores, gristmill and many houses, developed in a valley. Called **Spring Mill,** it has been fully restored and preserved within a state park.

In 1800, when the Indiana Territory, including what are now the states of Illinois, Wisconsin, Michigan and part of Minnesota, was created with Vincennes as its headquarters, Indiana contained about 5,000 people. Ten years later the number was about 25,000. Four years after Indiana became a state in 1816, population had swelled to nearly 150,000. Among the settlers were thousands of immigrants from Europe, including the Swiss who moved into the forests to develop woodworking and furniture-making. They named Switzerland County, and the river settlement of Tell City. Germans helped develop Terre Haute and the state's young capital of Indianapolis, becoming bankers and brewers and civic leaders. **New Harmony** on the Wabash was to become the site of two differently planned efforts of communal living, first by Germans, later by Scotch. Their efforts created one of the most charming village centers in the Midwest.

Throughout the last half of the nineteenth century the character of Indiana changed slowly, from rural-agricultural to a highly industrialized region. In 1905 the United States Steel Corporation selected a tract of sand dunes on the south shore of Lake Michigan as the site of a new steel city, Gary. The city became the core of a vast industrial complex devoted to steel, iron and chemicals, stretching 45 miles along the shore of the lake in the great Calumet region. Now this area has more than 500,000 people.

AGRICULTURE. Indiana's biggest crop is corn, and the inevitable companion of corn, hogs. Tomatoes, winter wheat, and other grains are widely grown. Orchards are extensive throughout the state (Johnny Appleseed, who started many of them in pioneer days, is buried in Indiana). The rich muck land in the northern half produces huge quantities of potatoes, cabbages, onions, peppermint, and spearmint. The state ranks high in soybean production.

In the west and southwest there are more than 200 coal mines from which more than 20 million tons of bituminous coal are dug each year. To the east of the coal mining region are the limestone quarries, accounting for more than 80 percent of the building stone used in the country. Major quarrying centers are around the two towns of Bloomington and Bedford.

INDUSTRY. Indiana's factories, more than 8,000 of them, are widely dispersed throughout the state, except for the concentration of steel and iron plants in the Calumet district. Industry leaders include Lilly Pharmaceutical Company of Indianapolis, which began as a drugstore and is now one of the largest pharmaceutical producers; Allison Engineering, Indianapolis, which has several plants for the manufacture of jet engines; and dozens of furniture factories throughout the state. Other large plants turn out automotive parts and appliances, prefabricated homes, canned tomatoes and vegetables, agricultural and roadmaking machinery, radio and television parts. Indiana also has several large meat packing plants.

CITIES. Of a total of nearly 3,000 settled communities, only about 250 have populations over 1,000; only six have more than 100,000; and only one over half a million.

BLOOMINGTON, 50 miles south of Indianapolis, is the center of a great limestone district. It is the site of **Indiana University** and its beautifully wooded campus.

EVANSVILLE, an industrial city, is located near **Lincoln Boyhood National Memorial** including the **grave of Nancy Hanks Lincoln,** mother of Abraham. The village of **Santa Claus** handles mail from and to all the world at Christmas.

FORT WAYNE (population 180,000) is about 100 miles northeast of Indianapolis. It developed from a French trading post and Revolutionary fort, from which it is named. The **grave of Johnny Appleseed** is in a local cemetery.

There are dozens of lakes in northeast Indiana, many with resort facilities, offering fishing and boating. On one, Maxinkuckee, is **Culver Military Academy.**

GARY, with a population of about 175,000, is the chief city of the Calumet steel producing region, on the shore of Lake Michigan just east of Chicago. East of Gary is a state park, preserving **giant dunes** and the flora found among them.

INDIANAPOLIS, capital and largest city in the state, is almost in its center, and is the hub of a network of rail lines, highways, and air traffic. It is also Indiana's chief industrial and business city. With a population of over 1.1 million in the metropolitan area, Indianapolis is the second largest city in the country not on navigable water.

It is famed for the **500-Mile Memorial Day automobile race**–staged on a two and one half mile oval track on the northwest side of the city. Other points of interest include the **Circle** with its Civil War Monument, in the center of the city; a **World War Memorial Plaza** with a great museum and monument; and the **national headquarters** of the **American Legion.** The spacious new campus of **Butler University** on the north side is worth seeing, as is **Fort Benjamin Harrison,** just northeast of Indianapolis. The **John Herron Museum** has a small but excellent collection and a good art school.

Northwest of Indianapolis, at Lafayette, is **Purdue University.**

NEW HARMONY, southwest of Vincennes on the Wabash, is the village where two successive groups tried to establish communistic colonies. Both movements failed but their historic old buildings remain.

SOUTH BEND (population about 125,000), site of a former Indian village, located just a few miles south of the

Michigan border, was the first point in Indiana to receive a name (from its situation on the St. Joseph River) when visited by the French explorer La Salle. South Bend is famed for **Notre Dame University,** located on the north side of town. Its football team is nationally known.

VINCENNES, on the Wabash 125 miles southwest of Indianapolis, is the oldest and historically most interesting city in the state. Fortified by the French in 1732, it was a frontier garrison and trading post, has a charming **French cathedral,** an impressive **memorial to George Rogers Clark,** who defeated the British at Vincennes in a decisive battle, and a moving **monument** to **Abraham Lincoln.**

SPORTS AND RECREATION. In Indiana, there are 17 state parks built around gorges, primitive wooded areas, lakes, along rivers, and other natural features. Some preserve historic buildings and monuments; many have excellent facilities for **fishing** and **boating.** In addition, there are hundreds of natural lakes in the northeast, as well as six important man-made lakes in the southern part of the state that offer boating and fishing.

SPECIAL EVENTS. The **Indianapolis 500-Mile auto race,** held on Memorial Day in the city's Motor Speedway, is witnessed each year by over 200,000 persons, and is the state's best-known event. Other important dates are **Creole King Ball,** Vincennes, January 6; **Apple Blossom Festival,** Brown County, May; **Indiana State Fair,** Indianapolis, late August or early September; **Pike County Catfish Festival,** Petersburg, mid-October; and **Indiana Day,** statewide, December 11.

Illinois

Among the eight states of the Midwest, Illinois is fourth in size, with more than 56,000 square miles, but first in population with more than eleven million people. The northern boundary is Wisconsin; on the east is the shore of Lake Michigan and Indiana, with the Wabash River near the lower tip. The western border is the Mississippi River, with Iowa opposite in the northwest and Missouri in the southwest. The short, winding, southern border is the Ohio River, with Kentucky opposite.

Illinois is shaped like a funnel. The greatest length of the state north to south is nearly 400 miles, and over 200 miles at its greatest east-west width.

In the nation, Illinois is the twenty-fourth state in area, fifth state in population. The name Illinois is a French corruption for Illini, meaning the land of great men or warriors. The state flower is the violet, the state bird the cardinal, and the state tree the bur oak. Illinois was the twenty-first state to be admitted to the Union, in 1818.

THE LAND. Although Illinois is now known as *"Land of Lincoln,"* its former name, *"Prairie State,"* gives a reasonably accurate description. Much of it is level, and in its natural state was covered with prairie grass. There are a few areas of low, rolling hills, and a few sections of natural forest. The extreme northwest has the highest point in the state, 1,235 feet, while the southern and lowest point, 279 feet, is the meeting of the Mississippi and Ohio rivers.

Stretching diagonally across the state, from the northeast to the southwest, is the Illinois River, linked to Lake Michigan by a canal, providing a deep water channel from the Great Lakes to the Mississippi. The combination of navigable river channels gives Illinois an unusual facility for commercial shipping.

THE CLIMATE. With little to break the sweep of the prevailing west-east winds, the weather of Illinois is subject to sudden sharp changes in temperature. Seasonal variations are also marked. Annual rainfall spread throughout the year averages from 30 to 35 inches, is heavier in the south. Chicago has an average January temperature of about 26 degrees, and an average of 75 degrees in summer. However, zero temperatures in the winter are not uncommon in the north; summer temperatures in the state not infrequently rise to over 100 degrees. The extreme southern tip of the state, an area known as Little Egypt, has unusually mild weather.

THE PEOPLE. The first people in Illinois, the Mound Builders, who built **Cahokia** mound near East St. Louis, had all disappeared when the French explorers, Father Marquette and Joliet, traveled down the Illinois River in 1673, to be followed by La Salle a few years later. The French established several missions and trading posts at La Salle, Marseilles, and Champaign. In 1810 there were about 12,000 people. Then the tide of migration began, chiefly families seeking easier farming than they had found in southern Indiana. Two years after Illinois became a state in 1818, the population was 55,000, and ten years later there were three times as many. During the mid-nineteenth century the invention of the reaping machine by an Illinois citizen named McCormick and the coming of the railways speeded settlement.

When the great streams of immigrants came from foreign countries, the Chicago area received first the Germans and Irish; later Italians, Poles, Hungarians, Lithuanians. Chicago, next to New York, now has the most polyglot population in the country. Many of these varied nationalities have made great cultural and economic contributions to the state.

AGRICULTURE. Bountiful crops of corn, soybeans, and wheat are grown yearly in the rich Illinois soil, whose level, unbroken areas make mechanized farming increasingly important. Almost two-thirds of the state's 30 million acres of farmland are devoted to corn, though cotton is grown in the rich river bottomlands of southern Illinois. The livestock industry—including dairy farming in the north and raising of hogs and cattle elsewhere, has become increasingly more important. As a result, Chicago is the largest meat processing and marketing center in the world.

Bituminous coal mines, extensive oil and gas fields are found in southern Illinois, while Hardin County, in the extreme southeast, accounts for 50 percent of the nation's supply of mineral fluorspar. Throughout the state are great beds of gravel and sand.

INDUSTRY. More than 18,000 Illinois factories, mills, packing and assembling plants make it one of the most important industrial regions in the world, with about 75 percent of the state's manufacturing concentrated in and around Chicago. Illinois leads the nation in making railway cars, telephone and radio equipment, sporting goods, printing, perfumes, cosmetics, tin cans. Chicago is near the top (next to New York) in the facilities and volume of selling and is first in mail-order selling. It is one of the nation's largest producers of steel and iron.

Elgin produces more watches than any city; Moline and Peoria are in top positions in making farm implements. Atomic energy for peacetime use is made at the Dresden Nuclear Power Station outside of Chicago.

CITIES. Apart from Chicago, only two cities in the state have a population of more than 100,000. In spite of this, more than 80 percent of Illinois' residents live in urban areas.

CAIRO (population about 6,000) is situated at the extreme southern tip of the state, at the junction of the Ohio and Mississippi rivers, protected from frequent floods by levees. The region, called Little Egypt, produces cotton for which Cairo is the shipping point.

CHAMPAIGN-URBANA. In east-central Illinois, dominating a region devoted to growing corn, is Champaign, with its companion city of Urbana, just east, the home of the **University of Illinois.** The huge campus, with some notable buildings and facilities, is worth seeing. The two cities together have a population of about 163,000.

CHICAGO. Second largest city in the nation in population (over three million), and second largest in area (after

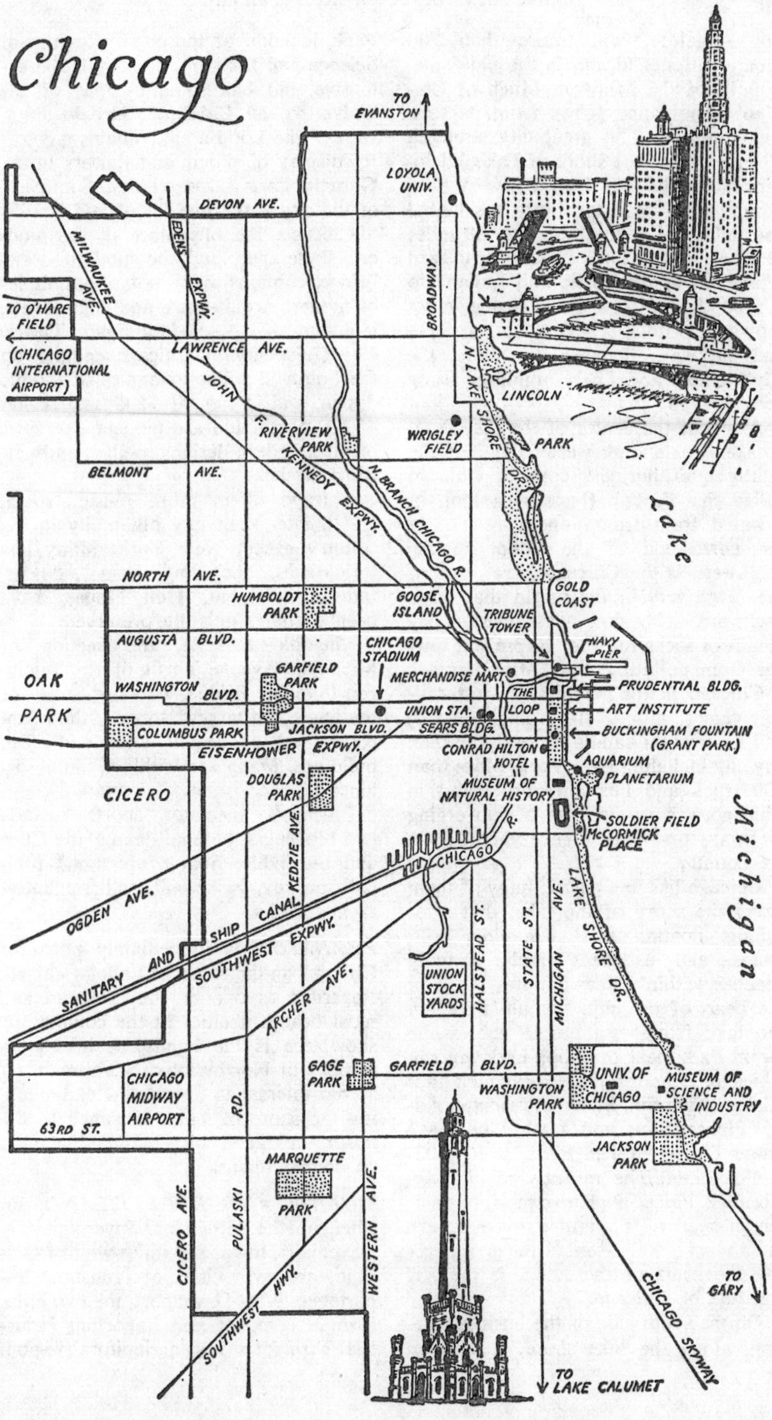
Chicago
TO EVANSTON
LOYOLA UNIV.
DEVON AVE.
EDENS EXPWY.
MILWAUKEE AVE.
BROADWAY
TO O'HARE FIELD
(CHICAGO INTERNATIONAL AIRPORT)
LAWRENCE AVE.
JOHN F. KENNEDY EXPWY.
N. LAKE SHORE DR.
LINCOLN PARK
RIVERVIEW PARK
WRIGLEY FIELD
BELMONT AVE.
N. BRANCH CHICAGO R.
Lake Michigan
NORTH AVE.
HUMBOLDT PARK
GOOSE ISLAND
GOLD COAST
TRIBUNE TOWER
NAVY PIER
AUGUSTA BLVD.
CHICAGO STADIUM
GARFIELD PARK
MERCHANDISE MART
PRUDENTIAL BLDG.
OAK PARK
WASHINGTON BLVD.
THE LOOP
UNION STA.
ART INSTITUTE
COLUMBUS PARK
JACKSON BLVD.
SEARS BLDG.
BUCKINGHAM FOUNTAIN (GRANT PARK)
EISENHOWER EXPWY.
CONRAD HILTON HOTEL
AQUARIUM
PLANETARIUM
CICERO
DOUGLAS PARK
MUSEUM OF NATURAL HISTORY
SOLDIER FIELD
McCORMICK PLACE
KEDZIE AVE.
CHICAGO R.
OGDEN AVE.
SANITARY AND SHIP CANAL
SOUTHWEST EXPWY.
HALSTEAD ST.
STATE ST.
MICHIGAN AVE.
LAKE SHORE DR.
UNION STOCK YARDS
ARCHER AVE.
GAGE PARK
GARFIELD BLVD.
CHICAGO MIDWAY AIRPORT
RD.
WASHINGTON PARK
UNIV. OF CHICAGO
MUSEUM OF SCIENCE AND INDUSTRY
63RD ST.
JACKSON PARK
MARQUETTE PARK
CICERO AVE.
PULASKI
WESTERN AVE.
SOUTHWEST HWY.
CHICAGO SKYWAY
TO GARY
TO LAKE CALUMET

Los Angeles), with more than 200 square miles, Chicago is the chief metropolis of the Midwest. Much of Chicago's dominance grows from its strategic position. The great city stretches 20 miles along the shore of Lake Michigan, facing the lake from the west. Suburban developments, both residential and industrial, take up another 30 miles of lake front in both directions, toward Wisconsin in the north, and Indiana to the southeast. The lake is the city's showcase, with a superb chain of parks and parkways flanking the shore, the city's tallest and finest buildings rising behind them.

At about the center of the lake front area and extending west from it is the tightly built business core of Chicago called the **"Loop"** (because a loop of elevated train tracks encircles it). At the north end of the Loop, angling southwest, is the **Chicago River,** one of the few rivers in the world that flows backward. The flow was reversed by means of locks in order to prevent sewage from polluting Lake Michigan.

Chicago is the world's greatest railway center, with 23 trunk line railways, and its airports handle more traffic than any city including New York. More than 500 truck and bus lines are based in Chicago, using a network of converging highways that lead to every corner of the country.

Chicago has fine parks, many of them along the shore of the lake, that offer fishing, boating and swimming, golf, tennis, and excellent public bathing beaches within a few minutes' walk of the heart of the city. **Lincoln Park,** on the lake front, has a fine zoo, while **Grant Park,** near the Loop in downtown Chicago, contains the **Chicago Natural History Museum, Shedd Aquarium, Adler Planetarium;** and farther up Lake Shore Drive, **Soldier Field,** a 101,000-seat stadium. The recently rebuilt **McCormick Place,** a giant exposition center, is nearby. It was destroyed by fire in January, 1967. Behind the park, facing the heart of the Loop, is the **Art Institute of Chicago.**

On the south side of the business section, along the lake shore, is **Jackson Park,** location of the city's **Museum of Science and Industry.** Nearby is the extensive and handsome campus of the **University of Chicago. Garfield Park,** west of the Loop area, contains a colorful display of plants and flowers in the **Garfield Park Conservatory.** Southwest of the city is the fine **Brookfield Zoo.**

Chicago, the birthplace of the modern skyscraper, and the modern drawbridge, contains many notable examples of modern architecture and engineering, including the 1,450-foot **Sears Tower.** The University of Chicago campus on the South Side has examples of Gothic design, and in the **"Gold Coast"** region of the north side are pioneer examples of ultramodern designs in glass and polished steel.

Chicago offers more music, opera, and theater than any other city in the country except New York. Many historic sites, including Jane Addams' famed settlement, **Hull House,** have been partially or fully preserved.

Magnificent Mile, the section of Michigan Avenue north of the Michigan Avenue Bridge, contains some of the finest and largest stores in the country, as well as elegant hotels and office buildings. Many are within walking distance of each other.

Chicago's spectator sports include two big-league baseball teams, the **Cubs** and the **White Sox; professional football, hockey, basketball,** and five **horse-racing tracks.**

EVANSTON is immediately north of Chicago on the shore of Lake Michigan. Regarded as one of the best run and most beautiful cities in the country, its showpiece is the handsome lake-shore campus of **Northwestern University.** Of scenic interest is **Sheridan Road** flanking the shore of Lake Michigan to the north, linking a succession of opulent residential towns.

MOLINE AND ROCK ISLAND, located on the Mississippi River opposite Davenport, Iowa, 130 miles west of Chicago, are twin cities of industrial importance. With Davenport, the two cities form a compact and important industrial core for a rich agricultural region.

Moline is known as the "plow city" because of a great farm machinery plant there. Rock Island takes its name from and is identified with the United States Rock Island Arsenal (established in 1862) on an island in the Mississippi. **Black Hawk State Park,** with a museum, is nearby. The two cities have a combined population of about 100,000.

PEORIA, 60 miles north of Springfield, in central Illinois, on the Illinois River (population over 125,000), is Illinois' third-largest city. It is a deep-water shipping point, with the Illinois River, its waters controlled by a nearby dam, making a big lake extending north for more than 30 miles. The lake provides excellent boating and fishing. Peoria is famed for its great factories, of which two turn out whiskey and roadmaking machinery (tours offered). The site of a pioneer French fort called **Fort Crève Coeur** is opposite the city on the east bank of the river.

ROCKFORD, a city of about 150,000 people 90 miles northwest of Chicago, with numerous manufacturing concerns, is the nation's second-largest machine-tool center. Using natural advantages of water power and fertile prairies, it has had steady growth since pioneer days.

SPRINGFIELD (population over 90,000), the state capital, is located in central Illinois, 175 miles southwest of Chicago. Seat of Sangamon County, and on the river of that name, Springfield is in the heart of a rich agricultural region and is the shipping point for bituminous coal from mines to the south. Its name is forever associated with Abraham Lincoln. His home, the only one Lincoln ever owned, has been preserved and is a popular visitors' attraction. The **Lincoln Tomb,** marked with a high spire and a statue of Lincoln in the front, contains the bodies of Lincoln, Mrs. Lincoln, and three of their four sons. It is one of America's most famous shrines. The **Centennial Building,** near the **state capitol,** includes much Lincoln material.

The restored pioneer village of **New Salem,** about 20 miles northwest of Springfield is where Lincoln lived for six years after coming to Illinois from Indiana.

SPORTS AND RECREATION. Throughout Illinois, thousands of acres of scenic beauty and areas of historic interest are set aside in 110 state parks, memorials, and conservation areas for the recreation of visitors. **Fishing, boating,** and **hunting** for geese, duck, and game make the state popular with outdoorsmen. Tourist attractions include **Starved Rock; Wild Bill Hickok Memorial;** the cities of **Galena** and **Nauvoo; Fort Kaskaskia** and **Pere Marquette state parks;** the **Cahokia** and **Dixon Indian mounds,** and many more. **New Salem State Park,** near Springfield, contains a reconstructed village, erected as a monument to Abraham Lincoln and furnished with actual articles used in the town in the 1830's. The **Lincoln Heritage Trail,** recently completed highway in Illinois, Indiana, and Kentucky, makes it easy for tourists to visit points of historic interest from Lincoln's time.

Chicago has excellent beaches, boating, fishing, and a diverse assortment of sights and facilities. Spectator sports, except for Chicago, are generally collegiate contests in **baseball, basketball** and **football.** Golfers find good courses scattered over the state.

SPECIAL EVENTS. In addition to Chicago's annual **International Live Stock Exposition,** held in November, yearly events include **Winter Carnival,** in Glen Ellyn, early January; **Golden Gloves Boxing Tournament,** in Chicago, early February; **Apple Blossom Tour,** in Calhoun County, late May; **Illinois State Fair,** Springfield, late August; **Grape Festival,** Nauvoo, early September; and **Illinois Valley Kennel Club Show,** Peoria, mid-November.

Michigan

Among the states of the Midwest, Michigan, with more than 58,000 square miles and over eight million people, is third in both size and population. It is the only state in the Union with two sections completely split by a deep-water channel. The lower peninsula, shaped like a large mitten, with 40,000 square miles, has most of the population. The upper peninsula, with 16,000 square miles, is shaped like a narrow, irregular triangle. Michigan has a shoreline of 2,232 miles.

Michigan was the twenty-sixth state to be admitted to the United States (1837). Among the states of the Union it ranks twenty-third in size, seventh in population. The state flower is the apple blossom, state bird the robin. The name is a corruption of an Indian word "michigama," meaning "large water." It is called the *"Wolverine State"* although there is no record proving that such an animal was ever found in Michigan. The name is thought to be originated by the Indians and French as an expression of contempt for outlanders arriving from the east in the early nineteenth century.

THE LAND. Most of the lower peninsula was smoothed down to low rolling hills and wide level areas by the glacial action which created the Great Lakes. But the glaciers touched and shaped only the eastern end of the upper peninsula. The western end is rugged, with wild tumbled hills, extension of the mountains of southern Canada, rising to nearly 2,000 feet in the Porcupine Mountains, the highest point in the state. The lowest level is on the shore of Lake Erie in the south, 572 feet above sea level. Much of the original forest was destroyed during settlement and subsequent development. Present forest areas, more than 19 million acres, are largely second growth, with a few patches of the original forest.

The shoreline of Michigan's lower peninsula is low, with many beaches, many with giant dunes. It is broken by bays and harbors, including **Grand Traverse Bay** on the Lake Michigan side and **Saginaw Bay** on the Lake Huron side. Three large bays and dozens of small ones fringe the rugged shore of the upper peninsula. On the east is Whitefish Bay, on the north, opening into Lake Superior, is **Keweenaw Bay,** and on the south, opening into Lake Michigan and shared with Wisconsin, is **Green Bay.**

Studded over both peninsulas are more than 11,000 large and small lakes. Offshore, in the Great Lakes, are hundreds of islands. The largest, in Lake Superior, is rugged, primitive **Isle Royale,** the only island national park in the U.S.A. Most famous is **Mackinac Island,** in the Straits of Mackinac. Other large islands are **Beaver** in Lake Michigan and **Bois Blanc** in the Straits of Mackinac.

The **Straits of Mackinac** connect Lake Huron and Lake Michigan. Soaring over the wide channel now is one of the **world's longest suspension bridges.** A strait called **St. Mary's River** winds between Canada and Michigan's upper peninsula, links Lake Superior with Lake Huron. Once set with wild rapids, it is now controlled by a series of giant locks, serving deep-water traffic. The third strait, with the **St. Clair River** at its north, **Lake St. Clair** in the middle, and the **Detroit River** in the south, links Lake Huron with Lake Erie. Detroit dominates its lower end, facing Canada from the west.

THE CLIMATE. Variations in climate between the upper and lower peninsulas are substantial. In the upper peninsula the mean average January temperature is about 15 degrees, the mean average July temperature 64. But Detroit has a mean average January temperature of 26 degrees, and an average for July of 74. Rainfall averages about 30 inches, well dispersed throughout the year (in the winter there are likely to be heavy snows). The northern peninsula has an annual precipitation of about 31 inches, much of it falling as snow in the winter.

Though the waters of the Great Lakes seldom freeze solidly in winter, smaller lakes, channels and rivers do freeze, providing ice sports and ice fishing. Michigan's deep snows provide fine skiing.

THE PEOPLE. The French explorer Étienne Brulé landed at Sault Ste. Marie in 1618. Within a few years a steady trickle of *voyageurs* and *coureurs de bois* were coming into Michigan. Sault Ste. Marie became the first permanent settlement in the area in 1668. In 1671 another settlement, to become the town of St. Ignace, was established. The Indians called the place Michilimackinac. (Later it was to become Mackinac.) For the French the lure of the forests was furs, and within a few years the annual shipment of pelts exceeded 200,000. In 1701, Detroit was established as a control point for the fur trade. The French established genuine colonies in Michigan, and in some cities today there are a number of old families of French origin.

After the opening of the Erie Canal in 1825, a steady stream of settlers moved in, chiefly from New England and New York. In 1830, seven years before Michigan became a state, the population was about 32,000. In 1840, it had jumped to more than 200,000.

German settlers maintained their own customs and language. In 1914 there were 200 church congregations in Michigan where services were conducted in German. Large numbers of Irish immigrated to Michigan, to become miners and laborers, and to work in the lumber camps that were beginning to ravage and destroy the state's proud forests. A special group were religious refugees from Holland. They established a colony in southwest Michigan, named their settlement Holland, drained marshland to provide some of the richest farms in the state. There are nearly 50,000 citizens of Dutch descent living in one county alone and the cultivation of tulips is a big local industry. Finns, Danes, Swedes, and Norwegians started settlements that have become cities today. Scandia societies preserve their cultures.

With the discovery of iron and copper in the northern peninsula, and the mining and shipping of it to help the rapid industrialization of the Midwest (a factor was the canalization of the rapids of Sault Ste. Marie to permit shipments from Lake Superior by steamer), large numbers of Polish miners were brought to Michigan. They worked the mines under the supervision of Cornish settlers, experts in deep mining techniques. Descendants of Poles now work in the great factories of southern Michigan. Hamtramck's population of about 27,000 is predominantly Polish.

As the auto industry boomed, laborers came from the Ukraine, Czechoslovakia, Lithuania, and Hungary, retaining many of the traditions of their former lands. Negroes and Mexicans swell the ethnic total.

AGRICULTURE. Michigan's farms have more than five million acres of land and a wide diversity of crops. Apples, grapes, peaches, pears are extensively grown. Michigan grows more cherries, beans, and pickle cucumbers than any other state, and ranks high in strawberries. Other important crops are winter wheat, soybeans, sugar beets, potatoes, hay, corn. Michigan's dairy industry, with more than a million milk cows, is one of the largest in the Midwest. In some specialty crops like peppermint and spearmint, Michigan ranks near the top in the nation, and in one, tulips (thanks to the Dutch settlers in and around Holland), it exceeds all other states. The Dutch also produce celery.

Michigan has the greatest inland fishing industry in the world, with 20 species, including trout, perch, carp, whitefish, pike and herring, regularly caught in the Great Lakes and shipped over the country. Smelt are often caught through the ice in the late spring in the northern areas.

INDUSTRY. Michigan has the most facilities for automobile production in the United States. Other important categories of manufacture are steel, paper, drugs, chemicals, machinery. In the making of furniture, in Grand Rapids, Michigan leads the country.

Many of Michigan's factories provide visitor tours. Kalamazoo excels in the production of paper, and Battle Creek in making breakfast cereals.

In recent years, iron ore and salt have become more important than copper.

Michigan is second in the production of sand, gravel and magnesium, and the production of salt, pumped from deep wells in the south-central area, chiefly around Midland, exceeds that of any state. The basis for a huge chemical industry, salt is used in more than 14,000 products. Limestone deposits are the basis for a big cement industry. A special mineral resource is gypsum of very high quality.

CITIES. Michigan is essentially a state of small towns and villages. Of some 3,300 communities in the state less than ten percent have more than 1,000 population, and only seven cities, Detroit, Grand Rapids, Lansing, Dearborn, Warren, Ann Arbor and Flint, have populations of more than 100,000.

DEARBORN, just west of Detroit proper, offers visitors a tour of the great **Ford Motor plants** and a visit to **Greenfield Village** and the **Henry Ford Museum,** with historic buildings, many authentically refurnished, in a setting of great charm. The museum building, a replica of Philadelphia's Independence Hall, has a remarkable collection of automobiles, farm implements, watches and musical instruments.

DETROIT began as a center for the fur-trading industry of the French, its site selected by its French founder Cadillac in 1701, because it could control traffic in the strait (*d'étroit*) which connected Lake Huron and Lake Erie. In 1900 it had less than 300,000 population. Now it has about 1.5 million, is the motor vehicle capital of the world (with the world's highest industrial wage), and the fifth city in size in the United States.

Though the original city plan was made by the same engineer who laid out Washington, D.C. (Major L'Enfant), no one paid much attention to the plan, so the city grew by chance and pressure into a vast sprawling area stretching west and north from the Detroit River. The river, with bridges spanning it and a tunnel going underneath, divides Detroit from Canada. By a quirk of geography, Detroit is the only city in the country from which you can enter Canada by going south. On the city's eastern side and to its northeast is **Lake St. Clair,** midway between Lake Huron and Lake Erie. Fine residences line its shores.

The **Detroit Institute of Arts** is one of the best museums in the country. **Belle Isle** is a 1,000-acre, six-mile-long playground and exhibit area in the middle of the Detroit River. Its exhibits include a **Museum of the Great Lakes.** A handsome new **civic center** has been developed along the riverfront in the downtown area, location of the city's tallest building, the **Penobscot Tower.**

Near Detroit is **Bloomfield Hills,** where there is a cluster of schools, institutes, museums and agencies all grouped under the heading of the **Cranbrook Institutions.** Many of the buildings are of striking and unusual design. On the grounds are some of the finest examples of statuary in America, some of it the work of Carl Milles.

West of Detroit is Ann Arbor, location of the **University of Michigan.** The university is famous for its extensive research facilities.

FLINT is Michigan's third largest city, with a population of nearly 200,000. It is 50 miles northwest of Detroit, to which it is linked by an express highway. The **General Motors Institute of Technology** is in Flint.

Along the shore of the Great Lakes there are excellent highways. Most towns and cities have complete facilities for boating and fishing; many are near state park areas, easily accessible to good beaches. The chief centers are **Traverse City** on Grand Traverse Bay; **Petoskey** on Little Traverse Bay; **Mackinaw City,** terminus for both the new bridge over the Straits of Mackinac and the ferry service to Mackinac Island; **Cheboygan,** terminus for a ferry service to Bois Blanc Island in Lake Huron; **Alpena** on Thunder Bay, and **Bay City,** at the head of Saginaw Bay. On the upper peninsula the chief resort centers are **St. Ignace,** old French fur-trading post and northern terminus for the Mackinac Bridge; **Escanaba** and **Menominee,** facing the huge arm of Lake Michigan called Green Bay, and on the Lake Superior shore, **Marquette** and **Hancock,** terminus for the ferry service to **Isle Royale,** Michigan's great wilderness national park. At the northeast tip of the northern peninsula is **Sault Ste. Marie,** with its system of great locks.

GRAND RAPIDS, with a population of more than 197,000 is about 150 miles northwest of Detroit and 30 miles east of the shore of Lake Michigan. Grand Rapids is pre-eminent in furniture manufacturing. There are a small but good art gallery, a public museum with assorted exhibits, a **museum of furniture** in the United States from Colonial times.

HOLLAND, 24 miles southwest of Grand Rapids, on the Black River, a few miles east of the shore of the lake, has a population of over 25,000, the largest colony of people of Dutch descent in the country. Each May, Holland's **Tulip Festival** draws crowds of visitors to see thousands of acres of blooming tulips and to watch Dutch ceremonies, which include street scrubbings and parades in native costumes.

MUSKEGON, 37 miles northwest of Grand Rapids, with a population of about 45,000, has a fine harbor at the mouth of the Muskegon River. Though a manufacturing city, it is also the shopping center for a chain of lakeside resorts, has full facilities for fishing and boating, with several good beaches nearby. An automobile ferry service offers a fast trip across Lake Michigan to Milwaukee, Wisconsin.

SPORTS AND RECREATION. Michigan's recreational facilities range from trackless areas of primeval wilderness, clothed in forest and set with lakes, to highly civilized resort centers with extensive facilities for **yachting, bathing, boating, fishing,** and **hunting.** Fishing in the Great Lakes and inland waters ranges from tiny smelt (dipped out in squirming basketfuls during spring smelt runs) to the giant muskellunge, found deep in Lake Superior's cold waters. Other fish caught are bass, perch, pike, rainbow trout, steelhead trout. Winter fishing through the ice, with colonies of fishing shanties springing up on frozen lakes, is common.

Hunting is extensive for both large and small game, but chiefly for white-tailed deer, as the deer population is well over a million. Limited elk hunting is permitted under restricted conditions in designated areas. Other game commonly found are bear, rabbit, fox, squirrel, beaver. Game birds that are plentiful include pheasant, partridge, grouse, duck, quail.

Few areas of the Midwest offer better facilities for boating and canoeing. Small craft of all kinds, both power and sail, are numerous on inland lakes and waters, and Great Lakes waters provide some of the finest cruising in the country. The **Mackinac race** for larger craft is held each summer from both Detroit and Chicago to Mackinac Island.

Michigan winter sports include **skiing** (Michigan claims the first ski-jumping tournament in the country in 1887, at Ishpeming. The ski slide on Pine Mountain at the city of Iron Mountain on the upper peninsula is the highest artificial ski slide in the world), **tobogganning, iceboating, ice-fishing.** Snow conditions are generally good and the season long in the northern part of the lower peninsula and throughout the upper peninsula.

Over the Straits of Mackinac is the **Mackinac Bridge,** one of the world's longest suspension bridges anchorage-to-anchorage, linking St. Ignace with Mackinaw City; Mackinac Island, crowned with a picturesque pioneer fort, **Fort Michilimackinac,** reconstructed at Mackinaw City; and the locks of the "Soo" at Sault Ste. Marie. Nature lovers find interest in the two great primitive areas of **Isle Royale** in Lake Superior and **Porcupine Mountain State Park.** More than 150 waterfalls dot Michigan's upper peninsula.

SPECIAL EVENTS of interest to the visitor are many, one of the most popular being **Holland's Tulip Festival** in May. Here residents dress in traditional Dutch costumes, hold parades, and sell items made by local craftsmen. **A Maple Syrup Festival** is held in Shepherd and Vermontville in April; **Michigan Week,** statewide in May; and the well-known **Music Festival** at Interlochen from June to August. Other dates of importance are **International Freedom Festival** in Detroit, July; **State Fair** in Detroit, late August; and **Automobile Show,** Detroit, November.

Wisconsin

Among the states of the Midwest, Wisconsin is sixth in size, with more than 56,000 square miles, and sixth in population, with over four million people. In the United States it is twenty-sixth in area, sixteenth in population. Wisconsin is irregularly shaped, its only straight border being the southern boundary with Illinois. The eastern border is the shore of Lake Michigan to the south, a diagonal land border in the

Wisconsin Vacationland

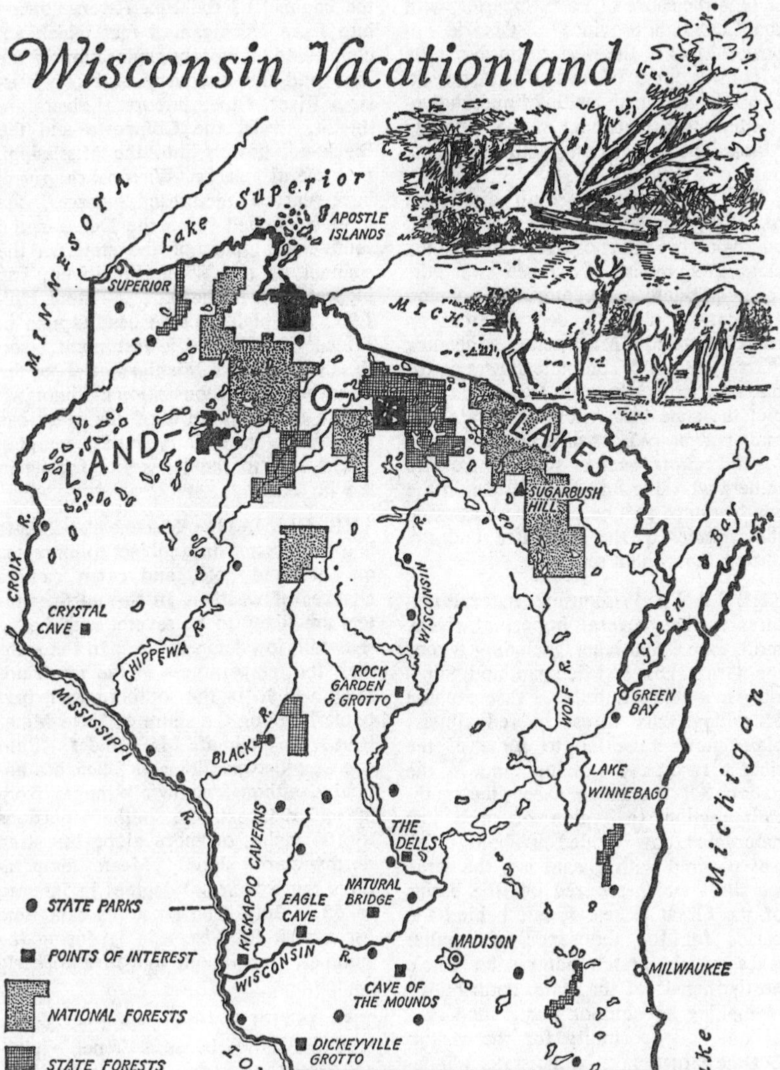

MINNESOTA
Lake Superior
APOSTLE ISLANDS
SUPERIOR
MICH.
LAND-O-LAKES
SUGARBUSH HILL
CROIX R.
CRYSTAL CAVE
CHIPPEWA R.
WISCONSIN R.
Green Bay
MISSISSIPPI R.
ROCK GARDEN & GROTTO
GREEN BAY
WOLF R.
BLACK R.
LAKE WINNEBAGO
Lake Michigan
KICKAPOO CAVERNS
THE DELLS
NATURAL BRIDGE
EAGLE CAVE
STATE PARKS
MADISON
POINTS OF INTEREST
WISCONSIN R.
MILWAUKEE
CAVE OF THE MOUNDS
NATIONAL FORESTS
DICKEYVILLE GROTTO
STATE FORESTS
IOWA
ILLINOIS
INDIAN RESERVATIONS

northeast where Wisconsin joins the northern peninsula of Michigan. The relatively short northern border of the state is the shore of Lake Superior, with the Canadian province of Ontario opposite. Most of the western border is the winding course of two rivers, the St. Croix in the north, with Minnesota opposite, and the channel of the widening Mississippi in the south, with Minnesota and Iowa beyond.

The greatest north-south dimension of Wisconsin is 315 miles, its greatest width—across the northern half of the state—289 miles. Wisconsin was the thirtieth state to enter the Union (1848). Its name is derived from an Indian word, Misconsing, meaning "Grassy Place." The state flower is the butterfly violet; the state tree, sugar maple; the state bird, robin; the state animal, badger. Wisconsin's nickname, the *"Badger State,"* came from the Cornish miners who dug into the hillsides in the southwestern part of the state and made their homes in the hills, like badgers, during the winter season.

THE LAND. Wisconsin's natural features include several important rivers, more than 8,500 lakes, including two of the Great Lakes, Michigan and Superior, low wooded hills, a vast expanse of rolling, once forest-covered alluvial plain, now converted to some of the richest farm and grazing land in the nation. All of the state except the southwest section (a region of once low mountains now eroded to bold hills) was covered with glacial ice, the same ice sheet which scoured out the basins of the Great Lakes. It left behind the basins for the thousands of smaller lakes which stretch across the whole northern half of the state, contributing to making an outdoor playground area of unique opportunity for the visitor. But the largest lake in the state, **Winnebago**, lies in the east-central part, 29 miles long, connected with Lake Michigan by the Fox River, leading into Wisconsin's Green Bay.

Wisconsin's largest river, shared with Minnesota and Iowa, is the Mississippi. Into it flow the Wisconsin, rising in the center of the state, winding south and southwest in a series of broad lake-like channels. Its channel is very close to the channel of the **Fox River,** flowing into Lake Michigan, a fact which accounted for the early exploration of the state and the discovery of the Mississippi River. Other important rivers are the **St. Croix,** the **Chippewa** and the **Black,** all flowing into the Mississippi. In several places Wisconsin's rivers have carved picturesque gorges, the most celebrated being the Dells, in the south-central part of the state, in the channel of the Wisconsin River. The highest point in the state is **Timms Hill,** 1,952 feet high, located near Ogema in Prince County; the lowest point is on the shore of Lake Michigan at about the point where Wisconsin joins Illinois.

The southern third of the state has rich farms and dairy lands, merging gradually into the lakes and forests in the far north.

THE CLIMATE. Wisconsin's climate is a continental one, subject to extremes of heat and cold, and often sudden changes of weather. In the north, winters are likely to be severe, with heavy snowfall, low temperatures. In the summer, the temperatures in the north are seldom high. In the southern part, particularly along the shore of Lake Michigan, the climate is milder. Rain averages between 28 and 32 inches annually, although snowfall ranges from 30 inches in extreme southern portions to 100 inches or more along the steep northwestern slopes. Mean temperatures range from 20 degrees in January to 68 in July. The most pleasant time for a visit to Wisconsin is during the summer, from about mid-June to early September.

THE PEOPLE. Wisconsin was discovered and settled because French explorers from Canada were seeking a "Northwest Passage" to China. The date was 1634, when Jean Nicolet sailed into Green Bay. Thereafter a trickle of French explorers and trappers followed. The most famed were the team of Jesuits, Marquette and Joliet, who paddled up the Fox River, made the short portage to the Wisconsin, and, sailing down that river, discovered the Mississippi. It was this portage that gave the state its great value to the French. To protect it, French forts and pioneer settlements were built, the chief and first being near Prairie du Chien in 1686, at the point where the Wisconsin joins the Mississippi. The fur trade went on for over 150 years, with the French naming places and features of the land: La Crosse, Eau Claire, Fond du Lac, Butte des Morts, Flambeau, Lac Vieux Desert. But there never were many French fur traders in Wisconsin. As late as 1820 there were only two settlements in the state, Green Bay and Prairie du Chien, each with about 500 people.

Subsequently, successive waves of immigrants began to fill the state, reducing the forest areas to farmed fields. First came settlers following the Mississippi north from southern areas into southwestern counties. They found that the great rolling hills of the region contained rich veins of lead. Within the next few years Cornish miners from Cornwall in England, more than 7,000 of them, moved to Wisconsin to work the veins. They built snug stone cottages like their homes in England, a whole street of them still standing in the town of Mineral Point. Yankee farmers moved into the southeastern part of the state. In 1840 the state's population, living almost entirely in the southern part, was about 30,000. Eight years later, 1848, when Wisconsin became a state, it had increased to more than 200,000.

By 1850 most of the population was either native-born or came from the British Isles. But the decades that followed brought large numbers of Irish, Norwegians, Germans, and Swiss, the latter establishing New Glarus. Germans settled along the Lake Michigan shore, giving the chief city of Milwaukee its beer-making industry and love of music and culture. Scandinavians helped develop the lumber industry in the northern forests.

Beginning about 1910, a large migration of Polish workers came, settling in industrial centers, such as Milwaukee and Racine. The last few decades have brought groups that form ethnic islands throughout the state. One county has a substantial group of Dutch and another county is predominantly Belgian. One offshore island has the only group of Danish-Icelanders in America. Green County is predominantly Swiss, produces more Swiss cheese than any region of the country.

In Wisconsin today more than 40 percent of the people are of Germanic origin. About 10 percent are of Polish ancestry and about 15 percent are Scandinavian.

A few of the varied peoples who have migrated to Wisconsin within the past 100 years left distinctive architectural marks on the land. One was a Florentine named Mazzuchelli, who built the first church in Wisconsin in 1831 at Green Bay. Another, Hercules Dousman, a fur trading agent, built the classic Victorian mansion named Villa Louis at Prairie du Chien in 1843. A third, a son of Norway, built a curious and characteristic Norse mansion at Mount Horeb. A fourth, one of the world's most gifted architects, Frank Lloyd Wright, left monuments to his special genius like the Johnson Wax office and factory at Racine, and his own remarkable home, Taliesin, near Spring Green.

AGRICULTURE. Wisconsin has more than 15 million acres of commercially important forest lands, and more than 20 million acres in farm and range land. It is the largest milk-producing state of the United States (more than 18 billion pounds annually), has more dairy cows than any state, and ranks first in production of hay and cheese, which is one of Wisconsin's best shopping buys. Potatoes are an important crop and Wisconsin ranks high in the production of cranberries. The Door Peninsula, which helps frame Green Bay, is one of the most important cherry-growing districts in the country. Wisconsin also produces half the canning peas of the country, and tobacco is grown in several southern counties.

Commercial mink farming is important in the state. Forest products, derived chiefly from white pine and native hardwoods, account for huge quantities of pulp used in paper and various plastics. Many of the commercial forests have second-growth stands, grown after the ruthless cutting of the original forests during the last half of the nineteenth century.

INDUSTRY. Although Wisconsin is not generally regarded as a dominant industrial state, it has some large-scale industries and important industrial concentrations in several cities. Breweries, chiefly in Milwaukee, produce more beer than any other state. Automobiles and automobile accessories rank high, as does farm machinery. Specialized plants of national importance produce malted milk and cheese, pack large quantities of meat, and make furniture, floor waxes, and polishes.

Although zinc and lead mines have not been depleted, little mining is done due to the low price of ore.

CITIES. Wisconsin is essentially an area of small towns and villages. Of nearly 2,700 communities in the state, only five have more than 50,000 people, and only two have a population over 100,000.

ASHLAND, at the head of big Chequamegon Bay, on Wisconsin's shore of Lake Superior, has a population of about 9,000. The city itself is a convenient base for the use of the cold clear waters of Lake Superior, stretching north and east. Just north in the lake is a cluster of islands called **Apostle Islands,** famed for colorful cliffs, picturesque home of fishermen. On one of them is an old mission built in 1832. The islands are a center for fishing and hunting, as well as cruises through the Apostle Islands and trolling for lake trout.

FOND DU LAC, located at the southern end of **Lake Winnebago,** largest in Wisconsin, has a population of about 35,000. Although primarily an industrial town, it is also a resort, with excellent facilities for the use of the lake's waters and shores. From the city a scenic highway rims the lake, providing interesting drives and easy access to resort villages that line the shore.

GREEN BAY, the oldest settled community in the state, is about 100 miles north of Milwaukee, in a strategic setting at the head of Green Bay, at the mouth of the Fox River. It has one of the finest harbors on the Great Lakes, serving various industrial interests, which include papermaking, meat packing, and cheese processing. Green Bay is a good base for visiting the shores of Green Bay, one of the most attractive summer vacation regions in the Midwest, offering superb boating and fishing. Within the city are several historic old buildings. Green Bay has received national fame as the home of a professional football team, the **Green Bay Packers.**

MADISON is the capital of Wisconsin and the state's second largest city (population over 173,000). From the visitor standpoint Madison is the most important city in the state. It lies among rolling, wooded hills, set with many lakes, 75 miles west of Milwaukee. The city itself is built on an isthmus between two lakes, whose wooded shores provide dramatic sites for homes and institutions. There are at least half a dozen other lakes within a short distance of the city, all providing fishing and boating, water sports in summer, skiing and ice skating in winter. In addition to being the state capital (the imposing **capitol building** is set on a hill, in a wooded park), Madison is also the seat of the **University of Wisconsin,** whose handsome buildings spread over a spacious lakeshore campus on the western side of the city. The campus itself, one of the most attractive in the country, is worth seeing and some of the buildings offer special exhibits. Nearby, the university maintains a 1,200-acre **arboretum.** Just west of the university is the **U. S. Forest Products Laboratory.**

Madison is an excellent base for visiting the more interesting sites and natural features of southern Wisconsin. About 55 miles northwest is the state's most celebrated scenic novelty, the

Wisconsin Dells, a series of cliff-walled gorges cut by the winding course of the Wisconsin River. Forty-five miles to the southwest is quaint and charming **Mineral Point.** This center for the once brisk mining of lead was settled by miners from Wales.

MILWAUKEE, with a population of about 717,000, is easily the largest city in Wisconsin, eleventh city in the nation. Eighty miles north of Chicago and 35 miles north of the Illinois state line in southeastern Wisconsin, Milwaukee spreads west from bluffs overlooking Lake Michigan. Although primarily a business center and a manufacturing city, it has some sights and facilities of interest, including several excellent restaurants which feature German and Polish dishes.

The city's industries include the largest breweries in the world (they have made Milwaukee famous), packing plants, diesel and gas engine and outboard motor plants. The breweries offer conducted tours with free samples.

Milwaukee is known for its excellent **city parks** as well as the **Performing Arts Center, Memorial Art Center,** a **public museum, conservatory,** many restored **old houses,** the recently developed **harbor and lakefront,** and the **county zoo.** A scenic drive runs along the shore of Lake Michigan to the north. The city is a good base for exploring the nearby area where, within an hour's drive, there are more than 150 lakes scattered over rich and rolling farmlands, offering fishing and boating.

WAUSAU, in the north-central part of the state, is the nearest city base and best outfitting point for the vast region of forests and lakes which extend across the northern end of Wisconsin. The lakes, more than 4,000 of them, are in two clusters. Part of the area is primeval wilderness, with almost no highways, a summer paradise for fishermen and campers.

SPORTS AND RECREATION. Within the forest areas of the northern part of the state there are more than 7,000 lakes, most offering good fishing. The waters of Lake Michigan and Lake Superior also provide **fishing** and **boating** opportunities. Altogether the state has more than 8,000 lakes, and more than 7,000 miles of navigable streams. Facilities provided for the use of them are complete, ranging from fishing camps in wilderness areas, to exclusive resorts near large city centers.

Fish found in the waters of Wisconsin include muskellunge, walleye, northern pike, bass, several species of trout, catfish (in the rivers). Wisconsin forests provide some of the best hunting in the Midwest, all controlled by license and seasonal limits. Hunters find deer, bear, fox, pheasant, duck, ruffed grouse, geese.

Points of historic interest are numerous, among them, the **Lincoln-Tallman Homestead** in Janesville; **Circus World Museum,** Baraboo; **Museum of Medical Progress,** Prairie du Chien; **Paul Bunyan Camp,** Carson Park. In the older, larger cities there are interesting historic houses as well as several buildings of architectural importance. The state's most famed scenic place is the river gorge of the Wisconsin called the **Dells.**

Wisconsin has some of the best and most extensive **winter sports facilities** in the Midwest, with **ski tournaments, ski jumping, snowmobile derbies, toboggan slides,** and **winter carnivals** in many areas, chiefly around Lake Geneva and in the northwestern part of the state. Madison is one of the few cities in the country where **iceboating** is a consistent winter sport.

SPECIAL EVENTS. In addition to the many winter festivals and snowmobile contests held throughout the state from October through March, other events include: **Madison Sports Show,** April; **Cherry and Apple Blossom Time,** Door County, May; **Old Milwaukee Days,** early July; **Wisconsin State Fair,** West Allis, August.

Minnesota

Of the eight Midwest states, Minnesota, with about 84,000 square miles, is the largest in area, but with about 3.8 million people it is seventh in population. Among the states of the United States its rank in area is twelfth, and in population nineteenth. It is the most northern of the Midwest states, with an irregular shape something like an hourglass. On its northern border are two provinces of Canada: Manitoba and Ontario. The eastern borders are Lake Superior, Wisconsin, and the Mississippi River. The ruler-straight southern boundary is with Iowa, the western border with North Dakota and South Dakota. The extreme length of the state is 406 miles; the width varies from 180 to 358 miles.

Minnesota was the thirty-second state to be admitted to the Union. Its name is derived from a combination of Indian words "minne-sota," meaning "sky-tinted water" to describe the appearance of the Minnesota River. The state flower is the lady's-slipper, the bird, the loon, and the state tree, the Norway pine.

THE LAND. Though the **Misquah Hills** in northeast Minnesota are the highest land in the Midwest (2,301 feet), most of the surface of Minnesota is relatively level, varying from slightly rolling land in the east to vast, flat, prairie lands in the west. The state's natural features, several of which are shared with adjoining areas, include large rivers, more than 10,000 lakes, one of the few extensive natural wilderness areas in the United States, vast reaches of forest land and prairie. An unusual feature of the state's topography is that within the northern part of Minnesota three national watersheds divide and three great river systems begin. From Minnesota some rivers flow north into the Hudson Bay, others flow into the Great Lakes, and several flow south to make the huge Mississippi system. The Mississippi itself has its source in northern Minnesota. A great tributary of the Mississippi is the **Minnesota River.** Among the thousands of the state's lakes, several are notable for size and character. They include island-studded Lake of the Woods, shared with Canada, 70 miles long by 60 miles wide, containing more than 14,000 islands. On the western shore of the lake, entirely cut off from the rest of Minnesota, is a curious orphan area called **Northwest Angle,** the farthest north part of the United States except Alaska.

The northern lake-wilderness area contains the low ranges of the Superior Highlands, including the Mesabi and the Misquah Hills, with the largest and the richest iron-ore deposits in the United States. The southern and western parts of the state are rich, rolling farmland. The forest areas, chiefly in the north, contain more than 19 million acres of timberland, some of it unexplored wilderness.

THE CLIMATE. Minnesota's climate is continental, with extremely cold winters and sometimes very hot periods during the summer. Temperature changes can be sudden and severe. Most of the northern part of the state is snow-covered for more than four months in the winter. Rainfall ranges from 25 to 29 inches, with less rain in the northern and western parts, and some of the southwest plains tending to be semi-arid. Average temperatures range from 8 degrees in January to 72 in July. Except for winter sports, the best time for a Minnesota visit is summer, from late June to early September.

THE PEOPLE. French trappers and missionaries, entering Minnesota from the Great Lakes, began visiting the area from about 1659, but established no settlements for many years. The first settlement was believed to have been made by the French about 1730, the village of Grand Portage. The French left no mark on the land and finally abandoned control to the British, who continued to maintain fur-trapping interests but made few settlements. American fur-trading interests took over from the British after the War of 1812 and the acquisition of northwest Minnesota by the United States as a part of the Louisiana Purchase in 1803. Fort Snelling at the Falls of the Mississippi was an American military outpost (now the site of Minneapolis) established in 1819 to protect fur traders from the Indians. They needed protection, for the fighting Sioux Indians deterred settlement of the state for many years. As late as 1850 the area of Minnesota had only about 6,000 people. Ten years later, two years after admission to the Union, it had 172,000 people. But then a migration boom began, first a lumber boom, served by steamboat traffic on the Mississippi and the building of railroads into the wilderness. Legendary hero of the lumberjacks was the fabulous Paul Bunyan. Two great pioneering developers were James Hill, who built railroads, and John S. Pillsbury, whose flour milling enterprises were the result of the settlement of the western plains. Many of the early settlers were Germans and Scandinavians. Whole communities took on the aspect and character of Scandinavian towns.

A new wave of migration, sparked by the discovery of rich iron deposits in the northern forests, and the completion of the locks at Sault Ste. Marie to permit ore shipments on the Great Lakes, began after 1884 when the first shipment of ore was made by lake steamer.

AGRICULTURE. Minnesota is essentially a farming state. Of its 30 million acres of farm and range land about 20 million are under cultivation. The state is a leading producer of grains: oats, corn, flaxseed, rye, wheat, potatoes, soybeans, as well as honey and turkeys. It produces more creamery butter than any other state and more sweet corn for processing, is first in the nation in the production of oats, third in flaxseed. The state's milk production from more than a million and a half cows ranks it next to Wisconsin in national production.

INDUSTRY. Flour and grain mills, located chiefly in Minneapolis and St. Paul, are the largest in the United States. Other important industry includes production of farm machinery, and a large paper mill at International Falls. St. Paul is known for publishing, and Rochester is the location of the Mayo Clinic and Hospital.

Minnesota's mineral wealth is concentrated in iron ore, with about 70 million tons of ore produced each year from the ranges in the northern forests near Lake Superior. It amounts to more than half the ore produced in the United States. The mines include the biggest man-made hole in the world, an open pit mine 400 feet deep, covering 1,300 acres, equipped with its own 55-mile railroad. The ore from Minnesota's mines is worth around $500 million each year. Getting the ore to smelters and mills involves a huge fleet of specially built ore boats, many of them more than 600 feet long.

CITIES. Most of the settled places in Minnesota are quite small towns and villages. Of the larger cities two, Minneapolis and St. Paul, known as the Twin Cities, are practically one community. A third, Duluth, is the great ore shipping center at the end of Lake Superior. Several smaller cities are important as bases and outfitting points in resort areas.

BEMIDJI, 140 miles northwest of Duluth (population 11,000), is chief center and outfitting point for a huge lake and forest wilderness area. Within the town, on the shore of the lake, which is closer to hundreds of other lakes, are the odd and amusing figures of **Paul Bunyan,** 18 feet tall, and his equally big Blue Ox. A point of special interest nearby is **Itasca State Park,** with 31,000 acres of forest wilderness, 25 miles to the southwest. Within the park are 157 lakes, providing a full range of resort facilities. One of the lakes, **Itasca,** is considered the source of the Mississippi River.

DULUTH is the third largest city in Minnesota (population, over 100,000). One hundred and twenty miles northeast of the Twin Cities, at the western end of Lake Superior and at the mouth of the St. Louis River, it has a commanding setting on 600-foot bluffs overlooking its great harbor (ice-bound four months of the year). A notable feature of the harbor is the towering **aerial lift bridge,** over 500 feet in length. The great Arrowhead country and the **Superior National Forest** lie to the north and northeast, and visitors can take daily excursion steamers to **Isle Royale** on Lake Superior. Within the town is **Skyline Parkway,** with a fine view of the city and lake. There is also a picturesque inclined railway. A **scenic drive** follows the shore of Lake Superior to the northwest and Grand Portage, a distance of 140 miles, while the excellent highway U.S. 61 closely follows the rugged shore of the lake. From Grand Portage a ferry operates in summer to nearby Isle Royale.

INTERNATIONAL FALLS (population 6,400) is at the mouth of the Rainy River and on the southern shore of huge **Rainy Lake,** extending into the lake and forest wilderness area of Canada. The town has big paper mills, but is of special interest to fishermen and sportsmen who want to fish and hunt in the maze of lakes and channels and primitive forest areas to the north in Canada.

MINNEAPOLIS AND ST. PAUL. The twin cities of Minneapolis and St. Paul, with a combined population of about 1.8 million people, lie on either side of the Mississippi River, which, crossed by several bridges, makes an irregular S-curve, with the downtown sections of each city opposite each other on its banks. Both are important manufacturing centers. Minneapolis has the five largest milling companies in the country, a big plant making agricultural equipment, another turning out precision instruments. It is the world's largest producer of hearing aids, fourth largest producer of clothing, particularly heavy outdoor wear. St. Paul, on the other hand, is fourth largest in publishing and printing, fifth in the production of cosmetics in the country, and the largest producer of refined petroleum products in the Midwest. Both cities are big transportation centers.

St. Paul, the state capital, has several handsome **capitol buildings,** and is the location of the **University of Minnesota's agricultural school.** In St. Paul's **city hall,** a gigantic figure of the **Indian God of Peace,** 44 feet high, can be seen.

The **Minneapolis Institute of Arts, Walker Art Center** and **Tyrone Guthrie Theatre** are cultural landmarks not only for the city but the entire nation. The main campus of the **University of Minnesota,** with a student population of 35,000, is located in the Minneapolis half of the Twins, on the banks of the Mississippi River. The city also has several attractive lakes within the city limits, their shores handsomely parked, and surrounded by fine residential districts. Most celebrated park, one well worth seeing, is **Minnehaha State Park,** just south of both cities on the bank of the Mississippi.

Hundreds of lakes, most of them offering fishing, boating and resort facilities, are within a few miles of the twin-city limits. Among them is big and beautiful **Lake Minnetonka,** 12 miles west of Minneapolis, which contains many islands and has a deeply indented, 97-mile shoreline with resorts scattered along it.

ROCHESTER, 65 miles southeast of the Twin Cities (population 40,000), is the most famed medical center in the United States, because of the development there of the huge **Mayo Clinic.**

SPORTS AND RECREATION. Minnesota's sights and facilities for the visitor nearly all relate to outdoor activities. The **Rune Stone,** at **Alexandria,** 150 miles northwest of Minneapolis, bears Scandinavian inscriptions said to have been carved on it by Norsemen visiting the area as early as 1362. The stone's authenticity has been disputed, but it attracts many visitors. An unusual national monument is **Pipestone,** about 200 miles southwest of Minneapolis. It preserves the red stone quarries from which Indians made peace pipes for centuries, as well as some oddly shaped and colored stones.

The superb **fishing** in most of the more than 10,000 lakes and thousands of miles of navigable streams includes

High Falls on the Pigeon River, Minnesota

Boyhood home of Dwight D. Eisenhower, Abilene, Kansas

Iowa farmland

University of Iowa, Iowa City, Iowa

4-H judging, Iowa State Fair in Des Moines

Rodeo in Burwell, Nebraska

Truman Library,
Independence, Missouri

Daniel Boone Home
near Defiance, Missouri

St. Louis, Missouri

bass, trout, muskellunge, pickerel, pan fish of various types. Boats and tackle are widely available, and guides can be hired. Excellent **boating** includes **sailing** and **canoeing,** for which the state has some of the best canoeing waters in the country. Few states offer better **camping** and **hunting** facilities. Deer, bear, moose, pheasant, and various small game birds are widely abundant in the forest regions.

Southern Minnesota is one of the best **winter sports** regions in the country, with many ski centers, ski jumps, and cross-country ski races. Ice skating is a top winter sport, with a **speed skating meet** held each year in **Minneapolis,** as a climax to a winter carnival period. Iceboating, tobogganing and ice fishing are popular.

The state's professional baseball team is the **Minnesota Twins,** and its pro football entry the **Vikings.**

SPECIAL EVENTS. Festivals throughout the year emphasize both the origins of Minnesota's people and the climatic and natural features of the land. Dozens of winter carnivals take advantage of the state's superb snow cover, the most celebrated being **St. Paul's annual ice carnival.** A popular event at the carnival is the **National Speed Skating Races.** Swedish people of **Duluth** have a **summer festival,** with costumes and folk dances. Germans in **Springfield** celebrate a **sauerkraut festival,** and **Sauk Center,** famed as the setting for Sinclair Lewis' "Main Street," has an annual **Sinclair Lewis Day.**

Iowa

Iowa, with slightly more than 56,000 square miles, is the fifth state in size among the states of the Midwest, with nearly three million people, eighth among the Midwest states in population. Among the states of the United States Iowa ranks twenty-fifth in size and in population.

Rectangular in shape, Iowa lies in the western tier of the Midwest states. All of its northern border is a ruler-straight line with Minnesota to the north. The entire eastern border is the Mississippi River, with Wisconsin and Illinois on the eastern shore. A straight-line southern border divides Iowa from Missouri. The western border is nearly all the curving course of the Missouri River, with Nebraska on the western bank. Above Nebraska on the west, divided from Iowa by the Sioux River, is South Dakota. The east-west length of Iowa is 324 miles, the north-south height of the state 210 miles.

Iowa was the twenty-ninth state to be admitted to the Union (1846). Its name is derived from a Sioux Indian word, and has a curious meaning—"one who puts to sleep." Iowa's nickname is the *"Hawkeye State,"* the state flower is the Carolina wild rose, the state bird, the goldfinch.

THE LAND. Most of Iowa is a gently rolling plain, rising almost imperceptibly from the east to the west, much of it once part of the vast natural prairie which extended from eastern Illinois to the foothills of the Rockies. High prairie grasses covered some of the richest soil in the world. The most rugged part of the state lies in the northeast corner opposite Wisconsin, in a section called Little Switzerland—where bluffs rise to 300 feet above the Mississippi River, and high rolling hills extend west from it. In the northeast corner (which also contains 1,675-foot **Ocheyedan Mound,** the state's highest point) there are a number of small lakes created by glacial action.

Iowa is the only state to be bordered by two navigable rivers—the Mississippi to the east and the Missouri to the west. The Des Moines River flows diagonally northwest to southeast, emptying into the Mississippi, as do the Iowa and Cedar rivers. Chief river flowing into the Missouri is the Sioux. Though more than 85 percent of the land area of Iowa was originally covered by prairie grass, the state did have about five million acres of forest land, chiefly in the east and along the river beds. About half of the original forest tracts remain.

THE CLIMATE. Iowa has a humid continental climate, with cold winters (and often very heavy snowfalls), hot summers and rainy springs. Temperature changes are sudden and temperature extremes common. Thus winter temperatures below zero are not unusual, nor are summer temperatures of more than 100 degrees. Rainfall ranges from 26 to 36 inches, with an average of about 31 inches. The average January temperature in Des Moines, the capital and approximate center of the state, is 20 degrees, the average July temperature, 75.

THE PEOPLE. Although Iowa is well-known for farming (30 percent of the labor force is employed in some phase of it), manufacturing is growing in importance. Figures show that 53 percent of all Iowans live in urban areas. In origin these people came from many countries of Europe and many states of the United States. As was general throughout the Midwest, the first to come were French trappers and explorers. Marquette and Joliet, coming south down the Mississippi, visited the eastern edge of the state in 1673. Fur traders began to follow them, though most of them headed farther west. One of the first to actually settle in Iowa was a Frenchman named Julien Dubuque, who developed Iowa's first industry, lead mining in the eastern hills. He gave his name to an important Iowa city near mines which he developed. The Louisiana Purchase of 1803 made Iowa a part of the United States, and it soon became a corridor for travel from the East to the West. When the tough cover of prairie grass was removed, the soil beneath proved so incredibly rich that settlers began to flock into the state to farm, the first coming from New England. They established village communities like those in New England.

In 1840 there were only 43,000 people in Iowa, but ten years later the population was nearly 200,000 and by 1860 was nearly 700,000. Among the first to come were Scotch miners, lured by coal mines opened in southern Iowa. Irish, Germans, Norwegians, Swedes, Dutch, Hungarians, Danes, Czechs came in numbers large enough to establish distinctive communities. A German group, members of the Amana Society, established several nearby communities, among the most prosperous in Iowa today. There are two distinctively Dutch communities, each of which celebrates its origin in Holland with an annual Tulip Festival.

The welding of divergent ethnic groups into a common social and economic order was uniquely successful in Iowa. Though Iowans have developed no special or characteristic architectural forms, they have made substantial contributions to art and literature.

AGRICULTURE. Ninety-five percent of Iowa's surface is in farmland, with 65 percent in cultivated fields, 30 percent in pasture. Iowa can justly claim to be the heartland of American agriculture, with 25 percent of the grade A soil in the United States. Iowa's production of corn ranks first in the nation along with Illinois. It ranks second in the production of soybeans and fourth in producing alfalfa. Iowa, "where the tall corn grows," as a favorite Iowa song declares, has done more to perfect and extend the cultivation of corn than any other state. Iowa leads the nation in hogs, is well-known for poultry and eggs, Western and native cattle fattened for the market. Other important crops are red clover, timothy, potatoes, onions, popcorn.

INDUSTRY. Although Iowa is basically an agricultural state, it has a number of important industries, many related to agriculture. These industries include manufacturing of farm machinery, and processing of agricultural products (Iowa has pioneered in several, such as the development of oils and other products from corn). Other products include railway or car equipment, washing machines, refrigerators, fountain pens, and drainage tile, used extensively to convert vast marshy areas of the state into productive farms.

Iowa has two important sources of mineral wealth: bituminous coal mined in the southern part of the state, and gypsum, of which it produces more than any other state.

CITIES. Iowa has no very large city, and only two with a population of more than 100,000. Seven cities have a population of 50,000 or more, and of the larger cities, the capital, Des Moines, is the biggest, followed by Cedar Rapids.

CEDAR RAPIDS, 25 miles north of Iowa City, is a commercial and industrial center. Its best known and one of its largest industries is the Quaker Oats Company. The city's local **art gallery** has a number of paintings by Grant Wood, celebrated Iowa artist.

DAVENPORT (population 100,000), on the western bluffs of the Mississippi River, 70 miles southeast of Cedar Rapids, is today a brisk and prosperous industrial center. There is a curious **roller gate dam** in the Mississippi nearby, and on an island in the river an important **U.S. arsenal.**

DES MOINES, with a population of about 200,000, is the capital city of Iowa. Located on the Des Moines River, near the center of the state, it is an important transportation link for rail, highway, and air travel, and is a key industrial area. Interesting to see are the massive and ornate **state capitol,** which has a commanding hilltop setting; a **historical memorial and arts building, library, civic center,** and **coliseum.** The largest and **most famous state fair** in the country, celebrated in the novel and motion picture "State Fair," is held each summer at the fair grounds on the east side of the city.

Des Moines is also the home of **Drake University,** a co-educational college set in a pleasant campus on the northwest side of town.

DUBUQUE, 70 miles north of Davenport on the Mississippi, one of the oldest settled places in the state, grew up as the result of pioneer lead and zinc mines nearby, some of which are still worked. Pioneer relics in or near the town are **an old shot tower,** the **grave of Julien Dubuque** just outside. One of the few ruggedly hilly towns in Iowa, the city has a curious inclined-plane elevator, which is amusing to ride. Nearby **Eagle Point Park** has a log cabin, said to be the oldest dwelling in Iowa. About seven miles away at **New Melleray** is one of four Trappist monasteries in the United States.

IOWA CITY, 100 miles east of Des Moines, though relatively small (population 46,000), is the seat of the **University of Iowa,** with a spacious and attractive campus, a feature of which is the **first capitol** of Iowa. Begun in 1840, it is a classic example of Greek Revival style. Iowa City is near the villages of the **Amana Society,** worth visiting to see the distinctive types of communal architecture.

SIOUX CITY, 200 miles due west of Waterloo, is on the state line opposite both South Dakota and Nebraska, and at the junction of the Missouri and the Sioux rivers. It has a population of 85,000, second largest in the state, and is a major market and meat packing center.

SPORTS AND RECREATION. Iowa has seven state forests and about 90 state parks. Most of them, however, provide facilities for local residents only. **Hunting** is fair in the autumn, particularly for pheasant, with duck and geese to be found in marsh areas. **Fishing** is only fair in small lakes and ponds stocked with perch, bass, and sunfish, and in a few streams trout are found. **Water sports** are popular on some of the larger lakes in the northwest area in summer. The state's most important spectator sports event is the **Drake Relays** held each April on the campus of Drake University in Des Moines.

SPECIAL EVENTS. In addition to the **Iowa State Fair** and the **Drake Relays,** other events of special interest are the **Cornell Music Festival** at Cornell College, Mt. Vernon, in May; **Tulip Festival** in Pella and Orange City, May; **Beef Cattle Show,** Fort Dodge, September; **Harvest Sunday,** statewide, Sunday before Thanksgiving; and **Boys' 4-H Annual Convention** in Ames, December.

Missouri

With nearly 70,000 square miles Missouri is second in area among states of the Midwest, nineteenth in area among states of the United States. With a population of over 4.6 million it is fifth among states of the Midwest, thirteenth among states of the United States.

Most southern of the western tier of Midwest states, Missouri is bounded on the north by a ruler-straight land border with Iowa. Its eastern border is the twisting course of the Mississippi River, with Kentucky opposite in the south, Illinois in the north. The southern border, except for a curious projection called the "Boot Heel," is a straight land border with Arkansas to the south. On the west, Missouri borders Oklahoma, Kansas, and the Missouri River.

The shape of Missouri is roughly rectangular, just over 300 miles east to west, and slightly less from north to south. Missouri was admitted to the Union as the twenty-fourth state in 1821. The name Missouri is derived from an Indian word meaning "those who have canoes." The state flower is the hawthorn, the state bird, the bluebird, and the state tree, the flowering dogwood.

THE LAND. Missouri's chief natural features are two great rivers, two clusters of rugged hills, and a wide strip of richly productive prairie land. The rivers are the Mississippi, a wide, important channel for commercial traffic which twists along the eastern edge of Missouri next to Illinois and Kentucky; and the Missouri, in the center of the state's eastern edge. The latter winds across Missouri, flowing west to east and dividing two distinctively different regions. At the Kansas line the channel of the Missouri turns northwest. Called the "Big Muddy" because of silt it carries, the Missouri has a commercial channel as far as Kansas City on the west.

The region north of the Missouri, once rolling prairie land rising slowly from east to west, is now rich farmland. South of the Missouri are the state's two clusters of rugged hills, the Ozark Highlands to the west and the St. Francois Mountains, actually an extension of the Ozarks, in the east. They cover about one-third of the area of the state and are characterized by abrupt wooded slopes, narrow valleys, with small, fast-flowing rivers. Several of the rivers have been dammed to make extensive and attractive lakes, the largest of which is the Lake of the Ozarks, near the center of the state. On the southern edge of the state other dams in rivers flowing south into Arkansas have created large lakes that extend into Missouri. The highest point in Missouri is 1,772-foot **Taum Sauk Mountain** in the southeast quarter of the state, in the St. Francois Mountains. Only a short distance southeast of the state's highest point is the lowest point, 230 feet above sea level on the St. Francis River. **Big Spring** is the largest single outlet spring in the United States, with a maximum flow of 846 million gallons each day.

THE CLIMATE. Missouri's size and position account for a range of climate and temperature change, with the average annual temperature 50 degrees in the northwest, 60 degrees in the southeast. Rainfall averages from 48 inches annually in the southeast to 32 inches in the northwest, and is fairly well distributed through the year. St. Louis and Kansas City have average January temperatures of 31 degrees, average July temperatures of 80 degrees. The state is generally quite humid, with several tornadoes yearly. The most pleasant time for a visit is late spring or early fall.

THE PEOPLE. Like so many states of the Midwest, Missouri was first explored by the French, and first settled by them. In 1673 Louis Joliet and Father Marquette, came down the Mississippi, followed a few years later by La Salle. (Spanish explorers under De Soto may have followed the Mississippi as far north as Missouri in 1541.) The French established the first settlements in Missouri, in 1735, at Ste. Genevieve on the Mississippi, and a few years later St. Louis, several miles to the north, as a base for fur-trading operations. The French discovered rich deposits of lead and zinc in southwest Missouri.

When Missouri became part of the United States in 1803, its settlement became the staging ground for the vast expansions in the west several years later. The expedition of Lewis and Clark began in and returned to Missouri. Most of the great western trails had their eastern terminus there, and from Missouri the wagon trains began their slow trek west. Later, great cattle herds were driven from the west into Missouri, most of them destined for the stockyards of Kansas City.

Early settlers were from eastern states. Large numbers came from the Carolinas and Virginia. Some of their descendants still live in the Ozark hills.

Some settlers took over the lead mines of the southwest, opened first by the French. During the third decade of the nineteenth century there was a wave of migration from Europe, chiefly from Germany. These settlers stayed mostly in St. Louis and Kansas City, New Hamburg and Altenburg. A later wave of settlement contained many Irish families. One group of Italians established Missouri's substantial but little known wine industry. Early Missourians included the political and social leader Carl Schurz; the celebrated writer Mark Twain, who as a boy named Samuel Clemens grew up in the Mississippi River town of Hannibal; and the outlaw Jesse James, whose house is still a landmark near Excelsior Springs. Daniel Boone owned a farm near St. Charles in Missouri, and General Grant once had a farm in the state.

The diversity of settlement of Missouri is reflected in the design of dwellings and buildings scattered over the state. There are many pioneer log cabins, Jesse James's birthplace being an excellent example. In St. Louis the old cathedral reflects the French look. Germans about 1850 began to build a distinctive type of one-and-a-half-story brick house, many of them still standing in St. Charles County. In the northern prairies Swiss settlers developed distinctive barns, while settlers from southern states built southern-style mansions.

AGRICULTURE. There are 32 million acres of farm and range land in the state, on 13 million of which crops are harvested. Biggest single crop is corn, raised chiefly as fodder for cattle, horses, hogs and mules. Corn grows in the north and west, an area which also produces large quantities of hay, winter wheat, oats, soybeans, potatoes. The state also produces, mostly in the southeast, important quantities of long staple cotton and melons. Livestock raising is an important collateral activity, with Missouri famed for the breeding of sturdy mules.

INDUSTRY. About 75 percent of Missouri's mills and factories are concentrated in the two large cities of St. Louis and Kansas City. St. Louis makes drugs, shoes, automobile parts, railroad cars, hardware, bricks, barber supplies, printing materials, clothing. It is the nation's chief processor of furs, is one of the nation's top cities in the brewing of beer. It leads in the wholesale distribution of dry goods and apparel, ranks second in the country (after Chicago) in handling food and tobacco.

Kansas City is a leading primary market for the processing of livestock, for the stocking and feeding of cattle. It ranks next to Chicago as a primary wheat market, second largest in the country (after Minneapolis) in making flour. It is also one of the country's chief assembly points for automobiles, has a huge maintenance base for airplanes, and major aircraft plants. An unusual product manufactured is corncob pipes.

Missouri is the nation's chief producer of both lead and zinc from mines in the southwest and in the east-central St. Francois Mountains. In the west and north there are extensive coal mines. Other important mineral resources of the state are limestone, granite, and marble for building stone; barite, fire clay, glass sand, nickel copper and cobalt; large quantities of recently discov-

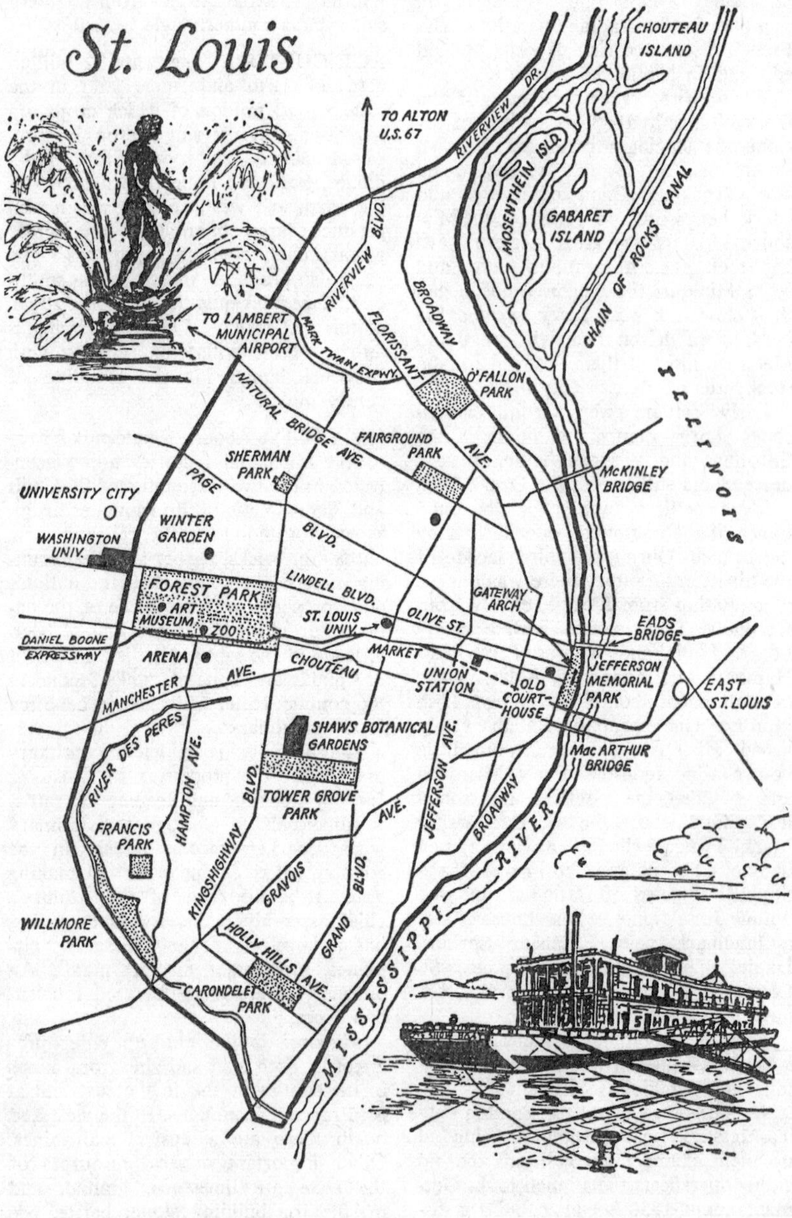
St. Louis
TO ALTON
U.S. 67
CHOUTEAU ISLAND
RIVERVIEW DR.
MOSENTHEIN ISLD.
GABARET ISLAND
CHAIN OF ROCKS CANAL
RIVERVIEW BLVD.
BROADWAY
FLORISSANT
TO LAMBERT MUNICIPAL AIRPORT
MARK TWAIN EXPWY.
O'FALLON PARK
ILLINOIS
NATURAL BRIDGE AVE.
FAIRGROUND PARK
AVE.
SHERMAN PARK
PAGE
McKINLEY BRIDGE
UNIVERSITY CITY
WINTER GARDEN
BLVD.
WASHINGTON UNIV.
FOREST PARK
ART MUSEUM
ZOO
LINDELL BLVD.
GATEWAY ARCH
ST. LOUIS UNIV.
OLIVE ST.
EADS BRIDGE
DANIEL BOONE EXPRESSWAY
ARENA
MARKET
JEFFERSON MEMORIAL PARK
CHOUTEAU
AVE.
UNION STATION
OLD COURT-HOUSE
EAST ST. LOUIS
MANCHESTER
RIVER DES PERES
HAMPTON AVE.
SHAWS BOTANICAL GARDENS
JEFFERSON AVE.
MacARTHUR BRIDGE
BLVD.
TOWER GROVE PARK
AVE.
BROADWAY
RIVER
FRANCIS PARK
KINGSHIGHWAY
GRAVOIS
BLVD.
GRAND
WILLMORE PARK
HOLLY HILLS AVE.
CARONDELET PARK
MISSISSIPPI

ered magnetite iron ore, manganese, and additional copper discoveries.

CITIES. Missouri is a state made up of small towns and villages; only four cities have populations in excess of 100,000. They are Kansas City, Springfield, Independence, and St. Louis.

JEFFERSON CITY, capital of Missouri, is just over 100 miles west of St. Louis on the south bank of the Missouri River (population 32,000). Points of interest include the **state capitol,** with the **state museum** on the ground floor; the **Jefferson Building;** the **state office** and **supreme court buildings;** the **governor's mansion;** the **Cole County Historical Society Museum;** and **Lincoln University.**

JOPLIN (population 39,000), leading city in the Ozark region for lead and zinc mines, is reached by a 60-mile drive from Springfield. A **mineral museum** can be found in the large city park.

KANSAS CITY, on the western edge of the state, almost due west of St. Louis at the junction of the Missouri and the Kansas rivers, is the second largest city in Missouri (population 510,000), twenty-seventh in size in the country. Kansas City is identified with the West and its development due to its beginning as an outfitting point for immigrant trains and settlers headed west.

The city has a notably fine **art gallery,** renowned for its collection of Chinese art; **Swope Park,** about 1,700 acres, with a good zoo. **Country Club Plaza** on the south side is a handsome new residential development. In the big stockyards, covering nearly 240 acres, authentic cowboys are always in evidence. Kansas City has professional football and baseball teams (the **Chiefs** and **Royals**) and a fine **philharmonic orchestra.**

ST. LOUIS, on the west bank of the Mississippi River at about the center of the eastern side of the state, is a metropolis with about 625,000 people, tenth largest city in the country. It produces more than 4,000 products in hundreds of factories, and is a center for transportation and wholesale distribution.

The older part of the city is along the river bank, from which the modern city spreads west for many miles. The newer residential sections, as well as a number of big, fine parks, are in the western part.

Points of interest near the Mississippi include the **Jefferson Memorial Park,** which preserves historic landmarks, and the **Gateway Arch,** an architectural marvel which soars to 630 feet. Also on the river is **Eads Bridge,** built in 1867 by Captain James Buchanan Eads. It was the world's first major steel structure and the first major Mississippi River crossing. In the heart of the downtown area is a recently developed **memorial plaza,** handsomely landscaped. Four miles west of the downtown section is 1,400-acre **Forest Park,** which has a Jefferson memorial, a good zoo, and a remarkable building called the Jewel Box which exhibits flowers. An unusual floral exhibit is **Shaw Gardens,** unique and famous for its plant curiosities.

For the visitor the city offers **river trips** in summer on a big, fully air-conditioned river steamer, spectator events that include **big-league baseball, professional football** (both teams called the St. Louis Cardinals) and a **municipal opera** with summer performances in **Forest Park. Anheuser-Busch Brewery** has visitor tours.

Ste. Genevieve (population 4,000) is the earliest permanent white settlement in Missouri (1735). Located 45 miles south of St. Louis, its old houses, a massive red brick church, and a walled convent should be visited.

Hannibal (population 18,000), located 100 miles northwest of St. Louis, is famed as the **boyhood home of Mark Twain** (Samuel Clemens). Twain's name is identified with a museum (his home), a lighthouse, a statue, and a bridge over the river.

SPRINGFIELD, about 120 miles southwest of Jefferson City (the road connecting the two cities leads past the **Lake of the Ozarks**), is the third largest city in the state (population 120,000) and the chief city in the Ozark resort region. It is the home of several small colleges, and is surrounded by the **Ozark hills.**

SPORTS AND RECREATION. The Ozark region, beginning south of St. Louis and angularly crossing the state to the southwest corner, contains 19 million acres of rugged terrain, in which are located eight major lakes offering **boating, fishing,** and all **aquatic sports.** Lake of the Ozarks, with a 1,375-mile irregular wooded shoreline and a complete complex of resort facilities, is Missouri's largest. Other important lakes are Table Rock, Taneycomo, and Bull Shoals, all in the White River Lakes System; and Clearwater and Wappapello lakes, both in the southeastern section. Fishing in the lakes is generally excellent. It is also good in some of the clear, fast-flowing Ozark streams, which provide float fishing, done with specially built "john" boats.

Hunting throughout the state is like that in many Midwestern states, with plentiful small game—rabbit, squirrel, and quail. Seasonal hunting of deer, waterfowl and wild turkey brings thousands of hunters to Missouri's private and public hunting areas.

For the sightseer there are good museums in the larger cities, and here and there throughout the state historic buildings, such as **Mark Twain's birthplace,** the **home of Jesse James,** a house said to have been built by **General Grant.** The **Truman Library** at **Independence** exhibits the papers and relics of former President Harry Truman.

SPECIAL EVENTS. Some of the best-known events in Missouri are the **National Intercollegiate Basketball Tournament,** in Kansas City, March; **Apple Blossom Festival,** in St. Joseph, May; **Mark Twain Fence Painting Contest** in Hannibal, July; **Ozark Empire Fair,** in Springfield, August; **Future Farmers of America National Convention,** Kansas City, October; **Silver Skates Tournament,** St. Louis, December; **La Guignolée Festival** (Old French New Year's celebration), in Ste. Genevieve and Old Mines, December 31.

The Plains States

Plains States

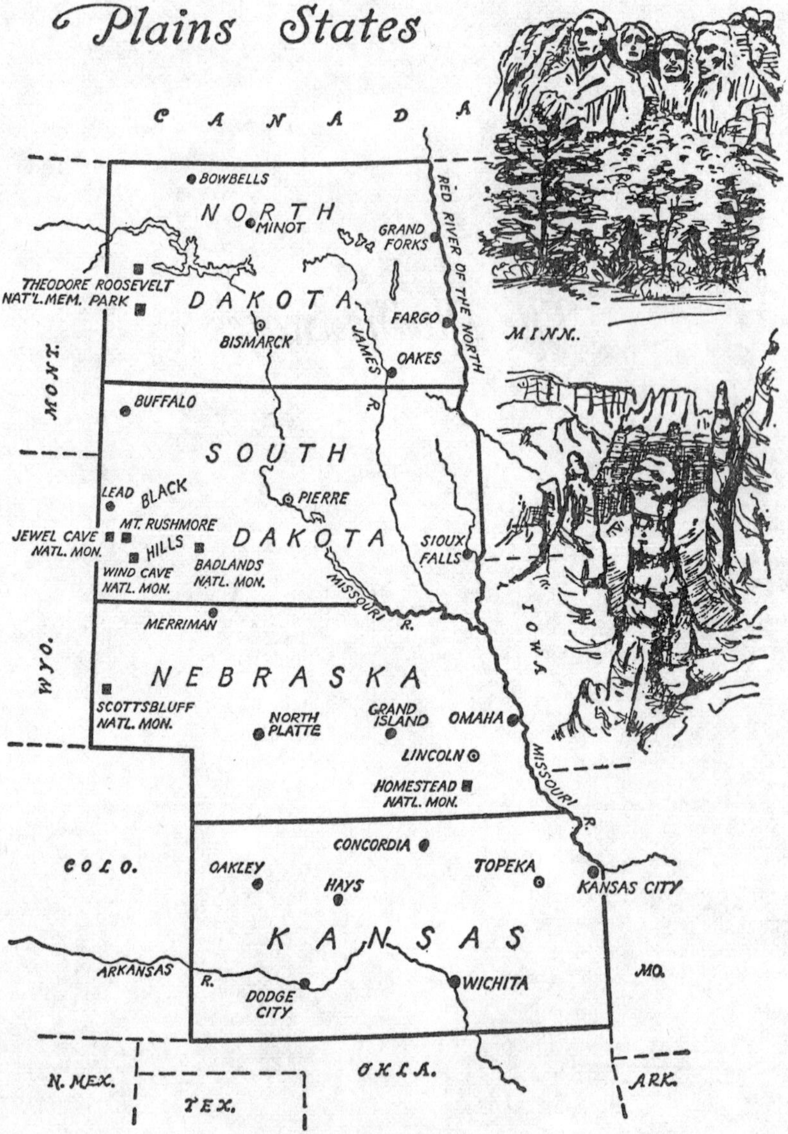

CANADA
NORTH DAKOTA
BOWBELLS
MINOT
GRAND FORKS
RED RIVER OF THE NORTH
THEODORE ROOSEVELT NAT'L.MEM. PARK
BISMARCK
FARGO
JAMES R.
OAKES
MINN.
MONT.
SOUTH DAKOTA
BUFFALO
LEAD
BLACK HILLS
PIERRE
MT. RUSHMORE
JEWEL CAVE NATL. MON.
WIND CAVE NATL. MON.
BADLANDS NATL. MON.
SIOUX FALLS
MISSOURI R.
IOWA
WYO.
NEBRASKA
MERRIMAN
SCOTTSBLUFF NATL. MON.
NORTH PLATTE
GRAND ISLAND
OMAHA
LINCOLN
HOMESTEAD NATL. MON.
MISSOURI R.
COLO.
KANSAS
CONCORDIA
OAKLEY
HAYS
TOPEKA
KANSAS CITY
ARKANSAS R.
DODGE CITY
WICHITA
MO.
N. MEX.
TEX.
OKLA.
ARK.

The Plains States

West of the Red River of the North and the Missouri River, a vast plain, comprising a belt of four states, extends from Canada south to the border of Oklahoma. Here the Midwest ends and the West begins. Indians once hunted buffalo where today fields of grain undulate. Snug farms, with white houses and red barns, are punctuated by forests of oil derricks, while towns and cities have replaced the log cabins and sod huts of a century ago.

The Great Plains are not level. The whole region rises imperceptibly toward the Rocky Mountains to the west, with the western part of the Dakotas turning into the fiercely rugged Black Hills. The Missouri and its broad tributaries water the northern plains, the Arkansas, the southern. Chalk bluffs, fossil beds, sand hills, rock pinnacles, and underground caverns add variety to the scenery. Temperatures, fairly constant throughout the area, range widely from 40-below winters to torrid 110-plus summers. Both extremes of the seasons are tempered by low humidity. Close to 25 inches of rain falls, most of it in the spring and early summer growing season; droughts, however, are not uncommon. Winds are brisk; dust storms, blizzards, and tornadoes are well-known. Yet sunshine is plentiful the year round, with frost-free days numbering from around 130 in North Dakota to about 200 in Kansas.

The first European visitors to the Great Plains were Coronado and his men in 1541, but it was not until the journey of Marquette and Joliet in 1634 that the real penetration began. During the latter seventeenth and early eighteenth century French fur traders roamed Kansas and Nebraska, and by 1743 entered the Dakotas. The Louisiana Purchase brought the whole region under United States control in 1803, and a year later Lewis and Clark made their historic exploration of the gigantic real-estate bargain. Settlers soon followed, especially in Kansas and Nebraska. By the 1840's Kansas was a jumping-off point for covered wagon trains headed farther west, and settlers were crowding into the Dakotas. Inevitably, trouble with the Indians followed, with raids and skirmishes all along the border. Inevitably, too, the Indians were pushed off the land and herded into reservations farther west and south.

Indian warfare was succeeded by equally bitter conflict among the white settlers. The Kansas-Nebraska Act, which had the effect of opening the new region to slavery, brought on fierce clashes between abolitionists like John Brown and the pro-slavery faction. "Bloody Kansas" won tragic fame.

After the Civil War, the new cattle-drive routes, like the Chisholm Trail, from the ranges to the railroad terminal, stirred fresh Indian trouble. When the Black Hills gold strike of 1874 sent a stampede of settlers into the Dakota country, another government treaty with the Indians evaporated.

Through the closing decades of the nineteenth century and the first years of the twentieth, Plains farmers battled drought, locust, plagues, and depressions. The two world wars were a boon to farming, and with the discovery of minerals—coal, zinc, lead, copper, granite, uranium, manganese, gas, and oil—industry developed.

Today some of the nation's most magnificent wheat and corn fields extend through the Plains States, together with acres of oats, rye, flaxseed, sugar beets, fruits, livestock, and dairying. Many manufacturing plants are directly linked to these agricultural pursuits—meatpacking, sugar and flour mills, fertilizer and farm equipment factories.

The pace is relaxed, with a practiced eye kept on the weather. When the crops are in and the first tingle of autumn is in the air, farmers, miners, and everyone else turns hunter. The pheasant, duck, and geese hunting throughout the region ranks with the best in the United States.

Larger cities, such as Omaha, have symphony orchestras, art museums, and other cultural attractions. Summer brings productions like the Black Hills' "Passion Play." Tourists seeking souvenirs of the Plains will find Sioux beaded belts, dolls, paintings, carved wood and pipestones, and two hundred different kinds of rock in South Dakota; Rosemeade pottery and pictures made from wildfowl plumage, prairie flowers, and grasses in North Dakota; wood carvings, metal crafts, ceramics, and paintings with a Swedish influence at Lindsborg, Kansas.

Regional cooking in the Plains States features American dishes: steak is king. A few restaurants have Continental cuisine, and in the Black Hills the visitor may partake of barbecued buffalo. But most establishments stress "good old American cooking."

North of Medora is the **Theodore Roosevelt National Memorial Park.** The 70,374-acre preserve is divided into three parts: the South Unit at Medora; the Elkhorn Ranch to the north; and the North Unit several miles south of Watford City. Highlights include the dramatic Badlands of colorful conical hills, buttes and tablelands; a burning lignite coal vein in the South Unit; remnants of petrified forests; varied flora, including yucca and cactus; a prairie dog town plus birds, deer, antelope, buffalo and smaller animals; museum at Medora; camping and picnicking.

West of Medora, the town of **Sentinel Butte**—named after a high promontory south of the community—is the site of **Father Cassedy's Home on the Range for Boys,** a non-sectarian establishment similar to Boys Town.

FARGO, on the Red River of the North, amid the prairies of eastern North Dakota, is the state's largest city. Founded in 1872 and named after William George Fargo of the famous Wells Fargo Express Company, the community is the chief distributing point between Minneapolis and Spokane; home of one of the nation's biggest wool marketing associations; major meat-packing and livestock hub; chief North Dakota manufacturing center; and terminal of three oil pipelines. The world's tallest man-made structure, the 2,063-foot KTHI-TV television tower, is located at Blanchard, N.D., just off Highway 81 between Fargo and Grand Forks.

On the northwestern edge stands **North Dakota Agricultural College,** whose experimental grain plots and animal farms have developed new species of great benefit to the country. The **Forsberg House** features early Americana from pioneer to Victorian days.

Downriver near Abercrombie lies **Fort Abercrombie Historic Site,** where the state's first U. S. Army post was established in 1857; the blockhouses, which figured in the 1862 Sioux uprising, have been restored, and tourists may use the camp grounds and picnic facilities. Farther along, the community of **Wahpeton,** is the setting for a **U. S. Indian School** and the **North Dakota State School of Science.**

GRAND FORKS is in the Red River Valley on the eastern fringe of the state, with **Grand Forks Air Force Base** about 14 miles west.

In town, are the **U. S. Bureau of Mines Lignite Research Laboratory** and the **University of North Dakota.**

MINOT, in north-central North Dakota, lies within the oil-rich Williston Basin and is rimmed by highly productive lignite coal strip mines. Started as a railroad tent town, it mushroomed so quickly that it was nicknamed "the Magic City." The city is home for an electronic railway yard, **Minot Air Force Base, a state teachers college,** and **Roosevelt Park and Zoo.**

Northwest of town, along the Mouse River, is **Upper Souris National Wildlife Refuge.** A bit farther west lies the **Des Lacs National Wildlife Refuge.** Northeast of Minot, **Lower Souris National Wildlife Refuge** is also along the Mouse River.

East of Westhope are the **Shallow Oil Fields.** At Bottineau, where the Turtle Mountains rise skyward, is the **Monument to the Four Chaplains** in memory of the chaplains who sacrificed their lives during World War II when the ship *Dorchester* went down.

On the Canadian border, the **International Peace Garden** represents a symbol of goodwill. Features include formal gardens, a cairn built of American and Canadian stone, amphitheater, picnic sites, cabins and a lodge.

A short distance west, the **Turtle Mountain Indian Reservation** marks the last retreat of the Chippewa Indians. Southward, near the town of Rugby, a cairn indicates the geographical center of North America.

South and southwest of Minot lie Garrison and **Garrison Dam.** The dam —more than 200 feet high and 12,000 feet long—forms a 200-mile-long lake with 1,600 miles of shoreline.

New Town, set up in 1952 to replace communities inundated by the dam-formed lake, now is headquarters for the Fort Berthold Indian Agency. Other regional lures are the scenic **Lost Bridge Drive** which skirts the Killdeer Mountains; a panoramic trip known as the **North Garrison Reservoir Drive** from New Town to Williston; **Twin Lake Park,** at Williston, with lagoons, zoo, picnic areas and other attractions; and the sites of old **Fort Buford** and **Fort Union.**

SPORTS AND RECREATION. Lakes and parks throughout the state provide excellent facilities for the sports lover. Near Bismarck are **Beaver Lake State Park,** offering swimming, fishing for perch and northern pike, and picnicking. Southwestward, near Glen Ullin, **Heart Butte Dam** forms a lake noted for its silver and large-mouthed bass. Along the 14-mile shoreline are four recreation areas, picnic spots, and boat docks.

In the area around Fargo, well-known facilities include the 250-acre **Chahinkapa Park** on the Red River, with a swimming pool, zoo, aviary, gardens, tennis courts, and an 18-hole golf course—half in North Dakota and half in Minnesota. Other parks of interest are **Little Yellowstone Park, Whitestone Battlefield State Park** (commemorating the 1863 battle between Sioux Indians and forces under the command of U.S. General Alfred Sully), **Bald Hill Dam; Jamestown Dam and Recreation Area; Spiritwood Lake,** and **Arrowwood National Wildlife Refuge.**

Grand Forks, in the eastern Red River Valley, is the location of **Turtle River State Park, Devils Lake, Roosevelt Park, Sully's Hill National Game Preserve, Homme Dam,** and **Selkirk State Historical Park,** where the state's first settlement was made.

Key recreation area near Minot is **Lake Metigoshe State Park,** in the heavily wooded Turtle Mountains, featuring excellent fishing, swimming, boating, camping, picnicking, and a museum displaying Indian relics.

SPECIAL EVENTS. Most well-known of the annual events in North Dakota are the **North Dakota Winter Show,** Valley City near Fargo, early March; **Planting Day,** the anniversary of Custer's departure on his last campaign, Bismarck, May 17; **Miss North Dakota Beauty Pageant,** Bismarck, June; **Sosondowah Amphitheatre** productions, held in Dickinson, July and August; **"Teddy Roosevelt's Life in North Dakota,"** an outdoor drama, presented at Burning Hills Amphitheater near Medora during July and August.

Rodeos are held in many of the towns in North Dakota during June, July and August, including Mandan, Fort Totten, Fargo, Sentinel Butte, New Town, and Fort Yates. Other events are **International Festival of Arts,** held in Dunseith in June; **North Dakota State Fair,** Minot, July; **Fort Ransom Wagon Train Caravan,** Jamestown to Mandan, in July; **Lipizzanian Stallion Horse Show,** Grand Forks, August.

South Dakota

When travelers think of South Dakota, two of the key attractions for them are the Black Hills and Mount Rushmore National Memorial, where the heads of George Washington, Thomas Jefferson, Theodore Roosevelt, and Abraham Lincoln have been carved into a granite mountain.

THE LAND. South Dakota is cut in half by the Missouri River, flowing southeastward through the state. To the west are the Black Hills, heavily forested mountains—called *Paho Sapa* by the Sioux because of their pine-dark woods—stretching over a region some 60 miles wide and 120 miles long. Black Hills National Forest blankets most of the area. Also in this western sector is Mount Rushmore, with its 70-foot-high faces carved some 600 feet above the valley.

The state becomes more level toward the east, with rolling hills and plains covering most of the state. South Dakota's highest point is Harney Peak near Custer which rises to 7,242 feet. Its area is 77,047 square miles, and it is bordered by North Dakota, Minnesota,

Iowa, Nebraska, Wyoming, and Montana.

THE CLIMATE. Extremes in temperature are not uncommon in South Dakota, but even in hottest weather, low humidity keeps the air comfortable. Temperatures often go to 100 degrees in summer, and drop below zero in winter. The averages, however, are 74 degrees in July, and 15 degrees in January.

THE PEOPLE. Because North and South Dakota were settled as one region, their early histories are virtually the same. Following the Lewis and Clark expedition, fur trappers entered the region. The first permanent settlement, a trading post, was built on the site of present-day Fort Pierre in 1817. Despite troubles with several Indian tribes in the 1830's, the fur trade thrived until the 1850's, when it suffered from both dwindling supply and declining demand.

At this point, the development of South Dakota's agriculture began. Land promoters bought up land in 1857, establishing the towns of Sioux Falls, Medary, Yankton, Bon Homme, and Vermillion within a few years. Severe difficulties with Indians, especially the Sioux, followed. The Sioux had signed a treaty with the government giving the United States land in southeastern South Dakota, but controversies over new roads and trespassing onto Indian reservations led to outbreaks.

Gold was discovered in 1874, and thousands of settlers poured in. Many who came in the gold rush stayed on as farmers. These were the days of Red Cloud, Sitting Bull, Calamity Jane, and Wild Bill Hickok, and this period between 1860 and 1890 was the most notorious in South Dakota's history.

By 1889, when the Dakota Territory was divided, and both North and South Dakota admitted to the Union, the Indian outbreaks had died down. However, a severe drought kept settlers away until the turn of the century.

In 1910 there were close to 600,000 residents in South Dakota, and its expansion continued in spurts until 1930 when the Depression, drought, and a grasshopper plague brought on the worst ten years in South Dakota's history.

The demand for agricultural products during World War II strengthened the economy and led to the development of industry. Today South Dakota's population is over 665,000.

AGRICULTURE. Close to 75 percent of South Dakota's farm income comes from livestock and livestock products, largely due to the excellent pastureland which covers over half the state. Field crops include alfalfa seed, flaxseed, spring wheat, grasses, corn, oats, rye and soybeans. In all, 80 percent of the value of goods produced in the state comes from farming.

INDUSTRY. Manufacturing is very light in South Dakota, accounting for only 15 percent of the value of goods produced. Food processing is the most important industry, along with lumber and wood products, and farm machinery. Mining is a small contributor to the economy, although South Dakota leads the country in gold production, and has valuable deposits of beryl.

CITIES. Sioux Falls, with 72,000 persons, is South Dakota's only large city. Over 60 percent of the people live in rural areas near farming regions.

CUSTER, on French Creek, was born to serve the gold rush of the 1870's, and it still contains gold, mica, gypsum, and beryl. The **Log Cabin Museum,** built in 1875, displays exhibits on natural history, minerals and the area's history.

North of Custer, the **Crazy Horse Memorial** stands as a gigantic mountain-top statue more than 500 feet high and over 600 feet long. Rock-rimmed **Sylvan Lake,** seemingly suspended in mid-air, is one of the Black Hills' most scenic lakes. At Hill City, the **1880 Steam Train,** a narrow-gauge operation, carries open tourist coaches from Hill City through the Black Hills to Keystone (summer only).

Gordon Stockade is a replica of a fortification erected by early gold-seekers;

the nearby **Anna Tallent monument** honors the first white woman in the region.

DEADWOOD, of frontier mining days, remains the seat of Lawrence County. **Adams Memorial Museum** exhibits mining equipment, Indian saddles, and early photographs. In **Mount Moriah** or **Boothill Cemetery** Calamity Jane Burke, Wild Bill Hickok, Potato Creek Johnny, Seth Bullock, and Preacher Smith are buried.

Broken Boot Gold Mine, one mile west, is an underground mine that produced for some 25 years prior to 1904 (guided trips made only in summer). Mount Roosevelt, farther on, is topped by a 35-foot-high circular tower known as the **Theodore Roosevelt Monument;** extensive views of four states may be seen from the summit.

At nearby Lead (pronounced Leed), the **Homestake Mine,** in operation since 1872, is the nation's largest gold producer. Vistas of the state, North Dakota, Montana, and Wyoming, may be seen from 7,071-foot **Terry Peak,** west of Lead; the summit can be reached via road or a 4,450-foot-long chair lift with a vertical rise of 1,100 feet.

U. S. Highway 14A runs northward for the 17-mile scenic **Spearfish Canyon Drive** past wooded slopes and towering gray and red limestone cliffs that hem in Spearfish Creek (good fishing). Tourist attractions include **"Passion Play of the Black Hills"; Spearfish City Park,** having an old Deadwood-Spearfish stagecoach and trout fishing; the **Old Spearfish Opera Company Melodrama** (summer performances in the Opera House), where the audience cheers the hero and hisses the villain; the **Federal Fish Hatchery,** in two units, where trout is raised; and the nearby **Theodore Roosevelt Game Refuge.**

MOBRIDGE, on the Missouri River in north-central South Dakota, was superimposed in 1906 on the location of former Arikara and Sioux Indian villages. In the **municipal auditorium** are **Indian murals** by Oscar Howe, which symbolize the region's Indian history and ceremonials. West of town, a hill marks the **burial site of Sitting Bull,** who was killed here in 1890 and was buried, until 1953, at Fort Yates, North Dakota. Southwest of Mobridge sprawls the huge **Cheyenne River Indian Reservation.**

PIERRE (pronounced Peer), in the middle of the state, fans out along the broad Missouri River. Now capital of South Dakota, it was first visited by the La Vérendrye brothers, in 1743. Fort Pierre, across the river, served the early nineteenth-century fur traders.

The domed **state capitol** contains numerous paintings and portraits dealing with state history. At the east end stretches **Capitol Lake** with wild waterfowl and shoreside Governors' Grove and Gate of the Counties. Opposite the capitol stands the column-fronted **Soldiers' and Sailors' Memorial Hall** which houses the State Museum, Department of History and State Historical Society. Exhibits cover such fields as Indians, history and natural history. **Riverside Park** provides swimming, camping or picnicking, and along the river is the **Pierre Indian School.** West of Pierre, at Murdo, the **Pioneer Auto Museum** displays a collection of vintage cars, wagons, and antiques.

RAPID CITY, on the mountain trout stream known as Rapid Creek, stands at the eastern edge of the Black Hills—between the mountains to the west and the prairies to the east. Rapid City is the home of the **South Dakota School of Mines and Technology. Mt. Rushmore National Memorial** is 25 miles south of the city.

The **Museum of Geology** at the School of Mines displays Black Hills' ores, minerals and rocks, and Badlands' vertebrate fossils. The **Sioux Indian Museum** features excellent exhibits of Indian art, costumes, and artifacts. **Dinosaur Park,** overlooking the city and on the scenic **Skyline Drive,** contains life-size, concrete replicas of giant prehistoric animals. Other sights include **Canyon Lake and Park,** owned by the city; **Rapid Creek Canyon Drive,** along the rim of a narrow gorge; and a nearby **state fish hatchery.**

Around Rapid City, **Black Hills Reptile Gardens,** south on U.S. 16, has a large reptile collection, while the **Highway Horseless Carriage Museum** deals with antique cars as well as rifles and pistols. At **Rockerville,** life of the region's first placer mining community has been re-created with false-fronted buildings typical of the pioneer gold period. The nearby **Stratobowl,** where an Army Air Corps balloon made a flight in 1934 to approximately 60,000 feet, and a year later reached a record 72,395-foot height, can be visited.

West of Rapid City are **Wild Cat Cave,** known for its frostwork crystal, flowstone and dogtooth spar crystal formations; and **Nameless Cave,** having odd crystal and rock forms. Near Piedmont, **Wonderland Cave** offers additional underground sightseeing.

Badlands National Monument, southeast of Rapid City and best reached via U. S. Highway 16A, appears as a fantasy of conical hills, ridges, ravines, spires, pinnacles and hundreds of other strange forms weathered by wind and rain. It is one of the world's most astounding examples of erosion; many of the formations are tinted in various colors. The area, too, has been a virtual mine for fossil remains of prehistoric animals. At campgrounds near Cedar Pass naturalists give nightly talks during summer.

SIOUX FALLS is the state's largest city. Clustering around an S-bend in the Big Sioux River, it was founded in 1857. Today, Sioux Falls serves as an important meat-packing, livestock, industrial and educational hub.

A meat-packing company, capacity of approximately 10,000 head of livestock, may be visited, as can **Pettigrew Museum** which displays Indian, pioneer and natural history items. Twin-spired **St. Joseph Cathedral** is one of the state's most impressive churches. **Sioux Falls College** and **Augustana College** comprise the city's most important institutions of higher learning. **Sherman Park,** where ancient Mound Builders once lived, has a zoo plus picnic and recreational facilities.

At nearby Vermillion, the **University of South Dakota Museum** shows Dakota Indian exhibits, pioneer relics, natural history and geological displays. Up the Missouri River, **Yankton** calls itself the oldest city in Dakota territory. **Yankton College** was the first in the region; upstream, **Gavins Point Dam** backs the elongated **Lewis and Clark Lake.**

Almost due west of Sioux Falls, the James River Valley town of **Mitchell,** home of **Dakota Wesleyan University,** has fine pheasant hunting. Unusual is the **Corn Palace,** decorated with pictures and designs formed by thousands of ears of natural-colored corn and grasses. North of Sioux Falls, the river creates a picturesque, red rock gorge at Dell Rapids.

SPORTS AND RECREATION. South Dakota is well-known for its recreational facilities, centered around the many lakes and parks in the state.

Around Custer is **Custer State Park,** 70,000 acres, providing a sanctuary for Rocky Mountain sheep and goats, deer, elk, and the largest bison herd in the United States. Other features include a zoo; a museum dealing with forestry, geology, and history of the area; lake trout fishing; boating and swimming, hiking, picnicking, horseback riding, and camping. **Wind Cave National Park,** adjoining Custer State Park, is known for its delicately formed boxwork and frostwork formations of crystals. Regular guided tours are conducted all year round. In that same area are **Hot Springs,** known for its natural mineral springs; **Angostura Dam and Reservoir,** and **Jewel Cave National Monument.**

Parks in the Mobridge area are **Lake Hiddenwood State Park** (sports fields, fishing, swimming, camping, and picnicking), **Shadehill Dam and Reservoir,** and **Llewellyn Johns Memorial.**

Lake Louise State Recreation Area, east of Pierre near Ree Heights, features a lake, fishing, hunting, picnicking, and camping in a 600-acre prairie section. Six miles north on the Missouri River, **Oahe Dam** backs up a reservoir all the way to North Dakota. Also in that region are **Farm Island State Park,** and **Fort Randall Reservoir,** which have a full range of facilities.

Points of interest around Sioux Falls are **Newton Hills State Park, Union County State Park, Fort Randall Dam, Palisades State Recreation Area, Lakes Madison** and **Herman,** and **Oakwood Lakes State Park.**

SPECIAL EVENTS in South Dakota include the **State Shorthorn Show and Sale,** Brookings, early May; **Antique Show,** Sioux Falls, early May; **Heart of the Hills Celebration,** Hill City, mid-July; **"Trial of Jack McCall for the Murder of Wild Bill Hickok,"** a play presented in Deadwood six nights weekly from June through August. **Black Hills Passion Play,** in Spearfish from mid-June to the first week in September; **Miss South Dakota Talent and Beauty Pageant,** June in Hot Springs; **Gold Discovery Days,** Custer, late in July; **Annual Black Hills Round-up** in Belle Fourche around July 4; **Sitting Bull Stampede,** Mobridge, July 4; **Fort Pierre Rodeo,** Pierre, July 4; **Days of '76,** held in Deadwood in August; **Black Hills Range Days, Rodeo, and Fair,** Rapid City, mid-August, and **Corn Palace Festival,** Mitchell, late September.

Nebraska

Nebraska, famous for its corn and beef cattle, is one of the nation's leading agricultural states. Visitors traveling through Nebraska will find lush grasses and rolling farmland that point up the nickname, the *Cornhusker State.*

THE LAND. Nebraska has an area of 77,227 square miles, runs 415 miles east to west and 205 miles north to south. The Great Plain covers almost 80 percent of the state, but rolling plateaus give a varied elevation from 840 to 5,426 feet above sea level. Nebraska's eastern and northeastern border is the Missouri River, with the North Platte and South Platte (which join in the town of North Platte to become the Platte River) being the other principal waterways.

THE CLIMATE. Quick changes in temperature are not unusual in Nebraska, and are often responsible for the violent thunderstorms, hailstorms, tornadoes, and blizzards which hit the state. Hot breezes from the Gulf of Mexico can make summer weather uncomfortable in eastern Nebraska. In July, temperatures average 78 degrees, and in January, 22 degrees, with rainfall ranging between 18–27 inches yearly (higher in the east).

THE PEOPLE. Pierre and Paul Mallet, Frenchmen exploring in 1739, were probably the first white men to cross Nebraska. After the Louisiana Purchase, it was explored by Zebulon Pike, and within a few years fur trading posts appeared along the Missouri in the early 1800's. The Oregon Trail was opened by fur agent Robert Stuart en route to the East. But because of its vast prairies and desert regions, the soldiers and trappers who traveled through Nebraska considered it unfit for farming.

The Kansas-Nebraska Act of 1854 created the Kansas and Nebraska territories, the latter including most of present-day Montana, North Dakota, South Dakota, Wyoming, and Colorado as well as all of present-day Nebraska.

Early settlers built sod houses and attempted to conquer the prairies. The 1862 Homestead Act, giving 160 acres of western frontier country to every settler, brought a rush of homesteaders; railroads were built west from Omaha, and in 1867 Nebraska became the thirty-seventh state in the Union.

After a brief setback in the 1870's when grasshoppers ruined the crops, a second wave of settlers began arriving. Demand for land raised prices and credit purchases became common, until drought in the 1890's collapsed the market.

Irrigation, cooperatives, and conservative farming methods helped strengthen the economy after 1900, and Nebraska began to prosper. Where crops could not be grown, cattle were raised.

After the Depression, attempts to bring in new industry were undertaken, and today this industrial expansion has helped shift the population of about 1.5 million toward the urban areas.

AGRICULTURE. Nebraska is one of the leading users of irrigation for farmland. Corn, the state's chief crop, brings in over $200 million alone each year, and wheat, hay, grain, oats, alfalfa, beans, and potatoes have prospered due to irrigation of the soil.

Livestock provides the largest part of Nebraska's farm income, especially beef cattle (the state is third behind Texas and Iowa in raising cattle). Feeder farms in eastern Nebraska fatten cattle for markets in Omaha. Hog-raising is another key area of agriculture.

INDUSTRY. Meat packing is the most important industry in Nebraska. Other areas of food processing are ice cream, butter, and dairy products, manufactured around Omaha and Lincoln.

Livestock feed, beer, chemicals, farm machinery, bricks, candy, clothing, and textiles are among the other industries in the state. Manufacturing as a whole contributes one-third of the value of goods produced in the state.

CITIES. Omaha, with over 300,000 residents, is Nebraska's largest city. Only nine other cities have more than 10,000 residents.

CHADRON, surrounded by canyons and buttes at the edge of White River Valley, is the seat of Dawes County. Wooded Pine Ridge forms the background, and nearby retreats in this northwestern corner of the state abound with deer. On the southern edge of town stands the campus of **Nebraska State Teachers College.**

Just east of town, the **Museum of the Fur Trade** reflects the color and lore of this period of American history. Essentials include dioramas and models of nineteenth-century Missouri River Basin operations; trade guns and other pioneer weapons; furs; replica of the James Bordeaux trading post established in 1846; and a garden with rare Indian crops.

Some nine miles south of the community, **Chadron State Park** covers 1,500 acres, containing Chadron Creek (brown and rainbow trout fishing), bridle and hiking trails, cabins, picnic areas, outdoor auditorium and a swimming pool. About 25 miles southwest, the town of Crawford is the focal point for seeing **Fort Robinson,** established in 1874. It was here in 1877 that Chief Crazy Horse was treacherously bayoneted to death while seeking a peaceful conference with Army officials. The old headquarters building now houses a museum dealing with the fort's history and the life of Plains Indians. The area, which has cabins and lodge facilities, is known for excellent deer, antelope, and wild turkey hunting in season.

HASTINGS, seat of Adams County, occupies a position in the middle of the huge Nebraska-Kansas wheat belt south of the Platte River. Founded in 1872, it now is a manufacturing locale and home of **Hastings College.**

The **House of Yesteryear** includes a pioneer grocery store, Indian items, firearms, pioneer attire and furnishings, old vehicles, farm equipment and natural history exhibits. **Prospect Park** contains an outdoor concert pavilion and recreation facilities. **Highland Park** features outdoor diversions plus the **Fisher Rainbow Fountain.**

At Minden, southwest of Hastings, **Harold Warp's Pioneer Village** shows a sod hut, school, the town's first church, old railroad depot, government land office, pony express station, general store and Indian fort, transportation equipment, furnishings and crafts shops. Outside Kearney, **Fort Kearney State Park,** with a stockade and blacksmith shop, marks the location of the old fort. A museum, interpretive center, picnic and campgrounds are also included.

LINCOLN, capital of Nebraska, fills a shallow basin amid a large irrigated agricultural region in the southeastern part of the state some 45 miles west of the Missouri River. Founded only a few years earlier, the community became the capital in 1867 after considerable controversy between "North Platters" and "South Platters"—those who wanted a capital site north, or south, of the Platte River.

The city is a major grain market, insurance hub and distribution locale for farm equipment. Here are the **University of Nebraska, Nebraska Wesleyan University** and **Union College.** Some five miles northwest is **Lincoln Air Force Base.**

The **Nebraska state capitol,** a skyscraper which is rated by architects as the fourth architectural wonder of the modern world, is a striking building with a 400-foot-high central tower topped by a 20-foot statue called The Sower. A statue of Abraham Lincoln, done by Daniel Chester French, stands at the west entrance. Several blocks away, the **University of Nebraska State Museum** boasts an excellent collection of fossil and modern elephant specimens, as well as the largest mammoth fossil skeleton in the world. Other visitor attractions are **Mueller Planetarium,** which presents regular sky shows, and **Sheldon Memorial Art Gallery.**

The **Nebraska State Historical Museum** deals with both Indian and pioneer subjects, and houses a notable reference library. The **Pershing Municipal Auditorium** has a colorful mosaic mural on its façade. **Antelope Park** entices with the city zoo and lovely sunken gardens. **Pioneers Park** contains wildfowl refuge lakes; herds of deer, elk and buffalo; the Pinewood Bowl Amphitheater; a memorial to Nebraska Indians; and Gaudet's life-size bronze figure of a buffalo.

Southeast on the Missouri River, Nebraska City—original location of Fort Kearney—is the center of a vast farm region. Of interest is 65-acre **Arbor Lodge State Park** with the 52-room mansion of J. Sterling Morton, the originator of Arbor Day. Highlights include antiques and early Nebraska relics, old-time vehicles, and an arboretum and rose garden. Near Beatrice on the Big Blue River is **Homestead National Monument,** which preserves the farm of Daniel Freeman, first person to file a claim under the 1862 Homestead Law. Features of the monument are an authentic homestead cabin, period furniture, museum and self-guiding sightseeing trail. West of Lincoln, the town of York is noted for its egg processing, while **East Hill Park** contains recreational facilities.

NORFOLK, in the low hills of the Elkhorn River Valley in northeastern Nebraska, is a sectional trade center for one of the state's most fertile agricultural areas. The livestock sales are interesting as are tours through the local cereal and flour mills.

White Horse Ranch, 20 miles north of Stuart, is where Albino show horses are trained and trick riding-horse acts are staged in summer.

NORTH PLATTE, on a narrow delta at the confluence of the North and South Platte rivers in central Nebraska, has grown, since 1886, from a construction camp to the seat of Lincoln County, a salient railroad division point and shipping hub for the state's oldest irrigated farm district. Livestock, wheat, sugar beets, and alfalfa are the main crops.

North Platte was once the home of Colonel William "Buffalo Bill" Cody. His ranch, "Scouts Rest," northwest of the city, has been reconstructed, furnished, and opened to the public as a part of **Cody Park.**

South of North Platte, **Wellfleet Lake Recreation Grounds** on Medicine Creek stresses camping, picnicking, hunting, and fishing. In the McCook area, **Red Willow, Enders, Medicine Creek, Sutherland,** and **Kimball** reservoirs supply opportunities for angling and other sports.

Near the South Dakota line, Valentine, seat of Cherry County and one of the region's best grazing districts, is the location of **Valentine State Fish Hatchery.** The **Fort Niobrara Big Game Refuge,** once a military reservation, now protects herds of Texas Longhorn cattle and American bison plus muskrat, weasel, mink, civet cat, skunk, raccoon, beaver, coyote, bobcat, elk, deer and birds; two exhibition pastures and a museum at the refuge headquarters provide close-up views. Southward, **Ballards Marsh Public Hunting Area** has excellent migratory fowl hunting in season, and fishing.

OMAHA, spreading along the west bank of the Missouri River and crawling up the nearby hills, occupies a position called the "Crossroads of the Nation" because of its role in westward expansion. Scene of a disastrous winter encampment for Mormons in 1846–47 and later a gold rush trading post, Omaha was incorporated in 1857. Shortly thereafter it became the starting point for the country's first transcontinental railroad.

The community, with more than 347,000 inhabitants, ranks as the state's largest city. It is the world's largest meat packer, butter producer, and has the biggest livestock market. It is a railroad hub for ten trunk lines; important manufacturing, distributing, financial and commercial center; a leading grain market; and home of **Duchesne College, University of Nebraska Medical School, Municipal University of Omaha,** and **Creighton University.**

Joslyn Memorial Art Museum, housed in an impressive pink Georgia marble structure, has lecture and music halls plus exhibits of the early West, Indian arts, and paintings from the Middle Ages to the present day. The **Union Pacific Museum** emphasizes development of the railroad. The public library shows the Byron Reed collection of rare coins.

The **Ak-Sar-Ben** (Nebraska spelled backwards) **Coliseum** is the scene of beef shows, coronation balls, hockey games, rodeos and horse racing. Twin-towered **St. Cecilia's Cathedral,** in Spanish Renaissance style, is the site of the beautiful **Our Lady of Nebraska Chapel.** Of the 45 city parks that cover some 2,100 acres, the most important are **Elmwood Park** (18-hole golf course, bridle paths, picnic grounds and springs); and **Levi Carter Park,** a game preserve with diverse wildfowl plus fishing and boating, pleasant landscapes, and drives.

Other sights include tours of meat-packing plants; municipal auditorium; municipal stadium, scene of the **College World Series, American Legion Little World Series,** and **Pop Warner Midget Football Bowl games;** the Czechoslovakian and Italian communities; **Union Stockyards;** and **Fort Omaha.**

On the northern edge of the city lies **Mormon Cemetery** in which some 600 pioneers, who died in the Mormon 1846–47 "Winter Quarters," are buried. A short trip south, next to Louisville, is **Louisville Recreation Grounds,** along the Platte River, with five sandpit lakes for swimming and fishing plus shore-side camping. Some ten miles west of Omaha, **Boys Town** is a haven for homeless boys.

SCOTTSBLUFF, in the North Platte Valley near the Wyoming state line, services another huge irrigated region of dairying, fattening cattle and sheep, canning and packing.

Southward are **Wildcat Hills Game Refuge** and **Wildcat Hills Recreation Grounds,** amid rugged, wooded terrain where elk, deer, buffalo and other wildlife roam. Southwestward, 3,500-acre **Scottsbluff National Monument** includes Scottsbluff, a prominent landmark on the Oregon Trail, some 800 feet above the North Platte River; a paved road with three tunnels to the bluff summit, from which there are extensive views of the North Platte Valley; remnants of the Oregon and Mormon trails; a museum at headquarters having numerous paintings and displays on Oregon Trail events, frontier history, buffalo hunting and local geology. Eastward, **Chimney Rock National Historic Site,** near Bayard, embraces another Oregon Trail landmark. Shooting some 350 feet skyward above the North Platte River, the odd red sandstone formation looks something like a huge, inverted funnel.

SPORTS AND RECREATION. Outdoor sports facilities can be found throughout Nebraska, especially around the many lakes and parks in the state.

East of Chadron, **Walgren Lake Recreation Grounds** and **Cottonwood Lake Recreation Grounds,** near Hay Springs and Merriman respectively, have facilities for camping, picnicking, and fishing. Visitors will find these facilities at **Alexandria Recreation Grounds,** near Lincoln; at **Blue River Recreation Grounds,** between Dorchester and Milford; at **Cottonmill Lake Recreation Grounds,** west of Kearney, and **Stolley State Park** (site of the old Fort Independence).

Parks around Norfolk, with a variety of facilities, are **Ponca State Park** and **Niobrara Island State Park.**

West of North Platte, the wheat and cattle community of Ogallala is taking-off point for **Lake McConaughy,** nine miles north. Formed by Kingsley Dam, it is the state's largest lake, and features all types of recreational facilities. Northward, **Nebraska National Forest** is one of the nation's oldest and largest man-made forests which supplies many of the Plains States with seedlings. In the area to the south, outside Anselmo, **Victoria Springs State Park** has mineral springs, picnic and campgrounds, cabins, boating, and fishing.

SPECIAL EVENTS. Most counties have a fair at some date in the late summer. These fairs feature livestock shows, games, rides, and exhibits. **Nebraska's State Fair** is held in Lincoln in early September.

In July are two important events, the **World Championship Steer Roping Contest,** in Ogallala, and the annual **Buffalo Bill Wild West Show,** commemorating the world's first rodeo, held in North Platte.

Concerts by the Omaha Symphony Orchestra are given in winter; there is horseracing at Ak-Sar-Ben Coliseum in Omaha during the summer. Ak-Sar-Ben is also the location of the **Livestock Show and Rodeo** in late September.

Kansas

Because it is the leading wheat producer in the country, Kansas has been nicknamed the *Breadbasket of America.* Dodge City, once the largest cattle market in the country, and fields of tall sunflowers are among this state's trademarks.

THE LAND. Kansas, midway point between the Atlantic and Pacific Oceans, is the location of the Geodetic Center of North America, in Osborne County, the reference point from which all government maps of the continent are drawn. The state's area is 82,264 square miles, and though relatively flat, has a high point of 4,039 feet at Mount Sunflower. Except for the Missouri River which forms its irregular northeast border, Kansas' boundaries are relatively straight. Most of the state is rolling plains which increase in elevation toward the west. About 150 lakes dot the state.

THE CLIMATE. Blizzards, thunderstorms, tornadoes, and hailstorms are not uncommon in Kansas, due to the rapid changes in temperature that can occur. Winters are cold, with temperatures averaging 32 degrees, and in July, they range from the high seventies to the low nineties. Snowfall averages 17 inches a year, with total precipitation varying between 18 inches in the west and 40 inches in the southeast.

THE PEOPLE. The first explorer to reach Kansas was Coronado, in 1541, but because no gold was found, the land was of little interest until the nineteenth century. Kansas was part of the Louisiana Purchase except for a small segment in southwest Kansas which was Spanish.

Peaceful farming-and-hunting Indians were the territory's principal inhabitants, augmented in 1825–42 when the government moved other tribes off eastern land and settled them on reservations in Kansas. At the same time white missionaries and settlers began to come, and the first permanent white settlement was established at Fort Leavenworth in 1827.

As homesteaders left the east and needed more land, the government again moved the Indians westward, this time to Oklahoma. Resettlement and encounters with warlike Plains Indians caused much bloodshed.

The territories of Kansas and Nebraska were created in the 1850's under "squatter sovereignty," letting the people work out their own regulations on slavery. The territories became the focal point of the nation as the settlers debated, passed laws, then grew more violent when towns were burned and those favoring slavery fought to protect their interests.

Finally, after several attempts at a constitution, one forbidding slavery was passed. But because the state was predominantly Republican, Democrats in Congress did not admit Kansas until 1861, when several southern states had seceded.

Kansas played an active part in the Civil War, and when it ended, opened land to freed slaves and settlers moving westward. Railroads were built, and cattle were brought to the trains from their Texas pastures; wheat was introduced by the Mennonites from Russia, and Dodge City became a symbol of the pioneer era.

Any long periods of dry weather greatly affected the farming economy of this new state, and in the 1880's and 1890's it became necessary for farmers to borrow money. The Populist Party grew up to bring about reforms in interest and freight rates, alcohol and child labor.

Mining of coal, zinc, and lead, and drilling for oil and gas in the twentieth century brought more money to the state. But through the two world wars, wheat farming grew to be the state's largest business.

The population has grown steadily toward the cities, and today stands at over 2.2 million.

AGRICULTURE. Wheat and beef cattle, raised together on land planted in the fall, used for grazing in winter and for wheat in spring and summer, have made Kansas one of the leading agricultural states in the country. They account for two-thirds of the state's farm income, followed by sorghum grains, hogs, and corn. Close to 92,000 farms cover the state, averaging over 544 acres each. Kansas was once the grazing land for large herds of buffalo, but most of them were killed by the 1880's.

INDUSTRY. Transportation equipment, food processing, machinery, stone, clay, and chemical products are the most important industries in Kansas, although manufacturing only accounts for two-thirds of the state's economy.

Farm machinery is a key industry, as are oil refining, flour milling, and meat packing. Petroleum is Kansas' most valuable mineral.

CITIES. Because of the growth of industry in Kansas, many residents have moved to the larger cities and urban areas to find employment. Kansas City, Topeka, and Wichita, all in eastern Kansas, are the most important cities.

DODGE CITY, on the Arkansas River, in the late 1880's was a wide-open cattle town. Dodge City today is a quiet trade and supply center for a livestock and wheat growing area. A monument, mock cemetery, museum, city hall and old Fort Dodge jail now are around **Boot Hill.** Old Front Street, once the toughest part of town, has been reproduced in a restaurant-saloon and outfitting shop. **Beeson Museum** displays Indian artifacts and pioneer items. **Fort Dodge,** a salient Santa Fe Trail outpost from 1865 onward, is now a state soldiers' home, and some of the 1867 stone buildings are still in use. **Point Rocks,** west of Dodge City, once served as a marker for the old U.S.-Mexican boundary.

Near Dodge City is Meade, where the **Dalton Gang Hideout Museum and Park** has 1887 furnishings, an escape tunnel, and a barn-museum with gun collection, pioneer objects and Indian relics.

Northwest of Dodge City is Scott

City, where **Scott County State Park** embraces the site of El Quartelejo, an ancient Indian pueblo, occupied about 1650–1720. Many of its relics are at the University of Kansas museum at Lawrence. Almost due north, **Pyramid Rocks,** southeast of Colby, present eroded chalk pinnacles which, like **Monument Rocks, Castle Rock** and the **Sphinx** nearby, contain reptilian fossils. At **Colby,** there is an authentic sod house.

Fort Larned, northeast of Dodge City, was an important Santa Fe Trail outpost from 1859–82. A few miles away, red sandstone **Pawnee Rock** was a guidepost and bears the names of Kit Carson and Robert E. Lee.

FORT SCOTT, near the Missouri state line in southeastern Kansas, began as a frontier military post and is now a shipping and manufacturing center.

Fort Scott Museum, in the white, two-story former Officers' Quarters, displays pewterware, candle molds, pioneer rifles and Civil War mementos. The **Fort Scott National Cemtery** was the first of its kind in the United States.

At Coffeyville, the **Dalton Defenders Memorial Museum** contains mementos of the Dalton gang and of the noted baseball pitcher, Walter Johnson.

The **Funston Memorial Home and Museum,** in Iola, was the boyhood home of General Frederick Funston, hero of the 1901 Philippine Campaign.

KANSAS CITY, on the Missouri River, ranks as the second largest city in Kansas. It is a leader in flour milling, meat packing, livestock marketing and soap manufacturing.

Here are the **University of Kansas Medical School** and **Junior College,** and **Central Baptist Theological Seminary.** Kansas City also has a well-developed parks system, including **Wyandotte Lake and Park** with many recreational facilities, and the **Wyandotte County Historical Museum.**

At nearby Osawatomie the **John Brown Memorial State Park** preserves the abolitionist's family's log cabin.

To the north, **Baker University** in Baldwin contains the **Old Castle Museum,** which exhibits Santa Fe Trail and university relics; and the **Quayle Collection of Bibles,** in Case Library, with volumes antedating the invention of printing. Northward, **Lawrence** is home of **Haskell Institute** (nation's largest U. S. Indian school) and the **University of Kansas** with its 120-foot-high campanile and carillon of 53 bells; **Museum of Art** (eighteenth century European art, Oriental arts, sculptures, prints, paintings, collection of medals, timepieces and plaquettes); **Dyche Museum of Natural History** (extensive accumulation of fossil remains, and mounted birds and animals in replicas of their habitats); and the **Snow Entomological Museum** (more than two million specimens of insects).

Fort Leavenworth, occupying 7,000 acres, is the oldest army post in continuous existence west of the Mississippi River. Established in 1827, it is now home of the **Command and General Staff College.** Points of interest are the **Fort Leavenworth Museum** (historic vehicles, guns and Indian artifacts); the former **territorial governor's mansion; old stone wall** with gun slots for cannon; **post chapel; wagon ruts** of the old Oregon and Santa Fe trails. **Leavenworth County State Park,** a rugged, wooded section, is a game sanctuary with nearly two hundred acres for lake fishing and boating.

In **Atchison,** a prominent industrial community, there are scenic drives in **Jackson Park;** vistas from **St. Benedict's College** on bluffs above the Missouri River (see also the Benedictine-style monastery and chapel); the **Atchison, Topeka and Santa Fe Monument.**

SALINA is one of the nation's largest flour milling centers. Guided tours of the mills may be arranged by appointment. **Kansas Wesleyan University** and **Marymount College** (women only); **Smoky Hill Historical Museum** in Oakdale Park (Stone Age man, Indians and pioneers); a historical museum in the **public library;** and the **Cathedral of the Sacred Heart** are all located in Salina.

Some four miles east of Salina, at **Indian Burial Pit,** archaeologists uncovered remains of 146 Indians plus shell necklaces, pendants, flint knives and pottery. The skeletons are exposed to view in the positions in which they were found. At **Abilene,** end of the famed Chisholm Cattle Trail, are the **Eisenhower Home** (daily guided tours), the boyhood home of General Dwight D. Eisenhower, and the **Eisenhower Memorial Museum Library and Chapel. General Eisenhower Park,** a 60-acre tract, has gardens, picnic grounds, swimming pool and Tom Smith Stadium.

Lindsborg, south of Salina, retains the Swedish characteristics of its founders. Studios of the **Lindsborg Artists Guild** (paintings, metalcrafts, ceramics and wood carvings) are located here—as is **Bethany College** (famous for its **Messiah Festival** during Holy Week) on whose campus stands the **Birger Sandzen Memorial Gallery.** Near Great Bend on the Arkansas River, **Cheyenne Bottoms**—a deep lake and four shallow ones—is a migratory waterfowl refuge which also has public shooting grounds and recreation areas.

Hays, an old cow town, is the location of **Frontier Historical Park** with a guardhouse and blockhouse of old Fort Hays established in 1865; **College Museum** (exhibits on history, geology, natural history and paleontology) on the Fort Hays State College campus; and **Fort Hays Experiment Station,** specializing in dry land problems. At nearby **Victoria,** the twin-towered **Cathedral of the Plains** (St. Fidelis Church) possesses choice stained-glass windows.

Northward, the town of **Osborne** is near the **Geodetic Center of North America.** Northwestward, **Kirwin Dam and Reservoir** comprise a large water recreation area. **Smith Center** has one of the two Dutch windmills still remaining in Kansas. Other attractions: **Pike-Pawnee State Monument** (site of a Pawnee village where Lieutenant Zebulon Pike raised the first American flag in Kansas in 1805); the **Hollenberg Ranch Pony Express Station** (said to be the only such station still in its original, unaltered state) at Hanover; **Ottawa County State Park** (game sanctuary, outdoor sports); and **Rock City** with some 200 odd formations.

TOPEKA is capital of the state, meat packer, grain miller, tire manufacturer, printer and publisher, insurance locale and medical center.

The imposing **Kansas State House** stands on a 20-acre square almost in the center of the city. Its interior contains murals by John Steuart Curry and David Overmyer. On the grounds are Merrill Gage's Lincoln Statue and "The Pioneer Mother." Across the street, the **Kansas Memorial Building** houses the Kansas State Historical Society with its museum and extensive library (including maps, pictures and old newspapers). **Mulvane Art Museum** (valuable American sculptures and paintings) is on the **Washburn Municipal University** campus. Of the 32 city parks, **Gage Park** stands out. In it are **Reinisch Memorial Rose and Rock Gardens.**

Other Topeka sights include **Munn Memorial,** marking the point where the old Santa Fe and Oregon trails divided; **Menninger Foundation,** the nation's foremost psychiatric center; the tremendous **Santa Fe Railroad repair shops;** and **Forbes Air Force Base.**

Emporia, home of **Kansas State Teachers College,** serves a large cattle and sheep grazing region in the Flint Hills. At Council Grove, the **Kaw Indian Mission** now is a state museum.

Fort Riley, first set up in 1853 as a Santa Fe outpost, is a base for the U. S. Army Aggressor Center and a "Pentomic" force. Tourist attractions: **Fort Riley Historical Society Museum,** featuring horse and cavalry, First Infantry Division and civilian displays; **First Territorial Capitol of Kansas,** constructed in 1855, rebuilt in 1928 and now a state museum; and **Camp Furston Monument** and **Leonard Wood Memorial.** Manhattan is the location of **Kansas State College.** Regional sights include the **Riley County Historical Museum** and the **Beecher Bible and Rifle Church** erected in 1862. Northward, the **Potawatomie Indian Reservation** blankets more than 7,000 acres near Holton; the July harvest season is marked by **ceremonial dances** plus a **crafts and agricultural fair.** Near Highland is the **Iowa, Sac and Fox Indian Museum.**

WICHITA, at the confluence of the Arkansas and Little Arkansas rivers, is the state's largest city. Its industry includes aircraft manufacturing, meat packing, grain milling, oil refining, and production of petroleum equipment; manufacture of lighting and heating units, air conditioners, and farm implements.

Wichita Historical Museum displays Kansas historical relics, old guns and Indian items. The **Wichita Art Museum** possesses the Naftger European print collection, Roland P. Murdock collection of American sculpture and painting, and an array of Beachy dolls. **Friends University Museum** deals with Africa, birds, a furnished log cabin and covered wagon. **Historic Wichita, Inc.,** is a developing re-creation of the 1872 cow town. Elsewhere, there are the **University of Wichita,** having a pioneer museum in the Forum and the **Walter H. Beech Memorial Wind Tunnel,** and **Wichita Zoo** in Riverside Park.

The town of **Medicine Lodge,** where the Five Tribes and the U. S. Government signed an 1867 peace treaty, became well known as the **home of Carrie Nation.** The structure, now a museum, is maintained by the W.C.T.U. Another visitors' attraction is the **Kansas State Fish Hatchery** near Pratt.

Hutchinson lies above one of the nation's richest salt fields–said to be about 4,000 square miles in area and more than 300 feet thick. Tours may be made through some of the salt mines and evaporating plants. The **Farmers Cooperative Elevator** is one of the nation's longest. **Newton** is the nation's largest Mennonite community and home of **Bethel College.** On the college campus, **Kaufman Museum** exhibits a pioneer Mennonite farm cabin, mounted birds and Indian artifacts.

SPORTS AND RECREATION. Almost every region in the state has at least one park or recreation area with facilities for boating, camping, fishing, swimming, and other outdoor sports. Among the most fully equipped parks are **Clark County State Park,** around a 337-acre lake near Dodge City; **Lake Meade State Park, Cimarron Crossing Park, Garden City,** and **Kearney County Lake,** all in the Dodge City area. Two of these, Lake Meade and Garden City, have game preserves.

Crawford County State Park, south of Fort Scott, features all sports and herds of buffalo, elk, and deer. Near Manhattan is **Turtle Creek State Park and Reservoir** which features boating. Kanopolis Dam on Smoky Hill River near Salina, backs a reservoir with a 30-mile shoreline.

East of Wichita, **Fall River Reservation** near Eureka covers some 2,000 acres. Sports include picnicking, camping, swimming, boating, fishing, and hunting. The oil refining center of **Arkansas City** has a rugged natural bridge formed by two huge rocks arching over a spring. About 12 miles farther east, **Cowley County State Park** has a full range of water facilities.

SPECIAL EVENTS in Kansas include the **International Pancake Race,** in Liberal, February; **Messiah Festival,** Lindsborg, April; **Southwest Kansas Square Dance Festival,** Dodge City, April; **Old Santa Fe Trail Rodeo,** Council Grove, July; **"Days of '49,"** Hanover, July; **Great Southwest Fair and Wheat Show,** Dodge City, mid-August; **Mid-America Fair,** Topeka, mid-September; **State Championship Drag Races,** Liberal, early September; **Kansas State Fair,** Hutchinson, late September; **Svensk Hyllningsfest** (Swedish festival), Lindsborg, every other October.

The Rocky Mountain States

Rocky Mountain States

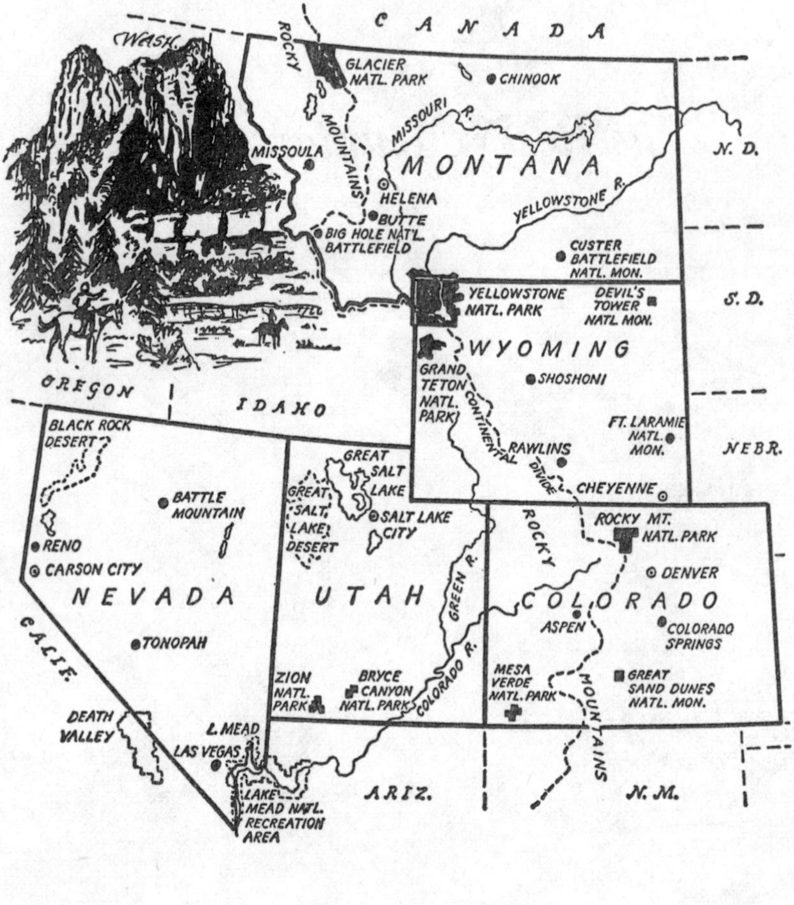
CANADA
WASH.
ROCKY MOUNTAINS
GLACIER NATL. PARK
CHINOOK
MISSOURI R.
MISSOULA
MONTANA
N. D.
HELENA
BUTTE
BIG HOLE NAT'L. BATTLEFIELD
YELLOWSTONE R.
CUSTER BATTLEFIELD NATL. MON.
YELLOWSTONE NATL. PARK
DEVIL'S TOWER NATL. MON.
S. D.
WYOMING
GRAND TETON NATL. PARK
SHOSHONI
OREGON
IDAHO
CONTINENTAL DIVIDE
FT. LARAMIE NATL. MON.
RAWLINS
NEBR.
BLACK ROCK DESERT
GREAT SALT LAKE
GREAT SALT LAKE DESERT
CHEYENNE
BATTLE MOUNTAIN
SALT LAKE CITY
ROCKY
ROCKY MT. NATL. PARK
RENO
CARSON CITY
DENVER
NEVADA
UTAH
GREEN R.
COLORADO
ASPEN
COLORADO SPRINGS
CALIF.
TONOPAH
COLORADO R.
MESA VERDE NATL. PARK
MOUNTAINS
GREAT SAND DUNES NATL. MON.
ZION NATL. PARK
BRYCE CANYON NATL. PARK
DEATH VALLEY
L. MEAD
LAS VEGAS
ARIZ.
N. M.
LAKE MEAD NATL. RECREATION AREA

The Rocky Mountain States

The Rocky Mountain States include some of the nation's most majestic vacationlands. Here, in a dry, somewhat rarefied atmosphere, sky-reaching mountains look down on stately forests, gurgling rivers, bright blue lakes, deep canyons, and placid valleys. Spreading over nearly 550,000 square miles, with fewer than four million permanent residents, this vast area abounds in grandiose scenery and splendid fresh-air recreation. Prehistoric pit houses of aboriginal Indians are neighbors of the uranium mines of the atomic age. Contrasts, odd sights, good fun, and hearty cuisine are hallmarks of the Rocky Mountain States.

Through Colorado, Montana, and Wyoming the Continental Divide winds southward along the peaks, sending waters on its western slopes tumbling toward the Pacific and those on its eastern slopes to the Atlantic. In the eastern parts of these states lie rolling plains and prairies, while the western parts jut upward in tall peaks interlaced with narrow canyons and broader valleys. Utah is principally a high plateau with mountain and canyon profiles. Nevada is alternating valleys and mountains, as if the land were sculptured by a giant trowel. Elevations range from 470 feet above sea level along the Colorado River in Nevada to over 14,000 feet in the Colorado Rockies (highest peak Mount Elbert, 14,433). More than 1,000 peaks in Colorado surpass 10,000 feet.

Sand dunes, arctic tundra, waterfalls, curious rock formations, hot springs, geysers, salt flats, earthquake faults, glaciers, natural bridges, and Great Salt Lake are among the natural wonders of the region. Man-made additions include ancient Indian cliff dwellings, Indian reservations, oil fields, and the nation's only wide-open gambling casinos. Buffalo herds are among the extremely varied and picturesque flora and fauna. Temperature readings swing from 64 below zero to 117 above, though the climate is generally mild, with plentiful sunshine and low humidity. Rainfall is very low, but large quantities of snow fall in the mountains.

Aside from an occasional fur trapper or explorer (usually French-Canadian) this whole vast region belonged to the Indians until well into the nineteenth century. The Louisiana Purchase made most of it American soil, the Mexican War adding the remainder. Two major elements contributed to the wave of colonization near the middle of the century–the Mormon emigration which Brigham Young led into Utah in 1847, and a succession of gold and silver strikes in all five states, which brought prospectors flocking, and founded a "wide-open" tradition that continues today in Reno and Las Vegas. Excellent grazing land attracted cattle and sheep ranchers. And as time went on the indefatigable prospectors turned up copper, oil, zinc, lead, gypsum, uranium, and other minerals important to modern industry.

Inevitably, trouble developed between the encroaching white men and the Indians who had roamed the plains from time immemorial. The years of raids, marches, skirmishes, and ambushes were virtually climaxed by the most famous battle of all the Indian wars–Custer's Last Stand, made on the Little Bighorn River in southeastern Montana.

Despite rapid growth in some centers, such as Denver, the Rocky Mountain States have retained most of their open spaces. They also have retained their tradition of Western hospitality–friendly, informal, easy-to-meet people. Another tradition every visitor notices: silver dollars are as prevalent as paper currency.

In Utah, Mormon culture has given the region a distinctive character. Music, education, literature, and the arts have all been fostered by the Church of Jesus Christ of Latter-Day Saints. Salt Lake City's Tabernacle Choir is a celebrated choral group. Denver and Colorado Springs are well-established cultural centers. Aspen, once a silver ghost town, now is renowned for its Summer Festival sponsored by the Music Associates of Aspen and the Aspen Institute for Humanistic Studies.

Today the Rocky Mountains area presents a balanced picture of industry and agriculture, hard work and recreation, cities and small towns, modern engineering wonders, and magnificent scenery–something for every visitor.

Montana

Because of the wealth of silver and gold found in its mountains, Montana has been nicknamed the *Treasure State*. It is one of the most popular outdoor vacationlands in the country.

THE LAND. With an area of 147,138 square miles, Montana is the fourth-largest state in the country. Its western half is rugged, where snow-capped Rocky Mountain peaks top 10,000 feet. The state's highest point, **Granite Peak,** towers 12,799 feet. Here is found Glacier National Park, with its breathtaking scenery, clear mountain lakes, and active glaciers.

In sharp contrast, eastern Montana is relatively flat, with rolling hills and wide valleys. The state's best farmland lies in this region.

Montana's rivers include the Missouri, Yellowstone, Kootenai, and Musselshell. The **Continental Divide** winds along the spine of the Rockies, separating waters running eastward to the Mississippi from those flowing westward to the Pacific.

THE CLIMATE. Weather varies markedly from east to west, with temperatures west of the Continental Divide being warmer in winter and cooler in summer than in the east. Temperatures average 12 to 31 degrees in January and 54 to 84 degrees in July. Snowfall is heavy in all parts of the state, with over 30 inches falling yearly in the northwest.

An unusual climatic feature of Montana is the *chinook* wind–warm dry air blowing down the eastern slopes of the mountains–which enables farmers to graze cattle on the ranges for short periods during the winter.

THE PEOPLE. Most of Montana was acquired in 1803 as part of the Louisiana Purchase. An area in the northwest corner was obtained from England in 1846.

In 1805, Lewis and Clark made their way through Montana as they opened a trail to the Pacific, and were probably among the first white men to explore the region. They were preceded by fur trappers and adventurers who sought new land, but no real settlements were made until 1858 when gold was discovered in Gold Creek in southwestern Montana. When other strikes followed, Montana was stampeded by gold seekers, with picturesque and lawless frontier towns springing up as fast as miners could come to fill them: Virginia City, Bannack, Diamond City, and others.

Until this point, Montana was part of the Idaho territory, but because the lawless mining camps and towns needed closer governing, the Montana territory was created by the government in 1864.

It was in the 1860's that cattle ranching was established, the first herd being brought up from Texas in 1866. The construction of railroads into Montana made cattle-raising even more prosperous, but an extremely cold winter in 1886–87 killed thousands of animals and reduced the industry considerably.

Throughout this time the Indians were being pressed farther and farther west, off land which had been their own. The site of "Custer's Last Stand" at the Little Bighorn in 1876 is a reminder of those fierce struggles.

Statehood was achieved in 1889, after Montana's population had grown to over 140,000. First silver, then copper was discovered in the hills and mountains. Rich veins of copper were responsible for the town of Anaconda, and men came from all parts of Europe to work in its mines.

In the twentieth century, new industries, especially food processing, were aided by good transportation facilities through the state and by dams and electric power. Although the Depression lowered demands for Montana's metals, World War II boosted the economy above pre-Depression figures, and the recent growth of tourism has brought much needed income to the state. Today Montana has about 695,000 residents, equally divided between urban and rural areas.

AGRICULTURE. Livestock accounts for over half of Montana's farm income, followed by crops such as wheat, barley, hay, sugar beets, and mustard seed (almost all of the country's mustard seed comes from Montana). Agriculture, concentrated in eastern Montana, brings in over $530 million annually—more than half of the value of goods produced yearly.

INDUSTRY centers around processing of foods, oil, forest products, and metals. Copper and aluminum wire, logs, paper, sugar, and flour are among manufactured products.

In spite of the early development of gold, silver, and copper, petroleum is now the leading mineral product. It is found largely in the eastern half of the state, and has a value of around $115 million yearly. Montana is a leader in the use of hydroelectric power, which provides extensive low-cost electricity to all industries.

CITIES. No cities have more than 100,000 residents, with Billings and Great Falls, the two largest at around 61,000 and 60,000 respectively. A main tourist attraction is the towns with almost no population at all—ghost towns where miners and prospectors led a rip-roaring life 100 years ago.

BILLINGS, on the Yellowstone River, is the state's largest city. The **Yellowstone Historical Museum,** near the Bill Hart statue, contains relics of the region's past. A scenic drive along the Rimrocks, 500 feet above the valley, may be made over the **Chief Black Otter Trail,** along which lies the grave of Luther Sage ("Yellowstone") Kelly, the Indian scout who brought the first news of "Custer's Last Stand." Another monument is the **Range Rider of the Yellowstone.**

Eastward, **Crow Agency** is headquarters for the 3,700-square-mile Crow Indian Reservation where summer Sun Dances are staged on special occasions. Nearby **Custer Battlefield National Monument** marks the site of the general's last stand on the Little Bighorn. The 70-mile **Beartooth Highway** climbs more than 5,000 feet and displays such scenery as the Beartooth Plateau and the rugged landscapes of Wyoming-Rock Canyon. About 14 miles north, a mountain trail leads to one-and-one-half-mile-long, three-quarters-of-a-mile-wide **Grasshopper Glacier,** named for millions of grasshoppers imbedded in its icy mass; they may be seen in alternating black lines along the front of an eight-foot ice sheet. **Gardiner,** northern and only year-round entrance to Yellowstone Park, is famous for its big-game hunting.

BUTTE, one of the state's largest cities, began in 1864 when prospectors found placer deposits in Silver Bow Creek, though it was another 12 years before the townsite patent was issued. Since then it has become known as the "richest hill on earth." First came the gold, then silver, and since 1885 copper, zinc, lead and manganese. There are more than 9,500 miles of underground excavations.

The **University of Montana** maintains the Montana School of Mines on whose campus is the **School of Mines Museum,** featuring fossils, minerals, and mine models. The **Berkeley Pit** operations may be viewed from an observation platform. Anaconda Company's Kelley Mine is open weekdays to persons over 16 years of age.

Anaconda, not far northwest, marks the smelter heart of this rich mineral district. Its Washoe Smelter (regular tours), having a 585-foot-high "Big Stack" with five-foot-thick walls—the world's biggest smokestack—refines copper ore. Nearby points of interest include **Washoe Park** with flower gardens and recreational facilities; forest trails into the **Pintlar Wilderness Area** and **Lost Creek Canyon,** a 2,000-foot-deep gorge located in a state park which has full camping facilities. Farther west—via 7,258-foot Skalkaho Pass—lies **Hamilton,** site of a U.S. public health laboratory. To the north, in **Stevensville,** is **St. Mary's Mission,** which has a museum and is the oldest mission in the Northwest.

Southeast of Hamilton, **Big Hole Bat-**

tlefield National Monument covers 200 acres around the scene of an 1877 fight between U.S. troops and Nez Percé Indians under the command of Chief Joseph. **Bannack State Monument** preserves the locale of the state's first territorial capital. This almost deserted former gold-rush town still has its hotel, jail, capitol and some of the log cabin homes.

In **Alder Gulch, Nevada City,** and **Virginia City,** buildings have been restored in authentic fashion, and the latter, the former territorial capital, with its wooden sidewalks and weathered façades, vividly reflects the mood of bygone days. Points of interest include the **Thompson-Hickman Memorial Museum,** exhibiting items of bygone days; the remodeled barn called the **Virginia City Playhouse** where nineteenth-century drama is presented in summer months. North of here and east of Butte, **Lewis and Clark Caverns State Park** shows delicately carved and colored limestone passageways, chambers and formations of the caverns, panoramic vistas of the Jefferson River Valley, the Gallatin and Madison mountains.

Heading east, **Three Forks** is the nearest town to **Missouri River Headwaters State Monument.** This section, first discovered by Lewis and Clark in 1805, contains the confluence of the Jefferson, Gallatin and Madison rivers. **Bozeman,** home of Montana State College, is headquarters for **Gallatin National Forest** with its numerous camp-picnic sites. It is also a gateway community for Yellowstone National Park. Another portal is **Livingston,** in Yellowstone River's Paradise Valley, edged by peaks of the Gallatin and Absaroka ranges. U. S. Highway 89, from here to Gardiner on the park's boundary, is exceptionally scenic. Still another entrance is **West Yellowstone.**

GREAT FALLS, second largest Montana city and seat of Cascade County, spreads across the Missouri River.

First recorded visit to the great Falls of the Missouri, which gave the community its name, was that of Captain Meriwether Lewis in 1805. Great Falls itself began as a planned city in 1883; its growth was aided by the development of hydroelectric power. Now it is a financial, industrial, wholesaling, distributing and trade hub amid a large wool and livestock region.

The **Charles M. Russell Gallery and Original Studio,** a memorial to this celebrated artist of cowboy and Indian scenes, displays a collection of his works, models and personal mementos. The **public library** has regional exhibits as well as a copy of the 1815-printed report of the Lewis and Clark Expedition. The **Anaconda Company,** which refines zinc and copper and which makes copper and aluminum wire, rods and cable, may be toured on weekdays. Some four and a half miles northeast of town, **Giant Springs** on the Missouri River flows at a daily rate of nearly 400 million gallons, having a year-round temperature of 52 degrees.

Northeast of Great Falls—past the site of old Fort Benton—stands **Havre,** a Milk River Valley distributing point near which is the **Northern Montana Agricultural Experiment Station.** South of this community is **Lewistown** on Big Spring Creek (excellent trout angling) amid a region full of ghost towns, battlegrounds, old forts, mountain lakes, and hunting for duck, pheasant, grouse, deer, antelope, elk, and bear.

HELENA, backed by low Mount Ascension and Mount Helena, gazes out on flat, irrigated Prickly Pear Valley which stretches east to the foothills of the Big Belt Mountains.

Late in the summer of 1864, four despairing prospectors stumbled into what they called "Last Chance Gulch" and, surprisingly, struck a bonanza in what is now the city's main street. The town boomed, became territorial capital in 1875 and the state capital in 1889. Since the original strike, some $20 million in gold has been mined in addition to considerable silver and lead.

The domed, granite **state capitol** is of interest for its first floor displays and historic paintings by Charles M. Russell, E. S. Paxson and other artists in

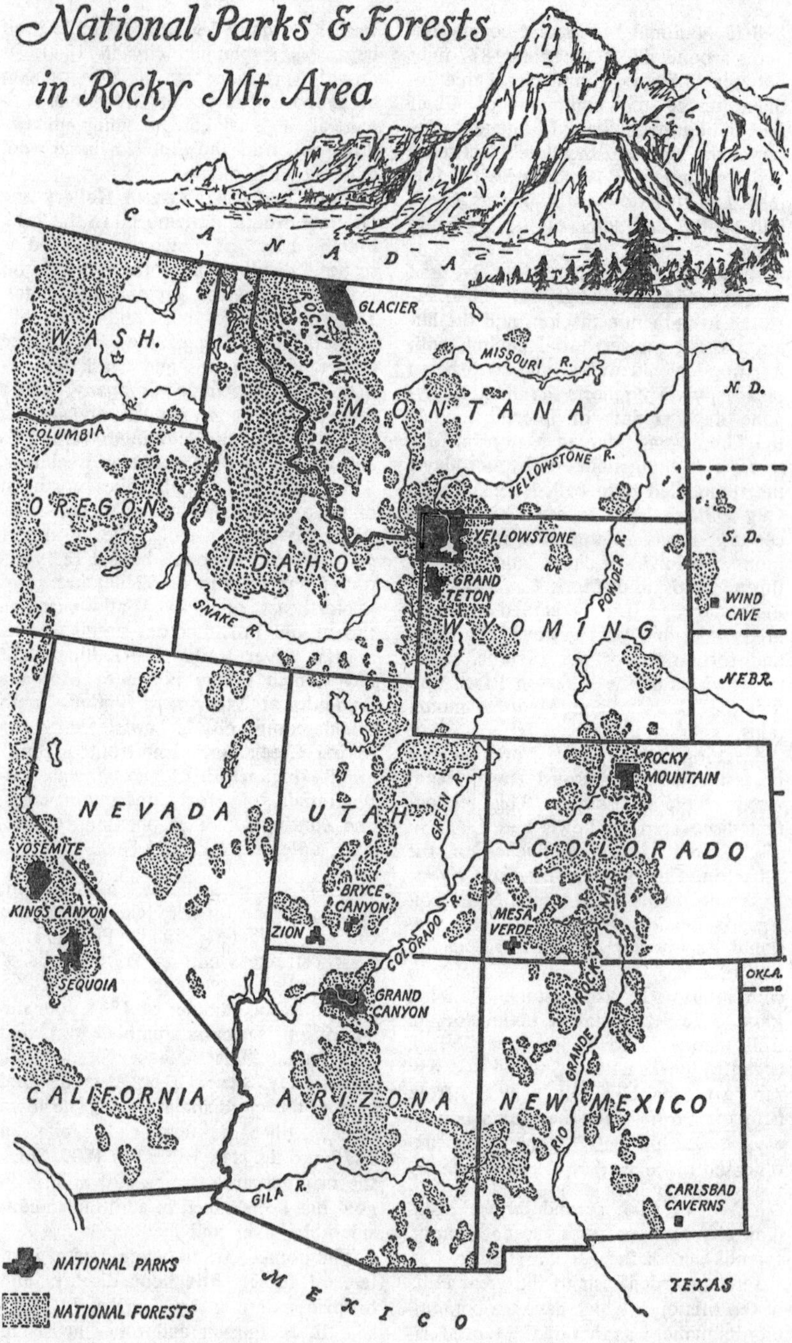
National Parks & Forests
in Rocky Mt. Area
CANADA
WASH.
COLUMBIA
OREGON
IDAHO
SNAKE R.
MONTANA
GLACIER
ROCKY MTS.
MISSOURI R.
YELLOWSTONE R.
N.D.
YELLOWSTONE
GRAND TETON
POWDER R.
S.D.
WIND CAVE
WYOMING
NEBR.
NEVADA
UTAH
GREEN R.
ROCKY MOUNTAIN
COLORADO
YOSEMITE
KINGS CANYON
SEQUOIA
BRYCE CANYON
ZION
COLORADO R.
MESA VERDE
GRAND CANYON
OKLA.
CALIFORNIA
ARIZONA
NEW MEXICO
RIO GRANDE
GILA R.
CARLSBAD CAVERNS
TEXAS
MEXICO
NATIONAL PARKS
NATIONAL FORESTS

the state. On the capitol grounds stands the **Montana State Historical Museum** and **Russell Art Gallery,** a prime showplace with the excellent State Historical Library, bronze sculptures and art works by Charles M. Russell, and the story of Montana in the form of minerals, Indian relics, dioramas and wildlife displays. During summer, a fascinating way to link the past and present is the **Last Chance Gulch Tour.** Two Helena structures—in addition to the so-called "Rococo House" of the 1880's and 1890's—are noteworthy: the **Algeria Shrine Temple,** a Moorish mosque design; and **St. Helena Cathedral,** a Gothic edifice modeled after the cathedral in Cologne, Germany, and having outstanding Bavarian stained-glass windows and Carrara marble decorations.

MISSOULA, at the mouth of the Hellgate Canyon, is the location of the **Aerial Fire Depot,** where the Forest Service's "smoke jumpers" are trained. The **Bonner Mill** of the Anaconda Company Lumbering Division offers weekday tours; the **Missoula Livestock Auction Company** has lively Thursday auctions. The city is also home of **Montana State University** and headquarters of **Lolo National Forest** (Lewis and Clark Trail, pack trips, wilderness areas, camping, picnicking, hunting, fishing, scenic motor trips and hiking).

SPORTS AND RECREATION. Montana is a sportsman's paradise. Clear lakes, cool forests, and towering mountains throughout the state provide excellent facilities for camping, fishing, hunting, swimming, boating, hiking, and bird-watching. Many parks maintain game preserves where elk, bison, antelope, waterfowl, and other wildlife can be seen in their native habitat. Others have facilities for winter sports, especially skiing and ice skating.

Among the most fully equipped parks and forests are **Beaverhead, Deer Lodge,** and **Gallatin national forests,** near Butte; **Fort Peck Recreation Area, Rock Creek State Park, Hell Creek State Park, Medicine Lake National Wildlife Refuge,** and **Bowdoin National Wildlife Refuge,** all near Glasgow.

Near Great Falls are **Lewis and Clark National Forest, Tiber Dam Recreation Area,** and **Helena National Forest,** location of the Continental Divide.

The state's, and one of the country's, most famous parks is **Glacier National Park** (West Glacier is the western portal), which covers more than one million acres including majestic mountains, over 50 glaciers, 200 lakes, frothy streams, and abundant wildlife. With adjoining Waterton Lakes National Park in Canada, it forms an international peace park. The 8,000- to 10,000-foot mountains are part of the Continental Divide, and rear sharply above the Great Plains to the East. In summer, thousands of wildflowers color the meadows and valleys, bringing a rainbow of color to the entire area.

Among the attractions of Glacier National Park are the 50-mile-long Going-to-the-Sun Road, 10-mile-long Lake McDonald, Sperry Chalet (from which Sperry Glacier can be explored), Avalanche Creek Campground, Granite Park, Flattop Mountain, Many Glacier Region, St. Mary Lake, Cut Bank, and Two Medicine Valley (dramatically glaciated valleys).

Eastern entrances to the park are St. Mary and East Glacier Park. About 12 miles northeast is **Browning,** headquarters for the Blackfeet Indian Reservation, and location of the Museum of the Plains Indians. Lakes and parks in this region are **Flathead Lake State Park, West Shore State Park, Yellow Bay State Park,** and **Kerr Dam.** Also in this area are **St. Ignatius Mission,** with unusual frescoes over 100 years old, and the **U.S. Bison Range,** where several hundred buffalo, mountain sheep, deer, and elk graze. **Hot Springs** is a health resort near St. Ignatius which has mineral springs with 120-degree temperatures, and mud baths.

SPECIAL EVENTS in Montana are highlighted by the **Annual Bucking Horse Auction Sale,** Miles City, May; **National Finals of Collegiate Rodeo,** Bozeman, June; **Montana State Square Dance Festival,** Kalispell, mid-June; opening of **Virginia City Opera house** for summer, June; **Ennis Annual Rodeo,** held on July 3rd and 4th; **Last Chance Stampede Rodeo,** Helena, late July; **North Montana State Fair and Rodeo,** Great Falls, August; **Annual Festival of Nations,** Red Lodge, mid-August; **Crow Indians Celebration and Rodeo,** Crow Agency, Billings, August; and the **Harvest Festival and Canadian Days,** Sidney, early October.

Wyoming

In giant Yellowstone National Park, stretching over 3,700 square miles of towering snow-capped mountains, clear lakes and streams, Wyoming possesses one of the world's great tourist attractions.

Wyoming was the first state to give the vote to women, hence its nickname, the *Equality State.*

THE LAND. The Continental Divide, moving southward from Montana, cuts through Wyoming from the northwest. In this western section of the state are some of the highest mountains in the country (the Rocky Mountains: Wind River Range, Absaroka Range, and the Bighorn Mountains), and some of the most spectacular scenery. Also in this area is a part of the Black Hills.

Several large basins lie between the mountain ranges, including Big Horn, Laramie, and Powder River. Three large river systems, the Missouri, the Colorado, and the Columbia have their beginnings in Wyoming's mountains.

In the eastern sector of the state are the Great Plains, where short grass and flat stretches of land provide excellent grazing for livestock. Here too are Wyoming's farms, made possible largely by irrigation.

THE CLIMATE. Temperatures and weather conditions vary greatly with altitude, although generally the climate is dry and sunny. In January readings of 22 degrees in central Wyoming and 12 degrees in Yellowstone Park are not uncommon, as are July readings of 71 and 59 degrees in those same areas.

Snowfall is extremely high in the mountains, sometimes reaching 260 inches a year. In contrast, 15–20 inches fall in the basins.

THE PEOPLE. Indians and occasional trappers were Wyoming's population until the early 1800's. After 1803, when the United States bought the Louisiana Territory from France, more fur traders moved westward, organizing camps where trappers could obtain supplies and food.

In 1834, Fort Laramie, the area's first permanent trading post, was established. Others sprang up as demand for furs increased, and settlers moved out to work the land.

By the 1850's a steady stream of families in covered wagons was heading westward. But the fierce Plains Indians, alarmed with the way the white men took over their land, began attacking wagon trains, leading to prolonged Indian warfare.

The discovery of gold in the 1860's brought even more homesteaders, and more Indian land was taken away. Treaties over northern land boundaries were made and broken, especially when gold was found in the Black Hills.

In southern Wyoming, however, more peaceful progress was made. The territory of Wyoming was created, railroad lines built, towns developed, and the cattle industry begun.

The granting of statehood in 1890 and the opening of mountain areas to tourists brought another flood of settlers. At this point new trouble arose, not with the Indians, but with owners of large cattle ranches who accused newcomers of stealing from their herds. The problem of cattle rustling led to considerable bloodshed in the early 1890's.

More settlers came as the word spread about Wyoming's excellent grazing land. Homestead acts in 1909, 1912, and 1916 provided free land, and the discovery of oil at Salt Creek Field near Casper in 1912 gave the economy a further boost. Later uranium and trona were found, and more industry was brought to Wyoming. In spite of this expansion, the state's population today is only about 332,000, second smallest in the country, with the majority living in or around the cities.

AGRICULTURE. Ranching is the leading agricultural pursuit in Wyoming, with over 80 percent of the farm income coming from livestock. The state is second in the country in wool production. Besides sheep, income producers are beef and dairy cattle, hogs and poultry.

Crops, largely raised on irrigated land, include hay, barley, and sugar beets.

INDUSTRY. Petroleum refining is Wyoming's leading industry, providing almost half of the state's manufacturing income. Refineries are located chiefly at Casper, Cheyenne, Cody, and Thermopolis. Minerals, natural gas, and foods are also processed in Wyoming. However, manufacturing as a whole only contributes 10 percent of the value of goods produced in the state.

CITIES. The largest city in Wyoming, Cheyenne, has little more than 40,000 residents. It is followed by Casper, Laramie, Rock Springs, and Sheridan, the latter with only 10,000 population. Most of the cities are in southern Wyoming.

CASPER, seat of Natrona County, is scenically situated at a large bend of the North Platte River in east-central Wyoming. Just south of town, pine-forested Casper Mountain rises about 3,000 feet above the community. Once an Oregon Trail outpost, the city is an industrial center.

Less than three miles west of the city, **Old Fort Caspar** illustrates what the frontier fort (originally Platte Bridge Station) was like. **Hell's Half Acre,** about 40 miles farther west, has been created by burned-out, subterranean coal beds and erosion. Covering 320 acres, this strange depression is a weird jumble of spires, towers, caverns, pits, pinnacles and dozens of fantastically shaped formations hiding numerous prehistoric fossils. **Alcova,** southwest of Casper, is the site of 700-foot-long **Alcova Dam** on the North Platte River. With Seminoe and Fremont dams and the 100-mile Casper Canal, it forms the **Kendrick Project,** aimed at reclaiming 60,000 central Wyoming acres for settlement. Farther along on State Highway 220, **Independence Rock** was named the "register of the desert" in 1840 by Father DeSmet. The granite monolith nearly 200 feet high covers more than 27 acres on the Sweetwater River's north bank, and is inscribed with the names of thousands of Oregon Trail emigrants who passed by it. North of Casper, the **Salt Creek Oil Field,** over 20,000 acres, ranks as one of the world's largest light oil producers. Between Casper and Douglas is **Ayer's Natural Bridge,** a 50-foot-wide, 30-foot-high stone span over La Prele Creek.

CHEYENNE, the state capital, started as an army-railroad settlement in 1867. The Wild West element lasted through vigilante days and on through the sheep and cattle wars. Much more subdued, Cheyenne now blows its top only once a year during its annual Frontier Days celebration. The sandstone **state capitol** –its gold dome some 145 feet above ground–dominates the city; of interest is its carved cherry woodwork. Nearby, the **state museum** contains western American Indian artifacts, the Wyoming Stock Growers Association collection, German war trophies, rare books, manuscripts and maps, paintings and other exhibits. An array of early range-life relics may also be seen at the Wyoming Stock Growers Association in the Bell Building. **Lions Park,** on the north edge of town, is a pleasant, popular place for its summer children's amusements, lawn games, fishing and picnicking.

Francis E. Warren Air Force Base, operational point for intercontinental ballistics missiles, marks the old Fort Russell cavalry outpost established in 1867; many of the old structures of the base may be visited. In summer, the **Frontier Riding Club** demonstrates calf-roping several nights weekly at its arena about five miles north of the city. The **Wyoming Hereford Ranch,** ten miles east of Cheyenne, rates as one of the world's largest producers of purebred Herefords. **Fort Laramie National Monument,** northeastward near Fort Laramie, protects the remains of the old Oregon Trail trading-military post. First founded by William Sublette in 1834, it became a military fort 15 years later.

CODY is near the Rattlesnake and Cedar mountains and Shoshone Canyon. The thick woodlands of Shoshone National Forest look down on the Shoshone River.

Named after Colonel William F. ("Buffalo Bill") Cody, the community is a gateway to Yellowstone National Park, 50 miles west. It also serves as headquarters for **Shoshone National Forest,** in the heart of the dude ranch country, where visitors can fish, hunt, camp, swim, and enjoy the vast wilderness areas of the forest. The largest of 15 forests in the Central Rocky Mountain Region, its highest elevation is 13,785 feet.

Buffalo Bill is remembered in two ways: his equestrian statue by Gertrude Vanderbilt Whitney, and the **Buffalo Bill Historical Center.**

JACKSON, an old cow town, looks out on the Grand Teton Range. A year-round resort for dude ranchers, fishermen, hunters, and skiers, Jackson is supply point for Jackson Hole ranchers, and southern gateway to Grand Teton National Park.

A 4,000-foot chair lift, operating all year, takes skiers or sightseers to the top of Snow King Mountain where the vistas of the town, Jackson Hole and Grand Tetons are magnificent. The **National Elk Refuge,** just north of town, is the winter home of a large elk herd that summers in the mountains; winter visitors may ride sleighs that distribute food.

Thayne is in the lovely Star Valley south of Jackson. Almost due east, the cow town of **Pinedale** at the foot of the Wind River Range is a take-off point for trout lakes, big game locales and the **Bridger Wilderness Area.** The latter, comprised of more than 380,000 acres of rugged landscapes in the Wind River Mountains, features camping, fishing, hunting, gay wildflowers, tundra-like expanses, deep canyons, rocky spires that draw mountain climbers, and dramatic waterfalls. East of Jackson, the old fur trappers' rendezvous of **Dubois** at the head of the Wind River Valley offers hunting (mountain sheep, deer, antelope, moose and elk), trout fishing, pack trips to Dinwoody Glacier Fields and Gannett Peak (state's highest point), camping, and winter sports.

LANDER, seat of huge Fremont County, lies at the eastern base of the Wind River Mountains, with the Popo Agie River running through it. The surrounding region is known for its sheep and cattle ranches, oil production, mining of uranium, gold, Wyoming jade, agate and mica; pack trips into the nearby mountains; and fine seasonal hunting and fishing. Both **Shoshone** and **Bridger national forests** shade the snow-topped Wind River Mountains to the west.

The **Wind River Indian Reservation,** north of town, is home for both Arapahoe and Shoshone tribes; items of interest are the late-July or early-August Sun Dances near Fort Washakie, the store, agency and mission buildings, and grave of Chief Washakie. Around **Riverton,** tours may be arranged through some of the uranium processing plants and a wood-treating firm that makes poles, railroad crossties and fence posts. **Ocean** and **Boysen lakes,** hunting areas and dude ranches make up the section's recreation. Farther north, U. S. Highway 20 runs through spectacular **Wind River Canyon** where odd formations on steep granite walls add spice to the drive. Near its end lies **Thermopolis,** a health resort on the Bighorn River, edged by **Hot Springs State Park.** Here are located the world's largest hot mineral springs—Bighorn Hot Springs—flowing at a daily rate of more than 18.5 million gallons; hundreds of other springs, hot waterfalls and terraces; indoor and outdoor pools; a zoo, roaming herds of elk and buffalo; picnic sites; and children's playground.

State Highway 28, south from Lander, is a scenic route that permits easy access to two ghost towns: **Atlantic City** and **South Pass City,** both former gold camps during the 1860's and '70's. Past Rock Springs, the coal-mining, lumber and livestock center of **Kemmerer** outfits hunters and fishermen headed for sports sections to the north; it is also headquarters for **Bridger National Forest.** A museum at city park exhibits a collection of native fish fossils some 40 million years old; the volcanic ash bed in which they were embedded is ten miles west. Southward is **Fort Bridger Historical Preserve**—nineteenth-century fort established by the fur trader and scout, Jim Bridger.

LARAMIE, between the Laramie Mountains and the Medicine Bow Range, came into being on the banks of the Laramie River in 1868 when it was designated a terminal for the Union Pacific Railroad. Previously, Fort Sanders, three miles south, was the local key point on the Overland Trail.

The city, home of the **University of Wyoming,** now is a trade hub for nearby sheep and cattle raising, timber and mineral activities. It also serves as headquarters for **Medicine Bow National Forest** offering fishing, deer hunting, pack and saddle trips, winter sports, camping and picnicking.

At the **University Library,** the Western Historical Collection and University Archives contains manuscripts, maps, photographs, pioneer relics, and Western historical research references. Also on the campus is an interesting geology museum.

A short drive east leads to the jagged-rock **Sherman Mountains,** where erosion has created striking scenery, and to **Pole Mountain Game Refuge.** State Highway 130 westward—the **Snowy Range Road**—provides an extraordinary motor trip filled with panoramas, fishing, hunting, camping, picnicking, skiing and delightful Medicine Bow National Forest settings.

SHERIDAN, in north-central Wyoming where Goose and Little Goose creeks unite, is overshadowed by the bumpy Bighorn Mountains, 15 miles westward. Once a cow town, Sheridan is the largest city in northern Wyoming.

On the west edge of Sheridan lies **Kendrick Park and Zoo,** popular for picnicking or seeing the collection of animals. Much farther west, about three-quarters of the way to Lovell, is the so-called **Medicine Wheel,** a large circle radiating in 29 spokes from a three-foot-high hub—all formed from limestone rock and believed to have been built by prehistoric sun-worshipers. To the south, **Greybull** boasts of Shell Canyon and Shell Falls. Heading eastward, around the sheep-cattle village of **Ten Sleep:** scenic Tensleep Canyon in the Bighorn Mountains; boating, swimming and angling on 267-acre Meadowlark Lake; and U. S. Forest Service picnic and campgrounds.

Completing the counterclockwise loop back to Sheridan—through **Big Horn National Forest**—one slips over 9,666-foot Powder River Pass to **Buffalo,** a cattle and sheep market in the area of former Indian wars and the Johnson County cattle war, around which are numerous dude ranches, a petrified forest, trout fishing and deer hunting.

Devils Tower National Monument, in the northeast corner of the state, is the location of an 865-foot-high stump-shaped cluster of rock columns formed millions of years ago by the cooling and crystallization of once molten materials. Other sights near the Belle Fourche River are a prairie dog village, a historical and geological museum, trails, campgrounds, and picnic setups.

SPORTS AND RECREATION. **Yellowstone National Park,** first-established, largest, and most noted of the federal preserves, blankets some 3,700 square miles, the main portion a volcanic plateau which ranges as high as 8,500 feet. U. S. Highway 20, the Cody Road, which winds past Shoshone Canyon and Buffalo Bill Dam, is one of the best approaches to the park.

Yellowstone, with a main season

from mid-June to mid-September, is a wildlife sanctuary populated by an abundance of birds and animals. Recreation includes trout fishing, boating, horseback riding, and hiking.

Especially worth seeing are the Shoshone, Heart Lake, West Thumb, Upper, Midway, Lower, and Norris geyser basins, where most of the park's 3,000 geysers and hot springs are located (including Old Faithful, Riverside, and Daisy); Mammoth Hot Springs, The Paintpots, where opal, quartz, and hot clay are combined to form colorful, bubbling apertures; Grand Canyon of the Yellowstone; Tower Creek Falls and nearby fossil forests; and Yellowstone Lake, with a 100-mile shoreline.

Grand Teton National Park's 485 square miles include some of the most breathtaking landscape in North America. Within the park are the alpine-like, glacier-carved Grand Teton Mountains with their jagged, horny peaks and intervening canyons; a dozen glaciers; eight large lakes; extensive fir, spruce, and pine forests; and summits ranging from 11,000 to nearly 14,000 feet above sea level. East of these peaks stretches 50-mile-long, six-to-ten-mile-wide Jackson Hole, hemmed in by high plateaus and mountains, and bisected by the swift Snake River. Here, in wild terrain, visitors may see elk, buffalo, shiras moose, deer, antelope, Canadian geese, and other wildlife.

Main park season is from mid-June to mid-September. Hiking and mountain climbing, trout fishing, horseback riding, pack trips, boat rides, and naturalist programs are popular diversions.

Trails include the Lakes Trail, Indian Paintbrush Trail, Cascade Canyon Trail, Skyline and Teton Glacier trails. Other points of interest are the Park Museum at Jenny Lake, Colter Bay Visitor Center, the log-built Church of the Transfiguration, and Bill Menor's Flatboat Ferry.

SPECIAL EVENTS in Wyoming include the **Big Horn Mountain Horse Show,** Casper, in June; **Days of '49,** Greybull, in June; **Cody Stampede,** Cody, July 4; **Pioneer Days Rodeo and Parade,** Lander, July 4; **Frontier Days and Nights,** Cheyenne, late July (parade features history of western transportation); **All-American Indian Days,** Sheridan, early August (featuring authentic ceremonial dances, arts and crafts, Miss American Indian contest, and other events); **Wyoming State Fair,** Douglas, August; **Gift of the Waters Pageant,** Thermopolis, early August; **One-shot Antelope Hunt,** Lander, early September; **Antelope Derby,** Rawlins, September.

Colorado

Famed for its skiing—Aspen, Custed Butte, Breckenridge—and its hot springs, Colorado is also one of the nation's most important and productive states, with mining, cattle, and manufacturing its chief industries.

THE LAND. A topographical map shows three distinct regions in Colorado—the Colorado Plateau to the far west, the towering Rocky Mountains and Continental Divide in the west-central area, and the Great Plains in the east. In the Rockies are Colorado's famous ski areas, national parks, famous Pikes Peak (14,110 feet), and Mount Elbert, highest point in the state at 14,433 feet.

Beginning in Colorado are the major tributaries of the Mississippi-Missouri River system—the Arkansas, South Platte, and Republican rivers. The Colorado is one of the state's most important rivers, while many lakes add to the state's beauty.

THE CLIMATE. The mountainous western sections of Colorado are generally cooler than the plains, with temperatures averaging at least ten degrees lower in the mountains. Because of the extremes in altitude within a short distance, temperatures and weather conditions can change rapidly as you travel through the state. In Colorado, as in Montana, a *chinook,* or warm wind, often blows down the eastern slopes, raising temperatures 20 or more degrees in winter.

THE PEOPLE. Most of Colorado became part of the United States with the Louisiana Purchase in 1803. The western section was obtained following the Mexican War in 1848. Shortly thereafter Zebulon Pike explored the region, discovering Pikes Peak.

Bent's Fort, built in 1833 by a fur company, was the first permanent settlement in Colorado. Few settlers came until 1858, when prospectors, traveling along Cherry Creek, near present-day Denver, found gold. In one year over 100,000 persons flocked in.

Land treaties with the Indians were ignored, and between 1860 and 1870, Indian warfare was continuous.

However, by the late 1870's, great strides were made in Colorado's development. Irrigation was begun in the east, the Denver Pacific Railroad brought train service, and in 1876 the territory was admitted to the Union.

Silver was discovered near Leadville and Aspen, and the state grew rapidly. A slump came in the 1890's when the government canceled its silver agreements, but because of advanced irrigation methods and another gold discovery, Colorado quickly recovered.

Oil was first discovered in the 1860's, but its commercial use did not come until 50 years later. It has since become one of the state's most important minerals.

Tourism has played a large part in the development of Colorado. Ski centers, camping facilities, and beautiful parks brought not only visitors, but new residents to the state. World War II's demand for defense and consumer goods, the mining of uranium, and the selection of Colorado for the site of the United States Air Force Academy have further swelled the state's population and economy, until today it has over two million residents, three-quarters of them living in urban areas.

AGRICULTURE. Livestock, grazed on the state's eastern plains, accounts for nearly two-thirds of the value of agricultural products in Colorado. Cattle are both grazed and fattened in the state.

Crops of importance are wheat, sugar beets, hay, vegetables, flowers, and fruits. In all, there are about 30,000 farms in Colorado. Irrigation has been responsible for most of the state's agricultural wealth.

INDUSTRY. Most of Colorado's industries are small, although together they account for over half of the value of goods produced in the state. Leading industries are food processing (meat packing, freezing, and canning), military weapons (missiles are made near Denver), chemicals, electrical and mining machinery, petroleum products, steel, and rubber products.

Mining is of vital importance to the entire state, with most income coming from petroleum and mineral fuels. Molybdenum (two-thirds of the U.S. supply is near Climax, Colorado), coal, natural gas, sand, and gravel are also key products.

CITIES. Denver, with over 500,000 residents, is by far Colorado's largest city. All three of the state's leading cities (Colorado Springs, Denver, and Pueblo) are located between the plains and the mountains, in central Colorado.

ASPEN. Once a prosperous silver-mining center, Aspen is now a year-round mountain resort, and one of the most popular ski centers in the West. Located near Leadville, across the mountains via 12,095-foot Independence Pass, **Aspen Highlands** and **Buttermilk Ski Area** serve all classes of skiers from novice to expert. The chair lift up **Aspen Mountain** and 11,300-foot **Ajax Hill** has an 8,840-foot lower section and a 5,600-foot upper, and is the world's longest chair lift. It operates for skiers during winter and for sightseers during summer and early autumn. **Maroon Lake** nestles beneath the summit of 14,126-foot **Maroon Peak,** southeast of Aspen.

COLORADO SPRINGS, near the foot of massive 14,110-foot-high **Pikes Peak,** has long been famous as a pleasure resort. The springs are located in nearby **Manitou Springs,** considered part of the same area, though there are two separate towns. Of the 14 mineral springs, the most well known is **Manitou Soda Springs.** Also in the area are the **United States Air Force Academy, Colorado College,** and headquarters of **Pike National Forest.**

In spite of its newness, the U. S. Air Force Academy is becoming the town's most celebrated attraction. Opened in 1958, the Academy is a four-year college which prepares cadets for a career as a commissioned officer in the Air Force upon graduation. Many striking buildings, set against the beautiful mountain scenery, make the Academy a worthwhile stop for travelers. The grounds, which contain picnic facilities, may be visited from 8 A.M. to sunset.

Another well-known sight is the 370-acre **Garden of the Gods,** a natural park beautified by vivid red, oddly carved sandstone formations (best viewed in early morning or late afternoon). **Cave of the Winds** is reached via a vista-filled drive through Williams Canyon, which is loaded with noteworthy formations of alabaster and onyx calcite. **Pikes Peak,** dominating the scene, may be climbed on foot, by car, or cog rail. The **Pikes Peak Auto Highway,** a toll road, is open (subject to snow conditions) from about May 1 to November 1, and **Pikes Peak Cog Railway** features "vista-top" cars that operate during approximately the same season. Both the road and railway afford exceptional panoramas. The **Mount Manitou Scenic Incline Railway** operates from June to October; at the summit, burros may be ridden to such points as Bottomless Pit, Eagle Cliffs and Mount Crest Crags.

The **Pioneers' Museum** houses both archaeological and historical items, while **El Pomar Carriage House Museum** displays vehicles, saddles and other riding equipment of the 1890's. The **Fine Arts Center**—in addition to an art school, studio and theater—has a museum and art gallery. **Van Briggle Art Pottery** features guided tours of its plant and exhibition rooms; adjoining **Monument Valley Park** is an appealing setting for a rock garden, tennis courts, swimming pool, and playgrounds.

Palmer Park, northeastward on Austin Bluffs, looks out on mountain views and has picnic sections, trails and scenic roads. Other spectacular places include **North Cheyenne Canyon,** adjacent to Stratton Park, where waterfalls such as Silver Cascades and Helen Hunt Falls set off eye-catching rock formations; and **Seven Falls** in South Cheyenne Canyon, best seen from Eagle's Nest reached via a cable car.

Panoramic motor drives abound in the Colorado Springs area. Interesting to see are **Broadmoor-Cheyenne Mountain Highway** (toll road), with **Cheyenne Mountain Zoo,** the **Shrine of the Sun memorial** to Will Rogers, and a summit lodge; **Rampart Range Road** (choicest views driving southward), which begins in the Garden of the Gods and runs north to Denver; and **High Drive** through North Cheyenne Canyon and Bear Creek Canyon.

Gold Camp Road, constructed on the former roadbed of the Cripple Creek Short Line railroad, runs for 36 dramatic miles from Colorado Springs past the ghost town of **Goldfield** and the semi-ghost of **Victor** to the old gold mining center of **Cripple Creek.** In addition to pioneer period buildings, Cripple Creek has two points of interest: the **Gold Bar Room** where summer melodramas are performed; and the **Cripple Creek District Museum.**

Both **Woodland Park** and **Green Mountain Falls** are recreational locales near Colorado Springs. **Santa's Workshop** is a children's entertainment spot.

DENVER, capital of Colorado, was founded in 1858 when prospectors washed gold out of Cherry Creek. Once a tough shack and tent town, Denver now ranks as the leading city of the Rocky Mountains region.

With a population of more than one million residents in the metropolitan area, Denver is the railroad, distributing, recreation and manufacturing hub of the Rocky Mountain region. Here are located the **University of Denver, Regis College,** and **Loretto Heights College.**

The Corinthian-style **Colorado State Capitol** commands the scene. Built of Colorado granite and onyx, it is topped by a gold-leaf dome where tourists may look out on a breathtaking panorama of the Front Range. Across the street, the **Colorado State Museum** contains exhibits on the state's pioneer days and early cliff dwellings, ethnology, geology, and history, plus trophies of Kit Carson. Nearby are the **state capitol annex, state office buildings,** and the **state service building,** all constructed from Colorado Yule marble. A civic center includes the municipal building, public library, Greek Temple, Voorhees Gate, and monuments such as the "Bucking Bronco," Kit Carson on a horse, and "On the Warpath."

The **U. S. Mint,** Denver branch, may be toured daily (no children under eight years of age). A few steps away, **Schleier Galleries** features prints, paintings, and etchings. **Chappell House** has changing exhibits from the art museum, an art school, a sizable collection of Indian art, and a children's museum; the **Clock Museum** exhibits odd and rare timepieces.

A good over-all view of Denver and its surroundings may be obtained from the enclosed lounge of the **Sky Deck** atop the First National Bank Building. **Cheesman Park,** too, has vistas of the Rockies (clear day views embrace 150 miles of the range from Longs Peak south to Pikes Peak); a dial and pointers at Cheesman Memorial enable visitors to locate and identify the mountains. At **Mountain View Park** one may look at a profile of the peaks worked in terrazzo; **Washington Park** emphasizes sports as well as lakes, flower gardens and pleasant drives. **Elitches Gardens** has a large amusement section and a summer theater and is known for its elaborate geometrical floral designs and its floral clock. **City Park** includes the Denver Museum of Natural History with its "safe-of-gold" exhibit, displays of minerals, meteorites, prehistoric skeletons, fossils, and native bird and animal groups in natural displays; the Habitat Zoo; a children's zoo; tropical bird house; an electric fountain illuminated in colors; Lorado Taft's 18-foot Fountain of State and other statues and fountains; tennis courts; adjoining 18-hole golf course; pools and gardens. Near the northern city limits are the **Denver Union Stockyards,** world's largest sheep-feeding market.

Golden, home of the noted **Colorado School of Mines,** presents a view of Lookout Mountain, on whose summit are **Colonel William F. "Buffalo Bill" Cody's rock tomb** and **Pahaska Tepee,** which houses the **Cody Memorial Museum.** The night view of Denver from here is especially spectacular. At **Idaho Springs,** center of an area with more than 200 mines producing a diversity of minerals from gold to zinc, the five-mile-long **Argo** or **Newhouse Tunnel,** world's longest mining bore, runs to Central City. In or near town are **Radium Springs; Alma Radon-Radioactive Mine;** the narrow-gauge **Colorado and Southern Railroad Locomotive #60 and a day coach,** now a monument to early railroad days; **Saint Mary's Glacier** near the ghost town of **Alice** (Saint Mary's Lake is at the glacier foot); and **Echo Lake,** a scenic, recreational locale. Impressive drives include **Mount Evans Highway,** highest paved road in the United States; **Squaw Pass Road,** which goes from Echo Lake to Bergen Park; and State Route 279 which runs through rugged **Virginia Canyon** to Central City.

Central City qualifies as one of Colorado's most famous gold mining camps. Of interest are **Teller House,** erected as a hotel in 1872 at a cost of more than $100,000, best known today for its portrait, "Face on the Barroom Floor"; the **Opera House,** which has four-foot-thick walls enclosing impressive crystal chandeliers and original furnishings (performances are given in summer); **Coeur d'Alene Mining Museum;** the 900-foot-deep **Glory Hole Mine; Old West Picture Gallery; Museum of Science and Industry; McFarlane Foundry;** and nearby, **Black Hawk, Nevadaville** and **Gregory Diggings.**

Denver

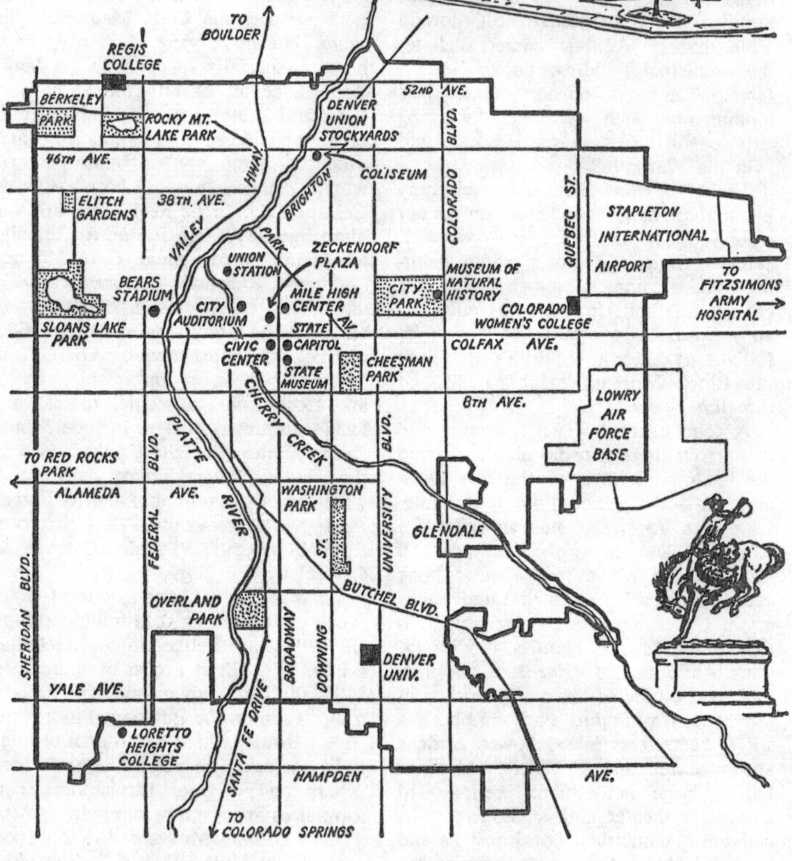

TO BOULDER
REGIS COLLEGE
BERKELEY PARK
ROCKY MT. LAKE PARK
DENVER UNION STOCKYARDS
52ND AVE.
46TH AVE.
COLISEUM
38TH. AVE.
ELITCH GARDENS
HWAY.
VALLEY
BRIGHTON
PARK
COLORADO BLVD.
QUEBEC ST.
STAPLETON INTERNATIONAL AIRPORT
ZECKENDORF PLAZA
UNION STATION
BEARS STADIUM
MILE HIGH CENTER
CITY PARK
MUSEUM OF NATURAL HISTORY
TO FITZSIMONS ARMY HOSPITAL
SLOANS LAKE PARK
CITY AUDITORIUM
STATE AV.
COLORADO WOMEN'S COLLEGE
CIVIC CENTER
CAPITOL
COLFAX AVE.
STATE MUSEUM
CHEESMAN PARK
CHERRY
CREEK
8TH AVE.
LOWRY AIR FORCE BASE
PLATTE
RIVER
FEDERAL BLVD.
UNIVERSITY BLVD.
TO RED ROCKS PARK
ALAMEDA AVE.
WASHINGTON PARK
ST.
GLENDALE
SHERIDAN BLVD.
OVERLAND PARK
BUTCHEL BLVD.
BROADWAY
DOWNING
DENVER UNIV.
YALE AVE.
SANTA FE DRIVE
LORETTO HEIGHTS COLLEGE
HAMPDEN AVE.
TO COLORADO SPRINGS

Georgetown's principal sights are **Hamill House,** constructed in 1867 at a cost of $50,000, with onyx fireplaces, parquet flooring, gold-plated doorknobs, camel's-hair wallpaper, and other luxurious features; and **Hotel de Paris,** erected in 1875, and now a museum that preserves rococo decorations, diamond-dust mirrors, a wine cellar, and French courtyard.

North of Denver, **Longmont's** mountain trout fishing and hunting (deer and ducks) are excellent. **Boulder,** site of the **University of Colorado,** sits below the summits of the towering Flatirons that jut about 1,000 feet above town. Some 28 miles west lies **Arapahoe Glacier,** goal of an annual summer hike. Most noteworthy is the **Flagstaff Scenic Highway** to the top of Flagstaff Mountain some 1,600 feet above Boulder. **Boulder Mountain Park** offers splendid views.

DURANGO, in the San Juan Basin of southwestern Colorado, is headquarters for **San Juan National Forest,** and is near Rio Grande and Uncompahgre national forests—all having wild areas, pack trips, big-game hunting, water sports, winter skiing and thick woods.

Southeastward, **Ignacio** is tribal headquarters for the Southern Ute Indian Reservation where the famous chiefs Ouray, Buckskin Charlie and Ignacio are buried. Eastward, the highway crosses 10,850-foot-high **Wolf Creek Pass.** Of all roads, U. S. Highway 550 northward—part of which is called the **Million Dollar Highway**—is the most breathtaking. It runs up the Animas River Valley, past the steep Hermosa Cliffs, lovely Electra Lake and other magnificent scenery to Silverton and Ouray. In summer months, **"The Silverton,"** a narrow-gauge operation, gives a parallel but different ride through the San Juan country to Silverton, taking a day to make the round trip.

Silverton is a former mining boom town nestling in a tight, peak-rimmed valley. The false-fronted structures along Blair Street have been used as settings for numerous movies; relics of bygone days include the gold-domed courthouse, an old hotel, museum, and the depot. The surrounding mountains—hiding such ghost towns as Gladstone and Eureka, rock hunting locales, big game and mountain trout waters—may be reached via jeep trips or hiking trails. Farther north, **Ouray** also snuggles in a huge amphitheater whose walls rise to meet 14,000-foot summits. Numerous old gold diggings—a few still in operation—honeycomb the nearby cliffs, while hot mineral baths and swimming pools draw seekers of health. **Box Canyon**—more than 200 feet high and 20 feet wide—is a spectacular, roofed gorge through which leap the frothy waters of Canyon Creek. Near town is 227-foot **Bear Creek Falls,** crossed by the Million Dollar Highway.

U. S. Highway 550 ends at **Montrose,** trading center for stock-raising, farming and mining activities around the Uncompahgre Valley. Sixteen miles northeast stands **Black Canyon of the Gunnison National Monument.** The preserve of more than 13,000 acres protects ten miles of the extremely narrow and awesome **Gunnison River gorge** that slashes through a high plateau. Four-mile-long roads skirt along each rim, affording frequent views of the rugged darkly colored and precipitous cliffs.

Mesa Verde National Park, established in 1906, is a huge, steep-sided tableland interlaced with canyons and crowned with thick piñon and juniper woods. Tucked among the canyon walls are scores of well-preserved cliff dwellings; a variety of other ruins dot the mesa top. Visitors may trace four cultural periods: the Basket Makers (A.D. 1–450); the Modified Basket Makers (A.D. 450–750), which brought the bow and arrow, pottery and houses; Development Pueblo Period (A.D. 750–1100), with kivas and sturdier structures; and the Great or Classic Pueblo Period (A.D. 1100–1300), during which the impressive cliff homes were built, and arts and crafts reached their peaks of development.

The park is open all year, but facilities are curtailed during the winter snow period of October or November to May. Main season facilities include well-equipped campgrounds; a good lodge; horseback trail trips; Navajo ceremonial dances; evening campfire programs; and guided tours of some of the ruins in company of well-trained ranger-archaeologists. Highlights are the **Archaeological Museum,** dealing with prehistoric Indian life in the area; **Ruins Road, Spruce Tree House,** the best preserved, having 114 rooms and eight kivas; **Cliff Palace, Square Tower House, Balcony House, Fewkes Canyon Ruins, Sun Temple, Far View House,** and **Pictograph Point Trail,** a three-mile hike from the museum.

Cortez, about nine miles west, is an alternate base for Mesa Verde exploration. To the southwest, a simple marker indicates the **Four Corners** where the Colorado, Utah, Arizona and New Mexico state lines meet.

ESTES PARK, set in a valley enclosed by snowy peaks rearing 13,000 to 14,000 feet skyward, is a popular year-round vacation center. In summer, nearby **Rocky Mountain National Park** is fully open.

Roosevelt, Routt and **Arapahoe national forests**—plus Estes Park itself—present trips to wild areas, hunting, camping, trout angling, hiking, scenic drives, skiing, skating, swimming, tennis and golf. **Lake Estes** offers fishing and boating.

East of Estes Park, the **Big Thompson Canyon Drive** (U. S. Highway 34) is considered one of the region's most outstanding canyon routes. It runs to **Loveland,** sometimes called the "Sweetheart Town" for its Valentine Day mailings, where mountain parks have nice picnic sites, and the New Loveland Museum houses local displays. **Fort Collins,** a big lamb-feeding center and the home of beautifully architectured **Colorado State University,** boasts of **Roosevelt National Forest** retreats; narrow **Poudre Canyon; Pioneer Museum,** old fort relics, gun collection and first log cabin in the area; **Horsetooth Reservoir,** all water sports plus shoreside picnicking; and **Fort Collins Mountain Park. Greeley** is the site of **Colorado State College.**

GRAND JUNCTION, seat of Mesa County and trading headquarters for the Grand Valley farmlands and mineral operations, at the confluence of the Colorado and Gunnison rivers, is headquarters for **Grand Mesa National Forest** and big-game hunting, fishing, boating and hiking.

Colorado National Monument, just west of town, qualifies as an outstanding example of erosion. Highlights of the 18,311-acre preserve include **Rim Rock Drive,** 1,000 to 2,000 feet above Grand Valley's floor and overlooking imposing formations along its 22-mile length; giant sandstone monoliths like 500-foot-high **Independence Rock;** odd formations such as **Window Rock, Coke Ovens** and **Devil's Kitchen.**

LEADVILLE, almost two miles above sea level and looking out on **Mount Elbert** and **Mount Massive** (the state's two highest peaks), began its fame over 100 years ago when prospectors washed out placer diggings in California Gulch. A rich silver strike created an even bigger boom, and by 1878, Leadville had a population of 30,000 (six or seven times the current figure).

Unlike many old camps, Leadville continues to produce; during the last century it has turned out more than $600 million worth of gold, silver, zinc, lead, iron and copper.

Healy House, constructed in 1878, is now a state historical museum with photos, maps, clothing, furniture and other relics of the 1870–80 heyday.

Cooper Hill, eight miles north of town, has good winter skiing as does **Climax,** where the huge Climax Molybdenum Company gouges out molybdenum in a gigantic operation (partially visible from the highway over 11,318-foot Fremont Pass). Scenic points include **Half Moon** and **Arkansas Falls** and **Turquoise Lake** and **Twin Lakes,** which are fishing holes.

Gilman, north of Leadville, is a White River National Forest zinc-mining town on Battle Mountain. Some 600 feet below the community, Eagle River cuts through a precipitous gorge. Fairplay, another old mining center east

ark Twain home and museum,
annibal, Missouri

irginia City, Montana

Indian cliff dwellings, Mesa Verde, Colorado

Temple Square in Salt Lake City, Utah

Bryce Canyon National Park, Utah

Uinta Mountain pack trip, Utah

Repairs on Mt. Rushmore, South Dakota

of Leadville, sits on the edge of South Park with its hunting and opportunities for packing into remote national forest wilderness areas. South of Leadville lies **Salida,** in the middle of the Rockies. Headquarters for **San Isabel National Forest,** this attractively situated community has a museum with regional exhibits, and a hot springs swimming pool supplied with water from **Poncha Hot Springs** in the mountains southwestward. The **Mount Shavano Trout Rearing Farm** is one of the world's largest. In winter, the mountain has the celebrated snow mass known as the "Angel of Shavano" on its side.

PUEBLO, in the Arkansas Valley of the south-central part of the state, turns out some 65 percent of all goods manufactured in Colorado. The **Colorado Fuel and Iron Corporation,** for example, is one of the biggest steel plants in the West. Pueblo's city park has tennis courts, golf course, zoo, picnic setups, Lake Joy, and playgrounds.

Westward via U. S. Highway 50, **Cañon City,** practically rimmed by mountains, sits at the head of the Arkansas Valley. Drawing cards in the immediate vicinity are **Museum of Natural History,** containing Indian artifacts, fossils and the DeWeese big game collection; and the three-mile **Skyline Drive** along a ridge some 800 feet above town. The winding, 35-mile-long **Phantom Canyon Highway** twists through a scenic gorge to Cripple Creek. West of Cañon City lies **Royal Gorge,** a narrow 1,100-foot-deep canyon on the Arkansas River; it is spanned by a suspension bridge and its bottom may be reached via a steep incline railway. Both south and west of here are **San Isabel National Forest** recreation sites and **Great Sand Dunes National Monument.** At **Fort Garland,** the adobe fort that was Colonel Kit Carson's last command has been restored and is now a state museum. To the northeast, **Rocky Ford** is famous for its big watermelons and cantaloupes. **La Junta,** in the irrigated Arkansas River Valley, has become most noted as the home of a Boy Scout group called the "Koshare Indians," who stage authentic Indian dances. The **Koshare Indian Kiva** contains exhibits of beadwork, pottery, wood carvings and Indian art as well as a curio shop.

STEAMBOAT SPRINGS, seat of Routt County, between Routt National Forest and the Yampa River valley to the west, has 157 springs (sulphur, iron, magnesia, saline, lithia, alkaline and other types). Local big game hunting is good, and winter sports are popular at Howelsen Hill and Emerald Mountain with lighted slopes for nighttime skiing.

The mineral springs supply both indoor and outdoor swimming pools as well as private baths at Heart Spring Bathhouse. Not far eastward, **Fish Creek Falls** tumble more than 200 feet; early summer is best for viewing. North of town, **Hot Springs** is a popular picnic place where 152 degree waters flow at a rate of 2,700 gallons per hour.

Southeast of town, **Green Mountain Lake** near Kremmling is celebrated for trout fishing, and the surrounding territory abounds with bear, elk, and deer. Another Middle Park community is **Hot Sulphur Springs** with mineral pools and baths plus nearby **Arapahoe National Forest.**

SPORTS AND RECREATION. State and national parks, with facilities for a variety of summer and winter sports, especially skiing, have made Colorado famous. In addition, most large towns provide tennis courts, a golf course, swimming pool, and in the mountain areas, facilities for skiing.

In the Denver area is **Arapahoe National Forest,** where winter sports are especially popular. Developments include **Winter Park, Arapahoe Basin, Loveland Pass,** and **Berthoud Pass. Evergreen,** in the same area, is a summer resort with full facilities.

Most famous of all Colorado's parks is **Rocky Mountain National Park,** covering some 260,000 acres of the Front Range, among the tallest mountains in North America. Rugged summits jut several thousand feet above valleys which themselves are some 8,000 feet high; glaciers, tundralands, flower-carpeted meadows, sharp cliffs, rough crags, and deep blue lakes provide a background for the park.

Attractions at the park, open from June to September, include **Hidden Valley**; **Moraine Park Museum**; and **Fall River Pass,** where there is an exhibit of high-altitude plant and animal life.

Trail Ridge Road (closed in winter) is one of the West's most spectacular roads, having a four-mile section at a height of more than 12,000 feet, with stunted trees and arctic tundralands. Other scenic roads are **Bear Lake Road, Longs Peak and Wild Basin Road,** and **Fall River Road.**

Trail trips include **Flattop Trail,** chief trans-park path from east to west; **Lawn Lake,** via Roaring River and backed by 10,950-foot Hagues Peak; **Loch Vale,** wild rocky terrain carpeted with gay wildflowers, rimmed by precipitous mountains like 13,150-foot Taylor Peak and cooled by Andrews Glacier; **Odessa and Fern lakes,** nestling in a canyon; **Glacier Gorge,** enclosed by Longs Peak, Thatchtop and McHenrys Peak, and graced by several lakes; **Longs Peak,** accessible by two trails full of astounding views; **Chasm Lake,** within the shadow of Longs Peak; **Wild Basin,** off-the-beaten-path lakes and scenery; and **Twin Sisters,** whose sharp-sided peak is reached via a zigzag trail.

On the western side of the national park, **Grand Lake** is another gateway to the preserve, with several noteworthy lures of its own. The village, on the lake's northern shore, is a highly popular resort with summer events ranging from National Park Service lectures and field trips to boat races, water skiing competitions and a buffalo barbecue. The mile-wide, one-and-one-half-mile-long lake, fed by glaciers, ranks as the state's biggest natural body of water; its trout fishing is excellent, and it has the highest registered yacht anchorage in the world. Other sports include boating, swimming, horseback riding, deer and elk hunting, hiking (several trails to high points and trout-angling lakes). Southwestward, **Shadow Mountain National Recreation Area** is a mountainlike sector covering nearly 30 square miles. Nearby **Granby,** in the Middle Park big-game hunting and fishing region, features dude ranch vacations.

In western Colorado, near Grand Junction, are **Uncompahgre National Forest, Grand Mesa National Forest, Mesa Grand winter ski area, Mesa Lakes recreation area, Glenwood Springs, Red Mountain ski course, White River National Forest,** and **Bridal Veil Falls.**

SPECIAL EVENTS. Some of the most popular annual events in Colorado are the **National Western Livestock Show, Horse Show, and Rodeo** at the Denver Stockyards, late January; **Aspen Winter Carnival,** Aspen; **National Junior Ski Meet,** Winter Park, late March; **Southern Colorado Music Festival,** Pueblo, late April; **Sheriff's Posse Rodeo,** Grand Junction, late May; **Summer Music Festival,** Aspen, June through August, drawing prominent artists, lecturers, scholars, and musicians to participate in forums, panel discussions, and concerts.

Gold Rush Days, Idaho Springs, mid-June; **Pikes Peak Invitational Golf Tournament,** late June; **Central City Opera and Play Festival,** Central City, July and August; **Annual Rooftop Rodeo,** Estes Park, late July to early August; **Spanish Trails Fiesta and Rodeo,** Durango, August; **Pikes Peak or Bust Rodeo,** August; **Colorado State Fair and Rodeo,** Pueblo, late August.

Utah

Almost two-thirds of Utah's one million population are Mormons, descendants of the migrants led by Brigham Young in 1847. The Mormon Tabernacle, one of Salt Lake City's most famous buildings, and the Great Salt Lake, five times as salty as the ocean, are two of the state's most well-known attractions.

THE LAND. The northeast boundary of Utah, shaped like a right angle, encloses two mountain ranges, the Wasatch and the Uinta, the latter being the only east–west section of the Rocky Mountains. In the Uinta Range, peaks tower as high as 13,000 feet.

To the west is the Great Basin, bordering Great Salt Lake and containing Great Salt Lake Desert, one of the driest regions in the country. Thanks to irrigation, some of the state's dry land, especially in central and southern areas, is productive farmland (over one-third of the state is desert).

The Colorado Plateau, with deep canyons, rugged hills, and high plateaus, contains some of the country's most unusual scenery.

THE CLIMATE. Differences in temperature of up to 20 degrees can be found in the extreme northern and southern sections of Utah. July averages in Salt Lake City range from 60 to 92 degrees; the January range is from 17 to 36 degrees. Extreme differences in snowfall can also be found (up to 400 inches in the ski areas are not uncommon, while the southern part of the state receives only a few inches).

THE PEOPLE. Cliff-dwelling Indians were Utah's first inhabitants. The first Europeans to reach the area were two Spanish Franciscan friars late in the eighteenth century. No interest was aroused in the region until the nineteenth century, following Jim Bridger's explorations in 1825. (He is thought to have been the first white man to see the Great Salt Lake.)

Twenty years later the Church of Jesus Christ of Latter-Day Saints—the Mormons—came west under the leadership of Brigham Young, in search of freedom from the religious persecution they had experienced in the East, largely due to their practice of polygamy.

The Mormons settled in 1847 near the Great Salt Lake, established several communities, irrigated and farmed the land. In spite of grasshopper plagues, the settlements prospered. At first they enjoyed peaceful relations with the Indians, but controversies over land ownership led to conflicts in the 1850's and '60's. These were finally settled on Brigham Young's advice that it would be less costly to feed the Indians than to fight them.

Utah's land became United States territory in 1847 after the Mexican War, almost at the moment of the Mormons' arrival. For the next generation the problem of polygamy prevented statehood.

Between 1850 and 1896, the federal government changed its policy toward Utah several times. After appointing Brigham Young governor of the newly created Utah Territory in 1850, it tried to take control away from the Mormons eight years later. It was hoped that the discovery of gold in 1863 would bring a rush of non-Mormon settlers, but this never fully materialized. Settlers did come, however; the Pony Express began carrying mail, railroad lines were built, and mining and farming helped the territory financially. Federal enforcement in Utah of the anti-polygamy law sent many Mormons to prison, and finally led to the outlawing of polygamy in Utah in 1895. Statehood followed in 1896.

In the next 35 years expansion of mining operations, increases in arable farmland (due to careful irrigation), and raising of beef cattle helped Utah's development. But whatever strides were made were almost totally wiped out by the Depression, and it took the intensive industrialization of World War II to put Utah back on its feet.

The federal government today owns and administers large quantities of Utah's farmland, forests, and mines, making the state heavily dependent on government aid. In spite of the decline in Utah's missile projects and value of mineral production, the tourist industry is keeping the state's income at a steady level.

AGRICULTURE. Utah is one of the leading sheep-raising states in the country. Cattle, calves, milk, turkeys, eggs, wool, and hogs are other key livestock products which account for nearly two-thirds of the state's farm income. Wheat is the leading field crop, followed by sugar beets, alfalfa seed, potatoes, cherries, and apricots. Over a quarter of Utah's land is used for farming.

INDUSTRY. Utah's key manufacturing industries, in order of importance, are primary metals (smelting, refining, and rolling; manufacture of basic metal products), transportation equipment, and processing of food and related products. The country's largest Swiss cheese factory is in Smithfield.

Copper is Utah's most valuable mineral, with Bingham Canyon Copper Mine, the largest open-pit copper mine in North America, a spectacular sight for visitors. Petroleum, gold, iron ore, uranium, lead, and zinc are also leading minerals.

CITIES. Salt Lake City, Ogden, and Provo are the only cities in Utah with more than 50,000 residents, although three-fourths of the state's population live in urban areas. Other towns of interest to travelers are Cedar City, Moab, Price, and Vernal.

CEDAR CITY, in southwestern Utah where mountains and plateaus stand two miles above sea level, began in 1851 as an iron mining community. It is the location of Dixie National Forest, known for winter sports, big-game hunting, lake and stream fishing, and guest ranches.

Cedar Breaks National Monument contains a huge, natural amphitheater with a rim elevation of 10,000 feet and a depth of 2,000 feet. The colored limestone cliffs, changing shade with the time of day and cloud cover, are tinted in many varied hues.

Zion National Park embraces one of the West's most grandiose gorges: multicolored, rock-temple-filled Zion Canyon, formed in part by the Virgin River. The canyon—one-half-mile wide and high—may be explored by motorists for about eight miles along its floor. The 12.5 mile **Zion-Mt. Carmel Highway** burrows through Zion Tunnel (three "picture window" overlooks permit remarkable chasm vistas), zigzags down the steep talus slope of Pine Creek Canyon via six switchbacks, and comes to park headquarters near the mouth of Zion Canyon. Twenty-six miles of trails meander to sections of the park not reached by road; a few are footpaths only, others are also bridle trails. The preserve, open year round, also has a museum, summer-season naturalist talks, and camping-trailer grounds.

Principal features of Zion are the park entrance, guarded by 7,795-foot-high **West Temple** and brownish-red **Watchman** towering more than 2,700 feet above ground; **Bridge Mountain** with a natural bridge on its side; **Great White Throne**—grayish-white and streaked with pinkish-red colorings—one of the park's most massive monoliths. Other attractions are **Temple of Sinawava,** a large amphitheater in the center of which are huge rock pillars called the "pulpit" and the "altar" (with the stone face of the "Guardian of the Temple"); the two-mile **Lady Mountain Trail; Angels Landing Trail; Canyon Overlook Trail;** the **Narrows Trail; Kolob Section;** and **Hurricane Fault.**

St. George, seat of Washington County, is the heart of Utah's "Dixie," a warm-summer, mild-winter region growing cane, pomegranates, figs, cherries, peaches and livestock. Sights include the **state's first Mormon Temple** (1869–77); **Brigham Young's winter home** (a unit of Dixie State Park) and other nearby structures; and **Shivwits Indian Reservation. Dixie State Park** contains red and yellow sandstone-walled Snow Canyon, a large ancient lava flow, and offers picnicking and hiking, while the historic **Jacob Hamblin Home** is in Santa Clara. Eastward, at **Kanab,** the **Museum of Southern Utah** emphasizes the Indians' cultural development. Due north, **Panguitch** is the largest community near **Bryce Canyon National Park. Kodachrome Flat** with tinted, odd-shaped rock formations, petrified logs and Grosvenor Arch Natural Bridge; and the **Panguitch-Escalante-Boulder Scenic Drive,** 120 miles long make interesting stopping points. Also to be visited are **Canyons of the Lower Escalante,** formed by the Escalante River and its tributaries into massive red sandstone walls with gently beautiful contours.

Bryce Canyon National Park, southeast of Panguitch, is reached via a drive through the stone sculptures of **Red Canyon.** Its 36,000 acres enclose a land of cream, pink, and red spires, domes, temples and figures. The area is a large horseshoe-shaped bowl cut by numerous huge niches, with fantastic rock forms carved out of 1,000 feet of the Paunsaugunt Plateau. A 20-mile road edges the rim and curves around to various points. A museum shows the area's history, geology, archaeology and biology. Though open year round, the main park season is mid-May to mid-October.

MOAB, seat of Grand County, is a hub for the surrounding uranium- and potash-mining district. **Arches National Monument,** a short drive northwest, covers some 34,000 acres of red rock terrain, 88 stone arches and numerous other fancifully shaped objects. **Canyonlands National Park** and **Dead Horse Point State Park** contain some of the most breathtaking scenery in the West. High cliffs, buttes, and mesas in various shades of red, with lush banks of the Colorado and Green rivers below, make this area a must for travelers. Also in Canyonlands are **Natural Bridges National Monument** (three natural stone bridges), and **Hovenweep National Monument** (six groups of ancient structures built by Pueblo Indians over 800 years ago).

Mexican Hat, near the Arizona line, is a Navajo trading post, and a gateway to Monument Valley. West of town, the **Goosenecks of the San Juan** are where the river has etched 1,200-foot-deep, awesome loops in the surrounding plateau. **Monument Valley,** covering several thousand square miles on both sides of the Utah-Arizona state line, has become famous for its giant red sandstone monoliths and spires rising several thousand feet above the surrounding plains of the Navajo Reservation. Monument Valley is best explored by jeep trips (arrangements may be made at Gouldings Trading Post or nearby towns). **Rainbow Bridge National Monument,** westward, is reached by horseback or boat. Its famous bridge is a rainbow-shaped, salmon-pink, nearly perfect arch more than 300 feet high and almost as wide.

OGDEN, Utah's second largest city, is located on the delta where the Ogden and Weber rivers meet between the Great Salt Lake to the west and the cloud-shattering Wasatch Range to the east. An old Indian hunting locale and fur traders-trappers rendezvous, Ogden became a Mormon site in 1847 and is now a major railroad, manufacturing, and military center for the Intermountain Region. The **Goodyear Cabin** in **Tabernacle Park** was built about 1841. Also in the park is the imposing white **Latter-Day Saints Tabernacle.**

Four miles south, the **John M. Browning Armory** has a special trophy room exhibiting the celebrated Browning Arms Collection. Near Huntsville, the **Abbey of Our Lady of the Holy Trinity,** a Trappist monastery, sells bread at the gate house, made from stone-ground flour.

Brigham City offers two sights: **Box Elder Tabernacle,** with a noted Reuter organ; and the **Intermountain School for Navajo Indians. Bear River Migratory Bird Refuge,** about 17 miles west, often contains some two million wild geese and ducks on its 60,000 acres; whistling swans may be seen during the autumn migratory period, and in summer months the area is the largest Rocky Mountain wildfowl breeding locale. **Inspiration Point,** near the summit of Willard Peak, looks out upon a vast panorama of the Salt Lake Basin, Bear River Valley, Idaho's Malad country and, on clear days, Nevada's eastern mountain ranges.

PRICE, on the river of the same name in central Utah, is the seat of Carbon County, home of **Eastern Utah College.**

South of Price, **Capitol Reef National Monument** is a 20-mile-long sandstone cliff with dome-shaped formations. Points to see are **Capitol Gorge,** a deep narrow canyon (about halfway down the canyon, on the north wall, are Basketmaker-period Indian petroglyphs); the self-guiding trail to **Hickman Natural Bridge;** cliff-enclosed Fremont River; and **Cohab Canyon. Fillmore,** over the mountains 150 miles southwest of Price, is the location of Utah's first state house, preserved in **Old Capitol State Park.** Built between 1851–55, the structure houses exhibits on pioneer implements, clothing, furniture, and dishes, the American Indian, and frontier period art.

PROVO is on the south bank of the Provo River between big Utah Lake and 11,054-foot Provo peak in the Wasatch Range. The surrounding farms raise the state's greatest output of raspberries, pears and apples.

Brigham Young University, founded in 1875, has several museums, a new library containing rare volumes and numerous new buildings. Public parks provide recreation, while the **Pioneer Memorial Park** has a replica of a pioneer cabin plus historic displays.

Northward, where American Fork stands near the 11,750-foot Mount Timpanogos, is the start of the **Alpine Scenic Drive,** a 45-mile mountain-encircling drive that twists up tight American Fork Canyon and past Aspen Grove, and **Timpanogos Cave National Monument.** On the north slope of the mountain, the monument's main feature is a 1,600-foot cavern, average temperature 42 degrees, with translucent white and pink crystals as well as dripstone still being formed. The road swings back to the city via **Provo Canyon,** along which are 430-foot Bridal Veil Falls, thrilling Sky Ride aerial tramway, picnic spots, and Deer Creek Reservoir.

SALT LAKE CITY, at the foot of the Wasatch Mountains, is Utah's largest metropolis and the state capital. To the west stretch the glistening expanses of the Great Salt Lake and alkaline flats, backed by the Oquirrh, Stansbury and more distant Nevada ranges.

Founded by Brigham Young and his Mormon followers in 1847, Salt Lake City became the heart of the State of Deseret and Mormon empire.

Temple Square, in the heart of the city, is the symbolic home of the Mormon religion. The new **Visitors Center** deals with Mormon history, natural sciences, the pioneer period and Mormon handicrafts. The six-spired, gray granite **Mormon Temple** (usually closed to non-Mormons) was built 1853–93 at a cost of $4 million; the **Tabernacle,** said to have the world's largest domed roof of its kind, seats 8,000 persons and contains the famous Great Organ.

The **state capitol**—made of Utah granite and marble, and containing historic, industrial, scenic and art exhibits—supplies vistas of the city and its surrounding terrain. The nearby **Pioneer Memorial Museum,** a replica of the former Salt Lake Theater, is rated as one of the best in the West. The **University of Utah** campus, covering several hundred acres, has the **University Anthropology Museum** (traces Utah residents from prehistoric times to the present); the **University Museum of Earth Sciences** (particularly good dinosaur skeletons); and the **University Museum of Fine Arts** (Hudnut collection of rare seventeenth-century tapestries, Louis XIV furniture and Rubens paintings).

The **Utah Historical Society** is housed in a mansion (circa 1899) formerly used as the governor's residence. Most interesting are the Society's library and state archives, and the dining room with its Italian tapestries and ornate, carved cherrywood panelings.

On the eastern outskirts, **Pioneer Monument State Park** marks the spot where Brigham Young declared, "This is the place," and Mormon pioneers first saw Salt Lake Valley. Not far from there, **Hogle Gardens Zoo** is an appealing place where a variety of animals is shown. The zoo is also the home of Shasta, the unique "liger" (cross between a lion and tiger). Other sights include **Brigham Young's grave** on First Avenue between A and State streets; **office building of the Latter-Day Saints Church** on the site of Deseret's first gold mint; **Lion House,** one of Brigham Young's homes; **Beehive House,** formerly the residence of presidents of the Mormon Church, built by Brigham Young and now open to the public; and the **Lockerbie Collection** of Utah minerals and rocks at **Westminster College.**

Great Salt Lake, northeast of the city, is a remnant of the prehistoric fresh-water sea—called Lake Bonneville—that once covered the greater part of northwestern Utah. The present lake—one of the earth's most saline bodies of water—has an average length of 75 miles and width of 30 miles, or about one-tenth the acreage of the original one. Deepest waters are now about 30 feet, and the salt content varies from 15 to 28 percent. From the shores of the lake stretch the alkaline reaches of the Great Salt Lake Desert, the old bed of the extinct lake. Of interest are swimming beaches; commercial salt operations; Antelope Island and others, which have bison, gulls and pelicans; the Southern Pacific Railroad's cutoff across the lake, where a 30-mile portion skips over rock-fill surrounded by water; **Promontory,** where **Golden Spike National Historic Site** marks the linking in 1869 of the eastern and western segments of the nation's first transcontinental rail route; and the Bonneville Salt Flats near Wendover where new world land speed records have been set nearly every year.

VERNAL, in northeastern Utah, is headquarters for **Ashley National Forest,** which has 13,528-foot King's Peak, highest in the state, and the Red Canyon of the Green River.

Utah Field House of Natural History deals with archaeology, geology, fossils and resources of the Uintah Basin. **Dinosaur National Monument** is just a short drive eastward.

This 209,744-acre preserve, partly in Colorado, has yielded numerous dinosaur skeletons and remains of many other prehistoric animals. Highlights include a visitor center and quarry where exhibits explain the sections and where dinosaur bones can be seen in the ground; Split Mountain, Whirlpool, Yampa and Lodore canyons—all cut by the Yampa and Green rivers; Castle Park near the confluence of the two streams; Echo Park at the junction; Jones Hole just below Echo Park; boat trips down the rivers; ancient Indian caves and stone writings; and camping at Echo Park and Split Mountain Gorge.

SPORTS AND RECREATION. **Lake Powell,** created in the Glen Canyon and San Juan River Gorge by Glen Canyon Dam, is one of the largest, most beautiful fresh-water lakes in western America. The lake is popular for boating, swimming, water-skiing, fishing, and sightseeing.

Excellent recreational facilities can be found in almost all parts of the state. **Brian Head Winter Sports Area,** near Cedar City, provides excellent skiing from November to May. Skiing is also popular at **Snow Basin,** 18 miles east of Ogden, and at **Beaver Mountain Ski Area** in Logan Canyon (here can be found year-round facilities for fishing and hunting).

Near Price, **Utah Lake** has water sports facilities and hunting for geese, duck, and other game birds. Also to be visited are **Mount Nebo Recreation Area, Devil's Kitchen,** and **Paupon Lakes Recreation Area.**

Wasatch National Forest, with headquarters in Salt Lake City, offers rugged outdoor sports and pack trips into the High Uintas Wilderness Areas. Southeast of the city, the former mining camp of **Alta** now is a thriving winter sports area in the Wasatch Mountains; full facilities and varied slopes draw all classes of skiers from early November to mid-May. The area also has been a Forest Service study section for avalanches; its Snow Rangers carefully watch dangerous snow conditions and eliminate them by explosives before avalanches can do damage. Over the mountain, at the head of Big Cottonwood Canyon, **Brighton** is a year-round resort at an altitude of nearly 9,000 feet; its winter ski facilities and season complement those in Alta. In summer, the Mount Millicent ski lift operates to show sightseers the vivid Wasatch Range scenery.

Wanship is the nearest town to **Wanship Dam,** backing 11,000-acre **Rockport Lake,** which attracts vacationists with its water-skiing, fishing and boating plus shoreside picnicking and cabin-lodge accommodations. About a half hour's drive southeast, **Kamas** is a departure point for Mirror Lake, edged by 11,947-foot Bald Mountain. Eastward, along the backbone of the Uinta Mountains to King's Peak, sprawls a high wilderness area with more than a thousand lakes, and camping spots.

SPECIAL EVENTS in Utah emphasize the outdoor, far-west aspects of the state. Among the most popular are the **Ute Indian Bear Dance Celebration** on the Uintah and Ouray Reservation, May, Whiterocks; **Dance Festival,** Salt Lake City, mid-June; **Annual Ute Stampede,** Nephi, early July; **Shakespearean Drama Festival,** Cedar City, three weeks in July; **Ogden Pioneer Days Rodeo,** late July; **Days of '47 Celebration and Rodeo,** statewide, mid-July; **Peach Days Celebration,** Brigham City, early September; **Utah State Fair,** Salt Lake City, mid-September.

Probably the state's most nationally-known event is the annual **"Messiah,"** presented just before Christmas at the Salt Lake City Tabernacle.

Nevada

Largely because of its legalized gambling, Nevada has become a major tourist center. The glittering casinos and plush night spots of Reno and Las Vegas are world famous. In spite of its high influx of tourists, however, Nevada has the fourth smallest population of any state.

THE LAND. Much of Nevada is barren and dry, with mountain ranges, valleys, buttes, and mesas blanketing most of the state. In the southwest are the Sierra Nevadas, one of the chief outdoor vacation regions, while in the center of the state are the Toiyabe and Toquima ranges. The state's highest point is at **Boundary Peak** (13,140 feet), along the western border.

Nevada lies almost entirely within the Great Basin, and most of its rivers, except the Virgin, Muddy, Owyhee, Bruneau, and Salmon, empty into it. The state receives such a small amount of rain that many rivers dry up during the dry season—June to December. Extensive projects to provide water have led to major dam projects, most spectacular being the Hoover Dam, which created Lake Mead, largest man-made lake in the United States.

THE CLIMATE. Nevada receives less rain than any other state (maximum seven inches), due largely to the Sierra Nevadas, whose lofty peaks cause clouds moving inland from the Pacific to drop much of their moisture in the form of snow. Snowfall in the Sierras often reaches more than 200 inches a year.

Temperatures in Nevada vary greatly from north to south, averaging 70 degrees in July in the mountains, and over 85 degrees in the south. In winter, the mountains average 24 degrees, southern Nevada, 43 degrees.

THE PEOPLE. Nevada's land became United States territory in 1848, when it was ceded by Mexico following the Mexican War. Before this date, Indian tribes, occasional fur trappers, and explorers had entered present-day Nevada (the Old Spanish Trail was opened by William Wolfskill in 1830).

Brigham Young and his Mormon followers founded a few trading settlements in Nevada in the early 1850's, and a handful of other settlers followed. The non-Mormons tried to persuade Congress to create a separate territory for them, or make them part of the California territory. But because they were so few, Congress refused to act.

Then in 1859 a fabulous vein of silver ore was discovered near present-day Virginia City by Henry Comstock. Treasure hunters and adventurers poured into the area, establishing lawless towns but bringing an overnight population explosion which led to territorial government.

Nevada favored the North in the Civil War, and could supply large quantities of badly needed silver. For these reasons, in spite of an insufficient number of residents, Nevada was admitted to the Union in 1864.

For the next 30 years Nevada's economy went up and down with the value of silver. Mines were producing only low-grade ore in the 1870's, and as the government's demand for silver fell, residents were forced to leave Nevada or take up ranching.

In 1900, however, new deposits of silver, copper, and gold were found, and a second rush was on. This time, railroad lines were brought in, enabling cattlemen to transport their livestock; land was irrigated, and by the time the United States entered World War I, Nevada's copper, tungsten, and other minerals were bringing top prices for wartime weapons construction.

Gambling, although widespread in early days, was not actually legalized until 1931. Large casinos were built, and Nevada's reputation as a tourist state spread rapidly. The state's divorce laws, requiring residence for only six weeks, have also brought thousands of people to Nevada each year.

AGRICULTURE. Livestock ranching is the leading source of agricultural income, with cattle, sheep, riding horses, poultry, and related products important. Crops, relying heavily on irrigation, are grown in the river valleys. These products include hearty grains such as barley, hay, wheat, and alfalfa seed. In limited areas, figs, grapes, melons, and some truck crops are grown.

INDUSTRY. Processing of minerals is the state's largest industry, after tourism. Smelters, mills, and kilns can be found around McGill, Henderson, and Battle Mountain. Meat packing plants are located in Reno.

Tourism brings in more than $730 million each year (compared with over $170 million for mining, $115 million for manufacturing, and $63 million for agriculture). Most valuable mined products are copper, gold, sand, gravel, mercury, gypsum, and petroleum.

CITIES. Las Vegas and Reno, the gambling centers of the United States, are Nevada's two largest cities. But of special interest to visitors are the cities of the past—the many ghost towns which grew up around the silver mines 100 years ago.

CARSON CITY, in Eagle Valley near the Carson River and the foot of the Carson Range, lays claim to being the smallest state capital city in the United States. First the Overland Trail post of Eagle Station, Carson City was formally laid out in 1858, became territorial capital in 1861 and the state capital three years later.

The **Nevada State Museum,** in the Old Mint Building, has a small mine exhibit in the basement, displays mummified Indian remains, basketry, coins, documents, guns, minerals, pioneer heirlooms and Nevada birds. East of town are **Carson Hot Springs** and the **Nevada State Prison,** where mastodon bones and giant sloth footprints were found.

Virginia City, the fabulous Western mining town in the 1870's, had one of the richest deposits of silver and gold ever discovered. Only a handful of the 110 saloons, 6 churches, 4 banks and other buildings of the boom period remain. Main points of interest are Sutro Tunnel; Piper's Opera House; the Museum of Memories; and Consolidated Virginia Mine, whose ore production has been valued at more than $200 million.

Southward, **Genoa** was the first permanent white settlement in the state; the restored **Genoa Fort, Stockade and Museum** was the scene of the first attempt at territorial government in 1859. Another early structure, containing ruins of the state's first military outpost, built in 1860, lies in **Fort Churchill State Park,** 23 miles north of the large-scale copper operations at Yerington. Near Hawthorne, **Walker Lake** is a celebrated trout fishing area. Old gold mining camps are hidden in the **Wassuk Range** and sections of **Toiyabe National Forest.**

ELKO, on the Humboldt River in the mountains of northeastern Nevada, is the state's chief cattle town. It is also

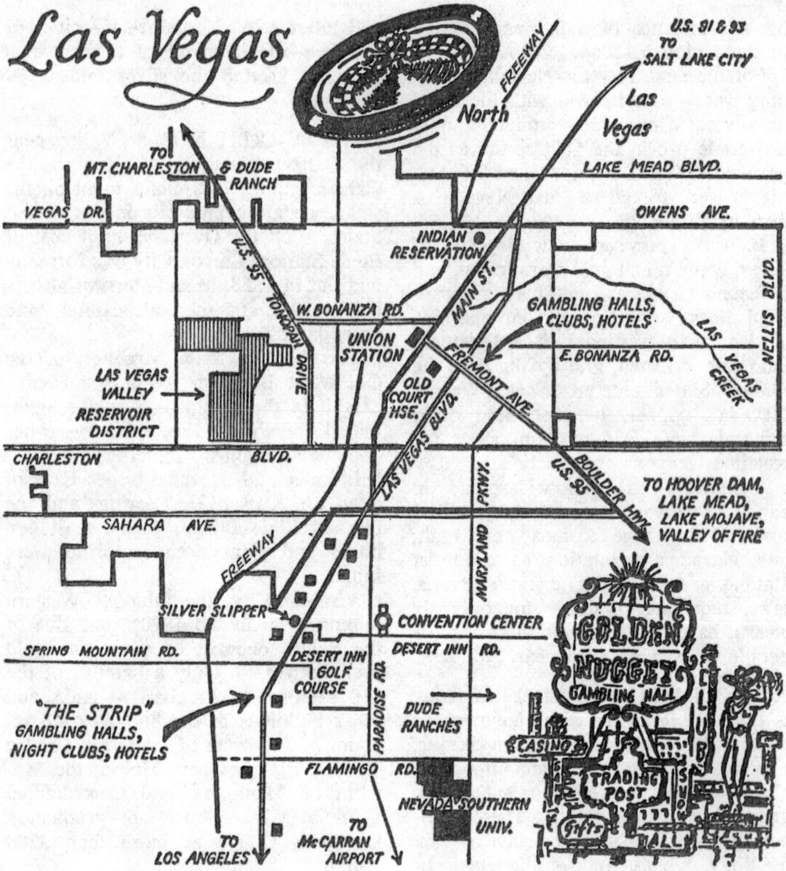

headquarters for **Humboldt National Forest.**

In the area are **hot springs and geysers** around Beowawe; **fossil beds** near Carlin; and such **ghost towns** as Cornucopia, Midas, Tuscarora, Jarbidge, Edgemont, Rio Tinto, and Metropolis.

ELY, among craggy cliffs in the Egan Range, sits amid a large region of alternating sagebrush valleys and scenic mountain ranges laced with gold, silver, copper, and lead deposits. Ely got its start in 1868 as a boom gold camp, now is the seat of White Pine County.

White Pine County Museum has extensive collections dealing with minerals, mining relics, old engineering equipment, and Indian crafts. Four miles west, the mile-wide, 650-foot-deep **Ruth Copper Pit** is one of the nation's largest open pit copper mines and the state's biggest producer of that mineral. The smelter at McGill, north of Ely, refines the ore. West of Ely, U. S. Highway 50, the Pony Express Highway, and branch roads lead to four other attractions: ghost town of **Hamilton,** a famous silver mining camp of the 1860's and '70's (other ghosts include Ward, Fort Schellbourne, Taylor, Lane City, Cherry Creek and Osceola); **Eureka,** another celebrated mining community; **Austin,** still another mining camp that retains many of its picturesque old buildings, near which Stokes Castle is an old three-story stone relic of an early era; and **Ichthyosaur Fossil Area State Park,** which has fossilized remains of large reptiles that once swam in a prehistoric sea covering the region.

LAS VEGAS, largest city in Nevada, spreads over a desert plain east of the Charleston Range. Big, brassy, and aglow with neon lighting, Las Vegas is a round-the-clock, year-round resort where emphasis is put on fun. Its casinos—with roulette wheels, slot machines, crap and poker games, faro, chuckaluck and other games of chance—operate twenty-four hours a day. Bars are open every hour, every day. Luxurious hotels on the "Strip" stage elaborate shows.

Though the "wide open" aspect draws most tourists, this seat of Clark County offers much more. Dry, sunny climate induces outdoor living, and many pools entice holiday seekers to swim or bask in the sun. The surrounding region is full of opportunities for scenic drives, hiking, mountain climbing, horseback riding, tennis, golf, boating, and outstanding bass fishing.

Whether or not one stays on the "Strip," the fabulously plush hotels and their floor shows certainly deserve attention; they are the city's highlights. Just east of the Strip is **Nevada Southern University.**

Southeastward—past the industrial community of Henderson—is **Boulder City,** gateway to the region's foremost attractions: **Hoover Dam** and **Lake Mead.** Hoover Dam, 726 feet high, plugging Black Canyon on the Colorado River, ranks as one of the world's greatest engineering projects. Built at a cost of $167 million (including expenditures for the power plant), the dam forms 115-mile long Lake Mead that backs upriver to the lower end of Grand Canyon. Parking overlooks on both sides of the canyon afford good dam views; the structure itself is crossed by U. S. Highway 93. An exhibit building contains a topographical model of the Colorado River basin, and recorded talks tell of the project's significance in terms of power production, irrigation, and other factors. Elevators descend more than 500 feet inside the dam and enable tour groups to inspect the interior and power plant.

Heading northwest from Las Vegas, **Beatty,** a mining town dozing in the Amargosa River Valley, is a gateway to **Death Valley National Monument,** mostly in California. Nearby is the ghost town of **Rhyolite,** where the most unusual of the few remaining buildings is the Bottle House, whose walls were made from hundreds of empty bottles laid on their sides. Farther north, two other old mining towns, **Goldfield** and **Tonopah,** are experiencing a revival.

RENO, on the Truckee River just east of the Carson Range, is another famous gambling community. Unlike Las Vegas, Reno has a well-settled, less boisterous appearance. A few blocks away from the downtown casino district is an area that looks like any typically American small city of the Midwest or East. The gambling, night-life and "wide-open" aspects of town are concentrated downtown.

Reno serves as headquarters for **Toiyabe National Forest** as well as the center of a widespread mining, farming, livestock and lumber region. It is also home of the main campus of the **University of Nevada.** Washoe County Courthouse, in spite of Reno's reputation as a divorce town, registers almost five times as many marriages as divorces.

The casinos are clustered around Virginia Street. The **Mining Museum** on the University of Nevada campus shows fine mineralogical, metallurgical, mining and geological collections, while the **Nevada State Historical Society** has exhibits on the state's past.

Fallon, east of Reno and near Lahontan Dam which impounds the Carson and Truckee river waters for irrigation, is popular with food lovers and hunters alike. In addition to being well-known for the "Hearts of Gold" cantaloupes raised nearby, Fallon is one of the nation's largest duck-hunting locales.

SPORTS AND RECREATION. Nevada provides all the ingredients for an outdoor vacation—dry climate, lakes and parks with facilities for **fishing, hunting, picnicking, camping, boating,** and **swimming;** towns and cities with public pools, **tennis courts,** and **golf courses;** game preserves; and breathtaking scenery.

In the Ely area are **Beaver Dam State Park, Cathedral Gorge State Park, Kershaw-Ryan State Park, Humboldt National Forest,** and **Lehman Caves National Monument** (a cave here is filled with colored limestone formations).

Outside Las Vegas are many excellent recreational facilities, most well-known being **Lake Mead National Recreation Area,** extending for 240 miles along the Colorado River from Grand Canyon south to a point below Davis Dam. Also near Las Vegas are **Boulder Beach, Las Vegas Bay, Echo Bay, Rogers Spring, Overton Landing,** and **Temple Bar.**

At Overton, 12 miles north, the Overton Museum displays Indian relics from an ancient pueblo now inundated by the lake.

West of Carson City lies **Lake Tahoe,** rimmed with tall forests and rippling mountains. **Sand Harbor State Park,** on its eastern shore, is popular for swimming. Near Elko, **Ruby** and **Jarbidge mountains, Humboldt National Forest,** and remains of the **Overland Trail** can be seen.

Toiyabe National Forest and **Mount Rose** are two popular areas near Reno, the latter having a well-equipped ski center. Another ski facility is the **Reno Ski Bowl** on Slide Mountain. Nearby is **Bowers Mansion,** typifying the home Comstock millionaires built after accumulating a fortune. Now a county park, the mansion has hot springs, swimming pool, and picnic area.

Northeast of Reno, **Pyramid Lake** is the state's largest natural body of water. Features of the 21-mile-wide, 32-mile-long lake are its mountain-desert location; the sharp pointed island that gives the lake its name; and flat Anahoe Island where some 10,000 large white pelicans breed in the federal bird sanctuary.

SPECIAL EVENTS. Among Nevada's most popular events are the **Annual Sports Car Club of America Rally,** Las Vegas, in mid-February; the **University of Nevada Winter Ski Carnival,** Reno, also in mid-February; **Appaloosa Show** and **Arabian Show,** both held in Las Vegas, April; **Silver State Square Dance Festival,** Reno, May; **National Basque Festival,** Elko, July.

Industrial Days Horseshow in Henderson, April, is considered one of the outstanding events of the year. Parades and street dances in western costumes highlight the festivities.

Also interesting are **Pony Express Days,** Ely, late August; the **Annual Nevada State Rodeo,** Winnemucca, late August or early September; and the **Nevada Day Parade and Pageant,** Carson City, October 31.

The Southwest

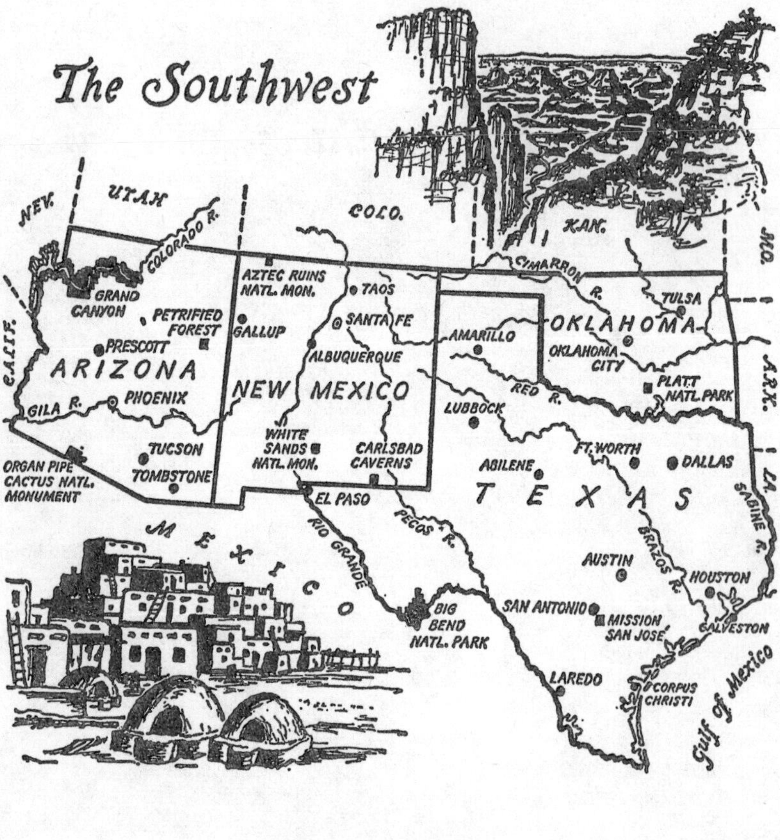
The Southwest
NEV.
UTAH
COLORADO R.
COLO.
KAN.
MO.
CALIF.
GRAND CANYON
PETRIFIED FOREST
PRESCOTT
ARIZONA
GILA R.
PHOENIX
TUCSON
TOMBSTONE
ORGAN PIPE CACTUS NATL. MONUMENT
AZTEC RUINS NATL. MON.
GALLUP
TAOS
SANTA FE
ALBUQUERQUE
NEW MEXICO
WHITE SANDS NATL. MON.
CARLSBAD CAVERNS
CIMARRON R.
TULSA
OKLAHOMA
OKLAHOMA CITY
AMARILLO
RED R.
PLATT NATL. PARK
ARK.
LUBBOCK
FT. WORTH
DALLAS
ABILENE
LA.
TEXAS
EL PASO
PECOS R.
RIO GRANDE
MEXICO
BIG BEND NATL. PARK
AUSTIN
BRAZOS R.
SABINE R.
HOUSTON
SAN ANTONIO
MISSION SAN JOSÉ
GALVESTON
LAREDO
CORPUS CHRISTI
Gulf of Mexico

The Southwest

Once consigned to the Indians as worthless, the American Southwest is today a rich and highly unusual region. The population (15 million) of its 572,000 square miles is growing more rapidly than that of any other part of the country. Where Spanish conquistadors vainly searched for gold, fabulous bonanzas of oil and gas now flow from the ground. Where hard-riding cowboys once herded cattle on the Long Drive, space scientists now push the frontiers of technology toward a new age.

This is not to say that the wide open spaces are disappearing. The magnificent vistas in which formations 50 miles off seem near at hand are still there. Bald, 12,000-foot-high mountains fringed with thick ponderosa pine and aspen forests rise within sight of unbelievable, mile-deep Grand Canyon. Jagged, twisted lava beds spewed by now-extinct volcanoes scar terrain that edges flower-bedecked meadows. Mesquite groves crowd spiny cactus while palm leaves fan backyard patios. Earth-moving rivers like the Colorado and Rio Grande—plus scores of sky-blue, man-made lakes and a few natural ones—water some of the most arid landscape in North America.

Diversity of climate makes the Southwest a year-round vacation land. In the southern areas visitors may broil in the summer heat of 110 degrees but bask in winter daytime temperatures of 65 or 75. In the northern and higher areas mercury readings may drop to zero, and in summer these regions provide a fine antidote to the heat of their neighbors.

For the most part the climate is dry and sunny. Oklahoma marks the transition zone between the subtropical climes of the South and the colder continental North. With eastern Texas, it is also the buffer between the more humid East and the drier West. The aridity becomes more pronounced as one travels west from San Antonio. Eastern sectors receive as much as five feet of rainfall annually, while western portions may get less than five inches.

The heritage of the Southwest begins with the Stone Age Indians of New Mexico and the desert dwellers who inhabited Ventana Cave west of Tucson some 10,000 and possibly 20,000 years ago. Near the dawn of the Christian era, the more advanced Basket Makers lived here. A gradual development began which may be seen at the ruins in Arizona's dramatic Canyon de Chelly National Monument. By A.D. 700 the Pueblo period had begun, reaching its climax around 1100–1300 in such places as Wupatki, Chaco Canyon, Aztec Ruins, Bandelier, and other national monuments.

In 1540, a year after Fray Friar Marcos de Niza had made a preliminary exploration into Arizona and New Mexico, Coronado led an expedition in search of the fabled Seven Cities of Cibola. Coronado did not find the Seven Cities, but he laid the foundation for Spanish rule over the vast region for nearly three centuries. Yet the future Southwest was very little colonized until after the Mexican War of Independence, when settlers from the United States began to arrive. Texas broke away from Mexico in 1836 (the time of the famous siege of the Alamo), and when the United States-Mexican War grew out of that conflict, Arizona and New Mexico were annexed along with Texas. Oklahoma was already part of the United States, thanks to the Louisiana Purchase.

Traces of the Spanish period are found in missions like Arizona's San Xavier del Bac or that of St. Francis in Rancho de Taos, New Mexico. Subtle blending of all three cultures—Indian, Spanish, and American—has formed an environment unlike any other in the country. Around Chimayo and Truchas, New Mexico, in the Penitente country between Santa Fe and Taos, visitors might imagine themselves in Old Spain. At adobe, multi-storied Pueblo de Taos, the Indian culture, modified somewhat by present-day mores, continues with ceremonials and other essential patterns of bygone days. The Hopis on their northern Arizona mesas perform their snake dances each August just as they have for centuries. Representatives of 67 different tribes still make Oklahoma "Indian Territory."

Visitors to New Mexico and Arizona in particular will be attracted by the products of the Indian crafts: Hopi Kachina dolls, Navajo rugs, Hopi and Pima or Papago basketry, silver and silver-and-turquoise jewelry in many forms from earrings to concho belts, and Pueblo pottery. Hand-tooled leather goods, Chimayo weaving, paintings by noted artists such as those around Taos, western fashions for the whole family, and odd foods like piñon nuts, prickly-pear jam, and cactus candy are also fun to buy.

The region's cuisine is typically American, for the most part, with emphasis on good steak, but there are strong overtones of both Spanish and Mexican cooking—tacos, chile, enchiladas, refried beans, served either hot or cold.

Arizona

Arizona has the largest Indian population of any state. Its name comes from the Indian, *arizonac*, or "small spring." One of the fastest-growing states in the country, Arizona is home of such famous natural wonders as the Grand Canyon, the Painted Desert, and the Petrified Forest.

THE LAND. Much of Arizona's breathtaking scenery is found in the northern half of the state, the Colorado Plateau. Here, at Grand Canyon National Park, the land is covered with deeply cut crevices and high peaks in colors ranging from black to red, lavender, brown, and sand, and stretching for 217 miles. Also here is the Painted Desert, with some of the most unusual natural formations and coloring in the country.

Fairly dry, mountainous land covers southern Arizona, location of Phoenix and Tucson, the state's most important cities. The ranges—Gila, Mazatzal, and Sierra Ancha—are fairly close together, with deep, narrow valleys between them. Desert covers the extreme southern and western area, but irrigation from the Colorado River, the state's most important body of water, has reclaimed a large portion of the land for farming.

At Four Corners is a monument indicating where the borders of Arizona, New Mexico, Utah, and Colorado meet —the only such point where four states touch. Mexico makes up Arizona's entire southern boundary.

THE CLIMATE. Rain falls where it is least needed in Arizona, with precipitation averaging around five inches in the southwest desert, and 30 inches in the highest mountain areas. Because of the range of heights, temperatures vary greatly from one part of the state to another, although the air is almost always dry. In southern Arizona, averages are 50 degrees in January, and 90 degrees in July.

THE PEOPLE. Arizona has been home to Indians since before the time of Christ, when Hohokam tribes were believed to have settled in the area. They were almost the only inhabitants until the sixteenth century, when Roman Catholic missionaries from Spain came to convert the Indians.

The Indians (mostly Apache and Navajo) were subdued by the Spaniards, but settlement was very slow. When Mexico achieved independence from Spain in 1821, Arizona became part of that new country. Twenty-seven years later, following the U.S.-Mexican War, the United States took over "New Mexico," including Arizona.

In spite of assertions that the land was worthless desert, settlers began trickling in. Because many were from the South, they favored the Confederacy when the Civil War broke out. The Union countered this danger by according territorial status in 1863.

Discovery of silver, copper, and gold, as well as suppression of the Indians by troops aided by frontiersmen like Kit Carson, brought rapid growth. Irrigation projects were undertaken, and large-scale farming and ranching developed.

During this period, Arizona had been unsuccessfully applying for statehood. Finally, in 1912, she was admitted as the country's forty-eighth state.

During the next generation, the federal government, through water development projects and promotion of tourist areas, helped Arizona's development. Copper mining grew in importance. World War II brought a heavy increase in population, as airbases and plants were built.

Since the war, the Indians have won the right to vote (1948), new industry has come to the state, and the total population has jumped to 1.7 million, increasing by almost 75 percent during the 1950's alone.

AGRICULTURE. Although the amount of cultivable land is small, crops account for about 60 percent of the value of farm products. The other 40 percent comes from livestock, largely beef cattle and sheep.

In the southwest, small truck farms grow melons, lettuce, grapes, oranges, and other citrus fruits which are shipped to northern markets in winter.

INDUSTRY. Arizona is one of the fastest-growing manufacturing states. Its goods have an annual value of over $900 million (agriculture's annual income is over $600 million; mineral production is over $1 billion).

Largest, most important of Arizona's industries are electronics and electrical machinery. Others employing large numbers of workers are aircraft manufacturing, food processing, and metal smelting. Plants are being built in small towns as well as the major cities, thereby adding to the growth of the entire state.

Arizona produces more than half the nation's copper, found in mines in almost every county in the state. Byproducts of the ore include gold, silver, and molybdenum.

Manufacturing on a smaller scale, but of special interest to travelers, includes goods made by the many Indian tribes of the state. In most reservations or nearby towns, colorful baskets, bowls, dolls, silverwork, rugs, pottery, leather goods, and paintings can be found.

CITIES. Phoenix, with a population of over 580,000, and Tucson, with over 260,000 residents, are Arizona's most important cities. However, the rapid influx of people is leading to growth of smaller areas such as Flagstaff, Glendale, Mesa, Prescott, and Scottsdale. Also of prime importance to Arizona are the many Indian reservations.

AJO, in the southwestern desert some 40 miles north of the Mexican border, is Arizona's oldest operating copper site. The mile-wide, 535-foot-deep pit remains one of the state's foremost mines. Nearby are the two-and-a-half-million-acre **Papago Indian Reservation,** beginning a dozen miles eastward; **Organ Pipe National Monument,** more than 300,000 acres of nature trails, rare organ pipe and senita cacti, and traces of the Camino del Diablo blazed by Father Kino, first missionary in Arizona.

CLIFTON AND MORENCI, at the southern end of the scenic **Coronado Trail** (U.S. Highway 666) in eastern Arizona, remain important because of low-grade copper ore. Regional magnets: trout fishing, hiking and big-game hunting in Gila and Apache national forests; the **Coronado Trail** to the north; **Safford National Wildlife Refuge; Swift Trail** motor road up 10,-720-foot Mount Graham; **Indian Hot Springs; Fort Apache Indian Reservation.**

FLAGSTAFF is pleasantly located amid towering ponderosa pines of Coconino National Forest near the base of the 12,000-foot-high San Francisco Peaks. Humphrey's Peak, at 12,633 feet, is the highest in Arizona.

Early pioneers were familiar with the site as a natural camping place with good water. It wasn't until the fourth of July in 1876, though, that a group of scouts raised a giant flagpole and gave the place its name. Today, Flagstaff is the region's largest city, seat of Coconino County, and the best base for sightseeing northern Arizona.

The **Arizona State College** campus and the **Museum of Northern Arizona,** three miles northwest on Fort Valley Road, are important to see. The Museum exhibits the area's archaeology, geology, natural sciences, and crafts and arts of the Hopis and Navajos. The **Arizona Snow Bowl** on the upper slopes of the San Francisco Peaks is a dependable winter ski area.

Lowell Observatory, one mile northwest of town, was the site from which the planet Pluto was discovered in 1930. It has reflectors and refractors of various sizes, and is open to visitors for one hour each weekday afternoon. **Schulz Pass Road** (partly unpaved) runs north between the San Francisco Peaks and Elden Mountains, then south to U.S. Highway 66 and west to town.

About 11 miles southeast is **Walnut Canyon National Monument** where, in a deep, horseshoe-shaped gorge fringed with tall ponderosa pines, more than 300 ancient cliff dwellings are sandwiched in the corrugated limestone walls. Sixteen miles northeast—four miles east of U.S. Highway 89—is **Sunset Crater National Monument,** with a 1,000-foot-high cinder cone formed about 1064 and having a rose-tinted summit.

About 45 miles northeast of Flagstaff is **Wupatki National Monument,** comprising nearly 36,000 acres, containing more than 800 Indian ruins looking out on the vast expanse of the distant **Painted Desert.** U.S. Highway 89 continues north through the **Navajo Reservation,** to the **Glen Canyon Dam** across the Colorado River, and gives glimpses of **Marble Canyon** and the **Vermillion Cliffs.** West of Fredonia, near the Utah line, is **Pipe Spring National Monument.** The South Rim's entrance to **Grand Canyon National Park** is reached via State Highway 64 off U.S. 89 near Cameron or the North Rim via State Highway 67 from Jacob Lake.

Oak Creek Canyon begins on U.S. 89A south of Flagstaff and continues for a dozen miles to **Sedona,** a growing artists' and writers' colony. Here the canyon opens up into a gorgeous, rock-rimmed amphitheater used as background for many Western movies. Some two miles south stands the **Chapel of the Holy Cross.**

INDIAN COUNTRY (North). The **Navajo** and **Hopi reservations** corner the northeastern part of the state. Navajo territory, larger of the two, completely surrounds Hopiland, and laps over into western New Mexico. It is a land of limitless horizons, stark mesas, eternity and inspiration; primitive Navajo hogans, Hopi mesa homes, traditional ceremonials and some of the old attire are parts of the scene.

Reservation Route 1 begins at **Tuba City** (Navajo school, hospital and trading post—ask to see the pawn silver vault at the trading post); near Tonalea, several roads lead to **Navajo National Monument;** the monument—split into three separate areas called **Betatakin** (most accessible), **Keet Seel** and **Inscription House**—contains some of the state's largest and most remarkable thirteenth-century pueblo cliff dwellings; just before reaching Utah, a side road enters **Monument Valley.**

Reservation Route 3 also begins at Tuba City. Just down the road is Moenkopi, a Hopi village in the Navajo Reservation. Most important communities are **Hotevilla** and **Old Oraibi** (oldest continuously inhabited site in the United States) on the Third Mesa, **Shongopovi** and **Mishongnovi** on the Second Mesa, and **Walpi** on the First Mesa. Of these, Walpi, dating back to before 1680, is the most picturesque. Hopi tribal headquarters are at **Keams Canyon,** just off the route. **Ganado** (site of a Presbyterian hospital and mission) has a notable collection of paintings on Hopi and Navajo scenes. Just west of here a road runs north to Chinle and **Canyon de Chelly National Monument.** This impressive preserve—where sheer, red sandstone walls rise as much as a thousand feet above the canyon floor and gigantic formations like Spider Rock stand taller than the Chrysler Building in New York City—shows Indian civilization from the early Anasazi Period, about 350, through thirteenth-century cliff dwellings.

INDIAN COUNTRY (South). Most important of the Indian lands in southern Arizona are the Fort Apache and San Carlos reservations north and east of Globe, the Gila River (or Pima) Reservation south of Phoenix, and the Papago Reservation west of Tucson. **The Fort Apache** and **San Carlos In-**

dian Reservations (both Apache domains) are contiguous sections bordered on three sides by Tonto, Sitgreaves, Apache and Gila national forests.

Headquarters for the Fort Apache preserve (with numerous trout fishing lakes and hunting sites below the Mogollon Rim and in the White Mountains around the lumber town of McNary) is **Whiteriver.** Near here are Fort Apache with its modern school and remnants of the frontier army post, **Kinishba Ruins**—partially restored—whose masonry structures formed a "melting pot" for Salt River, Little Colorado and Central Gila tribes around 1050–1350, and immense **Salt River Canyon,** traversed by U.S. Highway 60. **San Carlos,** headquarters for the adjoining Apache Reservation has periodic ceremonials and cattle auctions.

Sells is in the middle of the Papago Reservation between Tucson and Ajo. Northwestward, Gu Achi is the take-off point for **Ventana Cave,** where evidences of human habitation more than 10,000 years ago have been found, and for the nearby **Children's Shrine** or Well of Sacrifice that commemorates the sacrifice of four children to appease the gods during the Great Flood. Also on the reservation are 7,864-foot-high **Baboquivari Peak** and the **Kitt Peak Astronomical Observatory.**

North of **Jerome,** a rough dirt road runs past colorful, little-visited **Sycamore Canyon** country to **Williams,** another Grand Canyon gateway. U.S. 89A continues from Jerome to **Oak Creek Canyon.** Side roads en route lead to **Montezuma Castle National Monument,** a five-story, excellently preserved, cameo-like cliff dwelling built by thirteenth- and-fourteenth-century Pueblo Indians. **Montezuma Well** is seven miles northeast; there are small cave ruins above the 35-foot-deep lake. A few miles south of the monument is **Camp Verde** where the **Fort Verde Museum** deals with the pioneer-Apache era in the vicinity. Eastward, a breath-taking road twists over the mountains and beneath the precipitous **Mogollon Rim** (sometimes called the Tonto Rim) to Pine and Payson. About halfway between these towns is **Tonto Natural Bridge,** 400 feet long, 150 feet wide and up to 150 feet high.

KINGMAN, seat of Mohave County and northwestern Arizona departure point for Lake Mead, has a harshly scenic setting amid the Cerbat, Black and Hualpai mountains. A former mining camp, Kingman—on U. S. Highway 66—now is a shipping center for surrounding cattle and mineral pursuits. The **Mohave County Chamber of Commerce Tourist Center and Museum,** on the main highway, has exhibits on the region's past. Some 14 miles southeast in the Hualpai Range is **Hualpai Mountain Park** (at elevations of from 6,000 to 8,400 feet) with forest lodge, cabins, picnicking, and camping.

Eighty miles northwest of town stands 726-foot-high Hoover Dam which backs Lake Mead, focal point of the **Lake Mead National Recreation Area** (see Nevada).

NOGALES, on the Mexican border due south of Tucson, is a port of entry to the "land of *mañana.*" The twin-community—divided by a high wire fence that marks the boundary—also is the northern terminus for the West Coast Highway to Mexico City.

Started in 1880 as a trading post on El Camino Real, it was first known as Isaactown for its founder, then renamed Nogales (Spanish for the black walnut trees that grew in the area). **Coronado National Memorial** can be reached by the Montezuma Pass near Nogales.

PHOENIX, irrigated by water brought from dams along the Salt and Verde rivers, is an oasis in the desert-like Salt River Valley between the Phoenix and South mountains. It is the capital and the largest city of Arizona. The ancient culture was Hohokam—"The Departed Ones"—who built a thriving civilization, constructed the New World's first irrigation canals in the fruitful Great Pueblo period five to seven centuries ago, then vanished. Evidences of this Indian kingdom—in potsherds and ruins (best example is Pueblo Grande)—are still found throughout the valley. Modern Phoenix began in 1864 when John Y. T. Smith set up a hay camp to supply the U. S. Cavalry at Fort McDowell. Completion of **Theodore Roosevelt Dam,** the nation's first major reclamation project, in 1911 brought water to the valley.

To be visited in Phoenix are the **civic center,** Central Avenue and McDowell Road, with the million-dollar **Phoenix Public Library, Phoenix Art Museum,** having collections of Oriental and other world art, and the **Phoenix Little Theater,** one of the nation's most active drama groups. The **Heard Museum** has a lively approach to displays on world anthropology, southwestern Indian arts and crafts, and Spanish Colonial items. **Encanto Park** is a recreation area with palm-shaded, winding lagoons, expansive lawns graced with trees native to many parts of the world, two golf courses and other sports facilities. The State Fairgrounds, in addition to periodic fairs and shows, is the home of a **Mineral Museum.** The **state capitol** contains the State Department Library and Archives as well as Jay Datus murals depicting the progress of Arizona. **Arizona Museum** has displays of prehistoric items and pioneer relics, and **Pueblo Grande,** the best remaining Hohokam pueblo ruins around Phoenix.

Papago Park, with its strangely eroded red rock formations (including a Hole-in-the-Rock), is the setting for the **Desert Botanical Garden** whose 300 acres preserve hundreds of arid country plants. **South Mountain Park,** covering some 15,000 acres of Salt River or South Mountains, includes large ramadas, picnic tables and fireplaces, hiking trails, panoramic vistas such as that from 2,330-foot high Dobbins Lookout, a wide variety of plant and animal life, Indian stone writings, a Spanish inscription with a 1539 date, and odd rock formations.

See also the **Phoenix Indian School,** one of the nation's largest; the **Bayless Cracker Barrel Store;** the late **Frank Lloyd Wright's Taliesin West.**

U.S. Highways 60 and 70 run east from Phoenix through Tempe, home of **Arizona State University,** and Mesa (white **Mormon Temple,** patterned after the Temple of Solomon) to Apache Junction, about 30 miles east of Phoenix. This is the start of the **Apache Trail** (State Highway 88), one of the West's most dramatic drives. Highlights include **Canyon, Apache** and **Roosevelt lakes, Fish Creek Canyon,** 273-foot-high 1,125-foot-long **Theodore Roosevelt Dam,** and **Tonto National Monument,** one of the best preserved and most accessible cliff dwelling ruins, built by Salado Indians about the fourteenth century. **Superstition Mountain,** near the western terminus of the trail, is a prominent Arizona landmark and the supposed location of the Lost Dutchman Gold Mine.

Other Phoenix regional spots include the Yaqui Indian village of **Guadalupe** near the eastern end of South Mountain Park; **Luke Air Force Base** and the **American Institute for Foreign Trade** near Glendale; **Carl Pleasant, Bartlett** and **Saguaro lakes; St. John's Mission** at Komatke; and **Horse Thief Basin,** a city-maintained recreation area in the Bradshaw Mountains north of Phoenix.

PRESCOTT, the Territorial Capital among the fragrant pines of Prescott National Forest, is called the "Mile-High City." Prescott is the seat of Yavapai County. Cowboys and Indians are commonly seen in town. Its climate attracts vacationists all year round though summer is the most popular season.

In the center of town is the **Plaza** with the **County Courthouse** and the **equestrian Bucky O'Neill Monument** erected in memory of the organizer of Roosevelt's Rough Riders in the Spanish-American War. The **Sharlot Hall Museum** houses pioneer relics and a fine Indian collection. Nearby is the so-called **Governor's Mansion,** a log structure where the first Territorial Legislature met in 1864. Here, too, is the **grave of Pauline Weaver,** scout of the early West.

The **Smoki Museum** contains valuable collections of ceramics and other artifacts from the Fitzmaurice, King and Tuzigoot Indian ruins, ceremonial paintings and costumes, and a reproduction of a Hopi kiva.

TOMBSTONE, perhaps the most notorious Arizona frontier settlement, was named by Ed Schieffelin, the soldier-prospector who discovered the first rich silver lode in 1877.

Most of the interesting sights are clustered in an area of a few blocks around U.S. Highway 80. These include the **Bird Cage Theater,** a once boisterous honky-tonk built in 1881, where Eddie Foy and other stars of the period appeared; the old **Cochise County "Million Dollar Court House,"** erected in 1882, now the home of the public library and a museum in the former county jail; **Schieffelin Hall,** a former theater; the office of the **Tombstone Epitaph,** one of the frontier's most celebrated newspapers, still being published; **St. Paul's Episcopal Church,** oldest Protestant church in the state; the **O. K. Corral,** a collection of old vehicles on the site of the Earp-Clanton gunfight; City Hall; the Wells Fargo office; the gaping **Million Dollar Stope** (a tunnel into one of the old mines); and the **Rose Tree** planted in 1885 and covering a 66-by-70-foot arbor. On the north edge of town is **Boothill Cemetery.**

North of Tombstone, State Highway 86 between Benson and Willcox runs through **Texas Canyon,** an area of huge rugged boulders that hide enticing picnic-camping sites. South of here but reached from State Highway 181 is **Cochise Stronghold,** a former Apache citadel where the famous warrior, Cochise, is buried; its **Coronado National Forest** setting in rocky escarpments of the Dragoon Mountains makes it an appealing camping spot.

In the area are **Dos Cabezas,** an adobied-structured, semi-ghost town; the ruins of old **Fort Bowie** and nearby Apache Pass, which renegade Apaches favored in the late nineteenth century for ambushes; **Chiricahua National Monument,** the former Apache haunt known as the "Wonderland of Rock"; impressive **Cave Creek** and **Rucker canyons** near Portal; and **Skeleton Canyon,** off U.S. Highway 80 northeast of Douglas, where Geronimo made his final surrender in 1886.

TUCSON, spreading over the floor of an ancient sea where today most of the moisture lies in desert plant fibers or water taps, is Arizona's second largest city. The city, with a distinct Spanish flavor, has a more desert-like look than Phoenix—due in part to the lack of irrigation. It is a popular, fast-growing winter resort.

The campus of the **University of Arizona,** largest school in the state, is the key spot for in-town sightseeing. The **Arizona State Museum** has the world's most comprehensive collections of Southwestern archaeological relics (some more than 10,000 years old) plus exhibits of Indian crafts and ethnology of the Apache, Pueblo and desert tribes. Also of interest: **Steward Observatory,** having a 36-inch telescope; the **Arizona Pioneers' Historical Society** with an extensive Southwestern library and museum; the adobe brick **Wishing Shrine;** and the view of Tucson from the overlook on **A Mountain.**

Tucson Mountain Park, eight miles west, contains exceptional saguaro forests, a 35-mile scenic drive, 17 miles of hiking and bridle trails, picnic ramadas, Indian stone writings, and old mines. Here, too, are the unique **Arizona-Sonora Desert Museum** (a "living type" dealing with the Sonoran Desert); and **Old Tucson,** a movie-set replica of the town in 1860 and now a commercial operation.

South of the park stands **Mission San Xavier del Bac,** the "White Dove of the Desert." Founded by Father Kino, the present mission dates from 1783. It is considered the nation's most impressive Spanish-style mission.

WINSLOW, in the valley of the Little Colorado River on U.S. Highway 66, begun in 1882 as a Santa Fe Railroad division point, is a hub for lumbering, agriculture and cattle raising.

Some 22 miles west of Winslow, then six miles south of U.S. Highway 66, lies **Meteor Crater,** one of the earth's largest. Formed by a crashing meteor an estimated 40,000 years ago, the nearly circular crater is more than 4,000 feet wide and 570 feet deep with almost vertical sides and rim that rises about 150 feet above the surrounding plateau.

About 57 miles east of Winslow—past the town of Holbrook—is **Petrified Forest National Park** and part of the **Painted Desert** which extends northwestward to the Grand Canyon. Aside from views of the Painted Desert in the section north of U.S. Highway 66, features of the monument are the **Blue Mesa, Jasper, Crystal** and **Rainbow forests** where the best and most colorful specimens of petrified trees are seen; the **Rainbow Forest Museum,** having outstanding exhibits of polished petrified wood, crystals and fossils; **Newspaper Rock,** whose sides are inscribed with a large number of ancient Indian petroglyphs; 111-foot-long **Agate Bridge,** a single petrified tree spanning a 40-foot-deep arroyo; and **Agate House,** a partially restored Pueblo dwelling built 900 years ago from petrified wood; ruins of a fourteenth-century village at the **Puerco Station;** and badlands.

YUMA, on the Colorado River in the extreme southwestern corner of the state, is the hub of an irrigated agricultural domain covering nearly 200,000 acres. The largest city on the California-Arizona line, Yuma is also the driest and warmest.

Interesting to visit is the **Old Territorial Prison** on a bluff overlooking the Colorado. Constructed by convicts in 1876, it was the territory's first real prison; many of the notorious desperadoes of the late nineteenth century were incarcerated in its barred, adobe cells. The prison, abandoned as such in 1909, now is a museum with pioneer relics.

Area sights include the **Fort Yuma Indian Reservation** (on which there is a statue of Father Garces) across the river; the Sahara-like **sand dunes** along U.S. Highway 80 some 14 miles west of town; the **Imperial National Wildlife Refuge** on the Colorado northward; river fishing; ghost towns off State Highway 95; the **Kofa Game Refuge** in which lies **Palm Canyon,** home of the only native Arizona palms; and the border town of **San Luis.**

SPORTS AND RECREATION. A "must" for any visitor to Arizona is a trip through Grand Canyon National Park. Carved by the Colorado River (with an assist from other natural forces) into a myriad of colorful temples, buttes, crevices and plateaus, Grand Canyon varies from 4 to 18 miles in width. From the North Rim, it drops some 5,700 feet; the South Rim is about 1,200 feet lower. Only connection between the two rims within the park is the **Kaibab suspension bridge** (horse and foot only) near Phantom Ranch on the gorge floor.

There are scenic drives along both the North and South rims. The North Rim is closed by snow in winter, but the South Rim remains open year round. **Muleback trips** are made from both rims into the inner recesses of the canyon. Most popular one is the one-day ride down Bright Angel Trail (South Rim) to either the Tonto Plateau or the Colorado River at the very bottom of the gorge. There is also a two-day trip with an overnight stop at Phantom Ranch.

On the South Rim, a visitor center, one mile east of Grand Canyon Village, features dioramas, historic items and other exhibits on the geology and saga of the canyon and people associated with it (ranger naturalists are on duty to supply information, maps, pamphlets). **Yavapai Lookout,** the most comprehensive on the South Rim, has a topographical model of the gorge, high-powered binoculars trained on important points, naturalist lectures and exhibits on the region. Also on this rim are **Tusayan Ruin and Museum; Desert View Watchtower,** overlooking fine views of the canyon, river, Painted Desert and Kaibab Forest plus, in its interior, symbolic paintings by Fred Kabotie, noted Hopi artist; and **Hopi House,** where abbreviated "ceremonial" dances are staged each afternoon for tourists.

Cape Royal Drive, 22 miles long, shows off some of the best canyon vistas on the North Rim, plus views of Marble Canyon, the Little Colorado and the Painted Desert.

One of the newest communities in Arizona is **Lake Havasu City** on the Colorado River. It is famed as the new home of fabled **London Bridge,** which was assembled, piece by piece after arrival from London. **Lake Havasu** and the surrounding area offers excellent recreation opportunities.

Most towns and cities have nearby recreational facilities, from pools and lakes to tennis courts and golf courses. Of special interest in the Tucson area are **Sabino Canyon** (trout fishing, picnicking, and camping); **Mount Lemmon Recreational Area, Rio Rico,** and **Picacho Peak and Pass,** where the state's only Civil War battle was fought.

SPECIAL EVENTS. A variety of annual events are held each year in Arizona, many relating to the Indians and to the Old West heritage of the state.

In Flagstaff, the **Arizona Snow Bowl Ski Race** is held in mid-February and the **Southwest All-Indian Pow-Wow** on July 4. At Grand Canyon National Park an **Easter Sunrise Service** takes place at Shrine of the Ages, on the South Rim.

Many interesting events take place in the Indian Country, highlights being the **Hopi Ceremonials** in late August; the **Navajo Tribal Fair** at Window Rock in September; and the **Yaqui Ceremonials** in February.

Phoenix hosts the **Arizona National Livestock Show** in January; the **Wickenburg Gold Rush Days** and the **Annual Cactus Show,** both in February; **Phoenix World Championship Rodeo** in mid-March, and the **Arizona State Fair** in November. **Smoki Dances,** featuring snake dances with live bullsnakes, take place in Prescott in August, while **Helldorado Days** (gunfights and other events of the boom period) are in Tombstone in late October.

In Tucson, special events are highlighted by **La Fiesta de los Vaqueros** in late February; **Fiesta of San Francisco de Asis,** at Mission San Xavier on October 4; **Fiesta of San Francisco Xavier,** at the same mission in December, and **Las Posadas,** in the Mexican community the week before Christmas.

New Mexico

Indian pueblos, breathtaking canyons, missile bases, and atomic energy centers are among the contrasting elements of New Mexico. Fifth-largest state in area in the country, New Mexico is one of the most thinly populated, its eight residents to the square mile adding up to slightly more than one million.

THE LAND. New Mexico's area of 121,666 square miles is divided into four distinct regions. A small portion of the Rocky Mountains extends into northern New Mexico, its snows providing irrigation for the Rio Grande Valley below. To the east are the Great Plains. In the west is the picturesque Colorado Plateau, where weathered flat-topped hills—called *mesas*—as well as deep canyons, buttes, and cliffs, stretch for miles. Along the crests runs the southern continuation of the Continental Divide. Finally, there are the desert basins and scattered mountain ranges such as the Guadalupe, Organ, and Sacramento. And through the center of it flows the Rio Grande River, the state's most important body of water.

THE CLIMATE. Dry air and warm temperatures are typical of New Mexico, where readings in the mid-seventies are found in July. In winter, the north averages 35 degrees, the south, 55 degrees. Only about 20 inches of rain and snow fall yearly, mostly in the northern mountains.

THE PEOPLE. New Mexico has a rich Indian history going back at least 20,000 years. Remains of the advanced civilizations which flourished in the

Las Vegas, Nevada

Grand Canyon National Park, Arizona

London Bridge, Lake Havasu City, Arizona

Astrodome, Houston, Texas

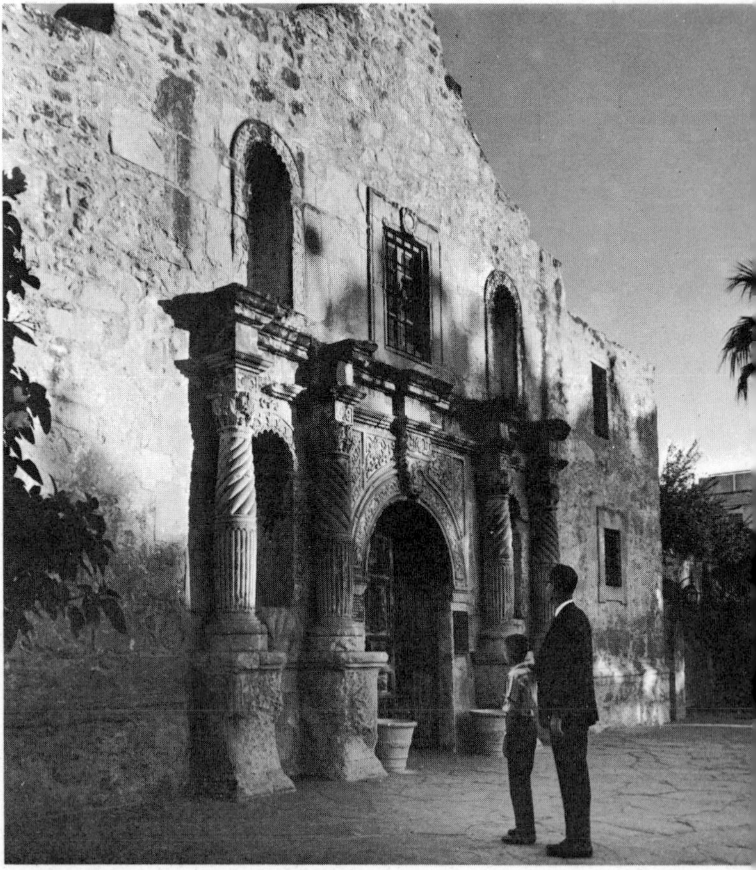

The Alamo, San Antonio, Texas

Mission of the Pueblo of Abo in Texas

Oil derricks in front of state capitol building

Ancient Cherokee ritual being reenacted at Tsa-La Gi Cherokee Indian Village near Tahlequah, Oklahoma

area can be seen in the form of well-constructed cliff dwellings–houses, apartments, and whole towns–which still stand.

The Spanish, exploring in search of the fabled "seven wealthy cities," claimed the land for Spain in 1539. The first settlement was established in 1598. Santa Fe became the capital of this new Spanish colony in 1610.

During the next 200 years, missionaries sought to convert the Indians, though clashes between settlers and Indians persisted here as elsewhere. Eventually a fairly peaceful relationship was maintained.

New Mexico became Mexican in 1821, but in 1848, United States troops occupied the land, which was annexed to the Union.

As a territory New Mexico developed slowly. Confederate troops overran most of the region in 1862, during the Civil War, but were soon defeated by Union troops.

When the railroads arrived in the 1880's, the territory experienced its biggest boom period. The cattle industry grew rapidly, settlers came from all parts of the country. Geronimo, last of the great Apache chiefs, surrendered in 1886. This brought to an end the Apache Wars and virtually terminated Indian resistance in the area.

Statehood was granted in 1912, but a long drought followed by the Depression hurt the economy, and it took the discovery of oil and potash, and the influx of atomic energy plants, to put New Mexico on its feet.

Because of the amount of government research being carried out in New Mexico, and because of the extensive mining operations in the state, New Mexico is now growing at a fast pace. Tourists are also coming in large numbers to visit the many scenic attractions, and to enjoy the dry, healthful climate.

AGRICULTURE. Because excellent grazing land covers so much of the state, sheep and cattle ranching is New Mexico's leading form of agriculture. However, more cropland is being made available through careful irrigation, facilitating the growth of cotton, wheat, sorghum grains, barley, and other products. In all, agriculture adds about $340 million to the economy yearly.

INDUSTRY. Because of great expansions in recent years, manufacturing has a value added of $185 million annually, or about 7 percent of the state's value of goods produced. Government atomic research accounts for most of this income, followed by petroleum refining, building materials (lumber), cement, chemicals, and food products.

Mining is the largest income-producer, outstripping agriculture and manufacturing combined. Petroleum makes up half of New Mexico's mineral production. Natural gas, with fields in both northern and southern New Mexico, and uranium, with more coming from New Mexico than from any other state, are next. Potash, copper, and gypsum are also mined in large quantities.

A small, but extremely popular, industry is carried on by the Indians of New Mexico, who make and sell a variety of products from basketry to silver goods and pottery.

CITIES. Albuquerque, with over 200,000 residents, Santa Fe and Roswell, are the three largest cities in New Mexico, although the latter two have populations of only about 41,000 and 33,000 respectively.

ALAMOGORDO, bursting into prominence with the birth of the Atomic Age, is in the desert-like Tularosa Basin of southern New Mexico. To the west lie gleaming white gypsum sand dunes backed by the serrated San Andres Mountains. Eastward, rise the Sierra Blanca and Sacramento mountains.

On July 16, 1945, the first atomic bomb in history was exploded at **Trinity Site** (closed to the public) northwest of the city. Just south of town is the **Air Force Missile Development Center,** Holloman Air Force Base, where a great deal of the nation's rocket research is done. The city is headquarters for **Lincoln National Forest,** for recreation and prime grazing area.

White Sands National Monument, 15

miles southwest, covers more than 140,000 acres, much of which are gleaming white gypsum sand dunes which rise from 10 to 60 feet high. The dunes are best seen via a scenic 16-mile loop drive from the museum administration building. **Cloudcroft,** in Lincoln National Forest, has one of the highest golf courses in the country. North of here stretches the 460,000-acre **Mescalero Apache Reservation** where ancient ceremonials are still performed periodically (inquire locally), as well as the ghost towns of **White Oaks,** and old **Fort Stanton,** originally established in 1855 to combat the Apaches. At Lincoln, the **Lincoln State Monument** preserves the old County Courthouse (now a museum) from which Billy the Kid made his escape in 1881. Nearby buildings include a rare *torreon* (defensive tower), La Paloma Bar and several other structures that figured in the Lincoln County cattle war of 1877–78. West of here, around Carrizozo, is the 1.5-mile-wide, 60-mile-long **Mal Pais**—a lava flow filled with deep crevices and odd, twisted shapes.

ALBUQUERQUE, largest city in New Mexico, sprawls across the broad Rio Grande Valley near the foot of the jutting Sandia Range. Westward rise the conical Five Volcanic Peaks, backed by 11,389-foot-high Mount Taylor.

The city, founded by the Spanish more than 250 years ago, is the industrial, financial, educational, transportation and military center of the state. It is headquarters for the U. S. Indian Service, **Cibola National Forest** and the Forest Services southwestern region. The **Sandia Military Establishment** and **Kirtland Air Force Base** are here.

Old Town, on the west side, marks the original settlement in 1706. Built around a Spanish-style plaza, its adobe structures (many of them shops and restaurants) reflect the atmosphere of that period. On the plaza's northwestern corner stands the twin-spired **Church of San Felipe de Neri** with an unusual spiral staircase built around a spruce tree.

The **University of New Mexico,** largest in the state, has a variety of adobe pueblo style buildings. **Rio Grande Park,** one of several, has a small zoo.

U.S. Highway 66 is the route west through **Laguna,** with squat adobe buildings, on the Indian reservation of the same name. About six miles farther on, unpaved State Highway 23 runs past the **Enchanted Mesa,** whose sheer rock walls jut some 430 feet above the brush-dotted plain, to Acoma, the so-called "Sky City" atop a 360-foot mesa. It claims, with Oraibi in Arizona, to be the oldest continuously inhabited village in the United States. Tourists reach it via a fairly steep sand trail or the original rock-step path cut into the mesa stone. Chief sight is **Mission San Esteban Rey,** begun in 1629. Every grain of sand plus the huge, hand-cut log ceiling beams had to be hauled up on Indians' backs; the altar, images of saints and paintings are of special interest.

South of Albuquerque, **Isleta Pueblo** (some pottery and silver goods) has the restored **Mission of San Antonio de Isleta,** originally built in the early seventeenth century. Southeast are **Quarai State Monument, Abo State Park,** and **Gran Quivira Monument.**

East of Albuquerque, in the **Sandia Mountains,** parts of the **Sandia Crest Drive** look out on some of the Southwest's most breath-taking vistas. The **Sandia Peak Ski Area,** at elevations from 8,700 to 10,500 feet, has skiing from about mid-December to mid-March; the piney summits are also ideal mild summer vacation retreats for desert-dwellers. **Paako Ruins,** near San Antonito, is another early pueblo abandoned before 1670. And a little less than 50 miles from the city—on U.S. Highway 66 near Moriarty—is the **Longhorn Ranch and Museum of the Old West.**

Northward, and crowding into Santa Fe's periphery, are a number of **Indian pueblos. Coronado State Monument** on State Highway 44, about two miles northwest of Mexican-like Bernalillo, marks Coronado's encampment from 1540–42; a rare painted kiva (large chamber used for religious ceremonies), Indian pueblo ruins, and a fine museum emphasizing Spanish Colonial life and ancient-modern Indian culture are nearby. Northward, past the Jemez Indian Reservation, is **Jemez State Monument** with the ruins of the Mission San Jose de Guisewa, founded about 1621–22.

Off the northeastern route–U.S. Highway 85–to Santa Fe is San Felipe, with its **Church of the Pueblo of San Felipe,** the third church on the site, erected about 1700. It is a splendid example of Spanish-Indian architecture. A short distance northward, **Santo Domingo** is unusual with its large kivas, adobe homes (where women often have turquoise necklaces or pottery for sale) and stick-edged corrals. Its **Church of the Pueblo of Santo Domingo,** built around 1886, has odd native paintings on its façade.

CARLSBAD CAVERNS NATIONAL PARK, in the foothills of the Guadalupe Mountains southwest of Carlsbad, contains–in addition to several smaller caves–prehistoric Indian sites and portions of pioneer trails, limestone stalagmites, stalactites, helictites and other formations begun 60 million years ago. It has 23 miles of explored passageways and chambers, of which about three miles are open to visitors. Scientists have explored as far down as 1,100 feet, but tourists go only to the 829-foot level. Entrance is made through a large natural arch some 40 feet high and 90 feet wide. Cavern temperature is a constant 56 degrees, and a sweater or jacket is advisable for comfort. The park is open year round.

Some 27 miles northeast at Carlsbad are **Carlsbad Museum's** mineral and Indian exhibits; mineral springs; the municipal beach; a wild bird game farm; seasonal hunting.

GALLUP, on U.S. Highway 66, 20 miles from the Arizona line, has an old frontier appearance. The **Museum of Indian Arts and Crafts,** in the city library, details the culture of Southwestern Indians.

Craggy **Shiprock Peak,** rising 1,400 feet above the desert plain, is a nearby landmark. Northwest of Shiprock, a monument marks the **Four Corners,** only point in the United States where four state lines meet. East of Shiprock, just outside the town of Aztec, is **Aztec Ruins National Monument.** The restored **Great Kiva** is the only one of its kind in the country; a museum exhibits artifacts found in the area. Some 65 miles due south, **Chaco Canyon National Monument** contains more than a dozen other prehistoric ruins, of which 1,000-year-old **Pueblo Bonito** (800 rooms and 32 kivas) is most impressive.

East of Gallup is **Kit Carson's Cave,** said to have been used by the scout during his 1864 campaign against the Navajos.

Around **Grants,** a uranium mining center, jagged lava beds (which hide a few perpetual ice caves) cover the terrain. From Grants, State Highway 53 swings south and west through **Cibola National Forest** to **El Morro National Monument** where **Inscription Rock** has Indian, early Spanish and American pioneer stone writings. Westward and due south of Gallup is the Zuni Reservation and the village of **Zuni,** known for its silver crafts and masked dances.

LAS CRUCES is an appealing town with a blending of Monterey, Spanish, and Pueblo architecture.

A short distance south of town is **La Mesilla State Monument** or Old Mesilla with its plaza and flat-roofed, adobied buildings–a scene straight out of Mexico. Main features of this settlement where Billy the Kid was brought to trial and the Gadsden Purchase was consummated are the **Gadsden Museum** and the **Wells Fargo Express Museum.** Eastward rise the fluted Organ Mountains, topped by 9,000-foot-high Organ Needle.

The region north and northwest of Las Cruces includes the typical old-time Spanish-Mexican village of **Dona Ana** with a church erected in 1834; the adobe ruins of **Fort Seldon,** established in 1865; the mineral hot springs resort of **Truth or Consequences; City of Rocks State Park** (picnicking, odd stone formations); the big **open pit copper mines** at Santa Rita; numerous ghost towns around Silver City; wilderness areas in Gila National Forest; and isolated **Gila Cliff Dwellings National Monument,** having three small ruins in 150-foot-high volcanic cliff.

SANTA FE, situated on a high rolling tableland dotted with piñon pines and backed by lofty Sangre de Cristo Mountains, is a most picturesque city.

Founded by Spaniards about 1610 on an old Indian pueblo, Santa Fe is said to be the oldest seat of government in the country.

To tour Santa Fe, start at "the end of the trail"—the Plaza—edged by La Fonda Hotel and numerous crafts shops. On the north side stands the **Palace of the Governors,** built around 1610, now a museum with outstanding displays of the region's past. Directly behind it, the **Hall of the Modern Indian** concentrates on Indian culture and crafts, and nearby, the Museum's **Fine Arts Building** collection includes works by local and internationally known artists.

Our Lady of Light Chapel, 1878, has a spiral staircase built without nails or any visible means of support. **Cathedral of St. Francis of Assisi** was the first cathedral in the Southwest. **Mission of San Miguel of Santa Fe** is perhaps the nation's oldest church, whose restored adobe walls house priceless paintings and ornaments. Other churches include **Chapel of Our Lady of Guadalupe** (founded in 1640, remodeled in 1883) with valuable paintings; and **Cristo Rey Church,** supposedly the nation's largest adobe building, with a notable hand-carved stone reredos (open hearth).

Out Old Pecos Road, not far from the downtown area, are the **Museum of Navajo Ceremonial Art,** which emphasizes sand paintings; and the **Museum of International Folk Art,** having lively displays of dolls, costumes, jewelry, ceramics, sculptures and other folk art from more than 50 nations.

A scenic drive (U.S. Highways 84–85) goes over Glorietta Pass to **Pecos State Monument,** which contains the ruins of an ancient five-story pueblo and also a 1617 Franciscan mission. Northeast of Las Vegas lies **Fort Union National Monument,** preserving the ruins of a post established in 1851.

San Ildefonso Pueblo, celebrated for its black pottery and ceremonial dances, contains several very large kivas. **Los Alamos,** famous for its atomic energy research, now is open to the public but there is little to see except a pleasant community. **Bandelier National Monument** protects pueblo and unique cave dwelling ruins constructed in soft tuff rock; largest, most accessible and different are those in **Frijoles Canyon** (self-guided walking tour, museum, lodge, campground). Farther northwest stretches **Valle Grande,** whose 18-mile-long, forest-rimmed meadowland comprises the world's largest extinct volcanic crater; and the **Jicarilla Apache Indian Reservation,** home of expert basket makers and horse and sheep raisers.

Around Espanola, about 25 miles north of Santa Fe, are **San Juan Pueblo, Santa Clara Pueblo, Puye Cliff Dweller and Communal House Ruins,** and the Spanish-American weaving village of **Chimayo** (see the primitive-style **Santuairo de Chimayo,** built of adobe in 1816 to protect earth that's thought to have miraculous powers) where the brightly colored Chimayo blanket is produced.

TAOS nestles in a lovely valley rimmed by the Sangre de Cristos, which rise to 13,161 feet at nearby Wheeler Peak, highest elevation in New Mexico. An old Spanish community, it is now a thriving art and writing colony. The adobe town actually is a three-part settlement: the central village of Don Fernando de Taos; Ranchos de Taos to the south; and the Indian Pueblo of San Geronimo (Taos Pueblo), north.

Begin at the **Plaza** with its old-time atmosphere and surrounding art studios, craft shops and restaurants. The **Kit Carson House,** one-half block east, where the famous scout lived from 1843–68, is furnished in period style and has both Indian and pioneer relics; **Kit Carson Memorial State Park** contains his and Mrs. Carson's graves. The

Millicent Rogers Foundation and Stables Art Gallery contains authentic articles of the early Spanish, Indian and American periods; the remodeled stable displays the works of 64 modern artists and all paintings are for sale. The **art museum** of the Harwood Foundation features temporary displays of noted Taos colony artists and permanent exhibits of Persian miniatures, paintings, Spanish and Indian art.

About two-and-one-half miles north of the Plaza stand the terraced, multistoried communal dwellings of **Taos Pueblo,** perhaps the most imposing of all. The **ruins of the Mission San Geronimo de Taos** were set up in 1598 and sacked during the 1680 rebellion.

About four miles south of the Plaza, the **Mission of St. Francis** or the Ranchos de Taos Mission, with its twin belfries, huge buttresses and adobe-walled *campo santo,* is one of the most impressive eighteenth-century Spanish missions. Its interior contains exceptionally old reredos, statues and Henri Ault's mysterious painting, "The Shadow of the Cross," on which the eyes of Christ seem to move and a luminous cross appears or disappears according to the amount of light.

Raton Pass, northeast, is a vista-filled gateway to Colorado. Southeast of the pass lie **Folsom Man State Monument,** where evidence of Stone Age man in America has been found, and **Capulin Mountain National Monument,** an extinct cinder volcanic cone rising 1,347 feet above the surrounding terrain. The spiral road to the crater rim is breathtaking, and trails allow closer glimpses of the 400-foot-deep, 1,500-foot-wide cup-shaped crater. South of Taos, U.S. Highway 64 runs through part of the **Rio Grande Gorge.**

SPORTS AND RECREATION. A variety of sports facilities can be found in New Mexico, where the clear, dry climate makes camping, hunting, fishing, and other outdoor diversions even more pleasant.

Near Alamogordo is **Ruidoso,** a piney, year-round resort with winter **skiing** and a full range of summer sports. **Bluewater Lake,** outside of Gallup, has **swimming, boating, picnicking, horseback riding, camping,** and **cabins. Hyde State Park,** outside of Santa Fe through Little Tesuque Canyon, is well-equipped with camping and picnic spots. Also in the area is **Santa Fe Ski Area,** with winter sports from mid-December to April.

Winter sports lovers visiting the Taos area will find **Taos Ski Valley** and **Sipapu winter sports area,** the latter open from December to March.

SPECIAL EVENTS. The majority of New Mexico's holidays and festivals are rodeos, Indian ceremonials, or related events. Indian dances and celebrations are held throughout the state all during the year, and most communities stage at least one rodeo or fair yearly.

Some of the highlights are the **Fiesta of San Felipe de Neri,** near Albuquerque in May; the **New Mexico State Fair,** in Albuquerque in September; the **Santa Fe Fiesta,** the state's biggest event, in Santa Fe each Labor Day weekend.

In Gallup, the **Inter-Tribal Indian Ceremonial** is held in August; the **San Geronimo Fiesta,** occurs in Taos the last week of September.

Texas

Texas, the *Lone Star State,* is famed for its picturesque history and its battle cry, "Remember the Alamo!" But today Texas is one of the country's most highly industrialized states, with petroleum refineries, chemical plants, and space exploration complexes dotting the sprawling countryside.

THE LAND. With an area of over 267,339 square miles, Texas is second only to Alaska in size. Its coastline on the Gulf of Mexico runs for 367 miles, and the state is bordered by Mexico, New Mexico, Oklahoma, Arkansas, Louisiana, and the Gulf.

Texas' famous Great Plains region in the northwestern corner contains one of the most oil-rich areas in the country, the Texas Panhandle. The Panhandle, a projection between Oklahoma and New Mexico, also contains some of the state's best farmland. Along the Gulf, the land is almost subtropical, providing excellent soil for hardwood trees and rice. The most mountainous area is in the extreme southwest, where an extension of the Rocky Mountains provides some of Texas' most breathtaking scenery.

The Rio Grande is Texas' largest, most important river, forming the 1,241-mile border between the United States and Mexico. Also important are the Colorado, Pecos, Red, and the San Antonio rivers.

THE CLIMATE in Texas varies from one end of the state to the other, with coldest readings found in the Northern Panhandle (January averages 35 degrees and July, 76 degrees). In southern Texas, warm, damp weather with temperatures of 60 degrees in January and 85 in July are not uncommon.

In eastern Texas, up to 46 inches of precipitation falls yearly, decreasing to under 8 inches in western Texas. Cold, strong winds accompanied by sleet and rain can sweep across the state in winter, often carrying soil with them. Whatever snow falls in Texas is found in the north.

THE PEOPLE. Because of fabulous reports of "seven golden cities," Texas was explored early in the sixteenth century by Spaniards Coronado and De Soto. Cavelier established Fort Saint Louis in 1685, but it was destroyed by Indians two years later. Spain, alarmed by the French explorations, sent in more expeditions and missionaries, building forts and missions such as San Antonio de Valero in 1718 (site of present-day San Antonio).

Texas became Mexican property in 1821 when Mexico broke away from Spain. Seeing Texas as a land ripe for settlement, Americans Moses Austin and his son Stephen soon after got permission to bring in settlers and found communities. They came in such large numbers that the Mexican government grew alarmed, and conflict led to open warfare in 1835.

It was during this war that settlers from San Antonio retreated to the Alamo, the chapel of an old mission, for protection. The entire garrison, including Davy Crockett and Jim Bowie, perished after a heroic resistance. Their example inspired their fellow Texans to win the victory of San Jacinto and ultimately their independence as the Republic of Texas, with Sam Houston as President. The population grew rapidly, and the republic applied for statehood. In spite of the wish of European nations that Texas remain independent, and fear of northern states that it would strengthen slavery, Texas became the twenty-eighth state in 1845. Mexico broke diplomatic relations with the United States immediately afterward, and less than a year later the Mexican War led to the acquisition of Arizona, New Mexico, California, and parts of several other states.

Texas seceded and joined the Confederacy during the Civil War, the last battle of which was fought on Texas soil. After a difficult Reconstruction period (including the rise of the Ku Klux Klan), Texas mushroomed rapidly. Settlers poured in, cattle became a giant industry, and Indian tribes were subdued. As railroad tracks were laid, farmlands were opened.

Oil and gas were discovered after the turn of the century, and Texas became even wealthier. Manufacturing developed, bringing roads, more urban growth, and shipping facilities.

Texas is still growing rapidly, with many new industries. Houston is the site of the Manned Spacecraft Center. The state's population is over 11 million, and increasing rapidly.

AGRICULTURE. Cotton, grown in central and northern regions, on the coastal plain, and in the Rio Grande Valley, is Texas' most important crop. Beef cattle, originally imported by the Spaniards, is second in importance.

Other field crops include sorghum, rice, pecans, and hay, while poultry and dairy products, horses and sheep, swell the livestock population. Shrimp are taken from the Gulf of Mexico in large quantities.

INDUSTRY. The chemical industry, bringing in 25 percent of Texas' manufacturing income, is the state's most important form of manufacturing. Located near Gulf Coast cities, the plants turn out such products as ammonia, hydrochloric acid and caustic soda. Food processing is next, with meat packing plants in the Fort Worth area contributing millions of dollars to the state's economy. Petroleum refining, wood products (lumber, furniture), transportation and electronic equipment, and printing are other key industries.

Mining accounts for one-third of the value of goods produced yearly in Texas, with petroleum the most important. More than 1.14 billion barrels of crude oil are brought up each year. Next is natural gas (40 percent of the nation's natural gas comes from Texas), sulphur, and helium.

CITIES. Houston, Dallas, San Antonio, Fort Worth, El Paso, Austin, and Corpus Christi are the largest cities in Texas, in order of population. Three-quarters of all Texans live in or around the state's urban areas.

ALPINE is a gateway to the rugged Big Bend country where game animals include black- and white-tailed deer, antelope, bear and panther. On the terraced campus of **Sul Ross State College,** see the **Big Bend Historical and Scientific Museum,** whose exhibits date back to cave dweller days.

Fort Davis, built to stave off Indian attacks in the 1850's and rebuilt in the 1880's using stone and adobe, is the highest community in Texas. Nearby is **W. J. McDonald Observatory** on Mount Locke, with its 83-inch reflecting telescope and visitor programs aimed at better celestial understanding (inquire locally about current arrangements).

Fort Stockton, a military post established more than a century ago, is right in the middle of Alpine. The **Crystal Pool** (a constant 71 degrees and formed by the flow of Comanche Chief Spring) marks the center of a park.

The once rough-tough cattle town of **Pecos,** now a melon-cotton shipping center known for its cantaloupes, has a replica of the **Judge Roy Bean saloon and courthouse.**

South of Alpine, **Big Bend National Park** covers more than 700,000 acres which include the state's last great wilderness. Open year round, its highlights are **Chisos Mountains** with rugged volcanic rock formations including pinnacles; dramatic **Santa Elena, Boquillas** and **Mariscal canyons,** formed by the Rio Grande; **Chisos Basin,** the section's chief development; hiking and horseback riding.

AMARILLO is a large, modern city rising abruptly above the expansive, short-grass prairies of the Staked Plains.

The **Canadian River,** north of the city, has numerous unpublicized pueblo ruins along its banks. Also in the area are the **Alibates Flint Quarries,** largest source of material (dating from 10,000 B.C.) for weapons and implements. **Boy's Ranch,** about 30 miles out, was founded in 1939 by Cal Farley to give "mavericks" a new start in life.

South of Amarillo, the community of **Canyon** is the home of **West Texas State College,** on whose campus is the **Panhandle-Plains Historical Museum** dealing with Southwestern culture and progress. About a dozen miles east, **Palo Duro Canyon State Park** features: 15 miles of scenic drives; 30 miles of hiking paths; 20 miles of bridle trails; narrow-gauge train ride; museum; petrified wood; some 30 different shades of color in spectacular canyon scenery.

AUSTIN, capital of Texas, spreads over a series of hills sliced by the Colorado River (not the Grand Canyon-cutting stream of the same name). Founded in 1839 as the capital of the Texas Republic, it is the sixth largest city in Texas. **Bergstrom Air Force Base** lies seven miles southeast.

Unique in America is Austin's "artificial moonlight"—the bluish glow of mercury-vapor lights from 27 towers

that rise 165 feet above the downtown area. They were erected in 1895.

The **state capitol,** a granite, domed edifice which is the largest state capitol in the country, was built in 1888, and has heroic murals by W. H. Huddle on the inside, and statuary on the surrounding grounds. Not far from the capitol, **The University of Texas** campus offers views of the city from the tower observation deck of the main building; and the **Eugene C. Barker Texas History Center** contains Frank Reaugh paintings.

The **Texas Memorial Museum** deals with historic, archaeological, biological and geological exhibits. **Elizabet Ney Museum,** former residence and studio of the sculptress, contains a collection of her works, while **O. Henry Museum** has items associated with the author. **Daughters of the Republic of Texas Museum** shows relics of Republic days, and **Daughters of the Confederacy Museum** displays mementos of that short-lived government. The **French Legation,** built about 1840, is the only structure ever erected in Texas by a foreign government. For a glimpse of ante-bellum days, visit the Southern-style **Governor's Mansion.**

The **LBJ Ranch,** Texas home of former President Johnson, is located 50 miles west of Austin. Built of native limestone and wood, and facing the Pedernales River, it has become one of the state's most popular tourist attractions.

BROWNSVILLE, 17 miles from the Gulf of Mexico, is an important point of entry to Mexico, a seaport, airport and railroad hub. **Fort Brown,** originally named Fort Taylor and established in 1846, was the primary townsite. **Resaca de la Palma,** north side of town, marks the scene of a Mexican War battle. **Port Brownsville** is the main harbor, with the shrimp and fishing fleet dominating the scene. **Ringgold Park** provides picnicking, shuffleboard and other outdoor recreation.

Matamoros, on the other side of the Rio Grande, is almost 200 years old. Paramount points of interest, aside from the Mexican influence, are the theater built during Maximilian's reign; market place; fort and cathedral. Northeast, on the Gulf, is **Port Isabel,** a prime shrimp and fish center where **Port Isabel Lighthouse State Park** with a tower built about 1852 and abandoned some 50 years later, can be visited. Just offshore lies **Padre Island,** a 120-mile-long sand strip with good beaches, fishing, camping, and picnicking.

CORPUS CHRISTI, on its landlocked bay just opposite the Gulf of Mexico, once was a haven for pirates such as Jean Lafitte. Kinney's Trading Post, set up in 1839, was virtually lawless, and even in later years, as Corpus Christi, it saw a bountiful traffic in contraband goods. Ranching, followed by gas and petroleum, created a more law-abiding atmosphere. A large naval air training station is located in the town.

South of Austwell stretches **Aransas National Wildlife Refuge,** the winter home of the last flock of whooping cranes in the world. Inland and southwest lies Kingsville, just outside of which is the famous **King Ranch** (nearly a million acres) where Santa Gertrudis cattle were first bred.

DALLAS, a leader in finance (the Dallas Cotton Exchange normally handles about two million bales of cotton annually), manufacturing, distribution, fashion, and culture, started as a trading post for Caddo Indians in 1840. The city has a celebrated symphony orchestra and **Dallas** and **Southern Methodist universities.**

Fair Park's 187-acre, $35-million exposition grounds are open as a city park except during the two weeks preceding the **State Fair of Texas.** In this area are **Cotton Bowl,** scene of the annual football classic; **Hall of State,** having a gigantic gold medallion, huge murals, statues and Museum of Texas History; **Museum of Fine Arts** with planetarium plus valuable paintings and sculptures; a **Museum of Natural History** exhibiting habitat displays of Southwestern animal and bird life, minerals and flora; the **aquarium** that shows off more than 4,000 fish and amphibians; **Health Museum,** featuring the "transparent man" that explains bodily functions, and a giant "hall-of-man" figure whose "heartbeat" reverberates throughout the building; the **State Fair Music Hall,** scene of summer musicals. The **John Neely Bryan Cabin** on the courthouse lawn is a replica of the city's first structure. In addition, city parks offer swimming, boating, picnicking, horseback riding and golf.

Six Flags Over Texas, a 115-acre entertainment center between Dallas and Fort Worth, features international musical shows, over 70 rides including trains and a riverboat, and many varied restaurants.

Denison, with an established reputation as a manufacturing city, is located north of Dallas, and is best known to tourists for the **birthplace of President Dwight D. Eisenhower** in the southeastern part of town. About four miles northwest is **Denison Dam** on the Red River.

EL PASO, "The Pass" on the Rio Grande, is the largest American city on the Mexican border and one of the most historic in Texas. Across the border from Ciudad Juárez, El Paso has a pronounced international flavor.

The **replica of Old Fort Bliss** stands opposite the parade grounds of the modern fort, now home of the U. S. Army Anti-Aircraft Artillery. The **Sun Bowl,** with its unusual Tibetan architecture, and the **Centennial Museum** (worldwide weapons, geological and hunting trophy collections), are both located at **Texas Western College.** The **International Museum** deals with early Indian artifacts, pioneer relics and the Spanish-Mexican period. A scenic drive (especially beautiful at night) can be taken to an overlook on **Mount Franklin.** Also to be seen are the **reptile gardens,** having rare Far East species; and **Sierra de Cristo Rey,** the statue of Christ (designed by Urbici Solar) atop Mount Cristo Rey near the international line.

Ciudad Juárez, commonly called Juárez, is the main sight in the area. Places to see are **Mission de Nuestra Señora de Guadalupe,** more than 300 years old; the bull rings known as **Plaza Monumental** (Mexico's second largest) and the **Plaza de Toros;** and the **Mexican markets** with their colorful variety.

Through the El Paso Valley, a three-hour drive visits **Ysleta** with its **mission Nuestra Señora del Carmen,** parts of which date to 1682; **Socorro,** whose mission, erected about 1681–83, is the oldest parish church in Texas; and **San Elizario** with a Presidio Chapel (1843) that replaced the original of 1683—on the site of the so-called Salt War.

FORT WORTH, with a good hold on petroleum, is more western than Dallas, and has the Southwest's biggest livestock, packing and grain operations. It is home of **Carswell Air Force Base,** aircraft manufacturers, and numerous colleges (**Texas Christian University** is the most noted).

Centennial Group includes the Municipal Auditorium, Will Rogers Memorial Coliseum, Memorial Tower, Art Museum and a half-dozen livestock exhibition buildings. The aluminum-domed civic theater, **Casa Mañana,** presents year-round entertainment. The **Fort Worth Children's Museum** has the "Live Animal Room," "Hall of Man," and the **Charles M. Noble Planetarium.**

Trinity Park, with **Botanic Gardens** at its southwestern end, is a lovely area filled with winding drives and bridle paths. Nearby, **Forest Park** contains a municipal zoo, children's zoo, aquarium, and sports facilities. "The Lord's Supper," a life-size wax replica of Da Vinci's renowned painting, tours of various meat packing plants, and Fort Worth International Airport are other area attractions.

GALVESTON, on Galveston Island in the Gulf of Mexico and connected with the mainland by causeway, is one of the Southwest's leading ports; more than 50 ocean-going vessels can be berthed at its docks. Galveston's popular **Stewart Beach** attracts many anglers for some 50 species of fish around the island.

The city saw maneuvering in both the Mexican and Civil wars, but its greatest blow came in 1900 when 110-mile-per-hour hurricane winds devastated the city and killed 6,000 persons. Strong sea walls have thus far prevented similar storm-caused tidal waves.

HOUSTON, largest city in Texas, is 50 miles from the Gulf of Mexico, but it ranks as a great seaport because of the industry-lined **Houston Ship Channel** to the Gulf.

The pride of Houston is the huge **Texas Medical Center,** a 164-acre section with 20 institutions. Nearby stands **Rice Institute,** on a splendid 300-acre campus. **University of Houston** provides guided tours of its campus. The Houston **Astrodome,** the world's first plastic-domed, air-conditioned stadium, gives Houston an all-weather sports and convention center, which is used for big-league baseball (it is the home stadium of the major league Houston Astros), professional football, and many other events.

Show place in the **Civic Center** is the **Sam Houston Coliseum,** with a 15,-000 capacity, which doubles as a convention and exposition hall and also contains a music hall. **Hermann Park**–having a children's lake stocked with fish and the Miller Memorial Theater for summer concerts–is a heavily-wooded, 600-acre beauty spot with riding trails, golf, tennis, picnicking and other pastimes. Within the park are the **Houston Zoological Gardens and Museum of Natural History.**

The **Museum of Fine Arts** emphasizes Oriental, European and American art. The **Noble house,** constructed about 1847, is the city's oldest and is furnished in period style. **Scenic drives** include the Azalea Trail past River Oaks estates; Riverside; Southmore Boulevard; and MacGregor Ways.

Huntsville, amid red, sandy, pine-covered hills, is Sam Houston's home town, and is also a college and lumber town with excellent swimming, fishing and hunting. On the south side lies **Sam Houston Park,** containing the general's old "steamboat house" in which he died, his law office and a museum with personal relics and mementos of the Texas Revolution. Some 21 miles east of Houston, is the 460-acre **San Jacinto Battleground State Park,** scene of the conflict that meant Texan independence from Mexico in 1836. The 570-foot-high stone **San Jacinto Monument** (elevator service to the tower) looks out on an impressive panorama; its base contains a museum which portrays the region's history. The battleship **U.S.S. Texas**–veteran of two world wars–is moored nearby.

LAREDO, the nation's chief port of entry on the Mexican border, was founded in 1755 and once known as "The Republic of the Rio Grande." The **capitol building** of the short-lived republic still stands at Martin Plaza. **Cactus garden** on San Bernardo Avenue should be visited.

Nuevo Laredo, across the Rio Grande, is known for shopping bargains.

NACOGDOCHES dates to early Indian times. The first white community was settled in 1716 with the founding of the Mission of Our Lady of the Guadalupe of Nacogdoches.

The **Old Stone Fort** on the Stephen F. Austin State College campus is now a museum. Interesting to see are **Nacogdoches University** and **Oak Grove Cemetery,** where four of the Texas Declaration of Independence signers are buried. **Angelina, Davy Crockett, Sabine** and **Sam Houston national forests** out of town provide recreational facilities.

SAN ANTONIO is one of the most attractive vacation spots in the Lone Star State. The remains of the **Alamo,** where the famous battle was fought in 1836, is the city's best known attraction. It remains militarily strategic with 3,300-acre **Fort Sam Houston,** Fourth Army headquarters; **Camp Bullis; Lackland, Brooks, Randolph** and **Kelly air force bases;** and the **Brooke Army Medical Center.** Symphony and opera groups, **Trinity University, San Antonio College, St. Mary's University** and other schools are located in San Antonio.

At the serpentine San Antonio River is the **Arneson River Theater** with the stage on one side of the stream and the audience on the other. Nearby are **La Villita,** the 200-year-old, quaint adobe Spanish "Little Town" where artisans practice arts and crafts, and the **Cos House** where, in 1835, Mexican General Perfecto de Cos signed the capitulation to the Texans.

The public library contains the **Hertzberg circus collection** with a room-size scale model of a complete circus, and 20,000 items of circus memorabilia. On the Main Plaza, dominated by **City Hall,** rises **San Fernando Cathedral** (present structure built in 1873) where Alamo defenders are buried. Nearby, on Military Plaza, stands the restored eighteenth-century **Spanish Governor's palace,** having handmade furniture and doors plus a rustic old-style kitchen of the period. The **Mexican community** has a colorful section with restaurants and shops.

Mission La Purisima Concepcion de Acuna was constructed on its present site in 1731. **San Jose Mission National Historic Site** embraces **San Jose y San Miguel de Aguayo Mission,** founded in

1720 (the Rose Window is a fine example of stone carving). **Mission San Juan Capistrano** has a restored chapel built in 1731 plus granary and church ruins. **Mission San Francisco de la Espada** houses a small Indian school in the restored section, whose church was erected here about 1731.

Breckenridge Park, covering some 360 acres in the northeastern portion of the city, is a travel bonanza. **San Antonio Zoological Gardens** with 2,000 specimens, barless bear pits, monkey island, hippopotamus pool and other features is especially worth visiting. **Witte Memorial Museum,** also in the park, exhibits art works, Texas natural history, foreign rooms portraying cultures from many lands, stamps and coins from most countries, and numerous other displays. The park also has sunken **Japanese gardens,** miniature train ride, lagoons, an outdoor theater, as well as golf, horseback riding, boating and picnicking. The **McNay Art Institute** exhibits modern French art.

Goliad, where the first Texan Declaration of Independence was issued, saw the massacre of 350 Texans who surrendered to Mexican promises of safe conduct; the deed inflamed the region even more than the Alamo battle three weeks before. **Goliad State Park** (monument, museum, camping and picnicking) commemorates the victims; south of the park stands **Mission Espiritu Santo,** begun in 1749, later restored and a museum added. **Presidio La Bahia Chapel** in Goliad still stands in its original state.

Sophienburg Memorial Museum exhibits historical items. Tourists seeking a dude ranch vacation should head for the **Bandera** area, one of the best in Texas for such a holiday. In Bandera, the **Frontier Times Museum** contains collections of early Texas and other pioneer relics. In **Fredericksburg,** the **Vereins Kirche,** an octagonal reproduction of the first church erected in 1847, is now a regional museum.

TEXARKANA, with the **Red River Arsenal** 17 miles to the west, is an important trading center split between Texas and Arkansas. **Gaddo Lake State Park** is popular for boating, fishing, and shoreside picnicking, while **Spring Lake Park** and **Lake Texarkana** feature fishing, boating, picnicking, and camping.

WACO, on the Brazos River, and named for the Hueco Indians, was first settled in 1849. **Lake Waco** offers swimming, fishing and boating; **Lake Whitney State Park** draws bass fishermen, campers, and picnickers, and **Cameron Park** has extensive recreational facilities. **Baylor University,** with the **Armstrong Browning Library,** offers the world's largest collection of original Browning works as well as some personal items, and the **Texas Collection** of state historic objects.

SPORTS AND RECREATION facilities can be found throughout the state, whether in the form of tennis courts, pools, and golf courses in the cities, or in rustic parks and clear lakes out on the hills and plains. Major league baseball, professional and college football are the state's most popular spectator sports.

In the Austin area are two popular recreation spots, **Lake Austin** and **Zilker Park,** both with facilities for **swimming, boating,** and **fishing.** Zilker Park also has **horseback riding, target shooting,** and **golf.** Up the Colorado are the **Highland Lakes, Inks Lake State Park,** and **Longhorn Cavern State Park,** one of the nation's largest caves. Spectators can watch underwater ballet from the **Aquarena,** a submarine theater located at the headwaters of the San Marcos River, in the vicinity of Austin.

Around Fort Worth are **Lake Worth** and **Eagle Mountain Lake** (both manmade); **Possum Kingdom Lake and State Park,** and **Mineral Wells,** a health resort.

Other facilities of note include **Padre Island National Seashore, Mustang Island, Port Aransas,** and **Aransas Pass,** all near Corpus Christi; **Port Arthur** and **Pleasure Island** near Galveston; and **New Braunfels, Landa Park,** and **Lake Dunlap,** in the San Antonio area.

SPECIAL EVENTS. Rodeos, fairs, and festivals are held in Texas throughout the year, the exact nature of them depending upon the region and its local customs (events with a Mexican flavor can be found along the southern border). The **State Fair of Texas,** held in Dallas every October, is the state's most important event.

In Galveston, the **Annual Shrimp Festival** is held in late April; the **South Texas State Fair** is held in nearby Beaumont in late October; and the **Shrimp Bowl** football game takes place in late December.

A **Pioneer Roundup** is held in Huntsville in April, **international flower and garden show** in Houston in March, and the **Bluebonnet Bowl,** also in Houston, in December are other events of note.

Special events in San Antonio include the **Grand Opera Festival** in February, with Metropolitan Opera stars; **San Antonio Rodeo** in February; **Fiesta San Antonio** in April; and concerts by the **San Antonio Symphony Orchestra,** November through March.

In other parts of Texas, key events include the following: **Southwestern Exposition and Fat Stock Show,** Fort Worth, late January; **Charro Days,** Brownsville, the week preceding Lent (when people wear Mexican attire, stage parades, concerts, and fireworks); **Buccaneer Days,** each spring in Corpus Christi, complete with pirate costumes, parade, dances, water pageant, and events depicting the city's early history; **Fort Griffin Fandangle,** held in Albany, June; **West of the Pecos Rodeo,** Pecos, early July; **Four-States Fair and Rodeo,** Texarkana, September; and the **Sun Carnival,** in El Paso in late December, including sports events, street dances, carnival queen coronation, and climaxed by the New Year's Day Sun Bowl parade and football game.

Oklahoma

Rolling wheatfields, towering oil pumps, Indian villages, and grazing cattle—all are typical of Oklahoma, one of the nation's major farming and mining states. This colorful state has been sung about in the musical, *Oklahoma!,* written about in John Steinbeck's *The Grapes of Wrath,* and visited by thousands of travelers interested in the nation's historical background.

THE LAND. Oklahoma's southern boundary is formed by the meandering Red River, one of the state's two most important river systems (the other, the Arkansas, flows in the southeastern part of the state). **Black Mesa,** in the northwestern High Plains region, is 4,978 feet high and the state's highest point. Although Oklahoma is known for its plains and hills—largely in the western part of the state—several mountain ranges (the Ouachita, the Wichita, and the Boston) also make up Oklahoma's landscape.

THE CLIMATE. Weather in Oklahoma is moderately warm and dry—typical of the south-central states. July temperatures climb into the low eighties, but in January usually average around 40. The state receives 25 inches of snow in the northern Panhandle, with as few as two inches falling yearly in the southeast.

THE PEOPLE. Oklahoma became United States territory when France concluded the Louisiana Purchase in 1803. Until then, it was known only to native Indian tribes, Spaniards seeking gold, a few trappers and explorers.

The first large-scale settlement was made in 1820 by Indian tribes—the Cherokee, Chickasaw, Choctaw, Creek, and Seminole—who were being moved westward by the government so their land in the Southeast could be opened to white settlers. Known as the Five Civilized Tribes, they established new homes, farms, schools, and eventually built a prosperous way of life.

After the Civil War, the need for homesteading land was critical. Although the government for a time refused to move the Indians and punished white trespassers, eventually action was taken to move the Indians again. All surrounding land was filled with settlers, and as soon as the Indians agreed or were forced to give up theirs, these homesteaders pounced on the newly opened areas. By 1889, new space was needed so badly that thousands of homesteaders actually waited on the border of Indian land in central Oklahoma until noon when a gun sounded, signifying that the land was open for settlement.

The Territory of Oklahoma, with the state's present dimensions, was opened in 1890, although maps showed two separate adjacent twin territories: Indian Territory and Oklahoma Territory. Settlers kept arriving by the thousands, and federal commissioners began preparing them, and especially the Indians, for statehood. After controversies over whether or not to make Oklahoma one large state (including both territories) were settled, statehood was granted in 1907.

During the territorial period farming developed rapidly and oil was discovered. Expansion continued through the 1920's when drought, the rise of the Ku Klux Klan, and a drop in farm prices brought severe economic difficulties, complicated by the Depression of the '30's.

Since World War II, when demand for oil and farm produce injected new funds into the economy, Oklahoma's growth has been steady. New construction, added water facilities, and industry have been in large part responsible for raising the state's population to close to 2.5 million.

AGRICULTURE. The beef cattle industry is the top agricultural income-producer in Oklahoma, with almost twice as many cattle in the state as people. The traditional range-riding cowboy, though in many areas replaced by enclosed feed lots, can still be seen. Other livestock include chicken, dairy products, and hogs.

Next in importance is winter wheat, the most valuable field crop, followed by cotton, peanuts, barley, hay, and soybeans. Fruits and truck crops are also grown.

INDUSTRY accounts for one-third of the value of goods produced in Oklahoma, as do agriculture and mining. The largest industries come from the processing of meat and produce, and from the refining of oil and natural gas. Tulsa and Ponca City are chief oil-refining cities.

Other areas of manufacturing are machinery, metal processing, transportation equipment, and glass.

Oklahoma's oil wells produce almost 200 million barrels of crude oil yearly, most of it coming from the Tulsa-Oklahoma City area. Natural gas is next most important mined product, then coal, gypsum, sand, gravel, and helium gas.

CITIES. In Oklahoma City, Tulsa, and Lawton live over half of Oklahoma's population. The state as a whole has only 30 cities with more than 10,000 people, largely concentrated in northeastern Oklahoma.

ANADARKO is headquarters for the **Southern Plains Indian Agency.** The federal building, decorated with eye-catching murals by Kiowa Indians, houses the agency which serves Oklahoma, Texas and Kansas tribes.

The **Southern Plains Indian Arts and Crafts Museum** features outstanding exhibits of weapons, ceremonial dress, daily life, and arts and crafts, while the adjoining **Indian Hall of Fame** honors famous Indians. North of town, 2,200-acre **Riverside Indian School,** founded in 1872, educates students from 13 different tribes.

Indian City, just south of town, consists of authentic (re-created) dwellings of the Apache, Wichita, Comanche, Caddo and Kiowa. Indians demonstrate the old ways, stage ceremonial dances, and fashion goods for sale.

ARDMORE is 20 miles south of the Arbuckle Mountains. In town are **Carter Seminary** (a U. S. Indian school), **Noble Research Foundation,** Oklahoma veterans' home and **Ardmore Air Force Base.**

CLAREMORE is the birthplace of Will Rogers, the humorist. One mile west of town is the **Will Rogers Memorial** which contains the tomb, mementos of Rogers, and educational, Indian and pioneer displays. The lobby of a hotel contains the **J. M. Davis gun collection** of nearly 61,000 items; **Lake Claremore** affords picnicking, boating, and fishing.

LAWTON is an old military post. **Fort Sill,** a few miles north, is now the U. S. Army Artillery and Missile Center, and in the **Apache cemetery** near Lawton is the grave of Geronimo.

Fort Sill Military Reservation, over 90,000 acres, was established by General Philip Sheridan in 1869. It includes **McLain and Hamilton halls,** which depict the lore of the artillery from 1638 to modern times; the ivy-covered **Old Post Chapel,** erected in 1870, one of the oldest churches in the state; the stone **Old Post Corral,** constructed in 1870 to protect horses and cattle from Indians, now a reconstructed blacksmith shop and trader's store.

MUSKOGEE, near the confluence of the Arkansas, Grand and Verdigris rivers, was an Indian country trade locale on the old Texas Road. **Bacone College** (a distinguished Indian junior college) and the **Five Civilized Tribes Indian Agency** are located in the town, which contains 22 parks.

Tahlequah, in the Ozark foothills, is the former capital of the Cherokee Nation, and is a good area for hunting and fishing. The **Murrell Home** was built in 1845. To the southeast is **Tsa-La-Gi,** a re-creation of an ancient Cherokee village, and a theater which presents "Trail of Tears" drama during the summer, commemorating the Cherokees' forced march to Oklahoma.

In Okmulgee, the **Old Creek Indian Council House,** constructed in 1878 as the capitol, now is a museum displaying weapons, pioneer documents and attire, and Indian craftwork. **Lake Okmulgee,** west of town, has picnicking, camping and fishing.

NORMAN is the state's chief college town. On the campus of the **University of Oklahoma,** the **University Museum** contains stuffed animals and birds; mounts of large reptiles in replicas of their usual habitat; Greek and Roman relics; and **Indian art.** The **W. B. Bizzell Memorial Library** has the Phillips Collection of books dealing with Oklahoma and the Southwest. The **art museum** houses the Woodruff Collection (European arts and crafts, old Indian basketry, Central American pottery, sixteenth- and seventeenth-century paintings) and the Wentz-Matzene Collection (Oriental art objects, precious stones, statues and old paintings).

OKLAHOMA CITY, capital city of the state, is also the largest with more than 366,000 residents. The community lies above two of the world's greatest high gravity oil fields. Derricks have sprouted everywhere—even on the state capitol grounds.

Founded in 1889, Oklahoma City became a thriving community of 10,000 persons in some six hours—thanks to the land-rush opening of Indian Territory. The big boom, however, came in 1928 when the first oil wells were opened. Now there are more than 2,000 of them. **Tinker Air Force Base,** the world's largest repair and supply depot, and the Civil Aeronautics Administration Center at Will Rogers Municipal Airport make the city an important aviation center.

A good, overall view can be had from the 32-story **First National Building** observation tower. Constance Warren's "Statue of a Cowboy" is in front of the south entrance to the **state capitol,** and the **Oklahoma Historical Society Building** houses comprehensive exhibits of Indian documents and relics.

The **Civic Center** includes City Hall, the Municipal Auditorium, County Building and Police Department. **Lincoln Park,** a 640-acre entertainment spot, has two 18-hole golf courses, the municipal zoo, a lake, outdoor theater, hiking and picnicking.

Other points: the **Church of Tomorrow** and **St. Luke's Methodist Church,** known for their arresting contemporary style architecture; the **Art Center;** tours of the **stockyards and meat packing plants;** the **National Cowboy Hall of Fame and Museum,** and fishing and boating on **Lakes Overholser** and **Hefner.**

Frontier City, about 12 miles northeast, is a children's amusement spot with old-time shops, train and stagecoach rides, periodic gunfights and other "Old West" activities. To the west, **El Reno** is the location of **Fort Reno,** sprawling over 9,600 acres, a pioneer army post in the early 1870's (now a federal and state agricultural and livestock experiment station); **State Game Farm,** pheasant and quail hatcheries; and the **Cheyenne and Arapaho Agency and School.**

PAWHUSKA, seat of Osage County, is situated amid cattle ranges, and is the tribal headquarters for the Osage Nation. Here, in 1909, the nation's first Boy Scout troop was formed. At the Indian agency, the **Osage Museum** shows Indian crafts, arts and costumes. North of Pawhuska is the 100,000-acre **Barnard-Chapman Ranch.**

TULSA, second largest city in Oklahoma, is considered the "Oil Capital of the World," due to its huge surrounding oil fields, offices of hundreds of oil companies, oil equipment manufacturers, petroleum research centers, and the **International Petroleum Exposition** staged every four years.

In 1879, Tulsa was a pony-express stop on the Arkansas River. The Atlantic and Pacific Railroad came three years later. Indian warfare, outlaws, lack of water, and arguments about the railroad right of way throttled growth, but discovery of oil in 1901 created the foundation for modern Tulsa. Located here are the **University of Tulsa** and the **United States Junior Chamber of Commerce.**

Industrial tours include guided trips through the Sunray Mid-Continental Oil Company and the Spartan Aircraft Factory which produces mobile homes. **Philbrook Art Center** has the Kress Collection of Italian Renaissance paintings, American Indian art, Indian pottery and baskets, period rooms, Chinese jades and other items. The **Gilcrease Institute of American History and Art** is a $12-million collection of Americana with rare documents and manuscripts, pre-Columbian gold and jade work, the world's largest array of Western paintings, including many by Charles M. Russell and Frederic Remington, early Indian relics, sculpture and other displays on the continent's past. The **Boston Avenue Methodist Church** presents a notable example of modern church architecture with four-story limestone walls surmounted by a 290-foot-high, illuminated tower.

SPORTS AND RECREATION. A variety of sports facilities are available in Oklahoma, especially for the traveler who enjoys the rugged outdoor sports of camping, hunting, and fishing.

Great Salt Plains and **Great Salt Plains Lake** are well-equipped facilities at Alva. Extensive salt flats, national wildlife preserve, **boating, fishing, swimming, picnicking,** and **water skiing** are among its attractions.

In the Ardmore, Oklahoma area are **Lake Murray State Park,** on a man-made lake; **Lake Texoma State Park,** which is on the Texas border; and **Platt National Park,** with 38 springs and a buffalo herd, as well as a variety of sports facilities.

Other popular recreation areas can be found at **Honor Heights Park, Fort Gibson Dam and Reservoir, Sequoyah State Park** (with hayrides, camping, all water sports), **Tenkiller Dam and Reservoir,** and **Greenleaf Lake State Park,** all near Muskogee.

In and around Tulsa are **Mohawk Park,** in the city; **Tulsa Garden Center** and **Tulsa Rose Garden,** also within the city limits; and **Grand Lake,** formed by Pensacola Dam on the Grand River.

SPECIAL EVENTS. Fairs, Indian celebrations, rodeos, and other similar events are very popular in Oklahoma. Especially so are "land openings" which commemorate the early pioneer days. The Oklahoma State Fair, held in late September in Oklahoma City, is considered one of the best-attended yearly events.

Others interesting to visit are the **Wichita Mountains Easter Pageant,** held in Lawton on Easter morning; the **Cimarron Territory Celebration,** Beaver, late May; **Oklahoma City Charity Horse Show,** in mid-May, and the **Indian Capital Rodeo,** Muskogee, June.

An **American Indian Exposition** is held at Anadarko in August; a **Will Rogers Memorial Rodeo** in Vinita, last week of August; **Cherokee National Holiday** at Tahlequah, September 2; **Osage Indian Celebration,** Pawhuska, late September; **Will Rogers Day,** Claremore, early November, and the **Statehood Day Observance,** state-wide, November 16.

The Far West

Far West States

CANADA
OLYMPIC NATL. PARK
SEATTLE
OLYMPIA
MT. RAINIER NATL. PARK
SPOKANE
WASHINGTON
MONTANA
IDAHO
Ocean
PORTLAND
COLUMBIA R.
SALEM
OREGON
RANGE
CRATER LAKE NATL. PARK
BOISE
CRATERS OF THE MOON NATL. MONUMENT
SNAKE R.
WYO.
UTAH
COAST
SACRAMENTO R.
LASSEN VOLCANIC NATL. PARK
NEVADA
LAKE TAHOE
SACRAMENTO
SAN FRANCISCO
YOSEMITE NATL. PARK
KING'S CANYON NATL. PARK
DEATH VALLEY
SEQUOIA NATL. PARK
Pacific
CALIFORNIA
JOSHUA TREE NATL. MONUMENT
ARIZ.
LOS ANGELES
SAN DIEGO
MEXICO
BARROW
Arctic
Ocean
CANADA
YUKON R.
NOME
FAIRBANKS
MT. McKINLEY
ANCHORAGE
JUNEAU
SEWARD
Bering Sea
Gulf of Alaska
ALEUTIAN IS.
ALASKA
KAUAI
NIIHAU
Kauai Channel
OAHU
MOLOKAI
Pearl Harbor
HONOLULU
LANAI
MAUI
KAHOOLAWE
Mauna Kea
HAWAII
Mauna Loa
Kilauea
HAWAII VOLCANOES NATIONAL PARK
HAWAII

The Far West

Six states are linked to each other by the waters of the Pacific Ocean—California, Oregon, Washington, Idaho (connected to the Pacific by the Snake River and its ocean port, Lewiston), Alaska, and Hawaii. This vast sea-linked community extends over 10,000 miles in length, and includes a quarter of the land area of the United States.

Few regions in the world can match the Far West for variety and number of natural wonders—a rain forest wilderness, groves of giant trees, glaciers creeping to the sea through towering fiords, raging rivers flowing through deep gorges, great craggy mountain peaks, active volcanoes, scorching deserts. Some of it—parts of Alaska, the southeastern corner of Oregon—are practically unexplored.

Almost any part of the region shows dramatic contrasts. A relatively short drive takes the visitor from Alpine-like Lake Coeur d'Alene in northern Idaho to the wild, mile-and-a-half-deep Snake River Canyon. On a highway in eastern California one can look west to the snowy crest of Mount Whitney, 14,494 feet above sea level, and east to Badwater, the blazing heart of Death Valley, 282 feet below sea level, lowest point in the country.

The Far West is one of the most productive regions in the world. In northern California, Washington, and Oregon are orchards, cattle ranges, limitless wheat fields; in the south, cotton and citrus fruit, the world's most extensive vineyards, and vegetable gardens. In Hawaii are vast plantations of pineapple, sugar cane, and coffee.

Exotic place names give clues to the region's historic background. In California most of the major cities have Spanish names—San Francisco, Los Angeles, San Diego, Sacramento. In the Pacific Northwest, such names as Coeur d'Alene and Grand Coulee are reminders of the French fur trappers who explored this as so many other areas of North

America. And in Alaska traces of Russian exploration are retained by such names as the Pribilof Islands.

Surprisingly, the Far West was opened up in all its far-flung reaches within a few short years. California's first Spanish mission dates from 1769, Captain Cook discovered Hawaii in 1778, the first Russian fur company settled in Alaska in 1784. Through war, purchase, treaty, and "manifest destiny" the whole region came under United States control in the period between 1803 (the Louisiana Purchase) and 1898 (annexation of Hawaii). In the twentieth century all six states have experienced a dynamic growth which has left its traces in a different kind of sightseeing attraction—Grand Coulee Dam, the Golden Gate Bridge, Hollywood.

Dwellings and other structures tell the story of the land's settlement. The Spanish contributed the chain of charming missions in California as well as the thick-walled, comfortable adobe houses. A New Englander in Monterey added galleries to a typical Yankee home and created the Monterey style. In northern California Russians descending the coast from Alaska built forts and churches which can be seen at Fort Ross. Chinese mine workers imported into California built joss houses and temples. French and Italian winemakers added stone wineries, and a quaintly charming little church in the form of a wine barrel. Lumber barons dotted the north with great Victorian mansions, while lumberjacks hewed out log cabins. Danish settlers in Southern California created a Danish village. In Los Angeles is what seems a typical street of a Mexican city.

Special tourist attractions abound: the Logging Jubilee and Salmon Derby in Washington, the Pendleton Rodeo and Floral Festival in Oregon, the Spud Festival in Idaho, and the Lei Festival in Hawaii. In California, the Jumping Frog Contest recalls the Gold Rush days and Mark Twain's famous story. Santa Barbara pays tribute to its heritage in Old Spanish Days, and in San Francisco's Chinatown firecrackers pop on Chinese New Year. Alaska stages the Midnight Sun Baseball Game every summer in Fairbanks.

The best way to plan a trip in this huge region is to pick appropriate cities as bases—San Diego, Los Angeles, San Francisco, Portland, Seattle, Spokane in the continental area, Honolulu in Hawaii, and Juneau, Anchorage, and Fairbanks in Alaska—and explore the towns and historic areas around them.

California

The nation's largest state in population and third largest in area, California is perhaps also the most diverse in scene, character, and climate. Its 158,693 square miles are immensely varied, and often dramatically beautiful. Its 20 million people spring from a variety of backgrounds, unusual even in the United States. The northern border of California is Oregon; on its west is the coast of the Pacific Ocean, a shore line of approximately 1,264 miles, which extends in a southeast-to-northwest direction. The result is that San Diego on the Pacific is actually farther east than Reno, Nevada. On the south the border is Mexico, and on the east are the states of Nevada and Arizona. The extreme width of California is 360 miles. California was the first state of the Far West to be admitted to the Union (1850). Its state tree is the California redwood, the state flower the golden poppy, and the state bird the valley quail.

THE LAND. The northern part is chiefly mountains and forests, with some of the finest stands of timber in the world, like the majestic groves of towering redwood trees. Mountain ranges with notable peaks like Shasta and Lassen Peak (the only active volcano in the continental United States) fill most of northern California, but the ranges divide toward the center. On the east they become the wild and magnificent Sierra Nevada, with dozens of great peaks, including **Mount Whitney** (14,494 feet). On the west the mountains, lower and superbly forested, crowd the coast, providing breathtaking scenic drives and forest playgrounds like the unique and lovely Monterey Peninsula and the redwood groves. Though California's rocky coast has few big natural harbors, it has dozens of pleasant coves, most of them flanked with beaches that are public parks. But there are three important natural harbors, and a man-made one. Southernmost of the harbors is **San Diego.** Next north is the busy harbor of **San Pedro,** entirely man-made. About the center of the coast is **San Francisco Bay,** guarded by its Golden Gate, rimmed by a chain of cities. It is a great natural harbor. Farthest north is **Humboldt Bay,** a shipping point for lumber and home of a big fishing fleet.

Behind the coastal mountains to its east is **Central Valley,** a rich alluvial basin about 400 miles long, from 40 to 60 miles wide. It is drained by the San Joaquin and the Sacramento rivers, which, after joining, flow into San Francisco Bay. Thanks to the largest and most complex system of irrigation in the world, the valley areas produce an incredible array of crops, year round.

South of the central valley, the mountain ranges join again to form the northern limits of Southern California. On its east lies a vast desert, areas of which, by ingenuity and irrigation, have been converted to richly productive fields. A part of the desert is a playground, another a great national monument preserving unique desert flora and fauna—**Death Valley.** The desert on the east is divided from the western half of Southern California by rugged mountain ranges that have become winter and summer playgrounds. Los Angeles spreads over a plain, south of which a lower cluster of mountains crowd to the coast, framing big **San Diego Bay.**

The lakes, though not numerous, are unusual. They include mile-high, incredibly deep and beautiful **Lake Tahoe,** among towering peaks on the California-Nevada border; the big, man-made reservoir in the shadow of **Mount Shasta; Clear Lake,** among pleasant northern forests; and in the extreme southeast, in the heart of the desert, the odd and salty body of water called **Salten Sea,** 241 feet below sea level.

Only two of California's rivers are large: the mighty, muddy, once truculent (now tamed) **Colorado,** on the eastern border, from which Southern California gets most of its water; the **Sacramento** with its San Joaquin tributary, fed by the melting snows of the high mountains, draining the Central

Valley. Southern California's newest, most important water source is the Oroville Dam on the Feather River. It is the highest (at 747.5 feet) dam in the U.S. But other rivers, particularly in the north, though relatively short, are important for scenic and recreational reasons. The **Russian River,** flowing through forests and vineyards, is one; farther north the **Trinity** and the **Klamath,** tumbling down from mountain wilderness areas, are a delight to sportsmen, ranking among the world's finest fishing streams. In the northeast, the **Feather River** is famed for its wild and beautiful canyon.

THE CLIMATE. California has several markedly different climates, and visitors can find any climatic condition within a few hours' drive of any point in the state. Thus rainfall on the north coast can be as much as 100 inches a year. In the southwest deserts it has been known to be as little as two inches, about as dry as a land can get. Areas of the Sierra Nevada get as much as 500 inches of snowfall in a year. The snow is the source of vast irrigation and complex water-supply systems of the state. It also provides some of the world's finest skiing grounds, including Squaw Valley, scene of the 1960 Winter Olympics. Death Valley claims to have had the highest temperature recorded on the North American continent—134 degrees. San Diego boasts the country's most equable climate, with an average for January of 55 degrees, an average for August of only 69 degrees. The Los Angeles area has a dry, Mediterranean type of climate, with only about 16 inches of annual rainfall, and almost perpetual sunshine. But in recent years parts of the Los Angeles area have suffered from periodic industrial smog. San Francisco has cool summers and mild winters. Temperature seldom gets above 70 degrees or falls below 50 degrees. San Francisco's much maligned fogs, erratic and occasional, may blanket one part of the city while nearby areas have sparkling clear skies. The city claims almost twice as many days of sun as days of cloud or fog.

In the north, the average for the coolest month is about 45 degrees; warmest month only about 60 degrees. But on high mountain slopes it is never warm; it may snow in June or even July, with the result that the mountain valleys draw huge crowds from the lower valleys where inland summer temperatures may average over 80 degrees.

THE PEOPLE. In the first half of the sixteenth century, Juan Cabrillo discovered the harbor of San Diego, and Sir Francis Drake landed near San Francisco Bay, but little was done to explore or settle the land for nearly 200 years. Then Russian immigrants began to settle along the northern coast, establishing forts and centers for the fur trade. Spanish settlement began in 1769 and continued for about 50 years, resulting in 21 missions, each about a day's ride from the next, the beginnings of such cities as San Diego, Los Angeles, Santa Barbara and San Francisco, and the naming of almost every natural feature in the southern half of California. The Spanish colonists traveled up and down the state over a Spanish road called El Camino Real. It still exists as U. S. Highway 101, with parts of it called by the old Spanish name, meaning the King's Highway.

A little more than 100 years ago, the Mexican War made California a state of the United States. Even before that immigrants had come over the eastern ramparts into the fertile California valleys. One of these immigrants, a Swiss named Sutter, discovered gold (1849) and the next year California became part of the United States. The two events brought settlers and prospectors from everywhere.

San Francisco became a roistering, polyglot boomtown overnight. The miners scrambled into the Sierra foothills, built a chain of settlements with odd and delightful names like Rough and Ready, Angels Camp, Chinese Camp, Fiddletown, Poker Flat, Poverty Hill. In their roaring heyday some of them had as many as 40,000 people. Most of the towns, either drowsing or fully asleep, are still there, linked (appropriately enough) by State Highway 49—the **Mother Lode Highway.** Visiting them makes a delightful motor tour for California visitors.

The completion of the railway, and the immigration boom which followed it, made some individual fortunes. Leland Stanford founded a great California university. Mark Hopkins gave his name to a luxurious hotel on Nob Hill (where the new millionaires lived). The cocktail lounge at its top provides a stunning view of the city.

Eliza Tibbets, by importing oranges from Brazil, started the citrus boom that filled the whole southern end of the state with citrus groves. It brought hundreds of thousands of new settlers from every part of the country, chiefly the Middle West. The annual Iowa picnic held each summer at Long Beach near Los Angeles often draws 75,000 picnickers.

Discovery of oil at Signal Hill in 1921 accelerated oil exploitation in California. Its production now is 35 million barrels of oil each year—making California the second biggest state in petroleum production.

In 1862 a Hungarian, Count Haraszthy, brought to California 100,000 cuttings of European grapevines and imported skilled vineyard and winery workers from France, Italy and Germany, to set out the vines and make wine. So California today makes 90 percent of all the wine made in the United States. The neat vineyards and the great stone wineries in Napa, Sonoma, Livermore and Santa Clara valleys have an Old World look.

During depression days of the thirties the dust bowl of the Southwest drove migrants into the state, to join the army of homeless part-time farm workers who helped harvest valley fields. With better times many of them became owners of well-watered land.

With the Second World War California became a training area and staging base for hundreds of thousands of members of the armed forces. At war's end many stayed in the state, and others returned soon with their families. So in the decade before 1950 California gained population faster than any other state.

Though in the past 50 years California has absorbed and fused millions of people from all states and most countries into a dynamic population whose members take pride in being called Californians, there are many picturesque ethnic islands.

At Solvang, near Santa Barbara, beside a charming old Spanish mission, is a complete **Danish Village,** home of a Danish colony. In Stockton there is a **Sikh temple** where the members of a colony from India worship, the only such temple in the country. In Oroville, an old gold mining center, is a **Chinese Buddhist temple,** and nearby Maryville has a Chinese joss house and temple. Near San Diego an extensive **Portuguese colony** of fishermen annually celebrate festivals of their land. So does another colony near San Leandro.

The largest single group of foreign-born ancestry have deep and old California roots. They are of Mexican origin, descendants of the Indians and Spaniards who first settled the state. In Los Angeles some streets resemble the streets of a Mexican village.

AGRICULTURE. California crops are produced on nearly 40 million intensively tilled acres; on more than six million acres with the aid of irrigation. Many aspects are fascinating: vineyards on rolling hills of Napa Valley; or blooming almond or citrus groves; groves of towering date palms; or the grotesque, gargantuan, special purpose gadgets designed to harvest cotton in fields that stretch to the horizon. California leads the nation in grapes, in peaches, persimmons, apricots, olives, dates, lemons, avocados, walnuts, almonds. It is second in oranges and cotton and near the production top in a dozen other crops. There are odd specialty crops like flower seeds and artichokes. One California town, Petaluma, claims to be the egg capital of the world; another, Salinas, the salad bowl. Most have several harvests each year.

INDUSTRY. An important aspect of California industry is concerned with

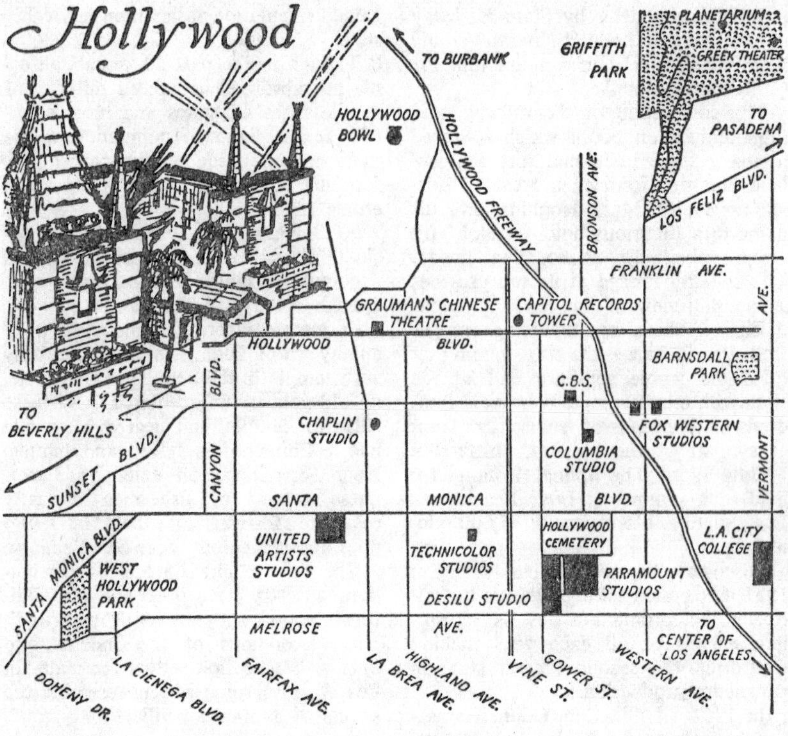

the processing and packing of the products of the fields, orchards and forests, and the harvest of the sea. Included are bottling and aging of wine. Grapes also produce raisins, and Fresno has the world's biggest plant for packaging them. Complex, specialized farming operations require special machines, which accounts for huge plants.

In the sunny south are three large, very different industries. One packages entertainment, with motion pictures and television; another produces most of the country's aircraft; and a third pumps oil from the earth and processes it. Canneries of coastal cities pack 40 percent of the commercial fish sold in the country. Among southern citrus groves is the West Coast's largest steel mill. On the coast is the world's biggest plant converting sea water to fresh. Mills in northern forest areas cut and process timber. Gold is still mined in the mountains or dredged from the streams, but so are about 60 other minerals, putting California among the first three mineral producing states.

CITIES. California has 20 cities with over 100,000 population, the largest being Los Angeles, which covers 464 square miles and has close to three million residents.

California's largest and oldest cities face the sea, or are near it. All of them have facilities in full range for the accommodation and interest of the visitor. So they make excellent bases for seeing and exploring the rest of California.

LOS ANGELES is the second largest city in the United States in area and third largest in population (almost three million). It spreads over an incredible 464 square miles of coastal plain and mountain foothills. Part of it towers a mile above the sea. The city began as a sleepy Spanish village (the original **Spanish square** is one of its sights) in

1781, when it was given the fascinating name of El Pueblo Nuestra Señora la Reina de los Angeles de Porciuncula (Town of Our Lady, Queen of Angels of Porciuncola). The city grew to its present enormous size in relatively recent years, partly by absorbing neighboring communities. One of these was **Hollywood,** legendary center of the film industry and modern TV production. On the fringe of the present city, or surrounded by it, are other communities which managed to keep their civic identity. Important ones are **Beverly Hills** and **Pasadena.**

Los Angeles proper spreads in a vast and confusing network of streets, reaching the sea at **Santa Monica,** another city not yet gobbled up. Mountains rise steeply behind, their foothill canyons favorite areas of exclusive residence, their upper slopes and forested crests a remarkable community playground.

Special sights and facilities include the **Old Spanish Plaza,** with reconstruction of a typical Mexican village. Nearby is the **Civic Center** and its towering 32-story City Hall, dominating a cluster of huge new buildings. Close beside it is the city's most remarkable structure, a four-level **freeway interchange,** with more traffic flowing into and over it than any place in the world (most of it at high speed). Near or in **Exposition Park** are a seven-acre rose garden, two big museums and the campus of the **University of Southern California. Hollywood** lies west of the main city center. Adjoining it is the world's largest city park—**Griffith**—over 4,000 hilly acres. Sights in Hollywood include the **Hollywood Bowl, motion picture** and **television studios** (many with frequently conducted tours), and two famous streets: **Hollywood Boulevard** and **Sunset Boulevard.** But the main show street of Los Angeles is **Wilshire Boulevard,** whose "Miracle Mile" is one of the most flamboyant shopping streets in the world. Just off of it is **Hancock Park,** where bones of prehistoric monsters are dug from ancient tar deposits. Close by is the **Farmers Market.**

Beyond Hollywood to the west is opulent **Beverly Hills,** with more fine estates (many the homes of stars) than any city. Equally elegant **Westwood Village** adjoins Beverly Hills to the west, boasts the handsome campus of the **University of California** at **Los Angeles.** A few miles west all highways come down to the sea at **Santa Monica,** renowned for its beach.

Other points of interest easily reached from Los Angeles over the freeway network include **Disneyland,** with the world's most remarkable exhibits of fantasy; **Hollywood Wax Museum,** in **Buena Park,** filled with wax likenesses of famous stars in their best-known roles; **Knotts Berry Farm** and **Ghost Town,** also near Buena Park. On the coast, **Long Beach** has the world's biggest pleasure pier; beside it is **San Pedro,** with a huge, busy, man-made harbor. Offshore 22 miles is the rugged resort island and playground called **Santa Catalina** (boating, fishing and water sports) where you may hunt wild boar and mountain goats.

Just east of Los Angeles, Pasadena has the famed **Rose Bowl,** and the celebrated **Huntington Library.** Nearby is **Mission San Gabriel Arcángel,** where wine was first made in California, and just beyond it **Santa Anita race track.** Several hours' drive by car east of Los Angeles, the remarkable desert city of **Palm Springs** is a winter resort and social center for the entertainment world. It has more swimming pools than any place else in the world, as well as the largest and longest single-lift passenger-carrying aerial tramway. The two trams, which cover 13,200 feet in 10 to 15 minutes, open previously inaccessible mountain terrain to snow sports in winter and spectator sightseeing, hiking, and cool temperatures in summer.

Accommodations in Los Angeles, scattered all over the city, include some of the finest, biggest and newest luxury hotels as well as motor courts that range from modest to elegant. Next to San Francisco the city has more good restaurants, many in outdoor settings, than any other city in the West.

SACRAMENTO, capital of the state

(population over 254,000), is on the left bank of the Sacramento River, an important shipping and distribution center. Near the middle of the city is **Capitol Park,** with a thousand varieties of trees and shrubs. The city's most interesting sight is **Sutter's Fort,** restoration of the house and garrison made famous in Gold Rush days. Sacramento has good hotels and motor courts, chiefly along the main east-west highways. They make convenient places to stay on trips to the high mountains on the east.

SAN DIEGO. In 1542 Cabrillo sailed into San Diego harbor. Settlement of San Diego began in 1769 when Father Junipero Serra established the first of the Spanish missions there. The city and the area around it claim the most equable climate in the United States. Long a resort center and a favorite place for retirement, San Diego is now a growing center, with a population of over 696,000 and booming industries. It is connected to the Mexican border 15 miles to the south by an express highway. Compact, clean, well planned, the city spreads over hills behind the bay.

Points of special interest within the city include **Balboa Park,** 1,400 acres, a zoo, art gallery, civic theater, natural history museum. Just back of the bay front is **Old Town,** with buildings going back to Spanish days. The bay front is shared by a handsome **Civic Center,** the **United States Navy,** and tremendous **aircraft plants.**

Across the bay, at **Point Loma,** reached by a scenic highway, is the country's smallest national monument, **Cabrillo National Monument,** where a tablet tells of California's discovery.

Sea World, one of the country's finest marine parks, is located in **Mission Bay Park,** just northwest of San Diego. Chief attractions are the **Theater of the Sea, Sea Grotto,** and **Lagoon.** Beyond the park is the suburb of **La Jolla,** celebrated for its fine homes and commanding setting among hills above the sea. Just north of the city is the charming **Mission San Diego de Alcala,** built in 1769, first of the mission chain. An easy drive from San Diego to the northeast is **Palomar Mountain** (6,126 feet), crowned by **Palomar Observatory,** at the crest of a scenic mountain road.

San Diego has good city-type hotels, but most visitors stay at excellent motor courts within the city proper and along the main highways leading in.

SAN FRANCISCO. About 350 miles northwest of Los Angeles, San Francisco has developed into a dramatic, beautiful and unusual city. The city proper, twelfth in size in the country, with over 715,000 people, fills the tip of a mountainous peninsula that has the ocean on the west, San Francisco Bay on the east. It is the core of a unique urban area with a necklace of towns and cities that surround the bay. In them live more than three million people.

The city, originally called Yerba Buena, was founded with the establishment of a Spanish presidio (fort) and a mission in 1776. (Both are still there.)

The discovery of gold in California made San Francisco a swarming, roistering boom city overnight. The first railroad completed across the continent made San Francisco the chief banking and commercial center of the West. A fire and earthquake destroyed most of the city in 1906, making possible the building of the handsome, solid and beautiful city visitors see today.

San Francisco is an exciting and rewarding place and an excellent base for exploring many of California's sights and facilities. The streets run steeply up and down and around a cluster of hills. A delightful way to travel over them is by gay, clanging cable car. Many points of interest are close together downtown, easily reached on foot or by short taxi and bus rides.

Ocean Beach, along the Pacific, has a fine zoo at one end, a historic restaurant at the other, big and beautiful **Golden Gate Park** in the middle. Golden Gate has unique facilities. North of the park, at the extreme tip of the peninsula, is the **Presidio,** the original Spanish garrison area and still an army base. From and above it soars the great span of the **Golden Gate Bridge,**

arching over the channel to the sea. Within the bay, fringing the waterfront, are successively an **aquatic park** with nautical museum, **Fisherman's Wharf,** home of the city's commercial fishing fleet, surrounded by colorful seafood restaurants. Just back of the waterfront and affording a fine view of it is **Telegraph Hill,** crowned by a tall tower. At its base is **Chinatown,** finest, biggest and most interesting Oriental community in the country. It is just below **Nob Hill,** with a group of famous hotels.

San Francisco's monumental **Civic Center** fills a ten-block area south of the main shopping section. From it streets lead to ramps that give access to the **Bay Bridge** (San Francisco–Oakland), eight-and-a-quarter miles long, actually a complex of bridges, trestles and tunnel. It offers the best and fastest way to reach cities and important towns across the bay. They include **Berkeley,** with the **University of California's** main campus, and **Oakland,** with a fine new Civic Center around a salt-water lake. The **east bay area** offers a chain of handsome parks along the mountains behind the cities.

A chain of redwood groves starts beyond the Golden Gate along the **Redwood Highway.** The historic and charming wine-growing areas of **Sonoma** and **Napa valleys** are northeast. South of San Francisco are **Palo Alto,** with **Leland Stanford University,** and **San Jose,** oldest incorporated town in California.

The **Monterey Peninsula** includes historic **Monterey;** quaint **Carmel;** and famous **Del Monte Seventeen Mile Scenic Drive,** which connects several of the finest golf courses in the world.

SANTA BARBARA, 85 miles northwest of Los Angeles, has a superb setting among hills, facing the sea, and one of the best climates in the West. It is a favorite place for retirement, with its many **fine gardens** (regular tours), where subtropical flowers and fruits grow luxuriantly.

Though Cabrillo discovered the site in 1542, the city was not founded until 1782, when one of its hills was selected as a mission site. Santa Barbara's **mission,** called **"Queen of the Missions,"** is beautiful and historic. A number of fine old adobe dwellings are in the downtown area, close by the huge and handsome **courthouse.** There is an excellent small harbor, flanked by a boulevard. West of the city, on a hill overlooking the sea, is one of the eight branches of the **University of California.**

Each summer, Santa Barbara dedicates a week of fun and fiesta to remembering its Spanish heritage. Most of the city's fine hotels are of the resort type, as are dozens of good motor courts along the waterfront and along main highways.

SPORTS AND RECREATION. For the active visitors who want more than to gaze at scenic wonders, California offers a wide range of sports and adventure. **Golf** is available everywhere. Nearly all California golf courses are good and some are celebrated for beauty and dramatic setting. In recent years California has become a **mecca for skiers.** High mountain slopes like **Squaw Valley** (scene of 1960 Winter Olympics) and **Shasta Snow Bowl,** offer skiing almost year round, and winter skiing is within a short drive of nearly every large center.

Fishing is excellent in lakes, rivers and offshore waters. California's state fish is the elusive and beautiful golden trout, caught in the waters of the high mountains. In the fast flowing rivers of the coastal ranges there are steelhead trout and salmon, and offshore waters yield tuna, sailfish and other species.

Boating is widely popular on the bigger rivers, lakes and such protected waters as **San Francisco** and **San Diego bays.** Spectator sports include **big-league baseball** and **football.**

California has more tennis courts and swimming pools than any area of the world, most of them in constant use. One community, the desert playground of **Palm Springs,** claims one pool for each twelve residents. For the lovers of the rugged outdoor life there are **pack trails** threading the high mountains, hundreds of fine **camping sites,** including many in the state park areas, offering beaches along 1,100 miles of scenic coast.

Visitors who enjoy camping or just looking at majestic scenery should visit California's many national parks and monuments, or national forest areas. All of them are accessible over more than 15,000 miles of state and federal highways. They include the great groves of tall trees, the **redwoods,** along the **Redwood Highway** north of San Francisco, and the **giant sequoias** within two big rugged national parks to the east. North in wild mountains are curious **lava beds** made by volcanic eruption. South of them is **Lassen Peak,** generally snow-crested, but still smoldering and active. **Yosemite National Park,** in addition to 757,000 wilderness acres of high mountain country, has what many call the world's most beautiful valley. In the south and southeast are **Death Valley,** an arid wonderland, and **Joshua Tree National Monument.** California's biggest and most beautiful lake, mile-high **Tahoe,** is set among national forests at the crest of the Sierra ranges.

SPECIAL EVENTS. One of the most colorful events of the year—and one of the best-known—is the **Tournament of Roses** and **Rose Bowl football game,** held in Pasadena each New Year's Day. Other dates of importance are the **Chinese New Year Celebration,** held in Los Angeles and San Francisco in January or February; **Easter Sunrise Service,** Hollywood Bowl; **Jumping Frog Jubilee,** Angels Camp, May; **Water Sports Carnival,** Long Beach, June; **Old Spanish Days Fiesta,** Santa Barbara, in mid-August; **Monterey Jazz Festival,** Monterey, in September; and the **Grand National Livestock Exposition,** at San Francisco's Cow Palace, November.

Oregon

Among states in the Far West, Oregon is third in area (after Alaska and California) with 96,981 square miles, tenth in size in the nation. In population it is third in the Far West, after Washington and California, with more than 2 million people.

Almost square in shape, Oregon has an average east-west width of 395 miles, an average north-south height of 295 miles. Its western limit is the Pacific Ocean. Much of its northern border is the great and beautiful Columbia River, with the state of Washington opposite. About half the eastern border, opposite Idaho, is the gorge of the maverick Snake River. The southern half of the eastern border is desert plateau, while the southern border is divided between California on the west and Nevada on the east. Oregon has been a state since 1859. The state flower is the Oregon grape; state tree, Douglas fir; state fish, chinook salmon; state bird, western meadowlark; nickname, *Beaver State.*

THE LAND. The surface of Oregon is generally rugged, sometimes immensely so. Through the state north to south run two parallel mountain ranges. Along the coast, often breaking down to the shore in picturesque cliffs, the mountains are low and heavily forested. About 100 miles east of the coast are the higher, wilder crests of the **Cascade Range,** with several peaks of more than 10,000 feet, and one, **Mount Hood** (the state's highest point), 11,235 feet. The Cascades are also densely forested, with the heaviest stands on the western slopes. East of the Cascade Range, stretching to the border of the state, is a semi-arid plateau, broken by mountain ranges. In the southeast the plateau is desert-like.

Oregon has several spectacular natural features. Shared with Washington to the north, they include the magnificent gorge of the great **Columbia River;** a remarkable chain of cliffs and beaches which make the **Pacific shore,** linked by one of the most scenic highways in the world; the majestic, craggy, generally snow-crested peak of Mount Hood, towering above the state's chief city, **Portland;** and high in the forested ranges of the Cascades in the south jewel-like **Crater Lake**—the blue heart of Oregon's only national park.

Between the Coastal and Cascade ranges is Oregon's most populous and productive valley, drained by the Willamette River. Along its banks live most of the state's population in cities and towns among fields and orchards.

Oregon's chief source of wealth derives from reserves of the land—the finest and biggest stands of timber in the country, spreading over 30 million acres. About one-half of the timber reserves are within national forests.

THE CLIMATE. Along the coast Oregon's climate is mild and moist, in part due to warm ocean currents. Rainfall, generally in the fall and winter, is about 75 inches a year. Portland, 100 miles in from the coast, has average January temperature of about 38 degrees, average summer temperature of only 67 degrees, with most of the rain in the fall and winter. But in the eastern half of the state, behind the range of the Cascades, the climate is so dry that average rainfall amounts to only a little more than ten inches a year, and summers are likely to be quite hot. From the visitor standpoint the best time of year is late spring, summer and early fall. A spectacular effect of the mild, moist climate in the western part of the state is the prodigal abundance of flowers of all kinds.

THE PEOPLE. Though the coast of Oregon was sighted and mentioned by Spanish navigators as early as the sixteenth century, no one did much about it until an American named Robert Gray sailed into and named the Columbia River in 1792. Soon after that, Lewis and Clark made the state famous with their report on its wealth and wonders. They pioneered the Oregon Trail.

Settlement came slowly, chiefly from members of wagon trains that had plodded across the mountains and prairie lands. They were intent on building homes in forest clearings, making farms in the rich valley lands. Many came from New England and gave such names to settlements as Portland, Salem, Medford, Albany, and Newport. Many came from the Middle West. They all used the abundant fine trees of the great forests in familiar ways, to build log cabins for their dwellings, and covered bridges over streams. Although the covered bridges are no longer being built, over 100, resembling those of New Hampshire, Pennsylvania, and Indiana, are still in existence throughout the state.

Later, after Oregon became a state (1859) and railways linked it to the East, the rate of settlement increased, but the lures remained the same: farms, forests, fish and furs. With the exception of fur trading, the same attractions account today for most of the Oregon economy.

AGRICULTURE. Oregon's huge, magnificent forests—of Douglas fir, spruce, hemlock, ponderosa pine—are the most important things that grow in the state and are the basis for a billion-dollar industry. Farm produce, with great orchards and wide fields in the valley between the mountains, is next. Beyond the mountains, in the dry east, farming, supplemented by irrigation (a million acres of irrigated land), accounts for great fields of grain. Cattle and sheep grazing are also important. Oregon grows some unusual crops, like peppermint, holly, lily bulbs, cane berries. Farmland accounts for 20 million acres.

INDUSTRY. Oregon is not a heavy manufacturing state, and its mills and factories are generally for products of the soil and sea. Woodworking plants and lumber, pulp and paper mills are many, some very big. Canning and packing of seafood, fruit and vegetables support many towns. Wool shorn from Oregon sheep goes to big woolen mills in both Portland and Pendleton. A relative newcomer, resulting from electric power resources, is the manufacture of aluminum.

CITIES. Oregon has no large cities, and only about five exceed 25,000 in population. Most centers are villages and hamlets with populations of less than 3,000. The state has a delightfully pastoral aspect.

ASTORIA (population, about 10,000), on the mouth of the Columbia River, 70 miles northwest of Portland, is where Lewis and Clark ended their epic journey and a few years later John Jacob Astor established **Fort Astoria** (1811), the state's first settlement. Both events are commemorated in a dramatic hilltop column, 125 feet high, with the history of the state spiraling around it in a colorful frieze. The city is an important base for the fishing industry. For the visitor it is the start of a dramatically scenic drive south along the coast.

KLAMATH FALLS (population, about 15,000) is on the eastern slope of the Cascades near the southern edge of the state. It is a resort center and highway junction, with good accommodations. There are more than 100 lakes nearby, including **Upper Klamath,** just north of town, largest body of fresh water west of the Rockies. Also to be visited is **Crater Lake National Park,** 55 miles northwest.

MEDFORD (population, about 28,000), in the heart of the Cascade Range and the southwest corner of the state, 75 miles west of Klamath Falls, is a center for hunting in nearby forests and fishing on the Rogue River. It is also a good base for visiting **Crater Lake National Park** to the northeast and **Oregon Caves National Monument** to the southwest. The **canyon of the Rogue River** to the west offers an exciting offbeat boating adventure.

PENDLETON (population, about 13,000), on northeast edge of the state, is the center of a sheep herding and cattle raising country. The sheep account for big woolen mills, the cattle for the town's most celebrated and exciting event—the annual **Pendleton Roundup,** a championship rodeo held each September.

PORTLAND, the largest city and the one most important to visitors, straddles the Willamette River, on the south bank of the Columbia, about 100 miles east of the coast. Seat of Multnomah County, it has a population of about 380,000, and is a modern, handsomely-built metropolis spread over a cluster of hills, one of which **(Council Crest),** 1,100 feet high, commands a stunning view of the whole area. The city has more than 100 parks, at their superb floral best in summer.

Portland's prosperity is solidly based on mills and factories that process timber, make aluminum, weave wool into cloth, pack fruits and fish products, and build ships.

For the visitor Portland is more important as a base than for itself. It has good hotels and motor courts. From the city several convenient trips reveal many of the state's outstanding sights.

It is an easy drive from Portland to the ocean, one highly scenic route following the Columbia, and another following the coast to the south, giving breath-taking views of beaches and cliffs.

SALEM, the state capital, with a population of about 68,000, is on the Willamette River and is a fairly important center for the processing of things grown in the rich valley that surrounds it. Worth seeing is the new white marble **capitol building,** where instead of the traditional dome a fluted marble cylinder carries a heroic symbolic figure, The Pioneer. A point of scenic interest nearby (26 miles east) is an 8,000-acre state park called **Silver Falls,** with six impressive waterfalls.

SPORTS AND RECREATION. Things for the visitor to do in Oregon are chiefly vigorous outdoor activities, or watching others be vigorous outdoors. **Fishing** is superb in both inland lakes and rivers and along the coast. **Hunting** for deer and elk is fine during a controlled fall season. Pheasant and quail are also abundant. There are **ski slopes** in more than a dozen centers, the most famous being Mt. Hood, where the sports season runs well into the summer. **Hiking trails** thread the mountains, the scenic and famous Skyline Trail twisting along the crest of the Cascades from Washington to California. Other popular sports include **golf-**

ing, swimming, boating, and **water-skiing.**

Particular sights of great interest include two highly **scenic drives:** the coast road (U.S. 101) from Astoria south for about 350 miles, with breathtaking views of cliff and shore. The highway links dozens of beaches and many state parks. The **Mt. Hood Loop,** including a drive up the **Columbia River Gorge** to The Dalles, is the state's greatest scenic drive. It goes past the 620-foot **Multnomah Falls** and **Bonneville Dam,** and makes several diversions before turning westward on U.S. 26 to Portland.

But perhaps the state's most notable visitor attraction is **Crater Lake National Park,** in the heart of the Cascade Range, 55 miles northwest of Klamath Falls. The 250 square miles of the park area, superbly wooded, with peaks rising to more than 8,000 feet, guard the unique and incredibly blue jewel of the lake itself. The lake surface is more than 6,000 feet above sea level, the shining blue waters 1,932 feet deep.

Oregon Caves National Monument, just north of the California border, near Medford, is a labyrinth of caverns in four levels spreading over about 500 acres.

SPECIAL EVENTS. The jobs that Oregonians have on the land are dramatized in occasions they observe every year. There is a **Timber Carnival** at **Albany** each summer; **Pendleton,** in the eastern cattle country, holds a big rip-snorting **rodeo** each September; one section celebrates the **pea harvest** with parades, and in Lebanon, strawberry picking time (early June) is the occasion for a **Strawberry Festival.** Portland's **Rose Festival** each June is the largest of the state's celebrations. Other occasions include the **Oregon Shakespeare Festival,** Ashland, mid-May to mid-September; **Oregon State Fair,** Salem, August; and the **McKenzie River White Water Boat Parade.**

Washington

Northwest corner of the United States, the state of Washington (which calls itself the *Evergreen State*) contains 68,192 extraordinarily varied square miles. Among the states of the country it ranks twentieth in area. With over three million people it is second in population in the Far West, twenty-second in the nation. Rectangular in shape, the average east-west width is 358 miles, the average north-south height 240 miles. On the west, Washington's boundary is the Pacific Ocean and the huge arm of the sea called Puget Sound. The northern boundary is the Canadian province of British Columbia, while the eastern border of Washington, with rugged mountains and a deep, wild river canyon, is Idaho. On the south is Oregon, sharing with Washington the gorge of the Columbia River. Washington became a state in 1889. The state flower is the rhododendron; state tree, the western hemlock; state bird, the willow goldfinch.

THE LAND. The surface of Washington, more than half of which is forested, has an unusual pattern of bold natural features, some of them unique. They include the vast, island-studded inland sea of **Puget Sound;** the largest rain forest in the United States; a chain of extinct volcanos that are now among the most majestic mountains in the country; alpine lakes of beauty and great size; and the **Columbia River,** large, powerful and beautiful. Harnessed by dams, it is the world's largest single source of electric power and irrigation water.

From west to east the topographic features of Washington are the forest wonderland wilderness of the **Olympic Peninsula,** with the Olympic Mountains clothed by a gigantic rain forest, the Pacific on one side, Puget Sound on the other; Puget Sound, 100 miles long, studded with wooded islands, and the Canadian island of **Vancouver** on its north; a chain of important cities on the east and south.

East of Puget Sound rise the massive,

forested ramparts of the **Cascade Range,** with an average elevation of 6,000 to 8,000 feet. Above the forests tower immaculate snow-crested volcanic peaks, all more than 9,000 feet in height, the highest being **Mount Rainier,** 14,410. Others are **Mount Baker** (10,778 feet), **Glacier Peak** (10,436 feet); and near the Oregon border **St. Helens** (9,677 feet), and **Mount Adams** (12,307 feet).

East of the Cascades is Washington's **Inland Empire,** the great valley of the Columbia River, which though semiarid, thanks to irrigation is now very fruitful. Leading from the valley, 55 miles into the Cascade Range, is narrow **Lake Chelan.**

Much of the eastern flank of the state is the tumbled massif of the western Rockies, the glaciers and snows of which feed into the Columbia River. The southeast corner of the state, extending into Oregon, is a high, arid plateau with vast fields of wheat, and great cattle ranges.

THE CLIMATE. Western Washington, with prevailing westerly winds and the coast washed by warm ocean currents, has a temperate marine climate, with cool summers and mild, somewhat rainy winters. Seattle has a mean average temperature range of from 64 degrees in July to 38 degrees in January. On the Olympic Peninsula just west of Seattle, the seaward slopes of the mountains have the heaviest rainfall in the United States, up to 140 inches a year.

But eastern Washington has a dry, continental type of climate, with rainfall not exceeding 20 inches a year and in some parts as low as six inches. Spokane, chief city of the eastern part of the state, has a mean July temperature of 74 degrees, a mean January temperature of 25. The best time to visit Washington is late spring, summer or fall.

THE PEOPLE. In the sixteenth century Spanish and English explorers skirted the coast of Washington, but it was 200 years later before the world had any knowledge of the land, or settlement of it began. Lewis and Clark described southern Washington in the journal reporting their explorations and three widely separated settlements occurred not long afterwards. The English established a fort, Vancouver, on the Columbia to help develop fur trade for the Hudson's Bay Company. On the other side of the state, Walla Walla became a supply center for nearby gold strikes, and American missionaries established a mission there in 1840. Roman Catholic missionaries established a mission on Puget Sound in 1839.

Mountain barriers and Indian wars deterred further settlement until railroad service opened in 1883. In the next ten years the population of the state quadrupled. Seattle became a great and increasingly cosmopolitan port, gateway to Alaska and the Far East. A few years later the Alaskan Gold Rush turned Seattle into a boom city. Lumbering and fishing began to develop as important industries, each drawing streams of settlers.

Both world wars stimulated the state's growth, with shipbuilding becoming vitally important. Dams on the Columbia began to provide an increasing resource for irrigation, drawing thousands of settlers to the central valley. The dams also gave a new resource of electric power, making many new industries feasible.

Washington's settlement has been so recent, and made up of so many different population strains, that no architectural tradition has been developed. Important structures there, most built within the memory of men now living, are more likely to be functional, such as the spectacular bulk of **Grand Coulee Dam,** or **Seattle's floating bridges,** and the **Pacific Science Center** in Seattle.

AGRICULTURE. In the early days of Washington's settlement, forest trees were considered a natural resource to be exploited. Vast tree farms are now the rule rather than the exception, and trees are a crop—the biggest in the state. Washington ranks next to Oregon in lumber production, chiefly softwoods, including Douglas fir, ponderosa pine, hemlock, spruce, white pine, maple. Another great harvest is from the rivers and the sea. Washington is fourteenth in the nation in total catch and ninth in total value of seafoods, including salmon, halibut, tuna, oysters, crabs, cod, and shark. Apples are grown in the central valley, while other important field and orchard crops include peas, strawberries, peaches, grapes, nearly all grown on irrigated land. There are large cattle and sheep ranches on the eastern slopes of the Cascades and great fields of wheat, particularly in the Palouse region of eastern Washington. Hops are an important specialty, as well as flower bulbs, such as daffodils.

INDUSTRY. In dozens of yards and plants, particularly around Puget Sound, the logs from the forests of Washington are converted into pulp, paper, and plywood. The same area is studded with processing, packing and freezing plants for fish and seafood. It is also a center for shipbuilding, which began with wooden ships, continues with steel. But perhaps the most important single product of the state today is kilowatts. Grand Coulee Dam is the greatest electric power producer in the world, but is only one of many dams in the state that are built to produce power. This vast flood of energy has resulted in new industries, one being the manufacture of aluminum. The great Hanford atomic energy plant on the Columbia is one of the largest. A new industry near Seattle makes military and commercial aircraft, including American jet transports.

CITIES. Most of Washington's approximately three million people live in the western third of the state, particularly around Puget Sound. Of the state's 22 cities of more than 10,000 population, over half are directly on Puget Sound or within a few miles of its waters. They include the capital, Olympia; the state's largest city, Seattle; and its third largest, Tacoma. Of the others, five are in the central valley on or near the Columbia River, and only two are in the eastern part of the state.

SEATTLE. This cosmopolitan metropolis of the Northwest (population, over half a million) has a commanding setting on a hilly isthmus between Puget Sound on the west and Lake Washington on the east. The city, which rises in terraces from the waterfront, is the center of a complex transportation network of air and rail lines and major highways. From it a system of ferries crisscrosses Puget Sound to link Seattle with dozens of communities that surround the bay, making Seattle a logical base for the exploration of the area.

By the Great Circle route Seattle is the closest point in the U.S. to the Far East and is the southern terminus for fast-developing travel to Alaska. From it, historic and beautiful **Vancouver Island** in British Columbia, is easily visited. Seattle has good hotels and motor courts.

Seattle Center, public entertainment area on the site of the 1962 World's Fair, is made up of key buildings and featured attractions left from that Fair. They include the **Monorail; Space Needle** observation deck and restaurant; **Pacific Science Center** (former Federal Science Pavilion); **amusement park;** and **Food Circus,** large building featuring international specialties.

Other sights of interest within the city include the campus of the **University of Washington,** with a 260-acre arboretum; two **floating bridges** over Lake Washington, world's longest; 42-story **L. C. Smith Building,** with observation balcony; **Volunteer Park,** with an art museum, one of the 46 parks in the city.

Near Seattle and easily reached from it are two national parks, **Rainier** on the southeast, and **Olympic,** dominating the peninsula to the west. The very British and quite charming city of **Victoria** is a four-hour ferry ride across the Sound. To the south, in **Tacoma,** is the nation's tallest totem pole, carved by Indians from a single tree; and the graceful **Tacoma Narrows Bridge,** nation's fifth-longest suspension bridge. Nearby is the state capital, **Olympia,** with its monumental capitol building set in one of the finest landscaped gardens in the West. Ferry trips in the Sound include visits to the **San Juan Islands,** 172 of them in all, some studded with pleasant resorts.

SPOKANE. At the picturesque falls of the Spokane River on the eastern edge of Washington, Spokane is regarded as the metropolis of Washington's Inland Empire. A new, brisk, attractive city with excellent accommodations of all types, it is a fine base for visiting the dramatic mountain wilderness region to the north and east, both in Washington and the panhandle of Idaho, and the rich Palouse River Valley to the south. Lake Roosevelt, formed by Grand Coulee Dam on the Columbia River, is an easy drive to the northwest, and northeast a few miles is a notable mountain resort on the slopes of Mount Spokane.

YAKIMA AND WENATCHEE. In the great central valley of Washington are the twin centers of **Yakima** in the south and **Wenatchee** to the north, each with excellent hotels and motor courts. Wenatchee, on the Columbia, center of a vast irrigated area and claiming to be the apple capital of the world, is an excellent base for visiting **Coulee Dam,** with the 150-mile-long lake backed up behind it, and a unique mechanism of irrigation operated from the dam. Equally accessible from Wenatchee is **Lake Chelan,** one of the world's most beautiful alpine lakes. Near Wenatchee is a fine five-acre **mountain garden.**

Yakima, on the Yakima River 100 miles southeast of Seattle, is a good base for visiting the tour center of the **Hanford Works of the U. S. Atomic Energy Commission,** located to the southeast on the Columbia River. A highway links Yakima to the north bank of the Columbia, where a scenic drive runs along that river to the west.

SPORTS AND RECREATION. Puget Sound has become one of the finest boating regions in the world. **Sightseeing boating trips** are available on it, as well as on the mountain lakes and some of the rivers. **Fishing** in coastal waters provides limitless sport, chiefly for salmon. But the fresh-water streams and lakes are crowded with trout.

The state's mountain slopes offer numerous top **skiing areas,** with dozens of lifts and runs. It is easy to arrange to play **golf** on any one of a number of excellent courses, and there are hundreds of miles of mountain trails.

No visitor to Washington should miss seeing the great snow peaks that thrust above the wooded slopes of the Cascades, most celebrated of which is Mount Rainier. The mountain rain forest wilderness of Olympic National Park, dominates the Olympic Peninsula. Puget Sound, with its hundreds of wooded islands, its deep water channels, is both a sight to see and a huge amphibious playground. In the mountains are alpine lakes, located in more than 100 state parks, the most beautiful and famous being Lake Chelan. Man-made sights include the vast bulk of Coulee Dam, several great and unusual bridges, and **Rocky Reach Dam,** near Wenatchee, where through a special viewing window, visitors can see salmon underwater.

SPECIAL EVENTS. Washington's international population is reflected in its variety of national festivals throughout the state. Best known is the **Highland Games Carnival,** sponsored by a large colony of Scots, which includes many events and contests reflecting the timber wealth of the state. Other annual occasions are the **Ski-Jumping Tournament** in Leavenworth, in January; **Apple Blossom Festival** in Wenatchee (located in Central Washington, where more apples are produced than any other region in the country), in May. **Seafair,** held in Seattle in early August, is the state's best-known event. It features water carnivals, parades, and races on Lake Washington.

Idaho

With completion of a new engineering feat, the Snake River-Columbia Waterway, landlocked Idaho now has its own ocean port at Lewiston, thus joining the other five Pacific Ocean states. Almost entirely mountainous, it contains 83,557 square miles, making it the thirteenth state in size in the country. But in population, with only about 700,000 people, it is forty-second in rank. The shape of Idaho is curious. The southern part is a rectangle 310 miles east to west, 175 miles north to south. But the upper part is a narrowing panhandle only 45 miles wide at the northern end at the Canadian border. The western border, divided between Washington and Oregon (about half of it the astonishing gorge of the Snake River), is 483 miles north to south. South of the ruler-straight southern border are the states of Nevada and Utah. In the east the winding state line, much of it the Continental Divide of the Rockies, is shared with Wyoming and Montana. Idaho was the forty-third state to enter the Union (1890). Its state flower is the syringa; state tree, western pine; state bird, the mountain bluebird.

THE LAND. The surface of Idaho is incredibly rugged, much of it almost uninhabited mountain wilderness. Most of the mountains are tumbled western ranges of the Rockies, with crests reaching from 8,000 to 12,000 feet. The state's highest point is **Borah Peak,** 12,662 feet. Idaho has two remarkable rivers, each of which cuts a deep and picturesque gorge. Flowing chiefly east to west through the center is the **Salmon River,** called the "River of No Return" because its rapids make passage along it possible only downstream. The state's great river is the **Snake,** which flows in a wide arc east to west through the southern part of the state, its course set with waterfalls. Its great dams provide power for industry and water for irrigation. Swinging north at the Oregon line, the Snake cuts the country's deepest and wildest canyon (almost one-and-one-half miles deep at some points). Other natural features of importance are some very fine big mountain lakes in the northern panhandle. The most important are **Coeur d'Alene, Priest** and **Pend Oreille,** home of the world's largest trout. A natural oddity in the south is an extensive area of strange volcanic formations and lava beds, partly preserved within **Craters of the Moon National Monument.** About 40 percent of Idaho's area is forested, 21 million acres of it public lands within 16 national forests. In one of these is the world's biggest stand of white pine.

THE CLIMATE. Idaho's climate is considered the dry continental type, quite cold in winter, often very hot in summer. Lack of humidity, and the prevailing west winds from the Pacific give the most populated areas an ideal four-season climate. The annual rainfall ranges from 8 to 20 inches, winter snowfall in the mountains from 40 to 100 inches.

THE PEOPLE. Until Lewis and Clark passed through the southern part of Washington along the valley of the Snake River, and reported its character, Idaho was a mountain wilderness known only to the Indians of the area. And though an isolated fur trading post, first in the Northwest, was established on one of the northern lakes in 1809, most of the state remained a wilderness for a long time. In 1860 a Mormon settlement, the first in the area, was established. Gold discovered the same year brought a trickle of adventurers into the state. But it remained a trickle until the last of the nineteenth century, when rich silver and lead deposits were found and a railway managed to thread the mountain gorges and tunnel through the ranges. After that, lumbering and sheep raising began to spread. When it was discovered that the volcanic soil of the Snake River Valley in the south was fine for crops, extensive farming, aided by irrigation, began.

Idaho still has one of the smallest populations in the Northwest section, with no large cities or heavily settled areas. Population strains, the result of migration from many states, are so diverse that they give no special character to the land—with two exceptions. In the earliest days (1809) a fur trading post was established on Lake Pend Oreille. Many of the trappers were French and gave French names to the land—like

Coeur d'Alene, Boise, Pend Oreille. In later years, on the high mountain meadows of central Idaho, sheepherding became important. To tend the great flocks, skilled sheepherders were brought in from the Basque country of southern France.

AGRICULTURE. Sheep and cattle raising is a main source of Idaho's agricultural income. First in line are potatoes, a celebrated specialty grown on Idaho's more than 25,000 farms. Other crops are alfalfa, sugar beets, hay, apples, wheat, beans, onions, and seed.

Timber, particularly western white pine, is one of Idaho's great resources. The vast forests include more than 50 huge tree farms, spread over more than 20 million acres, chiefly in the northern panhandle. They account for the world's largest white pine lumber mill at Lewiston, one of more than 250 mills in the state.

INDUSTRY. The mills and factories of Idaho are almost entirely devoted to processing potatoes, lumber, ores, packing vegetables, fruit, refining beets into sugar, and milling flour. Underground resources give Idaho high rank in mineral production, particularly lead, silver, zinc, copper, and gold. It is the only state supplying substantial quantities of antimony.

CITIES. Idaho has no large cities, although Boise, the capital, has a population of over 74,000. Including Boise, there are only 4 cities with 25,000 or more population, and most of the state's settlements are small towns, villages, and tiny hamlets.

BOISE, on the Boise River, a few miles east of its junction with the Snake, is a brisk and modern center for trade and transportation. Important highways, some of them quite scenic, fan out from it. High **Arrowrock Dam,** just east, has made the city the center of a huge irrigation district. Worth seeing in town is the relatively new **state capitol** of classic design, and the historical museum in **Julia Davis Park,** which contains priceless exhibits of the early days. Two nearby city parks, one containing a pioneer village with original cabins, the other with an illuminating fountain, adjoin one another at the Boise River. The city's **Basque community,** which stages a **summer festival** with traditional food, dancing, costumes, and merrymaking, is the largest in the United States. Points of nearby interest, some reached by scenic highways, are lake and mountain recreational areas to the north and northwest, including the southern end of the spectacular canyon of the Snake River.

POCATELLO (population over 42,000) is Idaho's second largest and most important industrial city. Here one may visit **Idaho State University,** widely acclaimed for its **Minidome,** the first indoor stadium built on a university campus. Midway between Sun Valley, Yellowstone, and the Grand Tetons, Pocatello has excellent vacation facilities, summer or winter.

COEUR D'ALENE (population 16,000), the most important town in the northern panhandle, is 32 miles east of Spokane. Its pleasant setting on the north shore of **Coeur d'Alene Lake,** in a rugged region of lakes and mountains of great beauty, makes the area popular with visitors. It is an easy drive north from Coeur d'Alene to celebrated **Pend Oreille,** home of the huge Kamloops trout. The city is a summer resort with full accessories, has excellent facilities for winter sports.

IDAHO FALLS is on the banks of the Snake River (population, 35,000). Hub of main highways, it is an important shipping and supply center for an irrigated area. The city has good accommodations, both hotels and motor courts, and is an excellent base for visiting nearby sights reached over main highways. Within the city is a handsome **city park** with a fine view of the river falls which give the town its name, and a notable new **Mormon Temple.** West of town is the **National Reactor Testing Station.** A few miles beyond the station is a picturesque natural bridge and the strange **Craters of the Moon**

National Monument, a wild area of lava beds and volcanic rock formations. Still farther west is the state's most celebrated resort, **Sun Valley.** The city is only 120 miles west of **Yellowstone National Park,** the edge of the park being in Idaho.

LEWISTON (population, 26,000), located on the western edge of the state, just at the point where the Snake River turns west into Oregon, is a good base for exploring the Snake River Gorge from the north, and the great, wild region of mountains and forests that fill the lower panhandle of the state to the east. Tourist accommodations are excellent. Lewiston began as a supply town for gold-seeking miners in the mountains to the east, now has the biggest lumber mill in the West, which offers conducted tours. Here also is the **Nez Perce National Historical Park. Moscow** (population, 14,000), home of the **University of Idaho,** about 50 miles north of Lewiston, has a wooded campus which is worth seeing.

SPORTS AND RECREATION. **Fishing** is superb in the Snake and Salmon rivers and the northern lakes. The catch is trout: rainbow, cutthroat, Dolly Varden, and Idaho's giant Kamloops. The wild, wooded mountains offer wilderness **pack trips,** and also provide fine **hunting** —deer, mountain goat, mountain sheep, bear, elk, moose. There are thrilling **river trips,** shooting the rapids of both the Snake and Salmon rivers. Spectator sports are chiefly **rodeos** and **roundups,** held in the summer. Excellent **winter sports facilities** can be found throughout the state.

SPECIAL EVENTS in Idaho include the **National Old Time Fiddlers Contest and Folk Music Festival,** held in Weiser every summer to re-create the song of the Oregon Trail; the annual **Shoshone-Bannock Indian Festival,** Fort Hall, August; **State Fair,** Boise, in August; numerous **snowmobile** and **skiing** competitions throughout the state, winter.

Alaska

Alaska is huge, its 586,412 square miles being more than twice the size of the next largest state, Texas; thus it ranks first in area in the United States. But it ranks fiftieth in residents, with only about 300,000 population.

Alaska's position on the globe is the most northern and western portion of the North American continent, much more western in location than is generally understood. Nome, Alaska, is farther west than Honolulu, Hawaii, and Attu Island, the most western of the Alaskan Aleutian island chain, is as far west as New Zealand. In latitude Juneau, Alaska, the capital, is about the same distance north as Stockholm in Sweden, and Point Barrow, northernmost point of Alaska, is about as far north as North Cape in Norway.

The northern limit of Alaska is the Arctic Ocean. Its eastern border, its only land border, is Canada, with the Yukon Territory in the north and the Province of British Columbia in the south. The southern border is the Pacific Ocean and the Gulf of Alaska. The western limit is the Bering Sea, with Siberia on its opposite shore. The southern limit of the Bering Sea is the chain of the Aleutian Islands, stretching in a great arc 1,200 miles southwest from the Alaskan mainland. The mainland of Alaska is separated from the mainland of Siberia by the Bering Strait, only 55 miles wide. Within the strait two islands, one owned by Alaska and the other by Siberia, are less than three miles apart.

The name of Alaska is derived from an Aleut Indian word spelled Alaxsxaq—"the vast or big land." Fortunately the Indian spelling has been corrupted to the present word—Alaska. The state flower is the forget-me-not; the state bird, the willow ptarmigan.

THE LAND. Alaska, with the island clusters and chains that extend from it, is one of the most remarkable and fascinating areas on the earth. Most of it is wilderness, but not a frozen wilder-

Alaska

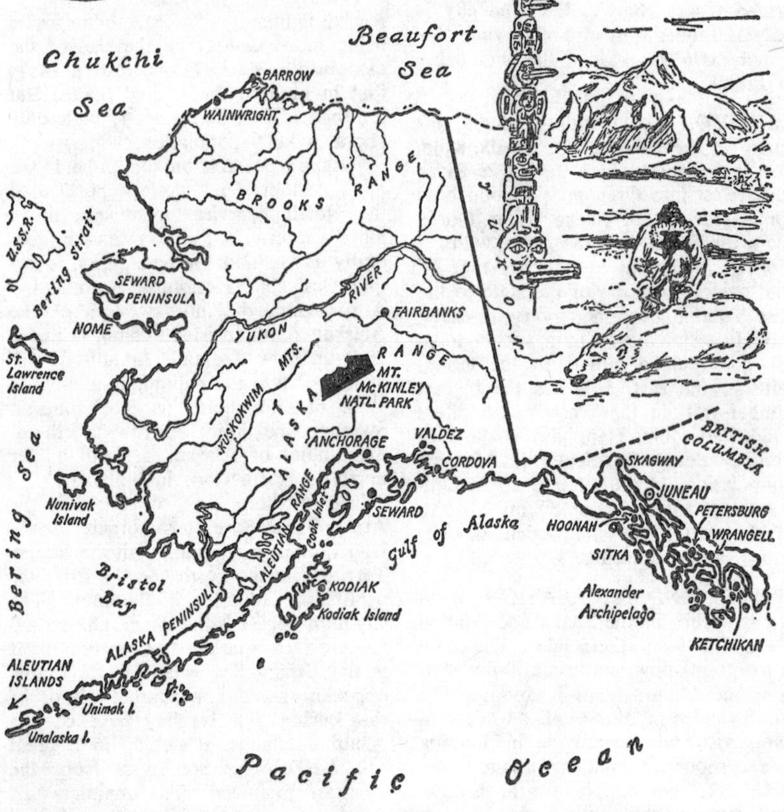

ness as many people seem to think. Few regions of the world have such extraordinary contrasts.

Actually the character of the land of Alaska divides into several distinct regions. In the extreme southeast stretches the long Panhandle, consisting of a narrow strip of mountainous, heavily wooded mainland masked by a chain of hundreds of islands, also rugged and forested. Channels thread the islands, the long north–south "Inside Passage" of protected deep water providing visitors an absorbing ocean voyage. In the Panhandle, near Yakutat, is the well-known glacier, **Malaspina,** which is as large as the state of Rhode Island.

West of the Alaskan Panhandle, facing the Pacific Ocean from the north, is south-central Alaska, dominated by the towering peaks of the Alaska Range, including **Mount McKinley,** highest on the North American continent (20,320 feet), set within **Mount McKinley National Park.** Southwest on the coast is the extraordinary and recently created Valley of Ten Thousand Smokes, preserved in **Katmai National Monument.** From the high, wild slopes of the mountains vast glaciers extend and creep toward the sea. The largest and most majestic cluster of them are within **Glacier Bay National Monument,** where the huge Muir glacier, two miles wide and 250 feet thick, is found.

The southern coast of Alaska is cut

by deep bays, surrounded by mountains. On or near the bays are many of the settled places in Alaska, including the largest city—**Anchorage.** Near the towns in the valleys between the mountain ranges are most of Alaska's few cultivated fields.

From the mountain masses of southwestern Alaska the mountain spine of the Alaska Peninsula extends southwest, starting with **Katmai Volcano,** below which lies the strange **Valley of Ten Thousand Smokes.** The peninsula tapers into the chain of the **Aleutian Islands,** sweeping southwest in a great arc, bleak and treeless, desolate and fogbound, some of the loneliest land fragments on the earth. They are the hazardous homes of once great herds of Alaskan sea otter. The chain ends far to the west with **Attu**—briefly occupied by the Japanese in World War II. Attu is 1,200 miles west of the southernmost end of the Panhandle.

North of the islands and the mountain masses of the south stretches the huge, almost empty heart of Alaska, divided into two strikingly different parts. Central Alaska lies between the northern slopes of the coastal ranges and the southern slopes of the **Brooks Range** far to the north. It is a wide plateau sloping to the west, drained by Alaska's two big rivers—the **Yukon** and the **Kuskokwim.** Though partially forested it is a plain area with endless grassy prairies through which slow flowing streams meander. To the old-time Alaskan, this is the true Alaska, the land of gold and legend. The chief city is **Fairbanks,** but its most celebrated town is **Nome,** facing the Bering Sea.

The Brooks Range, rising on the northern side of the central valley, with peaks above 9,000 feet, is the southern limit of a strange, frigid, never-never land—Arctic Alaska, a flat, frozen expanse where shallow streams twist north toward the Arctic Ocean, through endless miles of treeless tundra. Here, even in summer, the ground never thaws below a foot or two. It is the land of the Eskimo and the polar bear. The whole of Arctic Alaska is north of the Arctic Circle. Its most northern point, and therefore the most northern point of the United States, is **Point Barrow,** an Eskimo village.

The vast bulk of Alaska, above its island extensions east and west, is about 900 miles from north to south, 800 miles east to west.

THE CLIMATE. Just as Alaska varies enormously in character, so it varies in climate. Along the southern and the southeastern coasts and the island groups which flank them the climate is surprisingly mild, thanks to the Japan Current sweeping in from the west. Rainfall is heavy, in places as high as 150 inches a year. The temperature of Juneau is not much different from that of New York City, though the rainfall is much heavier. Average winter temperatures will be about 32 degrees, summer temperatures from 50 to 60 degrees.

In the southern coastal valleys, in and around Anchorage, it is cooler and drier, with greater extremes, summer and winter, more like the north-central plains area of the United States. The island chain to the westward has its own peculiar and unpleasant climate, cool and very foggy both summer and winter, pleasant only for its native inhabitants, the herds of seal. In the central valley it is still drier, with winter temperatures falling often to 30 or 40 degrees below zero and summer temperatures soaring at times above 85. Average rainfall in the valley regions is only about 15 to 20 inches a year. Arctic Alaska is what its name implies, cold most of the time, with a climate comparable to northern Norway. But the summer days of almost total daylight in various parts of the Arctic warm up the land a little, encouraging thousands of delicate flowers to bloom.

From the visitors' standpoint the best time to enjoy Alaska is during the summer months, when they will need about the same traveling wardrobe as for a holiday in Maine or Scotland.

THE PEOPLE. The world in general knew nothing about Alaska until after most places in the western world had been discovered, named, and settled. Alaska's discovery was made at last almost by accident. Peter the Great of Russia commissioned a Danish navigator named Vitus Bering to find a channel across the northern seas that would link Siberia with Europe. The assignment was given in 1725, but it was sixteen years later before Bering, cruising the coast of Siberia and the shores of the strait that now carries his name, found Alaska. That was in 1741.

Bering died without exploring or reporting his find, but members of his party collected specimens of animals from along the coast of Alaska and carried them back to Russia. They included the sea otter and the fur seal, whose home was the island chain extending from the western coast of Alaska. Furs were important in Russia, and the pelts brought to the Imperial Court by Bering's men were among the sleekest, softest and richest ever seen. So hunters and trappers from Siberia called *promyshlenniki* began to cross the fog-swept channel that separated Alaska from Siberia and to slaughter relentlessly the seals and sea otter. They were Alaska's first white explorers.

The wealth of furs in Alaska was so great that big Russian companies were formed to exploit it. One of them was responsible for the first settlement of Alaska, on Kodiak Island, just off the southwest coast, in 1784. Then the Russian government became officially interested, formed the Russian-American Company in 1799, made Aleksandr Baranov its manager. Baranov selected Sitka as his capital. It remained Russia's chief base in Alaska for many years, and is still today the most Russian-appearing community in the western world. From Sitka, Russian colonists extended their claims and control as far south as California.

Within a few years prior to the founding of Sitka, British exploring mariners Captain James Cook and Captain George Vancouver had both surveyed and reported areas of the coast. At about the same time Canadian fur traders began to come into Alaska from the east.

But long before the coming of the Russians to Alaska, islands on the shore and areas of the great mainland wilderness had been sparsely populated by Indian tribes. Along the western islands and southwest shore lived the friendly, trusting Aleuts. In the southeast Panhandle were the hard and hostile Tlinget and Haida tribes, while the Athapascan Indians lived in the wilderness of central Alaska. The Eskimos inhabited the far north. Little is known of the ethnic origin of the Indians in Alaska, but most anthropologists believe that in remote times they all crossed into Alaska from Mongolia and northern Siberia. All the tribes appear to be related in origin, language, and legend, though Eskimo and Indian languages are entirely different. Descendants of most tribes are still in Alaska, giving it a high percentage of native stock. The southern Indians are noted for their totem poles, while Eskimos are designers of the Kayak and carvers of ivory.

Baranov died in 1819, and thereafter Russian interest declined. The young United States of America proclaimed a Monroe Doctrine, aimed in part at the Russian hold on the northwest. Britain and the United States agreed to zones of influence which limited Russia still more.

But while Russia's interest in and profits from Alaska diminished, those of the United States increased. The West Coast fishing interests wanted control of the Alaskan waters. The Western Union Telegraph Company had a plan to lay a cable to Siberia, and thence to Europe, by way of Alaska. Toward the middle of the nineteenth century Russia began to liquidate, first selling its California holdings and claims to a Swiss immigrant named John Sutter. (It was on his farm in California that gold was later discovered.)

Pressures and trends came to a climax in 1867 when William H. Seward, Secretary of State for the United States, offered Russia $7.2 million for Alaska. (It has since been learned that Russia wanted to sell so badly that an offer of $5 million would have been accepted.) The deal was made within a matter of hours, signed at 4 A.M. It was promptly called "Seward's Folly," "Seward's Icebox," and, after the President, "Johnson's Polar Bear Garden."

The American flag went up at Sitka on October 18, 1867, and the whole vast new land was put in charge of a few army officers. Then, in 1880, gold was discovered near Juneau and a mild stampede of prospectors began.

Ironically it was not the discovery of gold in Alaska, but its discovery in the Klondike region of Canada to the east, in 1896, that caused the famous rush to Alaska. It was easier to reach the Klondike by way of Alaska than across the rugged wilds of Canada. Some of the prospectors returning from the Yukon, joined the Nome rush in 1899, and near Fairbanks in 1902. The sourdoughs made headlines all over the world. They took over Alaska. Few of them made much money from gold, but they created robust and colorful legends. Young writers like Robert Service, Jack London and Rex Beach made more money recording the exploits of the sourdoughs than the miners made from gold itself.

Today survivors of the sourdoughs, all tough old men, spin their yarns and live out their days at the Pioneers' Home in Sitka. Visiting these last survivors of a richly colorful historic episode delights tourists to Sitka now.

The era of modern Alaska officially begins with the establishment of local government in 1912, preceded by the moving of the capital to Juneau in 1906. The hysteria of individual gold prospecting was over. Gold mining was big business, done by great placer mines and dredging. Fishing became more important. Lumber interests began to use the timber from the forests. The Alaskan Railway from Seward to Fairbanks was begun in 1915.

The entry of the United States into World War II gave enormous impetus to Alaskan air travel, both civil and military, particularly long range intercontinental air travel. Alaska became the center for shorter routes between the United States and the Orient, and Europe. Alaska also became a first line of defense. Army camps, naval bases, air bases, sprang up. The Alaskan Highway was built to provide a land link. Thousands of young men, and many of their families, went to Alaska to help install the new bases and to man them. Engineers discovered that Alaska is incredibly rich in natural resources, in mineral wealth, in timber.

In June of 1942 Japanese amphibious forces landed on Attu and Kiska, in the westernmost Aleutians. In the following March a U.S. naval force defeated the enemy off the western Aleutians, the first battle fought on American soil since Appomattox. Of more than 300,000 military personnel stationed in the area during the war, many stayed or returned as civilian citizens.

Now, in Sitka, the Japanese have succeeded in a peaceful penetration. There Japanese capital has financed a pulp mill costing $55 million. Japanese steamers make Sitka a regular port of call to load the pulp needed in the manufacture of rayon.

Of Alaska's total population of a little over 300,000 about 55,000 are native in origin. Of these about half are Eskimo, many of whom speak English.

AGRICULTURE. Alaska is distinctly not an agricultural area. Of an estimated three million acres of arable land, only about 70,000 are being farmed. The chief crops are potatoes, truck vegetables, berries, dairy products. In the whole of Alaska there are only about 500 farms. In the Panhandle area the land is too steep for farming. Most of the farms are in the mountain valleys and near the coast in southcentral Alaska. Though in many of the valleys the soil is very rich, the growing season is relatively short. But high latitude makes each day of the growing season unusually long. The result: some crops grow very fast, attaining huge sizes. In Matanuska Valley near Anchorage, where the largest single concentration of farms exists, it is not unusual to find strawberries as big as peaches, cabbages that will weigh 30 pounds.

Other centers for farming are near Homer, south of Anchorage, on the Kenai Peninsula, where a combination of sheltered valley and mild temperatures make farming unusually productive, and in the valley of the Tanana near Fairbanks.

But only a small fraction of the food needed is grown in Alaska. Everything else is shipped in by boat, or flown in by air, or trucked in over the Alaskan Highway.

INDUSTRY. Though Alaska's agricultural production is negligible, the wealth of the land and the seas that wash Alaskan shores is huge, making food and wood processing industries very important. The biggest single developed resource is from fisheries, chiefly salmon, halibut, cod, herring, shellfish. It accounts for about $70 million a year in Alaskan income and gives work to about 25,000 fishermen and cannery workers.

Becoming important is the exploitation, under rigid government control, of Alaska's forest reserves, spruce and hemlock, ideally suited for pulp needed for paper, plastics and synthetic fibers. Two huge pulp mills, costing more than $100 million, are being developed.

Mineral resources are very extensive, nearly all, except gold, scarcely touched by development. In dollar value, gold no longer exceeds other minerals. More recently tapped resources are coal, iron ore, tin, copper and oil, most major companies having oil exploration teams in Alaska. As a result, huge oil and gas fields, chiefly in Prudhoe Bay off the Arctic slope region, have been discovered. The early trend of wholesale slaughter of the fur-bearing animals, practiced by the nineteenth-century trappers from Russia, has been reversed by controls under the Alaska Department of Fish and Game and the U. S. Fish and Wild Life Service. Today Alaska's herds of seal and sea otter are rapidly increasing.

In addition, sable, wolverine, muskrat, beaver, ermine, mink, fox, lynx, and marten are widely trapped and hunted. The ancient Indian crafts produce beautiful, authentically designed miniature totem poles, carved ceremonial masks, carved ivory, beaded slippers, baskets, drums and jewelry, set with locally produced jade, agate and petrified wood.

CITIES. The cities of Alaska are all small, each strikingly different in character. Some, like Anchorage, the largest, are quite new. Others, like the Russian capital of Sitka, are ancient. Each is an adaptation of economic and social needs to the special terrain of Alaska.

ANCHORAGE, on Cook Inlet at the head of the Kenai Peninsula, is many times larger than any other city in Alaska. It is, in fact, one of the fastest-growing cities in the world. Anchorage was founded in 1915 as permanent headquarters for the Alaskan Railway. In 1940 it had a population of 3,500. Ten years later the population had trebled and is in the neighborhood of 48,000. Anchorage is the traffic hub of Alaska for air and rail travel, an important stop on international air flights, with **Anchorage International,** just outside the city, ranking as one of the busiest airfields anywhere. Anchorage is a seaport, and a center for commercial fishing, and is western terminus for the **Glenn Highway,** connecting with the **Alaskan Highway.** Just outside of the city are **Fort Richardson,** and **Elmendorf Air Force Base,** U.S. military headquarters for Alaska.

Anchorage is the best base for sightseeing and travel to southcentral Alaska, the Remai Peninsula, and the lower interior. From Anchorage the **Alaskan Railway** extends 260 miles north to Fairbanks. Traveling the railway is a sightseeing adventure of unique character.

FAIRBANKS is northern terminus for the railway, and Alaska's second largest city. The present population is about 14,000, more than doubled in 15 years. It is the only city in Alaska which is a hub of several highways, including the Alaskan Highway. Like Anchorage, it is an international air travel center, with regular service to all points of Alaska and the rest of the United States. Fairbanks, founded in 1902 when gold was discovered in central Alaska, became the heart of the gold mining country.

More than any other city in Alaska the town has greater contrast in aspect between the old relics of gold rush days and the modern booming development of Alaska. Steamers from Whitehorse down the Yukon once made it a western terminus (the city is just south of the main channel of the Yukon on the Tanana River). River trips are still a sightseeing opportunity for visitors.

Fairbanks' chief point of interest is the new campus of the **University of Alaska,** at College, three miles northwest. **Eielson Air Force Base,** 25 miles southeast, is a huge new military installation. **Indian villages,** former old mining towns, of **Circle** and **Fort Yukon** nearby, are authentic and interesting. Both are centers for gardening, with fruit and flowers becoming enormous under the constant summer sun.

JUNEAU, capital of Alaska (population about 6,000), has one of the most striking settings of any Alaskan city. Two perpetually snow-capped mountains, Juneau and Roberts, tower behind it to the east, rising steeply from narrow Gastineau Channel. Some Juneau streets climb the mountain slopes so steeply as to defy motor vehicles. One of the city's historic sites is across the channel, linked to the town by a bridge on Douglas Island. It is the **Treadwell Mine,** the once-rich (now abandoned) mine from which millions of dollars in gold were taken. The city has mainline jet airport facilities and is an excellent base for visiting some sights of the Panhandle area. Eleven miles north, reached by a good highway, is **Mendenhall Glacier.** A boat or short air flight of about 75 miles connects Juneau with spectacular **Glacier Bay National Monument,** covering 3,600 square miles, from where one can see 20 glaciers creeping down from a vast icecap among 15,000-foot peaks, into a fiord 60 miles long and two miles wide on their way to the sea.

There are good shops in Juneau that sell authentic native craft articles, and in summer, visitors can ride an ore car through **Mt. Roberts.**

KETCHIKAN, a port on the Inside Passage, and most southern town of any importance in Alaska, lies 230 miles southeast of Juneau, on Revillagigedo Island. Ketchikan began as a supply base for miners lured north by the gold rush in the 1890's, and became the chief center and shipping port for Alaska's fishing industry. More recently one big new pulp plant was established there. The world's largest collection of totem poles is about two miles outside of town at **Saxman Park.** A little farther away at **Totem Bight** there are other totem poles and a ceremonial Indian house.

MATANUSKA VALLEY, with the largest and most profitable agricultural development in Alaska, is 40 miles northeast. There 10,000 acres each year produce vegetables, fruit, grains, and forage crops, everything growing, thanks to the long summer days, incredibly fast, often resulting in giant specimens.

Katmai National Monument, southwest 250 miles, accessible by plane, is a strange volcanic wonderland including Katmai Volcano, with a crater eight miles wide. Its eruption in 1912 created the **Valley of Ten Thousand Smokes,** part of the monument area. Off the coast just east of the Katmai Monument, easily accessible from Anchorage by air, is rugged and beautiful **Kodiak Island,** mecca for fishermen and big-game hunters, the only place where they can find the giant brown Kodiak bear, largest of the species.

Mount McKinley, 140 miles north of Anchorage, reached either by rail or highway, is Alaska's single most important and impressive sight. The majestic and immaculate snow peak (20,320 feet) is the highest point on North America, and the focal point of the superb, forested wilderness of 3,000-square-mile **Mount McKinley National Park.**

NOME, on the Seward Peninsula and the Bering Sea, has a population of about 2,000. It is one of the few cities in Alaska that is not growing rapidly, though once, in 1900, after gold had been discovered on the beach, it had a population of 30,000. Nome has regular air service and regularly scheduled summer steamer service. For the visitor it is of interest as the chief center for Eskimo life. The best Eskimo handicrafts are produced there in nearby villages, and can be bought in the shops of Nome. Several Eskimo villages are nearby. Each summer one Eskimo group sets up its tent village just outside of town.

SEWARD is at the head of Resurrection Bay, on Kenai Peninsula, 80 miles south of Anchorage, founded in 1902 as a supply base for the Alaskan Railway then being built. It became important as an army supply base during World War II, is still the principal ice-free port of entry to the interior of Alaska.

SITKA, Alaska's oldest town, has also been called its most beautiful. Though not on main travel routes, it is eminently worth visiting. It has a commanding setting on Baranof Island, a hundred miles southwest of Juneau. Snow-covered mountains tower over and surround it and deep blue ocean channels lead from it among the islands. The town was founded by Baranov in 1799, was first called Novo-Arkhangelsk (New Archangel). Later the name was changed to Sitka and it became headquarters of all the Russian activities in Alaska.

The Russian church, **St. Michael's Cathedral,** with its ancient little graveyard, is one of the most charming buildings in the western region. There is a fine museum of Indian crafts at the **Sheldon Jackson Junior College.** Nearby, on the site of World War II naval installations, is the **Mt. Egecumbe High School,** maintained by the Bureau of Indian Affairs. Sitka also has the **Pioneers' Home,** where the last of the sourdoughs live. But its most impressive sight is just south of town, the **Sitka National Monument,** where an excellent collection of Indian totems is preserved, along with an Indian stockade and a replica of a Russian blockhouse.

Sitka has a huge new pulp mill, financed by Japanese capital, a substantial fishing fleet, and canneries.

SKAGWAY, most northern city in southeastern Alaska, at the head of the fiord called Chilkoot Inlet, is 75 miles northwest of Juneau. It has something of the aspect of a pioneer frontier town, which it was when it began as a transfer point for miners bound for Yukon gold fields, over towering **White Pass** in Canada just north. In those days, about 1898, it had a population of nearly 20,000. Now it is southern terminus for the short White Pass and Yukon Route, which offers the passengers who ride on it one of the most dramatically scenic rail journeys in the world. Its northern terminus, **Whitehorse,** in Canada's Yukon, is the starting point for short excursions by river down the Yukon.

Over 500 miles west of Skagway is the Kenai Peninsula, thrusting south into the Gulf of Alaska.

SPORTS AND RECREATION. **Fishing** and **hunting** are superb, and in most of the larger centers facilities for doing both are easily available. Coastal waters swarm with salmon, and mountain lakes, generally reached by float planes, are alive with trout. Game for the hunter attracts those who want big specimens found under rugged conditions. They include moose, caribou, and Dall Mountain sheep, with moose most abundant. Bear range from the huge brown Kodiak and grizzly to the small black bear. In the north region **polar-bear hunting** is a special sport. Among game birds ptarmigan are the most widely distributed and abundant. Game fish, in addition to salmon, include the greyling, and the Dolly Varden trout.

Alaska's vast snow fields offer virgin slopes to skiers, two of the most popular organized facilities being the **Douglas Ski Bowl** in the mountains above Juneau and **Mt. Alyeska,** site of the 1963 U. S. National Alpine championships.

SPECIAL EVENTS. Many of Alaska's holidays, contests, and festivals center around her cold climate and snow. Ski competitions and dog sled races are popular annual occurrences. Among the best-known are the **Anchorage Fur Rendezvous Festival** in February; **Iceworm Festival** in Cordova, February; **Alaska Arts and Crafts Show,** Juneau, March; **Ice Pool Contest,** in Nenana, April or May; **Midnight Sun Baseball Game,** Fairbanks, June; and **Alaska Day Festival,** held in Sitka on October 18 to commemorate the day when Alaska was transferred from Russia to the United States in 1867.

Hawaii

Among the 50 states of the United States, Hawaii, the fiftieth, is unique in several ways. It is the only state which is a group of islands. It is more than 2,000 miles from the mainland of the United States, and, with the exception of southern Florida, is the only state with a subtropical climate.

Hawaii, a chain of islands near the center of the Pacific Ocean, has a land area of 6,450 square miles, about the size of the state of Connecticut. But the extent of the islands stretching out across the ocean is nearly 1,600 miles from one end of the chain to the other. The islands, volcanic in origin, are the peaks of a towering submarine mountain range. The Hawaiian Islands are more southern and more western than any other part of the United States. The most northern island in the chain is about as far north as Key West, Florida. The most southern, which is also the largest, is about as far south as Mexico City or Calcutta. The most eastern island in the chain is about as far west as the western coast of Alaska, or about 2,100 miles southwest of San Francisco, while the most western island is in about the same longitude as New Zealand.

Of the more than 130 islands in the Hawaiian chain only eight, which are also the largest, are clustered at the eastern end of the chain, sweeping in an arc from the southeast to the northwest about 400 miles. The rest of the chain, many islands little more than tropical atolls, stretches more than 1,600 miles to the northwest.

In area of land Hawaii ranks forty-seventh among the states. With a population estimated at just over 700,000, it is fortieth in the rank of states. The state flower of Hawaii is the hibiscus.

THE CLIMATE. The climate of the Hawaiian Islands is renowned for its perfection. The islands lie in a subtropical latitude, which means almost no seasonal change and general warm temperatures. But temperatures are moderated by currents from the cold Bering Sea and constant northeast trade winds. Thus the islands can boast a summer average of 78 degrees, a winter average of 72 degrees. The trade winds blowing against the mountain slopes yield enough rainfall, well-scattered through the year, to keep everything green. Locally the rainfall may vary markedly, island to island. Thus the verdant island of Kauai claims the wettest spot on earth—with an average rainfall of 407 inches each year. But one place on the island of Hawaii is almost a desert, with only nine inches of rainfall.

Local temperature variations are modified by altitude. Thus in the island of Hawaii, with its towering peaks, visitors may find Hawaii's characteristic balmy weather along the coast, but may shiver on the high mountain slopes. In winter snow is not uncommon around the peaks.

THE PEOPLE. The Pacific had been crossed many times and most of the lands around it had been explored before the world knew there was an inhabited archipelago in its very center. The first white man to discover the islands was Captain James Cook in 1778. He called them the Sandwich Islands, after the Earl of Sandwich. Captain Cook, making his first landing on the verdant island of Kauai, found the islands populated by about 300,000 natives. They were Polynesian in origin, and among the most advanced of all

Hawaii

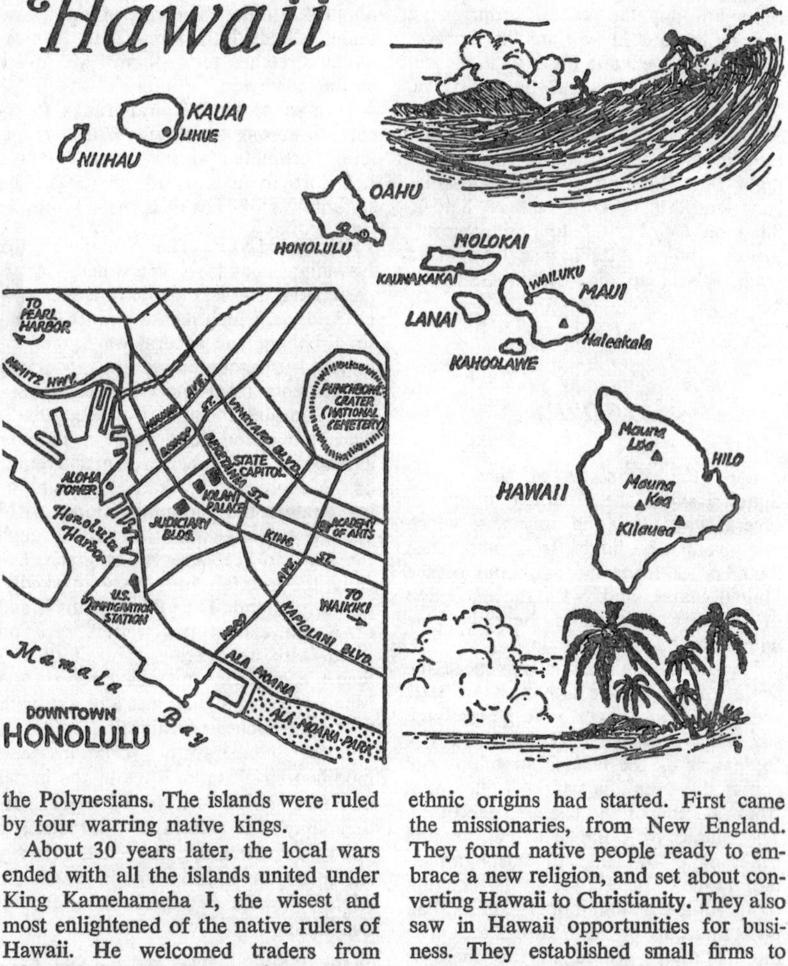

the Polynesians. The islands were ruled by four warring native kings.

About 30 years later, the local wars ended with all the islands united under King Kamehameha I, the wisest and most enlightened of the native rulers of Hawaii. He welcomed traders from other lands, promoted agriculture and commerce. His peaceful reign was the beginning of Hawaii's golden era. But it was an era of golden twilight, for the traders from abroad who brought goods from far lands and bought the exotic products of Hawaii in return also brought diseases for which the isolated Polynesian people had no natural immunity. Within 100 years the native population had dropped to 50,000. In the meantime the trends which were to make the Hawaiian Islands one of the most polyglot regions in the world in ethnic origins had started. First came the missionaries, from New England. They found native people ready to embrace a new religion, and set about converting Hawaii to Christianity. They also saw in Hawaii opportunities for business. They established small firms to trade with the rest of the world. They succeeded so well that the children of the missionaries are now the chief directors and owners of Hawaii's great companies, operating huge plantations and far-flung trading companies.

With the dwindling of the native population through the ravages of disease and the development of Hawaii's plantation fields, field labor was recruited from other lands. The first groups were Chinese, about 1850. Japanese, Koreans, Filipinos followed. Puerto Ricans, Germans, and Portuguese came later.

During this period Hawaii was a monarchy. Toward the end of the nineteenth century agitation for annexation to the United States began. For a brief period the islands were a republic. Annexation was accomplished in 1898, and in 1900 Hawaii became a Territory of the United States, under a governor named Sanford P. Dole. At that time two-thirds of the population were foreign-born aliens, most of them uneducated Orientals.

Impetus to the transition between an Oriental crossroads community and an integrated American society was given by the sudden impact of World War II, the bombing of Pearl Harbor by the Japanese, the establishment of the islands as one of the great military bases for the war and a staging ground for the whole Pacific Campaign. It brought to the islands many thousands of fighting men to man the installations, and hundreds of thousands more who stopped briefly in the islands in transit between the distant fighting fronts and home areas. With the war's end many stationed in the islands stayed to work and live; others who had sampled the benign climate and glimpsed the exotic charm of the islands, returned. With the war's end the fighting bases became great permanent military installations with a military personnel of about 50,000.

About 90 percent of the 700,000 people now living in the islands are either island-born or migrants from the United States mainland. Ethnic groups are of Polynesian, Asian, European and African extraction.

Hawaii's varied population is reflected in the food specialties which are served. These include *poi,* a paste made from taro root; roast pig, cocoanut. The islands have superb fruits; some of them, like the passion fruit, are quite rare. Others are guava, papaya, pineapple. There are also native nuts that are unusual. All are served at the popular *luau* feast.

AGRICULTURE. Farming in Hawaii is chiefly big business, a highly industrialized operation maintained by large companies. The two most important crops are cane for sugar, and pineapples. Of these sugar is the most important and the oldest Hawaiian product, accounting for about a million tons of sugar a year, requiring 17,000 workers employed by companies cultivating 230,000 acres. Pineapple production, more than $100 million worth each year, requires from 10,000 to 20,000 workers, depending on the season, and accounts for 75,000 acres. But more than a million acres of the island area are devoted to cattle ranching. The Parker Ranch on Hawaii alone has half a million acres, making it the world's second largest.

Hawaii is the only state in the United States where coffee is grown commercially. There are about 7,000 acres, chiefly in the Kona district of Hawaii, producing coffee. Tropical fruits and nuts are unique products of Hawaiian fields, particularly the Macadamia nut, grown on about 2,000 acres. Rare and exotic Hawaiian flowers are grown abundantly and regularly shipped to the mainland by air.

INDUSTRY. Most of the big industrial establishments in the Hawaiian Islands are concerned with processing or packaging the products of Hawaiian fields. They include sugar refineries, pineapple packing plants, coffee roasting and packing, packing of nuts and exotic fruits. Other factories are small and highly specialized. A large and growing industry is garment manufacturing, producing gay "aloha" shirts and other typically Hawaiian garments. A small plant makes ukuleles and other Hawaiian musical instruments. Other small plants make perfume and handicrafts.

THE ISLANDS. The islands of Hawaii, volcanic in origin, girdled with coral reefs, are mountainous. The mountains, thanks to a warm tropical climate and abundant rainfall, are covered with lush green plants and palms. But the islands of the group vary markedly in size, physical character, population and use.

HAWAII, often called the "Big Island," has given its name to the entire group. It has a land area of 4,030 miles, more than half the total land area of all the islands, and is roughly triangular in shape. The population, most of it concentrated in two towns and several villages, is about 63,000 people. Hawaii is about 90 miles long by 75 miles wide, and is geologically the youngest of the group. Two of its three mountain masses are active volcanos. **Mauna Loa,** is the world's biggest active volcano (13,680 feet). Even higher, dormant **Mauna Kea** is generally snow-capped, its peak rising 13,796 feet. Other physical features are dramatically varied. The coastline is rugged, picturesque, with few good harbors. On the slopes of the mountains are vast bamboo and giant fern forests. There are extensive lava flows, some quite recent, and a waterfall creating almost a perpetual rainbow. Upland slopes are cattle ranges, part of one of the world's biggest ranches. Near **Hilo,** the island capital, more than 22,000 varieties of orchids grow. On the opposite side of the island, the Kona coast is the only district within the United States where coffee is grown commercially. Much of the tropical, scenic splendor of Hawaii is preserved within **Hawaii National Park,** including the peak and crater of volcanic **Mauna Loa.** Good highways circle the island, linking all the towns and villages along the coast, with loops from the coastal roads giving access to the mountain slopes and ranch lands. Hiking trails lead to the mountain summits.

KAHOOLAWE, southwest of Maui and southeast of Lanai, about equally distant from each, contains 45 square miles of land but has no population at all. The island is about nine miles long and six miles wide, its highest point 1,444 feet. The soil, of volcanic origin, is poor, so about the only use ever made of the island was as a cattle range. It has recently been used as a practice bombing range by the Air Force.

KAUAI. The fourth largest in the Hawaiian chain, 555 square miles, is Kauai, the most isolated of the larger islands. The population is about 29,000. The island is roughly circular, about 32 miles in diameter, with a central mountain mass with peaks over 5,000 feet, and slopes dropping down to fertile coastal plains. Geologically it is the oldest of the islands, its once great craters and mountain cones eroded away. It is also the most fertile and most verdant of the larger islands and so is called the "Garden Island." The slopes of Mount Waialeale are the wettest places on earth.

An unusual natural feature are several deep canyons, one, **Waimea Canyon,** resembling the Grand Canyon of Arizona in its spectacular coloring and boldly eroded rock formations.

Kauai has the largest rivers on any of the Hawaiian Islands. One of them, **Wailua,** on the east coast, provides scenic sightseeing journeys through a lush tropical setting, including strange fern grottos.

The island's coastline is broken by small but good natural harbors, set with fine beaches. The principal commercial harbor, Nawiliwili, is just south of the county seat and chief town of Lihue. Most of the population live in small towns and villages near the shore, linked by a scenic highway. Another highway threads **Waimea Canyon,** providing spectacular views of its depths. Most of the cultivated land of Kauai is devoted to sugar and pineapple, with cattle grazed on the upland slopes.

Kauai is the oldest island of the Hawaiian group geologically and historically. Captain Cook made his first landing at Waimea Bay on the southern shore.

LANAI has a land area of 140 square miles, a population of about 2,200. The island is dominated by the mass of **Mount Lanaihale** rising 3,370 feet. Its slopes were long devoted to the grazing of cattle, but in recent years the entire island was purchased by a pineapple company and much of its area converted to a pineapple plantation. Most of the population is concentrated at Kaumalapau Harbor, with its modern port facilities, and at Lanai City, in the interior.

MAUI. Thirty miles northwest of the island of Hawaii, across Alenuihaha Channel, is the island of Maui. Second largest in size and population of the islands, it has a land area of 728 square miles, a population of over 45,000. Maui has a curious shape, two mountain masses at east and west peninsulas linked by a low isthmus only ten miles from north to south, from which the island takes its name as the Valley Island. Maui is dominated by the towering peak of **Haleakala,** rising 10,032 feet, part of **Hawaii National Park.** The coast of the island, broken with coves and bays, has some fine beaches. There are dramatically rugged headlands, and deep, wild gorges breaking down to the sea.

Most of the island's population, devoted to agriculture, live in the villages along the coast, the largest town and county seat being **Wailuku** near the western end. They work on sugar and pineapple plantations and on cattle ranches. Two small islands–Lanai and Kahoolawe–lie to the west of Maui, ten miles across the Auau Channel.

MOLOKAI, least developed of the larger islands, has a land area of 260 square miles, a population of about 5,000. The island is mountainous, with peaks rising to about 5,000 feet, is 37 miles long and 10 miles wide. Most of its area is devoted to cattle grazing and pineapple growing. The chief port is Kaunakakai, linked to other villages along the south shore by a highway, which extends across the island to the north coast and Hansen's Disease settlement at the village of **Kalaupapa.** A big water power development has been completed recently, adding many acres on Molokai to cultivation.

NIIHAU. Southwest of Kauai, 15 miles across Kaulakahi Channel, is the small island of Niihau. Privately owned, it has an area of 72 square miles, a population of about 250. It is 18 miles long and six miles wide, with a rugged spine of rocky hills rising to 1,281 feet in the north. Compared to the moist verdure of nearby Kauai, the island is arid. Its population, scattered among several tiny villages, is devoted to cattle grazing, and making the best rush mats in the islands.

OAHU. Third largest of the Hawaiian Islands (604 square miles), Oahu has four-fifths of the population of the islands, with over 600,000 people, most living in the capital city of **Honolulu.** Roughly triangular in shape, Oahu is 40 miles long and 26 miles wide. Two mountain ranges parallel the coasts on either side. On the northeast coast the Koolau Range, superbly forested, rises abruptly from the shore, its eastern flank a steep escarpment. The crest of the range is about 3,000 feet. On the western side of the islands rise the Waianae Mountains, with one peak of more than 4,000 feet. Between the mountains are fertile areas, chiefly Manoa and Nuuanu valleys, intensively cultivated. Unusual natural features of Oahu include **Pearl Harbor,** one of the few good natural harbors in the islands, and a great naval base; **Nuuanu Pali,** a cleft in the eastern mountains carrying a dramatically scenic highway; several extinct volcanos near the eastern end of which **Diamond Head, Koko Head** and **Punchbowl** are landmarks.

The coast of Oahu is rugged and picturesque, cut by many small bays with some notably fine beaches. Among them is **Waikiki Beach,** just outside of Honolulu. An excellent highway circles the island, often close to the shore, and so providing a most impressive scenic drive. Connecting highways thread the valleys, giving access to the extensive cultivated areas.

The most heavily populated part of Oahu is the eastern end, where Honolulu is an important port for world shipping and a hub of air travel. Most facilities for visitors are in or near Honolulu. Near it are the great military installations of the navy, clustered around Pearl Harbor, the army base of **Schofield Barracks,** and the air force base of **Hickam Field.**

The superbly forested mountain slopes of Oahu are maintained as a forest reserve, with extensive stands of native hardwoods, a largely undeveloped but important timber resource.

CITIES. There are only a few cities in the Hawaiian Islands of any size. Honolulu, on Oahu, capital of the state of Hawaii, with a population of more than 320,000, is about ten times larger than Kailua, the second largest city, on the same island. But there are a number of small towns and villages, many of them communities of unique charm. Each of the larger islands has at least one town which will serve as a convenient base from which the island can be explored.

HILO, chief city of the largest Hawaiian island, Hawaii, with about 30,000 population, is the third city in size among the islands. The city faces the natural harbor of Hilo Bay on the island's east coast. It is the chief port of the island and the second most important airport (after Honolulu) among all the islands. Hilo, which has good tourist facilities, is an excellent base for visiting the whole island.

Within the city and just outside it are several points of special interest, including **Rainbow Falls,** created in the Wailuku River, and **Hilo Florist Center,** for packing and shipping orchids, grown in fields around the city. Within the city, **Lyman Memorial Museum** has ancient Hawaiian relics. Not far from Hilo, easily reached on a good highway, is the **Kalapana Black Sand Beach,** beneath a large coco-palm grove. Hilo is a good base for visiting **Hawaii National Park,** which includes a forest of giant tree ferns; **Volcano House,** near Kilauea Crater, from which trails lead to the towering, smoldering crater of **Mauna Loa.** The vast **Parker Ranch,** in which an excellent resort hotel is located, spreads over upland grazing lands between the volcanic peaks in the center of the island. From Hilo a good highway leads around the island to the picturesque **Kona district** on the west coast, with its extensive coffee plantations, the ancient royal palace of Hawaiian kings, a monument where Captain Cook was killed and the first Catholic church in the islands. Easily reached from Hilo are dozens of lava flows, some quite recent.

HONOLULU. The most southern and farthest west city in the United States, after Nome, Honolulu has been the island capital for more than 100 years. On the southwest shore of Oahu, on a narrow plain, the city faces the sea, with the wooded Koolau Mountains behind. The older part of the city is closely built around the busy harbor, dominated by the **Aloha Tower** (which can be climbed for a fine view). From the older area new sections spread into the foothills of the mountains and along the shore. Just west is the **International Airport** and Hickam Field, headquarters for the Pacific Air Forces.

East of the city center, along the shore, is the famed Waikiki district, with its celebrated beach, rivaling Miami Beach in the exotic splendor of its great hotels.

Among outstanding sights are **Iolani Palace,** the Hawaiian capitol building, with the only throne room in the United States; the fine campus of the **University of Hawaii; Bishop Museum,** on Kalihi Street, with the world's finest collection of Polynesian relics. The city's **aquarium** has a stunning collection of tropical fish, while the **zoo,** in one of the city parks, has a unique collection of tropical birds. **Fisherman's wharf,** with the sampans for deep-sea fishing, is worth seeing, as is the city's small but colorful **Chinatown.** A typical native Hawaiian village is in **Ala Moana Park.** Just above the city, in the Punchbowl, is the **Pacific National Memorial Cemetery,** with graves of World War II war dead. Near Pearl Harbor is the **Oahu Sugar Mill** which offers tours.

The rest of the island can be easily explored from Honolulu over excellent highways which have superbly scenic stretches. Most celebrated of these is the Nuuanu Pali, a pass through the mountains, with a road dropping down an almost sheer cliff to the sea and the island's eastern shore. On the eastern shore are several fine beaches, some villages with tropical charm, a handsome **Mormon temple.** At the southern end of the island there is a superb beach in a dramatically rugged setting, within Koko Head Park.

LIHUE, on the "Garden Island" of Kauai, is the chief town and county seat. It is on the southeast coast, about two miles inland from Nawiliwili Harbor. The town has a population of about 3,000. From it a scenic road goes around the shore of the island, connecting villages and points of interest, giving access to the island's fine beaches.

WAILUKU, the county seat on the island of Maui, with a population of about 8,000, is located two miles inland from the north coast near the harbor of Kahului. A good road leads from the town to the rim of the crater of the extinct volcano **Haleakala.** Equally accessible a few miles west of Wailuku is lushly tropical **Iao Valley,** known for a volcanic freak–a needle of rock towering 1,200 feet above the valley floor.

SPORTS AND RECREATION. Few areas in the world match the **scenic drives** possible on the islands. Dozens of fine beaches provide the usual diversions, with such beaches as Waikiki offering Hawaiian specialties like **surfboarding, outrigger canoe racing** and **sailing.** Larger craft, capable of ocean navigation, offer **yachting.** Fishermen rate the offshore waters as among the best in the world, with facilities excellent and easily arranged. **Hunting,** good on most of the islands, is a seasonal sport. Game and game birds include dove, pheasant, wild pig, deer, goats, quail. (There are no squirrels, rabbits or snakes on the islands.)

Golfers have a choice among a number of good courses, particularly near Honolulu, the unique island climate keeping **golf** greens and fairways always emerald. An oddity in a subtropical land, **skiing** is sometimes possible on the high slopes of Mauna Kea, on the island of Hawaii.

Sightseeing from the air, made possible by a network of inter-island airways, provides striking views. There are good **hiking trails** on all the islands, with places for camping or picnicking.

SPECIAL EVENTS. Hawaiian festivals throughout the year suggest both the origin of Hawaiian customs in far countries and the rich abundance of Hawaiian lands and waters. Throughout the year there are **Hukilaus** or fishing festivals; in the winter the Chinese celebrate, with banquets and dancing, the **narcissus festival,** or the Oriental New Year; a **doll festival** is observed among the Japanese in the spring. Another Japanese occasion is a **Cherry Blossom festival; Lei Day** is typically Hawaiian, celebrated each spring. **Aloha week,** each fall, is called the "Mardi Gras of the Pacific."

Canada

Canada

Arctic Sea
QUEEN ELIZABETH ISLANDS
ELLESMERE
GREENLAND
PARRY ISLANDS
Beaufort Sea
DEVON I.
Baffin Bay
BANKS I.
ALASKA
Davis Strait
BAFFIN ISLAND
VICTORIA ISLAND
NORTHWEST TERRITORIES
Foxe Basin
YUKON
Mackenzie River
Great Bear Lake
WHITEHORSE
Atlantic
NEWFOUNDLAND
LABRADOR
Great Slave Lake
Hudson Bay
Pacific
BRITISH COLUMBIA
ROCKY MOUNTAINS
ALBERTA
EDMONTON
SASKATCHEWAN
MANITOBA
Lake Winnipeg
James Bay
QUÉBEC
PRINCE EDWARD ISLAND
NEWFOUNDLAND
ST. JOHN'S
VANCOUVER ISLAND
VICTORIA
VANCOUVER
REGINA
WINNIPEG
ONTARIO
QUÉBEC
MONTREAL
OTTAWA
NEW BRUNSWICK
NOVA SCOTIA
HALIFAX
SAINT JOHN
Lake Superior
TORONTO
Lake Ontario
Ocean
UNITED STATES
Lake Huron
Lake Michigan
Lake Erie
Ocean

Canada

"Dominion from sea to sea, and from the river even unto the end of the earth"—this scriptural quotation is Canada's motto. From the Atlantic to the Pacific, and from the St. Lawrence to the Arctic Circle, Canada is an area of nearly four million square miles. Much of it is inhabited only by scattered groups of Eskimos; much of it is an enormous archipelago of large and small islands divided by icy seas. Most of Canada's approximately 21 million people live and work along the southern border. The size of the country, with its many natural barriers of water, forest, and mountain, slowed the development of a national consciousness. But today, railways, highways, airlines, telephone and telegraph lines, radio, and television tie the people of the widely separated provinces more and more closely together.

The scenic and cultural variety of this huge, bilingual country draws many visitors from the United States, from the skiing season through the sudden rush of springtime, the languor of summer to the glorious autumn coloring, and the first snowfall that makes tracking easy for the hunter.

Millions of years ago mammoths roamed the reaches of the Yukon, and even earlier, dinosaurs wallowed in steamy swamps of Alberta, before the Ice Age doomed them. Perhaps 20,000 years ago some Asian tribes crossed Bering Strait, founded settlements, and slowly spread southward. These Indians, or Eskimos, had come to terms with their environment long before the European explorers intruded by the bays and rivers. Traces of Viking culture mark the arrival of the first of these around A.D. 1000. The Vikings' visit was only momentary, and not until Columbus opened the way to the explorers of sixteenth-century Western Europe did Canada's recorded history begin. The Venetian sailor John Cabot, sailing in the service of Henry VIII, may not have been the first to fish the Grand Banks, but he was the first to publicize these fabulous fishing grounds. Jacques Cartier explored the Gulf of St. Lawrence and "the great river of Canada," making careful notes of all he saw. In 1604 Samuel de Champlain brought French settlers to Acadia, and shortly after established a colony at Quebec.

French settlers were followed by English, whose main colonies lay farther south, but who succeeded in taking over Canada in the French and Indian Wars. A new influx of English-speaking settlers poured in after the American War of Independence, when thousands of Loyalists arrived to populate empty areas from Nova Scotia to Ontario.

In the meantime, explorers probed through the pack-ice of the Arctic, finding a way into Hudson Bay, where a fur trade flourished from 1670. More fur trappers and traders pressed westward, through the Rocky Mountains and into the western Arctic. Others rounded Cape Horn to explore the western coast. The War of 1812 with the United States, in which Canadians saw themselves threatened with annexation, for the first time gave the country a real sense of national unity.

Gradually the colonies won self-government, and in 1867—greatest date in Canadian history—achieved confederation. In the new Dominion of Canada (now simply "Canada") each province retained certain jealously guarded rights, which accounts for considerable variation in provincial laws. The country is officially bilingual, with the large French-speaking population concentrated mostly in Quebec. The twentieth century has seen the addition of new ethnic and religious groups from Europe, and even Asia—a visitor now sees Eastern Orthodox cupolas, Sikh and Buddhist temples, as well as Protestant and Catholic churches.

Industrial development has been spectacular, with the famed Klondike gold strike of the early years of this century followed by discovery of a vast range of mineral riches. Today Canada is a major exporter of industrial raw materials, and an important manufacturer of finished products. Yet the frontier is not far behind—a few hundred miles north of Toronto and Montreal, the old fur-trapping life is carried on.

Close to the United States, and speaking for the most part the same language, Canadians and Americans have developed close ties. There has been a constant flow of population back and forth across the border. Canadian currency has long been on the decimal dollar-and-cents basis. On the other hand, Canada measures gasoline by the Imperial gallon, one-fifth larger than the American. In spelling, Canadians steer a middle course between British and American usage.

In sports, cricket is still played in a few cities, but baseball is far more popular. Canada's top sports, however, are two specialties in themselves—Canadian football, a variant of American, and ice hockey, in which Canadian boys become so proficient that an American hockey player in the professional National Hockey League is practically unknown. Skiing, figure skating, and other winter sports are also widely popular, including curling, imported from Scotland. In summertime, devotees of sailing, canoeing, power boating, and swimming take advantage of the numerous lakes, rivers, and bays.

Fishing and hunting are premier attractions for visitors, as is outdoor living generally in this land of unspoiled wilderness and open spaces. Not only first-rate trout fishing, but Pacific and Atlantic salmon, walleye or northern pike, muskellunge or grayling, and Arctic char, a pink-fleshed fish very good to eat, provide unusual variety for anglers. Deer, bear, moose, and caribou may be hunted in many provinces, and antelope in Alberta and Saskatchewan. Mountain goat, bighorn sheep, and elk are hunted in Alberta and British Columbia. Even wild buffalo may be shot on a wilderness range in the Northwest Territories, outside the Wood Buffalo National Park. The vast marshes around the big interior lakes of Manitoba are famous for their duck and goose shoots. Waterfowl also breed farther west, but the prairies are more noted for their upland game birds. Ptarmigan and ruffed grouse (partridge) are found in all provinces.

But Canadian travel isn't limited to hunting, fishing, and sports. Canadian musicians and dancers are winning renown at home and abroad. A season of grand opera is produced in Toronto yearly, as well as a month of first-class ballet. Drama however, has the widest appeal, with professional theatre in the big cities, and Little Theatre groups throughout the country. Above all, the little town of Stratford, Ontario, named for Shakespeare's birthplace, has won world fame for its productions.

Local Canadian handicrafts are outstanding. The Canadian Handicraft Guild keeps a watchful eye on quality for its chain of shops, and craftsmen's associations insist on high standards. Cape Breton Island produces hooked rugs in delicate tones of woolen yarn, while Quebec's hooked rugs, of more vivid coloring, are made of wool cloth. Quebec also specializes in catalogne weaving–strips of cotton cloth woven into drapes, bedspreads, floor runners. Several provinces are known for silver and copper jewelry. Vancouver workmen incise silver with totemic designs of great beauty. Small specialized shops carry semi-precious stone–agate, jade, amethyst, garnet–either cut and polished or in the rough. In the Yukon, Indian-made moccasins, gloves, and jackets of caribou and moosehide are excellent buys. The soapstone carvings of the Eskimos are each individual creations, because the Eskimos dislike repetition. Raw furs or finished garments may be purchased from trappers, traders, and mink ranchers.

Newfoundland

This island province, farthest east in Canada, includes the coast of Labrador and is Canada's newest province. It is rugged, beautiful, and sparsely populated, and has a colorful history that goes back to the Viking days.

THE LAND. Newfoundland, with its 43,359 square miles, and Labrador, almost three times as big, have many dramatic landscapes, especially where the sea dashes against rockbound coast. Along the coast, the land is scalped of trees, since lumber is needed in boats and buildings, and regeneration is slow. Inland, especially in the west and in Labrador, are immense stands of spruce and balsam, poplar and white birch.

The **Cirque Mountain** in northern Labrador is 5,500 feet above sea level, and is the highest point in Newfoundland. Fiords, bays, and small islands add to the province's rugged coastline.

THE CLIMATE. Newfoundland is cool and often windy, with frequent storms typical of the province. The Labrador Current and strong arctic winds are responsible for keeping temperatures around 50–60 degrees in July and from 4–20 degrees in January, coldest readings found in Labrador. Large amounts of snow fall, especially in southern Labrador.

THE PEOPLE. Newfoundland was first discovered by Icelandic Vikings exploring southward around A.D. 1000. But this "land to the west" remained shrouded in legend until 1497, when John Cabot under English commission stumbled upon a "New-found-lande." Island tradition declares Cabot landed at Bonavista, and later dropped anchor in a landlocked harbor he named for St. John the Baptist. His description of waters teeming with fish roused European merchants, and their fleets won more wealth than the conquest of Mexico. Some crews wintered at St. John's, tending lofts of fishing gear, but Newfoundland was regarded merely as "a great ship moored off North America for the convenience of the cod fishery." England planted its flag on the island only in 1583. Sir Humphrey Gilbert called together the shipmasters then in port, and formally claimed the land for Queen Elizabeth I, the first of Britain's overseas possessions. Settlement was erratic, being prohibited at first, then plagued by heavy-handed skippers, and later by skirmishes with French squatters on the south shore. Settlements did grow slowly in coves on the ragged 6,000-mile coastline, "outports" linked only by sea. Residents engaged in fishery didn't bother with the interior of the island. Its forests, boulder barrens, bogs and turbulent rivers held little interest for them. A few Beothuck Indians lived there, but they died out.

Newfoundland won responsible government in 1855, but in 1934, financial difficulties compelled it to return to colonial status under a commission government. This unhappy situation ended in April, 1949, after Newfoundlanders voted for federation with Canada, thus becoming the tenth province of the Dominion.

Isolation preserved Old Country traditions, and Newfoundland speech is flavored with Irish and Devonshire accents. Until the ear is attuned, it may be difficult to understand a man from the outports. In Labrador "the liveyer may fadge to prepare a scoff of lobscouse" means "the man who lives here bustles about to prepare a quick meal of stew."

Little Heart's Ease, Come By Chance, St. Jones Within, Ireland's Eye and Pushthrough are only a few of the evocative place-names. In folksong, too, Newfoundland is richest of Canadian provinces, with such indigenous songs as "Killigrew's Soiree" and the familiar "Squid-Jiggin' Ground." Most of the approximately half-million people live on the Avalon Peninsula, farthest east of the North American continent. Marine Drive links the picturesque fishing villages of Logy Bay, Flatrock, Pouch and Portugal coves.

AGRICULTURE. Small farms, where

farmers grow mainly for their own consumption, dot the landscape, with chief products including hay, oats, potatoes, and a variety of other vegetables. Forestry, a thriving industry, takes up large areas of land.

INDUSTRY. Pulp and paper production in Newfoundland is more valuable to the province's economy than all other areas of manufacturing combined.

Fishing and fish processing is next in importance. Newfoundland is one of the top fishing regions in the world, and the catch includes cod, herring, salmon, and turbot, as well as seals although this has recently been restricted by the government.

Manufacturing of wood products, leather goods and cement, oil refining, mining for iron ore, copper, and gold all add to the economy.

CITIES. St. John's and Corner Brook are the only cities of note in Newfoundland. On the coast of Labrador live less than 5 percent of the province's population.

ST. JOHN'S. Newfoundland's capital and largest city grew up on the mile-long harbor that still provides safe anchorage for white-hulled Portuguese schooners and, in World War II, sheltered naval and merchant ships of all the Allied nations. St. John's population now is around 110,000, and its steep streets have been paved with its increasing prosperity. "Lower Path," a historic trail twisting along the waterfront, grew into busy **Water Street.** Its shops open their front doors to customers, their back doors on private wharves. Little history is visible in St. John's, whose wooden buildings were razed repeatedly in devastating fires. However, old batteries guarding the harbor mouth, **Queen's Own** on **Signal Hill** and **Chain Rock** below, may be visited. In wartime, a chain boom was stretched across the narrows to protect ships within. A stone signal station, **Cabot Tower,** was named as a memorial to the explorer, and is important in the coastal signal service. Here, in 1901, **Marconi** received the first transatlantic wireless message, and in 1919, from St. John's, the English aviators Alcock and Brown made the first daring flight across the Atlantic. At **Heart's Content** in **Trinity** Bay, the first transatlantic cable was landed successfully, later to be joined by many more cables. St. John's is the focus of administration, both secular and religious. Here are old churches and cathedrals, the **Legislative Building, Newfoundland Museum, Gosling Library.** The white buildings of **Pepperell Air Force Base** were the first U.S. military installations outside its own territory.

The largest settlement in the west is **Corner Brook,** an attractive small city of 27,000 inhabitants, centering around the very extensive pulp and paper operations. In little coves and havens of the shore and islands, fishermen work as they have for centuries, making and mending nets in foul weather, splitting and drying cod after a successful haul.

On **Labrador** one of the world's largest electric power projects is under construction at **Churchill Falls.**

Newfoundland is generally reached by car ferry from North Sydney, Nova Scotia. At **Port aux Basques** a narrow-gauge railway and a new highway start their meandering course across the island. Provincial parks and the **Terra Nova National Park** provide campgrounds, and hotels have been built. Other visitors arrive via the international airport at **Gander,** which has air, rail and road connections with the rest of the island. Large American air bases are located at **Argentia** and **Stephenville.** Steamship lines carry passengers from New York, Boston and Halifax, and from Great Lakes ports and Montreal, to St. John's, some calling at fishing and mining "outports" en route. Smaller vessels go up the northern peninsula and the Labrador Coast.

SPORTS AND RECREATION. Eastern brook trout, sea-run squaretails, browns and rainbows are the delight of anglers who "go **trouting.**" Over 100 licensed salmon streams offer excellent fishing for Atlantic salmon. Salt-water **cod-jigging** may be arranged through local fishermen. **Deep-sea fishing** for bluefin tuna has taken world records in recent years. **Hunters** find caribou on the barrens, moose, bear and smaller game in the forests; wildfowling for snipe, ptarmigan and waterfowl is also popular.

SPECIAL EVENTS. Newfoundland has an unusual number of public holidays. **Short motorboat tours** of the harbor are arranged through the Newfoundland Tourist Office. St. John's holds its famed **regatta** first Wednesday in August, on Quidi Vidi Lake.

DINING AND SHOPPING. Newfoundland has a distinctive cookery, though visitors are unlikely to sample it except by request. Fish-and-brewis, salt cod and hardtack soaked overnight, is a staple outport dish, not immediately palatable to newcomers. Cod tongues and cheeks are a delicacy. Seal-flipper pie is still popular, although seal-hunting has greatly diminished.

Crafts made from sealskin, such as paperweights, are interesting buys in Newfoundland. Hooked rugs, hand-knit and hand-embroidered products are of especially high quality.

Prince Edward Island

Completely pastoral, unexciting and relaxing, Prince Edward Island has colors to thrill any artist. Long ago, the Micmac Indians named it "Abegweit" —cradled on the waves—and so it seems to visitors flying from Moncton, New Brunswick, to Summerside or Charlottetown. Below are neat fields, hedged about with dark trees, red roads leading off to inlets of dazzling blue. With its population around 110,000, the island is neither crowded nor lonely.

THE LAND. Prince Edward Island is Canada's smallest province, less than 2,200 square miles, lying offshore from New Brunswick and Nova Scotia in the Gulf of St. Lawrence. Pretty rather than spectacular, the island province has a rolling landscape that nowhere reaches higher than 500 feet.

THE CLIMATE is warm and pleasant, skies are sunny, and temperatures in summer are in the upper sixties. The island's temperatures are actually warmer than the Canadian mainland.

THE PEOPLE. Jacques Cartier, making his first voyage to the New World in 1534, called at several places on this unnamed "low and lovely land," as he described it. Champlain, questing down the St. Lawrence in 1603, stopped long enough to label it Ile St. Jean. The name stuck for two centuries, then was changed to honor the gay Prince Edward who later fathered Queen Victoria. The French had uneven success with their colonization, though Acadians who left Nova Scotia after it became British did better for a while. Less than 20 Acadian families escaped the 1758 general deportation to France—but they have 15,000 descendants on the island today.

The island has scant military history, but it stars as the birthplace of Canada. In 1864, the four Atlantic colonies of Newfoundland, Nova Scotia, Prince Edward Island and New Brunswick agreed to discuss a maritime federation. Politicians from Upper and Lower Canada (Ontario and Quebec now) begged an invitation to the conference, which was held in Charlottetown. With broader vision, they made a startling proposal—political union of all the colonies of British North America. Such a radical suggestion couldn't possibly be accepted all at once, and the decision was reached only at a second meeting in Quebec City. On July 1, 1867, four provinces and the vast northwest territories became the Dominion of Canada. Prince Edward Island held out for six years.

AGRICULTURE. Nearly all the land is under cultivation, so that Prince Edward Island is often called "the Garden of the Gulf," its decomposed sandstone yielding bountiful crops. Many farmers have a sideline as well—lobstering, oyster-farming off his own acres, mink ranching, or raising race horses.

INDUSTRY. Little manufacturing takes place on Prince Edward Island, in part due to the cost of shipping goods to and from the mainland. Whatever industry does exist is based on processing the farm produce and fish. The island is one of the leading lobster and oyster producers in North America.

CITIES. Charlottetown is the only "city" of any size on Prince Edward Island, as most residents live in rural areas and villages.

CHARLOTTETOWN, the capital, often written as "Ch'own," grew up at the confluence of three rivers, where the French, too, built their chief settlement, Port la Joie. A pleasant city of some 18,000 inhabitants, Charlottetown is pretty, gracious and unsophisticated. Three good bathing beaches lie within five minutes' drive of any part of town, two of them in **Victoria Park,** which also contains picnic area, riding trails and **Government House.** A new theater for the performing arts, **Father of Confederation Memorial Center,** as well as the large white Colonial house, residence of the lieutenant governor of the Province, should be visited. Along the park roadway is **Fort Edward Battery,** with grassy earthworks and half a dozen old cannon. Farther along the harbor, some 200 acres have been landscaped as **Fort Amherst National Historic Park,** to include what remains of a fort named for the commander-in-chief of British forces at Louisbourg. With two colleges, two hospitals, government buildings, cathedral and basilica, Charlottetown is a natural hub of island life. The **Provincial Building** in Queen Square contains Confederation Chamber. That handsome room with its historic table and leather-covered chairs is something less than a shrine, but visiting Canadians are gratified to read in bronze lettering that the Fathers of Confederation who once sat here in conference "Builded Better Than They Knew."

A nine-mile ferry trip across Northumberland Strait links Prince Edward Island with New Brunswick, and another, of 14 miles, with Nova Scotia. The big modern train-ferry also carries automotive traffic and passengers.

The great and very real charm of Prince Edward Island is its atmosphere of relaxation, not least on its (literally) endless beaches. Although the island is only 140 miles long, it is so deeply indented as to have 1,100 miles of coastline, mostly sandy. Some 25 miles of beach are included in a **national park,** with an excellent golf course, and a tearoom that was once the home of the author of "Anne of Green Gables."

SPORTS AND RECREATION. **Harness-racing** is a favorite spectator sport on the island, and both Charlottetown and Summerside race tracks are in continuous use throughout the summer. Charlottetown even goes in for night-racing, and the sulkies whirl around the circuit under a battery of floodlights. The **Woodleigh Replicas,** scale models of famous British buildings such as York Minster, Ann Hathaway's cottage and Glamis Castle, form a delightful exhibit out of doors near Kensington.

SPECIAL EVENTS. One of the island's best-known events is the **Lobster Carnival** and **Livestock Exhibition,** held in Summerside in July. Also popular is **Old Home Week** in Charlottetown, taking place in mid-August, which draws harness-racing entries from Canadian and United States' stables. Other occasions to note are the summer arts festival; and the **Provincial Fur Show,** the latter held in Charlottetown in October.

DINING AND SHOPPING. Lobster and other freshly caught seafoods are the specialties of Prince Edward Island. The emphasis is on home cooking—soups, pastries, fresh fruits, and vegetables.

Visitors to the island will find excellent hand-loomed woolens, woodcraft, and other items such as pottery and furs.

Nova Scotia

The most developed of the Atlantic provinces, Nova Scotia has a rich historic background and full facilities for a relaxing seaside vacation. It is a leader in fishing and manufacturing, but has managed to retain its quiet villages, deserted beaches, and atmosphere of calm.

Canada's second smallest province packs considerable variety into some 21,000 square miles. Nova Scotia is a peninsula that is almost an island, plus an island now attached to the mainland. Only a narrow neck of marshland links Nova Scotia with New Brunswick at the Isthmus of Chignecto. Also part of Nova Scotia is **Cape Breton Island**, separated from it by the Strait of Canso. A rocky spine runs the length of the province, ribbing out into innumerable coves and harbors on the Atlantic and tidal inlets on the Bay of Fundy.

THE CLIMATE. Nova Scotia is one of the rainiest provinces in Canada, although showers can be brief, and warm, sunny weather is the rule. Best seasons for coming to Nova Scotia are late spring, summer, and early fall, when excellent hunting can be enjoyed. The seacoast is generally warmer than the interior.

THE PEOPLE. Perhaps the Vikings stopped off, and perhaps Cabot's landfall was actually Cape Breton Island. The records are vague. Unquestionably, Champlain explored the ragged south shore and into the Bay of Fundy in the summer of 1604. The following summer, he helped establish the Port Royal Habitation on the north bank of the Annapolis River. This farm flourished until destroyed in 1613 by marauding Virginians.

During one of the intervals when Acadia belonged to Britain, it acquired the name "Nova Scotia"–New Scotland. For a century French and English squabbled over Acadia, and in 1713, the mainland was finally ceded to Britain. The French kept on making trouble, from Ile St. Jean (Prince Edward Island) and Ile Royale (Cape Breton Island). To hold them in check, the garrison town of Halifax was built on Chebucto Bay, in 1749.

All through the years, the Acadians in Nova Scotia claimed to be neutral, but connived with the French forces. At the insistence of exasperated New Englanders, the British at last took action in 1755. Six thousand stubborn Acadians, still refusing the oath of allegiance, were shipped back to France or south to colonies on the Atlantic seaboard. In 1758, British and New England forces re-took the Fortress of Louisbourg on Cape Breton Island, and this time leveled it. With the end of the Seven Years War, New France became British. Before long, the American colonies revolted, and loyalists were expelled to colonies still under the British flag. Many came to Nova Scotia.

Today, the province's population is around 765,000, most being descendants of the original settlers.

AGRICULTURE. Nova Scotia has a mixture of occupations–mining, industry, fishing and farming. The soil is not very fertile, except around the Bay of Fundy, where the diked lands raise excellent crops. From an agriculture that depended on the sale of apples to Britain, Nova Scotia farmers switched to poultry, cranberry production, and cattle raising. Fishermen have turned from trawling on the Grand Banks to fishing for scallops, lobster and flounder.

INDUSTRY is by far the leading source of income for Nova Scotia. Its steel and iron mills, food-processing plants, and manufacturing facilities contribute over $150 million yearly to the economy. Transportation equipment, pulp and paper, shipbuilding and repair, automobile manufacture, and petroleum refining all add to the wealth of the province.

Mined products, in order of importance, are coal, gypsum, barite, salt, and copper.

CITIES. Halifax, capital of Nova Scotia; Dartmouth, across the harbor from it; and Sydney, located on Cape Breton Island, are the only cities in the province. Many small villages such as Yarmouth, Windsor, and Pictou are especially charming to visit.

CAPE BRETON ISLAND. The **Canso Causeway,** 7,000 feet long, links Nova Scotia with Cape Breton Island. The island is shaped rather like a lobster claw, the interior being the **Bras d'Or Lake.** The big claw contains most of the highlands, and is looped by the spectacular **Cabot Trail,** which begins and ends at **Baddeck,** closely associated with Alexander Graham Bell. Part of the trail runs through the **Cape Breton Highlands National Park,** a tract of moor and beach, golf links and salmon streams. For all its pockets of Acadian French, Cape Breton is predominantly Scottish. The Gaelic language, tartans and bagpipes are in everyday use. Watch for the **Gaelic Foundation** at St. Ann, which promotes the **Mod,** a week of Highland games each August; its **pioneer museum,** with relics of Giant MacAskill; its **weaving school,** which turns out authentic tartans.

The "thumb" of the lobster claw is less hilly, but more historic and more industrial: **Sydney,** with its great steel mills; **Glace Bay,** where coal mines run out far under the sea; **North Sydney,** where the ferry takes off for Newfoundland. On a bleak spit of land poking into the Atlantic are the foundations of the **Fortress of Louisbourg,** and remnants of its bombproof shelters. The museum contains an exact model of the fortress.

HALIFAX was originally built to curb the power of the French at Louisbourg, and has never lost its naval and military traditions. Capital of Nova Scotia, with a population of over 200,000, Halifax is one of the great ports of the world, one of the busiest in Canada, open in winter and of supreme value in wartime. The site chosen in 1749 was a knobby peninsula jutting out into Chebucto Bay, a magnificent body of water protected by an island and with a Narrows that could easily be defended. A garrison town for many decades, Halifax is reminiscent of the elegance and gaiety of those days. **Citadel Hill** is crowned with gray stone fortifications which never fired a hostile shot, and are now crowded with mementos of the past. **St. Paul's Church,** built in 1750, is the oldest Protestant church in Canada, and is still in active use.

Halifax does not live in its past, however. A busy mercantile life goes on along its waterfront and in the narrow sloping streets. Fishery establishments, rail terminals, oil installations bristle on both sides of the Narrows, now linked by the Angus L. Macdonald Bridge. Interesting to visit are **Dalhousie University; Northwest Arm,** narrow reach of salt water much used for boating; **Point Pleasant Park,** 200 acres of forest and heather, containing remains of several forts and a Martello tower; **Public Gardens,** downtown, 18 acres of dazzling flower displays, plus band concerts.

No part of Nova Scotia is very far from the rest, for the province is less than 400 miles long. Just across the peninsula from Halifax is the **Annapolis Valley,** cradle of much Canadian history. The **Port Royal Habitation** has been reconstructed, and its palisades rise only seven miles downstream from **Annapolis Royal.** This is a charming little town, with the historical attraction of **Fort Anne's** green ramparts, old powder magazines and historical museum. A bit farther east, near Wolfville, is **Grand Pré,** with its memorial to Longfellow's fictional Evangeline. Nearby **Windsor** has a blockhouse in the middle of its golf links, and **Haliburton Museum,** home of Canada's first humorous writer. All through this region, the various communities celebrate an unusual number of festivals, natal days and pageants. At the **Bear River Cherry Festival,** one may rent a cherry tree and gorge on fruit. **Cape Blomidon** (blow-me-down) **Lookoff** spreads a panorama of earth, sky and water, while on the shores below, rockhounds can search for agates and amethysts.

The south shore of Nova Scotia is decidedly picturesque with its innumerable bays, channels and islands. **Chester** and **Mahone Bay** are noted among yachtsmen, and treasure-hunters still probe **Oak Island** for the pirate loot of Captain Kidd. **Lunenburg,** once home of the *Bluenose* and other famous sailing schooners, is a busy port, though no longer crowded with masts. **Yarmouth,** where the ferry from Bar Harbor comes in, boasts an ancient stone covered with runic script. Experts have deciphered it as "Leif to Eric raises this monument." Other findings nearby suggest that possibly this may have been the site where Leif the Lucky wintered so long ago. Above Yarmouth, on the St. Mary's shore, French is the main language, and the rare ox may still be seen hauling loads of hay or pulling the plow. In the eastern section of the province, **Truro** is a hub for roads in all directions. Tourists find the road west along **Minas Basin** rewarding. Watch for **Five Islands,** the **Fundy tide, dikes.** A northern road leads from the Isthmus of Chignecto, over maple ridges along Northumberland Strait, to the energetic town of Antigonish, spearhead of the co-operative movement in the Maritimes.

SPORTS AND RECREATION facilities are largely aquatic, with many good bathing beaches, yacht and boating clubs in profusion. There are numerous **golf** courses. There is **hunting** for bear, white-tailed deer, abundant partridge; fresh-water **fishing** for trout and salmon, especially on Cape Breton Island, broadbill swordfishing in Cape Breton waters.

In Halifax, **plays** are performed at the Neptune Theatre, and **concerts** are given in the Public Gardens.

SPECIAL EVENTS. Kentville, **Apple Blossom Festival,** four days end of May; Antigonish, **Highland Games,** two days mid-July; Tatamagouche, **Nova Scotia Festival of Arts and Crafts,** three days early in August; St. Ann, **Gaelic Mod,** second week in August; Lunenburg, **Annual Fishermen's Reunion and Regatta,** five days in mid-September; Church Point, annual **Acadian Festival,** second week in August.

DINING AND SHOPPING. As in the other Atlantic provinces, seafood is the chief specialty of restaurants in Nova Scotia. British desserts such as trifle, and British fish chowder are especially popular. Nova Scotia smoked salmon, served in many countries, had its origins here.

Handicrafts from Nova Scotia—notably ship models, carved driftwood, homespun textiles, and Chédicamp hooked rugs—are considered among the finest in eastern Canada. Handicraft production is encouraged by the provincial government.

New Brunswick

Covered with lush forests, farmland, and waterways, New Brunswick is a seaside province located east of the state of Maine. Its fishing, hunting, and beach facilities are considered to be among the best in Canada.

THE LAND. The rectangular province of New Brunswick covers approximately 28,000 square miles, with a population strung out around the edges. Its interior is deep forests and mountains—an extension of the Appalachian mountain system. New Brunswick has a 750-mile coastline with many bays and coastal islands just offshore. Most of the farmland is found in the valleys of the St. John River (the province's most important) in the southeastern part of New Brunswick.

THE CLIMATE. Warm summers and clear, cold winters are typical of New Brunswick, although differences of 10–15 degrees between the warmer coast and the cooler interior can be found. Snowfall averages close to 100 inches yearly.

THE PEOPLE. The French were the first explorers in New Brunswick. Jacques Cartier cruised along the east coast in 1534, dropping anchor briefly in Miramichi Bay, and reveling in the summer heat of a vast harbor he named the Bay of Chaleur. Samuel de Champlain, King's Geographer, came next, scouting the Fundy shore. By remarkable mischance, only half of his party survived the winter of 1604–05 on a small island in the St. Croix River. However, he had already noted and sketched the mouth of a great river, and named it for St. John the Baptist. The river mouth was a natural site for fortification, with half a dozen rocky hills, and in time one fort after another was piled up there.

After Acadia was ceded to Britain in 1713, New Englanders came to New Brunswick. Following the American War of Independence, thousands of loyalists chose to move to this northern wilderness. The newcomers had balked at revolution, but they were determined not to be ruled from Halifax. So the colony of New Brunswick was established in 1784, and in 1867 it became a province of the Dominion of Canada.

With no particular line of demarcation, the population of over 620,000 is about evenly composed of Anglo-Saxon in the south and west, Acadian French to the north and east.

AGRICULTURE. Potatoes, apples, milk and dairy products, beef cattle, and hogs are chief products of New Brunswick. The farms average 186 acres in size, and bring in over $23 million yearly. Lobster and other seafood are important catches for New Brunswick fishermen.

INDUSTRY. Lumbering and wood processing in New Brunswick goes back to the seventeenth century when trees were cut for ship-building. Today more income is received from this industry than from all of agriculture combined, and pulp, paper, and other processing plants can be found in many large towns.

Recently discovered deposits of copper, lead, silver, and zinc have led to a mining boom (value of production increased to ten times its original value in five years). Coal, natural gas, and petroleum are also mined.

CITIES. Fredericton, the capital, and Saint John, the largest city, are the province's two best-known cities. But many of the small towns, found in the scenic countryside, are charming and should be visited.

FREDERICTON, the capital, is a quiet city of elm-lined streets, located at a bend of the St. John River. **Legislative buildings,** the **University of New Brunswick, Christ Church Cathedral** and the new **Beaverbrook Art Gallery** are its most notable structures. Loyalists had replaced Acadian settlers when St. Anne's Point was selected for the seat of government. In 1845, the town became a city by royal edict.

SAINT JOHN (population 100,000) is a city of history and character. In winter its ice-free harbor shares with Halifax the traffic shut out of the ice-filled St. Lawrence River. Here, too, is the ferry to Digby, Nova Scotia, to St. Andrews and Grand Manan Island. The history of Saint John begins with Champlain's sketchbook. Acadian fur trader Charles de la Tour built his fort where the city of Saint John now stands. When New France became British, some settlers from New England established themselves at the mouth of the river, augmented later by United Empire Loyalists. In 1785, Parr Town was incorporated as Saint John, the oldest incorporated city in Canada. Located on a peninsula bounded by two rivers and the Bay of Fundy, it is a city of magnificent views. The excellent **New Brunswick Museum** has exhibits of history and modern design. A **Martello tower,** built to defend the harbor during the War of 1812, has old firearms, loyalist relics, and handicrafts.

In New Brunswick, the world's highest tides flood past the herring weirs of Grand Manan up the **Bay of Fundy.** At St. John River, the salt tide forces back the fresh water pouring over an 11-foot drop, and the surging water boils upstream over the rocky barrier at the **Reversing Falls Bridge.** Rolling up the ever-narrowing Fundy Bay, the tide funnels into every bare inlet. It rises quickly on the pebbly beaches of **Fundy National Park,** 80 square miles of seaside playground, then rushes past sandstone "sentinels" at **Hopewell Cape,** and up the Petitcodiac River. A clock in **Tidal Bore Park,** Moncton, indicates the time to expect the crest of muddy water, a foot to four feet high.

Moncton is a bustling town, almost equally French- and English-speaking, and now outstripping Saint John in commerce. A few miles outside town is the **Magnetic Hill,** an optical illusion where the stream beside the road appears to run uphill, as does a car left in neutral gear, apparently against all laws of gravity.

East of Moncton is **Shediac,** where there are long beaches fronting on the Gulf, the road to Cape Tormentine and the ferry to Prince Edward Island. Southeast is Sackville, where the towering spikes of the Canadian Broadcasting Corporation's transmitters beam radio programs overseas. This **Isthmus of Chignecto,** with its diked haylands, was the home of many Acadians long ago, before they were moved to Louisiana. Of several forts in the area, **Fort Beauséjour's** embankments and remains have been established as a national historic park, and an excellent museum overlooks the windy Tantramar marshes.

North of Moncton, the road skirts the Gulf shore, passing through French fishing, lumbering and mining villages up to the Bay of Chaleur with its pulp mills.

A high lonesome road leads from the Bay of Chaleur at Campbellton across country to the valley of the St. John River at St. Leonard, where the river forms the boundary between New Brunswick and the state of Maine. Largely French-speaking, **Edmundston** is notable for its paper manufacture, **St. Leonard** for its hand-weaving, **Grand Falls** for its waterfall and hydroelectric power, and seed potato business. The very impressive **Beechwood hydroelectric power plant** farther south and its dam have changed the appearance of the Tobique River near Perth.

At **Hartland** is the longest covered bridge in the world, 1,282 feet, one of more than 200 still in use in New Brunswick. It is now overshadowed, though not altogether replaced, by a concrete bridge upstream, where the **Trans-Canada Highway** crosses the River St. John. Watch for the falls and gorge at **Pokiok.** At several points in the river valley, roads branch off to the Maine boundary. At Long's Creek, Highway 3 leads to the lake country in the southwest corner of the province, and gives access to **St. Andrews-by-the-sea** and the **Fundy Isles,** a famed resort region.

SPORTS AND RECREATION facilities include **boating** on bay, gulf, inland lakes and rivers; **golf; fishing** for trout and salmon in licensed rivers (many hunting and fishing lodges dot the wilderness, and a dozen game refuges form a wildlife reservoir); **hunting** for deer, bear (moose are protected), woodcock, partridge and black duck.

SPECIAL EVENTS. The year's biggest event is held on May 18, and commemorates the landing of American Loyalists in New Brunswick in 1783. Another special occasion is **Dominion Day,** July 1, celebrated throughout the province. A lobster festival in Shediac in mid-August and **National Acadian Day,** also in mid-August, are interesting for visitors.

DINING AND SHOPPING. Lush berries served with cream; fresh lobster, salmon, and oysters; and a special early-season green vegetable called "fiddlehead" are among the dining specialties in New Brunswick.

For the shopper, woven tartans and a variety of handicrafts are the best buys. In York County, potters, weavers, and jewelry and cabinet makers often open their studios to visitors.

Quebec

French origins, language, food, and customs distinguish Quebec from the British-oriented provinces of Canada.

Especially popular with tourists, Quebec gives a "little bit of France" to North America.

THE LAND. Quebec, largest of Canada's provinces, with nearly 600,000 square miles, reaches 1,200 miles north from Montreal to Hudson Strait. As in other provinces, settlement huddles in the south, and only scattered Eskimo and Indian encampments and trading posts are found along the northern coastline. The interior is bleak even for Montagnais and Naskapi Indians. The province of Quebec is rocky, except for occasional clay belts south of James Bay and the St. Lawrence Lowlands. (The St. Lawrence River is the largest, most important body of water in the province.) The Laurentian Mountains are rounded granite hills, oldest rocks in America, scoured and scored by long-gone glaciers. Most of the country is covered with spruce forest, dwindling in the north into "little sticks" and reindeer moss.

THE CLIMATE. For all its range of latitude, the climate differs only in degree throughout the land mass. It is sharply cold in winter with dazzling sunny days, followed by a chilly spring and hot short summer. The best seasons for a visit are spring and fall, when temperatures are moderate, and skies are usually clear.

THE PEOPLE. Jacques Cartier, the seaman from St. Malo, under commission from King Francis, was the first to set up the French flag in the New World. Having explored the Gulf of St. Lawrence in 1534, the following year he explored up the St. Lawrence River until rapids barred his way at the Indian village of Hochelaga, now Montreal.

Samuel de Champlain founded a settlement in 1608, which has grown into the city of Quebec. He ruled well, made long trips through the country, made friends with some Indians and enemies of others, brought priests from France for the comfort of his colonists and the conversion of the Indians. After him came governors, intendants and bishops, some with the good of the colony at heart, some for private gain. New France throve during a period with Frontenac as governor, Talon as intendant, and Laval as bishop. The fertile land along the St. Lawrence was settled gradually through disbanded regiments, bride ships, and missionary devotion. The feudal system was brought over from France. Local gentry or court favorites received large land grants, and settlers paid their rental in produce and services.

Some young men didn't care for this life, and became bushrangers, roving with Indians, even though the Church frowned. They proved invaluable to the development of the fur trade, which was New France's only source of cash for some years. In 1610, Henry Hudson, exploring for a passage to China, discovered instead the great inland sea of Hudson Bay, and there perished through mutiny. Other European explorers came after him, without finding much to interest them in its bleak shores. Only in 1669 did the North become important. Two French fur traders, Radisson and Groseilliers, being snubbed by New France and France, took their knowledge of new fur lands to the English court. After one successful voyage, the Hudson's Bay Company was formed in 1670, and naturally drew away some of the fur that formerly went to the St. Lawrence. The small battles in Hudson Bay were part of the greater struggle between the mother countries of France and England, and at times, all but one of the English posts were in French hands.

The conquest of Canada was part of that struggle, and after Quebec was taken in battle, New France became British by the treaty of 1763. By the terms of capitulation, Canada kept its boundaries, its French language, freedom of worship, educational system and civil code. This was considered generous by both sides, and the French proved loyal when American Revolutionary forces captured Montreal and attempted to take Quebec in 1775. Again in the War of 1812, American troops using the Lake Champlain-

Richelieu River route were repulsed at Châteauguay. For some years, there was considerable friction between the French of Lower Canada and the English settlers of Upper Canada. However, by confederation in 1867, they became the provinces of Quebec and Ontario, both subject to the larger powers of the Dominion of Canada.

The great majority of Quebec's 6 million people are French-speaking and Roman Catholic. Most city people are bilingual, and the visitor soon acquires a smattering of French if only from signs around.

AGRICULTURE. Milk and dairy products, hogs, beef cattle, poultry, and a variety of fruits and vegetables come from Quebec, where farm products are valued at more than $270 million yearly. Quebec is a leading producer of maple syrup and is an important forest and lumber supplier for North America.

INDUSTRY. Quebec is one of the leading industrial regions on the continent, with many plants concentrated in the Montreal area. No North American region produces as much electric power as Quebec.

Metal processing, pulp and paper, and food and beverages are the largest industries, with all manufacturing turning out over $3 billion in goods yearly. Within these three large areas of industry, products include aluminum, copper, newsprint, paperboard, soft drinks, cheese, and alcoholic beverages.

Mining, led by asbestos, copper, iron, and zinc, is valued at more than $255 million yearly.

CITIES. Quebec is an urban province, as close to three-fourths of the population lives in and around the cities. In them, as well as the small towns, the influence of France can be seen in the buildings and parks, felt in the way of life of the people, and tasted in the French food served in many restaurants.

MONTREAL. Located 160 miles west is Montreal, Canada's largest city, and second-largest French-speaking city in the world. About a third of Quebec's population is crowded into Greater Montreal, which has a population of over 2.5 million. One thousand miles from the Atlantic, Montreal is a great seaport, with 13 miles of docks, in use eight months of the year.

The city is located on Montreal Island at the junction of the Ottawa and the St. Lawrence rivers, and where the Lachine Rapids blocked Cartier's advance upriver in 1535. Champlain portaged his canoes around the rapids in 1613, but in 1821, a small 14-foot canal cut past them. Now the new deeper Lachine Canal forms part of the St. Lawrence Seaway. In 1642, a courageous band of settlers, nuns, and soldiers pushed upriver to the island with the ancient volcanic cone, Mount Royal, rising from the trees. They built their little wooden fort on the slope, and the settlers laid out their fields. In spite of repeated Iroquois attacks, the settlement grew to a small fur trading town named Ville Marie, and later to the great metropolis of Montreal.

The large square, **Place d'Armes,** with its monument to Maisonneuve, was a battlefield in 1644. Nearby is the handsome big **Notre Dame Church.** Down at the waterfront is the smaller, much older church of **Marguerite Bourgeoys, Notre-Dame de Bonsecours,** the sailors' church. Nearby is the famous **Bonsecours Market. St. Sulpice Seminary** and the two remaining round towers of their fort (1694) are the oldest buildings in Montreal. Near Bonsecours is **Château de Ramezay,** its three-foot-thick walls built in 1705. It was occupied by General Montgomery and the Revolutionary forces when the Americans captured Montreal in 1775, and was Benjamin Franklin's headquarters when he tried to persuade Canada to become the fourteenth state in the Union. The Château is now an interesting historical museum. From there one can see **Ile Ste. Hélène,** which Champlain named for his wife. It is reached by car or bus over the **Jacques Cartier Bridge,** and has an old log blockhouse built for defense against the Americans in the War of 1812. The island is a city park, with excellent restaurants, theaters, and a ringside view of the busy harbor. Excursion boats load at **Victoria Pier,** near Bonsecours Market, for a 25-mile trip around the waterfront.

The forested summit of **Mount Royal** overlooks the city that has grown up all around the base and halfway up its sides. On the other side of the mountain is the dome of the famous **St. Joseph Oratory,** a shrine to lay Brother André, once a janitor there. Across the street, in the **Musée Historique,** one may find a remarkably lifelike wax figure of Brother André, aged 92, among other notable figures in the history of Montreal. Two universities, famous hospitals, huge commercial enterprises, "Man and His World," the largest permanent exhibition anywhere, a new subway system, suburbs that may be wholly French or wholly English-speaking, all give Montreal a character of its own. Tawdry in some ways, sparkling in others, the despair of sober-sided citizens and the delight of visitors, Montreal is more wide open than any other Canadian city. It has many fine restaurants, good hotels, sidewalk cafés in summer, and a liberal attitude toward liquor. There are facilities for boating, golf, tennis, racing, football, baseball, and hockey.

Beginning about 30 miles north of Montreal, the Laurentian Mountains form a playground almost 100 miles wide by 50 miles deep. On the western fringe of the region is **Gatineau Park,** opposite Ottawa, and the playground for Canada's capital. The Laurentians, a rolling forested country with many little lakes and numerous hamlets, is one vast resort area. Many hotels are open year round. In summer, the emphasis is on fishing, golf, water sports including water skiing, summer theater and artist workshops. In autumn, attention turns to hunting—deer, partridge, ducks. The Laurentians are buried in snow from December to Easter, and are just as vividly alive then as in summer. Ski tows and ski schools proliferate, and there is a vast network of well-marked ski trails, including the 100-mile Maple Leaf Trail. Many of these resorts are highly sophisticated, but there is accommodation for every purse as there are slopes for all degrees of skill. There are week-long winter festivals, torchlight parades, and horse races on frozen lakes.

Lying south and east of Montreal is a plain with sudden mountains and long narrow valleys, which rise into hardwood country, Les Bois Francs, and the Appalachian Mountains. The Richelieu River flows northward from Lake Champlain, once providing a highway for Iroquois war parties, and later for liberating Americans. Two national historic parks stand as reminders, **Fort Chambly,** and **Fort Lennox** on an island in the river. The waterway is still navigable, thanks to canals, and enthusiastic boaters can take their craft from the St. Lawrence through into the Hudson River and the Atlantic. Farther east from Montreal is a resort region much favored by English-speaking Montrealers and American visitors. The resort life around **Lakes Memphremagog** and **Brome** is quite delightful.

QUEBEC CITY is the capital of Quebec Province, and Canada's most romantic city. It is a seaport, loaded with three-and-a-half centuries of history. For Quebec is the only walled city north of Mexico, and has Old World charm along with its practical everyday factories. Quebec's story begins with Cartier's arrival in 1535, when his three sailing vessels appeared as "winged canoes" to the Indians. Donnacona, chief of the Indian village of Stadacona, welcomed the white men, and urged them to stay. When Cartier spoke of ascending the river, Donnacona warned of dreadful beings, and even staged an attack of demons. The French went anyway, but they wintered at Stadacona. The village had vanished when Champlain arrived in 1608, but it was a good site for a settlement, and Champlain built his little Habitation close to shore under the towering Cape Diamond, and his wooden fort on top.

That is still the division of the city—Lower Town with its docks and factories and very narrow streets; Upper Town with its crenelated walls and gates; and the modern city which spreads back through the countryside, both on the heights and on the flats beside the St. Charles River. Unlike most Canadian cities, Quebec's most interesting features are crowded together, compressed into a relatively small area which may easily be covered on foot, though preferably not all in one day. The simplest and pleasantest way to explore Quebec is to take one segment at a time, map in hand, either on foot or rolling slowly along in a horse-drawn calèche.

Since history began in **Lower Town,** it is simplest to start there. Several streets slope down from the walled Upper Town to the wide thoroughfares and narrow old streets of Lower Town. That isn't a contradiction, for the margins of the St. Lawrence and St. Charles rivers have been built out since Champlain's time, so that the old streets of the Colonial period contrast with the heavy traffic on the truck routes. The historic part of Lower Town is immediately below the walls. From the **Rue des Remparts,** with its fine view over harbor and city, a break in the walls opens for Côte de la Canoterie, which leads down into **Sous-le-Cap,** reputedly the narrowest street in North America.

The narrow lane jogs into **Sault-au-Matelot,** where a tablet marks the spot where General Montgomery fell and Benedict Arnold was wounded on New Year's Eve, 1775. Another jog leads into **Notre Dame Street** and **Place Royale.** Here is the old (1688) church of **Notre Dame des Victoires,** its main altar carved like a fort. This is historic ground, where Champlain built his first little church, the original market-place of the settlement, and his two-story Habitation. Sous le Fort Street leads into **Petit-Champlain Street,** with its old houses, including the one occupied by Louis Joliet, the explorer. An iron staircase, **"Breakneck Steps,"** leads upward to **Côte de la Montagne** and to Upper Town. An easier way up is by incline elevator, through **Joliet's house,** to Dufferin Terrace above.

Upper Town was well-defended by the cliffs of Cape Diamond, and the low walls surmounting them. The plains to the west needed a wall 18 feet high. Even within the walls the ground is far from level, and the streets run together in a confusing way. **Château Frontenac,** a hotel built like a glamorous castle, stands on the site of Champlain's little fort and of Frontenac's Château St. Louis, the governor's residence. Château Frontenac is a landmark no one can misplace. In front of it stretches **Dufferin Terrace,** a boardwalk with a splendid view out over Lower Town and the St. Lawrence River, and the south shore, including the town of Lévis and its old battlements. In winter, the western end of the terrace is transformed into a toboggan slide. Immediately east of Château Frontenac is **Place d'Armes,** where horse-drawn calèches wait to carry sightseers around, and their drivers to tell stories in French-Canadian accents and with French-Canadian drollery.

One pleasant loop is to proceed up **Rue St. Louis,** passing the **Palais de Justice** (Court House of French Renaissance architecture). Left, at No. 23, is the **Duke of Kent house,** former residence of Queen Victoria's father, who was stationed there 1791–94; in this building the capitulation of Quebec was signed after the Battle of the Plains of Abraham. Right, a delightful old house built in 1677, with high, steep roof, is often wrongly referred to as Montcalm's headquarters. A jog to the right brings one to the **Ursuline Convent** grounds, covering seven acres. The convent, founded in 1639, is certainly among the oldest educational institutions for girls on the continent. In the chapel is the skull of General Montcalm. A little farther along the street, No. 6 is believed to be the narrowest house in North America, and just over 100 years old.

Turn onto **Rue des Jardins** (a reminder of Jesuit gardens) and to the right is the **Anglican Cathedral of the Holy Trinity,** with quaint headstones in the churchyard, and locked pews and a royal box inside. Left is the **Hotel de Ville** (city hall), its park adorned with a statue of Louis Hébert, the Paris apothecary who was also Champlain's

Golden Gate Bridge, San Francisco, California

Disneyland, California

Mount Rainier, Washington

Heart Lake in Big Horn Crags, Idaho

Crater Lake, Oregon

Astoria Column,
Astoria, Oregon

Alaska's famous Northern Lights

Dogteam racing in Alaska

friend. Hébert became Canada's first farmer, and this monument marks the location of his farmhouse. Turning right, you come to the complex of the **Basilica of Notre Dame,** 1647, the **Cardinal's Palace,** and the buildings occupied for 224 years by the **Quebec Seminary** and by the **Laval University.** (The university has modern buildings on the outskirts of the city now.)

Nearby is the **Musée Historique,** a waxworks museum of Canadian and American history. Opposite the Basilica is **Upper Town postoffice,** with the Golden Dog stone as its lintel. The dog gnawing a bone is a reminder of the long antagonism between the original builder and the infamous Intendant Bigot. Continue strolling past the break in the walls to **Rue des Remparts,** with its ancient cannon pointed over the river. Forming part of the walls, to the west is the **Citadel** on the highest point of Cape Diamond. An old French fortress, it was rebuilt by the British in 1823, and in 1943 was used by Roosevelt, Churchill and Mackenzie King of Canada for their famous Quebec Conference. Officially the Citadel is the Quebec residence of the governor-general of Canada, and is still garrisoned by the Canadian Army. Most parts may be visited by conducted parties.

Only a square mile of Upper Town lies within city walls, and less than half of Quebec City is located on the heights. Three gateways lead through the walls—the much-photographed **Porte St. Louis, Kent Gate** and **Porte St. Jean.** Porte St. Louis opens to the **Legislative Buildings,** set in green lawns, and to the **Plains of Abraham** (Champs de Bataille). The battlefield is now a park, where the fate of Quebec was fought out in 1759, and where Montcalm and Wolfe fell. A monument honors both French and English generals—but the lettering is in Latin to avoid any charge of favoritism. Look down over the steep cliff-side to **Wolfe's Cove,** where the British troops landed.

The sloping **Rue de la Fabrique** is a street of shops leading from the heights down into the main shopping district of the city, **Rue St. Jean.** St. Jean disperses traffic to the Beauport shore north of the St. Charles River, to the Isle of Orleans and west to Montreal.

Six miles east of the city, a graceful bridge soars over the north channel of the St. Lawrence to the **Isle of Orleans.** The island is only 20 miles long by 5 wide, but is such a notable example of old New France that it's worth a visit. Each of the half dozen parishes has a church noted for carving, for its bells, or for its history. Several old manor houses, especially **Manoir Genest,** bear cannon balls in their woodwork, souvenirs of the conquest. Any number of old farmhouses with swooping eaves have a gallery across the front, a false chimney at one end, and a windmill in the distance. Like Quebec City, the architecture of Ile d'Orléans is protected by law. **Ste. Pétronille** boasts a hotel and beach. Near the landward end of the bridge are the beautiful **Montmorency Falls,** dropping 274 feet from the cliffs like a bridal veil. Some 20 miles downriver from Quebec City is the famous shrine of **Ste. Anne de Beaupré,** a pilgrimage place for three centuries, and claimed as the most famous in North America. Other outstanding resorts along the St. Lawrence River are **Baie St. Paul** and **La Malbaie** (Murray Bay) and **Tadoussac.**

A road north of Quebec City leads to the **Zoological Gardens** (seven miles), and to **Lac Beauport** (ten miles), noted resort in both summer and winter. The road leads on through the vast **Laurentides Provincial Park,** a block of wilderness preserved for vacationing, and noted for its trout streams. This road leads to the Lake St. John country, loops around the lake through agricultural villages and industrial towns to Arvida, and its neighboring towns on the Saguenay River. **Arvida,** a pioneer in "company town" planning, is most attractively laid out. Great hydroelectric plants such as Shipshaw serve the aluminum mill and the pulp industries of other towns. The deep dark Saguenay runs through farming and forest lands, at the foot of immense cliffs, to join the St. Lawrence at

Tadoussac. Steamers from Montreal and Quebec make cruises to historic Tadoussac, and up the Saguenay, one of the pleasantest cruises in Canadian waters. The north shore beyond Tadoussac is very sparsely populated, an empire of pulp-and-paper mills linked by gravel road that now reaches to Seven Islands, the seaport of the great iron ore mines of Ungava and Labrador.

SOUTH SHORE AND GASPÉ. Along the south shore of the St. Lawrence River, the road leads through industrial towns and cities, through old seigneuries and historic parishes. Settlement seems almost continuous, with towns and villages as thick as beads on a string. Many French-Canadian families have summer homes in villages along the **St. Lawrence,** where the young people play tennis all day long, or sun on *les plages.* **St. Jean Port Joli** is rightly noted for its woodcarvings, with nearly every family in town engaged in this craft. Rivière du Loup and Rimouski are the only cities along the route. At the village of **St. Flavie** begins **La Gaspésie,** the actual **Gaspé Peninsula,** looped by a scenic highway where beetling precipices alternate with beaches. This is the northern end of the Appalachians, locally called the Shickshocks. Historic Gaspé town is located at the end of the peninsula, a large stone cross now recalling the wooden one erected by Cartier over four centuries ago. Most famous, however, is the charming village of **Percé,** with its pierced rock standing offshore like a ship moored to the land. Across the water is **Bonaventure Island,** whale-shaped, with colonies of gannets nesting on its steep cliffs. The south shore of the Gaspé Peninsula is bounded by the **Baie des Chaleurs** and is less rugged. At the Matapedia River (noted for Atlantic salmon fishing) the road turns northward across the neck of the peninsula, and back to St. Flavie.

SPORTS AND RECREATION. **Tennis** is played almost everywhere and **golf** is nearly as widespread. There is **skiing, snowshoeing, sleigh riding** in winter; **hunting,** particularly in the wild sections of the Laurentians and Gaspé; goose **shooting,** especially near James Bay; sport **fishing** for trout, salmon, and through the ice in winter; duck and partridge shooting in season.

SPECIAL EVENTS. **St. Jean Baptiste Day,** a public holiday, is held on June 24 while the date varies for **Corpus Christi** (Fête Dieu). Quebec City's big event is the **Winter Carnival,** celebrated at a movable date during the three weeks preceding Lent. The Carnival includes dog derby, costume balls, torch-light parades, curlers' bonspiel, ice-cutter races, and the exciting ice-canoe race over the dangerous ice floes of the St. Lawrence. The climax is a grand parade with buffoons and maskers, and with "Bonhomme Carnaval" the lord of all.

DINING AND SHOPPING. Excellent French cuisine can be found throughout Quebec, whether in the large cities or in more rural areas. Canadian pea soup, *cipaté* (hot meat pie), *Pâté de Noël* (famous Christmas dish of turkey, chicken, pork, mushrooms held firm in jelly and enclosed in richly glazed pastry), and *tourtière* (pork pie), are among the favorites.

Handicrafts, after being abandoned for many years, have again become popular and are of excellent quality. Best buys include carved wood, hooked rugs, textiles, ceramics, leatherwork, wrought iron, and other articles. Silver, woodwork, and jewelry are also good buys.

Ontario

With an abundance of resort areas, the longest provincial frontier, and bordering on six of the most populous states, Ontario receives the greatest number of American visitors, who come north for a general holiday, a change of shopping and scenery—including the autumn coloring—many for fishing in summer, and hunting in fall.

Ontario is the manufacturing and farming hub of Canada, and the location of such well-known sights as Niagara Falls and Stratford, where the noted Shakespeare Festival takes place each summer.

THE LAND. Ontario is the second largest of Canada's provinces, with 412,582 square miles. It stretches 1,000 miles from the Ottawa River to the Manitoba border, and from Lake Erie to salt water of Hudson Bay. The very irregular southern shore line is formed by the Great Lakes and their connecting rivers, while the Ottawa forms much of the boundary with Quebec. The province is shaped rather like a sculptured bust—the large head being Northern Ontario, the neck and shoulders, Southern Ontario.

THE CLIMATE. Winter in Ontario is sharply cold and clear, highlighted by sunny days and large quantities of snow. In the south the climate is much milder, therefore attracting more residents and industry. Summers range from cool in the north to hot in Southern Ontario. As much as ten feet of snow falls in the north yearly, but the average for the rest of the province is around seven feet.

THE PEOPLE. Samuel de Champlain's young explorer Étienne Brulé must be credited with seeing most of the Great Lakes first. Champlain followed his trail up the Ottawa in 1615, pushed across Lake Nipissing and down the French River to Lake Huron. That pathway into the wilderness eventually became the beaten highway of the fur brigades. Other French explorers blazed their trails along the lakes. La Salle paddled and portaged along the St. Lawrence River through Lakes Ontario and Erie, then overland into the Mississippi watershed. The trail along the north shore of the lakes was taken by loyalists leaving the new United States of America in 1783.

The first permanent settlement of Ontario, other than the Indians, began after the American War of Independence, with the coming of the United Empire loyalists to the unoccupied land beyond the Ottawa. These pioneers of British stock spread westward to Lake Ontario and the Niagara Peninsula, Lake Erie and the Detroit River. In 1791, the settlements were established as a separate province, Upper Canada (now Ontario), while Lower Canada (now Quebec) remained French-speaking, with its own code of civil law.

Niagara-on-the-lake (then Newark) was the capital for a few years, when it was considered too close to the American border, and the legislature was moved to Toronto (then called York). Free land was available to all comers, and immigrants came from the British Isles in numbers, with a few coming from the United States. One hundred years later, newcomers from Europe swarmed into Ontario en route to the Canadian West or waiting to get into the United States. Many found jobs and homes in Ontario, and settled down. Its 7,600,000 people form slightly more than a third of the national population.

AGRICULTURE. The rich soil and warm climate of Southern Ontario provide for the growth of a variety of crops, including alfalfa, hay, oats and other field crops; vegetables and fruits; and maple syrup, tapped from gray-barked maples in early spring.

More than two-thirds of Ontario's farm income comes from raising beef and dairy cattle, hogs, horses, and sheep. From these animals come eggs, butter, and milk. Fur farming takes place in the north.

INDUSTRY. Almost half of Canada's manufactured goods come from Ontario, where all goods have an annual value added of over $5.5 billion.

Ontario's chief industry is automobile manufacturing, with plants located in Hamilton, Windsor, Brampton, and other cities. Meat packing, electrical equipment manufacture, flour, feed, knitted and leather goods production are centered in Toronto, the province's major industrial area.

In Hamilton, iron and steel production is the largest industry, while Fort William, in Northern Ontario, is famous for its papermaking facilities. Other industries of importance to Canada are chemicals, oil refining, aircraft and electrical machinery manufacture. Forestry also accounts for a large portion of Ontario's income.

Almost as valuable to the economy as agriculture is mining, with more nickel, gold, and uranium coming from here than any other province.

CITIES. Ontario has more large cities than any other province, largest being Toronto, Ottawa, Hamilton, London, and Windsor. However, equally interesting for the visitor are the less built-up, more rustic regions of Georgian Bay and Northern Ontario.

GEORGIAN BAY. Nearly one-third of Lake Huron is a deep notch in the north shore formed by the Bruce Peninsula and Manitoulin Island, rimmed with sandy beaches and white limestone. **Manitoulin,** "home of the Great Spirit," is the largest fresh-water island in the world, and itself contains 100 sparkling lakes. From the French River south, Georgian Bay itself is ragged with harbors and inlets and channels, and at least 30,000 islands. This maze of islands ranges in size from Manitoulin down to reefs only large enough to hold a summer cottage. **Parry Sound, Point au Baril** and **Honey Harbor** are the main centers in this region.

Champlain named this bay "the Freshwater Sea." A few years later, near present-day Midland, courageous priests established Fort Ste. Marie, headquarters of the ill-fated Jesuit mission to the Hurons. It lasted until 1649, when as a result of the Indian wars, the priests were killed, Fathers Brébeuf and Lalement by torture. Pilgrims come for cures to the **Martyrs' Shrine,** a great church beside the Wye River. The foundations of the old stone fort have been excavated, and an authentic replica of a **Huron Indian village** constructed nearby. Archaeological finds of the region are in several museums, notably **Huronia House** in Midland.

Among many excellent beaches on Georgian Bay, **Wasaga's** unusual width and firmly-packed sand is notable. Its population, nonexistent in winter, bounces up to 65,000 in summer. In addition to sun-bathing, water-skiing and swimming in Lake Huron, there is the Nottawasaga River curving back of the beach. Here is **Museum Park,** where stands the hull of the British schooner *Nancy,* sunk in the War of 1812. Nearby **Penetanguishene** has an old fort, naval headquarters during that war, and rudder and hull of the warship *Tecumseh.* From nearby **Port McNicoll,** passenger ships carry travelers north to **Sault Ste. Marie,** through the locks and on to the head of **Lake Superior.** Excursion boats run from several ports in summer, notably a line from Owen Sound which circles Georgian Bay. At Tobermory, tip of Bruce Peninsula, a ferry crosses to Manitoulin Island.

HAMILTON AND NIAGARA FALLS. West from Toronto, and by heavy construction almost adjoining it, is **Hamilton,** the busy industrial "steel city of Canada." Its large deep harbor is valued by freighters. Especially interesting are the **Royal Botanical Gardens** on the outskirts of the city.

The **Queen Elizabeth Way** skirts around Hamilton, and the **Burlington Skyway** arches over its narrow harbor mouth, both on their way to the **Niagara Peninsula.** This famous fruit belt is a sea of blossoms in May and June, although orchards are being squeezed out by industry. This is a historic frontier, with several old forts manned in summer by high school boys in the scarlet uniforms of a bygone day. A floral clock at Queenston dramatizes the hydroelectric power generated at the nearby falls. The town of **Niagara Falls** is still the "honeymoon town." Visitors should see the **Oakes formal garden;** take the *Maid of the Mist* trips to the foot of the falls; the trip down behind the curtain of water; the Spanish aerial cable car trip over the whirlpool. The Niagara River eats its way back upstream a little each year, crumbling off the rocky lip as it crashes down more than 160 feet into its gorge. To the west, roughly paralleling the river, is the 25-mile **Welland Ship Canal.** It is a dramatic moment at the twin flight locks of **Thorold** to watch one freighter rising up through the locks and meeting another on its way down.

Beyond the Niagara Peninsula is the arrowhead of Ontario, the wedge between Lakes Erie and Huron, the richest soil of the province and the "sun parlor" of Ontario. The white sand beaches of both lakes have had a strong tourist appeal for many years. In recent years, **Storybook Gardens** has been opened near London, a child's wonderland of nursery rhyme scenes and characters. More important, the little town of **Stratford** on the Avon River has won fame with its Stratford Festival, a summer of Shakespearean plays, music, ballet and films. Considered Canada's leading contribution to the arts, Stratford's Festival is subsidized by the government.

NORTHERN ONTARIO. Lake Nipissing and the French River at the "neck" of the province form the rough division between Northern and Southern Ontario. The rocky northern portion of the province is densely forested, laced by innumerable lakes and rivers, fine country for fishing, hunting and canoeing, but only occasionally suited to agriculture, as in the Clay Belts. A number of Indians make a living by trapping in the northern woods, and by guiding hunters and fishermen.

North Bay on Lake Nipissing is a pivot of transportation lines—railway and highway west to Sudbury's nickel mines and to Sault Ste. Marie's steel mill and locks. Through North Bay runs a transcontinental railway and highway, while the Ontario Northland Railway has its head offices here. From North Bay, the Ontario Northland and Highway 11 strike north to the beautiful Timagami region of interlocking lakes and portages. **Lake Timagami** is dotted with over 1,200 islands. North lies the Clay Belt and the gold and silver mining district. At Cochrane, the road turns west while the railway continues north to Moosonee at the foot of James Bay. The mud flats of James Bay are noted among moose-hunters, and many Indian guides live at Moose Factory. The old log smithy here is believed to be the oldest building in Ontario, at the Hudson's Bay Company post.

The highway west from North Bay skirts the North Channel of Lake Huron, a vacation country of spruce, rocks and water, a description true of the entire **District of Algoma.** At **Sault Ste. Marie** look for a steel plant, paper mill, ferry to Sault Ste. Marie, Michigan; rapids on the St. Mary's River, locks on both sides of the river, the tiny remnant of the first "canoe" lock built in 1797, Hudson's Bay Company blockhouse of 1842. "The Soo" is a terminus of the Canadian Pacific Railway and starting point for the Algoma Central Railway, which winds north for 300 miles. Algoma is ruggedly beautiful, its scenery considered the finest east of the Rockies. The **Trans-Canada Highway,** too, runs along this east coast of Lake Superior, giving access to **Superior Provincial Park** at Agawa, to unexcelled hunting and fishing country. The highway hugs the shore most of the way from Sault Ste. Marie to Fort William and Port Arthur. Lake Nipigon, deep and cold and remote, pours its river down over cliffs to Lake Superior, its hydroelectric energy harnessed on the way. Fishing camps have sprung up in this region, along highways and railways and on lakes reached by airplane.

The twin cities of **Fort William** and **Port Arthur** form the gateway into Northwestern Ontario, whether one arrives by boat, plane, train or car. Only a small creek separates the two cities, which have grown together on drained marshland. Both have docks thrust out into **Thunder Bay.** One may watch grain ships loading at the towering concrete elevators, freighters loading red iron at the ore docks, rolls of newsprint being hoisted aboard a "laker." Behind the cities rise the strange flat-topped hills characteristic of this region. Mount McKay behind Fort William also guards the city's pure water supply. Out from Port Arthur to the north is the remarkable **Ouimet Canyon,** a gash between precipitous straight-sided mountains. **Orient Bay** and **Red Rock** are dramatically lovely, while **Pie Island** and **Sleeping Giant** are features of Thunder Bay.

Westward from the lakehead cities, beyond Kakabeka Falls, the road forks, the southern prong pushing into iron ore country and to **Quetico Provincial Park.** No cottages or resort lodges have been allowed in its nearly 2,000 square miles.

The other fork of the road, the Trans-Canada Highway, continues west, with occasional spurs of road leading north or south to settlements and lakes and sandy beaches known to only a few. One side road leads north to **Sioux Lookout,** to the lovely beaches of **Lake Minnitaki,** and the great irregular waters of **Lac Seul.** At the highway, **Eagle Lake** stretches a vast sheet of water near Vermilion, and is noted for its muskellunge fishing as much as for its beauty. **Dryden** is not just a paper mill, but a center for hunting and fishing camps as well. In the extreme west of the province is **Lake of the Woods,** with its 14,000 islands, and Kenora at its outlet. **Kenora** is a resort town unabashed, a center for hundreds of smaller lakes and more islands, and the base for chartered flights into remote fishing camps. There are boat excursions throughout the summer.

OTTAWA, capital city of Canada with over 525,000 people, grew up from a construction camp where the Rideau River falls into the Ottawa, and the Gatineau River flows down from the Laurentians opposite. It is a very beautiful setting, and Ottawa is gradually beautifying itself to keep pace. Furs brought the first commerce to the regions. Around 1800, a shrewd Yankee, Philemon Wright of Massachusetts, saw the possibilities of the lumber industry in the Ottawa valley. He settled in Hull, across the river from Ottawa, and both the town and Mr. Wright prospered. Ottawa did not exist until 1826, when the Royal Engineers came to build a canal linking the Ottawa River with Lake Ontario, and Lieutenant-Colonel John By saw the job completed. The settlement took his name. During the mid-nineteenth century, the two provinces of Canada squabbled constantly, not least over which city should become the capital. Bytown quietly changed its name to the more euphonious Ottawa, and presented itself as a candidate for the honor. Queen Victoria chose unknown Ottawa for the capital, in 1857. The choice was so bitterly opposed that it wasn't until 1865 that proclamation fixed the capital permanently at Ottawa.

The **Parliament Buildings** of pointed Gothic style in cut stone rise across from the rocky Nepean Point overlooking the Ottawa River. **Royal Canadian Mounted Police** stand on guard, and conducted tours go through the buildings every weekday. The **Peace Tower,** with its Memorial Chamber, Book of Remembrance, and peal of 53 bells, is noteworthy. Directly across Wellington Street is the large **U. S. Embassy.** Downstreet is **Confederation Square** with the somber beauty and dignity of the war memorial. Then the bridge over the **Rideau Canal** with its eight watery steps down to the Ottawa River, and **Bytown Museum** beside it. A very pleasant launch trip begins under the bridge, a tour of the Rideau Canal as it winds through the city between landscaped banks, beautiful driveways, under arched bridges. The spring flowering bulbs draw visitors from far away to see the unforgettable sight. There are also water cruises on the Ottawa River.

Château Laurier, rising beside the Rideau Canal, is the starting point for many bus tours of the city. Watch for **Dominion Archives; Royal Mint,** various embassies; the new city hall on Green Island above the Rideau Falls; the **prime minister's residence; Rideau Hall,** residence of the governor-general of Canada; **Rockcliffe Park,** with flowers all-year-round and acres of spring-flowering bulbs in naturalistic plantings; lookouts over the Ottawa River and Laurentian Mountains. The return trip crosses the Rideau River, passes **Laurier House,** home of Prime Ministers Laurier and later Mackenzie King; **Ottawa University; Laurier Bridge** over the Rideau Canal; and past the **National Museum.** The tour continues along **The Driveway** skirting the Rideau Canal to **Dow's Lake;** the arboretum at the **Central Experimental Farm;** then back along Wellington Street, past embassies and the Parliament Buildings. A delightful drive is to cross the **Champlain Bridge** as it hops from island to island across the Ottawa, drive east through Hull, and cross back into Ottawa over the **Chaudière Bridge** that spans the **Chaudière Falls.** The chief bridges between the cities are the **Alexandra Bridge** near the Parliament Building, and the new **MacDonald-Cartier Bridge.** Many citizens of Ottawa take the scenic **Gatineau Parkway** to **Gatineau Park** in Quebec. The Park makes up a section of the Federal District and is known for its lakes, hills, and trails.

The Rideau River winds through the city of Ottawa to fall curtain-like over a precipice into the Ottawa River. It drains the lovely Rideau lakes, and forms part of the Rideau Canal System. Lakes, rivers and canal-cuts stretch more than 120 miles from the Ottawa River to Lake Ontario. It was originally constructed as a military measure, so that gunboats could go from the lower St. Lawrence to Lake Ontario without running the narrow international waterway, where cannon could menace them from the south shore. A blockhouse stood guard at **Merrickville,** and is still in fine condition. At Kingston, **Fort Henry** protected the outlet of the canal, and even today "redcoats" in the British uniform of a century ago march in parade and fire ancient cannon.

The gray limestone city of **Kingston** is noted for **Queen's University** and the **Royal Military College,** Canada's equivalent of "West Point." In the St. Lawrence narrows below Kingston are the **Thousand Islands,** with summer homes, picnic sites and boat excursions. From Cornwall, special buses carry visitors around locks, powerhouse, dams, and parkways of the **St. Lawrence Seaway.** The **Long Sault Parkway** is a scenic new causeway linking a series of islands formed by the new lake. A large park has been developed to include **Upper Canada Village,** an outdoors museum of historic buildings.

TORONTO is the provincial capital for legislation and education, and the national center for finance and industry. With over two million inhabitants, the city stretches far along Lake Ontario, its harbor protected by low sandy islands. Streets and avenues spread back over an ancient lake bed, and over prehistoric beaches cut by rivers and ravines which are the city's most attractive natural feature. Canada's first subway runs north-south, with a second subway handling east-west traffic.

Big hotels with facilities for conventions, smart specialty shops, and immense department stores make Toronto much like any big American city. However, the view from the thirty-fourth floor of the Bank of Commerce shows a jungle of trees, with roofs poking up through the greenery. Wide thoroughfares stretch north from Yonge Street all the way to Lake Simcoe, according to the original plan. Broad University Avenue moves north, splits around the **Parliament Buildings** in **Queen's Park,** rejoins at the **Royal Ontario Museum.** The museum is noted for its exceptionally fine Chinese collection, part of it out-of-doors. This is the cultural heart of a highly commercial city, for the museum is closely linked with the **University of Toronto,** which practically surrounds it. The campus and leafy walks are very pleasant green spaces in a compactly-built city. A few blocks away, on Dundas, are the **Toronto Art Gallery** and the **Ontario College of Art.** The Art Gallery, like many small commercial galleries in the Bay-Bloor area, carries paintings by Canadians old and new, old masters and touring collections. The **Maple Leaf Gardens** and **Maple Leaf Stadium** provide the main spectator sports, the former being used occasionally even for ballet or opera. Horse racing has a long season.

The city's importance as a theatrical center is increasing, with the main CBC studios where radio and television shows are produced, the majority of Canadian film companies here, as well as a vigorous live theater. Toronto's **O'Keefe Centre for the Performing Arts** is considered one of the most beautiful theaters in North America. The great influx of Europeans since the war has brought talent, new ideas and a much more cosmopolitan atmosphere to Toronto. Some sections of the city have distinct national character—"The Village" is still bohemian in outlook; Chinatown persists, though shrunken; to stroll along College Street West sounds and smells like a visit to Italy. Kensington Market is still redolent of the Old World, with bagels and cottage cheese and live carp swimming in tanks, and five synagogues within a few blocks.

Guided bus tours of Toronto loop down Bay Street, home of high finance; past the piers, warehouses and yacht clubs of the waterfront; past the green ramparts of **Fort York** and its military cemetery; through the grounds of the **Canadian National Exhibition;** twist through the estates of **Rosedale** and call at picturesque **Casa Loma,** the composite castle built early this century.

SPORTS AND RECREATION. Facilities for football, baseball, hockey, soccer, horse racing, golf, tennis, swimming, water-skiing, boating, lawn bowling can be found throughout the province. There are skating, skiing and curling in winter; fishing almost everywhere; hunting in season.

Two of the province's most popular outdoor recreation regions, other than the north area and Georgian Bay, are the **Lakeland** section near Toronto and **Algonquin Park,** one of Ontario's largest, oldest, and best-known national parks.

Within an hour of Toronto, Lakeland stretches from Georgian Bay to the Haliburton Highlands and Kawartha Lakes, and is the lower edge of the Canadian Shield, an ideal summer playground. **Lake Simcoe** and nearby lakes offer full facilities for camping, boating, swimming, and fishing. At **Peterborough,** in the Kawartha region, is the famous hydraulic lift lock, largest in the world.

Algonquin Park, larger than the entire province of Prince Edward Island, is largely roadless, contains a game sanctuary, and permits fishing. Camping and canoeing are popular pastimes.

SPECIAL EVENTS. The **Canadian National Exhibition,** two weeks, end of August, early September—largest permanent annual exhibition in the world, with livestock, industry, midway, sports, grandstand; **Royal Agricultural Winter Fair,** mid-November, including horse show; **Blossom Week,** third week in May, Niagara Peninsula; **Niagara Grape Festival,** St. Catherines, late September.

DINING AND SHOPPING. English-style food is served throughout Ontario, although German, Chinese, French, and Italian dishes can also be found. Among the popular foods are shrimp, lobster, and other seafood; game meat, especially pheasant; baked alaska; and a variety of breads and cakes.

Eskimo carvings, parkas, boots, and handicrafts can be found in Toronto, as well as Indian totem poles, masks, ceramics, and metalcraft. Antique lovers will enjoy the many shops throughout the province where old furniture and glass can be found.

Manitoba

Lying directly north of Minnesota and North Dakota, Manitoba is one of Canada's Prairie Provinces. Its clear lakes, forests, and scenic landscapes make it a popular camping and outdoor sports region. "Manitoba" comes from the Indian *Manito Waba,* or "Great Spirit's strait."

THE LAND. With Manitoba, the Canadian prairies begin their wavering spread across the interior of the continent. This region long ago was scraped by glaciers, and lay under glacial lakes. They left behind a fine silt, deep and black, in what is now Manitoba, the lowest of the prairie steppes. Remnants of the glacial lakes remain in several large and thousands of small lakes in the province. Less than a quarter of the province is prairie, a wedge beginning at Lake of the Woods and slanting northwest past Lake Manitoba. The rolling wheatlands merge into marshland, then into spruce forest and the rocks of the Canadian Shield. In the north, the trees dwindle on the "little Barrens" and vanish on the salt-water shore of Hudson Bay.

THE CLIMATE. Although winters can be long and extremely cold, the crisp dry air makes them more pleasant. Summers are warm, with averages around 60 degrees. Up to 50 inches of snow falls yearly, and stays on the ground for four to five months.

THE PEOPLE. The fur traders Radisson and Groseilliers were among the first white men to explore west of Lake Superior, and discover the excellent trapping grounds south of Hudson Bay. They sold their knowledge to English businessmen, including King Charles II. After a successful expedition through Hudson Strait, the Hudson's Bay Company was formed in 1670, and established trading posts on the shores of this inland sea. Explorers paddled up long rivers to discover the prairies, reach the Barrens and the Rocky Mountains. The company had Indians bringing furs to their posts for 1,000 miles before the French penetrated the west. In the 1730's, La Vérendrye and his sons set up their trading posts along the Winnipeg, Red and Assiniboine rivers.

The company met further competition after New France became British, and free traders united as the North West Company. The rivalry was very keen, finally reaching the point of bloodshed. Lord Selkirk, gaining a controlling interest in the Hudson's Bay Company, decided to send poverty-stricken Scottish crofters into the Red River country where land was free and plentiful. Even their scant farming was resented by all the fur traders, but no one could resist the inevitable march of settlement. The two fur trading companies, both nearly exhausted by their long struggle, united under the old charter in 1821, and the Hudson's Bay Company has continued to prosper. In 1869, the company sold its vast land grant to the new Dominion of Canada. Homesteaders began to move into the Canadian west, and in time the provinces of Manitoba, Saskatchewan, and Alberta reached their present size.

When the white man arrived, he found Assiniboine Indians on the plains, Crees in the woodlands, Chipewyans and a few Eskimos in the north. French and English fur traders added to the stock with their European families, and with their children of mixed blood, the métis. The Selkirk settlers brought Scottish blood, and after the west was opened to settlement, throngs of homesteaders came from every country in Europe, from eastern Canada and the United States. Some communities are predominantly Icelandic, Ukrainian or German.

The Indians taught the newcomers woodcraft, brought furs and food to the trading posts, helped homesteaders farm the land, and even accepted the white man's religions. Many Crees are today excellent wheat farmers on their reserves, while others are laborers in the towns and cities. In the northern parts of the province, they are trappers, guides, tractor-freighters, mine workers, and commercial fishermen. No profession is barred to them, and the younger people are leaving the reserves.

AGRICULTURE. Manitoba's farmers grow wheat, barley, rye, buckwheat, corn, and other vegetables. Flaxseed, sunflowers, and mustardseed are grown largely for their oil. Beef cattle are raised, as are hogs, sheep, and dairy cattle. Fur farming in southern Manitoba and fishing in Lakes Winnipeg, Manitoba, and Winnipegosis are important occupations in this province.

INDUSTRY. Major industries in Manitoba include food processing (the largest), railroad repair, furniture and paper production, and nickel processing. Winnipeg is the manufacturing hub of the province, where flour mills, cement-making, clothing, and printing concerns are also located.

Mining is valued very highly in Manitoba, with major mineral deposits located at **Flin Flon** and **Thompson** within the Canadian Shield. Leading minerals are nickel, zinc, petroleum, copper, and oil.

CITIES. Of Manitoba's population of over 980,000, close to two-thirds live in cities and towns. More than half the people reside in Winnipeg, the capital.

WINNIPEG, capital of Manitoba, with a population of over half a million, prides itself upon the variety of languages spoken within its metropolitan boundaries. The city is located at "The Forks" of the Red and Assiniboine rivers, an ideal location for the fur-trading post it originally was. This is the historic heart of the city, site of four trading posts in turn, to which the stone gateway of **Upper Fort Garry** is a memorial. Rivers demand expensive bridging with urban growth, and Winnipeg has many bridges over the wide Red and the winding Assiniboine rivers, which add greatly to the beauty of the city. The **Legislative Buildings** are set in wide lawns on the banks of the Assiniboine, and the turreted **Fort Garry Hotel,** too, is reflected in its waters. Only a few traces of Winnipeg's past are still visible: **Ross House,** the first post office; **Seven Oaks House,** the oldest habitable house in Manitoba, near the site of the fur traders' massacre in 1816. Many years later came the **"Countess of Dufferin,"** a steam locomotive now in honored retirement in front of the **Canadian Pacific Railway station.**

Historical museums in the **Civic Auditorium** and in the **Hudson's Bay Company department store** are splendid for a backward glance at the history of western Canada. Actually, **St. Boniface,** the French-Canadian city across the river, part of Greater Winnipeg, is the senior partner. There a handsome monument perpetuates the exploits of La Vérendrye and his sons. After La Vérendrye came the traders of the North West Company and French-Canadian voyageurs, who married Indian women and produced the new race of mixed blood, called métis. Later came French-Canadian colonists from Lower Canada and some Swiss mercenaries, whose patron saint was St. Boniface. Today the city is decidedly cosmopolitan, with large French and English segments, and smaller groups of German, Polish, and Belgian citizens. Only a shaft of red granite marks the grave of the most colorful, controversial figure in the history of the Canadian west. Louis Riel championed the métis, who feared for their rights under the new Dominion of Canada. Riel captured Fort Garry, and flew the métis flag of the provisional government, but he prudently left before soldiers arrived from Ontario. Relics of Riel, Bishop Taché and others may be seen in the **Musée Historique** in the Basilica.

Visitors should head northward along the Red River for historic interest in **St. John's Cathedral,** for sports in **Kildonan Park.** About 12 miles north of the city is **Lower Fort Garry,** with its three-and-a-half-foot-thick stone walls, its bastions, and historic fur lofts. The fort is presently a country club, designated as a national historic park. Nearby is **St. Andrew's-on-the-Red,** the oldest stone church in western Canada, built in 1849. Still in continuous use for public services, its kneeling benches bear the original buffalo hide. In the same area is **St. Andrew's Lock,** the only lock in western Canada, with its dam in the Red River that raises or lowers boats nine feet.

A highway crosses the top of the dam, heading eastward to the **Seven Sisters Falls** and the 1,000-square-mile playground of **Whiteshell Forest Reserve** with its clear rock-bottomed lakes. Prehistoric rock "mosaics"—loose stones arranged in snake and serpent patterns—are found on the flat granite bedrock. A pleasant way of exploring Manitoba is the 600-mile, 6-day **cruise of the Red River** and **Lake Winnipeg.** The boat loads at **Selkirk,** steams out through the **Netley Marshes,** and into the lake. Calls are made to various trading posts, such as **Grand Rapids,** and to isolated settlements, including the **Icelandic Hecla** on an island, the Indian fishing village of **Warren's Landing,** and **Norway House** on the Nelson River.

Southwest of Winnipeg rise the **Pembina Hills,** rolling country of ponds, lakes, orderly woods and great sand dunes. **La Rivière** is a skiing resort in winter. Near Turtle Mountain, south of Brandon, is the **International Peace Garden,** 2,300 acres of landscaped parkland established jointly by Manitoba and North Dakota.

Brandon has a charming setting on the high bank of the serpentine Assiniboine River. Some 60 miles north is the sudden hump of **Riding Mountain.** About half of it has been reserved as a national park, with headquarters at **Wasagaming,** a pleasant resort town. Twenty miles from town is the wild animal enclosure, with herds of buffalo. The woods are full of mule deer and elk, but one must have sharp eyes to spot them. Boating, fishing, swimming and golf are the most popular sports.

The highway through the park continues north to **Flin Flon,** a mining and smelting town. The railway branches at **The Pas,** one spur leading to the new mining town of **Lynn Lake.** The older route heads northeast to **Hudson Bay** at Churchill. This northern settlement began and still continues as a fur-trading post and white whale fishery, carried on by Eskimos and Chipewyan Indians. A museum at the **Oblate Mission** displays artifacts of both races. A few miles out of town is **Fort Churchill,** which is used for Joint Services Arctic Testing by Canada and the United States. Older defenses are visible in the remnants of a battery on **Cape Merry,** and the star-shaped stone walls of **Fort Prince of Wales** across the Churchill River. This Hudson's Bay Company post took 33 years to build, and an hour to capitulate. Arrangements may be made locally for crossing the river in motor canoe, where the stone walls and rusted cannon are much as they were left when the French blew them up in 1782. **Sloops' Cove,** a mile or so upriver, bears the autograph of the distinguished explorer Samuel Hearne, dated 1767. On the **Churchill shore** is a cairn with a bronze plaque recalling the tragic Danish expedition under discoverer Jens Munck in 1619.

SPORTS AND RECREATION facilities include **swimming, boating** and **golf** in summer; **skiing, curling, ice-fishing, hockey** in winter. There is **fishing** for lake, brook and speckled trout, northern pike, walleye; **hunting** for moose, deer, upland game birds, duck (especially on marshes around Lakes Winnipeg and Manitoba), goose (around The Pas and York Factory).

SPECIAL EVENTS. Winnipeg—**Annual Red River Exhibition** late June; **Manitoba Music Festival,** May; **Winnipeg Bonspiel,** February; Brandon—**Livestock Fair** in April, **Provincial Exhibition** in July. The Pas—**Annual Trappers Festival** in late February, with Fur Queen, King Trapper and northern-style contests. Flin Flon—**Northern Trout Festival** in June; **rail excursion** to Churchill, August.

DINING AND SHOPPING. One of Manitoba's most popular foods is the Winnipeg Goldeye, a fish weighing less than a pound and found in the northern lakes of the province. It is considered a gourmet delicacy, and is served in many unusual dishes. Other fish and seafood, as well as a variety of meats, are also readily available.

Saskatchewan

Waving wheat fields, tall grain elevators, and oil rigs contrast with the new buildings and homes of bustling Regina and Saskatoon, Saskatchewan's leading cities. In this province alone, close to 60 percent of Canada's wheat supply is raised. The Cree Indians were responsible for naming the province after the winding river, *Kisiskadjewan* (meaning fast-flowing) which cuts through the state and is now called the Saskatchewan.

THE LAND. The southern half of

Saskatchewan's 251,700 square miles forms the second prairie steppe, and the sediment left by the long-gone glaciers is chocolate-brown in color. Flat plains, broken occasionally by little hills and sloughs and bluffs of trees, are the southern half.

Great river systems cross the province from west to east: the scalloped trench of the **Qu'Appelle,** the 1,205-mile-long **Saskatchewan River,** cutting a trench through wheatland, and the north branch through parkland, to meet east of Prince Albert. On the edge of the Canadian Shield, the **Churchill River** rushes over the rocks and widens into lake expansions. Far to the north are the vast **Lakes Reindeer** and **Wollaston,** and on the edge of the Barrens, **Lake Athabasca.** Saskatchewan is "the breadbasket" of Canada, although only half of it is prairie.

THE CLIMATE. Summer, when temperatures average in the mid-seventies and skies are usually sunny, is the best season for visiting Saskatchewan. In winter, 50 inches of snow is not uncommon, and temperatures may hover around zero. The chinook wind, with its masses of warm air, can raise these temperatures up to 20 degrees in a few hours, however.

THE PEOPLE. Fur traders explored waterways that led them all the way to the ice fields of the Rocky Mountains. In 1857, the British government sent out a major scientific expedition under Captain John Palliser. He brought back a thorough report, finding most of the country suitable for settlement, except for an area immediately north of the international boundary. "Palliser's Triangle" was too dry, he declared, but homesteaders settled there nonetheless —only to prove him right.

The surveyors used the American system of a square mile forming a "section," and this triggered the second Riel uprising. As in Manitoba 15 years earlier, the métis feared their long narrow strips of land running back from the Saskatchewan River were endangered. Ottawa, busy with other projects, paid no attention to queries and protests. The Indians faced starvation, with white men filling up the land and wantonly destroying the buffalo.

Eventually, the métis and Indians brought Louis Riel from Montana, and though he preached moderation and established a provisional government again, the situation soon got out of hand. Under Gabriel Dumont, the métis repulsed a force of Northwest Mounted Police sent against them; the Stoneys besieged Fort Battleford; the Crees massacred settlers at Frog Lake and kidnapped survivors. Soldiers from Ontario, local militia and the Mounted Police won the final engagement at Batoche, and the rebellion ended.

Riel and some other leaders were hanged, some were exiled. But their efforts were not in vain. The métis finally got their title to their lands, and treaties were made with the Indians. Since 1885, Saskatchewan's growth in agriculture, mining and industry has been peaceful.

AGRICULTURE. Wheat is the principal farm crop in Saskatchewan, with a total of around 280 million bushels harvested yearly. Although the province has over 64 million acres of farmland, they are not all used, thus helping to store moisture in the soil. Barley, flaxseed, rye, oats, and rapeseed are also key field crops.

The government has bought up dry land in the southwest, regrassed it, and turned it into community pastureland for beef cattle—another of the province's important farming activities.

INDUSTRY. Petroleum refining—centered in Moose Jaw, Regina, and Saskatoon—is the province's leading industry. Food products, as well as chemicals, helium, potash, natural gas, uranium, and other minerals are processed throughout Saskatchewan.

The two fastest-growing industries, however, are mining and forestry. Saskatchewan is a leader in the production of copper, gold, petroleum, uranium, zinc, and potash, the latter having developed into the major mineral product of the province.

Growth in forestry has been rapid, and new mills are being built which will more than triple the total forest income within a few years.

CITIES. In Regina, the capital, live over 140,000 people, but no city in the province is large enough to qualify as a metropolitan area. Other large towns are Saskatoon, Moose Jaw, Prince Albert, Swift Current, and North Battleford.

REGINA, originally capital of the Northwest Territories, became capital of Saskatchewan when the province was created in 1905. The site, chosen in 1882, and named for Victoria Regina, was no compliment to the Queen. It was the flattest stretch of prairie for many miles, treeless, with a muddy little creek meandering past a pile of bleached buffalo bones. The creek has been dammed to become **Wascana Lake,** mirroring white sails and the dome of the **Legislative Buildings.** Nearby is the provincial **Museum of Natural History,** very modern architecture housing excellent habitat groups. In the west end of the city is the **Royal Canadian Mounted Police training college,** which trains both men and horses. The stained-glass windows of the chapel bear red-coated Mounties, and the museum displays a crime collection.

About 25 miles north of Regina is the wavering furrow of the **Qu'Appelle Valley,** varying from one to several miles wide, and stretching through more than 200 miles of prairie. The walls of the valley are banked with trees, a sight of surprising beauty, especially after miles of driving on the plains above. The valley has beaches, fishing, boating on all the lakes and craft-shop courses at **Fort Qu'Appelle.**

Swift Current in the southwest is the brisk center of a cattle, wheat, oil region. Due south, half a dozen prairie dog "towns" are on **Frenchman's Creek,** the only ones in Canada. **Cypress Hills** straddle the provincial border, with lakes, river, forests, plains, and antelope on both sides. These hills formed a unique island in the glacial period, and still contain remnants of ancient life unknown nearer than Texas—a species of wasp, scorpions, horned toads and yucca plants. Cypress Hills, the home of Indian tribes, is visited for its **Sun Dance ceremonial sites.** Here many were massacred by American whisky traders in 1873, hastening the formation of the Northwest Mounted Police. **Fort Walsh,** in the hills, was headquarters for several years, and the rebuilt log buildings today serve as a remount station for the Royal Canadian Mounted Police.

Saskatoon is the second city of the province, home of the university and attractively located astride the South Saskatchewan River in parkland. The **Western Development Museum** houses antique plows that broke the prairie sod, steam engines that drove early threshers, and buggies that bogged down in glue-like mud. These implements go into action for a week during the annual **Pion-Era. North Battleford** has a similar museum, while **Battleford** across the river has a log-palisaded reconstruction of the fort besieged by Poundmaker's Indians. **Churches in St. Walburg** and surrounding areas boast exceptionally fine **murals,** done by the late international religious artist Berthold Imhoff, whose studio is near the village. The road continues north through **Meadow Lake,** plunges through forest to historic **Ile à la Crosse,** and on to **Buffalo Narrows** on **Churchill Lake.**

Another road north of Saskatoon leads to **Prince Albert,** and beyond that to the national park, farther still to **Lac la Ronge,** and north to **Lake Athabasca** at the top of the province. **Prince Albert National Park,** filled with rocks, trees, and waterways, occupies 1,500 square miles of the Canadian Shield. **Waskesiu,** a resort colony in the Park, has a buffalo enclosure nearby, while a pelican rookery at **Lake Lavallee,** reached by canoe and portage, is another feature of the area.

SPORTS AND RECREATION. There is **golf, boating,** and **swimming** in many small provincial parks and all large parks; **fishing,** especially in the larger parks, in Lac la Ronge, and farther north; **hunting,** for upland game birds (sharp-tailed grouse, Hungarian partridge, pheasant), duck and goose shooting in marshes and on stubble; in the south—deer, antelope, elk; in the north—bear, moose.

SPECIAL EVENTS. Regina—**Provincial Exhibition** first week in August; Saskatoon—**Pion-Era,** first week in July. Swift Current—**Frontier Days, three-day rodeo,** first week end in July; Frobisher—**field dog trials,** two weeks in September, beginning Labor Day. (The hunting dogs, mostly American, are trained on the plains of southeastern Saskatchewan and nearby Manitoba all summer. At Frobisher, they begin a series of field trials which go on from place to place until they reach Florida by May.)

DINING AND SHOPPING. A favorite dish in this province is Saskatoon berry pie, made with unusual, dark saskatoon berries that grow thickly on high bushes in the prairie provinces. They taste like a combination of black currants and blueberries. Other popular dishes include snow muffins and honey apple dumplings.

Alberta

Alberta is one of the richest provinces in Canada. Its oil wells bring in most of Canada's petroleum, while coal and other minerals, and farming heap more wealth onto the province. Alberta is also one of the most strikingly beautiful provinces, with the towering Canadian Rockies making a perfect background for clear lakes and lush green forests.

THE LAND. Alberta, 255,285 square miles, is the largest, most populous and most glamorous of the prairie provinces, and, like the others, bounded by the 49th and 60th parallels of latitude. Alberta is the final steppe of prairie land, rising into foothills, then into jagged peaks of the Rocky Mountains. The highest peaks of the Continental Divide form its bulging boundary with British Columbia. Several great rivers cross the province, plunging down from the glaciers of the Rockies, carving their deep trenches through the fertile soil of the plains—Oldman, Bow, Red Deer, North Saskatchewan, Athabasca and Smoky. Farther north is the Peace River, beginning deep within British Columbia, sweeping through northern Alberta to join the Slave River above Lake Athabasca.

THE CLIMATE. Because of its long, crisply cold but sunny winter season, Alberta has developed extensive winter sports facilities. Temperatures seldom climb above the freezing mark and frequently go below zero. Spring and autumn are short but pleasant seasons, and summer has temperatures in the mid-sixties.

THE PEOPLE. Eons ago, the interior of North America was covered with swamps where dinosaurs crawled and devoured. Their skeletons are still found in the Red Deer River Valley. The great lizards were vanquished by the ice age, as glaciers time and again scoured their way east of the sharp young Rockies. The bulldozer action of the glacier foot flattened out the land; the sea flowed in, its salt water gradually replaced by the fresh water of the great glacial lakes. The first humans of the plains were Indians, drifting south from Bering Strait. Herds of buffalo were their mainstay for both food and clothing. As a rule, the Indians were peaceable and helpful to the white explorers who eventually arrived.

Fur traders of the North West Company and of the Hudson's Bay Company thrust deeper into the wilderness until the amalgamation of the two companies in 1821 brought peace to the west. Anthony Henday, Alexander Mackenzie, Simon Fraser and David Thompson were outstanding prairie explorers, most of whom pushed on through the mountains to the Pacific. In the wake of the fur brigades came the missionaries—first Methodist and Oblate. They made peace between the warring tribes, and kept peace between white man and Indian.

Captain John Palliser made his famous scientific expedition through the west in 1857. Lieutenant William Butler brought back information for the Canadian government in 1870, especially recommending a federal police force. Three years later, the Northwest Mounted Police were ready for their long grueling trek across the plains. Their arrival in 1874 promptly put an end to the "whisky forts" on the southern border. With the Mounted Police and the missionaries there first, the homesteaders had neither the dread nor the adventure of a "wild west." There was, instead, a vast respect for Indians like Red Crow, chief of the Bloods, and for Crowfoot, the Blackfoot chief, both of them wise and dignified leaders worthy of all respect. The Northwest Mounted Police built Fort McLeod down in the south of the province, then Fort Calgary beside the Bow River. Another division reached Fort Edmonton, and built barracks in the vicinity at Fort Saskatchewan.

With law and order assured and a railway projected, settlers began to trickle in with their two-wheeled Red River carts and yokes of oxen. The land survey for the railroad brought tension among the Indians whose hunting grounds it crossed, but Father Lacombe was a tactful peacemaker. More critical, as in the two other prairie provinces, the land survey brought trouble with the métis. However, it never reached the point of violence in Alberta. The railway construction camps became the foundation for towns, and steel rails opened the country to ranchers, then to wheat farmers, to sheepmen in the dry southeast, to dairymen in the central parkland, and later to industrialists. By 1905, there were enough people in the districts of Alberta and Saskatchewan to change them into provinces.

Today the population of Alberta is more than half British in origin, though many other nationalities are represented—German, Ukrainian, French, Scandinavian, Russian, and a dozen more. English is the language used throughout the province, by the Crees and métis, by the newcomers from Europe, and by bilingual French-Canadians north of Edmonton.

AGRICULTURE. Fur, then cattle, then wheat and later oil, have laid the solid base for Alberta's burgeoning economy. The shortgrass plains of the south drew experienced cattlemen from the United States, adventurous Englishmen and Ontario farmboys. Wheat farmers found fertility in the light-brown soil. They battled drought with irrigation, higher altitudes with faster-maturing strains, and where wheat wouldn't grow nor cattle graze, they stocked the land with sheep.

Today, Alberta's farm income is growing steadily. Its crops, in addition to wheat, include barley, sugar beets, and vegetables.

INDUSTRY. Because of the size of Alberta's agriculture, food processing is the main area of manufacturing. Meat packing plants, breweries, sugar and oil refineries can be found throughout the province.

Alberta's mining production has an annual value of over $460 million, or more than either agriculture or manufacturing. Petroleum (as well as natural gas) is by far the most important mineral, followed by coal (demand for this mineral has dropped considerably in recent years), bentonite, and limestone.

Forestry is a rapidly growing industry in Alberta, where over $17 million in logs and pulpwood are cut yearly.

CITIES. Alberta's population of 1.5 million is largely urban, and the province has two cities with more than 200,000 residents—Edmonton and Calgary. But of special interest to visitors are the rural areas near these cities where an abundance of recreational facilities can be found.

CALGARY, second city of Alberta, is somewhat smaller than Edmonton, and growing almost as fast. It began as a Mounted Police post, became a trading center for the ranching community, swelled with construction workers when the Canadian Pacific Railway was being built in 1883. Located on the rolling prairie at the junction of the Bow and Elbow rivers, Calgary has an attractive setting, with the snow-capped Rockies visible on a clear day. It is also the highest, sunniest city in Canada. Calgary is headquarters for many oil companies who are now operating important oil and gas fields near Edmonton. Though an oil center, Calgary likes to think of itself as a "cow town," and one week a year overflows with Western spirit and ten-gallon hats. **The Calgary Stampede,** early in July each year, is a freewheeling rodeo. Contestants come from as far away as Texas, and infield events are the dramatic bronc-busting, chuckwagon racing, steer-decorating and calf-roping. Free hotcakes on the streets and square-dancing at the corners make this stampede distinctive. **Bowness Park,** and **St. George's Island Park,** with fenced animals, a children's zoo, and dinosaur park are interesting to visit. Nearly 50 concrete dinosaur models of excellent workmanship lurk in life-like manner in the grasses and shrubs of the park, where their prototypes actually roamed 50 million years ago. A glassed-in **fossils house** displays exhibits from the Badlands of the **Red Deer River,** where excavation still goes on, up- and down-river from Drumheller. This scarred, eroded wilderness of clay buttes, runnelled by rain, shaped by wind, with sandstone-capped hoodoos, is weirdly beautiful. In the layers of sediment, the history of millions of years may be read.

EDMONTON, with a population of about 437,000, is the capital, almost exactly in the center of the province. It grew out of the Hudson's Bay Company trading post, **Fort Edmonton,** a palisaded stockade on a terrace above the North Saskatchewan River. Edmonton's city planners laid out the town on the flat prairie on both high riverbanks, necessitating a number of bridges over the wide trench and its treed slopes. The flood-plain below was shrewdly reserved for parks, which are not disastrously affected if the river floods in spring.

Edmonton is a city of homes, but one of wide boundaries, and the result is rather like a number of villages, which avoids heavy congestion downtown. In fact, Edmonton's city limits, drawn during a boom period, were so wide when the bubble burst that the city airport grew up inside the town. Vacant lots have filled up, and the outskirts are now built-up with heavy industry. The oil strike at Leduc in 1947 and the fabulous finds since then have brought wealth. The eastern side of the city is grown up into **"petro-chemical valley,"** a maze of industries that use oil and/or its by-products. Most plants provide conducted tours of their operations for visitors.

With its central location, **Edmonton** is literally a hub of transportation, a gateway to the regions beyond. Scheduled and charter flights take off into the northland. Highways radiate in all directions, northeast, due north to **Athabasca** and **Peace River,** northwest to the **Alaska Highway.** The **Mackenzie Highway** now runs north of the Peace River country all the way to **Great Slave Lake,** the first highway to enter the Northwest Territories. From Edmonton, a railway runs to **McMurray,** where freight is shipped by barge down the **Athabasca River** and into the **Northwest Territories.**

Elk Island National Park, 35 miles east of Edmonton, grazes a herd of 1,000 buffalo, in addition to its camp and picnic facilities, golf and swimming. A Ukrainian pioneer house with thatched roofs, a replica of those built by immigrants, is furnished with handmade articles brought from the Ukraine. It is the first unit of a projected open-air museum.

Due west of Edmonton, the new trans-Canada highway leads into **Jasper,** the largest of Canada's national parks, and one of four safeguarding the ridgepole of the Rockies. Jasper's 4,200 square miles include tumultuous rivers in wide valleys, towering mountains, and immense forests. A blond fur trader, Jasper Howse, is well commemorated by park and townsite, the **Howse River** and **Yellowhead Pass.** The **Canadian**

National Railway penetrates Yellowhead Pass to reach **British Columbia,** and it operates a palatial summer hotel a few miles outside the graceless town of Jasper. Beside **Lake Beauvert** it is not unusual to find mule deer, elk or black bear roaming the golf course. East of town, **Maligne Canyon** and **Lake, Punchbowl Falls** and **Miette Hot Springs** are rewarding. South of town, **Angel Glacier** on **Mount Edith Cavell,** the **Valley of Crooked Pines, Sunwapta** and **Athabasca Falls** are noteworthy. The pass of the Athabasca skirted the mountain and glacier of that name, a well-beaten path until the railroad came. Straddling the Jasper-Banff-British Columbia boundaries is the **Columbia Icefield,** more than 100 square miles of ice and snow draped over the mountain tops. Only one of several tongues of the ice field, the **Athabasca Glacier** comes within a few hundred yards of the highway, and **snowmobiles** carry visitors well up on the creviced blue ice. The ice field spawns rivers that reach the Atlantic via the Saskatchewan, the Arctic via the Athabasca, and the Pacific by means of the Columbia.

The road rises southward and the peaks thrust higher and sharper from the narrower valleys of **Banff National Park.** They cup jade-green lakes, notably **Peyto** and **Lake Louise,** the latter the most-photographed in Canada, with mountains and **Victoria Glacier** mirrored in its changing waters. Accommodations at **Lake Louise** range from campground to luxurious château. Like Jasper, Banff is crisscrossed with trails for hiker or horseman. **Moraine Lake** may be reached by car from Lake Louise. Eastward, the **Banff-Windermere Highway** branches off at **Mount Eisenhower** to the **Kootenay Pass. Johnston Canyon** is the next breath-taking view. The town of **Banff** is a resort site and headquarters for the park administration. The hot springs on **Sulphur Mountain** were the origin of Canada's national parks system when, in 1882, the government reserved ten square miles to protect the springs. The park has grown to more than 2,500 square miles, and the hot springs still bubble healing sulphur waters at the **Cave** and **Basin,** and at **Upper Hot Spring.**

Half a dozen impressive mountains crowd closely around the townsite in the green valley bottom and can be climbed—**Norquay** by chair lift, and **Sulphur Mountain** by gondola lift. The town has an exceptionally good small **museum of Indian arts.** Crowded in summer with visitors and students at the **School of Fine Arts,** Banff has a small permanent population who delight in the winter's superb skiing.

Immediately east of Jasper and Banff national parks are the provincial forest reserves, conservation areas snuggled against the park outlines, and threaded by a gravel road. Actually a **fire rangers' road,** it is the highest engineered road in Canada, and open to the public. Beginning at **Nordegg** in the **Clearwater Forest** (noted for its elusive wild horses), the road winds south to **Coleman** in the **Crowsnest Pass,** crossing innumerable streams where the fishing is first-rate. Crowsnest Pass is the southernmost pass in the Canadian Rockies, now signaled by a concrete crows' nest, and noted for its string of coal-mining towns. Most notable is **Frank,** because of a disaster dramatized in "The Ballad of Frank Slide." On April 29, 1903, old Turtle Mountain "nodded its head," and 70 million tons of limestone crashed down on one end of the sleeping village. In 90 seconds, the slide killed 66 people, destroying dozens of homes and the coal mine, and burying the railroad under 100 feet of rocks as big as a house. Modern highway and railroad cross the debris, and decades of hauling broken rock for railway ballast have made little impression.

South of Crowsnest is **Waterton Lakes National Park,** where the mountains rise suddenly, without benefit of foothills. This smaller park is of unusually vivid coloring, with crimson rock and long gashes of green lakes. It adjoins the much-larger **Glacier National Park** in Montana, and in 1932 together they were named the **Waterton-Glacier International Peace Park,** to celebrate a century of goodwill along the border. Chief towns of southern Alberta are **Fort McLeod,** with its replica of the original Northwest Mounted Police fort; **Lethbridge,** industrial and ranching center; **Cardston,** with its marble **Mormon Temple; Medicine Hat,** in a coulee beside the South Saskatchewan, supplying hothouse flowers across the country.

SPORTS AND RECREATION. **Golf** is played almost everywhere. **Fishing** is excellent in mountain streams. There are big-game expeditions and **hunting** for upland game birds, duck, geese. Hiking may be done on your own or organized through **Skyline Trail Hikers.** Guides for mountain climbing may be arranged with the Alpine Club. **Trail-riding** is available by arrangement, on dude ranches, or with Trail Riders—four five-day outings per summer from Banff. In winter there is excellent **skiing,** especially in Banff, with various ski tows and lifts in the area.

SPECIAL EVENTS. **Calgary Stampede,** always the Monday and week after July 4; **Alberta Rodeo Circuit,** local rodeos before and after Calgary Stampede; **Banff Indian Days,** four days, the week end after Calgary Stampede; **Edmonton Exhibition,** "Klondike Days," July.

DINING AND SHOPPING. A variety of dishes—with the emphasis on beef—can be found in Alberta. Chinese, Italian, French, and Spanish restaurants are located in Edmonton and Calgary.

Souvenirs made from petrified dinosaur bone make interesting buys.

British Columbia

This most westerly of Canada's provinces is third largest, most varied in terrain and climate, and unquestionably one of the most beautiful regions on earth. Shaped rather like a Christmas stocking, the vamp nudges Alberta in the east, and Vancouver Island forms the heel. The chunky province of 366,255 square miles, nearly twice the size of Spain, has snow-peaked mountains rich in minerals, jewel-toned lakes for fishing and boating, leaping waterfalls with hidden power, grasslands studded with cattle, a ragged coastline of innumerable harbors, and rain forests with renewable resources of great timbers.

THE LAND. British Columbia is nowhere flat. The center of the province is a plateau within mountain ramparts, the Coast Range to the west, the Rockies cradling its other margins. The great rivers of British Columbia must force their way around these giant obstructions.

The Kootenay River loops south into the United States to get around the Selkirk Mountains, then returns north of the border to bulge into Kootenay Lake, and to power five hydroelectric installations before joining the Columbia. The Columbia, rising close to the Kootenay, makes a big bend around the top of the Selkirks, turns southward to expand into the lovely Arrow Lakes, meets the Kootenay, and pours south into Washington. The Thompson River is impressive on its own, but it soon loses its distinct personality when its green waters join the muddy Fraser. Like an angular S, the Fraser slashes across the province from Mount Robson to Vancouver.

Other rivers include the Bulkley, the Skeena, the Peace, the Stikine, and the Liard. Most of British Columbia's lakes are long and narrow . . . actually river expansions. Large southern lakes—Harrison, Okanagan, Kootenay, Arrow—are not crowded. Many more in the central and northern areas are comparatively unknown—Shuswap and Quesnel, Chilko and François, Stuart and Babine.

THE CLIMATE. Climate varies tremendously with altitude and latitude, depending also on the side of the mountain from which it is measured. The west coast of Vancouver Island drips with rain while Victoria at the tip goes short of water. Ocean Falls at the coast receives 187 inches of rain, while Kamloops over the mountains in the hot dry interior gets about ten inches. Farther east, in the Rocky Mountain complex, the weather is cool, while across the mountains the Peace River Block has short bright summers and long cold winters.

THE PEOPLE. First to reach this bounteous land were the Indians, whose ancestors crossed the land bridge from Asia in the dawn of history. Life was fairly easy, with abundant fish, meat and berries, so the Indians developed a complex social system, a culture superior to most others north of Mexico. Their laws of etiquette, decorative arts, dramas, and oral traditions were remarkable. So was their fighting ability. Thus they lived when the Spaniards sailed up the coast from Panama, and when the Russians sailed south from Bering Strait. In 1792, Captain George Vancouver was sent to accept surrender of the Spanish possessions on behalf of Britain.

The next year, Alexander Mackenzie became the first white man to cross the continent north of Mexico. Fur traders pushed westward through the mountain passes, down swift rivers, to establish trading posts on the Pacific. David Thompson of the North West Company reached the mouth of the Columbia a few days too late for his company—Fort Astoria was already rising there, an important detail when the boundary was being drawn. The Hudson's Bay Company built other trading posts—Forts Victoria and Langley at the south, to keep out Americans, and Forts Essington and Simpson near the Alaskan Panhandle, to warn Russians off the fur trade.

The boundary line west of the Rockies was drawn only in 1846, at the 49th parallel, a compromise between conflicting U.S. and British ambitions. James Douglas, governor of the Hudson's Bay Company trading post of Fort Victoria, was also governor of its Colony of Vancouver Island. But when gold was discovered in the creeks of the Cascades and the gravel bars of the Fraser River, Douglas insisted that all miners take out a license in the name of Queen Victoria. Actually, Douglas had no legal authority on the mainland, but his action preserved the country for British North America. In 1858, when gold-seekers thronged into the Cariboo, the mainland became the Colony of British Columbia, with James Douglas as governor.

The two Colonies united in 1866, rather uneasily. Confederation of the eastern Colonies in 1867 and the American purchase of Alaska persuaded British Columbia to enter Confederation in 1871, on promise of a transcontinental railway in ten years. It took 15 years to build the railway, completed by the drive of an American, William Van Horne. Called the Canadian Pacific, it was one of the world's first transcontinental railways.

The mountains isolate British Columbia from the rest of Canada psychologically as well as physically. To its people, the wide prairie and the forests of the Canadian Shield are an equally high barrier. Their interests flow southward along the natural lines of communication.

The great majority of the province's two million people live in the southwest corner around Vancouver and Victoria. About 40,000 Indians live on reserves, and perhaps as many more live away from them.

English, French, Scottish traders from eastern Canada, and "Boston men" (Americans) engaged in the fur trade brought their variety of speech with them. Mixed with the two dozen Indian tongues, this resulted in the Chinook jargon, now a "dead language" still traceable in speech and in place-names. Skookumchuck, for instance, means "powerful water." To these immigrants were soon added gold-seekers of every nation and condition. Railway construction demanded much cheap labor, and those who came often stayed to develop fishing, gardening (the Japanese), and other trades. Scandinavians helped to develop the logging and fishing industries, and today nearly every whaler is Norwegian. Americans launched the cattle industry in the Cariboo, and are still moving into ranching.

English capital went into orchards and mines, and continues in industrial development and housing projects.

AGRICULTURE. Because of the numerous mountain and forest areas little of the land is suitable for farming. Where crops are planted, however (in the Vancouver area around the Lower Fraser Valley), they thrive. Products from this area include fruits, a variety of vegetables and bulbs, and cattle. In the southern interior, irrigated lands grow fruits, while grain and livestock are most important in the northeastern region.

INDUSTRY. Wood processing (veneer and plywood) and food processing (packing of fish, meats, fruits, and vegetables) are the two key areas of manufacturing in British Columbia.

Forestry resources are abundant. British Columbia leads the country in production of wood products. Logs are cut and floated down to sawmills around Vancouver. Fishing is also a big industry.

Lead and zinc are the chief mined products, although a variety of other minerals, including copper, oil, and gas, contribute to the huge income earned yearly from mining.

CITIES. Vancouver and Victoria are the two largest, most important cities in British Columbia, although more visitors come to visit the outdoor wilderness than the towns. Rugged forests, steep mountains, and swiftly moving rivers make British Columbia an outdoor-lover's paradise.

THE MOUNTAINS. Several corridors penetrate the Rocky Mountain barrier, with **Crowsnest Pass** in the south leading through mining country—coal, gold, lead and silver—and into a tangle of mountains and lakes. These are threaded on the wavering **Kettle Valley railway line,** and **No. 3 Highway,** a very in-and-out and up-and-down route of great scenic beauty.

The next route through the mountains is the **Banff-Windermere Highway,** which crosses through **Kootenay Pass.** A road in Banff forks at the foot of **Mount Eisenhower,** and the south branch swings through the **Kootenay National Park,** 71 miles to the **Columbia River road.** Watch for panhandling black bears; **Marble Canyon,** 2,000 by 200 feet deep, with natural bridge and waterfall; **Vermilion Pass and River; Iron Gates,** natural portals of red sandstone; **Radium Hot Springs,** hot mineral waters in bathhouse and pool; and **Sinclair Canyon.** Just beyond the park boundaries are yellow sandstone hoodoos on the bank of the **Columbia River,** and in the Kootenay Valley, wide grasslands and lovely **Windermere Lake.**

On the summit of **Kicking Horse Pass,** a small creek divides, one branch heading east for the Atlantic, the other west to the Pacific. Nearby arches the sign, **"The Great Divide."** The Continental Divide also marks the provincial boundary and that of **Banff** and **Yoho national parks.** Yoho is one of three smaller mountain parks of special delight to alpinist and hiker. **Lake O'Hara** and the **Seven Sisters Falls,** tumbling down from **Lake Oesa,** are reserved for hikers and trail-riders. **Yoho Valley** and **Takkakaw Falls,** tumbling 1,248 feet, may be reached by car. Just off the **Trans-Canada Highway** is the **Natural Bridge** which **Kicking Horse River** has worn through the rock. The **Emerald River** flows in close by, and a motor road leads up its valley to the incredibly green **Emerald Lake.** A memorable sight in Yoho National Park is that of a railway train negotiating the world-famous **Spiral Tunnels.** A most ingenious engineering feat, the railway tracks form the figure **8,** one loop inside Cathedral Mountain, the other across the river inside Mount Ogden, at the same time changing their elevation by more than 100 feet in less than a mile.

Farther north in the Rockies is **Yellowhead Pass,** west of Jasper, with hoary **Mount Robson** overlooking its western end. Robson, at 12,972 feet, highest peak in the Canadian Rockies, is enclosed in a provincial park. A guest ranch below provides horses for the 18-mile trail ride up to the chalets on the north side of the mountain. Passing through the **Valley of a Thousand Falls,** fording the **Robson River,** visiting glorious **Emperor Falls, Berg Lake** and its **Tumbling Glacier**—this is a most beautiful ride to alpine meadows. Another road slopes southward from Yellowhead Pass, following the north branch of the **Thompson River,** through spectacular scenery to **Kamloops.**

Across the **Rocky Mountain Trench** rise the **Selkirk Mountains,** containing **Glacier National Park.** Railway and highway mount the steep valley of the **Beaver River** to the park, set among mountain peaks over 10,000 feet high. The region is noted for its wild life—bear, mountain goat, marmot—and above all for its fantastic 40-foot snowfall, highest in Canada. The heavy snowfall necessitated miles of snowsheds over the railway before the five-mile **Connaught Tunnel** was drilled through **Mount Macdonald.** The precipitous **Illecillewaet River** carves a valley for itself—and for human traffic—as it plunges down the western slope of the Selkirks, skirting **Mount Revelstoke National Park.**

A road hairpins up Mount Revelstoke, past the championship ski jump, to lookouts that provide breathtaking views over the mighty Columbia River and the town of Revelstoke on the flats below. Here a directional board points out peaks, glaciers, ranges and, west of town, **Eagle Pass.** Highway and railway wriggle through to **Craigellachie,** where the last spike was driven on a raw November day in 1885. Beyond it is A-shaped **Shuswap Lake,** noted for scenery, wild ducks, and more varieties of trout than anywhere else in British Columbia. Shuswap Lake drains into the South Thompson River, which flows from the cool forests of the mountains through country that makes a sudden dramatic change. The plateau is dry, very hot in summer, very cold in winter. To the south, the plateau is cleft by the blue of **Okanagan Lake** and **River. Kelowna,** a pretty, thriving town, sponsors the notion that a sea-serpent, the Ogopogo of Indian tales, may dwell in unplumbed depths of the lake. Near Vernon at the north is a second lake, **Kalamalka,** whose greens and purples are noteworthy.

The city of **Kamloops,** originally a trading post at the junction of North and South Thompson, is headquarters for the cattle country, the near-desert of sagebrush and pinewoods, grasslands, and clay buttes, of sparkling lakes up in the mountains and of dry canyons with astonishing rock pillars. Due north of Kamloops, the **Cariboo Mountains** contain innumerable lakes in forested hills, some in the **Wells-Gray Provincial Park,** others fanning out from **100-Mile House,** most of them accessible by road. A number of guest "ranches" in this vicinity could more accurately be termed fishing lodges. **Barkerville,** scene of the great Cariboo gold rush, lies east of Quesnel, and is gradually being restored to its early appearance. One may watch the hydraulic mining near Wells.

Farther north is the city of **Prince George,** a traffic crossroads. The Canadian National Railway runs through from Yellowhead Pass to the Pacific at **Prince Rupert,** paralleled by the **Skeena Highway.** The **Pacific Great Eastern,** British Columbia's own railroad, slices across the province from Vancouver in the southwest to the **Peace River Block** in the northeast, following the path of the **Hart Highway.** At **Dawson Creek,** the P.G.E. links with the **Northern Alberta Railway,** and the **Hart Highway** with the beginning of the **Alaska Highway.** This fabulous road to Fairbanks wavers across the "high, wide and lonesome" northeastern corner of British Columbia. The village of **Telegraph Creek** on the **Stikine River** is still served by flat-bottomed riverboat based at **Wrangell, Alaska,** which makes a weekly **scenic voyage** upriver through the **Coast Range.**

The main river of British Columbia is the **Fraser,** which begins in the Rockies near Yellowhead Pass and, in the shape of a giant meathook, gouges a path across the province. In the 70-mile **Fraser Canyon** watch for the green waters of the **Thompson** joining the silted Fraser at **Lytton;** the aerial car ferry at **Boston Bar; Hell's Gate,** a portal with fish ladders and viewing windows where you can watch salmon on their way upstream; nearby **Devil's Wash Basin,** a whirlpool; the bridges by which highways and railways switch to opposite sides of the canyon. At **Hope,** the Fraser makes a right-angle turn out of the Coast Range, to flow 100 miles to Vancouver.

VANCOUVER. The sawmill settlement on Burrard Inlet gladly changed its name from Granville to Vancouver, in order to become the terminal of the Canadian Pacific Railway in 1887. This was greatly to the annoyance of Victoria, on Vancouver Island, and the rivalry between the two cities has never completely cooled. Greater Vancouver includes the nearby municipalities, and is the third largest city in Canada, with about 985,000 residents. Vancouver revels in a beautiful setting, with Seymour and Grouse mountains rising straight from the salt water, and beyond, the famous Lions. Vancouver grew up on a mitten-shaped peninsula, between the Fraser and Burrard Inlet, with 1,000-acre **Stanley Park** as its "green thumb." Vancouver's safe harbor is Canada's gateway to the Far East and to the South Pacific.

Sightseeing buses show visitors around, a good way to get acquainted with a city that flings many bridges across **False Creek, Burrard Inlet,** and various arms of the Fraser. Vancouver is a trail-blazer in architecture, with its modernistic **public library, art gallery, civic auditorium** and the **city hall** perched upon a height well uptown. The guide will point out the **University of British Columbia** at Point Grey as you take in the **Marine Drive,** and downtown the flourishing **Chinatown,** third only to San Francisco and New York, with its markets, shops and excellent restaurants. Dooryards and public parks, including **Little Mountain** and **Stanley parks,** have lovely gardens.

Stanley Park has formal gardens, forest trails, a Lost Lagoon and lily-covered lake in the wilderness depths; a vest-pocket zoo, cricket pitch, bathing beaches, golf links, tennis courts and concrete checkerboard, outdoor theater and restaurants.

Harbor cruises, boarded at the entrance to Stanley Park, show a very lively scene with craft of many kinds—seiners and trollers, grain ships, ferries to Vancouver Island and liners from Australia, motorboats, tow-boats hauling slow-moving barges, oil tankers.

The **Lions Gate Bridge** is a delicate-looking span arching over Burrard Inlet, to serve communities on the north shore. **A Marine Drive** links many small pretty communities strung out along the inlet. At **Horseshoe Bay,** a new road turns northeastward with the P.G.E. Railway, up **Howe Sound to Squamish** and on to **Garibaldi Provincial Park.** Formerly reached only by rail, Garibaldi is a high, beautiful, little-known park with jade-green lakes and towering peaks, fine hiking country in summer, skiing country in winter.

A new road continues into the village of **Horseshoe Bay,** and there a ferry makes the hour-long trip across the rugged fiord of **Howe Sound.** Another hour-long ferry trip comes at **Jervis Inlet,** a beautiful arm of water running far back into the mountains. The road ends a few miles north of **Powell River,** a pulp-and-paper city, at a maze of channels and islands known to ardent salmon fishermen. The road has replaced the steamer service on which the residents formerly relied. Union steamships still ply the Inside Passage to the **Queen Charlotte Islands** and **Prince Rupert,** calling at isolated ports such as **Bella Coola** and **Ocean Falls.** Both **Canadian National** and **Canadian Pacific steamships** operate **cruises** from **Vancouver** and **Seattle** to **Skagway, Alaska,** a 7-day cruise of 2,000 scenic miles said to be unsurpassed anywhere.

VICTORIA AND THE ISLANDS. At the southern tip of cigar-shaped Vancouver Island is the capital city of Victoria, more than 185,000 citizens in the aggregate. With the snow-capped **Olympic Mountains** across **Juan de Fuca Strait,** Victoria is delightfully located. In fact, being on a point of **Saanich Peninsula,** the city seems to have salt water sparkling at the end of every street. The Inner Basin of Victoria Harbor, where ferries from Vancouver and Seattle berth, is flanked by the **Legislative Buildings** in their green lawns, and the fabled **Empress Hotel** amid its holly hedges. Victoria is sedate, very pretty, and deliberately English. Old buildings in Victoria are **Dr. Helmcken's house** (1852), now a museum, and **Craigflower School,** first school in British Columbia, near the head of Gorge Waters. About the same age are the totem poles standing in **Thunderbird Park** between the Empress Hotel and the **Provincial Museum.** Most are authentic poles or ceremonial figures moved from abandoned Indian villages up-coast. Others are replicas of weathered poles in the museum. The world's tallest totem pole was carved here recently, and erected in nearby **Beacon Hill Park.** Also in Thunderbird Park is an Indian dugout canoe, bought and refitted by Captain Voss, which made a voyage around the world.

Victoria's downtown street lamps are adorned with hanging flower baskets, precedent for such attractions in other cities. Victorians are, if possible, even keener about gardening than Vancouverites. **Beacon Hill Park** exhibits flowers outdoors winter and summer. Victoria gets less than half the rainfall of Vancouver, however, and gardens must be nursed through the hottest spells. The **Butchart Gardens** a few miles outside the city are among the world's five most famous private gardens. The late Mrs. Butchart created the Italian, English, and Japanese Gardens for family pleasure. She brought earth and imported plants to an ugly quarry to create her famous **Sunken Garden.**

The **Island Highway** swings westward from Victoria, then north over the Malahat, with its Lookout across the **Strait of Georgia** and the (miscalled) **Gulf Islands.** The scenic drive up-island continues, either close to the shore, through older settlements, or bypassing them on a new straighter highway. At **Nanaimo** look for **Petroglyph Park,** where quaint drawings were pecked in the flat rock ages ago by unknown Indians; the **octagonal log bastion,** once part of the Hudson's Bay Company fort, now a museum; a large chunk of coal, monument to a historic industry. Ferries operate to **Gabriola Island** and, more important, directly across the Strait to Vancouver. The **Island Highway** continues north past sandy beaches and summer resorts like **Qualicum,** to small towns and logging communities. Side roads ray to **Alberni** on the west coast, toward **Forbidden Plateau,** and at **Campbell River,** to **Strathcona Provincial Park** and **Buttle Lake.** The jagged chain of snowy peaks continues north, beyond the reach of roads. The west coast of Vancouver Island is beautiful and lonely, with craggy shores, Indian villages and long sandy beaches rarely footprinted. Canadian Pacific Steamships provide steamer service to this coast, a five-day round-trip that is delightful in fine weather.

SPORTS AND RECREATION. There are a variety of facilities available, including lawn **bowling, mountain climbing, skiing** even in summer, spectator sports. Yachting and motorboating are very popular on lake and salt water. **Fishing** is possible almost everywhere—trout and grayling inland; salmon derbies are practically epidemic along the coast in August; oysters, abalone, clams are for the gathering. There is **hunting** for everything from upland game birds, ducks, and geese to all varieties of North American big game.

SPECIAL EVENTS. Vancouver–**International Arts Festival,** three weeks in June–July; **Sea Festival,** July; **Pacific National Exhibition,** two weeks, August–September; **Chinese New Year,** February; Victoria–**May Day celebrations** (Victoria Day); **flower shows** in season in **Crystal Gardens; Yule Log and Boar's Head** traditional ceremonies, December 25. July 1 (Dominion Day) there is a **Cherry Carnival** at Osoyoos; **Barbecue,** Saturna Island; **Loggers Sports,** at Lumby. **Williams Lake Stampede** runs for three days around July 1.

DINING AND SHOPPING. Freshly caught salmon is a specialty in restaurants throughout the province, and is served in a variety of dishes. Visitors can also find Mexican, German, Danish, and many other international foods in British Columbia.

Good shopping values include British woolens, clothing, leather, and china; Irish linens; and antiques. Eskimo carvings, sweaters, basketry, and prints are other excellent buys.

Yukon Territory

The Yukon, a beautiful, rugged, and immense territory, became famous in the Gold Rush of 1898. Made more accessible by the Alaska Highway, the Yukon is a friendly, hard-working area where mining is still the chief industry.

THE LAND. Yukon Territory, 207,076 square miles, fills Canada's northwestern corner, and is up against the Alaska border and the Arctic Ocean. The Mackenzie Mountains divide Yukon from the Northwest Territories, and the 60th parallel from British Columbia. A contour map of Yukon makes it appear completely mountainous, but the southern interior is actually a great plateau, drained by the Yukon and its tributary rivers. The plateau extends almost to the Arctic Circle. Above it comes the Porcupine River system, which reverses its direction to flow past Old Crow Indian settlement, and join the Yukon River in Alaska. The Yukon is the great river system, rising in the Coast Range of British Columbia, gathering silted glacial waters and the clear cold green of lakes in its journey of more than 2,000 miles to the Bering Sea. The sharp snowy peaks of the St. Elias Range in the west are extensions of the Coast Range. These are the highest peaks in Canada, and include Mount Logan at 19,850 feet, second only to Mount McKinley in Alaska.

THE CLIMATE. June to September, when temperatures are in the mid-seventies, are the best months to come to the Yukon. In winter, below zero temperatures cover most of the territory. Snowfall varies between 40 and 80 inches yearly, most in the north.

THE PEOPLE. Little was known of the Yukon before the Gold Rush of 1898, and not much more before construction of the Alaska Highway in 1942. Hudson's Bay Company fur traders explored and named the rivers, set up trading posts at river junctions, including the first at Fort Selkirk in 1838. So little was the interior known that in 1867, when the United States purchased Alaska from Russia, the Hudson's Bay Company trading post of Fort Yukon was found to be about 100 miles on the wrong side of the Alaska-Yukon boundary line.

Gold-seekers panned their way north from the creeks of southern British Columbia to the Cariboo, then the Cassiar Mountains. By 1873, quite a number had reached Yukon, and by 1895, there were several hundred miners. On August 17, 1896, three men struck gold on Bonanza Creek near Dawson trading post, giving nearby prospectors just enough time to stake their claims before the stampede was upon them. The Klondike gold rush lasted several years, until gold was discovered in Alaska. Over $100 million in gold was washed out of Klondike creeks in eight years. Yukon has produced some $400 million in gold altogether, largely by modern hydraulic and dredging techniques. Equally valuable have been the silver, zinc and lead deposits at Keno Hill.

Some 17,000 people live in the Yukon. A very few nomadic Eskimos live along the Arctic coast. The Tlingits, or "Stick" Indians, of the interior are energetic, good hunters and craftsmen, whose young people are trying to retain their own culture and coexist with the white population. Many of these are miners—old-timers, prospectors and geologists, and those employed in actual mining operations. Some Yukoners remained in the backwash of highway construction, and went into business for themselves. A considerable tourist industry has grown up, not least in big-game guiding. Many residents are employed at large or small airfields dotted around the Territory, on road construction, or on the White Pass Railway and bus routes. Government has grown up to administer this valuable Territory.

AGRICULTURE. On the benchlands of the rivers, fertile volcanic soil raises excellent crops of vegetables, although frost is always a hazard. Because of the brief summers, farming is of no large-scale importance to the economy.

INDUSTRY. Yukon mountain ranges contain a wealth of minerals including gold, silver, zinc, lead, and asbestos. After being mined, ores are also processed in the Yukon. Tourism is a growing industry, due in large part to the construction of the Alaska Highway.

CITIES. Whitehorse is the only town with more than 1,000 residents, the others being small settlements which dot the territory. Most visitors, however, come to see the remains of the gold rush days.

DAWSON. A good graveled highway now replaces the winter trail from Whitehorse to Dawson, the former capital. Dawson, with only about 700 residents now, boasted 35,000 population during the gold rush days. It remained the capital until new administrative buildings were needed, and the capital was moved to Whitehorse. The town has a glamorous past, beginning as a fur-trading post at the junction of the Yukon and Klondike rivers. To visitors, it seems a true ghost town, with weathered frost-heaved old dance halls and gambling saloons. Visitors can stay at a hotel that is one of the few historic buildings to survive the years. The cabin in which bank clerk Robert Service lived when transferred to Dawson is kept in good condition. You can drive along the Klondike River to the placer workings, and from **Midnight Dome** view the headwaters of most of the rich creeks. The road is built on tailings from the gold dredges that inch their way along the gravel bars from which all the "easy gold" was extracted long ago. Some dredges can handle a million cubic yards of gravel a season (a yard of gravel weighs 3,000 pounds), and average only two or three cups of pure gold per week.

WHITEHORSE, terminus of the White Pass & Yukon Route, became a city in 1950, and capital of Yukon Territory in 1951, instead of remote Dawson. From the beginning, Whitehorse has been a distributing center and transportation hub—by river, then rail, then air, finally highway. A small fleet of paddle-wheel steamers operated until 1955. The railway terminated at Whitehorse below the dreaded Miles Canyon and Whitehorse Rapids, where some Argonauts lost their lives.

Interesting to see are **Old Log Church,** now Christ Church Cathedral, built 1900; the 1906 account books, initialed "R.W.S." by vestry clerk Robert W. Service, bank teller and poet of the gold rush. Among his rhymes was "The Cremation of Sam McGee," whose cabin is now a museum. Nearby stands an old stagecoach, used on the Whitehorse-Dawson winter Overland Trail; and an **Indian cemetery** with small "doll" houses over the graves. **McBride Museum,** in a two-story log telegraph office of 1899, contains Indian and gold rush mementos. Some 20 miles west of town, **Takhini Hot Springs** sports a large concrete swimming pool and lunch counter.

Some gold-seekers reached Yukon overland, but most poured off ships at Skagway, and pushed up through the mountain passes—Dyea, Chilkoot, Chilkat or White—blazing the Trail of '98. Their tracks can still be seen from the train windows of the White Pass & Yukon Route. This narrow-gauge railway runs more than 100 miles from the tidewater to Whitehorse on the Yukon River, and was built in 1898–1900 to carry miners and supplies. The difficult construction job was further complicated by workmen rushing off with the company tools to the gold fields. The little line was used to haul materials for the airfields of the Northwest Staging Route and later for the Alaska Highway.

Today its diesel locomotives still haul supplies in and concentrated ore out, as well as providing a scenic one- or two-day tour for visitors. The tracks rise abruptly from Skagway at sea level, and climb steeply for 20 miles. At **Dead Horse Gulch,** where 3,000 pack animals perished during the gold rush, the trail below the tracks is clearly visible on the mountainside. Waterfalls, roaring little streams, jagged peaks and dense forests mark this slope in Alaska. Once over the summit, there is a gentle descent through British Columbia to 20-mile **Lake Bennett,** where the gold-seekers whipsawed lumber into boats and rafts for the 550 river miles to the Klondike gold fields.

Along the Alaska Highway are many places of interest. At Lower Post, on the Liard River, the highway begins its 600 miles in Yukon, and at **Dry Creek** it enters Alaska for its final 300 miles to **Fairbanks.** Watch for **Fort St. John,** 1806 trading post now with flourishing gas wells; **Summit Lake,** at 4,256 feet, highest point on the highway as it crosses the Rocky Mountains; **Teslin,** at the center of 85-mile Teslin Lake, headquarters of Indian tribe; and, at **Champagne** on the old Dalton Trail, numerous gravehouses at the Indian cemetery.

SPORTS AND RECREATION. There is little organized sport, but good **hunting** for big-game trophies–moose, caribou, mountain sheep and goats, bear–and for upland and migratory game birds. **Fishing** is outstanding for grayling, lake trout, northern pike and rainbow trout.

DINING AND SHOPPING. Many visitors to the Yukon go camping along the way, and do their own cooking. Supplies are available in most towns, and several good restaurants, especially in Whitehorse, can also be found.

Indian-made moccasins, gloves and jackets of caribou or moosehide, raw furs, jewelry of mammoth ivory and gold nuggets are good buys in Yukon.

Northwest Territories

This somewhat illogically named "Northwest Territories" is a tremendous stretch of land, ice, and water reaching from the 60th parallel, between Hudson Bay and the Yukon, to the Arctic Ocean. With only two persons per 100 square miles, it is virtually uninhabited.

THE LAND. The tree line swoops down from the mouth of the Mackenzie River in the northwest to south of Churchill, Manitoba. The country is low-lying, of moss-covered rock with ponds and lakes among the boulders and bedrock of the Canadian Shield, broken here and there by clumps of spruce and occasional rivers. The Territories includes all the islands in Hudson and James Bay, and several Arctic islands on the Canadian mainland.

THE CLIMATE. Summer is brief throughout the Northwest Territories, though the sun shines brightly all through the night in regions above the Arctic Circle. In places, spring breakup does not come until June, and ice begins to form again in September. The milder climate of the Mackenzie River Valley promotes forest growth.

THE PEOPLE. For centuries, European explorers pushed among the islands and channels of the Arctic, searching for a northwest passage to Asia. They found instead a bleak country, and the friendly, peaceful Eskimos. Fur trading began in the Arctic within the present century, when the only fur, arctic fox, became valuable. However, in the forested regions the fur trade is much older. Alexander Mackenzie, the daring young fur trader, pushed northward to the Arctic Ocean on the 2,600-mile river now named for him. Toward the end of the nineteenth century, Britain ceded the Northwest Territories to Canada, and the Districts of Yukon, Mackenzie and Keewatin were drawn on the map.

Only 34,000 people live in this region

Canadian Northwest Territory

of 1,304,903 square miles, including most of Canada's Eskimos. Tribes of Indians live in the wooded regions around Great Bear and Great Slave lakes, and along the Mackenzie River to its delta. The white population of the Northwest Territories has long consisted of fur traders and trappers, Mounted Police and missionaries. Fur traders are still there, though much of their work is actually straight storekeeping. Hunting and trapping are now reserved for Indians and Eskimos, though many are also employed in mines, at airfields, and building the natural gas pipeline that will carry gas from Prudhoe Bay, Alaska to the Canadian provinces and the mainland. Government installations have multiplied in recent years–radio, military, weather, airports, administration.

The Northwest Territories hold great interest for the hardy traveler. Most travel nowadays is by air, either scheduled or charter flights or via the Great Slave Lake Railway which runs to Pine Point. The Hudson's Bay Company vessel *Rupertsland* carries a few passengers on its supply trips each summer to posts in the **Districts of Franklin and Keewatin.** The District of Franklin lies well above the Arctic Circle, comprising mostly the **Arctic Islands,** including the large **Baffin Island.** Its booming townsite, **Frobisher Bay,** has an important airfield, and is a metropolis of the **Canadian Arctic.** The **District of Keewatin** includes the west coast of Hudson Bay and its interior. Its most important settlement is **Chesterfield,** with hospital, schools, and government offices.

AGRICULTURE and forestry are of almost no importance to the economy of the Northwest Territories. Only the District of Mackenzie could support crops in any large quantities, and most food must be brought in from the Canadian provinces.

INDUSTRY. Mining, fishing, and fur trapping are the main industries. Iron, zinc, and lead mining is being exploited. Geologists expect to locate a big oil field in the Mackenzie Delta.

Whitefish and lake trout are caught in large numbers on Great Slave Lake. Trapping for fox, mink, muskrat, beaver, and seal also brings income to the Territories.

DISTRICT OF MACKENZIE is the most populous, has a more equable climate, and is most accessible of the Northwest Territories. The Mackenzie River forms a great thoroughfare to the Arctic Ocean, along which the natural gas pipeline is being built, with a network of large rivers and lakes feeding into it. Travel is by airplane, except for local motorboats and dog teams. Freight, supplied via the Alaska Highway, the Mackenzie Highway and by railway to McMurray on the Athabasca River, moves down the river network on barges. **Fort Smith** on the **Slave River** just within the borders is headquarters for the Northwest Territories.

Mackenzie Highway, first road into the Northwest Territories, pushes north from Peace River, Alberta, to Hay River on Great Slave Lake. Watch for gravehouses at **Indian Cabins Post;** 65-foot **Louisa Falls;** 106-foot **Alexandra Falls; Hay River** (old and new towns), headquarters for freight and commercial fishery. At the gold-mining town of **Yellowknife** (new and old towns), across the lake, one may visit a gold mine and possibly see a gold brick being poured. **Inuvik,** a "double town" which includes the town of **Aklavik,** which was moved because the latter's land was sinking, is far to the north, a sleepy settlement of Indians, Eskimos and whites, until the recent excitement of the pipeline made it a boom town. Farther down the Mackenzie River, at **Reindeer Station,** are corrals for herds of reindeer owned by government and Eskimos.

SPORTS AND RECREATION. There is little organized sport in the Territories, except at Yellowknife or Hay River, though the Territories are becoming increasingly popular for fishing. Several fishing lodges have sprung up, two in the District of Franklin. Fishing for grayling, arctic char, and lake trout is good. Visitors can arrange at a trading post to accompany Eskimos on a polar bear, walrus, seal, or whale hunt in season. Muskox are protected at all times, and many are found in the **Thelon Game Sanctuary** in Mackenzie District.

SPECIAL EVENTS. The most interesting events for visitors are a **tagging and tabulating roundup,** held in June at the Reindeer Station on Mackenzie River, and a **meat roundup** in December.

DINING AND SHOPPING. No foods of special interest are served in the towns, although Eskimo handicrafts (*mukluks,* the Eskimo decorated footwear; parkas, and soapstone carvings) can be found in many settlements.

Mexico
Central America
Bermuda
The Bahama Islands

Mexico

MEXICO
Cortez
Tijuana
Ensenada
Nogales
Juarez
Guaymas
Nuevo Laredo
Chihuahua
Monterrey
Matamoros
Gulf of Mexico
Durango
La Paz
Mazatlan
Tampico
Guadalajara
Veracruz
Manzanillo
MEXICO
Acapulco
Oaxaca
Pacific Ocean

Mexico

In almost every way Mexico is unusual. It is unusual in shape and setting, in physical character, culture. Climatic contrasts are extreme and dramatic.

In size Mexico spreads over more than 760,000 square miles, an area equal to one fourth of the continental United States, the third largest of the Latin American countries. Mexico's greatest width is its northern land border with the United States, a distance of a little more than 2,000 miles, stretching northwest to southeast. The narrowest point of Mexico is only 125 miles wide.

The shape of Mexico is that of a slightly bent triangle, with its broad base on the north, its apex to the southeast. The angling northern base has the state of California on the west, Arizona in the middle, and Texas on the east. Much of the border with Texas is the Rio Grande River, which, in Mexico, is called the Rio Bravo. On the western side of Mexico's northern U.S. border, a narrow, rugged peninsula called "Lower California" or, in Mexico, "Baja California," a rocky gnarled finger, extends 760 miles to the south. It has the Pacific Ocean on its west, the Gulf of California on its east. East of the Gulf of California and below it, the western limit of Mexico, extending northwest to southeast, is the shore of the Pacific Ocean.

The eastern limit of Mexico is the Gulf of Mexico. Thrusting into the Gulf from the narrow southern apex of the Mexican triangle is the broad peninsula of Yucatán. The southern land border of Mexico, flanking Yucatán and the narrow Isthmus of Tehuantepec, is British Honduras on the north, and below it, Guatemala. From the border of California on the north to the southern border of Guatemala is 1,600 miles. Mexico's Pacific coast line is more than 4,400 miles, and its eastern coast line is nearly 1,800 miles. From the northern tip of the peninsula of Yucatán it is only 125 miles to the tip of Cuba, and only 600 miles due north to Pensacola, Florida.

The area of Mexico is divided into 29 states, two territories, and a federal district. The states range in size from the huge area of Chihuahua in the north, 245,000 square kilometers (about 95,000 square miles). The smallest area is the federal district, with about 1,500 square kilometers. Within all of Mexico live over 50 million people, of which around seven million live in metropolitan Mexico City, the capital.

THE LAND

Mexico is framed by northern deserts, tropical jungles on the south, tropic seas on either side. Within that frame of desert, tropic jungle and shining ocean, the character of the land of Mexico is dramatic in the extreme. Its most important physical features are mountains that fill three-fourths of the area of the country, sweeping north to south along both coasts in rugged ranges. In the west, along the Pacific, often rising abruptly from the sea, are the wild and rugged ranges of the Sierra Madre Occidental. Swinging down the eastern coast is the great range of the Sierra Madre Oriental, less rugged and more verdant. Between the mountains and the sea on either side is a narrow, coastal, semi-arid region where elevations range from about 4,000 feet in the north to more than 8,000 feet in the south. Where the two great coastal ranges meet, rises a mountain mass from which towers a cluster of peaks, most of them former volcanoes. Among them are snow-crowned crests that rise to more than 18,000 feet above the sea. They include the beloved and majestic peak of Popocatépetl, and its neighbor, Iztaccihuatl.

Below this central mountain mass extends a lower range called the Sierra Madre del Sur, with a narrow coastal strip on the west which contains Mexico's most famed ocean resort, Acapulco. To the south is the tropical isthmus of Tehuantepec, where the land is only a few hundred feet above sea level.

Mexico has no important rivers. The few that it does have, which lie wholly within the country, tumble swiftly down from the mountains toward the sea, and are navigable only near the coast. Its largest and most celebrated river is shared with the United States, the wide and shallow Rio Grande.

Within the mountain area there are several lakes. The largest, Lake Chapala, nearly 50 miles long and about ten miles wide, lies at an elevation of 6,000 feet. The highest navigable lake in Mexico is Lake Pátzcuaro, about 13 miles long, which lies high in the mountains at an elevation of 6,717 feet. The most famous lake in Mexico is now little more than a dusty saucer in the high mountains. It was Lake Texcoco, the site of the present Mexico City.

The contrast of Mexico extends to the character of the surface of the land. Vast areas of northern Mexico, particularly along the border of the United States, are complete desert. Associated with the desert are high, grassy ranges, which are semi-arid and largely uncultivated. The rugged, tumbled western mountains, Sierra Madre Occidental, are cut with deep gorges and valleys called *barrancas*. The western coastal strip is semi-arid, but the east coast is humid and richly verdant. As the coasts converge toward the south, land becomes more and more tropical, ending in the lowland isthmus in an almost impenetrable tropical jungle.

THE CLIMATE

Since all of Mexico lies well within the tropical zone, it would be expected to have a tropical climate, and does have, in many areas. But the country's southern position is but one factor in its climate. Others are altitude and rainfall. Most of the people of Mexico live within altitudes ranging from 4,000 to 7,000 feet, in the high central plateau area, where the effect of altitude is to modify the tropical climate. Thus, Mexico City, for example, where the altitude is about 7,500 feet, has a climate perpetually springlike. Another factor is rainfall, which is very scant in some areas, creating the desert regions of northern Mexico. The rainfall increases to the south and to the east. Thus, in states like Tabasco in the south on the Gulf, the annual rainfall often exceeds 120 inches, making steaming tropical jungle. Rains in Mexico tend to be seasonal, generally most of the rain falling between June and September. Rainfall in the west coast is relatively slight, giving that area a hot, dry climate, very similar to southern California. All the coastal areas are hot and tropical year-round.

Climatically, Mexico City is pleasant to visit at any time. The sun shines almost every day, even in the season of rains, and nights are invariably cool. The rainy season in Mexico City usually begins in May, continues until early fall, but the rains are remarkably regular, generally beginning about four in the afternoon and lasting for around two hours. From October to May, it almost never rains. In January, the mean temperature average in Mexico City is 54 degrees; in June it climbs to an average of 64 degrees.

The east coast of Mexico is likely to be steamy and uncomfortable most of the time, and can be unbearably so during the summer season. The west coast, on the other hand, is quite dry and the humidity very low, but the summer temperatures become incredibly high. The best time to visit either coast is the late fall, winter, and early spring.

THE PEOPLE

The extraordinary differences between the people who now live in Mexico, in physical appearance, customs, and culture, is one of the fascinating aspects of the country. Mexico exhibits physical evidence of civilizations that go back several thousand years in the form of ancient temples and the ruins of once great cities. Mexico was civilized to a degree long before the birth of Christ. It is known that the cultivation of maize, which we call corn, began there perhaps 6,000 years ago, and that pottery was made and fabrics woven in Mexico almost that long ago.

No one knows where the people came from who first built their temples and villages in Mexico, although two theories have been brought forward. One is that nomadic tribes crossed the Bering Sea from Asia, slowly worked their way south, and settled in Mexico. Another is that the Asiatic peoples came to Mexico across the Pacific. There were dozens of different prehistoric tribes that left behind no record of their life or character, but some tribes were smarter, stronger, and more aggressive than others. They conquered or destroyed their neighbors and began to develop cities. The most remarkable of these were the Mayans, who migrated north from the jungles of Guatemala probably more than 3,000 years ago, and built cities in the region of Yucatán. The descendants of the Mayans still live in Yucatán, some speaking the Mayan language. The ruins of the cities their ancestors built there are among the exciting sights in Mexico. At the same time the Mayan empire was developing in southern Mexico, another tribe, called the Toltecs, warriors and hunters, came down from the north, and began to develop cities in the great central mountain plateau area. They built temples and palaces of remarkable design and character, ruins of which can still be seen.

After the Toltecs came the Aztecs, fighters with a greed for power who had little trouble conquering less warlike tribes. It is believed that their dominance of central Mexico began at about 1300. They established their capital in the valley of Mexico, the site of the present Mexico City, around the shores of Lake Texcoco. There they built one of the biggest and most beautiful cities in the world. Nothing in Europe could match it for splendor. About the year 1500 it is thought to have had more than 100,000 people, served by stone aqueducts carrying water from the hills, by concrete causeways linking islands of the lake. There were temples and palaces, flower gardens and fountains. In the year 1487, five years before Columbus sailed west to discover a new world, the Aztecs built and dedicated a new temple, largest and finest of them all. It is said that more than 20,000 slaves were sacrificed at its dedication.

Thirty-two years later, a Spanish adventurer, named Hernando Cortez (Sp., Hernán Cortés), landed on the east coast of Mexico at the site of the present city of Veracruz, which he named. He had with him about 500 soldiers, 11 ships, which he promptly burned, 16 horses, and ten cannon. He proposed with his tiny expeditionary force to conquer the empire of the Aztecs. He succeeded in doing so in about two years, in a conquest unequaled in the history of the world. His weapons were craft and deceit, ingenuity and the superstition of his enemies, luck, ambition, murder and torture, and an occasional contest of arms. He overthrew the Aztec empire and tortured to death its emperor, tore down the great new Aztec temple, and with its stones began the building of a vast cathedral.

For the next 300 years, Spain ruled and exploited Mexico, built colonial cities with cathedrals and palaces like those in Spain. Most of them are still there, adding to the fascinating range of architectural variety which visitors find in Mexico. The Spanish conquerors of Mexico and the thousands of colonists that followed them began to develop vast ranches. They dug into the mountains to find and bring out the silver and gold which lay within them. From Mexico, Spanish expeditions of soldiers and priests explored, claimed, and settled areas that are now Arizona, New Mexico, Texas, and California within the United States. They built the Spanish missions of California and Arizona, and established the beginnings of many cities in those areas.

But the Spanish rulers of Mexico were not much concerned with human rights. Ideas of liberty and revolution which began in the United States and France finally took root in Mexico and flowered into a revolution in 1810. Twelve years later Mexico became a republic, but stable government was a long way in the future. Revolution followed revolution. Army officers fought each other for control. Twice, foreign nations invaded Mexico.

The United States invaded Mexico in 1845. In the settlement of that contest, the United States gained from Mexico the whole western area of this country. France tried to invade Mexico, and sent an army and a puppet emperor there, the Austrian Archduke Maximilian, and his wife Carlotta. Maximilian ruled Mexico for a few years and left behind a charming palace and a handsome boulevard.

Following Maximilian, another series of revolutions and rule by dictators ended with a final revolution of 1910, out of which grew Mexico's present stable government. Starting then, the stability of Mexico has been relatively unbroken, and the development of the country has proceeded with dramatic acceleration, resulting in a brilliant renaissance in industry, agriculture, architecture and culture.

The remnants and relics of Mexico's long, often dark and troubled history, which can be seen by the visitor to Mexico today, are rich in color, drama, and variety. In many areas are native villages where live descendants of ancient Indian tribes, often little changed in more than 2,000 years. In the northern mountains there is a tribe of Indians called Tarahumara, who wear Oriental serapes and colorful turbans, play small, home-made violins. On the Yucatán peninsula, thousands of people live in thatched huts like those their Mayan ancestors built, and speak an almost pure Mayan dialect. The whole story of Mexico's colorful pageant of people is told in its architecture. There are still standing huge and dramatic examples of vast stone structures built by the ancient Mayan, Toltec and Aztec peoples. During the 300 years of Spanish rule, churches and palaces were built in the growing cities of Mexico in all the styles that were known in Europe, with some embellishments and characteristics that were typically Mexican.

There are fine examples in Mexico of Gothic and Romanesque design, of the fanciful plateresque, characteristic of the Spanish Renaissance, of the rich and unrestrained baroque, and finally of the theatrical and richly exuberant and excessively ornamented Churrigueresque design. In its modern period, Mexico has made more dramatic and imaginative use of modern structural methods and materials than almost any other nation, with dozens of brilliant examples of modern design, often standing side by side with ancient colonial buildings. Most colorful of these is the great new University of Mexico, where soaring wall surfaces are covered with glowing mosaics.

Through the centuries, the designers and builders of Mexico, Mexican craftsmen, added their own details and local modifications. One of these was the lavish use of colored tile in domes and towers and wall surfaces. Another was the perfection of the enclosed patio, and the extensive use of arcades. Examples of all these add endless fascination to travel in Mexico today.

AGRICULTURE

Another example of the contrast of Mexico is in the range in the character of things the land produces. The tropical lowland areas, particularly the east coast, produce commercial quantities of coffee, cacao, sugar cane, cotton, coconut, fruit, corn, rice, and tobacco. In tropical Yucatán, the principal crop is henequen, a fibrous cactus-type plant which results in 50 percent of the world's supply of sisal, from which cord and rope are made.

In the central plateau, with its more temperate climate, chief crops are coffee, sugar cane, maguey, from which Mexico produces its celebrated drink tequila; tobacco, various cereals, fruit, alfalfa, and cotton. Tremendous irrigation projects along the west coast of Mexico have turned that semi-arid region into the country's most productive cotton-producing regions, which also have a large production of wheat and vegetables, particularly tomatoes.

In much of the central highlands, cattle ranges predominate, and sheep raising is important. Irrigation, resulting from the damming of small rivers in the mountain areas, has created a number of important cotton-producing districts. Truck gardening, which began there during the days of the Aztec empire, occupies most of the arable land surrounding Mexico City. The humid tropical lowland areas produce a rich variety of tropical fruits and bananas. Coffee plantations are important on the lower slopes of the mountains in the tropical zone, with Mexico fifth largest producer of coffee in the world. The extensive pine forests higher on the mountain slopes account for valuable naval stores, and some timber.

Mexico's harvest of the seas is important. Fishing fleets based on both coasts account for important commercial quantities of shrimp, sardines, abalone, red snapper. A special marine harvest is shark liver. The most ancient and widely produced crop in all of Mexico, however, is maize, or corn, grown on small tracts all over the country, almost entirely a subsistence crop and the basis of the Mexican diet.

Mexico's mineral wealth is vast, much of it still undeveloped. From the earliest Spanish days, Mexico has been the world's largest producer of silver. It is found almost all over the mountainous area of the country, usually occurring with lead, zinc, and copper. In lead, zinc, antimony and mercury, Mexico is the third largest producer in the world, and it is also an important producer of gold.

Mexico's mountains contain vast reserves of coal and iron, many of them still untapped. Iron ore deposits are believed to exceed 300 million tons, but iron ore production is only about half a million tons annually. Coal, both bituminous and anthracite, accounts for a production of about one-and-one-half million tons annually. Another important mineral resource in Mexico is sulphur, from salt domes in the southern part of the country, with more than 800,000 tons of it produced annually. But Mexico's most important mineral resource is oil, primarily found along the east coast in the area of Tampico and Veracruz. The production and refining of it from wells and in plants completely owned by the government is huge, averaging more than 160 million barrels a year. Most of the oil produced in Mexico is used there.

INDUSTRY

Except for smelting and refining plants to process the mineral products of Mexico's mines, Mexico, until recently, had no large manufacturing establishments and was not regarded as a manufacturing nation.

But from earliest days, small village shops and craft centers produced a variety of handicrafts of distinctive design and character. Within the past 35 years, new factories in Mexico have begun to produce all sorts of goods, most of them consumed in Mexico, but an increasing number developed for export. About 40 percent of these new plants are located in or near Mexico City, with several other larger cities dominant in particular industries. Thus, Monterrey is a center for the nation's iron and steel industry; Puebla is the chief textile city, as well as producing great quantities of pottery and tile; the port city of Progreso in Yucatán produces more cordage products than any city in the world. New plants in various parts of the country are producing shoes, cotton, wool, and synthetic textiles, flour, beverages, particularly beer (with Mexico claiming two of the largest breweries in the world), cigars, soap, cigarettes, electrical appliances, refined sugar.

For the visitor, Mexico's village shops and craft centers produce a fascinating range of products. Their availability to local markets and village shops makes shopping in Mexico an endless adventure in discovery. No region in the western hemisphere offers the visitor more colorful, varied, and unusual shopping rewards. Outstanding in this field is silverware, widely available but with some cities, such as Taxco, famed for it. Other outstanding craft products made in important quantities in village shops and centers are pottery of all kinds, tile, copperware, leather goods, glass, jewelry, colorful fabrics, tinware, toys, and wrought iron.

CITIES

Most of the people of Mexico live in quite small villages and on farms and ranches in rural districts. Except for Mexico City, there are no very large cities. There are, however, a number of medium-sized cities and quite a number of cities of from 25,000 to 50,000.

ACAPULCO, 150 miles to the west, is dramatically situated, overlooking the Pacific Ocean from behind a big and beautiful bay. Acapulco has a long and colorful history. It was for many years the chief west coast port for shipping to Mexico from the Orient, with cargoes including female slaves (which the Spanish conquistadors seemed to fancy). But the evidence of the old Acapulco has almost entirely disappeared. The present city is quite new, modern, and striking in appearance, with a forest of resorts and hotels of all types, sizes, and price ranges, rising from along the shore of the great bay and climbing up the mountain slopes behind. The city has a delightful winter climate, several fine beaches, and offers some of the best sports fishing in the world. Its points of interest include about a dozen striking new hotels, with a variety of features and facilities to beguile the visitor.

CUERNAVACA is 37 miles to the south and connected to Mexico City by an express highway. A city with distinct charm, it has a fine climate, an interesting setting, and is both a resort and a luxurious suburb of Mexico City. In it are the handsome villas of the very rich, set in tropical gardens; one of the oldest and most interesting cathedrals in Mexico, and a celebrated public garden once part of the estate of the French silver tycoon, José de la Borda.

FORTÍN DE LAS FLORES, the center of the most luxuriantly floral regions of Mexico, is famed for the production of gardenias, orchids, and camellias. The little town has one celebrated resort with a famous swimming pool kept full of gardenias.

GUADALAJARA, about 300 miles northwest of Mexico City, is the second largest city of Mexico, with a population of over a million people. Gay and brisk, it is the capital of the rich, colorful state of Jalisco. The city dominates a productive, verdant mountain valley, at an altitude of more than 5,000 feet. It has a delightful springlike climate year-round. With some of the finest examples of Colonial architecture in Mexico, Guadalajara also has new buildings of striking modern design which contrast dramatically with handsome older structures. Most important of the classic Colonial buildings is the great **cathedral** set between four plazas, a huge and remarkable building combining four different architectural types in a medley of towers and domes. The city is colorfully filled with gardens and parks of tropical flowers. It is also noted for shopping opportunities, particularly for glass, textiles, leather goods, and pottery.

Guadalajara is the center of a green and pleasant mountain district with unusual natural features, including **Lake Chapala,** largest lake in Mexico. On its shores are several delightful small villages, one being a picturesque center for artists and writers called **Ajijic.** Another famous village near Guadalajara is **Tequila,** center for the cultivation of maguey, from which the drink tequila is made. Between Lake Chapala and Guadalajara is Mexico's biggest and most scenic waterfall, created by the Santiago River, second largest waterfall on the North American continent after Niagara.

MÉRIDA, one of the most remote and isolated of the larger cities of Mexico, is capital of the state of Yucatán, and chief city of the Yucatán peninsula. Seventh largest city in Mexico, it has a population of over 250,000, is regarded as one of the cleanest cities in the country, and is said to have more windmills than any city in the world, an estimated 20,000. Mérida's chief interest for the visitor, however, is as a base from which to explore the extraordinary Mayan ruins which lie to the south and east of the city, easily reached by good highways. Of these the most famed is the archaeological zone of **Chichén-Itzá,** 70 miles to the east, where two groups of amazing ancient buildings have been excavated, several well-restored. They are regarded by archaeologists as among the most remarkable ancient ruins in the world.

Equally remarkable is another group of Mayan ruins 50 miles south of Mérida, called **Uxmal,** believed to have been an aristocratic center of Mayan rule, with most buildings built between the seventh and the eleventh centuries in what is known as the "great classic period." On the east coast of the Yucatán peninsula, reached only by boat or aircraft, is a fascinating tropical island called **Cozumel,** which has been developed as a new resort center.

MEXICO CITY, or, as it is generally referred to among Mexicans, simply Mexico, is a remarkable metropolis in many ways, unique in several ways. It is the third largest city in the western hemisphere, after New York and Chicago. Greater Mexico City has a population of over seven million people (more than the nine next largest cities combined), and is the oldest large city in the western world. When it was conquered by Cortez in 1521 it is thought to have had a population in excess of 300,000 people. It is the highest great city in the world, with an average altitude of 7,349 feet, a factor which tends to give it a delightful and stable sunny climate. No other city has a setting even remotely like that of Mexico City. It fills the southern end of a great valley about 60 miles long and 20 miles wide, once the bed of Lake Texcoco. From that former lake bed, the mountains rise steeply around the city to the east, south, and west. They include the great, towering, and beloved volcanic peaks, always snow-crested, of **Popocatepétl** and **Iztaccihuatl,** both towering more than 17,000 feet. Within its flat valley, the great metropolis spreads over 500 square miles, with important suburbs, many of them quite new, climbing into the mountain slopes. Much of the city is old, going back to the days of Colonial Spain. There are hundreds of miles of old, narrow streets, flanked with Colonial buildings, and many miles of wide, handsome new boulevards and avenues. Part of the charm and contrast of Mexico City is that an ancient church or ornate Colonial palace may stand side by side with a towering new hotel or office building of gleaming glass and shining metal.

Though the city spreads over a great area, most of the places of interest to the visitor are relatively close together and easily accessible. Quite a number are within walking distance of each other near the center of what is both modern and ancient Mexico City. These include the Zócalo, or **Central Plaza,** with Mexico City's great **National Cathedral,** the largest Christian church in the country, facing it. Of ornate Spanish Renaissance style, it stands on the site of a huge pagan temple of the Aztecs. Nearby is the **National Palace,** location of the offices of the President of Mexico, where a celebrated mural depicting the story of Mexico can be seen over the main staircase.

Not far from the National Palace is Mexico's ornate **Palace of Fine Arts,** a relatively new building of classic design, which houses the National Theater, galleries, auditoriums, and ballrooms, made more dramatic by the fact that just across the street from it is Mexico's tallest building, a modern skyscraper towering more than 40 stories.

The show street of Mexico City is the wide, beautiful **Paseo de la Reforma,** which links the heart of the old city with Mexico City's finest park, **Bosque Chapultepec,** to the west. Paseo is the city's most celebrated street, flanked by new, modern buildings on both sides. A series of historic monuments stands in circles marking important intersections at the center of the avenue. **Chapultepec Castle,** in the center of the park, is one of the most historic buildings in the western world. It began as an Aztec temple and fort, was converted to its present appearance of elegance and charm by the ill-fated Emperor Maximilian. Other well-known attractions are the **National Natural History Museum,** at the northwestern section of Chapultepec Park; **National Museum of Modern Art,** also in the Park; the **Museum of Religious Art, City Hall** and the **National Pawnshop.**

Beyond the limits of Mexico City to the north, but easily visited from it, are two very different sights. One is an ancient pagan temple group, and the other the most sacred Christian shrine in Mexico. The temple group, called the **Pyramids of the Sun and Moon,** is the most extensive, impressive, and easily visited archaeological zone in Mexico. Believed to be more than 1,000 years old, it was built by the Toltecs, includes the Pyramid of the Sun, the Pyramid of the Moon, and the Temple of Quetzalcoatl, God of the Feathered Serpent.

The Christian shrine is the **Basilica of Guadalupe,** dedicated to the Virgin because, it is said, on this site the Virgin appeared to an Indian and directed that a church be built there.

On the opposite side of Mexico City to the south is one of Mexico's prettiest and gayest attractions, the celebrated floating gardens of **Xochimilco,** where flower-decked boats manned by singing boatmen thread their way among floating islands.

Not far away is Mexico City's most brilliant example of modern architecture, **University City,** new campus of the oldest university in the western world. In it 80 buildings of striking design are scattered over 600 acres. Some of them, glowing with colored mosaics, are dramatically beautiful. The University is near Mexico City's smartest and most modern residential suburb, **Jardines del Pedregal,** with dozens of opulent, dramatically designed villas. About midway between University City and the center of Mexico City is Mexico City's new sport city with the world's largest and finest **bull ring** and **Olympic stadium.** Bullfights are staged each Sunday afternoon with the finest and fiercest bulls competing against the most renowned matadors.

The extensive sightseeing opportunities of Mexico City are only one of its attractions for the visitor. Mexico City has dozens of excellent restaurants, many of them of dramatic design, featuring specialties in most of the great cooking styles of the world.

Night-clubbing in Mexico City is gay and tuneful, with top Latin American stars performing in more than a dozen places. **Golf** fans have the choice of several excellent courses. **Horse racing** takes place during the afternoons on a handsome new track in the western foothills; and almost every Sunday morning Mexican gentlemen cowboys appear in exciting **charreadas,** the Mexican version of a rodeo.

Mexico City is probably the best city in Mexico for shopping, with dozens of well-stocked establishments displaying all the best examples of Mexican craft and manufacture, generally at prices only slightly higher than they could be bought for in the cities where they are made.

MONTERREY is Mexico's third largest city, with a population of about 830,000. It is the capital of the state of Nuevo León, and, next to Mexico City itself, the chief industrial city of Mexico. It is famed for three products: steel, iron, and beer. The brewery where the beer is made offers a pleasant offbeat sightseeing adventure for the visitor. The largest brewery in Mexico, it stands in handsome landscaped grounds on the north side of the city, produces the famed Carta Blanca beer.

Two much-visited attractions near Monterrey are **Horsetail Falls,** a succession of cascades dropping down a mountain slope; and **García Caves,** said to be the largest and most beautiful in Mexico.

OAXACA, capital of the state of the same name, located on the Inter-American Highway, about 230 miles southeast of Mexico City, is the chief city and principal point of interest in southern Mexico. It dominates a pleasant mountain valley at an altitude of about 5,000 feet, has a population of about 156,000 people. Center of a coffee-growing and mining district, the city is famed for the craftsmanship of its silversmiths and potters, who turn out gold and silver ornaments of unique design, and a distinctive black type of pottery. It has one great church of distinction, **Santo Domingo,** regarded as one of the finest examples of baroque design in the western world.

Oaxaca is the nearest center from which two ancient and interesting ruins may be visited. They are **Monte Albán,** the remains of an ancient Indian capital city; and a group of ruins at **Mitla,** believed to have been a Zapotec religious capital. There, carvings on some excavated buildings are said to be the finest in the world.

PUEBLA, one of the oldest and most typically Spanish cities in Mexico, 85 miles southeast of Mexico City, is capital of the state of the same name. It dominates a rich valley, has large textile mills and cement plants, but is chiefly famed as a center for the making of fine tile and pottery, an industry started in the early days by the Spanish with craftsmen brought from Toledo in Spain. Tile made in the city adorns and faces many of its buildings, including the **cathedral,** one of the great churches of Mexico. An interesting opportunity is the exploration of several tile factories, which also make distinctive Spanish pottery. Neither of Mexico's large east coast cities, Tampico, on the north, and Veracruz, almost due east of Mexico City, offers much in the way of visitor interest, but on the road between Mexico City and Veracruz, in an area of lush tropical lowlands to the east of the mountains, is the one small city of unusual charm, Fortín de las Flores.

TAXCO, 70 miles southwest of Mexico City, is famed for the production of silver and its processing and manufacture in dozens of craft shops. Taxco, built among steep mountain slopes with climbing cobbled streets, is such a perfect example of a Colonial town that it is preserved as a national monument. Chief feature of the town is the twin-towered parish church, one of the finest examples of Churrigueresque styles in Mexico.

TEPOZTLÁN, an architectural gem maintained as a national monument by the government, is a village almost unchanged since Aztec days, with some residents of the town still speaking Aztec.

SPORTS AND RECREATION. Though sightseeing, since it offers an almost endless pageant of dramatically varied spectacles, is likely to be the principal activity of visitors to Mexico, there are important activities that can be indulged in for fun and adventure. These include some of the finest **sports fishing** in the world, with several cities on both the east and west coasts offering full facilities.

The most popular spectator sport in Mexico is the **bullfight.** Nearly every large city has a bull ring, with Mexico City having the largest and finest in the world. Fights are held invariably on Sunday afternoon and are almost the only thing in Mexico that begins on time. There are occasional **horse races,** with Mexico City having the finest horse track in the country. Most large cities of Mexico have a golf course, though the only really fine ones are in or near Mexico City.

Mexicans are ardent **baseball** fans, and there is a Mexican league with a number of teams. During the winter season, many big-time U.S. players appear in Mexico. The famous Basque game of **jai-alai** is played there, with two frontoms in Mexico City, one of which presents girl performers. Sportsmen consider Mexico one of the most interesting places in the western world in which to hunt. **Duck hunting** is fine in many areas, and the forested mountain slopes offer larger game including deer, wild boar, iguana. **Crocodile hunting** is an exciting offbeat sport practiced along the coast in the southern part of Mexico.

SPECIAL EVENTS. Mexico is famous for its colorful fiestas and local celebrations. Among its most noteworthy are the **Day of the Three Wise Men,** Santos Reyes Fiestas where Wise Men are local patron saints, held January 6; **Fiesta of Santa Prisca,** in Taxco, January 18; **San Sebastian Celebrations,** featuring ten days of carnivals and cowboy stunts, in San Luis Potosi on January 20; **Carnival Time,** held throughout Mexico from February 19–22; **San Marcos Fair,** the annual spring festival of Aguascalientes, taking place around Saint Mark's Day in late April.

Events later in the year include **Corpus Christi Day,** a traditional spring festival taking place throughout Mexico on June 13; **Guelaguetza Festival** in Oaxaca late July which dates from pre-Columbian times; the **Day of St. Miguel,** patron saint of horsemen, held in all places named San Miguel on September 29; and the **Day of Virgin of Guadalupe,** patroness of the Republic, held December 12. The professional bullfighting season commences in Mexico City in November.

DINING AND SHOPPING. There was long a persistent legend that eating in Mexico was dangerous, likely to produce disastrous results to the diner in the form of intestinal disorders as the result of drinking impure water or eating unwashed fruits and vegetables. The danger has long since passed in the larger centers, and in nearly all the restaurants or hotels where a visitor is likely to eat.

Many of these hotels and restaurants now have fine dining rooms serving excellent food in various types of cooking, including American. The result is that many visitors actually never eat Mexican food, which is a pity, since Mexico has excellent specialties of its own, served in good restaurants. Many of them are distinctive in origin, ingredients, and taste. Typical Mexican foods have developed from a number of influences, beginning with the diet of pre-Columbian Indians. Other influences were Spanish, Moorish, and French. Typical and interesting Mexican foods include the *tortilla,* a flat cornmeal pancake; *tacos,* a tortilla rolled around all sorts of special ingredients; *enchiladas,* another adaptation of the tortilla; *tamale,* another adaptation of the basic tortilla, wrapped in corn shucks or banana leaves and steamed. Almost basic to the Mexican diet are *frijoles,* which are brown beans cooked in various ways, often served with rice. A favorite dish is *mole de guajolote,* turkey served with a heavily spiced sauce. Another is *guacamole,* a salad made of avocado and onion. A favorite dessert is *flan,* or browned custard. Various regions and cities of Mexico have specialties of their own. Thus, Veracruz is noted for seafood soups; Oaxaca is famed for cheeses. Throughout the tropical regions of Mexico, tropical fruits are widely available. Most of Mexico's seaport cities have restaurants which feature seafood of various types, almost always fresh-caught.

Though Mexico does produce a few types of wine, it is seldom found on restaurant menus. But an almost invariable accompaniment to food in Mexico is beer, the two most famous and popular brands being Carta Blanca and Bohemia, which beer drinkers rank as some of the best brews in the world. The national drink of tequila is available everywhere and served in a variety of combinations. Few visitors, however, learn to like it.

Shopping in Mexico is a rewarding activity in which nearly all visitors engage. Few regions offer a greater and more colorful variety in craft products, including bags and purses in a great variety of styles, sizes, and materials; handmade baskets of straw with interesting designs and colors, available throughout the country. Unusual copperware, both utensils and ornaments, is produced in several centers. Fabrics in a wide range of pattern and material are available all over the country, nearly always hand-loomed. Mexican glass is distinctive both in color and design. One district is famed for producing lacquerware, one of the most ancient of the Mexican crafts. Excellent musical instruments, made in several sections, include flutes and drums, violins and guitars. The making of pottery is universal throughout the country, with all sorts of different designs, glazes, and shapes available. Along with pottery, tile is made, many types being notable for design and quality. An unusual novelty is tinware, produced in frames, lamps, ornaments of various types. But the greatest of all shopping opportunities in Mexico is fine, beautifully designed silver. It is offered in a wide range of design and grade, and is available almost everywhere, with the best examples and the largest stocks of it found in the silver center of Taxco and in Mexico City. Quaint and delightful children's furniture, toys, and dolls are made in various cities and towns.

Central America

CENTRAL AMERICA
MEXICO
BELIZE
Belmopan
GUATEMALA
Guatemala
HONDURAS
Tegucigalpa
San Salvador
EL SALVADOR
NICARAGUA
Managua
Caribbean Sea
COSTA RICA
San José
Pacific Ocean
PANAMA
Panama

Central America

Both topographically and culturally, the region called Central America is curious: a rugged, twisting neck of land which connects the North American continent with the continent of South America, about 1,200 miles to the southeast. The limits and boundaries of Central America are the mountains and tropical jungles of Mexico on the north and northwest, the Caribbean Sea to the east and northeast, the mountainous land border with the nation of Colombia in South America on the south, and the Pacific Ocean along the entire western and southwestern sides. The area contains nearly a quarter of a million square miles.

The population, for which no accurate figures are available, is estimated at between ten and twelve million people. They live in six republics and one British colony, which are from northwest to southeast: British Honduras, Guatemala, Honduras, El Salvador, Nicaragua, Costa Rica, and the narrow, curving Republic of Panama.

THE LAND

Physical features of Central America include two distinct ranges of mountains, towering thousands of feet above sea level, many with still active volcanoes. The mountain slopes on either side of the ranges drop down to coastal lowlands where high heat and humidity have resulted in great tropical forests. Several lakes, a rugged coastline with fine harbors, also characterize the land.

The mountain systems divide in about the center of Central America, within the state of Honduras. From the north they are an extension of the Sierra Madre Range of Mexico, with tumbled slopes and craggy peaks, the highest rising more than 13,000 feet. The second system begins in Honduras, extending in a spine of gradually higher slopes into

Panama. In the center of Panama there is an abrupt break, where now the Panama Canal cuts a channel to connect the Caribbean Sea and Pacific Ocean. From the Canal Zone, the mountain spine climbs to the high slopes of the South American Cordilleras. There are many small rivers that tumble swiftly to the sea, none of them navigable except for short distances beyond its mouth.

The surface character of the land varies sharply with altitude; the lowlands, chiefly flat, are covered with dense tropical growth, particularly on the Caribbean side. As the slopes rise into the mountains, the tropical trees are replaced by great stands of hardwood, and still higher, by pine forests, particularly in the north part. Some of the lowland areas are intensively cultivated and account for the largest production of bananas, in big plantations, in the world. Recently, irrigation projects in lowland areas account for extensive cotton plantations. The mountain slopes, often rising to a height of 5,000 or 6,000 feet, are chiefly devoted to coffee plantations.

THE CLIMATE

As the land surface of Central America varies sharply, so does the climate. The whole area lies in the heart of the tropics, and all the coastal sections are very hot, often quite humid. The prevailing winds from the east out of the Caribbean drench the eastern side with heavy rains, up to 200 inches a year. Less rain falls on the western slopes and on the lowlands of the Pacific, while some sections of the western coast are semi-arid, almost desert-like. Temperature variations are equally marked. Guatemala City, for example, more than a mile high in altitude, has a balmy and delightful climate year-round, with a temperature range in January of 61 degrees and in July of only 66 degrees. But Panama City and Managua, both at sea level, have an average range year-round of about 80 degrees and high humidity. Some sections, high in the mountains, have continually cold temperatures and occasional snow despite the tropical latitude.

THE PEOPLE

Before the Spanish exploration and conquest of the new world, the area of Central America was sparsely settled with nomadic tribes of Indians, largely primitive—with one exception. In the mountains of the north lived the energetic and clever Mayan people, who built their remarkable cities, the ruins of which are still to be seen in the jungles of Guatemala and British Honduras. But several hundred years before the arrival of the Spanish, the Mayans migrated north into Yucatán, now part of Mexico, leaving behind in the jungles small nomadic tribes of hunters and fishermen.

Columbus, who landed at Panama in 1502, was the first European to see the area of Central America. A few years later, 1513, an energetic, red-headed Spanish adventurer named Balboa led a small band of followers from what is now Haiti across Panama to discover the Pacific Ocean, and claim all the lands it washed in the name of the King of Spain.

Spanish settlement of Central America proceeded slowly and not very successfully after that. The Spanish sought gold and docile, sedentary farmers who could be exploited to raise commercial crops. They found neither in Central America. Exploration of the area, however, proceeded under different Spanish leaders, whose bands occasionally met and fought each other. Colonists who followed the explorers brought with them from Spain their grains, their animals, and their diseases. Only the diseases flourished, with the result that most of the Indian population was wiped out. One exception was in the wild mountains of Guatemala, where over half the population today is still of pure-bred Indian stock. Throughout the rest of the area, the Indians married freely with the Spanish colonists, producing the ethnic strain called Ladinos, characteristic of most of the area today. One exception to this was the highland region of Costa Rica, where almost all the Indians had died of disease, with the result that the present population is almost of pure Spanish ancestry. During the latter half of the nineteenth century, another ethnic strain was introduced: large colonies of Negroes, brought into the lowlands of the Caribbean coast to help plant and cultivate bananas, and into the Canal Zone to help dig that great waterway. Their descendants still live in both areas.

Guatemala

Most northern and most populous country of Central America, Guatemala is also the most varied in physical character and cultural background, and offers more of interest for the visitor than any of the other countries. Irregular in shape and varying greatly in surface characteristics, Guatemala contains about 42,000 square miles, an area approximately the size of Tennessee. Within that area live about five million people, or one third of all the people living in the Central American region. The country is dramatically rugged and of great scenic beauty.

Boundaries of Guatemala are Mexico on the west and north, British Honduras on the east, with Guatemala touching the Caribbean Sea in a narrow strip just below British Honduras. On the east is a rugged land border divided between Honduras and El Salvador. To the south and southwest is the Pacific Ocean. The capital of Guatemala is the high mountain-set city of Guatemala City. Its currency unit is the quetzal, named for a rare and beautiful bird, the national bird of the country.

THE LAND. Guatemala has two principal natural features: a high and rugged chain of mountains filling the whole southern and western area of the country, and a fairly flat, highly isolated region of tropical jungle filling the northern part between Mexico and British Honduras. Among the mountains there are dozens of peaks rising over 10,000 feet, the highest, Mount Tajumulco, rising to 13,845 feet. In these mountains is a string of volcanoes stretching all along the coast, some of them occasionally active, their peaks rising to above 12,000 feet. The area contains some of the most dramatically beautiful lakes in the western world, including **Lake Atitlán,** surrounded by volcanic peaks, and **Lake Amatitlán,** close to Guatemala City. The mountains rise abruptly from the Pacific shore, descend more gently toward the northern interior and the Caribbean. Earthquakes are frequent, although rarely violent, and there are many rivers, none important in size or for navigation. On the Pacific slope they drop swiftly to the sea in foaming torrents, but on the Caribbean side they meander slowly through the tropical jungle. Vegetation is relatively dense, varying from lush tropics in the coastal region to hardwood forests on the lower mountain slopes and pine forests higher up. In the heavily humid northern and eastern sections there are extensive tropical rain forests. The Pacific coastline of Guatemala extends for 200 miles, while the Caribbean coastline is only 70 miles long. Throughout the mountains are high valleys at levels ranging from 5,000 to 8,000 feet, and it is here that most Guatemalans live. The lowland area, just south of Mexico, contains about 15,000 square miles of wilderness, covered with a dense mahogany forest.

THE CLIMATE. Guatemala's climatic variations are extreme. The coastal areas are hot, tropical, and often very humid. Rainfall is heaviest in the east, nearly 200 inches a year in some areas, but the mountain areas, particularly at altitudes of from 5,000 to 7,000 feet, are springlike and pleasant year-round. Guatemala City, which lies at an altitude of about 5,000 feet, has a year-round springlike temperature of 68 degrees, varying only slightly. Guatemala has two very well-defined seasons—dry and rainy, with rain falling from May to October, and almost never from October to May. Some cities and towns higher in the mountains have a cooler climate, like the curious Indian city, high in the mountains at an altitude of about 8,000 feet, with the exotic name of Chichicastenango, which has a perpetually cool climate, with fires necessary every night, topcoats all day. The most pleasant time for a visit is during the dry season, with exception of the cooler months, December and January.

THE PEOPLE. Long before the Spanish conquest of Guatemala in the sixteenth century, the northern mountain slopes and parts of the northern jungle area were inhabited by a remarkable

Maya Indian civilization. They built extensive cities of which their ruins, swallowed in the jungle, are accessible today by commercial airline. Throughout the rest of the country, particularly in the mountains, live scattered Indian tribes, some with customs and costumes suggesting Oriental ancestors. Spanish conquest and colonization began in the early part of the sixteenth century, with expeditions coming south from Mexico. The Spanish, under the leadership of Pedro de Alvarado, established in Guatemala a special province of Spain which included the whole of Central America, with its capital city in the ancient city of Antigua. With the conquest complete, colonists began to filter into Guatemala from Spain, establishing most of the present towns and cities. They married freely with groups of Indians, resulting in the mixed heritage of mestizo, which characterizes most of the more settled areas today. But in the higher mountains there was little mixture, and the Indian tribes of ancient and unknown origin have retained their special customs and character almost unchanged.

The result is that today the population of the country, estimated at about five million, is more than 50 percent Indian of pure stock. They are divided into many distinctive tribes, each with its own costumes and customs, often very colorful. Although the official language of the country is Spanish, most of the Indians speak only a limited version of it. Their most familiar languages are the dialects that may go back thousands of years. Minor population elements in the country result from Carib Indians immigrating from the islands of the Caribbean Sea, as well as Negroes brought to work on the banana plantations. The culture of the cities, however, is essentially Spanish. Spanish influences in architecture and culture account for most of the buildings, both public and private. The prevailing religion is Roman Catholic, with a number of churches of charm and architectural interest. But in the high mountain villages where the population is entirely Indian, though the church buildings and religion are officially Catholic, many of the actual religious practices continue to be the ancient Maya-Guiché ones.

AGRICULTURE. Although forests cover 60 percent of the area of Guatemala, leaving a much smaller percentage fit for cultivation, a large part of the nation's economy is based on agriculture. Coffee, by far, is Guatemala's most important product—its plantations take up one-sixth of the cultivated area. Almost 80 percent of the coffee grown is for export, both to the United States and to the other Central American countries. Cotton and bananas are also important. An unusual crop, developed in the jungles of the north and east, is chicle, which comes from the sap of the zapote tree, and is used for making chewing gum.

Another unusual group of agricultural products are aromatic oils, chiefly citronella and lemon grass, distilled in many small plants scattered over the country. Of these oils, Guatemala is the largest producer in the world.

INDUSTRY. The only mineral of any importance is pure sulphur, derived from volcanic deposits, but lead, silver, and zinc are mined on a small scale. Manufacturing plants are growing rapidly, as trade among the Central American countries increases. There are dozens of small craft centers scattered throughout the country, where interesting fabrics are hand-loomed, baskets are woven, and gay straw hats of unusual design are made.

CITIES. Most of the people of Guatemala live in small villages and towns, or on separate farms and plantations. Guatemala City is the only fairly large city in the country.

ANTIGUA is 28 miles from Guatemala City and can be reached by a good highway. Once a rich and splendid Spanish city with a population of about 80,000 people, it was almost completely destroyed by a violent earthquake in 1773. The population today is about 13,000. Much of the city lies in picturesque ruin, including several of the great churches, but some of the more interesting old buildings have been beautifully restored. The **local market** is of special interest, has fine examples of hand-wrought silver, and colorful hand-woven fabrics. Antigua is the commercial center for a rich agricultural area producing coffee and sugar cane. **Coffee plantations,** several worth visiting, surround the area.

CHICHICASTENANGO, north of Lake Atitlán, reached by a winding, dramatically scenic mountain road, is the hub of a remnant of the Mayan-Quiché civilization. Its population of about 2,000 is almost entirely of pure Indian blood, with another 20,000 of the same tribe living in the rugged mountains all around. The town has a breath-taking setting, narrow, winding streets, and an aspect of great charm, with fine views of mountains from every corner. The native costumes, among the most colorful and splendid in Guatemala, suggest an Oriental origin for the tribe. Points of principal interest include the massive village church, **Santo Tomás,** where the devout practice both Christian and Indian rites, and the very large **native market** held in the open plaza before the church, where notable examples of distinctive native crafts are sold.

GUATEMALA CITY, the capital, with about 700,000 people, is the largest city in Central America. It dominates a broad mountain valley surrounded by forested peaks and is about 150 miles inland from the sea. The city has a clean, new look, partly the result of the fact that much of it was demolished by an earthquake in 1917 and then rebuilt in modern fashion or with copies of Colonial style. Of special interest is the **cathedral,** built in 1782, which escaped the 1917 earthquake. The most ornate and handsome building in the city is the huge **National Palace** completed in 1943, while an unusual church building worth seeing is the **Church of Santo Domingo,** gleaming white in color because milk and white of eggs were mixed with the mortar. An unusual sight is a huge **relief map** of the country in **Minerva Park.** There is an excellent **national museum** with a fine collection of relics, a notable **museum of natural history,** a fine **botanical garden.** Guatemala City is the best base in the country for visitors, with excellent facilities there for trips to nearby areas of interest.

LAKE AMATITLÁN, 17 miles south of the capital city, is a popular resort center and one of several of the country's beautiful lakes. It is about seven miles long and two and one-half miles wide, offers fishing, swimming, and boating. Coffee plantations are all around the shore, which is rimmed by a pleasant scenic drive flanked by picturesque chalets.

LAKE ATITLÁN, about 100 miles west of the capital over the Inter-American Highway, through a section of rugged and picturesquely beautiful mountains, is one of the most breath-taking lakes in the world. Its surface lies at an elevation of 5,100 feet. From its shores, wooded mountain slopes rise to the peaks of four towering volcanoes. The lake is about 17 miles long, 12 miles wide, with a broken shoreline of about 70 miles. On the shore are a dozen picturesque villages, several of them named for the Apostles, and each a center for a special native craft. The lake offers the best mountain resort facilities in Guatemala, with several excellent resort hotels, offering fishing, boating, and bathing, and a sightseeing boat trip on the lake itself.

QUEZALTENANGO, still farther west on the Inter-American Highway, is Guatemala's second largest city with about 45,000 people. Lying at an altitude of 7,656 feet, it has a cool climate. Though it has a handsome central plaza and an interesting native market, it has few other tourist attractions.

SAN JOSÉ, one of Guatemala's chief ports, is 75 miles south of the capital by highway, on the Pacific. Though there are small beach resorts nearby, the town and the area offer little of interest for the visitor.

TIKAL, with the crumbling remnants of the oldest known Mayan ruins in the world, was once the center of the great Mayan metropolis. To visitors with a strong archaeological interest, there are daily flights to this remote village from Guatemala City.

For the visitor, the principal activity in Guatemala is sightseeing, and there are good facilities for it based in the capital, with excursions by automobile and airplane to centers of scenic and resort interest. Most of the Inter-American Highway is good; stretches of it dramatically scenic. In addition to the larger and more important centers of interest, where there are good hotels, there are dozens of small towns and picturesque villages. The mountains and lakes themselves are colorful and picturesque. An adjunct to sightseeing is shopping for native crafts, often presented for sale in the village workshops where they are made. Most important among them are brightly colored fabrics of unusual design, all hand-loomed, of both wool and cotton. Various articles of straw, such as baskets and hats, are interesting and inexpensive.

SPORTS AND RECREATION. Facilities for most sports, including **tennis, golf, swimming, water sports, horseback riding,** and **cycling,** can be found in all parts of the country. Good **hunting, fishing,** and **camping** are also possible, for which equipment can be rented in the larger cities.

SPECIAL EVENTS. Guatemala's most interesting annual events are **Holy Week,** a colorful, traditional occasion celebrated throughout the country in mid-April; the **Fiestas Julianas,** in Huehuetenango July 12–18; and the **Santo Tomás Fair,** one of the year's most colorful fairs, taking place in Chichicastenango in December.

DINING AND SHOPPING. Dining opportunities in Guatemala are adequate, and often unusual. Many good restaurants in cities and resort areas offer dishes of Spanish and French character, and there are excellent native dishes of special interest, including coffee, which is of high quality and served everywhere, on every occasion. Tropical fruits are plentiful and unusually good.

British Honduras

This curious and remote region fills the eastern jungle flank of northeastern Guatemala, and is distinguished by its small population and abundance of dense forest-jungles. In an area of almost 9,000 square miles, about the size of New Hampshire, live over 122,000 people. The boundaries of British Honduras are the wilderness of northern Guatemala to the west, the equally primeval Mexican district of Quintana Roo to the north, the Caribbean Sea to the east, and Guatemala to the south. Its length, north to south, is about 170 miles, its width about 70 miles. British Honduras, which attained internal self-government in January 1964, is governed by a premier, his cabinet, and a house of representatives.

THE LAND. Except for low mountains rising to about 3,000 feet in the south and southwest, the country is flat. In the north the coast is only a little above sea level, much of it very swampy. There are some short jungle rivers, one of which, the Belize, is navigable by small craft for about 120 miles. Down this river great logs cut in the jungles are floated to the sea. The mountains to the southwest, extending into Guatemala, known as the Maya Mountains, are partly unexplored, but one section of them contains a ridge of superb pine forest rising to about 3,700 feet.

THE CLIMATE. Considering the lowness of the land and its tropical location, the coast, particularly in the north, is surprisingly comfortable. Trade winds blowing in from the sea keep the temperature down to tolerable levels, seldom above 96 degrees even in the hottest months. In winter the temperature in Belize, the largest city, may drop as low as 50 degrees, with an average of about 70 degrees. But interior regions away from the coast are very hot and uncomfortable, with high humidity and temperatures soaring to well over 100 degrees. There are marked variations of rainfall both seasonally and in different areas. The average in Belize is about 51 inches a year, most of it falling during the summer rainy season. But in the south the rainfall reaches 175 inches a year, much of it falling in drenching torrents. The heavy rains and high temperatures account for the fact that more than 90 percent of the land is covered by forests.

THE PEOPLE. Of the total population, the main racial groups are American Indians (Maya), Caribs, and Creoles (defined as either people of African extraction or those of mixed Spanish and Indian descent). Most of those of white ancestry were British, chiefly from the islands of the Caribbean. There are some Syrians and Chinese, some people of Latin extraction who have drifted in from neighboring Spanish-speaking areas, and in the north, a few Spanish-speaking descendants of the original Mayan tribes, who at one time are believed to have numbered nearly half a million. Very few people of unmixed white stock live in British Honduras.

The Spanish discovered British Honduras—as they did the rest of Central America—but they greatly disliked forests, and the vast and virtually impenetrable woodlands of the area baffled them. The accident of a shipwreck on the coast, involving an Englishman and his African slaves, resulted in the first real knowledge of the area and led, in 1786, following a treaty with Spain, to its colonization by British from Jamaica, where a brisk business was going on in logwood, the chief source of dyes. Later, after synthetic dyes had doomed the use of logwood for that purpose, Victorian England provided a profitable market for forest products. Mahogany had become the fashionable furniture wood of England and to "put your feet under mahogany" was a status symbol of the era. Guatemala, since it won its independence from Spain in 1821, has claimed British Honduras, but has not succeeded in obtaining it.

AGRICULTURE. Of the whole country, only about 600 square miles are under cultivation. Much cultivated land is in small patches, devoted to subsistence crops. Of the exported agricultural products, the most important are sugar, citrus, and forest products. Cattle farming and fishing are being developed, along with the cultivation of vegetables, cocoa, and bananas.

INDUSTRY. The great forests of British Honduras have the finest mahogany in the world, in virtually unlimited supply, thus mahogany and other woods provide almost the only employment of the people. Other trees beginning to produce export capital are the following: A special type of pine, called British Honduras pine, heavier and stronger than mahogany, is important. The sapodilla tree, a source for the latex from which chewing gum is made, is also fine for axe handles, doorposts, golf clubs. A local cedar is widely used for boats. Rosewood of great beauty is increasingly important in wood inlays for furniture. Most of the woods, generally cut during the first six months of the year, are cut into lumber in a sawmill in Belize, almost the only mill of any kind there.

CITIES. The only town of any size in the area is the former capital, **Belize**, with about 37,000 people. It is relatively primitive, filled with frame buildings covered with galvanized iron roofs. There are several acceptable hotels, however, comparing in quality and cost with resort hotels in some of the Caribbean islands. The capital is a newly built inland city, **Belmopan.**

SPORTS AND RECREATION. There is little for the visitor to do, although fishing off the coast is good, and jungle hunting for jaguar and deer is possible, but requires an amphibious safari to engage in it. There is a country club at Belize with a small golf course, where visitors are permitted to play. Some visitors find expeditions to the curious and extensive Mayan ruins in the jungle fascinating, but quite expensive special arrangements must be made to visit them. There are few roads worth mentioning into the interior and most of those that do extend a few miles are in such poor condition that they can be negotiated only by jeep or equivalent vehicle.

SPECIAL EVENTS in British Honduras are highlighted by the **Mestizo Villages' Fiestas,** taking place throughout the country from January to March. These fiestas are known for their colorful costumes, feasting, and street dancing. Also of visitor interest are the **National Festival of Arts and Crafts,** held during March and April; the **Virgin Del Carmen Fiesta** which takes place in July; and the **National Day Celebrations,** 14 days of celebrations climaxed on September 10.

DINING AND SHOPPING. Items of unusual interest to buy are snakeskins, peddled by the natives, who will also sell live iguanas, said to taste like chicken by those daring enough to sample them. Nearly all the rest of the food in the region is imported, none of it distinctive. The one exception is native lobster, which is excellent and abundant.

Honduras

With a land area of more than 43,000 square miles, Honduras is the second largest of the Central American countries, but is the most sparsely settled. The shape of Honduras is that of a rough and flattened triangle, with its base to the west, its stubby apex 400 miles to the east. The greatest north–south distance is 200 miles. Guatemala and El Salvador to the west, Nicaragua to the southeast and south are Honduras' neighbors. On its north side, Honduras has a 350-mile coast on the Caribbean Sea, its access to the Pacific being limited to the Gulf of Fonseca, which it shares with El Salvador and Nicaragua. Honduras, a republic, has its capital in the ancient mountain city of Tegucigalpa.

THE LAND. Honduras is almost entirely mountainous, with rugged ranges of volcanic peaks rising to more than 8,000 feet. Filling three-fourths of the area of the country, they reach their greatest height in the west on the north coast of the Caribbean Sea; the mountains rise abruptly from the sea in the western portion. To the east they disappear in a vast, humid, tropical lowland, called the "Mosquito Coast," filled with an almost impenetrable forest.

From the north coast to the south is a curious rift in the mountains, where the highlands drop to about 3,000 feet. Along it or near it are the important communities of the country. The principal rivers of Honduras, which empty into the Caribbean, are the Ulúa, the most important, navigable for a distance of about 125 miles; and to the east, draining the jungle area of the Mosquito Coast, the Patuca. Only about one-fifth of the land area of the country is used for any purpose, and almost 50 percent is covered with forest.

THE CLIMATE. Along the tropical coastal lowlands, the climate of Honduras is hot and very humid. Rainfall, maintained by a prevailing eastern wind, is extremely heavy, with the rainy season from May to December. The climate in the mountain valleys of the interior, however, is more temperate, with the capital having a pleasant, springlike year-round climate due to its altitude of more than 3,000 feet. Rainfall in the capital is heaviest during the summer months. The average temperature range in the interior is a low of 65 in January and a high of 75 in June. Temperature averages on the coast almost always exceed 85 degrees, often climbing to more than 100, accompanied by high humidity.

THE PEOPLE. Though the clever and civilized Mayan tribes at one time lived in northern Honduras and built city centers which today provide the country's most fascinating archaeological ruins, most of the area of the country, before the middle of the sixteenth century, was largely unsettled. Columbus visited the coast of northern Honduras briefly on his fourth voyage in 1502, but no attempt to explore the country came for many years thereafter until the Spanish, pushing down from Guatemala, discovered that there was silver in the mountains of Honduras, and began to settle the country. They founded Tegucigalpa near their mines in 1524, and later established a capital city at nearby Comayagua. Most of the settlements made in the country for several hundred years remained in this central mountain area. The settlers married freely with the few Indian tribes living in the country, with the result that today the entire population, with the exception of about one percent of pure Spanish ancestry, is of mixed Indian blood, called "mestizo." Another exception is along the northern coast, where the majority of the population is of African ancestry–descendants of Negroes brought into the country fairly recently to help work the banana plantations which flank that coastal area. The country has been a traditional setting for military adventurers and revolutionaries. A picturesque character was an American freebooter called William Walker, who attempted to "liberate" the country in 1860.

With the dominant cultural influences of Honduras being almost entirely Spanish, it is natural that most of the architecture worth noting is of Spanish Colonial design. It includes some impressive churches and public buildings, built by anonymous mestizo artisans.

AGRICULTURE. About seven out of ten people in Honduras are engaged in some form of agriculture. By far the most important crop is bananas, which are grown on great plantations along the northern coast and account for 60 percent of the nation's exports. The next largest crop is coffee, with the coffee plantations, or *fincas*, generally small, in the upland valleys of the west. Honduras has rich timber resources, particularly pine and mahogany. Tobacco is a commercial crop of some importance, as are coconuts. Cattle raising is also important.

INDUSTRY. Important products of the country are minerals, chiefly gold and silver. The country is third in rank, after Mexico and Peru, among silver-producing nations. Antimony is another important mineral. There are few manufactured products of any importance; however, clothing, textiles, cement, chemicals, and food products show growth.

CITIES. Honduras is essentially a rural land, with by far the largest number of people living in country districts, in small villages and towns, and on farms. The only city of any importance is the mountain capital of Tegucigalpa.

COMAYAGUA, ancient mountain capital, 75 miles northwest of the present capital on a winding mountain road, is another accessible city of interest. Founded in 1535, Comayagua was the capital of the area for 300 years. Some of the fine buildings of Colonial design which are still to be seen are relics of that period. They include the **university,** first in Central America; a massive **cathedral;** several **convents,** most of them dating to the middle part of the sixteenth century. The aspect of the town is picturesque in the extreme, with whitewashed one-story houses, narrow cobbled streets. An unusual local industry is the manufacture of firecrackers.

COPÁN, reached by a jungle trail through the mountains, 35 miles west of the village of Santa Rosa and just east of the border of Guatemala, is unusual and historically interesting. Under any circumstances, surface travel to Copán is difficult and tedious. A better way to get there is by air, with regularly scheduled flights from the capital. The present ruins, partially excavated and explored, spread over 15 square miles. They are the remnants of what was the first Mayan capital, and are regarded as some of the finest and most beautiful archaeological relics in the world. Several modern hotels, as well as a small but pleasant inn adjacent to the ruins offer accommodations and meals to visitors.

TEGUCIGALPA, with a population of about 253,000, is an old and picturesque city, situated in a mountain valley at an elevation of 3,200 feet. As it has no railways, connection to the rest of the world is by a winding mountain road and by air. The capital is 62 miles inland from the Pacific coast, and 125 miles from the Atlantic coast. Sharp-peaked mountains rise around it on three sides, the Picacho being the most notable. A river flowing through a steep gorge divides the town into two sections, where streets are mostly narrow and often winding, frequently steep. The chief show places of the city include two **parks;** overlooking one of them is a handsome **cathedral,** generally regarded as one of the finest in Central America. Not far away from it is the **national museum,** with a curious collection of odds and ends, including a scale model of the ruins of Copán. The city's **native market** is noisy and colorful, and is a good place to buy the native handicrafts of the country.

The only other cities of any importance in the country are the agricultural, industrial, and trading center of San Pedro Sula; and the banana ports of Puerto Cortés, Tela, and La Ceiba, all on the north coast. Puerto Cortés, a wholly owned community maintained by the United Fruit Company at the mouth of the Ulúa River, is located 200 miles from the capital, and has a population of 21,000. A second United Fruit port is Tela, 30 miles to the east. A third banana shipping port is La Ceiba, maintained by the Standard Fruit Company, 40 miles farther east on the coast. It has a population of about 33,000, some fine nearby beaches, but little else of interest. Offshore are the Bay Islands, historically famed as the point where Columbus first landed in 1502.

Of all the countries of Central America, Honduras has the least interest for the average visitor and provides the poorest visitor facilities. Sightseeing opportunities are limited to the country's two principal cities, the capital and the original old capital, and to the prehistoric Mayan ruins of Copán. There is a small and not very good golf course in the capital, where visitors can play by special arrangement. Fishing is good in the Caribbean off the north coast, but facilities for it are inadequate and difficult to arrange. It is also good in the Gulf of Fonseca on the Pacific Ocean side, but there again facilities are also inadequate and very primitive. Transportation facilities are limited, but improving, especially for automobiles, with completion of the Pan American Highway, and for air travelers, as increased flights are scheduled. Some of the mountain scenery is picturesque and dramatic, and is best reached by car.

SPORTS AND RECREATION. Arrangements for **golf** and **tennis** can be made through the Pan American office, which also has information on **hunting** and **fishing.** Spectator sports include **soccer, basketball,** and **baseball.**

SPECIAL EVENTS. Annual celebrations in Honduras are highlighted by the **Virgin of Suyapa Celebrations** (Patron of Honduras) in early February; **Holy Week,** in April; the **National Fair,** held in San Pedro Sula in mid-June; and **Independence Day,** with celebrations and parades, held yearly on September 15.

DINING AND SHOPPING. Dining and shopping opportunities are limited, although there are good restaurants in the larger cities, where the dishes are quite likely to be Spanish or European in type. The native dishes are similar to those found in Mexico and Guatemala, though not quite as highly spiced. There are abundant supplies of good native fruits, and on the coast to the north fresh fish is plentiful and good. Special shopping opportunities, generally in native markets, include good Panama hats, hand-woven handbags made of the same material as the hats. Some examples of native pottery and carved ornaments from local hardwoods are interesting and picturesque.

El Salvador

Though the smallest of the countries of Central America, El Salvador, which is often also called Salvador, is the most densely populated, the most industrialized, and the most prosperous. The area of the country is only slightly over 8,000 square miles, about the size of the state of Maryland. It is the only country in Central America which does not have access to both the Caribbean Sea and the Pacific.

El Salvador, lying just to the east of Guatemala, faces the Pacific Ocean from the north and has a 170-mile east–west coastline. Its northern neighbor is Honduras, a much larger country located across a rugged mountain frontier. To its east, across the wide Gulf of Fonseca, is Nicaragua. El Salvador, whose capital and largest city is San Salvador, is a republic.

THE LAND. Rugged mountains dominate El Salvador, crossing the country from west to east in two roughly parallel ranges, and rising to heights of more than 5,000 feet (the highest peak, Santa Ana, is 7,825 feet). Most of the peaks are volcanoes, although none are still active, including the famous Izalco, which had been well-known for its volcanic activity. Between the mountain ranges is a fertile plateau at an elevation of about 2,000 feet, where most of the people live and where most of the towns and villages are, including the capital city of San Salvador. North of the mountain ranges is the course of the country's largest river, the Lempa, rising in Guatemala and twisting along the northern side of the country, to swing south and empty into the Pacific; it has little value for navigation. In the mountains are several picturesque lakes, on the shores of which are popular resorts. The land of El Salvador is more completely used than that of any other country in Central America. Much of it is devoted to coffee plantations, some of the most productive and richest in Central America. The coast of El Salvador is rugged, with mountain slopes rising from the sea, and cliffs and headlands alternating with picturesque small beaches, some of black volcanic sand. Occasional cultivated fields along the coast produce cotton.

THE CLIMATE. The climate of El Salvador is tropical, but is more temperate in the higher altitudes, and generally hot and quite humid along the coast. The average in San Salvador is 73 degrees, with a range of only about five degrees. The hottest months are from February to May, while the rainy season runs from May to October, with an average of about 72 inches falling annually. But rains are not likely to be continuous, and there is sunshine nearly every day. Evenings throughout the country are generally cool. The best time for a visit is fall and winter.

THE PEOPLE. Like most of Central America, before the Spanish conquest the land was inhabited by migratory Indian tribes. Though conquered by the Spanish coming down from Mexico, and attached to Guatemala, the actual settlement of the country by Spanish colonists was very slow. The small number of Spanish settlers who did enter the country married freely with the Indians, with the result that a majority of the people there now are of mixed Spanish and Indian blood, called mestizo. The population, however, remained relatively small until the last half of the nineteenth century, when coffee began to be an important crop. After that, there was a great surge of migration to El Salvador, chiefly from Spain, resulting in a rapid population increase, with the early coffee planters nearly all of pure Spanish ancestry.

Today the population of about 3.5 million is divided between a small minority of pure Spanish families (generally the upper class), the people of mixed blood (about 92 percent of the population), and the people of pure Indian blood.

Spanish is the language of El Salvador, although some isolated Indian tribes in remote villages speak their native tongue. Most of the architecture of note is of the Spanish Colonial type, due to the dominant Spanish heritage of the people. There are, however, remnants of ruins of ancient Mayan settlements, including great historic temples and pyramids. The combination of Spanish origin and predominant Roman Catholic religion accounts for the number of colorful festivals held throughout the year, many featuring gay parades and colorful social activities.

AGRICULTURE. More than 58 percent of the people work on the land, while another 10 percent are engaged in processing or packing the products grown in the fields. Of the total land area, almost a fourth is under cultivation, much of the rest being unfit due to the mountains and forest areas. Two crops, coffee and cotton, account for about 90 percent of all exports.

Coffee is of high quality and is produced on plantations which cover nearly 300,000 acres in the highland areas. It accounts for almost 80 percent of the commercial crops. Next in importance is cotton of good quality, grown on about 90,000 acres along the coast. Most of the rest of the agricultural production is of mere subsistence quantity, grown on small, fairly primitive farms. An interesting specialty crop is sesame seed; another is balsam, a third is honey.

INDUSTRY. Mineral production is unimportant, with a few small mines producing gold and silver. But in industry, El Salvador is the most highly industrialized country in Central America, with more manufacturing plants than all the other countries. There is neither coal nor oil; power for its industries is electric, resulting from river dams. The biggest industries are food processing and textiles, with fairly large mills located in the chief cities. Other products made or processed on a substantial scale are straw hats, sisal bags, leather, shoes, beer, cigars, and cigarettes. Most items produced are consumed locally, though some exports go to neighboring republics.

CITIES. El Salvador has only one very large city, the capital, San Salvador, but it has a number of towns, as well as several sights of special interest outside the city areas.

LA LIBERTAD, easily reached from San Salvador over a good highway, 23 miles to the south, is the principal seaport of the country and its chief resort. Along the coast in both directions from La Libertad, a scenic highway links a series of beach resorts. The coast area is picturesque and rugged, with several resorts featuring black sand beaches.

SAN SALVADOR, 23 miles inland from the sea, lies in the central valley at an elevation of about 2,000 feet, and has a population of about 350,000. Above it towers the volcano San Salvador, from which the city takes its name. Most of the city has a brisk, modern appearance, with some fine residential sections on the slopes above the town, both west and south. There are several pleasant parks within the city limits, and at the base of the volcano to the northwest, is a fine resort hotel, one of the most notable in Central America. Just outside the city to the south is **Los Planes de Renderos,** a mountain ridge that has been converted to a picturesque and handsome residential district, the chief feature of which is a large and attractive park.

SANTA ANA, second city in size, is 34 miles to the northwest over the Inter-American Highway. It is a handsome metropolis, has a population of about 100,000, and is the acknowledged coffee capital of the country (one coffee mill within the city, El Molino, is the world's largest). Of interest to visitors are the public buildings and churches in Santa Ana, many of classic Spanish Renaissance design. Near the city are two scenic attractions, **Lake Coatepeque** and **Izalco,** the country's most famous volcano. The lake, 12 miles from town, and one of the most beautiful in Central America, has high mineral content in its water that is known for its therapeutic quality. The shores are lined with resorts, and the fishing is excellent. Although Izalco is no longer active, it is visited by thousands of travelers yearly, and is best seen from the nearby park of Atecozol, one of the country's most popular, best equipped, and scenically attractive resort areas. Not far away is another national park called **Cerro Verde,** regarded as the country's top visitor attraction. It is built at the crest of an extinct volcano at a height of 6,168 feet. A mountain road leads to the crest, where there is a good new hotel and a fine view of the surrounding country, including the nearby Izalco.

SANTA TECLA, on the highway just west of San Salvador, eight miles distant, is situated in a mountain-rimmed valley about 1,000 feet higher than the capital, and has a cooler climate. A suburban resort of much charm, it is the center of a rich coffee-producing region, and the closest community to the crater of **San Salvador volcano.** A mile wide and a half mile deep, the crest of the volcano, reached by a winding mountain road, is at an elevation of 6,373 feet. A park at the crater's edge provides dramatic views of the valley area below.

As with most Central American countries, the principal visitor interests are sightseeing and shopping. Sightseeing is most easily done from the capital, where there are excellent facilities for it. Most of the sights are based on natural features and novelties, such as the volcanoes and several national parks. The country itself is rugged and beautiful, and many smaller villages and towns are picturesque.

SPORTS AND RECREATION. Participant and spectator sports are limited and are almost entirely confined to the capital. They include a country club with a nine-hole **golf** course open to visitors by arrangement, one of the best **horse racing** tracks in Central America, and a national stadium where a variety of athletic contests are staged. **Deep-sea fishing** off the coast, **fresh-water fishing** in the lakes, and **hunting** for duck or alligator are popular.

SPECIAL EVENTS. **Holy Week,** taking place in early April, is the year's first major event. Others include **July Fiestas** and **August Fiestas,** held in towns and villages throughout the country during those months; **San Miguel's Carnival,** November; and **Our Lady of Guadalupe Fiesta,** with traditional celebrations held in San Salvador on December 12.

DINING AND SHOPPING. Dining opportunities are adequate but not notable. All the better hotels and resorts have good dining rooms, where the food tends to be either Spanish or French. Specialties of the area are tropical fruits, coffee, and fresh-caught fish.

Handicraft products, including pottery, native gourd bowls from Izalco, articles of tortoise shell and silver, baskets woven from coconut leaves are the best buys. Interesting fabrics of various kinds, including fine cotton and silk textiles, wool blankets and rugs of good quality and design are also excellent purchases.

Nicaragua

Nicaragua, with about 50,000 square miles, is the largest of the Central American countries, and has an area slightly larger than Louisiana. Triangular in shape, Nicaragua is bordered by Honduras on the north, the Caribbean Sea on the east, the Pacific Ocean on the west, and Costa Rica on the south and southwest. The longer coast dimension of the country, 350 miles, is along the Caribbean coast; the land border with Honduras also runs for 350 miles. Nicaragua's western coast on the Pacific is about 200 miles long, while the land border with Costa Rica runs 150 miles. Managua is the largest city, and capital of the country, which is a republic. The language is almost entirely Spanish, and the religion of the people is predominantly Roman Catholic.

THE LAND. In physical character, Nicaragua is unusual. Important natural features include more than 25 volcanoes, several still active, along the Pacific coast; a very large lake flanking the row of volcanoes; rugged mountain areas to the north and in the central part of the country; and a vast, relatively flat and uninhabited tropical jungle region along the Caribbean Sea to the east. Mountain peaks are somewhat lower than in other parts of Central America, with the highest one rising to about 7,000 feet.

The country, as does most of Central America, lies along a ring of volcanoes and seismic faults that encircles the Pacific from the Aleutians down through the western rim of the Americas to New Zealand and up through Japan, making it prone to geologic turbulence.

The most picturesque natural features are two connecting lakes—Lake Managua and Lake Nicaragua. The former, about 32 miles long and from 10 to 16 miles wide, has a surface 127 feet above the sea. A river called Tipitapa drains from Lake Managua and connects with even larger Lake Nicaragua. The two lakes and the river have often been considered as the basis for a route across the Isthmus of Nicaragua, connecting the Pacific Ocean with the Caribbean Sea, to provide a relatively low level waterway. The country as a whole is only sparsely settled, much of its mountain area covered by forests, and the whole eastern coast covered by a dense tropical jungle. Only about 16 percent of the surface area of the country is put to any useful purpose.

THE CLIMATE. The climate of Nicaragua is humid and tropical. Rainfall varies from a high of 200 inches a year on the low east coast area to about 60 inches a year in the vicinity of the capital of Managua. There are two distinct seasons, dry and rainy, with most of the rains falling between May and December. Temperature variations are slight from month to month, averaging well over 80 degrees in Managua, regardless of the time of year.

THE PEOPLE. Spanish conquistadors who marched into Nicaragua from Panama to the south as early as 1519 found a land fairly well populated with peaceful Indians engaged in farming. The fact that the Indians had golden ornaments suggested to the Spanish that the country was worth colonizing. They established several centers, particularly Granada, on the shore of Lake Nicaragua, and León farther to the northeast. Spanish colonists intermarried freely with the Indian people, with the result that most of the population today is of mixed Indian and Spanish blood, the ladino. There are relatively few people of pure Spanish blood. An important recent ethnic strain is the Negro, brought to the east coast by British and American interests to develop banana plantations and forest reserves. The total population of the country today is estimated at about 2 million. Of these almost three-fourths are completely illiterate. The Spanish colonization of Nicaragua accounts for the fact that most of the architecture of the country of any importance is in the Spanish Colonial style. Spanish traditions also account for numerous colorful festivals, nearly all of religious origin.

AGRICULTURE. Though Nicaragua has rich mineral resources, chiefly gold, copper, and silver, most of the people live on the land and all of the exports except minerals are either agricultural or are derived from the rich forest reserves. First in importance is cotton. Coffee is second and gold is third. Though the country is capable of producing fine crops on easily accessible areas, only 16 percent of the potentially arable land is under cultivation. But the cotton crop has been growing steadily. Coffee plantations lie to the south on the mountain slopes; the coffee is of high quality. Bananas, once quite important, are now decreasingly so, although plantations on the Pacific coast have begun growing them. Cacao is increasing in production, especially along the tropical east coast, formerly used for bananas.

Other crops important enough to be economic factors are rice, sugar, which has been increasingly important in recent years, and a limited amount of tobacco. A relatively new specialty crop is sesame. Forest products, derived from enormous and almost completely undeveloped reserves, are chiefly mahogany, cedar, and pine.

INDUSTRY. Nicaragua is developing industrially, although it is advancing slowly. There are several cotton mills, and one fairly large sugar refinery.

CITIES. Nicaragua has few cities of any size and only three important to the visitor. Most of the towns and villages lie in the western area among the mountains. On the tropical Caribbean coast there are a few scattered small settlements devoted entirely to commercial purposes. Managua, virtually destroyed by an earthquake December 23, 1972, is the country's chief city and is the capital.

BLUEFIELDS, the only town of importance on the east coast, is easily reached by good highway, ship, or by air. Located 180 miles from Managua, it has a population of about 15,000, and is the chief shipping port for bananas and cabinet woods. Off the coast, beyond Bluefields, are two dramatically beautiful small tropical islands called the Corn Islands, both popular resort areas for Nicaraguans.

GRANADA, chief city on the shore of **Lake Nicaragua,** is located 30 miles southeast of the capital. One of the oldest cities in Central America, it was founded in 1524, has an interesting setting on the lake shore at the foot of a volcano. Once a rich and colorful city, it still has buildings of charm and interest, all designed in the Colonial Spanish manner. The lake front nearby offers Nicaragua's best recreational facilities, including several beaches, linked by small resorts. There are boat docks, where boats for fishing and sightseeing may be hired.

The lake itself, largest in Central America, about 100 miles long and 45 miles wide, is unique in some ways and dramatically picturesque in aspect. Its western shore near Granada is fringed by a cluster of more than 300 small islands of great beauty. Formed from black volcanic stone, they are crested by clumps of tropical forest, separated by winding, picturesque channels. A sightseeing boat trip among them is a rewarding visitor opportunity. The lake is the only lake in the world known to be the home of salt-water fish, including sharks. Toward the center of the lake are two fairly large islands, on one of which are two volcanoes, one rising in a perfect cone to 5,000 feet.

LEÓN, second city in size in the country, with a population of about 44,000, and probably the oldest city in Nicaragua, is 50 miles northwest of Managua on the Inter-American Highway. It was founded in 1524, at about the same time as Granada, was the country's capital until 1852, and is still regarded as the cultural center of the country. León has an ancient air, winding, cobbled streets, low adobe houses, roofed with red tile, and several interesting buildings of Spanish Colonial design. They include the **cathedral,** of baroque design, the largest church in Central America, as well as several other Colonial churches and public buildings.

MANAGUA, the country's capital and the commercial center of the country since 1858, was also its newest city, having been completely rebuilt after a violent earthquake destroyed it in 1931. But this spacious, beautifully arranged new capital with its modern buildings, broad avenues and pleasant parks was hit by another disaster. Managua, which sits on top of a volcanic belt in a highly active area, was virtually leveled again by an earthquake, two days before Christmas in 1972.

Compared with other quakes, this one, measuring 6.3 on the Richter scale, was not severe. The effects were devastating, nevertheless. Because the city was built on compacted volcanic debris rather than solid rock, and because the exact center of the quake was nine miles under downtown Managua near the Lake Managua shorefront, most of its 1,200-acre commercial district was ripped apart and swallowed up by the quake.

The rebuilding of the city and efforts to return to normal for the population of over 250,000 will be slow and costly. Tourists will find travel here difficult for some time. The capital of Nicaragua may be moved to another city or to a new area considered safer from seismic disturbance.

TIPITAPA, a picturesque village on the shore of the lake, 14 miles from Managua, has a small resort built around hot springs, with a hotel and casino and a colorful native market. Of greater interest is a visit to Granada.

Though the potential of visitor interest in Nicaragua is substantial, much of it is undeveloped and present facilities for doing and seeing things of interest are scattered and inadequate. There are several small museums in the larger centers, and some buildings of architectural and historical interest. The most unusual sightseeing opportunities are the boat trips on Lake Nicaragua, but the boats available for such trips are small and special arrangements for their use must be made well in advance. Hotel facilities, particularly a new first-class hotel, are adequate.

SPORTS AND RECREATION. Cockfights and bullfights are very popular in Nicaragua, though baseball is the national sport. In the bullfights, the matador mounts and rides the bull, rather than killing it.

SPECIAL EVENTS in Nicaragua are highlighted by the **Independence Day** celebrations taking place throughout the country. Parades and civic ceremonies are the chief attractions of this holiday. The **Festival of Santo Domingo** is held in Managua, the capital, in early August, and Diriamba stages a **Festival of San Sebastian** in January. Special religious festivities are an integral part of the Christmas and Easter seasons.

DINING AND SHOPPING. Cooking styles are chiefly Spanish and French, and there are no local food specialties of unusual interest.

Shopping opportunities, particularly for native crafts, are moderately interesting in most of the native markets and in several good shops in the larger cities. Craft specialties of interest include jewelry and ornaments made of filigree gold, leather goods of various kinds, particularly from alligator hide.

Costa Rica

Costa Rica, next to the smallest of the Central American countries (after El Salvador), with a land area of 19,575 square miles, somewhat smaller than the state of West Virginia, has been called the Switzerland of Central America. Ruggedly picturesque, irregular in shape, it stretches northwest to southeast across the narrowing isthmus, with the Caribbean Sea on one side and the Pacific Ocean on the other side. The straight-line distance along the Pacific coast is about 300 miles, but the actual coastline is 630 miles, because of deep indentations and coastal peninsulas. The relatively straight Caribbean coastline is 125 miles. The country varies in width from 74 to 175 miles. Its neighbor to the north is Nicaragua, with that country's Lake Nicaragua forming part of the border. To the southeast, a border of wild, high, rugged mountains, is the Republic of Panama. The population of Costa Rica is estimated at about 1.8 million. The capital is San José. The country is a true democratic republic, with a stable government.

THE LAND. No country of Central America is more pleasantly picturesque and more colorful in aspect than Costa Rica. Most of the area of the land is filled with mountains, some of them quite high. Among them are so many volcanoes that they are a symbol on the national seal of the country. Among the mountains, individual peaks rise to more than 12,000 feet. The mountain masses are particularly rugged in the south-central part of the country, north of the border of Panama. Both coasts have lowland areas. On the Caribbean coast tropical jungles and swamps extend south from Nicaragua in a broad, fairly level plain narrowing toward the south. Most of the east coast is uninhabited, a land of steaming dense jungle, winding tropical rivers. On the west coast, the coastal shelf is narrower and, though still tropical, less humid. From that coast extend two big peninsulas, each with a bay on its eastern side. In the north is the peninsula of Nicoya. In the south is the peninsula of Osa.

An unusual feature of Costa Rica, which contributes much to that country's special charm, is the big rich upland valley called the *Meseta Central,* an area of more than 3,500 square miles at an altitude of from 3,000 to 6,000 feet, with an average elevation of about 4,000 feet. In this rich high valley, with a delightful springlike climate year-round, live most of the people of Costa Rica, and most of the towns and settlements are located here. The rich valley floor and the equally rich lower slopes of the wooded mountains rising above it are intensively cultivated. On the higher, cooler slopes are grazing areas for cattle and sheep.

THE CLIMATE. The climate of Costa Rica varies markedly with elevation and location. Though the whole country is in the tropical zone, by changing elevation it is possible to find almost any climatic character desired. The Caribbean coast, with high humidity and excessive rainfall, is uncomfortably torrid day and night. The lowlands on the Pacific side, however, are dryer and milder. The great central valley has a springlike climate year-round, with a dry, almost rainless season from December to April, but with a good deal of rainfall between May and November. Even during the rainy season the rainfall is sporadic and most days have sun. In the capital of San José and the area around it, temperature variations range less than 4 degrees from month to month, with an average around 70. Higher mountain slopes, which are divided between cattle and sheep ranges and forest areas, are often quite cool; occasional snow is not unknown near the crests of the high mountains. The fact that nearly 65 percent of the area of Costa Rica's surface is covered by forests adds a tempering effect to the climate.

THE PEOPLE. The character of the people who live in Costa Rica make it unique among the countries of Central America. It is the only country in that region where the population is almost entirely uniform, of European origin, chiefly Spanish. Most of the people live in the relatively cool temperate highland basin. The government of the country has been stable for many years, and spends three times more on education than it does on defense. There are more schoolteachers in Costa Rica than there are soldiers. Literacy is higher than in any other Central American country, and higher than in most Latin American countries. The country has a comparatively high standard of living and social services.

The special character of the population of Costa Rica is the result of factors of settlement and growth. Columbus saw the Caribbean coast of Costa Rica in 1502, and is said to have given it its name, "The Rich Coast." But the hostility of Indians discouraged settlement for many years, so that no settlement occurred until 1564, when the city of Cartago was founded. Settlers from Spain brought with them their animals, ideas—and diseases. Indians, enslaved to work on the haciendas of the early Spanish settlers, were not immune to European ailments and within a few years were almost entirely wiped out. The settlers had two alternatives: either to starve or go to work. They decided to work, and divided the land into small family farms, the only known case of its type in all of Latin America. The result has been a tradition of self-sufficiency and industry unique among Latin American countries. The original settlers numbered only 55 families. Two hundred years later, the entire population amounted to less than 3,000.

In the year 1800, however, with the introduction of coffee as a crop (Costa Rica being the first of the Central American republics to grow it), the population began to increase rapidly. Coffee made the country prosperous, made possible the building of railways, the gradual extension of highways, and the spreading of population from the high mountain valley centers to other regions. At the present time, out of a population of about 1.8 million, it is estimated that there are less than 5,000 people of Indian ancestry, descendants of the original Indian tribes. More than 98 percent of the population is white, of essentially Spanish descent, except for one district on the Caribbean coast, the region of Limón, where the population is about one-third of African origin, descendants of Negroes brought in during the nineteenth century to help develop banana plantations.

Costa Rica's Spanish heritage, combined with its brisk, pleasant climate and mountain terrain, has resulted in an unusual combination of architectural adaptation. Many of the older buildings, particularly churches, are of traditional Colonial Spanish design, but the most elegant and impressive building in the country is of classic French design of the mid-nineteenth century. On the mountain slopes not far from the capital are many villas which resemble Swiss chalets, and in the capital, as well as in several suburban communities, there are both private dwellings and public buildings of ultra-modern design. The country celebrates a long series of gay and colorful holidays and fiestas, most of them of Spanish origin.

AGRICULTURE. Costa Rica's sound economy and its evident prosperity are based primarily on agriculture, with more than half of the population engaged in it. There are three major crops. By far the most important is coffee, the cultivation and development of which led to the settlement of the country. Coffee grows on mountain slope plantations spreading over nearly 150,000 acres near the capital, in a rich soil based on volcanic ash. The second most important crop is bananas. As with coffee, Costa Rica was the first area in Central America to produce bananas for export. In the beginning the big banana plantations were on the Atlantic coast, but in recent years the production of bananas has shifted to plantations on the Gulf of Dulce in the southwest corner of the country. The third crop of importance is cacao, grown chiefly on derelict banana plantations on the Caribbean coast. A fourth important crop is abacá, also grown on former banana plantations. It is a plant from which manila hemp, used in making cordage, is produced.

Costa Rica has an unusually large number of cattle, particularly dairy cattle, and it is one of the few Central American countries where the dairy industry (based on mountain slope ranges above the coffee plantations) is important. Other crops important enough to be mentioned are tobacco, cotton (the basis of a local textile industry), forest products of various types, one of which is extensively used for plywood. An agricultural oddity is the commercial cultivation of flowers, many of which are exported by air to northern regions. Another unusual product is honey, with hundreds of farms maintaining hives.

INDUSTRY. Next to El Salvador, Costa Rica is the most industrialized country in Central America. There are about 8,000 factories of various types and sizes, most of them small and most of them engaged in manufacturing products consumed locally. The largest mills are devoted to textile manufacture, particularly cotton. There are almost no mineral resources of importance, but gold and silver are mined on a small scale on the Pacific slopes. Other metal ores found but not fully exploited are copper, iron, lead, mercury, nickel, and zinc. Large deposits of sulphur are known to exist, and are now being mined.

CITIES. Small Costa Rica, with its highly literate and prosperous population, has no really large cities, and only one, the inland capital of San José, even approaches being a big city. But there are dozens of pleasant small towns and villages, most of them concentrated in the upland central valley. The capital, with its central location, its easy access to the rest of the country, and its excellent facilities for accommodations and diversion, is, however, the chief center of visitor interest.

SAN JOSÉ, with a population of about 182,000, is one of the most handsome and modern cities in Central America. It spreads over a broad, fertile valley at an elevation of over 3,000 feet, with mountain slopes rising above and around, patterned with patches of forest and coffee plantations. There are many substantial suburban centers, with the result that more than 400,000 people live in the metropolitan district, within a few minutes' drive of the city center.

San José is brisk and clean, has a distinctive modern aspect, but with dozens of older, often charming, dwellings and public buildings going back to the Spanish period. It is the hub of the business, political, and cultural life of the country. The principal streets are broad. There are a half-dozen important parks, most of them filled with flowers.

In addition to being a convenient base for visiting points of interest in the nearby area, the city itself has some sights worth seeing, many of them close together, near the city center. Most important of these is the city's superb **National Theater,** echoing in design and detail on a smaller scale the Grand Opera House in Paris. Another is the **National Museum,** converted from a former fort on a hill at the eastern side of the city. Exhibits include displays relating to the culture and natural resources of the country. The **cathedral,** facing a central park, is massive and impressive without being architecturally notable. Most interesting of the city's several important parks is **National Park,** with various government buildings, including the nearby residence of the president. A building of great charm and unusual character in the downtown area is the **Union Club,** with one of the biggest and most interesting indoor aviaries, filled with gay and noisy tropical birds. The principal and the most attractive street of San José is Paseo Colón, which extends from the center of the business district to the western limits of the town, where there is a national stadium seating 20,000 people, and the National Airport, smaller of two airports which serve the country. The city maintains an excellent small national **zoo** in a picturesque ravine on the northeastern edge of town. The **National University,** with an interesting campus and some notable buildings, is regarded as one of the best in Central America.

San José is a convenient place for visiting several nearby points of interest. One of these is in the suburban town of **Alajuela,** second largest city in Costa Rica, with a population of about 25,000. Here is a curious resort called the **Ojo de Agua** (Eye of Water), a state-owned and -maintained public park built around a gushing spring which fills a large swimming pool, the whole set in handsomely landscaped grounds. On the edge of the town is Costa Rica's handsome airport, one of the best in Central America. Towering above is a volcano, **Poás,** with a crater a mile wide, said to be the largest in the world. Somewhat farther away, to the east, over the Inter-American Highway, is the old city of **Cartago,** founded in 1564, the capital of the country until 1823. Visitors flock there to see the most famous church in the country, the **Shrine of Our Lady of the Angels,** Patroness of Costa Rica. It houses La Negrita, the black, six-inch image of the Virgin which is said to have first appeared at the site in 1635. Outside the main church is a shrine to the Virgin with a bubbling spring said to have miraculous properties.

Northeast of Cartago, reached over a dramatically scenic highway which climbs forest slopes, is Costa Rica's most interesting and most visited volcano, the crater of **Irazú,** the crest of which towers over 11,000 feet, 34 miles from San José. The volcano is active, with dramatic clouds of steam rising from the crater, and sometimes rumbles alarmingly to delight and terrify visitors. A few miles from Cartago is a delightful valley center called **Agua Caliente** (because of its flowing hot springs), reached by a spectacularly scenic highway. In the valley are two ancient, picturesque missions, one in ruins; the other, still maintained as a place of worship, is said to have been founded over 300 years ago.

The only other city of importance in Costa Rica is the east coast port of **Limón,** with a population of about 30,000, a modern industrial port with little to interest visitors. It is built on the site of an Indian village which is believed to have been the point at which Columbus landed on his fourth voyage. Most of the population is Negro. The only points of interest include a palm-filled promenade, and a park noted for tropical flowers. A narrow-gauge railway links Limón with San José about 100 miles away. It offers one of the most unusual and **scenic rail journeys** anywhere.

SPORTS AND RECREATION. There are several small resorts to be visited, both close to the capital and off the coast. One of these, a mountain resort built in the center of a great coffee plantation, has the appearance of a Bavarian mountain lodge, with facilities for **swimming, tennis, golf,** and **riding.** There are other **golf courses** at San José and at Limón, **sea bathing** on both the Atlantic and Pacific coasts, and also **deep-sea fishing** from both coasts. A pleasant participant sport, with excellent facilities, is **horseback riding,** with horses for hire almost everywhere. Costa Rica features **bullfights,** generally a part of colorful fiestas, but the bullfights differ from those in other areas because no one, including the bulls, gets hurt. The opportunity for **hunting** is varied, with jaguar, puma, alligator, wild boar, deer, mountain goats, duck, partridge, quail.

SPECIAL EVENTS in Costa Rica are centered around the many festivals and feast days which are held in towns throughout the country. These include **St. Joseph** on March 19; **Labor Day,** May 1; **Corpus Christi,** mid-June; **St. Peter and St. Paul,** June 29; and **All Souls Day,** November 2. **Independence Day** celebrations take place September 15, while **International Soccer Football Games** are held in December in the National Stadium in San José.

DINING AND SHOPPING. Costa Rica, particularly San José, has an unusually large number of good restaurants. They tend to feature Continental-type food, representing various cooking styles of Europe, particularly French and Spanish, but there are also good German, Swiss, and American-type restaurants. There are no unusual or distinctive native dishes. The characteristic native food is Spanish in origin. Costa Ricans regard their coffee, an almost universal beverage, as one of the best in the world. The country has an abundance of fine tropical fruits, and along the coast and in some of the better restaurants of San José, fresh-caught seafood is plentiful and good.

There are excellent, modern stores, chiefly in San José, well stocked with merchandise from everywhere, particularly the United States and Germany. The most interesting craft articles, however, are beautifully tanned and finished leather goods, woodenware, ornaments carved and colored in a manner reminiscent of Switzerland, and tortoise-shell articles of various types. Native art translated to craft articles is distinctive, involving intricate geometrical designs worked out in vivid color.

Panama and Panama Canal Zone

The Republic of Panama, with its associated Canal Zone under the jurisdiction of the United States, is one of the most curious countries in the world in shape and character. A curved ribbon of rugged land, it is shaped like a slightly flattened S lying on its side. This ribbon varies in width from 35 to 113 miles, and has a length from west to east, measured down its center, of 400 miles. The geographic position of the country is uniquely strategic, a fact which, combined with its physical character, has determined its destiny. To its west is Costa Rica; to its east is Colombia in South America, a nation which originally owned the area of Panama; to its north is the Caribbean Sea, with the island of Jamaica about 600 miles away; to the south is the open Pacific Ocean.

The curious shape of the country accounts for two geographic oddities. First, when crossing the isthmus at the Canal Zone, to reach the Pacific from the Atlantic, travelers proceed to the east, and second, at Panama City, the sun rises in the east over the Pacific. The area of the country is over 29,000 square miles, not including the Canal Zone, which contains about 650 square miles. No Central American country has a smaller population. All of Panama's more than 1.4 million inhabitants live on one-fourth of the land.

THE LAND. The land of Panama, covered with mountains and lakes, is markedly varied in character. From Costa Rica in the west, a rugged range of steep and tumbled slopes, with peaks rising to more than 11,000 feet, fills the center of the isthmus. As the ranges proceed east, the crests become lower, slopes less abrupt, until at about the center of the isthmus a curious cleft or gap occurs. Within this gap is a large lake, fed by mountain rivers. The gap, the lake, and the rivers flowing into it have made possible the Panama Canal, which extends 50 miles across the isthmus, linking the Atlantic and the Pacific. To the east of the gap, through which the canal runs, rises another range of mountains, with steeper and higher slopes extending into the continent of South America at the Colombian border. Among them, the topography, flora, and fauna are characteristically South American. Heavily indented coasts on both sides of the ranges are covered with densely tropical forests, fringed with islands. Valleys within the mountain ranges are often richly fertile, the slopes of the mountains themselves covered with superb stands of tropical and hardwood trees. The length of the broken coastal line on the Pacific side is 767 miles, and on the Atlantic side, 477 miles, the longer Pacific coast due to the bold out-thrusting of a peninsula called Azuero. The offshore islands on either side, found near the center of the peninsula, are some of the most interesting and unusual tropical islands anywhere. On the Pacific side they have been converted to popular resorts; on the Atlantic side are the homes of an indigenous tribe of Indians. Very little of the land of Panama is cultivated. Only about 15 percent is farmed, and of that only a small part is under crops.

Most of the peninsula is linked by the route of the Inter-American Highway, which connects nearly all of the larger centers of population. It winds down the Pacific shore, from the border of Costa Rica, peters out to the east of Panama City, in a dense and largely uninhabited and unexplored tropical wilderness. It was from the crest of a peak in this area, called Darién, in 1513, that the redheaded and venturesome explorer, Balboa, first saw the shining waters of the Pacific Ocean.

THE CLIMATE. Except for some highland areas, the climate of all of Panama is tropical and humid, the mean average annual temperature being 80 degrees. Seasonal variations from that average are slight, divided between the so-called rainy and dry seasons. The rainy season occurs from mid-May to mid-December with total rainfall of 65 inches annually in the Pacific and 120 inches in the Atlantic regions. The Caribbean and Atlantic coasts are more humid than the Pacific coast; temperature variations between night and day are only about 15 degrees. Midday heat is usually high, which results in the universal custom of a two-hour siesta.

Some of the higher mountain valleys,

particularly on the Pacific side, have more pleasant and temperate local climates, and therefore have become resort refuges from the heat for permanent residents of urban areas. Because of the heavy rainfalls along the coasts, the tropical forests which flank them are among the most dense and luxurious in Central America.

THE PEOPLE. The history of Panama and the present high diversity of its people is almost entirely the result of attempts to use the isthmus as a route connecting the Atlantic with the Pacific. Everything that has happened in Panama since its first discovery by the Spanish mariner, Rodrigo de Bastidas, in 1501 (followed by Columbus the next year) has been an attempt to exploit and develop practical ways of getting from the Pacific to the Atlantic and vice versa. Those attempts began very soon after Balboa made his monumental journey across the isthmus, and, marching down from the mountains into the Pacific, claimed all the lands it washed for the king in Spain.

Old Panama, about five miles from Panama City, was founded in 1519 by Pedro Arias, a nobleman from Ávila, nominated as Governor by the Spanish Crown. Known as the "greatest city in the New World," Old Panama was used as a base for expeditions to various parts of the west coast of Central and South America. The fabulous treasures gathered on these forays were transported by pack animals over a 50-mile, stone-paved road to the Caribbean harbor of Portobelo for transshipment to Spain.

The existence of the treasure and the treasure ships made the isthmus the target for raids by pirates and such English mariners as Francis Drake and Henry Morgan. In 1673, two years after Morgan sacked the original city of Panama, the inhabitants began constructing their new Panama City on its present site, encircling it with a wall and building the fort "Las Bovedas" on a rocky promontory.

Piratical raids on treasure fleets and the city treasure bases continued for all the period of Spanish reign, up to about the middle of the eighteenth century. During the 82 years (1821–1903) that Panama was under the rule of Colombia, the city fell into a decline, with its Colonial buildings left in a state of disrepair and its streets grass-grown and neglected. In 1903 Colombia's military rule was overthrown and the new Republic of Panama began. Camino Real, or the King's Road, was little used until the middle of the nineteenth century when the discovery of gold in California made the passage of the isthmus once more important.

The gold rush to California resulted in a railway being built across the isthmus. The first train on it ran in 1853, and until the opening of rail travel across the United States, about 1870, the railway, a U.S. company, chiefly financed with U.S. money, was a huge financial success. Before it was built, a treaty with Colombia had been granted to the U.S. for transit rights across the isthmus, but the treaty presumed not a railway but a canal. The possibility of a canal had been explored as early as 1534, when a survey indicated that such a canal was not possible. But France actually attempted to dig a canal. French workers and engineers contributed a special ethnic note that is still in evidence, as well as some architectural relics of great charm in Panama City. The French attempt failed, but not for lack of engineering skill. The attempt was defeated instead by bad management, malaria, yellow fever, cholera, and other diseases. Many of the Negro workers brought in for the labor of digging remained in the area.

It was the possibility of a canal, notwithstanding the failure of the French, which led eventually to a revolution and the setting up of the Republic of Panama. The revolution was established with the support of the United States, which immediately made plans to do what it succeeded in doing some years later: dig the Panama Canal. To do so, the United States leased a ribbon of land across the isthmus forever.

The result of these struggles and changes over a period of 400 years, and the constant flow and flux of population elements which were involved in them, has given Panama today the most diverse and polyglot population pattern of any region in Central America. There are substantial numbers of Negroes, persons of mixed blood, as well as native Indians and Chinese whose forebears came to the isthmus during the canal-digging period and have remained to engage in trade and business. In addition, more than 50,000 indigenous Indians live as tribes on the offshore islands and in the mountain jungles to the east. One picturesque Indian tribe, the Cunas, inhabits a cluster of some 360 islands called San Blas, off the Caribbean coast, and lives much as their forefathers did centuries ago. Their brilliantly colored, hand-loomed costumes suggest patterns and styles of ancient Egypt. In the mountains to the east, the Indian tribes, living in stilted houses, are among the most primitive to be found in Central America.

Most of the present population of Panama lives either in Panama City or Colón or in their suburbs which flank the Canal Zone. Many of the Negroes living in Panama City are the descendants of groups of Negroes brought in as labor forces at various times, starting with slaves brought in during the sixteenth century. The West Indian Negroes were brought in for the building of the railway in 1850, and more came for the two canal ventures. Since then they have gradually been assimilated into Panama's population.

AGRICULTURE. The agriculture and economy of Panama is almost as curious as its shape and history. Imports are five times greater than exports, the gap being closed by invisible exports, almost all from the operation of the Canal in one way or another, ranging from direct payments from the United States to the government, to millions spent in the area every year by resident Canal workers and administrators.

The potential of Panama's agricultural resources is substantial, but the actual agricultural production is relatively small. Bananas, coming largely from the Pacific lowland areas are the chief crop. The second most important crop is the harvest of the sea, chiefly fresh shrimp, while a third agricultural product is cacao, developed on former banana land. Abacá, used in making rope, and coconuts are both produced in commercial quantities. There is a substantial amount of sugar grown, a considerable part of it refined in the country. Excellent coffee is grown in a limited way in the volcanic soils of western Panama. Other crops, nearly all of a subsistence character, are rice, a staple consumed by the entire population; as well as corn, beans, and potatoes. There has been a recent development of a cattle industry, and an increase in dairy farming.

INDUSTRY. One of Panama's great untapped resources is hardwoods from its superb forests, chiefly mahogany. Major deposits of copper and molybdenum were recently discovered. Other minerals, relatively unexploited, include gold, mercury, and a small bauxite deposit, being worked by a U.S. firm near the Costa Rican border. Almost no manufacturing plants turn out products for export. Those that exist make goods almost entirely for local consumption. There are several breweries and distilleries making both rum and whisky. One of the economic developments of importance was the establishment of a free trade zone in Colón, which permits manufacturers to maintain duty-free warehouses for transshipment from one country to another. A substantial economic resource is money left in the country by visiting tourists, most of whom are passing through the Canal or who stop over in connection with an international air flight.

CITIES. Panama has two fairly large cities, each of which has smaller satellite companions. They stand at either end of the Canal Zone and are historically, economically, and culturally associated with the long history of the Canal and the previous devices by which the isthmus was crossed. The chief and by far the largest is Panama City.

Iolani Palace, Honolulu, Hawaii

Dancers at Polynesian Cultural Center, Oahu Island, Hawaii

Waikiki beach, facing Diamond Head in Hawaii

Giant redwoods, northern California

Catalina Island, California

Lone Cypress,
Monterey, California

Mission San Carlos Borromeo (Mission Carmel),
Carmel, California

Sun Valley, Idaho

Basque sheepherder, Idaho

COLÓN, the second largest city in Panama, with a population of about 67,000, was originally founded as a base for the construction of the railway over the isthmus. Though Colón has some interesting Oriental shops, there is little to see in the town itself, but many attractions nearby. There is a pleasant beach drive leading from the town, and 20 miles away is the old port of **Portobelo**, a harbor which was used by Columbus in 1502. It is the oldest of the ruined Spanish settlements in Panama, and has some interesting forts, a former treasure house, and a quaintly curious cathedral with a statue of the Black Christ. Also near Colón is historic **Fort San Lorenzo**, near the mouth of the Chagres River, a dramatically set fortressed ruin perched on a high bluff overlooking the river mouth, reached by a highly scenic jungle road about 20 miles north of Gatun Dam. Not far from Colón, off the coast, are the colorful **San Blas Islands**, which afford visitors their most interesting offbeat excursion opportunity. They are reached by boat and by air, are magnificently tropical, with the finest coconuts in the whole area.

Outside the Canal Zone, there are many communities of interest for the visitor. The largest and most distant from Panama City is the western city of **David**, with about 35,000 people, capital of the rugged mountain province of **Chiriquí**, and the richest agricultural section of the country. Third largest city, founded in Colonial times, it retains an old-world Colonial aspect. Nearby are the highlands of Chiriquí, dominated by a volcanic peak more than 11,000 feet high. The area is noted for fine coffee and for the luxuriance of its tropical flowers.

PANAMA CITY, the capital, has a population of over 418,000. Although most of the present city is modern, it has several very old quarters (remaining from the first Panama City, begun in the sixteenth century), and is a curious blend of smart, new, modern sections; ancient, crowded Spanish districts; and swarming Oriental and Negro areas. The older part of the present city is close-built and crowded. The most interesting structures in its congested heart include those which surround the old **Plaza de Francia**, on the extreme south, a picturesque little plaza with monuments and buildings that commemorate the French attempt to build the Canal. Several fine Colonial buildings are nearby, including the **Palace of Justice**, and the **Dungeons of Las Bovedas**, built on a rock promontory. Not far away is the **National Cathedral**, a massive and ornate building of typical Spanish Colonial design. Of the old buildings, the most impressive is the **president's palace**, with a charming inner courtyard of Moorish design. The original Old Panama, actually four miles away from the present older quarter of the city, is linked to Panama City by a water-front drive, with the attractive new sections of the city lying in between. Among them, in addition to many handsome government buildings and tropical parks, is a large new resort hotel, set in extensive tropical gardens.

From many points in Panama City the course of the Canal to the west can be seen, and highways from the city cut in and out of the Canal Zone, with its two communities of **Balboa** and **Ancon** nearby. The facilities and communities in the Zone are neat, well landscaped, beautifully maintained. Administration buildings for the Canal Zone are on Balboa Heights; nearby are clubs and residences of those who administer the Canal and work on it. Balboa is an efficient, well-planned, attractive, wholly-owned government city. Some of the government buildings within it are interesting and worth visiting, having effective murals telling the story of the Canal and monuments commemorating those who helped build it.

The Canal itself is, of course, the most interesting single sight in Panama. Facilities for seeing it are convenient, including areas adjacent to each of the locks by which ships are lifted or lowered from one level to another. The Canal is actually a series of waterways dug to connect the big central **Gatun Lake** with the two coasts, with water

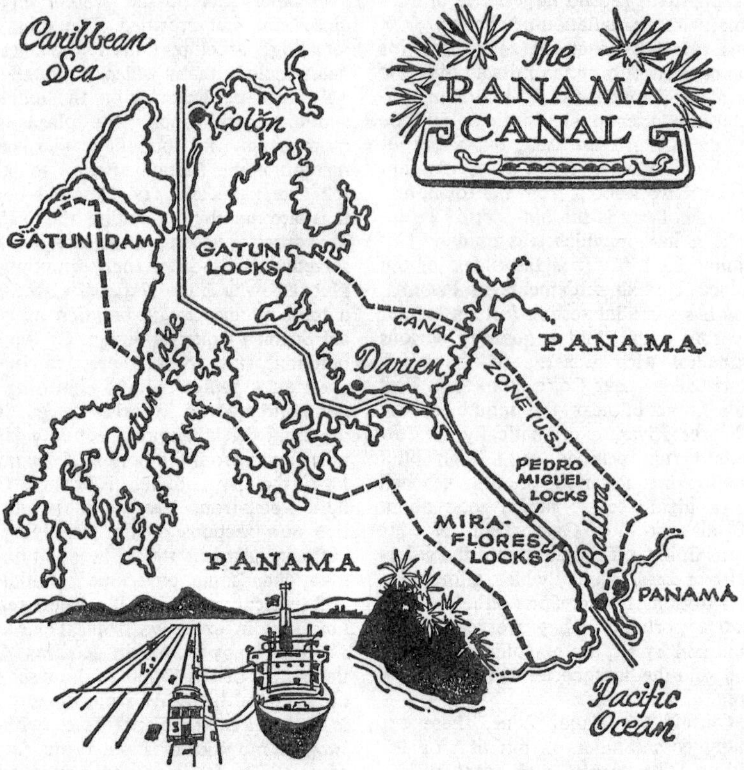

levels maintained in the Canal by locks and water maintained in the lake level by dams in tributary rivers. The distance shore to shore is just over 400 miles. Because of the curious shape of the Isthmus of Panama, the Pacific entrance is paradoxically 27 miles east of the Atlantic entrance. Transit usually takes seven to eight hours, traffic moving in both directions, as all locks are double. Each is 1,000 feet long, 110 feet wide, and 70 feet deep. The minimum depth of the Canal is 41 feet, and its deepest cut is the eight-mile-long **Gaillard Cut.** More than 14,000 ships pass through the Canal in a year's time. Although its shores are heavily forested with tropical jungles, many stretches of the Canal, particularly those in Gatun Lake, are highly picturesque.

One of the best ways to see the Canal, next to riding through it on a ship, is to take a trip on the curious railway that follows its course, a successor to the original railway which crossed the isthmus, built more than 100 years ago. The railway operates from terminals at either end, makes stops along the way, often closely follows the route of the channel, and cuts across a wide section of Gatun Lake on a bridge of islands. Near its western or Atlantic end, a point of principal interest on the Canal is **Gatun Dam,** controlling the waters of Chagres River, and the great locks which lead from the lake down to the sea and the Caribbean port of Colón.

The operation of the Canal, within its own U.S.-controlled zone, so completely dominates the Republic of Panama that it tends to preempt visitor interest. Although seeing the Canal and traveling upon it is one of the most important sightseeing opportunities in the country, there are many other places to visit. Boats make the 12-mile trip from Panama City to the offshore **Taboga Islands,** year-round resort of great beauty and tropical charm, offering fine fishing, swimming and lodgings. The islands are rustic, with no horses, cows, animals, or automobiles. A longer trip of several hours can be made to the **Pearl Islands,** 46 miles offshore, said to offer some of the finest fishing anywhere. They have high mountains and picturesque native villages, where residents live in bamboo huts.

SPORTS AND RECREATION. **Big-game fishing** for marlin, tuna, dolphin, pompano, and other fish off both the coasts of Panama is regarded as among the best, with boats and tackle readily available. There are **horse races** on Saturdays, Sundays, and most holidays at a handsome track near Panama City. The **golf club** of Panama City has an excellent 18-hole course where visitors with courtesy cards are welcome. Many sportsmen claim that interior Panama is a **hunter's paradise.** Mountain jungles abound with various species of big game, including jaguar, wild hog, deer, and a rich variety of wild fowl. Many of Panama's beaches on both coasts are superb, and facilities for using them are good. **Boating** is excellent in various sections, particularly at either end of the Canal.

SPECIAL EVENTS in Panama include the **Panama Open Invitational Golf Championship** in January or February; **Bullfighting** held from January to April; **Carnival,** highlighted by costume exhibitions, masquerades, and a coronation, Tuesday before Lent; **"La Pollera" Festival** of Panama's national costume, in July; and the **Mejorana Festival,** featuring a colorful song contest at Guarare in September.

DINING AND SHOPPING. Dining in Panama, particularly in Panama City and Colón, offers many interesting culinary adventures. Good restaurants feature French and Spanish cooking, with dishes served being typical of both countries. There are also excellent American and Chinese restaurants. Specialties typical of Panama include fried plantain, a banana-like vegetable; *sancocho, arroz con pollo,* and *seviche.* Tropical fruits and seafood are excellent and abundant.

Shopping opportunities in Panama, concentrated in Colón and Panama City, with some notably fine specialty shops in both places, include all sorts of Oriental jewelry and ornaments, articles of tortoise shell and leather, some distinctive pottery. A native craft product of unique interest is the brilliantly colored fabric woven by the San Blas Indians.

Bermuda

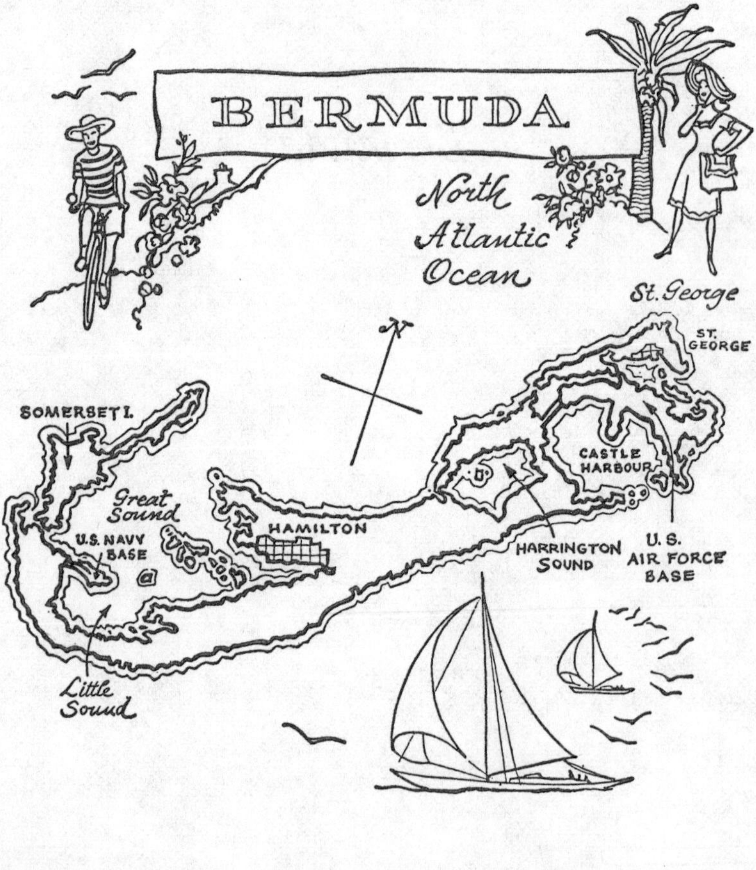
BERMUDA
North Atlantic Ocean
St. George
ST. GEORGE
N
SOMERSET I.
Great Sound
U.S. NAVY BASE
HAMILTON
CASTLE HARBOUR
HARRINGTON SOUND
U.S. AIR FORCE BASE
Little Sound

Bermuda

"The Bermudas"–also known as Somers Islands–can claim the distinctive boast in this island area of the Western Hemisphere that they were *not* discovered by Christopher Columbus. They can also boast that thousands of recent visitors have discovered them–discovered them to be one of the most completely ideal vacation playgrounds in this part of the world. Their atmosphere is one of happy and serene contentment, the climate is pleasing and healthy, the inhabitants friendly, gracious, and hospitable. Here one finds the "good life," the personification of "gracious living."

Situated 580 nautical miles east-southeast of Cape Hatteras, North Carolina, Bermuda is made up of about 300 coral islands and islets, the summits of extinct volcanoes, encircled on three sides by submerged coral reefs. Most are small rocky islets; only a few are inhabited. Bermuda is really half a dozen islands, Great Bermuda or Main Island being referred to as the mainland. Separated by narrow channels and joined to it by bridges or a causeway are the islands of St. George's and St. David's to the east; Somerset, Ireland, and Boaz to the west. The submerged reefs make for difficulty in navigational approach, but in spite of this, several large lagoons–Great Sound, Harrington Sound, Castle Harbour and St. George's Harbour–have made it possible for Bermuda to become famed as a haven for boating. There are no rivers or lakes. Bermuda will be eternally grateful to one Harry Watlington who was knighted for his discovery of the fact that wells could be drilled into the hillsides and that by branching off horizontally from these he could draw out a fresher water that floated on the brackish water underground. This is known as Watlington Water and is used for domestic purposes, while rain water is used for drinking purposes. Bermuda has no mountains. Gibb's Hill, a landmark because of the lighthouse on it, is only 240 feet high. Town Hill in Smith's Parish is a mere 20 feet higher than Gibb's and is the islands' highest point.

THE LAND

All of Bermuda is one big, well-kept flower garden. Whatever the season, there are different masses of bloom everywhere—fields of Easter lilies, mile-long hedges of oleanders—the variety is as profuse as the bloom. More than two million decayed cedars, killed by a blight in 1949, have been largely removed by now and the reforestation program is adding its green to the landscape. Nowhere in Bermuda can visitors be more than a mile from the dazzlingly lovely clear waters that surround it, from the intimate little coves or fine open stretches of beach where the sands are pink-tinted coral, ground powder-fine by the wind and the waves. The houses on the islands add another appealing and colorful note to Bermuda's landscape. They are made of limestone coral rock—cut from the ground—which is soft enough to be cut with a wood saw but, once exposed to the air, hardens with age, and are painted a pastel color, pink being the predominating choice. Bermuda roofs are world-famous. They are made of overlapping coral shingles about 10 by 14 inches and an inch thick. They are always painted white and by law are washed periodically with a coating of lime for sanitary purposes, since each household is dependent for its drinking water on the rains that are channeled over these shingles and funneled into a reserve tank below. A typical feature of the homes is a long flight of steps wider at the bottom than at the top and called "welcoming arms" steps. Another feature is the great chimneys. Windows are for the most part small-paned, and shutters, hinged at the top, swing up and out. Inside are fireplaces (ankle, knee, or waist level) and "tray ceilings"—an old-time air-cooling device. The separate little buildings added on to even modern homes in order to preserve the typical Bermuda style of architecture are known as "butteries" and formerly, before the days of the "fridge," were used to store food on the hanging shelves inside. They are without windows, having just a door, and air vents at the top of the walls, and are topped with a high-pitched coral-shingled roof. Houses throughout the islands are identified by name, not number.

No automobiles were permitted in Bermuda until World War II. In 1946 a law was passed permitting the use of public taxis and one private car to a family. When the owner of a private car wishes to dispose of it to buy another, he must have it destroyed or shipped out of the colony. If he sells it locally, he must wait one year before buying another. This is a safety factor designed to keep old jalopies off the road. Another safety factor is a 15-mile speed limit in towns, 20-mile limit in the countryside, a ruling that is strictly enforced and that adds greatly to the peacefulness of life, once one adjusts to it.

THE CLIMATE

The climate in Bermuda is semi-tropical. Summer temperatures prevail from late April to mid-November, with the warmest weather in July, August, and early September. Summer temperatures average around 80 degrees; while the days can be hot and humid in late summer, the evenings are comfortable. From mid-November to mid-April, temperatures range from the low 60's to the low 70's. January, February, and early March are the cooler months, but even during this period there are frequently warm days and the sea temperatures are in the 60's. There is no definite rainy season—just brief rains throughout the year.

THE PEOPLE

Bermuda's population of around 52,000 is approximately one-third white, which includes some Britishers (Bermuda-born citizens are called Bermudians, not Britishers) and U. S. Army and Navy personnel. There are a number of descendants of the originally indentured Portuguese, many of whom still speak that language and who constitute the majority of Bermuda's farmers. The people of African and mixed descent are a respected and integral part of the community. For a British colony, there is surprisingly little evidence of class distinction, the merchant or clerk being as honored as the professional man. The islands are charmingly British in feeling and tradition—"tea" is a proper ritual and government functions are carried out with great pomp and ceremony.

The language is English, with a distinctive Bermudian dialect. The Church of England predominates, though many other sects are represented. Primary education is compulsory, and provision exists for attendance between the ages of five and eighteen. There is no institution of higher education, but students are prepared for entrance to colleges and universities abroad. Schools for secretarial and manual training, handicapped children, delinquent boys and girls, and a hotel school are also available. Medical care is no problem—there are doctors, dentists, oculists, and a good hospital. The climate has proved efficacious for hay-fever victims.

There is little obvious evidence of poverty on the islands. All the population seems to have enough to eat and a house to live in. Bermuda has little unemployment, no income tax, and no inheritance or real-estate tax. All of this is a strong inducement to the tourist and the person wishing to establish permanent residency.

The islands were named for one Juan de Bermúdez, who is believed to have been shipwrecked there about 1503 and is credited with their discovery. They are shown on a map dated 1511 as "La Barmuda." In

1527, Philip II of Spain granted the islands to Hernando Camelo, a Portuguese, but there is no record of his having been there. However, crude markings, including the date 1543, found on a rock 70 feet above the south shore, are believed to have been made by men of a shipwrecked Portuguese or Spanish vessel. Henry May, an Englishman, was wrecked there in 1593 and spent five months on the island. A Captain Diego Ramirez is recorded as having been wrecked there in 1603, but was able to continue on his way.

The first settlement was not made until 1609 when Admiral Sir George Somers and his ship's company, who were headed for Virginia in the *Sea Venture,* were blown off their course during a violent storm and ultimately wrecked and wedged so securely in the reefs off Bermuda's shore that the ship remained upright, permitting the admiral and his 150 or so passengers to land with safety. They found the islands uninhabited. From the salvaged material of the *Sea Venture,* two ships were built—the *Deliverance* and the *Patience,* which sailed on to Jamestown within the year. Finding the Jamestown colony suffering from lack of food, the admiral returned to Bermuda for supplies and died there. His sea mates from then on referred to the islands as the Somers Islands. The Virginia Company, as a result of the report of the virtues of Bermuda, had their charter extended to include it and sent a group of colonists there in 1612 who founded the city of St. George. It soon sold out to a group who called themselves the Bermuda Company. In 1684, due to disputes between the companies, the King annulled the charter and Bermuda became a colony under the Crown and has remained so ever since. A British garrison occupied the colony from 1797 to early 1953. It returned later that year and was withdrawn again in 1957. U. S. Navy and Army bases were established in Bermuda on a 99-year basis in exchange for 50 destroyers. These bases are still active.

The United States has played an important part in the economy of Bermuda for many years. During the American Revolution, Bermuda traded salt and arms for food. During the following years, St. George's was a base for privateers who plundered supply ships during the War of 1812. It also served as a transshipment port for cargoes for the South and as a headquarters for blockade-runners during the U. S. Civil War. U.S. prohibition proved profitable for Bermuda, too, as it began in earnest the great tourist trade which is now so important to Bermuda's well-being.

Bermuda is a member of the British Commonwealth of Nations and is its oldest self-governing colony; in age, its Parliament is second only to the Mother Parliament in England, having been established in 1620. Though there is evidence on occasion of antagonisms in the old days due to the independent spirit of the Bermudians (they frequently jailed their Crown-appointed governors!), today there is a good working relationship between the Crown and its colony. Bermuda's external affairs are administered by a governor and commander-in-chief, who is appointed for three years by the Queen as her personal representative. He is responsible for external affairs, defense, internal security, and the police. Since the enactment of a new constitution in 1968, most executive powers are in the hands of a government leader, who is head of the majority party in the elected House of Assembly of the bicameral legislature. The House of Assembly has 45 members, elected every five years, five from each of the nine parishes; it usually sits three times weekly from October to June. Parish vestries are elected annually to handle local affairs; Hamilton and St. George each have a mayor and secretary.

AGRICULTURE

Agriculture plays a small part in the economy of the islands, but it is increasing, and a government wholesale marketing center has been set up. Citrus fruits, vegetables, and dairy products are produced, and Easter lilies are grown for export. However, the majority of foodstuffs are still imported.

INDUSTRY

Tourism is a most vital industry in Bermuda, accounting, directly or indirectly, for about 65 percent of the colony's economy. Bermuda's light industry includes manufacture of perfume, woodworking of cedar for both carpentry and ornaments, and some small boat-building and ship repair. Other light industries exist in the Freeport area where many foreign companies operate—pharmaceuticals, shampoo, essential oils, mineral water extracts, and toilet lotion are among the products manufactured there mainly for export.

CITIES

The only town of any size in Bermuda is Hamilton, the capital, which was named for Henry Hamilton, its governor from 1788–94. For visiting the capital or other parts of the island, bicycle, horse and buggy, bus, or taxi are the best means of transportation.

HAMILTON. The main attractions of the town are its many shops; and **Sessions House**, complete with a high clock tower, built in 1815 to house the Supreme Court and House of Assembly, who still meet there. Back of the **Cenotaph Memorial to the World War I Dead** is the **Colonial Secretariat** containing the offices of the governor, the colonial secretary and his staff and the meeting place of the legislative council. Nearby is the main **Perot Post Office.** The restored original Perot Post Office, established by him in 1848, is on the Par-la-ville grounds. Mr. Perot achieved fame by having conceived the idea of making up a sheet of stamps by hand and signing his name across them so that letters could be posted without his having to receive them personally; the Perot stamp is now a valuable collector's item. The large **Gothic Bermuda Cathedral of the Most Holy Trinity,** dedicated in 1894, was built of stones from five countries and has an excellent view from its tower. Roman Catholic **St. Theresa's Church** on Cedar Avenue is of interesting Spanish Mission architecture and has a fine carillon. The **Bermuda Library** in Par-la-ville Park also houses the Colonial archives and the permanent exhibition of the old china, silver, furniture and painting of the Bermuda Historical Society; this building was once the home of Mr. Perot. Other interesting stops are at colorful **Par-la-ville gardens,** the art gallery of the **Bermuda Society of Arts** in Hamilton's City Hall, the bandstand in **Victoria Park,** erected in commemoration of Queen Victoria's Golden Jubilee; and **City Hall,** a new building that serves as headquarters of the Corporation of Hamilton. **Government House** is back of Hamilton, while **Admiralty House** is farther out near Spanish Point. Also in this area is an old **ducking stool** which is said to have been used as late as 1671. Overzealous gossips were tied to the stool and dunked in the ocean to the apparent enjoyment of the populace.

To the east of Hamilton, en route to St. George, the **Botanical Gardens** in Paget warrant a visit. Beyond here in Smith's Parish is the eighteenth-century mansion **Verdmont,** restored by the Bermuda Historical Monuments Trust and furnished with very fine antiques. A little farther along is **Spanish Rock;** an inscription on it dated 1543 has led to the belief that Spaniards landed here before the islands were discovered by Sir George Somers. The government aquarium, containing more than 60 species of salt-water fish, also houses a small zoo, an aviary, and a museum containing treasures recovered from a Spanish ship which went down off Bermuda in the sixteenth century. **Devil's Hole** is a deep natural pool connected with the sea by a subterranean channel, where visitors are permitted to fish for tropical fish with bait but no hook. **Natural Arches** are on the bathing beach of the Mid-Ocean Golf Club. Heading north, one comes to the **Leamington** and **Crystal Caves,** which are electrically lighted and can be toured. Farther north, set in acres of gardens, is the **Lili Perfume Factory** where visitors can watch the entire process of enfleurage.

Across the causeway is **St. David's Island,** of interest for the **St. David's Lighthouse,** standing more than 200 feet above sea level on the southeastern end of the island; the **U. S. Army Base;** and the islanders themselves, who are a mixture of British, Indian, African and American and who speak a dialect all their own.

ST. GEORGE'S ISLAND. The **Bermuda Biological Station** is located on the island, as is the appealing quaint little old Colonial town of **St. George.** St. George was founded in 1612 and served as the capital until 1815. Its narrow lanes and alleyways have great charm and such intriguing names as Featherbed Alley, One Gun Lane, Tin Can Alley, Thread and Needle Alley, Shinbone Alley, Petticoat Lane and Old Maid's Lane. Bordering them are quaint old pastel-hued houses. Many of the original old stone buildings still stand, and restoration endeavors have added replicas of the stocks and pillory in old King's Square, old English signs over the shops, a costumed town crier, and many more. The old **State House** was the first building of stone ever erected on the island, and it is said that turtle oil and lime were used as mortar. **St. George's Historical Society Museum,** containing many fascinating relics of old Bermuda days, is in an old home built in 1725. Featherbed Alley Print Shop is in this same building, with a handmade working replica of a seventeenth-century press; its techniques will be demonstrated upon request.

Still standing is the **House of Joseph Stockdale,** who imported the first printing press and in 1784 founded the *Bermuda Gazette* which is still being published today. In **Somers Garden** is buried the heart of Sir George Somers, who was the first Englishman to land on Bermuda. His body was taken back to England—reputedly preserved in a keg of rum. The old **Henry Tucker House,** where the Duke of Clarendon, later William IV, lived as a Royal Navy officer, is now a museum with its original pieces of silver, china and furniture. Henry Tucker was colonial secretary of Bermuda and president of the council in the late 1700's. On Rose Hill, on the present site of the St. George Hotel, was the home of Hestor (Henrietta) Louise Tucker, who achieved fame and lives on in Tom Moore's "Odes to Nea." Tom Moore's home was on adjacent Old Maid's Lane. He was to become even more famous later on through his verses for "Irish Melodies" which include the deathless "Believe me if all those endearing young charms."

The **Old Town Hall** has been reconstructed in keeping with the original designs. Picturesque **St. Peter's Anglican Church,** at the top of a much-photographed wide flight of steps, was built in 1619 and was reconstructed in 1713, retaining the original altar, pulpit, font, and the gallery for the use of the slaves. Its communion service, still in use, is the one presented to the church in 1684 by King William III. **Old Rectory,** an eighteenth-century building, houses a branch of the Bermuda library.

Gate Fort, built between 1612 and 1615, guarded the entrance to the harbor. It was named for Sir Thomas Gates, one of the officers of the shipwrecked *Sea Venture* and later governor of Virginia. **Fort St. Catherine,** begun in 1613 and enlarged from time to time, has been carefully restored and is a sightseeing must. It contains a series of dioramas known as "The Bermuda Cavalcade" that depict the early history of the islands as well as replicas of Britain's Crown Jewels, and wax figures made by Tussauds of London. Offshore from here is Sea Venture Flat, the reef on which the famed ship of that name was wrecked, and below the fort, the beach where the survivors landed. **Tobacco Bay** is also nearby. It was here that the 100 barrels of gunpowder stolen from the government's arsenal in 1775 by Bermudians sympathetic to the American cause were loaded onto small boats and taken out to the American frigate that was to carry them up to the States to help George Washington force the British out of Boston. The perpetrators of the "crime" were never apprehended. **Gunpowder Cavern** on Retreat Hill has rooms and tunnels that cover over 29,000 feet. (The cavern now has a grill, bar, and dining room in it.) **Confederate Museum** has been set up in the reconstructed Globe Hotel, commemorating the period when American Confederate agents were in Bermuda arranging for the shipment of supplies to the U.S. during the Civil War. The hotel was built in 1700 by Governor Samuel Day to serve as his residence.

SOMERSET, to the west of Hamilton, is reached by road or by ferry across Great Sound. By road, travelers will pass **Christ Church,** a Scottish Presbyterian church built in 1719, and **Gibb's Hill Lighthouse,** erected in 1846, one of the few in the world constructed entirely of cast iron. There is a superb view of the islands both from its base and from the top of its tower. The **U. S. Naval Base** is situated on the peninsula that juts out into Little Sound just south of Somerset Bridge. **Somerset Bridge,** between Ely's Harbour and Great Sound, claims, and doubtless with justification, to be the smallest drawbridge in the world—an 18-inch plank in the center lifts to permit the passage of the mast of a sailboat. In Ely's Harbour are the **Cathedral Rocks**—erosion by sea and wind has formed arches in the coral rocks that resemble cathedral arches. Somerset itself lacks the historical points of interest of St. George's but is a delightful rural section of Bermuda in which to stay. It has swimming beaches, cottage colonies and guesthouses, a charming old church, and outstanding shops. **Fort Scaur** has been restored and its grounds serve as a picnic site and park; the **Springfield**

library occupies an old Bermuda house.

Bridges connect a series of little islands off the northern tip of Somerset. One of them, **Ireland Island,** was purchased by Britain in 1809 to serve as a naval station and dockyard. It was returned to Bermuda in 1950 and is a free-port area.

SPORTS AND RECREATION. **Swimming** in the ocean, harbor, sound, cove, and pool is excellent. The entire south shore is made up of open stretches of beach or sheltered coves, all delightful for swimming. A variety of boats is available for charter, including 16-foot sail-yourself models. There is fine **sailing** in Hamilton Harbour and Great Sound. Racing is very popular, particularly the famed Bermuda Fitted Dinghy Races, these being 14-foot deckless boats that carry up to 1,000 or more feet of canvas. There are scheduled sailing, cruiser, speedboat, deep-sea diving, and sightseeing cruises as well as glass-bottomed boat trips to the Sea Gardens. Yachting clubs welcome visitors from clubs in other countries. Instructors are available for the popular sports of **water-skiing, disc-riding, aquaplaning** in Hamilton Harbour, the Great Sound, or Mangrove Bay in Somerset; **helmet-diving** in Harrington Sound or off Shelly Bay.

Many wrecks of ships lie on the reefs as goals for **skin-diving** enthusiasts. Statistics list 335 varieties of fish in these reefs, and 267 varieties in the open sea, making **shore, surf,** and **deep-sea fishing** very popular. Many game fish records have been established during tournaments held in Bermuda waters, where fishing is good all year round, but especially from April to November. **Golf,** highlighted by weekly tournaments and important annual competitions, can be played on excellent and beautiful courses. Other popular sports are **tennis,** with courts readily available; **horseback riding,** and **bicycling.**

Spectator sports include **field hockey, badminton matches,** and **football** (soccer). There are summer competitions in **cricket,** with a two-day holiday at the time of the Somerset-St. George competition, a national institution since 1904; and in spring, **rugby**—American, Canadian, Royal Navy, and Bermuda teams participate during Rugby Week.

Dancing and **entertainment** are offered nightly except Sunday at hotels, some of the guest houses, and clubs. **Theater** is provided through periodic productions by a Little Theater group, and various movie houses and hotels show films daily. Frequent **concerts** are held under the auspices of the Bermuda Musical and Dramatic Society. **Art exhibits** are regularly held by the Bermuda Society of Arts in the Hamilton City Hall.

SPECIAL EVENTS. A succession of events that are of interest to the visitor takes place throughout the year. Among them are weekly summer **water carnivals,** held in winter at indoor pools; and **Gombey dancing** (African tribal dances brought over by the slaves and handed down from generation to generation). The dancers parade in the streets on Boxing Day, December 26, and at Easter.

Other interesting events are the **Floral Pageant,** a parade of floats in Hamilton in April; and the **Peppercorn Ceremony.** The Freemason's Lodge members of St. George's leased the former state house for a rental of one peppercorn annually when the capital was moved from St. George's to Hamilton in 1815. A peppercorn is still presented with great ceremony to the governor by the treasurer of the lodge in Kings Parade, St. George's, on the Wednesday closest to April 23. **Kiteflying** is a favorite recreation throughout Bermuda on Good Friday.

During the summer, **water-ski revues** can be seen Sunday afternoons at Lantana Cottage Colony and the Inverurie Hotel. Ceremonial occasions include sessions of Parliament, open to visitors, and the Cathedral service the Sunday before the opening of Hilary Court, when court officials attend in their court robes and assist in conducting the service. There are **dog shows,** an annual spring **agricultural exhibition;** and on November 5, Guy Fawkes Day, fireworks in Hamilton Harbour. Many of the hotels have yule-log parties and night beach parties.

DINING AND SHOPPING. Most of Bermuda's food is imported, but there are local tropical fruits and vegetables that differ from ours, such as paw-paws and cristophenes.

Most famed local dish is, perhaps, cassava pie, an essential for a Bermudian's Christmas dinner, with each household seeming to have its own recipe. The pie consists of pork and chicken in a pie crust made from the grated root of the cassava plant. Salt cod, potatoes, and fried banana are a common Sunday breakfast in Bermuda. Sweet-potato pudding is popular, and a must on November 5, Guy Fawkes Day. Fish head chowder is another favorite dish. Wedding cakes are unique in Bermuda, as two cakes are always served. The groom's cake is a plain poundcake decorated with gold leaf, symbolizing prosperity, and the bride's cake is a fruitcake decorated with silver leaf and topped with a tiny cedar tree which is transplanted to the lawn with great ceremony before the bride leaves her father's house.

As for drinks, everything is available. Swizzle Inn on Bailey's Bay has been famous for its own version of a rum swizzle.

Bermuda has enchanting shops with tempting merchandise that offer savings over U.S. prices of from 25 to 50 percent. There are no sales or luxury taxes. Personal shoppers are available to help visitors with their shopping.

Local handicraft includes appealing items from local woods—personal monograms can be made up in the form of lapel pins, cuff links, and buttons in 24 hours. There are attractive ceramics, dolls, seashell articles, perfumes, watercolors, and calypso recordings. Imports from Great Britain, the Continent, and the Orient can be purchased.

The Bahama Islands

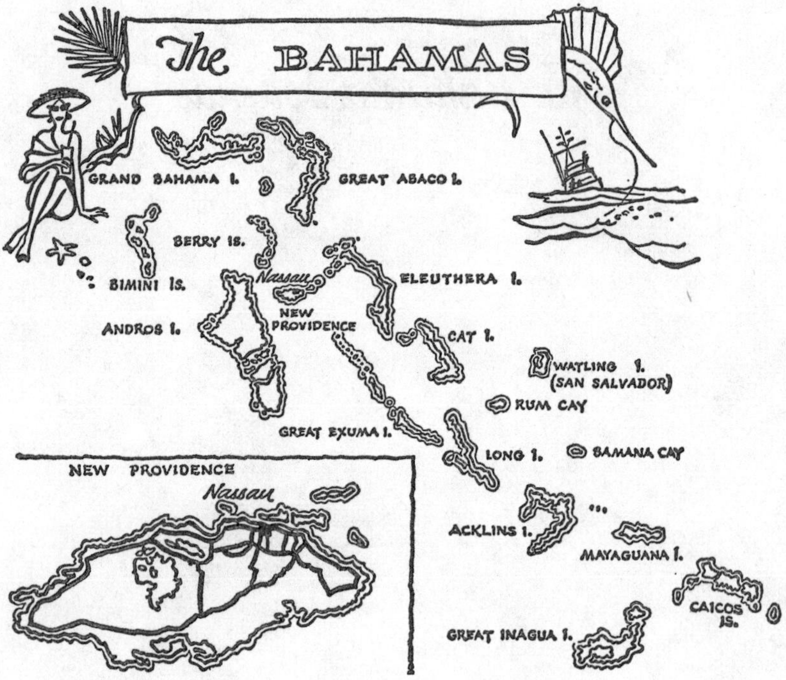

The BAHAMAS
GRAND BAHAMA I.
GREAT ABACO I.
BERRY IS.
BIMINI IS.
Nassau
ELEUTHERA I.
NEW PROVIDENCE
ANDROS I.
CAT I.
WATLING I.
(SAN SALVADOR)
RUM CAY
GREAT EXUMA I.
LONG I.
SAMANA CAY
NEW PROVIDENCE
Nassau
ACKLINS I.
MAYAGUANA I.
CAICOS IS.
GREAT INAGUA I.

The Bahamas

Convenience of location, a 12-month climate that permits year-round swimming and other water sports, the appeal of an English colony and its pomp and ceremony (such as the bewigged and robed chief justice inspecting the honor guard on the opening of the supreme court, and the nattily costumed police force that also serves as the fire brigade), the lack of inconveniences entailed by travel to some foreign ports (such as language barriers and currency conversion problems), and the superb fishing and cruising possibilities, have made the Bahamas one of America's favorite vacationlands.

THE LAND

The 700 oölitic limestone islands and more than 2,400 additional rocks and cays (pronounced keys) that make up the Bahama group are the summits of a submerged mountain range. They form a 760-mile arc from 50 miles off the east coast of Florida down to about the same distance from Haiti and Cuba, and are flat, with just slightly rolling ground, the highest point on any of them being 400 feet on Cat Island. Once heavily forested, many of the islands were stripped bare to make room for fields in which to grow cotton. Fine woods are still to be found on Andros, Grand Bahama and a few others, however; the soil is inclined to be shallow but fertile. The fact that the islands can be made into garden spots has been proved by the planting that has been done on the relatively few that are inhabited. There is a riot of color in the oleanders, the hibiscus, the bougainvillaea, royal poinsettias, and myriad of other flora. The profusion and variety of growth in the gardens of the Royal Victoria Hotel in Nassau are known the world over. There is a great variety of birds—flamingos, hummingbirds, parrots, wild geese, duck—while the waters teem with fish and turtle. The seas that surround the islands are somewhat shallow but with three well-defined channels—the Florida or New Bahama Channel between the northwest islands and Florida; the Providence Channels that run northeast and northwest, and from which runs the "Tongue of the Ocean" along the east coast of Andros; and the Old Bahama Channel between the southernmost Bahamas and Cuba. The water itself is pure, not being contaminated by silt brought into the sea by rivers, as there are no rivers in the Bahamas; the only fresh water that reaches into the sea is on Andros. High plateaus form the "Bahama Banks," covering thousands of yellow sandy square-miles under the surface of the water. Due to the effect of the sun shining through the crystal-clear water on this sand and on the coral formations at the bottom of the sea, and the varying depths of water, the gold and purples and blues and greens to be seen make these waters as breath-takingly beautiful as any you will ever see.

Nassau, the capital city, is on the 21 by 7-mile island of New Providence, stretching along the fine three-and-one-half-mile harbor, sheltered by Paradise Island. It is a pleasantly quaint little town with its Rawson Square and old public buildings patterned after those in New Bern, North Carolina. The old wooden or pastel-tinted coral houses with louvered windows and balconies overhanging the often walled-in streets—Georgian and Federal style architecture for the most part—produce a unity unmarred by modern architecture. Modern cars are permitted, however, and vie with the bicycles and fringe-topped surreys on the narrow little streets. The water front adds a delightful note of color and activity, for it is here that the inter-island vessels bring their cargoes. Quaint as the city is in many of its aspects, it is, at the same time, a decidedly sophisticated, modern resort with all that the word implies. For those who desire a quieter, more secluded vacation atmosphere there is a variety of most appealing "Out Islands" to visit, with accommodations ranging from the essence of comfort and modernity to the small and almost primitive.

THE CLIMATE

The Bahamas have a climate that is practically perfect all year round, claiming 360 days of sunshine a year. The average winter temperature is 72 degrees, the summer average 82 degrees. In late summer and early autumn, days can be hot and humid but the nights are always cooler, and there are brief rains throughout the year, slightly heavier from mid-August to October. Forty-nine inches is the average yearly rainfall. The "high" season is considered to be December to April, with hotel rates being substantially lower in the summer and fall.

THE PEOPLE

The original Indian inhabitants called themselves "Ceboynas" (also known as Siboney). It was Columbus who first called them Indians, thinking he had arrived in India. The population of all the islands today totals over 168,000 with approximately 100,000 living in Nassau. Bahamians are chiefly descendants of the English settlers, the American Loyalists and Confederates who came in the late seventeenth and eighteenth centuries, and the slaves from Africa, who now account for around 85 percent of the population. The original population has been augmented by the many British, Americans and Canadians who have chosen to establish residence in this peaceful mecca.

Twenty-eight religious denominations are represented in the Bahamas, which number, naturally, includes Church of England. There is a modern hospital in Nassau, good doctors, dentists and oculists. There are also medical facilities on the major Out Islands. The Bahamas are fortunate in that government costs are mostly paid for by customs revenue. There is no tax on incomes, inheritance or unimproved property, and on improved property the tax is small.

The Bahamians consider Christopher Columbus, who arrived in the Bahamas on October 12, 1492 to be their first tourist, the generally accepted spot being the island of San Salvador. The Spaniards at this time apparently did not consider the Bahamas worth colonizing but they did find a use for the Lucayan tribe of Arawak Indian inhabitants they found there. Within an eight-year period, they had rounded them all up and had either killed or transplanted them to work in the mines of Cuba and Haiti.

The islands were ignored for some time, although it is believed that Ponce de León stopped at some of them in his search for the Fountain of Youth. In 1629, Charles I of England granted the islands to Sir Robert Heath, thus establishing England's claim to them. The first settlers, a "Company of Eleutheran Adventurers" formed in England under the leadership of Sir William Sayle, did not arrive until 1648. Their name came from the Greek word "eleutheros," meaning free, and they gave this same name to the island on which they settled. Later, others settled on the island of New Providence, which rapidly increased in popularity because of its large and sheltered harbor. In 1670, Charles II granted New Providence and some of the other Bahamas to six "Lords Proprietors" of Carolina, headed by the Duke of Albemarle. This group eventually authorized the construction of a city and fort on the site of old Charles Town on New Providence which was to be called Nassau for William III, former Prince of Orange-Nassau. The city was not actually laid out until 1729, the attempted settlement having been attacked by the Spanish, the French, and then the Spanish and French together, as well as being repeatedly sacked by the pirates. Pirates and buccaneers had discovered that the secluded harbors of the Bahamas made excellent hideaways and headquarters, particularly Nassau's because of its two entrances. There was complete disorder on the island; even the governors took part in privateering and there was constant conflict between the government and the people.

In 1717 the Lords Proprietors surrendered the civil and military government to the Crown. The following year, England sent over Captain Woodes Rogers to act as the first royal governor, and a naval squadron and soldiers to aid him in trying to restore order to the area. His orders were to pardon all pirates who repented, to hang those who did not. The motto of the Bahamas became "Expulsis Piratis Restituta Commercia" (pirates expelled commerce restored), and was incorporated into the Bahamas' coat-of-arms established in 1728. During the American Revolution in 1776 an American naval force captured Forts Montagu and Nassau, in Nassau, without resistance. After seizing 100 or more guns and 15 barrels of powder, it departed, taking Governor Montfort Browne as hostage. The Bahamas were captured for a brief period by Spain in 1782 but within a year were restored to England by the Treaty of Versailles in return for east Florida. Peace came to the Bahamas, order was restored, a new Constitution set up, and in 1787 the Lords Proprietors surrendered their remaining rights to the government of the Crown for £12,000. The Loyalists came to the Bahamas with their families and slaves at the close of the American Revolution, bringing a temporary era of prosperity. This came to an end in 1838 when Britain freed the slaves and the plantation system of life collapsed. Nassau blossomed again during the U. S. Civil War when it became an important base for supplies for the Confederate blockade-runners, and also profited during the American prohibition period when it became a headquarters for bootleggers.

During World War II, Nassau served as an R.A.F. training base and an "air-bridge" to combat zones. In 1940, a U.S. seaplane base was granted the U.S. for 99 years at George Town, Great Exuma, but it is now inoperative. In 1950, the U.S. and Britain signed an agreement for long-range proving grounds for guided missiles in the Bahamas with a base at Cape Kennedy, Florida. Today there are missile tracking stations for spotting the rockets and missiles from Cape Kennedy on Grand Bahama, Eleuthera, and Mayaguana.

In January 1964, Great Britain handed over the reins of internal self-government to the Bahamas. Under the new constitution, the Bahamas has a ministerial system of internal self-government with a two-chamber Legislature—the House of Assembly and the Senate—and a cabinet with a Premier and 14 ministers. The governor, appointed by the Crown, acts on the advice of the cabinet except in the area of foreign affairs, national defense, and internal security (including police), where Britain still retains responsibility. An amended constitution signed into effect in 1968 gave the islands an increased degree of self-government. The colony is now known as the Commonwealth of the Bahamas.

AGRICULTURE

Fruits and vegetables are grown on the islands, some livestock is raised, and the combined poultry and dairy farm on Eleuthera is one of the largest in the world. Crawfish is one of the most important exports, as well as salt (from Inagua), lumber, tomatoes, and cascarilla bark.

INDUSTRY

Over half a million yearly visitors are making tourism a major industry of the Bahamas, and a large portion of the population is dependent on this tourist trade. The fine straw work, made from the palmetto fronds which are bleached, dyed, and woven into baskets, bags, and hats that are taken home by visitors yearly, amounts to a large part of tourist exports. Small industries are being encouraged. A few in operation produce such items as rum, liqueur, paper, textiles, cement, plastics, chemical bleaches, and rubber goods. The sponge industry had been the Bahamas' chief industry and export from 1841 to 1939, when it was completely wiped out by a blight. Now the sponge beds are being worked again under government supervision and have been operating on an ever-increasing scale since 1957.

NASSAU

In Nassau, **Rawson Square,** named for one of the islands' governors who served from 1864–69, is the center of activity and the location of its public buildings–**House of Assembly, Cabinet office, post office, police station,** and the **public library** that once was the islands' first prison and is a replica of a powder magazine at Williamsburg. The **Waterfront Market** across the street toward the waterfront, the **public straw market,** plus the **dock area** where the inter-island boats come in with their cargoes for the markets are the prize sights. Old **Vendue House** at the foot of George Street, which now houses the Electric Company offices, was built in 1800 and served as the slave market. A few blocks beyond the **Royal Victoria Hotel,** with its world-famous gardens, is **Queen's Stairway,** a series of 65 steps carved by hand by slaves out of solid limestone, (an original 66th has been covered over by the road at the top). They lead up to Fort Fincastle and were to be a means of escape to the sea. **Fort Fincastle,** built in 1783 and named for one of the titles of the then Royal Governor, Lord Dunmore, now serves as a signal station. Its shape resembles an old paddle-wheel steamer. Near here on Bennett's Hill is the **Water Tower** with an elevator that goes to the top, from which one can see a fine view of the city and harbor.

Government House is on a hill called Mount Fitzwilliam; the statue of Columbus in the center of the long flight of steps leading up to it was sculptured under the direction of Washington Irving in London and given to the colony in 1832. There is a **Gregory Arch** under one of the entrances to Government House which leads to **Grant's Town,** a native settlement founded by the slaves after their emancipation. West of town are the very beautiful **Ardastra Gardens,** where twice daily, flamingos are put through amazing "on parade" formations. **Fort Charlotte,** really three forts in one—Charlotte, Stanley, and D'Archy—was built in 1788 and is one of the largest on the island. Its passageways, dungeons, stairways and 88-foot deep well, were all hewn out of solid rock by slave labor. It is possible to drive out around the western tip of the island past the **race track,** Country Club, and a hotel area to the residential and club area of **Lyford Cay,** and around on the south shore, the exclusive **Coral Harbour Club** development.

In the interior are **Lake Killarney, Lake Cunningham,** and **Mermaid's Pool,** the latter connected subterraneously with the sea. East of town are **Fort Montagu,** built in 1741, captured briefly in 1776 by the U. S. Navy and again later on in 1782 by the Spaniards; and the remains of **Blackbeard's Tower.** The **St. Augustine's Monastery and College** has a lovely chapel; out in the grounds is a replica of Our Lady of Fatima. Livestock and vegetables are raised here, and there are truck gardens in the coral rock. Even non-swimmers like to cross the 300-foot stretch of the bay to Paradise Island to visit **Paradise Beach.**

OUT ISLANDS

The Out Islands of the Bahamas are easily accessible by air or sea from the Florida coast and from Nassau. Some can be visited in a day. Longer visits are recommended for those who are seeking delightful holiday spots that are less commercial in atmosphere than is Nassau. Best known of the Out Islands are the following:

ABACO, the most northerly of the Bahamian islands, is 70 miles long and varies in width from two and a half to seven miles. A water-cut called "Pen Curry" or "The Crossing" cuts the island into **Great Abaco** and **Little Abaco,** with numerous surrounding little cays considered a part of it. Small but comfortable accommodations are available at many points now, such as **Green Turtle Cay, Sandy Point,** at **Hopetown** on Elbow Cay. A colony of American yachtsmen reside at **Man-o'-War Cay** while many tourists go to the elaborate resort development at **Treasure Cay,** which offers miles of glorious beaches and superb bone fishing. Abaco was settled by Loyalists from New York City and Florida about 1783 and at one time was a great lumbering center. Most of the hardwoods have been destroyed by fires through the years but there are still great forest areas where wild hogs are hunted. Abaco has always been famous for its shipbuilding. The little settlements are growing rapidly in popularity with visitors who are discovering its fine swimming beaches, sheltered harbors for sailors, excellent fishing possibilities and hunting areas especially for duck.

ANDROS is the largest of the Bahamas, measuring approximately 40 by 100 miles. Cut by waterways known as Northern Bight, Middle Bight, and Southern Bight and by tidal creeks, it is actually three islands plus many smaller ones. Much of Andros has never been explored, being low and swampy; other parts are covered with forests of fine woods. There is a great deal of bird life on the island, providing excellent hunting. For the vacationing visitor or fisherman who is looking for superb bone fishing or deep-sea fishing in the 1,000-fathom "Tongue of the Ocean" outside the coral reefs, or lake or river fishing and other water sports, there are as informally luxurious and delightful accommodations at **Fresh Creek** as are to be found anywhere in the Bahamas. At **Pot Cay** in North Bight are less luxurious but also popular accommodations. Andros was settled about 1780

Neil Harbour near Cape Breton Highlands National Park, Nova Scotia, Canada

Moraine Lake in Banff National Park, Alberta, Canada

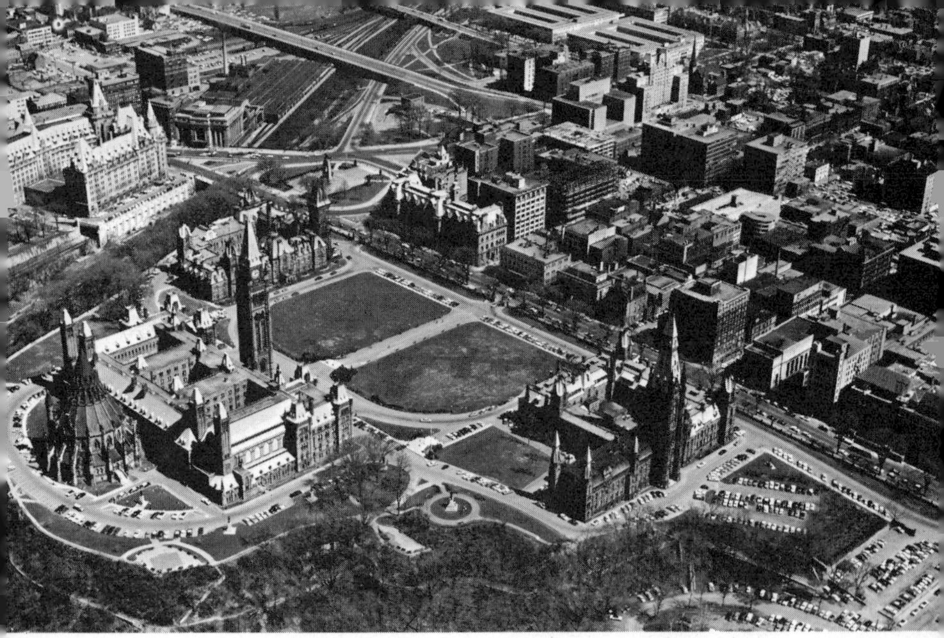

Parliament Buildings, Ottawa, Ontario

Entrance to Saint Lawrence Seaway from Montreal Harbor, Canada

Harbor at Acapulco, Mexico

Taxco, Mexico

Bull Fights in Mexico City, Mexico

Administration Building, University of Mexico, near Mexico City

Panorama of Guanajuato, Mexico

and the population now consists of nearly 8,000 people, most of them people of African descent. Some of their legends, highly imaginative and superstitious, deal with the "chickcharneys," tiny red-eyed men with three toes and three fingers who live in the tops of pine trees, the "luscas," half-dragon and half-octopus, who eat those who venture to pass their caves, and the "yahoo" who kidnap children.

The U. S. Navy, by agreement between the United States and Great Britain, has developed the Atlantic Underwater Test and Evacuation Center (AUTEC) at Middle Bight, south of Fresh Creek. An annual rental of $150,000 is paid to the Bahamas' government, with a consequent boost to the burgeoning economy of the Colony.

BERRY ISLANDS are a small chain of cays settled by English, Canadian, and American residents, many owning their own private cays. A small hotel and Yacht Club and marina on Frazers Hog Cay now make the excellent bone fishing, reef fishing, and deep-sea fishing of the area available to non-resident, non-yacht-owning visitors.

THE BIMINIS consist of a string of cays extending over a 45-mile stretch, only 55 miles off the coast of Florida across the Gulf Stream; off their eastern coasts is the Great Bahama Bank. The waters that surround these islands are what make the area a fisherman's paradise. **North Bimini** is the largest, is seven miles long and a few hundred yards wide. Two settlements, Alice Town and Bailey Town, practically merge into one and make up most of the island. Kings Highway, which goes along one side of the island, and Queens Highway on the other are little more than wide paved sidewalks but suffice for the traffic, which consists mostly of pedestrians and bicycles. There is a handful of little food and gift shops, a few bars and a number of modern accommodations. Four fully-equipped marinas, as well as the noted **Lerner Marine Laboratory** and **Marine Aquarium,** where valuable research work is being undertaken are also on North Bimini. This is a charming spot for the vacationer who wants a quiet pace and who is happy to fish, talk fishing or listen to fishing-talk morning, noon, and night. **South Bimini** has an airstrip, a modern resort and marina, and what is accepted as being the authentic "Fountain of Youth" of Indian legend, once sought by Ponce de León.

Great Isaac is a flat rock north of Bimini with a red-and-white-striped lighthouse that has been in operation for over 100 years.

Cat Cay is a beautiful, privately owned little two-mile-long island, located 12 miles south of Bimini, with a Cat Cay Club, luxurious homes, a golf course, tennis courts, pool, skeet range, fishing docks and a good harbor. Visitors are permitted only on invitation.

CAT ISLAND, just south of Eleuthera, contained fine estates in bygone days but they are in ruins now. The island offers good pasture land and is where local sailors stage an annual **Cat Island regatta.**

ELEUTHERA, called by Indians "Cigatoo," was the first of the Bahamas to be settled by Europeans. In 1648 a Company of Eleutheran Adventurers under the leadership of one William Sayle landed here from England and founded **Gregory Town.** On this island, which is less than 100 miles long and only five miles at its widest point, much of Nassau's food is grown. A colossal poultry farm and dairy at Hatchet Bay provide much of its produce. A beef experimental station is also nearby. The two chief settlements are **Rock Sound,** which offers luxurious and lovely accommodations, and the sleepy little capital settlement, 22 miles away, of **Governor's Harbour,** which has simple accommodations as well as luxurious and charming ones. Many people have built winter-vacation or permanent homes here in order to enjoy the island's tranquil, secluded atmosphere and its miles of unsurpassed beaches.

EXUMA ISLANDS, a long line of cays stretching over 100 miles, are considered the most beautiful of the Bahamas, and are surrounded by some of the loveliest multihued waters in the world. The area is a favorite with yachtsmen and duck hunters, with supplies and fuel available at **Staniel Cay** and at **George Town** on Great Exuma. Peace and Plenty Inn at George Town is named for a pioneer sailing vessel that brought the first settlers to the island. Only a few of the Exumas are inhabited. Winter-vacation homes have been built on some, and there are scattered, native settlements such as the one on Little Farmer Cay.

GRAND BAHAMA is an 83-mile-long island 60 miles off the coast of Florida. At its eastern end is a missile tracking station and vast pine woods; on the southwestern end, the phenomenally growing resort-industry complex at Freeport. Here are located the largest hotels in the entire Bahamas, offering full tourist and convention facilities. Industries are encouraged to build here by freedom from taxation for 30 years. No excise taxes or customs duties will be levied except on goods for personal consumption, as a result of a basic 99-year act passed in 1955.

A jet airstrip has been built to accommodate the increased flow of visitors, and intensive real estate development is in progress. The harbor is the best in the Bahamas, with full bunkering, storage, and ship-repair facilities. On the northwest end of Grand Bahama Island is the town of West End. Just outside town is the airport and a hotel-club which has a wide range of entertainment and convention resources.

GREAT INAGUA ISLAND is the southernmost island of the Bahamas. **Matthew Town** was once prosperous, then became a ghost town. Now, again, its salt pans are being worked. Approximately a quarter of a million tons of a very pure salt are produced annually; it is shipped to the U.S. and used in commercial chemicals. There are wild horses here, the largest flamingo rookery in the Bahamas, possibly in the world, with an estimated more than 40,000 birds. Also popular for duck shooting, the island has a few informal visitor accommodations.

HARBOUR ISLAND is an utterly enchanting hideaway with delightful accommodations. It is only about two and a half miles long, one and a half square miles in area, but that small area includes one of the oldest, most charming settlements, **Dunmore Town.** There is fine sailing in the protected harbor, good snorkeling, spear-fishing and skin-diving around the coral reefs that rim it, and a beautiful pink-tinted beach for bathers.

LONG ISLAND, 150 miles to the southeast of New Providence, straddles the Tropic of Cancer. The island's greatest development began with the arrival of the Loyalists; in the decades following their arrival, Long Island was one of the most prosperous of the Bahamas, its economy centering on cotton. Today the island is a heavy producer of corn, peas, avocados, bananas, and other produce for the Nassau market. It is also one of the leading Resort Island stock-raising areas, and its salt industry is being expanded.

ST. GEORGE'S CAY is at the northern tip of Eleuthera. Its settlement, **Spanish Wells,** is an industrious little agricultural community that grows fruits and vegetables for the Nassau markets. The 700 or so inhabitants, noted for their seamanship, are almost all descendants of the Loyalists who migrated there in the seventeenth and eighteenth centuries. Boats commute daily from Eleuthera. There are several hotels on the island.

SAN SALVADOR, known to the Indians as Guanahani, was the first landfall of Christopher Columbus in the Western Hemisphere (October 12, 1492). A large cross marks one of the three sites claimed by different factions to be the exact location of his landing. The island was later called Watling's Island, named for a pirate who, in spite of his profession, was so pious that he flogged his crew if they broke the Sabbath. There has been much controversy over which island was actually the one on which Columbus first landed. Well-backed theories in favor of other islands have been advanced but San Salvador still remains the popular choice. There are limited visitor accommodations, and a lighthouse, whose beam can be seen 19 miles out at sea. A Museum of the New World, made up of artifacts and curios relating to the 1492 voyage of Columbus, has been opened.

WALKER CAY is north of Grand Bahama and 110 miles from Palm Beach, Florida. This is a 90-acre little cay with a pleasant, comfortable, informal clubhouse and hotel that is popular with fishermen and with families. It has a pool, fine beach, good shooting and fishing.

SPORTS AND RECREATION. Chief activities on all the islands are outdoor sports, especially **swimming.** Best-known bathing site on Nassau is famous Paradise Beach on Paradise Island, to which small "bumboats" ferry people across the short expanse of water from the Prince George Wharf at Rawson Square in Nassau. A small entrance fee provides transportation for the half-mile across the island on Causerina Driveway to the beach, and use of the following facilities: dressing rooms, showers, thatched huts, beach umbrellas, chairs, and mats. There is a coffee shop, gift shop, bar, and snack bar nearby, and many hotels in the area have their own beaches and pools. **Water-skiing** and **skin-diving** instructors are available at Paradise Beach, Nassau Yacht Haven, Brown's Boat Basin, and several of the hotels. **Boating** is another popular sport, with all types of boats available for charter. Half-day, full-day, or longer cruises operate on schedule–sloops, cruisers, a 72-foot catamaran raft are used–and glass-bottomed boats go out to the Sea Gardens at the east end of the harbor. Weekly racing is popular in the winter season, highlighted by annual meets such as the **Out Island Regatta** at George Town, Exuma, which is a three-day race among commercial fishing boats of the Bahamas.

Fishing, be it light tackle casting, reef fishing, spearfishing, or deep-sea, is magnificent all year round. Many record game fish catches have been established during tournaments. **Hunting** for wild boar is possible on some of the Out Islands, with bird-shooting permitted during specific seasons. **Golf, tennis, horseback riding** are popular in Nassau and in several of the Out Islands. For spectator sports, Nassau offers **cricket, basketball, soccer, rugby, boxing, softball, horse racing,** and **polo** in the winter season, as well as **horse shows** and **dog shows.** International **sports car racing** on Oakes Field Course during "Speed Week," usually in early December, is very popular.

Occasional art exhibits are held, concerts are given during the winter season, musicals in the hotels, band concerts on The Green once a month are popular. The Governor's Hall in the British Colonial Hotel, which seats 500, has a series of musicals and dramas, and up-to-date films are shown in good movie houses.

Dancing is featured at the hotels, and in many night clubs ranging from good to poor. The Bahamas have their own version of a combination of calypso and drumming called "goombay." Nightclub entertainment includes goombay, as well as steel bands, fire dancers, and limbo dancers.

SPECIAL EVENTS. The most fascinating event of the year for visitors is "junkanoo," which lasts from dawn to 8 A.M. or later on the mornings of December 26, **Boxing Day,** and New Year's Day. Costumed people dance and parade up and down Bay Street to the accompaniment of goombay drums, "shak-shaks," and cow bells. Gambling is open to tourists during the winter season. The annual **Red Cross Fair** is an important social event held in the gardens of Government House.

DINING AND SHOPPING. Pigeon peas and rice are the local standby, while plantain, a type of banana, green turtle pie, and soup are favorite items. Seafood is good; conch (pronounced conk) is very popular as a cocktail, chowder, or in fritters. Delicious tropical fruits grow in the island, such as guavas, soursops, sapodillas, papayas, mangoes, from which ice creams are made. Cocktails are more expensive in bars than one would expect, considering the price of liquor in the Bahamas, but liquor is very inexpensive by the bottle.

Handicrafts include sisal or coconut fiber straw work; jewelry and ornaments of seashells, fish shells, tortoise shell; local recordings; imports—British cashmeres, woolens, leather articles, china, crystal, cutlery, and pipes; Oriental goods; silver; cameras and watches; perfumes and other items from various European countries.

The Caribbean

The Caribbean
FLORIDA
Bahamas
CUBA
Greater Antilles
JAMAICA
HAITI
DOMINICAN REPUBLIC
PUERTO RICO
Atlantic Ocean
Leeward Islands
Windward Islands
Caribbean Sea
Lesser Antilles
TRINIDAD
PANAMA
COLOMBIA
VENEZUELA

The Caribbean

Sun-drenched beaches, warm air, and swaying palm trees typify the West Indian islands of the Caribbean. On these islands, as varied as the countries—Spain, France, Great Britain, The Netherlands, Portugal—responsible for their early development, relaxation is the byword. Industrialization and urbanization have taken place on many of them, but with little sacrifice to the leisurely atmosphere and carefree life for which the West Indies are famous.

THE LAND

The West Indies are peaks of a partially submerged mountain chain—the Caribbean Andes—that once connected North and South America. They now form a 2,500-mile arc from Cuba, 50 miles off the tip of Florida, to Trinidad within sight of Venezuela. This arc forms a dividing line between the Atlantic Ocean and the Caribbean Sea.

Prior to the arrival in the New World of Christopher Columbus, the unexplored land between the Canary Islands and India was called Antilia. Columbus found not one mainland, but a series of islands, so Antilia was changed to the plural Antilles. The term "West Indies," which is synonymous with Antilles, resulted from Columbus' belief that he had reached India; he called the people he found on the island "Indians" for the same reason.

Two major island groupings—the Greater Antilles and the Lesser Antilles—are found in the Caribbean below the Bahamas. Within these two groupings are the islands of Cuba, Jamaica, Hispaniola (Haiti and the Dominican Republic), Puerto Rico, the U. S. Virgin Islands, the British Virgin Islands, the British West Indies, the Netherlands Antilles, the French West Indies, Trinidad, and Tobago.

THE CLIMATE

There is much contrast in climate between the islands, often on the same island. Caribbean climates are always comfortable–warm but not oppressive. A few days or weeks in late summer or early autumn can be hot and humid, but the heat is tempered by northeast trade winds. The nights are always cool. Rains are usually heavy, but brief, and vary from an average of around 50 inches in the low islands, such as Antigua, eastern Guadeloupe, Barbados, and Marie-Galante, to 100 inches and more, annually, on the mountainous islands such as Dominica. There is, in some areas, a brief wet season around April, but as a general rule the heavier rains fall between July and October.

Hurricanes, named for the Indian god, Huracán, meaning the "Despoiler, Lord of the Circular Tempest," threaten the middle or northern Antilles from August to October, but less often now than in past years. They can be spotted days in advance and preparations made against them, with time to spare.

THE PEOPLE

The earliest known inhabitants of the Caribbean, the Arawak Indians, are thought to have migrated from the mainland of South America. But they were all absorbed or killed less than a century before the arrival of Columbus, by the more ferocious Carib Indians. The Carib conquest of the Greater Antilles was interrupted by the arrival of the white man, and the Indians fought fiercely to retain what territory they did possess. It was not until the late eighteenth century that they were finally forced to give up domination of Dominica, St. Lucia, and St. Vincent. Today, the only remaining pure-blooded Caribs live on the British island of Dominica. The Caribbean Sea was named for these Indians and is pronounced correctly Carib-bé-an.

Christopher Columbus missed only a few of the islands during his several voyages to the Caribbean. He landed in 1492 in the Bahamas, eventually sailing on to discover Cuba and Hispaniola, and returned to Spain early the following year. On his second voyage, in 1493, he discovered Puerto Rico and some of the middle Lesser Antilles. In 1494 he explored the coast of Cuba, believing it to be part of the Asiatic mainland and discovered Jamaica and several other islands. He returned to Spain in 1496, leaving his brother Bartholomew in charge, and did not return again until 1498, when he discovered the more southerly islands, including Trinidad, and the mainland of South America. His disastrous fourth voyage in 1502 added Central America and Panama to his list of discoveries.

In spite of Spain's claim to the majority of the islands, the Spaniards made little attempt to settle many of them; they had no interest in those that lacked mineral resources or large areas of land suitable for cultivation, or in those too fiercely defended by the Caribs. In later years, however, possession of the islands was violently contended and fought over by the Spaniards, the French, the British, the Dutch and the Caribs. Since the Napoleonic Wars, the situation has remained a stable one. The main exceptions, of course, are the U. S. Virgin Island group, which was purchased from the Danes in 1917, and Puerto Rico which was ceded to the U.S. after the Spanish-American War and is now a member of the U. S. Commonwealth.

Today about 25 million people inhabit the islands of the Caribbean. There is a great mixture of race, creed, color, language and currency. Over ten million slaves were shipped from Africa to the American world, and their descendants constitute the major portion of the present population. Many of the East Indians and the Chinese and some of the Portuguese found on the islands today are descendants of those who were indentured to replace slave labor after the latters' emancipation in the early nineteenth century.

There have been great strides made since World War II in labor and political reforms. The war itself helped the unemployment situation; U.S. bases on some of the islands have been instrumental in upping wages. British and U.S. grants have helped improve living and working conditions. Efforts are being made by the islands to become more self-sufficient through diversified cultivation, new industries, development of mineral resources, and most vitally through tourism. But the economy is still largely agricultural. Sugar, brought to the islands in 1640 from Guiana by a Dutchman, is still the main crop of the West Indies. Cotton, cacao, coffee, coconuts, nutmeg, bananas, limes, arrowroot, livestock, charcoal and salt are also important.

Cuba

Long a favorite vacation ground for Americans, Cuba was closed to tourism in 1961 as a result of the Castro revolution. When and if normal relations are resumed, Americans are likely to find considerable changes in the island.

THE LAND. Cuba is the largest and westernmost island in the West Indies, 759 miles (northwest by southeast) by 135 miles (north by south). It lies 90 miles south of Key West, Florida, 50 miles west of Haiti, 120 miles east of the Yucatán Peninsula and about 85 miles north of Jamaica. Its more than 2,500 miles of coastline is indented with great numbers of fine harbors and bottleneck bays. The coastline varies from rocky terraced bluffs and rugged steep hills in the north to low sandy or swampy areas through most of the south.

The Sierra Maestra range, at the southeastern end of the island, the Trinidad Mountains, in central Cuba, and the Sierra de los Organos Range in the west are Cuba's chief mountain ranges. Cuba's highest peak is Pico Turquino, at 6,561 feet. It is in the heart of Cuba's richest mining region. Between and around the mountains are level uplands and low rolling plains with rich fertile soil. The soil is much poorer in the east central portion but this makes good pastureland for the cattle. There are over 200 creeks and rivers—some of them torrential streams during the rains, at other times dry. The 150-mile Cauto River is the longest one.

Cuba is rich in fine woods; over 40 choice cabinet woods grow here. There are literally thousands of varieties of flowering trees. Ceiba trees (the silk-cotton tree) grow to a height of 150 feet.

THE CLIMATE. There is little variation in Cuba's temperature; the average temperature ranges from about 71 degrees in winter to 82 degrees in summer. Trade winds and afternoon breezes help to keep summer more comfortable than in the United States. Santiago is one of the hottest points. The south coast is cooler than the north, the interior cooler than the coast. There are generally brief tropical showers on summer afternoons, but the heaviest rains come in May–June and September–October; they are heavier in the interior and in the west than on the rest of the island, and heavier on the north coast than on the south. Yearly average rainfall is only 54 inches. There are occasional hurricanes in late summer or fall, mostly in the western half of the country.

THE PEOPLE. On October 27, 1492, Christopher Columbus landed on the northern coast of Cuba, midway between the present sites of Gibara and Banes. He thought the island to be either Japan or China, and called it Juana. Later it was called Santiago and then Ave Maria, but eventually its original Indian name "Cuba" was adopted. The island was not settled by the Spaniards until 1511, when Diego de Velázquez came over from Hispaniola. By 1544 practically all the Indians had been annihilated by the Spaniards; what few were left were emancipated. Slaves from Africa were imported as early as 1523 but were not freed until 1886. Except for a brief spell of British domination in 1762–63, the island remained under the control of Spain until 1898.

Dissatisfied with Spain's authoritarian rule, independence movements started in the 1860's, culminating in 1895 when José Martí began a drive for independence. On the 25th of February, 1898, the U.S.S. *Maine,* which had been sent to Cuba to protect American interests, was blown up in the harbor at Havana; the true facts of the explosion are still a mystery.

Spain capitulated before the end of the year, and on December 10, by the Treaty of Paris, relinquished all claim to the island to the U.S. in trust for its inhabitants. In 1902 the Republic of Cuba came into being.

In spite of many changes of presidents and corruption on the part of politicos, Cuba thrived and prospered. Sugar prices soared and acres of valuable timber were cut and burned to make more space for sugar cane. There was an orgy of extravagance—marble palaces were built, magnificent clubs and gambling houses established. By 1920, new industry flourished and mining projects were begun. However, in 1921, a satiated sugar market ultimately resulted in a drop of prices, and Cuba's economy collapsed. It was to rise and fall innumerable times during the ensuing years under a series of inept and extravagant leaders whose rule was marked by terror, revolutions, and strikes.

The dictatorship of Major General Fulgencio Batista y Zaldivar began on March 10, 1952. Opposition to his regime began in earnest in 1953 under the leadership of a lawyer and former leader of student opposition, Fidel Castro Ruz. His "26th of July Movement" was a guerilla warfare by revolutionists that started in 1956. Batista fled to exile on January 1, 1959. Castro proclaimed Dr. Manuel Urrutia Lleó the Provisional President the following day, and four days later all former governors, congressmen, mayors and aldermen were removed from office. Pending elections, the country was governed by a "Fundamental Law" approved on February 8. Castro became Premier on February 16. The first land seizure, of nearly two-and-a-half million acres in Camagüey, was made on June 25. Castro resigned as Prime Minister in protest of the attitude of Dr. Urrutia Lleó, "attitude bordering on treason," as Castro expressed it. Dr. Urrutia then resigned, in turn accusing the "communists," as he called members of the new government, of treason. Castro resumed the premiership on July 26, and a Council of Ministers named Dr. Osvaldo Dorticos Torrado as the new president.

The same year, on August 10, Cuba severed diplomatic relations with the Dominican Republic. On January 3, 1961, the United States severed diplomatic relations with Cuba.

Today, the population of Cuba is about 8.5 million, of which about 75 percent are white people of Spanish descent. Most of the rest are Negro or mulatto. The original inhabitants of Cuba were the Arawak Indians, but most of them died out from overwork and disease after their enslavement by the Spanish.

Over half of the people live on farms or in small villages. Some earn wages only a few months of the year, during the *zafra* (sugar harvest).

The official language is Spanish, but English is widely spoken and understood. The majority of the population is Roman Catholic.

Primary education is compulsory and free. Cuba has several universities–Havana, founded in 1721, Marta Abreu in Santa Clara, Oriente in Santiago de Cuba, founded in 1947, and St. Thomas of Villanova, in Havana, founded in 1946.

AGRICULTURE. Cuba is chiefly agricultural. Most farms specialize in one product such as sugar, tobacco, coffee, or cattle, fruits and/or vegetables. Sugar is grown for the most part in the central and eastern portions of the island. Tobacco, the second crop, is grown chiefly in the western part of the island; the choicest tobacco in all the world is grown in the Vuelta-Abajo district. Coffee and cacao are grown mainly in the eastern Oriente province; some coffee is also produced near Cienfuegos. Sisal is to be found around Matanzas, cattle raising and dairying around Camagüey. Vegetables thrive profusely in the central and western sections, and such fruits as banana, date, pomegranate, plantain, papaya, avocado, and mango. Henequen and kenafara plants are grown to provide fiber for making rope.

INDUSTRY. Sugar refining and the manufacture of cigars and cigarettes are the leading Cuban industries. Food canning is also important. Other manufactured products include textiles, chemicals, shoes, twine and rope, rum, flour, cement, fertilizer, soft drinks, and furniture.

Cuba's mines produce iron, copper, barium, silica, platinum, gold, and silver. Its chromium and asphalt deposits are among the purest in the world; Cuba mines more manganese than any other Latin American country. There is a rich deposit of nickel in the east, and oil was discovered in 1954.

Cuba has forests of mahogany, cedar, ebony, logwood, and rosewood. Much of this is used to make cigar boxes and furniture; charcoal, one of the country's most important forest products, is used for cooking fuel. The royal palm furnishes thatch for the homes of the farmers.

CITIES. Cuba is divided into six provinces: Havana, Pinar del Río, Matanzas, Las Villas, Camagüey, and Oriente. The cities within them provide a rich background in the history of the island.

BAYAMO, 60 miles west of Santiago de Cuba on the Bayamo River, was founded in 1513. It was one of the leading Colonial towns and in those days an intellectual center; General García received his famed message from Andrew S. Rowan near here.

CAMAGÜEY, the capital of Camagüey Province, is about 350 miles from Havana. It was founded in 1514 as Santa María de Puerto Principe on the north coast, was moved inland to its present site in 1530 to escape the pirates. In spite of this, Henry Morgan also went inland at one point, locked the leading citizens in a church and proceeded to sack and plunder the town. The name was changed to its present one in 1889. The city contains many old historic spots, interesting Moorish-type mansions, **Nuestra Señora de la Merced** church, which dates from 1748, a fine museum, and residential sections. It is famous for its pastries and its cheeses.

CIENFUEGOS is 140 miles from Havana and is Cuba's most important commercial city and port. It has a plaza, an old fort—**Castillo de Jagua**—used as a protection against pirates in old Spanish days, a cathedral, a municipal palace, fine old homes, the most notable being the Moorish-style **Del Valle Palace.** Cienfuegos is on the south shore and has become a great fishing and sports center.

GUANABACOA, about 15 minutes from Havana, is a charming old Colonial town. There is a park on the **Hill of the Cross—La Cotorra Garden and Spring,** the Convent of St. Anthony, built 1755, the lyceum where José Martí made speeches, an **Indian tomb of Bichat** on the outskirts. This town was once used as a summer resort for Habañeros and their fine old Colonial mansions are still there.

HAVANA. Havana, the capital of Havana Province, as well as of the country, was first established on the site of what is now Batabano, on the southern coast of the island, in 1515. It was moved in 1519 to its present site, on the north coast facing the Atlantic and the Gulf of Mexico, to lie at the entrance of a superb, landlocked natural harbor, guarded by Morro Castle on one side and La Punta Fort on the other. The Almendares River separates the main section of the city from the suburbs to the west.

Havana is the social and political center of the country, with a population of over 1.5 million. There is an amazing mixture of the very old and the very new. Habana Vieja (Old Havana) still retains its old buildings, fortifications, and walls, its narrow little streets and tiny shops.

Surrounding it, and spreading into the hills, is the old Colonial Spanish section of town. In the suburban areas is the New Havana, with wide boulevards, skyscrapers, hotels, and apartment houses. The Havana Bay Tunnel connects the old city with the new.

La Punta Fortress at the entrance to the harbor, built in 1598, is one of Havana's most interesting sights. Nearby in Martires Park is the **Students' Monument.** Students were accused, in 1811, of violating the grave of a Spaniard named Castañón who was killed in a duel after writing an article slandering women. As a result of the violating of the grave, every fifth student of the group was shot, eight in all. A piece of the wall against which they stood facing the firing squad has been preserved with an eight-columned marble canopy over it. The **President's Palace** is an amazing building with a glass-tiled dome.

Beyond the **National Amphitheater** along the waterfront is **La Fuerza Fortress**—the first to be built in Havana. The Spanish governor, Hernando de Soto, ordered it built in 1537, but funds provided by Spain were insufficient so he ordered the work to be completed at his own expense after he sailed off to Florida in 1539. His wife, Isabel de Bobadilla, watched from a tower in La Fuerza for his return for five years and died of a broken heart when word was brought of his discovery of the Mississippi and his burial there. It served as the home of Spanish governors-general for many years, then as the National Library. Now it is a military museum depicting the island's history.

Ayuntamiento (the City Hall) is in Armas Park. Considered to be the finest example of Colonial architecture in the city, it was completed in 1790 and was the residence of Spanish governors-general. In later years it served as a city hall until the new one was built at the civic center. Now it is a museum.

Only a block away is lovely old **Cathedral Square.** Facing the central square where slaves were once sold is the **Colón Cathedral,** built in 1777, and palaces that once belonged to Spanish nobility.

Morro Castle is across the bay. It was built in 1587–97 with walls 20 feet thick, and towers above the sea for 125 feet. Its dungeons and the garroting room can be seen with ghastly wax figures to add to the horror of the spot. It also has a chute into the open sea, built originally as a garbage disposal but used also as a means, under various regimes, of dumping political enemies to the sharks waiting below.

The **capitol** is similar to the one in Washington, D.C., but a foot higher—all distances in the city are measured from the 24-carat diamond in the floor of its rotunda. **La Merced Church,** the **Palace of Fine Arts** and **National Museum** are also impressive. The **Plaza de la Republica,** a most striking civic center, has elevators which go to the top, giving a good view of the city. Also to be seen are elaborate **Colón Cemetery,** the **Zoological Gardens,** and the completely equipped **City of Sports.**

HOLGUÍN, northwest of Santiago de Cuba, is Cuba's third largest city and of importance industrially and commercially.

THE ISLE OF PINES lies, at its closest point, little more than 35 miles off the southern coast of Cuba. It was called *Camaraco* by the Indians, *Evangelista* by Columbus when he discovered it in 1494, and "Treasure Island" by some who claim it to have been the locale of the book of the same name by Robert Louis Stevenson. Today it is referred to by others as the Isle of Palms since the lovely specimens of palms here now outnumber the pines.

The island is 30 by 40 miles, about the size of Rhode Island. Most of the southern half is swamp, but the beaches on the south shore are beautiful. The northern area is also very scenic, with 1,500-foot marble mountains rising from flat plains and covered with dense vegetation, rolling hills, forests of pine, scores of magnificent royal palms, acres of citrus orchards, fields of colossal pineapples and even more colossal watermelons, and profuse truck gardens.

The climate ranges from a low of 58 degrees to a high of 90 degrees. Sea breezes help keep it comfortable even in summer.

The population are known as *pineros* and number around 20,000. A little more than half of this number live in the capital town of **Nueva Gerona,** less than a quarter of that number in the second town of importance, **Santa Fé.** The remaining residents are scattered among the other little settlements and on the plantations. English is spoken freely.

The only two "sights" outside of the beauty of the island itself and the sea are (1) the **house in which José Martí lived** when in exile on the island, recovering from his incarceration in El Morro for his revolutionary activities. In the garden there is a sundial dated 1868 that shows the time in Havana, Barcelona and Paris; (2) the **Presidio Modelo**—a model prison, with marble floors and marble stairways in its main building, solid mahogany table tops in its circular dining room that seats 5,000.

For the sportsman the island is sheer paradise. Quail shooting is excellent. Also available are dove, wild pigeon, guinea hen, duck, snipe, cocos, rail and wild boar. Bonefish are especially abundant here, and there are tarpon, ladyfish jacks, snapper, barracuda and so forth, plus the deeper-water specimens, in the surrounding seas.

MATANZAS, the capital of Matanzas Province, is a delightful 64-mile drive from Havana. The town was founded in 1693 and has produced so many of the country's poets, writers and artists that it has earned itself the title of the "Athens of Cuba." It is situated between the Yumurí and San Juan rivers and is a busy port and a growing industrial center.

PINAR DEL RÍO is the capital of the province of the same name, and 100 miles from Havana. It has a population of about 67,000. The province is the garden spot of Cuba, with glorious scenery of mountains, rivers, waterfalls, sea views, hundreds of caves, many of them still unexplored, freak stone columns called *mogotes* jutting up from the valley floor, rich agricultural land—heart of the tobacco center.

SANCTI-SPIRITUS, 240 miles from Havana, was founded in 1515 and moved to its present site in 1533. The town has some sixteenth- and seventeenth-century architecture with Moorish leanings, a museum, a theater whose façade is a replica of the Scala di Milan. In a church is a mysterious piece of sculpture called "Humility and Patience," carved by an unknown who came, carved his famed work, and left. This area is a cattle-raising center.

SANTA CLARA, the capital of Las Villas Province, almost 200 miles from Havana, is in about the center of the island on the site of old Cubanacan, to which Columbus sent emissaries, thinking they would find Kublai Khan, Emperor of China. The Spaniards moved their settlement here from the coast in 1689 to get away from the pirates. It is a commercial town but has nice old Colonial churches, a museum, a university, a square where band concerts are conducted at night and where young *villaclareños* promenade as of old.

SANTIAGO DE CUBA was founded in 1514 and was the capital of the island until 1556. It is now the capital of Oriente Province. Though not as large as some of Cuba's other cities, with a population of only 259,000, it is the second city of importance. Located on a pretty harbor and framed in by steep hills on three sides, it is an attractive city, a hodge-podge of architecture but nonetheless charming. It has a two-towered cathedral that is a fine example of Colonial architecture; it was built in 1522, suffered from fire, sacking and earthquake and had to be rebuilt three times. The **Bacardí Museum** is a fine building housing a collection of Indian relics, paintings, a replica of an eighteenth-century street with various types of Colonial houses in its patio, and shows the process of rum making. The **Provincial Palace** is across the street.

The **Santa Efigenia Cemetery** is now a national shrine because José Martí is buried in it; there is a special entrance to his impressive tomb. This is the home of the **University of Santiago de Cuba.** The **house of Cuba's famous poet José María de Heredia** can be visited, as can **San Juan Hill.** Seven miles south of the city is **Morro Castle,** the fort that was built at the entrance to the harbor in 1600, blown up by Henry Morgan in 1662 but rebuilt two years later; it is Cuba's greatest fortress.

Forty-five miles east of Santiago de Cuba is **Guantánamo;** it is 12 miles north of the bay that is the location of the U. S. Naval Base. Also to the east but on the north coast is **Baracoa,** the location of the first Spanish settlement on the island, 1512. It is scenically situated and has an eighteenth-century fort and church, but its chief attraction seems to be the fine collection of shells which can be found on its beaches. There is an annual rainfall in this area of 120 inches, but on days that are clear it is possible to see Haiti across the 50-mile stretch of the Windward Passage that lies between it and the island of Cuba.

TRINIDAD is connected to Cienfuegos by a fine scenic highway. Located on the south shore, Trinidad was founded in 1513, the third settlement established by the Spaniards. It is one of the most interesting and charming towns on the island of Cuba. In 1942, the government decreed that this should be a national monument and its old buildings preserved. There are narrow little streets, cobbled hundreds of years ago, old houses and palaces, the **Convent of San Francisco,** once used as a barracks by Spanish soldiers and now used for a school, **Serrano Square** where Cortés recruited his followers. Just outside of town is a ceiba tree to which Columbus is said to have moored his ships. Lovely views can be seen from La Vigia Hill.

VARADERO is 25 miles beyond Matanzas on narrow Hicacos Peninsula between the Bay of Cárdenas and the Atlantic Gulf Stream. It has many miles of fine white sandy beach and clear blue waters.

SPORTS AND RECREATION. Cubans as a rule do not swim during the winter months, but the water is delightful all year round (its winter temperature seldom falls below 70 degrees). There are many fine beaches, called *playas.* Most noted is Varadero's long Playa Azul **(Blue Beach),** so called for the blue of the sea and the sky. **Skin-diving** and **spear-fishing** are good all along the coast. Boating of all types is popular.

There is good lake and river **fishing;** good bass fishing at **La Laguna del Tesoro** (Treasure Lake) on the edge of the **Zapata Swamp** and at less accessible **Venero Grande** and **Venero Chico.** The waters off the coast of Cuba teem with hundreds of varieties of fish. Bone fishing is considered to be fine near Varadero and off the north coast keys and particularly off the Isle of Pines.

There is **hunting** for wild boar and some deer. **Shooting** is excellent—quail, dove, duck, pheasant, pigeon, and wild guinea hen.

Golf, tennis, and **bowling** are popular. Havana's 70-acre **Sports City** includes stadiums, sport fields, pools, tennis courts, and a children's playground. One spectator sport is **baseball**—this has been called the "national madness."

Boxing also enjoys great popularity, **wrestling** matches are held, and **basketball,** and **jai alai** are played in a three-walled court called a *frontón.*

Horseracing season is December to June. **Cockfighting** takes place in arenas called *vallas.* **Dog races** are held from July to October.

Much of the inspiration for Cuban music and dance has come from the Negro population. There are many rhythmic folk dances in the country, which include the habanera, guaracha, conga, danzón, rumba, mambo, and the zapateo, a popular rural dance. Music is provided by orchestras which often have ankle bells, bongo drums, gourds, bottles, hard sticks, earthenware jars, and castanets.

Cuba has its version of the Caribbean calypso, the *guajira* with improvised lyrics and accompaniment. The *guantanamera* uses the same melody but the words are changed daily to keep them up-to-date.

Dramas and musical shows are presented; there are many movie houses.

SPECIAL EVENTS. There are innumerable carnivals, fiestas, and holidays throughout the country. Among the more important are **José Martí's birthday,** January 28, with students' parades; **Grito de Baire,** February 24, the National Independence Day, commemorating the outbreak of the revolt against the Spaniards in 1895; **Havana Carnival,** celebrated for four weekends beginning before Ash Wednesday. There are public and private dances, and masked and costumed paraders. Highlights are the *comparsas,* Afro-Cuban pageants. Holy Week ceremonies are held in Havana on Good Friday. *Arroyo Areras,* a religious ceremony, takes place on Easter Sunday and Monday. Guïnes, 30 miles from Havana, presents a Passion Play.

The **death of José Martí** is commemorated on May 19. May 20 is the **Republic of Cuba** day, commemorating the day the Cuban flag was raised in 1902. There are parades and fiestas everywhere. **Carnival in Santiago de Cuba,** from July 24 to 26, celebrates the founding of the city. The **Twenty-sixth of July Movement anniversary,** on July 26, commemorates, with parades and festivities, the beginning of the Castro revolution.

On December 7, all **religious martyrs** are commemorated with a ceremony, held at the tomb of Antonio Marceo. **Parrandas de Noche Buena,** December 24 and 25, are Christmas choral serenades held in all parts of Cuba.

DINING AND SHOPPING. Many varieties of foods are available in Cuba. Seafood is excellent. *Pargo* (red snapper) is particularly good and *congrejos moros* (crabs and rice) are delicious. Local Spanish foods include *arroz con pollo* (chicken and rice), *congri* (black beans, rice and pork), *Moros y Cristanos*—"Moors and Christians"—(beans and rice without the pork). *Hot tamales* are grated fresh corn, pork and chicken; *paella a la Valenciana* is a casserole of rice with meat, chicken and seafood, vegetables and seasonings. The closest thing to the Creole calaloo is *caldo gallego. Lechón asado* is roast suckling pig and invariably delicious. Tropical fruits are numerous and delicious: *chirimoya* with a creamy pulp and black seeds, the *guanabana* with a prickly green skin, the papaya, called *fruta bomba* here, and the *platano manzano,* apple banana. Bananas are used in a variety of ways. There are mammees, anons, and 27 kinds of mangos.

Cuban coffee is famous, with *café con leche* being the standard breakfast coffee.

Refreshing drinks are made from various tropical fruits mixed with milk, sugar and ice and whipped, known as "refrescos." A *champola* is made with soursop; a strained pineapple and coconut milk drink with shaved ice is called a *piña colada;* unstrained, *piña sin colar.*

Rum is the national drink, as it is very good and very inexpensive. There are some eighty-odd brands of bottled sodas, two favorites being *Ironbeer,* a carbonated drink, and *Materva,* a pineapple-flavored maté.

Jamaica

"Crown Jewel of the Caribbean" . . . "New world elegance combined with old world charm" . . . "Fashionable playground of the international set." These are the phrases travel folders use to describe Jamaica, and with complete justification.

THE LAND. Jamaica has an area of 150 by 50 miles. Its scenery is varied and fascinating—lofty mountains rising to 7,400 feet, forbiddingly wild areas such as the Cockpit country (with giant forests, limestone cones, weirdly shaped rocks and bottomless sinkholes), fertile valleys, coastal swamps, radioactive hot springs, more than 100 rivers with numerous tributaries. (The Arawak Indian name for the island was "Xaymaca," meaning Land of Wood and Water.) Kingston's fine harbor, one of several that serve Jamaica, is the seventh largest in the world and is considered one of the finest natural harbors in use. There are over 2,000 types of flowering plants, about 450 species of fern—one variety growing to a height of 20 feet—and fine timber such as West Indian cedar, mahogany, mahoe, bulletwood, lignum vitae, guango, silk-cotton, spathodia—the list seems endless. The native pimento trees supply practically the entire world market.

Jamaica is one of the best established tourist resorts of the Caribbean. The pleasure-bound vacationer would find it difficult to think of anything that Jamaica could not supply. Its clean white beaches and crystal-clear protected waters have an average yearly temperature of 72 degrees. There is every conceivable sport on land and sea for daytime amusement, and touches of the exotic in the calypso singers and fire-breathing dancers for nighttime entertainment. The last word in creature comfort is supplied by a wide choice of luxurious hotels and, for those who prefer them, there are simple but charming little guesthouses, some isolated in the hills.

Jamaica has five distinct and distinctive resort areas: (1) **Montego Bay,** the international resort playground referred to as "MoBay." (2) **North Coast,** the Ocho Rios and points west area, with another string of hotels of varying degrees of plushness and simplicity, each with its own inviting stretch of white beach. At Ocho Rios there is a fine bay protected by a coral reef. (3) **Port Antonio** on the north coast to the east of Ocho Rios; its twin harbors are a favorite hangout for fishermen and yachtsmen. The town also serves as a banana loading port. (4) **Mandeville,** an appealing, scenic, quiet little English town 2,000 feet up in the hills with a perpetual springtime climate—a popular spot for retired British. (5) **Kingston,** the capital and only city of any size on the island—well-located on the Liguanea Plain of the southeast coast, backed by the Blue Mountains and facing the fine seven-mile-long harbor.

THE CLIMATE. Jamaica has almost perpetual sunshine, with temperatures varying greatly in different localities. The year-round average in the lowlands

is 77–82 degrees and it is somewhat cooler on the north shore than the south. Lowlands can be extremely hot and humid in the summer months, but the island is directly in the path of the trade winds and at night there are breezes from the hills. The hill areas are, of course, much cooler. Rainfall also varies from 32 inches in Kingston to 200 inches in the mountainous northeast, most of it falling during a three-week period in May–June and September–October. Storms can be torrential but usually are of brief duration.

THE PEOPLE. Jamaica is densely populated. Of its more than 1.9 million inhabitants, over 400,000 of them live in Kingston and its suburbs. The population is very mixed—predominantly the descendants of the slaves brought over from Africa by the Spanish and the British; also Britishers who came over from 1655 on, together with Irish and Scotch, Portuguese (including many Jews, who migrated here after Portugal became attached to Spain in the late sixteenth century); East Indians, who came as indentured laborers after 1845;

Chinese, who came for the same reason from Hong Kong after 1885; Syrians who ventured up from Venezuela, and also some Italians and Germans. In recent years, many people from the United States have built homes there.

The language is English, as is usual in these islands with a British heritage. An engaging local patois is spoken by some Jamaicans. It is a mixture of archaic English and African words. Many stories are told by Jamaicans about ghosts, known to them as "duppies," who live in the silk-cotton and almond trees. Fascinating tales are also told of very special legendary ghosts: a three-legged horse which appears on the highways between one and four in the morning before Christmas; a calf with eyes of balls of fire which wanders about annoying people on moonlight nights in the countryside; a cowherd who can be heard, in August, cracking his whip.

The religion of the island is predominantly Protestant, with the Anglican and Baptist churches heading the long list. Society of Friends, Roman Catholicism and Judaism are also represented. A relatively small local religion is called "Pocomania." Following a service led by their "shepherd," the congregation strives to achieve possession by the spirits through ever increasingly frenzied singing and dancing to the accompaniment of either drums or a roaring of the participants known as "trumping."

Columbus landed on Jamaica during his second voyage in May 1494 on the north coast at Discovery Bay, a spot he called Santa Gloria. On his return, nine years later, he was stranded and spent a year awaiting rescue. He and his men lived on their two battered ships which they fastened together on the beach and roofed over. Between illness and the hostility of the Arawak Indians, it was a harrowing year. Only the Indians' superstitions, encouraged by Columbus' knowledge of the date of an impending eclipse of the moon, finally brought them under control. The first genuine Spanish settlement was established by Juan de Esquivel, who was sent over in 1509 under orders from Diego, the son of Columbus, to act as governor. He founded the island's first capital, overlooking St. Ann's Bay, which he called Sevilla Nueva. Later, in 1535, Villa de la Vega was made the capital and remained so until 1872. This was first called Sant' Jago de la Vega under the British, and today is Spanish Town.

England captured Jamaica in 1655, and its title to the island was ceded by the Treaty of Madrid in 1670. Except for one brief raid, the British settlers were not bothered by foreign invasions. Their difficulty lay with slaves, imported by the Spaniards, who had taken to the hills when their owners were forced from the island. Until the end of the eighteenth century, this group, augmented by runaway slaves of the British, fought for their independence. The wild, rugged, almost impenetrable section to which they fled is called the Cockpit country. It was also called the "Land-of-Look-Behind" because the soldiers who strove, unsuccessfully, to capture them had to keep an eye in all directions against unexpected virtually invisible attack from within the dense terrain.

After many years of alternating war and uneasy peace, the island's government offered amnesty and permanent domain to those slaves who surrendered. In 1796, these guarantees were violated and some 600 slaves were shipped to Nova Scotia. Many who remained settled in an isolated mountainous reserve of 2,500 acres, and some of their descendants still live on this grant of land where they enjoy the rights of citizenship without taxation. They are beholden only to their chief, whom they call "Colonel" and who meets annually with the Governor of Jamaica on August first, to exchange amenities and to discuss grievances. Today there are an estimated 2,000 pure blacks who live for the most part in Accompong and Maroon Town in St. Elizabeth, adjacent to the Cockpit country. A few live in the difficult to reach mountain fastness at Moore Town in the eastern John Crow Mountains and in small settlements at Charles Town in Portland and Scott's Hall in St. Mary's. These people were and are known as "Maroons," a word probably based on the old Spanish word *cimarron,* meaning fierce, or the phrase *nègre marron* which was used for a fugitive slave who took to the woods.

Another highlight of Jamaican history was the period of the buccaneers, adventurers who flourished during the late sixteenth and all of the seventeenth century. Their name came from the *boucans* on which they smoked and dried their meat. After about 1670, they and the pirates–the two are practically synonymous–made Port Royal their headquarters. Governor Modyford of Jamaica, lacking a fleet of his own, actually appointed infamous Henry Morgan as vice-admiral of the buccaneer fleet and backed him in his raids on the Caribbean area. By the Treaty of Madrid, England and Spain agreed to stop buccaneering. Lusty, gusty Morgan was returned under arrest from his raid on Panama and taken to England to stand trial for his crimes, with the amazing result that he was sent back to Jamaica to serve as lieutenant-governor. This was undoubtedly an expression of England's appreciation of his aid in securing England's position in the Caribbean and the profits collected for England's benefit as well as his own.

Morgan held his post three times but ultimately, because of dubious practices, was deprived of his glory. He died in Port Royal in 1688 and is buried somewhere in the area. In 1692 an earthquake toppled most of Port Royal into the sea and subsequent hurricanes further damaged what was left of the city, making it necessary to transfer this commercial center to Kingston. Port Royal carried on as an important seaport, garrison town and naval station. In recent years underwater Port Royal has been the scene of exploration; one group of divers located a flight of steps leading to a taproom, bottles still intact upon the shelves.

The imported slaves were still another point of friction. A Royal African Company had been formed in 1672 and, with a monopoly on the slave trade, Jamaica became the greatest slave mart in the world. When the trade was abolished in 1807, there were over 320,000 slaves on Jamaica alone. In 1831–32 there was a revolt of the Negroes, who had been led to believe that the abolishment of the slave mart meant emancipation. An emancipation act was passed two years later, and after a four-year term of apprenticeship, the slaves were freed. This crippled the plantation owners; many estates were abandoned and trade in general dwindled. The economic situation was bad, and discontent among the ex-slaves came to a head with an uprising at Morant Bay in 1865. With time, the resultant general chaos was improved under Sir John Peter Grant (1866–74), who established a crown colony. Laborers were indentured from India whose presence, plus a rapidly growing banana trade with the United States, helped restore prosperity to the island.

Jamaica, a crown colony from 1816–1944, became an independent country in August 1962. Its parliament consists of the British monarch (represented by a governor general), a 21-member senate, and a 53-member house of representatives. The principal instrument of policy-making is the cabinet, charged with the general direction and control of the government, and responsible to parliament. It is comprised of a prime minister, who has executive power, and 11 other ministers.

AGRICULTURE. With half of the land under cultivation, most Jamaicans earn their living by farming. Leading crops include bananas, cacao, coconuts, coffee, sugar cane, and a variety of fruits. Exports are sugar, rum, liqueurs, bananas, citrus fruit, pimento spices and bauxite (Jamaica leads all other countries in the world in bauxite mining).

INDUSTRY. Many industries have been and are being established, such as cement, textiles, matches, cigarettes, cigars, and perfumes. More than 20 sugar factories produce over 350,000 tons of sugar annually, while distilleries bring out two million gallons of rum each year.

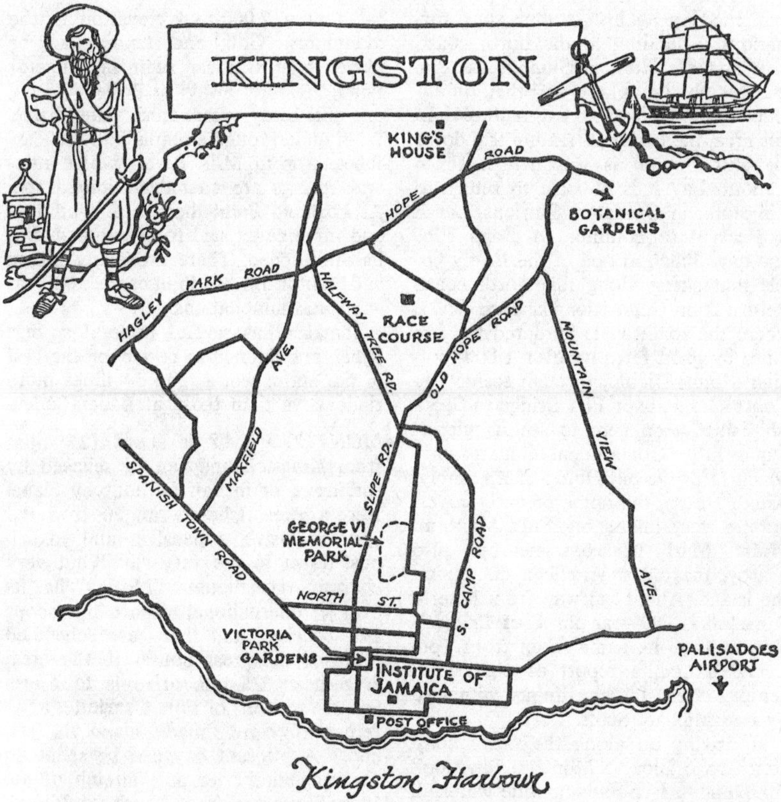

KINGSTON. Due to a disastrous earthquake in 1907, and a later fire, the center of the city has lost much of its old charm, and is not especially attractive. The residential sections do have some lovely old Georgian homes, however. **Royal Botanic Gardens, Hope,** covering 200 acres and located about five miles from town, is one of Kingston's high points. In town, the **Victoria Crafts Market** not only supplies all articles typical of a native market, but has an art gallery and cocktail lounge as well. **King's House,** the Governor's residence, can sometimes be visited by special permission. **Knutsford Park** has been developed into a "New Kingston" with a fine shopping district. Cigar, rum, china and perfume plants are open to the public. **University of the West Indies** is a few miles out in the foothills. Also to be seen are the gardens, pool and freeport shops of the famed **Myrtle Bank Hotel.** Kingston has several good museums and many hotels for the visitor who plans to spend time in the capital.

There are short scenic drives into the mountains from Kingston to **New Castle,** at 4,000-foot elevation, or **Strawberry Hill**—nice for tea—and a longer, curving but magnificent drive up to **Castleton Gardens.**

A perfect way to spend one day is to drive up to the north shore, with a choice of several available routes. The following is one of the most scenic and covers the high spots on this part of the island: Drive along the shore out of Kingston and up around the east coast. It is arid at first but becomes increasingly beautiful, with dense tropical growths and fine sea views of heavy surf crashing against strange rock formations. Rounding to the north coast, stop and see **Blue Lagoon,** a favorite spot for photographers, and then on another seven miles to **Port Antonio.** In this area, the two-hour rafting trip down the Rio Grande is worthwhile. From Annotto Bay it is possible to return to Kingston via Castleton Gardens, but it is pleasant to continue to **Ocho Rios** and have lunch at one of the lovely hotels that string along this north coast. Return from Ocho Rios via **Fern Gully,** where the roadway is bordered for five miles by giant fern; up over 1,800-foot-high Mount Diablo, through scenic **Rio Cobre Gorge,** over Flat Bridge to **Spanish Town.** Stop here to see its picturesque little Government Square onto which faces the old House of Assembly; King's House, the home of early governors; a very interesting **Folk Museum; White Marl Museum** nearby; also nearby, the oldest Anglican church on the island. About halfway from here to Kingston is 900-year-old **Tom Cringle's Cotton Tree,** its name taken from Tom Cringle's Log, a report of eighteenth-century West Indian life as witnessed by one Michael Scott.

If driving on along the north coast from Ocho Rios to Montego Bay, look for **Dunns River Falls,** a wide waterfall that cascades in gradual slopes down to the sea; the signpost that marks the site of the first Spanish settlement, **Sevilla Nueva; Runaway Bay**—the point from which Christóval Arnaldo de Ysasi, the last acting Spanish governor, took off in a canoe for Cuba; and **Discovery Bay,** where Columbus first landed in 1494. The remains of **Rose Hall,** the great house of the notorious Annee May Palmer, can be explored. Credited with murdering three husbands, many of her slaves, and the young girl with whom her own pet overseer had fallen in love, Annee Palmer was in turn murdered by one of her lovers. Needless to state the house is considered to be royally haunted.

MANDEVILLE can also be reached by car from Kingston or Montego Bay. This is the popular, but quiet resort located at a 2,000-foot elevation in the mountains. Golf and tennis can be played here. One can swim in Alligator Pond, 20 miles away; at Boilers Beach, one mile away, where fresh water erupts from underground streams into the Caribbean; or in Milk River, where mineral springs are channeled into a spa. At **Portland Point** there is a lighthouse and three caves said to be more than a half-mile deep. There are many hiking and motoring possibilities as well as good accommodations.

Jamaica has several mineral springs which are claimed to be among the best in the entire world, and 54 times more radioactive than those at Baden-Baden.

MONTEGO BAY is about 125 miles from Kingston and can be reached by car, train, or in half an hour by plane. Here are resort hotels ranging from the very exclusive, expensive, and luxurious, down to the very small but very charming guesthouses. "MoBay" has its own jet international airport, fine shops and beaches, and there are scheduled tours of the great houses in the area. A pleasant 25-mile drive is to **Lucea** and the remains of Fort Charlotte. (The return trip can be made inland via Jericho.) A pleasant day can be spent on the magnificent ten-mile stretch of the island's most perfect beach at **Negril,** destined to become a resort rival of MoBay's in the near future. Farther on is the fishing headquarters of Blue Water Club at Whitehouse Beach.

PORT ROYAL, headquarters of the buccaneers in their heyday, is only a few miles from Kingston out on the tip of the Palisadoes. Today primarily a fishing village, Port Royal's chief attraction is **Fort Charles,** largely designed by the old buccaneer, Henry Morgan, and commanded by Horatio Nelson, who came as a second lieutenant in 1779. A memorial to Nelson, "Nelson's Quarterdeck," is a part of the Fort, which has an excellent view of the Blue Mountains. To be seen at the Fort are the dockyard, the barracks, and the quarantine station. In the little town is **St. Peter's Church,** built in 1725, which has been restored but has retained the original carved organ loft and stairway. Silver ceremonial service pieces can be seen which were donated by Henry Morgan, as well as his two-quart silver beer tankard complete with whistle, which he blew when a refill was indicated. One can swim, boat, water-ski, eat, drink, and even stop overnight at **Morgan's Harbour Beach Club,** open to visiting travelers without membership. Old buildings such as Morgan's pitch-house, from which he caulked his ships, have been utilized in developing this resort inn.

SPORTS AND RECREATION. **Swimming** at beautiful private and public beaches, as well as hotel and club pools all around the island, is the most popular sport. Doctor's Cave Beach at Montego Bay, open to the public, is world-famous for its fine white sand and crystal-clear waters. A Doctor Alexander James McCatty donated this property for a bathing club in 1906, and the beach was given its name because so many doctors, who believed that the buoyant waters possessed healing properties, swam there. Dressing rooms, beach chairs and umbrellas, and food and drink are available. Average year-round temperature of the water is 79–84 degrees. Many hotels supply the necessary equipment for **snorkeling, skin-diving,** and **water-skiing,** and have *pedalos* for the use of their guests. The Caribbean water sports championship matches are held at Morgan's Harbour every August.

Boating is an increasingly popular sport, evidenced by the well-attended annual regattas, availability of charter boats (many hotels supply them for their guests), and excellent harbor anchorage for visiting yachtsmen. Several yacht clubs are open to visitors, and the glass-bottomed boat excursions are popular. The Phosphorus Lagoon boat excursion at Oyster Bay on the north shore on moonless nights should not be missed. Also to be seen are calypso singers paddling past some of the hotels and beaches at night with their "Show Boat" performances.

Fine mountain stream and river **fishing,** as well as spear and deep-sea fishing banks within 10–15 miles of shore, make Jamaica an angler's paradise. Popular spots are the California Bank, one of the finest, just south of Morgan's Harbour; banks at Port Antonio and outside the reef that protects Montego Bay. The Portland Fishing Club is at Port Antonio; Blue Water Fishing Club at White House Beach, Westmoreland.

Hunting for pigeon, snipe, dove and migratory birds is permitted from mid-August to February, teal duck in December. The big hunting thrill of Jamaica—too thrilling for most people—is shooting crocodile at night. Arrangements can be made through the Blue Water Club. Other available sports are **tennis, golf, horseback riding, mountain climbing.** Blue Mountain Peak, 7,402 feet high, and Cinchona, with the very old Cinchona Botanical Gardens at 5,000 feet elevation, are two popular hiking goals. Spectator sports include **horse racing, polo, cricket, soccer, football, boxing, bicycle racing, annual international tournaments in golf and tennis.**

"Rafting on the Rio Grande" is a popular two-hour pastime. Bamboo rafts with seats at one end for two or three passengers are poled down the rapids by expert native boatmen.

The **Institute of Jamaica** in Kingston is the cultural center. It has a science museum with relics of the old slave days, a noted reference library, lending library, a lecture hall, and a very small zoo in its gardens. Old and modern prints and paintings are exhibited there, and at various galleries and hotels throughout the island, where some are for sale. Jamaica has a musical society to promote interest in musical events. A military band plays at the **Myrtle Bank Hotel** on cruise-ship days and on Sundays in the **Royal Botanic Gardens, Hope.** Plays and concerts are given periodically, several amateur Little Theater groups perform regularly, and the island has air-conditioned and open-air movie houses featuring good productions. Kingston also has its Society for the Study of French Culture and is visited yearly by national dance companies.

Dances at the hotels are open to outsiders as well as to guests of the hotel and feature native entertainment with calypso singers and dancers.

SPECIAL EVENTS. The most interesting holiday celebration in Jamaica is **Independence Day,** first Monday in August. Other holidays of note are **Boxing Day,** December 26, and the **Queen's official birthday** in June.

DINING AND SHOPPING. Jamaica's fruits and vegetables include pawpaws, granadillas, soursop and sweetsop, naseberries, star apples and Otaheite apples, and various crossbreeds such as ortanique (orange and tangerine). Also, ackees, plantains, cassavas, cho-chos, kalalu (spinach), and breadfruit, whose tree was first brought to Jamaica by Captain Bligh of "Mutiny-on-the-Bounty" fame. Pepper pot is a popular soup made from Indian kale and kalalu, okra and finely chopped meat. Stuffed cho-chos, rice coco with cinnamon and brown sugar, cassava pudding, roasted breadfruit, and soursop ice cream are delicious. "Booby" eggs, hard-boiled and served as an hors d'oeuvre, are very good and have a somewhat gamy taste. These small eggs have a pink yolk and come from the Morant and Pedro cays, dependencies of Jamaica.

There are many unusual nonalcoholic drinks—"Matrimony," a blend of sweet oranges and pulp of the star apple; "sorrel," a Christmas drink made from the red sorrel leaf and stalk of its bush; "sour-sweet," crushed pulp of the soursop mixed with sweetened condensed milk, a pineapple drink of the peel fermented in a stone jug, and ginger beer.

Rum is the alcoholic drink of the island, in the usual forms of planters punch, sour, or Collins, or served with pineapple juice or milk with cinnamon or cloves. A good, light strong beer is made here, as are liqueurs—Tia Maria, with a coffee base; Sante, rind of citrus fruit steeped in white rum; Pimento Dram, pimento berries steeped in white rum.

Native craft is a specialty—straw and jippi-jappa articles, hand-painted textiles, ceramics, wood items, silver filigree jewelry—also Jamaican rums and liqueurs, cigars. Duty-free imports from all over the world—Swiss watches, German cameras, Danish silver, French perfumes, English woolens, gloves, cashmeres, tape recorders, radio and hi-fi equipment—are available. There are excellent tailors who will make up a suit in 72 hours or less, and good seamstresses.

There are in-bond shops at the airports, in the main cities and at some of the hotels. **Victoria Crafts Market** in Kingston is a must.

CAYMAN ISLANDS

The three islands, Grand Cayman, Cayman Brac and Little Cayman (all crown colonies), are situated about 175 miles west and slightly north of Jamaica. Their total population is a little over 10,000.

GRAND CAYMAN, the largest, is approximately 22 by 8 miles in size. It is completely flat but nonetheless attractive, with wooded areas, tropical vegetation and flowers. Its swampy interior breeds mosquitoes, which can be a nuisance during the summer and the fall months of rain, but they are nonmalarial and efforts have been undertaken to stamp them out. The beaches are unsurpassed, particularly the unbroken five-mile stretch at West Bay. A gigantic seven-by-six-mile coral reef protects a harbor called North (or Great) Sound that almost cuts through the island at its western end. Although there are 60 miles of good paved road, as well as others of hard-packed marl, bicycles are still the favorite means of transportation. All the settlements—West Bay, Bodden Town, East End, Northside, and Georgetown, the capital—are at the water's edge.

The people on Grand Cayman are predominantly Negro or of mixed blood, many being descendants of the first arrivals in 1741. Men on the island have been noted for centuries as seafarers and ship-builders, and the islands provide excellent timber for that purpose. Turtles are the raw material for a major industry. Columbus, who apparently did not consider the islands worth exploring when he passed near them in 1503, did take the time to name them "Las Tortugas," because of the quantities of turtles he saw. Their numbers have diminished over the years, however, and now the turtle fleet goes to Nicaraguan waters to corral their catch. When the fleet returns to Grand Cayman, the turtles are placed in crawls to fatten and eventually are processed for export. The hawksbill shells are considered best for articles to be made of tortoise shell; the female green turtle is used for edible purposes. Thatch rope, resistant to salt water, is also made for export. Cayman Island postage stamps are another source of revenue.

This being one of the truly "escapist" islands in the Caribbean, it is surprising to find excellent and modern accommodations. The Island is becoming increasingly popular with tourists so that it may, before too long, be out of the escapist class. From December to April the temperature averages 70–75 degrees, in summer about 10 degrees higher. Autumn is the rainy season, with an average yearly rainfall of about 60 inches. The island has a small but well-staffed hospital.

Grand Cayman was never occupied by the Spanish. It was annexed by Britain in 1655 and colonized by Englishmen from Jamaica in 1741. For years it had been a pirate hideout and buried treasures have been discovered there.

A dependency of Jamaica since 1863, an act was passed in 1958 giving statutory power for a new government, for the formal separation from Jamaica, and for the establishment of the Cayman Islands as a crown colony.

Interesting to see are **Fort George** on the waterfront; the ruins of **St. James Castle** on Great Pedro Point, said to have been frequented by Henry Morgan; **"Hell,"** near West Bay Town beyond Galleon Beach, an area full of jagged rocks and little coral peaks; the cannon at **Gun Bay** that were set up during the Napoleonic Wars.

CAYMAN BRAC. This is the most scenic of the three islands, a limestone plateau, protected by cliffs, with green pastures and coconut palms. It is about one by twelve miles in size, 60 miles northeast of Grand Cayman, and has a population of 1,700. Dairy and beef cattle are raised, fruits and vegetables are grown, and there is some small boat building. Copra is the chief export.

Cayman Brac can be reached by boat or plane from Grand Cayman. Attractive accommodations are provided by a small inn.

LITTLE CAYMAN is five miles west of Brac. It is one by nine miles in size and has about 50 inhabitants.

SPORTS AND RECREATION. Life on Grand Cayman is informal, out-of-doors, and relaxed. There is no real night life although dancing at the hotels and movies in the various settlements are popular. **Swimming** is possible at reef-sheltered sandy beaches around most of the island, as are **aquaplaning, surfboarding, skin-diving, snorkeling,** and **boating.** There are **glass-bottomed boats** for viewing the coral and fish, good deep-sea and spear **fishing** for tarpon in the lagoons, and **lobster progging** at night. **Hunting** for wild duck is best between January and March. Local schooners or catboats take passengers on their fishing expeditions or their round-the-island trips. A favorite tourist pastime is a scheduled all-day fishing and picnicking trip to Rum Point—named for an ancient rum carrier that was wrecked here and is still visible. Rum Point Deep-sea Fishing and Skin Diving Club provides food, drink, and rooms for those who wish to stay overnight.

Five-day regattas are held in late January before the schooner fleet sails to the turtle fishing grounds off Nicaragua. A British warship officiates, Georgetown is gaily decorated and it is a very festive occasion. Every year there is a **Cayman Islands Pageant** depicting the islands' history, the date varying from year to year. Treasure hunting is another possibility and there are pirate caves to explore.

DINING AND SHOPPING. Turtle steaks are the prize specialty, followed by conch and large crayfish, crab backs, calalou, fish stew, carrots cooked in coconut milk and the native almond pie.

Best buys are tortoise-shell articles, thatch-rope baskets, and hats.

TURKS AND CAICOS ISLANDS

These islands, geographically part of the extreme southeastern end of the Bahama chain, are 420 miles northeast of Jamaica. A 22-mile channel separates the Turks and Caicos islands. The group consists of islands of various sizes, the better known being Grand Turk, Salt Cay, and the South, North, East, and Middle Caicos. There is air service between Nassau and Grand Turk and an emergency landing strip in South Caicos.

The name "Turks" is derived from a form of cactus that grows with a flower that resembles a red fez. Most of the islands are uninhabited, the total population being around 3,800, of mixed European and African descent. Free compulsory education is provided for children from the age of 7 to 14 by both denominational and private schools, and there is a senior school on Grand Turk. The islands are rather barren but some sisal is grown. Salt raking is the chief industry and is government-controlled. Dried conches are processed and exported to Haiti, frozen crawfish to Miami.

A dependency of Jamaica since 1873, a 1958 act gave statutory power for formal separation from Jamaica. Since 1965, the islands have been governed by the Bahamas. The administration is in the hands of a British Crown-appointed administrator, aided by an executive council and the consent of a partially elected legislative council.

Haiti and Dominican Republic

Haiti and the Dominican Republic share the Caribbean Island where Columbus was shipwrecked in December 1492, and which was named Hispaniola, a corruption of the Spanish "La Española," by him. The western third of the island is Haiti (an old Indian word meaning mountainous land), and the eastern two-thirds belongs to the Dominican Republic.

Columbus claimed the island for Spain and built Fort La Natividad at a point near the present Cap-Haïtien. On his return the following year, he found the entire settlement had been massacred by the Arawaks. A new settlement site was chosen near the present Puerto Plata, now part of the Dominican Republic. This settlement which he named La Isabella, was the first real city in the New World.

The original La Natividad area was ignored by the Spaniards. A mixed group of English and French buccaneers settled on offshore Tortuga Island around 1625–30 and soon moved to Haiti's mainland. The French managed ultimately to assume power over the English and to repel attacks by the Spaniards, who were beginning to show renewed interest in the area. In 1697, by the Treaty of Ryswick, Saint Domingue (now Haiti) was ceded to the French, and the Spaniards called their remaining portion of the island Santo Domingo.

Slaves from Africa were imported to replace the Arawaks, who had been exterminated by the Spaniards. Intermingling of slaves and masters produced a class of mulattoes who, by a decree of Louis XIV, were considered to be free, not slaves, and as such were able to become owners of property including slaves. In 1789, the National Assembly of Paris granted political rights to "persons of color," but the French settlers on the island strenuously objected to this and there were bitter struggles be-

tween the two groups. At the request of the French settlers, English and Spaniards came to their aid and occupied a part of the island. Inspired by the Revolution in France, the slaves then rose in revolt against the cruelty of their masters, and on the night of August 14, 1791, they killed both whites and mulattoes and burned plantation houses and sugar-cane fields. It was a battle not of color but of slave against freeman.

Pierre Dominique Toussaint l'Ouverture (the last name being a nickname earned by the openings he managed to make in enemy lines) became leader of the rebel forces. Having achieved his own emancipation in 1793 by decree of the new French republican government, he proceeded to drive the Spaniards and English out of Santo Domingo because they still traded in slaves. As a reward, he was made Governor of Hispaniola by France. The mulattoes opposed his authority, and after successfully quelling their rebellion (aided by supplies and ships from the U.S.), he proclaimed himself dictator of the island. Napoleon sent General Charles Victor Emanuel Leclerc to replace him and there was more bitter fighting. A peace of sorts was made, but through treachery (he accepted what he was led to believe was a friendly invitation to talk with the French) they took Toussaint prisoner and deported him to France, where he died in prison after an uprising against France.

Jean Jacques Dessalines, a Negro general, then took over, and in 1804 drove out the would-be French conquerors, proclaimed the independence of Haiti, and later was crowned Emperor Jacques I. Hating both white and mulatto alike, he ruled with such force that he was assassinated two years later. Henri Christophe was then elected President without his consent. He returned to the northern part of Haiti, where he was in command, and later pronounced himself King Henri I. At the same time, the southern section became a republic with the mulatto Alexandre Sabès Pétion as President. Upon the suicide of Christophe in 1820, Pétion's successor, another mulatto named Jean Pierre Boyer, brought the entire island under his control. In 1821, the Spanish portion of the island declared its independence. Boyer invaded and conquered it, but in 1843 a revolution forced him out of that part of the island. Since that date, Hispaniola has been shared by Haiti and Santo Domingo, now called the Dominican Republic.

Thereafter followed a long period of continual revolts in the Dominican Republic, political chaos and disorder and the incurring of huge foreign debts in both countries. Foreign intervention was threatened by five European countries. Finally a U.S. representative was sent in 1905 to apportion the revenue and assure payment of foreign debts. Following another period of complete disorder, on the brutal massacre in 1915 of President Vilbrun Guillaume Sam of Haiti, U. S. Marines intervened to protect American interests and to restore order. U. S. Marines occupied the entire island on November 29, 1916 and established a military government.

Partial control was restored to the Dominican Republic in 1922 and a provisional government set up. In March 1924, a constitutional government took over and the U.S. occupation ended later that year by a treaty. In Haiti, after the landing of the Marines, a treaty offering a ten-year period of assistance in stabilizing the government and developing its natural resources, was signed between the U.S. and Haiti. At its expiration it was extended for another ten-year period. Predictably, in spite of the great improvements achieved in the way of sanitation, roads, and schools, the 19-year period of occupation by the U. S. Marines is still bitterly resented by many Haitians. In 1940, the U.S. relinquished its administration of Dominican Republic customs, but an American fiscal agent remained in charge of customs in Haiti until 1948, when the country's total debt to the U.S. was repaid.

In 1930, when Rafael Leonidas Trujillo Molina was elected President of the Dominican Republic, it was an impoverished country, and made even more so by a devastating hurricane three weeks after he took over. He assumed absolute control over the country for a continuous period up until 1961, except for the years 1938–42 when he permitted a lieutenant of the Dominica Party to hold the reins.

Trujillo was assassinated in 1961. In 1962 the people elected Juan Bosch as President, in the first free election in over 30 years. But in 1963, military leaders ousted Bosch. A three-man civilian *junta* (council) was set up. After a civil war and U.S. intervention free elections again have taken place in the Dominican Republic.

HAITI

Haiti is colorful, exciting and mysterious, and completely unlike any other country in the entire Caribbean. The beauty and grace of its women are world-famed, the *joie de vivre* of the poorest peasant is notoriously infectious.

THE LAND. The major portion of the mainland is densely wooded mountains with peaks rising to great heights, the tallest, Pic La Selle, being 8,793 feet. Between the three great mountain ranges lie the fertile plains of Artibonite, Central, Cul-de-Sac, and the Plaine du Nord. There are many swiftly flowing streams, the chief river being the Artibonite; Lake Étang Saumâtre covers

69 square miles. A new 18 by 20-mile lake in the Pèligre Canyon of the Artibonite Valley has been created by the building of the Artibonite Valley Dam. The coastline of cliffs is frequently broken by indented coves and harbors; in many places the mountains rise sheer from the sea. Many fine woods are to be found in the forests—mahogany, cedar, oak, pine, lignum vitae, satinwood, rosewood. In the arid areas are cacti and the dwarfed thorn tree.

THE CLIMATE. Haiti has a pleasant climate which varies with the locale rather than through seasonal changes. Average yearly temperature in Furcy, at a 5,000-foot elevation, is 66 degrees, in Port-au-Prince on the coast, 80 degrees. Port-au-Prince can be hot and humid in the summertime although sea breezes bring relief in the morning hours and land breezes in the evening ones. And one can always retreat to the fine hotels in the suburb of Pétionville 1,500 feet above the city. Nights everywhere in Haiti are always cooler. Haiti has two rainy seasons—April to June and August to October, May and September generally having the most rain. Rainfall varies greatly from semi-arid areas to a high of around 100 inches per year. The rains come in torrential downpours of brief duration and usually in the evenings. Haiti has had a few hurricanes but less than many of the other islands, being somewhat protected from them by the mountains. It has also suffered from earthquakes.

THE PEOPLE. Probably 95 percent of the population of an approximate 4.8 million are black; the balance are mulatto, descendants of old French settlers. There are, in addition, an estimated 5,000 foreigners, about ten percent of whom are white.

French is the official language of the country, but a Creole mixture of 17th century French, African dialects, and English, Spanish and Indian words is most commonly used. English is widely used and understood, the teaching of it being compulsory in all schools.

The people of Haiti are a proud and sensitive people, formal and scholarly. The "elite" minority is well-read and highly educated, very often receiving their higher education in Europe or the U.S. Consequently, they have accepted many of the values of their educational surroundings. Despite the poverty of the majority of the population there exists a relaxed, gay spirit which adds much to the atmosphere that makes Haiti appealing. One of the most engaging sights to be seen is the *marchandes*—peasant women—tramping the mountain roads to market with their easy gait and with huge loaded baskets on their heads, beside them the scores of burros, their panniers filled with the heavier produce.

A system of *plaçage* substitutes for the marriage ceremony which few of the peasants can afford. This means the placing of a common-law wife on a plot of ground; one man may place several common-law wives on his different pieces of ground. Haitians are a co-operative people: neighbor helps neighbor in the building of huts or tilling of the soil, a co-operative work-effort known as a *coumbite.* Drums throb day and night—by day to call the neighbors to a *coumbite* or to provide work-rhythms, at night for the peasant get-togethers known as *bamboches*—gay, informal parties or dances—and for their sacred voodoo ceremonies. (Although Roman Catholicism is Haiti's state religion, voodoo is the practiced religion of the peasant class.)

Education is free and compulsory—theoretically. Most peasants, however, have neither the money to buy school supplies nor the impetus to send their children the long distances necessary. Secondary education is provided by private schools, mostly Roman Catholic, and French lycées. The University of Haiti, the Faculty of Law, the Faculty of Medicine, and the Central School of Agriculture offer higher education. There are two normal schools for teachers, a military school for the training of Army officers.

Haiti was the first independent Negro republic in the world. Its constitution calls for a president elected for life who has a cabinet of 11 secretaries-of-state and five under-secretaries-of-state, a National Assembly of 67 deputies and 21 senators. Locally, Haiti is divided into nine departments. These in turn are subdivided into *arrondissements,* and again into communes each of which has a mayor who serves for four years. Women have the franchise and at 35 years of age have the right to hold public office.

AGRICULTURE. Fertile valleys produce coffee, bananas, sugar, sisal, cotton, cacao, maize, rice, millet, castor beans, essential oils. (The Artibonite Valley project for irrigation and flood control has done much to increase crops in that area.) Important exports, after coffee, are sisal fiber, raw sugar, molasses, and cocoa; essential oils, mahogany ware, cotton, baseballs, and bananas. Some bauxite and copper are mined, and other untapped sources of minerals such as gold, silver, copper, iron, and nickel are said to exist.

INDUSTRY. Tax exemption benefits and duty-free entry of raw materials have been a boon to the development of new industries. There are now a sugar mill, sugar refinery, and sugar factory; a distillery for alcohol and rum, cotton processing plants, lard factories, a textile mill, a cement plant. Aerated water, ice, bay rum, and edible oils are produced, as are shoes and mahogany products.

CITIES. Although there are several interesting cities to visit, Port-au-Prince is the largest and most well-known. Other towns are Cap-Haïtien, Kenscoff, and La Gonâve.

CAP-HAÏTIEN. First known as Le Cap, then Cape Français, then Cap Henri (so named for himself by Christophe), this is Haiti's most historic city and its second city of importance. It is 85 miles from Port-au-Prince on the north coast and is the trade center for the Plaine du Nord, where sugar cane, coffee, cacao, tobacco, bananas and sisal are grown. Founded originally by French buccaneers, it became the French capital in 1670 and in its surrounding areas, rich plantations were established for the growing of sugar, coffee and cacao. Under the French Cap-Haïtien was a gay, sophisticated, prosperous city known as the "Paris of Saint Domingue." Practically destroyed during the revolution, it was rebuilt by Christophe but again badly damaged in 1843 by fire and earthquake. Today it is a quiet, charming little town with narrow old streets, little parks, multi-hued French Colonial homes with wrought-iron balconies, patios, and high walls. At the **Place Notre Dame d'Armes,** with its old French fountain, is the Union Club with beautiful inlaid mahogany floors and a "liberation document" hanging on the walls, signed by President Roosevelt and President Vincent of Haiti in 1934, concerning the withdrawal of the U. S. Marines. Also facing the square are the old **City Hall,** the **Bishop's Palace,** the **Notre Dame Church,** the **Musée Paul E. Magloire.** Cap-Haïtien, like Port-au-Prince, also has its little Iron Market. Overlooking the harbor is the rubble of the Palace of Pauline Bonaparte Leclerc. At the harbor entrance are forts and a lighthouse.

Nearby is **Bois Caiman,** where the rebellion to free the island of French domination began in 1791. This same area was the birthplace of **Toussaint,** who was instrumental in organizing the fight for freedom. Outside the city gates is the site of the final battle for independence, where Dessalines defeated the French in 1803, on the Vertières battlefield. Ruins of various French fortifications can be seen along this north coast. A half hour's drive leads along the cliffs to **Ducroy** and **Cormiers beaches.** A resort center has been planned for lovely **Chouchou Bay,** farther on. About eight miles beyond Chouchou Bay are various Indian caves with interesting sculptures and paintings. **Labardie** is another good beach about 20 minutes' drive from Cap-Haïtien.

To the south of Cap-Haïtien are Haiti's most renowned attractions—the ruins of Christophe's **Sans Souci Palace** and the **Citadel.** Sans Souci Palace, built as a replica of the Sans Souci Palace of Frederick II of Prussia at Potsdam, is just beyond the settlement of **Milot.** Though much destroyed by an earthquake in 1842, it is still possible to visualize its former glory of four stories of rooms, a private theater, wide stairways, and its own cooling system produced by streams channeled beneath the structure. On the front wall is a plaque marking the spot where Christophe committed suicide with a golden bullet, the humiliation of falling, following a stroke, when attempting to mount his horse to review his troops being more than his pride could face. Fronting the palace are the pillars of the main gates and two little churches–one built for the use of Christophe and his family, the other for his people.

At Milot, one can hire horses for the two-hour, four-mile climb up to **La Citadelle de la Ferrière.** This is one of the great wonders of the world. Begun as a defense against Napoleon, its completion became a mad obsession of Christophe's. It was built by slave labor at a claimed loss of over 10,000 workers, who died from the effort expended in dragging up the mountain trail the materials needed to erect this monumental waste. There are five floors of dungeons, gun galleries, storerooms, quarters for the royal family, steep parapets. The walls rise from 100 to more than 200 feet and are ten feet thick. Still to be seen are an estimated 45,000 cannon balls, 375 cannon. It was designed to house 10,000 troops plus another 5,000 in case of emergency, with food supplies for a year. The Citadel was never put to the test as a refuge from attack. A monument in the courtyard marks the site of the lime pit in which Christophe was buried.

KENSCOFF, 16 miles from town via Pétionville, is located at a 4,500-foot elevation. Four miles beyond is Furcy, at 6,000 feet–four miles of magnificent mountain vistas, with **Pic La Selle** the highest peak at 8,793 feet. Coming or going, one should branch off the main road to **Boutillier** for a magnificent panorama of the mountains, the Gulf of Gonaïve, the Cul-de-Sac Plaine and Port-au-Prince.

LA GONÂVE, in the bay, is headquarters for sport fishermen. This is the island to which Faustin Wirkus, a U. S. Marine sergeant, went "absent without leave" to proclaim himself king. The story of his experiences, in the book *The White King of La Gonâve,* makes fascinating reading.

On the northern peninsula is **Saint Marc,** 60 miles north of Port-au-Prince. Eight hundred Haitians sailed from here to the U.S. to offer their services during the American War of Independence, their number including Henri Christophe, who later became King of northern Haiti. **Gonaïves,** north of Saint Marc, is of Indian origin. In its Place d'Armes, Dessalines proclaimed the island's independence in 1804; an independence memorial and a modern cathedral mark the spot. Toussaint was captured near here by the French. Much farther north offshore from the little town of Port-de-Paix is **Tortuga Island,** which has the largest collection of relics of the Arawak Indians to be found in the West Indies.

On the southern peninsula is the town of **Jérémie,** the birthplace of the father of Alexandre Dumas; **Les Cayes,** a port city where Audubon was born in 1785, where Simon Bolívar took refuge in 1815 and obtained military aid; and **Jacmel,** a nice old town with lovely nearby beaches. Jacmel, 60 miles south of the capital, was an old-time buccaneer hangout and is a present-day coffee center. To the east of Jacmel is the **Pine Forest,** an area that covers 150,000 acres and contains rare birds and tropical plants. En route, about 22 miles from Port-au-Prince, is **Lake Étang Saumâtre,** a hunter's paradise.

PORT-AU-PRINCE, the capital, was laid out in 1749, and has been the capital since 1807. The city curves around its fine harbor, the Bay of Gonâve, and sprawls up the encircling mountains from the reclaimed land of the Exposition Grounds (site of the 1950 World's Fair) on the waterfront, to the fashionable suburban area of Pétionville. The architecture of the city is a mixture of old but elegant wooden French colonial homes with balconies, slums of tumbledown thatched-roof "cailles" (huts) with dirt floors, and ultramodern structures. Sidewalks, arcaded against the sun, line the streets in the center of town; merchandise on crude stands is for sale on the sidewalk.

A boulevard named for Harry Truman runs through the Exposition Grounds, where many of the fair buildings have been converted to permanent use. The area has museums, restaurants, bars, shops, the **Théâtre de Verdure,** the model of the Sistine Chapel, and an outdoor mural depicting the history of the country. In town in a central recreation park and military field, the **Champs-de-Mars,** are statues of Haiti's noted men—Toussaint, Dessalines, Christophe, and Pétion. Here are the various government ministries, the Caserne Dessalines—headquarters of the army—as well as theaters and restaurants. At the **Place des Héros de l'Indépendence** is the mausoleum in which Alexandre Pétion and Jean Jacques Dessalines are buried. The three-domed **National Palace,** a replica of the Petit Palais on the Champs Elysées in Paris, is the official residence of the President. The **National Museum** houses a collection pertaining to Haiti's history: one of its chief pride-and-joy items is the iron anchor of the *Santa Maria,* flagship of Columbus. Most-photographed sight is probably the Moorish turrets of the **Iron Market** where native merchandise is sold. Most unusual and intriguing sight are the murals in the Episcopal **Cathedral of St. Trinité,** painted by noted Haitian artists, of Biblical scenes but with local landscapes inserted and voodoo figures added—even a policeman chasing a chicken thief. There is a pink and white, double-towered Catholic **Basilica of Notre Dame,** and an old seventeenth-century French Colonial church. The **Rhum Barbancourt Distillery,** six miles out at Damien, and the **Haitian-American Sugar Company** welcome inspection.

In Port-au-Prince the fascinating art of Haiti can be seen at the **Centre d'Art,** the **Foyer des Arts Plastiques,** the **Musée des Beaux Arts,** the **Musée du Peuple Haïtien.** Several hotels have outstanding paintings or murals by noted Haitian artists. There is a collection of Columbian, Indian, and African relics—including a fascinating collection of voodoo ritual items—in the **Museum of Ethnology.** The private collection of Kurt Fisher, which can be seen by appointment, contains articles pertaining to archaeology, history, numismatics, and ethnology, with literally thousands of voodoo items.

Periodic **music concerts** are given, often with visiting celebrities. There are open-air concerts Sunday evenings near the illuminated fountains in the Exposition Grounds. **Plays** are produced by the Comédie de Paris Troupe. The **Institute Français de Haiti** in the Exposition Grounds has its own theater, and at the **Théâtre de Verdure** wonderful performances of native dancing and drumming are given. Performances by the Dejean Chorus are also considered excellent.

SPORTS AND RECREATION. Most of the major hotels and clubs in Port-au-Prince have swimming pools. **Kyona Beach,** about a 40-minute drive to the north of Port-au-Prince, offers dressing rooms, a restaurant, fishing and overnight facilities. **Ile à Cabrit,** 20 minutes out of Port-au-Prince and a half mile offshore, has cabãnas, a snack bar, and a dance floor. Sixty-acre **Cacique Island,** across the bay from Port-au-Prince and the last refuge of the Arawak Indians in the Caribbean, has been developed as a water resort with complete facilities. **Carrefour Raymonds Beach,** about ten miles out of Jacmel, can be reached by car in four to five hours or 15 minutes by plane from Port-au-Prince.

Fishing, popular throughout Haiti, is best at Kyona Beach and La Gonâve (headquarters for deep-sea fishing). **Water skiing** and **spearfishing** are also excellent, as is **snorkeling,** best at the Sand Cay coral reef Submarine Gardens. Glass-bottomed boats, available for charter, go daily to Sand Cay in the Bay of Gonâve from Port-au-Prince.

Hunting is permitted all year round, but it is best from July to February (to be hunted are wild goat, wild boar, crocodile; a variety of birds, including duck, guinea hen, and pigeon). For the butterfly collector, Haiti is the place to be in late summer. Other sports include **golf, tennis,** and **horseback riding,** while the spectator can enjoy **soccer,** the national game; **baseball,** and **cockfighting,** popular throughout Haiti. All towns have their gagueres—cockpits. Other sporting events may take place at the Sylvio Cator Stadium in Port-au-Prince, which seats over 20,000.

Entertainment at night is largely at hotels and clubs, in the form of dancing and folk dancing shows. The government-controlled **International Casino** should be visited, and for an unusual experience, attend a voodoo ceremony, called *vaudou* in Creole, *vôdu* in French.

SPECIAL EVENTS. **Mardi Gras Carnival** is a very gay affair during the three days prior to Lent. There are parades of floats, bands, costumed people, and a costume ball. **Rara** is a Good Friday and Easter peasant carnival celebration, before the crop season. It is held in all parts of the country and can be seen along the road to Leogane, 22 miles from Port-au-Prince. In June there are religious processions in celebration of Corpus Christi. Official celebrations are held on **Independence Day,** January 1; **Pan American Day,** April 1, with official ceremonies; **Agricultural and Labor Day,** May 1, with a parade of workers and employees and an Agricultural Fair; **Army Day,** November 18, with a military parade; the anniversary of **Dessalines' death,** October 17, with official ceremonies; **Columbus' Discovery Day,** December 5, with official ceremonies.

DINING AND SHOPPING. Haitian, French Creole, and excellent French cooking are served, as are German and Italian dishes. Specialties to be tried include *pain patate* (sweet potato pudding), mango pie, *homard flambú* (flaming rock lobster), *grillo et banane pesé* (pork chops with plantain), *diri et djondjon* (rice and black dried mushrooms), and *ti malice* (a delicious sauce made of onions and herbs). Fine tropical fruits grow wild throughout Haiti, though rice and beans are the main dish of the peasants. Haiti is famous for its Barbancourt Rum (Five-Star is the best), while Clairin, a local rum, and champagnes of the area are excellent. When the French occupied the island, they found the soil and climate suitable for the production of brandy. They introduced the art of distilling and exported the results to France.

Shopping is a treat in Haiti and offers some of the best buys in the Caribbean; its free-port prices present a substantial savings over prices in the U.S. Fixed prices are usual in the shops but prepare to pay about a third of the asking prices in the markets. Prowl through the Iron Market—*Marche Vallières*—in Port-au-Prince. Less interesting from the shopping point of view, but a colorful sight, is the open-air market on the waterfront used by the poorer peasants.

Handicraft is particularly appealing in Haiti, is in good taste and of good quality—fine mahogany, paintings and sculpture, hand-loomed textiles, hand-woven and hand-dyed rugs, embroidered dresses and blouses, ceramics, good tortoise shell jewelry, voodoo drums, sisal hats, bags and place mats. Dolls and native recordings are other good buys. Imports include German cameras, Swiss watches, French perfume, English cashmeres, woolens and leather goods, Danish silver, Swedish crystal, and china.

DOMINICAN REPUBLIC

The Dominican Republic (*República Dominicana*) occupies the eastern two-thirds of the island of Hispaniola, which it shares with Haiti. The area on its side of the 193-mile borderline between the two republics is an approximate 235 miles (east–west) by 165 miles (north–south), with 600 miles of coastline.

THE LAND. Four-fifths of the country is mountainous, a series of massive ranges, with the highest peaks of the entire Antilles in the heavily forested Cordillera Central range, running the length of the country, southeast to northwest. The highest point in the country is Pico Duarte, 10,249 feet. The well-watered area north of the Cordillera is extremely fertile, and sugar, cacao, and coffee are grown there with great success. The largest lowland, Cibao, is in the north. The lowlands in the southeast also produce a great deal of sugar. More arid areas are found in the west and southwest. Of the many waterways, the Yaque del Norte, Yaque del Sur, Ozama, and the Yuna are the most important. Lago Enriquillo, 22 miles inland, is the principal lake. It is 27 by 8 miles, is about 150 feet below sea level and is saltier than the sea itself. The Republic's coastline has many excellent natural harbors and fine stretches of beach, particularly on the north shore. The flora is varied and luxuriant. Fine woods abound—mahogany (the national tree), rosewood, satinwood, grugru, palm, logwood, cypress, ironwood, pine, and oak. Important deposits of gold, copper, gypsum, rock salt, iron, petroleum, silver, bauxite and platinum have been found.

THE CLIMATE. The Dominican Republic is in the tropical zone, but the northeast trade winds keep it comfortable. It has an average 77-degree temperature in the lowlands, is cooler in the mountains. Rainfall is heaviest north of the Cordillera, averaging about 120 inches a year; the west and southwest area is arid. Rains usually come between May and November, with occasional hurricanes.

THE PEOPLE. The population of the Dominican Republic is over 4 million. About 33 percent of the people live in the cities, while 67 percent reside on farms or in small towns. Dress in the cities is much like that in the United States; in the country the men usually wear blue denim work clothes and the women, cotton dresses.

Most Dominicans are of Spanish, Indian, and Negro ancestry. Mulattos comprise about 70 percent of the population; about 15 percent are pure Negro; the other 15 percent are Europeans (chiefly from Spain).

Although Spanish is the official language of the country, English is largely used for business, and the tourist will have little difficulty in finding English-speaking people. English is an eight-year required subject in the schools. French and Portuguese are also offered to the students.

Primary education is free and compulsory for children from the age of 7 to 14. There are secondary schools and vocational schools. The University of Santo Domingo was founded in 1538 by the Dominican Fathers and is the oldest in the Western Hemisphere. Its present student body exceeds 4,000. A campaign against illiteracy has been in progress since 1941. The government has subsidized many new schools and trained many new teachers. Today about 64 of every 100 persons can read and write.

Roman Catholicism is the state religion but complete religious freedom exists.

AGRICULTURE. The Dominican Republic is chiefly agricultural. About four out of five people earn their living from the 15,500 square miles of fertile soil. Sugar, cacao, coffee, rice, molasses, bananas, leaf tobacco, corn, peanuts, rice, and oranges are the principal crops. Livestock also plays an important role; cattle, hogs, horses, goats, and poultry all enhance farm prosperity. Some farmers have their own small farms while others work on large plantations. There is also extensive forestry.

INDUSTRY. The main industry is preparation of sugar for export. There are many *centrales,* or sugar mills, throughout the country. Other products made in the Dominican Republic include rum, molasses, alcohol, cement, peanut oil, chocolate, tobacco products, cordage, textiles, furniture, animal feed, and meat packing. Sugar accounts for about half the country's exports, followed by cocoa beans, coffee, chocolate, tobacco leaf, and beeswax. Large deposits of nickel are mined and exported abroad.

CITIES. The major cities in the Dominican Republic offer the tourist a contrast between the lavish world of the Spanish conquistador and the bustle of a modern-day metropolis.

CONCEPCIÓN DE LA VEGA, 65 miles northwest of the capital, is an old Colonial city on the Camú River. It was founded by Bartholomew Columbus in 1495 on the other side of the river (the ruins of the old city and fort can still be seen), but was moved to its present site after the 1564 earthquake. Four miles north of here is the **Santo Cerro Shrine and Church** to the Virgin of Mercedes; it marks the site where the Virgin appeared to Christopher Columbus during the Vega Real battle. There is a good mountain resort hotel nearby.

PUERTO PLATA, the chief port on the north coast of the country, was founded by Christopher Columbus in 1503, and has become an important exporting, fishing, and processing center. The town produces matches and dairy products, is the home of the country's biggest chocolate factory, and is near a large resort area on the coast about 20 miles to the east.

SAN CRISTÓBAL, the birthplace of the late Generalissimo Trujillo, lies about 20 miles west of Santo Domingo. It is reached by an excellent highway and is near the site of the gold mines which lured the Spanish to the southern coast. The present town is new, the two major attractions being the murals painted by Vanetti and found in a mustard-yellow church with blue shutters, and the fabulous **La Casa del Cerro,** built by donations from the people of the country as a home for Trujillo, and presented to him in 1950. At **La Toma,** two natural pools are open to the public. Also of interest are the coffee and sugar plantations, rice paddies, and tobacco farms.

SAN PEDRO DE MARCORÍS is a port and center for the cultivation of sugar cane and shipping of sugar. It lies about 40 miles east of Santo Domingo along the coast.

SANTIAGO DE LOS CABALLEROS, in the Cibao region on the Yaque del Norte River, is the country's second city of importance. It is an ancient Colonial city, very Spanish in atmosphere, and a good place to see the more genuine Dominican life.

The city was founded in the early 1500's by Bartholomew Columbus but rebuilt on its present site after the 1564 earthquake. The decisive battle for independence was fought in Santiago in 1844.

This area is the most highly cultivated in the country, with extensive irrigation and rich soil. It has fine scenery, a healthy climate, and good hotels, one of which has a casino. There are many industries here and it is a distributing and processing center for the northern part of the country. Saturday is the best day to visit the market.

SANTO DOMINGO was settled in 1496 by Bartholomew Columbus and stands as the oldest city in the New World. Its original site was the east bank of the River Ozama, but in 1502 a plague of ants and a hurricane combined to make the higher west bank a more attractive location. The new city stretches west from the old Spanish town, along the waterfront, and into the rolling hills behind.

Modern Santo Domingo is a bright and beautiful capital city with magnificent boulevards and a permanent civic center, complete with mammoth outdoor theater, casino, and imposing public buildings. Many lovely parks grace the city, with Parque Infantil Eugenio Maria Hostos Park, on George Washington Avenue, devoted exclusively to children.

Some of the historical sites in town can be covered on foot. **Primate Cathedral,** oldest in the Americas, was built between the years of 1514 and 1540. Its Treasure Room contains magnificent relics. Just inside the main entrance is an elaborate marble, bronze and onyx monument to Christopher Columbus containing the remains of his body in a bronze casket that is opened to the public with three keys every October 12.

The **Administrative Council's Palace,** with a high clock tower, was built to serve as the first city hall in the eighteenth century. The **Tower of Homage** was built in 1503 and is the oldest stone fortress in the Americas; it now serves as a prison. The buildings around the tower, known as "La Forteleza," were built in 1787 and enlarged in 1942. **Casa del Cordón** is the first mud-walled, two-storied house built in the city, in 1502. The plaster cord above the door is the symbol of the Order of St. Francis.

St. Francis Church and Monastery, now in ruins, was the first monastery in the Americas, begun in 1504. Bartholomew Columbus was buried here, as was Alonso de Ojeda, the "Conqueror of Venezuela." **San Nicolás de Bari** was the first hospital in the Americas, built 1503–08; its ruins also may be visited.

Alcázar de Colón was the palace of Diego, son of Christopher Columbus. Started in 1509, it was completed in record time by 1,000 Indian laborers under the supervision of 22 master builders from Spain. Restoration efforts have been under way for many years and the palace is now officially open to the public. The original plans and designs were carried out to the last detail; the result is one of the most important contributions to historical restoration to be found in the Americas. Interesting to see is **Ceiba de Colón,** a large trunk of a silk-cotton tree on the bank of the Ozama River to which Columbus is said to have chained his ships.

Other points of interest, which require transportation, are on the other side of the river. **Church of the Rosary,** constructed in 1511–16, has since been rebuilt but it is called the oldest church in the Americas. The **Altar de la Patria,** a lovely national shrine at the Parque de la Independencia, contains the remains of the three men who began the movement for independence in 1844—Juan Pablo Duarte, Francisco del Rosario Sanchez, and Ramón Matias Mella. An eternal flame burns here in their memory. The **Jardín Zoológico** to the west of town is a beautifully landscaped little zoo.

SPORTS AND RECREATION. Most of the recreational areas of the Republic are in Santo Domingo, but resorts and hotels can be found in the mountains, along the coast, and in other cities.

Boca Chica is a small but popular shore resort 19 miles east of Santo Domingo. It offers shallow water for safe swimming and small boats, has a fine beach and excellent accommodations. At **Jarabacoa,** a small mountain village, the government has developed a beautiful resort hotel set in a pine forest. It claims an average temperature all year round of about 75 degrees and offers an assortment of facilities and activities. About 15 miles south on the same road is **Constanza,** where the government has built a Swiss-type chalet hotel. It is strikingly set and offers varied facilities, such as a nearby lake and a beautiful waterfall. About 20 miles east of Puerto Plata, along the Atlantic, the new resort area of **Sosua** has been developed. It has a new and pleasantly rustic hotel with an excellent beach and an attractive bay, and offers food with a Viennese accent.

Within Santo Domingo one can find numerous art exhibits, which are held in the National Gallery of the beautiful **Palace of Fine Arts.** Operas are also given in the auditorium of the Palace. A national symphony orchestra gives concerts throughout the year, and plays are produced periodically by a Little Theater group. The **Academy of Ballet** puts on productions in various theaters. One of the leading hotels has an outdoor theater where native folk-dancing exhibitions are given. There are good air-conditioned movie theaters.

Dancing with floor shows is available at hotels and night clubs. The *merengue* is the national dance. There are sophisticated casinos in Santo Domingo and at Santiago, and weekly lottery drawings at the Lotería Nacional building in the capital.

There are year-round events in Santo Domingo's fine sports stadium that seats 24,000. The **Perla Antillana Race Track,** in the northwest corner of Santo Domingo, is the scene of regularly scheduled polo matches, as well as an all-year-round season of horse racing. Other spectator sports include **baseball, dog racing, cockfighting, bullfighting,** and **water polo.** There is **tennis, golf,** and some **hunting; fishing** is excellent—stream, spear and deep sea. Sailboats and motorboats are available as well as fully-equipped deep-sea fishing boats. There is **swimming** in hotel and club pools and at beaches, and **waterski** facilities are available throughout the year. **Horseback riding** is popular in the mountains.

SPECIAL EVENTS. Island-wide services celebrate **Corpus Christi,** but each town and village has its own special annual Saints-Day celebration. Outstanding are the **Pilgrimage to Our Lady of Altagracia** at Higuey on January 21; **St. James Day** at Santiago on July 25, at Santa Cerro and Mercies on September 24; **St. Andrews Day** at Boca Chica on November 30. **Carnival** is held on Independence Day, February 27 and in Boca Chica there is an informal carnival the Saturday before Easter.

A **sports day parade** is held on June 5.

DINING AND SHOPPING. The food in the Dominican Republic is basically Spanish, but Continental and Chinese foods are also available. The old Spanish favorites, *arroz con pollo* (chicken and rice), *sancocho* (a soup-like stew), *casabe* (a tortilla-like hard bread made from grated dried yucca), *pastelitos* (meat-filled pastries), are all good here, as are seafood, and *sambumbia, asopao,* and *piñonate* (a coconut and milk dessert). A *cremita* is the Dominican version of an Eskimo Pie. Rum is the native drink.

Santo Domingo is rapidly becoming a shopping center comparable in values and range of wares with other cities of the Caribbean. Each of the first-class hotels has one or more shops offering souvenirs, imports of various types, as well as some locally designed and made handicrafts. There is free-port shopping at the Plaza. Mahogany pieces, tortoise shell, basketware, and embroideries are available. There are some small shops near the cathedral and also at the *Mercado Modelo,* which is indeed a model market, and is one of the most interesting and new additions to the old city. Modern and functional, it is a huge arched room with dozens of stalls and exhibits, selling everything imaginable.

Puerto Rico

Just a few hours away by air, the island of Puerto Rico occupies a unique position in the annals of United States history—that of a Commonwealth. North American in status and progress, it is completely Spanish in atmosphere and culture. To visit Puerto Rico is to have all the advantages and excitement of overseas travel but with none of the inconveniences: no passports or visas are needed, there are no differences in currency, and virtually no language problem, for although the primary language is Spanish, it is a rarity when the visitor encounters anyone who cannot speak English. Accommodations range from the YMCA to ultra-modern hotels at least as sumptuous as those on the U.S. mainland. This applies not only to San Juan but throughout the island. Puerto Rico has excellent restaurants; gay, sophisticated night clubs and gambling casinos; much of cultural interest and many historic sights. For a healthy outdoor existence, almost every type of sport is possible, except, of course, those which require snow and ice. To add to that feeling of being "at home abroad," the Elks, Rotary, Masons, Knights of Columbus, Lions, a

PUERTO RICO

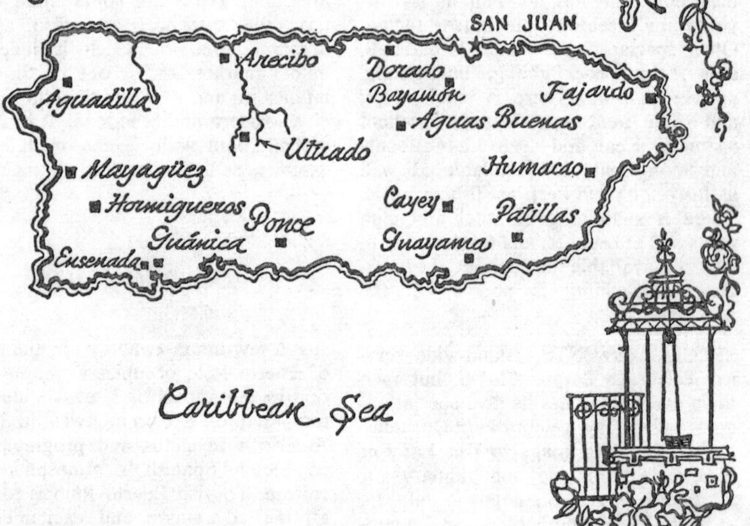

Woman's University Club, even the Boy and Girl Scouts are represented. Excellent schools, hospitals, doctors, and dentists are also available. The water is pure, the milk is pasteurized and dated, the food varied, and the liquor excellent. For anyone who wants a less sophisticated, quieter type of existence, there are secluded hide-away spots in beautiful settings.

THE LAND. Puerto Rico's 105 by 35 mile area contains vistas of unsurpassed beauty. Flat coastal plains slope back from fine golden-yellow sandy beaches to mountains that cover nearly three-quarters of the island's surface. Sierra de Luquillo and the Cordillera Central ranges cross Puerto Rico in an east-west direction, with Cerro de Punta rising to 4,398 feet, the highest point. The many rivers are navigable for only short distances but provide valuable irrigation and water power. There are quantities of limestone, clays and gypsum available for building purposes as well as a high-grade marble. Sugar cane is the chief crop, which in turn provides molasses for the important rum industry. Tobacco is grown in the east-central mountain area and coffee in the west-central mountains. Though second only to sugar in the area of cultivation, coffee is no longer a chief export. Puerto Rican sea-island cotton is of a high quality; the main vegetable exports are tomatoes, cucumbers, peppers, pineapples and coconuts. Numerous small islands include Vieques, Culebra, and Mona.

THE CLIMATE. Average all-year-round temperature is a delightful 76 degrees on the coastal areas, although cooler in the mountains. There is only about a six-degree difference between winter and summer; it is somewhat humid during the summer months but not unbearably so. Puerto Rico can claim practically perpetual sunshine as it has only about five sunless days throughout the entire year. Rainfall varies with the location from about 40 to 150 inches, with 200 inches in the **Caribbean National Forest** at El Yunque Mountain. There are brief rains throughout the year, slightly more frequent during May to December.

THE PEOPLE. Columbus discovered the island on November 19, 1493, on his second voyage, and called it San Juan Bautista in honor of St. John the Baptist. He landed on the northwest coast (at a spot that is now Aguadilla) but made no attempt at colonization. The first colonizers were the conquistadors under Ponce de León, in 1508, who founded Caparra near San Juan Harbor between the present Santurce and Bayamón districts—the second oldest city in the New World. Later, for reasons of defense, the settlement was moved to the site of the present "Old San Juan" on an island in the bay. Upon arriving, Ponce de León is said to have exclaimed, "*¡Qué puerto rico!*" ("what a rich port") and so named the area around the harbor. For some unknown reason, in the course of the island's history, the names of the capital and the island were transposed and Puerto Rico came to be used as the name of the island, and San Juan, that of its capital. Earlier, in 1514, the island was divided into two districts, each autonomous with its own administrators; the eastern section was referred to as Puerto Rico, the western section as San Germán.

The early years for the settlers were difficult ones. Hurricanes, more frequent then than now, did considerable damage; the Caribs staged raids from other islands; the British, French and Dutch all attacked, raided, burned and plundered from time to time, as did the pirates.

During the Spanish-American War in 1898, American troops landed on the south coast at Guánica and the Spanish troops retreated before them. Puerto Ricans refused to come to the aid of the Spanish and welcomed the U.S. troops. On October 18, the island was surrendered to the North Americans (and ceded to the United States by the Treaty of Paris). It remained under a U.S. military government for the next year and one-half.

One of the most dramatically impressive highlights of Puerto Rico's history has taken place since 1948—"Operation Bootstrap," an effort at economic development to make the island self-sufficient and to raise the standard of living. It has been highly successful—over 1,000 new industries have been developed with the result that, since 1956, industry has surpassed agriculture for the first time as the principal source of income. Tourism has also become an important "industry."

In April, 1900, Congress passed the Foraker Act which instituted civil government. As drawn up, the arrangement did not please the Puerto Ricans, nor did a subsequent Organic Act. An improved Act in 1917 made Puerto Rico a territory of the U.S. and granted U.S. citizenship to all who wanted it, but former status was permitted those who preferred it—only 288 persons chose to retain their old status. The first native-born governor was appointed in 1946 by President Truman, and in 1948 Puerto Rico for the first time elected its own governor.

On July 3, 1950, Puerto Rico was granted the right to draw up its own constitution. The island voted for commonwealth status and on July 25, 1952, the Commonwealth of Puerto Rico came into being. In November 1953, the U.N. passed a resolution granting self-government. In a referendum in 1967, Puerto Ricans favored continuation of commonwealth status, although movements for statehood and independence are growing. It has a governor, elected by direct vote of the people, a senate of

16 members and a house of representatives of 40 members, elected by direct vote at each general election, for four-year terms. It has its own supreme court plus minor courts. Puerto Rico has no voting representation in the U. S. Congress and thus pays no federal taxes. Autonomous in internal affairs, the U.S. shares responsibility for common defense and foreign relations.

The present population of about 2.7 million is made up of many people of mixed African–Spanish descent. Others are pure Spanish or African. The original Arawak Indians were destroyed in the 16th century. There are many Europeans and "continentals" (a term used by Puerto Ricans to indicate people from the U.S. mainland) who have come to establish businesses or just to enjoy the pleasures and advantages of living on this island. The islanders are known as "Puertorriqueños."

AGRICULTURE. Farming, with 80 percent of the land area used for crops, is the chief industry in Puerto Rico. Sugar cane is the most important crop, although income from dairy and livestock is greater. Other leading crops, in order of value, are tobacco, grown in the east-central mountains; fruit, especially pineapple; and coffee. Due to extensive use of soil over the years, thousands of tons of fertilizers must be added to the soil.

INDUSTRY. As sugar cane is the chief crop, industries based on sugar production are most important to the economy. There are mills which produce raw sugar, those which refine sugar, and others which make rum from molasses. Also of great importance to the economy is the tourist industry. To spur new growth in Puerto Rico, the government set up "Operation Bootstrap," a program of tax exemptions and building, in the 1940's. The program has added many diverse industries to the country.

CITIES. Although Puerto Rico has many towns and villages, there are only three large cities–Mayagüez, Ponce, and San Juan.

MAYAGÜEZ is the island's third-largest city, an important port, and center of the needlework industry. The Federal Agricultural Experiment Station, said to have the largest collection of tropical plants in the world, is just north of town, and is a branch of the University of Puerto Rico. Above the city is **Las Mesas Orchid Nurseries** with around 1,500 varieties. The city has good fishing, swimming, and accommodations. Slightly inland is **Hormigueros,** where on September 8 a pilgrimage is made on the knees of the faithful up a long flight of stairs to the Shrine of Our Lady of Monserrate. The church was built in the early seventeenth century on the spot where a peon working in the fields is reputed to have been saved from a charging bull by his prayer for help from the Virgin de Monserrate.

San Germán, the "City of Hills," is one of the earliest original settlements. Established in 1512 on the south coast, it was gradually pushed back from the sea because of attacking pirates and settled at its present site in 1570. Its most famed "sight" is the Cathedral de Porta Coeli (Gate of Heaven Church) with thick walls and massive doors as protection against the Indians. The original doors, altar, carved wooden pillars, and sounding boards of the pulpit were retained, and the church serves as a museum for old religious art objects. In a Catholic church in this city is a chandelier presented by Queen Isabella. The Inter-American University is also in San Germán.

PARGUERA. Around on the south coast is the charming little fishing village of Parguera with fine accommodations, fishing, boating, swimming. From here one can go out to the zoo and aquarium on **Magüey Island,** and out on **Phosphorescent Bay** in the evening, preferably during the dark of the moon. A little farther along the coast is **Guánica,** where the Americans landed in 1898 during the Spanish-American War–a monument at La Puntita marks the spot. There is a beautiful beach here with dressing rooms, and *cantinas* where food and drink are served. The

South Puerto Rico Sugar Central on the outskirts of Guánica welcomes visitors.

The balance of the trip could follow the southern coast via Ponce and Guayama and continue on up the eastern coast and back along the northern road into San Juan, or a cross-island scenic return to San Juan can be made from Ponce or Guayama. Special sightseeing tours by air are also available.

PONCE. A circle tour across the mountainous interior to **Ponce,** 79 miles from San Juan, can be made in a day if time is limited. There are many routes available, all of them scenic. One possibility would be via **Naranjito** and **Barranquitas,** birthplace and burial site of Luis Muñoz Rivera (1859–1916), one of Puerto Rico's great political leaders (his home has been made a national shrine and museum), and **Coamo**—a health resort, with curative hot mineral baths, dating back to the old Indian days.

Ponce is Puerto Rico's second largest city and an industrial port, as well as a coffee and sugar center. Its firehouse ("Parque de Bombas"), red-and-black striped with yellow and green ornamental trim, is a favorite with photographers. See the Ponce **Museum of Fine Arts** in a restored colonial mansion at 70 Cristina Street; the modern **Catholic University** and its modernistic church; in the **Cathedral of the Virgin of Guadalupe,** the altar painting of the Virgin as she appeared to a Mexican Indian; the beaches. For overnight visitors, a short drive to the northeast leads to **Doña Juana recreational area** and waterfalls; or a boat trip goes ten miles offshore to the **Isla Caja de Muertos.**

To return to San Juan, drive along the south shore to **Guayama,** which was founded in 1736. Between here and **Cayey** is one of the most scenic drives (16 miles) on the island, the **Jajome Highway,** over the northern range of the Cordillera Central. The road passes a replica of the Grotto of Our Lady at Lourdes, the summer residence of the Governor of Puerto Rico, and goes over red brick bridges made by the early Spaniards. About ten miles north of Cayey is **Cidra,** a Treasure Island resort, a popular vacation spot, with large spring-fed, bass-stocked lakes; swimming pools, and horseback trails. From here, one can continue to San Juan via **Caguas,** or **Aguas Buenas,** only a half-hour's drive out of San Juan, a favorite spot for people to come for lunch or dinner or for overnight. One-thousand-foot-high caves can be reached from there by foot or horseback, but they are wet and bat-filled, and torchlights and guides are recommended.

For travelers with enough time, the round-the-island tour is a must. Heading west from San Juan along the north coast, highlights would include the modern church at **Toa Baja;** the fabulous **Dorado Beach** and **Vega Baja** beach areas, nearby **San Vicente Sugar Central;** beach caves at **Mar Chiquita; Manatí,** where the summer pineapple harvest is a colorful sight (a side trip south of here to **Jayuya,** coffee country, passes unusual rock formations). From Manatí take the coastal route, via the old Spanish settlement of Barceloneta, to **Arecibo** (50 miles from San Juan). This is one of the island's oldest cities, dating from 1556, and is a popular swimming and fishing site. There are sugar centrals and rum distilleries in this area at which visitors are welcomed. **Poza del Obispo** is its best beach. Four miles east of town are caves with Indian drawings on the walls. **Arecibo Ionospheric Observatory,** which contains the world's largest radar-radio telescope, is in nearby barrio Esperanza, and is open to visitors. About 30 miles farther on is **Guajataca Beach,** one of the best on the island; food, drink, and overnight accommodations are available. At **Aguadilla,** a memorial cross marks the spot where Columbus is believed to have landed in 1493, though Aguada also claims this distinction. Aguadilla, a lovely place to stay overnight, has good swimming, fishing, and a casino.

SÁBANA GRANDE, nine miles to the east, is the site of the appearance of the Virgin in 1951 to three school children to whom she said that she would return in May. More than 100,000 people

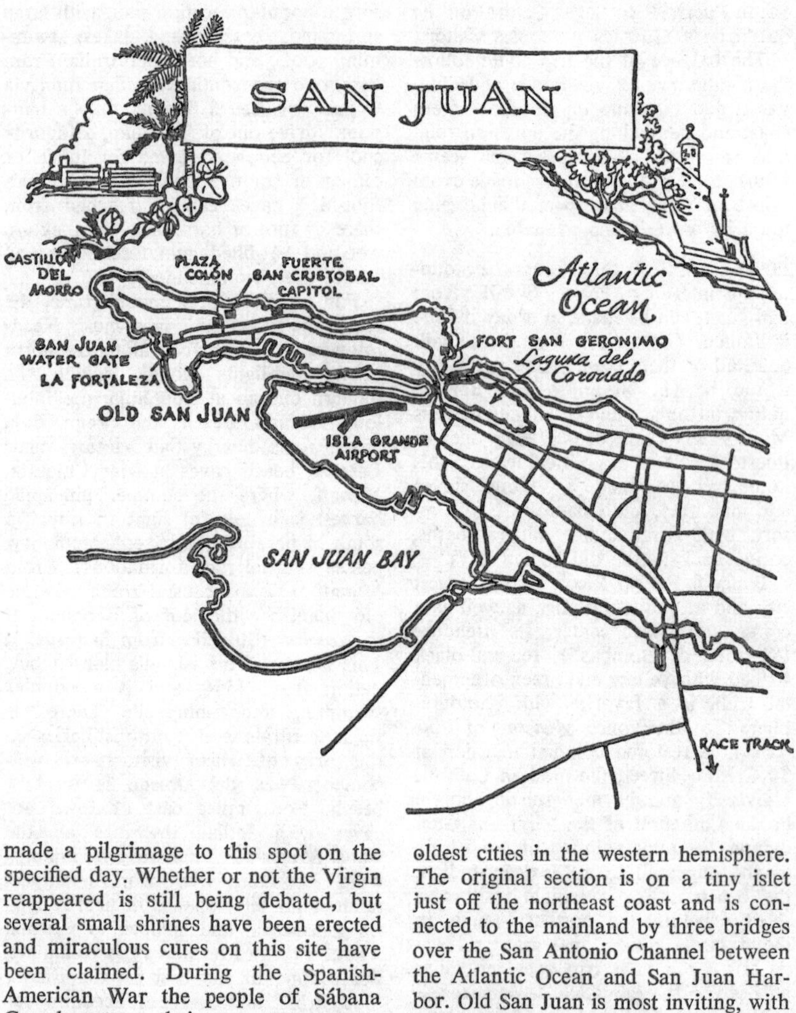

made a pilgrimage to this spot on the specified day. Whether or not the Virgin reappeared is still being debated, but several small shrines have been erected and miraculous cures on this site have been claimed. During the Spanish-American War the people of Sábana Grande set up their own government, an administration that functioned for 12 days.

West of San Germán and beyond **Cabo Rojo** are salt flats, and south of here, **Boquerón Bay,** which offers fine beaches, swimming and snorkeling and the facilities of Boquerón Yacht Club. The bay area served as a hideaway for the pirate Cofresí who, according to legend, haunts a nearby cave where he is said to have hidden his treasures.

SAN JUAN, the capital, is one of the oldest cities in the western hemisphere. The original section is on a tiny islet just off the northeast coast and is connected to the mainland by three bridges over the San Antonio Channel between the Atlantic Ocean and San Juan Harbor. Old San Juan is most inviting, with narrow little tree-shaded streets, some of them still paved with the original bluish glazed blocks brought over as ballast in the old Spanish sailing ships, and certain of them still lighted by the original beautiful old Spanish gas lamps—some mounted on posts, some on the façades of buildings. Its seventeenth-century, Spanish-Renaissance-style, pastel-colored homes and buildings are most appealing, with arches and balconies, wrought-iron grillwork at the windows, with handsome tile floors inside, inviting patios and gardens outside. The business section has no *mañana* spirit: large office buildings and fine shops line the crowded, noisy streets where there is always great activity. In spite of its aggressive North American business atmosphere, one still finds a delicious foreign flavor in the Spanish one hears on all sides, the street vendors who carry their wares in little carts or on their heads, the shouts of the myriad lottery-ticket salespeople, the whistle of the scissors grinder, the playing of his triangle by the Puerto Rican equivalent of a Good Humor salesman.

Spreading back over the mainland is the newer section of the city, chiefly the residential, resort hotel, and social club area, although commercial ventures and fine shopping centers have been established here. San Juan now comprises **Old San Juan,** the main banking and commercial center; **Condado,** a hotel and residential area; **Miramar,** across the lagoon; and the large and crowded **Santurce** district, with excellent shopping areas, deluxe movie houses, and residences. There are many suburban areas south and beyond here, including the former separate municipality of **Río Piedras.** Total population of the city, including the suburbs, is over 840,000.

In historic Old San Juan, the following are all within a radius of a half dozen blocks and can be covered on foot:

(1) **El Morro** (Fortress of San Felipé). The Spaniards made San Juan one of the best-fortified cities in this hemisphere, and El Morro, construction beginning in 1539, was their largest and strongest fort. Guided tours go through its passageways, dungeons, storerooms, and chapel (constructed with windows slanted in such fashion that no cannon ball could make a direct hit on the altar). Its 18-foot-thick surrounding walls rise 145 feet above the sea; its moat has been filled in to make a golf course.

(2) **San José Church** was first known as St. Thomas Aquinas, but the name was changed when it became Jesuit property in 1863. It was the first building in the city (1522) and is the oldest church in continuous use in the Americas. The very old crucified Christ on the side wall was so made that it could be removed in time of battle. An example of the early architecture used in this part of the world can be seen in the circular stairway and Gothic ceiling.

(3) The statue of **Ponce de León** outside the church in San José Plaza was cast from a bronze cannon captured in 1797 from the British and faces his original settlement across the bay at Caparra.

(4) **Casa Blanca** was built in 1523 as a residence for Ponce de León, who died before it was completed, but his descendants used it for 250 years. It is now the residence of the commanding general of Puerto Rican-based U.S. troops.

(5) **San Juan Gate** is the only remaining gate of the old wall. Visitors will want to walk through it to see the views of Casa Blanca, La Fortaleza and a portion of the old wall. Governors landed here in the old Spanish days and entered the city through this gate with much pomp and ceremony.

(6) The **Cathedral of San Juan Bautista** is a much revered church with a history of disaster. Originally constructed as a little thatch-roofed structure in 1512, it has suffered from earthquake and hurricane, was plundered during the occupation of the Dutch and in 1598 lost its bells and organ during the 157-day occupation of England's Earl of Cumberland, who stole them. The remains of Ponce de León are here; also, in a glass case is the body of a converted Roman soldier from the Catacombs of Rome which is considered a "first-class relic." The present Spanish Renaissance Church was built in 1542.

(7) **La Fortaleza,** also known as the Palace of Santa Catalina, was built originally (between 1533 and 1540) to serve as a fort. Burned by the Dutch during a raid in 1625, it was then rebuilt as it now stands. The home of Puerto Rican governors for over 300 years, it is open to the public and should

be visited. Restored in 1939–40, it still has the original marble floors and mahogany stairway with a fine dome over it, a Round Room where gold was stored, with a chute from the upper floors down which the gold could be dropped; and a little chapel. The blocks in the entryway served as ballast in the old Spanish ships which came over to collect treasure to take back to the mother country. The gardens are lovely.

(8) **San Cristo Chapel,** called the smallest public chapel in the world, has a superb altar of gold and silver repoussé work. It was erected in 1753 by General Tomás Mateo Prats as a memorial for Baltasar Montañez, whose horse galloped out of control down Calle Cristo and leaped over the 70-foot cliff at the end of the street to the rocks below. The horseman miraculously survived, having been thrown into a tree growing out of the cliff near its base.

(9) To the north of the Plaza de Colón is the **Castillo de San Cristóbal.** This fort, begun in 1631 and completed in 1771, was built as a protection against attack from the mainland; it was a 20-foot-thick fan of walls known by the Spanish word for fan, "El Abanico." Many legends are connected with the fort; a miraculous painting of San Cristóbal over a water cistern is said to have kept it always full of water even in times of drought, and there is a haunted sentry box from which a sentry was said to have been spirited away by the devil. The first shot of the Spanish-American War was fired from here at the *U.S.S. Yale*. At present it is used as a U. S. Army base.

(10) **Plaza de Colón** is in the center of Old San Juan and has a monument to Columbus erected in 1893 to commemorate the 400th anniversary of his discovery of Puerto Rico. This is a city bus terminal; bus stops are indicated by yellow posts or yellow paint on the curbing and marked *Parada* ("stop") and sections are zoned. Stop 12 means the whole area around that stop and these numbers are often given as an address; the Department of Tourism location, for example, is at Stop **22,** Santurce.

Take a bus or a taxi from Plaza de Colón and drive toward the mainland past the large white Renaissance capitol building, begun in 1925, and the **Muñoz Rivera Park.** A sixteenth-century *polvorín* ("powder house") near the entrance is now a national history museum; there are a small zoo and a children's playground nearby. **Sixto Escobar Stadium,** named for a Puerto Rican bantamweight boxing champion of the world (1938–40), seats over 14,000 and was used for many sports activities. It has largely been supplanted by the newer and larger **Hiram Bithorn Stadium** in suburban Hato Rey, which is the setting for popular night baseball games in Puerto Rico's Winter League.

Beyond the park, on a point, is **San Gerónimo Fort,** built in the eighteenth century to protect the part of Old San Juan that lies outside the walls surrounding the old city. It now houses the Museum of Military History. Bridges from this area lead to the mainland and outlying suburban and resort hotel districts. A little more than seven miles out is **Río Piedras.** To be visited are the **University of Puerto Rico** with its somewhat surprising baroque tower façade, and the 21 seals of the Americas, the seal of Puerto Rico and those of various universities, which decorate the steps and floor of the entrance of the main buildings; also the **Río Piedras Museum, art gallery** and **aquarium.** The Anglican Church here was the first Protestant church permitted by the Spaniards in this hemisphere (1870).

Several industries in these suburban areas welcome visitors, as does the Puerto Rican Pottery Company in San Juan.

A lovely 30-mile drive from San Juan leads to **El Yunque** ("the anvil"), a 3,496-foot elevation in a national rain forest filled with luxuriant tropical growth. Millions of tiny wild orchids, 30-foot-high ferns, and hundreds of varieties of trees and plants growing in their native state can be seen. In the forest are picnic sites, a restaurant, swimming pools, overnight facilities, and a watch tower. Also nearby is **Luquillo Beach,** two and one-half miles long and said to be one of the world's most attractive, with picnic sites, "change-huts," restaurant, bar, and boating. On the return to San Juan via Loíza Aldea, ferries are hand-poled across the Loíza River. With more time to spare, swing from Luquillo Beach around to the east coast to **Las Croabas,** a little fishing village and the sumptuous **El Conquistador Hotel** on the cliffs above–and south of here to **Fajardo,** a popular sailing and fishing center. Below Fajardo is **Punta Santiago,** Humacao Beach, with dressing-room facilities. Offshore is the little island of **Cayo de Santiago** where rhesus monkeys are kept for scientific research.

VIEQUES. Off Puerto Rico's coast is the island of **Vieques.** Geographically, Vieques and nearby **Culebra Island** are part of the Virgin Isle group and were once known as the Spanish Virgin Islands, having been under Spanish control from 1753 to 1898. They are now part of Puerto Rico. Vieques is in the process of being developed as a major resort area with a hotel, residences, golf, and yachting facilities.

Isabel Segunda is the main town and shows both the Spanish and French influences. There is a lighthouse on Punta Mulac and a fort looking down on the town. The island is attractive rolling hill country. Sugar and fruits are grown; the main industry is cattle raising and dairying.

SPORTS AND RECREATION. At least 50 world's **fishing** records have been broken in Puerto Rico, due to its excellent year-round facilities. Many tournaments, sponsored by the Club Náutico in San Juan, add to the competition. Fresh-water fishing is outstanding in the lakes and rivers; there are **skeet-** and **trap-shooting** ranges; and fowl season runs from mid-December to mid-February. **Sailing** in Puerto Rico's protected harbors is popular, with several yacht clubs providing boats for the use of visitors.

Glass-bottomed boat trips are made twice daily during most of the year from Boca de Cangrejos, which also offers **swimming,** fishing, and picnicking possibilities. There are beautiful beaches all around the island, most of which are protected from too-heavy surf and the big-game fish by offshore reefs. Many of the San Juan hotels and clubs have pools; there are fresh-water pools at El Yunque rain forest and throughout the island.

Other active sports include **water-skiing, skin-diving, snorkeling, golf, tennis, horseback riding,** and **bowling.** There are many chess clubs where visitors are welcome. Among spectator sports are **horse racing,** all year round at the El Comandante race track, called "the Ascot of the Caribbean," and located three miles out of town; **cockfights** at "galleras" throughout the island; **jai alai, boxing, soccer, tennis. Baseball** is very popular (enthusiasts are called *fanáticos*), and is the major spectator sport from October to February.

Legal gambling in the island's plush casinos is a popular pastime. The lottery is government-sponsored, with weekly, and some special drawings. The Government Lottery Building in San Juan is open to the public for inspection.

Art exhibits are held regularly at the **Institute of Puerto Rican Culture** at Plaza de Colón in San Juan. Also in San Juan there is an **Ateneo Museum** and a historical and industrial museum in **Muñoz Rivera Park.**

Plays are frequently given, usually in Spanish. A winter drama festival, featuring Broadway plays and casts in English; plays produced by a Little Theater Group; and ballet highlight the theatrical season.

Concerts, often featuring visiting celebrities, are given throughout the year. Open-air concerts, performed by the Puerto Rican Symphony Orchestra, are presented in Sixto Escobar Stadium; a Pablo Casals Music Festival takes place in late May–early June; and religious festivals provide opportunities to hear native music.

SPECIAL EVENTS. Puerto Rico has the same holidays as the United States, as well as several religious days. Each town and village has a special fiesta to honor its patron saint. The most important holidays are the following: January 6–**Three Kings' Day,** the actual Puerto Rican Christmas celebration, with parades throughout the island; January 11–**birthday of the philosopher Hostos;** March 22–**Abolition,** or **Emancipation Day,** with civic ceremonies, special exhibits, celebrations by various societies; June 23, 24–**St. John's Night;** July 17–**birthday of Muñoz Rivera,** with concerts, recitals, shows, and special exhibits. Also in July, on Santiago Apóstol Day, the town of Loíza Aldea has its famed "fiesta patronal."

July 25–**Commonwealth Day,** commemorating the day Puerto Rico voted for commonwealth status with the United States. Also on July 25 is **José Barbosa Day.** November 19–**Discovery Day,** celebrates Columbus' discovery of Puerto Rico in 1493.

DINING AND SHOPPING. Food is chiefly Spanish and North American, but there are also fine restaurants specializing in French, German, Italian, Hungarian, Chinese, and seafood. Popular Spanish dishes are *arroz con pollo* (chicken and rice), *lechón asado* (barbecued pork), *pasteles* (mashed plantain and chopped meat rolled in a plantain leaf and boiled), *asopao* (shrimp or chicken with rice–a liquid stew), *pastelillos* (dough filled with meat and deep-fat fried), *hallacas* (chicken or pork wrapped in banana leaves, on the order of a tamale), *arroz con dulce* (rice pudding).

Puerto Rican rum is excellent and inexpensive to buy. Most of the rum distilleries permit visitors to go through their plants.

Native crafts include straw and fiber baskets, rugs, and mats; *pava,* the straw hat worn by the sugar workers; needlework; sport clothes with Puerto Rican motifs; attractive pottery; wood, bamboo and leather articles; *esclaves* (slave bracelets), a thin band of silver or gold is added for each year of marriage and an etched band for each child; *pelisse* (string rugs); *santos,* antique primitive wooden figures carved by the early religious settlers; character dolls–over 50 varieties, depicting the types of workers on the island. Imports from all over the world are available but native crafts are definitely the best buys.

U. S. Virgin Islands

"Las Once Mil Virgenes," in memory of the 11,000 martyr-virgins who accompanied St. Ursula on her ocean voyage, is the name Columbus gave to the islands, cays and rocks that today make up the U. S. and the British Virgin Island groups.

The three U.S. islands are completely different, and can supply the vacationer with a variety of scenery and facilities. St. Thomas is gay and sophisticated, with a happy air of excitement, though it has its quieter, more secluded spots. St. Croix is unhurried and unsophisticated, peaceful and enchanting. St. John is pristine and primeval, with nothing in the world to offer except blissful relaxation and the chance to enjoy the beauty of the island, the fascination of its sea views, the luxurious perfection of its available accommodations.

THE LAND. The islands are splattered over an area of multihued water about 40 miles east of Puerto Rico. The total U.S. group covers 133 square miles and consists of more than 50 islets and cays and the three inhabited main islands of St. Thomas, St. Croix, and St. John.

Due to the rugged, hilly nature of the islands, and the composition of their rocks and soil, it is believed that volcanoes pushed the islands up from the ocean floor. Only the three major islands are large enough to support people.

The islands are readily accessible to the United States. Cruise ships stop at St. Thomas and St. Croix and even occasionally at St. John. St. Thomas and St. Croix have air service. From St.

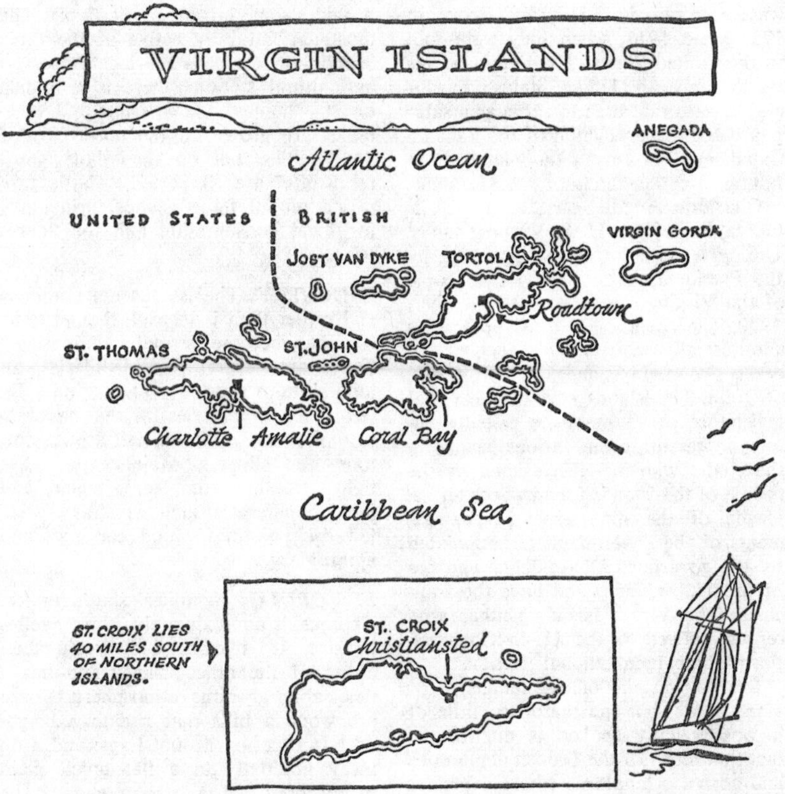

Thomas one goes the three miles to St. John by daily scheduled ferry-shuttle service from Red Hook, by chartered boats or on tours; to St. Croix by air, mail launch or schooner.

THE CLIMATE. With temperature ranges between 70 and 90 degrees all year round, the Virgin Islands are delightful in any season. Rainfall averages 45 inches yearly, with heaviest rains falling in spring and autumn.

In spite of the heavy rainfall, the islands have a water shortage due to increases in population and tourism. By law, each house must have its own cistern to catch rain water, the size of the cistern based on the area of the roof. There is a seawater distillation plant on St. Thomas, but water is still imported from Puerto Rico during droughts.

THE PEOPLE. The population of the islands is over 63,000, 80 percent of whom are black. On St. Thomas there are settlements of the French descendants of the Huguenot refugees who came from St. Barthélemy to escape persecution; a large group of Puerto Ricans lives on St. Croix. The natives of St. John are mostly Negro, but not descendants of former slaves, who were annihilated during the slave rebellions. Instead, they came for the most part from nearby British Tortola Island and brought with them their soft English accent. English has been the language of all the islands since the British occupation of 1802.

Although the British Virgin Islands have been under the British flag since 1671, the U. S. Virgin Islands belonged to Denmark between 1671 (St. John was acquired in 1717, St. Croix in 1733) and 1917, when they were sold to the United States. The purchase was made to give the United States a harbor and base in that area to serve as a safeguard for the protection of the Panama Canal, and to prevent the islands from falling into the hands of the Germans.

Charlotte Amalie, on St. Thomas, is the capital of the U. S. Virgin Islands. The governor, formerly appointed by the President, is elected by the people of the Virgin Islands, as of November, 1970. The governor in turn appoints an administrative assistant for each of the other two main islands, St. Croix and St. John. The islands have a unicameral legislature of 15 members called senators, representing the various islands in the chain, who are also elected by the people of the islands for two-year terms. Heads of the nine executive departments of the government are appointed by the governor. All residents who are 21 are U.S. citizens and have the franchise. The Virgin Islands neither send representatives to the U. S. Congress, nor participate in national elections.

Danish was the official language for many years, but the reason so little of it was actually spoken is due to the fact that many of the Danish plantations had absentee landlords whose overseers were frequently Scots. There is a colloquial dialect, quite different from that on other Caribbean islands, called "calypso" English—intriguing but difficult to understand. Some Spanish is heard on St. Croix.

Many religions are represented. Lutheran and Roman Catholic chiefly, but also Anglican, Christian Mission, Moravian, Methodist, Hebrew, Seventh-Day Adventist.

Educational facilities are comparable to the U.S. mainland and are compulsory up to 15 years of age. There are public and parochial schools through the twelfth grade, several private schools and the Virgin Islands College.

AGRICULTURE. Sugar cane and cotton, main source of the U. S. Virgin Islands' prosperity years ago, have decreased in importance, although sugar provides some income on St. Croix. The most agriculturally active of the three islands, St. Croix is the location of an agricultural station (there is a branch on St. Thomas). Some fruits and vegetables are grown on the north side of St. Thomas, but on the whole, most foodstuffs are imported. Cattle are raised on all three islands, principally for local consumption and for Puerto Rico.

INDUSTRY. The islands are commercial rather than industrial, though tourism has become a major "industry." There are several rum distilleries, an aluminum-processing plant on St. Croix, a few factories for the manufacture of concrete blocks, soft drinks, buttons, and slippers. Major exports are light rum, bay rum, some sugar, and local handicrafts such as straw work, jewelry, paintings, wood carvings, and embroidery.

ST. CROIX, 40 miles south of St. Thomas, is approximately 7 by 27 miles in size. It is more Old World than either of the other islands and has a delectably gracious atmosphere. There are wooded hills that rise to a height of 1,165 feet on Mount Eagle and drop away gradually to a flat green plain in the south. The eastern end of the island is quite arid and uninspiring but has a fine public beach and picnic site, **Cramer's Park,** and a beautiful sea view. The center of the island is given over chiefly to cattle raising and the cultivation of sugar cane. During the extravagant days of the reign of sugar, there were 375 lovely plantations. Many of these are still being occupied; the ruins of others dot the landscape, and their big stone windmills add flavor to the picturesque, pastoral effect of the island.

Christiansted, known locally as Bassin, is a captivating old Danish town situated on the northeast coast on a shallow sheltered harbor. It has often been termed the loveliest old town in the West Indies. The old stone buildings, the pastel-colored houses, the sidewalks arcaded against the sun, the wharf area

Mayan ruins at Tikal, Guatemala

Panoramic view of Guatemala City, Guatemala

National Theater, San José, Costa Rica

Corner of the Presidential Palace, Tegucigalpa, Honduras

View of Izalco, El Salvador

Fort St. Catherine, Bermuda, dating from the seventeenth century

The Basilica, in a modern residential section of Panama City, Panama

Gatun Locks, Panama Canal

Annual Peppercorn Ceremony, Hamilton, Bermuda
Front Street, Hamilton, Bermuda

where inter-island boats tie up at the little park right in the center of town, the quiet little streets, the two-wheeled carts drawn by sleepy little burros add to its charm.

Three blocks on the waterfront area have been made into a national historic site and include **Fort Christiansvaern,** built by the Dutch around 1734; the **Danish Post Office;** the **Steeple Building;** the first Lutheran Church, built in 1753 and now housing the **St. Croix Museum,** with a small but remarkable collection of pre-Columbian Indian relics, early Danish items, historical documents and maps; the old **customs house, public library,** and **government house.** The oldest section dates back to 1748. Reproductions of the original Danish Colonial furnishings, donated by Denmark, are on the third residential floor. One of the rooms on the second floor has mirror panels, each flanked by six hurricane lamps. These together with the four large chandeliers total 188 lights. A large white-satin banner stands at one end, its gold lettering reading, "Gracious gift of the Danish Government, commemorating 150 years of continuous diplomatic relations between Denmark and the United States and is a token of friendship and good will for the people of St. Croix."

Across the street is the **Alexander Hamilton store** in which he clerked as a young boy. Close to town is the monument to Hamilton's mother, **Rachel Sarah Fawcett Levine.** The monument was erected by Gertrude Atherton, the novelist, on a 50-foot strip of land on a private estate donated for the purpose by the owners and maintained by the government. Highly phosphorescent **Altona Lagoon** is said to have been Alexander Hamilton's favorite fishing spot. **Cannon and Parasol hills** offer fine views. **Salt River Bay,** five miles west of Christiansted, is where Columbus first landed on the island in 1493. Visit **Buck Island, Butler's Bay** and the fantastic **Underwater Trail** for snorklers.

Tours to some of the old plantation houses and open-house tours of ones still occupied provide some of the most interesting sights on St. Croix. Privately owned and occupied **Estate Bulow Minde,** built in 1838 and the former home of the Danish governor Peter von Scholten, who freed the slaves after their revolt in 1848, is one of the most notable. It has an eight-sided watchtower, a secret stairway and chapel.

The only other town on the island is **Frederiksted,** 14 miles away on the north coast, on a sheltered but deep and open roadstead. A disastrous fire in 1878 necessitated a complete rebuilding of the town and it now has some delightful examples of Victorian architecture. The one really old sight to be seen is **Fort Frederik,** built in 1760, which claims (as does the fort on the Dutch island of Statia) to have been the first to fire a gun salute to the new flag of the United States of America, in 1777. The proclamation abolishing slavery was read here in 1848. North of town is a noted and scenic highway lined with mahogany trees.

The history of St. Croix resembles that of the other two islands but with a few added complications. The ferocious Caribs had replaced the Arawaks by the time Columbus arrived in 1493. They called their island Ay Ay. Landing at Salt Water Bay, the Spaniards fought their first pitched battle in the Americas with native Indians. Columbus named the spot Cabo de las Flechas, Cape of the Arrows. He withdrew from Ay Ay to more peaceful locales after renaming the island Santa Cruz for the Holy Cross—a name that was changed many times with succeeding occupants until the French label St. Croix was finally settled upon.

French corsairs used the bays around 1600; the Dutch occupied the island in 1640, and were ousted by the British in 1645. The British established colonies there and they in turn were massacred by the Spanish in 1650. The French took over in 1651 and sold out to the Knights of Malta the same year. During the latter's few years of occupancy they built Government House and famed Judith's Fancy, although four years later they sold the island back to the French West Indies Company. Ten years after that the island became a colony, but in 1696 the entire settlement was forcibly removed to Haiti. In 1733 St. Croix was purchased by Denmark; Christiansted became the capital, and the island thrived on cotton, sugar and the fine light rum they made from it. It came to be known as the "Garden of the Danish West Indies" and life was lived in the most opulent, extravagant manner conceivable. A U.S. tariff on West Indian sugar, slave riots and the burning of plantations, the freeing of the slaves, all contributed to the decline of the island's prosperity and the removal of the Danish Virgin Island capital to St. Thomas. Slowly St. Croix is coming into its own again, due in large measure to the fact that tourists have become aware of its great charms and many who came as tourists have remained to build homes or to restore old ones and establish permanent residences.

ST. JOHN is a languid, unspoiled 19-square-mile piece of land three miles across Pillsbury Channel from St. Thomas. A ten-mile center-line road and mountain trails make accessible the heavily forested green hills of its interior that rise to a peak of 1,288 feet on Bordeaux Mountain. The foliage is lush and lovely—great giant ferns, wild orchids and a myriad of other blooms, 154 species of trees, 72 shrubs and herbs, some with such intriguing local names as "Bellyache Balsam." The western shores are almost arid and have eight varieties of cacti, one growing to a height of 20 feet. There are endless invitingly intimate little bays, beach after beach of pure white sand, the loveliest seascapes in the Caribbean, underwater coral formations that provide good snorkeling. This is the spot that Laurance Rockefeller found to be so beautiful that he bought and donated to the United States more than 9,500 acres to serve as **Virgin Islands National Park.**

Wildlife is unknown, unless sand flies could be counted in this category. The mongoose was imported from India long ago to rid the island of snakes. It succeeded in killing off all the snakes but also all other wildlife as well, including many of the birds, though there are still an estimated 150 types of birds to be seen here.

The atmosphere is refreshingly nontouristic. The population of over 1,000 are easygoing, relaxed, friendly human beings. Local natives spend their time collecting leaves from the bay trees on Bordeaux Mountain to be sent to the bay rum factory in St. Thomas, or making charcoal, also for St. Thomas, or weaving an extra fine quality of basket, or fishing. There is some cattle raising.

St. John is truly an escapist's dream—except for the prices, which are as modern and stateside as the accommodations.

To see the island, visitors can hike, horseback or donkey ride, jeep or take the "safari trip" in surrey-topped cars built with special-order shock absorbers and cushions to make the trip over the somewhat rugged road through the tropical magnificence of this national park somewhat more comfortable. At Hogshead Bay there are a few picnic tables and lavatories but only bushes for dressing rooms.

An ideal way to see the rest of the island is to sail or cruise around it, stopping off at the various and many bays. **Cruz Bay** is the main settlement on the island, with the resident commissioner's home and office, a few little stores, post office, school, police station for its two officers, a few houses and the attractive Gallows Point cottage colony. **Caneel Bay** is the setting for another Laurance Rockefeller project—a finely balanced combination of hotel luxury and informality, plus a choice of ten superb beaches. Beyond here is a famed-for-its-food guesthouse with cottages, also able to boast of a small but ideal beach.

On huge **Coral Bay,** considered to be the best harbor of refuge in the Antilles, is the island's largest settlement. It was used as a Danish port in 1780 and was then called Frederiksvoern. At **Mary's Point,** slaves threw themselves off the cliffs onto the rocks in Fungi Passage rather than be captured by the French troops from Martinique, who had come to the rescue of the Danish planters after a slave revolt in 1733. Petrographs still visible near **Reef Bay** are proof that the Arawak and Carib Indians once inhabited St. John. Columbus landed here in 1493.

Eventually the island was occupied in turn by the Dutch, the British, the Spanish, the French and the Danes, and its bays became hideout spots for the buccaneers. Sugar cane was grown in profusion and the plantation system thrived for the planters until the great slave rebellion in 1733, when plantations and cane fields were put to the torch.

ST. THOMAS, with a population of about 30,000, is 3 by 12 miles in size, with a ridge of mountains through the center. To the north, one looks out on the Atlantic Ocean and the panorama of British and U. S. Virgin Islands; to the south, over the Caribbean Sea and the picturesque harbor of its capital city.

Charlotte Amalie sits pertly on the edge of its islet-dotted, landlocked harbor, and its homes sprawl up the hillsides that rise sharply behind it to a height of 1,500 feet. The hillsides are three volcanic spurs called Frenchmans Hill, Denmark Hill and Government Hill—or, more engagingly, by their old nicknames, Foretop, Maintop and Mizzentop. Originally called Taphus by the Danes, the city was renamed Charlotte Amalie by King Christian V for his Queen when he took possession of the islands in 1666. St. Thomas became its official title in 1921 under U.S. ownership but it was changed back to Charlotte Amalie again in 1936. It is a gay, social, cosmopolitan town with a festive air. The Danish influence is shown in its street names, and its architecture reflects the influence of its various occupants—Dutch doors, French grillwork, Spanish patios, Danish roof lines. A modern Miami-type hotel shows the U.S. influence.

In Charlotte Amalie are several outstanding architectural structures selected by the Historical American Buildings Survey. One is **Fort Christian,** named for King Christian V of Denmark, built in mid-seventeenth century. It was the first building erected in St. Thomas by the Danes and served as the governor's residence, court house, parsonage and church and jail, all in one. Today it serves as the police station and jail. The courtyard is paved with slabs of gravestones, and there are dungeons and a torture chamber that can be visited. Another is **Bluebeard's Tower** —three stories high and with five-and-one-half-foot-thick walls. In 1934 workmen found an ironbound chest with old papers inside telling the story of Musa Ben Hasser (Bluebeard), similar to the story of Perrault. This, plus seven grave markers on the terrace (actually these are the graves of old-time residents on the island), gave rise to a belief that this was the true hangout of the pirate Bluebeard. Buildings added later for use as a private home have been restored and enlarged and are now used as a hotel. Built by the Danish government in 1689 as a fort, it was so used until 1734, after which time it was headquarters of the buccaneers.

Blackbeard's Castle, formerly called Fort Skytsborg, is believed to have served as the home of the notorious pirate, Edward Teach. Nearby **Government House** was begun in 1865. On the first-floor landing are murals of the landing of Columbus at Salt River Bay, St. Croix; the hoisting of the U.S. flag at Charlotte Amalie, St. Thomas; and a rum still. The governor's residence is on the third floor, a reception room on the second. Opposite Government House is **Quarters B,** once the German consulate, now government offices; it has a beautiful stairway taken from an old ship. **Hotel 1829** (the name comes from the date March 12, 1829, when the house was deeded over to a Mr. Lavalette, the original builder and a shipping man, and his wife Angela) is a good example of a nineteenth-century home, as is **Denmark Hill,** now the Danish consulate. **Grand Hotel,** opened in 1841, was the first hotel on the island.

Also chosen by the Historical Buildings Survey were several churches:

Dutch Reformed Church, one of the oldest established churches on the island; the **Lutheran Parsonage,** eighteenth century; **Frederick Evangelical Lutheran Church**—second oldest in the Western Hemisphere, its original seventeenth-century ecclesiastical silver still in use; the **Jewish Synagogue**—second oldest in the Western Hemisphere (claimed by some to be the first). It still keeps clean sand on the floor in old traditional style to commemorate the passage of the Jews out of the desert. There was a distinguished Jewish colony here at one time; in the seventeenth century one of the governors was a Jew. In more recent times, on July 10, 1830, the artist Camille Pissarro was born on the site of the Sears Roebuck building. His parents are buried in the **Jewish cemetery** in Charlotte Amalie. Across the street is an interesting old **Danish cemetery.** Out of town to the west is the **Nisky Moravian Mission;** the original church was built in 1777; the church, school, and seminary are good examples of Moravian Mission architecture.

Other points of interest to be seen in the capital city are the **Beretta shopping center** in the old stone warehouses by the waterfront, including the **Virgin Island Museum** (with an interesting collection of Indian relics, old Danish furniture, etchings, photos, costumes and documents of the seventeenth through nineteenth centuries); the **Street of 99 Steps; Emancipation Park,** where the abolition of the slaves was proclaimed in 1848; the **market place** on a Saturday, and a nearby **"wishing well"** imported over 200 years ago as a memorial for a merchant's son. **SS. Peter and Paul's Church** has a fine large white marble altar, paintings on the walls, while at **All Saints Anglican Church,** there is an organ which is over 100 years old.

Art lovers will want to see the murals in the **post office** by Stephen Dohanos, the art gallery in the Grand Hotel and at **Smith's Fancy,** whose owner Ira Smith is one of the colony's noted artists.

An around-the-island drive could be covered in less than half a day. En route, there are lovely seascapes of the other U. S. and British Virgin Islands. The road goes to popular **Morningstar Beach** on Eastern Point; near the **Moravian Mission** at Nisky; past the **Mandahl School** for delinquent boys to **Colki Point** off the main road, a small, favorite beach for skin-divers and snorkelers; through a mangrove swamp which is swarming with crabs (torching parties go out at night to collect them); and on to rectangular **Magens Bay,** one of the loveliest in the Caribbean, with a marvelously clean, long white swimming beach. Above the bay is **Louisenhoj,** the estate of the late Arthur Fairchild, who erected **Drake's Seat** up above the bay on the spot where Drake is presumed to have sat and charted the course of the channel since named for him. On the north coast on Magnolia Hill is an obelisk called **Venus Pillar,** erected in 1882 by Brazilian astronomers to celebrate the witnessing of Passagem to Venus on the sixth of December, and **Mafolie,** a settlement of French farmers who grow fruits and vegetables here for local consumption. Up on **Signal Mountain** is a hotel which overlooks Magens Bay and has a permanent orchid show. **Estate Dorothea** is an agricultural station that can be visited. Heading back toward Charlotte Amalie, one passes the airport and **Lindbergh Beach,** a large, modern hotel sprawling over a hillside and offering fine views of the harbors, and **French Town,** or Carenage, formerly called Cha-cha town. The inhabitants live quite separate lives from the rest of the people on St. Thomas and have a Norman-French dialect of their own. They are fishermen and handicraft workers; their trademark is a high-crowned straw hat known as a "cha-cha" hat. **St. Anne's Shrine** is on the hill beside their little St. Anne's Church.

The Dutch tried unsuccessfully to settle the island in 1657, as did the Danes in 1666 and again in 1672, this time successfully and permanently, except for a British period of occupation from 1801–02 and 1807–15. St. Thomas has always been a business and shipping center due to its fine harbor and facilities, convenience of location for ships coming and going between the various islands of the Caribbean, the Spanish Main area and the mother countries; the secluded bays and coves of the other Virgins that admirably served as hideaways for pirate ships (even the government turned its hand to privateering). The waterfront warehouses were always piled high with merchandise until the beginning of the nineteenth century and the coming of the steamship, after which ships could bypass St. Thomas on a direct path to their destinations. Now the area has the most cruise-ship calls in the world.

SPORTS AND RECREATION. There is **swimming** at pools and a wide choice of superb beaches on all three islands. **Water-skiing** instruction is available on all three, and the area is one of the finest for **cruising** in the Western Hemisphere. All types of boats are available for charter by the hour, day, week, or longer–cruisers, sloops, cutters, ketches, schooners. There are service facilities for private yachts and scheduled **boating tours**–glass-bottomed boats, round-the-island cruises, sunset harbor cruises, special tours from St. Thomas to St. John, to Tortola, and among the other U. S. and British Virgin Islands; to Buck Island from St. Croix; round-the-island and among the Virgin Islands from St. John. The Institute of Marine Biology takes visitors on three-hour biological collecting trips. Take a ferryboat from the Submarine Base dock over to Water Isle in the harbor and spend a day swimming, relaxing and enjoying a picnic lunch on the beach. **Hunting** is limited although big-game fishing is coming into its own. There is fine **deep-sea fishing** for sailfish, tarpon, dolphin, barracuda, small tuna, kingfish and yellowtail; line, net, and seine fishing–seining parties (fish fries) are fun, with local fishermen pulling in the seines. A **spear-fishing** school on St. Thomas offers instruction for beginners and trips for experts. On St. John there is a rod-and-spear club and an anglers' club at Maho Bay. Lobster and conch diving and spearing is often done by torchlight at night when lobsters come out in the shallow water to feed. Virgin Island waters have been rated the second-best marine area in the world for **snorkeling** and **skin-diving** (Great Barrier Reef in Australia holding first place). U. S. Navy frogmen have used this as a training base for many years. **Tennis** courts are on all the islands, **golf** courses on St. Thomas and St. Croix, **horseback riding** on all three. Spectator sports include informal **baseball, softball, cricket; horse racing** on St. Thomas and St. John, **donkey races** and **cockfighting** on St. Croix.

SPECIAL EVENTS. **Carnival,** a gay affair on St. Thomas during the last week in April, was originally a celebration of the cane harvest. A king and queen are crowned, and everyone dresses in costume and wears wild hats. There are parades, floats, street dancing, special "bamboula" (of African origin) dancers and quadrille dancers, steel bands, calypsos, Indian and Zulu mock stick-fights, a market fair. On Friday there are a children's parade and performances, on Saturday the adult parade and exhibitions, with "Mocko Jumbi," a costumed figure on stilts, as a reigning character.

St. Croix's greatest celebration is at Christmas time. A queen is chosen at a selection ball in mid-December. On December 23, she sails in a flower-decked barge to "Festival Village" on the Christiansted waterfront and is crowned. A coronation ball is held that night. The Village is opened officially Christmas Eve, and at dawn Christmas Day a community serenade is held on the old Danish parade ground. December 26 is the big day, with a children's parade in the morning, horse races in the afternoon, *aguinaldos* (Spanish Christmas caroling by the Puerto Ricans of the island) in the evening. On December 27 there is a steel-band contest and street dancing. The following day the people come in from outlying districts to do gig dances, and there is dancing and band music daily until New Year's Eve, which is called Old

Year's Day here. An old-fashioned fair is held in the open market place in Christiansted, prizes given, and costumed celebrations held. New Year's Day there is a grand parade of costumed groups in the morning in Frederiksted and in the evening by lantern light in Christiansted.

Christmas season is celebrated in a variety of ways on various days by the different nationalities represented on the islands. The Danes celebrate on December 24 with an "open house" at Denmark Hall, the Danish consulate. Annually at Christmas for the past quarter century a four-masted Danish Marine training vessel has made a cruise from Copenhagen to Charlotte Amalie with Danish cadets for holiday parties and a Government House reception. At Estate Contant on St. Thomas the winning island choir from the previous year sings before formally dressed guests on Christmas Eve. An annual choir-singing contest is held in Emancipation Park Gardens. The large Puerto Rican community on St. Croix celebrates the Day of the Kings on January 6 with a parade, and there are always steel bands and visitors from Antigua.

July Fourth is celebrated on both St. Thomas and St. Croix by street parades, costumed crowds, steel bands and water sports. On St. John there are donkey races and greased-pole climbing contests, boat races and fireworks.

Hurricanes were much more frequent and devastating years ago. Since 1726, July 25 has been a holiday called "Supplication Day" when church services are held to pray for escape from hurricanes, and another holiday called Thanksgiving Day, dating from 1726, has been held every October 25 in gratitude for escape.

DINING AND SHOPPING. All types of food are available at the many attractive hotel dining rooms and restaurants. *Kallaloo* (known as "calaloo" or "calalou" on other Caribbean islands) is a combination of ham, pork, seafood, spinach or greens, onion, okra, and seasonings, served over a plain *fungi*, which is a corn pudding. *Okra fungi* is a ball-shaped okra and cornmeal mixture served with boiled fish and onion sauce. "Cornmeal pap à la creole" is cornmeal, milk, sugar, cinnamon, butter, salt and raisins. "Whelks and rice" and turtle stew are popular.

Liquor is very inexpensive; all types of drinks are available. Many of the hotels have concocted their own specialties, such as banana daiquiri, bullshot (vodka and consommé), pineapple daiquiri, planter's punch, "hibiscus for two" (huge cocktail with a flower floating on top), "Harbormaster Swizzle," "rum fountail."

Shopping is sheer delight. Both the local handicraft and imports are excellent in quality, quantity and design. Savings are one-third, one-half, or better over U.S. prices. At the time the islands were purchased from Denmark by the U.S., it was agreed that they should continue as the free ports they had been for centuries, meaning that there are no luxury or excise taxes added. In addition, all goods made in the Virgin Islands are duty-free into the U.S. and do not even have to be declared. There is no more delightful a group of shops in the Caribbean area than on St. Thomas. The **Beretta center** just off the main shopping street, Dronningens Gade, has alluring shops in the charming setting of transformed centuries-old stone warehouses. Equally fine shops are to be found on St. Croix, but in lesser numbers, many of them branches of the St. Thomas shops. Handicraft is outstanding. Virgin Island locally-created fashion designs have achieved an enviable reputation, ready-mades or special orders of imported materials or locally designed and painted materials are particularly appealing. Local artists present opportunities to pick up delightful paintings. There are also straw work, seedwork, tortoise shell, character dolls; imports from all over the world—perfumes, silver, china, linens, cashmeres, Oriental silks, ivories and jewelry. One store carries a rare collection of books on the West Indies. Liquor prices are inexpensive and standardized.

British Virgin Islands

A group of more than 30 islands, including Tortola, Virgin Gorda, Anegada, and Jost Van Dyke, make up the British Virgin Islands. Previously undeveloped touristically, new hotels and resort areas are opening to make the islands excellent vacation spots.

THE LAND. Some of the islands are only rocky cays, while others are scenically breathtaking, with rugged hills rising from superb beaches to a maximum height of 1,780 feet. The land area covers 59 square miles, the islands being located 15 miles northeast of St. Thomas.

THE CLIMATE. Lying within the Trade Winds belt, the islands possess a pleasant subtropical climate. Maximum temperature seldom exceeds 90 degrees, tempered by steady breezes, and in winter months seldom falls below 70 degrees. Average annual rainfall is about 53 inches.

THE PEOPLE. The total population is over 10,000, most of whom live on Tortola. They are predominantly of African descent, but a few whites live in Road Town, Tortola, and in private homes scattered throughout the area. The native peoples are friendly and relaxed, although the circumstances of life on the islands are difficult. The shortage of water is a major problem. Many of the men who work on St. Thomas, where job opportunities and pay are better, have families in both places.

Discovered by Columbus in 1493, and named by him for St. Ursula's 11,000 virgin attendants, this group of islands was settled by the Dutch in 1648, taken over by the British in 1666, and settled by British planters from Anguilla in 1680. The group of British Virgin Islands is a Crown Colony.

AGRICULTURE. Fruit and vegetables are grown and exported to the U. S. Virgin Islands—in fact, Tortola is known as "The Vegetable Garden" of the Virgin Islands. Other exports include fish, charcoal, coconuts, and cattle.

INDUSTRY. There are no large industrial or commercial firms carrying on business in the Colony, and consequently, few opportunities for skilled or professional work. Small-boat building, several primitive rum distilleries, and some straw work are the industrial mainstays.

THE ISLANDS. With the growth of tourist facilities and construction of luxurious new hotels, many visitors are spending their entire vacations on the British Virgin Islands (before there were facilities, travelers came only on day trips from St. Thomas or St. John). A scheduled passenger boat makes the trip between St. Thomas and Tortola, and an airline makes regular stops.

ANEGADA ("drowned island") is somewhat isolated from the others and was once a pirate's hide out. A coral island with little soil on it, its few houses were built mostly of the timbers from ships that had been wrecked on the offshore coral reefs.

BEEF ISLAND is a tiny island just a few yards offshore in Trellis Bay, Tortola. A Trellis Bay Club offers natural anchorage and repair facilities to yachtsmen and all kinds of water sports. Rooms are available in the clubhouse and there are also beach cottages.

DEAD MAN'S CHEST is the rocky cay where Blackbeard (Edward Teach) marooned 15 of his men. The cay was purchased by Earl Baldwin in 1948 and presented to the colony in perpetuity.

GUANA ISLAND has fine beaches; good swimming, fishing, hunting, horseback riding. A clubhouse provides rooms for non-club members upon approval of application.

JOST VAN DYKE, which has several hundred inhabitants, was the location of a Quaker colony during the eighteenth century. William Thornton, who designed the capitol building in Washington, D.C., and Dr. John Lettsom, founder of the Medical Society of London, were born on this island.

NORMAN ISLAND is another of those islands claimed to have been Robert Louis Stevenson's Treasure Island. Pirate treasures have been found there.

SOMBRERO definitely resembles its name. Its shore is lined by cliffs 20 to 40 feet high, and to land one must climb a ladder to reach a rock platform at the top. It has no harbor, no beach, no good anchorage, no vegetation. It is uninhabited except for blue crabs and a few keepers of the red and white stone lighthouses that guide shipping through the Anegada Channel. There is a great deal of migratory bird life, particularly from April through July. Free resthouse facilities are available for overnighting, but visitors must take the food they will need. Drinking water is available. You can go and return the same day by boat from Anguilla–a four-and-one-half-hour trip–or, with a permit from the supervisor of lights in St. Kitts, go gratis on the fortnightly mail boat. Some old relics or fossils from the rocks may be found and you can swim in sea pools in caves.

At one point, Americans exploited phosphate deposits on the island until the British objected to this violation of territorial rights. The British continued working the phosphate deposits until 1893.

TORTOLA ("turtledove"), is the largest of the British Virgin Islands. **Road Town,** the only real town on any of the islands, serves as the capital. A mile-long road curves along the bay on the southern coast and a second road winds across the hills; numerous foot or horseback trails make the rest of the island accessible. New improved roads are continually being added. There are movies six nights a week and several new boutiques are open. Cables can be sent or received via U. S. St. John Island, and there is a post office. There are no tennis courts and no golf courses except those facilities provided by hotels. There is a hospital, medical laboratory and doctors. Schooling is provided by several government primary and secondary schools, and by denominational ones. Methodist, Church of England, Seventh-Day Adventists, Roman Catholic and Church of God religions are represented.

VIRGIN GORDA ("fat virgin"), ten by two miles at its widest point, is the second largest island of the group and is the location of several resort hotels, including **Little Dix Bay.** It has fine beaches, and at its southern point huge rock formations with caves called **The Baths,** some with sea pools in which one can swim. It is mountainous and has rich tropical foliage.

SPORTS include **deep-sea** and **spear fishing, snorkeling, boating** and **swimming, hiking, horseback** or **muleback riding, duck shooting** in winter, **pigeon shooting** in summer. There are caves to explore and pirate treasure for which to search.

SHOPPING. Native straw goods and needlework can be purchased on Tortola.

Leeward Islands

This group of islands, usually considered to be completely British, is made up of the British Leeward Islands (Antigua and its dependencies, Barbuda and Redonda; St. Kitts, Nevis, and Anguilla; and Montserrat); the Netherlands Antilles (page 483), and the French West Indies (page 494).

In the British Leewards, with the exception of Antigua, all are relatively undeveloped from a tourist's point of view. However, for the traveler who is satisfied with simple accommodations, simple foods, and more or less self-made, or at least self-inspired amusements, these islands are delightful to visit. Each island has its own administrator and a separate government made up of an executive and a legislative council.

LESSER ANTILLES

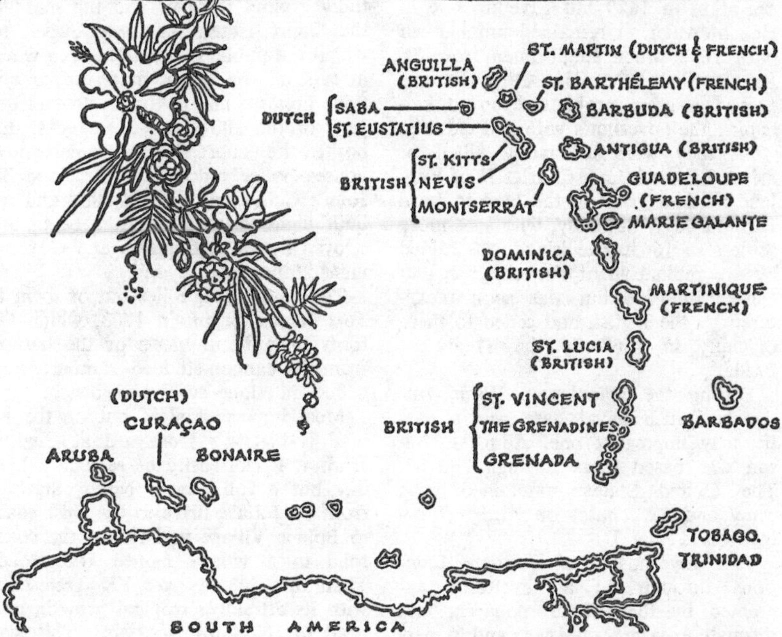

ANTIGUA

Antigua is the largest of the British Leewards but, even so, is only 14 by 10 miles in size and has a small population of over 65,000. The atmosphere is definitely on the quiet side, but peacefully and pleasantly so.

THE LAND. A batch of lovely tropical growth can be found in the southwestern Fig Tree Hill area. Here, too, is Antigua's highest point–1,330-foot Boggy Hill. Other than this, the land is mostly gently rolling countryside, much of which is given over to the cultivation of sugar cane. Antigua's beauty lies in its superb clean white beaches all around the island, its secluded little coves, wild surf in the rocky northwestern areas and some excellent harbors.

THE CLIMATE. This is considered one of the healthiest spots in the Caribbean and has a truly superb climate. The days average 80 degrees and are warm, sunny, and dry except for September and October, which can be very humid; May to October is considered the hot season. The rainfall varies from year to year but averages less than 45 inches, most of which falls between August and January. Antigua, largely dependent on the rainfall for its water, is sometimes faced with very real difficulties toward the end of the dry season. The slight rainfall accounts for the lack of lush tropical foliage found on most of the other islands, and also, no doubt, for the fact that it is more insect-free, even in the evenings.

THE PEOPLE. Discovered by Columbus on his second voyage in 1493, he named this island after the Church of Santa Maria la Antigua, in Sevilla, in which, before starting his trip, he had asked the blessing of the patron saint of travelers. The French attempted colonization in 1629 but gave up due to lack of water. It remained uninhabited until 1632, when Englishmen from St. Kitts settled here. The Carib Indians proved a great problem—even to kidnaping the governor's wife and children—but they were ultimately killed or driven off the island. Charles II of England made a grant of the land to Lord Parham de Willoughby, who sent more settlers in 1663. The island was raided by a combination of French, Irish and Caribs in 1666 but was soon recaptured by the British and ceded to them officially in 1667 by the Treaty of Breda.

During the Napoleonic Wars, Antigua's British naval base was a particularly important one. Admiral Nelson was based there during 1786–88. The United States maintained both army and navy bases on Antigua during World War II.

The government of Antigua functions through an administrator appointed by the British monarch, and through a prime minister, and a parliament consisting of an elected house of representatives and an appointed senate.

AGRICULTURE. More than 18,000 of Antigua's 70,000 acres are under cultivation, with sugar cane occupying some 14,000 acres of this area. Other produce includes herbs, sweet potatoes, mangoes, pumpkin, and okra.

INDUSTRY. Over two-thirds of Antigua's exports consist of sugar and sugar products. Almost 90 percent of the population is involved in sugar production. In addition, Antigua has a rum distillery, cotton gin, arrowroot, edible oil, and cornmeal factories.

ST. JOHN'S. The capital of St. John's, with a population of 24,000, is the only town of any size on the island. Built on a slight rise overlooking its large, shallow, and almost landlocked harbor, St. John's is a bustling little town with fine new buildings side by side with old Georgian structures which are still preserved.

Sightseeing attractions include the activity around the pier and the market; the **Court House** on Long Street, to which the public is admitted even when in session; the **fence,** made up of antique firearms and bayonets, around the yard of the 300-year-old barracks, opposite the court house, which now houses police offices; the Anglican **St. John's Cathedral,** built in 1834 and rebuilt eight years later after being destroyed by an earthquake, and **Government House** just beyond.

Two and a half miles out of town is **Fort James,** begun in 1703, which affords magnificent views of the harbor from its cannon-studded rampart, and a fine mile-long swimming beach.

Most important sight out on the island is **Nelson's Dockyard** at **English Harbor.** It can easily be seen in a half day but a full day is better. Starting from St. John's, drive to the west coast to Bolans Village and follow the coast road to a village named **Old Road.** Then turn inland over **Fig Tree Hill,** with its attractive tropical growth, and head for Nelson's Dockyard. This was built originally as a navy base in 1725; the present one was begun in 1746 and was abandoned as a dockyard in 1889. The Antigua government took it over a few years later but did not keep it up. In 1951, a "Society of the Friends of English Harbor" was formed, with the aim of restoring the area as a historical monument. The old barracks and paymaster's office, and the winches used for the careening of ships, all appear much as they must have looked during Nelson's time.

Up a hill overlooking the harbor is **Clarence House,** built in 1786 for Prince William Henry, later William IV of England, and now serving as a summer residence for the administrator. His flag flies when he is in residence. At other times one may enter and inspect the house. From here, on the road to Shirley Heights and the Ridge, are old eighteenth-century artillery quarters, various fortifications and barracks, the block house, and below, an old cemetery. There are several ruins on **Shirley Heights,** named for Sir Thomas Shirley, the Leeward Islands' first governor. From this vantage point, the islands of Guadeloupe and Montserrat can be seen in the distance. Returning via Ridge Road, you will come to **Dow's Hill,** with ruins of old quarters of the commanding general, and on the savannah below the residence of the first governor of Antigua can be seen. Nearby is **Bat's Cave,** said to extend for great distances underground and **Indian Creek,** where the Carib Indians presumably beached their canoes when they came to raid and kidnap as hostages the wife and children of Governor Warner. **Black Point** on Falmouth Harbor was where slaves were landed; the ruins of **Great Fort George** (1689) are on Monks Hill just beyond Falmouth.

Inland from All Saints, you can head back to St. John's, or go east and see the beautiful beaches on the east coast around **Half Moon Bay;** the Mill Reef Club is just to the north.

You can also swing north from St. John's to see the **Central Agricultural Station and Cotton Research Station** (phone ahead for permission to visit). Then go up around the north coast where several of the hotels are located, and down through the former U.S. army and navy bases to **Parham,** where there is an 1840 Italian-style church with a ceiling construction that resembles a boat hull in the process of being built. On the route back to St. John's you can visit **Gunthorpe's sugar factory.**

BARBUDA, one of the dependencies of Antigua about 40 miles north, is not a tourist spot but is a favorite with sportsmen. The **hunting** is good—wild pig, guinea fowl, duck, pigeon, wild deer (deer season January to April)—as is the **fishing,** which includes fine lobster and turtle.

Barbuda can be reached by air from Antigua. Leeward Islands Air Transport operates weekly flights, and charters can be arranged.

Barbuda, formerly known as Dulcina, is a coral formation, wooded and flat, its highest point being only about 200 feet. It was annexed by the British in 1628 and granted to a Codrington family in 1680. After some 200 years it became government property. Its capital is still called **Codrington.**

REDONDA, also a dependency at Antigua, situated 25 miles to the southwest, is slightly more than a half square mile of volcanic rock rising to a height of about 1,000 feet. It is uninhabited, and its sole interest lies in its unusual and absurd bit of history. In 1865 an Irishman, who considered himself a descendant of Irish kings, sailed past the island and decided to claim it as a kingdom for his newborn son. When the son was in his mid-teens, the father took him and a member of the clergy to the island and officially proclaimed him, the son, King Felipe I. They left the next day. (The Colonial Office in London actually did acknowledge the father's claim to the island.) King Felipe proceeded with time to appoint various of his friends as dukes. Before his death in 1947 he had appointed a friend of his, the poet John Gawsworth, to be his successor. Gawsworth became King Juan I and proceeded to appoint his own friends as dukes, many of whom are well-known writers of today. He "holds court" in England on his birthdays but has never even seen his "Kingdom."

SPORTS AND RECREATION. Sports include **cricket, football,** and **horse racing** twice a year at Cassada Gardens. Active sports are **tennis, golf, horseback riding, bowling. Deep-sea** and **spear fishing** are good. The coral reef at an offshore island, Prickly Pear, is a popular **skin-diving** and **snorkeling** spot. There is **hunting** on the island of Barbuda; **swimming** is excellent. Some of the hotels have boats for charter, while boats and yachts are available at Nelson's Dockyard, English Harbor. Cruising is good all year round, but May to July and mid-October to December are the best months. **Aquatic Sports Day** ("Dockyard Day") takes place at English Harbor on November 14, Prince Charles' birthday.

There are a handful of simple night clubs, and dances at the clubs and hotels. Special dance performances by dancers on the beaches can be arranged by your hotel. Steel bands are popular and excellent. Groups sometimes hire a steel band for dancing on Corbison Point Beach. There are also amateur theatricals and art exhibits.

DINING AND SHOPPING. The favorite native dishes of these islands are pepper pot, fungee, and coo-coo (cornmeal and okra); rice, souse (boiled pighead and trotters served with sliced cucumber, lime juice, and peppers). American, continental, and French cuisine are featured at resort hotels. Fresh lobster is caught at the nearby island of Barbuda.

Shopping possibilities are limited, but there are some attractive local handicrafts—pottery, fiber and straw articles, such as table mats, bags, belts, and tortoise-shell articles. There are some British imports and French perfume. Shops are on High Street, St. Mary's and Market Streets, and on others in this general area.

ST. KITTS

St. Kitts is very English, very appealing though rather unexciting. It is not a tourist spot and is in no way dependent on tourist trade, sugar having made it a booming little island. It does boast one of the better "sights" in all the Caribbean area—the New World's great fortress, **Brimstone Hill,** but otherwise there is little to see or to do other than just relax and enjoy the pleasing atmosphere and the polite and genuine friendliness of the people who live there.

THE LAND. Lofty mountains cross the island's area of approximately 68 square miles in a northwest-southeast diagonal, reaching their greatest height at 3,711 feet in awe-inspiring, frequently cloud-hidden **Mount Misery.** The mountain's peak stands high above its extinct volcano's tree-lined crater, which is 6,000 feet deep and two-and-one-half miles in circumference. The upper slopes of the mountains are densely forested. Fields of sugar cane and of cotton cover much of the fertile, well-watered stretches from the sea and up the lower slopes. The resultant vistas as seen when approaching the island by sea are most attractive.

THE CLIMATE. The months of September and October are hot, although the average temperature throughout the year does not exceed 79 degrees. Rainfall, though slight, often appears in torrential showers and varies from 48 to 70 inches in different sections of the island. While in the hurricane belt, St. Kitts has very few, the last recorded in 1928.

THE PEOPLE. The population of St. Kitts, about 38,000, is for the most part of mixed African-European descent. The white colony accounts for perhaps no more than one percent. All the people of the island seem to have a great dignity and charm that is responsible, no doubt, in large measure for the nostalgic feeling all visitors seem to experience on leaving the island after even a very brief stay. The language of the island is English. The religion is varied—Anglican, Roman Catholic, Seventh-Day Adventist, Methodist, Moravian, Pilgrim Holiness. Extremely fine and up-to-date government facilities supply compulsory education for children between the ages of 5 and 16, and there are, in addition, several private schools and one parochial school. Also the island maintains a good library with a collection of Indian relics.

St. Kitts was discovered by Columbus on his second voyage in 1493. The first white settlers, British, arrived in 1623 and almost simultaneously French colonists established settlements. For some years the two groups shared the island, living peacefully together, and even joining forces at one time to repulse an attempted raid by the Spaniards. By

1664, however, the French had gained complete control, and henceforth ownership changed back and forth between the two powers. In 1713 the Treaty of Utrecht ceded the island to England. Almost 70 years later France, in what might now be termed an amphibious operation, again took possession. The British had been forced to leave some of their cannon and ammunition at the base of Brimstone Hill and, their own artillery turned against them, the fort was obliged to surrender to the invading French. Two years later, in 1783, St. Kitts was again ceded to Great Britain under the terms of the Treaty of Versailles—and ever since the island has been in British hands.

St. Kitts is known as the "Mother Colony of the West Indies" because it was from here that colonizers went out to settle other islands. It has been known by several other names, the Carib Indian name Liamuiga, meaning "fertile isle," and St. Christopher, the name given the island by Columbus either in honor of himself or of the patron saint of travelers. Columbus is said to have thought that the rocky formation jutting up on Mount Misery resembled the picture of St. Christopher carrying the Christ on his shoulders. In the seventeenth century, the island was referred to as "Merwar's Hope," a name concocted from the first syllables of the last names of two men important to the history of St. Kitts, Sir Thomas Warner, the first settler, and a Mr. Merryfield, his financial backer. Today, it is known as St. Kitts, an abbreviation also employed by earlier settlers.

AGRICULTURE. Sugar and sea-island cotton are the main crops, with sugar, salt, molasses, and cotton the chief exports.

BASSETERRE, the capital of St. Kitts, is a lethargic and pleasant town located on the southeast coast. Its little port serves as a distributing center for nearby islands and has a colorful waterfront. The two main streets cross at the picturesque center of town known as the "Circus," with the often-photographed fountain clock tower. Motor traffic has increased considerably in recent years, though bicycles are the most popular means of transportation. Most of the buildings in town are of mid-Victorian stone construction with upper floors of wood, whereas the more usual construction in the outlying districts is all wood. Scattered about the island are some lovely old sugar plantations, including one about a mile from town that belonged to a seventeenth-century governor of the French Antilles with the imposing title of "M. le Chevalier de Poincy, Bailiff and Grand Cross of the Order of St. John of Jerusalem, Commander d'Oysemont et de Coutour, Admiral of the Fleet of His Majesty the French King of Brittany." To this gentleman is attributed the development of the magnificently beautiful flowering *poinciana regis,* the flamboyant tree now found throughout the Caribbean islands.

Visitors can see all of **Basseterre** on foot—the busy pier, and the colorful Treasury Building on the waterfront, the clock tower in the **Circus.** Private homes face **Pall Mall Square,** as does the old Roman Catholic **Cathedral of the Immaculate Conception** and the courthouse. Farther inland are **Government House,** and **St. George's Church,** built by the French Roman Catholics in 1670 and converted in 1713 into an Anglican church by the British.

A visit to the local movie house is an experience not to be missed. The movie may be well below par but the excitement and enthusiasm of the audience is well worth the price of admission. Circuit court can be attended when in session. See the changing of the police guard at 6:01 P.M. outside the Treasury Building in Basseterre.

One mile from town is the modern **Central Sugar Factory** which welcomes visitors. Hiking in the mountains is a popular pastime. Favorite goals are **Monkey Hill,** 1,319 feet, and **Sir Timothy's Hill,** a battleground of the French and English in 1690. An all-day combination car and horseback trip to **Dodan Pond** on Verchilds Mountain—a lake in the crater of an extinct volcano—is worthwhile. To climb **Mount**

Misery requires a full day via Belmont Estates, which can be reached by car, and from there an hour's horseback trip and a two-hour climb by foot will take you to the lip of its crater. Sulphur vapors seep from the northeast side of the mountain and there is a sulphur spring.

The prize trip on St. Kitts is a circumnavigation of the island which includes **Brimstone Hill.** The road takes you through **Bloody Point,** the site of the massacre, in 1626, of 2,000 Caribs who had been betrayed by a young Indian girl. Carib Indian inscriptions on rocks can be found some 50 yards off the main road up the gorge of the Pelham River. **Old Road Village** was the landing site of the original British settlers and the site of the first British settlement in the West Indies. There are remains of the walls of old Government House and more Indian inscriptions on a rock near Old Road in Wingfield Estate. Old **St. Thomas Church,** with its cemetery containing the tomb of Sir Thomas Warner, the first settler, is located in Middle Island. A little farther on and ten miles from Basseterre is 750-foot **Brimstone Hill,** the "Gibraltar of the West Indies." The hill received its name from the constant odor of sulphur around its base. It was a belief of the Indians that the hill was the top of Mount Misery, blown off during an eruption and deposited at its present site upside down. **Fort George,** on top of the hill, is a gigantic fortress built by the labor of thousands of slaves over a period of 100 years. Apart from the sights in the fort, the views of land and sea from Brimstone Hill would make the drive well worthwhile.

Farther along the coast are **Sandy Point** and St. Ann's Church. Driving on through various little fishing villages, one comes to a point called **Black Rocks**—strangely shaped masses of black lava on which the surf breaks and which you can see only by walking to the edge of the cliff. From here, you can cut back across the island to Basseterre past the **Government cattle farm,** open to visitors, and some of the old plantation homes.

Spare time on St. Kitts could be spent taking the Sunday excursion boat, or a chartered craft, to **Salt Pond Estate** to see the ponds where salt is raked, washed and packed.

SPORTS AND RECREATION. Beaches are not on a par with most Caribbean ones, but **swimming** is pleasant at Conaree Beach and Frigate Bay, both about two miles out of town. **Fishing** is good. Ramier pigeon and some migratory birds can be hunted during the summer months. Mountain monkeys are considered fair game since they are destructive to vegetable gardens.

DINING AND SHOPPING. Food is typically British, with some French creole. No rum is made on the island due to religious regulations, but it is put to good use in the local version of a delicious planters punch.

Native crafts include basketware, bags, hats, embroideries; tortoise-shell articles; pottery from Nevis.

NEVIS

This is an escapist's dream island with an insidious peace-on-earth atmosphere that affects and infects even the most restless of visitors. The relaxed pace of activities, the almost deserted streets of the dead-asleep little capital city, **Charlestown,** the quiet of the rustic countryside add to the belief that here time has really stopped.

THE LAND. Almost circular in shape, approaching it by boat from a certain angle, Nevis appears to be a perfect cone rising from the sea to a height of 3,596 feet, its summit usually smothered in clouds resembling a cap of snow. This, perhaps, is the reason why Columbus, who arrived here in 1493 and first called the island St. Martin, later changed the name to the Spanish word for snows—*nievas.* Or it may have reminded him of Las Nievas, a snow-capped peak in Spain.

Almost the entire island is hilly. The lofty central volcanic cone is called Nevis. To its north is 1,192-foot-high

Hurricane Hill, to its south 1,432-foot-high Saddle Hill–both connected to Nevis by "saddle." The mountains, covered with government-protected forests, slope down to the sea, and the lower lands are strewn with boulders that make cultivation difficult. Most of the island is surrounded by coral reefs.

THE CLIMATE. Of course there is no real snow in Nevis, whose average year-round temperature, 79 degrees, is somewhat higher than in St. Kitts from June to November. Rains average only 53 inches a year. The few streams on the island and a 60-acre catchment in the mountainous north and northwest sections supply the island with its water.

THE PEOPLE. The population of 14,000, mostly of African–European descent, are a courteous and friendly people. Church of England is their religion, for the most part, although several other denominations are present.

Nevis, part of a grant to the Earl of Carlisle in 1627, was first settled by the English under Sir Thomas Warner of St. Kitts. For such a placid little island as it is today, it has had a sadly tumultuous past. The first settlement was destroyed by Spaniards a year after it had been established. During the earthquake of 1680, Jamestown, Nevis' first capital, was engulfed by a tidal wave. In this tragedy there was only one survivor —an imprisoned pirate. In 1706 the island was sacked by the French who, among other items, captured and removed some 3,500 slaves. In 1780, the French took and occupied Nevis but returned it to England under the Treaty of Versailles in 1783.

Nevis has a warden under the jurisdiction of the administrator on St. Kitts. The old government house now serves as a hospital. Burros, horses, buses, and taxis serve as the primary means of transportation.

Nevis is isolated in feeling but accessible by daily scheduled launches or by a five-minute plane trip to Basseterre on St. Kitts, only 13 miles away. The two islands are separated at their closest point by a two-mile strait called The Narrows. Booby Island in The Narrows is so-called because of the pelicans, "booby birds" to the natives, that inhabit it.

AGRICULTURE. Sea-island cotton, ginned and baled on the island, is the main crop. Sugar and coconuts are also grown, largely on a sharecropping basis. Fruit and vegetables are raised, boats are built, and clay pottery is made at the village of Brick Kiln. Cotton, coconuts, cocoa, and livestock are exported.

CHARLESTOWN. Southeast of the pier in **Charlestown** is the house that claims to have been the **birthplace of Alexander Hamilton** (January 11, 1757).

Highlights of the pretty 20-mile drive around the island are **Pinney's Beach; Hurricane Hill,** with a few remains of an old fort at the top and from which there are five views; the lagoon and **Nelson's Well** at Clifton, where Admiral Nelson presumably watered his ships; the native village of **Newcastle,** with remains of the great houses; ruins of **Montpelier House,** where Nelson lived and married the widow Fannie Nesbit on March 3, 1787, now a cottage-type hotel. In **Fig Tree Church** is a monument Lady Nelson erected to her father and mother, and Nelson's signature to his marriage register is in the Parish House. **Morning Star** is the site where the English repulsed a dawn attack by the French. **Saddle Hill Fort** was one of Nelson's lookout posts. Some of the old great houses can be seen: **Eden Brown's Estate** is where its owner fought a famed duel and was killed before his home was completed, and **Golden Rock Great House** which has been made into a charming hotel.

SPORTS AND RECREATION. Four-mile-long, reef-protected **Pinney's Beach,** one mile from town, is the most popular bathing area. Near the beach there is a clubhouse with occasional dances in the evenings. There is rough surf on the western coast, but **swimming** is possible in some of the protected coves. Also popular are **boating, fishing, spear-fishing, snorkeling, tennis, cricket, horseback riding,** and **hiking.** In addition, there is some **bird shooting,** and hunting Indian relics is another popular pastime. The **thermal baths** of the old Bath House Hotel are still operating, with five baths of temperatures varying up to 107 degrees.

DINING AND SHOPPING. One of the local favorites is a planters punch. Items to buy include local handicrafts and pottery.

ANGUILLA

This is the ugly duckling of the Caribbean, an island of 16 by 3 miles. It has no tropical growth–just low shrub; no mountains–just a high point of 213 feet above sea level; no real towns–just three districts called Road, Valley and Spring; no rivers–just wells and catchments but little rain to catch. It does have miles and miles of some of the most perfect beaches in the Caribbean, particularly on the western side of the island and notably at **Rendezvous Bay,** and a superb view from the cliffs at **Road Bay.** It is a healthy island with no tropical diseases and with a cooler climate than St. Kitts.

At present, only a handful of tourists cross the waters between Marigot on the French side of St. Martin and Anguilla by the daily boat that plies between the two places, or take the 15-minute flight. People cruising these waters in their own or chartered boats have discovered that **"Snake Island"** has a peculiar charm all its own. Anguilla earns its nickname from its shape and not from a prevalence of snakes.

A few houses and cottages are available for rent, and rooms in private houses would probably be offered a visitor by some of the 5,000 inhabitants, all of whom are Negroes except for several white families. Understanding their version of English may present difficulties, but their friendly, relaxed hospitality is everywhere in evidence.

Anguilla's history is the usual one of much of the West Indies. It was discovered by Columbus (1493), settled by the British (1650), and later attacked by the Carib Indians, the French and the Irish. At one point, in 1689, the French raided it so often from St. Martin that all the inhabitants were evacuated to Antigua. However, it did manage to remain permanently under British control.

The island has its own warden under the jurisdiction of the administrator of St. Kitts.

Way offshore, a six-mile stretch of various islets form what is known as the Seal Islands Reef, which includes the Prickly Pear and Dog islands, both cultivated but not inhabited. Dog Island is so named because the sound made by the pounding of the surf oddly resembles the howling of a dog.

There is good **hunting** for duck and migratory birds for part of the year, with an open season from mid-July through January. There is good **game fishing,** but poisonous fish also live in these waters. **Swimming** is ideal, but the presence of some fish that might become inquisitive make it prudent to stay reasonably close to shore.

MONTSERRAT

Montserrat is a quiet, beautiful little island, its 11 by 7 miles of tropical scenery made up of green, fertile lowlands and rugged, heavily wooded volcanic peaks. One of them, 3,000-foot-high Chance Peak, has two active *soufrières* on its leeward slopes. It is a healthy island with a dry climate and an average temperature of 81 degrees, cooled by traditional trade winds. An average annual rainfall of 62 inches and springs provide an adequate water supply. Its capital town of **Plymouth,** on an open roadstead, is its only port of entry.

With a population of 14,000, the majority of whom are of African–European descent, the areas around St. Peters and Cudjoe Head contain descendants of the Irish settlers who came over in the seventeenth century. Only English is spoken, and occasionally one can hear an Irish brogue. Oliver Cromwell, who sent Irish settlers over in the seventeenth century, can be held responsible for this, for at one time there were 3,000 Irish families on the island. A shamrock adorns the center gable of Government House.

There are 15 primary schools in the colony and one secondary school situated in Plymouth. The Anglican, Roman Catholic, Wesleyan, Pentecostal, Pilgrim Holiness, Church of God, and Seventh-Day Adventist churches are represented.

Sea-island cotton, the main crop, sugar, vegetables, and fine fruits are grown. Cotton lint, lime products, and vegetables, chiefly tomatoes, carrots, cabbages, and sweet potatoes, are exported. The island has a government-run cotton ginnery and one rum distillery.

Stores in Plymouth can supply everyday needs. The island is easily accessible from Antigua (only 27 miles) and from St. Kitts and other islands by boat and by plane. A few freighters stop here as well as private yachts cruising in the area.

Montserrat, like the rest of the West Indian islands, was discovered in 1493 by Columbus, who named it Monserrado, after a mountain in Spain. In 1632, an expedition of Irish commissioned by Oliver Cromwell established a settlement, and though briefly captured and occupied by France in 1664 and again in 1782, since 1783 Montserrat has been a property of Great Britain.

While on holiday, one may **fish, swim, snorkel,** or enjoy scenic **sailing** on power boat trips around the island. On land, there is the spectacular Belham River Valley **golf** course, **tennis,** and **horseback riding.** For hikers and mountain climbers, Montserrat is a paradise with interesting sights such as Galway's **soufrière** and the Great Alp Water Falls. There is also a thermal spa in its natural setting within easy reach.

Being of volcanic formation, all its beaches, with the exception of two, are of non-flowing gray-black sand. One can swim at all the beaches on the island and also in streams and under waterfalls in the interior. There is **shooting** for pigeons in the mountains, and **hunting** for mountain chicken, an edible frog. A boat trip to Redonda provides good fishing. **Cricket, football,** and **netball** games are played.

Tourist attractions include a war memorial on the waterfront, a botanical garden, a public market, and a lovely garden on the grounds of Government House on a cliff overlooking the sea. Close by Plymouth are the ruins of Fort Barrington. Fort St. George is 1,200 feet above the town. It is a five-mile drive across the island to Harris' village. Montserrat has 80 miles of asphalt main roads and 70 miles of unsurfaced secondary roads which are suitable for traffic.

Netherlands Antilles

Six island territories, three leeward and three windward islands, make up the Netherlands Antilles. The Leeward Islands are Curaçao, Bonaire, and Aruba; the Windward Islands are St. Eustatius, St. Maarten, and Saba.

The Spaniards discovered the islands around 1500, but didn't take possession of any until 1527. The Dutch showed up in these waters around 1630, when the Dutch West Indies merchantmen dropped anchor at Sint Maarten, and in Statia in 1632. The islands changed hands several times, and although Peter Stuyvesant established a strong foothold as the island of Curaçao's first governor in 1643, the Dutch didn't hold the territories until 1816, when they became a part of the Kingdom of the Netherlands.

The Netherlands Antilles is administered by a governor representing the Queen. He is assisted by an appointive Advisory Council consisting of nine members, and he shares his executive powers with the Executive Council, consisting of seven members who serve a term of four years and who are appointed by the governor in concert with the legislature.

The legislative branch of the govern-

NETHERLANDS ANTILLES

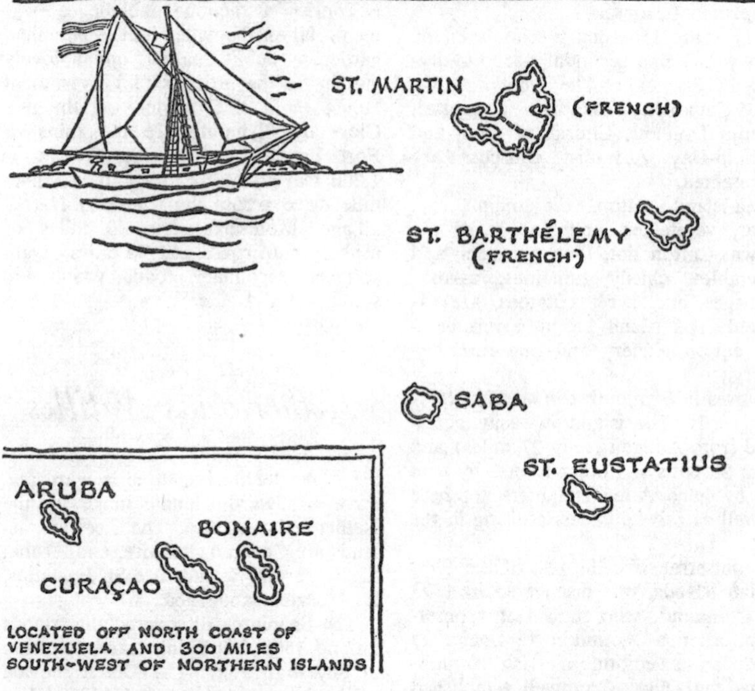

ment is called the "Staten"; it has 22 members and is elected by the people of the six islands through universal suffrage. The Legislative Council sits at Willemstad. Each island has its own government and a council, who have autonomy in local affairs and administer certain taxes. The island government is headed by a *gezaghebber,* appointed by the Queen, who is assisted by two to five "deputies."

ARUBA

The island of Aruba, believed to be the top of a submerged mountain, part of the Paraguana Range which terminates in Venezuela 15 miles away, is a land of contrasts. Only six miles wide and less than 20 miles long, it is generally arid, coral terrain.

Its barren north coast has steep cliffs and rough water, hardly navigable; the south coast, with a barrier of underwater coral reefs which provide a natural breakwater, teems with fine harbors, natural bays, inlets and white sand beaches.

THE LAND. The island is like no other in the West Indies. Lush tropical verdure is absent, except in tiny patches. The soil is volcanic rock; terrain is quite hilly in places, and on the higher ground, huge boulders and stones, like carved monoliths of animals and people, are in scattered profusion. The only conspicuous natural landmark on the island is the cone-like **Haystack Mountain,** which rises 500 feet out of the middle of Aruba.

Vegetation is skimpy on the island, being limited to the numerous varieties of cacti and the divi-divi (fan tree), a small, gnarled tree that grows straight to the point where it gives itself over to the never-ending northeastern trade wind. Its top streams out horizontally to the southwest. The countryside, or *kunuku* (a word meaning bare, barren, uncultivated), has areas where even the cacti and divi-divi cannot survive, which resemble some prehistoric world. In striking contrast, there are patches of vegetation and glossy palm trees.

On the southwest side is the pride of every Aruban—**Palm Beach,** a beautiful, fine-powdery ribbon of sand that stretches for miles. Gently sloped, it is rimmed with coconut palms and washed with clearest blue and green water.

Spanish seafarers were first to discover the Netherlands Leeward Islands, historians believe, including Aruba—a name derived from either the Guaranee Indian word *Oirubea,* which means companion, or the Carib Indian word *Oraoubao,* meaning island of shells.

THE CLIMATE. The island has a tropical but pleasant and healthy climate, with an average annual temperature of 82 degrees. Nearly 12 months of the year the northeast trade wind blows—a fact that accounts for the absence of mosquitoes, flies and other disease carriers. Malaria, yellow fever, and hay fever are unknown.

The coolest months are January and February; the warmest, August and September. Rainfall is scant, the average slightly over 17 inches annually. The rainiest months usually are November and December. However, even in the wettest months, the showers are of short duration and there is hardly a day without sunshine. In addition, Aruba is completely outside the range of hurricanes.

THE PEOPLE. On this small island there are nearly 60,000 inhabitants, of whom about 36,000 are Arubans, the descendants of the original Indians, Africans, the Spanish, and, later, the Dutch settlers. The remainder came from Holland, Surinam, Curaçao, Bonaire, and the Netherlands Windward Islands.

The Aruban is strong physically, a good worker, and quick to learn skills. He is intensely home-loving and industrious, and clings to his own patch of soil, no matter how unproductive, and to his small pastel-colored home.

The island-born population speaks a remarkable tongue called Papiamento. Opinions differ widely on the origin of Papiamento, but it is likely that original local Indian languages were influenced by those of foreign settlers. Apart from French, English, Dutch, and Portuguese (Portuguese Jews arrived in 1659), Papiamento has absorbed many expressions from African dialects brought over by the slaves, and, because of close contact with Venezuela, it is described by some as "Spanish with a Dutch remodeling job."

Dutch is taught in the schools, and is the official language. The trade language is mostly English and Spanish.

AGRICULTURE. In Aruba, agriculture concentrates mainly on the growing of sorghum or millet—the local name of which is *Maishi Rabo.* The flour is used generally for making a porridge and also a kind of pancake or *pan Bati.* Predominant, however, is *funchi,* a national dish made of imported coarse-grain corn flour. Most foodstuffs, fruits, and vegetables are imported to the island. In operation is a 24-acre hydroponic farm, using distilled seawater (from a seawater distillation plant).

INDUSTRY. The industrial economy of Aruba can be summed up in one word: "oil." In 1925, when the Standard Oil Company of New Jersey opened what is today the largest oil refinery in the world, Lago Oil and Transport Company, the island economy was changed from the slim one produced as a result of farming the cactus-like plant called aloe (a source of medicinals), to a burgeoning one, where some 80 percent of the population is directly or indirectly employed in the oil industry.

Background of this strange metamorphosis in an island which lacks oil or other fuel, as well as water and food-producing soil, lies in the discovery of perhaps the richest oil field in history under Lake Maracaibo, an arm of the sea reaching deep into Venezuela, 150 miles away. Vast sand bars made it impossible to bring in ocean tankers. The only solution was to haul out the crude oil in shallow-draft boats to a processing site. Aruba offered spacious harbors and was a healthful area.

CITIES. Aruba, famous for its excellent beaches and mountain areas, has two small cities, Oranjestad and San Nicolas.

Oranjestad, the capital city, is known for its neatness and cleanliness. Its orderly streets and efficient administration are most interesting. Distinctly Dutch in flavor, the city has gaily colored buildings and fine residential sections.

Over the harbor area is the old square tower of Fort William III, originally called Fort Zoutman. It overlooks the post office, police headquarters, and the modern government guesthouse. In front, fishing schooners are tied up alongside the piers of Lloyd Smith Boulevard. The long pier partially closes Paardenbaai (Horse Bay), the harbor of Oranjestad. Night life in Oranjestad is gay; entertainment is provided by local singers, dancers, and steel-band music.

San Nicolas (St. Nicholas, Sint Nicolas–three versions are common) is at the opposite end of the island. The city, second largest on Aruba, is an oil town, with a character all its own. It boasts some good beaches, a yacht club, the Exxon Club, which supplies entertainment for the oil workers, and the Aruba Gold Club.

SPORTS AND RECREATION. In Aruba's West Coast area, **Palm Beach** and **Eagle Beach**–miles of fine white sand–offer some of the finest year-round bathing to be had anywhere. Sailing and fishing along this coast, between shore and reef and even in open sea, are popular pastimes.

For the sightseer, the *kunuku,* Aruba's countryside, offers much of the unusual. It is dotted with neat, small houses in pastel colors. In the center of the island are quaint villages such as **Santa Cruz** and **Savaneta,** a fishing village on the south coast near San Nicolas. The contrasting cities of **San Nicolas** and **Oranjestad** are of keen interest: San Nicolas because of the huge oil-refinery operation and the *Seroe Colorado,* a modern American community with all its facilities; Oranjestad because of its old Dutch flavor.

The **Yamanota,** Aruba's so-called "mountain range," provides interesting Indian caves, the walls of which contain ancient, unfathomed inscriptions and drawings. Most fascinating is **Quadirikiri Cave.** Also in the *kunuku* are the giant monoliths, the most impressive of which are those at **Ayó.** Photogenic are the weird rock formations at **Canashito Hill,** the habitat of large flocks of bright green parakeets.

Balashi, a "ghost town" relic of Aruba's gold-mining days, is as barren as the oasis of **Boca Prins** on the north coast or the **Fountain Plantation** is lush.

The network of roads all over the island is excellent. Everywhere the visitor goes–on the road, off the road–in the *kunuku,* the soon-familiar, ever-present sight are the herds of wild goats, or *cabrites* (pronounced "*cabreetes*").

SPECIAL EVENTS. Big **native celebration** in Aruba comes at **New Year's** with an imaginary character known as "Dandee." The celebrants go from house to house, singing, playing drums, maracas, and the *wiri,* a unique, home-made instrument fashioned from a ribbed piece of steel. When scraped with a long nail, it produces a repetitive bell-like sound.

DINING AND SHOPPING. The food specialty of the islands is the Dutch-Indonesian dish called *rijsttafel.* The word itself is Dutch; no native Indonesian dialect has an equivalent for this name in its vocabulary. Literally translated, the word means "rice table." A complex series of dishes, it is an original native food in the sense that rice is the basis; all the other dishes go with it in varying tastes and an endless number of combinations.

Both cities on Aruba offer the tourist a wide variety of merchandise from all continents, displayed either in old bazaars or in neat modern shops. There are Swiss watches, French perfume, Delft Blue and silverware from Holland and England, Madeira embroidery, souvenirs from China and India, liquors and liqueurs of all types from all countries. Prices are "free port," often less than half what the tourist would pay in the U.S., because of extremely low import duties, or, on many articles, no import duty at all.

BONAIRE

Bonaire, second largest of the Leeward Islands, is the most easterly of the ABC islands, and about 30 miles east of Curaçao.

THE LAND. The island is hilly in the northern section. Its highest peak, Brandaris, rises to nearly 800 feet. The southern portion is flat, with characteristic *kunuku* vegetation. However, Bonaire has slightly more rainfall than Aruba and Curaçao.

THE CLIMATE. With a climate similar to that of Curaçao, Bonaire has an average temperature range between 76 and 90 degrees, August and September being the hottest months.

CITIES. The main village is **Kralendijk** (coral dike) on the west coast. It is situated in the southern part of the island, facing the three-mile-square island of Little Bonaire. (Little Bonaire is uninhabited except for the goats.) Kralendijk still preserves the typical character of a Colonial settlement of the days when the Dutch West India Company first took possession. Reminder of that period is the yellow-walled **Fort Oranje.**

Lining small **Wilhelmina Square** in Kralendijk, which is called the "Playa" by the natives, is the **Pasanggrahan,** a stately old Dutch mansion, formerly the Government Guest House, now a hotel. From the top of its long flight of stairs one has a view over the square and quadrangle of grass and flowers in which a small obelisk is inscribed: "1634–1934. In memory of 300 years of Dutch rule. Van Walbeek landed here July 26, 1634."

Driving from Kralendijk toward the rugged east coast of Bonaire, one comes to the **Fontein Plantation,** an oasis in a stretch of arid land. A natural fresh-water well is here, and various fruit trees and other tropical plants grow in abundance. Swimming is allowed in the large open concrete water tanks.

Not far from Fontein, at **Boca Onimo,** there is a fascinating grotto. Indian inscriptions and drawings on the walls and ceiling, carved by early Indians (as on Aruba), are believed to date from the twelfth century.

Idyllic spot is **Lac Lagoon,** a land-locked bay in the southeastern part of the island. On a small peninsula is a clear sandy beach with shade trees, ideal for a camp or a picnic. The Lac, with waters so clear that one can see coral on the bottom at a depth of 30 feet, is an outstanding spear-fishing, skin-diving spot. Across the mouth of the bay, and easily accessible over a good road, is another beautiful picnic area, called **Sorobon.**

In the southern part of the island when the salt industry was thriving, early salt ships were guided to their moorings by still-standing, 30-foot-high red, white and blue obelisks. Nearby are stone huts, only waist-high, which housed the slaves who worked the salt pan district.

In and around the square salt ponds, dotted with shining salt crystals, are a large variety of water birds: blue and white herons, snipes and sandpipers, various species of sea gulls, ducks, pintails, pelicans and, the most beautiful and fascinating of all, the flamingoes.

Every spring, thousands of the brilliant pink birds breed in Great Salt Lake. The flamingo colony can be observed at close range all year round. (Audubon Society visitors go to Bonaire with the sole purpose of watching these lovely birds.)

SPORTS AND RECREATION. Principal attractions on relaxed Bonaire include the clear-water **swimming, skin-**

diving, spear-fishing, deep-sea fishing along the entire north and east coast of the island, **game fishing** in the mouth of Lac Bay—sea bass, kingfish, sailfish, bonito, barracuda, snapper, perch, grouper, pompano and others. Sea crayfish and spine lobster can be speared in shallow water along the coast. Best season for fishing is September through February.

All spear-fishing and skin-diving equipment can be rented, as well as glass-bottomed boats, from which sea gardens, coral formations can be viewed and photographed. **Sailing** is another excellent sport on Bonaire, for the waters are sheltered.

SPECIAL EVENTS. Some of the more important holidays include **Queens Birthday,** on April 30, celebrating the birthday of the Dutch Queen Juliana, **Labor Day** on May 1, **Kingdom Day,** December 15, **Christmas Day** on December 25, and **Second Christmas Day** on December 26.

SHOPPING. Best buys are articles made of tortoise shell—combs and cigarette cases—and native-made coral and conch-shell ornaments.

CURAÇAO

Curaçao—30 miles west of Bonaire, 50 miles east of Aruba, and 38 miles off the coast of Venezuela—is the largest and most important of the six Antilles Islands. It is 38 miles long, seven miles wide at its broadest, two-and-one-half miles across at the narrowest point.

THE LAND. The island is volcanic rock base, overlaid in part with coral which has hardened into limestone, and in part with sandstone. On the southern coast are several bays, former valleys through which the sea has flowed. The longest of these is **Schottegat,** which winds its way into the surrounding hills and forms the magnificent harbor of the capital of the island, **Willemstad.**

The northern coast, exposed to the trade-wind-driven surf, is fringed with cliffs, and almost without bays. The best beaches are on the northeast top of the island at Knip Bay and West Point.

A dozen hills or so roll over the island, with **St. Christoffel Hill** the highest point at an elevation of 1,230 feet. The mountain range consists of limestone which at one place has caused a grotto formation (the Grotto of Hato). In the area is a commercially-exploited deposit of phosphate of lime.

Indigenous vegetation in the *kunuku* (sometimes spelled *cunucu*), or countryside, consists of varieties of drought-resistant plants, such as the amusing divi-divi trees, cacti, agaves and aloes. The countryside is barren, desert-like. Here and there on the island are patches of rich mold suitable for cultivation of vegetables and for small-scale fruit culture.

All over this area of rocky, dry soil, are the *cabrites,* the countless hordes of wild goats. All entrances to the villages also have game fences to protect them against the "invasion" of these goats. There are wild rabbits and some herds of wild mules, as well. Parakeets, multicolored hummingbirds, several kinds of pigeons and birds of prey, and songsters are plentiful.

In the caves along the north coast there are masses of bats, quick-footed lizards and newts. On the shores of the bays, the **iguana,** a lizard-like animal that sometimes grows to the size of a dog, is found. (In many a Curaçao kitchen this iguana is turned into a delicacy—either a delicious soup or a veal-like roast for dinner.)

The sea around Curaçao holds many kinds of edible fish, turtles, shrimps and lobsters.

THE CLIMATE. Average rainfall is 22 inches per year, the rainy season being from October to February. August and September are the hottest months; January and February are the coolest. Average temperature range is between 76 and 90 degrees. The variations in temperature between day and night are greater than the annual variation. The constant trade wind, with an average velocity of 16 miles per hour, brings coolness throughout the year.

THE PEOPLE. Curaçao was discovered on July 26, 1499, by Alonzo de Ojeda. Thirty years later, settlement was begun by the Spaniards, led by Juan de Ampues. In 1634, Dutch landed in Curaçao, banished the Spanish governor and about 400 Indians and Spaniards to Venezuela, and founded the Dutch settlement.

In 1643 Peter Stuyvesant was appointed Governor of Curaçao. Three years later he became, in addition to being Governor of Aruba, Bonaire and Curaçao, Governor of the New Netherlands and its capital New Amsterdam—the present city of New York.

During the Colonial period, Curaçao was the center of the slave trade in the Caribbean area. With the decline of the slave trade early in the nineteenth century, and the abolition of slavery by King William III in 1863, Curaçao lost much of its economic importance. The oil-refining industry in 1916 began a new era of prosperity.

AGRICULTURE. Because of the arid climate, agriculture is limited on the island, with only a small number of people engaged in farming and horticulture. Famous on the island are small orange trees which provide an essence, distilled from the skins of the oranges, used to make Curaçao liqueur.

INDUSTRY. Shell Curaçao Ltd. is one of the world's largest refineries. About 30 percent of the labor force in Curaçao is directly employed in oil refining. The oil refinery (in Aruba as well) makes the standard of living in the Netherlands Antilles higher than elsewhere in the Caribbean.

The central government as well as the island governments of the Netherlands Antilles is now doing all that is possible to attract more industries and hotels, and to stimulate tourism by granting tax holidays and by establishing free-trade zones.

Other industries on Curaçao include shipbuilding and repairing (there are two drydocks that can be classified as being among the best-equipped in the Caribbean area); the manufacture of chocolates, bonbons, caramels; woodworking; building; liquor distilling and production of non-alcoholic beverages; printing; making of furniture and drums.

Phosphate is the only important natural product of the Netherlands Antilles. It is mined at Santa Barbara by the Curaçao Mining Corporation, an English and Dutch corporation, and exported to the United States, Canada, and Holland.

A well-known export of Curaçao is orange peel, used in the distilling of the distinctive liqueur called "Curaçao." Most of the island's food is imported.

CITIES. Curaçao has only one city, Willemstad, although several tiny villages dot the island.

Willemstad, the capital, is a quaint bit of Holland transplanted to a tropical setting. Seen from the air, it presents a pattern of gabled, iron-red tile roofs; on the ground it is a colorful collection of gay, many-gabled houses of seventeenth- and eighteenth-century Holland. In addition to the older houses, there is modern architecture that uses the best of earlier designs.

Willemstad is a sightseer's dream, as nearly everything is within a few minutes' walking distance. The city is bisected by the harbor of **St. Anna Bay,** which looks like a Holland canal but is actually a natural channel leading from the sea into the huge landlocked basin behind the city. Branching off from this main channel is a smaller canal which turns off at right angles and cuts the city on that side of the channel again, so that it is divided into three distinct sections—**Punda, Pietermaai** and **Scharloo.** The section on the west side of the channel is **Otrabanda** which means "the other side." Pietermaai and Scharloo are residential sections; Punda, an older section of the city, contains shopping and business; Otrabanda is a combination of residences and business.

Life in Curaçao revolves around the **"Queen Emma,"** swinging pontoon bridge (dreamed up by an American consul years ago) across the bay, which separates the two parts of Willemstad.

It is the only way a car can get from one part of the city to the other (except for a ten-mile drive between Punda and Otrabanda). The bridge swings at every ship signal and then there is a concerted dash by motorists and pedestrians alike to make the bridge before it swings over to the side of the quay. A few hundred feet beyond the bridge a ferryboat takes passengers across, free, when the bridge is closed to traffic.

In the Punda section, **Old Fort Amsterdam** adjoins **Government House.** In the background, the white building of the old **Protestant Church** (built in 1769) is an excellent example of Colonial Dutch architecture. Nearby are the **legislative council** and **court house buildings,** and a statue of former Queen Wilhelmina.

On the same boulevard are the **Temple Emanu-el** and the **Masonic Temple.** Where it ends stands the **Church of the Rosary,** one of the many Roman Catholic churches in Curaçao. Not far away is the **Mikve Israel,** large synagogue which was built in 1732.

Near the synagogue, where fresh sand is sprinkled over the floor each day, and where the orthodox Jewish congregations of Curaçao have worshiped for over 200 years, is the **floating market**—a long line of small schooners from Venezuela—anchored almost on the sidewalk, loaded with fruits, produce and fish.

Along **Pietermaai Boulevard** are stately old Curaçao mansions. Spacious residential areas are grouped around a pond-like inlet of St. Anna Bay, the **Waaigat** (lagoon).

Scharloo is one of the most fashionable districts, composed of picturesque old Curaçao houses with shaded patios.

Ararat Hill (often referred to as the best piece of real estate on the island) is the site of the **Franklin D. Roosevelt House,** official residence of the United States consul general. The building was presented by the people of the Netherlands to the U. S. Government in 1950 in gratitude for aid in World War II. From here there is a magnificent view of the city.

Two important statues (in a historical sense) are in the Punda—that of Peter Stuyvesant and that of Simón Bolívar, who for many years lived in Curaçao and did much to cement relations between the island and neighboring Venezuela.

The old fortification of **Fort Nassau** on a 200-foot-steep hill, which can be reached by car, offers a splendid view and houses an excellent restaurant. The fort is now used as a shipping signal post.

West of the harbor—Otrabanda—and west of town, **Brionplein (Brion Square,** with a statue of Brion, Curaçao-born admiral [1782–1821] who fought beside Simón Bolívar), the road goes to the sea-front boulevard leading to Shell Oil's private club and beach of picturesque **Piscadera Bay.** On the way is the **Curaçao Museum,** built over a century ago as a military hospital. It is another typical example of stately eighteenth-century Dutch Colonial architecture. Inside can be seen beautiful furniture, decorations, paintings of the Colonial period and other valuable antiques. Another part is devoted to the new industrial and economic history of the island. A large garden contains specimens of all plants and trees indigenous to the island. Also at striking Piscadera Bay is an interesting **Marine Biological Institute and Aquarium.**

Nearby is fascinating **"The Isla"** (the island), town of the towering, shiny installations of the oil refineries. In this area is Juliana Village, one of the residential sections for the oil refinery employees. Not far from here (15 minutes' drive west of town) is a relic of the early Jewish settlement—a cemetery dating from 1650, the **oldest Caucasian burial ground** in the Americas. The tombstones, which lie flat on the ground, are lavishly carved in the seventeenth-century manner, and inscribed in Portuguese.

Through the *kunuku* settlements, toward the coast, one can drive to the old **"Savonet"** plantation at the base of Christoffel Mountain, and come out near the north coast. The last few hundred yards must be walked, as the ground is full of clefts and boulders.

High over the cliffs flies white foaming water which undermines the coral base, forming underwater caves and grottoes of great beauty, at **Boca Tabla** (Devil's Mouth Grotto) and other places.

In this area are the small village of **West Point,** high on the cliffs, with its **West Point Bay**—(the beach is excellent) and the old **"Knip" plantation,** the *kunuku* settlement of Lagoen. Here and there one may see the old-time industry of straw-hat weaving still being done.

North of town is **Rio Canario,** another residential section, consisting of neat, modern bungalows, for employees of the oil refinery.

East of town are **Mahaai, Van Engelen** and **Damacar,** modern garden suburban residential sections.

SPORTS AND RECREATION. Water sports are excellent on the island. **Swimming, waterskiing, snorkeling, skin-diving, sailing,** and **fishing** are most popular. Spectator sports include **baseball, soccer,** and occasional **tennis matches.** There are also **bowling, golf,** and **horseback riding.**

Dancing facilities—ballroom and folk —are provided for the visitor at several hotels and clubs. There are three movie houses and one drive-in theater in Willemstad. A Theatre for the Performing Arts, **Schouwburg,** is located about four-and-one-half miles out of the city. Its facilities include an 800-seat concert hall in which ballet, opera, drama, and musical comedy are performed, as well as concerts by symphonic orchestras.

SPECIAL EVENTS. Special days on the island include the **Birthday of Princess Margriet** on January 19, the **Birthday of Princess Beatrix** on January 31, and the **Birthday of Princess Christine** on February 18, all celebrated by military parades. **Carnival** is held for the four days before Ash Wednesday, with parties throughout the island. **Queen Juliana's birthday** is celebrated on April 30 and is an official holiday. **Memorial Day,** May 4, marks the death of World War II soldiers, commemorated at the War Monument. The **Miss Curaçao election** is held in June, the winner being sent to the Miss Universe Pageant in Miami Beach, Florida.

July 26 is **Curaçao Day,** on which most probably Alonzo de Ojeda, a companion of Christopher Columbus, discovered the island in 1499. **Columbus Day** (Día de la Raza) on October 12 is marked by cultural gatherings. **Kingdom Day and Antillian Flag Day,** December 15, commemorates the signing of the complete autonomy in the Knight's Hall in The Hague in 1954. The Netherlands Antilles flag was flown for the first time on this date in 1959.

DINING AND SHOPPING. Dutch cuisine, of course, is the specialty, with steaks a local favorite. Indonesian and Javanese dishes, as well as Chinese food, are featured in a number of restaurants, of which there are many. One can also get French, Italian and typical American meals.

One great specialty of the island is "Java Dog's Dish," listed on the menu as *Java Honde Portie*—filet mignon, surrounded by rice, onions, french-fried potatoes, and two fried eggs.

Another favorite is Nasi Goreng, a succulent dish of Javanese ancestry, consisting of fried rice, pork loin, shrimp, and chicken in casserole.

A specialty of the island is the Curaçao liqueur. It comes with two different labels, denoting different degrees of sweetness: orange label meaning very sweet and white label slightly sweet. It is flavored with the bitter Curaçao orange peel. The oil of the peel is extracted—two gallons of Curaçao liqueur can be flavored with the oil from a single orange!

Another favorite is Curaçao punch, made in a tall glass, using lemon or lime peel, canned peaches, rum, green curaçao, and ice, topped by a maraschino cherry.

Almost bereft of fresh water, Curaçao has solved its problem by building two sea-water distilling plants. These plants supply 250 million gallons per year, to which minerals are added for health and taste. Soon there will be 450 million gallons per year, supplemented by softened and purified well water.

Curaçao has long been a shopping mecca for cruise ships either stopping for a short time or staying over. The Punda is filled with shops of all sizes and architectural styles, and department stores selling free-port bargain items of endless variety. Among the featured bargains are exclusive jewelry; German and Japanese cameras and binoculars; Swiss watches; all conceivable kinds of fine bone china, tape recorders, porcelain and crystal from every European country; Hong Kong, Madeira and Irish hand-worked linen; Dutch, English and Danish silver hollow-ware and flatware; Scotch cashmere men's and women's sweaters, men's suits; Italian wool dresses; Dutch, Swedish and German stainless-steel flatware.

Always available are such "classic" lines as French perfumes, liquors and liqueurs from all European and Western Hemisphere countries; leather articles, Austrian petit-point bags, and products of local artisans. Air and ship passengers can purchase merchandise at prices 40 to 60 percent lower than retail costs in home cities.

ST. EUSTATIUS

Called "Statia," the island has an area of about 11 square miles; it is the second in size of the Windwards, but has the smallest population—about 1,000, mostly of English and Dutch descent.

From the sea, Statia, the most rustic of the islands, shows its two rocky, steep, extinct volcanic cones. The highest is "The Quill," which rises about 2,000 feet. There is an excellent harbor. The language is English, although a few have learned Dutch.

Much of the island's sad destiny is linked with the American Revolution. In 1776 Fort Oranje fired the first salute of a foreign nation to the rebel flag of the American colonies, flying from the brig *Andrew Doria.*

In 1780 the British fleet, under Admiral Rodney, sent forth a punitive expedition which looted the island and destroyed the capital by fire. The island never recovered from this attack. A population of over 20,000 in 1780 dwindled to 1,000.

Oranjestad, on the western coast at the base of a mountain, is the island's capital. Of interest to the tourist are the ruins of the old **Fort Oranje.** At the base of its flagstaff an inscription on a bronze plaque, given by President Roosevelt in 1939, commemorates the historic event of the first salute.

Next to the memorial plaque, a white memorial needle bears an inscription, important historically—"in commemoration of the stay at St. Eustace of M. A. De Ruyter, May 14–17, 1665."

Adjoining the fort stand the roofless ruins of the **Dutch Reformed Church** and the yellow brick remains of the **Jewish Synagogue** of a colony long since extinct. There are also remains of an old **Protestant Church** with a number of weather-beaten tombstones next to vaulted graves. One of them covers the grave of Jan de Windt, governor of St. Eustatius, Saba, and St. Maarten, who died on January 19, 1775.

Native handmade lace and native baskets make lovely souvenirs.

ST. MAARTEN

St. Martin (Sint Maarten) was discovered by Columbus on the name day of St. Martin of Tours. He found the island populated by Carib Indians "probably belonging to the same tribe as those on the neighboring island." He described them as "courageous, warlike savages, given to cannibalism . . ." The men hunted, fished, warred; the women worked the fields.

Holland first conquered St. Martin in 1631, but was forced to abandon it. In 1644, Peter Stuyvesant personally led an expedition to recapture it. It was during a skirmish with the Portuguese that he lost his leg.

The island is divided between the Netherlands Antilles and France. The northern part is French **St. Maarten.** The border dispute between France and Holland in 1648 was settled by having a citizen of each country walk around the island in opposite directions. The territory covered by each man then became the property of his country. The Frenchman covered more ground, but the Dutchman enclosed the then valuable salt ponds.

In 1948 a simple monument commemorating the 300 years of friendly relations between the two parts of the island was erected at the border line, on the road from Philipsburg, capital of the Dutch area, to Marigot, capital of the French territory.

St. Maarten (Martin) lies 100 statute miles east of the Virgin Islands and has the best anchorage of the three Windward Islands of the Netherlands Antilles. The island is hilly with a pleasant vegetation; highest peak in the Dutch part, 1,200 feet, is called **Sentry Hill.**

Philipsburg is the home of the greater part of the 5,000 population in the Dutch area. It lies on a narrow sand bar between the bay and the Great Salt Pond. Mountains spring up steeply from either side of the town; the Great Bay encircles the whole area.

Marigot, capital of the French section, is quite different from Philipsburg. Houses are smaller, not so neat, and have gingerbread decoration.

The language spoken most is English. Dutch is the official language in the Dutch section, and French is the official language in that section but is seldom used otherwise. There are several native dialects, but nothing at all of the Leewards' Papiamento.

No barbed wire, no guideposts or frontier guardhouses mar the peaceful border which merges rather than divides the French and Dutch parts of the island. Since all the waters surrounding the island and the roads across it are used jointly by French and Netherlands citizens, the groups are close in other ways: both celebrate **Bastille Day;** both celebrate the **Dutch Queen's birthday.** Biggest celebration occurs on **July 21,** the date slavery ended on the island. These all-out festivals include foot racing, horse racing, donkey racing, bicycle racing, boat racing, fireworks and public dancing and singing.

The top of **Mount William** offers a magnificent view over the Great Salt Pond, intersected by narrow dams. Silhouettes of Saba and St. Eustatius can be seen. On top of one of the two ranges which rise on either side of Philipsburg are the ruins of old **Fort Amsterdam.** To the north of Mount William the view ranges over the rolling hill country of the French part of the island, and to the left the slopes of Mount William and the hills opposite meet in a small green valley called Cul-de-Sac. Beaches are abundant, and **swimming, skin-diving** and **spear-fishing** are popular pastimes.

There is excellent **horseback riding** throughout the island. Horses are bred for export by both the French and the Dutch.

The western half of the island boasts a vast, picturesque bay called **Simpson Lagoon.** Near there is a small white settlement whose main occupation is fishing. Almost the entire western section of St. Martin encompasses a vast housing and hotel development project, covering an area of 2,000 acres, with 15 miles of water frontage, including some of the most attractive beaches in the Caribbean. The entire east coast of the French part has scenic bays and beaches.

Fishing is another attraction. Game fish are plentiful. All equipment and boats can be rented.

SHOPPING. In both parts of the island free-port privileges exist, for neither has duties or taxes on imported merchandise. In the French part, the visitors can find fine French wines and liqueurs, perfumes and cosmetics at unbelievably low prices. In Philipsburg, attractive locally-made wearing apparel is available. Items of tortoise shell, wood, Delft china, figurines and sporting goods are also good buys.

SABA

Saba is actually an extinct volcano rising from the sea in a broken cone to a height of 2,900 feet. The island is only about five square miles in area.

It is 29 miles from St. Martin, 19 miles from St. Eustatius. (Antigua is 40 and St. Thomas 120 miles away.) Saba can be reached only by sea.

The white population, comprising about 60 percent of the 1,200 total population, are supposed descendants from a long line of seafarers. The majority of the males on the island have found work in the oil refineries on Curaçao and Aruba. Many men born on Saba are seafarers, serving with the merchant marine of several nations. English and Dutch are spoken.

Since 1640 there have been Dutch settlers on the island. Early settlers cut stone steps in the rocky cliff from **Fort Bay**—a strip of black volcanic beach with rocks on either side—some 800 feet up, to the only flat spot on the island, called Bottom, where they founded their main village. Now a steep, winding concrete road (wide enough for one jeep) leads to Bottom, but the old step path is still traversable.

The people of Saba live within the crater of the volcano, clinging precariously to the walls in the little villages of St. Johns, Windwardside, and Hellsgate at about the 1,800-foot level. The chief town, Bottom, is not all the way down, but is at the 800-foot level.

Bottom is a transplanted Dutch village, which has neat white houses with red-tiled roofs, around which are carefully tended gardens. Its few narrow streets are spotlessly clean; houses are brightly painted. About half the island's population lives in Bottom. Bottom is also known as "The Promised Land," so called by a group of eight families by the name of Sagor who were moved from the West Coast and incorporated again in a single group under the same name—although the idea of the government was to break them up.

From Bottom to a small village, **Windwardside,** 1,000 feet above it, the visitor may ride a jeep up the spectacular single-track road. Windwardside has about two dozen houses. Stone walls frame the little streets on both sides. Over the low stone walls peer bunches of roses, pink and red hippocras and flaming poinsettias.

Hellsgate is the northernmost village on Saba. Here a few houses seem to cling to a rough, wind-swept slope, completely isolated. From Windwardside to Hellsgate, stone steps cut in the rocks make an impressive climb. On the right is a sheer drop to the ocean; on the left is the steep slope of the volcano.

Only tourist attraction on the island is the climb to the crater of the volcano. The visitor can find a guide easily. One unusual sight on the way is the tombstones that dot the yards of the tiny white houses. Because of the rocky earth and the steep ascents, one can be buried in one's own backyard.

As the climber goes higher, the trail leads through a lush tropical jungle with exotic plants and trees. Still higher, within the crater, is a banana plantation with hundreds of trees, deep green and graceful. It is the last fertile land on the island, giving Saba the name of "greenest" of the three Windward Islands.

SHOPPING. Lace made by the local people is excellent, and far below U.S. and European prices.

French West Indies

Three hundred miles southeast of Puerto Rico lies **Guadeloupe,** somewhat larger than its sister, **Martinique,** separated from Guadeloupe by British Dominica. The small island dependencies of Guadeloupe—**St. Martin, St. Barthélemy, Marie-Galante, La Désirade** and **Îles des Saintes**—are unique examples of insular communities, whose people are separated from their neighbors in the other islands by cultural differences, by occupation, or—like La Désirade—by purpose (it is a leper colony).

Both Martinique and Guadeloupe (including dependencies) are *départements* of France, having risen from territorial status in 1946. The laws, the customs, and underlying way of life are thoroughly French, although spiced

FRENCH WEST INDIES

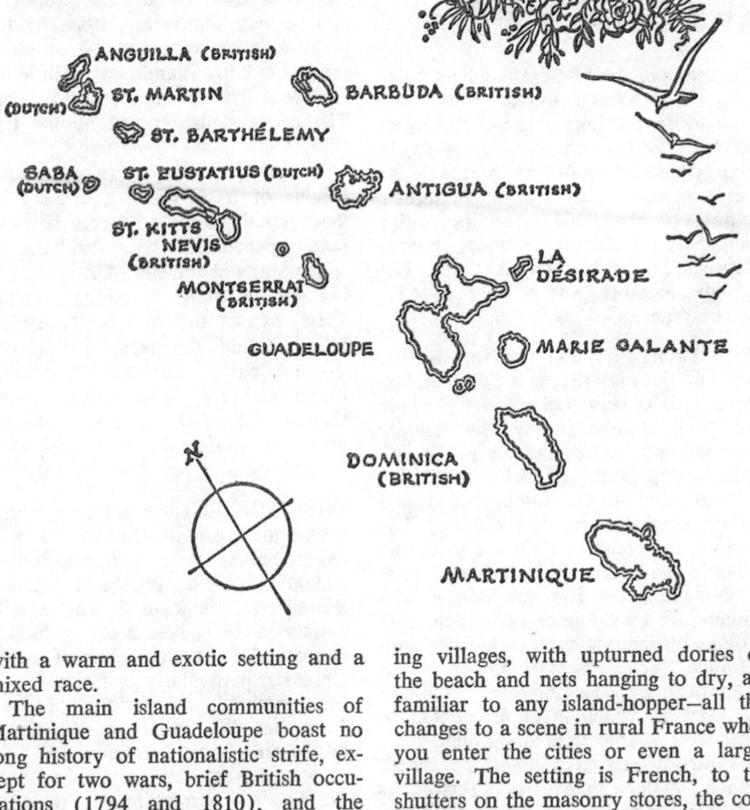

with a warm and exotic setting and a mixed race.

The main island communities of Martinique and Guadeloupe boast no long history of nationalistic strife, except for two wars, brief British occupations (1794 and 1810), and the struggles of early colonials with the indigenous Carib Indians. The spectacular and tragic eruption of Martinique's Mount Pelée volcano in 1902 and the birth there of Napoleon's Empress Josephine make Martinique the better known of the two islands.

There is one notable distinguishing feature of the two main islands. Although the countryside, with its fields of sugar cane, pineapple, and stunted banana and plantain trees, is typically Caribbean—the corrugated-tin and slatted-board shacks of the impoverished agricultural population; the seaside fishing villages, with upturned dories on the beach and nets hanging to dry, are familiar to any island-hopper—all this changes to a scene in rural France when you enter the cities or even a larger village. The setting is French, to the shutters on the masonry stores, the cobblestone of many streets, the balconied windows of Empire-style grand villas, and the ornate yet faded dignity of the Mairie or the Hotel de Ville. Until you reach the open-air produce markets, with the ever-present Caribbean fruits and vegetables, all the institutions and settings appear typically French—yet even the markets have their counterparts in every French village. The custom of the apéritif in the little French bars holds up, as does the rigid methods of civil servants in the Bureau des Postes.

French West Indians, excepting government officials or French businessmen or tourists from France, may speak a French patois called Creole. Although comprehensible in part to anyone speaking French well, there are some structural peculiarities.

GUADELOUPE

Guadeloupe, the "Emerald Island," lies between Dominica in the south and Antigua in the north, about 300 miles southeast of Puerto Rico. It is really twin islands—**Basse-Terre** and **Grande Terre**—spread out like a butterfly's wings and connected by a drawbridge that spans the narrow sea-water channel between, called the Rivière Salée. The islands together cover only a 687-square-mile area.

THE LAND. Basse-Terre, the western wing of the butterfly, is a volcanic formation. It is very rocky and the whole island is dominated by the densely forested mountainsides and peaks culminating in Soufrière. Basse-Terre, the official capital of Guadeloupe, is located at the southwest tip of the island. Lying off the south coast are two of the island's five insular dependencies, Marie-Galante and the Îles des Saintes. The others are La Désirade, a French leper colony off the east coast of mountainous Grande Terre; St. Barthélemy to the far north; and the northern portion of St. Martin, which is an island far to the north shared with the Dutch.

Grande Terre is a limestone island, much flatter than Basse-Terre. Its beaches are a dazzling white, especially on the south coast where there are some of the finest swimming stretches in the world. They are shaded with palms and clumps of bright bougainvillaea, and tropical lilies grow almost to the tide line. A coral reef encircles the island, helping to shelter the waters, and in the north are many lovely coral-tinted beaches. The interior of the island is mostly rolling plains.

Guadeloupe has been nicknamed "Emerald of the Caribbean" due to its dense forests and sparkling rivers. It has many features similar to the French Riviera, and is connected by scheduled plane service to Paris as well as by French passenger freighters en route to French Guiana and French Tahiti.

THE CLIMATE is always pleasantly warm all over Guadeloupe, though it can be very humid in parts. The temperature averages about 60 to 80 degrees on both islands, with little difference between summer and winter. The evenings are cooled by the trade winds.

It is much cooler in the mountainous heights of Basse-Terre, and there is a three-month season of torrential downpours punctuated with brilliant sun which starts at the end of August, trailing off in early November. Grande Terre escapes this and is dry all year round except for rare, fine showers which occur at intervals all over the island and especially under the rain shadow of Soufrière. It is coolest everywhere from December to March; warmest and driest from April to July.

THE PEOPLE. There are over 300,000 people living on Guadeloupe and its five dependencies, with concentrations of 60,000 at Pointe-à-Pitre and 14,000 in Basse-Terre, the capital. The rest live mainly in the coastal areas or tend the coffee and sugar plantations of the flatter parts, particularly in Grande Terre. The mountainous regions of Basse-Terre and the interior of the dependencies are almost uninhabited.

Nearly 90 percent of the population are Creoles, a mixture of French and African (with faint traces of the early Spanish settlers). The original Carib Indian inhabitants of Guadeloupe never surrendered to any of the invaders and they were killed off or fled to other islands. Slaves were brought from Africa to work on the plantations, and their descendants, interbred with the French colonizers, form the indigenous Creole population. About 10 percent are pure Negro.

There are about 5,000 Europeans on the island, mainly from France, employed in governmental services or working for the large sugar and coffee concerns. Others have set up shops and restaurants.

The people of Guadeloupe are known as *les bons gens*—and are famous for their honesty and hospitable friendliness. Many of the Creole women wear the traditional dress, especially at fêtes —a voluminous and brightly colored overskirt looped up over stiff white-lace petticoats. This is topped by a bandana, or madras, wound round the head with a high fan of material in front.

Guadeloupe was discovered by Christopher Columbus in 1493 just a few days after he had found La Désirade and Marie-Galante. He stopped his ships to take on fresh water in the Bay of Saint-Marie, on the southeast shore of Basse-Terre, naming the island Guadeloupe in honor of the monastery of Guadeloupe in Estremadura. Six days later he claimed the Îles des Saintes for Spain.

The Carib peoples who lived there, after having thrown out the original Arawaks, proved a difficult proposition for the Spaniards. They were never successfully conquered, and after two attempts to colonize, the island was abandoned in the beginning of the seventeenth century.

The French took over just 31 years later, in 1635, when Charles Lyenard de l'Olive landed and occupied the island. There were several exchanges between the English and the French, but the Peace Treaty after Napoleon's defeat at Waterloo in 1815 finally restored it to France.

In 1940 Admiral Robert took over Guadeloupe for the Vichy government —as he did Martinique. The island suffered from blockades, but this unhappy period was forgotten after the local "Liberation Commission" was given authority in 1943.

The island has been a full-fledged overseas department of France since 1946. It is represented in the French Parliament by its own elected senators and deputies, and the General Council on the island has all the same privileges and duties as its motherland counterpart. As in all French departments, the regional administrative chief is a prefect, appointed by the Minister for the Interior.

All the government buildings are in Basse-Terre, the official capital. Their French design, like the balconied houses, helps to give the city its look of a typical French provincial town.

AGRICULTURE. Guadeloupe is an almost entirely agricultural country. The chief crop is sugar cane, and the only important industries are sugar refining and rum-making, both at Pointe-à-Pitre.

The banana crop is also very important, and the enormous fronds of the banana trees help to give the islands their distinctive brilliant greenness. Some of the finest coffee in the world, as well as cacao, brilliant-blossomed vanilla and pineapples are other crops. Tropical fruits including mangoes, avocados, pomegranates and guavas are cultivated.

Although crops are exported (mostly to France), Guadeloupe is far from self-sufficient. Foodstuffs have to be imported, as well as textiles, construction materials and fuel.

The tourist industry is just beginning to be exploited, and the government offers tax concessions for development. Recent improvements of the harbor have increased the cruise-ship trade.

CITIES. Guadeloupe has only two cities of any size—Pointe-à-Pitre and Basse-Terre, the capital.

Pointe-à-Pitre, with a population of 60,000, is the largest of Guadeloupe's two cities, lying at the southern end of the Rivière Salée on the Bay of Le Petit Cul de Sac Marin. The airport at Le Raizet is just a mile outside.

The city was nearly destroyed by fire and hurricane in 1928 but no traces of havoc remain today. Since the dredging of the harbor it has steadily increased its importance as a commercial center and chief port. Its immediate surroundings are covered mainly with sugar plantations, with rum and sugar factories close by. The harbor, filled with sloops and schooners, is one of the most pleasant sections, and a hive of activity when a cruise ship puts in.

The **Club Nautique** has an office on the Quai Perrinon, abutting on the harbor, where arrangements for fishing and sailing trips can be made.

The main square, **Place de la Victoire,** is just a block away. During the "reign of terror" a guillotine stood here, and in 1794, 27 Royalists were executed. Today a fountain marks the spot. There is also an imposing war memorial, the chamber of commerce, and a cinema.

Rue Frebault, the main street, is nearby. The little boutiques here offer a wide variety of good French-style accessories for men and women. The open-air market with native stall-owners and their mounds of exotic fruits and vegetables and rolls of bright Madras cloth is picturesque. The cathedral in Pointe-à-Pitre is entirely made of pieces of iron crisscrossed and bolted together.

The **Le Raizet International Airport,** just ten minutes outside the city, should be visited. There are some well-designed murals, a free-port shop and an excellent restaurant. The shop has French perfumes, spirits, haute-couture fashions and a variety of goods flown direct from Paris.

As well as shopping facilities and French cuisine in Pointe-à-Pitre, there are dances every Saturday at the principal hotel. Cockfighting, the popular pastime of the West Indies, takes place at the **Gallodrome** every Sunday. There are frequent football matches and cycle races. Organized trips can be arranged through your hotel or at agencies in the Place de la Victoire.

Basse-Terre, the official capital of Guadeloupe (population 14,000), is the only other city in the islands. It is located near the southwest tip of the island of Basse-Terre, about 50 miles by road from Pointe-à-Pitre. All the government buildings are in Basse-Terre, and the city has a clean, neat look, topped by the towering mass of Soufrière, the active volcano, directly above.

The **Cours-Nolivos Square** is the main meeting place in town. A bust of Victor Schoelcher was erected there in 1904 in honor of his birthday centenary. Schoelcher, as Under-Secretary of the Navy and of the Colonies, was instrumental in securing the freedom of the slaves in the French islands, and has been highly honored ever since.

The market place and dock are near the Cours-Nolivos. Here the blond fishermen from the Île des Saintes wearing their coolie-like *selaca* hats, bring in their tuna catch.

There are several palm-shaded parks to rest in, a delightful seventeenth-century church to visit, and just outside the city is the historic **Fort Richepance.** It is erected on the site of the fort built in 1647 by Governor Houel to guard the capital from sea and land. The tomb of General Richepance is there, and also that of Governor Gourbeyre, who rode the 45 miles to Pointe-à-Pitre on horseback to give aid to the inhabitants after an earthquake and fire in 1843.

Basse-Terre is an excellent base for climbing and hiking expeditions to the interior. Information and guides are available from the Mountaineering Club. Arrangements for fishing and sailing trips can be made through the Yacht Club.

A round trip of the island, including a trip partway up the Soufrière volcano, can be accomplished in one day, if necessary. The winding road around the coast of Basse-Terre is about 100 miles long, and its surface is good.

Leaving Pointe-à-Pitre by the drawbridge which runs for four miles over the narrows of the Rivière Salée, you can continue down the east coast of Basse-Terre.

Petit Bourg is the first seaside town on the route. In the hills above it at Vernou there is a tiny inn whose restaurant is excellent. Passing through Goyave, you come to **Sainte-Marie,** where a monument commemorates the landing of Columbus at that point in 1493. At **Capesterre** there is a war memorial to the islanders who lost their lives in the two world wars. **Bananier** is noted for its beautiful beach.

Trois Rivières is the next stop, and the fascinating paintings and carvings done by the pre-Columbian Carib Indians should be seen. The setting is very soothing–a woody glade by the side of a running stream. Trois Rivières is also the starting place for sea trips to the **Îles des Saintes** and **Marie-Galante.**

Dole-les-Bains is the diminutive spa on the road turning inland to Basse-Terre. There is bathing in warm mineral springs, set in a background of red-blossomed vanilla trees, giant banyans and swinging lianas. The hotel-restaurant serves meals al fresco in this woodland setting. Basse-Terre, with Fort Richepance, is a few miles away.

An alternative plan, if time permits, is to branch onto a small coast road at Trois Rivières which leads south to the tip of the island. **Vieux Fort** is at the extreme point. Charles de l'Olive landed here in 1638 and took possession of the island with 500 men. The fragmentary ruins of the old fort can still be seen. Visitors can go back to the main road at Trois Rivières or continue around the coast into Basse-Terre.

The 50-mile drive from Basse-Terre to Pointe-à-Pitre round the north of the island passes several points of interest. **Le Baillif,** a few miles out of the capital, has the ruined tower of Père Labat, near the sea. Père Labat was a Dominican priest-explorer who did much to promote colonization of Guadeloupe. **Vieux Habitants,** a little farther up, has an excellent beach. There is also a hotel-restaurant, with cottage accommodations, a private beach and good French cuisine. **La Bouillante,** ten miles away, provides the wonderful sight of a gush of hot water from volcanic source spurting far into the sea. **Pigeon,** five miles up the road, has a beach of volcanic red sand beloved by Gauguin.

Past La Pointe Noire one arrives at **Deshaies.** This village, too, has a red beach dotted with palms and also a pleasant new hotel-restaurant. **Kahouanne,** at the extreme northern end of the west coast, also has first-class swimming from a red beach. Going east toward the bridge and Pointe-à-Pitre, you will pass through **Lamentin.**

One should not leave the island without at least a partial ascent of the mysterious jungle-covered volcano of **La Soufrière.** The 5,000-foot-high peak dominates the southern end of the chain of mountains that form Basse-Terre. It last erupted in 1799 but is still considered "active." If you wish to reach the summit itself you must take a guide with you, for the drivable road ends at Matouba, two steep hiking hours away, and there are some deceptive steaming bogs.

Leave Basse-Terre city by the mountain road, which climbs steeply for some way. **St. Claude** is a mountain station and suburb of the capital, five miles above the city. The prefect's residence is here and other imposing buildings. From here drive on and up through primeval forest of giant palm, jungle lianas, lush fern and mosses, crossing the Rivière Noire and the Rivière Rouge, glimpsing gorges and swift mountain streams through the trees. The road worsens as you get higher, until it ends at Matouba.

Matouba is a charming village inhabited by long-haired Hindus—East Indians believed to have come to Guadeloupe as servants of some British settlers. It is two hours' hiking distance from the top of the volcano.

The trip itself, considered best early in the day, affords a view of Guadeloupe, Dominica, and Montserrat, and goes through dense forests and jungle.

Le Gosier, 15 miles east along the road from Pointe-à-Pitre, is a charming village with tree-fringed beach, excellent for swimming. On the beachfront there is a restaurant and tourist landmark with terrace overlooking the beach. Specialties include stuffed land crab, langoustes au vin and a succulent chicken. Rooms in individual bungalows are available.

Pointe des Chateaux, on the extreme eastern tip of the island, looks like a rugged corner of the Breton cliff. From the giant rocks jutting out into the surf there is an excellent view of La Désirade, the mountains of Basse-Terre, Marie-Galante and the Îles des Saintes.

Le Moule, on the Bay of Bones, is the next stop particularly worth making, as one travels up along the east coast. This historic beach was the scene of many battles between Caribs, English and French in ancient times. Erosion of the cliff face by sea and weather has now revealed fossilized bones and skulls—not to mention those found in the sand, half-overgrown with brilliant tropical lilies.

From Le Moule you can continue by the same highway (No. 5), which turns east at this point, taking you across the rolling hills bordered with sugar plantations and little villages to Pointe-à-Pitre, about 45 minutes away.

An alternative and somewhat longer route is the secondary highway, No. 7, a few miles past Le Moule. This will take you northeastward through some quaint little villages until the road almost touches the east coast.

SPECIAL EVENTS. The **Mardi Gras Festival** is celebrated in February just before Lent. Every Sunday for weeks before the **Carnival** celebrations, groups of children roam the streets in masquerade. On the Monday before Ash Wednesday, the festivities really begin —people from all over town meet in the main streets to dance and sing. The celebrations continue until late at night and all day on Mardi Gras (or "Fat Tuesday"); teams of semi-professional dancers give exhibitions of traditional dances.

Unlike anywhere else in the world, except Martinique, the biggest day of the festival is Ash Wednesday, which is devoted to the mock wake, burning, and burial of Roi Bois-bois, the spirit of Carnival.

After the burning of the king, all the *pistes de danse* are open and there is dancing everywhere. Then a figure of Bois-bois is brought in, he is buried, and Carnival ends.

DINING AND SHOPPING. Many excellent restaurants feature French cuisine or Creole-style foods. Specialties to try are gumbos, stuffed inland crab, and a rum drink, *punch antillais*.

The main shopping center in Pointe-à-Pitre is in the Rue Frebault, where a line of little shops filled with French and local products can be found.

Local rum is on sale everywhere, but look for French wines, liqueurs, and perfumes—the prices are lower than in France. One can find a good selection of French luxury items such as gloves, lingerie, and silks and scarves, in the small boutiques.

For souvenirs, there are the *doudou* dolls in Creole costumes, and some skillfully made figures of shells and beads. Also interesting to buy are records of Creole songs, or a *selaca*, the distinctive hat worn by the fishermen of Îles des Saintes.

Beautiful baskets of all shapes and sizes, lace-making, the lovely white embroidered petticoats of the Creole national dress, and painted gourds, ceramics, and bright-woven Creole madras can be seen.

ÎLES DES SAINTES can provide a wonderful day's excursion. Boats leave Trois Rivières practically every day for the six-mile sea trip to the two inhabited islands, **Terre de Haut** and **Terre de Bas**, which provide a very different world from the mainland. The population (about 12,000) of the former is mostly descended from Norman and Breton stock. There has been much inbreeding and the inhabitants are very fair-skinned, some even with blond hair and blue eyes. The people of Terre de Bas are almost all pure Negroes—intermarriage has been rare although the two islands are so close together. Fishing is the chief occupation on both islands.

The islands, particularly more-accessible Terre de Haut, abound in good picnic and swimming spots. If you wish to stay overnight, there are hotel accommodations at Terre de Haut.

Curious hats, *selacas*, worn by the *Saintois* (as the male inhabitants of both islands are known) are made out of split bamboo and other straws. Fine white cloth is tightly stretched over the frame. The hats measure about 18 inches in diameter.

ST. BARTHÉLEMY, another strange community of Guadeloupeans, is to be found 100 miles to the north. It was first colonized by the French, but in 1784 passed into Swedish hands in return for certain trading rights. Almost

100 years later it was restored to France.

It is the only island in the West Indies where the Swedes have left their mark. Nearly all of the 2,000 inhabitants are white descendants of Breton and Norman settlers mingled with Swedes. The language, unlike the rest of Guadeloupe, is not the Afro-French Creole but a patois of French and Swedish, and some English is spoken. The main town is called **Gustavia** after the Swedish King Gustavus III, and its hotels have accommodations for tourists.

A distinctive feature is the frilled, lacy cap worn by the older women—an exact copy of those worn by the Norman peasants in the nineteenth century.

French cooking allied with the local tropical produce results in a wonderful variety of exotic and mouth-watering dishes. The food is good everywhere and not expensive.

Seafood is served in many ways, all spicy and delicious. Particularly try *chatrou,* an octopus stew; *matete,* spiced fricassee land crab on rice. Also there is a raccoon that is surprisingly good. Order in advance for broiled dove and skewered larks; or taste the more substantial *callalou,* which is a kind of luxurious stew of local vegetables.

Creole curry or *Colombo* must be sampled as should a red fish specialty spiced with an amazing hot pepper (called "Madame Jackass" in the local slang).

MARTINIQUE

The feeling of being in both a tropical and a foreign land is one of the charms of the island.

Martinique offers a genuine welcome by a hospitable populace, comfortable accommodations of French quality, excellent food and the art of relaxation.

THE LAND. Martinique is one of the largest islands of the Lesser Antilles chain that arches from Puerto Rico to the northeast coast of Venezuela to enclose the Caribbean. The terrain is varied, ranging from the low, desolate salt fields of the southern tip to heavily forested mountains in the north. Except for several varieties of European trees in the hilly regions, its vegetation is typically tropical, marked by tall ferns, bamboo trees, stately palms and the red mangroves which grow quite close to the heavily indented shoreline.

The island, approximately 425 square miles in area, is served by a network of roads that wind along the coast and through the dense jungles and mountain forests of the interior, passing Colonial-style mansions owned by the wealthy planters and the tiny thatched shacks of local farmers.

While there is not a great deal of animal or bird life, the island is literally covered with flowers—hibiscus, orchids, bougainvillaea and other varieties which bloom the year round.

Many travelers consider Martinique the loveliest island in the world—an opinion that's supported by such connoisseurs as Paul Gauguin and Lafcadio Hearn, both of whom were seduced by its beauty.

THE CLIMATE. Martinique has three principal seasons—the cool months between November and April; a hot, dry season between April and July; and a hot, rainy period from July to November—also the season for hurricanes.

The climate is warmer and more humid at sea level, temperatures ranging from 70 degrees in January to 90 degrees in October at Fort-de-France. 4,600-foot Mount Pelée is from 20 to 30 degrees cooler.

Martinique is the land of eternal summer, but the trade winds bring relief from the heat and nights are comfortable. Visitors should bring light summer clothing, preferably washable, and a light wrap for the cool evenings.

Informality of dress is the rule in Martinique. Men are not obliged to wear coats or neckties, even in hotel restaurants. Women wear beach dresses in town, but shorts are seldom worn.

THE PEOPLE. Martinique has a population of over 300,000, most of whom are descendants of African slaves. They are a vigorous, tall and stately people, carrying themselves with dignity and grace. The women are especially famous for their beauty. A percentage of the people are Creoles, the wealthy landowners, descended from Africans and the French colonials who settled there three centuries ago, and a sprinkling of French from France, the *métropolitains*.

Although the people of Martinique have been entitled to all the privileges of French citizenship since 1848, the island was not raised to the status of an overseas department until 1946. Its government is headed by a prefect, the chief administrative officer chosen by the Ministry of the Interior. He is assisted by a General Council whose members are elected by universal suffrage. Martinique is represented in the French Parliament by three deputies and two senators.

Martinique was discovered by Columbus in 1493. However, the great navigator didn't land on the island until 1502, then only to be driven off by the fierce Caribs, conquerors of the Arawaks, the original inhabitants.

No one showed any particular interest in the island until 1635, when two Frenchmen, De l'Olive and Du Plessis took possession of it in the name of France and declared it unsuitable for colonization. However, during the latter part of that year, a Norman captain by the name of Sieur d'Esnambuc, sailed down from Saint Christopher and founded the first settlement, Saint-Pierre.

Colonization was strongly resisted by the Caribs, and for 20 years the settlers fought them off, finally driving them into the inland jungles where they were killed off, one by one. With this threat removed, interest in Martinique increased, and in 1671 the French government bought the island from its private owners.

During the seventeenth and eighteenth centuries, an era of land-grabbing, control of Martinique passed from one European nation to another. Periods of occupation were brief, however, and had little or no influence on the essentially Gallic character of the islands or its inhabitants.

Diamond Rock, which juts out of the sea a few miles south of Fort-de-France, is a reminder of the early sea battles for possession of the island and control of the West Indies. It was fortified by the British with cannon and a force of over 100 men and was the scene for the savage Battle of Diamond Rock and the capitulation of the British. *Le Diamant* was registered as a fighting ship by the English navy, the only rock ever to win that distinction. It was well-equipped with barracks, a hospital and warehouse built in the caves of its sheer cliffs.

Martinique reigned supreme some two centuries ago as a leading Caribbean sugar center. Injustice and corruption of the colonizers prevailed as the island flourished. The capital city became a little Paris, three centuries in the building, with structures modeled after the Empire period.

Slavery, introduced after sugar and coffee became important factors in the island's economy, by 1815 had led to serious internal strife and one or two major insurrections. Finally, in 1843, the Negroes were emancipated and given full political standing with the French colonists.

French is Martinique's official language, supplemented by a picturesque patois known as "Creole"—a combination of Carib, English, Spanish, French and African words.

AGRICULTURE. Martinique has an agricultural economy based on sugar cane, bananas, pineapples, cacao and coffee. Sugar cane is the principal crop, most of which goes into the manufacture of rum. Sugar, rum and bananas, the principal exports, pour from the rich hinterlands into Fort-de-France, the capital and leading port.

The island is not self-supporting and must import practically everything to meet its requirements. The chief imports are wheat flour, chemical fertilizer and codfish.

CITIES. There are several cities of special interest to the visitor, Fort-de-

France, the capital, being the most important.

Fort-de-France, a pretty town of more than 90,000 inhabitants, is Martinique's capital. It likes to think of itself as Parisian, a pleasant self-deception which visitors find easy to accept as they sip an apéritif in a sidewalk café, walk along the narrow streets, or visit an intimate little shop stocked with French goods. The capital is built in a half-circle around a deep-water harbor.

Most of Fort-de-France's public buildings and statues are located in or near **La Savane Park,** as are the tourist bureau, airline offices, post office and main shopping area.

All activity in Fort-de-France stops promptly at noon while the populace takes a two-and-one-half-hour break for luncheon and leisure.

The city's night life for the most part is confined to after-dinner dances at hotels and private clubs. There are, however, frequent exhibitions of dancing, especially the famous béguine which was born here.

The market is a favorite haunt with tourists. Under its high arched roof, which covers an entire city block, all Martinique seems to gather.

Early in January, costumed groups begin to sing and dance in the streets, the signal for **Carnival,** big event of the year. The important days are the **Monday** and **Tuesday before Lent,** and **Ash Wednesday,** when Bois-bois (King Carnival) comes to the end of his reign and is burned in La Savane. Martinique and Guadeloupe, her sister island, are the only places in the world where Carnival is observed on Ash Wednesday.

It doesn't take long to exhaust the sightseeing attractions in Fort-de-France. However, the appeal of its lush countryside, threaded with a network of precipitous, curving roads, more than compensates.

If time permits, visitors may explore the entire island on organized tours, or they may hire a car with driver, rent a car, or, for the most fun of all, travel via the little red busses.

Saint Pierre. The twisting coastal road north from Fort-de-France leads to the ruined city of Saint Pierre (population 6,000), the classic sight of Martinique. Once called the "Paris of the Indies," today it is the Pompeii of the Western Hemisphere—the victim of **Mount Pelée,** which erupted with unimaginable fury on May 8, 1902 and in three minutes virtually annihilated the city, its 30,000 inhabitants and several surrounding villages. A second blast on May 20 completed the destruction.

Before the holocaust, Saint Pierre had been Martinique's first city—the capital and the financial and cultural center of the island—larger, busier and gayer than the Fort-de-France of 1902. Today, visitors can wander about the streets of the martyred city—now slowly rebuilding from the debris.

The ruins of an ancient church, recently uncovered, attest to the force of the explosion, as do the many items dug up from the rubble which are now on display at the Frank Perret Musée Volcanologique. From 1929–32, Mount Pelée showed renewed but less potent signs of life. Since then she has been more or less quiescent.

Tourists with only a day at their disposal can visit Saint Pierre and still have time to shop and sightsee in Fort-de-France. However, if they wish to go to the top of Mount Pelée, they should allow at least another half-day. Cars and horses can make it part of the way, but the adventurous who want to climb to the top must do so afoot. It takes about an hour and should be attempted only with an experienced guide. Guides, cars and horses are available at **Morne Rouge.**

Visitors in Fort-de-France can make the trip to Saint Pierre by car or boat. The latter keeps close to the shoreline so that passengers have a fine view of the high cliffs alternating with creeks and gulfs where small fishing villages nestle. The trip by car, however, follows one of the most picturesque roads on the island. It winds through **Schoelcher, Fonds Lahaye, Case Pilote, Bellefontaine,** and **Carbet**—coastal towns and villages where sturdy fishermen put out to sea in their uniquely styled boats, fashioned from a single trunk of the gum tree.

There are two alternate return routes from Saint Pierre. The shorter goes inland to the town of Morne Rouge, where visitors may, if they wish, stay overnight at the inn. It continues on through the lush tropical rain forest where gigantic tree ferns, mahogany and bamboo trees grow, then threads its way between steep ravines and over swift rivers to the thermal baths at **Absalon** and **Didier,** returning finally to Fort-de-France by way of **Balata.**

The other much longer route explores the extremely picturesque Atlantic Coast, where the sea is always rough and many cliffs and inlets mark the rugged coastline. At **Trinité** the long arm of the Caravelle Peninsula pushes its way into the sea. Here tourists may visit the ruins of the castle of M. Dubucq de Rivery. In the castle are the remains of an old dungeon—a tiny cell in which the prisoner could neither lie nor sit.

Many of Martinique's sugar and rum factories are located in this eastern section, which is heavily populated and quite wealthy.

In addition to Saint Pierre, tourists should be certain to see **Trois Îlets,** the birthplace of the Empress Josephine, the local girl who made good. This can make the visit a part of a tour that embraces the southwest coast, covering such towns as **Lamentin,** a large industrial center; **Ducos** and **Rivière Salée,** with their sugarcane fields; **Anses D'Arlet,** a fishing and holiday resort; and **Diamant,** with its magnificent beach and famous rock.

At Trois Îlets there is a small museum which guards historical documents and souvenirs of Josephine's childhood, and the church where she was christened in 1763.

Beyond **Rivière Pilote,** a village of thatched-roof bamboo huts, the route passes through the barren southern extremity of the island. Nearby is **Savane Des Petrifications,** one of the four known petrified forests in the world. The oppressively silent forest rises out of solidly baked ground. There are no landmarks or definite paths to follow, and anyone who wishes to explore it should hire a guide.

SPORTS AND RECREATION. Martinique, with its crystal-clear waters and sparkling black or white sand beaches, is a **swimmer's** paradise. Many of the best beaches are quite near Fort-de-France, among them the **Lido Hotel beach,** the **Hilton Hotel beach,** both just outside the city, and **Le Diamant,** only 15 minutes away. One of the best beaches on the island is at **Anse Mitan,** a 30-minute boat ride from the capital. **Ste. Anne's beach**—two miles of fine white sand—is a delightful day's outing from the capital. To reach it, one can drive through lush vegetation, sugar and banana plantations, and fishing villages.

The surf is mild on the leeward side of the island; vigorous on the windward coast. Tuna, dolphin, kingfish and bonito abound. There are facilities for underwater **fishing,** and **sailing** at the local yacht club.

Visitors can play **tennis** at the tennis club in Fort-de-France or at one of the hotels. There are **soccer** matches every Sunday at the stadium. **Cockfights** are a favorite sport.

Hunting is largely confined to wood pigeons and sea birds. However, hikers and photographers have magnificent opportunities to study Martinique's flora and fauna in the dense rain forests.

SPECIAL EVENTS. One of the big events of the year is the Bal Doudou, a sort of Beaux Arts Ball which is held in several parts of Martinique, but reaches its zenith at the select Tango Ballroom in Fort-de-France. **Carnival,** and the activities staged with it, is the other important event of the year.

DINING AND SHOPPING. Many hotels and restaurants offer an excellent French cuisine comparable to Paris, and a wine list of the best French wines, champagnes, liqueurs, and local rums. The latter is the basis for punch Martinique, considered one of the best tropical drinks ever invented.

Spicy regional specialties are also available and include such dishes as *callalou,* an herb soup; gumbos with rice and codfish; baked yams; salads of palm or coconut hearts; roasted wild goat; tortoise; crayfish the size of small lobsters; stuffed crab, and other seafoods prepared in a variety of ways.

Fort-de-France's principal shopping streets—Rue Saint Louis, Rue Victor Hugo, and Rue Schoelcher—lead off from La Savane Park. Here visitors can buy French perfumes, wines, liqueurs, and other imported luxury items at less than Paris prices. Martinique dolls in native costumes, ceramics, baskets, and other locally produced souvenirs are also good buys.

Women visitors will want to purchase the madras square which can be tied into becoming headdresses.

Windward Islands

Within the Windward Island group are five British islands—Dominica, St. Lucia, Grenada, St. Vincent, and the Grenadines. Barbados (see page 514), an independent member of the British Commonwealth, is the farthest east of any West Indian island, and is not included in the Windward group.

The string of 600-odd islets known as The Grenadines are dependencies of Grenada and St. Vincent. Carriacou and those islets adjacent to and south of it are under the jurisdiction of Grenada, and those north of Carriacou are administered by St. Vincent. The total estimated population of the entire group is over 340,000.

These islands are probably the most scenically beautiful of any in the Caribbean and certainly are among the least expensive to visit. Accommodations are simple but adequate and comfortable.

Each of these four islands has its own administrator, executive council and legislative council.

DOMINICA

Dominica is a botanist's paradise. Sixty percent of the island's surface of several hundred square miles is covered by rain forest, where an annual maximum rainfall of 250 inches has produced lavishly luxuriant tropical growth of the most unusual species to be found in the entire Caribbean. Except for its scenery, which certainly warrants a visit, Dominica has little to offer except peace and quiet. An airstrip on the northeast coast at Melville Hall has made the island reasonably accessible, and several new roads have made it possible to visit areas previously reached only by foot, horseback, or by coastal boats.

THE LAND. A range of forested mountains traverses the entire length of the island, from north to south, broken only by a narrow plain. There are impenetrable jungles, verdant valleys, rich lowland. Literally hundreds of large rivers and racing, raging mountain torrents and waterfalls add to the beauty of Dominica. Some of the birds living in all this tropical lushness are not to be found anywhere else in the world.

Hot springs, *solfataras* and subterranean vapors are proof of the island's volcanic origin. In the south, 2,300 feet up a mountainside, is Boiling Lake, of mud whose depth is unknown.

THE CLIMATE. Cool between December and March (average 72 to 84 degrees), it is dry from February to May. The hot period (78 to 86 degrees) is from August to October. June to October are the wettest months—annual rainfall varying from 70 inches on the leeward coast to 160 inches at the higher levels to several hundred inches in the rain forests. The porous soil quickly absorbs rains and leaves the air clear and fresh.

THE PEOPLE. Dominica, one of the least visited of all the Caribbean islands of any size, boasts a sizable population of more than 70,000.

The majority of the population is Negro, the balance being descendants of the early French and British settlers. Church of England, Methodist and Roman Catholic churches and chapels are found on the island. The language is

English, though a French patois is also spoken.

The only remaining group of Carib Indians in the world lives in the mountainous regions of Dominica. There are a few hundred left but probably less than 50 of these are pure-blooded. They live on a reservation at **Salybia,** where they make dugout canoes, shellwork, and water-tight baskets.

Columbus discovered Dominica on November 3, 1493, a Sunday, hence its name. The Caribs defended their island with such ferocity that it was one of the last in the Caribbean to be settled by foreigners. French and English made unsuccessful attempts to colonize and in 1660 they acknowledged St. Vincent and Dominica as property of the Caribs. In 1748, Britain and France declared the island "fair game," and finally the Treaty of Paris in 1763 formally awarded Dominica to England. However, French settlers managed to infiltrate by intermarriage with the Caribs and by 1778 had control of the island. Restored again to England in 1783, it was tossed back and forth between the two powers until 1805, when the French captured and burned Roseau. A ransom of £12,000 influenced the French to leave the island to the British. Dominica then (1872) was grouped with the Leeward Islands; in 1940 it became a part of the British Windwards and was a member of the West Indies Federation.

The island is divided into ten parishes and 18 districts. Roseau and Portsmouth have their town councils to handle local governmental affairs; other settlements have village boards or councils.

AGRICULTURE. The fertile soil of the lowlands yields excellent crops. Limes, lime oil, and lime juice (Rose's Lime Juice, world-famous, and a necessary ingredient of a Singapore gin sling, is made here), oranges, grapefruit, bananas, cocoa, copra, vanilla, coffee, spices, and tropical fruits—all are indigenous, the first five constituting major exports. Rum is distilled, tobacco cultivated; cottage industries produce local items; honey and wax are gathered.

ROSEAU, the capital, has a population of more than 11,000. It is on an open roadstead and is a simple, quaint, quiet little town. Roseau has a government house, a museum, a war memorial, and an old 1775 fort at the waterfront. Visitors should see the main square on Saturdays, and the lovely, spacious, and well-kept botanical gardens.

For magnificent views, drive 3,000 feet up in the mountains to **Freshwater Lake.** By going three or four miles south of Roseau to **Pointe Michelle** and on to **Soufrière Bay,** you can see hot springs and cook on the hot sands by the sea. Here there is an old fort and a fine view from a bluff.

Take the spectacular drive from Roseau inland to Marigot and along the coast to Portsmouth. Portsmouth itself has little to offer except its excellent harbor in **Prince Rupert's Bay.** There is an old English Fort Cabrits used by the British in 1805 to defend their position against the French. The island's best beaches and quaint fishing settlements can be found in this northern district.

Visit the **Carib Indian Reservation** either from Roseau, or drive across the northern tip of the island from Portsmouth past the fine beach on the north coast at Calibishie and down the east coast to **Marigot** and to Hattan Gardens, then you can go on to the Indian settlements of **Salybia** and **Battaka.** Allow one day for this trip. Alternate approaches are by boat and by horseback via Rosalie.

Guides are recommended for hiking. Incidentally, there are no poisonous snakes and the pythons are harmless.

From **Laudat,** five miles by car from Roseau, you have a choice of excursions: A two-hour hike to **Boeri Lake,** past twin waterfalls; a three-hour hike to the **Sylvania Citrus Estate** with 4,672-foot Morne Trois Pitons towering over it; a three-hour hike to the **Valley of Desolation** with hot springs and nearby Boiling Lake—bubbling mud, 300 feet wide (gases escaping from below frequently raise the level of the lake by several feet; the fumes from these gases are sometimes noxious); or a strenuous four-hour climb up Dominica's highest peak, **Mount Diablotin,** 4,747 feet.

SPORTS AND RECREATION. Most popular are **deep-sea** and **river fishing; hunting** of iguanas and agouti, wild pig, *crapauds;* **swimming** in rivers and natural pools, at the beach at Calibishie on the north coast, Scotts Head, at Canefield Cliff near Roseau, and by the Layou River, eight miles out of Roseau; **tennis, horseback riding, netball, cricket, football** in season. Occasional **dances** are held at the Dominica Club, the Union Club, and at the Aquatic Club near Roseau. A dramatic society produces periodic **amateur theatricals.**

DINING AND SHOPPING. Dominica is famous for its *crapauds*–frogs so large they are called mountain chickens. The crayfish are excellent. The local "calaloo" stew made of river crab is delicious. Dominican oranges are colossal, its limes world-famous and its grapefruit have excellent flavor.

Grass floor mats are made at the Convent of Roseau and at Dominica Handcrafts. The fiber squares that are sewed together to make rugs are found all over the Caribbean, but those of the very finest quality are made here. Basketware made from the larouman plant by the Caribs is utterly superb–the best is made by the men. One of their most popular is a waterproof basket with a lining of bolisier leaves between the outer and inner woven walls.

ST. LUCIA

Here is the island for anyone who just wants to sit down and relax in the sun in the midst of glorious tropical plants. It is quiet, peaceful, pleasant, and one of the loveliest of all the "Caribee Isles."

THE LAND. Second largest of the Windward Islands, St. Lucia has an area of 238 square miles. "Hewanorra," as it was called by the Carib Indians, is credited, without historical evidence, to have been discovered on Columbus' fourth and last voyage on St. Lucy's Day, June 15, 1502. Its mass of forested mountains rises from the sea to over 3,000 feet and its deep, rich valleys are profuse with dense magnificent tropical growth. Trademark of the island is its unique giant verdure-covered rock cones, Petit Piton, 2,461 feet high, and Gros Piton, 2,619 feet, which rise from the sea near the picturesque little town of Soufrière. Two miles inland from that town is a three-acre live crater into which you can actually drive your car. The volcano last erupted in 1776 but is constantly active, with boiling-hot sulphur springs, steam rising from potholes, a black water stream, hot vapors, gases, and sulphur fumes.

THE CLIMATE. The climate is quite ideal from late October to April, dry and sunny. February is the coolest month, July the hottest. Annual temperatures average 70 to 90 degrees, with nights much cooler than daytimes. Summers can be hot and humid but there are only three or four all-rainy days during the entire year. Rains vary with the locale from 55 to 160 inches and come in short showers, for the most part between June and November.

THE PEOPLE. The population numbers about 110,000. Mostly of African descent, there are also the descendants of the British and French settlers, a few Lebanese and a few Americans and Canadians who have chosen to make this island their home. Educational needs are provided by primary and secondary Roman Catholic and government schools. Religion is represented by the Church of England, Roman Catholic Church–nearly 80 percent of the people are Roman Catholics–and Salvation Army, Seventh-Day Adventist and Wesleyan groups.

English is the principal language of the island, but the peasants still use an African-French patois and the white descendants of the old French families speak French, Creole and English.

St. Lucia deserves and needs its present calm existence after its stormy, tumultuous past. England made the first known attempt at a settlement in 1605, but the would-be settlers were repulsed by the Caribs, who fiercely defended their island. The first recorded settlement was made again by the British in 1638, but three years later they, too, were driven out by the Indians. Both England and France claimed the island and tried to occupy it but by 1660 conceded defeat and signed a peace treaty with the Caribs which left the island in their hands provided the Caribs did not cause trouble elsewhere. Three years later, however, the French and English were again trying to establish themselves on the island, and for the next 150 years the island continued to change from one to the other—14 times, in fact. Finally, the British succeeded in the capture of St. Lucia in 1803, and France ceded it to England by the Treaty of Paris in 1814. Two U.S. air and military bases were established in 1940, one at Gros Islet in the north, one at Vieux Fort in the south. These were deactivated in 1950. The Vieux Fort base, Beane Field, was reactivated as a guided missile center in 1955. The Gros Islet base was restored to St. Lucia in 1959 and is now the site of a beautiful hotel.

Local governmental matters are handled by town councils in the main towns of Castries, Soufrière, and Vieux Fort. Smaller settlements have village councils.

CASTRIES, sitting on the edge of one of the finest landlocked harbors in the Caribbean, is the capital city of St. Lucia. As a result of two disastrous fires—the last one in 1948 wiped out nearly two-thirds of the city—today Castries is a neat, clean little town with modern stores and wide streets. There are still some old French stone buildings and old English brick ones that give a pleasing, non-modern tone. Although very English, the island still shows decided traces of French influence absorbed during the intermittent periods when the island was in French hands. This is seen in the names of the people, the names of towns, and particularly charmingly, in the costumes still worn by many of the older women. Be sure to see the Saturday Market on the waterfront, as well as an Anglican church built in 1834. On **Vigie Hill** (the word means "Lookout"), guarding the city to the north, is an old barracks and a lighthouse and a lovely view. Inland is the Government Agricultural Station and Nurseries, at **Union.** Climb or drive the mile and a half up **Morne Fortuné hill** behind Castries past the astonishing structure that is **Government House** to **Fort Charlotte.** The fort today is noted chiefly as the spot where the Duke of Kent, Queen Victoria's father, raised the Union Jack in 1794 on one of the several occasions when England had captured the island—only to lose it again and again. Back of the fort is a monument to the 27th Regiment, which captured the hill, and an old cemetery. The view from here of Castries and its spectacularly lovely harbor, particularly at sunset, defies description.

Drive north from Castries past some fine beaches to **Gros Islet** and go by boat to **Pigeon Island,** a half-mile offshore. There is an entrancing three-sided thatched-roof beach house open to the sea where drinks and food are served—a favorite stopping point for yachts cruising in the area. Overnight accommodations are available in little thatched-roof structures and in a few small houses. You can swim, fish, and boat from here, climb the little slope up to the ruins of **Fort Rodney** and see the pigeon cote where Rodney kept his carrier pigeons while spying on the movements of the French fleet before his famous victory over De Grasse in 1782.

Back on the mainland, an interesting 29-mile drive from Castries will take you south over the mountains to **Soufrière,** or you can go by coastal launch. Since the disastrous fire of 1955, Soufrière has been partially rebuilt. From the pier, you can get a good view of the town, fishing boats, and to the south, Petit Piton. Beyond here is Gros Piton.

Back of the town is the live crater of Soufrière, which definitely should be visited and which is safer than it sounds. Available are warm springs which chemical tests have proved to be equal to the curative springs at Aix-les-Bains. These baths were built as far back as 1785 by order of Louis XVI for the use of his soldiers garrisoned nearby.

Time permitting, instead of returning to Castries direct, take the 60-mile drive down around the southern coast and up past the Pitons through verdant hills to **Choiseul, Laborie** and **Vieux Fort,** once the capital of the island. If you have time to spare, you can rent pirogues here to paddle around the harbor. Drive on up the east coast past Beane Field Air Base, up along the sea to Micoud and the settlement of **Dennery.** Just beyond here is a banana sorting shed where bananas are collected for shipment to England on the little banana boat that comes twice a week. From here you climb up the **Barre-de-l'Isle** to a height of 1,200 feet and through a wildly lush rain forest of giant ferns and palms and bamboo. This road leads down through the banana valley of Cul-de-Sac, over Morne Fortuné to Castries.

SPORTS AND RECREATION. **Swimming** is excellent at various beaches around the island. Vigie Beach, less than a mile from the center of Castries, is a fine three-mile white beach. To the north, Choc Beach, Reduit Beach, the beaches on Rat Island and Pigeon Island are all good and readily accessible from Castries.

There is good **deep-sea** and **spear fishing, lobstering.** Pirogues (seaworthy canoes), sailboats, and launches can be chartered. There are scheduled launch trips to Soufrière and Vieux Fort. Other sports include **tennis, horseback riding, cricket,** and **hiking**—for which there are innumerable possibilities, including the famed Pitons.

SPECIAL EVENTS. Biggest event of the year is held the night before **Carnival,** when a carnival queen is selected. Carnival in St. Lucia is very elaborate. Much time is given to the costuming, and costumed groups enact tableaux in the park on **Mardi Gras.** December 13, **St. Lucia's Day,** is another festive holiday.

DINING AND SHOPPING. The food is typically West Indian and French Creole—*calaloo, pelau,* and crab backs are among the favorites. The lobsters are tremendous and delicious, as are the many varieties of fish.

Shopping possibilities are somewhat limited. There is local handicraft—best buys are the straw work. Good English imports include materials and shoes.

GRENADA

The 16-mile drive from the airport of "The Spice Island's" capital city of **St. George's** is reason enough to visit Grenada. It takes you through dense, lush, variegated tropical growth to an elevation of 2,000 feet and through a 5,000-acre forest reserve and wild bird sanctuary. In this area a trail leads from the main road to the 13-acre Grand Etang Lake in the crater of an extinct volcano and, closer to the capital, another side road leads to the ideally situated 60-foot Annandale Falls in a verdant tropical setting. This airport road and one that completely circles the island permit you to see its mountains and ravines, its main towns and its primitive little settlements, its sheltered black and white beaches and the surf pounding the magnificent white sand stretch of beach at Levera, on the north coast. Lake Antoine, in the northeast, sits in the crater of an extinct volcano. Nearby are rivers and streams and mineral springs. Except for a small amount of the lowland on the northeast coast and in the southwest, the island is completely mountainous. Mount Catherine is Grenada's highest peak—2,749 feet.

The view of St. George's and its harbor, whether approaching it from the sea or looking down on it from the hills that hem it in, is reputedly the most picturesque in the Caribbean.

THE CLIMATE. With an average temperature at 70 degrees between December and May, visitors can count on pleasant weather throughout that period. Temperatures rise to 90 degrees between July and October, and though these months can be somewhat hot and humid, almost perpetual trade winds keep it comfortable all year round. Rainfall varies from 30 to 60 inches in the lowlands, and goes up to 200 inches per year in the higher regions. Heaviest rains come during the fall, though they are not rare in July. Grenada is not in the hurricane belt, although it was hit by the freak hurricane Janet in 1955.

THE PEOPLE. Of the 100,000 population, only about two percent is white. Living standards seem to be somewhat better on this island. Many small holdings are owned by the peasants either through government grant or squatter's rights. There are numerous primary and secondary government and church schools. St. George's has a hospital, as does St. Andrews Parish, while rural areas have medical visiting stations. English and a French-African patois are spoken. More than half the population are Roman Catholics, a hangover from the days of the French occupations. Church of England, Church of Scotland, Methodist Church, Plymouth Brethren, Salvation Army and Seventh-Day Adventists have churches and meeting-houses.

Columbus discovered the island on August 15, 1498, and landed on its north shore in search of water. He first named it Concepción. For 150 years after his arrival, the Caribs managed to keep possession of their island. Some London merchants tried to establish a settlement in 1609 but had to abandon it because of difficulties with the Indians. The French purchased Grenada from the Caribs in 1629 with glass beads, knives, hatchets, and a couple of bottles of brandy as currency. From that date on, Grenada, like so many of its neighbors, changed back and forth between British and French control until 1783, when it was granted to England by the Treaty of Versailles.

It has its own local government under an administrator, executive council and legislative council, as do each of these islands; there are also several ministers. District Boards manage the local affairs within their districts, and the city of St. George's is administered by a mayor and municipal council.

AGRICULTURE. The many spices grown here, such as nutmeg, clove, cinnamon, ginger, sapote, and tonka bean, have given Granada the name "The Spice Island." Nutmeg, mace, and other spices, bananas and cocoa are the chief exports. Other exports consist of lime juice and oil, some Marie-Galante cotton, and cotton seed. Enough sugar is grown for local consumption only.

INDUSTRY. There are several small industries—cigarettes, soap, coconut oil and meal, aerated water and ice plants, and rum distilleries.

ST. GEORGE'S. A good first stop is **Fort George** at the harbor entrance, built by the French in 1705, now serving as a police barracks. There are fine views of the city and harbor from here. In the town are **Sendall Tunnel;** the market place on the main square; the photogenic **Roman Catholic Church** at the top of a very narrow, very steep little street; a pink Anglican **St. George Church** built in 1763. Drive out the Esplanade and turn in past Queens Park, a recreational sports field, past an old cemetery up to spacious Government House and along Richmond Hill Ridge to **Hospital Hills Fort,** from which vantage point the views are truly magnificent. Also in town, a small **botanic garden** should be visited.

A drive around the island to the north would take a half day, but it is preferable to allow more time. The road skirts the coast and goes through several little towns on the west coast, notably **Concord** and **Gouyave,** also called Charlotte Town, with red-roofed, weather-beaten houses teetering along the sea wall, a market, churches, and a "nutmeg pool" building, where you can see women cracking and sorting the seed. Gouyave is the important receiving depot where nutmeg is processed through various stages. The rivers you will cross, the hills, the black beaches, the rock-strewn beach at Victoria, the cacao beans out in the sun to dry on great trays on rollers so that they can be pushed under a flooring in case of rain, **Sauteurs,** with a cliff known as Caribs' Leap from which the remnants of the tribe chose to leap to their death rather than surrender to the French in 1652—all offer endless possibilities for the photographer. Beyond here, **Levera Beach,** with a protected swimming area, and the great expanse of beach on the open sea with colossal breakers, should not be missed by any visitor to Grenada. Farther on in this general section is **Lake Levera** in a volcanic crater and **Lake Antoine** farther inland. Down the east coast is the town of **Grenville,** with a most colorful market one block inland and a fish market right on the water. One road goes back to St. George's down and across the lower part of the island to Grand Anse. Unless you arrived by air and have already taken this other road from the airport to the capital, return by the scenic route across the island that goes past **Grand Etang** through the forest reserve and bird sanctuary and, time permitting, detour to **Annandale Falls.**

An approximate seven-mile drive from the capital will take you through flat grazing country and past the salt ponds to **Point Saline** on the southwest tip of the island. From the lighthouse at the end of the road there are lovely views looking back up the coasts, with white sands on one side of the narrow little peninsula, black sands on the other, and queer rock formations stabbing the brilliant blue water that fills the series of enchanting little coves.

If you arrived by ship, take the short round-trip drive from **St. George's** to **Grand Etang,** only 15 miles away. This is the 13-acre lake that lies in the crater of an extinct volcano in the midst of forests of cedar and gum. You can see the lake from "Lake House" at a 2,000-foot elevation, and nearby, take the trail that leads to the lake through jungle-like terrain. The air is clear and cool and delightful. Also to be visited is **Annandale Falls,** a high waterfall with a deep pool at its base—a popular swimming and picnicking site.

SPORTS AND RECREATION. **Swimming** and **snorkeling** are excellent, in surf or still water, and safe at practically all the beaches around the island except Pearl's Beach, where there is a strong current. Most popular beach is lovely Grand Anse Beach near St. George's, with a number of new hotels supplying food and drink and dressing-room facilities. There is deep-sea and fresh-water **fishing;** reef fishing at Glover Island off Point Saline; line casting from the 70- to 90-foot cliffs near Levera; good spear fishing at Levera Beach and at Levera and Green islands just offshore. Small boats are available for charter. In addition, there is a Grenada Yacht Club for those with boats, or you can go by ferryboat around the lagoon. A rowboat will take you to the Grand Anse Beach in half an hour from St. George's.

Ramier (a wild pigeon), mountain dove, and perdix are principal game. Best **hunting** is in the winter months. **Tennis** and **golf** are played, and **mountain hiking** is popular, especially at St. Catherine (2,749 feet), Morne Quaqua (2,412 feet), Mount Sinai (2,300 feet), and Grand Etang Lake (1,810 feet). **Fedon's Camp,** at 2,512 feet, is the site of the headquarters of Julien Fedon, the leader of the rebellion against British rule in 1795. A pillar serves as a memorial to the 48 British prisoners who were massacred here. Spectator sports include **cricket, football,** and **horse racing.**

SPECIAL EVENTS. **Carnival** takes place for two days prior to Lent. The residents are costumed, and there are street dances and parades.

Occasional dances are held at the hotels and clubs, and regularly at the Morne Rouge Beach Club. Periodic plays are put on by the Grenada Academy of Dramatic Art.

DINING AND SHOPPING. All the usual West Indian dishes are found in Grenada, such as pepper pot (boiled meat, casueripe, and peppers). The fish and lobster are excellent. Try the local tropical fruits, especially sapodilla.

Handicrafts include the usual straw

work, tortoise-shell and wooden articles. Best typical buy is a small basket of straw filled with a variety of spices grown on the island. British imports include textiles and cashmere sweaters.

ST. VINCENT

A little off the beaten track, relatively few tourists visit St. Vincent, but most of those who do return to it or at least wish that they could.

THE LAND. An 18-by-11-mile volcanic island, it is a mass of rugged mountains with 3,500-foot peaks and densely forested ridges, this last being Crown property. There are waterfalls and curative springs, the Rabaka River and a 4,048-foot volcano that has erupted three times in its recorded history—in 1715, 1812, and 1902. Coastal areas offer a series of sheltered bays and also surf-pounded black or yellow sandy beaches sometimes backed by red cliffs. Much of the northern interior, known as Carib Country, can easily be reached by car.

THE CLIMATE. St. Vincent is reputedly one of the Caribbean's healthiest islands. There is no malaria here; there are no wild animals either, nor are there many birds, though it does claim a certain type of talking parrot not found elsewhere. The climate is pleasantest from December to May, with temperatures ranging from 67 to 78 degrees. May to December is the wet season, with a rainfall of 60 to 100 inches annually on the coastal areas, 150 inches in the interior.

THE PEOPLE. The population of about 90,000 is chiefly Negro. The term "Black Caribs" refers to a mixture of shipwrecked or escaped African slaves and the original Carib inhabitants. Unfortunately, the reservation granted the Caribs in 1805 at Morne Ronde was in the direct path of the lava eruption of Soufrière in 1812 which virtually wiped out the Caribs. The descendants of the few survivors live in a small settlement at Sandy Bay on the windward coast. After slaves had been emancipated in 1838, Portuguese laborers were imported. A few years later East Indians were brought to the island, though the majority of them returned to India.

The language of the island is English, but an Afro-French patois is also spoken. Religion is represented by Church of England, Methodist, Roman Catholic, Seventh-Day Adventist, Pilgrim Holiness, Jehovah's Witnesses, Church of God, the Salvation Army.

Discovered by Columbus on January 22, 1498, St. Vincent's Day, this was the last West Indian island to be settled by Europeans, so ferociously was it defended by the Caribs. Both the Spaniards and the French claimed it, and in 1627 the King of England granted it to the Earl of Carlisle, but he did nothing with it nor did others who were proffered later grants. The Spaniards apparently lost interest in St. Vincent, and the French and English finally agreed to leave it to the Indians and to consider it neutral territory. This it remained until 1763, when it was ceded to England. The French captured it in 1779 but it was restored to England by the Treaty of Versailles in 1783. Twelve years later the French and Caribs combined forces in an attempt to oust the British, but after a violent year of burnings, plunder and murder, they were forced to again surrender to the British. An estimated 5,000 Caribs were then deported to the island of Ruatán in the Bay of Honduras. To the few who had managed to hide themselves in the hills, amnesty was granted in 1805.

Local governmental affairs are handled by a town board in Kingstown. Other settlements have their town boards or village councils.

AGRICULTURE. The chief occupation of the people of St. Vincent is farming, the finest quality of sea-island cotton being grown on the island. Bananas, coconuts, cocoa, copra, and ground nuts (peanuts) are important crops. St. Vincent is the largest exporter of arrowroot in the world.

KINGSTOWN, the capital, is scenically situated on a crescent-shaped bay sheltered by cliffs and wooded hills. It is a neat, flower-filled town with pastel-tinted, red-tile-roofed houses and stately eighteenth- and nineteenth-century homes.

In Kingstown, see the 14 acres of the **Botanical Gardens,** the oldest in the western hemisphere. Captain Bligh of *Mutiny on the Bounty* fame brought the breadfruit trees here in 1792, and they have so flourished that the island is called "The Breadfruit Isle." The **market** is particularly colorful and lively on Saturday, when the people from other settlements bring in their produce in canoes or sloops. The handsome **Government House,** the mixture of Gothic, Romanesque and Moorish architecture in **St. Mary's Cathedral,** and the murals in **St. George's Cathedral** are among the sights to see. **Fort Charlotte,** now a women's prison, is 600 feet above the town and two miles away. There are ruins of a fort on Cane Garden Point. The library has some interesting Carib relics.

Delightfully scenic short drives can be taken up the coast to **Layou,** about six miles from Kingstown, a small fishing village with a large black Christ on a cross in its church, and another seven miles beyond it the fishing village of **Barroullie.** Great celebrations follow the return of the whale-fishing expeditions that go out from there. En route you can see the arrowroot being harvested or planted and a cotton gin in action at appropriate seasons. Continue on up the coast to **Chateaubelair** and from there take a launch or sloop another nine miles up to the northwestern tip of the island to the 60-foot **Baleine Waterfalls.** There is nice pool bathing here close to the shore.

Visitors should see **Tyrrel Bay,** only three miles south of Kingstown, and go by rowboat the four miles from Calliaqua, a former capital, over to **Young's Island.** There is a strange 260-foot-high rock fortress, **Fort Duvernette,** with corridors and a winding stair of 365 steps, together with gun emplacements and lookouts all carved from solid rock.

One of St. Vincent's loveliest drives is a 28-mile trip through the farm area of Marriaqua Valley to **Mesopotamia Valley** in the hills back of Kingstown.

A somewhat longer coastal drive around and up the east coast would take you past the southern beaches, to the Argyle beach, and up to St. Vincent's second town of importance, **Georgetown.** Near here is the lava-filled **Rabaka River.**

All day is necessary for the climb to **Soufrière,** 4,000 feet high, far up in the north—with its lake-filled crater 1,100 feet below the peak. A car will take you to Georgetown on the east coast and up the Rabaka River route, or you can go by local boat to Dry River at Wallibou out of Chateaubelair, on the west coast.

SPORTS AND RECREATION. Villa Beach, Calliaqua, is a popular spot for **swimming,** as is the nearby island of Bequia. Launches or sloops sail the Grenadines; round-the-island sloops will take passengers. A government ferryboat plies back and forth between St. Vincent and Bequia.

There is **deep-sea** and **spear fishing**—the latter being particularly good at Young's Island just offshore at Calliaqua. Local fishing boats will take passengers along on their two-day to one week fishing trips among the Grenadines, or you can go whale fishing, usually a two-day outing, with the fishermen out of Barrouallie or Layou or Chateaubelair. These small whales are called "blackfish" by the natives. There are **snorkeling, tennis, golf,** and **horseback riding. Cricket** and **soccer** are played in Victoria Park. **Hikes** are possible from Kingstown, such as the three-hour hike up the 2,600 feet of Mount St. Andrew, inland and slightly north of Kingstown, and up Dorsetshire Hill, two and one-half miles from the capital.

DINING AND SHOPPING. Food is typically West Indian and French Creole. Try a "gru-gru swizzle." Gru-gru juice is a Carib Indian drink.

The best buy is local straw and fiber

handiwork. There is a limited selection of imports from England and Canada.

THE GRENADINES

These dependencies of Grenada and St. Vincent consist of some 600 pictorial islets dotting the 60 miles of dazzling sea between Grenada and St. Vincent. Some are fair-sized, others are mere rocks, and only a handful of them are inhabited. Most of them were French until the mid-eighteenth century and have retained a delightful French flavor. Beaches are unblemished and inviting, the surrounding waters multihued and clear. Swimming is excellent, as is fishing; naturalists will revel in the sea-bird life on the islands. Accommodations for visitors are extremely simple and visits of any duration are only for the escapist who requires no entertainment other than the enjoyment of sun, sea and sand.

No one who is traveling in this area of the Caribbean should miss the opportunity of at least cruising among the Grenadines. Scheduled schooner passage for a five-day cruise is available out of St. Lucia. Scheduled launches and sailboats make one-day cruises out of Grenada and St. Vincent. As a cruising ground for chartered boats and private yachts, the area is popular and captivating and at its best from April to June. High seas and winds are apt to make the going a bit rough during the midwinter months. Amphibious airplanes fly over the islands and make scheduled stops.

Among the Grenada dependencies are Carriacou, 30 miles north of Grenada, and all the islets adjacent to or south of Carriacou, such as Islet Ronde, Les Tantes, Isle de Gaille, Diamond Rock, Green, Sandy, and Levera islands. Largest and best known of all the Grenadines is seven-by-two-and-one-half-mile **Carriacou** with a population of around 7,000 that is a mixture of British, Scotch, French and African. These islanders are noted for their boatbuilding. Limes are an important crop; livestock is raised and an Antilles type of cotton is grown for export.

The island is lovely, with a picturesque coastline of a series of bays, fertile coastal flatlands, a central ridge of hills sloping up from the sea on the windward and leeward coasts—culminating in the 675-foot peaks of Belle Vue North and Belle Vue South, known locally as High North and Capeau Garré. A network of roads connects the various settlements, some of which are sprawled along the ridge of hills. **Hillsborough,** on the shores of Beausejour Bay (Grand Anse Bay), on the island's leeward coast, is the main settlement and port of entry. It has a hospital, shops, a reading room.

Among the St. Vincent dependencies are Bequia, Mustique, Mayreau, Canouan and Union Island. Total population of the St. Vincent dependencies is around 5,500. **Bequia** (Beck-wee) is best known due to its proximity to St. Vincent—the four and one-half miles between them is easily covered by small boats and a government ferryboat that runs daily. It is a favorite picnic and swimming goal for residents of and visitors to St. Vincent. Very good meals are served at its simple but attractive guesthouses. **Princess Margaret Beach** is one of the best on Bequia, while Long Bay offers another scenic beach. Fishing is good; night fishing by flashlight along the reef in Admiralty Bay is fun to watch or to try. There are wild pigeon and agouti for the hunter. **Port Elizabeth** on Admiralty Bay, called Morality Bay by the residents, is the main settlement. Cattle, sheep and a small amount of sea-island cotton are grown on Bequia's six square miles.

Barbados

Formerly known as "Little England," Barbados became independent on November 30, 1966. This new nation lies nearly 100 miles east of the general arc of Caribbean islands and is a nonvolcanic island sitting on a separate lit-

Bay Street in Nassau, Bahamas

St. James Parish Church in Annotto Bay, Jamaica

El Morro, Puerto Rico

Lime Cay, small island in Kingston Harbour, Jamaica

View near Road Town, Tortola, in the British Virgin Islands

View of the harbor at Port-au-Prince, Haiti

Emancipation Square in Charlotte Amalie, St. Thomas, U. S. Virgin Islands

Road leading to El Yunque, rain forest in Puerto Rico

The Pitons, St. Lucia, British West Indies

St. George's, Grenada, British West Indies

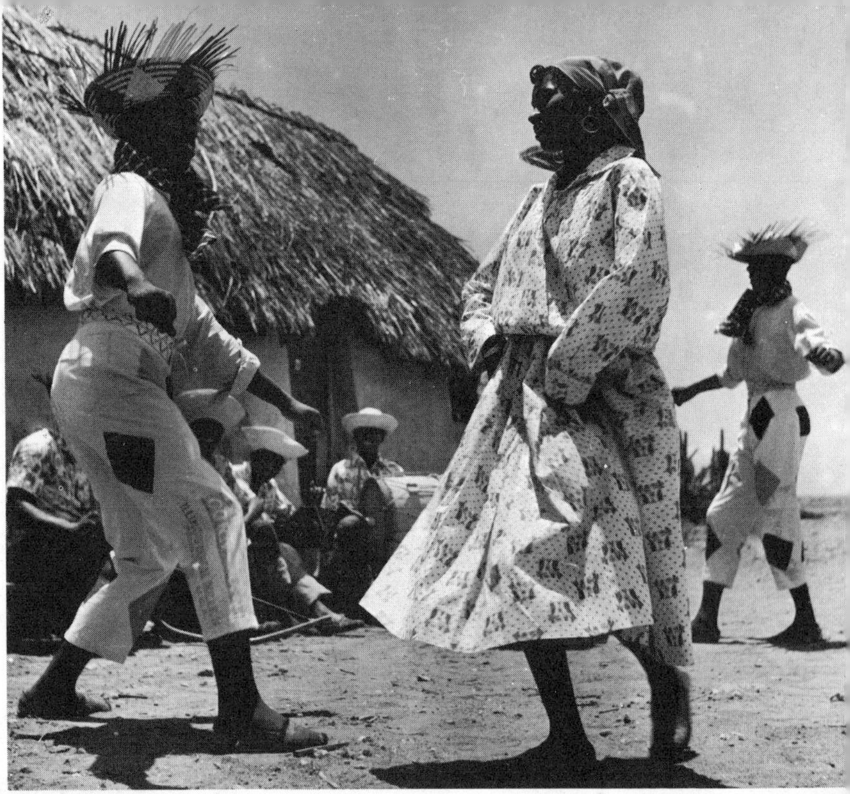

The "tumba," popular native dance in Curaçao, Netherlands Antilles

Curaçao, Netherlands Antilles

Guadeloupe, French West Indies

Bridgetown, Barbados

Fort-de-France, Martinique, French West Indies

"White Hall," Port of Spain, Trinidad

Beach along Carapuse Bay, Tobago

tle tableland of its own. It is particularly unique in that Columbus apparently missed the island altogether and it remained in British hands since they first settled here in 1627.

THE LAND. Barbados lacks the lush tropical growth of other nearby islands. About two-thirds of its 166 square miles in the south is soft, rolling, fertile countryside given over almost entirely to sugar cane, and the 46 acres of virgin forest still remaining are in the hills of the northern third. Though its highest point–Mount Hillaby–is only 1,104 feet above sea level, the magnificent vistas from this section give the impression that Barbados is far larger than its approximately 20 by 14 miles.

THE CLIMATE is practically ideal–one of the best and healthiest in the West Indies. It is tropical, but almost constant trade winds keep it comfortable except from July to September, when there may be several consecutive hot and humid days. There are only a few degrees of variation in temperature throughout the year. January to June is considered the dry season, though it actually does rain to some extent every month–usually heavy but brief showers. Average annual rainfall is around 45 inches at sea level, 75 inches at the higher elevations.

THE PEOPLE. The most colorful note of all is provided by the native people themselves, who call themselves "Bajans": boys with gleaming purple-black bodies diving for coins thrown from ships in the harbor; women in multicolored cotton dresses with enormous loads on their heads; gaily costumed peddlers known as "higglers," such as the biscuit man with red cap and bugle; the "Mawby women," who juggle an unwieldy spigoted container on their heads from which they pour into a glass or tin cup held at chest level a cool drink made of fresh bark from the Mawby tree; the harbor police, who still wear the identical white sailor shirt and tie and the high-crowned white sailor hat with the black name-band that were worn by the sailors back in the days of Admiral Nelson; traffic policemen, standing on their little sun-shielded platforms, wearing spotless white jackets and white sun helmets and blue trousers with a bright red stripe down the sides. When Parliament is in session, the daily opening procession of the speaker of the house, the mace-bearer, and the chaplain is a picture from the Old World. On special occasions, if you are fortunate, you will see the Regimental Fife and Drum Corps in their red and gold bolero jackets and baggy blue trousers and the mounted police in their uhlan helmets and leopard-skin tunics.

Barbados has a population of about 250,000, making this one of the most densely populated islands in the world –over 1,500 people to the square mile. More than 95 percent of these are Barbadians of African descent, with some white people of British descent and a smattering of residents from other countries. In a district in the north called Scotland, there are still a few descendants of the early indentured white servants–unwanted Scots and Irish, political and criminal prisoners, shipped over from England in the early nineteenth century, known then and now as "Red Legs." When the African slaves were freed in 1834, almost all of the land was privately owned and under cultivation, so that there was none available for them. As a result, most of them remained on the plantations as servants. Even today, many of the poorer farmers cultivate land rented from the wealthy white landowners.

The low average income of the Bajans is rising due to a lively fishing industry, booming tourist business and sugar refining. Barbados has one of the lowest illiteracy rates in the world. The people enjoy a British way of life in many ways although they are also expanding their regional and western hemisphere ties.

The language of the island is English, but the native dialect is a fascinating but hard-to-understand mixture of pure English, Cockney, Irish and Scotch plus local phrasing called "Bajan talk." The religion is chiefly Anglican and each of the 11 parishes has its own Anglican church. Also represented are the Roman Catholics, Methodists, Seventh-Day Adventists, Moravians and the Salvation Army.

Although remains of Arawak Indian settlements are still being found, the island was uninhabited when the white man arrived. One Pedro a Campos, a Portuguese, is believed to have landed here in 1536, and though he made no attempt at a settlement, he did leave hogs, whose descendants he intended to use should he return. He presumably gave the island its name from the bearded appearance of the fig trees there, which sent shoots down from their branches to take root again in the ground. A Captain John Powell, on his return to England from Pernambuco on a ship belonging to a London merchant, Sir William Courteen, did land there, planted a cross and carved on a nearby tree "James K. of E. and of this Island." On the strength of the captain's report, Sir William Courteen, under the protection of the Earl of Marlborough, sent some 80 adventurers, commanded by Captain Henry Powell, a younger brother, to develop a settlement on this spot. They built a fort which they called Plantation Fort and founded the town of James Town, now called Holetown. By 1628 their little settlement had grown to nearly 2,000 settlers.

In 1639 Barbados was permitted its own first Parliament, the second to be established in a British colony. Once the capital seat of the British Windward Islands, in 1885 Barbados was separated from the rest of the Windwards and became a colony in its own right with almost complete self-government. Today, as an independent nation, Barbados is the twenty-sixth member of the British Commonwealth. It is governed by a two-house Parliament, made up of a 21-member Senate appointed by the governor-general, and a 24-member House of Assembly, all elected by their constituents. The Prime Minister is the head of government. A governor-general represents the Queen, who still is regarded as the head of state. As is true in most Commonwealth nations, there is a cabinet, a privy council, and a supreme court.

AGRICULTURE. Over half of the soil of Barbados is cultivated, with sugar cane the main crop, followed by cotton and arrowroot.

INDUSTRY. Sugar refining has become a major industry in Barbados. Fishing and pottery are also important. There are a small petroleum refinery, rum distilleries, and a flying-fish freezing and processing plant. A variety of small industries include cigarettes, bay rum, edible oil, ice, lard, margarine, biscuits, macaroni, soap, and furniture. Other principal exports are excellent Barbados rum, cotton lint, and a syrup known as "fancy molasses."

BRIDGETOWN. Located in St. Michael's Parish, Bridgetown is the capital and only town in Barbados. Of all the other little settlements, only Speightstown could even warrant the title of village and its population is under 3,000. Bridgetown–so-named for the original little Indian bridge (since replaced) across an inlet connecting the harbor area with the rest of the island –is one of the most appealing, colorful, and picturesque towns in the Caribbean, with its busy wharf, narrow winding streets, pastel-colored homes (many made of coral blocks cut from the ground), and their charming gardens. The people and the atmosphere are the best "sight" in Bridgetown. Walk around **Trafalgar Square** area and watch the color and life around the wharves and the old screw dock at the Careenage in the center of town. In the square itself is the bronze **statue of Lord Nelson** by Sir Richard Westmacott, erected 27 years prior to its counterpart in London; the two incongruous Gothic-type public buildings, with their red awnings and green shutters, housing the Chambers of the Legislative Council and House of Assembly (which you may visit when in session); the granite **war memorial** obelisk, the **pottery market** and, to the south, the three-dolphin **garden fountain** and a cannonball tree.

Within walking distance inland, **St. Michael's Cathedral,** built in 1665 and rebuilt after the 1780 hurricane, is worth a visit. George Washington is said to have worshiped there when visiting the island with his brother Lawrence in 1751.

Broad Street is the main shopping street in Bridgetown. **Swan Street,** behind Broad and parallel to it, is another shopping street. **Luke's Alley fruit and vegetable market** is a colorful sight, and **Cheapside Market** should be visited on a Saturday night.

Even if you have only a day in Barbados, by all means make a tour of the island. Cars with drivers are available at very reasonable rates. Circling the island, going east from Bridgetown over Chamberlain Bridge out Bay Street, you will pass on the left the house where it is claimed George Washington lived during his visit. On the ocean side the **Royal Barbados Yacht Club** and **Barbados Aquatic Club** at the end of the esplanade, and **St. Anne's Castle,** now headquarters of the Barbados Regiment, can be seen. Inland from here is the **Savannah Club,** formerly garrison barracks, facing on the Savannah where the horse races are held. On its farther side is the **Barbados Museum and Historical Society.** The museum, started with a grant of £1,500 from the Carnegie Institute, is located in what was formerly a military prison. In a separate building behind the museum there is an art gallery where the exhibits are changed periodically.

Drive on through the resort sections of Hastings, Worthing, and St. Lawrence. Nearby is **Christ Church,** with the famed Chase family vault. The sea view farther up the coast, from the **Crane Hotel,** should not be missed, and beyond here be sure to see famed **Sam Lord's Castle,** now an inn. It is a beautiful mansion with superb plasterwork ceilings and paneled walls, priceless antiques, beautiful gardens and intriguing legends of old Sam Lord. Drive on to **Codrington College**—two of its avenues of colossal palms were planted by H.R.H. Prince Albert Victor and the late George V in 1879 when they were naval cadets. Codrington is a theological seminary. There are fine views of Conset Bay from here, and you should also see the interior of **St. John's Church.** In its grounds is the tomb of Fernando Paleologos, a churchwarden and vestryman in 1655–56, who descended from "Ye Imperial Lyne of Ye Emperors of Greece." The views from here are magnificent, as are the views from nearby **Hackelton's Cliff.** Go north of **Bathsheba** and see the glorious surf, to **Chalky Mount** and up Coggin Hill to a little village where you can watch the pottery-makers at work. From here you can drive to **Turner's Hall** and **Farley Hall,** "great houses" of the past, the latter noted also for the farley fern developed on its ground. Not far from here are caves with old Indian inscriptions. There are wild monkeys, readily seen at dusk, at **Cherry Tree Hill** and lovely views of the sea and the Scotland district. Past River Bay and Pico Teneriffe, at the northern tip of the island, are the **Animal Flower Caves.** Return to Bridgetown via the west coast through the little fishing village of **Speightstown,** down the exclusive **"Platinum Coast"** section with its beautiful homes and the finest of club-hotels. **St. James Church,** just below this area, is the oldest one on the island; its font is dated 1684. At **Holetown** a column marks the spot where the British first landed early in the seventeenth century.

With time to spare, there are various sights in the interior of Barbados. Among interior attractions, all within six or seven miles of Bridgetown, are **Coles Cave; Welshman's Hall Gully,** containing the only nutmeg grove on the island; **Gun Hill,** with a landmark of a lion sculptured in the white coral of the hillside by Colonel Henry John Wilkinson about 1868. The new **University of the West Indies** is located at **Cave Hill. Sugar factories** are interesting to visit during the grinding season. The **Mount Gay Rum Distillery** in St. Lucy Parish welcomes visitors.

SPORTS AND RECREATION. **Fishing,** both deep-sea and spear, is good all year round, but best between December and May. Sailboats and motorboats are available for hire, while small coastal boats and interisland cargo schooners also take passengers.

There are superb beaches, both on the leeward side where the water is calm, and on the southern coast where there is surf. On the south side, the Hastings, Worthing, and St. Lawrence areas are jammed with hotels, clubs, and guesthouses. Up the eastern (Atlantic) coast is the lovely beach area of Bathsheba.

Other sports include **snorkeling, skindiving, water polo, golf, tennis,** and **horseback riding.** Spectator sports are **horse racing** (three times a year, in March, August, and November, very gala occasions, lasting three or four days at a time), **cricket, football, basketball, hockey, polo matches** (every Saturday from June to January), **swimming competitions, boat regattas, annual "gymkhana" exhibitions.**

DINING AND SHOPPING. The great specialty is flying fish—baked, broiled, boiled, or fried, or as a flying-fish pie made of the fish, hard-boiled eggs, tomatoes, onions, yams, butter, Worcestershire sauce and sherry. *Chub* is almost equally popular and good. Other specialties are sea-eggs—seasoned with onion, lime, and pepper and steamed or fried; *poan*—grated coconut, pumpkin, corn flour, sugar, spices; *coocoo*—cornmeal porridge served with okra; *jug-jug*—boiled salt beef, salt pork, guinea peas, corn flour, served especially at Christmas time; *coulsies*—eggs, pumpkin, sugar and nutmeg steamed in plantain leaves. Also popular are baked crab backs, rum omelets, "pudding and souse," pepper pot.

Mawby juice is the native drink of mawby bark steeped with sugar and spices. Others are "raw liquor"—freshly crushed cane juice, iced (available January through June); *sangaree*—the island's famed spiced drink, the recipe for which has varied through the years (today it is usually made with a wineglass of Madeira, ½ tsp. of sugar syrup, ½ tsp. of curaçao or benedictine, glass filled with cracked ice and soda, slice of lime added and, when cold, nutmeg sprinkled on top); *bub*—rum, sugar and fresh milk; "black strap"—cracked liquor (cane juice subjected to intense heat), lime juice, rum, nutmeg; "corn and oil"—rum and falernum. Sorrel liqueur—fruit soaked in warm water with sugar and cloves and fermented in open bottles (a Christmas drink). Green swizzles, rum punches, gin slings and scotch are also popular.

Native handicrafts are pottery, basketware, tortoise-shell and sea-shell costume jewelry, needlework, wearing apparel, sea-island cottons, mahogany novelties, attractive wooden figures representing various types of Bajans, such as the Mawby women. Free-port shopping is now available, and the selection, particularly of British goods, is most appealing. Examples: English china, Royal Doulton figurines, cashmere sweaters, gloves, sport jackets, topcoats, woolen materials, tweeds, Liberty silks, Irish linens. Excellent light Barbados rum is very inexpensive.

Trinidad and Tobago

TRINIDAD

Columbus named this island La Trinidad for a group of three hills he could see from his anchorage off the southeastern coast. Today, it is the wealthiest and most important of the Eastern Caribbean islands. It is also one of the most interesting because of its cosmopolitan population of British, French, Spanish, Portuguese, Syrian, Chinese, East Indian and African.

THE LAND. The island of Trinidad covers an area of 1,864 square miles, about 65 miles north to south, and 48 miles east and west. But at one time, it was a part of the South American continent. Its two peninsulas in the northwest and southwest, which embrace the Gulf of Paria, are only a few miles from the Venezuelan coast; its ranges of hills, which reach their highest point in the north at 3,084 feet, are an extension of the Venezuelan ranges. As a result, the island's flora and fauna are quite different from the more northerly Caribbean islands.

Trinidad has real tropical jungles. There is greater scenic variety here than would seem possible in an island so small. Most of the island has level land, fertile soil, and thick forests. It has rugged mountains, open plains, miniature mud volcanoes, incongruous **Pitch Lake,** protected beaches and wild surf areas.

"Iere" ("Land of the Humming Bird") was the name given the island by the Carib Indians who once occupied it. These birds are still there. Trinidad is famous for them and for the keskidee birds that seem to repeat over and over the phrase *"Qu'est-ce qu'il dit?"*

THE CLIMATE. The island is tropical and hot, with an annual average temperature of 85 degrees. The nights are about 10 degrees cooler and it is, of course, even cooler in the hill areas. The summer months are often very humid. Trinidad averages 80 inches of rainfall a year, the wettest season being June to December, when there are torrential downpours, but as a rule these only last for an hour or so. In the island's recorded history, there have been only three hurricanes, the last in 1933. January through April are Trinidad's most comfortable months.

THE PEOPLE. Columbus first discovered Trinidad on his third voyage, in 1498, and claimed it for Spain. But no attempt was made to establish a settlement. Don Antonio Sedeño, from Puerto Rico, attempted colonization in the early 1530's, but the island really was not settled by the Spanish until 1577. Although the British, French, Dutch, and Spanish all fought for it during the ensuing 200 years or more, Trinidad actually changed hands less often than most of the other islands of the West Indies. Eventually, the British captured the island from the Spanish in 1797 without firing a shot, the Spanish governor having obligingly surrendered without argument. It was formally ceded by Spain in 1802 by the Treaty of Amiens and, until August 1962, when it became an independent nation along with Tobago within the British Commonwealth, belonged to Britain.

Under the "destroyers-for-bases" agreement of March 1941, 50 acres of land in Trinidad were leased to the United States for a period of 99 years. They were returned in 1967.

Tobago, for reasons of economic necessity and administrative purposes, became a ward of Trinidad toward the end of the nineteenth century. The two are now known as the Territory of Trinidad and Tobago. Negroes constitute more or less two-thirds of the territory's population of about 1 million. Englishmen, East Indians, descendants of African extraction, Dutch, French, Spanish, Portuguese, Syrians, Lebanese and Chinese, are the island's chief inhabitants. One of the intriguing sights, especially in Port-of-Spain, is the dress of the people: East Indian women in saris, Moslems in fezzes, Sikhs in turbans, and West Indians in traditional dress. On ceremonial occasions the mounted police add a colorful note with their white, spiked helmets and white jackets and blue trousers with the double white stripes down the sides.

English is the official and predominant language of the Trinidadians. Hindi and various other East Indian languages can be heard as well as Chinese, Syrian, Hebrew, Spanish, Portuguese and a French patois. Although France never actually occupied the island, so many immigrants settled in Trinidad to escape the Revolution that the French influence is very much in evidence. The names of towns indicate a cosmopolitan population: St. Mary's, Blanchisseuse, La Brea, Siparia (Arawak), Fyzabad (Hindustani).

AGRICULTURE. Trinidad's variety of natural resources gives it one of the most stable economies in the West

Indies. The government has several cattle farms for improving the livestock, and bananas, sugar cane, cocoa, coffee, oranges, and coconuts are grown.

INDUSTRY. Petroleum is one of the leading sources of the island's wealth. It is the chief natural resource and accounts for four-fifths of Trinidad's export revenue. There is an increasing number of other industries, such as sugar refining, textiles, glassware, copra products, cement, rum, beer, and cigarettes. Some of the other exports include cocoa, citrus fruits, fats and laundry soap, coffee, bananas, pitch, angostura bitters, molasses, and rubber.

Natural asphalt, a major resource, is taken from Pitch Lake, located on the southwest end of the island.

PORT-OF-SPAIN. The Spanish name Puerto España has been retained in its English version, Port-of-Spain, for the city that serves as Trinidad's capital. It is situated on the open roadstead of its sheltered harbor and backed by green hills. The tempo of its business section is surprisingly aggressive for a tropical town; there is a relaxed old-world atmosphere in its residential section with its wide tree-lined streets and fabulous eighteenth-century Spanish and nineteenth-century French mansions. The variety of architectural styles in Port-of-Spain is amazing: the Victorian Government House, the Moorish White Hall, the Scotch Baronial Stollmeyer's Castle, the Second Empire French Roodals residence, the Renaissance administrative building, "The Red House," Moslem mosques, and Hindu temples.

In Port-of-Spain's business section, you can walk to the few points of interest—the harbor, **Fort San Andres,** and the **Jama Masjid Mosque** to the east of Queen Street. Over on Woodford Square is the lovely Anglican **Holy Trinity Cathedral,** and **"The Red House,"** housing the government offices and the House of Representatives. On Charlotte Street is the native **Eastern Market.**

See **Queen's Park Savannah**—a 199-acre park with a race track, several playing fields, a rock garden, an old cemetery, and the weird old saman trees. The walk that circles the outer rim of the Savannah is known as "The Pitch."

Facing on the Savannah is the 63-acre **Royal Botanic Garden,** with a rare and superb collection of tropical trees, shrubs, and flowers, an orchid house, a zoo—small but with unusual specimens—a "Look-Out," tea pavilion, and the governor general's house. A few yards away is the **Concert Hall.**

Following around the Savannah counterclockwise are **Queen's Royal College**—a government secondary school housed in an ornate red and white building with a clock tower; some fantastically elaborate old mansions; the pink and white **U. S. Embassy;** famed **Queen's Park Hotel; Prince's Building**—and **Memorial Park.** A block away is the **Royal Victoria Institute Museum** with a small collection and a concert hall. The anchor in front of the building, literally "dropped" off Point Icacos on the southwestern coast by Columbus and dredged up in 1877, has been proved authentic.

There are beautiful vistas from the **Lady Young Road,** and the tower of the **Chapel of Our Lady of Laventille,** a four-mile drive out of the city to an altitude of 600 feet. The eighteenth-century Spanish **Fort Chacon** is to the north, the nineteenth-century British **Fort Picton** to the south.

Out Eastern Main Road is **San Augustine,** with the **University of the West Indies,** and **St. Joseph,** the site of the old Spanish capital where the Articles of Surrender were signed by the Spaniards and the British in 1797, and where the oldest church on the island still stands.

Turning from here into St. John's Road, an 800-foot climb leads to **Mount St. Benedict,** ten miles from Port-of-Spain, where there is a Benedictine Monastery open to male visitors, and a simple but spotlessly clean guesthouse offering isolated peace and quiet in which to enjoy its fine views.

A little farther out Eastern Main Road and just this side of Tacarigua, is

Caura Valley Road through the scenic valley of the same name.

Seven miles from Port-of-Spain and accessible by either car or boat is the **Caroni Swamp Bird Sanctuary**—10,000 acres of mangrove and marshland. Endless varieties of birds can be seen. The best time to plan to see these is just before the sun sets, when they fly home from their feeding grounds. The sanctuary is open to visitors for several months each year.

SPORTS AND RECREATION. **Maracas Bay** and **Las Cuevas Bay** on the north coast are Port-of-Spain's most accessible good beaches, but there are many others on Trinidad and the offshore islands. The most beautiful are on the northeast shore and east coast. Some of the hotels and clubs have pools and there is **swimming** at Blue Basin waterfall. Cabin cruisers and motorboats are available for charter; there is a Trinidad Yacht Club, and frequent regattas. Good deep-sea and spear **fishing,** as well as **hunting** for alligator (*cayman*), armadillo (*tattoo*), agouti, lappe, wild pig (*quenck*), and opossum (*manicou*). **Tennis, golf,** and **cricket** (from January to June), **football** (from July to December), **rugby, hockey, basketball, horse racing, water polo,** and **boxing** are also popular.

There is an **Art Center** where exhibits sponsored by the Trinidad Art Society are held. The National Museum and Art Gallery also offers exhibitions. Concerts frequently are given by visiting celebrities; there is a two-week biennial **Music Festival** in March.

The **Trinidad Theatre Workshop** offers productions regularly. Trinidad has its religious dances: its noted "jump-up"; its "shuffle", which requires no partner; and the "limbo" (without touching head or hands to floor the dancer bends backward under a stick held by two people who gradually lower it to a point sometimes a mere ten inches from the ground).

Steel bands originated in Trinidad, developing from the scarcity of available instruments during World War II, plus lack of necessary funds on the part of the people to purchase instruments. These instruments are literally steel oil drums, called "pans," cut to varying heights; through an intricate process, the tops are pounded into indentations of various sizes to produce a great range of notes when beaten with rubber-tipped sticks.

SPECIAL EVENTS. **Hosein** (Hoe-zay) is a Moslem festival with a colorful procession through the streets; it is held on the seventh to ninth day after the Mohammedan New Year.

February is **Carnival** month both in Trinidad and in Tobago. Although preparations begin after New Year, the true festivities begin with the Calypso Fiesta, in San Fernando, in mid-February. That same day the Children's Carnival Competition is held. A week later the Carnival Queen Competition is held in Queen's Park Savannah, followed by the Dimanche Gras Show, where the Calypso King and Queen of the Bands are chosen. The Carnival celebrations begin the two days prior to Ash Wednesday, beginning at dawn of the first day and ending at midnight on the second evening. There are street parades of costumed bands and steel bands, dancing, drinking, and eating.

The **Religious Feast of Corpus Christi** is held the first Thursday after Trinity Sunday; High Mass is held at the Cathedral of the Immaculate Conception in Port-of-Spain and then a public procession around Independence Square, with open-air benediction given. A provision was made in the treaty drawn up when Spain capitulated to England that this day would be set aside as an occasion for public worship by the island's Roman Catholics.

Other holidays include **May Day,** celebrated on May first with a public holiday and processions; **Whit Monday,** at the end of May, with athletic competitions; **Discovery Day,** a public holiday celebrated the first Monday in August (although Columbus actually arrived on July 31); **Diwali,** the Hindu Festival of Lights, in October; **All Saints Day** and **All Souls Day,** November 1 and 2, respectively, celebrated by illumination of cemeteries with candles; and **Christmas Day,** December 25.

DINING AND SHOPPING. Food is as varied as one would expect from the polyglot population. Specialties are a river fish called *cascadou* (or *cascadura*)—local residents claim that if you eat it, you will return to Trinidad; oysters; the West Indian *callaloo* soup, which is more like a stew, and *san coche.*

Pastelles are meat wrapped in a cornmeal mixture inside a banana leaf; crab backs have the crab meat removed from the shell, highly seasoned, and replaced in the empty back; *crabmatete* is crab meat and farina; *roti* is a highly seasoned meat, chicken or fish, wrapped in a big pancake. There are fine tropical fruits, such as pawpaw and sapodillas, and unusual vegetables, such as cassavas, tannias, eddoes. For unusual wild game, there is *lappe, quenck* (wild pig), *tattoo* (armadillo), and deer.

Rum is the local drink. A Trinidad rum favorite is a green swizzle made with Carypton. Planter's punches and rum and cokes are popular. Try a gin (or rum) and coconut water—the liquor is poured into a hole cut in a fresh coconut and drunk through a straw, or from a half-shell. Other local concoctions are soursop punch, granadilla punch, sorrel cocktail and poncha crema.

Native crafts include silver filigree work, gold (look for the Cascadura bracelets), ceramics, straw and fiber work, and articles of wood. One may purchase British imports—fine selections of the usual china, crystal, gloves, and woolens (fine tailoring is done in Port-of-Spain); French perfumes—prices are sometimes even less than in Curaçao; Oriental curios—ivories, brasses, wood; Indian saris and sandals; Chinese gowns; Trinidad rums; native recordings of steel bands and calypso music. Such items as perfume, cameras, watches, china, silk, woolens, linens, jewelry, gloves, and pipes may be purchased "in bond."

The Handicraft Co-operative Society with shops at Piarco Airport, the Trinidad Hilton Hotel, and King's Wharf Passenger Centre has articles for sale. Frederick Street and Independence Square is the main shopping area. Some East Indian shops can be found on the Western Main Road.

TOBAGO

On this island the atmosphere is relaxed and informal, the people natural and friendly, and the accommodations charming and modern. It is an ideal spot for the water-sports enthusiast, the writer seeking seclusion, and the artist and photographer looking for beauty.

Since 1962, Tobago has been, with Trinidad, a single independent nation and a member of the United Nations.

THE LAND. The island of Tobago lies approximately 21 miles northeast of Trinidad. It is somewhat fish-shaped, 26 miles long and 7.5 miles across at its widest point, and has an area of 116 square miles. It lies in a northeast to southwest direction, the flat southwestern end of the island giving way to a gradual rising of hills.

Down the center of Tobago, a volcanic range of mountains rises from the coral lowlands of its southern tip to a height of 1,856 feet in the northeast, with dense tropical growth in the central portion. Its coast is ringed by coves and bays, the largest of which is Man of War Bay, on the northeast coast, and picture-book beaches.

THE CLIMATE. Tobago, though tropical, has a healthy and pleasant climate, which is practically perfect from December to April, and is cooler and less humid than Trinidad during the other months. Most of its annual 70 inches of rain falls between August and December, but even then there is seldom an entire day of rain. Rains take the form of short, heavy showers followed by dazzling sunshine. The average annual temperature is 84 degrees during the day, 74 degrees at night.

THE PEOPLE. Columbus passed Tobago by in 1498, but did claim it for

Spain. Attempts at colonization were made by some Englishmen from Barbados and later by the Dutch in the early 1600's, but they were driven off by Carib Indians from nearby islands. Tobago holds the record for having changed hands more than any other island in the Caribbean, having been constantly taken, lost, and retaken by the French, the British, the Dutch and the Spaniards, and even a group from the United States. By mutual agreement, Tobago was finally declared neutral ground in 1748 and remained so for fourteen years until the struggle for control was renewed. It came into British hands in 1803 and England's possession was conceded by treaty in 1814. In 1898 Tobago was united with Trinidad as a single colony.

There are a few East Indians on the island, but the majority of the 36,000 people who live in this paradise are Negroes, many of whom live in houses on stilts, with carvings over the windows.

The official language is English, but people in some rural areas speak French and Spanish. Many of the natives speak all three.

During the past several years, with financial and technical assistance from some foundations and UNICEF, Tobago has been made a very healthy island. Malaria and other tropical diseases are now completely under control.

AGRICULTURE. Agriculture is encouraged by the government. There are sugar and coconut plantations. Cacao, copra, and bananas are important items; there is some livestock.

INDUSTRY. Some rubber is produced. There is also a cooperative lime factory, as well as an ice plant. Extensive forest reserves provide both hard and soft wood but petroleum is the economic lifeblood.

SCARBOROUGH (population 1,500) formerly known as Port Louis, is a typically tropical, relaxed little town. It sits on the edge of Rockly Bay and is backed by hills. In the center of the town the few streets are wide and clean. From them, steep narrow streets lined with weather-beaten little houses climb the slopes, and old Fort King George on the summit of a hill stands guard over all.

The most cheery spot in town is the market place, especially colorful on Wednesdays and Saturdays. The small **Botanic Garden** is well kept. **Government House** is a half mile out of town. The old white bridge with the ancient musket barrels for railings is called **Gun Bridge.** Walk or drive up the hill to **Fort George** at its 452-foot summit for a fine view of the harbor.

The perfect one-day drive from Scarborough is up around the southern coast and over to **Man of War Bay** at Charlotteville. The entire trip is fascinating —there are little settlements, a variety of churches, women washing their clothes in rivers, boys carrying baskets on their heads filled with the beans from the cacao to be dried and burned red by the sun in huge trays placed along the roadsides. At a coconut plant, men and women can be seen chopping the meat from the coconut shell for shipment to Trinidad, and piling up the shells, which will be used to make fiber in Scarborough. A **district agricultural station** is worth a visit, as is a **cacao propagating station** just beyond Delaford.

Speyside is a cozy fishing village where you can have lunch and a swim, or continue on up and across the tip of the island to a point where you will have a magnificent view of the marvelous two-mile-wide natural Man of War Bay and, on its edge and climbing back up the slopes, the town of Charlotteville, larger than Scarborough but less important.

SPORTS AND RECREATION. There are perfect beaches all around the island. **Pigeon Point Beach,** not far from Scarborough, is one of the loveliest and most popular, with dressing rooms available at the Aquatic Club where temporary membership is granted visitors.

Snorkeling is as ideal here as can be found anywhere. Even non-swimmers can enjoy it out on Buccoo Reef, a half-mile from shore. A motorboat takes you out to the three-mile-long reef, where the water is so shallow you can walk along the sandy stretches between the coral formations and lean over to watch the myriads of tropical fish through a glass-bottomed boat or your snorkeling mask, held just below the surface. **Fishing** is excellent—line fishing, trolling, bottom fishing, deep-sea and spear fishing. **Lobster catching** on the reefs by moonlight, **badminton, horseback riding, tennis,** and **hiking** are other interesting sports. Two-day **horse races** take place in late October or early November and again in late February or early March. **Goat races** are held the Tuesday after Easter.

Buses, taxis and drive-yourself cars are available for seeing the countryside, as are bicycles and horses. It is a short but pretty drive to **Plymouth,** a once thriving community. Now its grass-covered streets lead to the ruins of **Fort James,** Tobago's first fort, built by the Courlanders in 1642. En route your driver will doubtlessly insist you stop and look at a slab of stone that marks the grave of Betty Stivens, with the ambiguous inscription "—she was a mother without knowing it, and a wife without letting her husband know it except by her kind indulgences to him."

Farther on to the south is **Pigeon Point** with the island's most popular beach. On this end of the island, too, is what is claimed to be **Robinson Crusoe's Cave.** It is acknowledged that Daniel Defoe based his famous story on the experiences of Alexander Selkirk, who was marooned on Más-a-Tierra Island in the Pacific; but the descriptions of the island in the book and the location and the references to Trinidad certainly warrant the belief that author Defoe had Tobago in mind as the setting for his story.

There is a pretty little drive through the central interior part of the island toward Caledonia to **Mason Hall.** The growth in this section is tropical and luxuriant, the variety of flowering trees spectacular.

Little Tobago or **"Bird of Paradise Island"** is officially known as Ingram's Island. It lies a mile-and-a-half offshore from Speyside and is reached by motorboat from just south of the town. It was later purchased and abandoned by an English adventurer, and reclaimed by the government. In 1898 the island was bought by Sir William Ingram to serve as a sanctuary for 26 pair of birds-of-paradise he had commissioned someone to bring him from Dutch New Guinea. This was done in 1909. At the death of Sir William, his son donated the island to the country on condition that it be kept as a bird sanctuary. This has been done. Trees were planted of the type bearing fruit preferred by the birds-of-paradise, and the caretaker on the island sees that water is available to them at all times. The birds are so timid that relatively few people have ever seen them. It is particularly difficult during the winter months when the foliage is very dense. However, there are enough other birds on the island to warrant the trip for birdlovers, even if its main attraction fails to make an appearance.

SPECIAL EVENTS are almost all the same as those on Trinidad. (See page 521.)

DINING AND SHOPPING. Creole gumbo and *callaloo* soup are particularly good. Seafood is superb. Try conch in its various forms. Chinese food is served at several hotels.

The island abounds in fine tropical fruits and vegetables—sapodilla, pawpaw, shaddock, "mammy apple" and kenip, christophene, melongena, balata, granadilla, soursop, tannia, cassava, breadfruit.

Rum and gin are inexpensive. The favorite method of serving them to visitors is to pour the liquor in a hole cut in a ripe coconut, from which, mixed with the coconut water, it is drunk through a straw.

Best buys are the handicraft of straw work. British imports are limited in supply but good in quality.

South America

SOUTH AMERICA
VENEZUELA
GUYANA
SURINAM
FRENCH GUIANA
COLOMBIA
ECUADOR
BRAZIL
PERU
Pacific Ocean
BOLIVIA
Atlantic Ocean
PARAGUAY
URUGUAY
CHILE
ARGENTINA

South America

South America, a heart-shaped continent, is a land of incredible contrasts which has fascinated travelers ever since the earliest explorers. It has everything from crumbling ruins to modern cities, and from isolated Indian tribes to ultrasophisticated country clubs. Here can be found the awe-inspiring scenery of snow-capped volcanoes towering over quaint picturesque villages; the breath-taking panoramas of beautiful countrysides, seaside resorts and mountain spas; lovely emerald lakes and gigantic waterfalls, and vital and friendly people.

More visited by travelers every year, South America is a land of opportunity, a land of promise and a land of tomorrow that is undergoing a tremendous growth and population explosion.

THE LAND

Its seven million square miles, occupying about 12 percent of the land area of the earth—or roughly twice the size of Europe—are broken up into ten independent republics and three European colonies which are as unlike one another as their distinct topography, climate, racial origins, customs, ways, and even their language can make them. Even though nine of these countries share the same language, culture and political and social traditions (which are their common Spanish heritage), and 11 the same religion, each is uniquely different.

This is a continent of topographic and climatic variations which stagger the imagination and defy comparison; of rugged lofty mountains like the Andes, which stretch from the shores of the Caribbean to the tip of Tierra del Fuego; of dense jungles and tropical lowlands around the Amazon which extend almost clear across the continent; of bleak, wind-swept deserts like the Atacama, the largest dry area on earth; and of the vast and seemingly endless grassy plains of the lonely pampas.

THE CLIMATE

While two-thirds of South America lies in the Torrid Zone, with the remaining third in the South Temperate Zone, it generally enjoys a great diversity of climates, ranging from the warmer temperatures along the Caribbean and north Atlantic coasts and the Amazon lowlands to the colder climes in the Andean highlands and plateaus and the southernmost regions of Patagonia and Tierra del Fuego.

Since most of this continent is south of the equator, it's June in January; and visitors can go bathing in December, skiing in July, trout fishing in February, and deep-sea fishing off South America's Pacific coast practically any time of the year. In spite of a reversal of climates in the southern area, summers are cooler and winters milder than in North America.

THE PEOPLE

Most of the continent's over 186 million population is clustered around the metropolitan centers and large cities and generally falls into several distinct racial groups: those of predominantly European extraction, whose ancestors were the Spanish and Portuguese who first colonized these countries or migrated here during the last 100 years; the descendants of the Quechua and Aymara civilizations; other Indian populations; Negroes; and mixtures of all of these groups.

The largely European white populations, while spread throughout the continent, are largely concentrated in the southern countries of Argentina, Uruguay and Chile, with the indigenous races being found largely in Ecuador, Peru and Bolivia, and most of the Negroes inhabiting parts of Brazil, Venezuela and Colombia.

Most of these people speak either Spanish or Portuguese, with only slight variations, but other languages, such as Quechua in Peru, Aymara in Bolivia, Guarani in Paraguay, Guajiras in Colombia, and other native languages are heard throughout the land.

This continent was the site of pre-Columbian cultures and ancient civilizations which had reached a high degree of development in the arts and were already living in well-organized and populated communities prior to the coming of the white man; and their impressive ruins, works of art and colorful artifacts today constitute some of the area's outstanding tourist attractions.

Little is known about the earliest inhabitants of the coastal valleys of what is now northern Peru and the Andean highlands, although the most popular theory is that over the ages they migrated from Asia by way of the Bering Strait. But the ruins of the powerful Chimu empire at Chan Chan, the primitive but distinctive works of art of other ancients still being discovered, and the mysterious and impressive archaeological wonders of Tiahuanaco on the shores of Lake Titicaca offer mute testimony of the advanced stage achieved by these cultures. Some idea of the amazing social and political development attained by the sun-worshiping Incas, who came later to unify these people and extend their empire along the west coast of South America, is seen in the magnificent highways and artfully sculptured stone temples and fortresses in Cuzco and Macchupichu.

Many of the Indian tribes on the continent at the time of the Spanish and Portuguese conquest and colonization were either annihilated or driven into the forest wilderness. Descendants of the nomadic tribes which once roamed the Argentine pampas and harassed the Spanish settlers, like their indomitable red-skinned Araucanian brethren in Chile, today inhabit isolated communities and reservations in the southernmost regions of the continent. Yet the racial strains of other earlier civilizations, like the Aymaras of Bolivia, the Chibchas of Colombia, the Caras of Ecuador, the Tupis of Brazil and the Guaranis of Paraguay, may still be seen in some of the people.

There is an aura of the daring and adventurous days of the Spanish conquest and the splendid and romantic colonial period which followed in the historic buildings and magnificent churches and palaces which are still authentically preserved as a reminder of a glorious past. And the people's love of freedom and fierce struggle for independence are recalled in the many impressive monuments which revere the memory of patriots and liberators like Bolívar, San Martín, Sucre, O'Higgins, Murillo and Dom Pedro II.

From earliest times the great urban centers have been noted for their rich cultural and intellectual life where learning flourished and the arts reached their highest development and expression. Their diversity of races and cultures have given rise to an extraordinary artistic output and many outstanding artists in the fields of literature, painting, sculpture and music. Its rich literature stems from a colorful and intricate heritage which has produced some eminent poets, novelists and historians. Its impressive architecture from ancient to present times presents an arresting blend of the ancient, Gothic, Moorish, baroque, neo-classic and modern styles and designs not found anywhere else. Its notable art and sculpture show the influence of the continent's indigenous cultures, the Spanish Renaissance, and the abstract modern. And its music is as varied and colorful as the people themselves.

Colombia

Colombia, cornerstone in the mosaic of South American countries, borders on five other republics: Panama to the west, Ecuador and Peru to the south, Brazil and Venezuela to the east. The only South American country bordering on both the Atlantic and the Pacific, Colombia has some 2,000 miles of seacoast. Ports on the relatively undeveloped Pacific are Buenaventura and Tumaco, hot, humid, and seldom visited by tourists. On the Atlantic side, Colombia borders on the Caribbean Sea. Here balmy breezes relieve the heat and there are fine beaches. The deep-sea fishing is excellent. Historic forts and ruins, and buried treasures can be seen.

THE LAND. Colombia was known as the most isolated country in South America. The cause of the isolation that has had such a profound effect on Colombia is readily apparent to the airborne traveler. Four mountain ranges, the Eastern, Central, and Western Cordilleras, and the Baudó west of them, rise precipitously to averages of 10,000 to 14,000 feet. Several peaks are much higher, the Nevado del Huila being 18,865 feet, the Pico Cristóbal Colón, 19,029.

Many of the valleys between these ranges are covered with dense jungle growth. In some places, the adventurous tourist can switch from jungle hunting to mountain climbing in a matter of a few miles. Beyond the mountain ranges are the vast plains (*llanos*) and jungles (*selvas*) to the east, comprising more than half Colombia's 440,000 square miles. In the past there were a few isolated cattle ranges, but these have disappeared. Very little of this great wilderness has ever been explored beyond mapping expeditions and some oil exploration. To adapt it for settlement is a primary project of the government.

Nearly all of Colombia's 22 million inhabitants live on the plateaus and in the more shallow valleys of the Cordilleras. Climate is a matter of altitude. The tropical zone, with its dense jungles, extends from sea level to about 3,000 feet; subtropical from 3,000 to 7,000 feet; temperate, 7,000 to 10,000 feet; and cold above that, where the bleak *páramos* support only sparse and stunted trees.

THE CLIMATE. Seasons are somewhat arbitrarily divided into wet and dry, *invierno* (winter) being generally regarded as the wet season and *verano* (summer) as the dry. In the interior, especially Bogotá, December, January, and February are the most pleasant and driest months—the year-round temperature there averages 57 degrees. On the Caribbean coast, the dry season extends from October through March, and year-round temperatures are hot (75 to 80 degrees). In the tropical zones, it is always very humid.

Most population centers are in the temperate zones. The climate is generally pleasant, with clear, sunny days and magnificent cloud formations hovering around the mountain peaks.

THE PEOPLE. There are over 500,000 Indians representing almost 400 tribes in Colombia today, most of them living in the tropical or subtropical zones. In the northern jungles are the Motilones, still fierce and unconquerable. The Guambianos, inhabiting the valleys between the Western and Central Cordilleras, and the Paez, the Choco, and the Quillcinga, farther south, have kept most of their tribal customs.

Colombia also has about 500,000 Negroes, descendants of slaves brought here centuries ago. Most of them prefer the tropical weather of the port cities. About one-third of the population is classified as white. This group includes the descendants of early Spanish settlers and more recent immigrants. But the vast majority are racially mixed.

Spanish is the official language. The Colombian from Bogotá prides himself on speaking pure Castilian. In some places, words and phrases from local Indian dialects have become common idiom. The speech of the *costeño* or seaport resident seems the most difficult for a highlander to understand, for at the ports the greatest mingling of languages has taken place. In the cities the tourist will have little difficulty, even if his Spanish is limited. English is taught in most schools.

The educational system has been greatly improved in recent years, though about one-third of the population over seven years of age remains illiterate. This is partly due to the isolation of many small villages. In urban areas schools are good and elementary education is free. Secondary schools are primarily parochial. There are more than 150 colleges for training teachers, about 80 professional and technical schools, 26 art schools, and 28 universities, 14 of them located in Bogotá. The most important, the National University, was founded in 1572, but reorganized under its present name in 1935.

In 1501, Rodrigo de Bastidas explored the Caribbean coast and discovered the Magdalena River leading inland. He also discovered the fabulous wealth of the Indians. Spanish adventurers sent tons of gold and gems back to their motherland. The first colony to survive was established at Santa Marta in 1525. In 1538, Gonzalo Jiménez de Quesada established a colony named Santa Fé de Bacatá, soon shortened to Bogotá.

In 1740, Bogotá became the capital of the newly created viceroyalty of New Granada—a vast area including what is now Colombia, Ecuador, Venezuela, and Panama. The viceroy was overthrown and a United Provinces of New Granada established in 1808, but Spain, after many bloody battles, reconquered her colonies. In 1819, the royalists were overthrown by Simón Bolívar and his followers and the Republic of Gran Colombia established. In 1829 Venezuela seceded and Ecuador followed her example in 1831. Colombia was generally in a state of civil war until the secession of Panama in 1903 gave her sparring leaders a common foe in the United States. Liberals and Conservatives remained bitterly partisan, however. Their growing animosity culminated in the riots of 1948. More than 2,000 people were killed. The uneasy presidency of Laureano Gómez, a Conservative, ended in the military coup led by General Gustavo Rojas Pinilla in 1953. He in turn was overthrown in 1957. Colombia has enjoyed a period of relative peace and prosperity since 1958.

AGRICULTURE. Colombia ranks second in growth of coffee, after Brazil, and is a leader in the production of bananas, cacao beans, rice and sugar cane (all of which are exported). Although agriculture is the chief industry, less than 5 percent of the land is cultivated, with the average farm covering only five acres. Farmers still use primitive methods to grow crops for their consumption.

INDUSTRY. Though industry is not highly developed, food processing, aluminum, steel, chemical, metallurgical, and cement manufacturing plants have been established. In mining, Colombia's famed emerald mines are in their fourth century of operation. Gold and platinum are found in the same basins. Colombia's underground oil wealth ranks it as one of South America's leading oil-producing countries.

CITIES. Colombia's leading cities were among the first in the Western Hemisphere to be settled. Today they point up the contrast between modern new buildings and roads, and the older homes and villas of centuries ago.

BARRANQUILLA. Even the most hasty tourist will probably see Barranquilla. Atlantic ships dock here and planes for the capital land before going on to Bogotá. Largest port city of Colombia, it is also the newest by about 200 years. Its importance lies in its position astride the great Magdalena River, cargo highway to the interior. Ships can load and discharge cargo while safely moored in fresh water ten miles inland, and import-export trade flourishes. Customs and immigration headquarters for the country, Barranquilla has a population of over 816,000.

Barranquilla was "founded" in the early seventeenth century. It had been a fishing village and for a long time remained little more than that, its chief importance being as a transfer point for cargo brought by sea to Puerto Colombia, about ten miles distant, shipped by rail to Barranquilla and there transferred to river boats on the Magdalena. Eventually, however, the mouth of the Magdalena was opened to ocean-going traffic and Barranquilla became the most important port of the republic. It became capital of the department of Atlántico in 1905.

Like industrial river cities the world over, Barranquilla has blocks and blocks of warehouses along the waterfront, large factories and plants, and many office buildings. The marketplace is picturesque, with almost everything from fruit to flamingoes available. Fish is hawked direct from canoe to customer on the canal side of the market. Visitors will want to visit the library, the **Biblioteca del Atlántico,** at Carrera 39 and Calle 38-B, and the **Universidad del Atlántico** at Carrera 54 and Calle 68.

During the weeks before Christmas, there is a grand **Feria del Juguete,** a sort of all-purpose toy fair. Carrera 41 is jammed with colorful stalls and booths for this festival.

For fun and entertainment, many tourists go over to **Puerto Colombia,** its short distance making it virtually a suburb of Barranquilla. This sleepy, sandy, palm and cactus-studded former port is now a resort town. The hotels are good, the ocean swimming and fishing excellent.

BOGOTÁ. The city itself, with a population of 2 million, is a six-mile-long cluster of buildings sheltered by a ridge of mountains towering a precipitous 2,000 feet above. It was the center of a great Chibcha civilization, before Gonzalo Jiménez took over in 1538. The following year two more expeditions, driven inland by gold fever, arrived. Sebastian Belalcazar led a party of more than 100 Spaniards from Ecuador. Nicholas Federmann, representing German bankers, led jungle-toughened men over the Andes from the east. All had come in quest of El Dorado, and all had come in the right direction. For the legend arose from a mountain lake nearby, where, in a Chibcha ceremony, a gilded man dived in amid a rain of golden ornaments each year.

To tour the city, begin at the **capitol** in the center of the city, on the **Plaza Bolívar.** Here is a fine mural of the freeing of the slaves back in 1851. Colombians are proud of having put an early end to slavery. The glass-domed Elliptical Room (*El Salón Elíptico*), where state receptions are held, is architecturally interesting. The capitol itself occupies the site of the first houses built by Quesada's men more than four centuries ago. Quesada's remains now rest in the cathedral on the northeast side of the Plaza Bolívar, the site of the chapel he and his men built on arrival. Be sure to see the historical treasures on display in the sacristy there, and the beautiful silver altar of the Capilla de Nuestra Señora del Topo, behind the main altar. The cathedral itself was built in the late sixteenth century.

In the **Plaza,** surrounded by four fountains with decoratively colored lights, is the statue of Simón Bolívar, sculptured by the famed Italian, Pietro Tenerani. Within a dozen blocks are almost half of the city's Colonial churches. Half a block north on Carrera 7 is **El Sagrario,** housing some of the finest works of Vásquez de Arce y Ceballos.

To the east of the Plaza, on Calle 10, is **San Ignacio Church,** built in 1605, noted for the fine miniature paintings set in the goldwork of the altars and for the simplicity of line in its exterior architecture. Just around the corner and to the south on Correo 6 is the **Museum of Colonial Art,** with fine collections of Colonial furniture, silver and gold liturgical service, china and cooking utensils, and of early artists' works.

Back on Calle 10, in the next block to the east, is the **Teatro de Colón** or Columbus Theater. Its three circling balconies and galleries seat 3,000. Operas, ballets, and concerts are held here as well as plays. Across the street is the **San Carlos Palace,** where Bolívar lived, the window through which he jumped to escape assassins facing Calle 10 and marked by a plaque. Built in the sixteenth century, it was partially destroyed in the 1948 riots, but has been restored.

South of the Plaza, on Carrera 8, is the church of **Santa Clara,** noted for its Mudejar interior. Here too are paintings by both Gaspar and Baltasar de Figueroa. In the same block and across the street are the **Municipal Theater** and the **National Observatory.** Cross over one block to Carrera 7 and walk south half a block to the **Palacio Presidencial.**

Don't miss seeing the **San Francisco church** at the corner of Carrera 7 and Calle 15, which houses a veritable treasury of historic relics. Here also is the immense altar of gilded and polychromed wood carved by García de Ascucha and more paintings by Vásquez. The church itself was begun in the sixteenth century and completed in 1628, though additions have been built since then. Just north of the San Francisco, facing Santander Park, is **La Veracruz church** where several patriots were shot in the liberation. These heroes are buried within the church. Its chapel has been designated the National Pantheon.

The **Bank of the Republic,** just south of the San Francisco and separated from it by the broad Avenida Jiménez de Quesada, has priceless examples of ancient Chibcha art—grotesque golden masks and images, breastplates and jewelry.

Carrera 7, Septima, is the "main street" of Bogotá, famed for its outdoor forums. **Centenary Park** with its formal landscaping is separated by Septima and **Independence Park,** between Calles 25 and 26. Next to Independence Park, on

Calle 24, is the modern **National Library** with exhibition rooms featuring paintings, sculpture, and ceramics and a music room.

Just north of Independence Park is the **Plaza de Toros**—largest high-altitude bull ring in the world. North of the red brick bull ring is the **national park.**

Nearby, off Septima, is the treasure house **El Panóptico,** a former penitentiary now housing three excellent museums, Archaeological, Ethnical, and Historical. There are mummies thousands of years old, golden ornaments, some cast by the lost wax process; woven textiles and clay textile printers used by the Indians, replicas of ancient stone idols—the originals are generally left at their original sites—musical instruments, and all kinds of primitive utensils and hunting equipment. In the northwestern outskirts of the city is the magnificently modern **National University.**

Monserrate is the most famous landmark near Bogotá. This small white church perched in the mountains only two miles away from the heart of Bogotá is reached by cable car, in less than ten minutes.

An hour's car ride south from Bogotá leads to the Indian shrine, **El Salto de Tequendama,** a majestic 450-foot waterfall. Mist often obscures this spectacular plunge of the Bogotá River, but it wafts away in moments.

Thirty miles to the north are vast salt mines left when the mountain lake that once covered the site of Bogotá receded. At **Zipaquirá** you can drive into the mines for some distance. There is an underground lake, formed where salt was mined by the Chibchas.

To the west, half a day's drive, lie Girardot, Honda, and Puerto Salgar, ports on the **Magdalena River.** Here you can board former Mississippi River paddle-wheel steamers for the trip north to the coast. The steamers stop frequently for food and freight, and at low water points, yet reach the coast within a week. The trip upstream may take two weeks. Almost all travelers to Bogotá come by air today.

To the east, a day's drive brings you to **Villavicencio,** capital of the vast Meta Intendencia where plains and jungle stretch all the way to Brazil. The road winds among sheer drops of thousands of feet, but the scenery is magnificent.

To visit the archaeological excavations of **San Augustin,** it is necessary to fly from Bogotá to Garozón and take a bus from there. The bus may take as long as 12 hours, but it is about the only way you can reach San Augustin. It is well worth the effort to see the fabulous images of men, gods, embryos, birds, and snakes hewn from stone by a civilization vanished long ago.

CARTAGENA lies on a sandspit of the warm, shimmering Atlantic seacoast, the Spanish Main of history. This fortified city has withstood so many pirate, military, and naval attacks it has been called *"Ciudad Heroica."* Capital of the department of Bolívar, this port city has a population of about 230,000 and is a popular resort for Colombians and foreigners alike. Balmy breezes rustle the shading palms. There is surf swimming and deep-sea fishing as well as a wealth of historical interest in this city.

Columbus sailed along the entire coast on his last voyage. Pedro de Heredia founded Cartagena in 1533, although a great fire wiped out much of the settlement 12 years later. It was the shipping point for all treasure coming from the south. Cartagena's position on its landlocked harbor seemed almost impregnable thanks to Nature's fortifications alone. It wasn't. Drake successfully sacked the "pearl of the Indies" before fortifications were built back in 1586. Then vast fortifications were set up—at a reported cost of $70 million. It was sound investment. The city was never again taken, and annual shipments often amounted to more than the cost of the forts.

This superbly fortified city is built around both inner and outer sets of walls. Visitors can drive to the top of **La Popa,** highest observation point for many miles and only one mile from the outer walls.

The reconstructed fort of **San Felipe** lies between the city and La Popa. Its famous 12-gun battery of the Apostles helped fend off land attacks.

A delightful way to tour the narrow streets of the inner-walled city of Cartagena is by horse-and-carriage. The church and monastery of **St. Peter Claver,** the Jesuit who dedicated his life to helping slaves, is at the southern corner of the inner walled city, on Calle San Pedro. Two blocks north on this same street, the tourist finds himself on the **Calle de Los Santos de Piedra** (Stone Saints Street). The fine museum at No. 33 occupies what was formerly the residence of the bishops. Inside are fascinating old charts, early art, and historical exhibits. About a block west is the **House of the Inquisition,** on Calle Inquisición, where sixteenth-century trials were held. Cells, complete with chains, may be seen on the lower floor. Around the corner and north just over a block, on Calle Santo Domingo, is the church of **Santo Domingo,** rebuilt about 1560, after fire destroyed the original building which was built about 20 years earlier. The **Plaza del Ecuador,** inside the gateway separating the inner and outer walled cities, was the slave market.

Launch trips down the bay take a half-day round trip. Visitors will see the navy base, clear coral reefs, and at Boca Chica cross an authentic drawbridge into **San Fernando,** the fort guarding the entrance to the bay. Reconstructed on the original plans, it is well worth a visit. At **Turbaco,** 15 miles from Cartagena, are miniature mud volcanoes, erupting every half minute. The tourist with a yen for treasure-hunting should take a boat to **Islas del Rosario.**

MEDELLÍN. The nation's industrial center, Medellín is a popular vacation spot for Colombians. It is situated in the pleasant, fertile valley of the same name at an altitude of about 5,000 feet, protected on all sides by mountains. Its climate is sunny and warm; there are good golf courses and swimming pools.

The valley was discovered in 1541, but no settlement was attempted for another 100 years. In 1826, it became capital of Antioquia Department, but the period of explosive growth did not take place until the beginning of the twentieth century.

The **Cathedral de Villanueva,** on Calle 56 facing Bolívar Park, is said to be one of the ten largest all-brick constructions in the world. The stately, palm-bordered park is the site of Sunday morning open-air band concerts. The **Zea Museum,** No. 52, Carrera 47, houses exhibits of modern art as well as Colonial and Indian. Four blocks to the east, at Carrera 42 and La Playa, the **Palace of Fine Arts** holds lectures, concerts, readings and plays. More than half of all Colombia's gold production takes place in the department of **Antioquia,** and **Medellín's mint,** at Calle 52 and Carrera 53, stores literally stacks of gold bars, guarding them with dogs famed for their fierceness. Tulip trees line the streets, and thousands of species of orchids are on display. Large ponds with water lilies dot the countryside.

A long day's trip—about five hours each way by car from Medellín—brings you to the beautiful **Guadalupe River Falls,** where the rolling waters plunge more than 18 feet. Overnight stays in the inn can be arranged in advance. At the National Tourist Office visitors can arrange visits to orchid and coffee farms and to gold mines. You can also take a train from Medellín to **Manizales,** through the village of **Villamaría,** with its acres of carnations. Capital of the department of Caldas, Manizales is noted for its enormous Gothic cathedral, and a fine-arts building.

SANTA MARTA. Here, in 1525, was established the first European settlement to survive on this continent. Now capital of the department of Magdalena, Santa Marta has a population of about 137,000, but preserves a distinctly small-resort-town atmosphere. Unforgettable are the clear blue Caribbean waters that wash the clean sand shores and the snow-capped Pico Cristóbal Colón rising more than 18,000 feet behind the town.

Unfortunately there are few historic remains. Of the early forts, the **Castillo de San Fernando,** built in 1725, is the most interesting and has been partially restored.

Behind the statue of founder Bastidas, on the beach at the end of Calle 12, you can see in the shallow waters some of the foundation of the Santa Bárbara fort built in 1644. At the northern end of the bay are the ruins of the San Antonio and San Felipe forts, built in the early eighteenth century. You can also arrange to go by boat to the old fort on **Morro Grande,** a lighthouse rock featuring an observation tower for a beautiful view of Santa Marta.

Several miles out of town is the **Alejandrino** hacienda where Simón Bolívar died in 1830.

SPORTS AND RECREATION. Beautiful beaches, clear water, and sparkling sand make **swimming, water skiing,** and other water activities the most popular sports of the country. Many visitors enjoy **camping** and some take part in the frequent **hunting** safaris arranged from Barranquilla. Deep-sea **fishing** is another popular pastime.

SPECIAL EVENTS. Major events include **New Year's, Day of Kings** (January 6), **Labor Day** (May 1), **Colombian Independence Day** (July 20), **Bolívar's birthday** (July 24), **Columbus Day** (October 12), **All Saints' Day** (November 1), **Immaculate Conception** (December 8), and **Christmas. Holy Week,** the date depending upon Easter, is a special event. Festivals for various saints are frequent. Many celebrations are limited to specific churches and their congregations, and these make for a minor carnival spirit in some part of the city at almost any time.

One special event in Cartagena is unique to that area. On November 11, people who live near the seacoast flock to the city to celebrate the day that Cartagena won—and kept—her independence.

DINING AND SHOPPING. Cheese and chocolate almond soufflés are popular, as are French pastries and fruit compotes. But a dinner without hot tamales is rare. Fruits, melons, and berries are abundant. The *guayaba* and the green custard apple may be a new taste delight to visitors from the north because they are difficult to ship. *Agua de Panela* is an after-dinner drink of brown sugar and water, served with either milk or lemon, like tea. Soups and stews are regular fare. *Ajiaco* is a combination of boiled meats, peas, carrots, and potatoes, both white and yellow. Cream may be added after cooking. *Cuchuco* is a thick barley-and-meat-broth soup, seasoned with peppercorns. *Mazamorra* is a similar soup thickened with corn meal. *Chicha,* highly alcoholic, is the liquor of the poor. Cocktails and fine selections of wines can be obtained in any city.

The best buys are skins, hides, and leather goods; gold coins and trinkets, emeralds, wood carvings, colonial art, antique Spanish stirrups, and other early brasswork. The craftsmanship is excellent. It is illegal to buy uncut emeralds, but the cut ones are much less expensive in Colombia than elsewhere.

Venezuela

Venezuela borders Colombia on the west, Brazil on the south, and British Guiana on the east. The 1,800 miles of coastline that is the northern side borders the Caribbean Sea. In the central section, the magnificent mountains which rise abruptly almost at the shore provided Columbus with his first view of mainland in this hemisphere in 1498.

THE LAND. The two wings of Venezuela's butterfly pattern are separated by the broad Orinoco, eighth longest river in the world. With its more than 430 tributaries, it drains most of Venezuela's some 350,000 square miles. The

largest suspension bridge in South America spans the Orinoco. The northern wing of the country is generally divided into three sections.

The Maracaibo Lowlands in the northwest corner edge the 6,000-square-mile lake explored by Ojeda and Vespucci. Today Maracaibo's waters float a rainbow film of oil, and giant derricks line its edge. During the day, the oil company cruisers and speedboats darting from derrick to derrick remind you of a lake resort.

The Northern Mountains are the most important section of the country. Sixty percent of the total population of about 10 million lives in the garden valleys and plateaus of these rugged mountains, which make up only 10 percent of the country's area. Six of the seven largest cities are here. Caracas, only ten miles from the seashore, occupies a beautiful valley of the Ávila Range at an altitude of 3,000 feet. From 10,000 feet to the snow line are the alpine meadows, the *páramos.*

Beyond the Northern Mountains are the famed Orinoco Llanos. This strip of flat, treeless prairie is about 200 miles wide and separates the mountains from the Orinoco River. It makes up about one-third of the country's total area. Though still thinly populated, its development in recent years has been dramatic. For centuries home of the Venezuelan cowboys, the fierce and fearless *llaneros,* these plains were flooded with raging torrents during much of the wet season and often tinder-dry at other times. The new Guárico dam near Calabozo holds back the floods. Its vast reservoir can irrigate nearly 300,000 acres during the dry season.

The vast region south of the Orinoco River, about half of the country's total area, is known as the Guiana Highlands. In this land of mystery, setting for Sir Arthur Conan Doyle's *Lost World* and W. H. Hudson's *Green Mansions,* are rivers that flow in two directions, their schizophrenic sections joined by little streams. About 2 percent of the total population lives in this half of the country and it is still one of the world's least-known areas. It contains the world's highest waterfall—**Angel Falls**—an incredible cascade 15 times the height of mighty Niagara. Visitors can view it from an excursion plane. Here too are the strange *tepuis,* massive, flat-topped mountains with sides almost vertical, which so long barred land explorers from their jungle-choked valleys. The El Callao diamond mines in the northeast section were once the most famous in existence. The fabulous Cerro Bolívar, the mountain of iron discovered in 1947, has ore so rich it is almost malleable. Gold also is mined. The entire area, much of it unexplored except for low-flying airplanes, is believed to be fantastically rich in minerals.

In the center of this spectacular wilderness is **La Gran Sabana.** On this vast plateau are thousands of acres of fertile grassland, streams, and palm trees. The rolling levels are broken by occasional *tepuis,* from which spring crystal waterfalls.

THE CLIMATE. As in most Latin American countries, climate varies greatly with altitude. In the Maracaibo Lowlands, temperatures are hot, humid, and because of the encircling mountains, almost without a breeze. In that area, the average annual temperature is the highest in Latin America. Climate in the Northern Mountains, location of Caracas and several other major cities, is largely semitropical. From 7,000 to 10,000 feet there is a temperate zone. There is a dry season from December through April in the Orinoco plains, and a wet season from May to November.

THE PEOPLE. Venezuela has the most urban population in Latin America; over half of the inhabitants live in cities. Today they enjoy a high standard of living, compared to that of other low-income groups in Latin America.

More than half of Venezuela's inhabitants are of mixed Spanish-Indian descent. There are a few full-blooded Negroes in the port cities, though the descendants of early slaves have been largely assimilated in the mestizo group. That 20 percent of the population classified as white includes over one million Europeans who have immigrated since World War II, and descendants of early Spanish and German settlers.

Spanish is the official language though English is a second language to many and is taught in colleges and universities. The large number of U.S. citizens living in Venezuela—most of them connected with the oil industry—have also spread the English language.

Venezuela's early history was marked by disasters, natural and man-created. After its discovery by Columbus in 1498, and the explorations by Ojeda and Amerigo Vespucci the following year, every European adventurer wanted to come to the great pearl coast. The first settlement was on the island of Cubagua, surrounded by fabulously rich pearl beds. The first settlement on the mainland was made by Juan de Castellón at Cumaná in 1521. Seven years later the town of Coro was founded. That was the year, 1528, when Venezuela was turned over to the German banking family named Welser. Their blond troops swarmed over the rugged countryside, plundering every village and town. They committed atrocities even more barbaric than their Spanish predecessors, and Spanish priests who had been attempting to convert the Indians appealed to Charles V who, in 1556, revoked the grant to the Welsers.

Pirates and buccaneers frequently pillaged the coastal settlements and islands. For this reason, all foreign ships were forbidden in these waters for more than two centuries. Until the early nineteenth century, settlers could deal only with Spanish merchants. The colonists, most of whom had settled down to agriculture, had flourishing plantations of coffee, sugar cane, and cows, and resented Spain's trade monopoly.

There had been isolated uprisings as early as 1806, when Caracas-born Francisco de Miranda seized the port of Coro. Lacking sufficient backing, he had to flee, but that same year Simón Bolívar returned to Caracas from Europe. With Miranda and other idealistic Creoles, he formed the Sociedad Patriótica. Small revolts and large battles followed, and on July 5, 1811, the Congress of Venezuela declared its independence from Spain. A year later, Miranda was captured and Spain momentarily reclaimed Venezuela. Bolívar escaped to establish a second republic, with himself as president, in 1814, but he was forced to flee to New Granada again that same year. He led another army to triumph at the epic Battle of Carabobo in 1821. Later that year, the Republic of *Gran Colombia,* consisting of what is now Venezuela, Colombia, and Ecuador, was formed and Bolívar elected president. The federation was weak and loosely knit, and Venezuelans, under the leadership of General Páez, declared their country an independent republic in 1830. Páez ruled as president from 1830–34 and 1839–43, dictating the government from behind the scenes in the interim. In 1843, President José Tadeo Monagas took office, dismissed the Congress to prevent his own impeachment, and exiled Páez. His dictatorship lasted until 1857, though his younger brother served one term for him. The bloody Federal War followed, and though it technically ended in 1861 when General Páez returned to establish a dictatorship which lasted less than a year, the country was more or less in a constant state of civil war and revolt until 1909, when General Juan Vicente Gómez took control and established an absolute dictatorship. He ruled with the title of president or from behind the scenes until his death in 1935. Revolts ceased because all critics were thrown into prison and tortured.

Gómez was succeeded by his war minister, Eleázar López Contreras, who surprised many by relaxing the dictatorial controls and preparing the country during the transition period that led to the democratic government which followed. In 1940 a second political party, the Acción Democrática, was formed and, in a peaceful coup d'état, it took over the government in 1945. In the 1947 elections, universal suffrage was granted with the literacy requirement abolished, the parties being identified by the color of the ballot. The president was elected by direct vote, and novelist Rómulo Gallegos took office, but his government was overthrown by the army the following year. Colonel Marcos Pérez Jiménez took control, exiling the leaders of the Acción Democrática. This party did not participate in the 1952 elections, but when a more moderately liberal party's candidate was shown to be receiving a majority of votes, the Jiménez junta placed the nation under a state of siege and announced that Jiménez was the new president. His government was overthrown in 1958. In the new elections, Rómulo Betancourt was chosen President, and headed the government until his term expired in March 1964. Betancourt was the first Venezuelan president to serve his full term.

AGRICULTURE. Farming is the core of Venezuela's economy, with close to half of the country's population working the fields. Crops are primarily grown for internal consumption, though some coffee, sugar, cocoa, and tobacco are exported. The best farming is in the tropical zone, where coffee, cocoa, corn, rice, sesame, cotton, tobacco, and sugar cane are cultivated with modern agricultural methods. Due to the wealth of pastureland, Venezuela is a leading cattle-raising country.

INDUSTRY. Venezuela is the third-largest oil-producing country in the world, after the United States and the Soviet Union. Lake Maracaibo and the eastern region have the greatest petroleum deposits. Over three million barrels of oil a day are yielded from Venezuelan wells.

Though manufacturing has been growing slowly, the government has stepped in to help increase industrialization through money grants and high taxes on foreign manufactures. Leading industries include steel, chemicals, textiles, and consumer products such as cement, cigarettes, shoes, building materials, fats, and oils.

CITIES. Leading cities of Venezuela have grown up in the northern highlands, on or near the coast. They include Caracas (population, about 2 million), La Guaira, Puerto Cabello, and Cumaná.

CARACAS. Cruise passengers, who so often see only the port cities, will have no trouble visiting the Venezuelan capital, the most ultramodern city on the continent. It is less than half an hour's drive from either the port of La Guaira or the Maiquetía airport. The airport is six hours from New York on the nonstop flights.

As you approach the capital on the gently graded, multi-lane *autopista,* you may get the feeling that you are entering a full-scale model for the city of tomorrow, instead of a historic city dating from 1561. Its explosive growth is fairly recent, the population tripling between 1936 and 1960. That fact plus the country's great wealth has resulted in predominantly ultramodern architecture. In the center of the city is the famous **Avenida Bolívar,** 110 feet wide, ending in a great traffic circle at the foot of Calvary Hill. Traffic flows on two levels, and underground are parking facilities, stores, and a terminal that accommodates 500 buses.

The gleaming white **capitol** is an excellent place to start sightseeing. This sprawling edifice occupies an entire square, an area of two acres. It is built around a great oval patio, shaded by palm trees and brightened with tropical flowers. In the Elliptical Hall is Martín Tovar y Tovar's finest painting of the Battle of Carabobo.

Facing the south side of the capitol is the **Palace of the Academies,** fine Gothic buildings with beautiful gardens. Formerly housing Central University, the **National Library** is now located here. **Exposition Palace** houses the Bolívar Museum with its priceless relics of the independence movement on display. Here too is headquarters of the Academy of History. **San Francisco Cathedral** stands alongside.

Northeast of the capitol is the **Plaza Bolívar,** where big mahogany trees shade the mosaic walks. The enormous statue of the liberator is in the center of the park. Facing this plaza are the **Palace of Justice,** and on the north side, the main post office. On the west side is **La Casa Amarilla,** the presidential palace. Nearby is the birthplace of Bolívar, **Casa Natal,** which still belongs to his mother's family, the Palacios. Furnished with the original Colonial pieces, carved chests inlaid with satinwood, mahogany beds, peaked ceilings, tile floors, and the old grinding stones, it is religiously preserved. The tripledomed **National Pantheon,** formerly a church, contains the ashes of the liberator. The cathedral, the **Santa Capilla,** and the **Basilica de Santa Ana** are musts for the historically minded visitor.

But very little of the Colonial era remains in the dynamically modern metropolis. The broad **Avenida Urdaneta** (you cross it on the way from the Plaza Bolívar to the National Pantheon) is a shopping center featuring dresses from world-famed designers, native Indian pottery, and just about every other kind of merchandise imaginable. In the **Museum of Fine Arts** hang representative paintings from Venezuela's leading modern artists. The new **University City** boasts an Olympic Stadium seating 45,000, and a baseball stadium next to it with a capacity of 35,000. At the city's outskirts is the site of parades and other special ceremonies, the **Avenue of Heroes,** with an obelisk in memory of the independence leaders at one end, and fountains and lovely formal gardens at the other.

For a pleasant trip through the residential areas, start at **El Silencio,** the attractive, low-cost housing development at the foot of **Calvary Hill.** And while you are there, climb the hundreds of steps to the statue of Columbus at the top of the hill for a fine view of the city. Skirting the city are the new homes of the moderately well-to-do. **Mount Ávila,** above the city is reached by cable car.

The Caribbean shore of the small Federal District near Caracas is dotted with tropical resort towns. A broad boulevard which terminates at **Los Caracas** 40 miles from the capital, connects them with **La Guaira,** Venezuela's most important port. This vacation city, combining wonderful beaches with mountain trails for hiking and riding enthusiasts, was built by the government for low-income groups. The hotels and cottages charge moderate rates.

A short boat or plane hop brings you to the beautiful island of **Margarita,** about 450 square miles covering mountains, flatlands, rivers, lakes, and pretty, palm-studded beaches. The climate is excellent and there are hotels in the ports of **Porlamar** and **Pampatar,** and in the capital, **La Asunción,** a sleepy Colonial town. La Asunción is reached by car from the bustling port of Porlamar. Within its fine cathedral is the famous statue of the Virgin Mary robed with pearls.

Along the shores are little fishing villages. Pastel-hued *salinas,* or salt-evaporating basins, are located on some of the more barren stretches. The western region of the island, consisting of uninhabited desert and salt flats, is noted for the rumors of pirate treasure buried there and richly laden galleons sunk offshore.

Between Margarita and the mainland are **Cubagua** and **Coche,** islands noted for the size of the pearls found in their oyster beds. The commercial pearling fleet can harvest oysters only one year out of three, a conservation practice that has maintained a satisfactory pearl and oyster production for many years. Legally, pearls are sold only to the government, and visitors must purchase individual specimens from its agents, though pearl jewelry is available in private shops. There is some *escondido* pearling, of course, and tourists may be offered an illegal purchase (though quality is apt to be even more ridiculously low than the price).

A new city, **Ciudad Guayana** on the Orinoco River has a flight which takes you from the city of tomorrow to the most simple and primitive land of yesterday. A camp for visitors is close to **Angel Falls,** highest in the world (3,212 feet high) which can be seen from the plane. The traveler can sun on the pink sands of a quiet lagoon or swim in its rose-colored water, enjoy the sights and sounds of tropical forest from the relative safety of a riverboat, go exploring overland on horseback, and visit the primitive villages of the indigenous Indians. The fishing and wild-game hunting are excellent.

The broad, paved **Pan-American Highway** extends west from Caracas through such leading cities as Maracay, Valencia, Puerto Cabello, Barquisimeto, Mérida, and San Cristóbal, the Simón Bolívar International Bridge linking it to the Colombian Highway. Plane service is also very good.

MARACAIBO, capital of the state of Zulia, was founded in 1571. The vast inland sea of Maracaibo is hot and humid. However, air-conditioning is common in the many new buildings since, located at the mouth of the lake as the city is, the encircling mountains cut off the sea breeze. Strolling the lovely lakeside promenade is a popular twilight pastime. There are many broad boulevards and beautiful parks, and the newer part of the city, **Bella Vista** and its vicinity out toward the airport, is at a slight elevation and has a more pleasant climate. The national **University of Zulia** is the cultural center. The cathedral is the most important Colonial edifice. Like Caracas, Maracaibo is noted for its ultramodern skyscrapers, supermarkets, and fashionable stores.

A strange phenomenon of nature is the "Lighthouse of Maracaibo," the display of lightning that occurs almost every night in the region of the Catatumbo River in the southwest section of the lake. The interior of this region is best left unexplored. It is the land of the Motilone Indians, who are still hostile to outsiders.

From Maracaibo it is an hour's drive to **Coro,** founded in 1528. This sleepy, coastal capital of the state of Falcón was almost forgotten over the centuries. In the past few years it has been transformed into another oil boom town. Visitors from Maracaibo enjoy its fine white beaches and clear Caribbean surf.

MARACAY, capital of Aragua, is just 75 miles west of Caracas, facing the tranquil **Lake Valencia** on the south, and the hills of **Las Delicias** on the north. Its 1,500-foot elevation gives the city a pleasantly tropical climate. Former dictator Gómez made Maracay his unofficial capital, building the broad main boulevard, lining it with trees and gardens, and decorating it with statues and fountains. His, too, is the great Moorish bullfighting ring, an exact copy of the one at Seville, Spain. His opera house, in which some of the finest voices in Europe sang, remains unfinished. Another Maracay landmark is the Gómez mausoleum with its great triumphal arch. In the Las Delicias hills to the north is his country house, complete with zoo, and farther out, his uncompleted palace. Gómez also built the road from Maracay to the Turiamo naval base.

But perhaps the greatest Gómez landmark, and the most personally revealing, is a magnificent hotel with its formal park and fountain which he built for his highly informal revelries. Even this show place has been surpassed by the new government hotel, considered by travelers to be one of the most lavish in the world. The enormous swimming pool is spanned by a pair of bridges and has an artificial waterfall at one end. It has its own beautiful golf course, a fine stable housing 40 handsome mounts, a cinema, and a sumptuous night club. A dry moat surrounds its grounds to keep out jaguars and mountain lions. There is good hunting nearby.

There are also modest hotels in Maracay, and the real charm of the city lies in its Colonial character. It is in the center of a rich agricultural area, producing oranges, coffee and sugar.

MÉRIDA. Founded in 1558, the capital of the state of Mérida has been traditionally regarded as the cultural and religious center of Venezuela. Located on a spectacularly fertile alluvial terrace, seven miles in length, the city is surrounded by snow-capped peaks of the Andes, most of them rising over 13,000 feet. One, **Pico Bolívar,** 16,427 feet, is the highest in the republic. The new cableway to the summit of 15,-628-foot **Pico Espejo,** built by the government at a cost of $18 million, provides an unforgettably thrilling ride to fine ski slopes. The eight miles of cables carry passengers to a height two miles above the mile-high city in less than an hour. On the last lap the car skims over a deep abyss with the twin lakes, the **Anteojos,** at the bottom.

The city itself is a garden place, with narrow, cobbled streets lined with Spanish Colonial mansions and convents. The bright flowers provide a pleasant contrast to the pastel-colored buildings. **University of the Andes,** founded in 1785 as the Seminary of St. Bonaventure, is now one of the three national universities and the focal point of the city's cultural life. A fine eighteenth-century **cathedral** faces the plaza in the center of the city.

An interesting side trip through magnificent mountain scenery is provided by the little road down to **Barinas** at the foot of the mountains and the edge of the *llanos.* Barinas is a popular headquarters for jaguar hunters. A good road connects it with **Guanare** which contains a religious shrine.

From Mérida, the Pan-American Highway goes to **San Cristóbal,** passing through some precipitous and difficult terrain on this 185-mile stretch. The city of San Cristóbal is an important commercial center 60 miles from the Tachira River, the boundary between Venezuela and Colombia, spanned by the **Simón Bolívar International Bridge.**

Not on the Pan-American Highway,

but a fascinating place to visit, is Maracaibo, Venezuela's second largest city.

PUERTO CABELLO. This second largest port city has some remains of ancient fortresses. The narrow streets are lined with early Colonial houses, their balconies bedecked with flowers. Good hotels are on the nearby beaches.

From Puerto Cabello, the highway leads to **Barquisimeto,** capital of Lara State and third largest city in the republic. Highly industrialized, and a commercial center for the surrounding agricultural lands, it has been called the Chicago of Venezuela. From this city there is a road to the town of **Guanare.** The revered portrait of the patron saint of Venezuela, the Virgin of Coromoto, is housed in the ancient parish church. From Barquisimeto, the highway leads to Mérida.

VALENCIA. Thirty miles west of Maracay and situated on the same fine lake is the city of Valencia, founded in 1555. Here the feeling of old Spain is retained in the narrow Colonial streets. An early cathedral and the colorful market place stand on opposite sides of the central plaza. Outside the city is the national shrine of the **Battlefield of Carabobo.** An imposing monument towers over a reflecting pool, and a broad walk is lined with busts of national heroes. Nearby is a health spa featuring radioactive mud. Valencia is an industrial center with automobile assembly and manufacturing plants.

SPORTS AND RECREATION. **Aquatic sports** are among the most popular in Venezuela, with delightful bathing resorts scattered throughout the country. Near Orocopiche, Marcela, and Candelaria, excellent **fishing** can be found, as it can in the "Aro" Lakes. Boats can be chartered at Porlamar for superb fishing areas off Margarita. Large runs of kingfish, wahoo, and mackerel start early in the spring, followed by marlin, tuna, and broadbill swordfish periodically throughout the year. The tourist industry has made possible a sport-fishing fleet of small, modern cruisers with the latest fishing equipment. There is also unexcelled fishing off the Testigos and the Seven Brothers, two groups of lonely islets a day's run to the northeast and north.

Nuevo Circo de Caracas, in Caracas at the end of Avenida Bolívar, is where the **bullfights** are held from November through February. They feature some of the best matadors from Spain as well as from Latin America. **Horse races** are also a popular diversion. **Golf, horseback riding,** and **swimming** in lovely outdoor pools are features of luxurious government hotels in the capital. Also popular are the large **baseball** stadium and bullfighting arena across from the Plaza Urdaneta in Maracaibo.

SPECIAL EVENTS. Religious festivals are frequent and colorful, with **Christmas** and the 12 days prior to it constituting the year's greatest celebration. From twilight on, the sky is bright with fireworks, and the music of the *aguinaldos* or Christmas carols fills the air. Central figure in the pre-Lenten **Mardi Gras** is *La Burriquita*. The catchy rhythm of the "donkey songs" sung by the masqueraders sets the carnival tempo.

Non-religious national holidays include **Independence Day,** July 5, and Bolívar's birthday, July 24. They are also celebrated with parades and fireworks. The bullfights, scheduled from November to February, are always festive occasions.

In Mérida, the annual **festival of Mérida** is held on April 4, and thousands of visitors crowd the streets.

DINING AND SHOPPING. The avid gourmet in South America is apt to get very frustrated with recipes calling for a cup of dried, whole-kernel corn, a cow's foot, or a codfish head. Venezuelan cookery, while distinctly and delightfully Venezuelan, is geared to the modern efficiency kitchen, canned goods, and other conveniences. Most tamale recipes, for instance, require dried corn and corn husks. The Venezuelan chef makes a delicious tamale casserole from canned corn and "store bread," mixed with chicken, milk, eggs, butter, and other ingredients. *Mondongo* is a peppery tripe stew with bits of ham and vegetables and balls of corn meal. *Sancocho* is a meat soup given body by squash, sweet potatoes, and plantains. *Hallaca* is a type of meat pie, thickened with corn meal, and boiled in plantain leaves. It was common in Colonial days. Today, seasoned with sliced almonds, olives, and capers, it is served on special occasions such as Christmas Eve. Peasant corn bread is called *arepa. Queso de Venezuela* is a creamy casserole of cheese, chicken, and rice. Popular sweets are *bien me sabe,* a coconut custard on cake topped with meringue, and *queso de piña,* a rich pineapple custard. *Gorfiados* are twisted cinnamon rolls, moist with melted brown sugar, cream cheese, and topped with aniseed.

The tourist will have little difficulty locating the dish that is his personal favorite, no matter how distant the land of its origin may be. The local rums are good. Yet, land of riches that it is, Venezuela also offers the best imported wines, liqueurs, and other beverages.

The instruments used in Venezuela's colorful folk music are among the most popular souvenirs. There are small harps, beautifully made, the *quatro,* a little four-stringed guitar, and the Indian drums and *maracas.* Drums are made of hollowed-out logs with stretched hide over one end. The *maracas* are dried gourds with large seeds inside, mounted on wooden handles—in essence a rattle, but with a very pleasing sound. Pearls, so plentiful around Margarita and the other islands nearby, are also available in jewelry stores. Diamonds in the rough are an excellent buy, and uncut stones can enter the U.S. duty-free. Imaginative tourists planning to have them mounted in modern, abstract settings have created a small demand. Cut diamonds may cost more in Venezuela than in the visitor's home town, but in the rough, with the probable imperfections hidden, they should be low in price.

The Indian handicrafts of weaving and ceramics have been handed down. There are native woodcarvers of great skill. Some of the finest workmanship is found in the carvings of the *nacimiento,* the small figures arranged in the manger scene at Christmas time. Skins, hides, and leather goods are available.

Guyana

One of the Western Hemisphere's newest nations, Guyana received its independence from Great Britain on May 26, 1966. Until that date it was known as British Guiana and was one of three European overseas territories in South America. The official language is English.

THE LAND. Guyana, with an area of 83,000 square miles, is located in northeastern South America and is bordered by the Atlantic Ocean, Surinam, Brazil, and Venezuela. Most of the over 760,000 population lives along the coast where there is good farmland, in large part due to the system of canals and dikes which holds back the ocean. The Essequibo, which flows into the Atlantic, is the country's most important river.

THE CLIMATE. Guyana's temperatures are usually high, as the country lies entirely within the tropics. Its rainy seasons are mid-November through January, and April through July.

THE PEOPLE. As with Surinam and French Guiana (see page 546), colonization began in the early 1600's when the Dutch West India Company started settlements. Britain's control was officially established in 1814, although she had seized Guyana 18 years earlier. Slavery was abolished in 1834, and today over 35 percent of the population are of African descent. East Indians under contract to the sugar estates also were brought to Guyana in the 1800's, and this group, still dominating the sugar industry, now accounts for 50 percent.

In 1953, a constitution was approved to give greater self-government to the colony, and the first national elections were held that year. Since then, movements toward independence have been strong, despite racial conflicts and party controversies which threatened to make independence an impossibility. Independent since 1966, Guyana severed its ties with the British crown in 1970 and became a republic, but a member of the Commonwealth.

AGRICULTURE. Sugar is the leading crop of Guyana, with close to two dozen sugar estates spread throughout the country. About a third of the population works with the sugar crops. Also farmed on the rich coastal soil are rice, coconuts, coffee, plantains, mangoes, bananas, and cocoa.

INDUSTRY. The mining of bauxite and manganese brings more money to Guyana's economy than any other area of industry (the largest bauxite resources in the world are at Mackenzie). With the harnessing of several of Guyana's rivers for hydroelectricity, it is hoped that new industry will develop in the country. Earmarked for further development are pulp and paper production, food processing, and chemicals.

CITIES. Georgetown, the capital, is the most important city in Guyana, but trips to New Amsterdam and several of the villages are very worthwhile for visitors.

GEORGETOWN, capital of Guyana, is a city of broad, well-shaded streets and Victorian architecture. Most houses and other buildings are of wood instead of the typically Latin plaster or adobe. Some cement structures have gone up since the great fire of 1945. Fortunately, the beautiful **Anglican Cathedral,** said to be the world's tallest wooden building, survived that disaster. Other points of architectural interest include the twin-towered **Church of the Sacred Heart,** the **City Hall,** and the public buildings. The fine Guyana Museum was destroyed in the great fire but some sections have been reassembled in a new **museum.** The **botanic gardens** contain 180 acres, constituting one of the world's finest collections of palms and orchids. Its pools are filled with the giant Victoria Regia water lilies. Bright tropical birds and butterflies abound.

A fascinating side trip is the airplane excursion to **Kaieteur Falls** on the **Potaro River.** Five times higher than Niagara, this mighty cascade is 300 feet wide. The seaplane approaches the spectacle through a breathtakingly narrow, deep gorge, ten miles long, then lifts the visitor up and over the top to set down half a mile away. The trip can be made easily in a single day, with tourists following the jungle trail from the airport back to the falls to enjoy a basket lunch. From the falls you can visit the **Mahdia gold fields.** On the trip to the falls, the plane follows the **Demerara River,** passing over the world's largest bauxite-calcining kiln at **Mackenzie,** a jungle town which is the second largest community in Guyana, and can be reached by steamer. On the return trip, the plane flies past more than 30 other falls, some even higher than the Kaieteur, though less spectacular. Passengers ride low over bush villages as the plane follows the diamond-rich **Mazaruni River** to the **Essequibo** and rounds the short stretch of coastline back to Georgetown.

Rendezvous point for jungle hunters is **Bartica,** where there are hotels. It is reached by ferry (across the Demerara to **Vreed-en-Hoop),** train (to **Parika),** and steamboat (to Bartica). This used to be the easy part of the trip to the Kaieteur Falls, the final section involving 100 miles of rough jungle roads, a treacherous trip by boat, and a steep climb. The round trip, though no choice for comfort seekers, makes a highly adventurous week. With sufficient advance planning, the visit can still be made this way.

There are several small hotels in **New Amsterdam,** capital of the county of **Berbice.** A small Colonial town of about 14,000, it is easy to reach by train. Georgetown is also connected by rail with the villages of **Rosignol, Belfield, Mahaica,** and **Mahaicony,** but tourist accommodations range from rudimentary to nonexistent. Cars can be rented in Georgetown.

SPORTS AND RECREATION in Guyana includes **horse races, cricket matches** on the many fine cricket grounds, **football** and **field hockey, tennis,** and **golf.** An active **Theatre Guild** performs in Georgetown throughout the year.

SPECIAL EVENTS. Each year in early April, local teams meet in Georgetown for **cricket competitions.** Every few years, international matches are held, with teams coming from Australia, England, and the West Indies.

One of the nation's main events is the **National History and Arts Council,** held in October throughout the country. Among the events are competitions, art exhibits, concerts, and theater, all stressing the work and lives of the Guyanese people.

Also of interest to visitors are the biannual **music festivals,** with a children's music festival held in alternate years. **The League of Coloured People's Industrial Exhibition and Fair** is held in October.

DINING AND SHOPPING. Much of the food in restaurants is typically British, with some local specialties, the most important being pepper pot, a main dish of the Amerindians (American Indians). In pepper pot, the meat is cooked in a viscous liquid from the cassava called *cassareep.* This seasoning is a good food preservative, and enhances the flavor of the meat as it cooks.

Guava jelly and cassava bread are also popular, and *tannias,* a vegetable, have a distinctive taste. Corn, yams, sweet potatoes, and taro roots, known locally as eddoes, are other staples of diet.

The native Demerara rums are world-famous, and are served in a variety of punches. Imported quality brands of English beer are also popular.

Rum and guava jelly are very good buys. **Stabroek Market,** with its great Gothic tower, is a center for such Amerind curios as blowpipes, bows and arrows, beadwork, and baskets. The gold and silver jewelry made by these Indians is of excellent workmanship. Guyanese diamonds are of generally high quality, though small in size. Uncut diamonds are low-priced and can be taken into many countries duty-free. Cut diamonds are sold in jewelry stores.

The Guianas

Surinam and French Guiana, Europe's political orphans in South America, are two separate countries, similar to each other in topography and very different from the rest of the continent in culture and racial composition. Until May 1966, when British Guiana became the independent nation of Guyana, there were three of these overseas territories in South America.

THE LAND. They are bordered on the north by the Atlantic, on the south and east by Brazil, and by Guyana on the west. Larger geographically, as well as in size, population, and development, is Surinam or Dutch Guiana. The smaller, French Guiana, has an area of about 35,000 square miles, roughly a third that of France, and a population estimated to be about 48,000. The combined 90,000-square-mile area of the Guianas can be divided into three geographical sections. The narrow coastal strip where the majority of the inhabitants live is below sea level in many places, the ocean being held back by dikes, the land drained by canals. Beyond this is a strip of grassy savannah land, ridged with sand dunes. But most of the land is covered with dense jungle and ranges from hilly to mountainous.

Trees along the coast and in the jungles reach enormous heights. Leaves and blossoms are noted for their size. Orchids grow in giant clusters, some measuring 12 feet high. The brilliant colors of exotic flowers, rare birds, and butterflies make it a naturalist's paradise. The teeming wildlife includes jaguars and monkeys, deer, anteaters, tapirs, peccaries, and armadillos. On the larger rivers are colonies of the almost-extinct manatee. The jaguars frequently

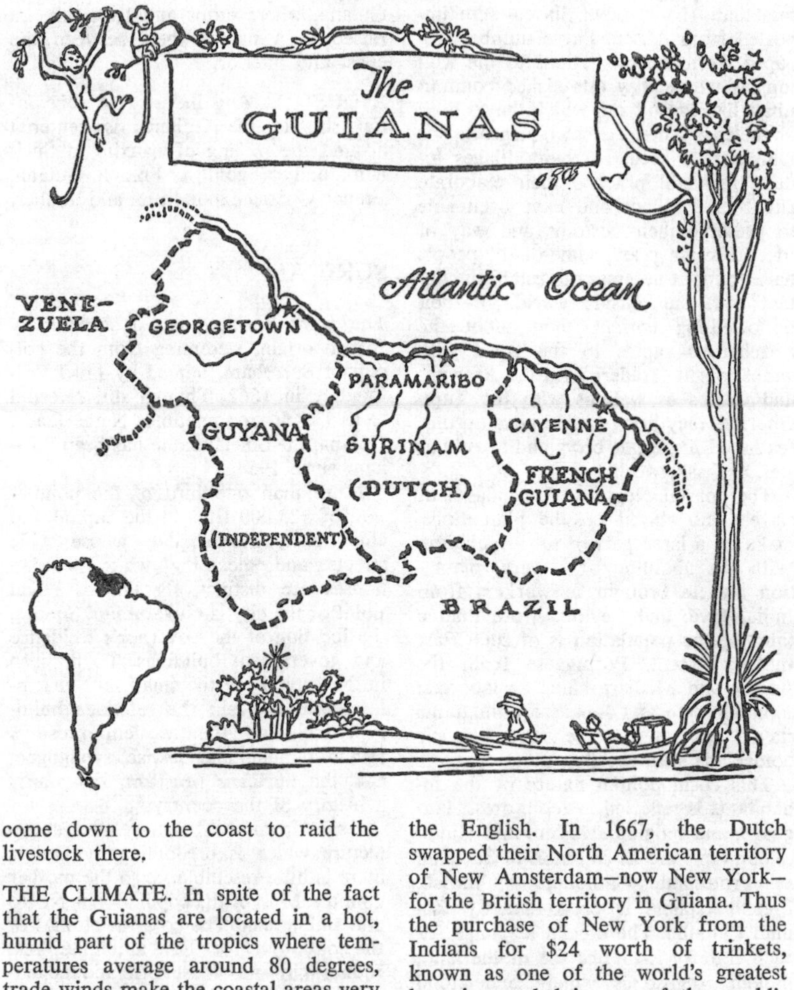

come down to the coast to raid the livestock there.

THE CLIMATE. In spite of the fact that the Guianas are located in a hot, humid part of the tropics where temperatures average around 80 degrees, trade winds make the coastal areas very cool and comfortable. The rainy seasons (when rainfall is frequent, though not incessant) are mid-November through January and April through July in Surinam, and November through January and April through June in French Guiana.

THE PEOPLE. The name Guiana derives from an Indian word, believed to mean "land of waters." The coast of the Guianas was settled by the Dutch in 1596, by the English 20 years later. The French arrived a few years after the English. In 1667, the Dutch swapped their North American territory of New Amsterdam—now New York—for the British territory in Guiana. Thus the purchase of New York from the Indians for $24 worth of trinkets, known as one of the world's greatest bargains, ended in one of the world's worst for the Dutch.

The first major settlement was made in what is now Surinam by Lord Willoughby, governor of Barbados, in 1654. Most of the colonists were English Jews. Soon others of that faith came from Italy, Brazil, and the Netherlands, seeking refuge. As more English, French, and Dutch settlements were made, the original inhabitants, including the Caribs and Arawaks, moved inland. These Indians in Surinam and French Guiana are thought to number less than 10,000 now. Slaves were imported from Africa. Large numbers escaped from the plantations to the wild jungles where they established communities like those from which they'd been abducted. These Bush Negroes or Djukas flourished. In their villages today, they still practice their elaborate rituals and taboos and have been able to preserve their customs and way of life. In recent years, some of the people have found it necessary to establish contact with the outside world. In their hollowed-log *corials,* they shoot the treacherous rapids to the coast with wares to sell. Traders with the Arawaks and Caribs as well as with the Tupi-Guarani, they bring Indian bead aprons, feathered headgear, bows and arrows as well as basketwork.

The coastal Negroes, descendants of slaves who stayed on the plantations, make up a large part of the population. With the abolition of slavery, plantation owners brought in workers from India, Java, and Ceylon. More than a third of the population is of such East Indian descent. Portuguese from the Azores and Madeira came as laborers; some Chinese and Japanese immigrants stayed, though most returned to their homelands with their earnings.

This cosmopolitan nature of the inhabitants is reflected in food, dress, language, and religion. Moslem and Hindu celebrations are as common in Surinam as Protestant, Catholic, or Jewish. French Guiana is predominantly Roman Catholic. The official language for each country is that of the motherland, though English is widely understood throughout and the Asiatics and Portuguese speak their native tongues as well. In Surinam a lingua franca called **Sranan Tonga** is also spoken. It is made up of Dutch, Spanish, Portuguese and English elements, and is also referred to as Tawki-Tawki.

AGRICULTURE. In Surinam, farm produce includes bananas, citrus fruits, coffee, cacao, rice, and sugar. Surinam is a leading producer of bauxite, used in aluminum production.

Farming is also important in French Guiana, where crops and livestock are raised in a narrow belt between the coast and interior.

INDUSTRY. Any industry of substantial size in the Guianas is centered around the mining of bauxite in Surinam, and of gold in French Guiana. French Guiana exports rum and lumber.

SURINAM

The name Surinam has a surprisingly British origin, stemming from the colony of Surryham, named by Lord Willoughby in 1662. Though still referred to as Dutch, or sometimes Netherlands, Guiana, the official name has been Surinam since 1954.

More than one-third of the population of 325,000 lives in the capital and chief port, **Paramaribo,** whose wide streets and gleaming white wooden houses are distinctively Dutch. Focal point of the city is **Government Square,** the location of the governor's residence and government buildings. To be seen in the capital are the small, but charming **Palm Garden;** the religious buildings including the Moslem mosque, Hindu temple, and Jewish synagogue; and the **Surinam Museum,** containing a history of the country.

Aside from the language and architecture which is predominately Dutch, there is little resemblance to the mother country. Most of the population is Negro and Indonesian. The colorful clothes of the coastal Negroes have a definite West Indian skirt-and-blouse form and the material is a bright mixture of cotton prints. The hats are fashioned of large printed handkerchiefs, pleated to form a wide band over the forehead, and widely flared in the back. Earrings, bracelets, and numerous strings of beads, shells, and corn, complete the costume.

The Indonesian clothes are equally colorful, with full skirts, beribboned "peasant" blouses, and stoles and boleros fashioned of beautiful batik prints. The jewelry is more often of silver and gold; even the poor Indonesian ladies are adorned with silver ear bangles.

Tourists can arrange to see Indonesian parties or weddings in Hindu temples. Cars can be rented in Paramaribo for visits to some of the bush villages of the Djukas that have road connections with the capital. Other Djuka and native Indian villages may be visited by launch. A fascinating side trip is that to the little village of **Moengo** on the **Cottica River.**

Visitors to Surinam should see the **open air museum** in Nieuw Amsterdam, located at the confluence of the Commewijne and Surinam rivers. This museum features a typical habitat of each of the many ethnic groups in the country. At Joden-Savannah, one can see the ruins of **Synagogue Berachah Ve Salom** and the graveyard of one of the oldest former Sephardic Jewish settlements in the Western Hemisphere.

Dining specialties include rice and seafood which are abundant and prepared in many delicious ways. Sweet honey cakes and pastries, often molasses-flavored, are popular desserts. All kinds of citrus fruits, plantains, bananas, and coconuts make up a large part of the diet. Chutney and curried fish dishes are typically Indonesian, while a rich, sweet potato pudding, corn breads, and a peppery succotash are credited to the coastal Negroes for their development. "Mutton," which may be the meat of goat instead of sheep on some menus, pork, and chicken are also served, but beef and fish are the main foods.

Beadwork and baskets, wood carvings, bows and arrows, and other handicrafts are made specifically for sale to visitors. Gold is no longer an important export, the only dredging left being done by hand by itinerant workers. It is used by the local Indonesians to make jewelry. The jewelry, batik prints, baskets, beadwork, and wood carvings are the best buys in Surinam.

FRENCH GUIANA

Least developed, smallest, and most humid of the Guianas, French Guiana covers 35,100 square miles and has about 48,000 inhabitants, half of them living in the capital, **Cayenne.** French Guiana has been a department of France since 1946, but largely due to its climate, little has been done for its development. Carts pulled by water buffalo are still an important means of transportation.

In Cayenne, tennis courts can be found in the **Place des Palmistes,** the park shaded by palm trees, which is faced by the hospital, the **Convent of the Sisters of St. Paul,** and government buildings. **The Church of St. Paul** has a beautiful carillon, and visitors should see the botanical gardens.

Saint Laurent, the other town of any importance, has a population of 3,000.

The most interesting part of French Guiana are the **Îles du Salut,** which include the infamous **Île du Diable** or **Devil's Island.** Plans have been made to convert the former penal colony into a resort. The sea breeze makes it far more pleasant than the mainland. There are lovely paths through grass and flowers and the rocky grounds are well-shaded with palm trees. In grotesque contrast to this idyllic setting are the preserved sheds and cells of the prison grounds, some still furnished with the tilted board "bed" and iron leg clamp which tortured those in solitary confinement. The tall watchtower and the quarters of Dreyfus are of historic interest, but the tricky currents of the shark-filled waters surrounding the island make it an unlikely spot for a beach resort. The deep-sea fishing nearby is good.

The language is French and most of the population is Roman Catholic, though the large East Indian segment observes its Hindu and Moslem holidays. Another population segment is the Amerindian, or indigenous Indian. Though much of the population is of Asiatic origin, and the land is as well suited to rice cultivation as that of Guyana and Surinam, very little rice is grown. Sweet potatoes, manioc or cassava, corn, bananas, and seafood are the principal foods. Two noteworthy dishes are saffron-flavored sausage and a delicious almond-chicken soup. Wines and liqueurs are imported, though rum is the most important export. An excellent rum is made by the Sisters of Saint Joseph of Cluny, who use the proceeds to finance the leper colony at **Acarouany** which was founded by them. As a secondary source of income, the sisters fashion exquisite flowers from the feathers of tropical birds. Their flowers and rum are two of the country's most popular souvenirs. Indian beadwork, baskets woven by the Djuka villagers, some wood carvings, and gold jewelry from Cayenne are also available. Gold is the chief export, with gold mining the main industry.

Brazil

Brazil is the fifth largest country in the world—inferior in size only to Russia, China, Canada and the United States. It has two waterfalls higher than Niagara and the largest river in the world—the Amazon—the mouth of which is wider than all of Belgium. The country's over 3,200,000 square miles occupy just a bit less than half of the South American continent and could cover most of the United States. If the "Vast Land," as it was called by early Portuguese settlers, were as heavily populated as Belgium, it would house all the people in the world. Brazil contains five regional territories—the Northeast, the state of Minas Gerais, the federal district, the state of São Paulo, and the state of Rio Grande do Sul.

THE LAND. The vast plateau which forms Brazil's main physical characteristic is 1,000 to 3,000 feet above sea level and is crossed by two long mountain chains. The Serra do Mar is a coastal range which terminates in the Organ Mountains near Rio de Janeiro at a height of 7,323 feet.

The inland range reaches a height of 9,145 feet at Itatiaia Peak. Less important is the central or Goiás mountain system, which has peaks about 4,000 feet high. Compared to the Andes, the highlands of Brazil can hardly be called mountains. Yet much of this vast rugged plateau lies above an altitude of 4,000 feet, which explains the temperate climate of a large part of the country that would otherwise be tropical.

In São Paulo, the rolling tableland that falls toward the west invites men toward the heart of the continent, as it did the early natives, the *bandeirantes*, who penetrated the far interior into the basins of the Paraguay and the Madeira.

The great river systems consist of the Amazon and La Plata and their tributaries. Of the 25,000 miles of navigable rivers, well over half enjoy the regular service of vessels. More than one-third of Brazil is drained by the Amazon and its more than 1,100 tributaries. The Amazon itself is navigable some 2,300 miles for ocean steamers to Iquitos, Peru. Southern Brazil is dominated by the La Plata system—the Paraguay, Uruguay, and Paraná rivers. But the most important navigable stream (for 1,000 miles) is the São Francisco, blocked near its mouth by the 260-foot Paulo Afonso Falls.

The vast Amazon Valley, with its dense equatorial forest known as the "hyleia," is one of Brazil's chief features. It can be divided into three natural regions: the Guianan Slopes in the north, which rise to a height of 9,433 feet at Mount Roraima; the Amazon Plain, which boasts the world's most luxuriant vegetation; and the Brazilian Upland Slopes in the south, which are covered by tropical forests comprised largely of brazil-nut and rubber trees.

The Amazon region by itself covers an area nearly as large as continental United States. The mighty "River Sea" tears whole islands from the jungle and floats them down the river. Torrential jungle rains and melting snows and glaciers of the Andes Mountains can make the river near Manaus rise and fall 60 feet, flooding an area the size of Poland. The valley is so thickly forested that its tangled trees make up 25 percent of the earth's forests. Of the mighty river's 1,100 tributaries, ten of them are longer than the Rhine. It is so

broad at its mouth that it contains an island larger than Switzerland.

THE CLIMATE. Brazil extends across three zones of climate. The first, in the equatorial region, has a mean temperature of 81 degrees. Frequent showers make the area bearable.

The second zone terminates at the Tropic of Capricorn and has a mean temperature of 74 to 80 degrees in the lowlands and 64 to 70 in the higher areas.

The third zone, which encompasses southern Brazil and Rio de Janeiro, is temperate, with a mean temperature of 62 to 66 degrees. The seasons are just the reverse of ours, with warm Februaries and cold Junes. The winters are quite dry and the summers tend to be wet.

THE PEOPLE. The Portuguese who settled Brazil gave the country its language, its Catholic religion and its basic racial types. Brazil is the second-largest country in area to be united by a single language. A distinct culture and nationality have been produced in the 400 years of amalgamation of the nation's major racial elements. All the main stocks, Indian, Caucasian, Negro, and Asian, are represented in the present population of about 100 million.

The fast growth of the white population in the cooler south has been due to a veritable stream of European immigrants. The most numerous immigrant stocks have been Italian, Portuguese, Spanish, Japanese, and German. Brazil has the largest Japanese colony in the world, and there are close to a million Italians in São Paulo alone.

Under the Portuguese the mixing of races went on from their first landings in Brazil. The result is visible today in the vast class of mixed races known as *caboclos.* Speeding the mixing in early Brazil, the second and third generation (Portuguese-Indian), known as *mamelucos,* enslaved their Indian neighbors.

The Indians of today inhabit the Amazon Valley and the Mato Grosso. The government has been concerned with resettling many unfriendly tribes since 1910 when the Indian Protective Service was established.

Thus, because the mixing of Europeans, Indians, and the Negroes brought as slaves from Africa has always been accepted in Brazil, the Brazilians of today vary greatly in racial characteristics. The populace ranges from blondes with blue eyes to dark-skinned Negroes and many strains between, yet overt racial discrimination is virtually unknown.

Brazil was discovered in the evening of April 22, 1500, by a Portuguese fleet commanded by Pedro Alveres Cabral. Cabral, however, had predecessors to dilute his honor of discovery just as Columbus had his Leif Ericson and others. The most important "prediscoverer" was Vicente Yáñez Pinzón, Columbus' commander of the *Niña,* who explored a portion of Brazil's Atlantic coast on behalf of Spain in 1498.

The absence of wealth which could merely be scooped up made Brazil unimportant. This supposed unimportance won time and peace for the land's development. It was spared the ravages of the conquistadors.

Cabral named the newly discovered land "True Cross" or Vera Cruz. The name was not widely accepted by the Portuguese and it was more common to refer to the country by the name of one of its early chief exports, *pau-brasil,* a red dyewood.

The country's lack of wealth made colonization attractive to practically no one. A partial solution was found by expelling criminals or *degregados* to the new land. The only sizable group of colonists to come on their own accord were the Jews, who were fleeing from the Inquisition. They organized the export of timber to Portugal and foreign countries.

It can be said that Portugal seriously decided to settle Brazil when it sent, on February 1, 1549, Governor Thomé de Souza with 600 soldiers, 400 criminals and six Jesuit priests. A temporary capital was established in Bahia, fortresses were built and the country's first prison indicated the law would be enforced.

Corruption was rampant in the Colonial system, which lasted to the early nineteenth century. Based on the actual slave system of the Negroes, and the virtual slavery of the Indians, the economic system consisted of huge estates run by slave labor.

The discovery of gold by the Paulistas in 1693 did something for the opening of the interior. With the exception of the Paulistas, who made frequent thrusts into the interior on treks called *bandeiras,* the bulk of the colonials had clung to the coastal belt. The forays of the rugged São Paulo frontiersmen, who were fond of taking whole families in a virtual traveling community in their wanderings, led to the subsequent discovery of diamonds. Whole coastal towns were evacuated overnight, and towns were created in the land of Minas Gerais.

Napoleon's campaign in Iberia made an empire of Brazil, for the royal family was forced to flee to the colony. The reforms made by the Marquis of Pombal had reverted the rights of the *donatarios,* heading the captaincies, to the crown, the Indians were given equality, and immigration encouraged. The capital had been moved back to Rio de Janeiro and Pombal had also banished the Jesuits from Brazil for engaging in commercial ventures.

Upon the arrival of Dom John, the regent, a new era commenced. Now, for the first time in history, a colony became the seat of a crown. Dom John opened the ports to all friendly nations, set up a ministry and council, a supreme court, treasury, and universities and libraries.

In 1817 a revolution in Pernambuco established a republic which lasted for ninety days before it was quelled by the king. In 1820, however, a revolution in Portugal caused Dom John to return to the mother country in 1821. High officials in Lisbon attempted to strip Brazil of the higher status it had gained as the seat of the empire. Dom Pedro, the king's son who had been left in Brazil as regent, was ordered back to Portugal. He refused. On September 7, 1822, after forming a ministry, he proclaimed the independence of Brazil. Three months later he was crowned emperor.

Portugal, headed by the father of the newly crowned emperor, did not offer much resistance. By 1823 all Europe recognized the independence, and two years later even Portugal offered official recognition.

Although Brazil made external agreements to abolish the slave trade, it never enforced them until 1853. It still required four giant steps to free all of the slaves—in 1871 a bill made newborn children of slaves free; in 1884 two states freed all their slaves; in 1885 all slaves over 60 were freed, and finally, in 1888, all slaves were completely emancipated. No compensation was given to the owners.

This loss of what the aristocratic slaveholders considered their capital equipment dealt a deathblow to the traditional social and economic system of northern Brazil. The great *fazendas* founded on the traditional slavery and sugar soon deteriorated. Some slaves remained on the land as wage earners, but few landholders considered the enterprise worthwhile. All of the uprooted, slaves and their idle masters, added to the perennial Brazilian problem of a nomadic population.

Although the country grew during Pedro II's reign—the population swelled, for example, from 4 to 14 million—and had prospered to a degree, there was much dissatisfaction. Many plantation owners who claimed ruin because of the emperor's liberal policies turned against him. The intelligentsia clamored for a republic and the clergy was vexed because several bishops had been punished. The heirs to the throne were unpopular, and, perhaps more important, the army was unhappy because Dom Pedro II kept it out of politics.

A revolt led by a military conspiracy in 1889 to make Brazil a republic, saw Dom Pedro II and his family banished after he formally abdicated. He died two years later.

Brazil was first declared a republic on November 15, 1889, when the empire, which lasted from 1822, was abolished. In all, four federal constitutions have evolved since the first one, based on that of the U.S., was written. The federal senate consists of three representatives of each state and the federal district, who are elected by majority vote. The chamber of deputies, which collaborates with the federal senate in exercising legislation, is composed of representatives of the people, elected on a proportional system. Executive power is vested in the president.

The last of the many Brazilian constitutions, adopted in 1946, sets forth a union of 22 states, five territories and one federal district. A popularly elected president holds office for a five-year term and may not succeed himself. Congress is composed of the Senate and the Chamber of Deputies, whose elected officials hold eight- and four-year terms respectively. All citizens are compelled by law to vote for congressmen on a secret ballot under a system of proportional representation.

AGRICULTURE. Brazil has survived two eras when the whole economy depended on one product. First the era of rubber, when Brazil supplied the whole world in the nineteenth and early twentieth centuries—until the British introduced the rubber tree to Malaya and West Africa—and the era of coffee, which was Brazil's near-total export product until the end of World War II. Coffee has been the keystone of the economic structure of Brazil for more than a century. Brazil is still the number one producer of coffee in the world and cotton has developed as a leading crop. The country also is a leader in growing beans, bananas, and cassava; ranks high in production of cacao, oranges, pineapple, and sugar cane; and is a leading producer of meat, cattle, and hogs.

Most of the food needed by its people is grown within the country; however, much land, especially in the interior, has not been developed. Brazilian farmers, using only one-tenth of the available farmland, rank among the world's leading food producers. Over half of the nation's workers are in agriculture.

In the Brazilian uplands the common fruit trees of the temperate zone do well. The banana, orange, and pineapple harvests leave a margin for export, while other tropical fruits are grown for local consumption. Brazil produces chocolate and tobacco in large quantities.

Brazilian forests are among the world's richest in oil-bearing fruits, gums, resins, essential oils, waxes, timber, cellulose, fibers and other products. Brazilian timber is of fine quality and ranges from wood so light that it can replace cork to the Brazilian pepper tree with a density one and one half times that of water. The greatest demand, however, is for the Paraná pine which grows in the southern states.

INDUSTRY. Manufacturing is the fastest-growing segment of the economy in Brazil. With the emphasis on goods used for other products (cement, steel), new factories are opening and expanding rapidly.

Textile manufacturing is one of the largest industries. Production includes cotton, wool, linen, and natural and artificial silk, jute and hemp goods. Brazil is also making rapid strides in other industries. Automobile and truck output has tripled. One of Brazil's aluminum plants is the largest in South America. Some additional products are glassware, matches, hardware, clothing, ceramics, plastics, and paints. The aircraft industry is the largest in Latin America.

For a wide variety of items, particularly machinery, crude petroleum, industrial chemicals, and wheat, Brazil is still dependent upon imports, however.

The United States is by far the principal market for Brazil's exports. Other markets are West Germany, Argentina, the United Kingdom, Italy and France. The principal suppliers of imports to Brazil are the United States, Argentina, Venezuela, West Germany, the Netherlands, the West Indies and France.

Brazil's mineral resources are being exploited, with more than 50,000 men working for large companies alone. In addition to gold, manganese, coal, zircon, quartz, and diamonds, there are deposits of tungsten, bauxite, nickel, mica, lead, zinc, silver, uranium, thorite, and others. Iron, however, is a major source of wealth. Brazil has about 33 percent of the world's estimated supply and much of it is of a very high quality. In addition to diamonds, a variety of precious and semi-precious stones are also found.

CITIES. Brazil is internationally known for its beautiful cities, in part due to the ingenious town planning of the Portuguese. Though Rio de Janeiro is the most well-known, many other cities, such as Brasília, the capital, are outstanding and should be visited.

BELÉM. Only two degrees below the equator and 90 miles up the Pará River is the city of Belém (Bethlehem), the capital of the state of Pará and the gateway to the Amazon. Belém is the main distribution point for the products of the Amazon Valley.

BELO HORIZONTE, a one-hour flight north of Rio, was Brazil's first planned city. Its history began in 1897 when Emperor Dom Pedro II decided to move the capital of the state of Minas Gerais (which means General Mines) from Ouro Prêto to this city because of its beauty and healthful climate.

From the beginning Belo Horizonte boomed, increasing its population 35 times in 50 years, bursting its planned boundaries and absorbing nearby satellite towns. Its architecture followed the French style until 1930 when it adopted the ultramodern Brazilian school of design as many other pioneering towns were doing.

Oscar Niemeyer, the internationally known Brazilian architect, is well represented in **Pampulha,** a suburb about 20 minutes from the center of town. Niemeyer built the remarkable lakeside yacht club, casino and restaurant and the much-debated Church of São Francisco—also known as the **Church of Saint Francis of Assisi.** It has beautiful blue tile murals by Portnari.

Other interesting points in and around the city are the **Feira de Amostras,** a permanent exhibit of the products of Minas Gerais; the experimental forestry and agricultural stations and the central park with its rare specimens of Brazilian flora.

Near this center of the country's mining industry are **Nova Lima** and **Sabará,** both old picturesque mining communities. The mine at Nova Lima has been operating since 1834. Men may visit its 9,000-foot pit, the second deepest in the world, but women are not welcome as the miners believe their presence invites disaster.

Minas Gerais is also the land of gems, and its precious and semi-precious stones can be bought cheaper in Belo Horizonte than in other parts of Brazil.

BRASÍLIA, with a population of 150,000, is located in the interior of the country on the plains of Goiaz. It is a planned city which was begun in April 1960 (the 460th anniversary of the discovery of Brazil).

Plans for this city were in the constitution for many years, but designs and construction were not begun until the 1950's. A totally modern city, Brasília's shape resembles an airplane, with a residential section at right angles to the government area. Very worth visiting is the striking **Plaza of the Three Powers,** which contains three slim skyscrapers, one each for the Congress, Supreme Court of Brazil, and Executive Department Office Building.

The city is bordered by a 19-mile-long artificial lake. The new residence of the President, the **Palacio da Alvorado,** should also be visited.

Excellent hotels and restaurants have been opened to accomodate visitors to Brasília, which is readily approached by new superhighways and by plane.

OURO PRÊTO is a living record of the country's Colonial period. The whole town is now a national monument, a gem of eighteenth-century baroque art and architecture. By law, all new construction must be in a similar style. The sole exception is an ultramodern hotel designed by architect Oscar Niemeyer.

The city was the center of a fabulous gold rush that began in 1690 and lasted for more than a century. The big years were 1735–80, when the seemingly inexhaustible supply of gold brought prosperity not only to Brazil and Portugal, but helped the sagging economy of Europe as well.

Piety and a love of ornamentation, plus a fear that the crown might usurp more than its rightful "fifth," were factors that led citizens to embellish the buildings with paintings, delicate carvings, statuary, gold leaf and gems. The same extravagance was lavished on the clergy, and today visitors can see ecclesiastical vestments of the period stiff with gold embroidery and glittering with precious stones.

Ouro Prêto's churches are a memorial to Aleijadinho (Little Cripple), who devoted his life to religious sculpture. The maimed Aleijadinho taught himself to carve with chisel and mallet strapped to his elbows. His statues, fountains and pulpits are considered to be the city's greatest treasure.

Ouro Prêto was a center of the Brazilian independence movement and the homes and headquarters of the insurgents are among the city's sights to see. Other historic landmarks are the **governor's palace,** now the National School of Mines with a fine collection of minerals and precious stones; the **municipal palace,** a historical museum and formerly the Colonial penitentiary, and the **Casa dos Contos,** the mint and assay office in gold rush days, now a post office.

PETRÓPOLIS, one of the favorite mountain resorts for the elite of Rio and São Paulo, provides one of the most interesting side trips from Rio.

The town, launched on its fashionable career when Dom Pedro II decided his court required a hot-weather retreat, is 45 serpentine road miles from Rio.

The **emperor's palace** has become the **Museum of the Empire,** housing the Brazilian crown jewels, empire furniture, paintings, and *objets d'art,* and is well worth a visit.

The drive is extremely scenic, providing an over-the-shoulder view of Rio that is spectacular as well as a unique engineering achievement. Hammered out of solid rock, but on a grade providing easy climbing by car, Rio and the semitropical fields behind can be seen. Sheer drops spread out magnificent valley vistas below. You pass through a tunnel, a chasm-spanning bridge, and circle the mountain's peak by a road built over the side.

Once around this bend, you see Petrópolis at 3,500 feet. Cobbled streets, Swiss chalets, and flowered slopes greet the eye.

Petrópolis is a city with a population of over 200,000 which more than doubles in the summer. It boasts 20-story office and apartment buildings, mills and industry, but still retains the feeling of rest and diversion. The pink and white palace served as the summer retreat for Brazil's emperors.

Floors of marble and inlaid wood are preserved by visitors wearing huge slippers. Rooms abound in the regal elegance of gold and silver table service, crystal, porcelain, silk tapestry and gilded furniture.

The throne room is preserved in all its elegance, and in an adjoining alcove rests the solid gold crown, weighing over four pounds and encrusted with 639 diamonds, 170 pearls and a famed 18-carat imperial diamond. The carriage house contains the sedan chairs and litters which were borne by slaves over the mountain roads.

One of the world's showplace hotels is set in the middle of tropical scenery nearby, including orchid-draped trees bordering the lake in front. Built in five years as the "Monte Carlo of South America," the great casino was closed soon after the hotel was opened after World War II, when Brazil banned gambling. Today, many Brazilians maintain apartments there in the summer as a private club. It is extremely ornate, boasting 20-foot-wide bird cages, indoor Roman pools, a theater, marble entrance halls and a veranda that must surely be the world's longest.

Petrópolis itself was founded by the Swiss and retains a Swiss-Bavarian air—the Germans have settled there too.

PÔRTO ALEGRE or *GAY PORT,* with a population of over 900,000 is the capital of Rio Grande do Sul. It is the third most important industrial city in Brazil and, like many other port towns, is built on hills sloping upward from the Guaíba River.

The city's invigorating climate and wealth of industry have attracted large numbers of Portuguese, Germans and Italians as well as other Europeans.

RECIFE, hub of northeastern Brazil, is the easternmost port in South America, with over 1 million population. Now the third largest city in the country, it was founded in 1548 by fishermen and sailors. The city gets its name from the broad, low reefs of coral which enclose the harbor. Recife has been called the "Venice of America" due to the rivers Capiberibe and Beberibe which cut the city into sections connected by many bridges and canals. It is from Recife that the massive Trans-Amazon Highway is being built. This highway will run some 3,100 miles to the Peruvian border and will open up the Amazon basin area.

RIO DE JANEIRO. Even Americans who have never been to Rio de Janeiro are familiar with its dramatic appearance. It is a crescent of land gently nestling in blue Guanabara Bay. On top of this crescent, 365 of the most sheer and rugged peaks, some of which zoom right up from the sea, can be found.

The names of the peaks—**Hunchback, Two Brothers, Parrot's Beak** and **Sugar Loaf**—are as aptly named as the atmosphere they create. The latter shoots out of the water to a point over 1,200 feet high. A short distance from the city's center, a cable-car ride to the top offers a sight you will never forget. The 60 square miles of land at the base of the peaks make up Rio de Janeiro, which means River of January. The Portuguese explorers thought the bay they found on New Year's Day was the mouth of a river.

It is a city of contrasts: mountains and wonderful beaches like Copacabana; block-wide streets like Avenida Getulio Vargas, and ancient twisting lanes no car can enter; mud and bamboo huts and avant-garde architecture; the whites of the clothing and buildings and the colors of the tropical flowers and fruits.

The traffic can get fairly out-of-hand however, with the profusion of privately owned buses, the *botas,* chauffeured by a reckless and fiercely competitive band of private entrepreneurs, and the solid front of the taxi drivers (who virtually know no laws except their own), one ventures abroad in the rush hours at his own peril.

Buses are mounted on truck chassis and painted in gay colors and confusing signs, according to the owner's taste. He can also choose virtually any route, and frequently takes unscheduled short cuts and alternate routes to save a few minutes.

The open-sided trolleys still run in the Copacabana and some other sections, and usually arrive at their scheduled destinations.

Although the weather may run to temperatures in the 70's and 80's all during the "winters" (June, July, and August), the many beaches are deserted completely by swimmers. But in the summer months (December, January, and February) Cariocas may swim twice a day and the beaches are packed.

Rio has broad boulevards surpassing those of most other major cities. The **Avenida Rio Branco,** stretching from one end of the city to the other, was constructed at the turn of the century, and the block-wide **Avenida Presidente Getulio Vargas** was made to cut perpendicularly across it during the war.

Soon after Avenida Rio Branco was built and well lined with trees, it was endowed with a number of stately, European-style buildings: the **municipal opera** with its regal stairs and rare Brazilian building stone; the **national library;** the **Palace of Justice;** and at the sea end of the Avenida, the senate or **Monroe Palace.** It was named after our doctrine-making president and was brought from St. Louis, where it served as the Brazilian pavilion at the Louisiana Purchase Exposition. Also on the Avenida is the **national art school,** which has an important collection of paintings. The boulevard is famous for its brightly illuminated movie district and, like many streets, its mosaic sidewalks.

Clinging precariously to the sides of some of the mountain peaks are the bamboo and mud or tin huts of the Negro slums. From these waterless primitive hovels devoid of electricity, unexcelled views of the city can be seen. One such community is right above the plushest of all beaches, Copacabana.

In contrast, located on other hills are some of the richest homes in Rio. Some are three stories in front and one in the rear. Others must be entered from the roof. Most of these houses, nestling against dense brush, represent the latest in building design.

The proximity of dense vegetation, the tremendous number of home gardens of tropical fruits and plants, and the parks and gardens of Rio scent the air heavily. The city is not large enough to have an atmosphere independent of the surrounding woods and sea.

The **Jardim Botánico,** situated on the slope of a hill, has a specimen of almost every one of the thousands and thousands of species of jungle flora. It had been said that only the botanical gardens in Batavia are more exciting in presenting the beautiful and bizarre products of nature. In this country of wood exports and rare wood items, one takes a special interest in the various species of the brazilwood trees, including the lignum vitae. Other stars of the *jardim* are the Victoria Regia lilies and the orchids.

On leaving the more than 100 acres of gardens, through the lanes of century-old towering royal palms, planted by King João VI, one is not surprised to learn that the first actual jungle zone is but an hour away.

Blocks and blocks of unsurpassed formal gardens along the **Beira Mar** near the Avenida Rio Branco form the bayside parks. Here, bordered with velvety lawns and shaded by the tallest palms, there are always artistic shapes of blazing flowers in bloom. In the evening the many fountains in the park are illuminated, changing the hues of this lively palette.

A walk to the end of **Rua Goncalves Dias** will result in a most pleasant and interesting visit to a large flower market, at the intersection of Rua Ouvidor, Avenida Rio Branco and Rua Miguel Couto. Nearby the bronze statue of a newsboy will be reminiscent of the Brussels Manniken.

Rio did not become the capital until 1763, and as a result its grand buildings are younger than those in the former capital of Bahia. There are only a few churches which were built in Colonial times. Here, as in most of Brazil, the church interiors are heavily gilded and extraordinarily ornate.

Our Lady of Candelaria, at the foot of Avenida Presidente Vargas, impressively dominates the heart of the city, while the regal **convent church of the Franciscans** on Santo Antonio Hill is a good example of Brazilian ornateness. This church, which contains a chapel of the Third Order, is fitted with hand-carved jacaranda wood which has been heavily gilded. It is reached by taking an elevator from the Rua Santo Antonio to the top of the hill.

An interesting church is the **Temple of Positivism** at 74 Rua Benjamin. It is the world's leading temple of the cult of Positivism, which attracted support from many of the founders of the republic. The first Brazilian flag, painted on cardboard, was made by the Positivists and is on display here. Men who are outstanding examples of the doctrine are honored with pictures and statues like saints. One of these is George Washington.

The church and monastery of **São Bento** near Praça Maua was built in 1589 to serve as a fortress, as well as a church. It stands alone on a hill; the interior of the church is one blaze of gold. The wood paneling has been completely covered with a thin coat of gilt, and every contour and surface reflects the colored light.

Although only five minutes away from the Avenida Beira Mar, the sea, air, winds and temperature are all different at **Copacabana,** the beach of beaches. All the rest of Rio is on the vast Bay of Guanabara, but at one end of the horseshoe bay stand the steep Sugar Loaf and Morro do Leme peaks which jut right into the sea. Copacabana is on the other side of these peaks and on the Atlantic Ocean rather than the bay. The beach is reached by two tunnels cut through Leme Hill.

Copacabana is actually a city within a city, with its night clubs, bars and movies along its three-and-one-half-mile stretch of white sand bordered by the sea on one side and skyscrapers on the other.

The beginning of Copacabana, called Leme, has become very elegant and fashionable. By walking 60 yards from the beach, one of Rio's most modern shopping districts can be found.

The sprawling cafés, famous hotels, and even the music, give Copacabana its own special cosmopolitan atmosphere. There are no stores or commercial traffic at the beach. This gigantic white strip, which can easily accommodate over 100,000 sun-lovers, is devoted exclusively to relaxation and fun.

Just 100 yards from the beach is a lake, **Lagoa do Freitas,** which is completely surrounded on three sides by mountains. The fourth side is made up of the patch of streets which terminate in **Leblon** and **Ipanema** beaches. Besides being a city of skyscrapers, mountains, flowers and light, Rio is also a city of beaches.

Many of these are just as wonderful as Copacabana; Ipanema is considered to be more stylish by some. Little **Urca Beach** is the smallest, but has the whitest sand; **Botafogo Beach** is the most perfect crescent; **Gavea Beach** has a nearby golf club as its main attraction.

The side streets of Rio, that tangled lacework which no car can enter, comprise, for many, one of the city's greatest attractions. This is **old Brazil** with a touch of old Portugal. The streets, packed to capacity with men, women, children, and more children, are bordered with open shops.

There is an emphasis of basic trades and an absence of mass production and the automobile in this area. The houses are old, the children lively and the streets go recklessly in illogical directions. Some end at a huge rock or, just as possibly, lead onto one of the supermodern Avenidas.

One street might terminate with a group of huts nestling among palm trees while another will meet the Rua Ouvidor or the Florida of Buenos Aires with their fashionable shops, some specializing only in handkerchiefs, another only in stockings. At one unexpected turn there is a former palace; another reveals the bay. This maze of streets—bursting with shoppers, its craftsmen in their small ancient shops in the shadows of the skyscrapers, at the edge of luxury—is a most fascinating aspect of Rio. Although there are many fine stores on the avenidas Rio Branco and Presidente Vargas, most of the shopping is done on these small streets.

Here one buys the jewelry, silverware, precious and semi-precious stones, the novelties and gifts made out of rare woods or reptile skins and the omnipresent novelties decorated with butterflies. The fatigued shopper may be interested yet forewarned to learn that the law requires all cafés to serve drinking water free of charge, but bottled water is recommended. And he should know that many cafés will serve a *cafézinho* before any formal request has been made. There is a legal maximum on the price of coffee.

The newest museum in Rio is the **Museu de Arte Moderna** on the Esplanada do Castelo. The building is an art work in itself and houses a formidable collection of modern art.

The **Museu Historico Nacional** on the Praza Marechal Ancora is the place to see old Portuguese architecture on the outside and furniture and artifacts of Colonial days inside.

The **Museu da Cidade** on the Parque da Cidade on top of Gravea hill makes an interesting excursion culminated with a wonderful view. The museum houses collections of the municipality.

The **Museu do Indio** on Rua Mata Machado has a wonderful collection of the tribes of Brazilian Indians.

Also interesting to visit is Maracanã Stadium, where soccer and basketball are played. Soccer is the number one sport, and the stadium, seating over 150,000 is one of the largest in the world. It can also accommodate 50,000 standees.

An interesting trip is via a trolley or *bonde* up to **Sylvestre hill.** The open streetcar climbs up the Moro Santo Antonio and then over the Colonial aqueduct, as if flying through the air, to Santa Thereza.

The almost vertical **Sugar Loaf** mountain is over 1,200 feet high and is reached by a basket car on a cable which makes a mile-long ride through the air. The trip is done in two stages with the first being on Urca Hill. This is the peak which separates the main crescent of Rio Bay from the crescent of Copacabana.

Corcovado, which at its 2,330-foot peak supports the world-famous **statue of Christ the Redeemer,** is to Rio as the Eiffel Tower is to Paris. The colossal concrete statue, created by Heitor da Silva Costa, was inaugurated in 1931 when the inventor Marconi pulled a switch in Italy which illuminated the statue for the first time. The 1,200-ton figure stands 125 feet high and the outstretched hands span 92 feet. The summit can be reached by auto or cable car and presents, as does Sugar Loaf, an unforgettable view.

SALVADOR or *BAHIA,* with a population of over 800,000, is situated in the center of Brazil's long seacoast. The capital of the state of Bahia, it is often called the City of Churches. The city is dotted with many old buildings and fortifications which date from the sixteenth century, when the town was called São Salvador da Bahia de Todos os Santos and was the national capital.

From the waterfront the city rises

over a sheer cliff 200 feet high. The city's two distinct levels are connected by cable cars, elevators and several roads. The docks and commercial buildings are on the lower level while the residential section, hotels and main shopping district overlook the bay from the upper level.

The tradition of Bahia is imbued with the folklore of Africa as evidenced in the music, dances and voodoo rituals in which the present-day descendants of Sudanese slaves partake. The Negro women wear distinctive clothing.

Among the interesting places to visit are the **Museum of Sacred Art,** operated by the University of Bahia in the seventeenth-century church and convent of the Discalced Carmelites of Santa Teresa; the **San Francisco Church and Monastery;** the gardens of the governor's palace.

SÃO PAULO, with its over 6 million Paulistas and thousands of factories, is the largest city in Brazil. Having enjoyed being the agricultural capital of the country for most of its history, São Paulo is now the industrial center, with even coffee taking a back seat. Situated 300 miles from Rio de Janeiro on a 2,400-foot-high plateau, it has an average temperature of 66 degrees.

São Paulo was founded by Jesuit priests who penetrated the interior to convert the Indians. The first Mass in the new settlement was said on January 25, 1554, and the name of the patron saint of the day was adopted for the colony. In 1558 it became a village and in 1681 it was made the capital of the province. The roaming *bandeirantes* who originated from and depopulated the town stunted its growth, but they helped build the country by exploring the interior on their mass forays.

Dom Pedro uttered his famous "Liberty or death" independence speech just outside of the city in 1822. A hundred years after the declaration, the **Ipiranga Independence Memorial** was inaugurated on approximately the same site where it was made. The memorial consists of 130 different pieces of stone and bronze and stands in the Ipiranga Parque. Dom Pedro's remains are in the crypt below the monument, which is guarded night and day by soldiers in dress uniform.

The **Paulista Museum** stands in the same park. It contains relics of history with special emphasis on the Imperial period. The São Paulo **Museum of Art** has an important collection of native and foreign painters. It also houses a 20,000-volume library, exhibition salons and modern art.

The city has a number of daily newspapers, movie houses, radio and television stations, five museums and a 200,000-volume library.

Among the most interesting parks are the **Parque do Estado** with more than 30,000 different species of orchids; the **Parque da Cantareira,** containing a tree nursery and a museum which exhibits the tremendous variety of wood originating from the state; the **Agua Branca Parque** featuring a collection of birds and fish; and **Parque Ibirapuera,** with industrial exhibits.

One of the chief attractions of the city is **Butantan Institute,** which is commonly called the Snake Farm. It is a world-famous research center specializing in serums and antitoxins with more than 10,000 snakes, scorpions and spiders.

In São Paulo you can enjoy German, Italian, and Japanese cuisine, among others. There are good red wines produced in Brazil, and Chilean white wines are imported. The beer, which is justly celebrated, is produced by German Braumeisters from the old country.

Only 38 miles from the industrial capital of São Paulo is the island port city of **Santos.** Most of Brazil's coffee and industrial products are shipped from here.

Santos, which has grown since 1534, when it was founded, to a population of over 200,000, is also a prime seaside resort. The coffee stock exchange with its fascinating tasting tables is of special interest to visitors. To the west of São Paulo is the huge hydroelectric complex of **Urubupunga,** among the largest of its kind in the world.

TERESÓPOLIS, named for Theresa Christina, Dom Pedro's wife, lies just a short drive (via a modern scenic highway) beyond Petrópolis. It is quieter and more rustic than its twin resort, and offers many spectacular views of the mountains which ring Rio de Janeiro—including the needle-like peak called the "Finger of God."

AMAZON VALLEY. At one time a "Green Hell" of fact and adventure, the Amazon Valley is the world's largest remaining natural zoo, and a vast network of fascinating water highways branching off the "River Sea" into a truly lost world of natural wonders. Fraught with danger from the man-eating piranha fish and crocodiles below, and the giant anaconda snakes in the branches above, exploring the region is not for the fainthearted.

The first explorer of the region, a Spaniard, Francisco de Orellana, entered the valley from the Andes in 1541. His expedition took eight months to reach the mouth of the Amazon; along the way he claimed to have seen a race of "Amazon women" (after the Greek legend), who could fight harder than ten Indian men and who guarded a city of treasure. He was the first and last person to see them, but that is how the river got its name.

The river is navigable by ocean-going freighters for a distance greater than New York to Ireland. It boasts a fascinating capital **Manaus** 1,000 miles upriver that was founded in the late nineteenth and early twentieth centuries. The ravaging floods tear whole acres of shore land and send them floating down the river complete with trees and wildlife, while the river floods areas equal to half of Europe.

Of the world's 22,767 known plant species, over 19,000 have been found here, while some 1,200 rivers churn with over 1,800 species of fish, including the voracious piranhas (less than a foot long) and the manatee (or sea cow).

The *matto da varzae,* one of the two kinds of jungles, is the true "Green Hell," consisting of dense matted vegetation of palm and other soft wood, mixed with an impenetrable undergrowth and vines. This is the flood plain. *Tierra firme* is the high ground, where the trees are hardwood and there is little undergrowth, although the sun seldom penetrates to the floor of this highland rain forest.

Until recently, even after four centuries, the Amazon region had fewer inhabitants than the island of Puerto Rico. Cortés and Jimenez de Quesada had searched for El Dorado and, like those that followed, found neither golden nuggets nor temples to plunder. The Jesuit, Father Acuna, who entered the valley from the Andes in 1659, even praised the climate, and considered the land a "paradise," but few took his word. The *bandeirantes,* intrepid wanderers of São Paulo, penetrated the interior in a search for riches, but found nothing.

The Portuguese entered the valley in larger numbers in the eighteenth century, seeking slaves and other jungle products. The penetration from Belém, at the river's mouth, continued in the nineteenth century and settlements grew on the river. But it was the rubber boom of the late nineteenth and early twentieth centuries that lured men to the interior, in spite of dangers, and the city of Manaus was built 1,000 miles up the river. The building of the **Trans-Amazon Highway** has created new boom towns along its route.

You can view the Amazon's shoreline from the deck of a comfortable ocean-going steamer that makes the trip from Belém, near the river's mouth, to Manaus. Or you can take the smaller river boats operated by the Brazilian government. Another alternative is flying directly to Manaus, a modern city of over 250,000 population, from which side trips into the interior by river launches can be arranged.

By boat you will see a shoreline, teeming in jungle fauna, trading settlements, and Indians in their dugout canoes plying between the settlements, where all the houses are perched on stilts above the swampy land. High point is the trip through the **"Narrows,"** where the ship winds through lanes of yellow flood with equatorial forests within 20 or 30 yards on either side and continues for 100 miles among the **"Thousand Islands."**

Belém (or Pará), the best starting point, is about 75 miles from the sea on the banks of the Rio Pará, where the Amazon is about 40 miles wide. You can see the jungle here in safety; the **Bosque,** a public garden, is an area of jungle left untouched, except for paths cut to disclose the weird and beautiful interior. Giant trees mingle with bamboo and lush undergrowth, and a cave of bats alongside a jungle pond makes a contrasting sight to the colorful parrots, parakeets, and chattering monkeys.

The **Goeldi Museum** features a unique collection of Amazonian plants, and the zoological gardens contain caged jungle fauna, from the baby coati to giant South American leopards (onca), as well as countless birds of fantastic plumage.

At the quayside market of the **Old Town,** the dark-skinned, and often fair-haired, natives sell authentic jungle craftwork, curious pipes, baskets, as well as snakeskins and alligator skulls.

During the trip upriver you may see gorgeous butterflies fluttering over the open decks in the daytime, and giant moths at night. You will hear thousands of chattering monkeys, especially around dusk, and you may pass through several jungle storms, lightning and torrential rains.

After five or six days, the boat turns from the yellow Amazon into the blue-black waters of the **Río Negro** for the nine-mile trip to Manaus.

Manaus is far from a ghost town, but the **Opera House** (modeled after the Opéra in Paris) no longer features the leading stars of the world. Today the town is the collecting point for Amazonian products like rubber, Brazil nuts, lumber, cacao, and aromatic plants and fruits. Although modern buildings include many handsome cafés, the society of the rubber-rich is not much in evidence these days. Here you will see traders, hunters, and trappers—people of all colors and races. You may still view the striking collection of Brazilian paintings in the Opera House, and study more of the life of the jungle in the **Amazon Museum.** The **customs house** is another landmark—it was imported stone by stone from England in 1910. Manaus is also the world's largest floating port, built to allow for a 30 to 40-foot rise or fall of the river.

From Manaus you can continue by motor launch up the Río Negro to explore an **igarape** (like the bayous of Louisiana), the waters completely covered with vegetation, combining with the jungle background to form an umbrella and carpet of millions of trees and flowers. In this region you pass the floating stores maintained for the crocodile and snake hunters. You may see them at work, stalking the giant amphibians, or see the snake hunters with a giant anaconda. Experienced Indian guides can take you farther by canoe to **Indian villages** deep in the jungle.

You may be shown a river crossing, where the tiny, yet man-eating piranha fish used to prey in swarms. To cross the river in days past, the Gauchos had to wound a horse, then send it half a mile up the river. The fish, sensing blood, would follow the wounded animal by thousands. It took the vicious school of flesh-eaters only three minutes to convert a horse to a skeleton, but this was sufficient respite to get the cattle across the river.

Iguazú Falls (which dwarfs Niagara) are certainly one of the world's most magnificent scenic views. They have only been known to the western world since the early nineteenth century. Today the mammoth falls can be reached by two airlines and a train which goes to **Foz do Iguaçu** (the Portuguese spelling). Many visitors will prefer to drive.

A new bridge links Brazil and Paraguay at the falls. Paraguay maintains the free zone city of **Paranagua** on the border. Also, to accommodate tourists, a $10 million hotel has been erected on the Brazil side.

The cataracts can be viewed from several vantages, descending to the water's edge at some points in the gorge, and climbing up the footpaths until you are alongside the falls as they plunge over the abyss. You can hear the thunderous roar of the falls 15 miles away, and as you approach by road through the jungles of the Mato Grosso, almost feel their presence. The new hotel, set in a clearing, offers a panorama of a mile or so of the 21 separate falls.

Southwest of Rio de Janeiro, in back of the mountains, the Paraiba River flows 2,500 feet above sea level. It goes past **Volta Redonda,** in which South America's largest steel plant is located; it flows by **Rezende** and the **Brazilian West Point** and the **Black Needles Range** with peaks at 9,000 feet. These mountains border the **National Park of Itatiaía** with its primeval treasures. The river travels on past **Campos de Jordao,** a mile-high plateau decked with picturesque umbrella pines and favored with a temperate climate. The visitor today has easy access to this wonderful valley via a modern express highway or air-conditioned streamlined trains, en route to Rio from São Paulo.

SPORTS AND RECREATION. All types of aquatic sports are popular on Brazil's excellent beaches. Fishing is also a well-followed sport. Big-game hunters go to the Mato Grosso region in the Amazon to shoot jaguar, mountain lion, and crocodile.

All types of individual and spectator sports are available, especially in Rio and the larger cities.

SPECIAL EVENTS. **Carnival** in Rio is the wildest, gayest festival held anywhere. For three days and three nights preceding Ash Wednesday, there is singing and dancing and parading everywhere in town. New carnival dances and songs, which have been rehearsed for months, are formally introduced. The streets are covered with confetti. The whole city becomes a festive hall, and the population at all-night balls and masquerades everywhere releases its inhibitions.

The weather in February is perfect for Carnival. February is the middle of the Brazilian summer, and the temperature at four in the morning will not be much below a delightful 75 degrees.

By noon on the Saturday before Ash Wednesday most work is at a standstill. More and more people, dressed in masquerade, flock onto the Avenida Rio Branco, Rio's main street. Wild-feathered Indians, colorful Bahianas laden with shiny beads, men dressed as women, and women dressed as men join the milling crowds singing and dancing down the avenue under the brilliant decorations that have been going up for the previous weeks.

The samba beat grows stronger as night falls on Saturday. Tom-toms are heard, tambourines and the weird *cuica.* A *cuica* resembles a long drum, usually made out of a keg, with a resined string attached to the inside of the head. When this is pulled, it gives a resonant croak like a cross between a bass fiddle and a bullfrog.

A special **Carnival costume ball** is held every year in Copacabana. The most brilliant and dazzling of Brazil's elite meet together to join in the fun.

Early on Sunday morning groups of people begin to congregate once more on the main streets of the city. This is the day for people to go visiting and show off their costumes. Sunday afternoon is mainly devoted to the parade or *corso,* a procession of beautifully decorated floats which wends its way through the city.

On Monday night an enormous costume ball is given at the Teatro Municipal under the auspices of the city fathers. The theater, which is Brazil's largest and most elegant one, is specially renovated each year for the occasion and converted by her leading architects into an immense ballroom.

The election of the Queen of the Carnival is one of the high spots of the evening, and regularly nearly two million people try to force their way in.

After three days and nights, the streets of the city are once more filled with merrymakers on Tuesday. The last tons of streamers and confetti are thrown and dances are given all over the city in the final outburst of wild celebrations that marks the end of the Carnival.

DINING AND SHOPPING. Brazilian food is roughly divided into the specialties from three areas: Creole cookery, at its best in Bahia in the north or old Brazil; Gaucho cuisine, the favorite of southern Brazil, or specifically a barbecue called *churrasco;* and the cosmopolitan cookery of Rio and São Paulo that features every type of European menu, notably Italian, Swiss, German and French (in São Paulo even Japanese specialties are readily available).

Churrasco is barbecued meat–beef, lamb, chicken, and pork–roasted over live charcoal and seasoned with a specially prepared brine. Typical of southern Brazil, it is popular all over the country and can be found in Rio or São Paulo in any "Churrascaria." It is usually served on long skewers directly from the pit, the customer slicing his cuts directly from the skewer. Potato salad, sliced tomatoes and onions are served as well as a farina (flour-like) side dish.

Vatapá is a Bahian specialty served in many ways. Generally it consists of fish or chicken and shrimps, prepared with manioc or rice flour. It is seasoned with coconut milk, pepper, and oil of peanuts and palm.

Feijoada is Bahian, consisting of black beans and meat (pork, smoked bacon, sausage, ham, or beef–in any or all combinations) cooked in a sauce flavored with herbs and onions. *Cozido* is Creole cookery, consisting of all kinds of vegetables and beef boiled in water.

There are also many kinds of spicy hashes called *picadinhos,* famed for the piquance of accompanying sauces.

Desserts are noted for sweetness, being prepared mainly from eggs, milk, sugar and coconut or cacao. Many Brazilian fruits offer a unique taste, like *fruta do conde* (custard apple), *mamao* (papaya) and mangoes.

In addition to ever-present *cafézinho* (like espresso coffee) and chocolate, there are many drinks prepared from the coconut, guarana berries, and fruits. The beer is of good quality; the native wines are excellent.

Semi-precious stones are sold in Brazil at prices well below those of the U.S. and Europe. Especially abundant are aquamarines, topaz, and amethysts, but there are many others as well. Some visitors will prefer to purchase unset stones.

Fine tartaruga sculpture from Recife, small wood carvings from the interior, charm bracelets and cocktail picks decorated with uncut semi-precious stones are of special interest.

Bahian dolls in colorful traditional costumes, flowers made of feathers, and a tremendous assortment of boxes inlaid with rare Brazilian woods have always been popular. Some unique items are black-magic charms, which are sold in antique stores, silver stirrups for wall decorations and church figurines in silver and wood.

Women like the hand-embroidered, top-quality blouses, the magnificent embroidery and lace work from Fortaleza and the ever-popular alligator handbags and accessories.

Of greater interest to men are the Amazonian Indian arrows, daggers and spears. Diamonds and other precious stones found in Brazil are good buys.

Ecuador

Ecuador, the little republic straddling the equator (for which it was named), is a land superbly endowed with everything a tourist could possibly wish for in the way of spectacular mountain scenery, artistic and architectural wonders, and colorful Indian life.

Despite its name and location in the tropical belt, its climate varies from the torrid heat of its coastal and interior lowlands to the cool, bracing, and, at times, frigid air of the Andean highlands. A little world within itself, its diverse topography includes volcanoes and jungles, fertile valleys and barren paramos, picturesque villages and met-

ropolitan cities, mountain spas and seaside resorts.

THE LAND. Jutting out into the Pacific on South America's northwesternmost hump, this wedge-shaped country is bounded on the north by Colombia and on the east and south by Peru. Its land area never has been exactly determined but is estimated to be over 100,000 square miles—more than New York, New Jersey, and Pennsylvania combined. This, however, does not include Galápagos Islands and the unexplored eastern section, which together total more than 170,000 additional square miles.

Two rugged ranges of the high Andes Mountains, not more than 40 miles apart, extend the length of the country, dividing it into three distinct geographical regions. In the lofty fertile valleys, or basins, between this double row of towering snow-covered peaks and ridges, comprising about 15 percent of the land area, is where most of the country's cities and two-thirds of its 6 million population is concentrated. The rest live mostly in the cities and towns along the coastal tropical lowlands; while the eastern Oriente, with more than half of the land, remains practically undeveloped and unpopulated except for a few Indian tribes.

THE CLIMATE. Although Ecuador's climate is measured by the kilometer, and it is wise to be prepared for extremes, the weather of the highlands is temperate the year round, with the rainy winter season from October to May and the dry summer season June to September. On the coast, the rainy season is from December to May.

THE PEOPLE. Several different racial and cultural elements are found in Ecuador, where the population is about 40 percent Indian, 40 percent mixed Indian–European, 10 percent European (mainly Spanish) origin, and 10 percent Negro. The majority of Indians live in the Andean highlands. Generally speaking, there is no true Ecuadorian type, and even the people differ from region to region and village to village. Those on the coast are completely different in speech, temperament, and mannerisms from those who inhabit the highlands; and nowhere is this difference more noticeable than between the inhabitants of Quito and Guayaquil. The Guayaquileño is usually frank, energetic and independent, speaks with a tropical drawl and has a more liberal attitude toward life than his highland brethren. The Quiteño is more reserved, proud, ingenious, generous, charming, and hospitable, and speaks in quick, syllabic tones. Although Quechua is spoken widely in the Andean communities, Spanish is the official language.

Long before the Spaniards landed in Ecuador it was inhabited by many different indigenous tribes, such as the Chibchas, Chimu, Cañari, Puruha, Palta, Zarga, Yunca, Quitu, Huancavilcas, Purvas, Cara. Some of these, such as the Otavalos in the highlands, the Colorados on the coast, and the Jívaros in the Oriente, have preserved their customs and way of life to this day. The others, such as the Caras, who had conquered Quitus before them, were in turn conquered by the superior forces of the Incas, who extended their empire as far as Colombia. The kingdom of Quitu became the northern capital of the Inca empire and later, during the Spanish colonization, a renowned center of art and culture in the New World.

Early in the nineteenth century Ecuador was a center of liberal political activity and one of the first countries to revolt against Spain on August 10, 1809. It won its independence when Antonio José de Sucre defeated the Spanish forces at the Battle of Pichincha in 1822. After eight years as part of the Republic of Gran Colombia under President Simón Bolívar, it withdrew to become the sovereign independent Republic of Ecuador, in 1830. Today, it has a republican form of government similar to the United States. Its president and vice-president are elected for four years and cannot be re-elected until another four-year term has expired. Voting is compulsory for men over 18 years of age and optional for women. The most prevalent religion is Roman Catholic, but there are Evangelist and Baptist churches, Witness of Jehovah temples and Jewish synagogues as well.

AGRICULTURE. Although less than five percent of the land is cultivated, agriculture ranks as one of the leading industries in Ecuador. Chief crops grown in the coastal lowlands for export are bananas (Ecuador's second leading export), cacao, rice, sugar cane, and coffee. Wheat, vegetables, corn, and barley are raised for local consumption along the coast and in the Andes highlands.

Forests play an important part in Ecuador's economy, with that country growing more balsa than any other. Valuable trees include the ivory palm, silk cotton tree, and the rubber tree.

INDUSTRY. Few factories are in operation in Ecuador, the main products manufactured being cotton goods, shoes, drugs, chemicals, flour, soap, nails, and liquors. Oil has recently been discovered in the Amazon region and petroleum is now Ecuador's main export.

CITIES. Several large cities and many small towns fill Ecuador. Of chief visitor interest are Guayaquil, the country's largest city; Quito, the capital; and Cuenca, the leading export city.

AMBATO, the "Garden City" of Ecuador, is a city of about 55,000 population in the center of a rich agricultural valley surrounded by mountains. Few travelers to Ecuador ever see this charming city of lovely homes, beautiful gardens and orchards, about 8,000 feet above sea level, unless they make the trip from Quito by road or train. But those who do are usually rewarded by the delightful climate, charming Colonial atmosphere and the colorful Monday market.

Indians from the surrounding countryside come into town to sell their varied fruits and handicrafts. Ambato is also famous as the birthplace of Juan Montalvo, one of Latin America's greatest writers, whose memory is enshrined with a mausoleum, museum and library in the home in which he lived and worked. The town is known as the starting point for fortune hunters seeking the lost treasures of the Incas which, according to maps that keep cropping up now and then, may be hidden in the vicinity.

One of the most popular excursions is the trip by bus or train to the resort town of **Baños,** about 30 miles from Ambato. Its mineral springs and thermal baths attract many tourists and vacationists from Ambato and Quito. The mountain scenery here and at **Pelileo,** on the way, is spectacular. A short walk from Baños are the falls of the **Cascada Inés María,** which were formed by a volcanic eruption from Tungurahua. **Topo,** a tiny settlement about 20 miles by bus from Baños, is another interesting side tour with some remarkable mountain scenery, waterfalls, turbulent rivers, and tropical vegetation to be seen on the way. Beyond it is the jungle wilderness of the Oriente section. To travel on from here to Mera and Puyo, in the dense valley of the Rio Pastaza, special permission from the Ministry of Defense is required.

BABAHOYO, a tiny town on the river of the same name, about 117 miles from Guayaquil, can be reached from that seaport by road and on an overnight boat from Guayaquil. It is the center of a rich cacao and fruit region.

One of the best ways to see the country is to fly between Guayaquil and Quito one way and make the return trip by train. Whether you go from Guayaquil to Quito, or vice versa, you will have one of the most impressive train rides over some of the most amazing topography in the world. The trip takes about 12 hours in air-conditioned trains that go from lofty snow-covered Andean peaks to the tropical lowlands and through great valleys and savannas and wind-swept plateaus. Starting at Guayaquil, the train departs from **Durán,** a short ferry ride across the Guayas, the coastal terminal of the railroad. It travels across the flat tropical lowlands, crisscrossed here and there by an intricate network of inland waterways. This is the fertile **Guayas Valley,** where the big sugar and rice plantations are located.

At **Bucay,** about 900 feet above sea level, the train takes on a more powerful engine to begin the slow steep climb up the **Andes.** Shortly after leaving **Huigra,** it creeps along a narrow ledge hugging the mountains and canyons and climbs the famous **Nariz del Diablo** (Devil's Nose) by a series of switchbacks up the steep, almost perpendicular side of the mountain. The train then zigzags along over bridges, tunnels and across deep chasms and gorges, climbing from an altitude of 4,800 feet at Huigra to almost 11,000 feet, about 100 miles farther on. This is bleak, desolate *páramo* country where nothing grows except stiff clumps of wild grass and cactus. Snow-capped peaks of Chimborazo (20,577 feet), Carihuairazo (16,496 feet), Altar (17,728 feet) and Tungurahua (16,685 feet) are seen in this region that is known as the **Avenue of Volcanoes.**

North of **Riobamba,** center of a rich agricultural region of rolling farmlands and giant eucalyptus trees, the train climbs to the highest point on the railroad, **Urbina Pass** (11,841 feet), and crosses the second range of Andes before coming to **Ambato.** En route it passes near the Ecuadorian–U.S. satellite-tracking station and over the topmost ridges of the Andean cordillera. Tiny villages of mud houses and straw-thatched roofs pass in review outside the train's window, and here and there an occasional shepherd leads his herds across the meadows. Their bright red ponchos contrast vividly with the luxuriant green countryside. From the frigid heights the train soon passes into a more temperate climate and the balmy air is fragrant with the smell of the fertile soil. Every half-hour or so the train stops at a station, giving the traveler an opportunity to view the countryside and the unusual vegetation. Train hawkers line the stations with all kinds of fruit, from pineapples and papayas to granadillas and naranjillas. From there it goes over barren, rugged country to the growing industrial city of **Latacunga** and the nearby volcanoes of **Cotopaxi** (19,339 feet—probably the highest active volcano in the world), **Illiniza** (17,400 feet), **Quilindaña** (16,134 feet) and **Quilotoa** (13,057 feet) before descending into **Quito.**

CUENCA, in a mountain-ringed flowery plain 8,000 feet above sea level, is one of Ecuador's most interesting cities which to this day proudly preserves its old-world atmosphere and tradition. Known as the "Straw Hat Capital of America," this third largest city in Ecuador has a population of more than 60,000. While the making of straw hats is still the city's principal industry, accounting for more than 50 percent of the country's output, the city's intellectual and cultural attractions have made it the "Athens of Ecuador." This has been the birthplace of many of the country's literary luminaries, eminent lawyers and brilliant diplomats and statesmen. Its university has a rich academic tradition and is one of the most progressive in the country. Its many churches are Colonial art treasures second only to those of Quito, and remnants of an even older civilization are seen in the old cathedral whose stone lintel was taken from an Inca palace. The "new" **Gothic cathedral,** which was begun over 80 years ago and is still under construction, will be one of the largest in the hemisphere when completed—although no Cuencano will hazard a guess as to when that will be.

A city which seems to bask in its golden past, its quaint Colonial atmosphere is enriched by the soft marble used in many of the buildings and the inscribed murals on patio walls of some of the older structures. Among its many traditions is the procession of the **paseo del niño,** when the town's children parade in their colorful costumes.

Cuenca was founded in 1557 by Gil Ramirez Dávalos on the ruins of Tomebamba, an Inca city which has been the birthplace of the Inca Huayna Capac. The weather is usually warm and sunny throughout the year, although the nights are often chilly and require warmer clothing. Its principal local holiday is November 3, when Cuenca celebrates its independence.

The heart of the town is **Plaza Calderón,** named for the young Cuencano who gave his life in the fight for independence. Facing it is the arcaded Colonial building which was the seat of the Royal Audience and was later visited by Bolívar, Sucre and other heroes of the independence. Also on this plaza is the impressive marble building of the **University of Cuenca.** Outstanding examples of the Colonial art which flourished during the seventeenth and eighteenth centuries are the **Church of La Concepción,** whose convent dates from 1599, and the **Church of Las Carmelitas,** built in 1682. Other churches worth visiting for their art treasures are **San Blas, San Francisco, Santo Cenaculo,** and **Santo Domingo.** In the **municipal museum** is an interesting archaeological collection of the pre-Inca Cañari civilization. The ruins of **Tomebamba** also can be visited. The silversmiths and cabinetmakers are noted for their fine craftsmanship.

Side trips to the various parts of this fertile valley can be made by car and bus. **Paute** and **Gualaceo** are noted for their semitropical fruits and markets, and as gateways to the primitive **Oriente region.** The trip into the Oriente is not recommended unless you wish to rough it. It takes about three days by muleback to Méndez, a Salesian mission settlement in Jívaro country. Four days from here is Macas, on the Upano

River, and five days further is the tiny village of Arapicos. The Jívaros, one of the primitive tribes of this region of eastern Ecuador, are hunters who use poisoned darts and arrows and shrink the heads of their enemies. They are generally considered friendly and hospitable and will not attack strangers unless provoked.

Azogues, about 19 miles from Cuenca, is known for its fine straw hats and Friday market. **Biblián** has a Friday market and shrines to the Virgin of El Rocio (dew) and the Sacred Heart of Jesus, which are worshiped by the Indians with pilgrimages. **Cañar,** about 60 miles from Cuenca, is a typically Indian community which once belonged to the powerful and intelligent Cañari tribe. Near here are the ruins of **Incapirca,** a castle built by the last Inca, Huayna Capac, in the fifteenth century, of which the only remains are a large stadium-like oval showing the excellent stonework construction of the Incas.

ESMERALDAS is a major seaport on the northern coast in the heart of a rich tropical region and is a principal outlet for petroleum, bananas, rice, rubber, tobacco and cacao. While somewhat off the tourist trail, although it can be reached by ship, plane or railroad from the principal cities, it has become more popular with travelers since the completion of the Quito-Esmeraldas highway. This was where a group of Spanish explorers under the command of Bartolomé Ruiz first landed on the coast of Ecuador in 1526. The gold and emeralds taken from the Indian city of Atacames, which is still in existence, brought Pizarro down that same year and gave the region the name of Esmeraldas (Land of Emeralds). However, very little gold and no emeralds at all have been found there since then. Two islands, **La Tola** and **La Tolita,** are the site of numerous burial mounds (*tolas*) where remnants of ancient Indian civilizations, gold artifacts, molded figurines and stone axes have been discovered. Swimming and canoe trips up the **Esmeraldas River** through lush, virgin forests are popular.

GUAYAQUIL, at the foot of Santa Ana Hill, sprawls lazily along the left bank of the muddy river Guayas about 35 miles from the Gulf of Guayaquil. But despite its indolent tropical appearance, this is Ecuador's largest city and chief seaport, a busy metropolis of more than 740,000 people.

The city one sees today is relatively new and modern, having been largely rebuilt in recent years, after being twice destroyed by Indians, pillaged and burned by pirates, demolished by earthquakes and burned to the ground on five separate occasions. The old bamboo and wooden houses so characteristic of the old city have given way to new concrete buildings, anywhere from four to ten stories high, and pleasant flower-filled parks and gardens. Its wide avenues, palm-fringed plazas, sidewalk cafés and portal-shaded walks give the city a modern, casual atmosphere.

Travelers are usually fascinated by the ebb and flow of traffic along its waterfront as the exotic cargoes of the tropical lowlands and jungles nearby are floated down the river in canoes, rafts, and dugouts and loaded on ocean-going steamers. The sweet fragrance of chocolate permeates the air of the city as cacao beans are strewn over street pavements to dry and be thrashed about by barefoot workers. And no traveler who visits Guayaquil ever comes away without first browsing around the open-front shops and bazaars for some fine bargains in hardwood salad bowls, Panama hats and tortoise-shell articles. The varied flora of the country may be seen in the luxuriant botanical garden.

Guayaquil's gloried past is recalled in the many monuments scattered throughout the city to all the liberators who spent considerable time here helping this country and the rest of South America attain its independence. The conquistadors, too, are well represented in stone and marble, as are the nation's distinguished men of letters. But one monument that has become a unique tourist attraction is that of Lord Byron, which was sent here in error and stayed because the city fathers could not afford the cost of returning it.

Although it is believed that Sebastián de Benalcázar, one of Pizarro's lieutenants, first established a settlement on what is now Guayaquil, the present city was founded in 1537 by Francisco de Orellana after several unsuccessful attempts. It was named Santiago de Guayaquil in honor of both the saint on whose day it was founded and the Indian chieftain Guayas and his wife Quil, who according to legend committed suicide when the conquistadors invaded their country. Their statue now stands at the southern end of the Malecón. Since its founding the city has survived attacks by Indians and pirates, several earthquakes, fires and plagues. The revolt of the people of Guayaquil, in 1820, marked the beginning of the independence movement in Ecuador. It was here that the famous meeting between the two liberators Simón Bolívar and José de San Martín took place in 1822. Shortly after that, San Martín retired to private life and Bolívar continued as supreme commander.

The city has its own university, a national conservatory of music, an Ecuadorean fine arts association, an institute of historical research, several libraries, and a municipal museum which has an interesting archaeological collection.

The best place to start on a tour of the city is at the **City Clock Tower,** at the southern end of the Malecón bordering the Guayas. Across the Malecón are the **governor's palace** and the **city hall.** Inside the central arcade of the city hall is a carved wooden totem pole called **"Palo de Brujo"** (sorcerer's pole), an unusual archaeological relic of an ancient coastal civilization that inhabited this area. The **Guayaquil Yacht Club** is a few blocks farther on this busy waterfront promenade. Nearby is the **Quito-Guayaquil** railroad station. A little farther on is **La Rotonda,** the city's most historic landmark, which faces the Ninth of October Avenue. Its semicircular colonnade forms an impressive background for the statues of Bolívar and San Martín clasping hands on the spot where their historic meeting took place. The equestrian statue of **Bolívar** graces **Parque Semmario.** Across the way from the customs house, at the northern end of the Malecón, is the **Plaza Colón** and a statue of Francisco de Orellana, which honors his memory and the site of the city's founding. Here at the foot of Santa Ana Hill is the ancient fort of **La Planchada,** which for many years defended the city against Drake and other famous pirates of the day. The **Church of Santo Domingo,** Guayaquil's oldest, founded in 1640, is just a short walk from Plaza Colón. Along the Guayas around the base of the hill is the charming old residential section of **Las Peñas,** whose houses show the influence of Venice in their architecture. Here also is the national brewery, which makes one of the finest beers in South America. An excellent view of the city may be had from the hill, where on a clear day you can see the snow-capped peak of Chimborazo. The heart of the city is **Parque Centenario,** whose monument was erected on October 9, 1920, to commemorate the 100th anniversary of the city's independence. This tall monument to the heroes of the independence, which is crowned by a statue of liberty, was the last masterpiece of the Spanish sculptor Agustin Querol. Also of unusual interest is the **cemetery,** an imposing necropolis of elaborate mausoleums, and row upon row of crypts, in a beautiful setting of formal gardens and royal palms.

A short excursion outside the city limits will take you to the thickly forested tropical lowlands of the country, with its banana and sugar-cane plantations, balsa-wood mills, cattle ranches and orange groves. The salt deposits at the extreme end of **Santa Elena Peninsula** are also interesting to see. **San Vicente,** about a half-hour's drive from Salinas, is a small resort known for its hot sulphur springs, frequented by people suffering from rheumatic ailments. There is also a full day's trip on the **Daule River** by regular steamer or chartered boat, where you can enjoy a picnic on a local hacienda.

The rivers around Guayaquil offer several short trips to nearby towns and glimpses of magnificent scenery and native life. There are also several beach resorts nearby: **Playas, Salinas,** and **Punta Carnero.**

IBARRA, another typical mountain town, and the northern terminal of the railroad, is best known for its fine wood-carving industry and silversmiths. Not far from town, at **Caranqui,** are Inca ruins believed to have been the birthplace of the last Inca emperor, Atahualpa and his mother, the Princess Paccha. Near here also is the **Laguna Yaguarcocha** ("Lake of Blood") where the Incas tossed the bodies of the brave Caras warriors who preferred to be slaughtered to the last man rather than surrender. **Cotacachi** is the site of the hot springs of Tuctara, Yanayacu and Ambi. Also near here are the 150-foot falls of **Peguche.**

JIPIJAPA, about 22 miles from Manta, was once the most important hat-making center in Ecuador, and, consequently, straw hats are still called Jipijapas in most Spanish-speaking countries. Today, this town is the country's largest coffee producer.

LOJA, a subtropical town at the confluence of the Zamora and Malacatos rivers, is moderately warm and humid all year round despite its 7,000-foot altitude. The rivers empty into the Amazon, and one of the great roads of the Incas which joined Cuzco and Quito can be seen in the rolling hills around the town. Its university is famous for its faculty of law. This is the center of the quinine industry; quinine is produced from the bark of the cinchona tree cultivated in the vicinity. It is also the site of a pilgrimage to the Virgin of the Swan on November 18. The Oriente section not far from here was once important gold-panning country and the site of the rich city of Sevilla de Oro, which was founded by the Spaniards but has vanished mysteriously. There is a Franciscan mission in Zamora.

MANTA is a busy seaport on the Pacific Ocean which is primarily noted for its exports of cacao, tagua, coffee, and toquilla straw hats from the nearby towns of Montecristi and Jipijapa, where the world-famed "Panama" hats come from. The hats are woven in the morning, when the weather is damp, and a single hat may take anywhere from one week to three months to make, depending on the quality. The finer the weave, the better the hat. Some are so finely woven that they can be passed through a small finger ring. Not on the regular tourist path, Manta has some excellent beaches and deep-sea fishing. Thirty miles north of Manta is the **Bahía de Caráquez,** a seaport known mainly for its beautiful scenery.

MONTECRISTI, a town of about 5,000 population, seven miles from Manta, is best known as the center of the straw-hat industry, which is also its principal tourist attraction. The hat manufacturers enjoy showing travelers how the fine toquilla straw hats are made. **Portoviejo,** about 17 miles east of Montecristi and linked by road with Guayaquil, is another straw-hat center and an old Colonial town dating from 1628. The original city of Portoviejo was founded on the coast in 1535 but moved inland to make it less vulnerable to pirate attacks.

OTAVALO, a cluster of red-roofed adobe buildings and cobblestone streets about 8,000 feet above sea level, is the site of an Indian settlement which predates the Incas. Famous for their fine quality homespun worsteds and woolens, which resemble fine English tweeds, the Otavalos are one of the earliest and most enterprising communities of weavers and traders in South America. Their colorful **Saturday fair,** which begins at daybreak, when the Indians from the nearby communities come into town to trade and sell their woolen fabrics, ponchos, shawls, rugs and blankets, is one of the most famous and oldest on the continent. There is bathing and swimming at **Laguna de San Pablo** in the shadow of several volcanoes, and an impressive view of the surrounding countryside from the 15,000-foot mountain of **Imbabura.**

QUITO is set like a many-faceted jewel of glistening church domes and spires in a picturesque valley of green-terraced slopes and red rooftops, crowned by the slumbering, snow-capped volcano of **Mount Pichincha.** Located almost on the equator at an altitude of more than 9,000 feet, this lofty Andean capital enjoys an ideal temperate climate.

No other city has preserved its air of antiquity and Colonial charm as fully as Quito. A walk through Quito is a pleasant excursion into the past, where life still moves in the quiet tempo of long ago. Its narrow cobblestone streets, picturesque plazas and squat stone houses are in the finest Spanish Colonial tradition. Its 50-odd churches and many monasteries are rich treasure chests of Colonial art and architecture. This city of 500,000 is the political and cultural heart of the country. Its university is one of the oldest institutions of higher learning in South America; it includes an astronomical observatory, a conservatory of music and a school of fine arts. Quito's museums contain outstanding collections of archaeological relics and historical manuscripts and art treasures. But Quito isn't just a city that lives in the past. A building boom has given the city a modern face lifting and broad new avenues, stately private residences, ultra-new office buildings and hotels. The Ecuadorian capital today boasts fine educational facilities, good hospitals and clinics and excellent shopping facilities where you can buy anything from Indian handicrafts to fine Swiss watches and nylon stockings.

Quito is an outstanding city for tourists. Snow-capped volcanoes surrounding the city provide incomparable scenic views; the richly ornamented interiors of its churches are awe-inspiring. The poverty of the Indian population is in striking contrast with its rich residential areas and elegant sophisticated society. It has excellent golf and tennis facilities in its ultramodern country club and Jockey Club. Spectator sports are bullfighting, horse racing and soccer. It is a city which experiences the four seasons each day—spring in the morning, summer at noon, fall in the evening and winter at night—and where days and nights are almost equal in length the year around.

Believed to be the oldest capital in South America, Quito's true age and prehistoric origin are cloaked in mystery. Long before the Spaniards came, this was the capital of the ancient kingdom of the Quitus, which was conquered by the Caras around A.D. 1100. The Incas conquered the Caras in the late fifteenth century, and made Quito their northern capital. The present city was founded by Sebastián de Benalcázar in 1534 on the ruins of the old Inca capital, and called Villa de San Francisco de Quito. At that time it covered an area of about 30 square blocks, which consisted of four parishes, five churches, one butcher shop and 1,000 inhabitants. After a short period under Gonzalo Pizarro, who was appointed governor of Quito, the city became a Colonial art center of considerable note. It was here that the first blow for Ecuadorian independence was struck in 1809 when the president of the Audiencia was jailed by the revolutionists. But the revolt was quickly put down, and it wasn't until 1822, when Antonio José de Sucre won the battle on the slopes of Pichincha, that Ecuador was assured its freedom. Quito became the capital of the new Republic of Ecuador in 1830.

Plaza de la Independencia, in the center of town is the best place to start a tour of the city. An impressive monument honors Quito's revolutionary heroes. Facing it is the **government palace,** a low two-story stone building extending across the entire block with the mountain Pichincha in the background. The **city hall** is across the plaza; under its arcades are many shops and stalls with all kinds of merchandise. Diagonally across is the green-domed cathedral, on whose outside walls are the names of the founders of Quito; inside is the tomb of the liberator Marshal Antonio José de Sucre. Opposite it is the **archbishop's palace.**

One of the great advantages about touring Quito is that practically everything is within walking distance. Just off the plaza on the west corner is the

Central University. A short walk down this street, Garcia Moreno, to the next corner is the **Church of La Compañia.** Its elaborately sculptured baroque façade shows the strong Moorish influence, and is one of the finest of its kind in the hemisphere. Its gold main altar, gold-plated side altars, gilded ceilings and handsomely sculptured wood and stone statues make this one of the most richly decorated churches in South America. Two blocks away is the **Church of San Francisco,** Quito's largest and unquestionably the most important repository of Colonial art treasures in Ecuador. Founded the same year as the city itself by Friar Jodoco Ricke and completed in the seventeenth century, its impressive façade in Italian Renaissance design was made of stone taken from a local Andean quarry. The bell towers on either side are distinctly Spanish. Among its famous art masterpieces are the 12 pillars around the nave with the carved wood statues of the apostles by the renowned Indian sculptor Caspicara, and some fine oil paintings by Miguel de Santiago, one of South America's greatest painters and founder of the famous seventeenth-century Quito School of Art. Here also is a magnificent gold altar, and a replica of Our Lady of El Pilar, whose original is in the cathedral of Saragossa, Spain. The monastery adjoining the church was the first built by this order in South America, and set the style for similar buildings throughout the continent. In its cloisters, around a Spanish fountain and patio, is one of the finest collections of Colonial art. Among the most notable works seen here are the series of oil paintings, depicting the life of St. Francis, by Miguel de Santiago and some of his pupils; his Immaculate Conception and Life of the Virgin Mary, and an Adoration by Rubens. In the library are 12,000 volumes, half of which are bound in old parchment. The monasteries can be visited only by men.

Two blocks west is Calle 24 de Mayo, site of the **Indian market,** which is usually teeming with life and color and native handicrafts from all areas of the country. Following this street south to Calle Flores will bring you to the **Church and Monastery of Santo Domingo** on the plaza of the same name. The church has been rebuilt several times and lost most of its antiquity, but the monastery shows strong Oriental influence in its elaborate wood carvings and has an impressive collection of Colonial and religious art.

The **Calle de la Ronda** nearby is a narrow, winding, cobblestone street, barely wide enough for the smallest of the new cars, and the oldest street in Quito. In the **Monastery of San Agustín,** two blocks from Independence Plaza, is where most of the heroes of the revolution are buried and where Ecuador's Declaration of Independence was signed. A stone trap door leads to a lower chamber where those who led the first rebellion were imprisoned and later massacred.

The **Monastery of La Merced,** near the center of the city, displays the twin of London's Big Ben. The **Church and Monastery of San Diego** have seen little change since they were constructed out of massive chunks of stone three centuries ago, and its original carved doors, ancient hinges and huge locks are still in use. The paintings of the Saints in the Sacristy have been "dressed" in rich fabrics sewed onto the original canvases.

The little **Church of Belén,** on the other side of town, was built between 1546 and 1573.

The **National Museum of Fine Arts** has a rare collection of coins, some fine examples of Ecuadorian paintings and sculptures, and an exhibit of Colonial furniture. The **Museum of Modern Art** in the Casa de la Cultura has on display some excellent contemporary water colors, oils, sculptures and other works of local artists, a unique musical museum and a fine exhibit of hand-woven fabrics by native craftsmen. There is also a valuable collection of paintings and sculptures by local artists in the Museum of Colonial Art.

One of the most popular tours from Quito is the trip to **Panecillo** ("little bread roll") **Hill,** which overlooks

Quito and offers some magnificent views of the city and the surrounding countryside. The Incas worshiped their sun-god atop this hill.

The residential districts of San Diego, Mariscal Sucre and Cristóbal Colón have lovely homes and gardens in varied styles of architecture ranging from the Oriental to the modern. Another scenic must is the drive around the outskirts of the city, with its superb panorama and a spectacular view of **Guápulo** below. The town of Guápulo itself is about 20 minutes by car from Quito, in the fertile valley of Tumbaco in the shadow of the volcano Cayambe. The little church here was the first one in Ecuador and contains a beautiful hand-carved pulpit, a solid silver font, a sixteenth-century statue of Our Lady by Diego de Robles, and several fine paintings by Miguel de Santiago.

The roads leading out from town follow the great **Inca highway,** linking Quito with Cuzco and other Indian settlements in Peru, Chile and Argentina to the south and to northern Ecuador and Colombia, and are now part of the Pan-American Highway system. The one to the north has been paved and broadened to permit tourists to visit the **Equator Monument** at Oyamburo, about 15 miles from town. This impressive granite monument honors the French scientific mission which here, in 1736, located the imaginary line which divides the two hemispheres. One branch leads to **Otavalo, Ibarra,** and **Tulcán** on the Colombian border. The road leading south parallels the railroad and leads to **Latacunga, Ambato, Riobamba, Guayaquil, Cuenca** and other cities.

The **Valley of Los Chillos,** a 20-minute drive southeast of Quito, is a fertile region of rolling hills and farms and great scenic beauty. Of special interest are the old haciendas which date back to Colonial days, the village of Sangolquí and the mineral springs of Tingo María. **Machachi,** mountain resort town an hour's drive from Quito, has excellent picnic facilities, scenic mountain views, and thermal baths and swimming pools. The Guitig mineral water drunk in the fine restaurants and hotels throughout the country is bottled here and the cheese made in the area is delicious. Near the town are burial mounds of an ancient pre-Inca civilization.

RIOBAMBA, a historic old Colonial town, occupies a spectacular setting close to 9,000 feet high in the shadow of several volcanoes. Founded in 1534 on the site of what is now Cajabamba, it was moved to its present location after it was destroyed by a landslide in 1797. The town has several lovely flower-filled parks and plazas, some magnificent views of the active volcano Sangay and the three peaks of Altar, and outstanding examples of Colonial art and architecture. It was here that the conquistadors Almagro, Alvarado and Benalcázar met during the early days of the conquest.

TULCÁN is the most northerly city on the Pan-American Highway, which leads to Colombia about four miles away. The Carchi River, the country's northern frontier, is crossed by the natural bridge of Rumichaca. The grotto of the Virgin of Peace under the bridge contains colorful stalactites and a crudely carved rock statue of Our Lady on a small altar.

THE GALÁPAGOS ISLANDS, an archipelago of 12 large and several hundred smaller volcanic islands occupying a 3,000-square-mile area about 650 miles west of Ecuador, are one of the least explored regions of the world. This is said to be one of the healthiest spots in the world, and may someday become a popular vacation resort. Some of its unique flora and fauna are found nowhere else.

Discovered in 1535 by the Bishop of Panama, Tomás de Berlanga, the islands were named for the giant land tortoises found there. Eventually they became known as the "Enchanted Islands" because of the strange and mysterious way in which ships were attracted and repelled by the tides. For the next 300 years they were visited only by pirates, seeking a hide-out or fresh water and food, and by an occasional whaler. Charles Darwin spent five weeks there in 1835, and out of this living laboratory which he called "a little world within itself" came some of his first theories of evolution which went into his book, *The Origin of Species,* 20 years later. During World War II, the Galápagos were a military air base from which American planes patrolled the Panama Canal and its adjacent defenses.

Besides their Spanish names, most of the islands have English ones given to them by pirates and whalers. The largest is **Albemarle** or Isabela, about 1,600 square miles. Only seven of the islands are populated and only two of them, **San Cristóbal** and **Santa Cruz,** have water. The former, once a penal colony, has the greatest population, 1,500, and is the seat of the local government. It also has electricity, a church, a general store, and a freezing plant where tuna, cod, and lobsters are cleaned, frozen, and shipped to the mainland. Santa Cruz has a population of about 600 English-speaking people. The islands' total population, about 2,000, equals the number of volcanoes.

Its vegetation is exotic and rare, including innumerable varieties of orchids and giant cacti, climbing plants, trees, and many semitropical fruits. On the equator, but also in the path of the cool Humboldt Current, the Galápagos enjoy even, temperate weather throughout the year, with warm sunny days and cool nights.

Its animal life includes many species of birds, penguins, flightless cormorants, the famous land tortoises, sea lions, seals, and land and marine iguanas.

Most remarkable is the way in which nature reverses itself here, with such wildlife as birds and reptiles being absolutely tame, while dogs, pigs, goats, horses, and cattle left on the islands become so wild and vicious that they must be hunted. The fishing is said to be among the best in the world, and commercial fishing fleets operate off these waters which teem with tuna, grouper, blackfish, devilfish, lobster, manta ray and shark. The Ecuadorian government has plans to make the Galápagos a health and vacation resort. These islands can be reached by cruise ship from Guayaquil.

SPORTS AND RECREATION. Spectator sports are popular in Ecuador, especially from May to December (the soccer, baseball, and basketball season). Soccer is played at night in Capwell and Modelo stadiums in Guayaquil. From November to January professional soccer teams from other South American countries come to play exhibition games against local teams. The "Chaza," a popular game similar to squash, is played in Quito and other mountain towns with a ball and wooden racket.

Excellent beaches can be found throughout the country. Near Guayaquil are the beach resorts of **Playas, Posarja,** and **Salinas.** Playas, about an hour's drive on a well-paved road, is noted for its excellent deep-sea fishing, fine surf-bathing and sailing. Duck and deer are numerous in the area. Posarja, southeast of Playas and near the island of Puna, is also a popular beach resort. Salinas, about 100 miles from Guayaquil, is Ecuador's largest and best seaside resort. On a beautiful crescent-shaped beach, it boasts the best deep-sea fishing and bathing facilities in the country. Here is the best fishing for black marlin, swordfish, and sailfish off the coast of Ecuador from April to December. A popular pastime with tourists and vacationists here is the collecting of rare seashells which are washed ashore.

SPECIAL EVENTS. All religious feast days and festivals are observed in this traditionally Catholic country. Especially noteworthy are the **Holy Week** observances.

March is the beginning of the **National Symphony's concert season.** Other important dates include April 13, **Juan Montalvo's birthday;** May 1, **Labor Day;** May 24, **Anniversary of the Battle of Pichincha;** June 5, **Corpus Christi;** June 29, **S.S. Peter and Paul** (festivals, processions, and bullfights in many towns); July 24, **birthday of Simón Bolívar;** August 8, **Festival of Guápulo,** in Quito; August 10, **Ecuador's Independence Day** and opening day of congress; August 15, **San Jacinto de Yaguachi;** September 23, 24, **Virgin of Las Mercedes,** in Quito; October 12 is **Columbus Day** and **Day of the Montuvio** (when the native races of the country are honored); November 21, **Feast Day of the Virgin of El Quinche,** in El Quinche; December 6, **Anniversary of Founding of Quito** (one week prior to this is the beginning of the formal bullfight season); December 28, **Día de los Inocentes** (Fool's Day), similar to April Fool's Day and lasting until January 6.

DINING AND SHOPPING. Ecuadorian cuisine is usually well-spiced and fairly exotic but a gourmet's delight. While the dishes vary in their content and preparation in the different regions of the country, *choclo,* the large Indian green corn, is used frequently with most dishes. So also is rice, another staple of this country. One of the most typical dishes is *locro,* a soup made with corn, potatoes and cheese. *Llapingachos* are another Ecuadorian specialty, prepared as an omelet with fried potatoes, cheese and an egg on top. Other popular items found both on the coast and in the highlands are *humitas,* corn tamales wrapped in green corn leaves; and *empanadas,* meat pies with rice, cheese and onions added.

The coastal cities are known for their rich variety of seafood, which comes from the abundant waters of the Gulf of Guayaquil and the Pacific Ocean. The *langostino* or *camarón,* a large sweet shrimp, is frequently served as an appetizer. The *ceviche de corvina,* a marinated white fish, is also popular.

Ecuador is also noted for its many tropical and semitropical fruits, of which papayas, mangoes, chirimoyas (custard apples), mamey, avocados, naranjillas, and bananas are only a few. Since this is the biggest banana-exporting country in the world, this fruit occupies a prominent place on most menus and dishes. The *naranjilla,* which can best be described as a cross between a tomato and a tangerine, makes one of the best-tasting non-alcoholic refreshments in Ecuador. The chocolate, which is also produced here, is especially rich and flavorsome. Travelers will also find such intoxicating Indian beverages as *pisco, chicha, aguardiente,* and *mayorca,* a hard liquor distilled from sugar cane and flavored with anise; one of the finest beers in the continent in Guayaquil; and a mineral water, Guitig, is not only refreshing but is said to be good for the liver.

The best buys are in Indian handicrafts, antiques and art objects, which make shopping a richly rewarding experience. Here, the visitor will find a wide assortment of hand-woven, hand-carved and hand-painted articles made by expert local craftsmen and artists. Among them are fine hand-woven rugs in modern, Incan, and pre-Incan designs, as well as ponchos, blankets, shawls, and scarves.

The homespun worsteds made by the Indians of Otavalo compare with the finest quality woolen fabrics to be found anywhere, and actually look very much like the tweeds made in England and Scotland.

Here visitors can purchase the most delicately woven toquilla straw hats, which are mistakenly called "Panama" hats, although they are made here; and a wide variety of straw articles.

The many shops and bazaars in the big cities have irresistible bargains in guayacán wood salad bowls, balsa- and orange-wood hand-carved dolls in native dress, alligator handbags and wallets, modern paintings and Indian miniatures, and all kinds of souvenirs made out of tagua nut (vegetable ivory). But the tourist will do just as well shopping around the native fairs and Indian markets in the towns and villages.

Peru

Peru, once the center of the great Inca Empire and later Spain's most impor-

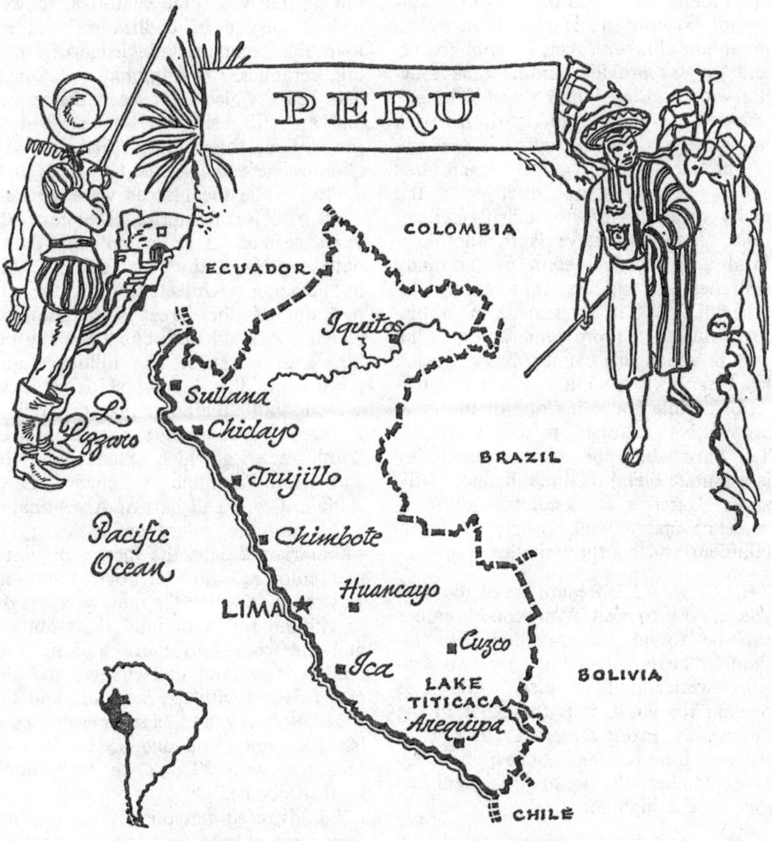

tant viceroyalty in South America, combines the irresistible allure of its ancient civilizations, rich Colonial heritage, modern sophistication and scenic grandeur to captivate the visitor.

THE LAND. Bounded on the north by Ecuador and Colombia, on the east by Brazil and Bolivia, on the south by Chile, and on the west by the Pacific Ocean, this third largest country in South America occupies an area of one-half million square miles—about the size of three Californias—of the most diverse land on the continent.

Geographically, Peru can be roughly divided into three distinct and principal areas: the long, narrow ribbon of rainless desert along the coast; the high plateaus and lofty mountains of the Andes running the length of the country's central section, where more than half of its 13.6 million population and most of its mineral wealth is located; and the largely undeveloped and unsettled tropical rain forests and jungles in the interior, comprising more than 60 percent of the land.

Gifted with such a diversity of topographic extremes, this country offers the tourist a variety of compelling natural attractions and a year-round vacation land. Its 1,400-mile coastline is dotted with many fine beaches and seaside resorts, and stretches of the blue Pacific Ocean just offshore offer sportsmen some of the finest deep-sea fishing in the world. Its majestic snow-covered peaks are a scenic delight to the growing number of vacationists and a challenge to mountain climbers. And its wild forests and jungles provide venturesome tourists with exciting hunting and fishing.

No other country in South America has more to offer the tourist in the way of archaeological wonders than this country which is still discovering the many mysteries of its ancient civilizations. Also impressive is the architectural and artistic wealth of its many churches and palaces, representing another period of its long and colorful history. But even more remarkable is the way in which this country has managed to preserve its ancient customs and traditions while becoming one of the most progressive nations on the continent. The Peru which the traveler sees today is a unique blend of three distinct civilizations, offering every comfort and convenience and a wide variety of entertainment and sports activities.

THE CLIMATE. Regardless of the time you choose to visit Peru, good weather can be found for traveling. For although the country has only two seasons, winter and summer, while it is one on the coast, it is the other in the mountains. From December to May is the best time for the beaches; and May to September, the weather is ideal for touring the highlands.

THE PEOPLE. The people of Peru are basically conservative, courteous and formal. About 45 percent of the population is Indian. The official language is Spanish, but English is spoken widely in most of the key cities and resort areas. Quechua, the ancient tongue of the Incas, is also spoken in the highland communities by more than three million people.

There is little information about the origin of the earliest inhabitants of what is now Peru, but there seems to be general agreement that the Chavin civilization appeared on the continent in the coastal area between Piura and Pisco somewhere between the third and the seventh centuries. The emergence of the Nasca-Paracas culture in the south and the Chimu-Mochica in the north, during the next three centuries, showed a high degree of civilization and remarkable technical knowledge of building, ceramics, weaving, and metallurgy. The relics which have been discovered and are still being unearthed attest to the skill of these ancient artisans. The Chimus were master potters and goldsmiths, while the Nascas were weavers of rich, colorful fabrics. The next 400 years seemed to be completely dominated by the Tiahuanaco culture, with its amazing architecture, and the expansion of the great Inca Empire, which flourished until conquered by the Spaniards in 1533. The influence and power of the sun-worshiping Incas spread until their empire covered a 2,500-mile area along the west coast of South America which extended all the way from Colombia to Ecuador, Peru, Bolivia, Chile, and part of Argentina.

As absolute rulers of a theocratic, totalitarian society, the Incas conquered and colonized this territory. Everyone was made to work; the men were taught to till the soil and build their houses, and the women to spin and knit. The land was worked collectively, and the crops shared with the Sun God and the state. Robbery and slander were punished severely, and one of the favorite greetings was: "Don't be lazy, don't steal, don't lie."

So advanced was this civilization that they were able to farm on steep mountainsides, use *guano* (sea-bird droppings) for fertilizer, devise intricate systems of irrigation, and control soil erosion. But most amazing is their artful and ingenious use of stone in construction.

For more than 300 years, 14 Incas ruled Peru with a marvelous system of organization and wise laws. Their civilization was all the more remarkable when one realizes that the Incas had no form of writing and no knowledge of the wheel. Yet they built great highways to link the four corners of their empire, and invented a decimal counting system based on sets of knotted cords. They also devised solar and moon calendars.

Their strong and centralized system

ironically was their one weak link and led to their eventual conquest. When Francisco Pizarro landed at Tumbes in 1532, the Incas had just ended a long and bloody civil war. Atahualpa had just wrested control of the empire from his half brother, Huascar, the legitimate Inca, and was busy consolidating his gains. Greatly outnumbered by the Inca legions, Pizarro and less than 200 men tricked the Inca into an ambush at Cajamarca and later killed him. Marching on to Cuzco, they were hailed as heroes and avengers until they sacked and plundered the city, which was too far inland to serve the sea-going Spaniards.

Following Pizarro's assassination in 1541 came a period of bloody revolts and dissensions between the Indians and their Spanish masters. The relatively peaceful era which ensued for the next 100 years ended when the discontented Indians were led into an abortive revolt by Tupac Amaru II in 1780. Another uprising among the Indians, this time with the support of the colonists, who resented the high taxes, restrictions of trade, and their inferior role to the Spanish rulers, followed in 1814.

In 1820, help came from the liberator José de San Martín, who, with the aid of the Chilean fleet under the command of Lord Cochrane, landed in southern Peru. He proclaimed the country's independence in Lima less than a year later, on July 28, 1821. In 1824, Bolívar and Sucre defeated the last remnants of the Royalist troops at the Battle of Junín and the Battle of Ayacucho; but it wasn't until two years later, when the Spanish capitulated in Callao, that the country was completely liberated.

Today, Peru is a constitutional republic headed by a president who is elected every six years. The country is divided into 23 departments which are subdivided into 140 provinces. The departments are represented in Congress by senators and the provinces by deputies.

AGRICULTURE. Farming, especially on the coast, is one of Peru's most important industries, and employs 60 out of every 100 Peruvians. The country's chief exports, sugar and cotton, are agricultural products, while other crops grown include rice, fruit, vegetables, tobacco, cocoa, and barbasco (a vine with poisonous roots which is used in insecticides). Although the most productive farms are on the coast, mountain farms grow corn, broad beans, barley, wheat, potatoes, and tomatoes.

Mining provides almost half of Peru's exports. The work is done so high in the mountains that Indians must be employed who are used to the high altitudes.

INDUSTRY. Only 16 of every 100 Peruvians work in industry, which is limited by lack of trained technicians, adequate transportation, and electric power. The fishing industry is paramount to the economy, with fishmeal being the major product. Forestry is also important.

CITIES. Although the majority of Peruvians live in small towns and villages, there are a number of cities with a population of 20,000 or more. Most of these are along the coast, or away from the mountains, where fear of earthquakes keeps buildings low and spread out.

AREQUIPA, in a beautiful fertile valley at the foot of the snow-topped volcano El Misti, is Peru's third largest city. Its pinkish-white buildings, which have made it known as the "White City," were constructed from *sillar,* the solidified lava of nearby volcanoes. Its spectacular setting, 7,500 feet above sea level, sunny, invigorating, dry climate, tree-fringed boulevards, flower-filled gardens and patios, and quaint Colonial atmosphere make it one of the country's most popular vacation stopovers for travelers to the land of the Incas. Indian runners (*chasquis*) who toted fresh fish from the coast to the Inca's table in Cuzco and stopped here to rest gave the city its name. For in Quechua *Ari quepay* means "here, rest." Heeding this ancient advice, today's travelers come here to take it easy and get away from it all, and about 200,000 people live here permanently.

For the sightseer, a tour of the twin-towered cathedral and **Church of La Compañia,** with its beautifully carved façade, the flower-filled **Plaza de Armas** around which the city was planned, and the many lovely homes and gardens in the suburb of **Tingo** is recommended. For swimming, there is the popular mountain resort and hot springs of **Jesús,** on the slopes of **Picchu-Picchu,** about a half hour's drive by car. On the slopes of **Chachani,** about an hour and a half by car, are the thermal baths of **Yura** and **Socosani,** and the ruins of **Churajon.**

The bustling market is the place to go for some excellent bargains in Indian ceramics, vicuña and alpaca rugs, and a wide assortment of silver handicrafts at very low prices.

AYACUCHO, site of the famous battle which ended Spanish dominance in Peru, is a historic old Colonial city about 9,000 feet above sea level and 160 miles from Huancayo. Churches and the cathedral are rich in Colonial art and baroque architecture. This is a good place to buy Indian handicrafts and ceramics, of which the most popular is the little replica of the twin-towered cathedral.

CAJAMARCA, now an important mining town north of Trujillo and inland about 9,000 feet up the mountains, is where Pizarro captured the Inca Atahualpa and held him for ransom. The room which the Inca promised to fill with precious metals to as high as he could reach is shown to visitors, but the red line on the wall was a later addition. Also see the thermal springs where the Inca bathed.

CALLAO, a finger of land jutting out over the Pacific, is the country's chief seaport and maritime gateway to Lima. It boasts one of the best-equipped harbors on the west coast of South America, a submarine and naval station and a variety of industries ranging from flour mills and breweries to lumber mills and iron foundries. It was from here that the treasures of Peru were shipped back to Spain. Raided by pirates and destroyed by an earthquake in 1746, it was the last stronghold of the Spanish in South America, who held out in the Reál Felipe fortress for two years until they capitulated in 1826. The historic pentagonal fort is now a military base and has an interesting war museum.

The sea bird which furnishes Peru with a natural fertilizer, guano, and constitutes one of the country's principal industries, can be seen by visiting either of two islands a short distance offshore from Callao.

CUZCO, a "sacred city" of adobe houses and red-tiled rooftops in a peaceful green valley 11,400 feet above sea level, is the archaeological capital of South America and one of the continent's most outstanding tourist attractions. This is a city which has seen the birth and death of an empire and where time seems to have stood still. Poncho-clad Indians still lead their llama herds over narrow cobblestone streets, and hold their open market in the city squares. Every street has a story or a legend; and the engineering skill and craftsmanship of these ancient artisans is seen in the perfectly matched stone walls of homes and temples.

For Cuzco was the center of the Inca Empire, with four great highways leading from here to its four provinces, and its name appropriately means "navel" in the ancient Quechua tongue, still widely spoken here. According to one legend, and there are several as to the origin of Cuzco, it was here that around A.D. 1100 the children of the Sun, Manco Capac and his sister-wife Mama Ocllo, sank a golden staff into the ground and watched it disappear. This was the sign of fertility foretold by their Sun-God, and here they built their temple to him. Manco Capac, the first Inca, then went north and his wife went south to unite the various tribes and form their empire. The **Plaza de Armas** in the center of town was the sacred square of the Incas. Known as Huacay Pata (Weeping Lane), it was where the

Inca held court and reigned over gay festivals and colorful ceremonies. This was also where the conquistadors conducted their executions. Diego Almagro was garroted here following his defeat by the forces of his former partner, Francisco Pizarro.

Cuzco was one of the most populous cities on the continent and about twice as large as it is today. At the time of the conquest, as the treasure-trove of the empire, it received all the wealth from the four corners of the realm, which poured into its sacred temples and palaces. But shortly thereafter, the Spaniards had plundered the gold and silver treasures and destroyed most of the city to build their own churches, monasteries and houses. The Cuzco one sees today dates back to 1650 when an earthquake almost wiped out the city. The churches and monasteries of Cuzco are museums of Colonial art and architecture and everywhere one sees doorways and walls from the time of the Incas. The **Church and Convent of Santo Domingo** were built on the site of the most sacred Inca structure in Cuzco, the Temple of the Sun. The Inca walls of the ancient temple are in bizarre contrast with the two-story cloisters of the Catholic convent. Cuzco was also an art center of considerable renown during the seventeenth and eighteenth centuries when the Cuzqueño school of painting flourished. Today it is again a cultural center and the site of the **University of Cuzco,** a liberal and progressive institution of higher learning.

For visitors not accustomed to the high altitude, touring by car is suggested. Starting from the **Plaza Mayor,** the cathedral, a somber twin-towered structure, was one of the first buildings constructed by the Spaniards in 1560. It was built completely from granite taken out of Inca structures and was reconstructed in 1668, following its destruction during an earthquake. Among its priceless possessions are a beautifully carved wooden choir and pulpit, and a main altar richly ornamented with silver. In addition to some fine oils, one said to be an original Van Dyck, it has a gold monstrance encrusted with every known jewel and precious stone.

To the left of the cathedral is the **Church of Jesus and Mary** with an unusual façade and an altar of hammered silver. On the right of the cathedral is the **Church of the Triumph,** which was erected by Hernando Pizarro and his two brothers to commemorate their victory over Manco Inca in 1536. Excellent examples of Cuzqueño art are inside **La Compañia,** the Jesuit church at right angles to the cathedral on the plaza, one of the finest examples of Colonial architecture in the New World. Its interior is richly ornamented and there are many beautiful paintings by Marcoa Papata and Cipriano Gutierrez.

La Merced, across the street from the tourist hotel, is one of the most original churches in Cuzco. It has a Moorish patio and many indigenous characteristics in the design of the altars. Fine paintings decorate the interior; one is said to be by Rubens. Its library contains some 17,000 volumes and a document with Pizarro's signature. Its solid gold four-foot monstrance weighs 44 pounds and is encrusted with thousands of diamonds, pearls, emeralds and rubies. The mortal remains of Diego Almagro, his son, and Gonzalo Pizarro are believed to be buried in a crypt under the main chapel. Other churches of unusual interest are **San Blas,** with its exquisitely carved pulpit; **San Antonio,** with some fine oil paintings depicting seventeenth-century life in Cuzco; **Santa Clara,** with an altar consisting of hundreds of small mirrors and a wood carving of the siege of Cuzco; **San Pedro,** which was built completely out of stone taken from Inca ruins; **Belén,** with its gold and silver altar; **San Francisco,** with its ancient organ and handsome wood-carved choir; and **Santa Ana,** which contains excellent paintings of the Corpus Christi procession in Cuzco.

The **University of Cuzco** is located near the airport. Of interest also is the **house of Garcilaso de la Vega,** the Inca historian and chronicler who wrote the "Royal Commentaries," the most complete treatment of the Inca civilization, and the **Admiral's House,** a sixteenth-century house in Renaissance style built with Inca stonework.

Not far from town are other remnants of this ancient civilization. Overlooking the city is the fortress of **Sacsahuamán** (pronounced "sexy woman"). Here, giant boulders have been brought from a distance of several miles and arranged strategically in such a way that a handful of men could defend the fort against greater numbers. At **Tampo Machai,** which means place to rest, is another fort, or outpost, where a fountain of water emerges mysteriously out of the stones and is believed to have been flowing continuously for several thousand years. At **Kkenco** (Zigzag), the remnants of a big amphitheater, altar and sacrificial stone built by the Incas still stand. **Puca Pucara** (Red Fortress) is where the Incas built a subterranean passage that led all the way back to Cuzco into the Temple of the Sun.

No excursion to Cuzco would be complete without a side trip to **Machu Picchu,** the lost city of the Incas. Once the secluded haven of the sacred virgins of the sun, this sky-top sanctuary in the valley of the Urubamba is the goal of thousands of tourists.

Yet until 1911, when a young Yale professor, Hiram Bingham, hacked it out of the centuries of vegetation, not a living soul knew where it was. Even the Spanish conquistadors who had gone over the area with a fine-tooth comb in their mad quest for gold had failed to get wind of the hidden citadel, so closely guarded was this secret.

Overlooking a deep gorge, and the turbulent, seething Urubamba River below, is a sight any traveler to these parts will long remember. Massive stones have been artfully carved and ingeniously fitted together, without the aid of mortar, to withstand the ravages of time and the elements. Only a civilization which had attained a culture well in advance of its time could have achieved such baffling perfection. Equally mystifying is how these giant stones could have been carried up to the top of the mountain, for the Incas had not learned the secret of the wheel.

HUANCAYO is a quaint Colonial town and tourist resort especially famous for its **traditional fair,** which was started by the Spanish soldiers over 130 years ago so they could obtain food and supplies from the Indians. This fair takes place on Sunday mornings on the Calle Reál, the city's main street, which was part of one of the main roads built by the Incas to connect Cuzco with Quito. Pizarro marched on this road on his way to Cuzco, as did the liberators Bolívar, Sucre and Arenales when they brought freedom to the inland countries. It is one of the best places to buy handmade alpaca and llama rugs, blankets, and silver jewelry. The **Convent of Ocopa,** near town, has a museum, library and some outstanding murals. **Geophysics Institute,** about nine miles from town, records seismic and cosmic ray observations.

IQUITOS, a bustling city of 76,000, is the last big port on the Amazon River for ocean-going steamers sailing down to the Atlantic. Commercially important since the rubber boom days at the turn of the century, it is an industrial center and shipping gateway for the products of the region. Lately, it is becoming increasingly popular with tourists wishing to sail on the Amazon and visit the nearby jungle areas. Also of unusual interest are the community of Belén, the aquarium and museum and the market. Rainfall here is very heavy, causing the Amazon tide to rise 30 feet.

One of the most interesting and exciting trips in Peru is a ride on the **Central Railway,** which begins at **Callao** and ends at **Huancayo.** This is the highest standard-gauge railroad in the world and an engineering marvel. The brain child of Henry Meiggs, an American engineer from Catskill, New York, the Central Railway climbs 27 feet a minute into the high Andes, and reaches an elevation of 15,806 feet. Its 258 miles of route are interspersed with 40 stations, 55 bridges, 68 tunnels and 22 zigzags or switchbacks. The trip from **Lima** to **Oroya,** a town of chimneys and smelters in the rugged cordillera, takes five hours and follows the Rimac and its tributaries. It passes through a fertile, subtropical region of cotton and sugar plantations and in less than half an hour climbs into the foothills of the Andes. It then follows a tortuous, roller coaster pattern through small Indian villages and towns, over sleepy valleys and around lofty mountains. It goes through Santa Clara, Chosica, San Bartolomo, Surco, Matucana, San Mateo, Chicla, Casapalca, Ticlio, Morococha, Pachachaca and Oroya. Near Ticlio, it reaches its highest point and crosses through the **Galera Tunnel,** 15,693 feet high, before starting its slow descent to Oroya, at 12,225 feet, and on to Llocllapampa, Jauja, Humali, Matahuasi, Concepción, San Geronimo and Huancayo.

One of the highlights of the railroad trip is **Infiernillo** (Little Hell) canyon, where a railroad bridge spans a gorge from the mouth of one tunnel into another. A spur of the railway runs north from Oroya to the mining center of **Cerro de Pasco,** 14,306 feet. Near here, at **Goyllarisquisga,** is the highest coal mine in the world.

JAUJA, about 50 miles south of Oroya, almost became the capital of the country because of its splendid climate. Founded in 1534, it is now a famous health resort.

LAKE TITICACA, the highest navigable body of water in the world, is more than a key tourist attraction, it is a natural phenomenon. From its lofty perch 12,500 feet above sea level, this giant body of water remains a source of mystery and wonder and a challenging adventure for travelers. They say that its crystal-clear water will never freeze or cause steel to rust, and that the immense gold chain which the Incas hid from the Spaniards may be lying in its depths. One of the strangest sights in this remote sky-top lake are the steamers which ply the route between Puno, Peru and Guaqui, on the Bolivian side. Although these ships were built in Scotland and England and sailed to Mollendo under their own steam, they had to be dismantled completely and hauled by mule across the deserts and mountains to the edge of the lake, where they were reassembled again. Today, a cruise on these freight ships is one of the highlights of any tour through the region. The native sailboats are also a popular tourist diversion. For the sportsman, there is excellent trout fishing in Lake Titicaca, where 20-pound rainbows are not unusual, and there is also some fine duck hunting in the area.

LIMA, on a flat, arid plain between the purple foothills of the Andes and the blue Pacific Ocean, is a busy, modern and proud capital of more than 3 million inhabitants (including suburbs) which still preserves its traditional customs.

For more than three centuries, this "City of Kings" was the seat of the viceroyalty and the center of Spanish power in the New World. It was here on the banks of the Rimac River that the Spanish conquistadors erected their first adobe buildings and divided the spoils and the treasures they sent back to Spain. Even before that it had been an Indian settlement.

Its indigenous antecedents are ever present in the hills that surround it and in the dusty remnants of ancient civilizations in and around town. A walk through the old section "below the bridge," with its carved wooden balconies, rococo palaces and romantic promenades, is like stepping into another era of long ago.

One of the most typically Spanish cities in the western hemisphere, Lima is noted for its monumental plazas and historic buildings, its beautiful churches and palatial homes, and its broad, tree-lined boulevards and fashionable residential districts. Its mild climate, traditional old-world atmosphere, Colonial art treasures, modern comforts and conveniences, and courteous, friendly citizens long have made this city a favorite with travelers.

Lima has gradually grown out toward the sea and now covers an area of some 40 square miles. Some of its suburbs, such as **Miraflores,** are veritable cities in themselves, with their own shopping areas, restaurants and nocturnal diversion.

The best place to start a tour of the city is at the historic **Plaza de Armas,** in the heart of downtown Lima. Pizarro's equestrian statue looks out toward this central square. The **government palace** facing the plaza is on the original site where Pizarro built the house that was to serve as his fortress and where he was to meet his end at the hands of his assassins. It was converted into a palace for the viceroys who followed him in ruling this wealthiest, most important of all of Spain's colonies. The present building dates from 1938 and houses many historic mementos of the old conquistador. A fig tree planted by Pizarro in the palace patio still gives fruit.

Turning clockwise, you will see the exquisitely hand-carved wooden balconies of the **archbishop's palace.** Next to it is the twin-towered neo-classic façade of the cathedral, built with stone brought from Panama. The original cornerstone was laid by the founder of Lima, but it has been partly reconstructed several times since. Pizarro's mummified remains can be seen in a glass casket in the small chapel near the entrance. Its walls are covered with inlaid gold mosaics honoring the intrepid "Thirteen Men of Gallo" who conquered Peru. Equally interesting are the silver-covered main altar, the hand-carved wooden statues of the saints, the image of Our Lady donated by Charles V, and some valuable oil paintings.

The old mint, where the golden treasures of the Incas were melted into ingots and stored, has since given way to modern shops and restaurants, which now line Colonial arcades on the northern side of the plaza. But the **city hall,** on the eastern side of the plaza, is on the exact spot where Pizarro placed the old cabildo. The present building, though built in 1945, has a pair of gigantic wooden balconies in keeping with the Colonial architecture around the plaza. Its library includes the original manuscripts of every municipal act since the city was founded.

Just behind the palace is the railroad station, which leads into the highland interior of the country, and the **Rimac River,** with its old Colonial stone bridge separating the old section of Lima. This is where the 200-year-old **Plaza de Acho,** the oldest and most famous bullfight arena on the continent, is located. Nearby is the **Palace of La Perichole,** a pink-hued rococo dream-mansion built by an amorous viceroy, and now a part of Lima's **Museum of the Viceroyalty.** Next to it is the **Alameda de los Descalzos** (barefoot promenade), a lovely garden walk, so called because it led to the Convent of the Barefoot Padres.

Crossing the Rimac to the main section of town, you'll see the baroque façade of the **Church of San Francisco,** founded in 1535 and famous for its gold, jeweled monstrance, vaulted, carved ceiling and painted mosaics in the monastery. Its catacombs were rediscovered in 1951, and the cloisters are adorned with a series of paintings representing the life of St. Francis. Other notable churches nearby include **La Merced,** on the spot where the first mass in Lima was said. Its imposing reddish-stone façade with twisted columns houses some outstanding examples of Colonial art and a fine paneled ceiling. The **Church of Santo Domingo,** whose twin towers have been one of Lima's more famous landmarks, dates back to 1549. It is specially significant because this is where the University of San Marcos was started, and because the mortal remains of the first saint of the Americas, Saint Rose of Lima, and those of San Martín de Porres and Juan Masias are kept in bronze urns in one of the altars. The statue of the saint was presented to the church by Pope Clement in 1669.

The **Church of San Pedro,** the largest in Lima, has a beautifully hand-carved wooden choir and vestry. It is also where several viceroys have been buried. Its bell, called "the little grandmother," is one of the oldest in the hemisphere and tolled the Declaration of Independence.

The **Sanctuary of Santa Rosa,** a

modest little church, is where Saint Rose was born and where she ministered to the sick and aided the poor. **Las Nazarenas Church** has a main altar which exhibits the "Lord of the Miracles," a painting of Christ by a Negro slave on a section of wall that withstood a devastating earthquake.

On the **Plaza Bolívar,** formerly the Plaza of the Inquisition, the court where heretics were tried is now used by a military council but may be visited. The statue of the Venezuelan liberator stands in the plaza in front of the congressional building.

National Library, which was founded by San Martín, sacked during the war with Chile and almost completely destroyed by fire in 1943, still has many unduplicated original volumes recording the Spanish conquest and explorations in this hemisphere. The **Torre Tagle Palace,** now Peru's Foreign Ministry, is one of the city's finest examples of Spanish Colonial architecture.

University of San Marcos, oldest in the Western Hemisphere, was founded more than 100 years before Harvard. Within its unimpressive exterior functions one of the world's most advanced institutions of higher learning. Next to it is the **Pantheon of the Heroes of Peru,** with some outstanding paintings by José Sabogal.

Plaza San Martín, Lima's most elegant plaza in the center of the shopping, theater, hotel, restaurant and entertainment district, is the brightest spot in town at night when the multicolored neon signs are turned on. It is linked with the quiet, austere Plaza de Armas by the city's main street, **Jirón de la Unión,** a narrow strip along five blocks of shops and movie theaters.

From the plaza, the broad avenue of La Colmena runs out to the **Plaza 2 de Mayo,** which commemorates the battle on that day in 1866 against the Spanish fleet which attacked Callao in a fruitless effort to win back the city. The tall marble column in the plaza is on the spot where the walled city had its principal gateway leading to the port of Callao, seven miles away.

Old Lima ends and modern Lima begins at the **Paseo Colón,** a broad avenue and popular promenade lined by gardens and attractive homes which bisects Plaza Grau. Bordering it is the **Parque de la Exposición,** with its **National Art Gallery** and some fine collections by outstanding Peruvian artists.

The **National Museum of Archaeology** in town and the **Museum of Anthropology** in Magdalena Vieja have valuable collections of relics and specimens of Inca and pre-Inca cultures. The **Museum of Peruvian Culture** has similar exhibits of pre-Colombian civilizations. Documents and mementos of the heroes of the independence are preserved at the **National Museum** and the **Bolivarian Museum,** where Simón Bolívar lived. The **Museum of the Viceroyalty** occupies the House of the Inquisition and the Quinta de Presa, a palace built by the Viceroy Amat for his Peruvian "Du Barry," La Perichole.

Among the more popular sights near Lima are the residential districts of **San Isidro, Miraflores,** along the coastal drive to the beaches of **Barranco, Chorrillos, La Herradura,** and the **Inca Museum** in Magdalena Vieja. Another is the ruins of **Pachacámac,** about 12 miles from town, which is said to have been the largest Indian settlement there when the Spaniards came. You can also drive to **Chosica,** about 30 miles away in the foothills of the Andes, where the sun is almost always shining no matter how overcast it may be in Lima. For bathing and aquatic sports there is **Ancón,** a charming old seaside resort 26 miles north of Lima and easily reached by car on a broad, well-paved super-highway.

A little farther away by car or train are **La Oroya, Huancayo,** with stopovers at **Matucana, San Mateo** and **Río Blanco** in the highlands of Peru. About 130 miles to the south on the Pan-American Highway is **Pisco,** a seaside resort on the coast which is famous for its fine weather and beaches and the popular national drink made from the grapes grown here. This is also a whaling and commercial fishing port. Nearby is **Paracas,** another popular beach resort near the site of an ancient pantheon where a pre-Inca civilization buried its noble dead centuries and perhaps thousands of years ago. The hotel fronting Paracas Bay is near the spot where San Martín first landed in Peru. **Ica,** about 45 miles from Pisco, is also known for its vineyard, cotton plantations and an archaeological museum. Nearby is **Huacachina,** a well-known spa in the midst of sand dunes, whose waters have great therapeutic value and are hailed by many. **Nasca,** some 90 miles from Ica, is another oasis town whose warm dry weather attracts many vacationists.

Following the **Pan-American Highway** north from Lima you can drive along the coast past **Ancón** to **Pativilca,** where you can see the well-preserved ruins of the Chimu fortifications of **Paramonga.** The mountains come down to the sea along the coast from here to **Chimbote,** a growing port city in a rich coal and iron ore region. But the best way to fully appreciate the beauty of the mountain scenery in this area is to take the valley road from Pativilca to **Huallanca** through the spectacular and awe-inspiring **Callejón de Huaylas.** This is a valley corridor between the black and white cordilleras of the Andes with some of the most magnificent mountain panoramas and picturesque Indian villages in the world. The 22,205-foot snow-capped peak of Huascarán, the highest mountain in Peru, can be seen from Yungay. Cañon del Pato thunders through a pass between the two cordilleras at the northern end of this mountain corridor. **Huaraz,** a tiny hamlet of little houses and narrow streets, is the gateway to this Swiss-like region of Peru, whose outstanding event is the **Exaltation of the Cross** on September 14. About a half hour out of town are the hot springs and the grottoes of **Chancos,** whose waters and steam baths are credited with miraculous healing powers. Also nearby, about 65 miles from Huaraz, are the stone monster **ruins of the pre-Inca Chavin civilization.**

PIURA is a proud and historic old city of over 100,000 on an oasis formed by the Piura River at the edge of the Sechura Desert. There are excellent examples of Colonial art in the church of La Merced. Piura is the birthplace of Admiral Miguel Gran, hero of the War of the Pacific, when Peru and Bolivia fought Chile.

PUCALLPA, on the Ucayali River, is a small jungle port of some 46,000 people. It is joined with Lima by road and with Iquitos by river boat and relies principally on its lumber industry and the rubber gathered in the area. Boat trips to Iquitos take four days and go right through the heart of the jungle past yucca and banana plantations, Indian villages, and all sorts of exotic flora and wild fauna.

PUNO, at the edge of Lake Titicaca, is where tourists transfer from the railroad to the lake steamer which takes them to Guaqui, on the Bolivian side. It is also famous for archaeological ruins at Sillustain, Juli, Pomata, Chucuito, Sonderhuasi and Pucara, where the ceramic ceremonial bulls are made, and for the picturesque Indian villages nearby.

TACNA, Peru's southernmost city, is a community of growing commercial importance about 1,800 feet above sea level, with the snow-covered peak of Mount Tacora visible in the distance. It can be reached by rail from Arica, plane from Lima, and via the Pan-American Highway from Chile or Peru.

TALARA, a tiny settlement of neat frame houses, squat round oil tanks and steel towers on the sun-baked desert coast of northern Peru, is the country's most important oil center. The town gets its water piped in from 25 miles away, and every blade of vegetation is artificially irrigated. As a model community for petroleum industry workers and their families, it enjoys every modern convenience and recreational facility. But its greatest tourist attraction is found at nearby **Cabo Blanco,** one of the world's most renowned fishing areas. Here fishermen catch black marlin that weigh more than half a ton. The big-

Fortress of San Félipe, Cartagena, Colombia

Bogotá, Colombia

Sweet-water canal in New Nickerie, Surinam

Angel Falls, Venezuela

Rio de Janeiro, Brazil

Brasília, Brazil

Statue of Simón Bolívar in Guayaquil, Ecuador

Marketplace in Otavalo, Ecuador

Machu Picchu, Inca Fortress in the Andes of Peru

Sunday marketplace in Pisac, Peru

Legislative Palace, Montevideo, Uruguay

Spanish-Colonial church near La Paz, Bolivia

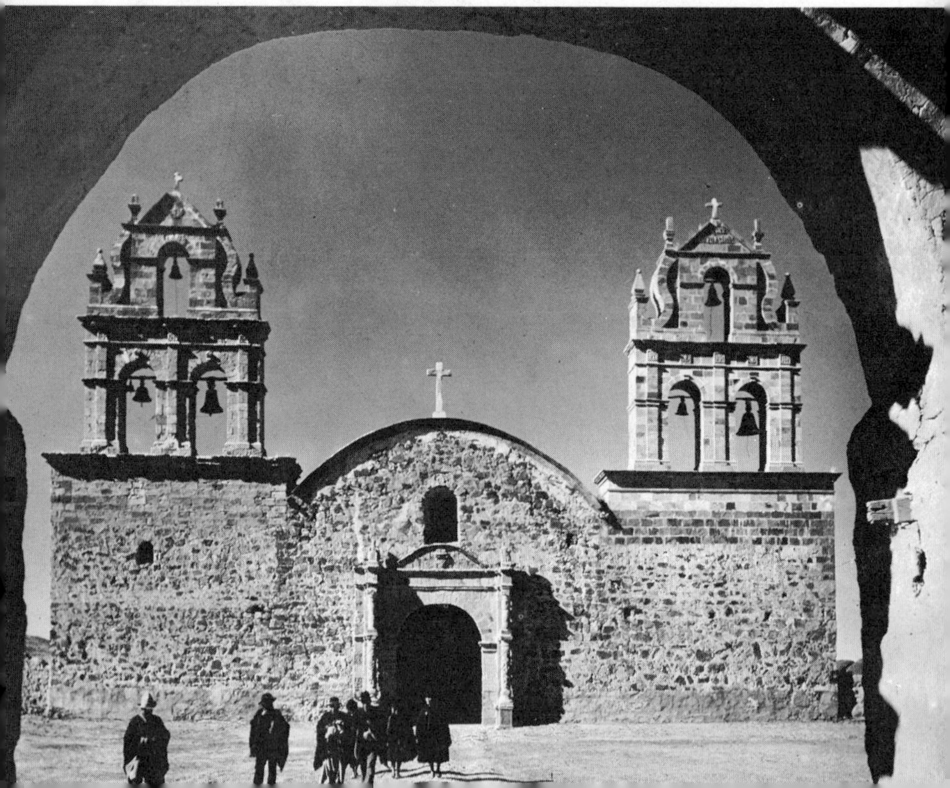

Grotto of San José, Viña del Mar, Chile

View of Santiago, Chile from Cerro San Cristobal

Buenos Aires, Argentina

A trademark of Argentina—the Gaucho

gest fish ever caught on a rod and reel was a monster black marlin weighing 1,560 pounds which was hauled out of these waters in 1953. The Cabo Blanco Fishing Club is headquarters for internationally famous big-game fishermen who come to try their luck here with broadbill swordfish, striped marlin, rooster fish, bonito, tuna and dolphin. The fishing is said to be good throughout the year, but June through September is best for swordfish and black marlin.

TINGO MARÍA, at the edge of the jungle on the shores of the Huallaga River, is a thriving colony which is fast becoming one of Peru's most fertile food-producing regions and a popular tourist resort. This is frontier country that is still being pioneered. The town has sprung up within the last twenty years in the wake of a highway that has been driven through the jungle to the east. There is now a hotel for tourists, a landing field, postal and telegraphic service, schools, a sawmill and even home-finance offices that offer credit to farmers. It is visited by thousands annually, both for business and pleasure. Among its many diversions are fishing, paddling a canoe over swift currents, hunting trips into the jungle, or just relaxing in the quiet of this primitive region and soaking up the tropical sun.

TRUJILLO, at the edge of the Moche River, about eight miles from the coast, is a traditional old Colonial city of churches, exquisitely carved Moorish balconies and pleasant Andalusian patios recalling the Spanish Colonial period. Of special interest are its beautifully landscaped **Plaza de Armas** and part of the old wall which defended the city against pirates, the artistic wealth within its churches, cathedral and the stately Colonial residences. This fourth largest city in Peru was founded by Pizarro, in 1535, who named it after his home town in Spain.

Its outstanding tourist attraction is the ruins of **Chan-Chan,** once the capital of the great Chimu or Mochica Empire, conquered by the Incas about A.D. 1400, and looted later by the Spaniards. More than $15 million worth of treasure is said to have been taken from the burial grounds there. Freak torrential rains have washed away most of the old city, which was built of adobe, in this arid region; and all that remains today for visitors to see are some of the burial mounds, parts of the temples and palaces, bright-colored bas-reliefs, and crumbling walls which once lined streets and buildings of this ancient settlement. The mummies of these early inhabitants, gold and silver ornaments, masks, robes and many other articles which they used may be seen in the **Larco Herrera Museum** on the sugar plantation of Chiclin, about 21 miles from Trujillo.

SPORTS AND RECREATION. Bullfighting in Peru is considered the best on the continent, attracting famous *toreros* from Spain, Mexico, and South America. Lima's 200-year-old bull ring, **Plaza de Acho,** is the most well-known ring in Peru. **Soccer** is the other top sport, with matches often held in the **Estadio Nacional.** Other popular spectator sports include **horse racing** and **cockfights.** Visitors will find facilities for **golf, tennis, horseback riding,** and **polo** in the cities; and **bathing, sailing, water-skiing** and **surfboard riding** at beach resorts up and down the coast.

SPECIAL EVENTS. In a traditionally religious country such as Peru, all Church holidays are celebrated fully. The two major ones are the **Fiesta de Santa Rosa de Lima** on August 30, which honors Peru's patron saint; and the **Procession of the Lord of the Miracles** on October 18, during the October Fair. Other important events include **St. John's Day,** June 24, known as the **Day of the Indian; Fiesta de Amancaes,** near Lima (a week-long celebration featuring the folk music and dancing from the days of the Incas); **National Independence Day,** July 28 and 29; **Day of the race,** October 12 (honoring the memory of Columbus and the coming of spring south of the equator); and November 27's commemoration of the **Battle of Tarapaca.**

In Cuzco, the **Inti Raymi Festival** on June 24 celebrates Midwinter's Day. This is a colorful pageant in which hundreds of Indians in authentic costumes perform the ceremony of crowning their Inca and present the typical dances of the various regions of the country. The **Fiesta of the Virgin of Cocharcas,** held in Huancayo the week of September 8, draws many tourists and is marked with gay festivities and colorful traditional dances.

DINING AND SHOPPING. Peruvian food is distinctive, flavorsome, usually highly seasoned, and varied according to the city or region of the country, although the fine restaurants of Lima provide a wide variety of international dishes.

In the old Spanish tradition, Peruvians eat dinner late, about 10 P.M., and tea is not only a popular custom and a social event but a nutritious necessity.

Ceviche, a highly seasoned appetizer, usually consisting of fresh raw fish marinated in lemon juice and garnished with a raw onion and *aji* (hot chili), is one of the most typically Peruvian dishes. *Ceviche de corvina* (sea bass) is one of the most popular, but it is also prepared with shrimps and other seafood. Among the top favorites with most tourists are the *anticuchos,* beef heart squares prepared with vinegar and *aji* and strung out on split bamboo skewers broiled over coals. These are usually eaten with large Indian corn on the cob and Peruvian sweet potatoes. They are also prepared with fish, shrimp and mussels, or *mixto,* a combination of all. *Soncochado* is a meat and vegetable stew. Most seafood, such as the *corvina, camarones* (shrimp) and *conchitas* (scallops), is especially good in Lima.

Peruvian fruits are varied and delicious and include pineapple, papaya and *chirimoya.* Avocados, which are known as *paltas* in Peru, are plentiful and tasty when in season, and frequently served in salads and sandwiches. Especially recommended are the Chinese restaurants, known as *chifas,* which offer a wide selection of tasty and unusual Oriental dishes.

For outdoor picnics, the equivalent of our cookout is the *pachamanca,* an ancient Peruvian *luau* or barbecue dating back to the Incas, which usually consists of chicken, pork, beef, sweet potatoes, corn and yucca cooked over hot stones in a closed pit.

Since corn is indigenous to Peru, there are many varieties of it found there. *Chicha morada* is a soft drink made from purple corn. But there is also an alcoholic *chicha* which looks brown and is drunk by the people in the highlands. Other liquors include *algarrobina,* a typical Peruvian cocktail made of *pisco* and *algarrobina* (syrup of the *algarroba* tree).

Other specialties are *causa limena,* small yellow potatoes, found only in Peru, mashed in olive oil and *aji,* with shrimp, fresh cheese, boiled egg, corn on the cob, lettuce and olives; *chupe de camarones,* a typically Peruvian soup made of milk and potatoes, shrimps, eggs and *aji;* and *papas a la Huancané,* boiled yellow potatoes, covered with a sauce of fresh cheese and *aji* and garnished with boiled eggs and lettuce. The Peruvian *tamales* consist of seasoned ground corn stuffed with bits of pork or chicken, hard-boiled eggs, olives, raisins and almonds, wrapped in banana leaves. For dessert try *picarones,* Peruvian doughnuts made of *yucca,* flour and eggs, fried in lard and served with molasses; or *mazamorra morada,* a jelly-like dessert made of purple corn, flour and dried fruits. *Pisco,* a distilled grape brandy, is the national drink. And *pisco* sour, the popular Peruvian cocktail, is made with the white of an egg, lemon juice and clear syrup.

Peru is a shopper's paradise where the present-day adventurer, as his predecessor of long ago, will find many treasures to take home.

Silversmiths still practice their ancient skills, and some rare but remarkably inexpensive jewelry in silver and gold may be obtained in the fine shops of Lima. The city's main shopping street, Jirón de la Unión, and the narrow side streets leading from it are where you will find many bargains in handsome tea sets, jewelry, hand-tooled leather, Inca and pre-Inca *huacos* (relics), and Colonial and modern art. There are also many souvenir and handicraft shops with an irresistible assortment of products made by Indians of the different regions of the country. Among the more popular items are the llama and alpaca slippers, ceramic ceremonial Pucara bulls and Ayacucho churches, vicuña rugs, masks, spears, gourds and other items made by the indigenous people of the more primitive areas of Peru. Most of these Indian products are usually found to be of better quality and less expensive when bought at the fairs and market places of Cuzco, Huancayo and other Indian villages and towns.

Bolivia

Bolivia, the land of the ancient Aymaras in the geographical center of South America, is one of the least known and least developed countries on the continent and yet one of the most fascinating to visit. Here, amid the ruins of what may have been the oldest civilization in this hemisphere, one sees fabulous mountain cities, breathtaking scenery and unusual tourist attractions.

THE LAND. This fifth largest country in South America is completely landlocked, surrounded by Brazil on the north and east, Chile and Peru on the west, and Paraguay and Argentina on the south. Its almost 500,000 square miles—over twice the size of Alaska—are inhabited by only about 4.8 million people, less than the population of the state of Massachusetts.

Since the Andes come to their widest range here and cover about half the land area, almost 80 percent of the people live in the mountains and *altiplano,* more than 10,000 feet above sea level on the very roof of the world. Through the centuries these people have worked the mines.

East of this lofty, barren and frigid plateau, the rugged Andes break up into a weird topography of innumerable canyons, steep gorges and fertile subtropical valleys known as the Yungas. Farther east and to the north are the rain forests and jungles of the Amazon basin in the Bení and Santa Cruz, and the grazing lands and lowland plains of the Chaco, which together cover more than two-thirds of the country.

With such a rich diversity of land, the country has everything from towering snow-crusted mountains more than 20,000 feet high to lush subtropical valleys constituting a natural wonderland. The only thing it lacks in the way of a tourist attraction are beaches and seaside resorts. But it makes up for this with an incredible array of remarkable attractions running the gamut of ancient ruins, Colonial art treasures, historical relics, intriguing native customs, charming resorts, unusual sports, comfortable hotels, and some of the greatest shopping bargains on the continent. The country also boasts two capitals, one of which is the highest in the world.

THE CLIMATE. The best time for a visit is during the dry season, from April to November, although a variety of weather conditions can be found at all times, depending upon the altitude. Along the western plateau (location of La Paz, and the most popular part of the country), temperatures average 45 degrees. Temperatures stay near 50–55 degrees in the Yungas regions, and the lower eastern area has a hot, humid, semitropical climate.

THE PEOPLE. Bolivia is the country with the largest Indian population in South America. About 54 percent of the people fall largely into two distinct types: the Aymara, whose ancestors were the Colla; and the Quechua, descendants of the Incas. The former, who are found only on the *altiplano,* are coarser in appearance, language and demeanor and are usually somewhat sullen and sad. Their ancestors are believed to have been the earliest known inhabitants of Bolivia and were found by the Incas living among the ruins of

Tiahuanaco. The Quechua, who also live in the *altiplano* and in the valleys, and are the most numerous, are physically stronger and of a gentler nature. They also seem to have become better adjusted to the white man's civilization. Many other tribes, such as the Chiquitos, Siriones, Mojos, and the Chiriguanos, are found in the jungle interior of the country, but these seldom come in contact with civilization and are practically unknown. About 25 percent of the population is mixed and about 13 percent is white, mainly of Spanish extraction. The official religion is Roman Catholic.

Little is known of the early Tiahuanaco civilization which settled on the southern shores of Lake Titicaca perhaps thousands of years ago. But all the archaeological evidence which has been unearthed since then clearly indicates that this primitive culture did exist a long time ago and was followed by a second and more advanced Tiahuanaco culture around A.D. 600. The crude primitive art of the first Tiahuanaco period and the exquisite refinement of the second, whose influence spread throughout the country and as far as Peru, Ecuador, Chile and Argentina, may be seen today on the southern shore of Lake Titicaca. What became of these ancient people, or why their civilization should suddenly end three centuries later in A.D. 900, is a mystery.

The Incas found the Collas in a low stage of civilization living among the ancient ruins of Tiahuanaco when they extended their empire there in the thirteenth and fourteenth centuries. This land of the Collas remained a part of the Inca Empire until the Spanish conquest, and a prized possession of the

King of Spain when its silver treasures were discovered at Potosí.

As stories of its fabulous wealth spread during the late sixteenth and seventeenth centuries, cities were founded, lands appropriated and the Indian population unscrupulously enslaved. By the eighteenth century the oppressive rule of the Spaniards had resulted in many Indian uprisings, attacks on the cities, and the beginning of a growing feeling of discontent that would eventually lead to open rebellion.

One of the first nations to declare its independence and the last to be liberated, Bolivia gave its first cry for liberty at La Plata, in 1809. That same year, Pedro Domingo Murillo led a bloody but abortive revolution in La Paz. Other attempts to liberate the country later also failed; and it wasn't until after Antonio José Sucre's decisive victory at the Battle of Ayacucho in 1825 that the country won its independence from Spain.

The new republic took its name from the liberator Simón Bolívar, who became its first president and gave the country its first constitution.

In recent years the country has made some headway in its efforts to improve the lot of the people, to achieve a more diversified economy and more stable political atmosphere.

AGRICULTURE. Although eastern Bolivia is known for its lush lowlands and excellent soil, most farming is done on the dry, unproductive western plateau by Indians, who are, for the most part, unwilling to leave their ancestral home or adjust to the lowland climate. About one-half of the people in Bolivia make their living by farming, but only two percent of the land is cultivated. Chief crops from the highlands are corn, barley, and many varieties of potatoes. Pigs and sheep are raised. Many other crops are farmed, including grapes, nuts, coffee, cocoa, peppers, and rice. In the lowlands, semi-wild cattle graze. Llamas produce wool for the Indians and are used as their farm animals.

INDUSTRY. Mining is, by far, the most important industry in Bolivia, with 12 percent of the world's tin coming from Bolivian mines. Other minerals include lead, silver, bismuth, and copper.

Few skilled laborers, with the exception of miners, and a lack of steel and power, have meant slow development of manufacturing in Bolivia. Most manufactured products are for consumer use.

CITIES. Four cities, La Paz, Cochabamba, Santa Cruz, and Oruro, have populations of more than 80,000. Most of the cities in Bolivia are in the west, at altitudes from 8,000 to 13,000 feet.

COCHABAMBA basks luxuriantly in the benign climate of a broad, fertile plain, sheltered by a cluster of blue mountains halfway between the *altiplano* and the tropical lowlands in the heart of Bolivia. Ranking second in population and importance, it is the country's most popular tourist and vacation resort.

Although easily accessible by air from the United States and other countries in South America, this 8,500-foot-high city in the Yungas is relatively unknown to all but a few international travelers. But its many attractions and diversions, unspoiled Colonial atmosphere, fine hotels and lovely resorts, and delightful semitropical weather the year round are a welcome sight to many travelers who flock here by car, train and plane from other Bolivian cities.

Visitors are usually impressed by the clean, orderly appearance of this city, with its old Spanish-style homes, flower-filled patios, tree-lined promenades and plazas, tall modern buildings, smart shops and well-paved streets. There are many sights to please the eye in and around Cochabamba, but none more so than the gaily colored skirts and stovepipe white enameled straw hats worn by the native women. You can tell a Cochabamba woman by her hat, for the taller the hat, the more important the individual, and the band denotes the town she comes from. Other attractions here are the fabulous home of the Bolivian "Tin King," Simón Patiño; the priceless collections in Colonial art within the city's churches; and the handsome souvenirs in silver and gold jewelry and hand-woven goods which can be obtained here. Best time to visit Cochabamba is from April to October, when it is summer and the weather is dry.

The city was founded in 1574 by Sebastian Barba de Padilla, who gave it the name of Villa de Oropeza. Its name was changed to Villa de Cochabamba in 1786, and it has also been called "City of Tunari," for the tall mountain which rises over it. Cochabamba men and women distinguished themselves during the battle of independence, and a monument to the women who took up arms by the side of their men stands on La Coronilla Hill overlooking the city.

The best place to start on a tour of Cochabamba is at the **Plaza 14 of September,** around which the city is laid out. A tall column monument honors the city's heroes in the independence movement in the center of this palm-fronded plaza, whose four sides are lined with Colonial arcades. Facing the plaza is the cathedral, with its saber-scarred doors bearing evidence of the horror that took place there when the city's patriots were butchered inside. Magnificent sculpture, showing the Repentance of St. Peter, Our Lord of the Column, Our Lady of Lourdes, the Crucifixion, and St. Sebastian, is found within. Opposite the cathedral on the other side of the plaza is the **city hall** and the library; and in the streets around it, the entertainment and shopping districts of the city. Other tourist attractions are the **University of San Simón,** the stadium, the **Acha Theater,** the museum with its interesting collection of historical relics, and the beautiful man-made **Cuellar Lagoon.** Also worth visiting for their Colonial art and architecture are the churches of **Santa Teresa, San Francisco, La Compañia,** and **Santa Clara.** The tourist should not fail to see the many promenades and plazas, such as **El Prado, Cuellar Lagoon, Parque Colón,** and the resorts of **Cala-Cala, Vinto, Quillacollo,** just outside the city. Usually included in the tour of the city is the drive to **La Coronilla,** atop San Sebastian Hill, where one sees the monument to the heroic women of Cochabamba and a splendid view of the city's red-tiled rooftops, pink churches and the surrounding mountains. Also on this tour is the **Palacio Portales,** at Pairumani, the former home of Simón Patiño, which has been converted into a museum and is open to the public. This impressive palace has a solid copper roof, and its interior is decorated in a variety of styles and designs which include French, Spanish, Turkish, Moorish, and Chinese bric-a-brac blended in surprising harmony.

Just outside the city limits are some excellent facilities for horseback riding, a favorite sport here. The lovely countryside in this valley is dotted with orchards of grapes, peaches, oranges, bananas and *chirimoyas* (custard apples), and old Colonial villas and homes. There are also good facilities for deer hunting in the not too distant forests. The nearby resorts of **Caya-Cayani, Cala-Cala, Liriuni,** and **Chaparé** are only a few of the many popular vacation spots, mineral springs and colorful towns found around Cochabamba. There are picturesque fairs at **Quillacollo, Punata,** and **Cliza,** which are noted for their largely Indian populations. And longer camping tours to the jungle can be arranged here, as well as overland trips by car or train to Sucre and Santa Cruz. A 313-mile all-weather highway links Cochabamba and Santa Cruz.

LA PAZ, a gleaming gray city of faded rooftops guarded by the towering snowy crest of Mount Illimani, lies at the bottom of a fertile valley in the shelter of a narrow rocky canyon which is two-and-one-half miles above sea level. While the high altitude and the thrilling spectacle of this picturesque city may combine to leave the traveler somewhat breathless on arrival, a visit to La Paz can be a most pleasant experience if taken unhurriedly.

This lofty city of steep streets and breath-taking vistas, 12,000 feet high, is the highest capital in the world. Unmindful of the altitude, which makes it unnecessary to have a fire department and even difficult to keep a match burning, its over 700,000 inhabitants carry on their normal activities which make this the country's most important city, its political and cultural capital (although Sucre is the official capital). On the *altiplano,* overlooking the city at 13,404 feet, is the highest commercial airport in the world.

For more than 400 years, La Paz has been a center of commerce and industry, and a haven for travelers. On the main route between the rich silver mines of Potosí and the viceregal capital of Lima, its sheltered location at the edge of the bleak *altiplano* made it a natural stopping place for treasure-laden caravans. Today, its invigorating mountain air, magnificent scenery, colorful Indian life, and inexpensive but comfortable living have made it a popular stopover and gateway for tourists crossing Lake Titicaca on the tour of the Land of the Incas.

Like most South American cities, La Paz has its old and modern sections. The dividing line between the two is the Choqueyapu River (also known as the La Paz River), which is seldom seen but often heard as it rumbles through deep crevasses, under old dwellings and high-walled bridges. The time-worn houses in the old section of town appear helter-skelter in a potpourri of confusion, while the streets wind, twist, and climb precipitously over the crooked landscape.

In striking contrast, the modern section of La Paz is seen bordering the smart, broad Avenida 16 de Julio, otherwise known as the Prado, a fashionable *paseo,* or promenade, of mosaic sidewalks and flower beds lined with ultramodern buildings and smart shops. The city's architecture is an incongruous combination of venerable Colonial buildings, squat two-story houses, and modern steel and glass skyscraping apartments and hotels. The snow on the mountains is not only decorative but utilitarian; waterfalls of melting snow beyond the city limits drive the generators which provide electricity for La Paz.

The life around town is one of its principal attractions. Derby-hatted Indian women in their billowing skirts and shawls and poncho-clad men create an unusual pageantry of color.

Although there are many excellent sporting facilities, most travelers arriving here are just content to walk slowly around the city's colorful streets, enjoying the magnificent scenery, taking long draughts of the pure healthy mountain air, visiting the Indian market and shopping to their hearts' delight for the most fabulous bargains in Indian handicrafts on the continent. April to November is the dry season here and the best time to visit La Paz. The rainy season is from December to March.

The earliest inhabitants of this hidden valley of the Choqueyapu River were the ancient Collas, or Aymara Indians, who still make up the bulk of the population. This was a tiny Inca settlement when Captain Alonzo de Mendoza founded the city in 1548 and named it Ciudad de Nuestra Señora de la Paz (City of Our Lady of Peace) to commemorate a peace treaty between the warring conquistadors. But its early belligerent history belied its peaceful name, and it became the site of many Indian uprisings against the Spaniards. During the latter part of the eighteenth century, this was the scene of great revolutionary activity. In 1809, a rebel band led by the patriot hero, Pedro Domingo Murillo, took over the Spanish garrison and proclaimed the country's independence. Their victory, however, was short-lived when the Spanish retaliated by crushing the revolt and executing the leaders of the revolution. The city was officially renamed La Paz de Ayacucho in honor of the battle that finally drove the Spanish out of South America. Although La Paz is recognized as the commercial, industrial and transportation hub of the country and both the President and the executive branch of the government have their offices here, Sucre continues to be, as it has been since the birth of the republic, the official capital and the place where the Supreme Court holds its sessions.

To visit the city, it is strongly recommended, unless you are not easily affected by the altitude, that you do little walking or climbing when you first arrive. The city is laid out in a checkerboard pattern. The heart of town is the **Plaza Murillo,** which honors the memory of Bolivia's independence hero. Around this plaza are the capitol, or legislative palace, in the style of the Renaissance; the **government palace,** where the President lives, and the cathedral, which took 100 years to build.

In the streets adjacent to the plaza is the commercial center of the city, where most of the fine shops and stores are located. **Calle Mercado** is the main business street; **Avenida Camacho** is the site of the Central Market, where Indian merchants in their colorful apparel come to trade their produce and handicrafts. The city's most elegant street is the **Prado,** or Avenida 16 de Julio, which runs from the statue of Bolívar in the Plaza Venezuela to the statue of Sucre in the Plaza Franz Tamayo.

La Paz also has its share of old Colonial churches and historic buildings. The **Church of San Agustín** on Calle Mercado was begun by 12 friars sent over from Spain by Charles V in 1562. The sixteenth-century **Church of Santo Domingo** has several beautiful altars; in the **Church and Monastery of San Francisco** are some of the finest examples of Colonial art and architecture in La Paz. Several architectural styles are seen in the present building, which dates from 1778. Its baroque façade contains some Inca patterns around the framework, and the bare stone walls are unmistakably Gothic. The hand-carved wooden altars and pulpits are in the finest Colonial tradition, reminiscent of the work to be seen in the churches of Cuzco. This monastery has a collection of religious oil paintings and a lovely garden. The oldest building in La Paz is found on **Calle Goizueta,** in back of the Plaza Alonso de Mendoza, said to have been laid out by the city's founder. Facing the plaza is the oldest church, **San Sebastian,** originally dedicated to San Pedro in 1548, the same year the city was founded. Some sections of the original structure still can be seen. An outstanding example of Spanish Renaissance architecture is the school for girls on Calle Ingavi, which was formerly the residence of the Marquis de Villaverde and still displays the family coat of arms.

The **military museum,** on the Prado, contains a valuable collection of arms and some interesting exhibits of the nation's military glories. Not far from the Prado is the **National Museum of Tiahuanacu,** on Calle Don Bosco, designed in the architectural style of the ancient civilization whose arts and crafts are displayed inside. The museum also has a fine library.

La Paz is noted for its fine curio shops and open markets. Best bargains are found in vicuña and alpaca furs, rugs, and blankets; fine gold and silver jewelry; wood carvings and paintings; religious objects and statues; porcelain, miniatures, hand-woven woolens and *chullos* (knitted caps); native dolls, and Indian handicrafts.

For traveling around the city and countryside, taxis are plentiful and inexpensive. One of the most popular tours takes in the old section, the market, **Tiahuanacu Museum,** the cathedral, **Church of San Francisco,** the **House of Villaverde,** and the residential areas and beautiful suburbs of **Miraflores** and **Sopocachi,** where most of the larger homes and many of the foreign embassies are located. There is an excellent view of the city and surrounding mountains from **El Monticulo Park** here. **Obrajes** is another, and newer, suburb of La Paz in a delightful green valley, surrounded by the gray and red cliffs of the canyon, about 1,000 feet below the capital. La Paz, by its central location, is the natural starting point for many tours in the vicinity, to **Lake Titicaca, Copacabana, Tiquina, Tiahuanacu, Chulumani** in the Yungas, and the hot springs of **Urmiri.** The full-day trip to the famous pre-Inca ruins of **Tiahuanacu,** about 50 miles away, is a must for the tourist to La Paz. Near the mud huts of the village can be seen the ancient ruins of the two civilizations that flourished here. The "Gateway to the Sun," with its strange half-man, half-bird figures whose meaning remains a mystery, is the site's main tourist attraction. But the Inca steps and sacrificial stone, as well as the older stone monuments on Apacana Hill, are also noteworthy. The village's modern church and several other structures were built with stones from the original settlement. Also recommended is the tour of Copacabana, a town on a peninsula in Lake Titicaca and the site of Bolivia's most famous pilgrimage. The rough-hewn but inspiringly beautiful statue of the Virgin of Copacabana, to which many miracles have been attributed, may be seen in the seventeenth-century church. Thousands of pilgrims journey here on August 2 to participate in the Fiesta de Copacabana, but the town's ancient customs, Indian lifestyle and incomparable scenic views make it a year-round tourist attraction. Close by are the Islands of the Sun and the Moon, sacred in Inca mythology as the birthplace of the children of the sun.

A trip across 12,500-foot-high **Lake Titicaca,** the highest navigable lake in the world, is an unforgettable experience and the way many tourists make the trip from La Paz to Cuzco and the Land of the Incas. The steamships which navigate this inland sea between Guaqui on the Bolivian side and Puno in Peru–a 12-hour trip–have overnight accommodations for travelers. Built in England and Scotland, they had to be completely dismantled at the seaport of Mollendo, Peru, and hauled by muleback up the mountains to be put together once again at the lake. The sunrise at this altitude is a thrilling spectacle of the most vivid colors.

Another side trip out of La Paz is the two-day trip to the jungle. Travelers descend through beautiful semitropical valleys to the resort town of **Chulumani,** about 80 miles east of La Paz, in the heart of the Bolivian **Yungas.** This fertile valley, about 5,400 feet above sea level, is noted for its delightful climate. Other towns in the vicinity are **Coroico, Coripata,** and **Irupana. Termas de Urmiri,** in a valley about 60 miles slightly southeast of La Paz, has fine mineral springs and hot baths.

North of La Paz, and accessible by road, is **Sorata,** a tiny resort town at the foot of Mount Hanko-Huma, which attracts many of the citizens of La Paz on weekends. There are also picnic facilities and sailing on native balsa (tortora reed) boats at **Puerto Perez,** on the shores of Lake Titicaca.

Corocoro, about 70 miles to the south in a valley of the *altiplano,* is the center of an important copper mining region.

ORURO, perched high in the *altiplano* about 12,000 feet above sea level, is a thriving mining community on the steep slopes of the Uru-Uru Mountain. It is an important rail center, noted principally as the country's chief mining region for tin, silver and wolfram, but very seldom visited by tourists.

Officially founded by the Spaniards in 1606, Oruro was first settled in 1595 by Father Francisco Medrano, who discovered rich silver deposits nearby. The climate of Oruro is usually cold and windy, and the average temperature is 50 degrees. Best time to visit is from May to September, when weather is dry, as December to March is the rainy season.

Of tourist interest are Oruro's lovely promenades and important public buildings, including the **Palais Concert,** the **Consistorial Palace,** the **Palace of Justice,** a fortress built by the Spaniards during the revolution, and two unusual and colorful markets. There is also an 18-hole golf course. But its most important tourist attraction takes place here on the Saturday preceding Ash Wednesday, when some of the Indians don their colorful spangle costumes and devil masks for the **Diablada** procession and dance. This religious festival, which dates back to Colonial times and is traditionally performed by the miners of this region, is a sort of morality play set to strange ancient music and exotic dances in which Good triumphs over Evil. When the impressive ceremony is over the Virgen del Socavon, patron saint of miners, blesses the proceedings and all beg her forgiveness for their past sins and chant a hymn in Quechua.

Nearby attractions are the former Patiño tin mines at **Huanuni** and **Uncia.** South of Oruro also are **Lake Poopó,** Bolivia's second largest lake; and the villages of **Challapata** and **Huari,** the latter noted for its famous fair during the two weeks following Holy Week. Indians from the surrounding areas come in to trade and sell their handicrafts and produce.

POTOSÍ, a Colonial jewel of old Spanish houses and narrow winding streets at the base of the great silver hill Cerro Rico, looks today almost as it did several hundred years ago when it was the silver capital of the world. High in the cold, wind-swept *altiplano,* at 13,255 feet, this fabled city is today an important tin-mining center of 55,000 population. But in its silver heyday, in the seventeenth century, this was the largest metropolis in South America with a population of over 160,000. Many of the old buildings, palatial homes, churches and monasteries are rich storehouses of the art and architecture of the Colonial period. Some of the outstanding examples are the **Church of San Lorenzo,** whose main entrance is elaborately carved in the style of the Spanish Renaissance; the Romanesque design of the **Church and Monastery of San Benito;** the **Casa de la Moneda** (mint), where most of the coin of the Spanish realm came from; the **palatial home** of the richest man in Potosí, **José Quiroz,** who owned the mine; and the original **Cabildo,** or town hall.

In Quechua, the word *potosí* means noise, which lends credence to the legend and prophecy of its origin and eventual founding by the Spaniards. Hearing a rumble from within the great silver mine, the Incas took this to be a command from the Sun God that the treasures were to be left alone for someone else who would come later, and stopped work immediately, naming the hill Potosí. The prophecy came true in 1545 when Juan de Villaroel y Santandia found the mine and founded the city a year later.

Worth visiting are the catacombs of the fabulous silver hill **Cerro Rico,** which is reputed to have given the Spanish King one-fifth of more than three-and-a-half billion silver pesos, and is represented on the Bolivian coat of arms. Some of the artificial lakes made by the Indians to furnish water power to run the mines are still in use, supplying water for the city, considered an engineering marvel. About a mile west of the city is the **Ingenio del Rey** (the King's Mine) with the Spanish monarch's coat of arms set in a solid block of stone. Still standing is the original paymaster's house and the ruins of the old jail. Also nearby is **Agua del Castilla,** where the old Porco mines were worked before Potosí was discovered.

SANTA CRUZ, on the banks of the Piray in the lush tropical lowlands of the state of Santa Cruz, is a roistering, colorful frontier town and the gateway to the country's wild interior. While the city's streets and rustic appearance may recall the old Wild West to first-time visitors, its quaint palm-filled plazas and gardens, old Colonial atmosphere and the traditional hospitality of its genial citizenry will make a stay here a pleasant experience. Not the least of the city's charms are its beautiful women, who constitute about two-thirds of the population.

A rich agricultural region, the *llanos* around Santa Cruz produce many of the country's varied crops, and most of its cattle, and is the site of extensive oil exploration. Its dense forests are known to contain a wide variety of game, including jaguar.

In the way of sightseeing attractions, the city has several Colonial churches, exotic tropical foliage, and the gay music and dance of its *carnavalitos.* For those who wish to rough it, there are several excursions to the nearby forests.

The town of Santa Cruz de la Sierra dates from 1595. An earlier settlement was founded by Ñuflo de Chavez in 1557 some distance from here but had to be abandoned because of the constant Indian raids.

SUCRE is set in a high, fertile valley which seems to be isolated from the rest of the world by the iridescent hills which surround it and give the city an unreal appearance of belonging to another era. Although this is the country's legal capital and the seat of its Supreme Court, its remoteness and inaccessibility in earlier years have caused it virtually to be replaced by La Paz as the functioning government capital. This long isolation has also preserved the city's rich Colonial atmosphere, traditional ways, and quaint Colonial charm, despite the fact that Sucre can be reached easily today by car, railroad or airplane.

One of South America's oldest and most interesting cities, it was founded in 1538 by Pedro de Anzurez Redondo, one of Pizarro's lieutenants. First called Chuquisaca, then Charcas, and later La Plata, its present name honors the country's liberator. This "City of Four Names" has a proud tradition of culture and learning dating back to Colonial days when it was the seat of the Audiencia de Charcas, the governing authority for Upper Peru. Its **University of San Francisco,** founded in 1624, is one of the country's outstanding institutions of higher learning, and its libraries and museums are noteworthy. The heart of the city is **Plaza 25 de Mayo,** a garden-filled square with a fountain and a small pavilion. Bolivia's declaration of independence was signed in the **legislative palace,** which was formerly a Jesuit monastery. Inside may be seen many historic relics of the revolution and the swords of Bolívar and Sucre. The country's Supreme Court holds sessions in the **palace of justice,** which also contains a public library with some 15,000 volumes and valuable manuscripts. Its **government palace,** a three-story marble building, is said to be one of the most magnificent in Bolivia, while the seventeenth-century cathedral is noted for its outstanding Colonial art and architecture. About 8,500 feet above sea level, the city enjoys a climate which seldom goes above 80 or below 45 degrees.

TRINIDAD is a typical jungle town in the Beni, and gateway to the dense rubber-producing region nearby. It dates from 1556, when it was founded by some intrepid Spanish explorers and is a Colonial city which attained some measure of prominence. Its architecture and art treasures are interesting to see, and the gay **Fiesta of the Trinity** is marked with ancient dances and a religious procession.

Other Bolivian cities worthy of note include **Uyuni,** a tiny mining town at the edge of the salt marshes of the *altiplano,* about 12,000 feet above sea level. Never a tourist center, it has an interesting market. **Pulacayo** is known for its rich silver mine at Huanchaca, one of the largest in the world. **Tupiza,** in a broad valley of the river Tupiza, is famous for its varied fruits. **Tarija** is a charming Spanish Colonial town on a flat plain in the midst of rugged canyons, noted for its Andalusian antecedents and the beauty of its women. Its outstanding tourist attractions are its cathedral and various churches, and its lovely plazas. **Villazón,** Bolivia's most southerly town, is its southern rail terminus on the Argentine border.

SPORTS AND RECREATION. One of Bolivia's outstanding sports arenas is the 50,000-seat stadium in La Paz, where international **soccer** matches are held. The stadium also has facilities for **baseball, basketball, swimming,** and **tennis,** as well as several restaurants and reception halls. Also in La Paz, visitors can see **horse racing, bullfights,** and just outside the city, play **golf** at the highest golf course in the world. Drives of more than 300 yards are not uncommon. There are excellent **fishing** areas in Bolivia, especially around Lake Titicaca, where 20-pound rainbow trout are often found.

For winter sports, the highest resort in the world is on **Mount Chacaltaya,** 16,800 feet above sea level, and an hour's drive from La Paz. The **ski** season runs from June to September. You can also motor out from La Paz to

Mount Illimani, whose 21,000-foot snow-covered peak towers majestically over the city.

SPECIAL EVENTS. January 20–25, **Indian Holiday,** in La Paz (Indians come into town, camp in the streets and outskirts, and dance in their colorful costumes); January 24–29, the **Alacitas Fair,** Plaza San Pedro in La Paz (Indians come to barter and sell their handicrafts); February 2, **Festival at Copacabana,** on the shores of Lake Titicaca (honors Our Lady of the Candelaria, drawing pilgrims and devout from all parts of the continent who dance in bizarre costumes to music dating back to pre-Inca days); March 23, **anniversary of the founding of Sucre,** in Sucre; March, **Romerias,** at Obrajes, near La Paz (fairs attended by Indians in picturesque costumes).

Carnival and **Holy Week** are especially significant and colorfully observed due to the religious nature of the people, and to the large devout Indian population. Other events include April 14, **Pan American Day,** ceremonies in many of the large cities; May 1, **Labor Day,** marked with speeches, parades, and much excitement; May 27, **Anniversary of the Battle of Coronilla,** in Cochabamba; June 5, **Corpus Christi** (religious processions, story of Adam and Eve reenacted by Indians in small villages); July 16, **Virgen del Carmen,** patron saint of La Paz, and date of the city's proclamation of freedom; August 5–7, **Fiesta of Copacabana** (celebrated by Indians in ancient costumes who perform pre-Inca dances and processions); August 5–11, **Independence Day,** celebrated in carnival-like atmosphere.

August 17, **Flag Day;** September 24, **Festival of Santa Cruz,** in Santa Cruz; November 1–2, **All Saints' Day** and **All Souls' Day;** November 7–14, **week-long celebration at Copacabana;** November 10, **Miner's Fiesta,** Oruro; November and December, **regattas** on Lake Titicaca.

DINING AND SHOPPING. Bolivian food varies with the region of the country, but in general is spicy and hot. In the cities of the high *altiplano,* where the climate is chilly, tiny chunks of beef or chicken dipped in very hot sauce and known as *picantes* are a popular delicacy. Another favorite is the *chuño,* a boiled dinner of tiny dehydrated frozen potatoes, scrambled eggs, meat or fish, mixed with cheese.

The *valdiviano con huevos* is a thick, hot soup made with eggs, which is especially welcome in the cooler climates. The *plato paceño,* consists of corn, potatoes, beans and cheese.

There are also *empanadas* (meat pies), which are found throughout the country, although their ingredients and spiciness may vary according to the region; *humitas,* tasty corn-meal tamales; *parilladas,* mixed grills; and *aji de carne,* a spicy treatment of pork or beef, similar to the pepper steak.

Travelers will find a rich variety of tropical and semitropical fruits in Bolivia, but most of these are more frequently available in the cities of the Yungas and the lowlands, rather than on the *altiplano.* The country is also noted for its excellent beer, which is brewed in La Paz; the fine Cinti and Muyurina wines of Cochabamba; and the hard corn liquor, Chicha, of the Indians in the highlands.

Bolivia is famous for its Indian markets and curio shops, where you can buy anything from a vicuña coat to a sea-shell miniature, and for the fabulous bargains in silver and gold bracelets, chains, brooches, rings and remarkably fine filigree jewelry.

In the way of native handicrafts, travelers will find a variety of souvenirs in hand-knitted woolen goods, alpaca furs, hammered silver, wooden figurines, and ceramics, as well as some excellent hand-carved wood sculptures, paintings and antiques.

Paraguay

Unlike modern, tourist-filled Uruguay—with which it is often confused—Paraguay is probably South America's least-

developed republic. One of the continent's two inland countries, it had been relatively inaccessible until the advent of the airplane. But even with air links to the world, it remains insular and isolated.

THE LAND. Paraguay is divided by the Paraguay River into the eastern and the Chaco regions. Covering over 150,000 square miles (about the size of Montana), it is one of South America's two inland nations. Bolivia is at the northern border, Brazil is on the east, with Argentina on the south and west. Most people live in the eastern region, in the low marshy areas near the Paraná River where the soil is fairly rich. The Chaco region, lying west of the Paraguay River, covers about two-thirds of the country.

THE CLIMATE. With temperatures averaging 50 degrees in winter and 85 degrees in summer, Paraguay's climate is not unlike Florida. There is no marked rainy season, though there may be frequent thunderstorms in summer.

THE PEOPLE. Paraguay is unlike any other South American country in that the popular language remains an indigenous language—that of the Guarani Indians, many of whom intermarried with early Spanish settlers. Spanish is the official language, but the great bulk of the population speaks Guarani, although educated Paraguayans are bilingual. The first Spaniards arrived in 1526 and in 1537 Asunción was founded. It was not until 1811 that the country became independent of Spain, but since that time very little progress has been made in either internal development or representative government.

The population remains sparse—just over two million—and the standard of living is low. The rate of illiteracy is

26 percent and education is compulsory until the age 14. In recent years, new hotels have been built in Asunción which offer excellent accommodations to the traveler. The capital is eminently worth a visit, and the handsome people—many of them a fine blend of Guarani and European—are gracious and hospitable.

AGRICULTURE. Only about three percent of the land is cultivated, as farmers usually raise only enough crops to feed their own families. Primitive tools and methods are used, which make the land (most of it around the Paraguay River) less productive than it could be. Chief crops are cotton, cocoa, bananas, coconuts, beans, corn, tobacco, and rice.

Breeding cattle is an important factor in the economy, with over 20,000 cattle raised on each of Paraguay's dozen or so large ranches. Quebracho, a hard wood used to obtain tannin, comes from Paraguay's forests.

INDUSTRY. Due to lack of adequate transportation, technicians, and power, Paraguay has made little progress in developing its industries. What industries it has are small, such as workshops which make pottery and leather goods, and plants which prepare packaged foods. The waterfalls along the Paraná River could provide more than enough electric power, and work on a major hydroelectric project is underway.

CITIES. Asunción is the only city of any size or real import, the others (Concepción, Encarnación, and Villarrica) being smaller and less developed.

ASUNCIÓN, the capital (population 415,000), can be reached by plane from either Rio de Janeiro or Buenos Aires. It remains a town where shawl-wrapped women carrying black umbrellas ride donkeys sidesaddle through the main thoroughfares, and wash their clothes by beating them on stones along the banks of the river.

The handful of mid-twentieth-century buildings contrast starkly with the elaborate Colonial style of the other buildings, and indeed of the town itself, being rectangular in plan, with wide avenues lined with trees and flowers converging on imposing plazas.

Important monuments include the **Pantheon,** modeled after Napoleon's Tomb in Paris, and the resting place of Lopez, an early dictator, two unknown soldiers, and other noted Paraguayans; the **national palace,** built along Italian lines of architecture; the **Godoy Museum of Art and National History,** the **congressional palace,** the Spanish-design cathedral, and the luxurious headquarters of the **national police** and the **army general staff.**

There are less than 20,000 pure-blooded Indians in the country and many are in government reservations, or **campos.** One, near Asunción, can be visited on guided tours. Excursions can be made also to other nearby towns, the most comfortable of which is **San Bernardino,** on **Lake Ypacarai** 30 miles distant, the leading resort of the country. A new highway now provides the best route to **Iguazú Falls** on the Brazil border.

Villeta is an interesting cotton town, **Caacupé** a small resort, and **Villarrica,** the second city of the republic—90 miles from Asunción—is delightfully set on a hill surrounded by orange groves, and is dominated by a particularly fine cathedral. **Concepción,** the main city of the north, lies 250 miles from Asunción and can be reached by river boat—a way of travel which affords a fascinating view of the countryside, with its tobacco and yerba maté (tea) plantations, grazing lands, and dense forests.

SPORTS AND RECREATION. Hunting is Paraguay's most popular sport, with sportsmen coming from many countries to hunt jaguar, deer, game, and wild hogs.

SPECIAL EVENTS. Paraguay's annual activities of visitor interest are highlighted by the **Festival of San Blas,** patron saint of Paraguay and of the city of Ita, where special festivities and folkloric shows take place. The Festival is held in early February. **National Independence Celebrations** are held throughout the country May 14 and 15; and **Immaculate Conception of the Virgin of Caacupé Festivities,** including pilgrimages, religious celebrations, and traditional fiestas, take place in Caacupé in early December.

DINING AND SHOPPING. Meat and vegetables are staples in the Paraguayan's diet. A favorite dish is a meat stew, called *puchero*.

Lace, coming from the village of Itaugua, is an excellent buy.

Uruguay

Uruguay is the smallest republic in South America. Despite its size, the country has a chain of beach resorts that extends for 200 miles up the coast, an excellent vacationland with wide stretches of sandy beaches.

THE LAND. Uruguay covers 72,172 square miles; its greatest length is about 340 miles, its greatest width about 300 miles, and there is a 600-mile coastline. It is bounded by Brazil on the north, the Atlantic Ocean on the east, and is separated from Argentina on the south and west by the Río de la Plata and the Uruguay River.

Uruguay has three land regions: the Coastal Lowlands, a narrow stretch of sand dunes along the Atlantic coast and the Río de la Plata; the Highlands, rising from the eastern coast and running from the Brazilian border to the southern coast (the country's highest point, the 1,644-foot **Mirador Nacional,** is in the Cuchilla Grande), and the Pasturelands, covering about four-fifths of the country.

The major rivers are the Uruguay in the west and the Negro, in central Uruguay.

THE CLIMATE. Uruguay's climate is dry and temperate, and though close to 45 inches of rain falls yearly, severe droughts can occur. Temperatures run from about 45 degrees in winter to 80 degrees in summer. There is rain all year round, with the heaviest rainfall in May and October.

THE PEOPLE. Juan Díaz de Solís led the first white landing party on Uruguay's shore in 1516; but on arriving, Solís and his crew were killed by the fierce Charrúas Indians, the first inhabitants of the country.

The Portuguese established the first white settlement in Uruguay in 1680—a fort built at Colonia, across the Río de la Plata from Buenos Aires. To offset the Portuguese colonization, Spain founded Montevideo, in 1726, and by 1777, the Spanish had driven the last of the Portuguese out of the country.

The movement for Uruguayan independence from Spain was begun in 1810 but in 1820, Brazil seized control of Uruguay. Five years later she broke away and united with Argentina for protection against Brazil. Finally in 1828 both Brazil and Argentina recognized Uruguay as an independent republic.

After years of civil war and controversies between the Blancos and Colorados for political control, stability was attained in 1865.

In 1903, the country's greatest President, José Batlle y Ordóñez, was elected. He soon put the government in control of the banks, improved the labor laws, gave credit and aid to farmers, and encouraged the construction of new harbors, factories, homes, and public buildings. Convinced that too much presidential power had caused the many revolutions, he worked for a new constitution, which was adopted in 1917. The present-day constitution, ratified in 1951, is based on his principles.

Today, about 20 percent of Uruguay's 2.9 million people live in small towns or on farms and ranches. About 80 percent of the population lives in Montevideo. Because the early settlers drove out almost all the Charrúas Indians, less than one-tenth of the population is Indian.

The language is Spanish, and French is spoken widely. Since World War II, the influence of English has been growing. About 90 percent of the people

can read and write. The law requires all children to attend elementary and high school, and provides free colleges for those who wish to attend.

There is complete separation of Church and State, although Roman Catholicism is the predominant religion.

AGRICULTURE. Livestock, particularly sheep and cattle raising, is the chief industry of Uruguay; wool, meat, and hides constitute the main agricultural export. There are many ranches (*estancias*) dedicated mainly to the selection and improvement of cattle. Wheat is grown on about half the farm land; alfalfa, barley, citrus fruits, corn, and oats are also grown. During recent years there has been tremendous growth in dairy farming. The government helps the farmers by subsidization.

INDUSTRY. Meat packing and tanning are the main manufacturing industries. Others include beverages, clothing, foods, furniture, glassware, leather goods, linseed oil, and tobacco.

Uruguay imports more goods than it exports. Imports include raw materials, automobiles, cotton, fuel, iron, steel, and machinery, while wool and meat are the main exports. It trades mostly with Brazil, Britain, West Germany, and Argentina. Uruguay joined the Latin American Free Trade Association in 1960.

CITIES. Uruguay is divided into 19 departments, each with its own capital city. Of these, Montevideo is the most important, as the cultural, recreational, and commercial center of the country.

MONTEVIDEO is the capital and largest city of Uruguay, with a population of 1.4 million. It is located on the eastern bank of the Río de la Plata, 135 miles southeast of Buenos Aires. The Old City (*Ciudad Vieja*) is on a small peninsula, on the west side of the city. The New City (*Ciudad Nueva*) lies east of it. Spanish settlers founded Montevideo in 1726, and the city suffered many sieges during Uruguay's struggle for independence.

The chief industry is meat packing, and the city handles three-quarters of Uruguay's exports. Companies of many countries have offices, factories, and packing houses here.

The capital has preserved very little of its Colonial past. Focal point of its non-resort activity is the **Plaza Independencia,** dominated by the handsome **Presidential Palace,** which has the distinction of being guarded by only two soldiers. Nearby is the old but elegant **Teatro Solís.**

Uruguayans are almost as proud of their **Legislative Palace** as they are of their representative government. The palace, most elaborate such edifice on the continent, is built almost entirely of native marble, topped with gold. The meeting place for both chambers of government, it contains beautiful murals showing historic feats of Uruguay, a complete library, and a central aisle of marble and bronze, known as "America's Hall," bordered by granite pedestals supporting busts of the "Fathers of the American Independence."

There is, as well, an old and lovely cathedral. There are scores of handsome, well-designed modern office-buildings and apartment houses lining wide boulevards, many pleasant sidewalk cafés, and beautiful parks.

PAYSANDÚ. With a population of about 47,000, Paysandú is the fourth largest city in Uruguay, and capital of the department of the same name. Lying on the east bank of the Uruguay River, about 300 miles northwest of Montevideo, Paysandú is an important meat-packing and railroad center. The city's chief products include meat, soap, and shoes.

SALTO. Located 60 miles northwest of Paysandú is Salto, with a population of about 55,000. An important trading center for farmers and ranchers of northern Uruguay, it is sometimes called the "City of Oranges" because of its large orange and tangerine groves.

Other smaller cities include **Mercedes,** a livestock center and resort; **San José,** with one of the best and largest of the country's churches; **Rivera,** divided by a street from the Brazilian town of Santa Ana do Livramento; and **Treinta y Tres,** a thriving agricultural community.

SPORTS AND RECREATION. Beaches and resorts such as Montevideo, Carrasco, and Punta del Este make the country a favorite South American vacationland. Solís, Santiago, Vazquez, Atlantida, and many other river and coastal cities are popular for their fishing and boating.

Of the vacation areas, **Punta del Este** is perhaps the most famous. It is a curved peninsula on the extreme southeast of the country, 130 miles from Montevideo. The temperatures range from about 75 in summer to about 50 during the winter months. On the water, there is a 25-mile strip of beaches, including **La Pastora, Marangatu, Pine Beach, Marconi, El Grillo, Arcobaleno, La Brava, Chiberta, San Rafael, Draga, Barra,** and others.

Montevideo's beaches provide a haven of relaxation in contrast with city life. **Ramírez** is the site of the most opulent waterfront hotels, and features a casino. There are also an open-air theater, golf links, children's playgrounds, and other recreational facilities. Other beaches are **Pocitos,** the city's best and oldest, five minutes from Montevideo; **Buceo,** site of the Uruguayan Yacht Club and the Icthyological Museum; **Malvin,** featuring an open-air cinema; **Verde,** with its *Club Naútico de Carrasco;* **Carrasco,** a residential and seaside resort with magnificent private homes and gardens; **La Mulato, Miramar,** and **Pajas Blancas.**

Sports (*deportes*) play an important part in Uruguayan life. In the **Estadio**

Centenario, the open-air stadium in Montevideo, *fútbal* (soccer in the United States), the national sport, is played. The Uruguayan team has been four times world champion. There are also national **rowing** and **cycling** teams. Other sports include **tennis, basketball, swimming, golf, boating, fishing,** some **hunting**–partridge and rabbit–**boxing,** and **horse racing** at **Maroñas Park** in Montevideo. The government runs a **lottery** and **casino,** the latter featuring roulette and baccara. Revenue from this is used to support education and city hospitals.

There are also a national ballet, **Balle del Sodre,** a **Compania Nacional de Teatre** (National Theatre Company) and an **Orcestra Simfónica del Sodre** (National Symphony Orchestra).

SPECIAL EVENTS. Uruguay celebrates its most colorful festival, **Carnival,** during the three days before Lent. Although the official celebration is only three days, the festivities continue throughout the entire month of February, with floats, carnival figures, grotesque costumes, street dancing and parades, masked balls, and fiestas.

The *Gauchos* (cowboys) of Uruguay's ranches can be seen each March during the annual **Semana Criolla** (Creole Week). This can best be likened to an urban rodeo. *Gauchos* converge on Montevideo from miles around in their elaborate outfits: beautifully woven, subtly colored *ponchos;* flattop, wide-brimmed hats; magnificent silver spurs; baggy *bombachas* (trousers); and high leather boots. There are exhibitions of riding and steer breaking, horse shows, and musical programs, featuring the *Gauchos'* traditional folk songs, sung to guitar accompaniment.

Other important holidays include **Día de los Reyes** (Day of the Kings), on January 6, commemorating the visit of the three kings to Christ. Uruguayan children receive presents on this day, making their Christmas season longer and more festive. April 19 celebrates the **Desembarco de los Treinta y Tres** (Landing of the Thirty-Three), who crossed the Río Uruguay, beginning the independence movement.

May 1 is **Labor Day,** a legal holiday. **Batalla de las Piedras** (Battle of Las Piedras Day) is celebrated on May 18 with parades and festivities. It commemorates one of the largest battles fought against Spain in the war for independence. **July 4** is celebrated in honor of the United States. **Jura de la Constitución** (ratification of the Constitution) is a legal holiday, on July 18, and is celebrated with parades. October 12, **Día de la Raza** (Day of the Race) commemorates Christopher Columbus.

DINING AND SHOPPING. Beef is a diet mainstay in Uruguay, and is complemented by Italian and French specialties. Popular dishes include *pavesa,* a delicious beef broth topped with poached egg, and *asado con cuero,* or beef barbecued in its hide. An *estancia* (outdoor stand) is an ideal place to sample Uruguay's two national drinks: *yerba maté,* a South American tea, drunk from gourds through specially designed sippers, and *grappa,* Uruguay's highly potent version of aquavit.

Shopping is exceptionally interesting in Montevideo. Fur coats of Uruguayan nutria cost considerably less than in the United States. Worthwhile, too, are sweaters and scarves of Uruguayan cashmere and lamb's wool, and such locally processed leather goods as handbags, wallets, belts, jackets, compacts, and briefcases in alligator and calfskin. Semi-precious stones can also be bought for good value.

Chile

Chile, a long strip of land stretching along the west coast of South America more than half the length of the continent, is a country of incredible geographic contrasts, incomparable scenic beauty and varied tourist attractions.

THE LAND. Hemmed in by the formidable snow-covered cordillera of the

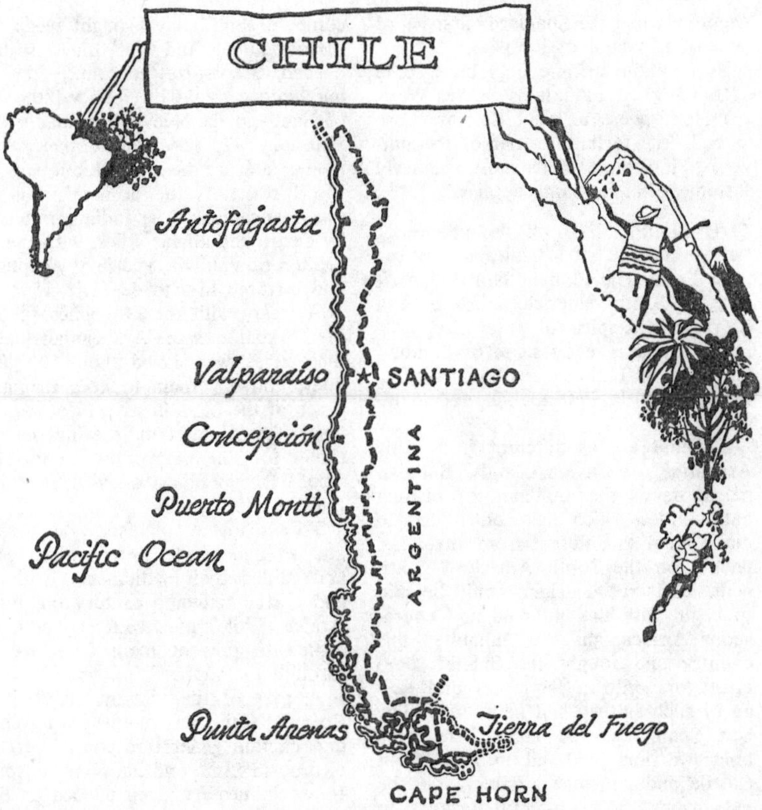

Andes on the east, and the vast limitless Pacific Ocean on the west, the country's 292,257 square miles—equal to the combined areas of Washington, Oregon and California—extend from Peru in the north to the southern tip of the continent.

It is a country of rich natural resources, and topographic and climatic extremes, which can be generally subdivided into three principal areas: the dry, sun-baked, rainless north, where most of Chile's wealth in nitrates and minerals is found; the fertile agricultural central region, where many of the nation's vineyards and industries are located and where 90 percent of its 8.8 million population is concentrated; and the rain-drenched, densely forested and largely unknown, undeveloped and unpopulated south.

THE CLIMATE. The seasons in Chile are the opposite of those in the United States, with the warmer climates in the north and the colder in the south. The northern desert areas require light tropical clothing; the central part around Santiago, light, medium-weight suits and dresses, sweaters and topcoats all year round; and the harsher, colder climate in the south, heavier winter clothing, and raincoats and umbrellas, even in summer.

The name of the country by an amazing etymological coincidence means in the language of the Incas exactly what it sounds like in English. In Quechua, the word *chiri* means cold or snow. In Aymara, *chilli* connotes "the ends of the world." It was both of these things to the Indians who inhabited the warmer, more northerly lands of South

America when the Spaniards first heard tales of this land of icy peaks.

But, although Chile may have some of the highest mountains in the Western Hemisphere in what Bolívar chose to call "the farthest corner of the universe," it is only in its most southerly extremes that its name applies.

THE PEOPLE. Of all the people of Latin America, the Chileans are the least Latin. Called the "North Americans of South America," they have a characteristic spirit of enterprise, self-reliance and a ready sense of humor—and such un-Latin names as O'Higgins, Pratt, Edwards, Petrinovitch, and Brunson.

Chileans are as different from their Argentine, Peruvian, and Bolivian neighbors as the amalgam of distinct nationalities which has contributed to make them so different from any other people on the South American continent. Their racial origins could be said to begin with the untamed and courageous Araucanians who inhabited this country and fought the Spanish conquistadors with a fierceness and savagery such as they had never seen. The first Spaniards who came here were bold warriors and adventurers from Castile and Andalusia. Later came the industrious and resourceful Basques, to be followed by successive migrations of English, Irish, Germans, French, Italians and Yugoslavs into the Chilean melting pot. They helped to shape the Chilean character and personality and make this the most homogeneous country in South America.

Although Magellan was the first white man to see what is now Chile when he sailed through the straits which bear his name, it wasn't until 1536 that Diego de Almagro led an expedition of 100 Spanish conquistadors and several thousand Indians from Peru into Chile. The Spaniards, like the Incas before them, found a tribe of hostile Araucanians, instead of the gold they were seeking, and quickly returned, bitterly disappointed. Five years later Pedro de Valdivia followed the same Inca road into Chile; but this time the Spaniards had come to stay. They brought seeds, domestic animals and everything else they needed to colonize the country, including women. Valdivia founded the city of Santiago de Nueva Estremadura on February 12, 1541, and other settlements later as he pushed on past the Bío Bío River, the no-man's land of the Araucanians. The Indians retaliated by destroying all his cities, with the exception of Valdivia, and finally captured and tortured him to death in 1554.

A treaty with the Mapuches (people of the land), as the Araucanians called themselves, was signed about 100 years later, allowing them to keep the lands south of the Bío Bío River. But war between the colonists and the Indians continued for 300 years; and not until 1877 would these Indians allow settlers into their territory.

To add to the colonists' woes, British and French pirates infested the coast and raided their settlements from the end of the sixteenth century on. Punta Arenas, Chile's most southerly city, was settled to prevent them from passing through the strait.

A part of the viceroyalty of Peru, Colonial Chile was ruled by a governor and captain general responsible to the viceroy in Lima and the King of Spain. It proclaimed its independence on September 18, 1810, under the leadership of General Bernardo O'Higgins.

The Spanish forces resumed control of the country in 1813 and held it until 1817, when San Martín marched his army across the Andes to join with O'Higgins and defeat them in the Battle of Chacabuco on February 17. The independence of Chile was assured a year later, in April 1818, after the Battle of Maipú, just outside Santiago, but it took five years more before the Chilean Navy under Admiral Lord Cochrane could break Spain's grip on Chile. O'Higgins became supreme dictator and ruled Chile for five years, giving it its first constitution and a navy, abolishing slavery, opening schools and libraries, promoting trade and agriculture.

Chile's present constitution dates from 1925, and provides for a republican form of government. After the

War of the Pacific (1879–83), which was fought against Peru and Bolivia for control of the great nitrate fields, Chile extended its territory to include the provinces of Antofagasta and Tarapacá.

A leader in social legislation, Chile set up the first social security system in the Western Hemisphere, which today ranks as one of the best in the world. Its preventive medicine law provides some measure of medical insurance for most Chileans. It was also one of the first countries to abolish slavery in 1823.

AGRICULTURE. Large dairy farms fill great amounts of central Chile. Also, vineyards cover about 250,000 acres and a good deal of wine is exported. In spite of this, agriculture supplies only about 10 percent of the gross national product. About 30 out of every 100 Chileans live on farms, many of which they now own, due to a government-sponsored agrarian reform program which was begun in 1965.

Chief crops include wheat, oats, corn, rice, beans, peas, and potatoes, with cattle, hogs, and sheep the most important livestock. Excellent lemons, peaches, grapes, apples, and oranges are also grown.

INDUSTRY. Chile, one of the leading manufacturing countries in Latin America, has three main industrial centers—Santiago, Valparaíso, and Concepción. Here are manufactured consumer goods (food products, clothing, and home appliances), and steel (Huachipato, near Concepción, has one of the most modern steel plants in the Western Hemisphere). Over one-fifth of the country's working force is employed in manufacturing.

Mining is Chile's most important industry, with copper, iron ore and nitrates accounting for 75 percent of the value of all exports. One of the top copper-producing countries in the world, Chile also mines large quantities of natural sodium nitrate, crude iodine, and coal.

CITIES. The leading cities of Chile include Antofagasta, Concepción, Santiago, Valparaíso, and Viña del Mar.

ANTOFAGASTA is a city of pleasant plazas, attractive walks and gardens around a crescent-shaped harbor which is sheltered by the mountains surrounding it. Founded in 1870, following the discovery of nitrate nearby, it has become the nitrate and copper capital of Chile. Its cosmopolitan population, numbering over 125,000, includes a sizable British colony and adequate representation from Spain, Yugoslavia, Greece, Italy and China.

Large freighters lie at anchor in the quiet bay while they take on their rich cargoes of nitrates from the area and copper from **Chuquicamata,** the largest open-pit copper mine in the world. The giant anchor on one of the hills overlooking the city was painted in 1886 to honor the first ship which entered this harbor. It seldom rains here and the climate is temperate and dry, with the best season being from May to September. An excellent beach is at **Mejillones,** about 40 miles north, where there is also an 18-hole golf course.

The wild, arid **Atacama Desert** northeast of Antofagasta was described by Darwin as "the largest dry area on earth" and is one of the most fantastic regions on the face of the globe. Nature seems to defy man to live in this desolate wasteland which has been aptly described as a "valley of the moon." Yet this area around Chuquicamata contains the world's richest known reserves of copper, iron, sulfate, nitrate and many other minerals. Within the past 40 years, an entire mountain has been dug away, and the hole from which these treasures have been taken is now more than a mile and a half long, half a mile wide and over 700 feet deep. Most of the copper and minerals produced here are exported, providing more than 80 percent of Chile's foreign-exchange income.

Pre-Inca ruins said to date back from 6,000 to 8,000 years are seen in **Lasana, Turi** and **San Pedro de Atacama,** formerly fortified towns in the north of Chile near the Bolivian frontier. At San

Pedro de Atacama near the Bolivian border a Jesuit priest has uncovered arrows and spears, crude pottery, and the mummified remains of an ancient civilization that may have existed here more than 6,000 years ago. The legend also persists that an immense gold chain and bull guards the treasure of an Inca buried nearby in an icy lake atop an extinct volcano.

ARICA, a patch of green palm trees and squat houses at the edge of the rainless, sun-baked desert of Atacama, is Chile's most northerly seaport. This busy commercial city is also a rich repository of history and legend. From its quaint little plaza you can see the harbor that was shelled by Sir Francis Drake. Dominating the city is **El Morro,** a cliff jutting out over the Pacific, which was the site of an important battle between Chile and Peru for control of the rich nitrate fields. Other tourist attractions are the little iron church of **San Marcos,** whose construction was supervised by Gustave Eiffel who designed the famed Paris landmark; the old American steamship **Wateree** which sailed a mile and a half inland across the desert during the great tidal wave of 1862 and is still there for all to see; and the **Virgin of the Drowned One,** whose sad legend is related to those who visit this grotto on the side of El Morro. This is also where you'll find a unique nine-hole golf course without a single blade of grass—all sand. Railroads connect this busy international port of over 90,000 people with Peru and landlocked Bolivia, which imports and exports about half of her economic needs through Arica. The **Pan-American Highway** comes down along the coast from Peru and branches off from here through desert towns south to Santiago and across the Andes through Uspallata Pass to Mendoza in Argentina.

CONCEPCIÓN, on the banks of the Bío Bío River not far from the sea, sheltered on three sides by the wooded hills which surround it, is one of the southern region's most attractive cities. It is also the third largest city in Chile, with a population of over 190,000, the "Capital of the South of Chile," and an important industrial center. Founded in 1550 by Pedro de Valdivia, on the site where the town of Penco is today, Concepción was capital of the country during the sixteenth century and a military outpost to be taken and destroyed by the fierce Araucanian Indians again and again. It was also attacked repeatedly by pirates and completely demolished by an earthquake in 1751. Rebuilt on its present site, it again suffered another earthquake in 1939, and again was reconstructed. Most of the new buildings are *asimico*—earthquake-proof. While the weather is invariably pleasant during the summer months from October to March, it rains heavily here during the winter from April to September.

To best see Concepción, go to the top of **Caracol Hill,** in the center of town, where you will see a spectacular view of the city, its lovely bays and lakes and the Bío Bío River flowing out to the sea. The residential district with its beautiful estates and clubs borders **Pedro de Valdivia Avenue.** Modern buildings, commercial houses and theaters are seen in the business area around the **Plaza de Armas.** Two of the outstanding sights here are the **University of Concepción,** in the suburb of La Toma, which is mainly financed by the city's lottery, and the **Gregorio Fuente murals** in the railroad station.

Other nearby places of interest are Chile's biggest coal-mining center at **Lota,** on a cliff overlooking the ocean, where the ore is mined; the naval base and seaport of **Talcahuano** with the steel mills of **Huachipato** nearby; the attractive seaside resorts of **San Vicente, Penco, Tomé, Dichato** and **Laraquete;** and the 150-foot **Falls of Laja.** There is fine trout fishing around **Laraquete.**

COQUIMBO, nine miles south of La Serena and on the same sheltered bay, is the winter quarters of the Chilean Navy. There are fine beaches to the south near the port of Guayacán. The little town of **Andacollo** near here is the site of one of the most colorful religious ceremonies and rituals on the continent, the **pilgrimage to the Virgen del Rosario,** around Christmas time.

IQUIQUE, a bustling seaport near the country's nitrate and iodine mining center, is gaining new prominence as the site for some of the finest deep-sea fishing in the world. The waters near here abound with swordfish, yellow-fin tuna, striped marlin and broadbill, to name a few, and many records have been broken. Weather conditions are ideal. There is seldom any rain or fog, rarely any wind, and the sea is invariably calm. Most anglers use the boats and facilities of the Iquique Yacht Club, which is less than 100 yards from their hotel. There is excellent bathing at the beach from November to March and fine mineral springs at Termas de Mamiña, in the foothills of the Andes about 60 miles from town. A monument to Arturo Prat, Chile's naval hero, commemorates the battle he fought off Iquique in 1879, and marks the center of the city.

LA SERENA (*San Bartolomé de La Serena*) is a historic old coastal town at the mouth of the Elqui River which is noted for its Colonial architecture, beautiful gardens and orchards and charming resort atmosphere. Founded in 1544 by one of Valdivia's captains, destroyed by Indians and sacked by pirates, it has been completely rebuilt into one of the country's most attractive cities. This was where Chile declared its independence from Spain on February 27, 1818, and where its eminent poetess Gabriela Mistral was born. The road along the coast to the port of Coquimbo takes you to the popular beach of **Peñuelas** with its casino and exhibition grounds where rodeos are held in February and March.

OSORNO, another important tourist center in the heart of the Chilean lake region, is a pleasant Colonial city which strongly reflects the German influence of its inhabitants. It is also known for its annual cattle expositions. Nearby are the **Falls of Pilmaiquén,** which cascade down from a height of 100 feet; **Lake Ranco,** and its tributary streams where the trout fishing is good; and the resort and mineral springs of **Puyehue** with its comfortable and luxurious stone hotel.

Good skiing is provided on the slopes of **Mount Osorno,** on the shores of the area's largest body of water, **Lake Llanquihue. Puerto Varas,** at the southern end of the lake, is a placid little city in the midst of tall mountains. It is also the starting point for a thrilling trip by bus and auto across the border into Argentina. The trip begins with a bus ride around the lake to **Ensenada,** skirting the hills to **Petrohué** at the edge of **Lago Todos Los Santos** (All Saints Lake). Theodore Roosevelt called this "the most beautiful lake in all the world." From here the trip continues by boat across the lake to **Peulla** and the Argentine frontier, with some spectacular lake and mountain scenery on the way as the mountains of Puntiagudo, Techado and Tronador pass in review. From Peulla it is by bus again to **Casa Pangue** to clear Chilean customs; and then by winding road across the border and on to **Puerto Frias,** on **Lake Frias,** to clear Argentine customs. The rest of the trip through the Argentine lake region is an equally spectacular boat trip across this lake, bus to **Puerto Blest,** and boat again across **Lake Nahuel Huapi** to **Bariloche.**

There are good hotels in most of the key cities in the Chilean lake region and adequate accommodations in some of the more remote areas. The food is typically Chilean, which means that it is excellent. And in the way of fun and diversion, there is fishing, swimming, boating, hunting, riding, mountain climbing and skiing. Here also, according to the rod and reel experts, is where you'll find some of the finest fresh-water fishing in the world. The many lakes, rivers, and streams such as **Lake Villarrica, Lake Riñihue, Lake Ranco, Lake Rupanco,** and the **rivers Rahue, Bueno, Fui, Trancura** and the **Toltén,** are among the best for fishing.

PUERTO MONTT, a panorama of trim, shingled houses and little farms, looks out over the Gulf of Reloncavi at the southern terminus of the Chilean state railways. Big ocean-going freighters lie like sleeping giants in its picturesque harbor, waiting to take out their cargoes of timber, wool and leather to other areas of the country and the world. This could be aptly described as the end of the earth, for south of here is an inland sea, and travel has to be by ship through a maze of channels and islands to the Pacific Ocean. From here south it is one green island after another, in what is known as the vast glacial archipelago of **Chilóe.** Its labyrinth of gulfs, channels and islands is indicative of the many hardships of the first mariners who ventured here, with such foreboding names as the Gulf of Troubles, Useless Bay, Delirium Point, Island of Deceit, Adventure Pass, Island of the Devil and Port of Famine. Although these coasts were thoroughly explored and charted by Charles Darwin on his famous voyage of the *Beagle*, the area is still practically unknown. Chile's newest province, **Aisén,** was founded here as recently as 1928 and is noted for its glaciers and icebergs.

PUNTA ARENAS, on the stormy, wind-swept Strait of Magellan, is the world's most southerly city, about 1,700 miles south of Valparaíso. Over 65,000 people live in this capital of the province of Magallanes, which is noted primarily for its thriving wool industry and as the site of the biggest sheep farming company in the world. Founded in 1849 as a penal colony, the city has grown into a prosperous, orderly community of attractive little houses, lovely parks and well-paved streets. Although there are no railways, it is connected via a good road with Río Gallegos in the Argentine and can be reached by plane from Santiago or ship from Valparaíso. It has good facilities for ice skating and skiing during the winter and fine fishing in the summer. It also has a race track, a nine-hole golf course and a museum with exhibits of the wildlife and Indian lore of the region. For spectacular scenery, an excursion to **Última Esperanza** (Last Hope), the beautiful region of fiords, snow-capped mountains, and serene lakes, is recommended. There are also trips to other areas **in Tierra del Fuego.** At **Fort Bulnes** is an old Chilean fort that protected the city against pirates in other days. The weather in this region is windy and cold most of the year.

SANTIAGO is a thriving modern metropolis of over 2.5 million inhabitants which enjoys a spectacular setting on a broad fertile plain in the shadow of the towering snow-topped Andes. At an altitude of close to 2,000 feet and sheltered from inclement weather by the mountains which surround it, the city enjoys an ideal temperate climate and invigorating atmosphere practically all year round. It has been the capital since 1818. Although its tall skyscrapers and crowded streets are indicative of its importance as the industrial, commercial and cultural center of the country, the city is noted for its many tourist attractions and the effusive charm and friendliness of its citizens. Its fine restaurants rank with the best on the continent, and its varied and cosmopolitan cuisine is a gourmet's delight. There are the usual night clubs, cabarets and theaters and some unusual ones, such as a 200-year-old Colonial inn where Chileans go to recite poetry and sip mulled wine.

One of the city's major attractions for travelers and residents alike is its central location near mountain and seaside resorts. The ski fields of **Portillo, Farellones, La Parva** and **Lagunillas** and the seaside resorts of **Viña del Mar, Concón, Santo Domingo** and **Tejas Verdes** are only a matter of hours away. Just outside the city are the vineyards and the *fundos* (farms), where you can see how Chile's famous wines are produced and watch the colorful, poncho-clad *huasos.*

Essentially a modern city, Santiago has not forgotten its Colonial past. Everywhere one sees evidence of another era when this was a picturesque town of narrow streets, one-story stucco buildings, pleasant parks and formal gardens. The broad, tree-lined **Avenida Bernardo O'Higgins** is a veritable hall of fame with statues of the great men of the country on each block. The colorful ceremony of the changing of the guard takes place every day in front of the presidential palace.

The first colonists laid out their city around the **Plaza de Armas,** between the Mapocho River and Avenida Bernardo O'Higgins, and this is where most of the principal buildings are still situated. On one side of this large tree-filled plaza are the **archbishop's palace** and the cathedral. The latter contains many religious and artistic treasures, such as the chapel of the Holy Sacrament, a replica of the one in SS. Peter and Paul in Rome, and the chandelier which lighted the meetings of congress following the liberation of Chile. Facing the plaza also are the post office and city hall. Shops, restaurants and night clubs line the arcades on the other two sides. A block to the west of the plaza is the magnificent palm-studded **congressional palace.** The streets radiating from the plaza in the business district known as El Centro are lined with fine shops, big department stores, good hotels and excellent restaurants. On Agustinas, three blocks from the plaza, is the **Municipal Theater** where outstanding musical and dramatic programs are presented. Two blocks up this street is the little hill of **Santa Lucía** which has been preserved as a museum and park. The huge statue of Valdivia stands at one end of the park, looking down from the terraced parapets and rocky gardens on the city he founded. The museum has an interesting collection of folk art and primitive firearms used by the Spaniards. The astronomical observatory on this hill was the first in Chile.

Two blocks from here, along Avenida O'Higgins, is the **National Library,** and next to it the **Museum of Natural History,** which has one of the finest archaeological collections of the Colonial period and the War of Independence. The red brick **Church of San Francisco,** the oldest church in Santiago, is two blocks farther. Inside is the small statue of Our Lady which Valdivia always carried with him. On the next block along this same avenue, which is also known as the Avenida de las Delicias (Avenue of Delights), are the **University of Chile** and, across the street, the **Club de la Union,** an exclusive men's club and gathering place of Santiago's elite.

Farther west on the avenue are the big skyscraping government buildings of the **Barrio Civico,** where the country's civic and administrative offices are located. The **Casa de la Moneda,** a two-story Colonial building which took almost 20 years to build and was once the mint, is across the Plazas Bulnes and Libertad. This is now the government palace where the President lives and works. Not far from here on Calle Nueva York is the country's stock market. **Parque Cousiño,** at the western end of town, is a large recreational area with a small lake, facilities for practically all kinds of sports and a popular playground and athletic field. This is where the **Independence Day Parade** is held on September 18. Nearby are the handsome gardens and buildings of the **Club Hipico,** one of the finest race tracks in South America. Also in Santiago is the Catholic University of Chile.

Other interesting attractions around the city are the thickly forested **Parque Forestal** where the **Palace of Fine Arts** is located and art exhibitions are held throughout the year; the **National Museum of Natural History,** with the incredibly well preserved mummy of the Inca child found on the summit of a 17,000-foot mountain near Santiago, and some of the armor worn by the first Spaniards; and **Cerro San Cristóbal,** overlooking the city. The statue of Our Lady of San Cristóbal graces the summit of this 1,000-foot-high, pine-tree-covered hill, which offers some splendid views of the city and a restaurant near the top reached by foot, car or funicular railway.

One of the most breathtaking sights in the world is the view from your plane as you cross this city. The icy crest of 22,834-foot **Cerro Aconcagua,** the highest mountain in the Western Hemisphere, is usually discernible in the midst of this rugged mountain terrain of massive snow-covered rock and deep purple canyons. On a wind-swept pass below stands the lonely figure of the **Christ of the Andes,** a symbol of eternal peace and good will between Chile and Argentina.

The two most popular excursions out of Santiago are to the beaches on the coast in the summer and the ski resorts in the Andes in the winter. Both are relatively near and take only a few hours by car or train. **Viña del Mar,** which takes its name from a vineyard planted near the sea by one of the early conquistadors several centuries ago, is one of the most delightful seaside resorts in South America. The vineyard is still bearing fruit outside the city limits in a fragrant, fertile valley. Thousands of tourists and local vacationists come here each year from December to March for the summery weather, sunswept beaches, excellent resort hotels, handsome race track, and a luxurious gambling casino. This playground on the Pacific sprawls leisurely on the sloping hills overlooking the ocean amid handsome villas, stately mansions and palm-studded, well-paved streets. This is Chile's own Cote d'Azur, the Chilean Riviera, where a smart, cosmopolitan, carefree crowd gathers in the summer, and the briny breezes are perfumed with the smell of jacaranda, honeysuckle, oleander and wisteria.

Viña has facilities for all kinds of sports from water-skiing and horseback riding to golf and cricket, international polo matches and yachting. Its outstanding attraction and showplace, however, is its magnificent casino, where, in addition to more roulette tables than in Monte Carlo, you will find a lavishly decorated dining room, a restaurant and bar, a library and reception room, and a boîte and cabaret with continuous dancing. Other sightseeing attractions are the open-air museum and botanical gardens at **Quinta Vergara,** with an excellent art collection, fine arts school, and a unique assortment of tropical flora; and the aquarium at the **Oceanographic Institute** of the University of Chile at nearby **Montemar.** In the way of hotels, some of the finest in the country are found in Viña. Many wealthy people of Santiago move to Viña during the summer. As would be expected, bathing in and around Viña is excellent —although the Humboldt Current offshore keeps the water cool and invigorating throughout the year. The best beaches are at **Salinas** and **Concón,** about ten miles north of Viña. The restaurants are excellent along the way. Farther north is the Bucanero, a seaside hotel at **Coquimbo** which was a former pirate stronghold. Two points of interest in Viña are **Parque Vergara** and **Parque del Salitre.**

Zapallar, about a four-hour drive north of here, is perhaps one of the most beautiful beaches in Chile. It is in a small secluded bay surrounded by pine trees and lovely gardens. The nearest beach resort to Santiago is **Rocas de Santo Domingo,** which is south of Viña and Valparaíso. Its strikingly beautiful rock formations and nearby pine and eucalyptus forests make it especially attractive to summertime travelers. **Tejas Verdes,** with its first-rate swimming pool in a garden setting near here, is also a popular vacation spot. Up the coast about halfway from Santiago to Valparaíso is **Algarrobo,** one of the few good beaches with a sheltered bay.

From June to mid-October, which is winter in Chile, ski resorts not far from this modern, mountain-ringed but seldom snowed-in capital become a mecca for skiers from all over the world. Although skiing in Chile is a relatively new sport, believed to have been introduced by British engineers building the trans-Andean railroad, the idea has quickly caught on and skiing here is now a popular pastime. The nearest ski resort is at **Farrelones,** about an hour and a half by car from the center of Santiago. Perched on the side of 7,300-foot Mount Colorado, it offers some of the best ski slopes, adequate facilities, including a 6,000-foot chair lift, and some of the most spectacular scenery in Chile. Its six-mile downhill run, known as La Gran Bajada (The Great Descent), will more than satisfy most skiers when it comes to thrills and spills. Another resort nearby is **La Parva,** about two miles from Farrelones, with equally fine skiing within its 2,000 acres.

But the resort that attracts most of the international set and especially skiers from the United States is **Portillo.** High in the Chilean Andes, more than 9,000 feet, and only about four miles from the Argentine border, this sky-top ski resort offers every convenience in a big seven-story hotel and ski conditions that are unexcelled. Towering mountains shelter the treeless slopes right in front of the hotel and make it possible for skiers to shed heavy clothing and ski in their shirt sleeves. One of the longest runs here is a three-mile dash which ends at Juncal, the next stop on the railroad, where skiers can take the train back to Portillo. There are also several world championship courses with 5,000- and 6,000-foot runs and little climbing, as well as a full-day ski excursion to the statue of the Christ of the Andes. Other ski resorts in the vicinity are **Lagunillas** and **Los Valdes.** Portillo is about five-and-one-half hours from Santiago on the trans-Andean railroad which continues across the cordillera to Mendoza and Buenos Aires in Argentina. The trip also can be made by car in the summer. Nearby are the **Baños de Jahuel,** a health resort at 4,000 feet, known for the therapeutic qualities of its mineral waters and superb mountain scenery, which attract many vacationists. Aconcagua, the highest mountain in the western hemisphere, can be seen from here. **Los Andes,** at 2,400 feet, is a charming mountain town in the heart of a rich agricultural and wine-producing area and an important railroad juncture for international travelers who must change trains here. **Río Blanco,** where the rivers Blanco and Juncal join to form the Aconcagua River, is a popular vacation resort.

Chile's central valley, in the heart of the country, is a very fertile and picturesque area which extends itself between two mountain ranges and is dotted with pleasant towns and delightful resorts. These are some of the principal ones: **Rancagua,** about 51 miles south of the capital and the site of one of O'Higgins' famous battles with the Spaniards, is near the **Baños de Cauquenes,** a health resort and mineral springs said to have been frequented by the two liberators. **San Fernando** is a tiny agricultural town about 32 miles from Santiago that still conserves its Colonial traditions. **Curicó,** another 35 miles farther south in the heart of Chile's cattle country, is noted for its fine leather handicrafts and the festive spirit of its citizens. Its main plaza is a typical Colonial landmark. **Talca,** 150 miles or so from Santiago, is the center of one of the greatest wine-producing regions of Chile and equally well known for its varied and delicious fruit. Some of the best trout fishing is found in **Laguna del Maule** nearby. **Linares,** a picturesque spot 30 miles south of Talca, is noted for its medicinal hot springs and baths of *panimavida.* **Chillán,** about 65 miles south of Linares, is the site of one of the more famous spas of the country. The town, which was the birthplace of Bernardo O'Higgins, was destroyed by an earthquake in 1833. It was rebuilt nearby, destroyed by another earthquake in 1939 and again reconstructed. There is good skiing on the slopes of the Volcano Chillán.

TEMUCO, in the heart of what was formerly Araucanian territory, is the gateway to the Chilean lake region. The city abounds in native lore; and Indians from the surrounding villages come here to barter and sell their produce and handicrafts. There are good buys in pottery, silverware, ponchos and choapinos. Of special interest are the government-organized fiestas for the Indians of the region to preserve their folklore. Prizes are awarded for athletic skills and oratory. A good view of the city and the Cautin River Valley can be had from **Ñielol Hill.** This overlook also has a fine rustic restaurant at the summit.

VALDIVIA, a city of rivers near the sea, to which the Spanish conquistador gave his own name in 1552, is today a prosperous agricultural and industrial center. Its pronounced German atmosphere makes it appear more like a town in Bavaria than the Spanish Colonial city which the Araucanians could not destroy. The old Spanish forts and cannons which guarded this early settlement from Indians and pirates still can be seen at **Niebla** and **Mancera** nearby. Its seaport of **Corral** was the scene of one of the major naval battles in the War of 1812. Situated in an area of unsurpassed natural beauty, the city is near lovely lakes, good beaches, inland waterways and cool green forests. It has adequate facilities for bathing and boating, as well as skiing on the slopes of the **Mocho** and **Choshuenco volcanoes** and sightseeing excursions to nearby mountains and old Spanish ruins.

VALPARAÍSO, Chile's second largest city and most important seaport on the west coast of South America, occupies a setting of unparalleled scenic beauty as it nestles against the hills which surround its horseshoe bay. Since its founding in 1536 by the Spanish captain, Juan de Saavedra, this colorful seafaring city has been the port of call of vessels from the four corners of the earth, and its narrow cobblestone streets and picturesque waterfront still echo with the tales and adventures of famous intrepid mariners like Drake and Cochrane.

Completely devastated by the earthquake and tidal wave of 1906, Valparaíso has been practically rebuilt and today little remains of Colonial interest or antiquity. A part of this old section is seen in the area known as "The Port," which is centered around the little stucco church of La Matriz. The old tenements of "El Baron" district, named after Ambrosio O'Higgins, father of Chile's national hero, are near here. Most of the other buildings are not more than 50 years old. The newest section is also the business district, which stands in the center of town on a flat piece of land reclaimed from the sea. In general, the climate is mild, with the summer heat made tolerable by the fresh ocean breezes, but occasionally the north winds blow cold. Since most of the town is perched on the surrounding hills, funiculars (cable cars) provide the logical means of transportation.

A tour of the city usually begins at the statue of Arturo Prat, Chile's naval hero, in the **Plaza Sotomayor.** This is the city's main square, where the Intendencia, or **Palace of the Governor,** is located. The passenger landing terminal is also here, as is the **port railway station,** where you can board the train to Santiago.

Calle Prat, heart of the financial district, crosses the plaza and continues around Cerro Alegre (Happy Hill). It then becomes **Calle Esmeralda,** where most of the principal shops are located. Another key artery is **Calle Cochrane,** named after the father of the Chilean Navy, which runs into Plaza Echaurren and the **Church of La Matriz.** The broad **Avenida Pedro Montt,** with its many fine restaurants and theaters, leads to the lovely residential section of **El Almendral** (the Almond Grove). The market place is found on tree-lined **Avenida Brasil,** which is also the site of a monument commemorating the centenary of Chilean independence. The statues of Lord Cochrane and William Wheelwright, the North American who helped develop the country's transportation, are also displayed prominently. The first sidewalks, which were laid out by Don Ambrosio O'Higgins, are seen in the polished stone slabs on the **Subida de la Concepción.** The city has such an international air that even the streets and hills seem to have an individuality and nationality of their own. Pythagoras, Chopin, and Rousseau are street names. Cerro Alegre with its Anglican church is typically British, while Cerro Concepción is German and has a Lutheran church. Avenida Errazuriz leads north along the coastline to Viña del Mar. Avenida Altamirano goes south around the lighthouse at Punta de Angeles (Angels' Point) to the quiet beach of **Las Torpederas.** Chile's proud naval tradition is seen in the **naval academy** which overlooks the bay, and in the **Valparaíso naval museum** which contains many interesting nautical exhibits and displays. Its newspaper, *El Mercurio,* founded in 1826, is the oldest in South America. The seafood in and around Valparaíso is the finest in Chile, if not in all of South America.

The beach resorts of **Viña del Mar, Salinas** and **Concón** are a short distance north along the coast, and there are also many tiny fishing villages and modest hotels along the scalloped coastline where the tourist can spend a pleasant vacation. The **University of Santa María,** where students are trained in technical skills and sciences, is located near Viña. Going south from Valparaíso, a fine paved highway leads to the **Miradero** (Lookout), where Bernardo O'Higgins is said to have watched the Chilean fleet put out to sea to fight the Spaniards in Peru, near Alto del Puerto; **Placilla,** where a decisive battle in the war of 1891 took place; **Casablanca,** a vacation spot with good hotels and restaurants; **El Retiro,** another vacation resort 12 miles inland, near the town of Quilpué.

The **Juan Fernández Islands,** an archipelago of three islands, lie about 400 miles due west of Valparaíso and can be reached by ship in about six days. One of them, **Más a Tierra** (Closer to Land), is believed to have been the famous Robinson Crusoe Island where Alexander Selkirk spent five lonely years and inspired Daniel Defoe to write his immortal classic. Visitors to this island will see the cave on the beach where Selkirk lived and also his lookout on El Yunque peak, and hear stories of hidden pirate treasure. A plaque was placed here to Selkirk's memory in 1868 by the officers of the British warship, *Topaze*. The only town on this island is San Juan de Bautista, which overlooks Cumberland Bay, where the German battleship *Dresden* lies 70 fathoms deep. Its over 400 inhabitants live a simple existence hunting wild goats and fishing for cod, weighing as much as 200 pounds, and the giant lobsters which they send to the mainland. The two other islands which comprise the archipelago are tiny **Santa Clara** and the largest of the group, **Más Afuera** (Farther Out), which has served as a penal colony for political prisoners. Named for the Andalusian navigator who discovered them in 1574, the Juan Fernández Islands were once the hangout for pirates who played hide-and-seek with the Spanish Armada and raided the mainland. The best time of the year to visit them is from November to March but the climate is generally mild all year round.

VILLARRICA, on the western bank of the beautifully wooded lake of the same name, dates back to 1552. **Pucón,** on the eastern bank, and connected by road and lake boats with Villarrica, is the site of some fine hotels and excellent lodges. Both cities draw trout fishermen to the lake and nearby streams for some of the finest rainbow and brown trout fishing in the world. The smoking volcano of Villarrica forms a magnificent backdrop, and facilities for swimming, boating, water-skiing, golf and tennis are excellent. Regular bus service connects Pucón with **Bariloche** in the Argentine lakes via **Junín de los Andes** and **San Martín.** The route follows the Trancura River and winds along the flanks of several volcanoes, by **Lake Quilleihue** near the border of Argentina, and through Tromen Pass into Argentina.

There is also some fine trout fishing and magnificent scenery in and around lakes **Calafquén, Pellaifa, Panguipulli, Pirehueico, Neltume** and **Riñihue.**

SPORTS AND RECREATION. Chile is a true sportsman's paradise and a vacationland par excellence. As one would imagine, in a country with a 3,000-mile mountain range and a 4,000-mile coastline, there is no shortage here of mountain or seaside resorts and sports. For the seeker of sun and surf, few beaches can rival Viña del Mar, Chile's own Riviera, and adjacent resorts. For the mountain climber there is a challenging array of rugged terrain extending from the northern frontier to the southern lake region where he can roam to his heart's content. Chile's famed spas and mineral springs long have been an attraction for travelers from all over the hemisphere.

When it comes to **skiing,** there are few countries that can offer better slopes or finer snow than the Chilean Andes just outside Santiago. The skiing here is said to be the best in the hemisphere.

For the **fishing** enthusiast, one of the most abundant deep-sea fishing grounds in the world is located in the broad blue stretch of the Pacific Ocean off the coast of Chile. Throughout the year these waters teem with game fish to test the skill of the most adroit fishermen. The biggest broadbill swordfish ever caught was hooked off Tocopilla, and striped marlin, yellow-fin tuna, oceanic bonito, and dolphin can be picked up almost any time the bait is presented.

If your preference in fishing is of the fresh-water variety, the Chilean lakes region is a true paradise. The season officially runs from October 15 to April 15.

In the same area there is also good quail, dove, and partridge **hunting; boating** through crystal lakes and exciting rapids; mineral springs and baths; and restful vacationing and sightseeing in a natural wonderland of virgin forests and towering snow-clad volcanoes.

Not to be overlooked are the equestrian sports. Chileans are proud of their horses and horsemanship, as anyone will testify after seeing a performance of the Cuadro Verde de Carabineros (Green Dragoons of the Mounted Police), one of the world's outstanding equestrian teams, or watching a *huaso* (Chilean cowboy) at a rodeo stop a charging steer dead in its tracks.

SPECIAL EVENTS. The first big event of the year is **Día del Roto** (Day of the Chilean Worker), observed on January 20. Other important dates are the **Founding of Santiago** on February 12; **Valdivia Week,** commemorating the founding of Valdivia, celebrated from February 12–18 with special dances, competitive sports, and a torchlight procession; and the **Battle of Maipú,** which gave Chile its independence, on April 15. **Navy Day**, celebrated on May 21, commemorates the Battle of Iquique; the traditional **Cristo de Mayo** procession is held on May 13; and the **Patron Saints of Fishermen,** on June 29, is marked with colorful fiestas and religious pageants in coastal towns. The **Patron Saint of the Chilean Army** is honored on July 16, and the nation's independence day is September 18. Special athletic events include the **international ski championship** competition, held at Portillo on August 15, and Chile's famous **rodeos,** presented during July, August, and September. **Día de Carmen,** Chile's patron saint, falls on September 16, when there are processions and fiestas throughout the country.

DINING AND SHOPPING. Chilean cuisine is truly cosmopolitan and as varied as the tastes of the people in the different provinces. The restaurants in Santiago are among the finest in the hemisphere; and there are few places in the world where you can find such an abundance and diversity of fine foods, fruits and wines. The seafood here is superb: *erizos* (sea urchins), *locos* (a giant scallop), oysters, *ostiones* (shellfish), conger eels, *corvina,* and lobsters from the Juan Fernández Islands.

Some of the more typical dishes are the *pastel de choclo* (a delicious combination of corn, meat, chicken and assorted vegetables baked in a clay bowl), *cazuela de ave* (chicken stew in casserole with large chunks of chicken, a whole ear of corn, vegetables and rice), *empanadas de horno* (meat turnovers with a filling of raisins, chopped onions, peppers and olives), *humitas* (a tamale-like concoction of sweet corn meal wrapped in corn husk and boiled), *pancho villa* (a casserole dish consisting of beans, corn and poached eggs cooked in beef juice and spiced with garlic), *papas rellenas* (fried mashed-potato patties filled with chopped meat or cheese and onions dipped in beaten egg), *plátano dulce* (bananas sprinkled with cracked meal, cinnamon and powdered sugar, placed in a pan greased with melted butter and baked slowly in the oven). *Paltas* (avocados) are used extensively in the Chilean diet in salads, sandwiches, appetizers, as a complete meal, and are often stuffed with shrimp and mayonnaise dressing. *Alfajores,* Chile's national sweet, is a tiny round cake made of sugar and milk and topped with freshly grated coconut.

Principal beverage is wine, naturally. Chile is the second greatest wine-producing country in South America and its wines are world-famous. Wine is served in homes and restaurants throughout the country and is as indispensable at the table as a fork or spoon. The first vines were planted by missionaries in the sixteenth century to assure themselves wine for the sacraments. All classes and types are now produced, but the sauternes are best and Undurraga vineyard best known. Vintage years have no significance because the weather is always ideal.

Another popular national beverage is the *chicha,* a dry-sweet refreshment made from the freshly crushed grapes which have started to ferment. *Cazuela en frutilla,* large ripe crushed strawberries in burgundy or in *chirimoyas* (chilled white wine), are popular.

Best buys are in handicrafts, handwrought copper merchandise, trays and candlesticks; black pottery jars; *choapinos* (soft-napped wool rugs); wool blankets, belts, and scarves; maté gourds; stirrups, spurs; saddles and other articles of the *huaso;* fine cowhide belts and bags; carved wooden figurines and statues from Easter Island; musical instruments of chestnut wood from the Island of Chiloé; and of course, fine Chilean wines.

Argentina

Argentina, the second largest country in South America, is a land of spectacular natural beauty, astonishing contrasts, and myriad attractions as varied as its topography and climate.

THE LAND. Cradled between the broad Atlantic Ocean and the rugged Andes Mountains, Argentina is more than a million square miles in area—roughly about one-third the size of the continental United States—and stretches across the southeastern corner of the continent from the densely forested, swampy tropics of the Gran Chaco in the north to the frozen fiords of sub-Antarctic Tierra del Fuego in the extreme south.

Within this vast area are such a seemingly endless variety of scenic wonders and tourist attractions as the magnificent waterways along the Uruguay, Paraguay, and Paraná rivers; lovely national parks and famed seaside and mountain resorts; its towering snow-covered Andean cordillera; a coastline which extends for 2,500 miles from the Río de la Plata to the Strait of Magellan; and the wide, desolate pampas, which covers nearly a quarter of a million square miles in the heart of the country. Two-thirds of the nation's over 23 million population is concentrated in the big cities which rim this great expanse of flat, fertile farmland where most of the country's wealth in cattle and grain is found.

The social, political, cultural, and commercial center of this young, vigorous, and dynamic nation is Buenos Aires, one of the largest cities in the world. "B.A.," as most travelers refer to it, is the most cosmopolitan city in South America.

From here, it is only a matter of hours by plane or slightly longer by train, bus, or auto to the remotest corners of this bountifully endowed country, which is still relatively unknown to the vast majority of tourists. In the northwest provinces of Salta and Jujuy, about 1,000 miles from the fashionable and sophisticated social swirl that is Buenos Aires, descendants of an ancient civilization live in the same primitive simplicity today as they did centuries ago. In Misiones, to the northeast, the great falls of Iguazú National Park are a breath-taking spectacle, and the forests are thick with exotic vegetation. To the west, thousands of acres of grape-laden vines near Mendoza give ample evidence of Argentina's claim to being the biggest wine-producing country in the Americas and the fifth in the world, and its eternally snow-clad cordillera of the Andes is a challenge to mountaineers and a delight for winter sports enthusiasts. In the east it has the seaside resorts of Mar del Plata with more than five miles of beach front, hotels, restaurants and what is said to be the largest gambling casino in the world. In the

south is Bariloche, gateway to the Chile-Argentine lake region, Argentina's vacation playground where you can ride, ski, fish, hunt, or just take in the fascinating scenery of this natural wonderland. Farther south in Patagonia, which gets its name from the large feet of the Patagones Indians who once inhabited this region, is a rugged vacation area for the sportsman.

THE CLIMATE. In the central part of Argentina the climate is generally mild and temperate, making it a most pleasant and attractive place to visit all year round. The seasons are just the opposite of those in the United States, with spring taking place from September through November, summer from December through February, autumn from March through May, and winter from June through August. This means that you can go swimming in December and skiing in July, sailing in January, trout and salmon fishing in February, stag, bird and boar hunting in March, to the opera or a concert in August, a polo match in September, and to the horse races any Saturday or Sunday throughout the year.

THE PEOPLE. According to a recent census, over 97 percent of the population of Argentina is of European origin and emigrated within the last century. Spaniards are the most numerous, with Italians a close second. Few persons are of Indian or other non-Caucasian strains. The official language is Spanish, though English is widely spoken.

The legendary gaucho, the colorful, hard-riding, tough, lawless and ruggedly independent nomad who roamed the pampas—like the American cowboy—is almost a thing of the past. But the tradition lives on in some of the large *estancias* where modern gauchos still dress in *bombachas,* ponchos, and black felt hats, round up the cattle and do other ranch chores as they did in days gone by. The Indians who once inhabited this part of South America, too, are practically extinct today, with the exception of those still found in the Chaco region and a few others on the island of Tierra del Fuego. The ruins of the Calchaquis, who, like the Incas, lived in stone houses, can be seen in Tilcara, about 50 miles from Jujuy. And descendants of the tall, handsome Ona tribe, believed to have been the giant hunters described by Magellan, are still to be seen on the island of Tierra del Fuego. So also are some Yahgans, whose ancestors fished these waters. But there is hardly a trace of the Puelchean, Tehuelchean, and Araucanian tribes who once hunted guanaco and ostrich on horseback across the plains of Argentina and were virtually exterminated by the Argentine Army in 1881, when the first white settlers came.

The first European to set foot on what is now Argentina was the Spanish explorer Juan Diáz de Solís, who in 1516 sailed into the tidal estuary of the Río de la Plata and was promptly killed by hostile Indians. In 1520 Ferdinand Magellan anchored briefly in the same river before continuing southward to discover the strait which now bears his name and separates Tierra del Fuego from the mainland.

In the sixteenth century Argentina was the goal of many adventurers who believed this great "silver river" would lead them to the treasures of the New World. The first European settlement on El Plata, as Argentina was originally called, was founded by Sebastian Cabot in 1527. He was followed shortly thereafter by Diego García, who had been a member of the Solís expedition. However, starvation, Indian massacres and quarrels between the two explorers sent their expeditions back to Spain and frustrated the realization of any permanent colony for many years.

In 1536 Pedro de Mendoza established a settlement near the present site of Buenos Aires and gave it the imposing name of Puerto de Nuestra Señora del Buen Aire (Port of Our Lady of the Good Air), after the patron saint of the sailors, and not, as is popularly believed, because one of the first sailors to step ashore exclaimed, "How good the air of this land." Although the Indians were friendly at first they eventually turned on Mendoza and forced him to abandon the settlement; and it wasn't until 1580 that Juan de Garay founded Santa María de Buenos Aires.

For centuries Buenos Aires was nothing more than a Spanish military outpost of little note whose inhabitants depended largely on smuggling for their very existence. It became the seat of the viceroyalty of the Río de la Plata, comprising the present territory of Argentina, Uruguay, Paraguay, and part of what is now Bolivia, in 1776.

The city has a proud and glorious history in its struggle for liberty and freedom. In 1806 and again in 1807 it repelled several British invasions; and on May 25, 1810, with Napoleon's brother on the throne of Spain, the people of Buenos Aires deposed the viceroy and declared their allegiance to the government of imprisoned King Ferdinand VII. On July 9, six years later, under the leadership of the liberator General José de San Martín, the United Provinces of the Río de la Plata declared their independence.

Bernardino Rivadavia became the first president of the Argentine confederation in 1826 and the new nation progressed rapidly. Commercial treaties were signed with other nations, banking institutions were established, construction of schools, universities and hospitals was begun, and cattle were imported.

But before long the powerful feudal landowners resented the centralized control of the government in the hands of the aristocracy of Buenos Aires and the country soon was divided between these two opposing factions. This disunity led to the resignation of Rivadavia and a time of political indecision and civil strife which ended with the coming to power of the colorful and controversial dictator, Juan Manuel de Rosas, who, ironically, was responsible for uniting Argentina while seeking local autonomy for the landowners. He was overthrown by one of his allies, José de Urquiza, in 1852; and a year later the present constitution, which is broadly patterned on that of the United States, was adopted.

The struggle for power between the city and the province of Buenos Aires and the rest of the country continued until 1880, when La Plata replaced Buenos Aires as the capital of the province of Buenos Aires. This separation of the federal capital from the province led to closer relations and greater equality between the various provinces, but did not abate the friendly political and economic rivalry between the industrial hub of the country and the agricultural provinces.

Argentina today is a republic composed of 23 provinces, a federal district, and one territory which comprises Tierra del Fuego, the South Atlantic Islands and the Antarctic. Its liberal constitution provides for a federal union of the provinces, which retain all powers except those reserved for the national government. The president and vice-president are elected for six years and may not be re-elected. The legislative branch of the government is vested in a congress which consists of a chamber of deputies and a senate. The judicial branch consists of a supreme court and the national tribunals in the federal capital and in the provinces.

AGRICULTURE. The pampas' 250,000 square miles make up the bulk of Argentina's farmlands, which produce 95 percent of all wheat, corn, flax, and grains, 75 percent of its cattle, half of its sheep, and a large proportion of its hogs.

North of the pampas, in the Chaco region, are cotton fields and quebracho forests which supply the tanning industry with the extract tannin. Sugar cane fields of Tucumán and Salta are to the west, as are the fruit and vineyard regions of Mendoza and San Juan. One-third of the country's sheep are raised in Patagonia.

INDUSTRY. Though industrial growth was slow, due to lack of sufficient electricity and fuel, Argentina is now self-sufficient in the production of foodstuffs, and is supplying an increasing amount of consumer durable and non-durable goods which formerly were imported. The major industries are the iron and steel plants; automobiles; meat packing plants; food processing factories, flour and oilseed mills, machinery manufacturing and assembly plants, textile, chemical, pharmaceutical and cement plants, and tanning and leather goods industries. In addition, Argentina is the world's fourth-largest wool producer.

A major factor in the country's industrial growth has been exploitation of iron ore deposits in Sierra Grande. In addition to these resources, petroleum and natural gas are the main products of Argentina's rapidly growing mining industry.

CITIES. Over two-thirds of the citizens of Argentina live in cities, giving the country one of the largest urban populations in South America. In Buenos Aires and its suburbs alone live one-third of the entire country's residents.

BARILOCHE, a resort town hugging the southern shore of Lake Nahuel Huapi, is the gateway to 3,000 square miles of one of the most diverse and spectacular regions of unspoiled natural beauty in the world. Its charming Swiss-like atmosphere, fine resort hotels and excellent location at the edge of **Nahuel Huapi National Park** make it a principal vacation center.

Tales of fabulous treasures and blond giants who had learned the secret of eternal youth spurred the conquistadors in their mad search for this enchanted city more than four centuries ago. Neither the treasures nor the youthful blond giants was ever found. But the wish to stay young still draws many to the healthful climate, magnificent scenery, excellent fishing, hunting, boating, mountain climbing and skiing, and the many other natural treasures for which this area has since become famous. Besides the usual sports activities and diversions which you would expect to find in such a popular mountain resort, the area also offers some outstanding sightseeing excursions. One of the most popular is the trip by boat and bus from Bariloche through the fabulous lakes region to Puerto Varas on the Chilean side and on through the Chilean lakes. Another is the boat ride on **Lake Nahuel Huapi to Victoria Island** where tame guanaco, deer and other game roam. The Parks Commission has a forest research station there.

The **Patagonian Museum** in Bariloche offers a remarkable exhibition of the archaeology, ethnology and natural and political history of this area.

BUENOS AIRES is a modern, bustling, progressive, and prosperous metropolis that sprawls leisurely on the flat, fertile southern bank of the broad and muddy Río de la Plata, about 125 miles from the Atlantic Ocean. Its cluttered skyline, busy modern harbor and giant grain elevators offer unmistakable proof that this is the capital, chief seaport, and most important industrial and commercial city in Argentina.

It is also the biggest city south of the equator and one of the largest in the world. A modern metropolis of 3.8 million people, "B.A." has the tallest skyscrapers in South America, and the widest avenue in the world.

Its fine restaurants, excellent hotels, elegant shops, and a wide variety of amusements and entertainment have made it a favorite stopover for tourists circling the continent. Known as the "Paris of the Western Hemisphere," it also has been compared to Chicago, Madrid, London and Berlin; but it is unique in many respects.

It is a city of contrasts and contradictions; of simple pleasures and sophisticated diversions; of broad, tree-lined boulevards and narrow, winding, cobblestoned streets; of beautiful women and flirtatious men; and of superhighways and modern subways, horse-drawn carts and old taxicabs.

Its citizens, known as *porteños* (of the port) to distinguish them from their rural kin, have the vibrant vitality and bold independent spirit so characteristic of this young nation, tempered with the self-assurance and sophistication of the true cosmopolite.

The **Plaza de Mayo** in the heart of the city is the central point from which to start on your tour of the city. Within easy walking distance are the smart shops, theaters, business and financial districts, and the principal monuments and landmarks. Here, facing the monument to Argentine independence, you will find the historic **cabildo** (town hall), where the first cries for liberty and freedom were heard in 1810; the **Greco-Roman Cathedral,** where the sarcophagus of the liberator General José de San Martín lies in state; the **Casa Rosada** (Pink House), or Government Palace; the **Intendencia,** the mayor's offices; and the **Banco de la Nación,** the principal bank.

Two short blocks north of the cathedral is the **Church of La Merced,** where you can hear one of the finest organs in the country and look over archives that date from 1601. On the other side of the plaza, in the old Colonial section of **San Telmo,** is the Jesuit church of **San Ignacio,** which looks today as it did two centuries ago. Here, too, is the battle-scarred **Church** and **Convent of Santo Domingo,** where the British held out until forced to surrender the city. The mausoleum of Manuel Belgrano, another leader in Argentina's independence movement, is in front of the church. Not far from here is **Casa Liniers,** the house of Captain Santiago de Liniers, who recaptured the city from the British and later became viceroy.

Sidewalk cafés and trees line the **Avenida de Mayo** as it runs from the Plaza de Mayo to the **Plaza del Congreso,** where the nation's capitol and congressional buildings are located. It cuts across the broad **Avenida Nueve de Julio,** said to be the widest avenue in the world. Its big circular plaza is not only impressive but practical. A towering obelisk commemorates the city's founding, and beneath it a large municipal garage provides enough parking space for 2,000 cars. A few blocks north of the plaza is **Calle Florida,** one of the city's busiest and most elegant shopping streets, which is closed to vehicular traffic from 11:00 A.M. to 8:30 P.M. to allow pedestrians to use the street and window-shop in a leisurely way. At one end of this usually crowded narrow street is **Plaza San Martín.** The equestrian statue of the liberator marks the place where he organized his famous Mounted Grenadiers and the city was defended against the second British invasion. The austere red brick clock tower at the foot of the plaza was a gift from the British colony of Buenos Aires. Also starting from the plaza is **Avenida Santa Fe,** the leading thoroughfare of opulent shops and lovely homes which goes out to Palermo.

Nearby **Recoleta** is one of the city's most attractive residential sections. A drive along Avenida Alvear will take you past the **National Museum of Fine Arts,** the **United States embassy,** and many palatial homes and modern apartment buildings. The **statue of Alvear** by the French sculptor Emile Bourdelle in the Paseo de la Recoleta is one of the loveliest in the city. The **Recoleta Cemetery** itself is a necropolis of marble mausoleums and ornate monuments.

The city's largest public park is **Palermo,** where tourists will find many pleasant walks, roads, bridle paths, lakes and gardens, tennis courts, a golf course, race track, polo fields and an outdoor theater. A replica of the house in Boulogne-sur-Mer, France, where San Martín spent the last days of his life is now a national shrine here. Other attractions are the authentic **Andalusian Patio** brought over from Spain, the **exposición rural,** where Argentina's great annual livestock show is held in August, and the **Botanical and Zoological Gardens.** There are more than 150 other parks throughout the city.

A performance at the **Teatro Colón** is a must during the winter season. So also are the concerts in the **open-air theater** at Palermo, the Buenos Aires Symphony Orchestra, and popular plays and ballets at the **Municipal Theater.** The **Cervantes National Theater of Comedy** offers a repertoire of classical and modern works. Some of the other outstanding theaters are the **Odeón,** which presents French plays as well as some Argentine productions, and the **Teatro Grupo sur o Mievo Teatro,** an experimental theater, which offers a selection of the best old and new plays at low prices.

Of the many museums and art galleries in Argentina, the largest and most important one is the **National Museum of Fine Arts,** with a fine collection of old masters, some of the earliest paintings done in this hemisphere, and a rare exhibit of Argentine wood carvings. The **National Historical Museum** has a rich collection of exhibits relating to the history of Argentina. **Bernandino Rivadavia Museum of Natural Science** contains many archaeological, botanical and marine curiosities, while the **Ethnographic Museum of the School of Philosophy and Letters** has more than 35,000 items of prehistoric Argentina. The **Isaac Fernández Blanco Museum of Hispano-American Art** is an attractive Colonial exhibit of the artwork and relics of the period. **José Hernández Municipal Museum of Art and Folklore** has many displays of the folklore of the nation and the work of local artists. Others worthy of a visit are the **Sarmiento Historical Museum,** the **Mitre Museum and Library,** and the **Museum of the Cabildo and the Revolution of May.** The **University of Buenos Aires** also should be visited.

One of the city's outstanding tourist attractions is its colorful, predominantly Italian waterfront district of **La Boca.** This is the city's bohemian section and the site of the **Boca Museum** founded by Benito Quinquela Martín, one of Argentina's best-known painters.

But by far the most popular form of diversion for most tourists is found in the many restaurants, *confiterias,* cafés, cabarets, *boîtes* and theaters which have made this city both a gourmets' paradise and the show place of the continent.

There are many guided sightseeing tours of the city and its environs which are readily available to tourists. For the boating enthusiast one of the most popular is that to the **Tigre,** the delta of the Paraná River, about 18 miles from the city. On weekends the numerous islands and channels are teeming with pleasure craft of all types.

Another trip that is well worth the hour ride is to an *estancia,* or cattle ranch, on the pampas just outside the city limits. Here, in the real grass roots of Argentina, life is of a different tempo.

CÓRDOBA, in the midst of grain fields and fruit orchards between the pampas and the Andes mountains, is one of those curious anachronisms that still manages to maintain the mood and tempo of Colonial days in this modern age. Founded in 1573 by Captain Don Jerónimo Luis de Cabrera, this third largest city of Argentina and the capital of the province has a population of 635,000. Its springlike climate, unsurpassed scenery, quaint Colonial charm, and fine resort hotels have made this an all-year-round vacationland.

Everywhere one sees signs of the splendor and grandeur of a bygone era when this was a center of religion and learning in the New World and known as the "city of culture." Its university, founded in 1613, was the first in the country. Many of its churches, especially the Jesuit-built **La Compañia,** are architectural marvels of the period.

The cathedral, which is almost as much a museum as it is a place of worship, was begun in 1680 and took almost 80 years to finish. One of the finest examples of Colonial architecture in the New World, it contains a valuable collection of original frescoes by outstanding painters of the day. Other relics of the past are the old **cabildo,** the **Obispo Chapel,** the **Provincial Museum,** which was once the palace of the last viceroy, and the **Colegio Nacional de Monserrat,** founded in 1695, whose library is the product of three centuries of work. In the **Church of Santo Domingo** you will see the flag which San Martín carried on his march across the Andes, and an altar of the Virgin which dates back to 1592. Its priceless collection of church jewels is shown to the public only on October 7, the day of the Fiesta of the Virgin of the Rosary.

El Pilar, one of the first churches erected in Córdoba, is an outstanding example of pure Colonial architecture. The **Church of La Merced** is famous for its hand-carved Colonial pulpit and candelabras. The modern section of **Alta Córdoba,** on the other side of the Río Primero, has broad avenues, new apartment houses and office buildings, lovely homes, fine theaters, and a zoo.

In the rolling hills which surround Córdoba, visitors will find numerous delightful hotels, charming villas, inns, and resorts with good food and comfortable accommodations.

Mar Chiquita (Little Sea) is a popular resort town with many hotels along its lakeshore on the fringe of the pampas. It is excellent for inland saltwater bathing, and easily reached by train or bus from Córdoba.

CORRIENTES, about 25 miles below the juncture of the Paraguay and Alto Paraná rivers, is a city of over 100,000 people whose proximity to the jungle of the Gran Chaco is seen in the lush tropical vegetation and hot climate. The city was founded in 1588 by Alonzo de Vera and is today the capital of Corrientes Province. A tourist must is the miraculous cross in the **Church of La Cruz.** Indians who tried to burn it are said to have been struck down by lightning from a cloudless sky. **Plaza Cabral** has a statue of the sergeant who saved San Martín's life in the Battle of San Lorenzo.

JUJUY is a picturesque old town almost a mile above sea level in a warm subtropical valley of the snow-topped Andes. Long before the Spaniards came, this was a Quechuan Indian village whose famous hot springs were frequented by the Incas. The **"baths of the kings,"** as the springs are still known, are about ten miles out of town; and Indian traders in striking ponchos still come down out of the surrounding hills to barter their handicrafts as they did centuries ago. This is one of the rare places in Argentina where Indians are very much a part of the scenery and follow their ancient customs. A Spanish settlement since 1592, Jujuy is rich in the heritage of old Spain and in Colonial art and architecture. The outstanding example is the hand-carved pulpit in the chapel, a work of art without equal in the country. Another tourist attraction is the doorway where General Lavalle was shot and killed in 1848, located on the street which bears his name. Other nearby places of interest are **Humahuaca** and **Tilcara**, where colorful Indian villages are found. At **La Quiaca**, about 11,000 feet high in the bleak and barren *puna* near the Bolivian frontier, the Indians wear their typical white homburgs and the climate is cool throughout the year.

LA PLATA, the capital of the province of Buenos Aires and an important city in its own right, is about 35 miles from Buenos Aires. Planned and constructed in 1880 to replace Buenos Aires as the provincial capital, it has a fine university, an interesting museum of natural history, some large meat-packing plants and petroleum refineries, and a windmill manufacturing company. The race track here is open all year round.

At **San Antonio de Areco**, about 70 miles from Buenos Aires, the gaucho has been immortalized in the **Gaucho Museum** of the Guiraldes *estancia*. This is where Ricardo Guiraldes wrote his classic "Don Segundo Sombra." The restored buildings include a *pulperia* (country store), a chapel and a coach house.

The picturesque resort town of **Chascomús**, on the road from Buenos Aires to Mar del Plata, attracts many vacationists, swimmers, boating enthusiasts and pejerrey fishermen to its salty lake waters. Its **Pampas Museum** in another restored *estancia*, which once belonged to General Pueyrredón, houses many noteworthy exhibits.

LUJÁN, the Lourdes of Argentina, about 40 miles from Buenos Aires, is a pleasant day's journey. Pilgrims from near and far come here to pay homage to Our Lady of Luján, the patron saint of Argentina, on May 21. On that day in 1630 the oxcart carrying the statue of the Virgin to Peru stopped here and could not be budged. A chapel was built on the spot and the town grew around it. The statue of the Virgin can be seen on the high altar of the imposing Gothic basilica, which has replaced the original chapel. The **Old Cabildo** contains a Colonial and Historical Museum with many interesting exhibits of the firearms and furniture of the period as well as some ancient manuscripts. The first steam locomotive to chug across the pampas is on display in the **Transport Museum.**

MAR DEL PLATA, on the gently sloping hills of the Atlantic coast about 250 miles from the capital, is the country's principal seaside resort and summer playground. Founded in 1868 by several wealthy Argentine ranchers looking for a place to rest, this sun-swept city of pleasure today numbers more than 800 hotels and boardinghouses. The resort's population swells from 150,000 to over a million during the busy summer season from December to Easter when people flock here for the sun and the surf. Not the least of the reasons for its popularity is its huge, rambling casino, said to be the largest of its kind in the world. This gay, ornate palace, which is operated by the government, covers two city blocks and can accommodate about 20,000. One room has 70 tables for roulette, baccarat, *vingt-et-un* (21) and craps. Other facilities include a skating rink, a gymnasium, basketball courts, swimming pool, a recreation hall, a movie theater, hotel and night club.

Its five miles of beaches leave nothing to be desired in the way of bathing facilities. There is also a boardwalk for promenading, pony carts for sightseeing, and some fine seafood restaurants and first-rate night clubs. The city's shopping street is Calle San Martín. Farther south along the coast are other beach resorts: **Miramar**, with a fine golf course overlooking the sea; **Necochea,** the second largest beach resort, with some beautiful rock formations; and **Quequen.** Good fishing for pejerrey, corbina, and Spanish mackerel is found all along the coast.

Other nearby points of interest are the *estancias* at **Chapadmalal** and **Ojo de Agua,** famous as a breeding place of Argentine race horses, and the mineral springs of **Copelina.**

MENDOZA, in an irrigated valley of vineyards and fruit orchards about 2,500 feet above sea level, is a splash of green in the arid sun-baked hills of the purple Andes. This historic city, which was founded in 1561 and named for the then governor of Chile, is on the main route between Argentina and Chile. It was from here that San Martín set out on his march across the Andes with 40,000 men to liberate Chile. Primarily known as the wine center of Argentina, Mendoza's dry, mild climate attracts many tourists and vacationists. The city was practically destroyed in 1861, following an earthquake and fire, and has been almost completely rebuilt. It is a modern city of low one-story buildings, pleasant gardens and trees.

Cerro de la Gloria, a public park on a hill with a monument to San Martín, commemorates his victorious march across the Andes. The monument is topped by a large bronze condor (vulture) and the Goddess of Liberty and circled by a grove of eucalyptus trees. The park also has a zoological garden, where live condors are kept in captivity.

Other attractions include the **Government Palace,** in the center of Independence Plaza, and the **Historical Museum,** housing some of San Martín's personal belongings. The **Moyano Museum of Natural History** has a fine collection of Argentine plants and animals. But the big attraction here is the **Fiesta de la Vendimia** in early April, to celebrate the grape harvest festival. This is marked with gay dancing, a colorful procession and the coronation of the queen of the festival on Cerro de la Gloria. Nearby are the resort towns of **Cacheuta, Potrerillos** and **Villavicencio,** known for their thermal springs, lovely mountain scenery and fine hotels.

PARANÁ, the capital of Entre Ríos Province, lies on the east bank of the river of the same name. One of the handsomest cities in the country, this was the capital of Argentina from 1853 to 1862. Among its notable attractions are the beautiful plaza in the center of town, with its fountains and a statue of San Martín; the fine Colonial art work in the interior of the cathedral; the beautiful **Urquiza Park,** with the enormous statue of General Urquiza and the bas-relief depicting the Battle of Caseros where the tyrant Rosas was defeated. The population numbers 100,000.

POSADAS, a modern town of over 70,000 people at the confluence of the Alto Paraná and the Paraguay rivers, is the jumping-off point for a visit to the famous **Iguazú Falls.** These cataracts, set in a tropical forest where orchids grow in wild profusion, surpass in grandeur both Niagara and Victoria falls and are more than two miles wide. Not far from Posadas are ruins of old Jesuit missions in Guarani territory, from which the province of Misiones gets its name. Outstanding tourist attraction is the grass-covered ruins of **San Ignacio Mini,** one of the largest mission villages of the early eighteenth century. Here the Jesuit priests trained the Indians to farm the land and develop their arts and handicrafts. Trips around the falls can be made on foot, by canoe or horseback. There is also some fine dorado fishing in the **Alto Paraná,** where 40-pound catches are recorded.

ROSARIO, a busy industrial and commercial port on a high bank of the Paraná River, is the second largest city of Argentina. Over 700,000 people live in this city of wide streets and beautiful boulevards. But the overpreponderance of grain elevators, factories, meat-packing houses, and extensive dock and railroad facilities show it to be more of a grain shipping port than a tourist center. The two bronze female figures holding a stalk of wheat and an ear of corn atop the Minetti building are symbolic of the city's main economic interest. A race track, several boating clubs, a golf course, and the salt-water Springs of Saladillo are enjoyable.

SALTA is a pure Colonial gem of terracotta rooftops and white towers in a fertile valley of the rocky, barren Andes which has changed little since its founding in 1588. Its 120,000 inhabitants cherish their traditional ways and still build today in the same style as they did four centuries ago. In the ancient cathedral in the central plaza of the town are the images of the Virgin and the Lord of the Miracle, which are said to have brought an end to a terrifying earthquake when they were paraded through the streets. A **fiesta** marking that day, September 13, 1692, is celebrated in Salta each year.

SANTA FE is a beautiful old city, rich in Colonial architecture, which sits astride the west bank of the Paraná River. In the center of a very fertile region, it is the capital of Santa Fe province, and a university city with a population of 275,000. It was near here that Sebastian Cabot in 1527 founded the first settlement in El Plata, a tiny fort he called Sancti Spiritus. Santa Fe was founded in 1573 by Juan de Garay on his voyage from Asunción down the Paraná to re-colonize Buenos Aires. Among its many historic buildings is the **cabildo,** where the nation's constitution was adopted by the Congress of 1853. The crucifix on which the delegates swore their allegiance to the constitution is in the sacristy of the Church of San Francisco. Local painters hold their exhibitions in the **Museum of Fine Arts** on Calle General.

TUCUMÁN, on a green fertile plain at the foot of the towering Sierra de Aconquija, is the busiest and most populated city of northern Argentina and rightfully called the "Garden of the Country." The melting snow of the high mountains forms the streams which irrigate more than a million acres of sugar cane, the principal produce of the city's quarter of a million inhabitants. It was here at the **Casa Histórica** that the Congress of the United Provinces of Río de la Plata met to draft Argentina's Declaration of Independence. Its restoration and the many Colonial treasures found here recall this colorful period in the country's past. The statue of General Belgrano in the plaza which bears his name commemorates the decisive battle he fought on this very spot in 1812. The **house of Bishop Colombres,** who introduced sugar cane to Tucumán, is worth a visit. So also is **Villa Nogues,** an hour's trip up the mountains, where most of the wealthy residents of Tucumán live.

USHUAIA, a tiny settlement of steep narrow streets and wooden houses with corrugated-tin roofs overlooking Beagle Channel, has the distinction of being the most southerly town in the world. Its close to 2,000 inhabitants comprise a sturdy breed of hard-working people who make their living out of raising sheep, cutting timber, fishing and trapping, and are virtually isolated by heavy blizzards in winter.

First colonized in 1868 by an Anglican pastor, Thomas Bridges, this town in the shadow of the ice-crested Andes became the capital of Tierra del Fuego in 1883. It is also the site of a prison for dangerous criminals.

In the way of tours and tourist attractions, there are several excursions on foot, horseback, or by car from here to the bays of **Lendegaia** and **Lapataia,** the **Olivia Falls, Fagnano Lake** and the **glaciers** of the **Martial Mountains.** To climb the 4,900-foot summit it is necessary to contact the Andean Club of Ushuaia. This is also the gateway for a boat trip to the Argentine possession in the Antarctic continent.

SPORTS AND RECREATION. A variety of sports activities take place in Argentina throughout the year. **International car races, polo matches** and **regattas,** as well as **horse racing** at **Palermo** and the turf track of **San Isidro** (both in Buenos Aires) are said to be the best on the continent. **Pato,** a cross between polo and basketball, was introduced by the gauchos in the seventeenth century, and outlawed as too dangerous until a few years ago. But the national pastime is **soccer,** and top-ranking teams in and around Buenos Aires draw as many as 100,000 spectators to **River Plate Stadium.**

Football matches for the national championship are played on Sundays from April to December; **rugby** on Saturdays and Sundays from April to October; and **polo** every Sunday from September to December. Other popular sports include **golf, tennis, swimming, horseback riding, surfing, rowing,** and **sailing. Hunting** and **fishing** are also excellent. **Alta Gracia,** about 30 miles south of Córdoba, is a popular summer and winter resort with good fishing, hunting, golf, and swimming.

SPECIAL EVENTS. The **opera season,** at the Teatro Colón in Buenos Aires, runs from May 25 to the latter part of September. Other special events include May 1, **Workers' Day;** May 25, **national anniversary of the Cabildo Abierto of 1810** (first Argentine government); June 20, **national flag day;** July 9, **parade of the armed forces** on Argentina's independence day; August 17, **anniversary of the death of the liberator General San Martín.** The **exposición rural,** held in August at the rural exhibit in Palermo Park, is the principal agricultural show of the year, when the finest-blooded cattle, horses, sheep, and pigs compete for prizes.

DINING AND SHOPPING. Argentina is probably the best-fed nation in Latin America, if not in the world. The average Argentine consumes 200 pounds of beef a year. The Argentine capital has epicurean delights and fine restaurants of every nationality to please even the most discriminating diner.

Meat in this carnivorous land is as plentiful as the great herds that graze on the pampas, and prices compared to U.S. standards are low. This is one of the reasons why *bife* (steak) is a staple food on the Argentine diet, and all sorts of chops and choice cuts are featured in restaurants, dining rooms, *confiterias* and even sidewalk cafés throughout the country. Other typical Argentine specialties are *parrillada*—a mixed barbecue consisting of a cut of beef, pork and blood sausages, kidneys, liver, and *chinchulines* (intestines); *cabrito* (roast kid); *escabeche* (chicken, fish or partridge marinated in vinegar); *puchero* (boiled dinner consisting of a brisket of beef, slice of salt pork, sausages, and several vegetables); *bife a caballo* (steak on horseback—a steak with two fried eggs on top); *empanadas* (fried or baked meat pies); and *mollejas* (sweetbreads). For some truly authentic Argentine food, journey out to an *estancia* (ranch) and enjoy an *asado,* an Argentine barbecue, and drink the bitter tea that is known as *maté.*

Most Argentines begin their day with a light breakfast consisting of a *café con leche* (coffee and milk) or tea with *tostadas* (toast). Their lunch generally includes soup, salad, fish or eggs, the inevitable meat entree, dessert and coffee, and plenty of wine or beer. From 4:30 P.M. to 5:00 P.M. is teatime. This quite often will run into the vermouth hour from 6 P.M. to 8 P.M., when many Argentines leave work and have a leisurely drink or snack and take in a movie, theater or a concert before dinnertime, from 9 P.M. to 10:30 P.M.

Té compléto (high tea) and the "vermouth" (cocktail) are usually taken in a *confiteria,* which is a unique Argentine institution that can best be described as a combination English tearoom, cocktail lounge, French café, American bar and ice-cream parlor, with a delicatessen thrown in for good measure. Some of these are rather modest little lunchrooms, where only the most essential viands are purveyed, but others are grandiose marble palaces.

Nothing typifies the Argentine's love of fine food and zest for good living more than the *confiterias* of Buenos Aires. However, if you want to see a totally different aspect of Argentine life, then you must also visit the modest inns and restaurants and the *pulperias* (country stores) in the little inland villages and towns of the country.

Argentina is a shopper's paradise where you can buy practically anything and everything from silver antiques and hand-woven vicuña ponchos to alligator handbags and nutria coats. And Buenos Aires is the place to come for excellent buys in leather and woolen goods, fine luggage, handmade shoes, and a variety of items for both men and women made out of alligator, calfskin, pigskin, snakeskin, and antelope. Its main shopping street, Santa Fe, is where you'll find the big department stores and smart dress shops, rare books and china, fine jewelry and a wide assortment of native handicrafts.

Photographic Credits

Picture Editor: Patricia Fink

VOLUME I

We gratefully acknowledge the cooperation and assistance of the following persons and organizations:

Alaska Travel Division, Department of Economic Development and Planning
American Airlines
Arizona Development Board
Bahamas Ministry of Tourism
Barbados Tourist Board
Bermuda News Bureau
Brazilian Government Trade Bureau
British Information Services
Canadian Government Travel Bureau
Canadian Pacific Railway
Caribbean Tourist Association
Chicago Convention and Tourism Bureau
Colombian Government Tourist Office

Commonwealth of Kentucky, Travel Division
Commonwealth of Puerto Rico
Consulado del Uruguay
Curaçao Information Center
Embassy of the Argentine Republic
Florida State News Bureau
French Government Tourist Office
Georgia Department of Industry and Trade
Haiti Government Tourist Bureau
Hawaii Visitors Bureau
Henry Ford Museum, Dearborn, Michigan
Idaho Department of Commerce and Development
Illinois Information Service
Instituto Costarricense de Turismo
Iowa Development Commission
Jamaica Tourist Board
John Crane, Colonial Williamsburg, Virginia
John F. Kennedy Center for the Performing Arts
Kansas Department of Economic Development
Lan-Chile Airlines
Las Vegas News Bureau
Laurence Laurie & Associates, Inc.
Lincoln Center for the Performing Arts (Bob Serating)
Maine Department of Economic Development
Marineland of Florida
Massachusetts Department of Commerce and Development
Minnesota Department of Business Development
Mississippi Agricultural & Industrial Board
Missouri Tourism Commission
Montana Highway Commission
Monterey Chamber of Commerce
National Film Board of Canada
National Park Service

Nebraska Game Commission
New Hampshire Office of Vacation Travel
New Jersey Department of Labor and Industry
New Mexico Department of Development
New York State Department of Commerce
North Carolina Department of Conservation and Development
Oregon State Highway Commission
Pan American Grace Airways
Pan American Airways
Port of New York Authority
Rhode Island Development Council
South Carolina State Development Board
South Dakota Department of Highways
Southern California Visitors Council
Standard Oil Company (New Jersey)
State of Alabama Bureau of Publicity and Information
State of Oklahoma (Mike Shelton)
Surinam Tourist Bureau
Texas Highway Department
Trinidad and Tobago Tourist Board
United Nations
United States Military Academy
U. S. Virgin Islands News Bureau
Utah Tourist & Publicity Council (Hal Rumel)
Utah Travel Council
Venezuelan Government Tourist Bureau
Vermont Agency of Development and Community Affairs
Walker-Missouri Commerce
Washington Convention and Visitors Bureau
Washington State Department of Commerce and Economic Development
Yale University News Bureau

Index

R.